Museum of Anthropology, University of Michigan
Memoirs, Number 37

Life on the Periphery

Economic Change in Late Prehistoric Southeastern New Mexico

edited by

John D. Speth

Ann Arbor, Michigan
2004

Printed in the United States of America
ISBN 0-915703-54-8

Cover design, by Katherine Clahassey, inspired by the painting *Trading at the Pecos Pueblo*, by Tom Lovell.

The University of Michigan Museum of Anthropology currently publishes three monograph series: Anthropological Papers, Memoirs, and Technical Reports, as well as an electronic series in CD-ROM form. For a complete catalog, write to Museum of Anthropology Publications, 4009 Museums Building, Ann Arbor, MI 48109-1079.

Library of Congress Cataloging-in-Publication Data

Life on the periphery : economic change in late prehistoric southeastern New Mexico / edited by John D. Speth.
p. cm. -- (Memoirs ; no. 37)
Includes bibliographical references.
ISBN 0-915703-54-8 (alk. paper)
1. Henderson Site (N.M.) 2. Pueblo Indians--Antiquities. 3. Pueblo pottery--Pecos River Valley (N.M. and Tex.) 4. Plant remains (Archaeology)--Pecos River Valley (N.M. and Tex.) 5. Animal remains (Archaeology)--Pecos River Valley (N.M. and Tex.) 6. Pecos River Valley (N.M. and Tex.)--Antiquities. I. Speth, John D. II. Memoirs of the Museum of Anthropology, University of Michigan ; no. 37.
GN2.M52no.37 L55 2003
[E99.p9]
978.9'4--dc21

2003010294

The paper used in this publication meets the requirements of the ANSI Standard Z39.48-1984 (Permanence of Paper)

Contents

Part IV. Ethnobotany

Part V. Skeletal Indicators of Diet

Part VI. Concluding Remarks

FIGURES

Tables

To
Matthew and Karen Henderson,
Calder and Candy Ezzell,
Jay and Carrie Hollifield
and
The Archaeological Conservancy
for their efforts in preserving the fragile
archaeological record of southeastern New Mexico

to
Elmer (Skip) and Jane Garnsey
who helped launch our work with prehistoric
bison hunters in southeastern New Mexico

and to the memory of
Robert H. (Bus) Leslie
in recognition of his pioneering contributions
to our knowledge of the region's prehistory

Acknowledgments

The work at the Henderson Site was made possible through the generous permission of Matthew and Karen Henderson, who owned the ranch where the site is located. Although they have since sold the ranch, their deep concern and interest in the archaeology of southeastern New Mexico led them to donate both the Henderson Site (LA-1549) and nearby Bloom Mound (LA-2528) to The Archaeological Conservancy for long-term protection and management. It was a pleasure to name the Henderson Site in Matt and Karen's honor, since it and Bloom Mound survived largely as a result of their efforts to preserve the fragile archaeological record of the area. Their interest, enthusiasm, and friendship always made the fieldwork a true pleasure and added in countless ways to the success of the project. We are forever grateful.

Calder and Candy Ezzell, who now own the ranch, have continued the same tradition of warm, open hospitality, interest, and friendship, and it is through their vigilance that both Henderson and Bloom Mound continue to survive undisturbed by the vandalism and pot hunting that has become so prevalent throughout southeastern New Mexico. Working on the 2C\ Ranch, as it is now called, has been a wonderful experience, and stands as a high point in the lives of all those who have participated in the fieldwork.

We would also like to express our gratitude to The Archaeological Conservancy, and in particular to Mark Michel, President, and James B. Walker, Southwest Regional Director, for their continuing efforts and enthusiasm in securing the protection of both Henderson and Bloom. We are grateful as well for their patience and understanding over these past many years waiting for the appearance of this long-overdue volume.

Throughout the project, we benefited immeasurably from Robert H. (Bus) Leslie's firsthand knowledge of the prehistory of southeastern New Mexico. He generously gave us open access to his extensive site files, helped us identify the sources of our lithic raw materials and type some of the unusual projectile points found with the Feature 36 burial, and spotted the deposits in the East Plaza that proved upon excavation to be the site's most impressive bison-roasting feature. The discovery of this feature totally altered our view of the subsistence practices of the Henderson villagers, since we had encountered very few bison remains elsewhere in the site. Most of all, Bus shared with us his knowledge and insights about southeastern New Mexico prehistory, for which we are extremely indebted. With his untimely death in 1992, southeastern New Mexico lost one of its most dedicated prehistorians. He is greatly missed.

Thanks also go to Jane Holden Kelley of the University of Calgary. It was her enthusiasm, expertise, and guidance, many years ago, that launched us in the direction that ultimately led to our work at both Henderson and Bloom Mound.

Many people have been involved in the project at various stages, and their help is gratefully acknowledged. The field crews worked long and hard hours, in the day excavating the site and in the evening washing and labeling the masses of material that we recovered during the five seasons. In the 1980-1981 field seasons, which lasted three months each, these included Michelle Hegmon, Andrea Hempel, Lee Horne, Dave Killick, Dana Lepofsky, Bryce Little, Claire McHale, Gretchen Neve, Lisa Oneal, Christine Peschel, Juan Ramirez, Tom Rocek, Cathy Rudelich, Priscilla Schuster, Andrea Sinclair, Gil Stein, Molly Sutphen, Carlos Tabares, Wirt Wills, and Lisa Young. Many others visited us for shorter periods during the course of the project and joined in the excavations. These included Elsa Burrowes, Dick Ford, Jane Kelley, Bus Leslie, Jeff, Mary, and Apphia Parsons, Dave Snow, Regge Wiseman, and Henry Wright.

Once the field school got started in 1994, many other students participated in the excavations and helped to make the project a success, including Ben Adams, Steve Archer, Kristi Arntzen, Dana Beehr, Gwen Bell, Anna Bloch, Jennifer Bragg, Sue Carroll (Roberts), Margaret Chavez, Rebecca Dean, Erica Gooding (Cameron), Marie Harris, Ellen Haskell, Carrie Heitman, Lisa Kelley, Marc Levine, Dana Limberg, Carl Matthews, Ken McGraw, Tatum McKay, Heather Miljour, Diane Miller, Cara Monroe, Amelia Natoli, Diane Nethaway, Sara Olson, Stephanie Pinsky, Richard Raffaelli, Julie Raybon, Angela Schmorrow, Laura Staro, Christina Waskiewicz, Chris Watt, Kim Wyllie, and Laurie Zimmerman.

Special thanks go to my field assistants—Sev Fowles, Gina Powell, Julie Solometo, Tineke van Zandt, and Chip Wills. They put up with some difficult field conditions, including not only the obvious—temperatures frequently in excess of 100° F and not a stitch of shade on the site—but also crowded living quarters, less than ideal "cuisine," long working hours, tiring weekend field trips, vermin of all sorts, and many other hardships. They also added greatly to the fun of doing fieldwork in southeastern New Mexico, for which we are all grateful.

Many of the field school students, and others, both undergraduates and graduates alike, got involved in the lab analyzing various classes of material from the site, and several wrote reports on their work or more extensive undergraduate Honors theses or predoctoral papers. Among these are Steve Archer, Kristi Arntzen, Gwen Bell, Sarah Bennett, Julia Blough, Jennifer Bragg, Sue Carroll (Roberts), Rebecca Dean, Frank De Mita, Jessica De Young, Cynthia Dillard, Kendall Eccleston, Sev Fowles, Julie Fremuth, Linda Gebric, Erica Gooding (Cameron), Marie Harris, Ellen Haskell, Michelle Hegmon, Lauren Herckis, Debra Holmes, Amy Lawson, Jennifer Lo, Mindy Martin, Carl Matthews, Tatum McKay, Diane Miller, Paula Murphy, Amelia Natoli, Gretchen Neve, Jim Noone, Laurie Ochsner, Sara Olson, Esther Osgood, Stephanie Pinsky, David Pohl, Ramona Quesada, Richard Raffaelli, Julie Raybon, Dennis Renaud, Tom Rocek, Angela Schmorrow, Brent Shaffer, Sudha Shah, Valerie Smulders, Julie Solometo, Miriam Stark, Laura Staro, Allison Stupka, Tom Suchyta, Matthew Syrett, Chris Watt, Chip Wills, Kim Wyllie, and Laurie Zimmerman.

Special thanks go to the many people who helped over the years in processing the hundreds of flotation samples from Henderson. These include Pui Ying Ching, Tom Cornelius, Yun-Kuen Lee, Claire McHale, John O'Shea, Gina Powell, Ken Sasaki, Tom Rocek, David Yoon, and Cal Will. We also thank Lisa Huckell for her analysis of the 1980-1981 paleoethnobotanical remains, and for the detailed synthetic study of Henderson's plant remains recently completed as a PhD dissertation at Washington University by Gina Powell. This document greatly enhances our understanding of Henderson's economy in the thirteenth and fourteenth centuries. We thank Steve Archer and Marie Harris for their detailed studies of Henderson's charcoal remains, and Mollie Toll, Sandy Dunavan, Heather Trigg, and Dick Ford for their valuable advice and assistance on botanical matters at various stages along the way.

Housing in Roswell has always posed a problem. It's not easy to find someone who is willing to rent to a "foreigner" from up north, a bearded foreigner no less, looking for a two-month lease for 10-15 students, all living under one roof. We are grateful therefore to Roy McKay, President of McKay Oil Corporation, for taking a gamble on us and renting the field school two adjacent houses year after year. We are also very grateful to the administration of Eastern New Mexico University's Roswell campus for allowing us to shower and eat there. We would particularly like to acknowledge the generosity of Frank Gonzalez, manager of the gym where we showered, and Frances Dubiel, facilities coordinator, who made it possible for us to eat in ENMU's cafeteria.

The first version of this tome was composed at Michigan using a mainframe computer and an obscure word-processing program known as "TextEdit," a cumbersome program that was used by only a handful of institutions in North America. When the University of Michigan pulled the plug on its mainframe, we found ourselves with hundreds of pages of text and complex tables, and no way to translate them into a form that could be used by a desktop computer. Renato Kipnis saved us from the nightmarish prospect of having to retype the entire manuscript, by writing a complex series of macros to translate the original document into a version that could be read by a Mac. Without Renato's help, this monograph might never have seen the light of day.

The final editing and layout of the manuscript were accomplished with the invaluable assistance of Sally Mitani, the Museum's editor. Kay Clahassey, the Museum's artist and photographer, did most of the figures. The two together designed the cover. The final product owes a great deal to their efforts and professionalism.

Funding for the earlier stages of the Henderson research was provided by a grant from the National Science Foundation (BNS-7924768). Supplemental funds were generously provided by the Museum of Anthropology, the Department of Anthropology, the Michigan Memorial-Phoenix Project (No. 616), and the Horace H. Rackham School of Graduate Studies (No. 387965), all of the University of Michigan. With the creation of the field school in 1994, much of the work was funded by student tuition payments and room-and-board fees, and by generous support provided by John G. Cross, Associate Dean for Budget and Administration, in the University of Michigan's College of Literature, Science and Arts. Portions of the manuscript were completed while I was a Weatherhead Resident Scholar at the School of American Research in Santa Fe, New Mexico. The scholarly environment provided by the SAR was an ideal context in which to bring a substantial part of this work to completion.

John D. Speth
University of Michigan
November, 2003

Part I

The Village

1
Introduction

John D. Speth
University of Michigan

This volume is the second report on the Henderson Site, a late prehistoric (ca. A.D. 1250-1400) pueblo-like community on the western margin of the Pecos Valley near Roswell in southeastern New Mexico. The first volume (Rocek and Speth 1986), while presenting a general overview of the site and the University of Michigan's excavations there in 1980 and 1981, focused primarily on the human burials and associated grave offerings found beneath the floors of several of the rooms. This second volume presents further documentation on this intriguing site, focusing this time more explicitly on the subsistence practices, and related technologies, of the village's inhabitants.

Much of the data presented here specifically concerns the large and exceptionally well-preserved faunal assemblage that we recovered from Henderson. It must be pointed out, however, that this volume cannot be considered a final report on the site or even on its fauna. Not surprisingly, detailed analyses of the type presented here have proved to be so time-consuming that were we to wait until all of the faunal and other artifactual material had been analyzed in a comparable fashion, no report would be forthcoming in the foreseeable future. Moreover, as our analyses on the 1980-1981 material progressed, we became increasingly aware of major gaps in our knowledge about the site, and in 1994 we returned to Henderson for three more seasons of excavation (1994, 1995, 1997). Needless to say, analysis of these additional materials, while vastly improving our understanding of the site, also further delayed completion of this report.

Most of the faunal remains identifiable to species or body part (including birds as well as fish bones larger than one-quarter inch) have been analyzed and are reported on here (nearly 24,000 specimens). The major exceptions are the bones of rodents other than gophers and prairie dogs, reptiles other than tortoises, and amphibians (and fish bones less than one-quarter inch), although somewhat surprisingly we encountered relatively few microfaunal remains (including rodents) at Henderson, even though several hundred flotation samples were processed. The largest class of faunal remains that are not dealt with here are several thousand mostly small shaft fragments that are not identifiable to either species or body part. While analyses of these remains, sorted into approximate body-size classes, would undoubtedly produce useful insights into site taphonomy, butchering and processing techniques, and so forth, the task of coding all of this material would delay publication for many more years. Rather than run the risk of Henderson joining the burgeoning ranks of unpublished archaeological projects, we have decided to publish the faunal studies that are now at hand, even if not all aspects are as yet complete.

In 1996 we began experimenting with the seriation of Henderson's El Paso Polychrome jar rims, and found that we could construct an internal chronology for the site that was not possible with the radiocarbon and archaeomagnetic dates (see Chapter 3). To our surprise and delight, the chronology made possible by the seriation demonstrated that the site had grown in two major phases, starting out as a linear or possibly "L"-shaped room block in the "Early phase" and then evolving in the "Late phase" into a larger "E"-shaped structure, a form it maintained until the time of its abandonment.

Prior to the seriation, we had been largely unable to examine processes of change, because we simply did not find stratified deposits of sufficient depth to make this possible. Our principal hope had been the discovery of several deep earth oven complexes, each containing over a meter of fire-cracked rock and trash. However, the discovery of unburned turkey and red-wing blackbird burials placed as closure offerings at the bottom of some of these features demonstrated that vertical stratigraphy was of little significance. The earth ovens very likely had been entirely emptied out following their last firing, closure offerings placed at the bottom, and then backfilled.

Thus, we lacked traditional vertical stratigraphy, but the seriation gave us horizontal, or spatial, stratigraphy. And by comparing the artifacts and fauna from different parts of the site, we suddenly found ourselves confronted with a veritable gold mine of information about change—change in subsistence and economy, change in exchange patterns, and even local resource degradation. But our new-found wealth of temporal information also created somewhat of a dilemma from the publication end of things, because several of the core chapters had already been completed when we began to work with the seriation. Our solution to this problem has varied somewhat, depending on the specific nature of each chapter. For example, in several cases we simply added a section at the end of the chapter headed something like "Temporal Perspective." This allowed us to discuss the principal findings that were made possible by the seriation, without having to substantially rewrite the entire chapter. In one case—the chapter dealing with the medium ungulates—we have written an entirely new chapter to supplement the one that had already been completed many years ago. And of course some of the chapters were written much more recently and these have largely or fully incorporated the insights made possible by the seriation.

We did make one decision, however, that is less than ideal but was an expedient necessitated by time. When we first began writing up the 1980-1981 materials, we made a monumental effort to include long appendices at the end of each chapter with complete tabulations of the basic data, including not only a table with site-wide totals but also separate tables for each major provenience (e.g., East Bar, Center Bar, East Plaza, etc.). These tables are still included in this volume, but we have made no similar attempt with the materials excavated in 1994, 1995, and 1997. Were we to present complete data tables now, broken down not only by provenience but also by phase, this study would never see the light of day.

Yet another important reason for getting this volume published now, despite the fact that a number of its components are not entirely complete, is because the "newness" would be further compromised with each additional year of delay. Some of the chapters have already been in my hands for more than a decade, so it is clearly time to get them into print without further delay.

We recognize that some of our interpretations and conclusions will have to be modified, and some perhaps rejected entirely, as other phases of the analysis are brought to completion. This unfortunately is inevitable. But the data we already have on hand is fascinating and informative in its own right, shedding light on the prehistory of an area of the Southwest that is still largely *terra incognito*. So we present here those studies that are now done, and we hope that in a few more years we will be able to present a third volume, and bring the Henderson work another step nearer to closure.

A few comments on the structure of the present volume are needed to help the reader wade through the often extremely dense data presentations. Our philosophy in a report of this type is to present as much data as we possibly can, tabulated and cross-tabulated in a variety of different ways. The goal is to provide a database, in essence a kind of archive, that other scholars, now and in the future, can rework according to their own interests and research questions. Obviously, it is impossible to anticipate all the different sorts of data that scholars will one day want. Nevertheless, there are certain fundamental kinds of information that are almost certain to be important. These include basic counts, measurements, and descriptive summaries, broken down by major categories and classes as well as by major spatial and temporal units.

Such detailed data tabulations, however, are primarily of importance to local specialists. Archaeologists in other parts of the Southwest and Southern Plains are likely to be interested in a report on the Henderson Site not for its details per se but for the comparative insights the report provides that may help illuminate developments elsewhere. Thus, to make it easier for the nonspecialist to extract these kinds of insights from the report without first having to wade through page after page of data tabulation and analysis, each chapter provides a synopsis at the end that pulls together the chapter's most interesting and important observations and conclusions. The final chapter of the volume attempts to draw all of these synopses together into a single coherent synthesis.

References Cited

Rocek, T. R., and J. D. Speth
1986 *The Henderson Site Burials: Glimpses of a Late Prehistoric Population in the Pecos Valley*. Technical Report 18. Ann Arbor, MI: Museum of Anthropology, University of Michigan.

2
The Henderson Site

John D. Speth
University of Michigan

Introduction

The Henderson Site (LA-1549) is a moderate-sized E-shaped pueblo-like community located about 10.5 mi (17 km) southwest of the modern city of Roswell in Chaves County, southeastern New Mexico (Fig. 2.1).[1] The site, which dates to the late thirteenth and fourteenth century, is situated at an elevation of 3,890 ft (1,186 m) on the easternmost of a series of low, northeast-trending limestone ridges that form the western border of the broad Pecos Valley lowlands. The Hondo River, a major western tributary of the Pecos, breaks through this last limestone ridge just north of the site and then flows northeast through Roswell before turning southeast and joining the Pecos (Fig. 2.2).

Since a previous report on the Henderson Site burials (Rocek and Speth 1986) has already described the nature and layout of the site in some detail, and has also provided basic information on excavation and recording techniques, only a brief review of these issues will be provided here, with emphasis given to those aspects that are new or that have been revised since the appearance of the first report. Some repetition is necessary, however, in order to put the new material in context.

Excavations were conducted at Henderson by the University of Michigan Museum of Anthropology during two three-month field seasons in the summers of 1980 and 1981. Renewed excavations at the site, in six-week seasons, were undertaken again in 1994, 1995, and 1997. An area of 314 m^2 was opened in the five seasons, amounting to less than 14% of the total site area (including the room blocks and the two plazas enclosed between the arms of the "E"). Of this total, 236 m^2 were excavated in the room blocks themselves, and 78 m^2 in plaza and other non-room areas. Excavations were conducted using a one-meter grid system. A permanent (cement) base datum (datum A) was arbitrarily placed just off the site near its southwest corner. The grid system was laid out with one axis roughly parallel to the long bar of the "E" (Main Bar), and the other parallel to the short bars (West Bar, Center Bar, and East Bar). Datum A was assigned coordinates 500N500E (i.e., 500 m north of, and 500 m east of, an arbitrary, and imaginary, reference point far to the southwest of the site). This was done to simplify recording procedures by keeping all of our excavation units within the same quadrant (to the northeast of the imaginary zero-zero reference point). Each one-meter grid unit received its designation from the coordinates of its northeast corner (e.g., grid square 500N500E is the one-meter unit immediately southwest of datum A). Datum A was also arbitrarily assigned an elevation of +100.00 m. All elevations (including artifact proveniences) were shot in with a transit and recorded in meters above or below datum A.[2]

Early in the 1980 season, every item was individually labeled with complete provenience information. This quickly proved to be far too cumbersome and time-consuming, and a new procedure was adopted in which every discrete provenience, such as a bag of material from a single level in a single one-meter grid square, was assigned a unique, sequential lot number. For example, lot number 274 was assigned to grid square 515N534E, level 101.00-100.90 m). Only these lot numbers were then written on each object. By the end of the 1981 field season, we had used a total of 2,333 lot numbers. We continued to use this system in subsequent field seasons, beginning arbitrarily at 3,000 in 1994, continuing without a break to 4,112 by the end of the 1995 season, beginning again at 5,000

Figure 2.1. Location of Henderson Site (LA-1549), Bloom Mound (LA-2528), Rocky Arroyo (LA-25277), and Garnsey Bison Kill (LA-18399) in southeastern New Mexico.

in 1997 and terminating the Henderson lot numbers at 5,669 at the end of the 1997 season. In 2000 we commenced work at the nearby quasi-contemporary site of Bloom Mound, and arbitrarily began the lot number system there at 6,000.

The lot number system greatly streamlined the labeling of artifacts, but has the obvious limitation that should the lot number records be lost or destroyed, most of the basic provenience information would also be lost. To prevent this from happening, we decided to create a permanent record of the lot numbers by publishing the complete file. The first 2,027 lot numbers were originally published as an appendix in Rocek and Speth (1986). Since the appearance of that publication, a number of errors have been noted. In addition, we decided that it would be useful to publish the full provenience information for each lot number, including our spatial designations, such as East Bar, Main Bar, etc. In Appendix 2 at the end of the chapter (Table A2.1) we present all 5,669 lot number records for Henderson, including the corrected and updated entries for the first 2,027 numbers. The lot numbers for Bloom Mound will be published elsewhere.

Henderson is an E-shaped, adobe village containing perhaps as many as 100 to 130 rooms (Fig. 2.3, the problems with estimating the number of rooms at Henderson is addressed in Chapter 21). The Main Bar is oriented approximately 60° west of true north, with the short bars (West, Center, East) extending out to the southwest or away from the Hondo. The open spaces enclosed between the Main Bar and the short bars form two roughly square plazas, the West Plaza between the West and Center Bars, and the East Plaza between the Center and East Bars. The pueblo, including plazas, covers a maximum area of approximately 2,640 m^2 (0.26 ha or 0.65 acres). The area occupied just by the room blocks is about 1,830 m^2 (0.18 ha or 0.45 acres). Since room outlines were often very difficult to determine from the surface, even with extensive shovel-stripping, the area occupied by rooms was estimated from the contour map of the site, arbitrarily selecting as the structure's perimeter the point where the ground surface first rises appreciably above the surrounding terrain. Since portions of rooms may have collapsed or eroded outward, the actual area of the structure is probably less than 1,830 m^2. Reducing this figure by 20% produces a more conservative and probably more realistic areal estimate of about 1,460 m^2 (0.15 ha or 0.38 acres) for the architectural portion of the site. The plazas occupy an additional 810 m^2 (West Plaza 390 m^2; East Plaza 420 m^2).

The discovery in 1994 that much of the Main Bar may consist of small, square, semi-subterranean structures rather than large, rectangular, above-ground dwellings, and the discovery of several such "pit structures" in areas we thought were plaza, may suggest that the architectural portion of the site is somewhat larger than 1,460 m^2. Reducing the 1,830 m^2 figure by 20% may be excessive.

The area and volume of sediment excavated in the five seasons of work at the site, broken down by major proveniences, are summarized in Table 2.1. These data provide an important baseline for standardizing count data in terms of items per cubic meter of sediment, and are relied upon extensively in later sections of this report.

Most of the rooms in the Main Bar of the "E" appear to be nearly square, with slightly rounded corners, and average about 3 m to 4 m on a side (see Fig. 2.4). The floors of these rooms were set well below the original ground surface (generally more than 25 cm), giving them the appearance of shallow pitrooms. Four upright posts set near the corners supported the roof. Upright limestone slabs were set at ground level and served as the base for the adobe superstructure. Sometimes these footings consisted of double rows of upright slabs oriented parallel to the wall, but at other times the stones were placed in a single line, either oriented perpendicular to the wall or lying flat. Fragments of deliberately broken metates (invariably made of limestone) were sometimes incorporated into these footings. The roofs appear to have been flat and entry was through a hatch. We encountered no unambiguous traces of doorways. Most rooms had multiple floors, each separated from the floor beneath by 5 cm to 10+ cm of deliberately introduced ashy fill. At least two of the excavated structures in the Main Bar started out as domestic dwellings (as suggested by the presence of a hearth in each) and were then converted into storage structures that lacked fireplaces.

Interestingly, what constituted the "original ground surface" at Henderson, both in the Main Bar and elsewhere in the vil-

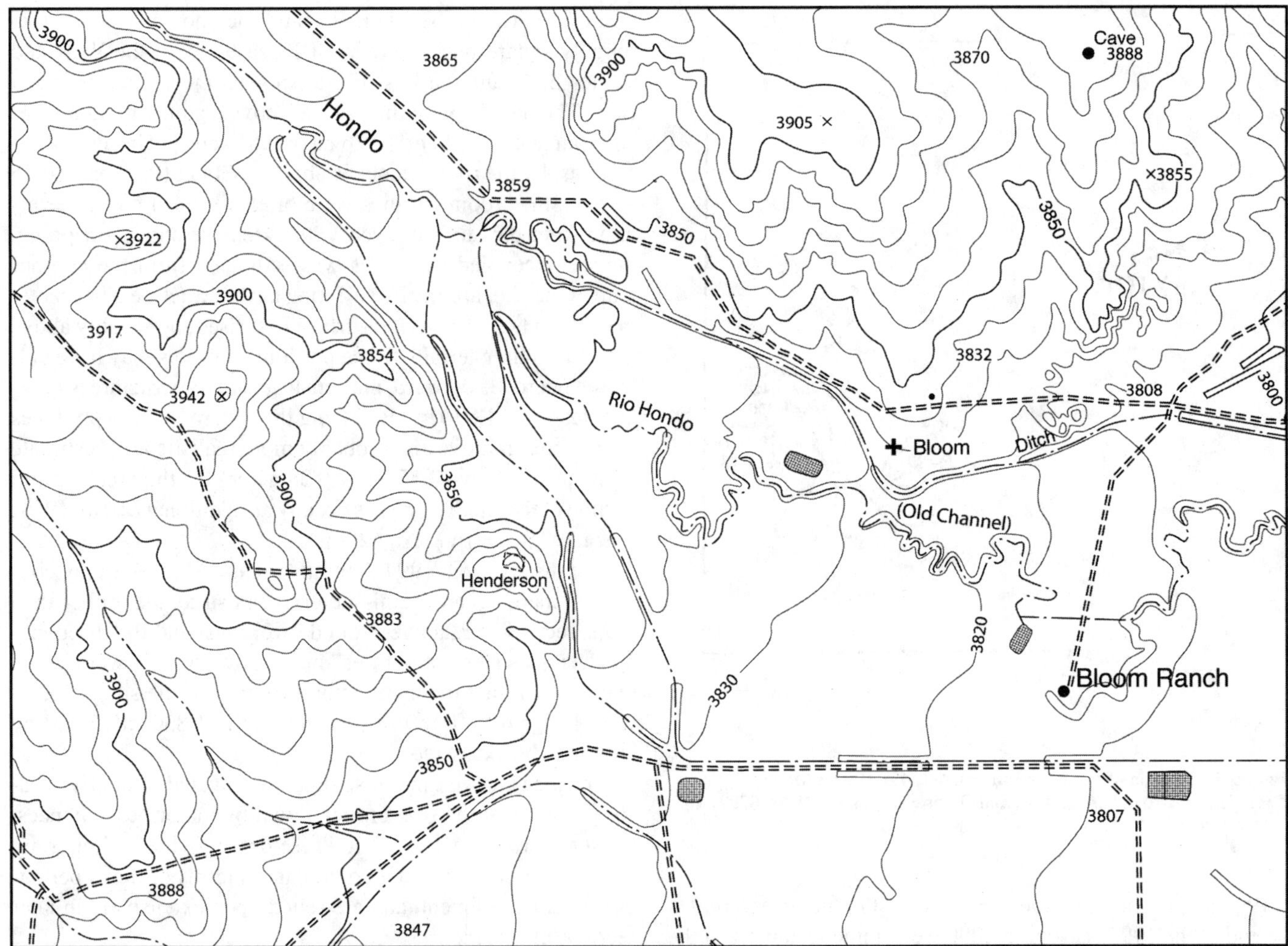

Figure 2.2. Point where Hondo River breaks into Pecos Valley, showing location of Henderson Site (LA-1549) and Bloom Mound (LA-2528) (adapted from USGS Hondo reservoir 7.5 Minute Quadrangle, Topographic Series, 1949 edition).

lage, was often artifact-rich midden dumped on to what had once been plaza surface. Thus, the upright limestone slabs were often set on earlier cultural fill, not on sterile pre-occupation deposits. As a consequence, the basal portion of many of the walls was unconsolidated midden faced with a thin veneer of plaster. Unfortunately, this veneer was seldom preserved, except along a narrow strip right at the base of the wall where the wall bonded with the floor plaster. This meant that, even when the upright slabs of a room were clearly visible on the modern surface, as they sometimes were, it was nevertheless exceedingly difficult to trace the walls down to the floor. We eventually abandoned the idea of exposing walls from the surface downward, and instead targeted the floor first and then identified the position of the walls by locating the point where the floor plaster curved up to bond with the wall.

The rooms in the smaller, southward-extending bars of the "E" were rectangular rather than square, with square rather than rounded corners. These rooms often are much larger than those in the Main Bar, averaging 3 m to 3.5 m in width by 5 m to 6 m in length (see Figs. 2.5, 2.6). Their floors were set at or only slightly below the original ground surface. As in the Main Bar structures, upright limestone slabs were placed at ground level to serve as a base for the adobe walls. Again, entry was through a hatch in the roof. Except in the Center Bar, many of the rooms had been eroded down to the limestone footings. Fortunately, the primary floors in these rooms, most of which were at least 5 cm thick and quite well plastered, were reasonably well preserved, and pothunters generally abandoned their digging when they hit the uprights, leaving primary floors, and subfloor features such as burials, largely intact. Most, if not all, of the structures at Henderson appear to have been one story, although the relatively high relief in the central and northern portions of the Center Bar makes it possible, though unlikely, that a few of the rooms in this part of the site may have had a second story.

Seriation of the rims of El Paso Polychrome jars, which is discussed further in Chapter 3, reveals that the Main Bar and

Table 2.1. Area and volume of principal excavation units at Henderson Site.[a]

Excavation Unit	Area (m^2)	Volume (m^3)
TOTAL EXCAVATION	314.0	182.6
Great Depression (trench K)	12.0	9.1
East Plaza (trenches B, C, D)	35.0	16.2
trench B	4.0	0.8
trench C	23.0	11.9
trench D	8.0	3.5
East Plaza (East)	14.0	11.3
East Plaza (South)	2.0	0.6
West Plaza (trench G)	8.0	1.9
North Plaza (trench N, test A)	7.0	4.3
Main Bar East (trenches E, J)	58.0	37.0
Room M-1	10.1	10.9
Room M-2	9.2	6.2
Room M-3	5.4	3.4
Main Bar West (trench O)	8.0	3.9
West Bar (trench M)	12.0	6.8
Center Bar (trench F)[b]	41.0	25.8
Room C-1	5.0	2.1
Room C-2	11.2	4.9
Room C-3	7.0	3.1
Room C-4	8.3	6.7
Room C-5	9.1	8.8
Room C-6[b]	0.5	0.2
East Bar (trench A)	117.0	65.7
Room E-1	16.0	5.1
Room E-2	14.9	5.1
Room E-3	13.2	5.1
Room E-4	18.3	10.0
Room E-5	18.2	8.1
Room E-6	5.5	1.6
Room E-7	7.2	6.2
Room E-8	9.5	5.3
Flotation (1980-1981)[c]	—	1.2
Flotation (all seasons)[d]	—	2.5

[a]Areas given for rooms refer to portion excavated, not to total floor area of original room; room volumes exclude subfloor features.
[b]Excludes large "pothunter's" pit (centered on Room C-6) at north end of trench F (Room C-6 values given are for grid square 520N533E only).
[c]A total of 303 flotation samples were taken in 1980-1981 (1,174.5 liters; average 3.88 liters per sample; range 0.2-19.0 liters). Proveniences sampled included most excavation levels, floor contacts, and all features.
[d]A total of 782 flotation samples were taken in all five seasons of excavation (2,511.4 liters; average 3.21 liters per sample; range 0.2-19.0 liters). Proveniences sampled included most excavation levels, floor contacts, and all features.

"Great Depression," and possibly also the West Bar, predate the Center Bar and East Bar, as well as the fill in the East Plaza. Over time the village shifted from a linear, or L-shaped, room block (Main Bar and perhaps West Bar) consisting of small, square, pitroom-like dwellings, to an E-shaped community, and several (most?) Main Bar structures were converted to store rooms. The large, rectangular Center Bar and East Bar rooms were then used as dwellings. The seriation also suggests that the East Bar is the youngest room block at the site, probably remaining in use after occupation declined sharply, or ceased altogether, in other parts of the site.

Four, and sometimes six, upright posts, each roughly 10 cm in diameter, supported the roof of each structure. According to Archer (1994), most structural beams were ash (*Fraxinus* sp.), although a few were *Acer* (either box elder, *A. negundo*, or bigtooth maple, *A. grandidentatum*). Hearths tended to be located along the midline of the rooms, though often not at their geometric center. At least one hearth was found in each of the rooms we tested. Ash pits or heating pits were also found along the midline axis, again offset from the center. Several of the hearths in the East Bar had distinct adobe collars, while elsewhere in the site hearths were either semi-spherical, with no trace of a collar, or less formal, shallow, basin-shaped pits. The occurrence of collared hearths in the East Bar, the last portion of the site to be occupied, and at Bloom Mound, which appears to postdate Henderson slightly, suggest that this form of fireplace may have chronological significance in the Roswell area. None of the hearths in the rooms was lined by stones and no ventilator shafts or deflectors (adobe or stone) were found.

Most of the rooms had evidence of multiple floors separated by up to several centimeters of trash or sterile fill. Primary floors typically were well made, whereas younger floors tended to be thin and poorly plastered. Many of these younger floors, in fact, were so ephemeral that we often had to establish their reality in profile before attempting to trace them horizontally. In many instances, walls showed evidence of replastering and rebuilding, with additions not uncommonly using adobe that differed in color and composition from the original wall segments. No traces of paint or colored plaster were found on walls or floors. Only one of the sampled rooms, a badly eroded structure at the south end of the Center Bar (Room C-2), showed clear evidence of burning. The evidence consisted of charred roofing beams and reeds lying more or less directly on the floor.

The sampled rooms had not been abandoned hastily; none had useable items left *in situ* on the floor. Even metates were seldom left in place. In fact, most metates, despite their massive size and limited wear, had been deliberately broken and either discarded or incorporated as uprights in the walls (see Chapter 17). Floors were generally clean, "floor-contact" artifacts were usually materials that had been dumped into the structures soon after their abandonment. Stubs of unburned upright support beams in Room E-4 in the East Bar remained in place; in most of the other rooms that we sampled, the beams had apparently been salvaged prehistorically as no trace of decayed wood was found in the postholes.

Most of the sampled rooms had one or more burials beneath the floors in ovoid, steep-sided pits. Some of the burial pits had been deliberately sealed beneath the primary floor, while others showed no trace of a plaster seal and may have been intrusive from a younger floor in the room. Subfloor pits, other than those used for burials, were not very common. Moreover, most of the nonburial pits were small, cylindrical features that would have been unsuitable for large-scale storage of foods. Some of these in fact may have been postholes that were abandoned and sealed under a new floor when a room was remodeled. A few of

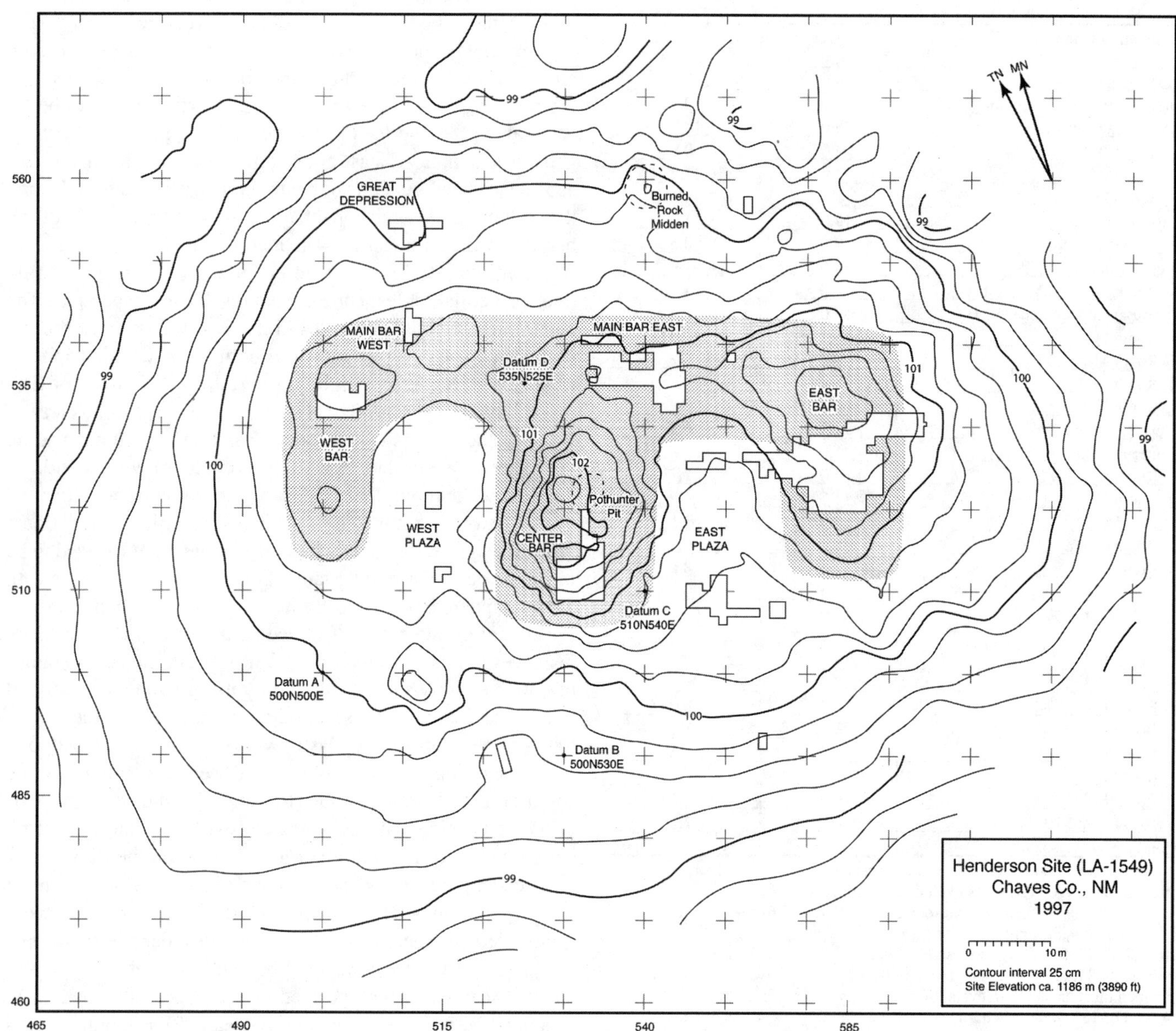

Figure 2.3. Contour map of Henderson Site (LA-1549), showing all major excavation units.

these cylindrical pits had been deliberately "plugged" by placing a piece of adobe near the top of the pit. The plug was largely or entirely symbolic, however, as it was normally much smaller than the diameter of the mouth of the pit and it never formed a clear bond with the surrounding floor surface or with the adjacent walls of the pit. While most of these pits were empty, a few contained items that had been cached, most notably grooved stone axes and manos.

The subfloor burials recovered in 1980 and 1981 (all from the Center Bar and East Bar) were the primary focus of the previous monograph on the Henderson Site (Rocek and Speth 1986), and only a brief summary is presented here.[3] Eleven bodies were found in ten discrete burial features in the Center and East Bars (one feature contained two individuals—an adult female and a fetus). The burials include one fetus, two infants, and eight adults. Of the adults, four were male, four were female. The immature individuals could not be reliably sexed. Six of the ten burial features were found in a single room (E-4) in the East Bar. Most of the burials were placed on their right sides or their backs, with legs flexed. One individual was placed on his left side, another on his back and left side. No clear association was found between burial orientation and age, sex, spa-

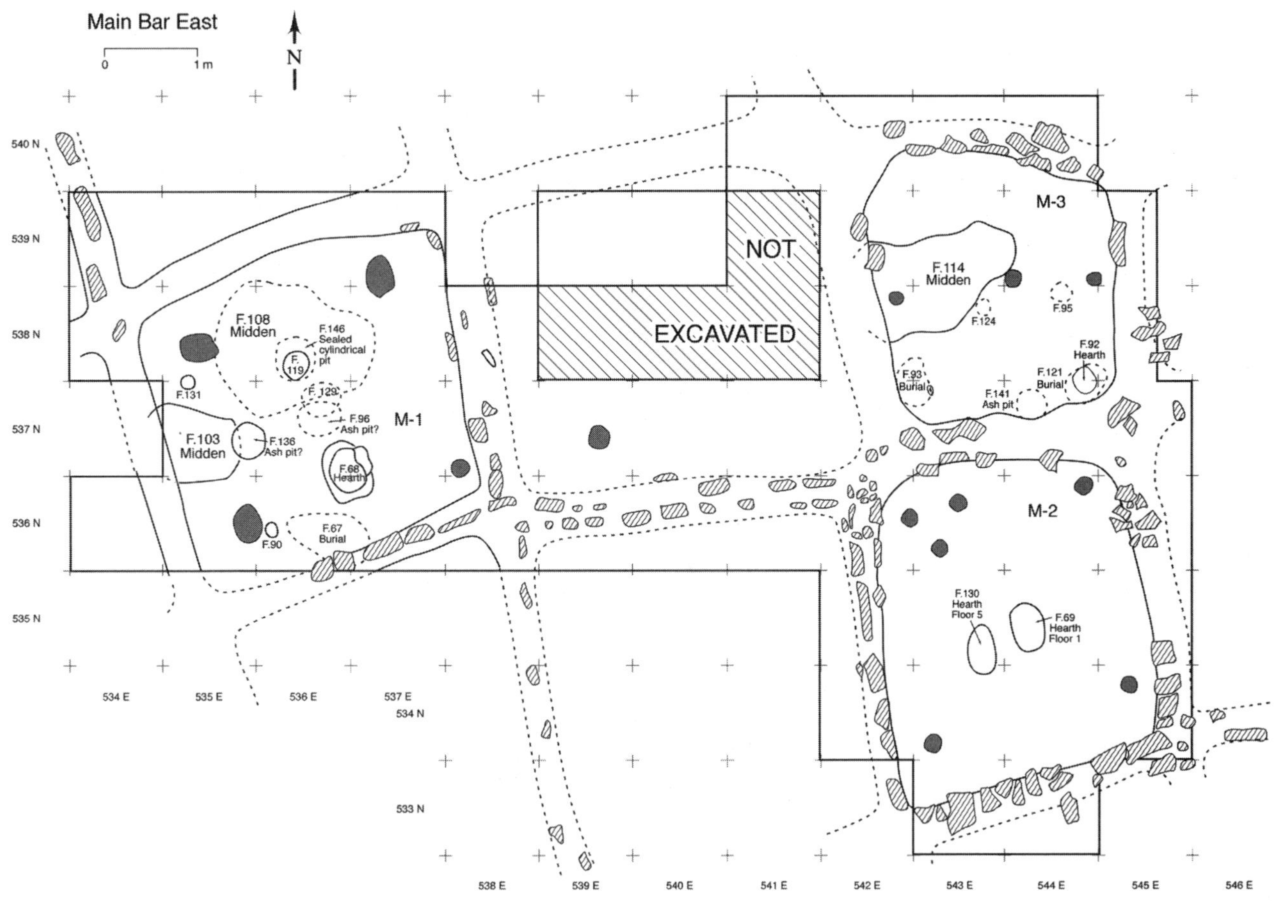

Figure 2.4. Main Bar East (trenches E and J), showing excavated rooms and features.

tial placement, or stratigraphic placement, although this may simply be a result of small sample size. Bodies tended to be placed relatively close to and parallel to walls. At least seven of the individuals bore traces of some sort of mat wrapping. The absence of matting on the remaining four may be an artifact of preservation.

Six individuals were accompanied by grave goods, including: pottery vessels (a small Lincoln Black-on-red bowl, small Chupadero Black-on-white jar nested within the Lincoln bowl, large Heshotauthla Polychrome bowl); coiled basketry; a variety of disc-shell beads, pendants, and other personal ornaments; caches of projectile points, many of archaic stylistic affiliation and made on Plains lithic materials including Alibates and Edwards Plateau chert (one, a "turkey-tail," was made on Tiger chert derived from southwestern Wyoming—see Whittaker et al. 1988); bone "awls" or "hairpieces" and tortoise-shell "gaming pieces"; and miscellaneous lithic items. Two wooden "prayer sticks" were also encountered; one was rod-like with a round or square cross-section to which were attached numerous *Olivella* beads, the other was thin and flat and cut into the form of a stylized corn plant. Grave goods were absent with the two youngest individuals (fetus and a roughly 3- to 6-month-old infant) and with the oldest individual (more than 40 years old), and most abundant with a 2.5- to 3.5-year-old child.

Chronology

While the general temporal placement of the Henderson Site is reasonably clear, there are several chronological issues that could not be resolved at the time of the publication of the first monograph on the site (Rocek and Speth 1986:8-23). These issues are discussed more thoroughly here and a series of new radiocarbon dates, all run on the accelerator, are presented and

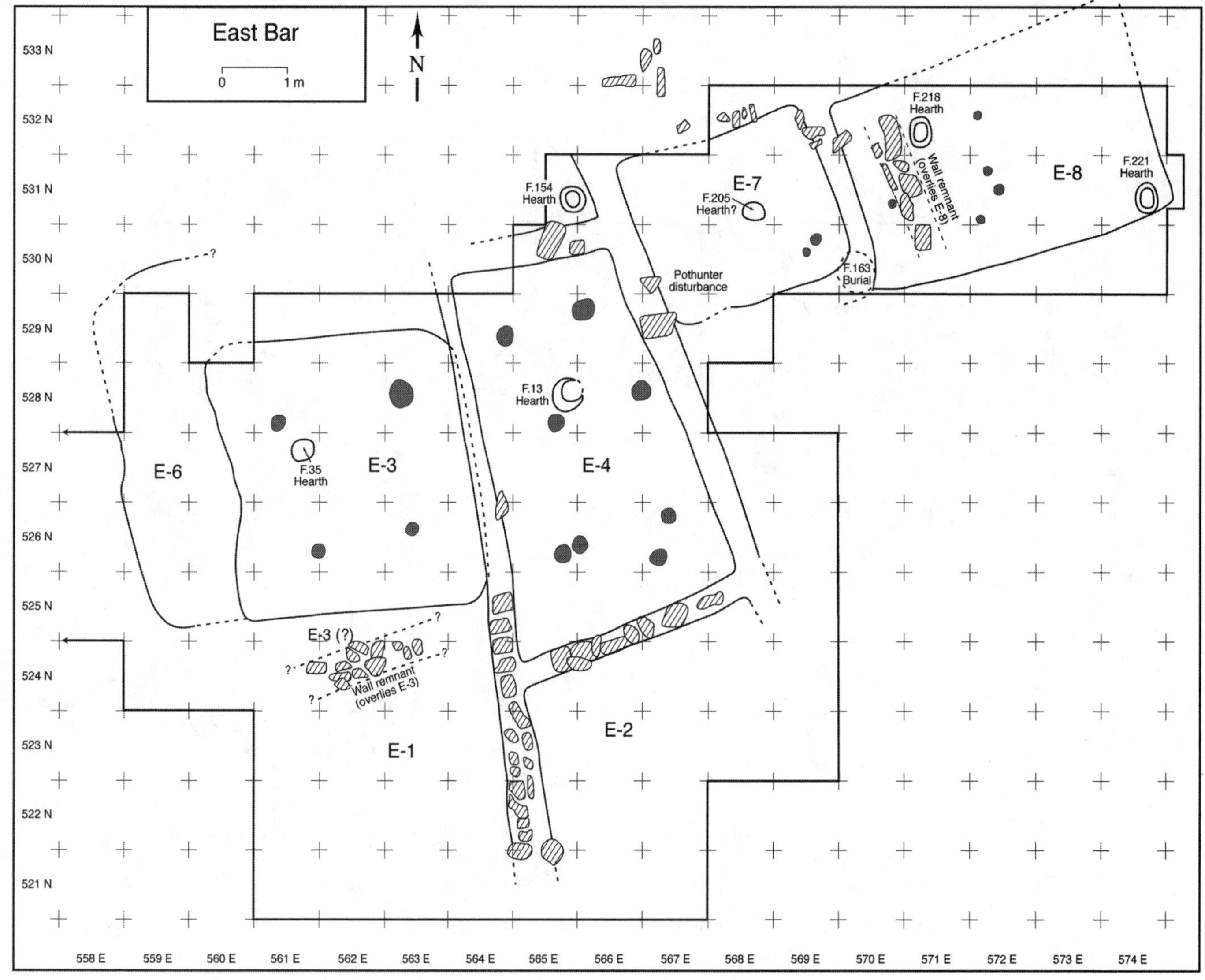

Figure 2.5. East Bar (trench A), showing excavated rooms and features.

evaluated. We also find it necessary to revise the phase terminology presented in the 1986 publication.

As discussed in Rocek and Speth (1986), the site's ceramic assemblage, as well as fourteen conventional radiocarbon dates and six archaeomagnetic dates, all clearly bracketed the age of the site between roughly A.D. 1200/1250 and 1400/1450. The ceramics are dominated by El Paso Polychrome, Chupadero Black-on-white, and Lincoln Black-on-red, typical of so-called "Lincoln phase" sites in southeastern New Mexico (Kelley 1984; Wiseman 1976), with lesser amounts of Three Rivers Red-on-terracotta, Gila Polychrome, Corona Corrugated, Heshotauthla Polychrome, St. Johns Polychrome, and trace amounts of several other types (see Chapter 3).

The abandonment date is compatible with the projectile point assemblage, in particular the virtual absence of Harrell points, small triangular side-notched arrow points with a third notch located centrally in the base (Bell 1958; Parry and Speth 1984). Out of several hundred identifiable arrow points and point fragments, only a single Harrell base was recovered—in the East Bar area—and it was encountered in the upper few centimeters of highly disturbed surficial deposits (see Chapter 15). In the Southern Plains area of southeastern New Mexico and the Texas panhandle, Harrell points probably do not become common until about A.D. 1450 (Parry and Speth 1984:31-32).

The fourteen conventional radiocarbon dates, all run by Beta Analytic, Inc., were ^{13}C fractionation-corrected and then calibrated using several different schemes available at the time (Ralph et al. 1973; Damon et al. 1974; Stuiver 1982; Klein et al. 1982). While all of the calibration schemes led to similar conclusions, we relied most heavily on the Stuiver calibration because it seemed to provide the most internally consistent results. The radiocarbon dates appeared to fall into two clusters,

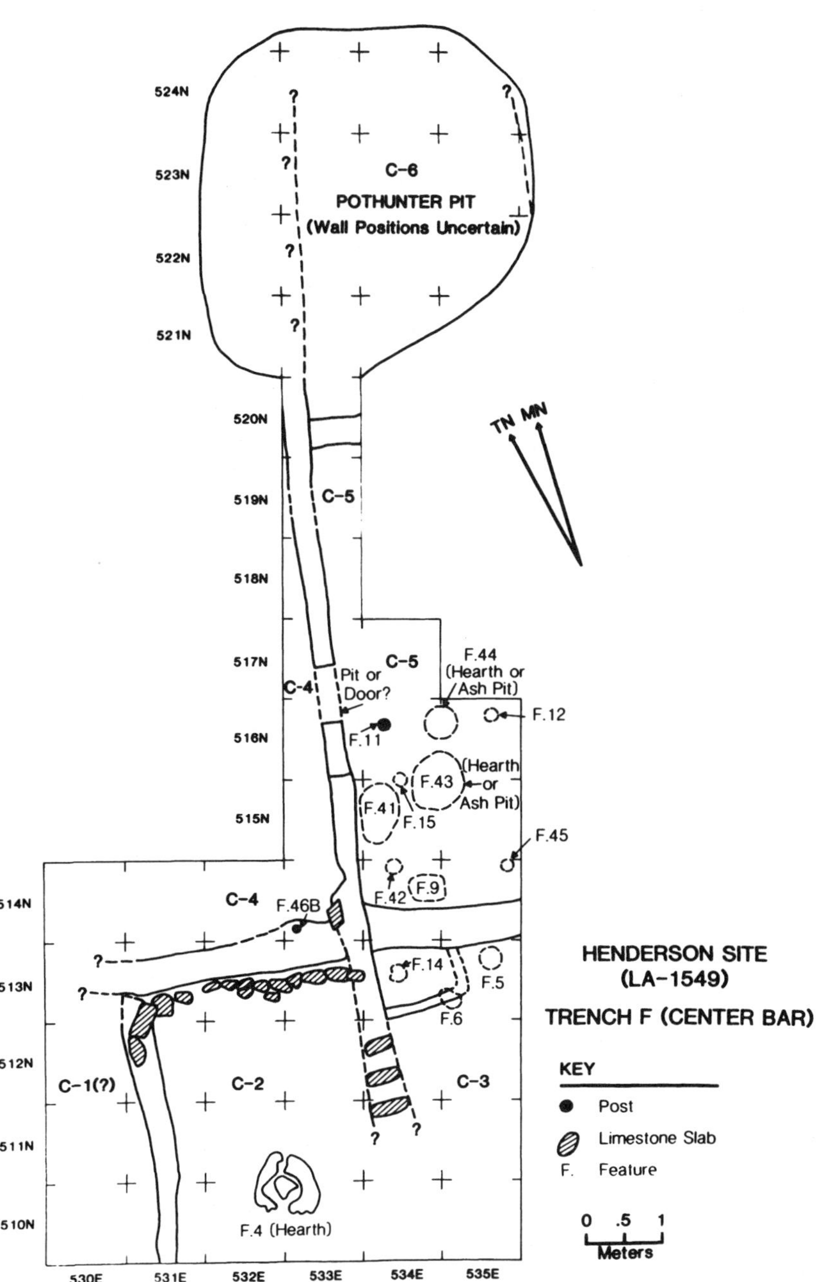

Figure 2.6. Center Bar (trench F), showing excavated rooms and features.

the first prior to about A.D. 1300, the second in the late 1300s or early 1400s.

In 1986 we referred to these two clusters of dates as the "Early" and "Late" phases of occupation, although we stressed the tentative nature of these designations. One obvious source of uncertainty stemmed directly from the calibration process itself. Some of the radiocarbon dates when calibrated corresponded to two or more calendrical dates, and it became necessary to draw on other information to decide which of the possible outcomes was the most reasonable. Another source of uncertainty stemmed from the fact that we were forced in several instances to date structural beams which may have been recycled prehistorically and which may also have been missing a substantial number of outside rings. Thus, the dates provided by these samples may be older than the events we sought to date (the so-called "old wood" problem discussed by Smiley 1985). Moreover, in a few cases we were forced to pool dispersed pieces of charcoal from arbitrary excavation levels to obtain sufficient material for dating. The reliability of these pooled samples was also open to question.

To circumvent the problems arising from "old wood" and "pooling," we submitted eight additional samples, seven consisting of burned maize cob fragments and one consisting of a single burned maize kernel, for accelerator (AMS) dating. These

Table 2.2. New accelerator dates from Henderson Site: provenience and sample description.

Lab. No.[a]	Grid Sq./ Level Elev. (m)	Locus	Sample Description
Beta-16126	509N549E 99.70-99.60	East Plaza	Burned maize cob fragment from lower half of East Plaza trash deposit.
Beta-16127	509N550E 99.60-99.50	East Plaza	Burned maize cob fragment from lower half of East Plaza trash deposit.
Beta-16128	509N549E 99.80-99.70	East Plaza	Burned maize cob fragment from lower half of East Plaza trash deposit.
Beta-20116 (ETH-2908)	509N547E 100.00-99.90	East Plaza	Burned maize cob fragment from upper half of East Plaza trash deposit.
Beta-20117 (ETH-2909)	508N551E 100.10-100.00	East Plaza	Burned maize cob fragment from upper half of East Plaza trash deposit.
Beta-25362 (ETH-3783)	526N566E 101.25-101.15	East Bar	Single burned maize kernel from fill between Floors 1 and 2, Room E-4.
Beta-25363 (ETH-3784)	528N567E 101.35-101.25	East Bar	Burned maize cob fragment from fill on or directly above Floor 2, Room E-4.
Beta-25364 (ETH-3785)	527N567E 101.40-101.30	East Bar	Burned maize cob fragment from fill above Floor 2, Room E-4.

[a]All samples for accelerator dating were submitted to Beta Analytic, Inc., Coral Gables, Florida where they were assigned "Beta-" sample numbers; samples were then forwarded to the Eidgenossische Technische Hochschule in Zurich for accelerator dating and assigned separate "ETH-" numbers (those provided to the authors by Beta Analytic are included in table). Chemical pretreatment and target material preparation were done at Beta Analytic.

new samples and their dates are summarized in Tables 2.2 and 2.3. The first table presents the relevant contextual information for the newly dated samples; the second summarizes the actual dates obtained by accelerator dating, calibrated in June 1999 according to the most recent calibration scheme (Stuiver and Reimer 1993; Stuiver and Becker 1993; Stuiver et al. 1998). For completeness, the fourteen previously published conventional radiocarbon dates are also included in the second table, and recalibrated according to Stuiver and Reimer (1993) to make them comparable to the accelerator determinations.

Before discussing the chronological implications of these dates, certain of the calibration results shown in Table 2.3 deserve specific comment. Beta-3333, for example, yielded three possible calibrated dates: 1334, 1336, and 1400. In subsequent discussion, we use only the A.D. 1400 date, because Beta-3332, which came from the same hearth, yielded a single calibrated date of A.D. 1406. The contents of the hearth—burned twigs—were divided and submitted to Beta as two separate samples. Beta-8320 from the East Plaza midden accumulation also yielded three possible calibrated dates: 1302, 1369, and 1382. In this case, we use the earliest of the three, A.D. 1302, because numerous other samples from the same deposits show that the midden accumulated between about A.D. 1260 and A.D. 1300. Similarly, Beta-14067, from the fill of a shallow hearth on the primary floor of Room C-5, produced three calibrated dates, and we again use the earliest one (A.D. 1304) because other dates from the fill of the structure clearly show that it was in use and abandoned sometime close to A.D. 1300. Finally, Beta-14071, pooled charcoal from the East Plaza, also produced three possible calibrated dates (1163, 1173, 1180), and in this case all appear to be too early. While the sample contained twigs, which should not have posed an "old wood" problem, the sample also incorporated larger "chunks" of wood charcoal that might have been interior fragments of construction beams, perhaps even beams that had been recycled from elsewhere. Hence, in subsequent discussion, Beta-14071 is treated as an outlier.

Turning now to the implications of the results shown in Table 2.3, it is clear that the majority of dates, regardless of provenience, fall within the middle to late thirteenth century. Moreover, the archaeomagnetic dates presented in Rocek and Speth (1986:23) remain entirely consistent with these recalibrated radiocarbon determinations. Thus, it seems safe to conclude that a major occupation at the Henderson Site did, in fact, take place during the last third of the thirteenth century, the period we referred to in 1986 as the "Early phase" (Rocek and Speth 1986).

The existence of a more ephemeral "Late phase" occupation (or reoccupation) is also supported by the recalibrated dates. Two radiocarbon dates from Feature 31, a rock-encircled hearth sitting atop, and immediately postdating, the massive trash accumulation in the East Plaza (see Fig. 15 in Rocek and Speth 1986:32), as well as two radiocarbon dates from East Bar Room E-4 and one archaeomagnetic date from Center Bar Room C-2, all date within the first few decades of the fifteenth century. Whether the site was abandoned entirely between the two occupational episodes cannot be determined with the data at hand.

Since the majority of the dates appear to fall within a relatively brief span of time in the thirteenth century, and for the most part within the latter half of that century, the calibrated average of the radiocarbon dates should provide a more precise estimate of the temporal placement of the East Bar, Center Bar, and East Plaza. The average can actually be calculated in several different ways, each providing a slightly different estimate for the mean age of the site (see Table 2.4). For example, one can average just the eight new AMS dates, thereby circumvent-

Table 2.3. Conventional and accelerator dates from Henderson Site (LA-1549): uncalibrated and calibrated dates.

Lab. No.[a]	Grid Sq./ Elev. (m)	Locus	Uncal. (BP ± 1σ)[b]	Calibrated (± 1σ)[c]
Beta-2851	528N567E 101.05 (F. 18)	Room E-4	460±80	1410 (1436) 1480
Beta-3332	512N550E 100.13-100.00 (F. 31)	East Plaza	550±30	1331 (1406) 1418
Beta-3333	512N550E 100.13-100.00 (F. 31)	East Plaza	570±30	1326 (1334,1336,1400) 1410
Beta-3334	526N564E 100.64	Room E-3	1000±40	1000 (1021) 1145
Beta-3335	526N564E 100.64	Room E-3	700±30	1281 (1290) 1298
Beta-3336	527N567E 101.06	Room E-4	530±30	1402 (1412) 1427
Beta-3337	528N562E 100.75-100.70	Room E-3	740±30	1266 (1280) 1288
Beta-8320	508N549E 99.50-99.40	East Plaza	640±40	1295 (1302,1369,1382) 1393
Beta-14067	515N534E 100.60 (F. 43)	Room C-5	630±40	1297 (1304,1367,1385) 1396
Beta-14068	511N532E 101.15-101.05	Room C-2	1080±110	784 (981) 1029
Beta-14069	516N535E 101.00-100.80	Room C-5	750±40	1259 (1278) 1288
Beta-14070	527N566E 101.00 (F. 24)	Room E-4	850±40	1161 (1212) 1242
Beta-14071	509N549E 99.80-99.70	East Plaza	880±40	1059 (1163,1173,1180) 1216
Beta-14072	516N535E 101.20-101.00	Room C-5	690±40	1282 (1293) 1379
*Beta-16126	509N549E 99.70-99.60	East Plaza	680±80	1276 (1296) 1393
*Beta-16127	509N550E 99.60-99.50	East Plaza	750±80	1218 (1278) 1298
*Beta-16128	509N549E 99.80-99.70	East Plaza	670±80	1278 (1297) 1396
*Beta-20116 (ETH-2908)	509N547E 100.00-99.90	East Plaza	900±80	1024 (1160) 1221
*Beta-20117 (ETH-2909)	508N551E 100.10-100.00	East Plaza	730±85	1222 (1282) 1380
*Beta-25362 (ETH-3783)	526N566E 101.25-101.15	Room E-4	795±85	1163 (1257) 1287
*Beta-25363 (ETH-3784)	528N567E 101.35-101.25	Room E-4	815±80	1160 (1222) 1282
*Beta-25364 (ETH-3785)	527N567E 101.40-101.30	Room E-4	710±80	1259 (1287) 1385

[a]All samples submitted for accelerator (AMS) dating (Beta lab numbers preceded by asterisks) were submitted to Beta Analytic, Inc., Coral Gables, Florida where they were assigned "Beta-" sample numbers; samples were then forwarded to the Eidgenossische Technische Hochschule in Zurich for accelerator dating and assigned separate "ETH-" numbers (those provided to the authors by Beta Analytic are included in table). Chemical pretreatment and target material preparation were done at Beta Analytic.

[b]Uncalibrated BP dates. Conventional dates corrected for ^{13}C-fractionation; half-life (5,570 years), age referenced to AD 1950 (see Rocek and Speth 1986 for fractionation data for conventional radiocarbon determinations).

[c]Calibrated AD dates. Each date includes the calibrated one-sigma range, separated by actual calibration date(s) in parentheses. For example, the date of AD 1295 (1302, 1369, 1382) 1393 indicates three possible calibrations (AD 1302, 1369, 1382) and a one-sigma range of AD 1295-1393. Calibrations were performed in June 1999 using The University of Washington, Quaternary Isotope Lab, Radiocarbon Calibration Program, Revision 4.1.2 for the Macintosh (Stuiver and Reimer 1993; Stuiver et al. 1998).

Table 2.4. Conventional and accelerator dates from Henderson Site (LA-1549): calibrated average dates.

Samples	*n*	Calibrated Average	
		AD ±1σ[a]	AD ±1σ[b]
All AMS dates	8	1216 (1277) 1297	1260 (1277) 1284
East Plaza AMS dates	5	1219 (1279) 1298	1261 (1279) 1288
East Bar AMS dates	3	1194 (1267) 1293	1220 (1267) 1283
All AMS and conventional dates	22	1258 (1282) 1297	1278 (1282) 1285
Excluding 2 oldest dates (Beta-3334, 14068)	20	1276 (1289) 1380	1284(1289) 1295
Excluding dates pre-AD 1250 (Beta-3334, 14068, 14070, 14071, 20116)	17	1282 (1297) 1389	1294 (1297) 1377
Excluding dates pre-AD 1250 and 4 youngest dates (Beta-2851, 3332, 3333, 3334, 3336, 14068, 14070, 14071, 20116)	13	1264 (1285) 1378	1281 (1285) 1292

[a]Average sigma used in calibration calculated by taking simple grand mean of individual sigmas. Each date includes the calibrated one-sigma range, separated by actual calibration date in parentheses. For example, a date of AD 1276 (1289) 1380 indicates a calibrated date of AD 1289 and a one-sigma range of AD 1276-1380. Calibrations were performed using The University of Washington, Quaternary Isotope Lab, Radiocarbon Calibration Program, Revision 4.1.2 for the Macintosh (Stuiver and Reimer 1993; Stuiver et al. 1998).
[b]Average sigma used in calibration calculated according to method described in Long and Rippeteau (1974:209). Calibrations were performed using The University of Washington, Quaternary Isotope Lab, Radiocarbon Calibration Program, Revision 4.1.2 for the Macintosh (Stuiver and Reimer 1993; Stuiver et al. 1998).

ing the problems of "old wood" and pooled samples. The calibrated average of these dates points to occupation of the East Plaza and East Bar centered on A.D. 1277. The five AMS dates from the East Plaza by themselves yield a calibrated average date of A.D. 1279, while the three from the East Bar produce a slightly older average of A.D. 1267. If one takes the least conservative approach, which is to average all 22 of the radiocarbon dates run thus far from Henderson, to ignore the possible existence of two occupational phases at the site, but to include two obvious outliers (Beta-14068, A.D. 981, and Beta-3334, A.D. 1021) that are almost certainly too old, the result—A.D. 1282—is very similar to the AMS-based estimates. A more reasonable approach is to exclude the two outliers, computing the average on the remaining 20 dates. This precaution nevertheless produces a very similar estimate of A.D. 1289. An even more cautious approach is to drop the two outliers plus the other three samples with dates prior to A.D. 1250 (Beta-3334, 14068, 14070, 14071, 20116). The new estimate is A.D. 1297. However, if there are in fact two distinct phases of occupation at the site, then it would make sense to also drop the four early fifteenth-century dates (Beta-2851, 3332, 3333, 3336). The remaining 13 dates yield a calibrated average for the Henderson "Early phase" occupation of A.D. 1285. In sum, if the calibration curves are reasonably on target, it seems safe to conclude that the principal ("Early phase") occupation at Henderson falls between about A.D. 1260 and A.D. 1300, with some brief use, or reuse, of the site around A.D. 1400. The actual duration of these two occupations is unknown, but neither is likely to have lasted more than about 35 to 50 years.

In 1996 we began experimenting with the seriation of Henderson's El Paso Polychrome jar rims, initially simply to see whether our rims had similar profiles to rims from sites of broadly comparable age in the El Paso area, where seriation of this ceramic type was first shown to have chronological significance (Carmichael 1985, 1986; Seaman and Mills 1988; West 1982; Whalen 1993; see also discussion on El Paso Polychrome in Chapter 3). Not only were our rim profiles very similar to those from the El Paso area more than 200 km to the southwest of Roswell, an interesting finding in its own right, but to our surprise our rim profiles, when quantified by a "rim sherd index" (RSI) that expresses the ratio of maximum rim thickness to minimum vessel wall thickness, fell into two distinct clusters, the later one including the rims from the Center Bar, East Bar, and East Plaza, and the earlier one including the rims from the Main Bar, Great Depression, and perhaps also the West Bar and West Plaza.[4] This made it clear that a major occupation had occurred at Henderson prior to what we had referred to as the "Early phase" on the basis of the 1980-1981 excavations (Rocek and Speth 1986). Thus, in order to avoid confusion in the future, we find it necessary to revise the phase sequence (see Table 2.5). Henceforth, "Late " will refer to the occupation that took

Table 2.5. Revised phase nomenclature for Henderson Site.

Rocek and Speth (1986)	This Volume	Provenience
—	"Early phase"	Main Bar, West Bar(?), West Plaza(?), Great Depression
"Early phase"	"Late phase"	Center Bar, East Bar, East Plaza, Main Bar[a]
"Late phase"	"Terminal phase"	Center Bar, East Bar, East Plaza

[a]Some structures in the Main Bar apparently continued in use into the Late phase.

Figure 2.7. East Plaza (trenches B and C) earth oven complex, showing sloping bedrock floor of depression and large quantities of fire-cracked rock.

Figure 2.8. Close-up of East Plaza (trench C) earth oven complex, showing large quantities of fire-cracked rock and bison bone.

place during the latter part of the thirteenth century (ca. A.D. 1270-1300+), and "Terminal phase" will refer to the ephemeral occupation (or reoccupation) of the village around A.D. 1400. The temporal placement of the newly defined "Early phase" remains uncertain, but almost certainly falls within the mid-1200s (perhaps ca. A.D. 1250-1270). Additional ^{14}C dates will be submitted in the near future to clarify the chronological placement of the Main Bar, Great Depression, West Bar, and other proveniences and features thought to date largely or entirely to the newly defined "Early phase."

Plaza vs. Room Block Trash Deposits

During the nearly three months of fieldwork at Henderson in 1980, excavation concentrated almost entirely on the East

Figure 2.9. Heavy-duty limestone tools associated with bison bone in East Plaza earth oven complex.

Bar and Center Bar room blocks, and yielded only limited deposits of stratified trash. While the burials that we found beneath the floors of several of the rooms provided extremely valuable information about mortuary practices, essential chronological data, and some tantalizing insights into the diet and subsistence practices of the village's inhabitants (Rocek and Speth 1986), one of our principal objectives in excavating at Henderson was to recover economic data. Adequate data were clearly not forthcoming from the rooms, with the notable exception of Room C-5, which produced nearly a meter of ashy stratified trash. Moreover, while there was clear evidence of extensive sheet midden on the slope behind (to the north of) the pueblo, we did not sample these deposits because they appeared to be shallow and disturbed by erosion, trampling by grazing cattle, and burrowing rodents.

Thus, in 1981 we began to sample several obvious depressions around the site in the hope of finding one or more trash-filled kivas or pitrooms. Unfortunately, most of these depressions proved to be shallow natural swales in the underlying limestone bedrock that were nearly devoid of cultural material. The one exception was a large depression at the southern end of the East Plaza which supported a relatively large mesquite bush (East Plaza, trenches B and C). Robert H. Leslie, an avocational archaeologist from Hobbs, New Mexico, pointed out that in his experience a mesquite of this size would require a considerable amount of subsurface fill to accommodate its deep root system. Given the location of the depression within the East Plaza, we thought it would be an excellent candidate for a kiva.

Testing proved otherwise, and instead revealed a deep, elongated natural depression (very likely a shallow karstic sink hole) in the limestone bedrock that had repeatedly served as the locus for a massive earth oven complex. The depression was filled with nearly a meter of dark black ashy midden, thousands of kilograms of fire-cracked rock (mostly limestone), and thousands of bison, antelope, smaller mammal, bird, and fish bones, as well as ceramics, lithics, and other trash (see Figs. 2.7, 2.8). Because the East Plaza earth oven complex contained such an abundance of economic data, much of our effort during the 1981 season was devoted to sampling this important deposit.

The East Plaza midden contained a very distinctive assemblage of expedient "heavy duty" limestone chopperlike and cleaverlike tools, many of which had been used and then tossed into the earth oven feature and burned (see Figs. 2.9, 2.10). These tools included many rounded limestone cobbles that had been flaked along part of their perimeter, sometimes unifacially, sometimes bifacially, resulting in tools very similar to classic Oldowan choppers. Others were large, irregular chunks and blocks of limestone, with a few flakes removed from one of their naturally more acute edges. Unretouched limestone flakes also occurred in the midden. Some of these appear to have been deliberately removed, perhaps in the preparation of the choppers, while others are more likely just spalls that were detached from a block of limestone while it was being used. A few of the more massive flakes may be by-products of metate manufacture, which we believe occurred on site, utilizing the local bedrock limestone (see Chapters 16, 17). Although with the data at hand we cannot demonstrate that the chopper- and cleaverlike tools were used for butchering the huge quantities of bison and antelope in the midden, this is the most plausible explanation for their presence and abundance. Tools of this sort were only rarely encountered elsewhere on the site, the only notable exceptions being in the middens overlying the former plaza surface exposed beneath Room C-5 in the Center Bar (particularly at the base of grid square 517N534E), and in the Great Depression just north of the Main Bar.

We opened a total of 27 m^2 in the East Plaza depression, comprising 23 contiguous one-meter squares (trench C) and a small adjacent block of four one-meter squares (trench B). Be-

Figure 2.10. Limestone flakes associated with bison and antelope bones in East Plaza earth oven complex.

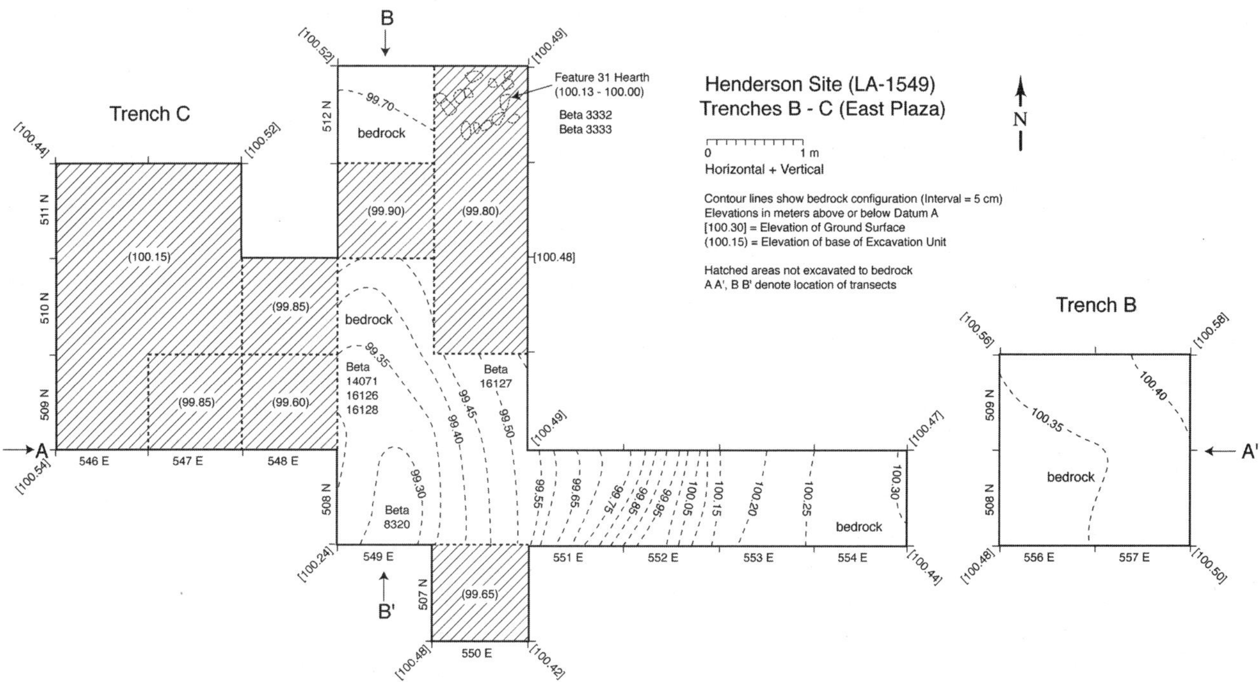

Figure 2.11. Plan of trenches B and C in East Plaza (see Fig. 2.3 for location of trenches).

cause of their proximity, these two trenches are treated as a single unit in all subsequent discussion. The layout of these trenches is shown in Figure 2.11, and stratigraphic sections are shown in Figure 2.12. Only 14 of the squares were excavated down to bedrock. The remaining 13 squares were terminated prior to completion because of unusually heavy rains that nearly filled the trench with water, although most of these squares stopped within 10-20 cm of bedrock.

The processes by which the East Plaza depression came to be filled with trash and fire-cracked rock are fascinating, as subsequent sections of this report will make evident. The nature of the problem can be briefly summarized as follows. Some

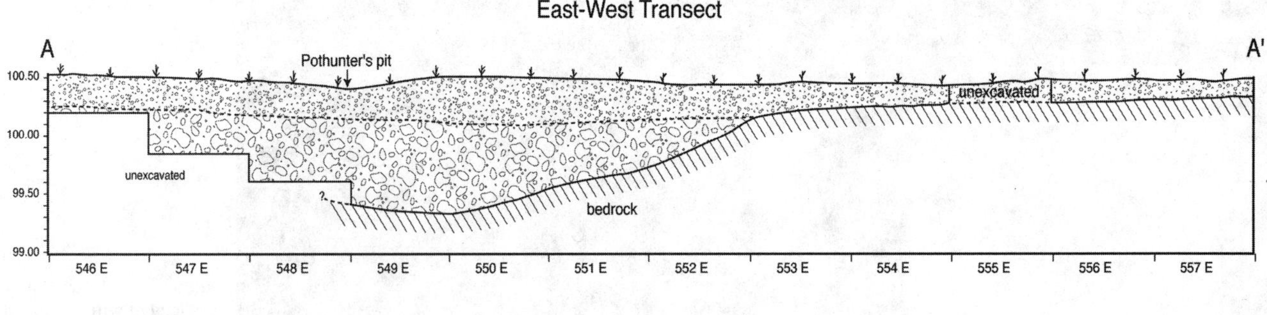

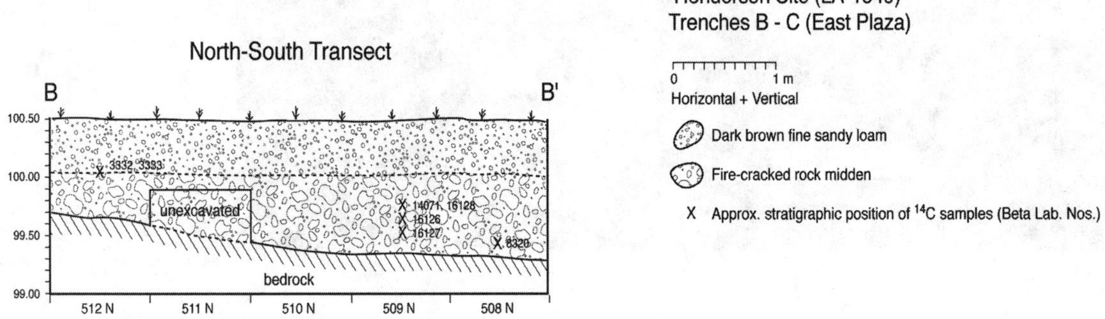

Figure 2.12. *A*. Transverse stratigraphic section through trenches B and C in East Plaza. *B*. Longitudinal stratigraphic section through trench C in East Plaza.

classes of cultural material occur in nearly identical proportions in both Plaza trash and room trash. This implies that trash from the same, or at least very similar, sets of activities sometimes ended up in abandoned rooms, while on other occasions it found its way into the East Plaza depression. Since the distance separating the East Plaza from adjacent room blocks is only 10 m to 15 m, this is hardly surprising. There are also some classes of material that are found only, or predominantly, in the East Plaza midden, suggesting that certain activities were carried on primarily in or around the earth oven complex, or at least that their residues tended to be disposed of there. Most notable among these are fire-cracked rock and bison bones. Both were rare in the rooms, so much so that if we had not sampled the East Plaza we might have concluded (erroneously) that bison hunting was an insignificant subsistence activity of the Henderson villagers.[5] Again, this result may not be particularly surprising, as one would hardly expect the butchering and processing of an animal that weighs in excess of 500 or 600 kg to have occurred in the rooms. But there are many other differences between the trash from the two contexts that are subtle and interesting, and underscore the fact that the fill in the earth oven complex is not merely a carbon copy of the fill that ended up in nearby abandoned structures. For example, even among the smaller-bodied animal taxa, there are significant differences in skeletal completeness, burning frequency, average marrow utility, and average body size. These and other differences point to the more "public" and "communal" nature of the activities and events that took place in and around the East Plaza earth oven complex.

Augering and small-scale testing in the West Plaza revealed no evidence of deposits like those encountered in the East Plaza. Instead, everywhere we sampled we encountered bedrock within 15-20 cm of the modern surface. However, in 1994 we explored a large, nearly circular depression north of the Main Bar near its west end that also proved to be filled with over a meter of fire-cracked rock and animal bones (Figs. 2.13, 2.14). Dubbed the "Great Depression" (trench K), this massive earth oven complex appears to have been contemporary with the "Early phase" occupation of the Main Bar. Like its later counterpart in the East Plaza, this earth oven complex also contained masses of fire-cracked rock and bison bones, as well as bones of smaller mammals, birds, and fish, plus substantial quantities of ceramics and lithics. Limestone choppers and other heavy-duty butchering tools were also common. Interestingly, at the base of the Great Depression, we encountered the unburned, articulated burial of a human infant (which we reburied within the basal deposits), as well as two complete unburned turkey (*Meleagris gallopavo*) burials, presumably "closure offerings" that were interred at the time the earth oven complex was abandoned. Birds were also used as closure offerings elsewhere on the site. For example, an unburned articulated skeleton, not yet formally identified but probably turkey (*Meleagris gallopavo*), was found at the base of a fire-cracked rock–filled earth oven or drying complex directly adjacent to, and stratigraphically beneath, Room M-2 in the Main Bar. In addition, the unburned articulated skeleton of a red-winged blackbird (*Agelaius phoeniceus*) was found beneath a small ash deposit placed directly upon the

Figure 2.13. "Great Depression" (trench K) excavation, showing sloping bedrock floor of depression and large quantities of fire-cracked rock.

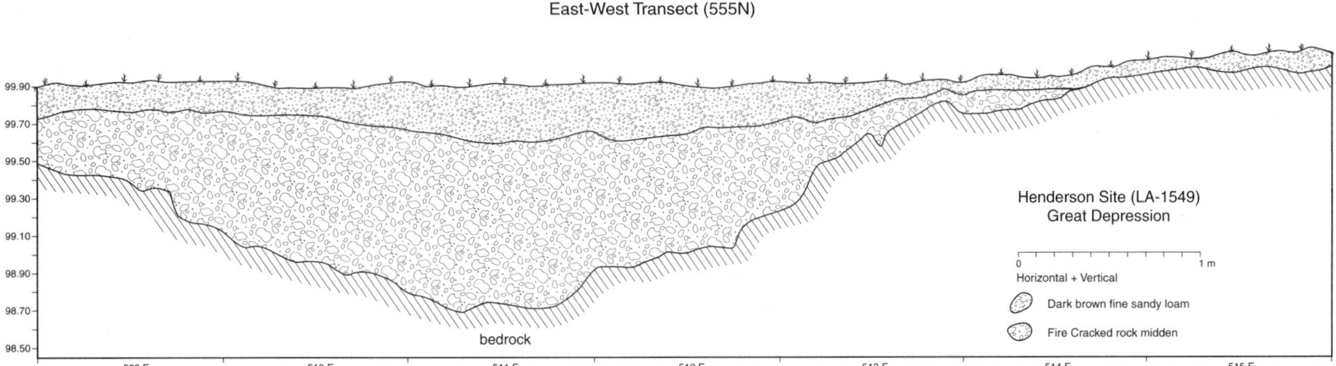

Figure 2.14. Transverse stratigraphic section through trench K in "Great Depression."

limestone slab seal of a cylindrical storage pit located in a plaza surface stratigraphically beneath Room M-2.

We encountered no comparable closure offerings in the East Plaza earth oven complex but, as we sampled less than 30% of this feature, it is entirely possible that similar offerings occurred there as well.

Synopsis

The Henderson Site (LA-1549) is a small E-shaped adobe pueblo situated on a ridge that borders the western edge of the Pecos River valley, about 17 km southwest of Roswell, Chaves County, southeastern New Mexico. The Hondo River, a major western tributary of the Pecos, cuts through this ridge directly north of the site. Excavations were conducted there in 1980 and 1981 and again in 1994, 1995, and 1997, by the University of Michigan. A preliminary report on the burials recovered in 1980-1981, but which also provides an overview of the site and the excavations, has already appeared (Rocek and Speth 1986). This volume expands on this preliminary overview, focusing particularly on evidence relating to the subsistence practices of the villagers.

Based on an extensive series of both conventional and AMS radiocarbon dates, as well as on several archaeomagnetic dates and the ceramic assemblage, the major Henderson occupation can be placed with some confidence in the last third of the 1200s.

There is also evidence for a second, somewhat later occupation at Henderson, dating to the late 1300s and perhaps extending into the first decade or so of the 1400s. This second occupation appears to have been more ephemeral than the earlier one, but this may be a function of the portions of the site that have been sampled to date.

Work at Henderson in 1994, 1995, and 1997 revealed that the Main Bar of the "E" was occupied prior to the construction of the Center Bar and East Bar (the internal site chronology is based largely on the seriation of El Paso Polychrome jar rims). Based on the results of the newer excavations, we have found it necessary to revise the phase designations to avoid problems in future publications. Hence, the period when the Main Bar was constructed we now designate as the "Early phase" (ca. A.D. 1250-1270). The occupation in the latter part of the thirteenth century, which we previously called the "Early phase," we now rename the "Late phase" (ca. A.D. 1270-1300). And the ephemeral occupation (or reoccupation) of Henderson around A.D. 1400, which we called the "Late phase," we now refer to as the "Terminal phase."

The pueblo, which covers an area of about 0.65 acres (0.26 ha), contained perhaps as many as 100 to 130 adobe rooms. Most if not all of the pueblo was one story. Rooms in the Main Bar tend to be square with rounded corners, averaging 3-4 m on a side, with primary floors set well below the original ground surface. Rooms in the Center Bar and East Bar are rectangular with square corners, averaging about 3 m in width by 5 and sometimes even 6 m in length, with primary floors set at or only slightly below ground level. In all rooms, entry appears to have been through a hatch in the roof. Too little work was done in the West Bar to determine the nature of the rooms in this part of the village. No kiva or other special-purpose structure was found. Rooms appear to have been abandoned systematically, leaving little or no cultural material on the floor. Only one of the sampled rooms showed evidence of extensive burning.

The burials recovered in the 1994, 1995, and 1997 field seasons have not yet been studied in detail. Most were infants or young children buried in subfloor pits. None were buried with ornaments or other accompaniments. In 1980 and 1981, 10 subfloor burial features were found containing a total of 11 bodies (1 fetus, 2 infants, and 8 adults, of which 4 are male, 4 female). Bodies were flexed, usually on their right side or back, and often wrapped in matting. Grave goods included personal ornaments of marine shell, turquoise, and other materials, as well as pottery, basketry, bone tools, projectile points (many of Alibates and Edwards Plateau chert from west Texas and one of Tiger chert from southwestern Wyoming), and two wooden "prayer sticks," one a plain rod wrapped in a strand of *Olivella* shells, the other flat and cut into the shape of a stylized corn plant. Grave offerings were absent with the youngest (fetus and 3- to 6-month-old) and oldest (40+ year-old) individuals, and were most numerous with a 2.5- to 3.5-year-old child.

Deeply stratified trash deposits were not common at Henderson, but a deep natural karstic depression in the bedrock underlying the south end of the East Plaza (trenches B/C), and another near the northwest end of the Main Bar (Great Depression, trench K), contained almost a meter of dark ashy midden filled with masses of fire-cracked rock, thousands of bison bones, and crude limestone chopperlike tools, as well as large quantities of other trash, including bones of deer, antelope, lagomorphs, birds, fish, and thousands of sherds, lithics, occasional mollusks, and so forth. Several radiocarbon dates, both conventional and accelerator, from the East Plaza complex demonstrate that this feature dates to the latter half of the thirteenth century, and is therefore a Late phase feature associated with the Center Bar and East Bar room blocks. No absolute dates have been run as yet on materials from the Great Depression, but seriation of El Paso Polychrome jar rims suggests that this feature predates the one in the East Plaza and is contemporary with the Early phase occupation of the Main Bar. The formation processes that produced the deposits in the East Plaza and Great Depression are not entirely clear, but their contents differ in numerous subtle but significant ways from the contents of fill deposited in abandoned rooms. These differences underscore the more public or communal nature of the activities and events that took place in and around these large earth oven complexes.

Notes

1. Although we use the term "pueblo" to refer to the Henderson community, as well as to other quasi-contemporary communities in the Roswell area, we do so only in the architectural sense of a village composed of tightly packed rooms sharing adjacent walls. Our use of this term does not imply ethnic, linguistic, or biological affiliation with historically known Puebloan groups farther to the west in New Mexico or Arizona.

2. A second datum point (datum D) was also permanently established with cement. This datum is located at 535N525E at an elevation of 100.89 m relative to datum A. Other datum points were employed during the excavations, but were not permanently set in cement.

3. The burials from the 1994, 1995, and 1997 field seasons have yet not been fully studied, but consisted mostly of infants and children, and a single unusually (pathologically?) small adult male (in a shallow pit directly beneath the primary floor in Room M-2 in the Main Bar East). None of these burials were interred with grave goods or ornaments of any sort.

4. In its original formulation, the RSI was the ratio of the maximum thickness of the rim, taken 2 mm from the edge, divided by the minimum thickness of the sherd body, taken 15 mm from the edge (Carmichael 1985, 1986; Whalen 1993). Because so many of our rim sherds are small, the 15-mm rule would have forced us to exclude many of the El Paso rims, making it difficult to date several of Henderson's major proveniences. Thus, to maximize our sample sizes for as many areas of the site as possible, we employed a less-than-ideal variant of the index. We divided the maximum thickness of the rim, wherever that occurred on the rim, by the minimum thickness of the body of the sherd, again regardless of distance from the edge. This version of the RSI is "noisier" than the original formulation, because on the smallest sherds the minimum thickness is seldom uniform near the rim, but instead decreases the farther one moves from the edge. Nevertheless, the seriation results are matched closely by a subsample

of rims measured according to the original guidelines published by Carmichael and Whalen. Moreover, we obtain nearly identical results when we use only maximum rim thickness, a parameter that can be measured with reasonable confidence regardless of sherd size (see Chapter 3, for a more detailed discussion of the seriation).

5. Driver (1991:200ff) observed a similar spatial distribution of larger mammal bones at the Robinson Site, a roughly contemporary Lincoln phase pueblo located on the eastern slopes of the Sacramento Mountains north of Capitan, New Mexico. At Robinson, deer and antelope—the most common larger mammals—were found primarily in contexts outside of the main room block, particularly in the village's central plaza area and in various external trash deposits. The rooms had higher frequencies of lagomorphs and prairie dogs.

References Cited

Archer, S.
1994 Species Identification of Large Wood Samples from Henderson Pueblo (LA-1549), Chaves County, New Mexico. Unpublished manuscript.

Bell, R. H.
1958 *Guide to the Identification of Certain American Indian Projectile Points*. Special Bulletin 1. Oklahoma City, OK: Oklahoma Anthropological Society.

Carmichael, D. L.
1985 Transitional Pueblo Occupation on Dona Ana Range, Fort Bliss, New Mexico. In: *Views of the Jornada Mogollon: Proceedings of the Second Jornada Mogollon Conference*, edited by Colleen M. Beck, pp. 45-53. Eastern New Mexico University, Contributions in Anthropology 12. Portales, NM: Eastern New Mexico University Press.

Carmichael, D. L.
1986 *Archaeological Survey in the Southern Tularosa Basin of New Mexico*. Historic and Natural Resources Report 3. (University of Texas at El Paso, El Paso Centennial Museum, Publications in Anthropology 10.) Fort Bliss, TX: United States Army Air Defense Artillery Center, Directorate of Engineering and Housing, Environmental Management Office.

Damon, P. E., C. W. Ferguson, A. Long, and E. I. Wallick
1974 Dendrochronologic Calibration of the Radiocarbon Time Scale. *American Antiquity* 39(2):350-66.

Driver, J. C.
1991 Assemblage Formation at the Robinson Site (LA46326). In: *Mogollon V*, edited by P. H. Beckett, pp. 197-206. Las Cruces, NM: COAS Publishing and Research.

Kelley, J. H.
1984 *The Archaeology of the Sierra Blanca Region of Southeastern New Mexico*. Anthropological Paper 74. Ann Arbor, MI: Museum of Anthropology, University of Michigan.

Klein, J., J. C. Lerman, P. E. Damon, and E. K. Ralph
1982 Calibration of Radiocarbon Dates: Tables Based on the Consensus Data of the Workshop on Calibrating the Radiocarbon Time Scale. *Radiocarbon* 24(2):103-50.

Long, A., and B. E. Rippeteau
1974 Testing Contemporaneity and Averaging Radiocarbon Dates. *American Antiquity* 39(2, Part 1):205-15.

Parry, W. J., and J. D. Speth
1984 *The Garnsey Spring Campsite: Late Prehistoric Occupation in Southeastern New Mexico*. Technical Report 15. Ann Arbor, MI: Museum of Anthropology, University of Michigan.

Ralph, E. K., H. N. Michael, and M. C. Han
1973 Radiocarbon Dates and Reality. *MASCA Newsletter* 9:1-20.

Rocek, T. R., and J. D. Speth
1986 *The Henderson Site Burials: Glimpses of a Late Prehistoric Population in the Pecos Valley*. Technical Report 18. Ann Arbor, MI: Museum of Anthropology, University of Michigan.

Seaman, T. J., and B. J. Mills
1988 What Are We Measuring? Rim Thickness Indices and Their Implications for Changes in Vessel Use. In: *Fourth Jornada Mogollon Conference (October 1985): Collected Papers*, edited by M. S. Duran and K. W. Laumbach, pp. 163-94. Tularosa, NM: Human Systems Research, Inc.

Smiley, F. E.
1985 *The Chronometrics of Early Agricultural Sites in Northeastern Arizona: Approaches to the Interpretation of Radiocarbon Dates*. Ph.D. dissertation, University of Michigan, Ann Arbor, MI.

Speth, J. D.
1991 Some Unexplored Aspects of Mutualistic Plains-Pueblo Food Exchange. In: *Farmers, Hunters, and Colonists: Interaction Between the Southwest and the Southern Plains*, edited by K. A. Spielmann, pp. 18-35. Tucson, AZ: University of Arizona Press.

Spielmann, K. A.
1991 *Interdependence in the Prehistoric Southwest: An Ecological Analysis of Plains-Pueblo Interaction*. New York: Garland.

Stuiver, M.
1982 A High-Precision Calibration of the A.D. Radiocarbon Time Scale. *Radiocarbon* 24(1):1-26.

Stuiver, M., and B. Becker
1986 High-Precision Decadal Calibration of the Radiocarbon Time Scale, A.D. 1950-2500 B.C. *Radiocarbon* 28(2B):863-910.

Stuiver, M., and B. Becker
1993 High-Precision Decadal Calibration of the Radiocarbon Time Scale, A.D. 1950-6000 B.C. *Radiocarbon* 35(1):35-65.

Stuiver, M., and G. W. Pearson
1986 High-Precision Calibration of the Radiocarbon Time Scale, A.D. 1950-500 B.C. *Radiocarbon* 28(2B):805-38.

Stuiver, M., and P. J. Reimer
1986 A Computer Program for Radiocarbon Age Calibration. *Radiocarbon* 28(2B):1022-30.

Stuiver, M., and P. J. Reimer
1993 Extended ^{14}C Data Base and Revised CALIB 3.0 ^{14}C Age Calibration Program. *Radiocarbon* 35(1):215-30.

Stuiver, M., P. J. Reimer, E. Bard, J. W. Beck, G. S. Burr, K. A. Hughen, B. Kromer, F. G. McCormac, J. v. d. Plicht, and M. Spurk
1998 INTCAL98 Radiocarbon Age Calibration 24,000-0 cal B.P. *Radiocarbon* 40:1041-83.

West, K.
1982 *A Study of El Paso Brown Rim Form.* Master's thesis, Department of Sociology and Anthropology, University of Texas at El Paso. El Paso, TX.

Whalen, M. E.
1993 El Paso Plain Brown Rims As Chronological Markers? New Data on an Old Question. *Kiva* 58(4):475-86.

Whittaker, J. C., A. Ferg, and J. D. Speth
1988 Arizona Bifaces of Wyoming Chert. *Kiva* 53(4):321-34.

Wiseman, R. N.
1976 *Multi-Disciplinary Investigations at the Smokey Bear Ruin (LA-2112), Lincoln County, New Mexico.* Monograph 4. Las Cruces, NM: COAS Publishing and Research.

Appendix to Chapter 2
Henderson Lot Numbers

Introduction

At the beginning of the first field season in 1980, we attempted to label almost every artifact (bone, lithic, ceramic, etc.) with complete provenience information. This information included the Museum of New Mexico site number (LA-1549); grid square (followed for point-provenienced items by a sequential field item number and quadrant within the 1 m square, when appropriate; e.g., 515N533E/1/ W); and stratigraphic level (usually an upper and lower value in meters above or below Datum A = 100.00 m). Where a single, precise elevation for an item was shot in with a transit, a 1 cm range is coded in this appendix (e.g., 100.91-100.90 m).

It quickly became apparent that this labeling procedure, while ideal in terms of the long-term curation of the materials, was far too cumbersome and time-consuming, and virtually impossible on very small items. We therefore initiated an alternative system in which a single, unique, sequential lot number was assigned to each discrete provenience, usually a bag of material from a single excavation level in a single 1-m grid square. Lot numbers were written directly on every item using indelible ink covered, where necessary, by clear nail polish, on the bags themselves (which were saved as a backup record until final publication of the complete system), in a master notebook, and in a computer file. Lot numbers were assigned in the order that bags were received; as a consequence, they do not correspond in any straightforward manner to provenience or level. Thus, a permanent, published record of the lot numbers and their associated provenience information is vital to assure that archaeologists in the future can reanalyze the Henderson material with full access to all essential data.

Lot numbers 1 through 2027 were published as Appendix 17 in Rocek and Speth (1986). However, all subsequent numbers up to the last one used at the Henderson Site in 1997 (Lot 5669) remain unpublished. These are now presented in full in Table A2.1. The first 2,027 numbers are republished here as well, with a number of errors corrected and with provenience information provided.

Lot Number System

Table A2.1 records the following information.

Col. 1. *Sequential Lot Number* (there are small gaps in the sequence because a few lot numbers were dropped or inadvertently never assigned; e.g., nos. 660-669).

Col. 2. *Grid North* (in meters).

Col. 3. *Grid East* (in meters).

Col. 4. *Upper Level* (in meters above or below Datum A = 100.00 m).

Col. 5. *Lower Level* (in meters above or below Datum A = 100.00 m).

Col. 6. *Provenience* (e.g., Center Bar, East Bar, Great Depression, etc.)

Col. 7. *Flotation Volume* (volume of sediment sample, in liters, processed by flotation).

Table A2.1. Lot number system used between 1980 and 1997 at the Henderson Site (LA-1549)

Lot No.	Grid N	Grid E	Upper Level	Lower Level	Provenience	Flot. Vol.
1	522	534	102.25	102.24	Center Bar	.
2	526	565	101.15	101.05	East Bar	.
3	521	562	101.15	101.05	East Bar	.
4	513	534	101.15	101.05	Center Bar	.
5	525	561	100.90	100.85	East Bar	.
6	525	561	100.94	100.93	East Bar	.
7	523	567	101.25	101.15	East Bar	.
8	522	566	101.25	101.15	East Bar	.
9	526	564	101.54	101.25	East Bar	.
10	526	565	101.25	101.15	East Bar	.
11	515	533	101.80	101.70	Center Bar	.
12	511	535	101.15	101.05	Center Bar	.
13	513	535	101.45	101.35	Center Bar	.
14	510	534	101.15	101.05	Center Bar	.
15	513	530	101.70	101.65	Center Bar	.
16	527	563	100.95	100.85	East Bar	.
17	526	563	101.05	100.88	East Bar	.
18	527	563	101.05	100.95	East Bar	.
19	525	563	101.54	101.25	East Bar	.
20	526	566	101.15	101.05	East Bar	.
21	522	564	101.46	101.25	East Bar	.
22	528	564	101.15	101.05	East Bar	.
23	528	565	101.05	100.95	East Bar	.
24	512	535	101.10	101.05	Center Bar	.
25	524	562	101.06	101.05	East Bar	.
26	512	531	101.45	101.40	Center Bar	.
27	515	534	100.70	100.65	Center Bar	.
28	513	534	101.15	101.05	Center Bar	.
29	515	533	101.40	101.30	Center Bar	.
30	523	535	100.72	100.54	Center Bar	.
31	525	566	101.55	101.25	East Bar	.
32	512	532	101.78	101.77	Center Bar	.
33	514	530	101.65	101.55	Center Bar	.
34	510	533	101.00	100.99	Center Bar	.
35	510	530	101.00	100.99	Center Bar	.
36	516	533	100.75	100.70	Center Bar	.
37	521	565	101.15	101.05	East Bar	.
38	521	563	101.39	101.25	East Bar	.
39	524	562	101.25	101.15	East Bar	.
40	512	533	101.30	101.25	Center Bar	.
41	513	535	101.50	101.45	Center Bar	.
42	515	533	101.70	101.60	Center Bar	.
43	513	533	101.89	101.80	Center Bar	.

Lot No.	Grid N	Grid E	Upper Level	Lower Level	Provenience	Flot. Vol.
44	525	564	101.30	101.25	East Bar	.
45	515	533	101.60	101.50	Center Bar	.
46	510	534	101.28	101.15	Center Bar	.
47	521	563	101.25	101.15	East Bar	.
48	513	533	101.65	101.60	Center Bar	.
49	524	561	101.36	101.25	East Bar	.
50	514	533	101.55	101.45	Center Bar	.
51	522	561	101.34	101.25	East Bar	.
52	525	562	100.90	100.85	East Bar	.
53	515	535	101.07	101.06	Center Bar	.
54	514	535	101.00	100.90	Center Bar	.
55	514	535	101.45	101.35	Center Bar	.
56	525	566	101.55	101.25	East Bar	.
57	523	562	101.25	101.15	East Bar	.
58	514	535	101.50	101.45	Center Bar	.
59	516	533	101.55	101.45	Center Bar	.
60	514	532	101.70	101.60	Center Bar	.
61	522	563	101.25	101.15	East Bar	.
62	526	564	100.90	100.80	East Bar	.
63	525	562	100.93	100.92	East Bar	.
64	522	563	101.25	101.15	East Bar	.
65	516	533	101.75	101.65	Center Bar	.
66	513	534	101.40	101.30	Center Bar	.
67	512	532	101.55	101.50	Center Bar	.
68	511	530	101.30	101.20	Center Bar	.
69	525	565	101.15	101.05	East Bar	.
70	514	534	100.37	100.36	Center Bar	.
71	512	530	101.50	101.40	Center Bar	.
72	523	564	101.25	101.15	East Bar	.
73	513	533	101.55	101.50	Center Bar	.
74	514	531	102.04	101.95	Center Bar	.
75	525	565	101.54	101.53	East Bar	.
76	512	535	101.30	101.25	Center Bar	.
77	514	534	101.35	101.25	Center Bar	.
78	514	530	101.90	101.85	Center Bar	.
79	514	535	101.35	101.25	Center Bar	.
80	510	532	101.20	101.15	Center Bar	.
81	522	561	101.15	101.05	East Bar	.
82	511	532	101.15	101.10	Center Bar	.
83	512	530	101.70	101.60	Center Bar	.
84	515	535	101.20	101.10	Center Bar	.
85	512	530	101.60	101.50	Center Bar	.
86	523	561	101.25	101.15	East Bar	.
87	523	561	101.15	101.05	East Bar	.
88	523	562	101.15	101.05	East Bar	.
89	510	533	101.20	101.15	Center Bar	.
90	513	530	101.55	101.45	Center Bar	.
91	516	533	102.09	101.75	Center Bar	.
92	515	535	101.20	101.10	Center Bar	.
93	513	534	101.35	101.25	Center Bar	.
94	515	534	100.70	100.65	Center Bar	.
95	523	562	101.25	101.15	East Bar	.
96	525	564	101.25	101.15	East Bar	.
97	512	535	101.16	101.05	Center Bar	.
98	512	530	101.45	101.40	Center Bar	.
99	514	535	101.70	101.60	Center Bar	.
100	513	530	101.70	101.65	Center Bar	.
101	512	530	101.40	101.35	Center Bar	.
102	512	532	101.50	101.45	Center Bar	.
103	512	533	101.25	101.20	Center Bar	.
104	512	533	101.25	101.20	Center Bar	.
105	512	533	101.23	101.22	Center Bar	.
106	512	531	101.40	101.35	Center Bar	.
107	514	534	101.55	101.45	Center Bar	.
108	526	564	101.25	101.15	East Bar	.
109	525	566	101.25	101.15	East Bar	.
110	526	562	100.94	100.93	East Bar	.
111	526	562	100.90	100.89	East Bar	.
112	529	566	101.73	101.60	East Bar	.
113	526	562	100.92	100.91	East Bar	.
114	527	562	101.10	101.00	East Bar	.
115	513	535	101.45	101.35	Center Bar	.
116	545	602	98.82	98.81	Surface	.
117	556	537	100.26	100.25	Surface	.
118	514	535	101.75	101.65	Center Bar	.
119	542	594	99.27	99.26	Surface	.
120	529	566	101.40	101.30	East Bar	.
121	510	530	101.10	101.00	Center Bar	.
122	510	533	101.02	101.01	Center Bar	.
123	517	533	101.89	101.60	Center Bar	.
124	522	565	101.35	101.25	East Bar	.
125	522	565	101.25	101.15	East Bar	.
126	523	565	101.15	101.05	East Bar	.
127	513	534	101.55	101.45	Center Bar	.
128	524	569	101.30	101.20	East Bar	.
129	514	534	101.45	101.35	Center Bar	.
130	514	530	101.50	101.40	Center Bar	.
131	512	530	101.55	101.50	Center Bar	.
132	515	534	100.65	100.60	Center Bar	.
133	524	565	101.15	101.05	East Bar	.
134	512	532	101.35	101.30	Center Bar	.
135	525	562	101.30	101.25	East Bar	.
136	525	563	100.95	100.90	East Bar	.
137	522	561	101.07	101.06	East Bar	.
138	512	534	101.35	101.30	Center Bar	.
139	513	534	101.45	101.35	Center Bar	.

Lot No.	Grid N	Grid E	Upper Level	Lower Level	Provenience	Flot. Vol.
140	512	530	101.50	101.45	Center Bar	.
141	525	564	101.15	101.05	East Bar	.
142	512	532	101.60	101.55	Center Bar	.
143	524	535	100.82	100.57	Center Bar	.
144	514	532	101.95	101.90	Center Bar	.
145	529	566	101.60	101.50	East Bar	.
146	512	532	101.25	101.15	Center Bar	.
147	517	534	101.25	101.05	Center Bar	.
148	520	533	102.08	101.65	Center Bar	.
149	511	533	101.30	101.25	Center Bar	.
150	517	534	100.64	100.60	Center Bar	.
151	513	533	101.89	101.88	Center Bar	.
152	524	567	101.51	101.25	East Bar	.
153	511	533	101.25	101.20	Center Bar	.
154	515	535	101.20	101.10	Center Bar	.
155	511	533	101.20	101.15	Center Bar	.
156	523	561	101.15	101.05	East Bar	.
157	526	566	101.25	101.15	East Bar	.
158	521	566	101.15	101.05	East Bar	.
159	512	533	101.35	101.30	Center Bar	.
160	515	535	102.04	101.60	Center Bar	.
161	512	535	101.41	101.35	Center Bar	.
162	516	534	100.70	100.65	Center Bar	.
163	529	565	101.30	101.20	East Bar	.
164	516	535	101.40	101.30	Center Bar	.
165	517	533	100.95	100.85	Center Bar	.
166	526	567	101.25	101.15	East Bar	.
167	513	535	100.95	100.85	Center Bar	.
168	515	535	101.20	101.10	Center Bar	.
169	523	566	101.09	101.08	East Bar	.
170	517	534	100.75	100.65	Center Bar	.
171	521	567	101.25	101.15	East Bar	.
172	526	566	101.57	101.25	East Bar	.
173	526	569	101.30	101.20	East Bar	.
174	526	562	101.30	101.20	East Bar	.
175	528	567	101.35	101.25	East Bar	.
176	525	568	101.30	101.20	East Bar	.
177	529	566	101.50	101.40	East Bar	.
178	522	563	101.44	101.25	East Bar	.
179	526	562	100.91	100.90	East Bar	.
180	510	530	100.76	100.75	Center Bar	.
181	526	562	100.82	100.81	East Bar	.
182	514	533	102.08	101.85	Center Bar	.
183	512	534	101.30	101.25	Center Bar	.
184	526	565	101.56	101.25	East Bar	.
185	522	561	101.10	101.05	East Bar	.
186	526	568	101.55	101.25	East Bar	.
187	527	566	101.27	101.15	East Bar	.
188	516	534	101.10	101.00	Center Bar	.
189	528	567	101.43	101.35	East Bar	.
190	521	563	101.15	101.05	East Bar	.
191	514	535	101.55	101.45	Center Bar	.
192	523	567	101.47	101.25	East Bar	.
193	526	562	101.30	101.20	East Bar	.
194	526	562	101.29	101.28	East Bar	.
195	523	563	101.25	101.15	East Bar	.
196	513	534	101.55	101.45	Center Bar	.
197	528	564	101.05	100.95	East Bar	.
198	522	563	101.15	101.05	East Bar	.
199	514	530	101.95	101.85	Center Bar	.
200	528	563	101.35	101.25	East Bar	.
201	510	530	101.40	101.30	Center Bar	.
202	516	534	100.64	100.63	Center Bar	.
203	525	562	100.85	100.81	East Bar	.
204	525	564	101.05	100.95	East Bar	.
205	514	530	101.85	101.75	Center Bar	.
206	527	563	100.95	100.85	East Bar	.
207	526	563	101.25	101.15	East Bar	.
208	526	564	101.15	101.05	East Bar	.
209	513	535	100.69	100.45	Center Bar	.
210	521	567	101.15	101.05	East Bar	.
211	515	534	100.70	100.60	Center Bar	.
212	516	533	100.90	100.85	Center Bar	.
213	516	534	100.64	100.63	Center Bar	.
214	526	562	101.20	101.10	East Bar	.
215	528	567	101.57	101.56	East Bar	.
216	527	566	101.38	101.37	East Bar	.
217	510	531	101.20	101.10	Center Bar	.
218	526	562	100.93	100.92	East Bar	.
219	526	562	100.95	100.94	East Bar	.
220	513	534	101.50	101.45	Center Bar	.
221	525	562	101.05	100.90	East Bar	.
222	525	563	101.05	100.95	East Bar	.
223	514	535	100.70	100.63	Center Bar	.
224	522	564	101.25	101.15	East Bar	.
225	524	562	101.35	101.25	East Bar	.
226	513	530	101.65	101.55	Center Bar	.
227	528	567	101.35	101.25	East Bar	.
228	526	567	100.90	100.84	East Bar	.
229	527	566	101.65	101.55	East Bar	.
230	528	567	101.45	101.35	East Bar	.
231	528	566	101.05	100.95	East Bar	.
232	514	534	100.47	100.38	Center Bar	.
233	513	530	101.51	101.50	Center Bar	.
234	525	568	101.40	101.30	East Bar	.
235	528	567	101.25	101.15	East Bar	.

Lot No.	Grid N	Grid E	Upper Level	Lower Level	Provenience	Flot. Vol.
236	529	566	101.30	101.10	East Bar	.
237	525	567	101.30	101.20	East Bar	.
238	527	566	101.38	101.37	East Bar	.
239	537	500	100.76	100.75	West Bar	.
240	528	567	101.45	101.35	East Bar	.
241	526	562	101.40	101.30	East Bar	.
242	527	566	101.20	101.10	East Bar	.
243	523	566	101.25	101.15	East Bar	.
244	524	569	101.19	101.10	East Bar	.
245	526	567	101.15	101.06	East Bar	.
246	512	533	101.70	101.60	Center Bar	.
247	526	563	101.95	101.94	East Bar	.
248	524	568	101.20	101.10	East Bar	.
249	527	561	101.30	101.10	East Bar	.
250	527	561	101.10	100.90	East Bar	.
251	526	562	101.00	100.90	East Bar	.
252	527	566	101.45	101.35	East Bar	.
253	528	564	101.15	101.10	East Bar	.
254	515	533	102.10	102.00	Center Bar	.
255	527	561	101.49	101.20	East Bar	.
256	527	566	101.25	101.17	East Bar	.
257	527	566	101.35	101.25	East Bar	.
258	528	567	101.02	100.90	East Bar	.
259	512	535	101.35	101.30	Center Bar	.
260	527	561	101.37	101.36	East Bar	.
261	527	567	101.40	101.30	East Bar	.
262	527	567	101.29	101.28	East Bar	.
263	522	566	101.15	101.05	East Bar	.
264	516	534	100.90	100.85	Center Bar	.
265	522	567	101.42	101.25	East Bar	.
266	521	566	101.46	101.25	East Bar	.
267	527	569	101.30	101.29	East Bar	.
268	515	535	100.70	100.65	Center Bar	.
269	516	534	101.60	101.40	Center Bar	.
270	520	533	101.65	101.45	Center Bar	.
271	512	532	101.65	101.60	Center Bar	.
272	528	566	101.68	101.25	East Bar	.
273	517	534	100.85	100.75	Center Bar	.
274	515	534	101.00	100.90	Center Bar	.
275	521	567	101.37	101.25	East Bar	.
276	523	566	101.15	101.05	East Bar	.
277	522	567	101.25	101.15	East Bar	.
278	527	567	101.20	101.19	East Bar	.
279	526	567	101.58	101.25	East Bar	.
280	529	566	101.10	101.00	East Bar	.
281	526	562	100.84	100.80	East Bar	.
282	527	566	101.23	101.22	East Bar	.
283	522	566	101.25	101.15	East Bar	.
284	523	567	101.47	101.25	East Bar	.
285	515	533	101.30	101.20	Center Bar	.
286	516	534	101.20	101.00	Center Bar	.
287	519	533	101.65	101.40	Center Bar	.
288	526	568	101.25	101.15	East Bar	.
289	527	564	101.58	101.25	East Bar	.
290	525	562	100.99	100.98	East Bar	.
291	519	533	100.60	100.40	Center Bar	.
292	516	534	101.20	101.00	Center Bar	.
293	512	533	101.60	101.55	Center Bar	.
294	512	533	101.40	101.30	Center Bar	.
295	516	534	101.60	101.40	Center Bar	.
296	511	532	101.25	101.20	Center Bar	.
297	519	533	101.65	101.40	Center Bar	.
298	527	563	101.57	101.25	East Bar	.
299	519	533	101.65	101.40	Center Bar	.
300	527	563	101.92	101.91	East Bar	.
301	526	562	100.61	100.60	East Bar	.
302	524	562	101.15	101.05	East Bar	.
303	527	567	101.20	101.15	East Bar	.
304	528	562	100.82	100.81	East Bar	.
305	525	561	100.91	100.90	East Bar	.
306	528	562	100.92	100.91	East Bar	.
307	528	562	100.96	100.95	East Bar	.
308	527	567	101.15	101.11	East Bar	.
309	527	567	101.51	101.50	East Bar	.
310	527	567	101.64	101.50	East Bar	.
311	527	567	101.51	101.50	East Bar	.
312	527	567	101.64	101.50	East Bar	.
313	528	564	101.45	101.35	East Bar	.
314	528	564	101.10	101.00	East Bar	.
315	527	566	101.36	101.35	East Bar	.
316	527	566	101.42	101.41	East Bar	.
317	527	566	101.35	101.34	East Bar	.
318	528	567	101.35	101.25	East Bar	.
319	529	565	101.40	101.30	East Bar	.
320	524	569	101.40	101.30	East Bar	.
321	527	562	100.78	100.77	East Bar	.
322	527	562	100.79	100.78	East Bar	.
323	527	562	100.79	100.78	East Bar	.
324	529	566	101.50	101.40	East Bar	.
325	529	566	101.30	101.20	East Bar	.
326	527	567	101.31	101.30	East Bar	.
327	527	562	101.00	100.90	East Bar	.
328	522	563	100.90	100.80	East Bar	.
329	527	566	101.20	101.10	East Bar	.
330	522	563	101.00	100.90	East Bar	.
331	530	565	101.75	101.50	East Bar	.

Lot No.	Grid N	Grid E	Upper Level	Lower Level	Provenience	Flot. Vol.
332	527	562	100.86	100.85	East Bar	.
333	528	563	100.87	100.86	East Bar	.
334	526	561	101.00	100.80	East Bar	.
335	526	561	100.90	100.89	East Bar	.
336	528	563	100.83	100.82	East Bar	.
337	528	563	100.83	100.82	East Bar	.
338	527	569	101.60	101.56	East Bar	.
339	526	561	100.95	100.94	East Bar	.
340	524	569	100.91	100.90	East Bar	.
341	528	563	100.79	100.78	East Bar	.
342	526	561	100.97	100.96	East Bar	.
343	527	562	100.84	100.83	East Bar	.
344	527	569	101.30	101.20	East Bar	.
345	528	563	100.90	100.80	East Bar	.
346	528	563	101.25	101.15	East Bar	.
347	524	569	101.30	101.20	East Bar	.
348	528	563	101.35	101.25	East Bar	.
349	529	566	101.10	101.00	East Bar	.
350	527	562	100.70	100.60	East Bar	.
351	528	567	101.16	101.02	East Bar	.
352	527	567	101.50	101.49	East Bar	.
353	527	567	101.46	101.45	East Bar	.
354	527	566	101.43	101.42	East Bar	.
355	527	562	100.91	100.90	East Bar	.
356	527	566	101.35	101.25	East Bar	.
357	527	566	101.25	101.20	East Bar	.
358	527	567	101.50	101.40	East Bar	.
359	526	562	101.10	101.00	East Bar	.
360	529	565	101.50	101.40	East Bar	.
361	526	561	101.20	101.00	East Bar	.
362	526	561	101.38	101.20	East Bar	.
363	527	563	100.80	100.70	East Bar	.
364	530	565	101.50	101.30	East Bar	.
365	528	563	101.05	100.95	East Bar	.
366	525	561	100.70	100.61	East Bar	.
367	526	562	100.80	100.70	East Bar	.
368	527	563	101.24	100.84	East Bar	.
369	527	563	101.24	101.00	East Bar	.
370	527	565	101.15	101.08	East Bar	.
371	526	564	101.60	101.50	East Bar	.
372	527	564	100.80	100.50	East Bar	.
373	528	563	100.81	100.80	East Bar	.
374	527	565	101.17	101.10	East Bar	.
375	527	565	101.01	101.00	East Bar	.
376	527	564	101.00	100.99	East Bar	.
377	523	534	101.14	101.13	Center Bar	.
378	523	568	101.21	101.20	East Bar	.
379	529	563	101.30	101.29	East Bar	.

Lot No.	Grid N	Grid E	Upper Level	Lower Level	Provenience	Flot. Vol.
380	523	564	101.08	100.90	East Bar	.
381	527	565	101.08	100.99	East Bar	.
382	528	567	101.15	101.05	East Bar	.
383	530	565	101.75	101.50	East Bar	.
384	524	569	101.00	100.90	East Bar	.
385	523	569	101.36	101.10	East Bar	.
386	526	547	100.74	100.60	East Plaza (D)	.
387	526	562	100.70	100.60	East Bar	.
388	528	563	100.95	100.10	East Bar	.
389	528	563	100.71	100.70	East Bar	.
390	527	561	100.78	100.77	East Bar	.
391	523	565	101.18	101.17	East Bar	.
392	527	561	101.76	101.75	East Bar	.
393	527	549	100.77	100.60	East Plaza (D)	.
394	526	548	100.60	100.50	East Plaza (D)	.
395	527	561	100.80	100.70	East Bar	.
396	526	566	100.96	100.90	East Bar	.
397	526	547	100.34	100.33	East Plaza (D)	.
398	527	550	100.44	100.43	East Plaza (D)	.
399	527	549	100.36	100.35	East Plaza (D)	.
400	523	564	101.04	101.03	East Bar	.
401	526	547	100.31	100.30	East Plaza (D)	.
402	526	566	101.02	101.01	East Bar	.
403	526	550	100.51	100.40	East Plaza (D)	.
404	526	565	101.57	101.56	East Bar	.
405	527	549	100.60	100.50	East Plaza (D)	.
406	527	548	100.78	100.50	East Plaza (D)	.
407	526	548	100.74	100.60	East Plaza (D)	.
408	526	564	101.29	100.76	East Bar	.
409	525	563	100.85	100.70	East Bar	.
410	526	549	100.40	100.30	East Plaza (D)	.
411	528	561	101.80	101.76	East Bar	.
412	528	561	100.58	100.57	East Bar	.
413	527	564	101.25	101.24	East Bar	.
414	528	561	100.58	100.57	East Bar	.
415	523	568	101.15	101.14	East Bar	.
416	526	566	100.90	100.80	East Bar	.
417	528	561	100.58	100.57	East Bar	.
418	527	569	101.26	101.25	East Bar	.
419	526	562	100.60	100.37	East Bar	.
420	526	562	100.81	100.80	East Bar	.
421	528	561	100.58	100.57	East Bar	.
422	527	564	100.80	100.50	East Bar	.
423	526	564	100.91	100.90	East Bar	.
424	529	560	101.50	101.49	East Bar	.
425	528	561	100.58	100.57	East Bar	.
426	528	561	100.58	100.57	East Bar	.
427	528	561	100.58	100.57	East Bar	.

Lot No.	Grid N	Grid E	Upper Level	Lower Level	Provenience	Flot. Vol.
428	528	561	100.58	100.57	East Bar	.
429	528	561	100.58	100.57	East Bar	.
430	528	561	100.58	100.57	East Bar	.
431	528	561	100.58	100.57	East Bar	.
432	528	561	100.58	100.57	East Bar	.
433	528	561	100.58	100.57	East Bar	.
434	528	561	100.58	100.57	East Bar	.
435	500	555	100.26	100.25	Surface	.
436	529	563	101.31	101.30	East Bar	.
437	523	564	101.25	101.24	East Bar	.
438	502	552	100.31	100.30	Surface	.
439	527	562	101.40	101.30	East Bar	.
440	501	498	99.91	99.90	Surface	.
441	527	550	100.51	100.50	East Plaza (D)	.
442	526	550	100.41	100.40	East Plaza (D)	.
443	527	561	100.76	100.75	East Bar	.
444	572	561	100.78	100.77	Surface	.
445	526	547	100.41	100.40	East Plaza (D)	.
446	528	561	100.58	100.57	East Bar	.
447	522	563	101.01	101.00	East Bar	.
448	527	562	100.81	100.80	East Bar	.
449	526	549	100.35	100.34	East Plaza (D)	.
450	528	561	100.90	100.89	East Bar	.
451	527	561	100.78	100.77	East Bar	.
452	528	565	101.06	101.05	East Bar	.
453	527	567	101.07	101.06	East Bar	.
454	527	549	100.54	100.53	East Plaza (D)	.
455	527	549	100.50	100.49	East Plaza (D)	.
456	528	567	101.07	100.77	East Bar	.
457	526	549	100.29	100.28	East Plaza (D)	.
458	526	549	100.42	100.41	East Plaza (D)	.
459	528	565	101.05	101.04	East Bar	.
460	528	565	100.99	100.98	East Bar	.
461	528	565	101.03	101.02	East Bar	.
462	527	565	100.99	100.98	East Bar	.
463	527	567	100.80	100.70	East Bar	.
464	527	563	100.84	100.83	East Bar	.
465	529	565	101.44	101.43	East Bar	.
466	527	563	100.78	100.77	East Bar	.
467	528	561	100.75	100.74	East Bar	.
468	523	563	101.10	101.00	East Bar	.
469	526	550	100.30	100.28	East Plaza (D)	.
470	526	550	100.26	100.25	East Plaza (D)	.
471	528	561	100.77	100.76	East Bar	.
472	527	550	100.37	100.36	East Plaza (D)	.
473	527	566	101.23	101.22	East Bar	.
474	510	550	100.51	100.50	East Plaza (BC)	.
475	526	550	100.70	100.28	East Plaza (D)	.

Lot No.	Grid N	Grid E	Upper Level	Lower Level	Provenience	Flot. Vol.
476	526	561	100.75	100.74	East Bar	.
477	527	564	101.19	101.18	East Bar	.
478	527	550	100.35	100.34	East Plaza (D)	.
479	527	563	100.70	100.60	East Bar	.
480	527	550	100.35	100.34	East Plaza (D)	.
481	526	561	100.79	100.78	East Bar	.
482	526	548	100.29	100.28	East Plaza (D)	.
483	528	562	100.78	100.77	East Bar	.
484	527	561	100.82	100.81	East Bar	.
485	526	550	100.54	100.53	East Plaza (D)	.
486	528	563	100.80	100.60	East Bar	.
487	528	563	101.55	101.45	East Bar	.
488	528	563	101.48	101.47	East Bar	.
489	526	547	100.50	100.40	East Plaza (D)	.
490	526	549	100.50	100.40	East Plaza (D)	.
491	526	549	100.74	100.61	East Plaza (D)	.
492	528	563	100.80	100.70	East Bar	.
493	527	567	101.20	101.09	East Bar	.
494	527	564	101.14	101.13	East Bar	.
495	529	565	101.60	101.50	East Bar	.
496	527	565	101.08	101.05	East Bar	.
497	528	562	100.60	100.55	East Bar	.
498	526	561	100.70	100.60	East Bar	.
499	528	563	101.67	101.55	East Bar	.
500	528	563	101.57	101.56	East Bar	.
501	526	548	100.40	100.30	East Plaza (D)	.
502	523	568	101.42	101.20	East Bar	.
503	526	547	101.60	101.30	East Plaza (D)	.
504	527	550	100.77	100.60	East Plaza (D)	.
505	526	569	101.40	101.29	East Bar	.
506	526	548	100.40	100.30	East Plaza (D)	.
507	527	564	101.15	101.05	East Bar	.
508	528	563	100.70	100.60	East Bar	.
509	527	550	100.71	100.70	East Plaza (D)	.
510	528	562	100.70	100.60	East Bar	.
511	527	566	101.00	100.88	East Bar	.
512	527	562	100.70	100.60	East Bar	.
513	525	568	101.51	101.40	East Bar	.
514	529	566	101.60	101.50	East Bar	.
515	528	567	101.67	101.55	East Bar	.
516	527	548	100.40	100.30	East Plaza (D)	.
517	526	549	100.60	100.50	East Plaza (D)	.
518	508	550	100.30	100.10	East Plaza (BC)	.
519	528	563	101.15	101.05	East Bar	.
520	524	568	101.30	101.20	East Bar	.
521	527	550	100.40	100.30	East Plaza (D)	.
522	526	567	101.06	101.05	East Bar	.
523	507	550	100.28	100.20	East Plaza (BC)	.

Lot No.	Grid N	Grid E	Upper Level	Lower Level	Provenience	Flot. Vol.
524	529	565	101.72	101.60	East Bar	.
525	509	550	100.53	100.30	East Plaza (BC)	.
526	527	568	101.60	101.40	East Bar	.
527	507	550	100.48	100.30	East Plaza (BC)	.
528	523	563	101.05	100.90	East Bar	.
529	526	550	101.41	101.30	East Plaza (D)	.
530	527	564	100.98	100.88	East Bar	.
531	526	546	101.79	101.60	East Plaza (D)	.
532	527	550	100.60	100.50	East Plaza (D)	.
533	527	563	100.70	100.60	East Bar	.
534	526	567	100.69	100.59	East Bar	.
535	526	550	100.28	100.20	East Plaza (D)	.
536	509	550	100.30	100.10	East Plaza (BC)	.
537	527	549	100.50	100.40	East Plaza (D)	.
538	527	550	100.77	100.60	East Plaza (D)	.
539	526	547	100.40	100.30	East Plaza (D)	.
540	530	565	101.30	101.20	East Bar	.
541	527	563	100.90	100.80	East Bar	.
542	527	566	101.10	101.00	East Bar	.
543	526	563	100.80	100.70	East Bar	.
544	529	566	101.73	101.60	East Bar	.
545	527	566	101.55	101.45	East Bar	.
546	524	568	101.48	101.30	East Bar	.
547	526	548	100.50	100.40	East Plaza (D)	.
548	528	561	101.30	101.00	East Bar	.
549	529	561	101.66	101.30	East Bar	.
550	527	562	101.53	101.40	East Bar	.
551	527	548	100.50	100.40	East Plaza (D)	.
552	526	563	100.88	100.80	East Bar	.
553	512	549	100.00	99.90	East Plaza (BC)	.
554	509	550	100.10	99.90	East Plaza (BC)	.
555	508	548	99.61	99.60	East Plaza (BC)	.
556	508	549	99.61	99.60	East Plaza (BC)	.
557	512	549	100.00	99.90	East Plaza (BC)	.
558	510	549	100.10	100.00	East Plaza (BC)	.
559	511	550	100.00	99.90	East Plaza (BC)	.
560	512	549	100.10	100.00	East Plaza (BC)	.
561	511	550	100.00	99.90	East Plaza (BC)	.
562	509	549	99.90	99.80	East Plaza (BC)	.
563	510	549	99.90	99.80	East Plaza (BC)	.
564	510	549	99.90	99.80	East Plaza (BC)	.
565	508	550	100.12	99.98	East Plaza (BC)	.
566	509	549	99.70	99.60	East Plaza (BC)	.
567	509	550	99.68	99.67	East Plaza (BC)	.
568	508	550	99.80	99.68	East Plaza (BC)	.
569	509	549	99.70	99.60	East Plaza (BC)	.
570	509	549	99.64	99.63	East Plaza (BC)	.
571	510	549	99.90	99.80	East Plaza (BC)	.
572	511	550	99.79	99.78	East Plaza (BC)	.
573	509	550	99.75	99.74	East Plaza (BC)	.
574	509	549	99.80	99.70	East Plaza (BC)	.
575	509	550	99.73	99.72	East Plaza (BC)	.
576	509	549	99.59	99.58	East Plaza (BC)	.
577	511	550	99.90	99.80	East Plaza (BC)	.
578	511	550	100.00	99.90	East Plaza (BC)	.
579	508	549	99.64	99.63	East Plaza (BC)	.
580	510	549	100.00	99.90	East Plaza (BC)	.
581	507	550	99.90	99.80	East Plaza (BC)	.
582	512	549	99.90	99.80	East Plaza (BC)	.
583	511	550	100.10	100.00	East Plaza (BC)	.
584	509	549	100.00	99.90	East Plaza (BC)	.
585	510	550	100.10	100.00	East Plaza (BC)	.
586	510	550	100.30	100.10	East Plaza (BC)	.
587	511	550	100.10	100.00	East Plaza (BC)	.
588	508	549	100.10	100.00	East Plaza (BC)	.
589	509	550	100.10	100.00	East Plaza (BC)	.
590	529	564	101.73	101.40	East Bar	.
591	529	564	101.44	101.43	East Bar	.
592	525	569	101.47	101.40	East Bar	.
593	511	550	100.10	100.00	East Plaza (BC)	.
594	509	549	100.10	100.00	East Plaza (BC)	.
595	509	549	100.30	100.10	East Plaza (BC)	.
596	526	550	100.28	100.27	East Plaza (D)	.
597	509	550	100.10	99.90	East Plaza (BC)	.
598	509	548	100.30	100.10	East Plaza (BC)	.
599	509	550	99.90	99.60	East Plaza (BC)	.
600	509	549	100.00	99.90	East Plaza (BC)	.
601	509	550	99.64	99.60	East Plaza (BC)	.
602	509	549	99.60	99.50	East Plaza (BC)	.
603	510	549	99.70	99.60	East Plaza (BC)	.
604	510	549	99.70	99.60	East Plaza (BC)	.
605	509	550	99.70	99.60	East Plaza (BC)	.
606	510	549	99.70	99.69	East Plaza (BC)	.
607	510	549	99.80	99.70	East Plaza (BC)	.
608	510	549	99.80	99.70	East Plaza (BC)	.
609	512	549	99.90	99.80	East Plaza (BC)	.
610	508	550	99.70	99.60	East Plaza (BC)	.
611	510	549	99.70	99.60	East Plaza (BC)	.
612	512	549	99.90	99.80	East Plaza (BC)	.
613	509	548	99.90	99.80	East Plaza (BC)	.
614	509	548	100.10	100.00	East Plaza (BC)	.
615	509	549	99.58	99.57	East Plaza (BC)	.
616	512	549	99.90	99.80	East Plaza (BC)	.
617	512	549	99.90	99.80	East Plaza (BC)	.
618	512	549	99.90	99.80	East Plaza (BC)	.
619	512	549	99.90	99.80	East Plaza (BC)	.

Lot No.	Grid N	Grid E	Upper Level	Lower Level	Provenience	Flot. Vol.
620	509	549	99.60	99.50	East Plaza (BC)	.
621	508	551	99.90	99.80	East Plaza (BC)	.
622	508	551	99.76	99.75	East Plaza (BC)	.
623	512	549	99.83	99.82	East Plaza (BC)	.
624	512	549	99.90	99.80	East Plaza (BC)	.
625	509	548	100.10	100.00	East Plaza (BC)	.
626	512	549	99.90	99.80	East Plaza (BC)	.
627	512	549	99.90	99.80	East Plaza (BC)	.
628	510	549	99.70	99.60	East Plaza (BC)	.
629	510	549	99.80	99.70	East Plaza (BC)	.
630	510	549	99.95	99.94	East Plaza (BC)	.
631	510	549	99.80	99.70	East Plaza (BC)	.
632	510	549	99.80	99.70	East Plaza (BC)	.
633	510	549	99.80	99.70	East Plaza (BC)	.
634	509	549	100.52	100.51	East Plaza (BC)	.
635	529	563	101.73	101.40	East Bar	.
636	528	550	100.50	100.40	East Plaza (D)	.
637	523	568	101.20	101.10	East Bar	.
638	527	549	100.40	100.30	East Plaza (D)	.
639	526	564	100.76	100.63	East Bar	.
640	508	552	100.02	99.95	East Plaza (BC)	.
641	512	549	99.90	99.80	East Plaza (BC)	.
642	510	549	99.90	99.80	East Plaza (BC)	.
643	510	549	99.80	99.70	East Plaza (BC)	.
644	510	549	99.80	99.70	East Plaza (BC)	.
645	509	550	99.80	99.70	East Plaza (BC)	.
646	508	552	100.17	100.16	East Plaza (BC)	.
647	512	549	99.90	99.80	East Plaza (BC)	.
648	510	550	100.01	100.00	East Plaza (BC)	.
649	510	549	99.80	99.70	East Plaza (BC)	.
650	511	550	100.00	99.90	East Plaza (BC)	.
651	526	549	100.40	100.30	East Plaza (D)	.
652	527	567	101.21	101.20	East Bar	.
653	510	549	99.80	99.70	East Plaza (BC)	.
654	510	550	100.01	100.00	East Plaza (BC)	.
655	511	550	100.10	100.00	East Plaza (BC)	.
656	511	550	100.00	99.90	East Plaza (BC)	.
657	512	549	99.80	99.78	East Plaza (BC)	.
658	527	562	101.40	101.30	East Bar	.
659	527	567	101.25	101.24	East Bar	.
670	529	561	101.30	101.10	East Bar	.
671	510	541	100.76	100.75	Surface	.
672	507	550	100.28	100.10	East Plaza (BC)	.
673	507	550	99.80	99.70	East Plaza (BC)	.
674	509	548	99.70	99.60	East Plaza (BC)	.
675	511	549	99.90	99.80	East Plaza (BC)	.
676	509	550	99.60	99.50	East Plaza (BC)	.
677	509	550	99.50	99.40	East Plaza (BC)	.
678	510	550	99.90	99.80	East Plaza (BC)	.
679	510	550	100.00	99.90	East Plaza (BC)	.
680	510	549	99.70	99.60	East Plaza (BC)	.
681	510	550	100.00	99.90	East Plaza (BC)	.
682	510	549	99.60	99.56	East Plaza (BC)	.
683	508	552	100.02	99.88	East Plaza (BC)	.
684	512	550	100.09	100.00	East Plaza (BC)	.
685	512	550	100.00	99.90	East Plaza (BC)	.
686	512	549	99.80	99.70	East Plaza (BC)	.
687	512	550	100.00	99.90	East Plaza (BC)	.
688	509	549	99.60	99.50	East Plaza (BC)	.
689	508	549	99.64	99.60	East Plaza (BC)	.
690	508	549	99.60	99.50	East Plaza (BC)	.
691	510	549	99.70	99.60	East Plaza (BC)	.
692	510	549	99.70	99.60	East Plaza (BC)	.
693	509	549	99.50	99.40	East Plaza (BC)	.
694	508	550	99.60	99.50	East Plaza (BC)	.
695	510	549	99.63	99.62	East Plaza (BC)	.
696	511	549	99.90	99.80	East Plaza (BC)	.
697	508	549	99.64	99.63	East Plaza (BC)	.
698	509	548	99.80	99.70	East Plaza (BC)	.
699	507	550	99.80	99.70	East Plaza (BC)	.
700	510	550	99.80	99.70	East Plaza (BC)	.
701	507	550	99.70	99.60	East Plaza (BC)	.
702	509	547	99.90	99.80	East Plaza (BC)	.
703	512	550	100.00	99.90	East Plaza (BC)	.
704	509	549	99.60	99.50	East Plaza (BC)	.
705	512	550	99.90	99.80	East Plaza (BC)	.
706	509	547	100.00	99.90	East Plaza (BC)	.
707	510	550	99.67	99.66	East Plaza (BC)	.
708	508	550	99.70	99.60	East Plaza (BC)	.
709	509	548	99.60	99.50	East Plaza (BC)	.
710	510	550	99.90	99.80	East Plaza (BC)	.
711	508	556	100.35	100.34	East Plaza (BC)	.
712	508	556	100.37	100.36	East Plaza (BC)	.
713	510	550	99.90	99.80	East Plaza (BC)	.
714	511	549	99.90	99.80	East Plaza (BC)	.
715	509	548	99.90	99.80	East Plaza (BC)	.
716	529	565	101.10	101.00	East Bar	.
717	529	565	101.10	101.00	East Bar	.
718	523	568	101.10	101.00	East Bar	.
719	508	551	99.90	99.80	East Plaza (BC)	.
720	509	548	99.90	99.80	East Plaza (BC)	.
721	510	549	99.74	99.73	East Plaza (BC)	.
722	510	549	99.60	99.56	East Plaza (BC)	.
723	510	549	99.50	99.44	East Plaza (BC)	.
724	510	549	99.60	99.56	East Plaza (BC)	.
725	508	551	99.80	99.70	East Plaza (BC)	.

Lot No.	Grid N	Grid E	Upper Level	Lower Level	Provenience	Flot. Vol.
726	508	551	99.91	99.70	East Plaza (BC)	.
727	508	551	99.70	99.60	East Plaza (BC)	.
728	508	553	100.30	100.20	East Plaza (BC)	.
729	508	554	100.47	100.30	East Plaza (BC)	.
730	510	548	100.48	100.30	East Plaza (BC)	.
731	526	547	100.30	100.24	East Plaza (D)	.
732	509	550	99.70	99.60	East Plaza (BC)	.
733	511	549	100.51	100.30	East Plaza (BC)	.
734	507	550	99.70	99.60	East Plaza (BC)	.
735	507	550	99.70	99.60	East Plaza (BC)	.
736	509	548	99.70	99.60	East Plaza (BC)	.
737	526	550	100.36	100.35	East Plaza (D)	.
738	527	550	100.30	100.20	East Plaza (D)	.
739	527	567	100.79	100.70	East Bar	.
740	509	549	100.10	100.00	East Plaza (BC)	.
741	490	523	99.10	99.00	South Trench(H)	.
742	528	561	100.64	100.54	East Bar	.
743	509	550	100.10	99.90	East Plaza (BC)	.
744	509	550	99.60	99.50	East Plaza (BC)	.
745	511	549	100.00	99.90	East Plaza (BC)	.
746	511	549	100.00	99.90	East Plaza (BC)	.
747	510	548	100.30	100.10	East Plaza (BC)	.
748	527	564	101.58	101.25	East Bar	.
749	509	549	100.00	99.90	East Plaza (BC)	.
750	526	546	101.60	101.50	East Plaza (D)	.
751	508	549	99.90	99.80	East Plaza (BC)	.
752	527	561	100.70	100.60	East Bar	.
753	510	546	100.30	100.10	East Plaza (BC)	.
754	509	548	99.90	99.80	East Plaza (BC)	.
755	509	549	100.10	100.00	East Plaza (BC)	.
756	509	548	99.90	99.80	East Plaza (BC)	.
757	526	567	100.70	100.60	East Bar	.
758	528	561	100.74	100.64	East Bar	.
759	508	553	100.47	100.30	East Plaza (BC)	.
760	526	550	100.61	100.50	East Plaza (D)	.
761	510	548	100.48	100.30	East Plaza (BC)	.
762	508	554	100.30	100.20	East Plaza (BC)	.
763	528	562	101.00	100.90	East Bar	.
764	510	550	99.80	99.70	East Plaza (BC)	.
765	527	567	101.00	100.88	East Bar	.
766	512	549	99.80	99.70	East Plaza (BC)	.
767	512	549	99.90	99.80	East Plaza (BC)	.
768	509	549	100.10	100.00	East Plaza (BC)	.
769	526	563	100.70	100.60	East Bar	.
770	512	550	100.00	99.90	East Plaza (BC)	.
771	510	532	101.15	101.05	Center Bar	.
772	512	550	100.10	100.00	East Plaza (BC)	.
773	512	532	101.45	101.40	Center Bar	.
774	510	549	100.20	100.10	East Plaza (BC)	.
775	509	550	99.70	99.60	East Plaza (BC)	.
776	511	550	100.10	100.00	East Plaza (BC)	.
777	508	551	99.80	99.70	East Plaza (BC)	.
778	515	534	100.60	99.90	Center Bar	.
779	509	557	100.58	100.40	East Plaza (BC)	.
780	509	547	100.10	100.00	East Plaza (BC)	.
781	509	547	100.30	100.10	East Plaza (BC)	.
782	529	567	101.21	101.20	East Bar	.
783	508	551	99.90	99.80	East Plaza (BC)	.
784	509	548	99.80	99.70	East Plaza (BC)	.
785	508	551	99.90	99.80	East Plaza (BC)	.
786	509	550	99.61	99.60	East Plaza (BC)	.
787	510	550	100.10	100.00	East Plaza (BC)	.
789	508	549	100.00	99.90	East Plaza (BC)	.
790	508	549	100.00	99.90	East Plaza (BC)	.
791	510	546	100.30	100.10	East Plaza (BC)	.
792	526	561	101.00	100.80	East Bar	.
793	510	546	100.54	100.30	East Plaza (BC)	.
794	510	550	100.10	100.00	East Plaza (BC)	.
795	511	550	100.10	100.00	East Plaza (BC)	.
796	528	562	101.60	101.30	East Bar	.
797	511	550	100.50	100.30	East Plaza (BC)	.
798	527	568	101.60	101.40	East Bar	.
799	527	568	101.40	101.30	East Bar	.
800	526	567	100.79	100.69	East Bar	.
801	508	549	99.90	99.80	East Plaza (BC)	.
802	508	556	100.40	100.30	East Plaza (BC)	.
803	526	561	100.80	100.70	East Bar	.
804	523	569	101.36	101.14	East Bar	.
805	527	569	101.40	101.30	East Bar	.
806	528	561	100.57	100.15	East Bar	.
807	508	551	99.80	99.70	East Plaza (BC)	.
808	509	547	100.10	100.00	East Plaza (BC)	.
809	509	548	99.60	99.55	East Plaza (BC)	.
810	511	549	99.90	99.80	East Plaza (BC)	.
811	510	550	99.80	99.70	East Plaza (BC)	.
812	509	551	99.90	99.80	East Plaza (BC)	.
813	510	548	99.60	99.55	East Plaza (BC)	.
814	511	550	100.00	99.90	East Plaza (BC)	.
815	509	549	99.60	99.50	East Plaza (BC)	.
816	510	530	101.05	101.00	Center Bar	.
817	512	533	101.30	101.20	Center Bar	.
818	527	563	101.27	101.15	East Bar	.
819	517	534	100.85	100.65	Center Bar	.
820	515	535	101.30	101.20	Center Bar	.
821	514	535	100.80	100.70	Center Bar	.
822	514	535	100.90	100.80	Center Bar	.

Lot No.	Grid N	Grid E	Upper Level	Lower Level	Provenience	Flot. Vol.
823	516	534	100.85	100.80	Center Bar	.
824	527	563	101.57	101.25	East Bar	.
825	516	535	101.20	101.00	Center Bar	.
826	510	531	101.25	101.20	Center Bar	.
827	516	534	100.80	100.75	Center Bar	.
828	518	533	101.65	101.40	Center Bar	.
829	516	535	101.20	101.00	Center Bar	.
830	517	534	101.05	100.95	Center Bar	.
831	524	566	101.54	101.25	East Bar	.
832	510	532	101.15	101.05	Center Bar	.
833	516	535	102.02	101.60	Center Bar	.
834	510	530	100.76	100.75	Center Bar	.
835	515	534	102.04	101.60	Center Bar	.
836	525	567	101.55	101.25	East Bar	.
837	524	564	101.52	101.45	East Bar	.
838	515	535	101.30	101.20	Center Bar	.
839	517	534	100.95	100.85	Center Bar	.
840	528	565	101.15	101.05	East Bar	.
841	517	533	101.15	101.05	Center Bar	.
842	517	534	101.25	101.15	Center Bar	.
843	509	548	100.51	100.50	East Plaza (BC)	.
844	513	530	101.51	101.50	Center Bar	.
845	511	532	101.35	101.30	Center Bar	.
846	510	530	101.10	101.05	Center Bar	.
847	526	564	101.06	101.05	East Bar	.
848	525	566	101.15	101.05	East Bar	.
849	524	563	101.15	101.05	East Bar	.
850	515	535	101.10	100.90	Center Bar	.
851	516	535	101.00	100.80	Center Bar	.
852	523	563	101.35	101.25	East Bar	.
853	511	530	101.30	101.25	Center Bar	.
854	520	533	102.08	101.65	Center Bar	.
855	517	534	101.35	101.25	Center Bar	.
856	525	561	101.05	100.90	East Bar	.
857	511	532	101.25	101.15	Center Bar	.
858	514	534	101.10	101.00	Center Bar	.
859	511	532	101.35	101.25	Center Bar	.
860	514	534	101.08	101.07	Center Bar	.
861	512	530	101.70	101.65	Center Bar	.
862	515	534	101.00	100.90	Center Bar	.
863	510	531	101.36	101.35	Center Bar	.
864	517	533	101.05	100.85	Center Bar	.
865	525	567	101.25	101.15	East Bar	.
866	510	533	101.10	101.09	Center Bar	.
867	516	535	100.63	100.62	Center Bar	.
868	526	568	101.55	101.25	East Bar	.
869	512	534	101.50	101.45	Center Bar	.
870	511	535	101.15	101.14	Center Bar	.

Lot No.	Grid N	Grid E	Upper Level	Lower Level	Provenience	Flot. Vol.
871	523	562	101.42	101.35	East Bar	.
872	516	535	101.60	101.40	Center Bar	.
873	522	561	101.15	101.05	East Bar	.
874	521	561	101.15	101.05	East Bar	.
875	516	535	101.20	101.00	Center Bar	.
876	524	563	101.25	101.15	East Bar	.
877	521	564	101.25	101.15	East Bar	.
878	515	535	102.04	101.60	Center Bar	.
879	526	563	100.95	100.90	East Bar	.
880	510	532	101.30	101.25	Center Bar	.
881	524	564	101.15	101.05	East Bar	.
882	523	565	101.45	101.35	East Bar	.
883	523	565	101.36	101.35	East Bar	.
884	511	535	101.25	101.15	Center Bar	.
885	509	548	100.10	100.00	East Plaza (BC)	.
886	539	551	101.40	101.20	Main Bar East	.
887	511	549	100.20	100.10	East Plaza (BC)	.
888	522	535	100.72	100.54	Center Bar	.
889	512	549	99.90	99.80	East Plaza (BC)	.
890	510	548	100.10	100.00	East Plaza (BC)	.
891	509	550	99.80	99.70	East Plaza (BC)	.
892	510	550	99.90	99.80	East Plaza (BC)	.
893	526	546	100.40	100.30	East Plaza (D)	.
894	523	562	101.05	101.04	East Bar	.
895	511	535	101.32	101.25	Center Bar	.
896	521	562	101.37	101.25	East Bar	.
897	514	534	101.35	101.25	Center Bar	.
898	509	546	100.30	100.10	East Plaza (BC)	.
899	507	550	100.28	100.10	East Plaza (BC)	.
900	522	565	101.15	101.05	East Bar	.
901	513	534	100.99	100.85	Center Bar	.
902	509	548	99.70	99.60	East Plaza (BC)	.
903	512	549	100.00	99.90	East Plaza (BC)	.
904	508	550	100.10	100.06	East Plaza (BC)	.
905	509	549	99.90	99.80	East Plaza (BC)	.
906	510	550	99.90	99.80	East Plaza (BC)	.
907	508	550	99.80	99.70	East Plaza (BC)	.
908	515	535	101.90	101.70	Center Bar	.
909	508	549	99.40	99.33	East Plaza (BC)	.
910	512	533	101.40	101.35	Center Bar	.
911	512	549	99.90	99.80	East Plaza (BC)	.
912	517	533	101.75	101.60	Center Bar	.
913	510	530	101.15	101.10	Center Bar	.
914	511	531	101.25	101.15	Center Bar	.
915	517	533	101.30	101.15	Center Bar	.
916	526	565	100.75	100.70	East Bar	.
917	512	534	101.45	101.40	Center Bar	.
918	510	531	101.35	101.30	Center Bar	.

Lot No.	Grid N	Grid E	Upper Level	Lower Level	Provenience	Flot. Vol.
919	509	548	100.51	100.50	East Plaza (BC)	.
920	510	549	100.00	99.90	East Plaza (BC)	.
921	522	564	101.46	101.25	East Bar	.
922	524	564	101.25	101.15	East Bar	.
923	523	564	101.15	101.05	East Bar	.
924	513	534	100.95	100.85	Center Bar	.
925	513	531	102.03	101.90	Center Bar	.
926	513	534	101.55	101.50	Center Bar	.
927	524	563	101.35	101.25	East Bar	.
928	510	549	99.70	99.60	East Plaza (BC)	.
929	511	549	99.90	99.80	East Plaza (BC)	.
930	526	562	101.49	101.40	East Bar	.
931	508	552	101.02	100.95	East Plaza (BC)	.
932	509	549	99.70	99.60	East Plaza (BC)	.
933	511	549	99.90	99.80	East Plaza (BC)	.
934	509	549	99.70	99.60	East Plaza (BC)	.
935	510	549	99.90	99.80	East Plaza (BC)	.
936	512	549	99.90	99.80	East Plaza (BC)	.
937	512	549	99.90	99.80	East Plaza (BC)	.
938	511	547	100.20	100.10	East Plaza (BC)	.
939	509	548	99.70	99.60	East Plaza (BC)	.
940	509	550	99.80	99.70	East Plaza (BC)	.
941	511	550	100.00	99.90	East Plaza (BC)	.
942	510	549	99.56	99.50	East Plaza (BC)	.
943	508	552	100.15	100.14	East Plaza (BC)	.
944	512	549	99.80	99.70	East Plaza (BC)	.
945	507	550	100.20	100.10	East Plaza (BC)	.
946	529	562	101.40	101.20	East Bar	.
947	512	549	99.90	99.80	East Plaza (BC)	.
948	508	548	100.30	100.10	East Plaza (BC)	.
949	509	547	100.50	100.30	East Plaza (BC)	.
950	509	550	99.90	99.80	East Plaza (BC)	.
951	510	533	101.06	101.05	Center Bar	.
952	508	549	99.80	99.70	East Plaza (BC)	.
953	509	548	100.51	100.50	East Plaza (BC)	.
954	509	557	100.58	100.40	East Plaza (BC)	.
955	509	547	100.10	100.00	East Plaza (BC)	.
956	513	535	101.35	101.25	Center Bar	.
957	508	552	100.20	100.10	East Plaza (BC)	.
958	523	569	101.10	101.00	East Bar	.
959	508	549	99.60	99.50	East Plaza (BC)	.
960	511	550	100.10	100.00	East Plaza (BC)	.
961	514	534	100.63	100.50	Center Bar	.
962	527	563	101.15	101.05	East Bar	.
963	508	551	99.90	99.80	East Plaza (BC)	.
964	510	550	100.30	100.10	East Plaza (BC)	.
965	517	533	100.85	100.75	Center Bar	.
966	524	561	101.25	101.15	East Bar	.
967	521	567	101.15	101.05	East Bar	.
968	513	530	101.85	101.80	Center Bar	.
969	517	534	101.25	101.15	Center Bar	.
970	524	562	101.15	101.05	East Bar	.
971	515	534	101.60	101.40	Center Bar	.
972	527	562	101.20	101.10	East Bar	.
973	522	562	101.25	101.15	East Bar	.
974	513	533	101.50	101.40	Center Bar	.
975	525	566	101.25	101.15	East Bar	.
976	512	535	101.30	101.25	Center Bar	.
977	508	550	100.53	100.30	East Plaza (BC)	.
978	529	562	101.73	101.43	East Bar	.
979	512	532	101.45	101.40	Center Bar	.
980	523	567	101.25	101.15	East Bar	.
981	522	565	101.25	101.15	East Bar	.
982	512	533	101.55	101.50	Center Bar	.
983	508	552	100.02	99.80	East Plaza (BC)	.
984	512	550	100.09	100.00	East Plaza (BC)	.
985	512	532	101.60	101.55	Center Bar	.
986	526	563	100.64	100.63	East Bar	.
987	510	546	100.54	100.30	East Plaza (BC)	.
988	521	566	101.21	101.15	East Bar	.
989	508	551	99.80	99.70	East Plaza (BC)	.
990	512	550	100.54	100.30	East Plaza (BC)	.
991	509	547	100.30	100.10	East Plaza (BC)	.
992	509	548	99.70	99.60	East Plaza (BC)	.
993	511	532	101.60	101.55	Center Bar	.
994	521	515	100.20	100.10	West Plaza	.
995	508	549	99.50	99.40	East Plaza (BC)	.
996	510	550	100.10	100.00	East Plaza (BC)	.
997	510	550	100.00	99.90	East Plaza (BC)	.
998	509	548	99.80	99.70	East Plaza (BC)	.
999	524	563	101.25	101.15	East Bar	.
1000	522	534	102.25	102.24	Center Bar	.
1001	526	550	100.76	100.60	East Plaza (D)	.
1002	524	566	101.15	101.05	East Bar	.
1003	522	534	101.49	101.48	Center Bar	.
1004	514	532	101.80	101.70	Center Bar	.
1005	524	569	101.10	101.00	East Bar	.
1006	525	566	101.51	101.50	East Bar	.
1007	522	534	102.25	102.24	Center Bar	.
1008	509	547	100.00	99.90	East Plaza (BC)	.
1009	507	550	99.80	99.70	East Plaza (BC)	.
1010	513	535	101.05	100.95	Center Bar	.
1011	507	550	99.80	99.70	East Plaza (BC)	.
1012	510	550	100.50	100.30	East Plaza (BC)	.
1013	508	549	100.20	100.10	East Plaza (BC)	.
1014	510	549	99.90	99.80	East Plaza (BC)	.

Lot No.	Grid N	Grid E	Upper Level	Lower Level	Provenience	Flot. Vol.
1015	507	550	99.80	99.70	East Plaza (BC)	.
1016	510	550	100.00	99.90	East Plaza (BC)	.
1017	509	548	99.70	99.60	East Plaza (BC)	.
1018	512	532	101.79	101.78	Center Bar	.
1019	522	565	101.46	101.35	East Bar	.
1020	509	548	100.48	100.30	East Plaza (BC)	.
1021	508	550	99.40	99.35	East Plaza (BC)	.
1022	522	561	101.20	101.10	East Bar	.
1023	524	567	101.51	101.25	East Bar	.
1024	508	550	99.50	99.40	East Plaza (BC)	.
1025	510	550	99.90	99.80	East Plaza (BC)	.
1026	522	515	100.30	100.20	West Plaza	.
1027	526	546	101.50	101.40	East Plaza (D)	.
1028	515	534	101.60	101.40	Center Bar	.
1029	508	550	99.70	99.60	East Plaza (BC)	.
1030	507	550	99.80	99.70	East Plaza (BC)	.
1031	512	550	100.30	100.10	East Plaza (BC)	.
1032	510	549	100.00	99.90	East Plaza (BC)	.
1033	507	550	99.90	99.80	East Plaza (BC)	.
1034	509	549	99.80	99.70	East Plaza (BC)	.
1035	510	549	99.90	99.80	East Plaza (BC)	.
1036	529	560	101.05	101.00	East Bar	.
1037	509	550	99.80	99.70	East Plaza (BC)	.
1038	509	548	99.60	99.50	East Plaza (BC)	.
1039	560	540	100.35	99.92	Ring Midden (I)	.
1040	510	550	99.80	99.70	East Plaza (BC)	.
1041	508	549	99.80	99.70	East Plaza (BC)	.
1042	511	550	100.30	100.10	East Plaza (BC)	.
1043	513	534	101.50	101.45	Center Bar	.
1044	525	564	100.95	100.90	East Bar	.
1045	510	530	101.39	101.30	Center Bar	.
1046	512	534	101.30	101.20	Center Bar	.
1047	511	550	100.30	100.10	East Plaza (BC)	.
1048	525	561	101.05	100.90	East Bar	.
1049	511	530	101.45	101.40	Center Bar	.
1050	513	533	101.80	101.75	Center Bar	.
1051	521	563	101.15	101.05	East Bar	.
1052	507	550	99.70	99.60	East Plaza (BC)	.
1053	528	563	100.56	100.24	East Bar	.
1054	526	561	100.61	100.60	East Bar	.
1055	511	550	100.00	99.90	East Plaza (BC)	.
1056	510	549	99.60	99.51	East Plaza (BC)	.
1057	508	549	100.41	100.20	East Plaza (BC)	.
1058	508	550	100.30	100.10	East Plaza (BC)	.
1059	511	534	101.35	101.30	Center Bar	.
1060	509	550	99.50	99.40	East Plaza (BC)	.
1061	509	547	100.00	99.90	East Plaza (BC)	.
1062	508	551	99.70	99.60	East Plaza (BC)	.

Lot No.	Grid N	Grid E	Upper Level	Lower Level	Provenience	Flot. Vol.
1063	510	549	99.50	99.44	East Plaza (BC)	.
1064	511	547	100.20	100.10	East Plaza (BC)	.
1065	510	549	99.50	99.44	East Plaza (BC)	.
1066	512	549	100.00	99.90	East Plaza (BC)	.
1067	525	561	100.81	100.70	East Bar	.
1068	522	534	102.25	102.24	Center Bar	.
1069	509	556	100.40	100.30	East Plaza (BC)	.
1070	510	548	100.12	100.00	East Plaza (BC)	.
1071	509	550	99.60	99.50	East Plaza (BC)	.
1072	517	533	101.75	101.60	Center Bar	.
1073	509	548	100.51	100.50	East Plaza (BC)	.
1074	511	549	100.00	99.90	East Plaza (BC)	.
1075	527	564	101.25	101.15	East Bar	.
1076	526	564	101.25	101.15	East Bar	.
1077	523	563	101.15	101.05	East Bar	.
1078	516	535	100.80	100.70	Center Bar	.
1079	510	548	100.00	99.90	East Plaza (BC)	.
1080	508	549	99.60	99.50	East Plaza (BC)	.
1081	525	562	101.05	100.95	East Bar	.
1082	517	534	101.05	100.85	Center Bar	.
1083	528	567	101.45	101.43	East Bar	.
1084	512	532	101.70	101.65	Center Bar	.
1085	522	515	100.42	100.30	West Plaza	.
1086	510	530	101.30	101.20	Center Bar	.
1087	526	550	100.18	100.10	East Plaza (D)	.
1088	527	565	101.15	101.08	East Bar	.
1089	513	530	101.80	101.75	Center Bar	.
1090	508	549	99.50	99.40	East Plaza (BC)	.
1091	524	567	101.51	101.25	East Bar	.
1092	528	565	101.25	101.15	East Bar	.
1093	514	531	101.85	101.75	Center Bar	.
1094	510	532	101.25	101.20	Center Bar	.
1095	511	531	101.60	101.55	Center Bar	.
1096	508	556	100.34	100.23	East Plaza (BC)	.
1097	528	562	100.90	100.80	East Bar	.
1098	528	565	100.99	100.98	East Bar	.
1099	526	563	100.63	100.37	East Bar	.
1100	510	532	101.06	101.05	Center Bar	.
1101	527	561	100.80	100.77	East Bar	.
1102	508	556	100.51	100.40	East Plaza (BC)	.
1103	508	552	100.20	100.14	East Plaza (BC)	.
1104	508	550	99.60	99.50	East Plaza (BC)	.
1105	508	557	100.53	100.40	East Plaza (BC)	.
1106	516	535	102.06	101.60	Center Bar	.
1107	509	549	99.60	99.50	East Plaza (BC)	.
1108	512	550	100.09	100.00	East Plaza (BC)	.
1109	509	549	100.00	99.90	East Plaza (BC)	.
1110	516	535	101.20	101.00	Center Bar	.

Lot No.	Grid N	Grid E	Upper Level	Lower Level	Provenience	Flot. Vol.
1111	511	549	100.51	100.30	East Plaza (BC)	.
1112	511	550	100.00	99.90	East Plaza (BC)	.
1113	511	550	100.00	99.90	East Plaza (BC)	.
1114	522	514	100.40	100.30	West Plaza	.
1115	523	564	101.25	101.15	East Bar	.
1116	512	534	101.30	101.25	Center Bar	.
1117	522	567	101.25	101.15	East Bar	.
1118	525	564	101.15	101.05	East Bar	.
1119	515	534	101.42	101.41	Center Bar	.
1120	509	556	100.56	100.40	East Plaza (BC)	.
1121	512	532	101.30	101.25	Center Bar	.
1122	521	565	101.25	101.15	East Bar	.
1123	527	563	101.30	101.20	East Bar	.
1124	522	566	101.15	101.05	East Bar	.
1125	517	533	101.60	101.50	Center Bar	.
1126	513	535	100.85	100.75	Center Bar	.
1127	510	550	100.00	99.90	East Plaza (BC)	.
1128	509	550	100.10	99.90	East Plaza (BC)	.
1129	510	549	99.90	99.80	East Plaza (BC)	.
1130	511	534	101.25	101.15	Center Bar	.
1131	511	549	100.30	100.20	East Plaza (BC)	.
1132	512	535	101.15	101.05	Center Bar	.
1133	509	546	100.10	100.00	East Plaza (BC)	.
1134	511	533	101.45	101.40	Center Bar	.
1135	520	533	101.65	101.45	Center Bar	.
1136	514	535	101.65	101.55	Center Bar	.
1137	522	565	101.15	101.05	East Bar	.
1138	510	548	100.10	100.00	East Plaza (BC)	.
1139	511	533	101.50	101.45	Center Bar	.
1140	509	548	99.90	99.80	East Plaza (BC)	.
1141	517	534	100.69	100.68	Center Bar	.
1142	514	535	101.10	101.00	Center Bar	.
1143	516	534	102.09	101.60	Center Bar	.
1144	517	534	102.00	101.60	Center Bar	.
1145	517	534	100.95	100.85	Center Bar	.
1146	527	548	100.50	100.40	East Plaza (D)	.
1147	508	552	100.45	100.30	East Plaza (BC)	.
1148	522	567	101.15	101.05	East Bar	.
1149	527	561	100.80	100.60	East Bar	.
1150	513	530	101.15	101.05	Center Bar	.
1151	508	551	99.70	99.60	East Plaza (BC)	.
1152	522	515	100.20	100.10	West Plaza	.
1153	522	534	102.25	102.24	Center Bar	.
1154	511	547	100.54	100.30	East Plaza (BC)	.
1155	526	563	101.54	101.25	East Bar	.
1156	524	564	101.45	101.35	East Bar	.
1157	514	533	101.75	101.65	Center Bar	.
1158	508	550	99.60	99.50	East Plaza (BC)	.

Lot No.	Grid N	Grid E	Upper Level	Lower Level	Provenience	Flot. Vol.
1159	526	563	101.05	100.88	East Bar	.
1160	521	565	101.15	101.05	East Bar	.
1161	510	533	101.09	101.08	Center Bar	.
1162	523	565	101.35	101.25	East Bar	.
1163	528	562	101.30	101.00	East Bar	.
1164	514	534	100.90	100.80	Center Bar	.
1165	515	534	101.30	101.20	Center Bar	.
1166	516	535	101.40	101.30	Center Bar	.
1167	521	561	101.28	101.15	East Bar	.
1168	509	546	100.10	100.00	East Plaza (BC)	.
1169	528	567	100.55	100.45	East Bar	.
1170	516	535	101.20	101.00	Center Bar	.
1171	508	551	100.49	100.30	East Plaza (BC)	.
1172	511	530	101.35	101.30	Center Bar	.
1173	517	533	101.05	100.95	Center Bar	.
1174	529	566	101.20	101.10	East Bar	.
1175	521	567	101.15	101.05	East Bar	.
1176	515	534	100.75	100.70	Center Bar	.
1177	507	550	100.10	100.00	East Plaza (BC)	.
1178	509	548	99.80	99.70	East Plaza (BC)	.
1179	509	547	100.00	99.90	East Plaza (BC)	.
1180	514	534	101.75	101.65	Center Bar	.
1181	528	565	101.68	101.25	East Bar	.
1182	508	551	100.10	100.00	East Plaza (BC)	.
1183	528	562	100.80	100.70	East Bar	.
1184	527	565	101.62	101.25	East Bar	.
1185	510	549	100.30	100.20	East Plaza (BC)	.
1186	508	553	100.20	100.10	East Plaza (BC)	.
1189	516	534	101.40	101.20	Center Bar	.
1190	524	565	101.25	101.15	East Bar	.
1191	509	550	100.10	99.90	East Plaza (BC)	.
1192	510	549	100.20	100.10	East Plaza (BC)	.
1193	516	535	100.80	100.70	Center Bar	.
1194	515	535	100.90	100.70	Center Bar	.
1195	512	530	101.65	101.60	Center Bar	.
1196	510	549	100.51	100.30	East Plaza (BC)	.
1197	521	561	101.15	101.05	East Bar	.
1198	508	549	99.70	99.60	East Plaza (BC)	.
1199	515	535	101.10	100.90	Center Bar	.
1200	516	535	101.40	101.30	Center Bar	.
1201	523	563	101.25	101.15	East Bar	.
1202	517	533	101.30	101.15	Center Bar	.
1203	508	550	99.90	99.80	East Plaza (BC)	.
1204	507	550	100.10	99.79	East Plaza (BC)	.
1205	510	533	101.25	101.20	Center Bar	.
1206	517	533	101.50	101.40	Center Bar	.
1207	516	535	101.20	101.00	Center Bar	.
1208	517	534	101.60	101.35	Center Bar	.

Lot No.	Grid N	Grid E	Upper Level	Lower Level	Provenience	Flot. Vol.
1209	526	565	101.56	101.25	East Bar	.
1210	507	550	99.80	99.70	East Plaza (BC)	.
1211	523	566	101.51	101.25	East Bar	.
1212	510	550	100.10	100.00	East Plaza (BC)	.
1213	509	550	99.90	99.80	East Plaza (BC)	.
1214	514	534	100.63	100.45	Center Bar	.
1215	514	534	100.60	100.59	Center Bar	.
1216	523	535	100.72	100.54	Center Bar	.
1217	527	565	101.25	101.15	East Bar	.
1218	508	551	100.30	100.20	East Plaza (BC)	.
1219	515	535	101.60	101.40	Center Bar	.
1220	509	548	99.70	99.60	East Plaza (BC)	.
1221	512	549	100.10	100.00	East Plaza (BC)	.
1222	510	547	100.52	100.30	East Plaza (BC)	.
1223	511	550	100.00	99.90	East Plaza (BC)	.
1224	509	548	99.80	99.70	East Plaza (BC)	.
1225	511	549	100.10	100.00	East Plaza (BC)	.
1226	510	548	99.90	99.80	East Plaza (BC)	.
1227	509	550	99.90	99.80	East Plaza (BC)	.
1228	509	549	100.30	100.10	East Plaza (BC)	.
1229	529	563	101.00	100.80	East Bar	.
1230	509	549	99.61	99.50	East Plaza (BC)	.
1231	507	550	100.00	99.90	East Plaza (BC)	.
1232	512	550	100.30	100.10	East Plaza (BC)	.
1233	523	569	101.20	101.00	East Bar	.
1234	512	534	101.58	101.50	Center Bar	.
1235	509	548	99.70	99.60	East Plaza (BC)	.
1236	511	550	99.90	99.80	East Plaza (BC)	.
1237	508	550	99.70	99.60	East Plaza (BC)	.
1238	521	565	101.44	101.25	East Bar	.
1239	522	563	101.15	101.05	East Bar	.
1240	508	550	100.00	99.90	East Plaza (BC)	.
1241	528	562	100.79	100.65	East Bar	.
1242	510	549	100.00	99.90	East Plaza (BC)	.
1243	510	535	101.16	101.05	Center Bar	.
1244	515	534	101.20	101.00	Center Bar	.
1245	510	548	100.00	99.90	East Plaza (BC)	.
1246	509	550	99.70	99.60	East Plaza (BC)	.
1247	511	531	101.35	101.30	Center Bar	.
1248	509	549	99.80	99.70	East Plaza (BC)	.
1249	526	569	101.53	101.40	East Bar	.
1250	514	533	102.04	101.85	Center Bar	.
1251	525	563	101.15	101.05	East Bar	.
1252	509	549	100.51	100.30	East Plaza (BC)	.
1253	511	549	100.20	100.10	East Plaza (BC)	.
1254	508	551	100.49	100.30	East Plaza (BC)	.
1255	510	534	101.15	101.05	Center Bar	.
1256	512	549	100.54	100.30	East Plaza (BC)	.

Lot No.	Grid N	Grid E	Upper Level	Lower Level	Provenience	Flot. Vol.
1257	517	534	101.15	101.05	Center Bar	.
1258	525	561	101.25	101.15	East Bar	.
1259	512	549	100.10	100.00	East Plaza (BC)	.
1260	525	562	100.70	100.67	East Bar	.
1261	527	567	101.20	101.10	East Bar	.
1262	511	549	100.20	100.10	East Plaza (BC)	.
1263	508	549	99.80	99.70	East Plaza (BC)	.
1264	521	564	101.42	101.25	East Bar	.
1265	509	548	100.00	99.90	East Plaza (BC)	.
1266	525	561	100.85	100.80	East Bar	.
1267	529	564	101.40	101.20	East Bar	.
1268	510	548	100.00	99.90	East Plaza (BC)	.
1269	510	547	100.20	100.10	East Plaza (BC)	.
1270	509	549	99.80	99.70	East Plaza (BC)	.
1271	529	563	101.00	100.80	East Bar	.
1272	510	533	101.15	101.10	Center Bar	.
1273	515	534	101.85	101.80	Center Bar	.
1274	521	535	100.73	100.52	Center Bar	.
1275	512	550	100.00	99.90	East Plaza (BC)	.
1276	509	549	99.60	99.50	East Plaza (BC)	.
1277	522	562	101.38	101.25	East Bar	.
1278	510	548	100.00	99.90	East Plaza (BC)	.
1279	527	562	100.80	100.70	East Bar	.
1280	528	564	101.25	100.98	East Bar	.
1281	527	562	100.60	100.55	East Bar	.
1282	508	550	100.00	99.90	East Plaza (BC)	.
1283	517	534	101.15	101.05	Center Bar	.
1284	511	549	100.10	100.00	East Plaza (BC)	.
1285	527	563	100.60	100.50	East Bar	.
1286	524	564	101.35	101.25	East Bar	.
1287	528	565	101.68	101.15	East Bar	.
1288	509	548	99.50	99.40	East Plaza (BC)	.
1289	513	534	100.95	100.85	Center Bar	.
1290	524	565	101.45	101.35	East Bar	.
1291	515	535	100.75	100.70	Center Bar	.
1292	517	534	101.15	101.05	Center Bar	.
1293	514	534	101.25	101.10	Center Bar	.
1294	523	563	101.15	101.05	East Bar	.
1295	513	534	101.05	100.95	Center Bar	.
1296	518	533	101.65	101.40	Center Bar	.
1297	513	535	100.75	100.65	Center Bar	.
1298	526	566	101.02	100.35	East Bar	.
1299	514	535	101.10	101.00	Center Bar	.
1300	512	533	101.30	101.20	Center Bar	.
1301	515	535	100.90	100.70	Center Bar	.
1302	528	565	101.25	101.15	East Bar	.
1303	523	561	101.25	101.15	East Bar	.
1304	523	563	101.25	101.15	East Bar	.

Lot No.	Grid N	Grid E	Upper Level	Lower Level	Provenience	Flot. Vol.
1305	516	534	101.60	101.40	Center Bar	.
1306	508	551	100.49	99.91	East Plaza (BC)	.
1307	516	534	101.60	101.40	Center Bar	.
1308	527	565	101.62	101.25	East Bar	.
1309	524	563	101.40	101.35	East Bar	.
1310	510	532	101.15	101.05	Center Bar	.
1311	514	535	101.10	101.00	Center Bar	.
1312	522	562	101.25	101.15	East Bar	.
1313	517	534	101.05	100.95	Center Bar	.
1314	529	563	101.20	101.00	East Bar	.
1315	511	530	101.51	101.50	Center Bar	.
1316	513	530	101.25	101.15	Center Bar	.
1317	527	566	101.01	101.00	East Bar	.
1318	513	533	101.76	101.75	Center Bar	.
1319	513	533	101.50	101.40	Center Bar	.
1320	521	566	101.46	101.25	East Bar	.
1321	525	564	101.40	101.35	East Bar	.
1322	530	565	101.21	101.20	East Bar	.
1323	511	550	100.20	100.10	East Plaza (BC)	.
1324	521	562	101.25	101.15	East Bar	.
1325	515	534	101.40	101.30	Center Bar	.
1326	511	549	100.10	100.00	East Plaza (BC)	.
1327	522	566	101.46	101.25	East Bar	.
1328	527	564	101.05	100.99	East Bar	.
1329	528	561	101.00	100.80	East Bar	.
1330	516	534	101.00	100.90	Center Bar	.
1331	526	566	101.27	101.25	East Bar	.
1332	510	548	99.90	99.80	East Plaza (BC)	.
1333	511	549	100.30	100.20	East Plaza (BC)	.
1334	509	549	99.70	99.60	East Plaza (BC)	.
1335	512	549	100.00	99.90	East Plaza (BC)	.
1336	508	549	99.60	99.50	East Plaza (BC)	.
1337	522	562	101.15	101.05	East Bar	.
1338	509	546	100.30	100.10	East Plaza (BC)	.
1339	513	534	101.05	100.95	Center Bar	.
1340	515	533	102.00	101.80	Center Bar	.
1341	515	534	101.20	101.00	Center Bar	.
1342	511	546	100.30	100.20	East Plaza (BC)	.
1343	522	570	101.04	100.90	East Bar	.
1344	512	549	100.30	100.20	East Plaza (BC)	.
1345	509	550	99.80	99.70	East Plaza (BC)	.
1346	528	564	101.62	101.25	East Bar	.
1347	525	563	100.90	100.85	East Bar	.
1348	511	547	100.30	100.20	East Plaza (BC)	.
1349	508	549	99.80	99.70	East Plaza (BC)	.
1350	526	564	101.66	101.25	East Bar	.
1351	508	551	100.20	100.10	East Plaza (BC)	.
1352	509	547	99.90	99.80	East Plaza (BC)	.

Lot No.	Grid N	Grid E	Upper Level	Lower Level	Provenience	Flot. Vol.
1353	508	551	100.49	99.91	East Plaza (BC)	.
1354	525	563	100.70	100.65	East Bar	.
1355	507	550	100.00	99.90	East Plaza (BC)	.
1356	513	534	101.25	101.15	Center Bar	.
1357	508	551	100.10	100.00	East Plaza (BC)	.
1358	529	564	101.20	101.00	East Bar	.
1359	521	515	100.42	100.30	West Plaza	.
1360	527	562	100.90	100.80	East Bar	.
1361	509	548	99.70	99.60	East Plaza (BC)	.
1362	513	530	101.65	101.60	Center Bar	.
1363	510	549	100.10	100.00	East Plaza (BC)	.
1364	516	535	101.30	101.20	Center Bar	.
1365	507	550	99.80	99.70	East Plaza (BC)	.
1366	523	564	101.45	101.35	East Bar	.
1367	527	561	100.76	100.75	East Bar	.
1368	521	565	101.25	101.15	East Bar	.
1369	528	565	101.25	101.24	East Bar	.
1370	522	564	101.46	101.25	East Bar	.
1371	528	566	101.25	101.15	East Bar	.
1372	508	549	99.60	99.50	East Plaza (BC)	.
1373	510	550	100.30	100.10	East Plaza (BC)	.
1374	525	569	101.35	101.30	East Bar	.
1375	509	548	100.51	100.50	East Plaza (BC)	.
1376	539	551	101.20	101.00	Main Bar East	.
1377	509	550	99.80	99.70	East Plaza (BC)	.
1378	510	549	99.80	99.70	East Plaza (BC)	.
1379	510	550	100.10	100.00	East Plaza (BC)	.
1380	509	548	99.90	99.80	East Plaza (BC)	.
1381	560	540	100.35	99.92	Ring Midden (I)	.
1382	512	549	100.20	100.10	East Plaza (BC)	.
1383	523	562	101.35	101.25	East Bar	.
1384	510	549	100.20	100.10	East Plaza (BC)	.
1385	511	549	100.00	99.90	East Plaza (BC)	.
1386	528	566	101.15	101.05	East Bar	.
1387	526	568	101.15	101.05	East Bar	.
1388	508	552	100.30	100.20	East Plaza (BC)	.
1389	511	550	100.00	99.90	East Plaza (BC)	.
1390	507	550	99.70	99.60	East Plaza (BC)	.
1391	511	547	100.54	100.30	East Plaza (BC)	.
1392	510	547	100.30	100.20	East Plaza (BC)	.
1393	509	550	99.80	99.70	East Plaza (BC)	.
1394	511	531	101.55	101.50	Center Bar	.
1395	509	549	99.60	99.50	East Plaza (BC)	.
1396	515	534	101.40	101.30	Center Bar	.
1397	518	533	102.10	101.75	Center Bar	.
1398	507	550	100.10	100.00	East Plaza (BC)	.
1399	510	550	100.10	100.00	East Plaza (BC)	.
1400	523	565	101.15	101.05	East Bar	.

Lot No.	Grid N	Grid E	Upper Level	Lower Level	Provenience	Flot. Vol.
1401	524	562	101.35	101.25	East Bar	.
1402	510	549	99.90	99.80	East Plaza (BC)	.
1403	516	535	100.70	100.65	Center Bar	.
1404	517	533	101.05	100.95	Center Bar	.
1405	514	535	101.55	101.45	Center Bar	.
1406	510	549	100.30	100.20	East Plaza (BC)	.
1407	512	550	100.00	99.90	East Plaza (BC)	.
1408	508	556	100.30	100.32	East Plaza (BC)	.
1409	528	567	101.25	101.15	East Bar	.
1410	523	566	101.15	101.05	East Bar	.
1411	515	535	100.70	100.65	Center Bar	.
1412	509	556	100.40	100.30	East Plaza (BC)	.
1413	523	565	101.25	101.15	East Bar	.
1414	508	550	99.80	99.70	East Plaza (BC)	.
1415	511	550	99.90	99.80	East Plaza (BC)	.
1416	509	550	99.70	99.60	East Plaza (BC)	.
1417	510	549	100.00	99.90	East Plaza (BC)	.
1418	509	549	99.70	99.60	East Plaza (BC)	.
1419	509	549	99.60	99.50	East Plaza (BC)	.
1420	511	546	100.51	100.30	East Plaza (BC)	.
1421	509	549	99.90	99.80	East Plaza (BC)	.
1422	516	535	101.20	101.00	Center Bar	.
1423	510	550	99.90	99.80	East Plaza (BC)	.
1424	512	549	100.10	100.00	East Plaza (BC)	.
1425	509	550	100.10	99.90	East Plaza (BC)	.
1426	508	550	99.90	99.80	East Plaza (BC)	.
1427	524	565	101.35	101.25	East Bar	.
1428	517	533	100.75	100.65	Center Bar	.
1429	513	534	101.35	101.25	Center Bar	.
1430	525	563	100.45	100.35	East Bar	.
1431	526	549	100.74	100.60	East Plaza (D)	.
1432	515	534	100.64	100.63	Center Bar	.
1433	511	549	100.01	100.00	East Plaza (BC)	.
1434	510	549	100.00	99.90	East Plaza (BC)	.
1435	512	535	101.15	101.10	Center Bar	.
1436	510	549	99.70	99.60	East Plaza (BC)	.
1437	522	570	101.14	101.04	East Bar	.
1438	510	548	99.90	99.80	East Plaza (BC)	.
1439	511	550	100.00	99.90	East Plaza (BC)	.
1440	525	566	100.35	100.25	East Bar	.
1441	513	535	100.27	100.23	Center Bar	.
1442	514	533	101.45	101.35	Center Bar	.
1443	519	533	102.11	101.75	Center Bar	.
1444	511	549	100.00	99.90	East Plaza (BC)	.
1445	509	548	99.90	99.80	East Plaza (BC)	.
1446	508	550	100.12	100.00	East Plaza (BC)	.
1447	508	549	100.20	100.10	East Plaza (BC)	.
1448	510	530	100.76	100.75	Center Bar	.

Lot No.	Grid N	Grid E	Upper Level	Lower Level	Provenience	Flot. Vol.
1449	526	564	101.54	101.25	East Bar	.
1450	508	550	99.90	99.80	East Plaza (BC)	.
1451	523	565	101.45	101.35	East Bar	.
1452	517	534	101.05	100.95	Center Bar	.
1453	512	549	100.54	100.30	East Plaza (BC)	.
1454	510	549	100.20	100.10	East Plaza (BC)	.
1455	511	549	99.90	99.80	East Plaza (BC)	.
1456	512	535	101.25	101.20	Center Bar	.
1457	526	563	101.15	101.05	East Bar	.
1458	515	533	101.58	101.57	Center Bar	.
1459	512	531	101.50	101.40	Center Bar	.
1460	510	546	100.30	100.10	East Plaza (BC)	.
1461	507	550	99.90	99.80	East Plaza (BC)	.
1462	508	551	100.10	100.00	East Plaza (BC)	.
1463	524	562	101.20	101.15	East Bar	.
1464	516	534	100.65	100.63	Center Bar	.
1465	525	562	101.15	101.05	East Bar	.
1466	560	540	100.35	99.92	Ring Midden (I)	.
1467	517	534	101.60	101.35	Center Bar	.
1468	527	561	100.80	100.60	East Bar	.
1469	539	551	100.00	99.80	Main Bar East	.
1470	527	561	100.77	100.60	East Bar	.
1471	515	535	100.75	100.70	Center Bar	.
1472	516	533	101.35	101.10	Center Bar	.
1473	509	547	100.00	99.90	East Plaza (BC)	.
1474	522	535	100.54	100.53	Center Bar	.
1475	509	557	100.40	100.30	East Plaza (BC)	.
1476	511	535	101.15	101.10	Center Bar	.
1477	515	533	102.00	101.80	Center Bar	.
1478	517	534	101.35	101.20	Center Bar	.
1479	514	534	101.70	101.60	Center Bar	.
1480	526	565	100.80	100.70	East Bar	.
1481	514	535	100.90	100.80	Center Bar	.
1482	521	515	100.14	100.00	West Plaza	.
1483	514	534	101.00	100.90	Center Bar	.
1484	513	532	101.50	101.40	Center Bar	.
1485	526	566	101.02	100.95	East Bar	.
1486	511	532	101.30	101.25	Center Bar	.
1487	509	548	100.10	100.00	East Plaza (BC)	.
1488	512	549	99.90	99.80	East Plaza (BC)	.
1489	523	565	101.25	101.15	East Bar	.
1490	560	540	100.35	99.92	Ring Midden (I)	.
1491	525	564	100.90	100.80	East Bar	.
1492	518	533	101.65	101.40	Center Bar	.
1493	510	549	100.51	100.30	East Plaza (BC)	.
1494	522	565	101.35	101.25	East Bar	.
1495	528	562	100.56	99.87	East Bar	.
1496	524	561	101.30	101.10	East Bar	.

Lot No.	Grid N	Grid E	Upper Level	Lower Level	Provenience	Flot. Vol.
1497	507	550	99.80	99.70	East Plaza (BC)	.
1498	522	534	100.58	100.57	Center Bar	.
1499	523	569	100.97	100.96	East Bar	.
1500	508	550	99.70	99.60	East Plaza (BC)	.
1501	522	565	101.35	101.25	East Bar	.
1502	516	533	102.09	101.80	Center Bar	.
1503	525	563	100.55	100.45	East Bar	.
1504	511	546	100.51	100.30	East Plaza (BC)	.
1505	522	564	101.42	101.25	East Bar	.
1506	508	549	100.00	99.90	East Plaza (BC)	.
1507	523	563	101.15	101.05	East Bar	.
1508	523	568	101.42	101.20	East Bar	.
1509	539	551	101.20	101.00	Main Bar East	.
1510	527	565	101.62	101.25	East Bar	.
1511	513	535	101.05	100.95	Center Bar	.
1512	539	551	100.20	100.00	Main Bar East	.
1513	514	534	101.00	100.90	Center Bar	.
1514	523	569	101.00	100.90	East Bar	.
1515	512	530	101.40	101.35	Center Bar	.
1516	516	533	101.00	100.90	Center Bar	.
1517	490	523	99.10	98.90	South Trench(H)	.
1518	514	530	102.06	102.00	Center Bar	.
1519	528	561	101.59	101.30	East Bar	.
1520	522	562	101.15	101.05	East Bar	.
1521	526	567	101.15	101.05	East Bar	.
1522	523	562	101.15	101.05	East Bar	.
1523	513	534	100.85	100.72	Center Bar	.
1524	523	563	100.80	100.70	East Bar	.
1525	509	547	99.95	99.90	East Plaza (BC)	.
1526	525	562	100.82	100.70	East Bar	.
1527	516	534	101.40	101.30	Center Bar	.
1528	514	531	101.95	101.90	Center Bar	.
1529	518	533	101.75	101.65	Center Bar	.
1530	522	514	100.30	100.20	West Plaza	.
1531	514	534	101.65	101.55	Center Bar	.
1532	521	515	100.31	100.20	West Plaza	.
1533	521	563	101.25	101.15	East Bar	.
1534	512	533	101.45	101.40	Center Bar	.
1535	508	551	99.91	99.70	East Plaza (BC)	.
1536	525	562	100.67	100.60	East Bar	.
1537	514	535	101.60	101.50	Center Bar	.
1538	539	551	101.40	101.20	Main Bar East	.
1539	511	533	101.20	101.19	Center Bar	.
1540	508	552	100.00	99.71	East Plaza (BC)	.
1541	516	533	102.09	102.08	Center Bar	.
1542	522	563	101.10	101.00	East Bar	.
1543	529	565	101.20	101.10	East Bar	.
1544	510	548	99.90	99.80	East Plaza (BC)	.
1545	513	535	100.75	100.65	Center Bar	.
1546	516	534	102.09	101.60	Center Bar	.
1547	510	550	99.90	99.80	East Plaza (BC)	.
1548	516	535	101.00	100.80	Center Bar	.
1549	511	549	99.90	99.80	East Plaza (BC)	.
1550	513	535	101.25	101.15	Center Bar	.
1551	513	535	101.35	101.25	Center Bar	.
1552	509	547	99.95	99.90	East Plaza (BC)	.
1553	524	566	101.54	101.25	East Bar	.
1554	515	534	100.55	99.86	Center Bar	.
1555	529	563	101.40	101.20	East Bar	.
1556	512	550	99.90	99.80	East Plaza (BC)	.
1557	512	531	101.70	101.65	Center Bar	.
1558	513	535	101.69	100.65	Center Bar	.
1559	527	561	100.75	100.74	East Bar	.
1560	522	561	101.25	101.15	East Bar	.
1561	523	563	100.90	100.80	East Bar	.
1562	517	533	101.40	101.30	Center Bar	.
1563	516	533	101.75	101.65	Center Bar	.
1564	515	535	101.60	101.40	Center Bar	.
1565	526	564	101.15	101.05	East Bar	.
1566	511	550	99.90	99.80	East Plaza (BC)	.
1567	525	563	100.90	100.85	East Bar	.
1568	515	535	101.40	101.30	Center Bar	.
1569	529	564	101.20	101.00	East Bar	.
1570	512	531	101.50	101.45	Center Bar	.
1571	524	564	101.06	101.05	East Bar	.
1572	515	534	101.40	101.20	Center Bar	.
1573	511	532	101.15	101.05	Center Bar	.
1574	523	561	101.34	101.25	East Bar	.
1575	522	567	101.15	101.05	East Bar	.
1576	513	534	101.65	101.60	Center Bar	.
1577	510	533	101.06	101.05	Center Bar	.
1578	513	532	101.70	101.60	Center Bar	.
1579	514	534	101.55	101.45	Center Bar	.
1580	525	561	101.15	101.05	East Bar	.
1581	510	532	101.15	101.05	Center Bar	.
1582	513	532	101.60	101.50	Center Bar	.
1583	508	550	99.70	99.60	East Plaza (BC)	.
1584	529	563	100.80	100.60	East Bar	.
1585	524	563	101.40	101.35	East Bar	.
1586	513	534	101.45	101.35	Center Bar	.
1587	515	534	100.75	100.70	Center Bar	.
1588	516	533	101.10	101.00	Center Bar	.
1589	523	562	101.15	101.05	East Bar	.
1590	513	531	101.60	101.50	Center Bar	.
1591	513	535	101.45	101.40	Center Bar	.
1592	515	534	100.80	100.75	Center Bar	.

Lot No.	Grid N	Grid E	Upper Level	Lower Level	Provenience	Flot. Vol.
1593	527	567	101.10	101.00	East Bar	.
1594	527	550	100.20	100.00	East Plaza (D)	.
1595	512	531	101.82	101.70	Center Bar	.
1596	528	562	100.56	99.87	East Bar	.
1597	527	567	101.01	100.32	East Bar	.
1598	522	515	100.10	100.00	West Plaza	.
1599	523	564	101.50	101.45	East Bar	.
1600	512	549	100.30	100.20	East Plaza (BC)	.
1601	526	566	100.96	100.95	East Bar	.
1602	526	565	101.05	100.95	East Bar	.
1603	513	535	100.45	100.27	Center Bar	.
1604	508	551	99.60	99.50	East Plaza (BC)	.
1605	523	564	100.90	100.80	East Bar	.
1606	524	567	101.25	101.15	East Bar	.
1607	515	534	100.90	100.85	Center Bar	.
1608	513	534	101.70	101.65	Center Bar	.
1609	508	550	99.70	99.60	East Plaza (BC)	.
1610	517	533	101.50	101.40	Center Bar	.
1611	523	565	101.52	101.45	East Bar	.
1612	514	533	101.35	101.25	Center Bar	.
1613	512	535	101.20	101.15	Center Bar	.
1614	525	567	101.15	101.05	East Bar	.
1615	511	546	100.20	100.10	East Plaza (BC)	.
1616	508	557	100.40	100.30	East Plaza (BC)	.
1617	512	530	101.82	101.70	Center Bar	.
1618	523	564	101.35	101.25	East Bar	.
1619	524	565	101.54	101.45	East Bar	.
1620	560	540	100.35	99.92	Ring Midden (I)	.
1621	510	548	99.80	99.60	East Plaza (BC)	.
1622	526	566	100.79	100.78	East Bar	.
1623	510	549	99.80	99.70	East Plaza (BC)	.
1624	560	540	100.35	99.92	Ring Midden (I)	.
1625	512	533	101.60	101.55	Center Bar	.
1626	513	531	101.70	101.60	Center Bar	.
1627	513	530	102.03	101.90	Center Bar	.
1628	525	564	101.15	101.05	East Bar	.
1629	515	534	101.20	101.00	Center Bar	.
1630	510	530	101.20	101.15	Center Bar	.
1631	516	534	102.09	101.60	Center Bar	.
1632	528	567	101.68	101.25	East Bar	.
1633	508	553	100.20	100.10	East Plaza (BC)	.
1634	526	563	100.88	100.80	East Bar	.
1635	510	530	101.20	101.10	Center Bar	.
1636	522	561	101.25	101.15	East Bar	.
1637	522	566	101.15	101.05	East Bar	.
1638	515	534	100.90	100.85	Center Bar	.
1639	513	531	101.50	101.40	Center Bar	.
1640	514	533	101.65	101.55	Center Bar	.

Lot No.	Grid N	Grid E	Upper Level	Lower Level	Provenience	Flot. Vol.
1641	513	535	100.95	100.85	Center Bar	.
1642	514	532	102.01	102.00	Center Bar	.
1643	511	532	101.45	101.40	Center Bar	.
1644	513	535	100.85	100.75	Center Bar	.
1645	510	530	101.30	101.25	Center Bar	.
1646	509	548	100.51	100.50	East Plaza (BC)	.
1647	527	562	101.40	101.30	East Bar	.
1648	527	562	100.53	100.52	East Bar	.
1649	514	535	100.70	100.60	Center Bar	.
1650	522	565	101.46	101.35	East Bar	.
1651	511	531	101.35	101.25	Center Bar	.
1652	515	533	102.10	102.00	Center Bar	.
1653	515	535	102.04	101.40	Center Bar	.
1654	513	535	101.15	101.05	Center Bar	.
1655	512	531	101.40	101.35	Center Bar	.
1656	527	565	100.90	100.80	East Bar	.
1657	516	534	100.75	100.70	Center Bar	.
1658	525	564	101.45	101.40	East Bar	.
1659	523	563	101.46	101.35	East Bar	.
1660	527	565	100.95	100.90	East Bar	.
1661	517	533	100.85	100.65	Center Bar	.
1662	527	561	100.58	100.53	East Bar	.
1663	526	568	101.25	101.15	East Bar	.
1664	513	534	101.24	101.23	Center Bar	.
1665	513	535	100.66	100.42	Center Bar	.
1666	523	535	100.92	100.58	Center Bar	.
1667	523	561	101.25	101.15	East Bar	.
1668	525	567	101.25	101.15	East Bar	.
1669	514	531	101.45	101.35	Center Bar	.
1670	517	534	100.60	100.30	Center Bar	.
1671	522	562	101.05	101.02	East Bar	.
1672	514	533	101.85	101.75	Center Bar	.
1673	524	565	101.25	101.15	East Bar	.
1674	515	533	101.40	101.30	Center Bar	.
1675	526	550	100.28	100.27	East Plaza (D)	.
1676	517	533	100.65	100.64	Center Bar	.
1677	527	567	101.10	101.00	East Bar	.
1678	525	566	100.70	100.65	East Bar	.
1679	513	530	101.85	101.80	Center Bar	.
1680	527	565	101.05	100.95	East Bar	.
1681	512	550	100.13	100.04	East Plaza (BC)	.
1682	560	540	100.35	99.92	Ring Midden (I)	.
1683	514	534	100.80	100.70	Center Bar	.
1684	527	561	100.80	100.70	East Bar	.
1685	523	566	101.25	101.15	East Bar	.
1686	516	533	100.90	100.85	Center Bar	.
1687	526	565	101.25	101.15	East Bar	.
1688	527	567	101.10	101.06	East Bar	.

Lot No.	Grid N	Grid E	Upper Level	Lower Level	Provenience	Flot. Vol.
1689	514	534	100.38	100.37	Center Bar	.
1690	515	535	100.61	100.60	Center Bar	.
1691	523	568	101.20	101.10	East Bar	.
1692	525	566	100.75	100.70	East Bar	.
1693	510	549	99.80	99.70	East Plaza (BC)	.
1694	514	535	101.75	101.65	Center Bar	.
1695	507	550	99.90	99.80	East Plaza (BC)	.
1696	511	534	101.35	101.30	Center Bar	.
1697	511	531	101.25	101.15	Center Bar	.
1698	517	533	100.85	100.75	Center Bar	.
1699	510	550	100.10	100.00	East Plaza (BC)	.
1700	511	531	101.35	101.25	Center Bar	.
1701	526	567	101.01	100.32	East Bar	.
1702	514	532	101.90	101.85	Center Bar	.
1703	511	533	101.53	101.50	Center Bar	.
1704	522	534	102.25	102.24	Center Bar	.
1705	524	562	101.41	101.35	East Bar	.
1706	525	566	101.15	101.05	East Bar	.
1707	524	564	101.01	101.00	East Bar	.
1708	511	535	101.07	101.06	Center Bar	.
1709	526	563	101.15	101.05	East Bar	.
1710	516	533	100.85	100.80	Center Bar	.
1711	514	534	101.85	101.75	Center Bar	.
1712	516	533	100.80	100.75	Center Bar	.
1713	525	567	101.15	101.10	East Bar	.
1714	523	534	100.63	100.55	Center Bar	.
1715	528	561	100.80	100.74	East Bar	.
1716	526	568	101.15	101.10	East Bar	.
1717	526	567	100.88	100.79	East Bar	.
1718	522	534	102.25	102.24	Center Bar	.
1719	509	547	100.00	99.90	East Plaza (BC)	.
1720	528	565	100.98	100.80	East Bar	.
1721	508	551	100.00	99.90	East Plaza (BC)	.
1722	521	566	101.25	101.15	East Bar	.
1723	525	562	101.15	101.05	East Bar	.
1724	514	533	101.55	101.45	Center Bar	.
1725	526	565	101.05	101.00	East Bar	.
1726	514	534	100.65	100.64	Center Bar	.
1727	513	533	101.90	101.80	Center Bar	.
1728	515	535	101.21	101.20	Center Bar	.
1729	529	564	100.96	100.66	East Bar	.
1730	513	531	101.90	101.80	Center Bar	.
1731	527	567	100.88	100.79	East Bar	.
1732	517	534	100.95	100.85	Center Bar	.
1733	512	531	101.65	101.60	Center Bar	.
1734	527	561	100.90	100.80	East Bar	.
1735	516	535	100.80	100.70	Center Bar	.
1736	511	531	101.40	101.35	Center Bar	.

Lot No.	Grid N	Grid E	Upper Level	Lower Level	Provenience	Flot. Vol.
1737	510	530	100.76	100.75	Center Bar	.
1738	525	566	100.90	100.88	East Bar	.
1739	516	534	100.25	100.24	Center Bar	.
1740	509	549	99.40	99.30	East Plaza (BC)	.
1741	527	567	101.10	101.06	East Bar	.
1742	513	535	100.69	100.68	Center Bar	.
1743	527	564	101.24	100.94	East Bar	.
1744	528	561	101.00	100.80	East Bar	.
1745	526	565	100.95	100.90	East Bar	.
1746	512	535	101.08	101.07	Center Bar	.
1747	526	564	100.95	100.90	East Bar	.
1748	523	566	101.11	101.10	East Bar	.
1749	516	534	101.60	101.40	Center Bar	.
1750	525	566	100.88	100.80	East Bar	.
1751	526	566	100.95	100.94	East Bar	.
1752	525	562	100.91	100.90	East Bar	.
1753	514	534	100.38	100.37	Center Bar	.
1754	526	566	101.02	100.95	East Bar	.
1755	516	535	100.64	100.63	Center Bar	.
1756	526	561	100.60	100.37	East Bar	.
1757	516	533	101.55	101.45	Center Bar	.
1758	522	534	102.25	102.24	Center Bar	.
1759	525	561	101.10	101.05	East Bar	.
1760	527	567	101.01	100.32	East Bar	.
1761	513	534	101.65	101.60	Center Bar	.
1762	514	530	101.60	101.55	Center Bar	.
1763	528	564	101.05	100.95	East Bar	.
1764	511	532	101.50	101.45	Center Bar	.
1765	513	530	101.80	101.75	Center Bar	.
1766	513	534	101.05	100.95	Center Bar	.
1767	514	531	101.75	101.65	Center Bar	.
1768	511	533	101.40	101.35	Center Bar	.
1769	511	530	101.25	101.20	Center Bar	.
1770	524	561	101.25	101.15	East Bar	.
1771	511	532	101.55	101.50	Center Bar	.
1772	525	563	101.15	101.05	East Bar	.
1773	514	531	101.90	101.85	Center Bar	.
1774	511	533	101.45	101.40	Center Bar	.
1775	525	565	101.30	101.25	East Bar	.
1776	513	530	101.45	101.35	Center Bar	.
1777	514	530	101.95	101.90	Center Bar	.
1778	512	531	101.65	101.60	Center Bar	.
1779	522	534	102.25	102.24	Center Bar	.
1780	513	530	101.35	101.25	Center Bar	.
1781	523	562	101.15	101.05	East Bar	.
1782	512	532	101.40	101.35	Center Bar	.
1783	514	531	101.85	101.75	Center Bar	.
1784	514	534	101.90	101.75	Center Bar	.

Lot No.	Grid N	Grid E	Upper Level	Lower Level	Provenience	Flot. Vol.
1785	516	534	101.20	101.00	Center Bar	.
1786	525	565	101.25	101.15	East Bar	.
1787	515	534	101.30	101.20	Center Bar	.
1788	511	530	101.35	101.30	Center Bar	.
1789	512	530	101.60	101.55	Center Bar	.
1790	526	563	100.93	100.92	East Bar	.
1791	523	564	101.25	101.15	East Bar	.
1792	512	532	101.55	101.50	Center Bar	.
1793	525	565	101.15	101.05	East Bar	.
1794	512	532	101.55	101.50	Center Bar	.
1795	511	531	101.30	101.20	Center Bar	.
1796	513	533	101.76	101.75	Center Bar	.
1797	513	530	101.60	101.55	Center Bar	.
1798	515	533	101.50	101.40	Center Bar	.
1799	515	533	101.80	101.70	Center Bar	.
1800	511	531	101.50	101.45	Center Bar	.
1801	512	534	101.50	101.45	Center Bar	.
1802	512	534	101.35	101.30	Center Bar	.
1803	514	530	101.75	101.65	Center Bar	.
1804	522	565	101.46	101.35	East Bar	.
1805	524	561	101.25	101.15	East Bar	.
1806	525	564	101.15	101.05	East Bar	.
1807	516	534	101.40	101.30	Center Bar	.
1808	512	534	101.40	101.35	Center Bar	.
1809	512	535	101.30	101.25	Center Bar	.
1810	514	531	101.90	101.85	Center Bar	.
1811	512	532	101.40	101.35	Center Bar	.
1812	513	534	101.05	100.95	Center Bar	.
1813	526	563	100.93	100.92	East Bar	.
1814	513	533	101.76	101.75	Center Bar	.
1815	515	534	100.70	100.65	Center Bar	.
1816	516	535	101.30	101.20	Center Bar	.
1817	516	535	101.60	101.40	Center Bar	.
1818	524	565	101.45	101.35	East Bar	.
1819	515	534	101.60	101.40	Center Bar	.
1820	515	534	101.20	101.00	Center Bar	.
1821	513	532	101.90	101.80	Center Bar	.
1822	521	566	101.46	101.25	East Bar	.
1823	514	534	100.80	100.70	Center Bar	.
1824	513	531	101.70	101.60	Center Bar	.
1825	521	566	101.46	101.25	East Bar	.
1826	516	534	101.20	101.00	Center Bar	.
1827	522	534	102.25	102.24	Center Bar	.
1828	515	535	101.20	101.10	Center Bar	.
1829	524	563	101.25	101.15	East Bar	.
1830	523	563	101.46	101.35	East Bar	.
1831	516	535	101.40	101.30	Center Bar	.
1832	513	535	100.95	100.85	Center Bar	.
1833	516	535	101.30	101.20	Center Bar	.
1834	512	531	101.55	101.50	Center Bar	.
1835	513	530	101.51	101.50	Center Bar	.
1836	512	535	101.30	101.25	Center Bar	.
1837	513	535	100.95	100.85	Center Bar	.
1838	521	535	100.73	100.52	Center Bar	.
1839	522	534	102.25	102.24	Center Bar	.
1840	527	562	100.70	100.60	East Bar	.
1841	510	530	100.76	100.75	Center Bar	.
1842	508	556	100.35	100.34	East Plaza (BC)	.
1843	525	562	101.25	101.15	East Bar	.
1844	513	530	101.51	101.50	Center Bar	.
1845	523	566	101.51	101.25	East Bar	.
1846	515	534	101.00	100.90	Center Bar	.
1847	516	535	100.53	100.48	Center Bar	.
1848	513	533	101.80	101.75	Center Bar	.
1849	525	565	101.45	101.40	East Bar	.
1850	521	564	101.15	101.05	East Bar	.
1851	522	534	102.25	102.24	Center Bar	.
1852	512	534	101.30	101.25	Center Bar	.
1853	526	568	101.15	101.10	East Bar	.
1854	522	534	102.25	102.24	Center Bar	.
1855	515	534	101.40	101.30	Center Bar	.
1856	522	534	102.25	102.24	Center Bar	.
1857	512	534	101.45	101.40	Center Bar	.
1858	514	534	101.25	101.10	Center Bar	.
1859	512	534	100.58	100.48	Center Bar	.
1860	522	563	101.15	101.05	East Bar	.
1861	514	531	101.85	101.75	Center Bar	.
1862	524	563	101.40	101.35	East Bar	.
1863	514	535	101.50	101.45	Center Bar	.
1864	525	561	101.25	101.15	East Bar	.
1865	513	535	101.45	101.40	Center Bar	.
1866	524	566	101.54	101.25	East Bar	.
1867	510	533	101.35	101.30	Center Bar	.
1868	513	532	101.80	101.70	Center Bar	.
1869	512	532	101.55	101.50	Center Bar	.
1870	516	534	100.75	100.70	Center Bar	.
1871	513	532	101.40	101.35	Center Bar	.
1872	526	566	101.15	101.05	East Bar	.
1873	513	533	101.89	101.70	Center Bar	.
1874	516	533	102.10	101.35	Center Bar	.
1875	514	531	102.04	101.95	Center Bar	.
1876	513	533	101.80	101.65	Center Bar	.
1877	517	533	101.89	101.75	Center Bar	.
1878	524	563	101.35	101.25	East Bar	.
1879	512	534	101.40	101.35	Center Bar	.
1880	526	564	101.25	101.15	East Bar	.

Lot No.	Grid N	Grid E	Upper Level	Lower Level	Provenience	Flot. Vol.
1881	525	563	101.25	101.20	East Bar	.
1882	513	535	101.45	101.40	Center Bar	.
1883	512	533	101.50	101.45	Center Bar	.
1884	514	535	101.25	101.10	Center Bar	.
1885	524	567	101.25	101.15	East Bar	.
1886	525	563	101.25	101.20	East Bar	.
1887	523	566	101.25	101.15	East Bar	.
1888	522	534	102.25	102.24	Center Bar	.
1889	524	563	101.35	101.25	East Bar	.
1890	512	533	101.78	101.70	Center Bar	.
1891	513	532	101.50	101.40	Center Bar	.
1892	517	534	101.04	101.03	Center Bar	.
1893	511	533	101.45	101.40	Center Bar	.
1894	512	532	101.82	101.70	Center Bar	.
1895	511	530	101.40	101.35	Center Bar	.
1896	514	534	101.25	101.10	Center Bar	.
1897	522	534	102.25	102.24	Center Bar	.
1898	512	531	101.60	101.55	Center Bar	.
1899	521	563	101.15	101.05	East Bar	.
1900	514	531	101.35	101.25	Center Bar	.
1901	516	533	101.65	101.55	Center Bar	.
1902	512	532	101.60	101.55	Center Bar	.
1903	512	534	101.30	101.20	Center Bar	.
1904	514	535	101.25	101.10	Center Bar	.
1905	526	566	101.15	101.05	East Bar	.
1906	516	533	101.45	101.35	Center Bar	.
1907	522	562	101.15	101.05	East Bar	.
1908	518	533	101.43	101.42	Center Bar	.
1909	514	535	101.35	101.25	Center Bar	.
1910	513	534	101.05	100.95	Center Bar	.
1911	521	562	101.25	101.15	East Bar	.
1912	522	562	101.38	101.25	East Bar	.
1913	522	566	101.15	101.05	East Bar	.
1914	516	535	102.06	101.60	Center Bar	.
1915	522	562	101.15	101.05	East Bar	.
1916	513	535	101.25	101.15	Center Bar	.
1917	521	566	101.25	101.15	East Bar	.
1918	520	533	102.08	101.65	Center Bar	.
1919	510	532	101.20	101.15	Center Bar	.
1920	525	563	101.20	101.15	East Bar	.
1921	523	564	101.15	101.05	East Bar	.
1922	515	535	101.90	101.30	Center Bar	.
1923	514	531	101.75	101.65	Center Bar	.
1924	524	564	101.06	101.05	East Bar	.
1925	522	567	101.42	101.25	East Bar	.
1926	518	533	101.75	101.65	Center Bar	.
1927	527	565	101.25	101.15	East Bar	.
1928	518	533	101.65	101.40	Center Bar	.
1929	523	561	101.25	101.15	East Bar	.
1930	515	534	101.00	100.90	Center Bar	.
1931	522	534	102.25	102.24	Center Bar	.
1932	523	566	101.15	101.05	East Bar	.
1933	521	567	101.15	101.05	East Bar	.
1934	516	534	100.70	100.65	Center Bar	.
1935	528	564	101.66	101.25	East Bar	.
1936	520	533	101.65	101.45	Center Bar	.
1937	522	567	101.42	101.25	East Bar	.
1938	522	561	101.25	101.15	East Bar	.
1939	522	534	102.25	102.24	Center Bar	.
1940	524	563	101.35	101.25	East Bar	.
1941	528	565	101.68	101.25	East Bar	.
1942	513	535	101.15	101.05	Center Bar	.
1943	512	532	101.82	101.70	Center Bar	.
1944	514	535	101.00	100.90	Center Bar	.
1945	510	532	101.20	101.15	Center Bar	.
1946	513	533	101.50	101.40	Center Bar	.
1947	512	535	101.15	101.05	Center Bar	.
1948	513	532	101.50	101.40	Center Bar	.
1949	524	565	101.45	101.35	East Bar	.
1950	513	532	101.40	101.35	Center Bar	.
1951	522	564	101.46	101.25	East Bar	.
1952	516	534	101.60	101.40	Center Bar	.
1953	515	535	101.90	101.30	Center Bar	.
1954	514	534	100.90	100.80	Center Bar	.
1955	510	532	101.25	101.20	Center Bar	.
1956	528	565	101.68	101.25	East Bar	.
1957	525	567	101.15	101.05	East Bar	.
1958	517	534	100.85	100.75	Center Bar	.
1959	514	532	101.80	101.70	Center Bar	.
1960	513	535	100.95	100.85	Center Bar	.
1961	516	535	102.06	101.60	Center Bar	.
1962	514	534	101.10	101.00	Center Bar	.
1963	513	532	102.00	101.90	Center Bar	.
1964	512	531	101.55	101.50	Center Bar	.
1965	523	561	101.25	101.15	East Bar	.
1966	516	535	102.06	101.60	Center Bar	.
1967	517	533	101.40	101.30	Center Bar	.
1968	515	535	100.90	100.70	Center Bar	.
1969	515	534	101.40	101.30	Center Bar	.
1970	514	531	101.45	101.35	Center Bar	.
1971	511	532	101.40	101.35	Center Bar	.
1972	513	533	101.76	101.75	Center Bar	.
1973	525	565	101.40	101.35	East Bar	.
1974	515	534	100.75	100.70	Center Bar	.
1975	513	533	101.75	101.70	Center Bar	.
1976	516	535	102.06	101.60	Center Bar	.

Lot No.	Grid N	Grid E	Upper Level	Lower Level	Provenience	Flot. Vol.
1977	523	567	101.25	101.15	East Bar	.
1978	515	535	101.30	101.20	Center Bar	.
1979	524	564	101.25	101.15	East Bar	.
1980	516	534	102.09	101.60	Center Bar	.
1981	514	534	101.25	101.10	Center Bar	.
1982	524	565	101.45	101.35	East Bar	.
1983	513	534	101.60	101.55	Center Bar	.
1984	520	533	102.08	101.65	Center Bar	.
1985	513	531	101.80	101.75	Center Bar	.
1986	513	530	101.45	101.35	Center Bar	.
1987	514	532	101.50	101.40	Center Bar	.
1988	527	565	101.13	101.10	East Bar	.
1989	516	534	100.65	100.60	Center Bar	.
1990	514	532	101.60	101.50	Center Bar	.
1991	525	564	101.35	101.30	East Bar	.
1992	513	533	101.70	101.65	Center Bar	.
1993	511	531	101.45	101.40	Center Bar	.
1994	514	533	100.70	100.62	Center Bar	.
1995	527	565	101.25	101.15	East Bar	.
1996	521	535	100.80	100.56	Center Bar	.
1997	525	565	101.35	101.30	East Bar	.
1998	513	533	101.76	101.75	Center Bar	.
1999	511	534	101.30	101.25	Center Bar	.
2000	516	535	102.06	101.60	Center Bar	.
2001	515	534	101.60	101.40	Center Bar	.
2002	513	533	101.60	101.55	Center Bar	.
2003	513	530	101.90	101.85	Center Bar	.
2004	513	535	100.95	100.85	Center Bar	.
2005	515	535	101.10	100.90	Center Bar	.
2006	513	530	101.45	101.35	Center Bar	.
2007	513	531	101.75	101.70	Center Bar	.
2008	511	533	101.35	101.30	Center Bar	.
2009	512	531	101.40	101.35	Center Bar	.
2010	513	534	101.05	100.95	Center Bar	.
2011	527	565	101.15	101.05	East Bar	.
2012	518	533	101.65	101.40	Center Bar	.
2013	513	530	101.75	101.70	Center Bar	.
2014	525	564	101.10	101.09	East Bar	.
2015	516	534	100.65	100.60	Center Bar	.
2016	513	530	101.35	101.25	Center Bar	.
2017	511	531	101.45	101.40	Center Bar	.
2018	517	534	102.00	101.60	Center Bar	.
2019	514	531	101.65	101.55	Center Bar	.
2020	514	530	101.85	101.80	Center Bar	.
2021	514	531	101.55	101.45	Center Bar	.
2022	525	564	101.30	101.25	East Bar	.
2023	514	530	102.00	101.95	Center Bar	.
2024	525	563	101.30	101.25	East Bar	.
2025	513	535	101.15	101.05	Center Bar	.
2026	513	533	101.76	101.75	Center Bar	.
2027	513	535	101.09	100.95	Center Bar	.
2028	523	564	101.25	101.15	East Bar	1.0
2029	513	534	100.71	100.58	Center Bar	2.0
2030	525	564	101.15	101.05	East Bar	.3
2031	515	535	100.70	100.65	Center Bar	2.0
2032	516	534	100.57	100.52	Center Bar	.3
2033	509	548	99.70	99.60	East Plaza (BC)	2.5
2034	508	549	99.80	99.70	East Plaza (BC)	1.5
2035	512	550	99.90	99.83	East Plaza (BC)	1.0
2036	510	549	99.50	99.47	East Plaza (BC)	3.0
2037	509	549	99.50	99.40	East Plaza (BC)	2.0
2038	524	565	101.10	101.05	East Bar	4.5
2039	516	533	101.35	101.10	Center Bar	5.0
2040	510	550	100.01	100.00	East Plaza (BC)	2.5
2041	509	556	100.40	100.30	East Plaza (BC)	2.5
2042	511	546	100.30	100.20	East Plaza (BC)	2.5
2043	514	534	100.67	100.65	Center Bar	4.0
2044	515	534	100.71	100.70	Center Bar	4.5
2045	511	550	100.00	99.90	East Plaza (BC)	3.5
2046	507	550	99.80	99.70	East Plaza (BC)	2.0
2047	509	550	99.90	99.80	East Plaza (BC)	2.5
2048	511	549	100.30	100.20	East Plaza (BC)	3.5
2049	515	534	100.70	100.65	Center Bar	5.5
2050	526	565	100.90	100.85	East Bar	16.0
2051	512	550	100.10	100.00	East Plaza (BC)	4.0
2052	511	547	100.20	100.10	East Plaza (BC)	3.0
2053	513	534	101.05	100.95	Center Bar	5.0
2054	509	550	99.80	99.70	East Plaza (BC)	2.5
2055	509	549	100.00	99.90	East Plaza (BC)	3.0
2056	517	534	100.95	100.85	Center Bar	6.0
2057	517	533	100.95	100.85	Center Bar	5.5
2058	516	535	100.63	100.62	Center Bar	4.0
2059	516	535	100.63	100.58	Center Bar	1.5
2060	508	551	100.30	100.20	East Plaza (BC)	3.0
2061	528	563	100.56	100.40	East Bar	5.0
2062	508	550	99.80	99.70	East Plaza (BC)	2.0
2063	509	548	100.00	99.90	East Plaza (BC)	3.5
2064	509	549	99.60	99.50	East Plaza (BC)	2.0
2065	508	550	99.90	99.80	East Plaza (BC)	3.0
2066	508	552	99.88	99.80	East Plaza (BC)	3.0
2067	512	550	100.10	100.00	East Plaza (BC)	2.0
2068	526	565	100.60	100.50	East Bar	9.0
2069	512	549	100.00	99.90	East Plaza (BC)	4.0
2070	508	557	100.40	100.30	East Plaza (BC)	3.0
2071	507	550	99.90	99.80	East Plaza (BC)	2.0
2072	508	550	99.90	99.80	East Plaza (BC)	2.0

Lot No.	Grid N	Grid E	Upper Level	Lower Level	Provenience	Flot. Vol.
2073	512	550	100.00	99.90	East Plaza (BC)	3.5
2074	509	546	100.10	100.00	East Plaza (BC)	3.0
2075	526	567	101.04	100.95	East Bar	6.0
2076	510	532	101.08	101.02	Center Bar	2.5
2077	509	547	99.60	99.50	East Plaza (BC)	3.0
2078	508	550	99.40	99.38	East Plaza (BC)	3.5
2079	510	550	99.80	99.70	East Plaza (BC)	3.5
2080	512	550	99.90	99.80	East Plaza (BC)	5.0
2081	512	550	100.09	100.00	East Plaza (BC)	5.0
2082	508	549	99.60	99.50	East Plaza (BC)	2.0
2083	509	550	100.10	99.90	East Plaza (BC)	3.0
2084	527	567	100.88	100.80	East Bar	4.0
2085	511	546	100.20	100.10	East Plaza (BC)	2.5
2086	510	546	100.30	100.10	East Plaza (BC)	1.5
2087	507	550	99.80	99.70	East Plaza (BC)	2.5
2088	510	548	100.10	100.00	East Plaza (BC)	2.0
2089	512	549	99.84	99.83	East Plaza (BC)	4.0
2090	509	547	100.10	100.00	East Plaza (BC)	3.5
2091	508	549	99.50	99.40	East Plaza (BC)	2.0
2092	525	566	100.95	100.90	East Bar	3.0
2093	516	534	101.20	101.00	Center Bar	6.0
2096	523	562	101.15	101.05	East Bar	.3
2097	516	535	100.28	100.23	Center Bar	1.0
2098	510	548	99.90	99.80	East Plaza (BC)	2.0
2099	525	564	101.15	101.05	East Bar	1.0
2100	515	534	100.65	100.64	Center Bar	6.5
2101	508	556	100.40	100.30	East Plaza (BC)	2.5
2102	510	549	99.70	99.60	East Plaza (BC)	4.0
2103	509	548	99.80	99.70	East Plaza (BC)	2.0
2104	525	562	100.90	100.89	East Bar	4.0
2105	509	550	99.70	99.60	East Plaza (BC)	4.0
2106	510	549	100.20	100.10	East Plaza (BC)	3.0
2107	508	551	100.10	100.00	East Plaza (BC)	3.0
2108	512	549	100.00	99.90	East Plaza (BC)	4.5
2109	508	550	99.70	99.60	East Plaza (BC)	2.0
2110	517	534	100.85	100.75	Center Bar	4.0
2111	510	548	100.00	99.90	East Plaza (BC)	2.0
2112	525	561	100.85	100.80	East Bar	4.0
2113	528	563	100.56	100.40	East Bar	2.0
2114	525	566	100.50	100.45	East Bar	5.5
2115	513	535	100.66	100.46	Center Bar	8.0
2116	525	567	101.05	100.95	East Bar	3.5
2117	516	535	101.30	101.20	Center Bar	8.0
2118	526	566	100.95	100.90	East Bar	3.5
2119	522	535	100.45	100.40	Center Bar	4.5
2120	516	534	100.39	100.34	Center Bar	.2
2121	516	535	100.63	100.62	Center Bar	2.0

Lot No.	Grid N	Grid E	Upper Level	Lower Level	Provenience	Flot. Vol.
2122	528	565	100.98	100.93	East Bar	1.5
2123	507	550	99.70	99.60	East Plaza (BC)	3.0
2124	512	549	100.20	100.10	East Plaza (BC)	2.5
2125	516	535	100.70	100.65	Center Bar	10.0
2126	508	550	99.60	99.50	East Plaza (BC)	4.0
2127	528	563	100.56	100.40	East Bar	3.5
2128	525	566	100.45	100.40	East Bar	6.0
2129	517	534	101.05	100.95	Center Bar	10.0
2130	510	550	100.00	99.90	East Plaza (BC)	1.7
2131	522	535	100.49	100.48	Center Bar	4.0
2132	523	562	101.05	101.03	East Bar	2.0
2133	514	534	100.37	100.36	Center Bar	2.5
2134	514	534	100.42	100.38	Center Bar	3.0
2135	525	566	100.65	100.50	East Bar	5.0
2136	511	532	101.26	101.08	Center Bar	5.0
2137	517	534	100.75	100.65	Center Bar	5.0
2138	516	533	101.35	101.00	Center Bar	3.5
2139	526	567	101.05	101.04	East Bar	4.5
2140	516	534	100.85	100.80	Center Bar	3.0
2141	515	534	100.85	100.80	Center Bar	3.0
2142	516	535	100.48	100.43	Center Bar	2.0
2143	516	534	100.44	100.39	Center Bar	1.0
2144	517	534	101.15	101.05	Center Bar	9.5
2145	525	561	101.05	100.90	East Bar	4.0
2146	516	534	100.65	100.63	Center Bar	8.0
2147	526	565	100.75	100.70	East Bar	19.0
2148	515	535	101.20	101.10	Center Bar	7.0
2149	523	535	100.58	100.55	Center Bar	3.0
2150	517	534	100.85	100.75	Center Bar	5.0
2151	516	533	101.05	101.02	Center Bar	3.5
2152	516	534	100.65	100.63	Center Bar	3.0
2153	515	535	100.75	100.70	Center Bar	3.0
2154	522	534	100.55	100.49	Center Bar	4.0
2155	516	534	100.64	100.59	Center Bar	1.0
2156	525	566	101.08	101.05	East Bar	.5
2157	516	534	100.59	100.54	Center Bar	.5
2158	515	534	100.70	100.65	Center Bar	5.0
2159	515	534	101.20	101.00	Center Bar	5.0
2160	516	535	100.53	100.48	Center Bar	1.5
2161	516	535	100.63	100.58	Center Bar	.5
2162	515	534	100.90	100.85	Center Bar	3.5
2163	526	567	100.85	100.80	East Bar	2.0
2164	526	567	100.85	100.80	East Bar	1.0
2165	525	567	100.85	100.80	East Bar	.3
2166	526	565	100.70	100.60	East Bar	8.0
2167	526	566	100.85	100.80	East Bar	.5
2168	525	566	100.85	100.80	East Bar	1.5
2169	523	563	101.05	101.03	East Bar	7.0

Lot No.	Grid N	Grid E	Upper Level	Lower Level	Provenience	Flot. Vol.
2170	516	533	100.95	100.92	Center Bar	5.5
2171	516	534	100.90	100.85	Center Bar	4.0
2172	517	534	100.66	100.64	Center Bar	8.0
2173	516	533	100.79	100.75	Center Bar	3.0
2174	525	566	100.90	100.70	East Bar	2.0
2176	514	535	100.66	100.64	Center Bar	2.0
2177	516	533	100.72	100.70	Center Bar	2.0
2178	517	534	100.85	100.75	Center Bar	5.0
2179	525	566	100.85	100.80	East Bar	5.0
2180	514	534	100.50	100.40	Center Bar	5.0
2181	517	534	101.35	101.25	Center Bar	9.0
2182	527	562	100.57	100.55	East Bar	.5
2183	528	562	100.77	100.70	East Bar	4.0
2184	529	563	101.17	101.16	East Bar	1.0
2185	527	561	100.73	100.70	East Bar	2.0
2186	523	563	100.97	100.96	East Bar	2.0
2187	527	561	100.73	100.72	East Bar	2.0
2188	527	561	100.57	100.56	East Bar	2.5
2189	527	565	101.10	101.08	East Bar	1.0
2190	527	561	100.74	100.73	East Bar	.5
2191	527	566	100.99	100.92	East Bar	3.0
2192	527	561	100.76	100.75	East Bar	2.0
2193	529	566	101.30	101.20	East Bar	1.0
2194	527	561	100.70	100.60	East Bar	.5
2195	525	567	100.85	100.80	East Bar	4.0
2196	515	534	100.75	100.70	Center Bar	3.0
2197	516	533	100.90	100.85	Center Bar	3.0
2198	513	535	100.27	100.23	Center Bar	3.0
2199	525	563	101.05	100.95	East Bar	5.0
2200	525	567	100.85	100.80	East Bar	2.0
2201	526	565	100.70	100.65	East Bar	10.0
2202	526	565	101.00	100.95	East Bar	14.0
2203	525	566	100.85	100.80	East Bar	7.0
2204	525	562	100.85	100.80	East Bar	5.0
2205	516	535	100.90	100.84	Center Bar	10.0
2206	526	567	100.98	100.97	East Bar	10.0
2207	521	535	100.59	100.57	Center Bar	5.0
2208	513	535	101.05	100.95	Center Bar	4.0
2209	513	535	100.95	100.85	Center Bar	4.5
2210	523	564	101.15	101.05	East Bar	2.0
2211	516	534	100.54	100.49	Center Bar	1.0
2212	516	534	100.49	100.44	Center Bar	1.0
2213	517	533	100.67	100.65	Center Bar	7.0
2214	525	562	100.75	100.74	East Bar	4.0
2215	517	534	100.95	100.85	Center Bar	5.0
2216	517	533	100.75	100.65	Center Bar	6.0
2217	507	550	100.10	100.00	East Plaza (BC)	2.0
2218	529	565	101.20	101.19	East Bar	2.0
2219	512	549	99.90	99.80	East Plaza (BC)	4.5
2220	526	565	100.70	100.60	East Bar	9.0
2221	525	566	100.75	100.70	East Bar	6.0
2222	525	567	100.90	100.85	East Bar	3.0
2223	525	566	100.85	100.80	East Bar	1.5
2224	513	535	100.75	100.65	Center Bar	7.0
2225	516	534	100.85	100.75	Center Bar	5.0
2226	527	565	100.70	100.60	East Bar	5.0
2227	514	535	100.63	100.50	Center Bar	3.0
2228	526	562	100.90	100.89	East Bar	2.0
2229	529	563	100.69	100.68	East Bar	1.0
2230	529	566	101.40	101.30	East Bar	2.0
2231	515	534	100.75	100.70	Center Bar	3.0
2232	529	566	101.40	101.30	East Bar	3.0
2233	526	563	100.62	100.58	East Bar	.2
2234	510	532	101.15	101.05	Center Bar	10.0
2235	516	534	101.00	100.90	Center Bar	5.0
2236	515	535	101.10	100.90	Center Bar	9.0
2237	513	535	100.45	100.27	Center Bar	5.5
2238	525	566	101.00	100.95	East Bar	6.0
2239	525	562	101.05	100.90	East Bar	5.0
2240	521	535	100.65	100.56	Center Bar	5.0
2241	525	566	100.90	100.85	East Bar	3.5
2242	515	534	101.00	100.90	Center Bar	6.0
2243	513	535	100.85	100.75	Center Bar	6.5
2244	525	566	100.80	100.75	East Bar	8.0
2245	516	535	100.70	100.65	Center Bar	8.0
2246	523	535	100.70	100.65	Center Bar	2.0
2247	526	565	100.85	100.80	East Bar	15.0
2248	525	562	100.90	100.85	East Bar	3.0
2249	511	533	101.15	101.10	Center Bar	.5
2250	526	564	100.90	100.80	East Bar	3.0
2251	515	535	100.90	100.70	Center Bar	8.0
2252	513	535	101.05	100.95	Center Bar	5.0
2253	514	534	100.67	100.65	Center Bar	5.0
2254	515	535	100.65	100.63	Center Bar	6.0
2255	526	567	100.90	100.85	East Bar	2.0
2256	516	534	101.00	100.90	Center Bar	5.5
2257	526	566	100.90	100.85	East Bar	4.0
2258	516	535	101.20	101.00	Center Bar	7.0
2259	525	564	101.03	100.93	East Bar	2.5
2260	511	533	101.15	101.10	Center Bar	3.0
2261	513	535	100.95	100.85	Center Bar	4.0
2262	525	566	100.70	100.65	East Bar	6.0
2263	526	567	101.05	101.04	East Bar	5.0
2264	525	564	100.95	100.90	East Bar	4.0
2265	516	535	101.32	101.30	Center Bar	3.0
2266	528	565	100.98	100.97	East Bar	3.0

Lot No.	Grid N	Grid E	Upper Level	Lower Level	Provenience	Flot. Vol.
2267	526	565	101.00	100.95	East Bar	6.0
2268	517	534	100.75	100.65	Center Bar	4.5
2269	510	532	101.15	101.05	Center Bar	2.0
2270	523	564	101.15	101.05	East Bar	1.5
2271	525	563	100.90	100.85	East Bar	2.5
2272	525	561	100.90	100.85	East Bar	2.0
2273	526	567	100.82	100.81	East Bar	2.0
2274	515	534	100.70	100.65	Center Bar	2.0
2275	522	535	100.50	100.45	Center Bar	5.0
2276	525	566	100.95	100.90	East Bar	12.0
2277	525	566	100.80	100.75	East Bar	3.0
2278	513	534	100.95	100.85	Center Bar	3.0
2279	517	534	101.25	101.15	Center Bar	12.0
2280	526	566	100.90	100.80	East Bar	3.0
2281	517	534	100.64	100.63	Center Bar	1.0
2282	516	535	100.70	100.65	Center Bar	9.0
2283	515	535	100.70	100.65	Center Bar	6.0
2284	516	534	100.90	100.80	Center Bar	5.0
2285	525	566	100.90	100.85	East Bar	4.0
2286	526	566	100.85	100.80	East Bar	1.0
2287	513	535	100.46	100.42	Center Bar	4.0
2288	516	534	100.75	100.70	Center Bar	4.0
2289	527	562	100.55	100.52	East Bar	2.0
2290	509	549	99.80	99.70	East Plaza (BC)	2.0
2291	527	561	100.57	100.45	East Bar	2.3
2292	511	549	100.10	100.00	East Plaza (BC)	3.5
2293	507	550	100.00	99.90	East Plaza (BC)	2.3
2294	510	550	100.00	99.99	East Plaza (BC)	2.5
2295	509	549	100.10	100.00	East Plaza (BC)	1.5
2296	510	549	100.20	100.10	East Plaza (BC)	2.0
2297	509	557	100.40	100.30	East Plaza (BC)	2.8
2298	512	549	100.10	100.00	East Plaza (BC)	4.0
2299	516	535	100.43	100.38	Center Bar	2.5
2300	525	563	100.95	100.90	East Bar	5.0
2301	523	534	100.63	100.62	Center Bar	5.0
2302	513	535	100.64	100.45	Center Bar	10.0
2303	516	535	100.38	100.33	Center Bar	5.0
2304	525	566	100.75	100.70	East Bar	5.0
2305	526	565	100.80	100.75	East Bar	15.0
2306	509	550	99.60	99.50	East Plaza (BC)	4.0
2307	509	548	99.70	99.60	East Plaza (BC)	2.0
2308	509	548	100.10	100.00	East Plaza (BC)	3.0
2309	511	549	100.20	100.10	East Plaza (BC)	3.5
2310	510	549	99.60	99.50	East Plaza (BC)	3.5
2311	511	550	100.10	100.00	East Plaza (BC)	1.5
2312	527	562	100.80	100.70	East Bar	4.0
2313	527	561	100.57	100.45	East Bar	3.5
2314	525	562	100.90	100.89	East Bar	3.0
2315	528	562	100.77	100.70	East Bar	5.0
2316	527	566	101.17	101.10	East Bar	3.0
2317	510	549	100.00	99.90	East Plaza (BC)	3.0
2318	510	550	99.90	99.80	East Plaza (BC)	1.5
2319	521	515	100.30	100.20	West Plaza	3.0
2320	510	549	99.90	99.80	East Plaza (BC)	4.0
2321	510	547	100.30	100.20	East Plaza (BC)	3.0
2322	510	549	99.80	99.70	East Plaza (BC)	2.5
2323	528	563	100.56	100.40	East Bar	5.0
2324	512	549	99.80	99.70	East Plaza (BC)	4.0
2325	511	549	100.00	99.90	East Plaza (BC)	4.0
2326	508	551	100.20	100.10	East Plaza (BC)	4.0
2327	510	549	99.56	99.50	East Plaza (BC)	3.0
2328	508	551	99.80	99.70	East Plaza (BC)	2.5
2329	509	547	100.00	99.90	East Plaza (BC)	3.0
2330	512	549	99.90	99.80	East Plaza (BC)	2.5
2331	508	549	99.64	99.60	East Plaza (BC)	2.0
2332	516	534	100.50	100.47	Center Bar	.5
2333	516	534	100.47	100.42	Center Bar	.3
3000	537	536	101.10	101.05	Main Bar East	.
3001	538	537	101.10	101.05	Main Bar East	.
3002	537	537	101.10	101.05	Main Bar East	.
3003	538	536	101.10	101.05	Main Bar East	.
3004	536	536	101.10	101.05	Main Bar East	.
3005	539	543	101.05	101.00	Main Bar East	.
3006	538	543	101.05	101.00	Main Bar East	.
3007	537	543	101.10	101.00	Main Bar East	.
3008	536	543	101.10	101.00	Main Bar East	.
3009	555	512	99.90	99.80	Great Depression	.
3010	555	513	99.90	99.80	Great Depression	.
3011	539	543	100.96	100.95	Main Bar East	.
3012	555	514	99.90	99.80	Great Depression	.
3013	538	537	101.05	100.95	Main Bar East	.
3014	537	537	101.05	100.95	Main Bar East	.
3015	538	536	101.05	100.95	Main Bar East	.
3016	536	543	101.00	100.90	Main Bar East	.
3017	536	536	101.05	100.95	Main Bar East	.
3018	537	536	101.05	100.95	Main Bar East	.
3019	538	543	101.00	100.90	Main Bar East	.
3020	555	511	99.90	99.80	Great Depression	.
3021	537	543	101.00	100.90	Main Bar East	.
3022	539	543	101.00	100.90	Main Bar East	.
3023	538	537	100.95	100.90	Main Bar East	.
3024	537	537	100.95	100.90	Main Bar East	.
3025	538	536	100.95	100.90	Main Bar East	.
3026	536	543	100.90	100.85	Main Bar East	.
3027	555	514	99.80	99.70	Great Depression	.
3028	538	537	100.90	100.80	Main Bar East	.

Lot No.	Grid N	Grid E	Upper Level	Lower Level	Provenience	Flot. Vol.
3029	555	511	99.80	99.70	Great Depression	.
3030	537	543	101.25	101.10	Main Bar East	.
3031	555	512	99.80	99.70	Great Depression	.
3032	555	513	99.80	99.70	Great Depression	.
3033	537	536	100.95	100.85	Main Bar East	.
3034	537	537	100.90	100.85	Main Bar East	.
3035	536	536	100.95	100.85	Main Bar East	.
3036	537	543	100.90	100.85	Main Bar East	.
3037	538	543	100.90	100.85	Main Bar East	.
3038	538	536	100.90	100.80	Main Bar East	.
3039	536	542	101.25	101.00	Main Bar East	.
3040	536	541	101.20	101.00	Main Bar East	.
3041	555	513	100.00	99.70	Great Depression	.
3042	538	537	100.80	100.70	Main Bar East	.
3043	536	540	101.20	101.00	Main Bar East	.
3044	536	536	100.85	100.75	Main Bar East	.
3045	536	539	101.20	101.00	Main Bar East	.
3046	537	537	100.80	100.70	Main Bar East	.
3047	555	514	99.70	99.60	Great Depression	.
3048	536	541	101.20	101.00	Main Bar East	.
3049	537	536	100.85	100.75	Main Bar East	.
3050	555	513	99.70	99.60	Great Depression	.
3051	555	512	99.70	99.60	Great Depression	.
3052	555	511	99.70	99.60	Great Depression	.
3053	536	542	101.00	100.83	Main Bar East	.
3054	536	541	101.00	100.90	Main Bar East	.
3055	555	514	99.60	99.50	Great Depression	.
3056	538	538	101.20	100.90	Main Bar East	.
3057	536	544	101.25	100.90	Main Bar East	.
3058	538	536	100.80	100.70	Main Bar East	.
3059	536	544	101.11	101.06	Main Bar East	4.0
3060	536	544	101.06	100.96	Main Bar East	4.0
3061	555	513	99.60	99.50	Great Depression	.
3062	536	540	101.00	100.90	Main Bar East	.
3063	536	537	101.20	101.02	Main Bar East	.
3064	555	511	99.70	99.60	Great Depression	.
3065	554	513	99.94	99.70	Great Depression	.
3066	536	536	100.75	100.65	Main Bar East	.
3067	536	541	100.90	100.80	Main Bar East	.
3068	555	511	99.60	99.50	Great Depression	.
3069	536	539	101.00	100.90	Main Bar East	.
3070	555	512	99.60	99.50	Great Depression	.
3071	537	536	100.75	100.65	Main Bar East	.
3072	538	538	100.90	100.70	Main Bar East	.
3073	555	513	99.50	99.40	Great Depression	.
3074	530	601	99.25	99.24	Surface	.
3075	536	540	100.91	100.90	Main Bar East	.
3076	536	540	100.90	100.89	Main Bar East	.
3077	537	540	101.20	101.00	Main Bar East	.
3078	537	541	101.20	101.00	Main Bar East	.
3079	536	536	100.65	100.55	Main Bar East	.
3080	537	538	101.20	101.00	Main Bar East	.
3081	536	536	100.65	100.55	Main Bar East	4.0
3082	536	537	101.02	100.90	Main Bar East	4.0
3083	555	511	99.50	99.40	Great Depression	4.0
3084	555	511	99.50	99.40	Great Depression	.
3085	554	513	99.70	99.50	Great Depression	.
3086	554	513	99.70	99.50	Great Depression	4.0
3088	538	536	100.80	100.70	Main Bar East	4.0
3089	536	544	100.90	100.85	Main Bar East	.
3090	536	544	100.90	100.78	Main Bar East	4.0
3091	536	539	100.90	100.85	Main Bar East	.
3092	536	539	100.90	100.85	Main Bar East	4.0
3093	555	513	99.40	99.30	Great Depression	.
3094	555	513	99.40	99.30	Great Depression	4.0
3095	537	605	98.23	98.22	Surface	.
3096	537	541	101.00	100.90	Main Bar East	.
3097	537	540	101.00	100.90	Main Bar East	.
3098	537	538	101.00	100.90	Main Bar East	.
3099	537	538	101.00	100.90	Main Bar East	4.0
3100	538	536	100.70	100.60	Main Bar East	.
3101	536	537	100.90	100.80	Main Bar East	.
3102	536	537	100.90	100.80	Main Bar East	4.0
3103	555	513	99.30	99.20	Great Depression	.
3104	555	513	99.30	99.20	Great Depression	4.0
3105	536	538	101.20	101.00	Main Bar East	.
3106	536	536	100.55	100.40	Main Bar East	.
3107	536	536	100.55	100.40	Main Bar East	4.0
3108	538	536	100.70	100.60	Main Bar East	4.0
3109	537	542	101.25	101.00	Main Bar East	.
3110	537	536	100.61	100.57	Main Bar East	2.0
3111	555	511	99.40	99.30	Great Depression	.
3112	555	511	99.40	99.30	Great Depression	4.0
3113	538	536	100.61	100.57	Main Bar East	4.0
3114	537	540	100.90	100.85	Main Bar East	.
3115	537	540	100.90	100.85	Main Bar East	4.0
3116	537	541	100.90	100.85	Main Bar East	.
3117	537	541	100.90	100.85	Main Bar East	4.0
3118	537	536	100.65	100.50	Main Bar East	.
3119	537	536	100.65	100.50	Main Bar East	4.0
3120	537	538	100.90	100.80	Main Bar East	.
3121	537	538	100.90	100.80	Main Bar East	4.0
3122	555	510	99.90	99.60	Great Depression	.
3123	555	512	99.50	99.40	Great Depression	.
3124	555	512	99.50	99.40	Great Depression	4.0
3125	554	513	99.50	99.40	Great Depression	.

Lot No.	Grid N	Grid E	Upper Level	Lower Level	Provenience	Flot. Vol.
3126	554	513	99.50	99.40	Great Depression	4.0
3127	538	536	100.60	100.50	Main Bar East	.
3128	538	536	100.60	100.50	Main Bar East	4.0
3129	538	537	100.70	100.60	Main Bar East	.
3130	538	537	100.70	100.60	Main Bar East	4.0
3131	536	537	100.82	100.79	Main Bar East	1.0
3132	537	537	100.70	100.60	Main Bar East	.
3133	537	537	100.70	100.60	Main Bar East	4.0
3134	537	542	101.00	100.80	Main Bar East	.
3135	537	542	101.00	100.80	Main Bar East	4.0
3136	537	541	100.85	100.80	Main Bar East	.
3137	537	541	100.85	100.80	Main Bar East	4.0
3138	537	540	100.85	100.80	Main Bar East	.
3139	537	540	100.85	100.80	Main Bar East	4.0
3140	536	537	100.80	100.60	Main Bar East	.
3141	536	537	100.80	100.70	Main Bar East	4.0
3142	555	511	99.30	99.20	Great Depression	.
3143	555	511	99.30	99.20	Great Depression	4.0
3144	537	537	100.80	100.40	Main Bar East	.
3145	536	537	100.70	100.60	Main Bar East	4.0
3146	537	541	100.80	100.70	Main Bar East	.
3147	537	541	100.80	100.70	Main Bar East	4.0
3148	537	541	100.70	100.60	Main Bar East	4.0
3149	537	540	100.80	100.70	Main Bar East	.
3150	537	540	100.80	100.70	Main Bar East	4.0
3151	537	540	100.70	100.60	Main Bar East	4.0
3152	536	538	101.00	100.90	Main Bar East	.
3153	536	538	101.00	100.90	Main Bar East	4.0
3154	554	513	99.40	99.30	Great Depression	.
3155	554	513	99.40	99.30	Great Depression	4.0
3156	538	537	100.60	100.50	Main Bar East	.
3157	538	537	100.60	100.50	Main Bar East	4.0
3158	537	541	100.79	100.78	Main Bar East	.
3159	538	536	100.50	100.40	Main Bar East	.
3160	538	536	100.50	100.40	Main Bar East	4.0
3161	537	537	100.61	100.60	Main Bar East	.
3162	555	510	99.90	99.60	Great Depression	4.0
3163	536	538	100.90	100.80	Main Bar East	.
3164	536	538	100.90	100.80	Main Bar East	4.0
3165	555	510	99.60	99.40	Great Depression	.
3166	555	510	99.60	99.40	Great Depression	4.0
3167	555	512	99.40	99.30	Great Depression	.
3168	555	512	99.40	99.30	Great Depression	4.0
3169	537	537	100.60	100.50	Main Bar East	.
3170	537	537	100.60	100.50	Main Bar East	4.0
3171	537	541	100.75	100.74	Main Bar East	.
3172	537	541	100.70	100.60	Main Bar East	.
3173	537	540	100.70	100.60	Main Bar East	.

Lot No.	Grid N	Grid E	Upper Level	Lower Level	Provenience	Flot. Vol.
3174	555	511	99.20	99.10	Great Depression	.
3175	555	511	99.20	99.10	Great Depression	4.0
3176	538	536	100.39	100.38	Main Bar East	.
3177	538	537	100.50	100.40	Main Bar East	.
3178	538	537	100.50	100.40	Main Bar East	4.0
3179	554	513	99.30	99.20	Great Depression	.
3180	554	513	99.30	99.20	Great Depression	4.0
3181	536	537	100.67	100.64	Main Bar East	1.5
3182	536	538	100.80	100.65	Main Bar East	.
3184	537	536	100.50	100.40	Main Bar East	.
3185	537	536	100.50	100.40	Main Bar East	4.0
3186	537	542	100.80	100.70	Main Bar East	.
3187	537	542	100.80	100.70	Main Bar East	4.0
3188	555	511	99.10	99.00	Great Depression	.
3189	555	511	99.10	99.00	Great Depression	4.0
3190	536	537	100.60	100.50	Main Bar East	.
3191	536	537	100.60	100.50	Main Bar East	4.0
3192	557	553	99.70	99.50	North Plaza (Test E)	.
3193	558	553	99.70	99.50	North Plaza (Test E)	.
3194	555	511	99.00	98.90	Great Depression	.
3195	555	511	99.00	98.90	Great Depression	4.0
3196	537	538	100.80	100.65	Main Bar East	.
3197	537	538	100.80	100.65	Main Bar East	4.0
3198	557	553	99.50	99.30	North Plaza (Test E)	.
3199	558	553	99.50	99.30	North Plaza (Test E)	.
3200	555	510	99.40	99.30	Great Depression	.
3201	555	510	99.40	99.30	Great Depression	4.0
3202	554	513	99.20	99.10	Great Depression	.
3203	554	513	99.20	99.10	Great Depression	4.0
3204	554	512	99.60	99.10	Great Depression	.
3205	537	537	100.50	100.40	Main Bar East	.
3206	537	537	100.50	100.40	Main Bar East	3.0
3207	539	536	101.10	100.80	Main Bar East	.
3208	539	537	101.10	100.80	Main Bar East	.
3209	537	542	100.70	100.60	Main Bar East	.
3210	537	542	100.70	100.60	Main Bar East	4.0
3211	537	540	100.61	100.59	Main Bar East	2.0
3212	537	541	100.60	100.50	Main Bar East	.
3213	537	541	100.60	100.50	Main Bar East	4.0
3214	555	512	99.30	99.20	Great Depression	.
3215	555	512	99.30	99.20	Great Depression	2.0
3216	555	511	98.90	98.80	Great Depression	.
3217	555	511	98.90	98.80	Great Depression	4.0
3218	537	539	101.20	100.90	Main Bar East	.
3220	537	540	100.60	100.50	Main Bar East	.
3221	537	540	100.60	100.50	Main Bar East	4.0
3222	554	513	99.10	99.00	Great Depression	.
3223	554	513	99.10	99.00	Great Depression	4.0

Lot No.	Grid N	Grid E	Upper Level	Lower Level	Provenience	Flot. Vol.
3224	537	542	100.60	100.50	Main Bar East	.
3225	537	542	100.60	100.50	Main Bar East	4.0
3226	539	539	101.10	100.80	Main Bar East	.
3227	555	509	99.91	99.60	Great Depression	.
3228	537	537	100.37	100.36	Main Bar East	.
3229	555	511	98.80	98.70	Great Depression	.
3230	555	511	98.80	98.70	Great Depression	4.0
3231	554	513	99.00	98.90	Great Depression	.
3232	537	540	100.56	100.54	Main Bar East	2.0
3233	539	536	100.80	100.70	Main Bar East	.
3234	539	536	100.80	100.70	Main Bar East	4.0
3235	539	537	100.80	100.70	Main Bar East	.
3236	539	537	100.80	100.70	Main Bar East	4.0
3237	537	542	100.50	100.40	Main Bar East	.
3238	537	542	100.50	100.40	Main Bar East	4.0
3239	554	512	99.93	99.60	Great Depression	.
3240	536	537	100.50	100.40	Main Bar East	.
3241	536	537	100.50	100.40	Main Bar East	4.0
3242	555	512	99.20	99.10	Great Depression	.
3243	555	512	99.20	99.10	Great Depression	4.0
3244	537	538	100.65	100.55	Main Bar East	.
3245	537	538	100.65	100.55	Main Bar East	4.0
3246	554	513	98.90	98.80	Great Depression	.
3247	537	540	99.50	99.40	Main Bar East	.
3248	537	540	99.50	99.40	Main Bar East	4.0
3249	539	539	100.80	100.70	Main Bar East	.
3250	539	539	100.80	100.70	Main Bar East	4.0
3251	536	537	100.39	100.38	Main Bar East	.
3252	537	538	100.55	100.45	Main Bar East	.
3253	537	538	100.55	100.45	Main Bar East	4.0
3254	539	537	100.70	100.60	Main Bar East	.
3255	539	537	100.70	100.60	Main Bar East	4.0
3256	537	542	100.40	100.30	Main Bar East	.
3257	537	542	100.40	100.30	Main Bar East	4.0
3258	537	541	100.50	100.40	Main Bar East	.
3259	537	541	100.50	100.40	Main Bar East	4.0
3260	555	510	99.30	99.20	Great Depression	.
3261	555	510	99.30	99.20	Great Depression	4.0
3262	539	540	101.15	100.80	Main Bar East	.
3263	536	537	100.38	100.37	Main Bar East	.
3264	536	537	100.38	100.37	Main Bar East	.
3265	536	537	100.38	100.37	Main Bar East	.
3266	539	536	100.70	100.60	Main Bar East	.
3267	539	536	100.70	100.60	Main Bar East	4.0
3268	537	538	100.45	100.35	Main Bar East	.
3269	537	538	100.45	100.35	Main Bar East	4.0
3270	536	543	100.85	100.70	Main Bar East	.
3271	536	543	100.85	100.70	Main Bar East	4.0

Lot No.	Grid N	Grid E	Upper Level	Lower Level	Provenience	Flot. Vol.
3272	555	509	99.91	99.60	Great Depression	4.0
3273	537	541	100.47	100.40	Main Bar East	2.0
3274	555	510	99.20	99.10	Great Depression	.
3275	555	510	99.20	99.10	Great Depression	2.0
3276	555	512	99.10	99.00	Great Depression	.
3277	555	512	99.10	99.00	Great Depression	2.0
3278	537	536	100.80	100.40	Main Bar East	.
3279	537	542	100.68	100.67	Main Bar East	.
3280	538	538	100.70	100.55	Main Bar East	.
3281	538	538	100.70	100.55	Main Bar East	4.0
3282	554	512	99.70	99.60	Great Depression	4.0
3283	538	538	100.55	100.35	Main Bar East	.
3284	538	538	100.55	100.35	Main Bar East	4.0
3285	537	539	100.80	100.70	Main Bar East	.
3286	537	539	100.80	100.70	Main Bar East	4.0
3287	539	537	100.60	100.50	Main Bar East	.
3288	539	537	100.60	100.50	Main Bar East	4.0
3289	536	543	100.70	100.60	Main Bar East	.
3290	536	543	100.70	100.60	Main Bar East	4.0
3291	536	538	100.65	100.50	Main Bar East	.
3292	536	538	100.65	100.50	Main Bar East	4.0
3293	555	510	99.10	99.00	Great Depression	.
3294	555	510	99.10	99.00	Great Depression	4.0
3295	539	536	100.60	100.50	Main Bar East	.
3296	539	536	100.60	100.50	Main Bar East	4.0
3297	536	543	100.70	100.65	Main Bar East	1.5
3298	555	509	99.60	99.50	Great Depression	.
3299	555	509	99.60	99.50	Great Depression	4.0
3300	536	535	101.20	101.00	Main Bar East	.
3301	555	512	99.00	98.90	Great Depression	.
3302	555	512	99.00	98.90	Great Depression	4.0
3303	539	537	100.50	100.40	Main Bar East	.
3304	539	537	100.50	100.40	Main Bar East	4.0
3305	539	536	100.50	100.40	Main Bar East	.
3306	539	536	100.50	100.40	Main Bar East	4.0
3307	536	543	100.60	100.50	Main Bar East	.
3308	536	543	100.60	100.50	Main Bar East	4.0
3309	536	538	100.50	100.40	Main Bar East	.
3310	536	538	100.50	100.40	Main Bar East	4.0
3311	537	539	100.70	100.60	Main Bar East	.
3312	537	539	100.70	100.60	Main Bar East	4.0
3313	555	510	98.90	98.80	Great Depression	.
3314	555	510	98.90	98.80	Great Depression	4.0
3315	539	536	100.39	100.38	Main Bar East	.
3316	536	534	101.25	101.00	Main Bar East	.
3317	536	535	101.00	100.80	Main Bar East	.
3318	536	535	101.00	100.90	Main Bar East	4.0
3319	539	535	100.80	100.40	Main Bar East	.

Lot No.	Grid N	Grid E	Upper Level	Lower Level	Provenience	Flot. Vol.
3320	555	512	98.90	98.80	Great Depression	.
3321	555	512	98.90	98.80	Great Depression	4.0
3322	536	544	100.80	100.60	Main Bar East	.
3323	536	544	100.80	100.60	Main Bar East	4.0
3324	537	539	100.67	100.50	Main Bar East	4.0
3325	537	539	100.50	100.31	Main Bar East	3.5
3326	538	534	101.25	100.90	Main Bar East	.
3327	536	534	101.00	100.80	Main Bar East	.
3328	536	534	101.00	100.80	Main Bar East	4.0
3329	536	535	100.90	100.80	Main Bar East	4.0
3330	554	511	99.92	99.60	Great Depression	.
3331	553	511	99.96	99.60	Great Depression	.
3332	554	512	99.60	99.50	Great Depression	.
3333	554	512	99.60	99.50	Great Depression	4.0
3334	538	535	101.20	100.90	Main Bar East	.
3335	555	509	99.50	99.40	Great Depression	.
3336	555	509	99.50	99.40	Great Depression	4.0
3337	538	534	100.80	100.60	Main Bar East	.
3338	538	534	100.80	100.70	Main Bar East	4.0
3340	536	535	100.80	100.60	Main Bar East	.
3341	536	535	100.80	100.70	Main Bar East	4.0
3342	536	535	100.70	100.60	Main Bar East	3.0
3343	554	512	99.50	99.40	Great Depression	.
3344	554	512	99.50	99.40	Great Depression	4.0
3345	539	534	101.15	100.90	Main Bar East	.
3346	553	511	99.96	99.60	Great Depression	4.0
3347	536	534	100.80	100.60	Main Bar East	.
3348	536	534	100.80	100.70	Main Bar East	4.0
3350	555	509	99.40	99.30	Great Depression	.
3351	555	509	99.40	99.30	Great Depression	4.0
3352	538	535	100.90	100.70	Main Bar East	.
3353	538	535	100.90	100.80	Main Bar East	4.0
3354	538	535	100.80	100.70	Main Bar East	4.0
3355	537	539	100.60	100.50	Main Bar East	.
3356	537	539	100.60	100.50	Main Bar East	4.0
3357	554	511	99.92	99.60	Great Depression	4.0
3358	553	511	99.60	99.50	Great Depression	.
3359	553	511	99.60	99.50	Great Depression	4.0
3360	536	535	100.60	100.40	Main Bar East	.
3361	536	535	100.60	100.50	Main Bar East	4.0
3362	536	535	100.50	100.40	Main Bar East	4.0
3363	555	509	99.30	99.20	Great Depression	.
3364	555	509	99.30	99.20	Great Depression	4.0
3365	555	509	99.20	99.10	Great Depression	4.0
3366	536	544	100.65	100.64	Main Bar East	.
3367	537	535	101.25	100.90	Main Bar East	.
3368	536	544	100.60	100.45	Main Bar East	4.0
3369	536	544	100.45	100.35	Main Bar East	4.0

Lot No.	Grid N	Grid E	Upper Level	Lower Level	Provenience	Flot. Vol.
3370	536	544	100.33	100.32	Main Bar East	.
3371	536	544	100.30	100.29	Main Bar East	.
3372	553	512	99.94	99.60	Great Depression	.
3373	554	512	99.40	99.30	Great Depression	.
3374	554	512	99.40	99.30	Great Depression	4.0
3375	539	535	101.15	100.90	Main Bar East	.
3376	536	544	100.29	100.28	Main Bar East	.
3377	536	544	100.35	100.28	Main Bar East	4.0
3378	536	544	100.24	100.23	Main Bar East	.
3379	554	511	99.60	99.50	Great Depression	4.0
3380	536	544	100.28	100.23	Main Bar East	2.5
3381	554	511	99.60	99.50	Great Depression	.
3382	536	544	100.80	100.60	Main Bar East	.
3383	538	535	100.70	100.50	Main Bar East	.
3384	538	535	100.70	100.60	Main Bar East	4.0
3385	538	535	100.60	100.50	Main Bar East	4.0
3386	553	511	99.50	99.40	Great Depression	.
3387	553	511	99.50	99.40	Great Depression	4.0
3388	539	535	100.90	100.80	Main Bar East	.
3389	539	535	100.90	100.80	Main Bar East	4.0
3390	536	543	100.60	100.44	Main Bar East	.
3391	536	543	100.60	100.44	Main Bar East	.
3392	537	537	100.40	100.39	Main Bar East	.
3393	536	544	100.60	100.50	Main Bar East	1.0
3394	536	544	100.60	100.50	Main Bar East	1.0
3395	536	543	100.60	100.50	Main Bar East	1.0
3396	536	543	100.60	100.50	Main Bar East	1.0
3397	538	536	100.34	100.25	Main Bar East	4.0
3398	539	537	100.37	100.14	Main Bar East	4.0
3399	538	536	100.33	100.24	Main Bar East	4.0
3400	554	511	99.50	99.40	Great Depression	.
3401	554	511	99.50	99.40	Great Depression	4.0
3402	539	537	100.14	100.01	Main Bar East	4.0
3403	537	537	100.80	100.40	Main Bar East	.
3404	536	535	100.39	100.26	Main Bar East	4.0
3405	553	511	99.40	99.30	Great Depression	.
3406	553	511	99.40	99.30	Great Depression	2.0
3407	537	535	100.85	100.84	Main Bar East	.
3408	539	537	100.01	99.86	Main Bar East	4.0
3409	538	535	100.50	100.40	Main Bar East	.
3410	538	535	100.50	100.40	Main Bar East	4.0
3411	539	535	100.80	100.70	Main Bar East	.
3412	539	535	100.80	100.70	Main Bar East	4.0
3413	538	535	100.37	100.36	Main Bar East	.
3414	536	535	100.26	100.16	Main Bar East	4.0
3415	537	535	100.90	100.70	Main Bar East	.
3416	537	535	100.90	100.80	Main Bar East	3.0
3417	537	535	100.80	100.70	Main Bar East	4.0

Lot No.	Grid N	Grid E	Upper Level	Lower Level	Provenience	Flot. Vol.
3418	538	536	100.25	100.17	Main Bar East	4.0
3419	538	536	100.17	100.15	Main Bar East	4.0
3420	538	536	100.15	100.06	Main Bar East	4.0
3421	553	511	99.30	99.20	Great Depression	.
3422	553	511	99.30	99.20	Great Depression	4.0
3423	537	538	100.37	100.06	Main Bar East	4.0
3424	539	535	100.70	100.40	Main Bar East	.
3425	538	536	100.40	100.31	Main Bar East	4.0
3426	538	536	100.31	100.22	Main Bar East	4.0
3427	553	511	99.20	99.10	Great Depression	.
3428	553	512	99.94	99.60	Great Depression	4.0
3429	553	511	99.20	99.10	Great Depression	4.0
3430	554	512	99.30	99.15	Great Depression	.
3431	554	512	99.30	99.15	Great Depression	4.0
3432	538	534	100.50	100.40	Main Bar East	.
3433	538	536	100.22	100.14	Main Bar East	5.0
3434	537	536	100.36	100.25	Main Bar East	4.0
3435	538	536	100.14	100.12	Main Bar East	4.0
3436	537	536	100.25	100.18	Main Bar East	4.0
3437	536	534	100.70	100.50	Main Bar East	.
3438	536	534	100.70	100.60	Main Bar East	4.0
3439	538	536	100.33	100.06	Main Bar East	.
3440	555	511	99.60	99.10	Great Depression	.
3441	554	511	99.40	99.30	Great Depression	.
3442	554	511	99.40	99.30	Great Depression	4.0
3443	540	542	101.05	100.80	Main Bar East	.
3444	540	543	101.05	100.80	Main Bar East	.
3445	538	535	100.36	100.26	Main Bar East	4.0
3446	537	535	100.70	100.40	Main Bar East	.
3447	537	535	100.70	100.60	Main Bar East	4.0
3448	537	535	100.60	100.50	Main Bar East	4.0
3449	537	535	100.50	100.40	Main Bar East	4.0
3450	553	512	99.60	99.50	Great Depression	.
3451	553	512	99.60	99.50	Great Depression	4.0
3452	538	535	100.26	100.18	Main Bar East	4.0
3453	538	535	100.18	100.14	Main Bar East	4.0
3454	538	535	100.14	100.12	Main Bar East	4.0
3455	538	535	100.12	100.09	Main Bar East	3.0
3456	536	534	100.57	100.52	Main Bar East	3.6
3457	538	535	100.39	100.30	Main Bar East	4.0
3458	538	535	100.30	100.16	Main Bar East	4.0
3459	538	535	100.16	100.10	Main Bar East	3.0
3460	538	535	100.39	100.13	Main Bar East	4.0
3461	538	535	100.13	100.12	Main Bar East	.
3462	536	534	100.60	100.50	Main Bar East	4.0
3463	553	512	99.50	99.40	Great Depression	.
3464	553	512	99.50	99.40	Great Depression	4.0
3465	554	511	99.60	99.20	Great Depression	.
3466	537	537	100.80	100.40	Main Bar East	.
3467	537	537	100.40	100.35	Main Bar East	1.0
3468	553	512	99.40	99.30	Great Depression	.
3469	553	512	99.40	99.30	Great Depression	4.0
3470	554	511	99.30	99.20	Great Depression	.
3471	554	511	99.30	99.20	Great Depression	4.0
3472	536	542	100.90	100.80	Main Bar East	.
3473	538	537	100.40	100.35	Main Bar East	1.0
3474	539	537	100.40	100.35	Main Bar East	1.0
3475	536	537	100.40	100.35	Main Bar East	1.0
3476	539	536	100.40	100.35	Main Bar East	1.0
3477	536	543	100.80	100.60	Main Bar East	.
3478	537	535	100.40	100.35	Main Bar East	1.0
3479	538	535	100.40	100.35	Main Bar East	1.0
3480	536	535	100.40	100.30	Main Bar East	1.0
3481	537	536	100.40	100.30	Main Bar East	1.0
3482	536	536	100.40	100.35	Main Bar East	1.0
3483	553	512	99.30	99.20	Great Depression	.
3484	553	512	99.30	99.20	Great Depression	4.0
3485	554	512	99.15	99.10	Great Depression	.
3486	554	512	99.15	99.10	Great Depression	5.0
3487	536	534	100.50	100.40	Main Bar East	.
3488	536	534	100.50	100.40	Main Bar East	4.0
3489	537	536	100.38	100.30	Main Bar East	4.0
3490	539	542	101.20	100.88	Main Bar East	.
3491	540	541	101.05	100.70	Main Bar East	.
3492	553	512	99.20	99.10	Great Depression	.
3493	553	512	99.20	99.10	Great Depression	4.0
3494	554	512	99.06	99.05	Great Depression	.
3495	537	536	100.34	100.29	Main Bar East	4.0
3496	554	511	99.20	99.10	Great Depression	.
3497	554	511	99.20	99.10	Great Depression	4.0
3498	537	536	100.29	100.28	Main Bar East	4.0
3499	537	536	100.28	100.26	Main Bar East	3.0
3500	553	512	99.20	99.10	Great Depression	.
3501	554	511	99.21	99.20	Great Depression	.
3502	554	512	99.10	99.00	Great Depression	.
3503	554	512	99.10	99.00	Great Depression	4.0
3504	537	536	100.26	100.25	Main Bar East	4.0
3505	537	536	100.25	100.18	Main Bar East	4.0
3506	553	512	99.40	99.10	Great Depression	.
3507	554	512	99.02	99.01	Great Depression	.
3508	554	511	99.10	99.00	Great Depression	.
3509	554	511	99.10	99.00	Great Depression	4.0
3510	537	537	100.36	100.26	Main Bar East	.
3511	554	512	99.00	98.90	Great Depression	.
3512	554	512	99.00	98.90	Great Depression	4.0
3513	554	511	99.00	98.90	Great Depression	.

Lot No.	Grid N	Grid E	Upper Level	Lower Level	Provenience	Flot. Vol.
3514	554	511	99.00	98.90	Great Depression	4.0
3515	554	511	99.60	98.90	Great Depression	.
3516	537	537	100.80	100.40	Main Bar East	.
3517					Number Not Used	.
3518	512	515	100.30	100.10	West Plaza	.
3519	512	514	100.30	100.10	West Plaza	.
3520	513	515	100.30	100.10	West Plaza	.
3521	513	515	100.10	99.90	West Plaza	.
3522	513	516	100.30	100.10	West Plaza	.
3523	513	516	100.10	99.90	West Plaza	.
3524	504	500	100.00	100.00	Surface	.
3525	535	543	101.15	101.00	Main Bar East	.
3526	534	543	101.15	101.00	Main Bar East	.
3527	533	543	101.15	101.00	Main Bar East	.
3528	537	544	101.15	101.00	Main Bar East	.
3529	535	504	100.83	100.60	West Bar	.
3530	535	505	100.79	100.60	West Bar	.
3531	534	504	100.82	100.60	West Bar	.
3532	533	505	100.76	100.60	West Bar	.
3533	534	505	100.78	100.60	West Bar	.
3534	533	505	100.60	100.50	West Bar	.
3535	536	543	101.15	100.87	Main Bar East	.
3536	536	543	100.87	100.60	Main Bar East	.
3537	534	505	100.60	100.50	West Bar	.
3538	535	504	100.60	100.50	West Bar	.
3539	533	504	100.78	100.60	West Bar	.
3540	535	505	100.55	100.50	West Bar	.
3541	533	505	100.50	100.40	West Bar	.
3542	535	504	100.50	100.40	West Bar	.
3543	534	505	100.50	100.40	West Bar	.
3544	533	505	100.40	100.30	West Bar	.
3545	535	543	101.00	100.90	Main Bar East	.
3546	535	543	101.00	100.90	Main Bar East	2.0
3547	535	505	100.50	100.40	West Bar	.
3548	533	543	101.00	100.90	Main Bar East	.
3549	533	543	101.00	100.90	Main Bar East	2.0
3550	534	543	101.00	100.90	Main Bar East	.
3551	534	543	101.00	100.90	Main Bar East	2.0
3552	537	544	101.00	100.90	Main Bar East	.
3553	537	544	101.00	100.90	Main Bar East	2.0
3554	532	504	100.74	100.60	West Bar	.
3555	533	504	100.60	100.50	West Bar	.
3556	534	505	100.40	100.30	West Bar	.
3557	535	543	100.90	100.82	Main Bar East	.
3558	535	543	100.90	100.82	Main Bar East	2.0
3559	532	504	100.60	100.50	West Bar	.
3560	537	544	100.90	100.80	Main Bar East	.
3561	537	544	100.90	100.80	Main Bar East	2.0

Lot No.	Grid N	Grid E	Upper Level	Lower Level	Provenience	Flot. Vol.
3562	533	505	100.30	100.20	West Bar	.
3563	533	543	100.90	100.76	Main Bar East	.
3564	533	543	100.90	100.76	Main Bar East	2.0
3565	534	543	100.90	100.77	Main Bar East	.
3566	534	543	100.90	100.77	Main Bar East	2.0
3567	534	505	100.30	100.20	West Bar	.
3568	533	504	100.50	100.40	West Bar	.
3569	535	505	100.40	100.30	West Bar	.
3570	537	544	100.80	100.70	Main Bar East	.
3571	537	544	100.80	100.70	Main Bar East	2.0
3572	532	504	100.50	100.40	West Bar	.
3573	533	505	100.17	100.00	West Bar	.
3574	533	505	100.00	99.90	West Bar	.
3575	533	505	100.00	99.90	West Bar	2.0
3576	535	543	100.83	100.80	Main Bar East	.
3577	534	543	100.83	100.80	Main Bar East	.
3578	533	543	100.94	100.93	Main Bar East	.
3579	533	543	100.95	100.94	Main Bar East	.
3580	533	543	101.02	100.80	Main Bar East	.
3581	533	543	101.10	100.94	Main Bar East	.
3582	534	503	100.78	100.60	West Bar	.
3583	533	503	100.78	100.60	West Bar	.
3584	535	505	100.31	100.20	West Bar	.
3585	532	503	100.78	100.60	West Bar	.
3586	537	544	100.70	100.60	Main Bar East	.
3587	537	544	100.70	100.60	Main Bar East	2.0
3588	535	505	100.20	100.10	West Bar	.
3589	533	543	100.94	100.80	Main Bar East	2.0
3590	535	505	100.10	100.00	West Bar	.
3591	535	505	100.30	100.29	West Bar	.
3592	531	503	100.70	100.60	West Bar	.
3593	535	542	101.20	101.00	Main Bar East	.
3594	534	542	101.19	101.00	Main Bar East	.
3595	535	504	100.38	100.37	West Bar	.
3596	532	503	100.60	100.40	West Bar	.
3597	534	544	101.17	101.00	Main Bar East	.
3598	531	503	100.60	100.40	West Bar	.
3599	533	503	100.60	100.40	West Bar	.
3600	535	505	100.80	100.40	West Bar	.
3601	534	542	101.00	100.80	Main Bar East	.
3602	532	503	100.40	100.30	West Bar	.
3603	535	505	100.24	100.10	West Bar	.
3604	536	536	100.39	100.38	Main Bar East	.
3605	535	542	101.00	100.80	Main Bar East	.
3606	536	536	100.39	100.38	Main Bar East	.
3607	536	537	100.39	100.38	Main Bar East	.
3608	533	503	100.40	100.23	West Bar	.
3609	537	536	100.39	100.38	Main Bar East	.

Lot No.	Grid N	Grid E	Upper Level	Lower Level	Provenience	Flot. Vol.
3610	535	544	101.20	101.00	Main Bar East	.
3611	535	542	100.84	100.82	Main Bar East	.
3612	534	503	100.60	100.50	West Bar	.
3613	537	537	100.39	100.38	Main Bar East	.
3614	532	503	100.30	100.20	West Bar	.
3615	534	544	101.16	101.00	Main Bar East	.
3616	531	503	100.40	100.30	West Bar	.
3617	534	544	101.00	100.80	Main Bar East	.
3618	532	503	100.20	100.00	West Bar	.
3619	533	503	100.23	100.05	West Bar	.
3620	536	536	100.38	100.37	Main Bar East	4.0
3621	534	503	100.50	100.30	West Bar	.
3622	532	503	100.00	99.80	West Bar	.
3623	531	503	100.30	100.20	West Bar	.
3624	536	536	100.37	100.35	Main Bar East	4.0
3625	536	536	100.35	100.33	Main Bar East	4.5
3626	536	536	100.33	100.30	Main Bar East	4.0
3627	536	536	100.30	100.26	Main Bar East	4.0
3628	536	536	100.26	100.18	Main Bar East	4.0
3629	536	536	100.26	100.18	Main Bar East	.
3630	535	544	101.00	100.80	Main Bar East	.
3631	535	544	100.90	100.80	Main Bar East	2.0
3632	535	545	101.24	101.00	Main Bar East	.
3633	535	544	100.91	100.76	Main Bar East	2.0
3634	543	512	100.67	100.50	Main Bar West	.
3635	543	511	100.64	100.50	Main Bar West	.
3636	542	511	100.67	100.50	Main Bar West	.
3637	542	512	100.67	100.50	Main Bar West	.
3638	536	544	100.70	100.70	Main Bar East	.
3639	543	511	100.50	100.40	Main Bar West	.
3640	535	544	100.80	100.80	Main Bar East	.
3641	541	512	100.66	100.50	Main Bar West	.
3642	536	536	100.38	100.16	Main Bar East	.
3643	543	511	100.40	100.30	Main Bar West	.
3644	543	512	100.50	100.40	Main Bar West	.
3645	542	511	100.50	100.40	Main Bar West	.
3646	543	512	100.40	100.30	Main Bar West	.
3647	534	545	101.00	100.80	Main Bar East	.
3648	536	545	101.18	101.00	Main Bar East	.
3649	535	545	101.00	100.80	Main Bar East	.
3650	542	512	100.50	100.40	Main Bar West	.
3651	543	511	100.30	100.20	Main Bar West	.
3652	541	511	100.66	100.50	Main Bar West	.
3653	543	512	100.30	100.20	Main Bar West	.
3654	540	511	100.70	100.50	Main Bar West	.
3655	537	536	100.39	100.38	Main Bar East	.
3656	542	512	100.40	100.37	Main Bar West	.
3657	541	512	100.50	100.40	Main Bar West	.

Lot No.	Grid N	Grid E	Upper Level	Lower Level	Provenience	Flot. Vol.
3658	533	544	101.18	101.00	Main Bar East	.
3659	536	545	101.00	100.80	Main Bar East	.
3660	540	511	100.50	100.40	Main Bar West	.
3661	538	544	101.15	101.00	Main Bar East	.
3662	539	544	101.12	101.00	Main Bar East	.
3663	536	536	100.39	100.38	Main Bar East	.
3664	539	543	100.93	100.70	Main Bar East	.
3665	536	543	100.80	100.60	Main Bar East	.
3666	539	544	101.00	100.80	Main Bar East	.
3667	535	543	100.80	100.80	Main Bar East	.
3668	534	544	100.80	100.73	Main Bar East	2.0
3669	538	543	100.87	100.70	Main Bar East	.
3670	543	511	100.20	100.10	Main Bar West	.
3671	535	543	100.76	100.70	Main Bar East	.
3672	535	543	100.76	100.70	Main Bar East	2.0
3673	534	544	100.76	100.70	Main Bar East	.
3674	534	544	100.76	100.70	Main Bar East	2.0
3675	535	544	100.77	100.70	Main Bar East	.
3676	535	544	100.77	100.70	Main Bar East	2.0
3677	538	543	100.87	100.70	Main Bar East	.
3678	540	544	101.09	100.80	Main Bar East	.
3679	538	544	101.00	100.80	Main Bar East	.
3680	534	544	100.69	100.69	Main Bar East	2.0
3681	539	544	100.80	100.70	Main Bar East	.
3682	535	544	100.69	100.69	Main Bar East	2.0
3683	535	543	100.82	100.69	Main Bar East	2.0
3684	534	544	100.76	100.69	Main Bar East	.
3685	534	544	100.69	100.68	Main Bar East	.
3686	535	544	100.69	100.68	Main Bar East	.
3687	535	544	100.76	100.69	Main Bar East	.
3688	539	543	100.70	100.56	Main Bar East	.
3689	544	511	100.57	100.20	Main Bar West	.
3692	534	545	100.76	100.67	Main Bar East	.
3693	534	545	100.76	100.53	Main Bar East	.
3694	534	543	100.76	100.58	Main Bar East	.
3695	535	543	100.76	100.71	Main Bar East	2.0
3696	538	543	100.70	100.60	Main Bar East	.
3697	535	543	100.80	100.71	Main Bar East	.
3698	535	543	100.71	100.69	Main Bar East	.
3699	540	543	101.15	100.85	Main Bar East	.
3700	539	544	100.70	100.60	Main Bar East	.
3701	535	543	100.69	100.68	Main Bar East	2.0
3702	540	543	100.85	100.60	Main Bar East	2.0
3703	538	543	100.66	100.60	Main Bar East	2.0
3704	544	511	100.20	100.10	Main Bar West	.
3705	537	543	101.15	100.80	Main Bar East	.
3706	538	544	100.80	100.70	Main Bar East	.
3707	540	542	101.15	100.80	Main Bar East	.

Lot No.	Grid N	Grid E	Upper Level	Lower Level	Provenience	Flot. Vol.
3708	538	543	100.60	100.56	Main Bar East	.
3709	534	545	100.80	100.72	Main Bar East	.
3710	533	543	100.80	100.76	Main Bar East	.
3711	533	543	100.76	100.70	Main Bar East	.
3712	534	542	100.85	100.76	Main Bar East	.
3713	534	542	100.76	100.70	Main Bar East	.
3714	539	544	100.80	100.57	Main Bar East	.
3715	539	543	100.80	100.57	Main Bar East	.
3716	538	543	100.82	100.57	Main Bar East	.
3717	537	543	100.80	100.57	Main Bar East	.
3718	538	545	101.00	100.80	Main Bar East	.
3719	539	544	100.80	100.57	Main Bar East	.
3720	535	545	100.75	100.75	Main Bar East	.
3720	538	542	100.80	100.70	Main Bar East	.
3721	537	542	100.80	100.57	Main Bar East	.
3722	539	544	100.87	100.86	Main Bar East	.
3723	535	545	100.75	100.74	Main Bar East	.
3724	535	543	100.70	100.69	Main Bar East	.
3725	535	545	100.70	100.63	Main Bar East	2.0
3726	539	545	101.16	101.00	Main Bar East	.
3727	537	545	101.20	101.00	Main Bar East	.
3728	538	542	100.70	100.57	Main Bar East	.
3729	537	545	100.90	100.57	Main Bar East	.
3730	538	545	100.80	100.57	Main Bar East	.
3731	536	545	100.70	100.70	Main Bar East	.
3732	534	543	100.70	100.61	Main Bar East	1.3
3733	534	543	100.70	100.68	Main Bar East	.
3734	540	542	101.00	100.57	Main Bar East	.
3735	537	545	101.05	101.04	Main Bar East	.
3736	535	543	100.70	100.58	Main Bar East	.
3737	537	545	101.00	100.90	Main Bar East	.
3738	537	543	100.57	100.57	Main Bar East	.
3739	534	543	100.71	100.46	Main Bar East	.
3740	539	544	100.60	100.29	Main Bar East	4.0
3741	538	542	100.55	100.23	Main Bar East	2.8
3742	537	543	100.57	100.53	Main Bar East	.
3743	538	543	100.59	100.53	Main Bar East	.
3744	537	544	100.60	100.55	Main Bar East	.
3745	538	544	100.60	100.55	Main Bar East	.
3746	535	543	100.70	100.63	Main Bar East	.
3747	535	544	100.70	100.63	Main Bar East	.
3748	536	536	100.39	100.25	Main Bar East	.
3749	535	545	100.70	100.65	Main Bar East	.
3750	539	543	100.69	100.60	Main Bar East	.
3751	537	544	100.60	100.49	Main Bar East	4.0
3752	534	544	100.70	100.65	Main Bar East	.
3753	534	543	100.73	100.65	Main Bar East	.
3754	534	544	100.73	100.65	Main Bar East	2.0

Lot No.	Grid N	Grid E	Upper Level	Lower Level	Provenience	Flot. Vol.
3755	535	542	100.70	100.65	Main Bar East	.
3756	537	542	100.53	100.38	Main Bar East	.
3757	534	545	100.73	100.65	Main Bar East	.
3758	536	536	100.25	100.10	Main Bar East	.
3759	537	542	100.38	100.30	Main Bar East	.
3760	535	543	100.66	100.58	Main Bar East	4.0
3761	534	543	100.66	100.60	Main Bar East	.5
3762	534	542	100.64	100.63	Main Bar East	1.0
3763	535	544	100.65	100.60	Main Bar East	.
3764	535	544	100.65	100.60	Main Bar East	2.0
3765	535	543	100.65	100.60	Main Bar East	.
3766	535	543	100.65	100.60	Main Bar East	2.0
3767	543	512	100.15	100.05	Main Bar West	.
3768	538	544	100.55	100.53	Main Bar East	.
3769	535	545	100.65	100.60	Main Bar East	.
3770	536	536	100.10	100.00	Main Bar East	.
3771	535	542	100.65	100.60	Main Bar East	.
3772	534	543	100.65	100.60	Main Bar East	.
3773	534	543	100.65	100.60	Main Bar East	2.0
3774	534	544	100.65	100.60	Main Bar East	.
3775	534	544	100.65	100.60	Main Bar East	2.0
3776	538	544	100.55	100.45	Main Bar East	.
3777	538	537	100.38	100.30	Main Bar East	.
3778	536	536	100.07	100.00	Main Bar East	2.0
3779	538	543	100.54	100.53	Main Bar East	2.0
3780	542	512	100.40	100.30	Main Bar West	.
3781	538	543	100.54	100.47	Main Bar East	.
3782	539	544	100.55	100.50	Main Bar East	.
3783	538	537	100.38	100.28	Main Bar East	2.0
3784	541	511	100.50	100.40	Main Bar West	.
3785	537	536	100.39	100.30	Main Bar East	.
3786	542	512	100.30	100.20	Main Bar West	.
3787	534	545	100.65	100.60	Main Bar East	.
3788	534	543	100.60	100.60	Main Bar East	.
3789	537	536	100.33	100.24	Main Bar East	4.3
3790	542	512	100.20	100.10	Main Bar West	.
3791	534	543	100.59	100.45	Main Bar East	.
3792	534	543	100.59	100.45	Main Bar East	2.0
3793	535	544	100.58	100.49	Main Bar East	.
3794	535	544	100.58	100.49	Main Bar East	2.0
3795	488	527	99.40	99.39	Surface	.
3796	534	544	100.71	100.66	Main Bar East	.
3797	536	542	100.62	100.59	Main Bar East	2.0
3798	539	543	100.55	100.52	Main Bar East	.
3799	537	535	100.39	100.38	Main Bar East	.
3800	539	542	101.08	100.90	Main Bar East	.
3801	543	511	100.20	100.10	Main Bar West	.
3802	543	512	100.20	100.10	Main Bar West	.

Lot No.	Grid N	Grid E	Upper Level	Lower Level	Provenience	Flot. Vol.
3803	537	543	100.80	100.70	Main Bar East	.
3804	535	542	100.83	100.77	Main Bar East	.
3805	535	542	100.77	100.72	Main Bar East	.
3806	534	544	100.76	100.72	Main Bar East	.
3807	534	544	100.72	100.70	Main Bar East	.
3808	534	543	100.70	100.72	Main Bar East	.
3809	534	543	100.72	100.70	Main Bar East	.
3810	540	544	100.80	100.57	Main Bar East	2.0
3811	538	542	101.16	100.80	Main Bar East	.
3812	540	544	100.80	100.57	Main Bar East	.
3813	537	542	100.93	100.62	Main Bar East	.
3814	538	544	100.70	100.65	Main Bar East	2.0
3815	537	543	100.70	100.57	Main Bar East	.
3816	538	544	100.70	100.57	Main Bar East	.
3817	535	545	100.80	100.77	Main Bar East	.
3818	535	545	100.77	100.70	Main Bar East	.
3819	538	545	101.20	101.00	Main Bar East	.
3820	534	544	100.72	100.70	Main Bar East	2.0
3821	539	542	100.80	100.70	Main Bar East	.
3822	539	542	100.90	100.80	Main Bar East	.
3823	534	544	100.71	100.58	Main Bar East	.9
3824	537	537	100.38	100.32	Main Bar East	.
3825	537	537	100.32	100.20	Main Bar East	.
3826	541	511	100.40	100.30	Main Bar West	.
3827	534	543	100.59	100.45	Main Bar East	.
3828	534	543	100.59	100.45	Main Bar East	2.0
3829	536	536	100.00	99.95	Main Bar East	.
3830	534	543	100.58	100.49	Main Bar East	2.0
3831	535	544	100.54	100.49	Main Bar East	1.0
3832	535	544	100.58	100.49	Main Bar East	.
3833	534	544	100.66	100.56	Main Bar East	.5
3834	536	542	100.62	100.47	Main Bar East	.
3835	534	543	100.58	100.39	Main Bar East	.
3836	534	544	100.60	100.54	Main Bar East	.
3837	536	543	100.59	100.50	Main Bar East	1.2
3838	534	544	100.59	100.40	Main Bar East	2.0
3839	534	543	100.59	100.48	Main Bar East	2.0
3840	534	543	100.59	100.48	Main Bar East	.
3841	538	536	100.39	100.35	Main Bar East	.
3842	537	535	100.39	100.29	Main Bar East	.
3843	537	535	100.39	100.37	Main Bar East	2.0
3844	536	543	100.58	100.49	Main Bar East	.8
3845	535	543	100.57	100.47	Main Bar East	2.0
3846	534	544	100.62	100.56	Main Bar East	1.0
3847	536	544	100.61	100.48	Main Bar East	1.8
3848	541	511	100.30	100.20	Main Bar West	.
3849	538	535	100.39	100.27	Main Bar East	.
3850	535	543	100.57	100.32	Main Bar East	.

Lot No.	Grid N	Grid E	Upper Level	Lower Level	Provenience	Flot. Vol.
3851	535	544	100.58	100.36	Main Bar East	2.0
3852	535	544	100.58	100.36	Main Bar East	.
3853	535	543	100.59	100.43	Main Bar East	1.2
3854	535	545	100.59	100.57	Main Bar East	.
3855	539	543	100.56	100.50	Main Bar East	.
3856	537	535	100.29	100.24	Main Bar East	.
3857	537	535	100.29	100.24	Main Bar East	2.0
3858	538	536	100.17	100.14	Main Bar East	.
3859	539	543	100.52	100.47	Main Bar East	.
3860	535	543	100.60	100.60	Main Bar East	.
3861	538	536	100.35	100.30	Main Bar East	.
3862	538	536	100.35	100.30	Main Bar East	4.0
3863	534	543	100.60	100.55	Main Bar East	2.0
3864	535	543	100.60	100.55	Main Bar East	2.0
3865	535	544	100.60	100.55	Main Bar East	2.0
3866	534	543	100.60	100.55	Main Bar East	.
3867	535	543	100.60	100.55	Main Bar East	.
3868	535	544	100.60	100.55	Main Bar East	.
3869	541	512	100.40	100.30	Main Bar West	.
3870	542	511	100.40	100.30	Main Bar West	.
3871	538	536	100.30	100.18	Main Bar East	4.0
3872	538	536	100.30	100.12	Main Bar East	.
3873	539	543	100.52	100.41	Main Bar East	2.0
3874	541	512	100.30	100.20	Main Bar West	.
3875	539	543	100.41	100.28	Main Bar East	.
3876	539	543	100.41	100.28	Main Bar East	2.0
3877	535	544	100.57	100.54	Main Bar East	.9
3878	538	536	100.30	100.25	Main Bar East	.
3879	542	511	100.30	100.20	Main Bar West	.
3880	535	542	100.60	100.55	Main Bar East	.
3881	534	544	100.60	100.55	Main Bar East	2.0
3882	534	544	100.60	100.55	Main Bar East	.
3883	542	511	100.30	100.20	Main Bar West	.
3884	535	542	100.56	100.51	Main Bar East	.
3885	538	543	100.53	100.40	Main Bar East	.
3886	513	516	99.93	99.93	West Plaza	.
3887	537	536	100.25	100.20	Main Bar East	.
3888	534	543	100.69	100.61	Main Bar East	.
3889	535	543	100.55	100.45	Main Bar East	.
3890	535	543	100.55	100.45	Main Bar East	2.0
3891	536	543	100.60	100.55	Main Bar East	.
3892	536	543	100.60	100.55	Main Bar East	2.0
3893	534	543	100.56	100.54	Main Bar East	2.0
3894	538	544	100.59	100.54	Main Bar East	.
3895	534	543	100.48	100.46	Main Bar East	2.0
3896	534	543	100.55	100.45	Main Bar East	.
3897	534	543	100.55	100.45	Main Bar East	2.0
3898	538	536	100.25	100.20	Main Bar East	.

Lot No.	Grid N	Grid E	Upper Level	Lower Level	Provenience	Flot. Vol.
3899	538	536	100.25	100.20	Main Bar East	2.0
3900	537	536	100.20	100.15	Main Bar East	.
3901	537	536	100.20	100.15	Main Bar East	2.0
3902	536	542	100.60	100.55	Main Bar East	.
3903	535	542	100.60	100.55	Main Bar East	.
3904	535	542	100.60	100.60	Main Bar East	.
3905	534	544	100.75	100.65	Main Bar East	.
3906	533	502	100.71	100.50	West Bar	.
3907	537	536	100.39	100.15	Main Bar East	.
3908	538	536	100.20	100.15	Main Bar East	2.0
3909	538	536	100.20	100.10	Main Bar East	.
3910	538	543	100.38	100.30	Main Bar East	2.0
3911	538	543	100.38	100.30	Main Bar East	.
3912	535	544	100.55	100.45	Main Bar East	.
3913	535	544	100.55	100.45	Main Bar East	2.0
3914	536	542	100.55	100.45	Main Bar East	.
3915	536	542	100.55	100.45	Main Bar East	2.0
3916	534	543	100.47	100.09	Main Bar East	2.0
3917	534	543	100.47	100.09	Main Bar East	.
3918	534	544	100.59	100.30	Main Bar East	2.0
3919	534	544	100.59	100.30	Main Bar East	.
3920	537	544	100.45	100.35	Main Bar East	.
3921	533	502	100.50	100.30	West Bar	.
3922	537	536	100.15	100.10	Main Bar East	.
3923	537	536	100.15	100.10	Main Bar East	2.0
3924	538	536	100.22	100.18	Main Bar East	.
3925	538	536	100.22	100.18	Main Bar East	3.3
3926	534	544	100.37	100.30	Main Bar East	2.0
3927	536	544	100.59	100.55	Main Bar East	.
3928	537	536	100.10	100.00	Main Bar East	.
3929	537	536	100.10	100.00	Main Bar East	2.0
3930	535	545	100.61	100.47	Main Bar East	1.3
3931	534	544	100.55	100.45	Main Bar East	.
3932	534	544	100.55	100.45	Main Bar East	2.0
3933	534	545	100.59	100.55	Main Bar East	.
3934	533	502	100.30	100.25	West Bar	2.0
3935	533	502	100.30	100.25	West Bar	2.0
3936	533	502	100.30	100.25	West Bar	.
3937	536	544	100.55	100.50	Main Bar East	.
3938	536	544	100.55	100.45	Main Bar East	.
3939	536	544	100.55	100.45	Main Bar East	2.0
3940	538	543	100.56	100.16	Main Bar East	.
3941	533	502	100.25	100.22	West Bar	.
3942	533	502	100.25	100.22	West Bar	.
3943	533	502	100.25	100.22	West Bar	4.0
3944	534	543	100.47	100.43	Main Bar East	2.5
3945	534	545	100.62	100.58	Main Bar East	.6
3946	538	543	100.56	100.16	Main Bar East	2.0
3947	536	543	100.47	100.35	Main Bar East	2.0
3948	535	545	100.65	100.60	Main Bar East	.
3949	534	545	100.59	100.51	Main Bar East	.
3950	539	544	100.60	100.55	Main Bar East	.
3951	534	545	100.59	100.51	Main Bar East	2.0
3952	536	544	100.63	100.63	Main Bar East	.
3953	534	545	100.59	100.51	Main Bar East	2.0
3954	534	545	100.57	100.28	Main Bar East	.
3955	538	543	100.53	100.50	Main Bar East	.
3956	535	543	100.55	100.45	Main Bar East	.
3957	534	545	100.51	100.36	Main Bar East	2.0
3958	535	543	100.45	100.45	Main Bar East	.
3959	537	535	100.40	100.27	Main Bar East	.
3960	538	537	100.34	100.20	Main Bar East	.
3961	537	536	100.02	99.90	Main Bar East	.
3962	535	543	100.47	100.39	Main Bar East	4.0
3963	537	535	100.44	100.29	Main Bar East	.
3964	538	544	100.56	100.50	Main Bar East	.
3965	535	543	100.47	100.34	Main Bar East	3.0
3966	537	536	100.02	99.88	Main Bar East	2.0
3967	539	544	100.52	100.29	Main Bar East	1.8
3968	538	535	100.44	100.30	Main Bar East	.
3969	537	536	99.88	99.80	Main Bar East	.
3970	533	542	101.15	101.10	Main Bar East	.
3971	534	545	100.55	100.47	Main Bar East	.
3972	536	545	100.81	100.72	Main Bar East	.
3973	536	544	100.47	100.20	Main Bar East	.
3974	534	545	100.53	100.53	Main Bar East	.
3975	536	545	100.72	100.60	Main Bar East	.
3976	535	543	100.47	100.45	Main Bar East	.
3977	536	535	100.44	100.30	Main Bar East	.
3978	534	543	100.47	100.45	Main Bar East	.
3979	534	543	100.47	100.45	Main Bar East	2.0
3980	536	545	100.60	100.43	Main Bar East	2.0
3981	534	545	100.57	100.28	Main Bar East	.
3982	534	545	100.55	100.45	Main Bar East	.
3983	538	535	100.20	100.10	Main Bar East	2.0
3984	537	535	100.20	100.10	Main Bar East	.
3985	536	544	100.47	100.40	Main Bar East	.
3986	536	544	100.47	100.40	Main Bar East	2.0
3987	534	543	100.45	100.42	Main Bar East	1.5
3988	535	545	100.46	100.37	Main Bar East	1.6
3989	537	535	100.10	99.91	Main Bar East	2.0
3990	537	535	100.27	100.18	Main Bar East	.
3991	538	537	100.20	100.10	Main Bar East	.
3992	534	544	100.45	100.42	Main Bar East	.
3993	534	544	100.44	100.24	Main Bar East	2.0
3994	534	544	100.44	100.24	Main Bar East	.

Lot No.	Grid N	Grid E	Upper Level	Lower Level	Provenience	Flot. Vol.
3995	534	543	100.42	100.20	Main Bar East	2.0
3996	536	544	100.45	100.42	Main Bar East	.
3997	537	535	100.20	100.10	Main Bar East	.
3998	537	544	100.48	100.38	Main Bar East	.
3999	537	537	100.22	100.13	Main Bar East	.
4000	536	535	100.39	100.20	Main Bar East	.
4001	537	544	100.48	100.38	Main Bar East	2.0
4002	553	551	99.94	99.74	North Plaza (Test B)	.
4003	535	543	100.45	100.42	Main Bar East	.
4004	535	544	100.45	100.42	Main Bar East	.
4005	536	544	100.43	100.16	Main Bar East	3.5
4006	534	544	100.45	100.42	Main Bar East	.
4007	554	560	100.16	99.98	North Plaza (Test D)	.
4008	537	536	100.35	100.00	Main Bar East	.
4009	534	545	100.50	100.43	Main Bar East	.
4010	535	544	100.44	100.36	Main Bar East	.
4011	538	543	100.50	100.35	Main Bar East	.
4012	538	536	100.24	100.24	Main Bar East	.
4013	534	544	100.40	100.26	Main Bar East	1.5
4014	538	536	100.24	100.00	Main Bar East	.
4015	534	544	100.42	100.19	Main Bar East	.
4016	554	560	99.98	99.95	North Plaza (Test D)	.
4017	536	544	100.42	100.19	Main Bar East	.
4018	536	544	100.19	100.12	Main Bar East	2.0
4019	538	536	100.10	100.09	Main Bar East	.
4020	538	537	100.30	100.10	Main Bar East	.
4021	554	544	100.09	99.89	North Plaza (Test C)	.
4022	534	543	100.42	100.40	Main Bar East	.
4023	536	537	100.39	100.27	Main Bar East	.
4024	535	544	100.36	100.19	Main Bar East	2.0
4025	535	544	100.36	100.19	Main Bar East	.
4026	536	537	100.27	100.20	Main Bar East	.
4027	538	536	100.02	100.00	Main Bar East	2.0
4028	535	544	100.34	100.27	Main Bar East	.3
4029	554	544	99.89	99.69	North Plaza (Test C)	.
4030	534	545	100.42	100.37	Main Bar East	.5
4031	534	543	100.34	100.28	Main Bar East	.3
4032	534	545	100.42	100.40	Main Bar East	.
4033	554	544	99.69	99.49	North Plaza (Test C)	.
4034	536	544	100.43	100.37	Main Bar East	.
4035	536	537	100.20	100.10	Main Bar East	.
4036	538	536	100.00	99.80	Main Bar East	2.5
4037	538	536	99.80	99.78	Main Bar East	2.0
4038	538	536	99.80	99.75	Main Bar East	2.0
4039	538	536	99.75	99.69	Main Bar East	2.0
4040	537	543	100.80	100.60	Main Bar East	.
4041	539	537	100.40	100.30	Main Bar East	.
4042	539	537	100.30	100.20	Main Bar East	.

Lot No.	Grid N	Grid E	Upper Level	Lower Level	Provenience	Flot. Vol.
4043	539	537	100.04	100.00	Main Bar East	.
4044	539	537	100.04	100.00	Main Bar East	2.0
4045	536	544	100.44	100.32	Main Bar East	2.0
4046	536	544	100.44	100.32	Main Bar East	.
4047	536	544	100.29	100.25	Main Bar East	1.8
4048	513	532	101.80	101.70	Center Bar	.
4049	513	533	101.70	101.65	Center Bar	.
4050	524	566	101.54	101.25	East Bar	.
4051	525	565	101.15	101.05	East Bar	.
4052	514	531	101.75	101.65	Center Bar	.
4053	514	530	101.45	101.35	Center Bar	.
4054	525	564	101.45	101.40	East Bar	.
4055	513	530	101.45	101.35	Center Bar	.
4056	525	561	101.30	101.25	East Bar	.
4057	521	563	101.15	101.05	East Bar	.
4058	525	565	101.45	101.40	East Bar	.
4059	524	566	101.35	101.25	East Bar	.
4060	525	561	101.25	101.15	East Bar	.
4061	522	566	101.15	101.05	East Bar	.
4062	525	563	101.15	101.05	East Bar	.
4063	513	530	101.80	101.75	Center Bar	.
4064	512	531	101.55	101.50	Center Bar	.
4065	516	533	101.45	101.35	Center Bar	.
4066	512	534	101.58	101.48	Center Bar	.
4067	511	533	101.45	101.40	Center Bar	.
4068	514	532	101.95	101.85	Center Bar	.
4069	513	532	101.50	101.40	Center Bar	.
4070	513	534	101.60	101.55	Center Bar	.
4071	514	535	101.25	101.10	Center Bar	.
4072	513	531	101.70	101.60	Center Bar	.
4073	513	532	101.50	101.40	Center Bar	.
4074	514	532	101.30	101.25	Center Bar	.
4075	513	530	101.90	101.85	Center Bar	.
4076	525	565	101.45	101.40	East Bar	.
4077	524	566	101.54	101.25	East Bar	.
4078	528	565	101.54	101.25	East Bar	.
4079	511	534	101.30	101.25	Center Bar	.
4080	525	561	101.38	101.25	East Bar	.
4081	528	565	101.68	101.25	East Bar	.
4082	512	534	101.58	101.48	Center Bar	.
4083	528	535	100.68	100.25	Center Bar	.
4084	512	530	101.55	101.50	Center Bar	.
4085	512	534	101.58	101.48	Center Bar	.
4086	513	532	102.00	101.90	Center Bar	.
4087	514	530	101.55	101.45	Center Bar	.
4088	513	533	101.80	101.75	Center Bar	.
4089	513	534	101.45	101.35	Center Bar	.
4090	511	533	101.20	101.15	Center Bar	.

Lot No.	Grid N	Grid E	Upper Level	Lower Level	Provenience	Flot. Vol.
4091	511	533	101.35	101.30	Center Bar	.
4092	514	534	101.40	101.35	Center Bar	.
4093	514	531	101.90	101.85	Center Bar	.
4094	525	565	101.40	101.35	East Bar	.
4095	514	535	101.35	101.25	Center Bar	.
4096	514	535	101.75	101.65	Center Bar	.
4097	517	533	101.89	101.75	Center Bar	.
4098	514	535	101.35	101.25	Center Bar	.
4099	513	533	101.80	101.65	Center Bar	.
4100	513	535	101.15	101.05	Center Bar	.
4101	525	564	101.55	101.45	East Bar	.
4102	512	532	101.40	101.35	Center Bar	.
4103	513	534	101.65	101.60	Center Bar	.
4104	512	530	101.60	101.55	Center Bar	.
4105	513	531	101.75	101.70	Center Bar	.
4106	525	563	101.49	101.40	East Bar	.
4107	514	531	101.75	101.65	Center Bar	.
4108	513	531	101.30	101.15	Center Bar	.
4109	512	534	101.58	101.48	Center Bar	.
4110	512	530	101.60	101.55	Center Bar	.
4111	526	567	100.79	100.78	East Bar	.
4112	528	565	100.88	100.78	East Bar	.
5000	541	535	101.04	100.84	North Plaza (Test A)	.
5001	541	536	101.05	100.85	North Plaza (Test A)	.
5002	541	537	101.05	100.85	North Plaza (Test A)	.
5003	531	566	101.72	101.40	East Bar	.
5004	530	567	101.70	101.40	East Bar	.
5005	531	567	101.72	101.40	East Bar	.
5006	530	568	101.70	101.50	East Bar	.
5007	531	568	101.70	101.40	East Bar	.
5008	528	560	101.42	101.10	East Bar	.
5009	528	559	101.42	101.10	East Bar	.
5010	527	559	101.31	101.10	East Bar	.
5011	527	560	101.31	101.10	East Bar	.
5012	526	559	101.26	101.10	East Bar	.
5013	530	569	101.60	101.40	East Bar	.
5014	531	569	101.65	101.40	East Bar	.
5015	541	535	100.85	100.70	North Plaza (Test A)	.
5016	541	536	100.85	100.70	North Plaza (Test A)	.
5017	541	535	100.85	100.70	North Plaza (Test A)	2.0
5018	541	536	100.85	100.70	North Plaza (Test A)	2.0
5019	531	566	100.40	100.33	East Bar	.
5020	531	566	101.40	100.33	East Bar	2.0
5021	530	567	101.43	101.33	East Bar	.
5022	530	567	101.43	101.33	East Bar	2.0
5023	530	566	101.45	101.05	East Bar	.
5024	542	537	100.96	100.85	North Plaza (Test A)	.
5025	530	565	101.17	101.16	East Bar	.
5026	530	565	101.16	101.05	East Bar	.
5027	528	560	101.10	101.00	East Bar	.
5028	528	559	101.10	101.00	East Bar	.
5029	527	560	101.10	101.00	East Bar	.
5030	527	559	101.10	101.00	East Bar	.
5031	526	560	101.10	101.00	East Bar	.
5032	530	569	101.39	101.30	East Bar	.
5033	530	569	101.39	101.30	East Bar	2.0
5034	528	560	101.10	101.00	East Bar	2.0
5035	541	535	100.70	100.60	North Plaza (Test A)	2.0
5036	541	536	100.70	100.60	North Plaza (Test A)	2.0
5037	531	567	100.39	100.33	East Bar	.
5038	531	567	100.39	100.33	East Bar	2.0
5039	542	537	100.85	100.70	North Plaza (Test A)	.
5040	530	566	101.70	101.43	East Bar	.
5041	541	534	101.07	100.85	North Plaza (Test A)	.
5042	530	569	101.30	101.20	East Bar	.
5043	530	569	101.30	101.20	East Bar	2.0
5044	527	560	101.00	100.75	East Bar	.
5045	527	560	100.76	100.75	East Bar	.
5046	527	560	100.78	100.77	East Bar	.
5047	530	567	100.33	100.23	East Bar	.
5048	529	567	101.67	101.43	East Bar	.
5049	531	567	101.40	101.30	East Bar	.
5050	528	560	101.00	100.90	East Bar	.
5051	528	559	101.00	100.90	East Bar	.
5052	527	560	101.00	100.90	East Bar	.
5053	527	559	101.00	100.90	East Bar	.
5054	526	560	101.00	100.90	East Bar	.
5055	530	566	101.44	101.43	East Bar	2.0
5056	541	536	100.60	100.50	North Plaza (Test A)	.
5057	541	536	100.60	100.50	North Plaza (Test A)	2.0
5058	530	564	101.70	101.43	East Bar	.
5059	531	570	101.50	101.20	East Bar	.
5060	526	560	101.00	100.90	East Bar	2.5
5061	530	570	101.50	101.40	East Bar	.
5062	527	560	101.00	100.90	East Bar	2.2
5063	527	559	101.00	100.90	East Bar	2.0
5064	528	559	101.00	100.90	East Bar	2.0
5065	528	560	101.00	100.90	East Bar	2.0
5066	529	567	101.45	101.35	East Bar	.
5067	530	566	101.43	101.33	East Bar	.
5068	541	535	100.60	100.50	North Plaza (Test A)	.
5069	541	535	100.60	100.50	North Plaza (Test A)	2.0
5070	527	560	100.61	100.56	East Bar	.
5071	542	537	100.74	100.68	North Plaza (Test A)	.
5072	530	566	101.33	101.23	East Bar	.
5073	528	560	100.90	100.80	East Bar	.

Lot No.	Grid N	Grid E	Upper Level	Lower Level	Provenience	Flot. Vol.
5074	528	559	100.90	100.80	East Bar	.
5075	527	559	100.90	100.80	East Bar	.
5076	526	560	100.90	100.80	East Bar	.
5077	526	559	101.22	101.00	East Bar	.
5078	530	570	101.40	101.30	East Bar	.
5079	531	570	101.40	101.30	East Bar	.
5080	530	564	101.43	101.33	East Bar	.
5081	528	560	100.90	100.85	East Bar	2.0
5082	530	566	101.23	101.13	East Bar	.
5083	529	567	101.15	101.14	East Bar	.
5084	525	560	101.50	101.00	East Bar	.
5085	527	558	101.50	101.00	East Plaza (East)	.
5086	527	560	100.90	100.75	East Bar	.
5087	530	566	101.14	101.04	East Bar	.
5088	541	534	100.85	100.70	North Plaza (Test A)	.
5089	541	534	100.85	100.70	North Plaza (Test A)	2.0
5090	530	570	101.30	101.12	East Bar	.
5091	531	570	101.30	101.20	East Bar	.
5092	526	560	100.90	100.75	East Bar	.
5093	527	560	100.70	100.68	East Bar	1.5
5094	530	566	101.10	101.05	East Bar	.
5095	530	564	101.32	101.22	East Bar	.
5096	530	566	101.23	101.22	East Bar	.
5097	528	560	100.85	100.75	East Bar	.
5098	542	536	100.97	100.85	North Plaza (Test A)	.
5099	528	560	100.85	100.84	East Bar	.
5100	528	560	100.85	100.75	East Bar	2.0
5101	530	564	101.22	101.12	East Bar	.
5102	530	564	101.40	101.39	East Bar	.
5103	530	567	101.33	101.30	East Bar	.
5104	526	560	101.75	101.60	East Bar	.
5105	527	560	101.75	101.60	East Bar	.
5106	541	535	101.05	100.50	North Plaza (Test A)	.
5107	541	534	100.70	100.60	North Plaza (Test A)	.
5108	541	535	100.50	100.40	North Plaza (Test A)	.
5109	541	534	100.70	100.60	North Plaza (Test A)	2.0
5110	541	535	100.50	100.40	North Plaza (Test A)	2.0
5111	527	559	100.90	100.80	East Bar	.
5112	528	560	100.77	100.60	East Bar	.
5113	528	560	100.77	100.60	East Bar	2.0
5114	531	569	101.64	101.40	East Bar	.
5115	529	568	101.65	101.40	East Bar	.
5116	526	560	101.75	101.58	East Bar	.
5117	541	536	100.50	100.40	North Plaza (Test A)	.
5118	541	536	100.50	100.40	North Plaza (Test A)	2.0
5119	530	566	101.00	100.95	East Bar	.
5120	527	558	101.00	100.90	East Plaza (East)	.
5121	531	568	101.68	101.40	East Bar	.

Lot No.	Grid N	Grid E	Upper Level	Lower Level	Provenience	Flot. Vol.
5122	530	564	101.30	101.10	East Bar	.
5123	529	568	101.46	101.45	East Bar	.
5124	527	557	100.90	100.80	East Plaza (East)	.
5125	541	534	100.60	100.50	North Plaza (Test A)	.
5126	541	534	100.60	100.50	North Plaza (Test A)	2.0
5127	541	535	100.40	100.30	North Plaza (Test A)	.
5128	541	535	100.40	100.30	North Plaza (Test A)	2.0
5129	541	536	100.40	100.30	North Plaza (Test A)	.
5130	541	536	100.40	100.30	North Plaza (Test A)	2.0
5131	530	566	100.85	100.84	East Bar	.
5132	530	566	100.85	100.83	East Bar	2.0
5133	529	567	101.07	101.06	East Bar	.
5134	529	567	101.41	101.40	East Bar	.
5135	528	560	100.90	100.60	East Bar	.
5136	527	559	100.80	100.70	East Bar	.
5137	527	557	101.16	100.00	East Plaza (East)	.
5138	529	568	101.40	101.30	East Bar	.
5139	530	565	100.70	100.50	East Bar	.
5140	529	567	101.43	101.42	East Bar	.
5141	541	536	100.25	100.16	North Plaza (Test A)	2.0
5142	541	535	100.30	100.20	North Plaza (Test A)	.
5143	541	535	100.30	100.20	North Plaza (Test A)	2.0
5144	530	564	101.05	101.04	East Bar	.
5145	541	534	100.50	100.40	North Plaza (Test A)	.
5146	541	534	100.50	100.40	North Plaza (Test A)	2.0
5147	530	568	101.50	101.40	East Bar	.
5148	527	556	101.10	100.90	East Plaza (East)	.
5149	527	559	100.70	100.60	East Bar	.
5150	527	558	100.80	100.70	East Plaza (East)	.
5151	529	564	101.05	100.95	East Bar	.
5152	531	568	101.40	101.30	East Bar	.
5153	525	560	101.00	100.75	East Bar	.
5154	525	560	100.75	100.58	East Bar	.
5155	531	565	101.50	101.43	East Bar	.
5156	541	534	100.40	100.30	North Plaza (Test A)	.
5157	541	534	100.40	100.30	North Plaza (Test A)	2.0
5158	541	534	100.30	100.20	North Plaza (Test A)	.
5159	541	534	100.30	100.20	North Plaza (Test A)	2.0
5160	541	534	100.30	100.20	North Plaza (Test A)	2.0
5161	525	559	101.13	101.00	East Bar	.
5162	530	568	101.40	101.30	East Bar	.
5163	531	565	101.43	101.34	East Bar	2.0
5164	527	558	100.70	100.60	East Plaza (East)	.
5165	530	570	101.40	101.20	East Bar	.
5166	541	534	100.30	100.20	North Plaza (Test A)	.
5167	529	565	100.95	100.85	East Bar	1.0
5168	531	570	101.10	101.01	East Bar	.
5169	541	533	101.06	100.85	North Plaza (Test A)	.

Lot No.	Grid N	Grid E	Upper Level	Lower Level	Provenience	Flot. Vol.
5170	526	559	101.00	100.90	East Bar	.
5171	527	557	101.00	100.90	East Plaza (East)	.
5172	527	560	100.75	100.60	East Bar	.
5173	531	565	101.43	101.35	East Bar	2.0
5174	527	559	100.90	100.80	East Bar	.
5175	531	568	101.35	101.20	East Bar	.
5176	531	565	101.34	101.25	East Bar	.
5177	531	565	101.43	101.35	East Bar	.
5178	527	559	100.90	100.80	East Bar	2.0
5179	526	559	101.00	100.90	East Bar	2.0
5180	530	571	101.40	101.30	East Bar	.
5181	541	534	100.28	100.27	North Plaza (Test A)	.
5182	531	571	101.40	101.30	East Bar	.
5183	541	533	100.85	100.70	North Plaza (Test A)	.
5184	541	533	100.85	100.70	North Plaza (Test A)	2.0
5185	526	559	100.90	100.85	East Bar	.
5186	530	569	101.40	101.20	East Bar	.
5187	530	571	101.30	101.20	East Bar	.
5188	531	568	101.22	101.21	East Bar	.
5189	527	556	100.90	100.80	East Plaza (East)	.
5190	531	571	101.30	101.20	East Bar	.
5191	530	572	101.34	101.20	East Bar	.
5192	530	571	101.20	101.10	East Bar	.
5193	530	568	101.45	101.35	East Bar	.
5194	529	568	101.45	101.35	East Bar	.
5195	527	560	100.90	100.80	East Bar	.
5196	541	533	100.70	100.60	North Plaza (Test A)	.
5197	541	533	100.70	100.60	North Plaza (Test A)	2.0
5198	528	559	100.90	100.80	East Bar	2.0
5199	531	569	101.50	101.32	East Bar	.
5200	528	565	100.92	100.91	East Bar	.
5201	541	536	100.85	100.20	North Plaza (Test A)	.
5202	524	559	101.13	101.00	East Bar	.
5203	529	559	101.49	101.20	East Bar	.
5204	528	559	100.80	100.79	East Bar	.
5205	527	557	100.90	100.80	East Plaza (East)	.
5206	532	567	101.70	101.50	East Bar	.
5207	531	571	101.20	101.12	East Bar	.
5208	531	571	101.20	101.12	East Bar	2.0
5209	527	556	100.80	100.70	East Plaza (East)	.
5210	530	569	101.32	101.22	East Bar	.
5211	530	569	101.32	101.22	East Bar	2.0
5212	530	570	101.13	101.12	East Bar	.
5213	531	570	101.21	101.20	East Bar	.
5214	531	569	101.21	101.20	East Bar	.
5215	530	572	101.20	101.12	East Bar	.
5216	531	568	101.36	101.14	East Bar	2.0
5217	531	568	101.36	101.24	East Bar	.

Lot No.	Grid N	Grid E	Upper Level	Lower Level	Provenience	Flot. Vol.
5218	528	559	100.79	100.68	East Bar	2.0
5219	528	559	100.79	100.68	East Bar	.
5220	541	533	100.60	100.50	North Plaza (Test A)	.
5221	541	533	100.60	100.50	North Plaza (Test A)	2.0
5222	530	569	101.22	101.12	East Bar	.
5223	527	555	100.96	100.80	East Plaza (East)	.
5224	530	569	101.12	101.02	East Bar	.
5226	530	569	101.40	101.12	East Bar	.
5227	530	568	101.36	101.26	East Bar	.
5228	541	537	100.85	100.70	North Plaza (Test A)	.
5229	528	559	100.79	100.70	East Bar	.
5230	531	568	101.14	101.04	East Bar	2.0
5231	531	568	101.14	101.04	East Bar	.
5232	527	556	100.70	100.60	East Plaza (East)	.
5233	532	567	101.50	101.40	East Bar	.
5234	530	569	101.32	101.12	East Bar	.
5235	530	567	101.22	101.12	East Bar	.
5236	530	567	101.22	101.12	East Bar	2.0
5237	531	568	101.34	101.33	East Bar	.
5238	541	533	100.85	100.50	North Plaza (Test A)	.
5239	541	534	100.85	100.20	North Plaza (Test A)	.
5240	541	535	100.96	100.20	North Plaza (Test A)	.
5241	530	569	101.32	101.20	East Bar	.
5242	530	573	101.26	101.05	East Bar	.
5243	530	574	101.26	101.10	East Bar	.
5244	531	568	101.32	101.31	East Bar	.
5245	527	555	100.80	100.70	East Plaza (East)	.
5246	527	557	100.80	100.70	East Plaza (East)	.
5247	529	559	101.30	101.20	East Bar	.
5248	532	570	101.60	101.40	East Bar	.
5249	530	568	101.12	101.04	East Bar	.
5250	531	568	101.34	101.12	East Bar	.
5251	531	565	101.22	101.07	East Bar	.
5252	530	568	101.34	101.12	East Bar	.
5253	526	560	100.90	100.80	East Bar	.
5254	527	556	100.60	100.50	East Plaza (East)	.
5255	530	574	101.08	101.00	East Bar	.
5256	529	567	101.00	100.80	East Bar	.
5257	526	560	100.90	100.80	East Bar	2.0
5258	541	533	100.50	100.40	North Plaza (Test A)	.
5259	541	533	100.50	100.40	North Plaza (Test A)	2.0
5260	493	555	99.76	99.50	East Plaza (South)	.
5261	492	555	99.66	99.50	East Plaza (South)	.
5262	532	570	101.40	101.30	East Bar	.
5263	528	559	100.70	100.60	East Bar	.
5264	527	556	100.60	100.50	East Plaza (East)	.
5265	528	559	100.70	100.60	East Bar	2.0
5266	530	574	101.00	100.90	East Bar	.

Lot No.	Grid N	Grid E	Upper Level	Lower Level	Provenience	Flot. Vol.
5267	530	568	101.27	101.14	East Bar	.
5268	530	570	101.10	101.06	East Bar	.
5269	530	573	101.05	101.00	East Bar	.
5270	530	570	101.06	101.00	East Bar	.
5271	531	569	101.40	101.30	East Bar	.
5272	524	560	101.24	101.00	East Bar	.
5273	527	556	100.50	100.40	East Plaza (East)	.
5274	541	533	100.40	100.30	North Plaza (Test A)	.
5275	541	533	100.40	100.30	North Plaza (Test A)	2.0
5276	542	536	100.85	100.70	North Plaza (Test A)	.
5277	530	573	101.00	100.90	East Bar	.
5278	530	568	101.27	101.14	East Bar	.
5279	530	570	101.03	101.01	East Bar	2.0
5280	531	574	101.13	101.00	East Bar	.
5281	528	559	100.88	100.58	East Bar	.
5282	527	556	101.03	100.90	East Plaza (East)	.
5283	529	559	101.20	101.10	East Bar	.
5284	531	569	101.30	101.20	East Bar	.
5285	531	569	101.20	101.10	East Bar	.
5286	527	556	101.00	100.90	East Plaza (East)	.
5287	527	557	101.05	100.90	East Plaza (East)	.
5288	527	555	100.93	100.80	East Plaza (East)	.
5289	527	556	100.90	100.80	East Plaza (East)	.
5290	527	555	100.80	100.70	East Plaza (East)	.
5291	527	557	100.90	100.80	East Plaza (East)	.
5292	527	556	100.80	100.70	East Plaza (East)	.
5293	527	555	100.70	100.60	East Plaza (East)	.
5294	527	557	100.80	100.70	East Plaza (East)	.
5295	527	556	100.70	100.60	East Plaza (East)	.
5296	527	556	100.60	100.57	East Plaza (East)	.
5297	527	555	100.60	100.50	East Plaza (East)	.
5298	527	557	100.71	100.70	East Plaza (East)	.
5299	492	555	99.50	99.40	East Plaza (South)	.
5300	493	555	99.50	99.40	East Plaza (South)	.
5301	532	569	101.31	101.21	East Bar	2.0
5302	530	568	101.16	101.05	East Bar	.
5303	526	557	100.99	100.80	East Plaza (East)	.
5304	526	556	100.99	100.80	East Plaza (East)	.
5305	531	570	101.10	101.01	East Bar	2.0
5306	531	570	101.10	100.93	East Bar	.
5307	531	570	101.10	101.00	East Bar	2.0
5308	531	570	101.10	101.00	East Bar	.
5309	532	569	101.36	101.30	East Bar	.
5310	530	568	101.07	101.05	East Bar	2.0
5311	526	555	100.90	100.70	East Plaza (East)	.
5312	526	560	100.80	100.70	East Bar	.
5313	526	560	100.80	100.70	East Bar	2.8
5314	527	558	101.10	101.00	East Plaza (East)	.

Lot No.	Grid N	Grid E	Upper Level	Lower Level	Provenience	Flot. Vol.
5315	526	558	101.10	101.00	East Plaza (East)	.
5316	531	570	101.10	101.01	East Bar	2.0
5317	531	570	101.10	101.01	East Bar	.
5318	531	568	101.58	101.20	East Bar	.
5319	530	568	101.06	100.97	East Bar	.
5320	531	574	101.00	100.90	East Bar	.
5321	526	560	100.70	100.60	East Bar	.
5322	530	568	101.08	100.90	East Bar	.
5323	525	555	100.90	100.70	East Plaza (East)	.
5324	530	568	101.00	100.90	East Bar	.
5325	526	556	100.80	100.61	East Plaza (East)	2.0
5326	525	555	100.70	100.60	East Plaza (East)	.
5327	530	568	100.90	100.80	East Bar	.
5328	531	573	101.27	101.10	East Bar	.
5329	531	572	101.32	101.20	East Bar	.
5330	526	560	100.60	100.59	East Bar	.
5331	530	568	100.85	100.85	East Bar	.
5332	525	558	101.11	100.90	East Plaza (East)	.
5333	526	555	100.70	100.60	East Plaza (East)	.
5334	530	568	100.80	100.72	East Bar	.
5335	530	569	101.20	101.00	East Bar	.
5336	525	557	100.99	100.80	East Plaza (East)	.
5337	525	555	100.60	100.50	East Plaza (East)	.
5338	526	556	100.80	100.70	East Plaza (East)	.
5339	527	559	100.80	100.70	East Bar	.
5340	530	569	101.00	100.90	East Bar	.
5341	530	568	100.72	100.68	East Bar	2.0
5342	527	559	100.70	100.58	East Bar	.
5343	531	573	101.10	101.00	East Bar	.
5344	531	572	101.03	100.94	East Bar	.
5345	527	558	100.90	100.85	East Plaza (East)	.
5346	527	558	100.90	100.80	East Plaza (East)	2.0
5347	531	572	101.20	101.10	East Bar	.
5348	532	568	101.33	101.20	East Bar	.
5349	531	569	101.20	101.10	East Bar	.
5350	529	559	101.10	101.00	East Bar	.
5351	531	568	101.08	100.98	East Bar	2.0
5352	531	568	101.08	100.98	East Bar	.
5353	525	555	100.50	100.40	East Plaza (East)	.
5354	531	572	101.19	101.09	East Bar	.
5355	532	568	101.20	101.10	East Bar	.
5356	526	559	100.80	100.70	East Bar	.
5357	526	559	100.70	100.60	East Bar	2.0
5358	531	568	101.08	100.98	East Bar	2.0
5359	531	573	101.00	100.90	East Bar	.
5360	531	570	101.10	101.09	East Bar	.
5361	532	568	101.10	100.00	East Bar	.
5362	527	558	100.86	100.75	East Plaza (East)	2.0

Lot No.	Grid N	Grid E	Upper Level	Lower Level	Provenience	Flot. Vol.
5364	531	572	101.10	101.00	East Bar	.
5365	527	558	100.86	100.76	East Plaza (East)	.
5366	531	569	101.00	100.90	East Bar	.
5367	531	569	101.00	100.90	East Bar	2.0
5368	532	568	101.00	100.90	East Bar	.
5369	531	568	101.20	101.00	East Bar	.
5370	525	558	100.90	100.80	East Plaza (East)	.
5371	526	555	100.60	100.50	East Plaza (East)	.
5372	531	573	100.95	100.90	East Bar	2.0
5373	526	559	100.80	100.70	East Bar	2.0
5374	527	558	100.90	100.80	East Plaza (East)	.
5375	531	572	101.05	100.84	East Bar	.
5376	531	573	100.91	100.90	East Bar	.
5377	526	557	100.84	100.83	East Plaza (East)	.
5378	526	558	100.90	100.80	East Plaza (East)	.
5379	525	557	100.80	100.70	East Plaza (East)	.
5380	526	556	100.70	100.60	East Plaza (East)	.
5382	531	567	100.30	100.20	East Bar	.
5383	530	567	101.50	101.30	East Bar	.
5384	531	568	100.95	100.90	East Bar	.
5385	526	556	100.70	100.60	East Plaza (East)	2.0
5386	531	572	101.05	100.95	East Bar	.
5387	525	555	100.40	100.35	East Plaza (East)	.
5388	531	568	101.10	100.75	East Bar	.
5389	531	567	101.20	101.10	East Bar	.
5390	531	567	101.21	101.16	East Bar	.
5391	526	557	100.80	100.70	East Plaza (East)	.
5392	527	558	100.80	100.70	East Plaza (East)	.
5393	529	567	101.36	101.28	East Bar	.
5394	530	567	101.30	101.20	East Bar	.
5395	531	567	101.21	101.18	East Bar	.
5396	531	572	100.98	100.77	East Bar	.
5397	529	559	101.06	100.90	East Bar	.
5398	530	567	101.20	101.10	East Bar	.
5399	531	572	100.97	100.90	East Bar	.
5400	531	572	100.91	100.90	East Bar	.
5401	531	572	100.97	100.92	East Bar	.
5402	531	572	100.95	100.91	East Bar	.
5403	529	559	101.06	100.90	East Bar	2.0
5404	526	557	100.80	100.70	East Plaza (East)	2.3
5405	530	567	101.10	101.00	East Bar	.
5406	531	569	101.10	101.00	East Bar	.
5407	525	558	100.80	100.70	East Plaza (East)	.
5408	526	555	100.50	100.40	East Plaza (East)	.
5409	530	567	101.00	100.90	East Bar	.
5410	524	559	101.00	100.90	East Bar	.
5411	526	556	100.60	100.50	East Plaza (East)	.
5412	531	569	101.00	100.90	East Bar	.
5413	526	558	100.80	100.70	East Plaza (East)	.
5414	531	571	101.11	101.00	East Bar	.
5415	526	558	100.80	100.70	East Plaza (East)	2.0
5416	531	567	101.10	101.00	East Bar	.
5417	531	567	101.10	101.00	East Bar	.
5418	525	559	101.00	100.90	East Bar	.
5419	527	558	100.70	100.60	East Plaza (East)	.
5420	527	558	100.70	100.60	East Plaza (East)	2.0
5421	527	560	100.80	100.70	East Bar	.
5422	527	560	100.70	100.60	East Bar	.
5423	532	569	101.20	101.00	East Bar	.
5424	529	567	101.34	101.20	East Bar	.
5425	532	567	101.40	101.20	East Bar	.
5426	524	559	100.90	100.80	East Bar	.
5427	531	571	101.00	100.90	East Bar	.
5428	529	568	101.26	101.17	East Bar	.
5429	530	569	100.80	100.70	East Bar	.
5430	526	555	100.40	100.35	East Plaza (East)	.
5431	532	568	101.35	100.90	East Bar	.
5432	532	569	101.35	101.20	East Bar	.
5433	532	567	101.20	101.10	East Bar	.
5434	529	559	100.90	100.80	East Bar	.
5435	526	557	100.70	100.54	East Plaza (East)	.
5436	525	557	100.70	100.60	East Plaza (East)	.
5437	525	557	100.70	100.60	East Plaza (East)	2.0
5438	525	558	100.70	100.60	East Plaza (East)	.
5439	526	556	100.50	100.40	East Plaza (East)	.
5440	526	558	100.70	100.60	East Plaza (East)	.
5441	527	558	100.60	100.50	East Plaza (East)	.
5442	526	555	100.40	100.35	East Plaza (East)	1.0
5443	525	558	100.70	100.60	East Plaza (East)	2.0
5444	525	559	100.90	100.80	East Bar	.
5445	526	558	100.70	100.60	East Plaza (East)	2.0
5446	532	567	101.00	100.90	East Bar	.
5447	527	558	100.60	100.50	East Plaza (East)	2.0
5448	532	571	101.44	101.30	East Bar	.
5449	532	572	101.34	101.20	East Bar	.
5450	532	568	101.50	101.35	East Bar	.
5451	532	569	101.20	101.07	East Bar	.
5452	526	556	100.50	100.40	East Plaza (East)	2.0
5453	526	556	100.50	100.40	East Plaza (East)	2.0
5454	525	558	100.64	100.46	East Plaza (East)	2.0
5455	529	559	100.80	100.70	East Bar	.
5456	529	559	100.80	100.70	East Bar	2.0
5457	532	569	101.07	100.90	East Bar	.
5458	526	556	100.50	100.40	East Plaza (East)	2.0
5459	526	556	100.50	100.40	East Plaza (East)	.
5460	531	569	100.31	100.30	East Bar	.

Lot No.	Grid N	Grid E	Upper Level	Lower Level	Provenience	Flot. Vol.
5461	530	570	100.91	100.90	East Bar	2.0
5462	530	569	101.00	100.80	East Bar	.
5463	525	558	100.64	100.46	East Plaza (East)	.
5464	529	559	100.70	100.60	East Bar	.
5465	525	559	100.80	100.70	East Bar	.
5466	532	573	101.28	101.10	East Bar	.
5467	532	571	101.30	101.20	East Bar	.
5468	530	569	101.00	100.80	East Bar	.
5469	530	569	101.00	100.80	East Bar	.
5470	532	572	101.20	101.10	East Bar	.
5471	527	558	100.50	100.40	East Plaza (East)	.
5472	526	556	100.50	100.40	East Plaza (East)	.
5473	526	556	100.50	100.40	East Plaza (East)	.
5474	531	569	101.28	100.98	East Bar	.
5475	525	559	100.70	100.60	East Bar	.
5476	525	557	100.60	100.50	East Plaza (East)	.
5477	524	559	100.80	100.70	East Bar	.
5478	525	557	100.60	100.50	East Plaza (East)	2.0
5479	526	558	100.60	100.50	East Plaza (East)	.
5480	527	559	101.10	100.60	East Bar	.
5481	527	555	100.50	100.40	East Plaza (East)	.
5482	526	558	100.60	100.50	East Plaza (East)	2.0
5483	531	569	101.10	101.00	East Bar	.
5484	527	558	100.45	100.40	East Plaza (East)	2.0
5485	532	571	101.20	101.10	East Bar	.
5486	524	559	100.79	100.78	East Bar	.
5487	532	572	101.10	101.00	East Bar	.
5488	532	569	101.00	100.90	East Bar	.
5489	526	554	100.84	100.60	East Plaza (East)	.
5490	526	556	100.45	100.40	East Plaza (East)	2.0
5491	532	573	101.11	101.00	East Bar	.
5492	526	557	100.70	100.60	East Plaza (East)	.
5493	527	557	100.60	100.50	East Plaza (East)	.
5494	531	567	101.30	100.90	East Bar	.
5495	527	555	100.40	100.30	East Plaza (East)	.
5496	525	558	100.60	100.50	East Plaza (East)	.
5497	525	557	100.50	100.40	East Plaza (East)	2.0
5498	525	557	100.50	100.40	East Plaza (East)	.
5499	532	571	101.08	101.00	East Bar	.
5500	526	558	100.50	100.40	East Plaza (East)	.
5501	526	558	100.50	100.40	East Plaza (East)	2.0
5502	525	558	100.60	100.50	East Plaza (East)	2.0
5503	532	572	100.95	100.94	East Bar	.
5504	531	567	101.30	100.90	East Bar	.
5505	531	567	101.13	101.01	East Bar	.
5506	532	573	101.00	100.90	East Bar	.
5507	532	573	101.00	100.90	East Bar	2.0
5508	526	556	100.40	100.30	East Plaza (East)	.
5509	526	556	100.40	100.30	East Plaza (East)	2.0
5510	532	572	101.00	100.90	East Bar	.
5511	527	555	100.30	100.20	East Plaza (East)	.
5512	527	554	100.70	100.60	East Plaza (East)	.
5513	532	571	101.00	100.90	East Bar	.
5514	532	571	101.00	100.90	East Bar	2.0
5515	527	555	100.30	100.20	East Plaza (East)	2.0
5516	532	571	100.91	100.90	East Bar	.
5517	532	573	100.91	100.90	East Bar	.
5518	532	573	100.91	100.90	East Bar	.
5519	531	571	101.06	101.05	East Bar	.
5520	531	571	101.06	101.05	East Bar	.
5521	531	573	100.91	100.90	East Bar	.
5522	530	569	100.91	100.90	East Bar	.
5523	532	573	100.91	100.90	East Bar	.
5524	525	558	100.50	100.40	East Plaza (East)	.
5525	525	558	100.50	100.40	East Plaza (East)	2.0
5526	527	556	100.50	100.40	East Plaza (East)	2.0
5527	531	572	100.91	100.90	East Bar	.
5528	527	553	101.20	100.60	East Plaza (East)	.
5529	525	557	100.99	100.40	East Plaza (East)	.
5530	531	568	100.91	100.90	East Bar	.
5531	531	569	100.91	100.90	East Bar	.
5532	531	574	100.91	100.90	East Bar	.
5533	527	559	100.58	100.50	East Bar	.
5534	527	559	100.58	100.50	East Bar	2.0
5535	525	557	100.40	100.30	East Plaza (East)	.
5536	525	557	100.40	100.30	East Plaza (East)	2.0
5537	530	572	101.10	100.90	East Bar	.
5538	530	572	101.10	100.90	East Bar	.
5539	527	556	100.40	100.30	East Plaza (East)	.
5540	527	556	100.40	100.30	East Plaza (East)	2.0
5541	530	571	101.00	100.90	East Bar	.
5542	526	554	100.60	100.45	East Plaza (East)	.
5543	527	556	100.30	100.20	East Plaza (East)	2.0
5544	527	556	100.30	100.20	East Plaza (East)	.
5545	525	559	100.56	100.55	East Bar	.
5547	527	555	100.50	100.40	East Plaza (East)	.
5548	527	556	100.57	100.50	East Plaza (East)	.
5549	531	575	101.08	100.95	East Bar	.
5550	531	569	100.91	100.90	East Bar	.
5551	531	568	100.91	100.90	East Bar	.
5552	527	556	100.50	100.40	East Plaza (East)	.
5553	527	557	100.60	100.50	East Plaza (East)	.
5555	531	575	100.95	100.90	East Bar	.
5556	532	573	100.91	100.90	East Bar	.
5557	527	556	100.49	100.48	East Plaza (East)	2.0
5558	526	557	100.60	100.50	East Plaza (East)	.

Lot No.	Grid N	Grid E	Upper Level	Lower Level	Provenience	Flot. Vol.
5559	532	567	101.40	100.90	East Bar	.
5560	532	573	100.91	100.90	East Bar	.
5561	531	567	100.91	100.90	East Bar	.
5562	529	559	100.78	100.70	East Bar	.
5563	527	553	100.60	100.50	East Plaza (East)	.
5564	527	555	100.40	100.35	East Plaza (East)	.
5565	526	559	100.60	100.57	East Bar	.
5566	527	557	100.60	100.50	East Plaza (East)	2.0
5567	531	574	100.92	100.90	East Bar	.
5568	530	569	100.91	100.90	East Bar	.
5569	526	554	100.45	100.35	East Plaza (East)	2.0
5570	527	557	100.60	100.50	East Plaza (East)	.
5571	529	559	100.70	100.60	East Bar	.
5572	526	559	100.54	100.53	East Bar	2.0
5573	527	556	100.40	100.35	East Plaza (East)	.
5574	532	570	101.44	101.10	East Bar	.
5575	532	573	100.91	100.90	East Bar	.
5576	530	569	101.10	100.90	East Bar	.
5577	532	570	101.40	101.15	East Bar	.
5578	532	573	101.40	100.90	East Bar	.
5579	526	557	100.50	100.40	East Plaza (East)	.
5580	526	557	100.50	100.40	East Plaza (East)	2.5
5581	531	571	101.24	101.15	East Bar	.
5582	525	559	100.55	100.40	East Bar	.
5583	525	559	100.40	100.30	East Bar	.
5584	530	567	100.91	100.90	East Bar	.
5585	530	569	100.91	100.90	East Bar	.
5586	531	571	101.15	100.90	East Bar	.
5587	531	571	101.15	100.90	East Bar	.
5588	525	559	100.30	100.20	East Bar	.
5589	527	557	100.50	100.40	East Plaza (East)	.
5590	527	557	100.50	100.40	East Plaza (East)	2.0
5592	526	559	100.50	100.24	East Bar	.
5593	532	570	101.15	100.90	East Bar	.
5594	532	570	101.15	100.90	East Bar	.
5595	527	558	100.70	100.60	East Plaza (East)	.
5596	531	569	100.91	100.90	East Bar	.
5597	531	573	100.91	100.90	East Bar	.
5598	530	567	101.10	100.90	East Bar	.
5599	527	560	100.75	100.60	East Bar	.
5600	527	554	100.60	100.50	East Plaza (East)	.
5601	525	555	100.35	100.30	East Plaza (East)	.
5602	527	558	100.60	100.50	East Plaza (East)	.
5603	531	570	100.87	100.80	East Bar	.
5604	530	567	100.93	100.90	East Bar	.
5605	527	553	100.50	100.40	East Plaza (East)	.
5606	525	559	100.24	100.10	East Bar	.
5607	527	556	100.35	100.30	East Plaza (East)	.
5608	527	553	100.50	100.40	East Plaza (East)	2.0
5609	527	556	100.35	100.30	East Plaza (East)	2.0
5610	527	559	100.60	100.50	East Bar	.
5611	525	557	100.30	100.20	East Plaza (East)	.
5612	525	557	100.40	100.22	East Plaza (East)	.
5613	532	572	100.90	100.84	East Bar	.
5614	530	571	100.91	100.90	East Bar	.
5615	526	555	100.35	100.30	East Plaza (East)	.
5616	526	557	100.40	100.30	East Plaza (East)	.
5617	527	558	100.50	100.40	East Plaza (East)	.
5618	527	558	100.40	100.30	East Plaza (East)	.
5619	530	570	101.12	101.00	East Bar	.
5620	532	572	100.84	100.81	East Bar	.
5621	530	570	100.97	100.90	East Bar	.
5622	527	553	100.40	100.30	East Plaza (East)	.
5623	527	553	100.40	100.30	East Plaza (East)	2.3
5624	527	559	100.50	100.40	East Bar	.
5625	532	571	100.91	100.90	East Bar	.
5626	531	572	100.91	100.90	East Bar	.
5627	529	567	101.30	100.90	East Bar	.
5628	526	560	100.91	100.90	East Bar	.
5629	527	554	100.50	100.40	East Plaza (East)	.
5630	526	554	100.35	100.30	East Plaza (East)	.
5631	530	572	100.89	100.80	East Bar	.
5632	531	568	100.91	100.87	East Bar	.
5633	525	557	100.20	100.10	East Plaza (East)	.
5634	530	567	100.93	100.90	East Bar	.
5635	531	568	100.87	100.81	East Bar	2.0
5636	531	568	100.87	100.81	East Bar	.
5637	529	559	100.60	100.56	East Bar	.
5638	527	553	100.30	100.20	East Plaza (East)	2.0
5639	527	553	100.30	100.20	East Plaza (East)	.
5640	531	568	100.93	100.90	East Bar	.
5641	532	571	100.91	100.90	East Bar	.
5642	527	558	100.30	100.20	East Plaza (East)	.
5643	527	558	100.30	100.20	East Plaza (East)	2.0
5644	526	555	100.30	100.20	East Plaza (East)	.
5645	531	570	100.90	100.86	East Bar	.
5646	530	567	100.91	100.90	East Bar	.
5647	525	557	100.20	100.10	East Plaza (East)	2.0
5648	527	557	100.40	100.30	East Plaza (East)	2.0
5649	527	557	100.40	100.30	East Plaza (East)	.
5650	528	559	100.60	100.55	East Bar	.
5651	531	571	100.86	100.81	East Bar	.
5652	527	557	100.50	100.40	East Plaza (East)	.
5653	532	570	100.90	100.81	East Bar	.
5654	531	570	100.93	100.77	East Bar	.
5655	530	571	100.91	100.90	East Bar	.

Lot No.	Grid N	Grid E	Upper Level	Lower Level	Provenience	Flot. Vol.
5656	531	574	100.85	100.82	East Bar	.
5657	527	557	100.40	100.30	East Plaza (East)	.
5658	527	557	100.40	100.30	East Plaza (East)	2.0
5659	532	569	100.91	100.90	East Bar	.
5660	531	574	100.82	100.77	East Bar	.
5661	532	569	100.95	100.90	East Bar	.
5662	526	555	100.30	100.15	East Plaza (East)	2.0
5663	526	555	100.15	100.05	East Plaza (East)	.
5664	527	554	100.40	100.20	East Plaza (East)	.
5665	532	568	100.90	100.81	East Bar	.
5666	532	569	100.90	100.81	East Bar	.
5667	531	575	100.79	100.77	East Bar	.
5668	531	574	100.75	100.70	East Bar	1.5
5669	532	573	100.91	100.90	East Bar	.

3

The Pottery of the Henderson Site

The 1980-1981 Seasons

Regge N. Wiseman
Museum of New Mexico

Introduction

Two seasons of excavation at the Henderson Site (1980-1981) yielded nearly 35,000 sherds, weighing about 105 kg or slightly over 230 lb. The average density of sherds for the excavation as a whole was just over 436 sherds per m^3 of deposit.[1] Despite the large number of sherds, the majority are very small, averaging only 3 g per sherd). The small sherd size in part reflects a recovery strategy using a quarter-inch screen (though the very smallest sherds have not been included in this analysis). It probably also reflects the predominance in the assemblage of very thin-walled and fragile El Paso Polychrome cooking and storage jars, which may have been especially prone to breakage during use, and which may have been further fragmented by trampling and other site formation processes. The 1980-1981 excavations yielded only three whole (or entirely restorable) vessels, all from two subfloor burial pits beneath the primary floor in East Bar Room E-4: a small Chupadero Black-on-white jar nested within a small Lincoln Black-on-red bowl, both placed with a young child in Feature 3, and a large Heshotauthla Polychrome bowl inverted over the face of a young adult female buried along with a fetus or newborn in Feature 40 (see Rocek and Speth 1986 for illustrations of these vessels).

The Henderson assemblage includes at least 27 named pottery types (Table 3.1). Six of these types—El Paso Polychrome, Chupadero Black-on-white, Three Rivers Redware (Three Rivers Red-on-terracotta and Lincoln Black-on-red), Corona Corrugated, and Jornada Brown—are almost certainly of local or regional manufacture (Wiseman n.d.a). Others were probably imported from northern Mexico (five types), southwestern New Mexico (four types), western New Mexico (five types), and the Rio Grande of north-central New Mexico (five types). As is common in Jornada-Mogollon sites, the local/regional types are a clear majority of the assemblage (n = 33,010 or 95%). Missing entirely from the assemblage are cordmarked or other obvious Southern Plains ceramic types (e.g., Lintz 1986), or types originating in extreme southeastern New Mexico, such as Ochoa Indented (e.g., Corley 1965; Leslie 1979).

The Local Pottery

Perhaps the most surprising aspect of the assemblage is that El Paso Polychrome is the dominant type (Table 3.1) both in frequency and weight. Jar sherds are by far the dominant vessel form. Both middle and late period jar rims are present in the assemblage (Way 1979; Whalen 1981), though late period rims outnumber middle period 157 to 45 (77.7% to 22.3%). No early period rims (Way 1979; Whalen 1981) are present. Interestingly, many of the El Paso Polychrome jar exteriors were coated with soot which had to be scrubbed off with a brush to reveal the underlying design. This implies that these jars, despite their painted decorations, often served as cooking vessels, and were routinely placed in or near the fire. In addition, although El Paso Polychrome jars (as well as jars of other types) may have been used for storage, none was found set permanently beneath the floors of rooms. Most of the El Paso Polychrome sherds, and therefore most of the vessels, may have been made in the El Paso district, some 200 km to the southwest. It is difficult to envision how this could be the case, however, since so many

Table 3.1. Summary of pottery from the 1980-1981 seasons at the Henderson Site (LA-1549).

Pottery Type/Ware	Counts		Weight	
	No.	%	grams	%
El Paso ware	18,432	53.1	47,608	45.1
Polychrome (no rims)	3,875		10,833	
Polychrome rims	470		2,864	
unpainted body (all polychrome?)	14,087		33,911	
Chupadero Black-on-white	5,782	16.7	23,290	22.0
jar	5,162		20,149	
bowl	620		3,141	
Three Rivers redware	5,214	15.0	16,010	15.2
Three Rivers Red-on-terracotta	536		2,516	
Lincoln Black-on-red	1,010		4,820	
undifferentiated, unpainted body	3,668		8,674	
Corona Corrugated	3,522	10.1	12,848	12.2
jar	98			
bowl	13			
undifferentiated body	3,411			
Jornada brownware group	60	0.2	719	0.7
Jornada Brown	54			
South Pecos Brown	6			
Playas Ware	82	0.2	265	0.3
Chihuahua polychromes	31	0.1	97	0.1
Babicora Polychrome	16			
Carretas(?) Polychrome	2			
Villa Ahumada Polychrome	1			
Ramos Polychrome	3			
unidentified	9			
Alma/Casas Grandes plainware	11	< 1.0	—	< 1.0
Salado polychromes (Pinto/Gila/Tonto)	118	0.3	365	0.3
jar	80			
bowl	38			
Salado plain utility(?)	4	< 1.0	—	< 1.0
White Mountain redwares	306	0.9	1,528	1.4
St. Johns Polychrome	9			
St. Johns/Springerville B/r	41			
Springerville Polychrome	8			
Pinedale/Heshotauthla Polychrome	53			
Pinedale/Heshotauthla B/r	132			
Cedar Creek Polychrome	5			
undifferentiated body sherds	58			
Seco Corrugated	30	0.1	—	< 1.0
indented	28			
plain body(?)	2			
Rio Grande whitewares	3	< 1.0	—	< 1.0
Santa Fe Black-on-white	2			
Wiyo Black-on-white	1			
Rio Grande Glaze A	130	0.4	657	0.6
Los Padillas Polychrome	5			
Agua Fria Glaze-on-red	111			
Arenal Glaze-Polychrome	9			
undifferentiated body	5			
Unidentified sherds[a]	991	2.9	2,173	2.1
b/w and whiteware	88			
redware	54			
brownware	5			
miscellaneous	7			
unknown/too small to identify	837			
Total	34,716	100.0	105,560	100.0

[a]Does not include tiny sherds from flotation samples.

vessels are represented in the assemblage. Perhaps El Paso Polychrome was made in communities closer to the Pecos Valley, as Kelley (1984:127) has suggested. Clearly, an in-depth study of this pottery type is needed.

Three other types and wares round out the primary pottery assemblage at the site—Chupadero Black-on-white, Corona Corrugated, and Three Rivers ware. Paste and temper studies indicate that most of the Henderson Chupadero was made in southeastern New Mexico. Very little appears to have been imported from the primary production center in the Gran Quivira country 160 km northwest of Henderson (cf. Hayes et al. 1981; Kelley 1979).

Corona Corrugated is the primary late prehistoric utility ware of the Gran Quivira country (Hayes et al. 1981). It is also one of the hallmarks of Lincoln phase sites in the Sierra Blanca area west of Roswell (Kelley 1984).

Three Rivers Redware is dominated by unpainted bowl sherds. Of the painted sherds, Lincoln Black-on-red is more common than Three Rivers Red-on-terracotta. It is worth noting, however, that most of the Henderson Lincoln is more aptly termed "black-on-terracotta," since red values according to Munsell chart comparisons are scarce in the assemblage. This variant, while expectable on the basis of the original description (Mera and Stallings 1931), is unusually common at Henderson.

Imported Pottery

The variety, specific types, and regions represented by the imported pottery are normal for a late prehistoric Jornada-Mogollon site (Lehmer 1948; Kelley 1984). Because the dominant local and regional pottery types are long-lived or poorly dated or both, the imported types are especially important for dating sites as well as for looking at exchange networks. Starting with northern Mexico and working progressively northward, four major groups of pottery are represented.

The Chihuahua polychromes represent the Casas Grandes culture of northern Chihuahua, Mexico, and, perhaps, far southwestern New Mexico. These are Babicora Polychrome, Carretas Polychrome, Villa Ahumada Polychrome, Ramos Polychrome, and Playas Red Incised (included within the Playas ware category in Table 3.1).

The Salado polychromes represent southwestern New Mexico and southeastern Arizona. I have not as yet definitively

Table 3.2. Dated intrusive pottery types found in southeastern New Mexico in chronological order.

Pottery Type	Date (AD)	Reference
Mimbres b/w (Style 3)	1000-1150 1000-1250+ ?	Anyon et al. (1981) Brody (1977:66)
"Late" Red Mesa B/w	1050-1125	Breternitz (1966)
Babicora Polychrome	1060-1340 1150-1300	DiPeso et al. (1974) Phillips (1989)
Carretas Polychrome	1060-1519 1150-1519	DiPeso et al. (1974) Phillips (1989)
Villa Ahumada Polychrome	1060-1519 1150-1519	DiPeso et al. (1974) Phillips 1989
Ramos Polychrome	1060-1519 1150-1519	DiPeso et al. (1974) Phillips (1989)
Playas Ware	1060-1519 1150-1519	DiPeso et al. (1974) Phillips (1989)
Chupadero Black-on-white	1100-? 1150-? 1175-1545	Wiseman (1982) Breternitz (1966) Hayes et al. (1981)
Three Rivers Red-on-terracotta	1150-1300 or 1350	Breternitz (1966)
St. Johns Polychrome	1175-1300	Breternitz (1966)
Santa Fe Black-on-white	1175-1425	Habicht-Mauche (1993)
Springerville Polychrome	1200-1325	Breternitz (1966)
Corona Corrugated	1225-1460	Hayes et al. (1981)
El Paso Polychrome ("Early") El Paso Polychrome ("Late")	1100-1250 1250-1400	Whalen (1981)
Wiyo Black-on-white	1250-1350	Habicht-Mauche (1993)
Pinto Polychrome	1260-1300	White (n.d.)
Pinedale Polychrome	1275-1350	Breternitz (1966)
Heshotauthla Polychrome	1275 or 1300-1400	Smith et al. (1966)
Gila Polychrome	1300-1400 1350-1400	Breternitz (1966); White (n.d.) Reid and Whittlesey (n.d.)
Cedar Creek Polychrome	1300-1400	Carlson (1970)
Los Padillas Polychrome	? 1300-1325 ?	Warren (1979)
Lincoln Black-on-red	1300-1400	Breternitz (1966)
Rio Grande Glaze A Red	1315-1425+ ?	Warren (1979); Earls (1987)
Arenal Glaze Polychrome	? 1315-1350 ?	Warren (1979)
Largo G/y or Polychrome	1400-1450	Warren (1979)

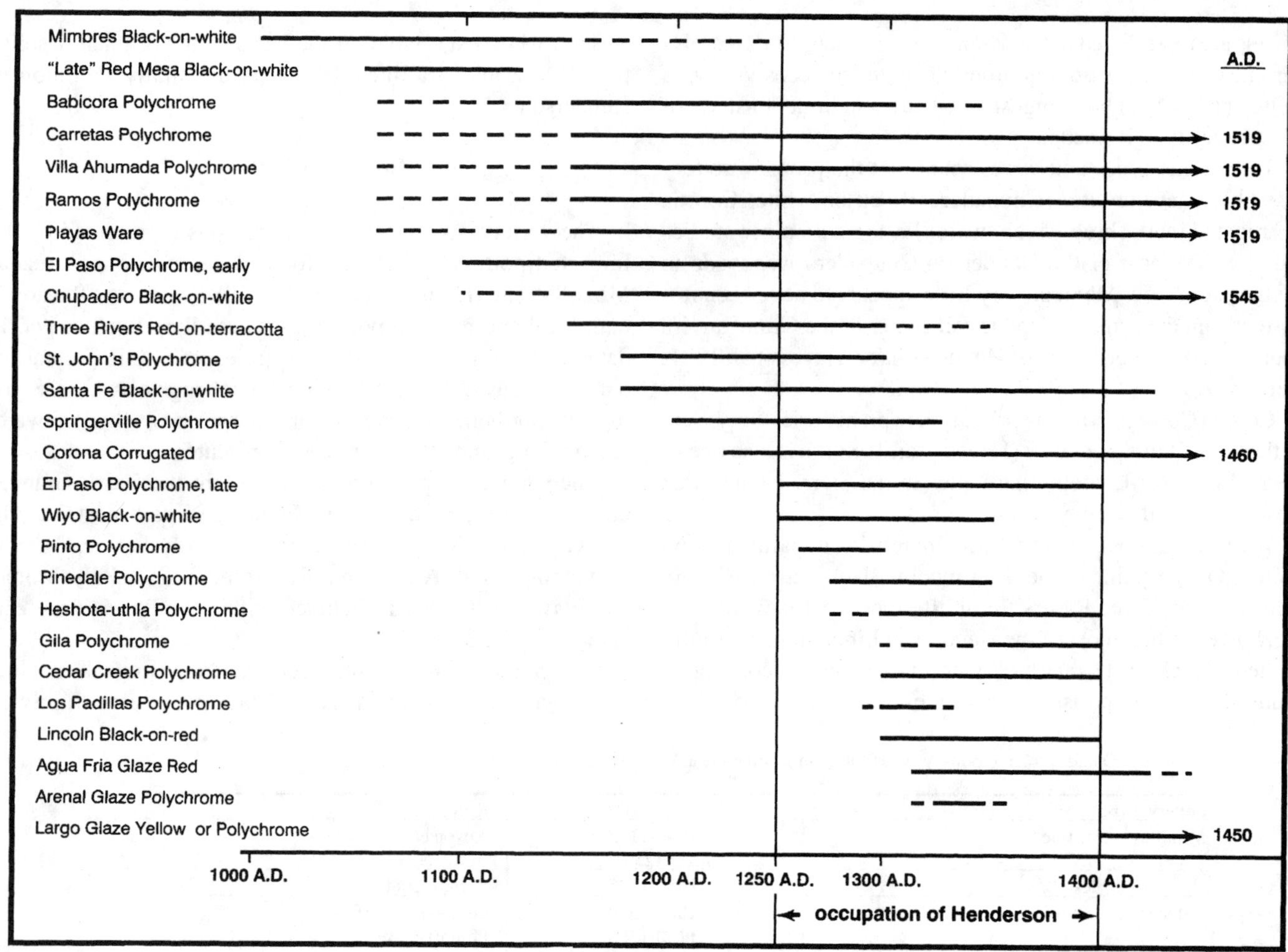

Figure 3.1. Date of the Henderson Site occupation based on the estimated temporal span of the ceramic types recovered during the 1980-1981 excavations.

separated out the three main types, but it looks as if the earliest one, Pinto Polychrome, is represented by perhaps as many as one to two dozen sherds, most of them from jars. Gila Polychrome appears to be the best represented and includes most of the bowl and jar sherds. Only two sherds of Tonto Polychrome, both from the same jar, have been noted in the 1980-1981 collections. However, because the sherd sizes in the assemblage are generally small, it is conceivable that this type is underrepresented in the tallies.[2]

White Mountain redwares represent the Western Pueblo Anasazi of west-central New Mexico and east-central Arizona. A few sherds can be confidently assigned to three types: St. Johns Polychrome, Springerville Polychrome, and Cedar Creek Polychrome. The bulk of the sherds, however, can only be assigned to one of the combination groups, or the unidentified group, because they possess too few distinct attributes.

Santa Fe Black-on-white, Wiyo Black-on-white, and Rio Grande Glaze A sherds represent the Rio Grande Anasazi. Santa Fe was made as far south as Albuquerque, but Wiyo came from farther north in the Santa Fe region. I suspect most of the glaze sherds probably came from the Albuquerque to Socorro stretch of the Rio Grande Valley and/or the Chupadera Mesa and northern Jornada del Muerto basin to the east.

Dating the Occupation with Pottery

In the Southwest, pottery has long been used to date sites, especially in the absence of materials datable by more direct means. While a number of other techniques can be brought to bear for dating Henderson, it is still useful to gain temporal perspective from the pottery. But because of the peculiar nature of the local and regional types of the Jornada-Mogollon, we must use a combination of both positive and negative information for this purpose.

Henderson produced numerous imported pottery types, many dated elsewhere in the Southwest (Table 3.2). While these solidly document occupation sometime during the mid-1200s to the mid-1300s (Fig. 3.1), we must rely on the absence of certain pottery types to estimate the beginning and ending dates of the occupation.

Two early pottery types that are absent at Henderson—Mimbres Black-on-white and Red Mesa Black-on-white—are well documented at a number of other sites in southeastern New Mexico. Mimbres has been recovered from Garnsey Spring Campsite and Los Molinos in the Roswell area (Parry and Speth 1984; Wiseman n.d.d), at several sites along the Pecos River between Roswell and Fort Sumner (Jelinek 1967), and at Crockett Canyon, Bonnell, LA-30949, and elsewhere in the Sierra Blanca (Farwell et al. 1992; Kelley 1984; Del Bene et al. 1986; Wiseman 1991). Red Mesa is especially common at several sites along the Pecos River between Roswell and Fort Sumner (Jelinek 1967) and has also been recovered at Garnsey Spring Campsite (Parry and Speth 1984). Neither type has been found at Henderson.

Both Mimbres Black-on-white and Red Mesa Black-on-white predate A.D. 1150 in their original regions of manufacture, though Brody (1977:66) has suggested that Mimbres may have been made as late as A.D. 1250 east of the Mimbres heartland. A third pottery type, early El Paso Polychrome (Way 1979), has a rim form altogether missing at Henderson. The rim form is dated between A.D. 1100 and 1250 by Whalen (1981). Taking the absence of these three pottery types into consideration, it is fairly certain that the initial occupation of Henderson took place after A.D. 1200 and perhaps after A.D. 1250.

Pottery evidence for an occupation end date at Henderson is also based on negative evidence. Largo Glaze-on-yellow and Largo Glaze polychrome (Rio Grande Glaze B or II) are absent. While these types are rare in southeastern New Mexico, I noted one sherd at the Robinson Site, a Lincoln phase pueblo situated on the east slopes of the Jicarilla Mountains in central Lincoln County, New Mexico. Glaze B was found at Gran Quivira (Hayes et al. 1981) and at a site near Lubbock, Texas (Watts 1963).

It might also be noted that the entire Rio Grande glaze series, including many types postdating A.D. 1400, has also been recovered from Gran Quivira as well as from numerous sites on the Southern Plains (Hayes et al. 1981; Watts 1963). Clearly, late-dating pottery was being widely distributed throughout eastern New Mexico and adjacent parts of Texas. If Henderson had been occupied after A.D. 1400, it would not be unreasonable to expect some of these types to show up, particularly considering that the 1980-1981 collections number nearly 35,000 sherds. We can only conclude that Henderson had been abandoned by about 1400.[3]

Description and Discussion of Specific Pottery Types

Chupadero Black-on-White

Chupadero Black-on-white (Mera 1931; Hayes et al. 1981; Warren, in Hayes 1981; Wiseman 1982) is the second most common pottery type in the 1980-1981 collections at Henderson. Despite Jelinek's (1967) suggestion that Chupadero may have originated in the Middle Pecos region of eastern New Mexico, the type almost certainly first developed in central New Mexico (Mera 1931; Wiseman 1986) some time between 1050 or 1100 and 1175 (Kelley and Peckham 1962; Breternitz 1966). During the 1200s and 1300s, Chupadero was also made in the Sierra Blanca region of southeastern New Mexico (Warren 1992; Kelley 1979).

Chupadero Black-on-white is best known for its distinctive globular, narrow-mouth jar or olla form, and its extremely wide geographic distribution. It has been found as far north as the Santa Fe region, as far west and southwest as Casas Grandes in northern Mexico, and as far east as central Kansas (Habicht-Mauche 1993; DiPeso et al. 1974; Wedel 1982). Most of the tree-ring dates for Chupadero are from trade contexts in various Galisteo Basin sites south of Santa Fe (Breternitz 1966).

The analysis of the 1980-1981 Henderson Chupadero Black-on-white focused on tempering materials and possible sources, rather than other attributes such as slip, paint, and surface finish. The samples of Chupadero sherds drawn for paste analysis differed for bowls and jars. The bowl sample ($n = 184$, or 29.6% of total bowl sherds) consisted of all sherds large enough to grasp with the fingers after removing an edge fragment for examination of the paste. Jar sherds ($n = 482$, or 9.3% of total jar sherds), being much more numerous, were selected for large size and overall preservation of other attributes, especially designs.

In most instances, the pastes and tempers of the Henderson sherds are familiar, though the ranges in texture, color, friability, grain size, and temper profusion are highly variable. It is possible that one variety was made at Henderson, as briefly described in the following paragraphs. As is typical of pottery sherds recovered from sites in southeastern New Mexico, most sherds are much too small to analyze design style.

Although it is premature to name a new variety of Chupadero until a more thorough study can be completed, the attributes of paste color and texture will provide a convenient starting point in the process. The pastes of the suspect sherds are frequently light brownish-gray to light orange in color, the two colors often being zoned with the orange next to the exterior surface and brownish-gray next to the interior. These colors suggest oxidation late in the firing process.

The paste texture of these sherds is generally more ragged or friable, probably reflecting the types of clays being used. Broken edges are ragged for Chupadero and are reminiscent of the White Mountain redwares in coarseness. Since the tempering material of these sherds is primarily crushed sherd, this attribute does not outwardly differ from the majority of the Chupadero sherds at Henderson or elsewhere in southeastern New Mexico. As so often proves to be the case, the paste colors and texture do not depart radically from those more typical of Chupadero; they merely represent extremes in the fairly broad ranges of colors and textures typical of the type.

The tempering materials of the Chupadero sherds comprise four main types and five minor types and groups. These are described in order of abundance in the following paragraphs (see Table 3.3).

Table 3.3. Summary of Chupadero Black-on-white temper types.

Temper Type[a]	No. of Bowl Sherds	No. of Jar Sherds	% of Analyzed Sample
Sherd and crystalline rock	7	231	36
Crystalline rock, ±sherd, dark minerals	107	91	30
50/50 sherd and rock	22	91	17
Caliche and sherd	42	61	15
Pueblo Colorado(?) temper	5	—	1
Gran Quivira(?) temper	1	4	1
Too fine to distinguish @ 30× (Gran Quivira temper?)	—	2	< 1
Crystalline rock with sand or sandstone	—	1	< 1
Vitrified	—	1	< 1
Total	184	482	100

[a]Analysis sample constitutes 11.5% of total Chupadero sample (29.6% of bowl sherds and 9.3% of jar sherds).

Sherd and Crystalline Rock. The temper in these sherds is predominantly crushed sherd and differs from the following group in that the crushed sherd particles clearly outnumber the crystalline ones. The implication is that these vessels were tempered with crushed sherds that contained crystalline rock temper. The crystalline rock is predominantly, if not solely, the Capitan monzonite and quartz monzonite described below.

Crystalline Rock, Sherd, and Minor Dark Accessory Minerals. The dominant, perhaps sole, tempering constituent of these sherds has been called Capitan aplite or alaskite granite by A. H. Warren (1992), and Capitan monzonite and quartz monzonite by David H. Hill (pers. comm.). The main constituent is a crushed, leucocratic, crystalline igneous rock, the dominant minerals being porcelaneous white and clear feldspars, with or without small amounts of quartz. Minor amounts of crushed sherd and/or various mafic minerals were noted in many of the sherds and may signal the presence of similar-appearing crushed rocks such as biotite felsite from the Gran Quivira region and perhaps others. The crushed-sherd temper grains vary from fine to coarse (0.5-1.0 mm) and are often dark grayish-brown (from utility vessels?). It is difficult to tell whether the mafics came with the crushed sherds or with the crushed rocks.

Ten bowl sherds have crystalline temper grains that are so finely ground that it is almost impossible to see them at a magnification of 30 diameters; they appear to be white to clear and mostly can be seen only as glints of light under 30-power magnification. The problem is compounded by the very fine-grained, very light-gray to white clay body of the sherds. Mafic particles, mostly in the form of small flecks and books of dark brown-black or black biotite, are occasionally identifiable, but one has to look closely to make certain that these items are actually mineral fragments and not small linear vesicles in the clay.

50/50 Sherd and Rock. The primary constituent of this temper appears to be crushed sherd tempered with crushed rock. Sherd grain size can vary considerably. The crushed rocks appear to be mainly Sierra Blanca igneous rocks composed primarily of feldspars, mostly white and off-white. Gray feldspar also commonly occurs in small frequencies, as do bits of caliche and dark accessory minerals, though these minerals do not occur in all sherds of this temper type.

The gray feldspar occurs in two varieties. One, from Sierra Blanca in Lincoln County, has large, well-formed crystals that are solid gray to rosy-gray or lavender and may or may not have surface rosettes. The other variety of gray feldspar has translucent crystals that are somewhat lighter gray. The origin of this second type of feldspar is uncertain and is discussed more fully under Playas Incised.

Caliche and Sherd. In most instances, the dominant constituent of this temper type is finely ground, ivory-colored caliche or calcium carbonate with variable amounts of crushed sherd. In a few sherds the caliche is a minor constituent, and often in these instances it is more coarsely ground. Large caliche grains near the exterior surface tend to cause the surface clay to spall off, exposing the caliche grains on the vessel surface. Crushed sherd grains can vary greatly in size and often appear black and bubbly. Probably derived from crushed sherds, crystalline fragments and mafics are often present in small amounts.

Pueblo Colorado(?) Temper. A few sherds have what I believe to be the temper attributes of pottery made at the village of Pueblo Colorado in the Saline-Medano country of central New Mexico. These temper grains are generally very finely ground, profuse in number, and are often sintered or black and bubbly in appearance.

Gran Quivira(?) Temper. One sherd has the light brownish-gray clay body and caliche and clay pellet temper Warren (in Hayes et al. 1981; Hayes 1981) ascribes to the village of Gran Quivira in central New Mexico.

Temper Too Fine to Distinguish at 30×. These sherds have gray pastes and very fine temper. They may or may not be Gran Quivira products (cf. description of Gran Quivira paste in Appendix 1 of Hayes et al. 1981).

Crystalline Rock(?) with Sand or Sandstone Temper. The quartz grains in one sherd are rounded as though weathered as a sand or sandstone, rather than being attributable to the quartz fraction of Capitan quartz monzonite. Warren (1992) notes the presence of sand or sandstone temper in some Chupadero sherds from the Smokey Bear Ruin (LA-2112), but she offers no ideas as to origin or significance. She also describes a sandstone temper in some Chupadero at Gran Quivira (Appendix 1, in Hayes et al. 1981).

Vitrified (Temper Indistinguishable). The vitrification of one sherd has fused the temper grains with the clay body, making them indistinguishable under ordinary magnification.

Corona Corrugated

Corona Corrugated is the principal indented corrugated utility ware in prehistoric components at Gran Quivira (Hayes et al. 1981). Although Kelley (1984) does not use that name, it is also the principal corrugated pottery in Lincoln phase sites of the Sierra Blanca region. Corona replaced Jornada Brown in both regions as the utility ware companion of Chupadero Black-on-white.

Almost all of the Henderson sherds fit the type description in Hayes et al.'s (1981) report on Gran Quivira, though they do not embody the total surface treatment variation of the Gran Quivira type materials. The Henderson sherds also diverge from the Gran Quivira Corona in temper and vessel form. At Gran Quivira, the most common tempering material is quartz mica schist, whereas at Henderson it is crystalline rock (mostly Capitan alaskite). This difference reflects the areas of manufacture. At Gran Quivira, bowl forms are apparently absent (Hayes et al. 1981), while at Henderson they are comparatively common, though still scarcer than jars.

The analysis of the Corona Corrugated was limited to temper and vessel form (see Table 3.4). The following discussions of tempering materials relate to slightly less than half of the Corona Corrugated sherds; the rest were too small for temper analysis.

Crystalline Rock (Capitan Alaskite and Similar Rocks). The most common temper in the Henderson Corona includes minerals belonging to at least three different rock types and perhaps more—Capitan monzonite/quartz monzonite (A. H. Warren calls this rock aplite or alaskite granite), biotite felsite (see Warren, in Hayes et al. 1981), and perhaps vitric tuff/pumice. This last one, tuff/pumice, is questionable. In many instances, the white to clear minerals of these rocks are so finely ground that they are difficult to identify and segregate without the assistance of petrographic techniques.

Table 3.4. Corona Corrugated temper types.

Temper Type[a]	Body Sherds	Rim Sherds		% of Sample
		Jar	Bowl	
Crystalline rock	1,389	90	13	88
Quartz/quartz mica schist	168	7	—	10
Sand/sandstone	13	—	—	1
Gray feldspar and crystalline rock	—	1	1	< 1
Miscellaneous	17	—	—	1
Total	1,587	98	14	100

[a]1,699 sherds were analyzed; an additional 1,823 sherds were too small to analyze for temper.

The basic mineral suite is dominated by crystalline white to off-white to clear minerals that include feldspars, perhaps quartz, with or without small quantities of mafics such as biotite, magnetite, and hornblende. Large particles of Capitan monzonite/quartz monzonite are identifiable as aggregates of small, equigranular porcelaneous white feldspar crystals, often with occasional clear feldspar and/or quartz crystals that are poorly formed and/or twinned beyond easy recognition of crystal forms; small flecks of biotite may or may not be present.

The range in paste colors of these sherds causes problems for the identification of temper type. The dark brown, dark yellow-brown, and black carbonaceous pastes are particularly troublesome. The temper particles are so finely ground that in the dark pastes temper particles can be ascertained only by the glint of crystal faces or by the observation of particles at the margins of the clay where the carbon has been burned out. Thus, it is practically certain that yet other rock types (though probably closely related to those mentioned above) are subsumed in the crystalline rock category.

Before moving on, the points of origin of the two main crystalline tempers should be noted. Capitan monzonite/quartz monzonite derives from Capitan Mountain and two or so major peaks in the nearby Jicarilla Mountains to the west and north. D. V. Hill (pers. comm.) notes that monzonite comes generally from the eastern end of Capitan Mountain and quartz monzonite from the western end of Capitan Mountain and, presumably, from the peaks in the Jicarillas. Biotite felsite is documented from the vicinity of Gran Quivira (Warren, in Hayes et al. 1981). It is not currently known whether other sources are closer to Roswell.

The source, or sources, of the vitric tuff/pumice, if in fact this material is in some of the Henderson Corona, is unknown at the present time. Warren (Hayes et al. 1981) mentions a tuff temper that she attributes to the Jemez Mountains north of Albuquerque, but this almost certainly does not apply to the Henderson pottery because of the great distance involved.

Quartz/Quartz Mica Schist. According to Warren, the primary tempering materials of Corona Corrugated at Gran Quivira are quartz mica schist and angular quartz with white feldspar (in Hayes et al. 1981). The actual mineralogical composition of the temper in a Henderson sherd can vary from high quartz (either as numerous large individual crystals or aggregates of finely twinned crystals) with little or no mica to quartz fragments with plentiful mica. Occasionally, other detritus also is observed, including tiny pieces of what appears to be gray limestone but in reality may be the ground mass of a quartz rhyolite or simply chunky fragments of unground clay.

Several sherds of Corona Corrugated are tempered with quartz sand or sandstone composed of rounded quartz grains. Warren (in Hayes et al. 1981) reports a variety of sandstones in the Gran Quivira sherds she examined. The quartz grains in the

Henderson sherds are mostly equigranular and rounded to subrounded.

A small number of Corona sherds are tempered with a crystalline rock like that described above except for the addition of minor amounts of singular translucent gray feldspar crystals. Warren (Hayes et al. 1981) mentions a temper variety involving quartz and white feldspar, but her material probably differs from that observed in the Henderson sherds. The gray feldspar may indicate a Sierra Blanca origin, but this is not certain.

Of the 1,699 analyzed Corona Corrugated sherds, only 112 are rim sherds, 98 from jars and 14 from bowls. Hayes et al. (1981) state that Corona Corrugated rims are moderately outcurved, which is true for the Henderson rims as well. Interestingly, Hayes reports only jars, not bowls. Corona bowl sherds, including a nearly complete vessel from the Baca Site north of Lincoln, New Mexico (Wiseman 1975), are known from the Sierra Blanca country.

El Paso Polychrome

El Paso Polychrome (EPP), including unpainted body sherds, is easily the most common pottery recovered by the 1980-1981 excavations at the Henderson Site, both by count and weight (see Table 3.1). The type is generally believed to be a product of the El Paso region of far west Texas, south-central New Mexico, and northern Mexico (Stallings 1931). In addition to its distinctive appearance and obvious widespread importance, El Paso Polychrome also has micro-interval dating potential in the changes in rim-profile shape (e.g., Whalen 1981).

Some of the El Paso Polychrome from Henderson has well-polished surfaces. These sherds recall H. P. Mera's (1943) brief mention of a type he called Jornada Polychrome. Mera believed this type, with its Jornada Brown paste and simple red and black designs, was the inspiration for true (unpolished) El Paso Polychrome. The polished polychrome sherds from Henderson, however, are on more typical El Paso pastes, leading me to include them under El Paso Polychrome.

The analysis of the Henderson EPP sherds followed that established for the Fox Place (another late prehistoric village along the Hondo channel between Henderson and the city of Roswell), and involved consideration of temper group, paste, surface finish and design style (where possible), presence/absence of charring on the vessel exterior, vessel form and size, and rim profiles. Sherds presumed to be the unpainted lower body sherds of EPP are described under El Paso Brown (EPB).

Temper analysis is restricted to a partial description of the mineral constituents, with special attention to the presence/absence of gray feldspar. Although there is now some reason to question the accuracy of the interpretation, at one time gray feldspar was believed to be the one mineral that could be attributed to the Sierra Blanca region of New Mexico (see comments under the discussion of Playas pottery).

A thorough treatment of El Paso Polychrome designs has not been attempted here for one major reason—too few large sherds and no complete or nearly complete vessels were recovered from Henderson. In general, El Paso vessels are so fragile that few complete or nearly complete specimens have been recovered anywhere. The few that have been recovered are scattered among a number of museums and private collections. Vernon R. Brook examined a number of complete vessels in the 1970s, but he has not yet published a report on his study.

Three general types of temper were noted in the Henderson EPP sherds: (1) feldspar and quartz, (2) feldspar and quartz with gray feldspar, and (3) other. The detailed observations presented here were made on both jar ($n = 200$) and bowl ($n = 16$) rim sherds.

The bulk of the temper (n = 167, 77%) is of the same, or closely related, rocks that constitute what is believed to be the primary temper of the EPP made in the general El Paso district of far west Texas and south-central New Mexico. This temper is dominated by off-white feldspars with minor amounts of slightly frosted, subrounded quartz grains and tiny fragments of dark (mafic) accessory minerals. The quartz content varies from essentially none or very little to fairly substantial, yet in many instances the parent rocks appear to be the same. Hornblende lath fragments are sometimes identifiable. In many instances, fragments of the parent rocks are observed, clearly showing the constituents in aggregate. The basic rock types appear to be granite and possibly monzonite.

The category "other" is the second most common temper group with 39 rim sherds (18%). This catchall category includes a mixture of rock types, most probably being igneous in origin.

Eleven rim sherds (5%) contain gray feldspar that, according to A. H. Warren (pers. comm.), may be from the Sierra Blanca country of southeastern New Mexico. In most instances, the gray feldspar is a minor constituent in a temper dominated by off-white feldspars and other minerals, but in four instances, it is the dominant form.

The paste runs the usual gamut for the type. Mostly it is black and "sandwiched" by reddish or brownish margins next to the surfaces. Less often, but still common, the paste is medium gray-brown or even reddish. Temper grains vary from conspicuous to barely observable by the unaided eye.

Surface finish was not routinely monitored. However, surfaces are generally unpolished or perhaps slightly polished, but a few are well polished.

The pigment quality varies considerably in the assemblage. The reds vary from a bright orange-red to dark red bordering on magenta. The blacks vary from very dark gray to solid black. In some cases the colors adhere well, but in others they adhere poorly, allowing the brown clay body to show through the paint.

The Henderson sherds are so small that only three distinct vessel forms can be discerned with any degree of certainty—jars, bowls, and ladles.

Orifice diameter was gauged on a cardboard template scribed with arcs at two-centimeter intervals. Many rim sherds have insufficient arc to permit reliable estimation of orifice diameter and were not measured. Jar orifice diameters range from 10 to 30+ cm, with at least two modes, one at 14 cm (range 10–16

Table 3.5. Rim sherd index (RSI) values for Henderson Site and other nearby late prehistoric villages in the Roswell area.[a]

Site	Provenience	RSI	
		n	Mean (mm±1σ)
Fox Place	All	50	1.36±0.24
Henderson	Early phase (all)	184	1.56±0.35
	Early phase (Great Depression)	46	1.59±0.34
	Early phase (Main Bar East)	102	1.59±0.36
	Early phase (Main Bar West, West Bar, West Plaza combined)	21	1.43±0.27
	Late phase (all)	582	1.82±0.53
	Late phase (Center Bar)	138	1.80±0.52
	Late phase (East Bar)	189	1.89±0.54
	Late phase (East Plaza B/C)	142	1.73±0.51
	Late phase (East Plaza East)	38	1.83±0.43
	All proveniences combined	766	1.76±0.50
Rocky Arroyo	All	23	1.84±0.42
Bloom Mound	All	81	2.25±0.72

[a]RSI values presented here are the maximum thickness of the rim, wherever that occurs on the rim, divided by the minimum thickness of the body of the sherd, again regardless of distance from the edge.

Table 3.6. Matrix of *t*-test results for comparisons of mean RSI values from Fox Place, Henderson (Early and Late phase), Rocky Arroyo, and Bloom Mound.[a]

	Fox Place	Hen. (EP)	Hen. (LP)	Rocky	Bloom
Fox Place		**t = 3.86 p = .0001**	**t = 6.07 p < .0001**	**t = 6.17 p < .0001**	**t = 8.39 p < .0001**
Hen. (EP)			**t = 6.09 p < .0001**	**t = 3.44 p < .001**	**t = 10.37 p < .0001**
Hen. (LP)				*t = 0.185 p = .85*	**t = 6.56 p < .0001**
Rocky					**t = 2.60 p = .01**
Bloom					

[a]Boldface = statistically significant; italics = not statistically significant. Abbreviations: Hen. (EP), Henderson (Early phase); Hen. (LP), Henderson (Late phase); Rocky, Rocky Arroyo; Bloom, Bloom Mound.

cm) and one at 30+ cm (range 20–30+ cm). Twenty-five sherds were measured.

Bowls are of at least two types: deep with nearly straight, slightly expanding upper walls, and hemispheres with slightly restricted orifices. The latter bowl type is also called a "seed bowl" or "seed jar." These vessels are painted on the exterior but not on the interior, which means that, in the absence of rims, we are unable to distinguish between body sherds of these vessels and jars. Only one bowl rim sherd was sufficiently large to measure orifice diameter. This sherd indicates a deep bowl with straight, slightly expanding upper walls, more than 30 cm in diameter.

A single ladle fragment has a scar where the handle once attached. The ladle is rare in El Paso Polychrome.

El Paso Polychrome Rim Profiles. Since the mid-1970s, much attention has been paid to the profile of El Paso Polychrome jar rims, in an effort to derive temporal information (e.g., Carmichael 1985, 1986; Seaman and Mills 1988; Way 1979; West 1982; Whalen 1981, 1993). In its original formulation, the profile of the rim was quantified using a rim sherd index (RSI), which was the ratio of the maximum thickness, taken 2 mm from the edge of the rim, divided by the minimum thickness of the sherd body, taken 15 mm from the edge. However, because so many of Henderson's EPP rim sherds are small, use of the 15-mm rule would exclude at least 15% of the rims, making it difficult, if not impossible, to date several of Henderson's major proveniences. Thus, in order to maximize the sample sizes for as many areas of the site as possible, a less than ideal variant of the RSI is used here, in which the maximum thickness of the rim, wherever that occurs on the rim, is divided by the minimum thickness of the body of the sherd, again regardless of distance from the edge. This version of the RSI is obviously "noisier" than the original formulation, because on the smallest sherds the minimum thickness is seldom uniform below the rim, but instead tends to decrease the farther one moves from the edge. Nevertheless, the seriation results closely match a subsample of rims measured according to the original guidelines published by Carmichael and Whalen. Moreover, similar results are obtained when only maximum rim thickness is used, a parameter that can be measured with reasonable confidence regardless of sherd size. And, as we will see below, even the minimum thickness, despite its limitations, faithfully replicates the seriation produced by the RSI.

We first began to experiment with the seriation of Henderson's El Paso Polychrome jar rims in 1996, initially to see whether the rim profiles were similar to those from sites of broadly comparable age in the El Paso area, where seriation of this ceramic type was first shown to have chronological significance (Zimmerman 1996). Not only were Henderson's rim profiles similar to those from contemporary sites in the El Paso area, a distance of more than 200 km, but the site's RSI values fell into two distinct clusters, the later one including the rims from the Center Bar, East Bar, and East Plaza, and the earlier one including the rims from the Main Bar, Great Depression, and probably also the West Bar and West Plaza (the last two proveniences have very small samples of measurable rims). The seriation results, using all of the measurable rims recovered from Henderson between 1980 and 1997, are summarized in Table 3.5. Also included in the table are mean values for several nearby communities, providing a tentative chronological ordering of the major late prehistoric villages in the Roswell area.

Table 3.6 summarizes the results of standard unpaired *t*-tests, which evaluate the significance of the differences in mean RSI values between pairs of sites. The means all differ significantly from each other, with the single notable exception of Henderson's Late phase and Rocky Arroyo. These two occupations appear to be contemporary, or at least substantially overlapping. Obviously, the chronological ordering produced by the

RSI values, while suggestive, should be viewed cautiously, since the seriation for Rocky Arroyo, Fox Place, and Bloom Mound treats these sites as though they each reflect a single point in time. In reality, the occupations at all of these sites may have overlapped to some extent. Nevertheless, the seriation results do suggest that the ages of the principal occupations at these communities were somewhat different, with Fox Place being the earliest and Bloom Mound the latest.

Not surprisingly, the rims from sites that are thought to be younger on the basis of their mean RSI values are thicker, on average, than those from earlier sites (see Table 3.7). Perhaps more surprising, however, is that as EPP rims become thicker, their bodies become significantly thinner (see Tables 3.7 and 3.8). In fact, despite the potential "noise" inherent in the way we have measured minimum sherd thickness, it nevertheless beautifully replicates the seriation produced by the RSI. The declining vessel wall thickness of Roswell area EPP jars echoes and amplifies observations made by Whalen (1994:88) in the El Paso area that after A.D. 1000,

> vessel wall thickness diminished, remaining relatively low throughout the prehistoric sequence. Vessel wall thickness seems to have been at its lowest in the late Pueblo period.

Whalen (1994:88-89) attributes this downward trend in vessel wall thickness to a growing concern for improved heating efficiency of Pueblo period cooking vessels, during a period when residential mobility decreased making durability of vessels less of a priority (see also discussion in Seaman and Mills 1988). Whether similar pressures were at work in the Roswell area, or the similarities instead reflect frequent import of vessels from sources in the El Paso area, or close social interaction among potters in the two areas, are interesting issues that remain to be explored.

Table 3.7. Maximum and minimum thickness values (means) for El Paso Polychrome rim sherds from Fox Place, Henderson (Early and Late Phase), Rocky Arroyo, and Bloom Mound.

Site	Max. Rim Thickness (mm±1σ)	Min. Body Thickness (mm±1σ)
Fox Place	6.60±1.04	4.99±1.15
Henderson (Early phase)	7.18±1.15	4.76±1.02
Henderson (Late phase)	7.66±1.21	4.47±1.16
Rocky Arroyo	7.54±1.07	4.32±1.18
Bloom Mound	7.69±1.15	3.72±1.12

Table 3.8. Matrix of *t*-test results for comparisons of minimum thickness values (means) for El Paso Polychrome rim sherds from Fox Place, Henderson (Early and Late Phase), Rocky Arroyo, and Bloom Mound.[a]

	Fox Place	Hen. (EP)	Hen. (LP)	Rocky	Bloom
Fox Place		*t = -1.40 p = .16*	**t = -3.02 p = .003**	**t = -2.30 p = .02**	**t = 6.22 p < .0001**
Hen. (EP)			**t = 2.98 p = .003**	**t = 1.93 p = .05**	**t = 7.39 p < .0001**
Hen. (LP)				*t = 0.63 p = .53*	**t = 5.45 p < .0001**
Rocky					**t = 2.22 p = .03**
Bloom					

[a]Boldface = statistically significant; italics = not statistically significant. Abbreviations: Hen. (EP), Henderson (Early phase); Hen. (LP), Henderson (Late phase); Rocky, Rocky Arroyo; Bloom, Bloom Mound.

Playas Incised

The Playas group of pottery products is one of those nagging problems that has so far defied solution. Years ago I defined a Sierra Blanca variety of Playas (Wiseman 1981), one that seemed clearly to have been made in the Sierra Blanca country of Lincoln County, southeastern New Mexico. The distinction was based on the presence of a mostly opaque, gray feldspar that derives from a syenite of unspecified source or sources in the Sierra Blanca. As will be seen in the section on Three Rivers Red-on-terracotta and Lincoln Black-on-red, the makers of those two types frequently used this gray feldspar, presenting the possibility that, to some degree, all three types—Playas Sierra Blanca var., Three Rivers, and Lincoln—were made by the same potters.

The clue about this feldspar, and its parent rock syenite, and its source in the Sierra Blanca, was taken from periodic comments made to me over the years by A. H. Warren and, to a lesser extent, from personal observation of pottery temper distributions in the region. Hand specimens of the syenite contain mostly opaque, gray feldspar, usually as relatively large, well-formed, single and intertwined crystals, with or without hematite staining and rosettes. The crystals are often lavender. Occasional grains of hornblende or similar mafic also occur, but these are comparatively uncommon.

When gray feldspar is the only constituent in a sherd, it is fair to say that its temper derives from Sierra Blanca gray syenite, as it is virtually the only constituent of Sierra Blanca gray syenite. But as so often happens in pottery analysis, temper identifications can be rendered more difficult if the potters used weathered products (stream sands) for temper rather than parent rocks. Under these circumstances, Sierra Blanca gray feldspar particles become mixed with constituents of other rock types that often predominate within a sherd. This is where the problem begins for the analyst.

On periodic visits with A. H. Warren over the years, I made a point of asking whether she had seen any gray feldspar like that of the Sierra Blanca gray syenite in either pottery or rocks from other sources. The reason for the question, of course, was to determine whether the gray feldspar continued to be a good indicator of the Sierra Blanca source or whether problems had appeared which might weaken its interpretive value. None had, until recently.

The problem sherd is one of the Playas type sherds in the Archaeological Research Collections, Laboratory of Anthropology, Museum of New Mexico in Santa Fe. The sherd in question is one of many type sherds sent to the lab in the 1960s by the Amerind Foundation in Dragoon, Arizona. The snipped edge of the sherd displays two individual crystals of gray feldspar very similar to those so typical of the Sierra Blanca syenite. The only possible difference is that the crystals are slightly rounded, probably from weathering. But this could also be expected in weathered Sierra Blanca syenite.

All other Casas Grandes type sherds with snipped edges were then examined, but none had the gray feldspar. Thus, although opaque-gray feldspar of apparently non-Sierra Blanca origin has been found in this one instance, the problem does not appear to be serious. However, we do need to find the new source in order to assess the overall implications. I am quite satisfied that the sherd in question was made in the State of Chihuahua, because the other attributes (sherd thickness, overall temper size, slip color, surface finish) are characteristic of the Casas Grandes region, for the sherd fits in every other way with the companion type sherds sent by Amerind Foundation. The problem now centers on the question of weathering products that contain both opaque gray feldspar and other weathering products such as off-white feldspars.

Another question has arisen. How many regions produced Playas pottery? The variety of pastes and tempers in the Casas Grandes type sherds, and the variety of pastes and tempers in the Henderson examples suggests to me that this type (or family of types) was made in many places, using a wide a variety of materials. The situation is reminiscent of the Salado polychromes (e.g., Crown 1994). There is a certain amount of overlap between the Casas Grandes type sherd collection and the Henderson collection, but not nearly as much as might be expected. The published description of Playas pottery was also consulted. Pertinent passages from that work are presented below, along with my comments.

In the paragraphs that follow, I first describe each characteristic of the Amerind Foundation's Playas type sherds in the Archaeological Research Collections, Laboratory of Anthropology, Museum of New Mexico, Santa Fe. I then present DiPeso et al.'s (1974) descriptions and comments. After that, I comment on the applicability of DiPeso et al.'s descriptions to the Henderson sherds.

Temper. The tempering materials are variable but mainly fall into two basic types of rocks: (a) volcanic rocks like tuffs and rhyolitic tuffs, and (b) angular, clear quartz (sandstones?). Although the tempering particles of some sherds can be characterized as coarse (diameter >1 mm), fine and medium grains, usually in some profusion, are much more common.

DiPeso et al. (1974:149):

> Many of the non-plastic inclusions were opaque white (7.5YR 9/0) in color, and crystalline particles, often translucent in nature, were quite frequent, sometimes constituting a major quantity of these inclusions. Gray particles made up another large fraction, but black, red, pink, and gold grains occurred only sporadically.

Comments. It is tempting to make simple equations between DiPeso et al.'s terms and mine; that is, the white, gray, and pink particles are probably feldspars; some of the black ones are hornblende, augite, and/or magnetite; and other black and all gold particles are biotite. The implications of the gray particles and DiPeso et al.'s comments are troublesome vis-à-vis the comments earlier about the gray feldspar of Sierra Blanca syenite. We must assume that A. H. Warren would have examined some of the Casas Grandes sherds, noted the gray feldspars, and mentioned them in her discussions about the Sierra Blanca material.

Paste Color. Paste colors are usually clear, indicating attainment of good firing temperatures and/or durations (good by Southwestern standards, that is). Light grays, light reds, and light browns are common. Medium grayish browns and medium grayish reds, indicating less effective firings, are less common. Dark grays and blacks, indicating much residual carbon from insufficient firing temperatures and durations, are uncommon.

DiPeso et al. (1974:149):

> Ranged from reddish-brown (5YR 5/4) and reddish-yellow (5YR 6/6) to light brown (7.5YR 6/4) when carbon streak or smudging (as in Ramos Black combination) not present. Typical color, reddish-yellow.

Comments. In the terminology I am using throughout this discussion, 5YR 5/4 refers to medium reddish brown, 5YR 6/6 refers to medium reddish yellow, and 7.5YR 6/4 refers to light to medium brown.

Paste Color Zonation. Paste color zonation may be an important distinction between Playas made in the Casas Grandes area and in the U.S. Although the Casas Grandes–made Playas has zoned pastes as described, the colors are generally lighter and clearer. My impression is that the pastes of non-Casas Grandes Playas are darker (more often dark gray and black) and less clear, indicating poorer firing success that left more carbon in the non-Casas Playas pastes.

DiPeso et al. (1974:149):

> Zoning from reddish-yellow surfaces to a gray interior core typical. This core color varied from a light gray (7.5YR 5/0, 6/0; 10YR 5/1) through a grayish-brown (10YR 5/2, 6/2) and dark gray (7.5YR 4/0, 10YR 4/1) to a very dark gray (7.5YR 3/0) and was found in about half of the sample of the Standard Variant.

Comments. These values, based on Munsell chart comparisons, indicate clear or well-fired colors. Given the examples among the type collection, we might be justified in assuming that Casas Grandes Playas sherds on average are well-fired and

Table 3.9. Playas decorative variations at Henderson by temper type (frequencies).

Temper	Decoration						
	Inc	Punc	Ind	Cord	Pln	Rim	Total
Coarse off-white feldspar	6	20	6	1	1	3	37
Coarse off-white feldspar and quartz	6	10	1	4	—	—	21
Off-white feldspar with some gray feldspar and minor minerals	5	—	—	—	—	—	5
Tuff(?)	9	4	1	—	1	1	16
Quartz sandstone(?)	1	—	—	—	—	—	1
Aplitic igneous rock	—	—	—	—	1	—	1
Miscellaneous	3	1	—	1	1	—	6
Total	30	35	8	6	4	4	87

Inc = incised; Punc = punctate; Ind = smeared indented and/or pseudo-smeared indented; Cord = cordmarked; Pln = untextured ("plain"); Rim = rim sherds (usually lack texturing).

the colors are clear and amenable to comparison with Munsell chips. However, my experiences in general, and with Henderson Playas sherds in particular, show that clear, well-fired paste colors are rare and not amenable to characterization in Munsell terms. Additionally, zoned pastes are uncommon to rare in the Henderson sherds (see discussions below).

Vessel Wall Thickness. Although the type sherds include the usual wide range of wall thickness, the average thickness of the Casas Grandes sherds is much more like that of historic period Pueblo and Spanish pottery in New Mexico. That is, thicknesses of 6-8 mm are common, while thicknesses <6 mm are less common.

DiPeso et al. (1974:148):

Bowls: 0.3 cm. to 1.0 cm.; average, 0.6 cm. Jars: 0.3 cm. to 1.0 cm.; average, 0.5 cm.

Comments. The written descriptions generally agree with my observations of the type sherd collection, except that the thickness of jar sherds according to DiPeso et al. is more in line with my measurements of Henderson sherds and less like my impressions of the comparative collection. The pastes of the type collection are reminiscent of ancestral northern Tewa Biscuit wares, hence my characterization of Casas Grandes Playas being thick on average. However one tries to characterize and compare the two collections, qualitative differences do exist, and are, I believe, significant. I believe this to the point of suggesting that the Henderson vessels were most likely made in southeastern New Mexico, not northern Mexico.

Playas Pottery from Henderson

The 87 sherds of Playas recovered in 1980-1981 from Henderson represent a range of tempers, surface decoration, colors, and presence/absence of a slip. I monitored temper type, and using it as the baseline attribute, compared surface decoration, paste color, and vessel wall thickness. These four attributes seem most useful in establishing relationships within the ware and among areas of manufacture. Each of these is discussed in turn, then compared with the data from the Amerind Foundation type collection at the Museum of New Mexico and the written description in DiPeso et al. (1974). The fundamental question here is whether the Henderson Playas was made in the Roswell/Sierra Blanca region or in northern Mexico.

Temper. Several tempering materials are represented in the Henderson Playas sherds. The three most common are coarse off-white feldspar (43%), coarse off-white feldspar and quartz (24%), and tuff (18%) (see Table 3.9). The first two could be from the same or closely related geologic sources. The tuff is a tentative identification, but the material closely resembles (and may be the same as) the welded tuffs seen in various Mogollon pottery types made in southwestern New Mexico and northern Mexico. I suspect that the coarse off-white feldspar tempers derive from the Sierra Blanca country of southeastern New Mexico, but this has not been established.

Minor temper types identified in the Henderson sherds include off-white feldspar with some gray feldspar and mafics (6%), angular-quartz sandstone (1%), aplitic igneous rock (probably Capitan alaskite, 1%), and a variety of miscellaneous rocks (7%). Of these, the off-white feldspar with some gray feldspar and mafics and aplitic igneous rock suggest an origin in southeastern New Mexico (but see earlier comments about the Amerind Foundation type collection). I suspect that some of the miscellaneous tempering materials, and perhaps the angular-quartz sandstone tempers, indicate manufacture outside southeastern New Mexico but I have no idea where.

Unfortunately, because the Amerind Foundation temper descriptions lack mineralogical specificity, I cannot evaluate my temper identifications relative to DiPeso et al.'s (1974) temper description for Casas Grandes Playas.

Decoration. Of the four types of surface decoration, incised-line designs (35%) and punctate designs (40%) dominate the assemblage. Minor design techniques include various manifestations of smeared-indented (9%) and cordmarked (7%) techniques. Sherds lacking decoration (plain sherds, 5%; rim sherds, 5%), generally represent those portions of vessels (rims, necks, bottoms) left undecorated.

Table 3.10. Playas paste colors at Henderson by temper type (frequencies).

Temper	Color							
	1	2	3	4	5	6	7	Total
Coarse off-white feldspar	—	—	—	—	—	11	26	37
Coarse off-white feldspar and quartz	—	—	—	—	—	7	14	21
Off-white feldspar with some gray feldspar and minor minerals	—	1	—	—	1	2	1	5
Tuff(?)	9	—	—	1	—	3	3	16
Quartz sandstone(?)	—	—	—	—	—	—	1	1
Aplitic igneous rock	—	—	—	—	—	1	—	1
Miscellaneous	2	—	1	—	—	2	1	6
Total	11	1	1	1	1	26	46	87

Color categories, from lightest to darkest: 1 = light to medium yellow-red; 2 = medium brown with yellow-red; margins (i.e., zoned); 3 = medium gray; 4 = dark reddish-gray; 5 = dark gray-brown with medium reddish-brown margins (i.e., zoned); 6 = dark gray-brown; 7 = black

Table 3.11. Playas vessel wall thickness at Henderson by temper type (frequencies).

Temper	Thickness (mm)						
	3	4	5	6	7	8	Total
Coarse off-white feldspar	—	6	12	13	4	2	37
Coarse off-white feldspar and quartz	2	6	10	3	—	—	21
Off-white feldspar with some gray feldspar and minor minerals	—	1	—	3	1	—	5
Tuff(?)	1	1	13	—	1	—	16
Quartz sandstone(?)	—	1	—	—	—	—	1
Aplitic igneous rock	—	1	—	—	—	—	1
Miscellaneous	—	3	1	1	1	—	6
Total	2	19	36	19	7	2	87

The Henderson Playas has some interesting correlations between decorative techniques and temper types (Table 3.9). Since coarse off-white feldspar temper and coarse off-white feldspar with quartz temper are mineralogically similar, perhaps coming from the same source, and they have similar decoration frequency patterns, they are treated as a single temper type referred to as "coarse feldspar" in this discussion. The two types together comprise 67% of the Henderson Playas assemblage. Tuff(?)-tempered sherds, at 18%, comprise the other large component of the assemblage.

In looking at temper types within decoration categories, we find that punctation, or indentation, and cordmarking are more common to the coarse feldspar group. Incised decorations are represented more equitably among the temper types, but the majority are on tuff(?)-tempered sherds.

In looking at decorative treatment within temper categories, punctate designs are the most common designs among coarse feldspar sherds. Incised designs are the most common decorative treatment among tuff(?)-tempered sherds.

Comparison of paste color with temper type also shows interesting trends (Table 3.10). First, sherds with light- to medium-colored pastes (categories 1-3) occur primarily in tuff(?)-tempered sherds. Three of the thirteen have miscellaneous tempers, and one is tempered with off-white feldspar with some gray feldspar and minor minerals.

Second, sherds having dark-colored but relatively clear pastes (most of the carbon removed by firing, categories 4-5) are few in number and occur in tuff(?)- and off-white feldspar-tempered pastes.

Third, the bulk of Henderson Playas sherds have the dark, cloudy pastes of categories 6 and 7. Of these, six are tuff(?)-tempered, three are miscellaneous-tempered, and three are off-white feldspar-tempered. That leaves 62 dark, cloudy pastes that occur only in sherds with coarse feldspar, coarse feldspar and quartz, and aplite tempers.

These paste-color/temper associations suggest that three temper categories—tuff(?), off-white and gray feldspars with minor minerals, and miscellaneous—primarily involve sherds that have been imported from some area to the southwest, probably northern Mexico. I suspect the majority of sherds that have coarse tempers of off-white feldspars—with or without quartz—were probably made in southeastern New Mexico.

Sherd thickness by temper type is less revealing (Table 3.11). The range in the Henderson Playas sherds is 3-8 mm, with a slightly left-skewed mode at 5 mm. The majority of sherds are 4-6.9 mm thick. Only nine sherds are 7-8.9 mm thick, and two-thirds of these have what we believe are southeastern New Mexico tempers. Tuff(?)-tempered sherds, with one exception, are all less than 6 mm thick, the average thickness of the Amerind Foundation type sample.

Three Rivers Red-on-Terracotta and Lincoln Black-on-Red

These two related types probably are distinct from one another. Three Rivers has red designs on a light orange background, and Lincoln has black designs on a red background. While these distinctions hold in most southeastern New Mexico pottery assemblages, the Henderson sample clearly departs from the norm in one way—most Lincoln sherds have black designs on light orange surfaces.

While the original description (Mera and Stallings 1931) indicates the ultimate difference between the two types is paint color (red vs. black), rather than surface color, the overall terracotta color of the Henderson Lincoln is so striking that it essentially characterizes the pottery from this site. Why so few sherds of red-fired and/or red-slipped Lincoln occur at Henderson is a subject that is worth pursuing, though this cannot be done with the collections and background information currently at hand. The analysis here is restricted to a detailed comparison of the Henderson Three Rivers with the Henderson Lincoln.

Because the average sherd size for both types at Henderson is between a quarter and a half dollar, the analysis of the designs involves only rim sherds that are large enough for below-rim lines to be reliably counted and measured. The use of rims also permits me to gauge whether or not vessels are represented by more than one sherd in the sample.

The 203 rim sherds were divided into those having Lincoln-style (band) designs versus those having Three Rivers-style designs. Three Rivers designs have multiple, parallel, narrow lines that follow around the rim of bowl interiors and occasionally dip down across the bottoms of bowls rejoining the rim on the opposite side. The following attributes were monitored as follows.

Painted Line Widths. Line widths were measured to the nearest half millimeter in order to document whether or not Lincoln-style lines are thicker than Three Rivers lines.

Surface Colors. Surface colors were monitored for the reasons discussed above. The Munsell system was used to determine color. All determinations were made under fluorescent lights in the lab.

Vessel Wall Thickness. Lincoln, on average, is thicker than Three Rivers. Since the terminal coil of these bowls is frequently not well thinned, at least not as thin as the lower coils, wall thickness measurements were made 10 mm below the lip. Because thickness can vary within the same coil, as well as between coils, the range on any given sherd was determined to the nearest half millimeter.

Temper. Tempering materials, highly variable in the Sierra Blanca region, were approached somewhat cavalierly. Few details were monitored, and the temper is characterized in general terms. Two minerals and mineral suites—gray feldspar and Capitan alaskite (also known as "granite," aplite, and monzonite)—were noted as present or absent. The gray feldspar, mostly being from Sierra Blanca gray syenite, is described above under Playas pottery. Capitan alaskite is described under Chupadero Black-on-white and Corona Corrugated.

In many instances, both gray and off-white feldspars occur together in sherds. I cannot be certain at this time whether this represents yet another type of Sierra Blanca syenite (a good possibility), or a mixture of the weathering products of different colors of syenite rocks. Some tempers consist solely of off-white or ivory-colored feldspars, often stained with hematite. Accessory mafic minerals that occur in varying degrees, or not at all, include biotite (black or gold), hornblende (black or, rarely, dark reddish-brown), hematite (as stain or as small, earthy bits), and magnetite.

As usual, a small number of sherds contain exotic tempers. Some contain occasional particles of a well-rounded, soft-looking, granular material reminiscent of nonglassy pumice or tuff. Other materials are even more mysterious, particularly when the pastes in which they occur are very dark to black in color.

Only rim sherds received the full analysis, and only bowls are represented.

Painted Line Widths. One hallmark of Three Rivers Red-on-terracotta is its running-parallel-line bundle motif. These bundles or groups of two to five narrow lines move in mostly rectilinear patterns around and across the interior surfaces of bowls. Curvilinear patterns of lines and scrolls are sometimes found. Small solids in the form of series of obtuse-angled triangles along outer lines of line bundles and checkerboards of squares or diamonds as fillers for large spaces between line bundles are fairly common. In all of these, the basic element is the narrow line, an element that becomes slightly wider to become the primary element of Lincoln Black-on-red.

The narrow line is so integral to Three Rivers and Lincoln designs that I thought it might be instructive to study line width in the two types at Henderson, particularly since paint color is the primary discriminating difference between the two types in that assemblage. Line widths were measured to the nearest half millimeter, taking several readings on each line as width varies along most lines. Rather than obtain an average for each line, I recorded width as a range and analyzed the values in the same way described below in the study of vessel wall thickness.

The comparative results (Fig. 3.2) confirm initial impressions. Overall line width for Three Rivers is 1.0-4.5 mm, and 0.5-8 mm for Lincoln. Both have strong single modal peaks at 2 mm, indicating a strong relationship between them. The Lincoln curve, however, also has two ancillary modes at 4 mm and 5 mm. The sherds representing the ancillary modes bear other characteristics, such as redder surface colors.

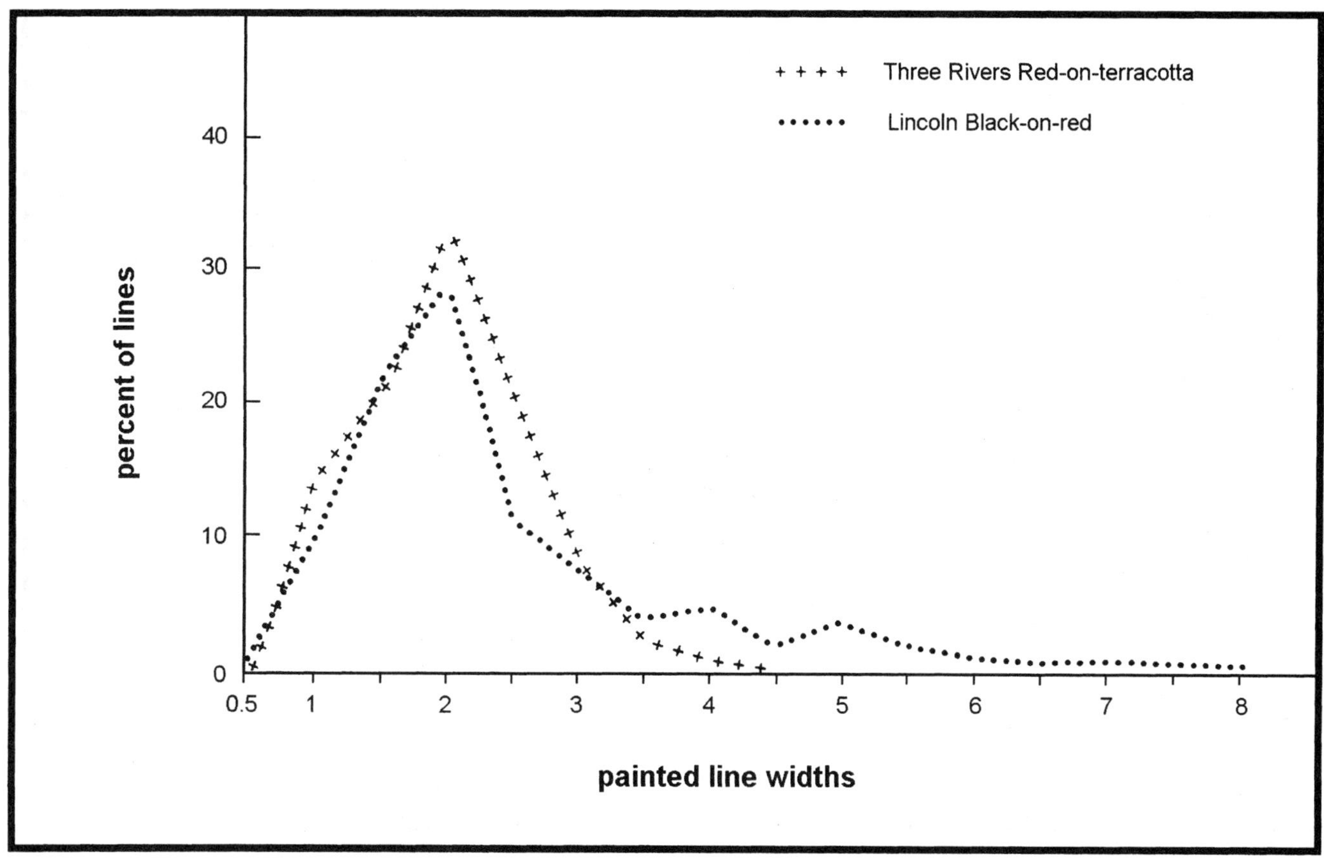

Figure 3.2. Comparison of line widths in decorations on Three Rivers Red-on-terracotta and Lincoln Black-on-red bowls from the Henderson Site.

Surface Colors. The inquiry into surface colors derives from the similarity of Henderson Three Rivers Red-on-terracotta and to Lincoln Black-on-red. This contrasts with the usual situation in Sierra Blanca sites where Lincoln surfaces are a stronger red color. Unfortunately, we currently lack systematic descriptions of the Sierra Blanca examples and must resort here to a comparison of the Three Rivers and Lincoln sherds from Henderson. Surface colors, both interior and exterior, were estimated according to the Munsell system for the rim sherd sample. Although we normally think of the colors in terms of red versus orange, discussion of color according to Munsell revolves around degree of red and degree of yellow.

In using the Munsell chart system, I found that the chips applicable to the Henderson material are all within the yellow-red (YR) colors. The fully red (R) and fully yellow (Y) colors are not applicable. The results are most interesting (Fig. 3.3). The most immediate revelation is that bowl interior surfaces of both types are often brighter in hue than exterior surfaces and lack fire-clouding and burning. This is expectable since the interiors were painted and had to receive the most attention if good results in design/background contrast were to be achieved.

Regarding interior surfaces, the colors of both types overlap as expected. In the reddest category among the Henderson materials (2.5YR), Lincoln is somewhat redder overall than Three Rivers. Otherwise the trends in both are very similar.

Exterior surface color trends, including frequencies of fire-clouding and burning, are virtually identical for both Three Rivers and Lincoln.

High frequencies of fire-clouded exteriors signify a consistent lack of protection from settling of firing fuel and, presumably, a lack of concern about exterior surface appearance. Burned exteriors suggest that some vessels were placed close to heat sources, perhaps for warming vessel contents.

Vessel Wall Thickness. Another impression gained in handling Three Rivers and Lincoln sherds is that Three Rivers is generally thinner than Lincoln. Accordingly, sherd thickness was monitored during the analysis. Because individual sherd thickness often varies, thickness was recorded as a range, rather than as an average.

In Figure 3.4, ranges are scored every half millimeter. That is, if a sherd has a range of 4.5 mm to 6.5 mm, it is scored five times—4.5, 5.0, 5.5, 6.0, and 6.5 mm. Since some sherds have a uniform thickness (whether from small size or evenness of thinning), they would be underrepresented by being scored only once. As partial compensation, each sherd with an even thickness is scored twice. Thus, a sherd having an even thickness such as 6.0 mm is credited with a "range" of 6.0 mm to 6.0 mm. I recognize that this approach emphasizes variation in thick-

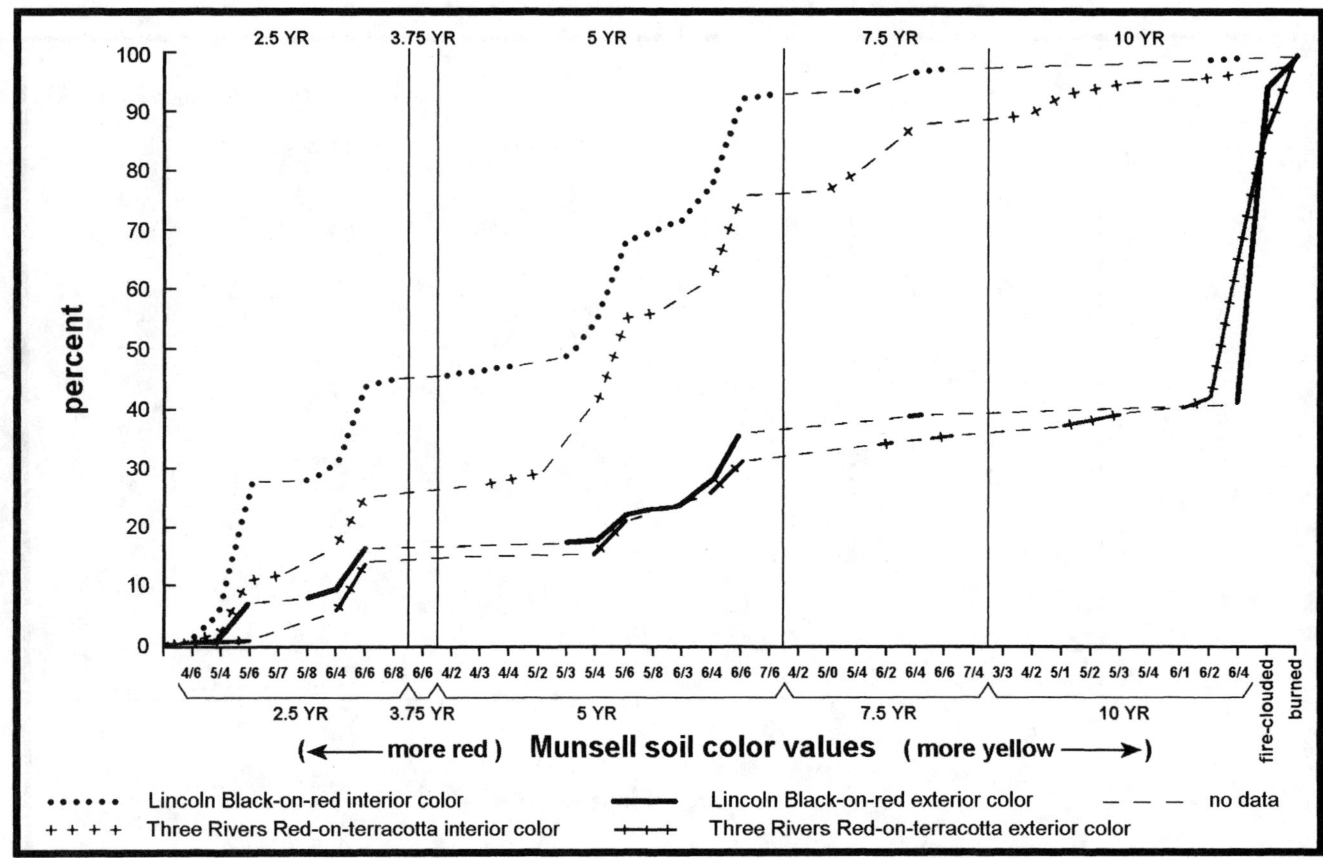

Fig. 3.3. Interior and exterior surface colors (Munsell system) of Three Rivers Red-on-terracotta and Lincoln Black-on-red bowls.

ness, but this is precisely the characteristic that I wish to evaluate.

Figure 3.4 shows that the overall ranges of wall thickness for both Three Rivers and Lincoln are the same at 4 mm to 8 mm. However, Lincoln is consistently thicker than Three Rivers, about 0.5 mm on average. This difference evidently relates to greater effort in meshing the coils and thinning the walls of Three Rivers bowls.

One way of assessing this interpretation is to look at the degree of variation in thickness. To do this, I scored each sherd for the number of .5 mm increments encompassed by its thickness range. If the range of a given sherd was 4.5-6.5 mm, then a score of 5 was given. In this exercise, sherds having a single thickness, such as 5.5 mm, were scored only as a one.

The results (Table 3.12) indicate that, if anything, the walls of Lincoln bowls were more consistently, evenly, thinned than those of Three Rivers bowls. Thus, some reason other than persistence in meshing and thinning of coils accounts for the fact that the walls of Lincoln bowls are generally thicker than the walls of Three Rivers bowls.

Temper. The same suite or suites of tempering materials were used for both Three Rivers and Lincoln; all appear to have come from the Sierra Blanca, Capitan, and Jicarilla mountains in Lincoln County, New Mexico. In many instances, the tempering particles are so finely ground that petrographic techniques are needed to identify the various minerals and the source rocks. Consequently, the temper analysis employed here focuses on certain key minerals that are identified mainly by color—gray feldspar, porcelaneous white feldspar, and ivory or off-white feldspar.

In some cases, such as Sierra Blanca hornblende syenite with its distinctive gray feldspar, I can be certain of the parent rocks, but in others I defer to future study. Dark accessory minerals

Table 3.12. Comparison of vessel wall-thickness ranges for Henderson Three Rivers and Lincoln bowls (see text for explanation).

0.5 mm Increments in Thickness Range	Three Rivers Red-on-terracotta		Lincoln Black-on-red	
	No.	%	No.	%
1	10	12	102	48
2	53	61	62	29
3	20	23	45	21
4	3	3	1	0.5
5	—	—	1	0.5
6	1	1	—	—
Total	87	100	211	99

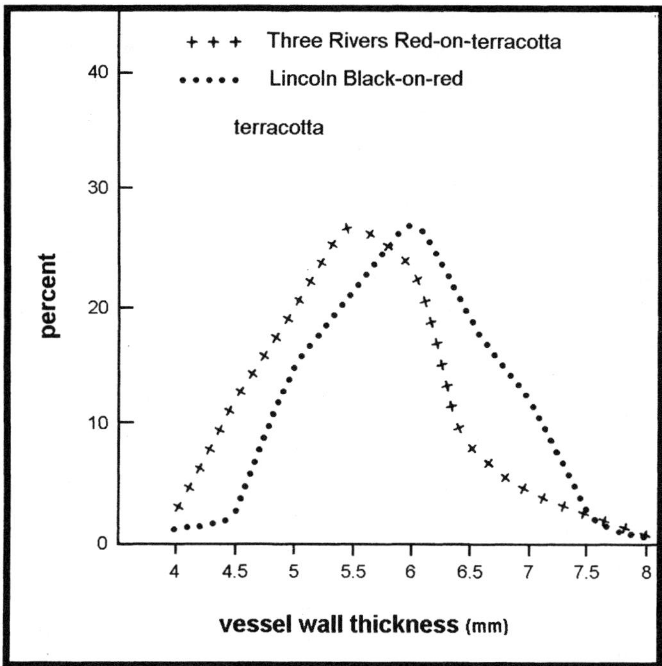

Figure 3.4. Vessel wall thickness (mm) of Three Rivers Red-on-terracotta and Lincoln Black-on-red bowls.

are present in some sherds, and in a few, they are more common than any of the feldspars. Biotite, hematite, magnetite, and hornblende, among others, are present in the igneous rocks of Lincoln County.

A 30-power binocular microscope was used to identify the primary minerals and to estimate subjectively their abundance. Abundance is characterized as dominant or codominant (D), present but not dominant (x), or absent (-). These are then compared for Three Rivers and Lincoln with the data grouped according to whether gray feldspar is dominant, present, or absent (see Fig. 3.5)

Key aspects of the tempering materials relative to Three Rivers and Lincoln from Henderson are: (1) gray feldspar as a sole dominant (D--) is more common in Lincoln (21% vs. 3%); (2) gray feldspar as a codominant with one or both other feldspars (DD-, DDD, D-D) occurs mainly in Three Rivers (28% vs. 0.5%); (3) gray feldspar as a minor constituent with other minerals as dominants (x--) occurs in 9% of Lincoln, but is absent in Three Rivers; and (4) white and ivory feldspars as codominants with minor gray feldspar (xDD) are common in both Three Rivers and Lincoln, but are clearly more so in Three Rivers (34% vs. 24%). Otherwise, all other categories of temper are about equally represented in the two pottery types.

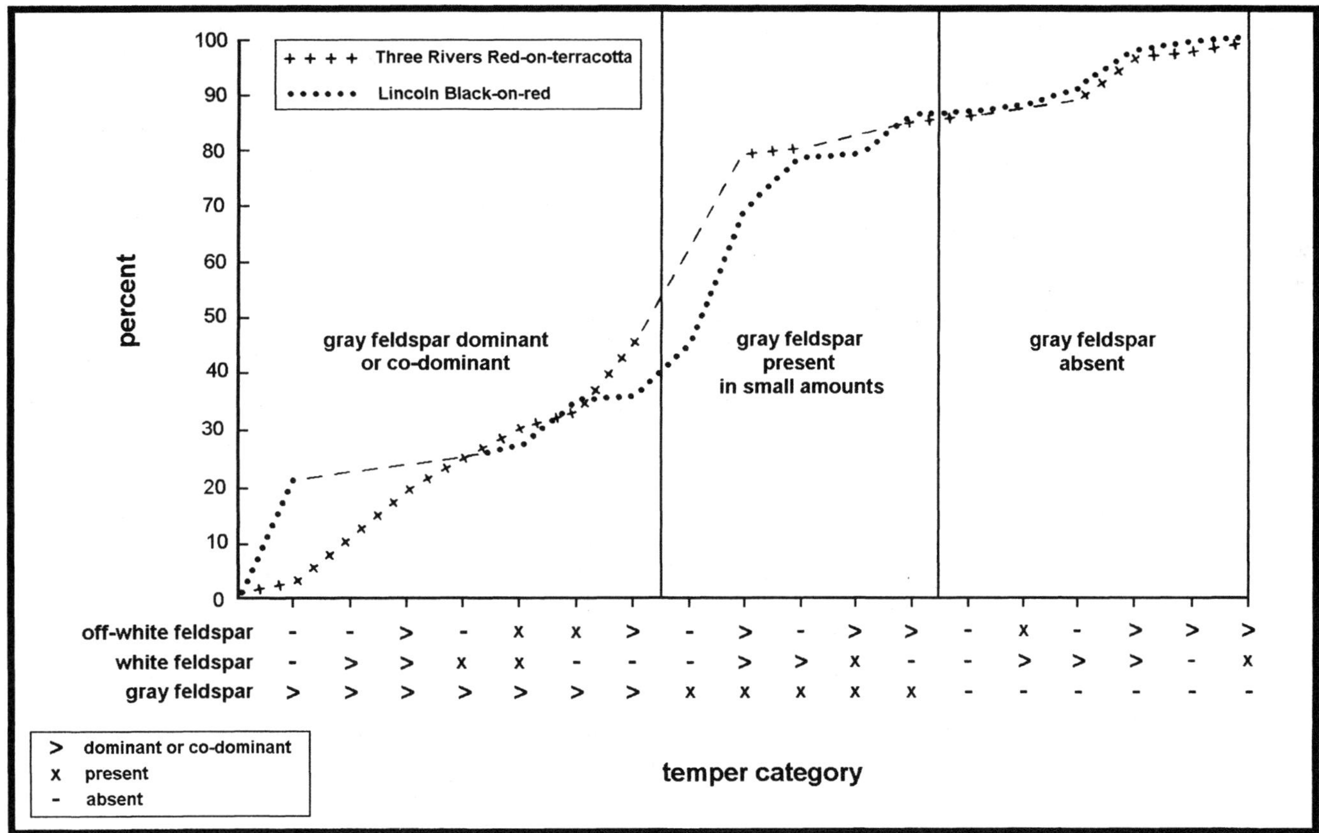

Figure 3.5. Abundance of off-white, white, and gray feldspar temper in Three Rivers Red-on-terracotta and Lincoln Black-on-red bowls from the Henderson Site.

I conclude from this that gray feldspar, probably mainly represented by Sierra Blanca gray hornblende syenite, was used much more frequently in the production of Lincoln Black-on-red. Now all that remains in this regard is to pinpoint the source of that rock type within the Sierra Blanca region. Also, tempers dominated by white or ivory (off-white) feldspars, and possessing few if any other minerals, constitute a major temper for both Three Rivers and Lincoln. Here again, more work, especially geological field work, will be necessary to sharpen our focus on source area.

This study of the Three Rivers and Lincoln sherds from the Henderson Site has looked in some detail at several aspects of these two pottery types. While the results essentially confirm the obvious, that the two types are closely related (Mera and Stallings 1931), we have gained a better understanding of that relationship. Lincoln Black-on-red derived from Three Rivers Red-on-terracotta, a process that appears to be encompassed within the Henderson assemblage. What remains now is to delve into the manufacturing processes—and perhaps social processes—that account for the changes.

Why and how did pottery makers at some point during the manufacturing span of Three Rivers shift the paint color from red to black, the surface color toward a more consistent and truer red, and the design style to a band that left the bowl bottoms free of design? Current replicative research elsewhere in the Southwest (E. Blinman, pers. comm.) indicates that a shift in paint color involving the same compound (hematite), while maintaining or amplifying the redness of the vessel surface, requires an increased sophistication in selecting, preparing, and manipulating the firing of materials.

At the present time, we accept Mera and Stallings's (1931) suggestion that the changes represented by classic Lincoln essentially reflect an attempt to copy the Rio Grande glazes. The inception of Lincoln generally coincides with the appearance of Agua Fria Glaze-on-red (a black glaze-painted, orange- to red-surfaced pottery) in the Sierra Blanca area west of Roswell.

But unlike Mera and Stallings, I do not see the Sierra Blanca peoples as having successfully reproduced a glaze-on-red pottery that is essentially indistinguishable from that made in the Rio Grande districts of central and north-central New Mexico. Rather, the failure to achieve a true glaze without overfiring the vessels to the point of sintering, contorting, and discoloring the vessels, all point to valiant but failed attempts at producing a true copy.

Distinguishing between Sierra Blanca products and the Rio Grande glazes is easily accomplished by examining the exterior surface finish on bowls. Lincoln bowls never lost the slightly undulating surfaces, often marked by lusterless polishing streaks that appear as densely packed shallow grooves. In contrast, Rio Grande glaze bowls are most often characterized by evenly thinned vessel walls and well-polished surfaces on which the individual polishing grooves have been eliminated by reworking the surface to a single smooth curve.

Tempering material is the one, though unspecified, criterion that may have led Mera and Stallings (1931) to conclude that the Lincoln potters achieved a glaze product that is virtually indistinguishable from Rio Grande products. To the unaided eye, or under slight magnification, both Lincoln and some Rio Grande glazes contain crushed rock composed of white or white and black particles (see A. H. Warren in Hayes et al. 1981, Hayes 1981). This is due to the fact that the rocks in both types of pottery are mineralogically similar. Differentiation of these materials, especially of the parent rocks and their sources, requires petrographic analysis.

The Henderson Pottery Assemblage in Regional Context

The pottery assemblage from Henderson is remarkable for the dominance of El Paso Polychrome, whether measured in numbers or overall weight (Table 3.1). Chupadero Black-on-white runs a slow second, followed by Three Rivers ware (here, both painted and unpainted Three Rivers and Lincoln sherds grouped together), Corona Corrugated, and brownwares (primarily Jornada Brown).

A review of the literature for other sites in southeastern New Mexico, including those assignable to Kelley's (1984) Bonnell, Corona, and Lincoln phases (36 proveniences in 14 sites), and Jelinek's (1967) 18 Mile, Mesita Negra, and Early McKenzie phases (13 proveniences in 13 sites), is instructive. The time period covered is approximately A.D. 900 to 1350 or 1400. The phase assignments and dates of each site are given in Tables 3.13 and 3.14. Summaries of the pottery assemblages for each site and provenience are provided in Tables 3.15, 3.16, and 3.17 and Figure 3.6.

Several trends in the frequencies of the primary pottery types are evident across southeastern New Mexico. First is the dominance of plain brown types, especially Jornada Brown, in the early periods in all areas. It is this brownware base that led to the characterization of the prehistoric cultures in southeastern New Mexico as "Mogollon."

During the later occupations, especially after A.D. 1200, the pottery assemblages of each region are characterized by different dominants even though all assemblages share the same basic set of types. For the most part, the dominants of each region reflect nearby source areas. This tendency was first noted by Lehmer (1947) in imported pottery types in Jornada-Mogollon sites. The tendency also forms the basis for the definition of Kelley's (1984) phase sequences for the Sierra Blanca country. These tendencies have become even more apparent with the collection of new data, as follows. The statements/observations generally apply to sites postdating A.D. 1200. They raise some intriguing questions, some old and some new. Some of these questions are outlined in the "comments" after each observation.

Figure 3.6 (*opposite*). Pottery assemblages from sites in southeastern New Mexico.

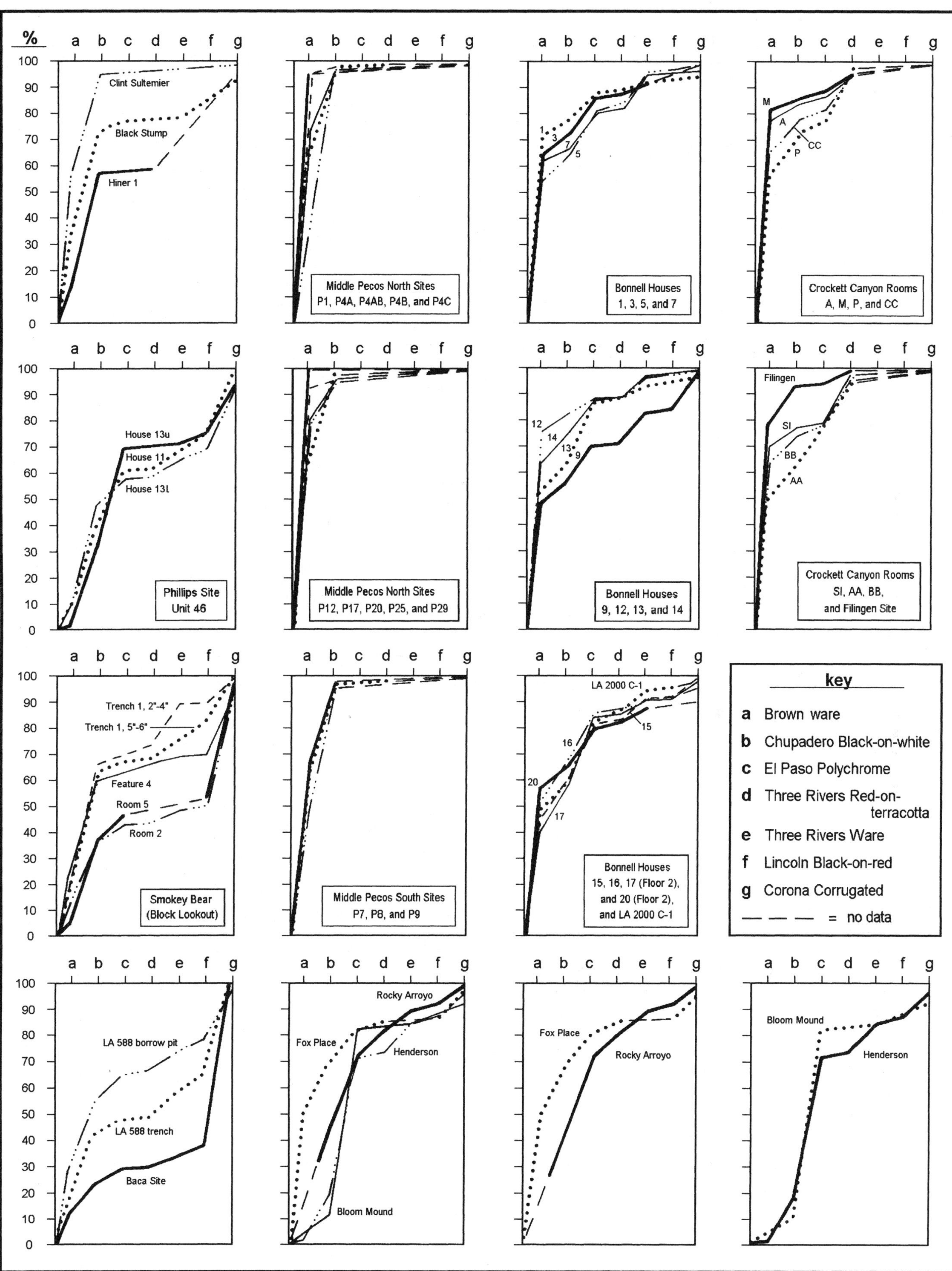
%
a b c d e f g
Clint Sultemier
Black Stump
Hiner 1
Middle Pecos North Sites
P1, P4A, P4AB, P4B, and P4C
Bonnell Houses
1, 3, 5, and 7
Crockett Canyon Rooms
A, M, P, and CC
House 13u
House 11
House 13l
Phillips Site
Unit 46
Middle Pecos North Sites
P12, P17, P20, P25, and P29
Bonnell Houses
9, 12, 13, and 14
Filingen
SI
BB
AA
Crockett Canyon Rooms
SI, AA, BB,
and Filingen Site
Trench 1, 2"-4"
Trench 1, 5"-6"
Feature 4
Room 5
Room 2
Smokey Bear
(Block Lookout)
Middle Pecos South Sites
P7, P8, and P9
LA 2000 C-1
Bonnell Houses
15, 16, 17 (Floor 2),
and 20 (Floor 2),
and LA 2000 C-1
key
a Brown ware
b Chupadero Black-on-white
c El Paso Polychrome
d Three Rivers Red-on-terracotta
e Three Rivers Ware
f Lincoln Black-on-red
g Corona Corrugated
= no data
LA 588 borrow pit
LA 588 trench
Baca Site
Rocky Arroyo
Fox Place
Henderson
Bloom Mound
Fox Place
Rocky Arroyo
Bloom Mound
Henderson

Table 3.13. Sites in southeastern New Mexico used for pottery assemblage comparisons.

Sub-Region/Site/Coll. Type[a]	Phase/Dates	Reference
Corona:		
Clint Sultemeier 1 (e)	Corona phase	Kelley (1984)
Black Stump Canyon (s)	Corona phase	Kelley (1984)
Hiner 1 (e)	Lincoln phase	Kelley (1984)
Capitan/Jicarilla Mountains:		
Phillips Unit 46 (e)	Lincoln phase (late)	Kelley (1984)
Smokey Bear (Block Lookout) (e)	Lincoln phase	Kelley (1984); Wiseman et al. (1976)
Baca (Baca Sawmill) (e)	Lincoln phase	Wiseman (1975)
LA-588 (Salas component of Priest Canyon Site) (e)	Lincoln phase	Wiseman (1975)
Sierra Blanca Slope:		
Crockett Canyon (e)	middle Glencoe phase[b]	Farwell et al. (1992)
Filingen (e)	middle Glencoe phase[b]	Farwell et al. (1992)
Bonnell (e)	late Glencoe phase	Kelley (1984)
LA-2000 C-1 (e)	late Glencoe phase	Kelley (1984)
Middle Pecos North:		
P1 (s)	Early McKenzie phase	Jelinek (1967)
P4A (s)	Late 18 Mile phase	Jelinek (1967)
P4AB (s)	E. Mesita Negra phase	Jelinek (1967)
P4B (s)	L. Mesita Negra phase	Jelinek (1967)
P4C (s)	Late McKenzie phase	Jelinek (1967)
P12 (s)	(Phase not given)	Jelinek (1967)
P17 (s)	E. Mesita Negra phase	Jelinek (1967)
P20 (s)	Early 18 Mile phase	Jelinek (1967)
P25 (s)	Early McKenzie phase	Jelinek (1967)
P29 (s)	E. Mesita Negra phase	Jelinek (1967)
Roswell (Middle Pecos South):		
P7 (s)	Roswell phase	Jelinek (1967)
P8 (s)	Roswell phase	Jelinek (1967)
P9 (s)	Crosby phase	Jelinek (1967)
Bloom Mound (e)	Lincoln phase(?)[c]	Kelley (1984)
Rocky Arroyo (e)	late 1200s-1300s	Wiseman (n.d.b)
Fox Place (e)	late 1200s-1300s	Wiseman (n.d.c)
Henderson (e)	late 1200s-1300s	Wiseman (this report)

[a]Collection types: e = excavation; s = surface (survey).
[b]Assignment by R. N. Wiseman based on medial position of pottery assemblage relative to Kelley's (1984) early and late Glencoe Phase assemblages.
[c]Provisional assignment by Kelley (1984).

1. Plain brown pottery, accompanied by Chupadero Black-on-white and related types, remains the dominant pottery in sites of the Middle Pecos North and Middle Pecos South as defined by Jelinek (1967). All other pottery types, whether of the "primary" types (brownware, Chupadero, Three Rivers ware, Corona Corrugated) or the "imported" types, constitute only a tiny fraction of the assemblages from these sites.

Comments. The pottery assemblages from the north and south areas of Jelinek's Middle Pecos region are strikingly similar to the pottery assemblages of Kelley's (1984) Corona phase sites in the northern Sierra Blanca region (Capitan Mountain north to Gallinas Mountains), and to Caperton's (1981) "jacal" sites in the Chupadera Mesa region of central New Mexico. Except for the fact that the Middle Pecos sites are smaller on average than sites of these two more westerly regions, the similarities in pottery types, pottery tempers, and architecture are so great that it is difficult to imagine that the cultural manifestations are not identical.

One of the points of disagreement that must be settled in this matter is whether several pottery types named by Jelinek were actually made in the Middle Pecos as he implies. I think that the key lies in the tempering materials, most of which evidently are of igneous origin, with the nearest major sources being in the mountains to the west. A few igneous dikes do occur in the Middle Pecos region, but as far as I am aware, the mineralogy of those dike rocks is incompatible with the tempering materials documented in the pottery.

Since Corona phase sites and Caperton's jacal sites are both larger and more numerous than Jelinek's Middle Pecos sites, the normal assumption would be that the manifestation developed first in central New Mexico and spread eastward to the Middle Pecos country. If true, then it remains to be established whether this movement of culture was accomplished by the movement of people or by the adoption of the traits by peoples indigenous to the Middle Pecos Valley.

Table 3.14. Dates of phases in Table 3.13.

Region/Phase	Dates AD	Reference
Sierra Blanca North[a]		
Corona phase	1100-1200 (early Pueblo III)	Kelley (1984) Wiseman (1985)
Lincoln phase	1200-1450 (mid-Pueblo III to Pueblo IV)	Kelley (1984) Wiseman (1985)
Sierra Blanca South[b]		
early Glencoe phase	1100-1200 (early Pueblo III)	Kelley (1984) Wiseman (this report)
middle Glencoe phase	1200-1300 (late Pueblo III)	Kelley (1984) Wiseman (this report)
late Glencoe phase	1300-1450 (Pueblo IV)	Kelley (1984) Wiseman (this report)
Middle Pecos North		
Early 18 Mile phase	???-900	Jelinek (1967)
Late 18 Mile phase	900-1000	Jelinek (1967)
Early Mesita Negra phase	1000-1100	Jelinek (1967)
Late Mesita Negra phase	1100-1200	Jelinek (1967)
Early McKenzie phase	1200-1250	Jelinek (1967)
Late McKenzie phase	1250-1300	Jelinek (1967)
Middle Pecos South		
Crosby phase	(pre-dates Roswell Phase)	Jelinek (1967)
Roswell phase	1250-1300	Jelinek (1967)
Lincoln phase (?)	1250-1400	Kelley (1984)
Roswell Area		
Phase affiliations not assigned to Rocky Arroyo, Fox Place, and Henderson.	All three sites have radiocarbon dates in latter half of the 1200s and 1300s.	Henderson dates (see Chapter 2); dates for Rocky Arroyo and Fox Place not published.

[a]Kelley (1984) gives dating estimates for her Sierra Blanca phases in terms of the Pueblo I-V system developed by A. V. Kidder for the Anasazi culture of the Four Corners region. Wiseman (1985) suggests calendrical dates based on clues provided by Kelley (1984) and pottery types associated with her sites.

[b]Although Kelley (1984) detected temporal differences among her Glencoe phase sites, she did not believe that these differences warranted the establishment of separate phases, hence the use of lower case letters for "early" and "late." Based on the results of the Crockett Canyon Project (Farwell et al. 1992), Wiseman recognizes the usefulness of a middle Glencoe period based on the presence of Three Rivers Red-on-terracotta but an absence of Lincoln Black-on-red. The calendrical dates suggested here by Wiseman are based on pottery types. It should also be noted that Kelley (1984) leaves room for the possibility that the earliest Glencoe sites may have little or no painted pottery other than red-slipped brown pottery. Since brown ware pottery is now being documented early in the first millennium AD in the El Paso region, it seems likely that the beginning date of the early Glencoe Phase in the Sierra Blanca will have to be adjusted earlier as well. A site well dated to the second half of the first millennium by tree-ring and radiocarbon determinations was recently excavated near Mescalero (Del Bene et al. 1986).

2. Chupadero Black-on-white and related types are most common in Lincoln phase sites surrounding the Capitan, Jicarillas, and Gallinas mountains of central and northern Lincoln County and less common in sites to the south and east. Chupadero is also the major painted pottery type in pre-Glaze A times in the Chupadera Mesa (Gran Quivira) region of central New Mexico.

Comments. As mentioned earlier, the dominance of Chupadero Black-on-white in both regions may simply be a matter of proximity. However, given strong ceramic and architectural similarities between the two regions and the fact that they adjoin each other, it is reasonable to suggest that the remains belong to the same or closely related peoples.

Rautman (1990, 1993) examined the climatic data for both the Chupadera Mesa and the Sierra Blanca regions and found that when conditions were favorable for agriculture in one, it was often less so in the other, and vice versa. By implication, if we can assume that such shifts in climate patterns can result in at least partial shifts in populations of humans, are we perhaps seeing an archaeological manifestation of population expansion and contraction in the Corona and Lincoln phase remains in southeastern New Mexico?

Or did a group of people carrying Corona phase ("jacal") culture move permanently out of central New Mexico and take up residence in the Capitan/Jicarillas region, with their culture later to "evolve" into the Lincoln phase? This possibility is supported in one major difference between the pottery assemblages of the Capitan/Jicarillas region and the Chupadera Mesa/Gran Quivira region. This difference is the importance of Three Rivers Red-on-terracotta and Lincoln Black-on-red in sites of the two regions—common in the Capitan/Jicarillas and rare in the Chupadera Mesa/Gran Quivira (compare Fig. 3.6 with Table 19 in Hayes et al. 1981). In contrast, Heshotauthla Polychrome from western New Mexico and Biscuit A and B (Abiquiu Black-on-gray and Bandelier Black-on-gray) from northern New Mexico, areas that are at least twice as far from Gran Quivira as the Capitan/Jicarillas mountains, are much better represented at Gran Quivira than Three Rivers and Lincoln.

3. Corona Corrugated, as a companion type to Chupadero Black-on-white, is also most common in sites surrounding the Capitan, Jicarillas, and Gallinas mountains of central and northern Lincoln County and less common in sites to the south and east. Corona Corrugated, in replacing Jornada Brown as the primary utility pottery in those areas, heralds the inception of the Lincoln phase (Kelley 1984).

4. Jornada Brown was the dominant utility pottery in late Glencoe phase sites along the eastern slope of the Sierra Blanca proper in central and northern Otero County and in south-central Lincoln County.

Comments. This fact, in combination with other factors such as architecture, led Kelley (1984) to suggest that the differences between these sites and those of the Corona and Lincoln phases are sufficient to define separate phase sequences. Because sites belonging to both the late Glencoe phase and the Lincoln phase lie within short distances of each other along the same (Rio Bonito) and adjacent (Rio Ruidoso) drainages, it is a simple, almost axiomatic step to suggest that the two actually represent different ethnic groups with similar cultural remains and a history of contacts and interactions. Kelley (1984) suggests this is so, and I concur.

5. Three Rivers Redware—including Three Rivers Red-on-terracotta, Lincoln Black-on-red, and unpainted body sherds of these types—is most common in late Glencoe phase sites in the Ruidoso and Rio Bonito drainages of northern Otero and southern Lincoln counties and in southern Lincoln phase pueblos in the Capitan and Jicarilla mountains of southern and central Lincoln County.

Comments. Three Rivers Redware clearly developed from Jornada Brown. The shift from the latter to the former simply involved increased oxidation during the latter stages of firing, finer grinding of the temper, and, of course, painted designs. The popularity of Three Rivers Red-on-terracotta and Lincoln Black-on-red in southern Lincoln phase sites (those around the Capitan and Jicarilla mountains), along with the probability that at least some of them were producing these pottery types, suggests to me that these people, after migrating out of central New Mexico, had become full-time residents of the region, rather than migrants who shifted back and forth between the two regions. Kelley (1984) lists several architectural, artifactual, and burial traits suggesting the same thesis, though some of these are no longer applicable.

6. Most importantly for purposes here, El Paso Polychrome is the dominant pottery type at both Bloom Mound and the Henderson Site, where it evidently served as the primary utility pottery for cooking and storage. Plain brown pottery and Corona Corrugated are present only in small amounts at these sites.

Comments: This parallel with El Paso phase sites in the El Paso region is remarkable. Kelley (1984) took note of this fact, plus the presence of copper bells and certain kinds of ornaments at Bloom Mound, and suggested that Bloom was part of a trade network between Pecos Pueblo to the north and the El Paso district to the southwest. Pecos, of course, is known for its major role in trade between various Plains groups and Southwestern pueblos at the time of the Spanish entry into the Southwest in the mid-sixteenth century. I suggest that both Bloom Mound and the Henderson Site, rather than being way stations or satellites of Pecos, were probably trading centers. After all, Bloom and Henderson saw their heyday and evidently were abandoned prior to the ascendancy of Pecos some time in the 1400s.

Long-Distance Exchange

The presence of a variety of ceramic types from source areas located several hundred kilometers to the southwest and west of Roswell underscores the importance of interregional exchange. Unfortunately, all of the material recovered in the first two field seasons at Henderson (1980-1981), which has been the focus of this chapter, comes from Late phase contexts (Center Bar, East Bar, East Plaza). Early phase contexts (Great Depression, Main Bar East) were not sampled until the 1990s. Thus, the ceramic assemblage that I have described in detail in this chapter cannot, by itself, elucidate the dynamics of the exchange system over time. However, rather than deferring the temporal analysis until all of Henderson's ceramics have been analyzed, I use an interim approach here that focuses on a much more manageable subset of the ceramic data. Specifically, what I have done is to code all of the rim sherds for all ceramic types, both local/regional and extraregional, as well as all of the body sherds for the extraregional types. This far more manageable data set yields some surprising results.

The total number of rim sherds (all seasons) for all ceramic types at Henderson is 2,678. Of these, 137 or 5.1% are from vessels of extraregional origin, a proportion that is nearly identical to the value obtained from just the 1980-1981 assemblage, as summarized in Table 3.1 above. When the rim data are looked at chronologically, extraregional rims constitute 1.4% ($n = 8$) of the total Early phase rims ($n = 570$), and 6.1% of the total Late phase rims ($n = 2{,}108$; $t_s = 5.57$, $p < .001$).[4] Thus, there is a significant increase in the proportion of extraregional ceramics at Henderson during the Late phase, or after about A.D. 1270. The striking nature of this change is brought out more clearly if one looks only at the extraregional types. Of the 137 rims, only 5.8% occur in the Early phase and 94.2% in the Late phase. A similar result is obtained when all of the extraregional ceramics

Table 3.15. Summary of primary pottery types for selected southeastern New Mexico sites.[a]

Site	Ceramic Type						
	Brown	Chup	EPP	TR R/t	TR ware	Lincoln	Corona
Hiner 1, Rooms 1, 3, 4	14	43	< 1	1	—	—	37
Black Stump	34	39	4	1	< 1	—	15
Clint Sultemier 1	57	38	< 1	—	—	—	—
Phillips, Unit 46							
House 13u	2	30	38	< 1	< 1	4	19
House 13l	9	39	10	1	6	5	22
House 11, 20" floor	8	32	21	< 1	7	7	24
Block Lookout/LA-2112							
Room 2	13	23	7	1	4	2	45
Room 5	6	31	10	—	—	6	46
Tr. 1, 2-4'	24	42	4	4	15	< 1	9
Tr. 1, 5-6'	26	37	4	1	8	7	16
F. 4, Str. 1	24	36	3	3	3	1	23
Baca Site	12	11	6	1	4	4	63
LA 588							
Borrow Pit	15	27	6	< 1	9	7	35
Trench	29	26	10	2	6	5	18
Crockett Canyon							
Room A fill	78	6	4	8	—	—	—
Room M fill	82	4	3	7	—	—	—
Room P fill	58	14	6	20	—	—	—
Room CC fill	66	12	4	14	—	—	—
Room S1 fill	71	7	2	18	—	—	—
Room AA fill	51	13	4	27	—	—	—
Room BB fill	65	10	4	17	—	—	—
Filingen	80	14	< 1	5	—	—	—
Bonnell							
House 1	71	7	10	1	3	< 1	< 1
House 3	64	8	14	2	4	—	7
House 5	54	10	17	3	12	1	2
House 7	61	5	14	2	13	—	2
House 9	47	8	14	1	11	2	14
House 12	75	7	6	1	4	< 1	2
House 13	52	11	23	2	9	< 1	1
House 14	63	12	12	2	7	2	1
House 15	44	15	22	2	8	< 1	7
House 16	51	15	19	2	3	2	3
House 17, Floor 2	39	17	28	< 1	5	1	7
House 20	56	8	15	3	5	—	5
LA-2000 C-1	47	11	24	4	8	1	—
Middle Pecos North							
P1	71	25	—	—	—	—	—
P4A	95	-	—	—	—	—	—
P4AB	95	3	—	< 1	—	—	—
P4B	62	34	—	< 1	—	—	—
P4C	26	71	—	—	—	—	—
P12	80	16	—	—	—	—	< 1
P17	78	17	—	—	—	—	—
P20	100	-	—	—	—	—	—
P25	66	32	—	—	—	—	—
P29	93	3	—	—	—	—	—
Middle Pecos South							
P7	60	37	< 1	1	—	—	< 1
P8	47	48	—	2	—	—	—
P9	63	35	—	—	—	—	—
Bloom Mound, Room F	3	8	71	< 1	< 1	4	5
Rocky Arroyo, F. 2, Str. 3	—	44	27	10	8	3	7
Fox Place	50	19	12	4	—	1	10
Henderson	< 1	17	53	2	11	3	10

[a]Values are percent of count. The sites are grouped by region. The first group includes Corona and Lincoln phase sites in the Sierra Blanca highlands and vicinity of Corona (Kelley 1984; Wiseman 1975; Wiseman et al. 1976). The second group comprises Glencoe phase sites in the Sierra Blanca highlands (Kelley 1984; Farwell et al. 1992). The third group belongs to the northern part of the Middle Pecos region (Jelinek 1967). The fourth group involves the Roswell vicinity (Jelinek 1967; Kelley 1984; Wiseman, n.d.b, n.d.c, and this report).

Table 3.16. Summary of trade pottery recovered at selected southeastern New Mexico sites (Part 1).[a]

Site	Ceramic Type						
	RM	Wing	Mimb	Reser	Cebol	Soco	Kwa
Hiner 1, Rooms 1, 3, 4	—	—	—	—	—	—	—
Black Stump	—	—	—	—	—	—	—
Clint Sultemier 1	—	—	—	—	—	—	—
Phillips, Unit 46							
House 13u	—	—	—	—	—	—	—
House 13l	—	—	—	—	—	—	—
House 11, 20"-floor	—	—	—	—	—	—	—
Block Lookout/LA-2112							
Room 2	—	—	—	—	—	—	—
Room 5	—	—	—	—	—	—	—
Tr. 1, 2-4'	—	—	—	—	—	—	—
Tr. 1, 5-6'	—	—	—	—	—	—	—
F. 4, Str. 1	—	—	—	—	—	< 1	—
Baca Site	—	—	—	—	—	—	—
LA 588							
Borrow Pit	—	—	—	—	—	—	—
Trench	—	—	—	—	—	—	—
Crockett Canyon							
Room A fill	—	—	—	—	—	—	—
Room M fill	—	—	—	—	—	—	—
Room P fill	—	—	< 1	—	—	—	—
Room CC fill	—	—	< 1	—	—	—	—
Room S1 fill	—	—	—	—	—	—	—
Room AA fill	—	—	—	—	—	—	—
Room BB fill	—	—	—	—	—	—	—
Filingen	—	—	—	—	—	—	—
Bonnell							
House 1	—	—	< 1	—	—	—	—
House 3	—	—	—	—	—	—	—
House 5	—	—	< 1	—	—	—	—
House 7	—	—	—	—	—	—	—
House 9	—	—	< 1	—	—	—	—
House 12	—	—	< 1	—	—	—	—
House 13	—	—	< 1	—	—	—	—
House 14	—	—	< 1	—	—	—	—
House 15	—	—	< 1	—	—	—	—
House 16	—	—	—	—	—	—	—
House 17, Floor 2	—	—	< 1	—	—	—	—
House 20, Floor 2	—	—	—	—	—	—	—
LA-2000 C-1	—	—	—	—	—	—	—
Middle Pecos North							
P1	< 1	< 1	—	—	< 1	—	—
P4A	5	—	—	—	—	—	—
P4AB	2	—	—	< 1	< 1	< 1	—
P4B	2	—	—	< 1	< 1	< 1	—
P4C	1	—	—	—	—	—	< 1
P12	—	—	< 1	—	—	< 1	—
P17	1	—	—	—	< 1	< 1	—
P20	—	—	—	—	—	—	—
P25	—	—	—	—	—	—	—
P29	2	—	< 1	—	< 1	—	—
Middle Pecos South							
P7	< 1	—	—	—	< 1	—	—
P8	< 1	—	—	—	—	—	—
P9	—	—	—	—	< 1	—	—
Bloom Mound, Room F	—	—	—	—	—	—	—
Rocky Arroyo, F. 2, Str. 3	—	—	—	—	—	—	—
Fox Place	—	—	—	—	—	—	—
Henderson	—	—	—	—	—	—	—

[a]Values are percent of count. The sites are grouped by region as explained in Table 3.15. Pottery types in this table are: RM = Red Mesa Black-on-white; Wing = Wingate Black-on-red; Mimb = Mimbres Black-on-white; Reser = Reserve Black-on-white; Cebol = Cebolleta Black-on-white; Soco = Socorro Black-on-white; and Kwa = Kwahe'e Black-on-white.

Table 3.17. Summary of trade pottery recovered at selected southeastern New Mexico sites (Part 2).[a]

Site	Ceramic Type						
	SF/Wy	BiscA	StJ	Hesh	GlazA	Salad	Mex
Hiner 1, Rooms 1, 3, 4	—	—	< 1	< 1	< 1	< 1	—
Black Stump	—	—	—	—	—	—	—
Clint Sultemier 1	—	—	—	—	< 1	< 1	—
Phillips, Unit 46							
House 13u	—	—	—	—	< 1	—	< 1
House 13l	—	—	< 1	—	< 1	—	—
House 11, 20"-floor	—	—	< 1	—	—	< 1	—
Block Lookout/LA-2112							
Room 2	—	< 1	—	—	3	< 1	—
Room 5	—	—	< 1	—	< 1	—	—
Tr. 1, 2-4'	—	—	—	—	—	—	—
Tr. 1, 5-6'	—	—	< 1	—	—	—	—
F. 4, Str. 1	< 1	—	—	< 1	< 1	< 1	—
Baca Site	—	—	—	< 1	< 1	< 1	—
LA-588							
Borrow Pit	—	—	—	—	—	—	< 1
Trench	—	—	—	—	—	—	—
Crockett Canyon							
Room A fill	—	—	—	—	—	—	—
Room M fill	—	—	—	—	—	—	—
Room P fill	—	—	< 1	—	—	—	—
Room CC fill	—	—	< 1	—	—	—	—
Room S1 fill	—	—	—	—	—	—	—
Room AA fill	—	—	—	—	—	—	—
Room BB fill	—	—	—	—	—	—	—
Filingen	—	—	—	—	—	—	—
Bonnell							
House 1	—	—	—	—	< 1	—	< 1
House 3	—	—	—	—	—	—	—
House 5	—	—	—	—	—	—	—
House 7	—	—	—	—	< 1	< 1	—
House 9	—	—	—	< 1	< 1	—	< 1
House 12	—	—	—	—	—	—	—
House 13	—	—	—	—	—	—	< 1
House 14	—	—	< 1	—	—	—	—
House 15	—	—	< 1	—	< 1	—	< 1
House 16	—	—	< 1	—	< 1	—	—
House 17, Floor 2	—	—	—	—	—	< 1	—
House 20, Floor 2	—	—	—	—	—	—	—
LA-2000 C-1	—	—	—	—	—	—	—
Middle Pecos North							
P1	—	—	—	—	—	—	—
P4A	—	—	—	—	—	—	—
P4AB	—	—	—	—	—	—	—
P4B	< 1	—	—	—	—	—	—
P4C	< 1	—	—	—	—	—	—
P12	—	—	—	—	—	—	—
P17	—	—	—	—	—	—	—
P20	—	—	—	—	—	—	—
P25	?	—	—	—	—	—	—
P29	—	—	—	—	—	—	—
Middle Pecos South							
P7	—	—	—	—	—	—	—
P8	—	—	—	—	—	—	—
P9	—	—	—	—	—	—	—
Bloom Mound, Room F	—	—	—	—	< 1	< 1	—
Rocky Arroyo, F. 2, Str. 3	—	—	< 1	—	—	—	—
Fox Place	—	—	< 1	—	-< 1	< 1	< 1
Henderson	< 1/< 1	< 1	< 1	< 1	< 1	< 1	< 1

[a]Values are percent of count. The sites are grouped by region as explained in Table 3.15. The pottery types in this table are: SF/Wy = Santa Fe Black-on-white/Wiyo Black-on-white; BiscA = Biscuit A (Abiquiu Black-on-gray); StJ = St. Johns Black-on-red or Polychrome; Hesh = Heshotauthla Black-on-red or Polychrome; GlazA = Agua Fria Glaze-on-red (Rio Grande Glaze A Red); Salad = Salado polychromes (Pinto, Gila, Tonto); Mex = Mexican polychromes (Babicora, Ramos).

are considered, body sherds as well as rims. Of the 1,560 extraregional sherds, 95 (6.1%) come from Early phase contexts and 1,465 (93.9%) come from Late phase contexts. In other words, long-distance ties to the west and southwest, at least as reflected in ceramics, increase explosively during the Late phase; evidence of a parallel increase in Late phase westward-focused exchange of dried bison meat, as reflected by the proportional representation of ribs and vertebrae, is presented in Chapter 4.

Interestingly, the proportional frequency of extraregional ceramics, when looked at chronologically, mirrors the ordering of sites in the Roswell area produced by the seriation of El Paso Polychrome jar rims: Early phase Henderson 1.4%; Late phase Henderson 6.1%; Bloom Mound 12.5% (29 of 203 rims).[5] In other words, the extraregional exchange, that expands dramatically during the Late phase at Henderson, continues to expand during the subsequent occupation at Bloom Mound.

Synopsis

Two seasons of excavation (1980-1981) at Henderson produced nearly 35,000 sherds, weighing about 105 kg. The average density of pottery for the excavation as a whole was just over 436 sherds per m^3 of deposit. Despite the large number of sherds, the majority are very small (average only 3 g per sherd). The small sherd size in part reflects a recovery strategy using a quarter-inch screen. It probably also reflects the predominance in the assemblage of very thin-walled and fragile El Paso Polychrome cooking jars, which may have been especially prone to breakage during use and which may have been fragmented further by trampling and other site formation processes. The 1980-1981 excavations yielded only three whole (or entirely restorable) vessels, all from two subfloor burial pits in East Bar Room E-4 (a small Chupadero Black-on-white jar nested within a small Lincoln Black-on-red bowl, both placed with a young child in Feature 3, and a large Heshotauthla Polychrome bowl inverted over the face of a young adult female who was accompanied by a fetus or newborn in Feature 40).

The Henderson assemblage includes at least 27 named pottery types. Six types are almost certainly of local or regional manufacture: El Paso Polychrome, Chupadero Black-on-white, Three Rivers Redware (Three Rivers Red-on-terracotta and Lincoln Black-on-red), Corona Corrugated, and Jornada Brown. Others were probably imported from northern Mexico (5 types), southwestern New Mexico (4 types), western New Mexico (5 types), and the Rio Grande of north-central New Mexico (5 types). The local/regional types are a clear majority of the assemblage (n = 33,010 or 95%). Missing entirely from the assemblage are cordmarked or other obvious Southern Plains ceramic types, or types originating in extreme southeastern New Mexico, such as Ochoa Indented.

Jars constitute by far the most common vessel form at the site. Of these, El Paso Polychrome sherds, mostly from jars, clearly predominate, comprising 53% (by count) of the total ceramic assemblage. Interestingly, although the jars are decorated, most have a heavy exterior coating of soot which largely or entirely obscures the painted design. This implies that these vessels, despite their decoration, were used in preparing food, routinely being placed near or directly on the fire. The locus of manufacture of the Henderson El Paso Polychrome jars is uncertain and remains an intriguing problem for future research. They may have been imported from the El Paso district some 200 km to the southwest, although given their large numbers in the village, and their comparatively fragile walls, this seems improbable. A local or regional source is more likely.

Chupadero Black-on-white (also mostly jars), Corona Corrugated (again mostly jars), and Three Rivers Redware (predominantly Lincoln Black-on-red bowls), all thought to be locally or regionally made, comprise an additional 42% of the assemblage. Imported ceramics represent less than about 3% of the total.

While the ceramic evidence does not help clarify the issue of whether the Henderson occupation was continuous or broken into two or more distinct periods, it is fully compatible with the chronology established by radiocarbon and archaeomagnetic dating. The ceramics reveal no evidence that the village was occupied prior to A.D. 1100/1150 nor after about A.D. 1400.

Analysis of the total sample of rim sherds recovered from all five seasons of excavation at Henderson reveals that extraregional ceramic exchange with communities located hundreds of kilometers to the west and southwest increased explosively in the Late phase, and continued to increase during the subsequent occupation at nearby Bloom Mound.

Acknowledgments

Our understanding of the extraregional ceramics recovered in the 1990s has benefited from the work undertaken as part of an undergraduate honors thesis by Diane Miller (1998), as well as lab analysis projects undertaken by Heather Miljour and Julia Blough. Our understanding of the El Paso Polychrome jar rim seriation has also benefited from a lab analysis project undertaken by Valerie Smullers.

Notes

1. The total volume of sediments excavated at Henderson in 1980-1981 was 79.56 m^3.

2. In 1995 a fully restorable Tonto Polychrome jar was found broken on a "Late phase" upper floor of Room M-2 in the Main Bar.

3. As noted in Chapter 2, the presence of only one Harrell point out of several hundred identifiable points also indicates that Henderson was abandoned prior to about A.D. 1450.

4. Test of equality of two percentages based on arcsine transformation (Sokal and Rohlf 1969:607-10).

5. Recovered by University of Michigan excavations at the site in 2000.

References Cited

Anyon, R., P. A. Gilman, and S. A. LeBlanc
1981 A Reevaluation of the Mogollon-Mimbres Archaeological Sequence. *Kiva* 46:209-25.

Breternitz, D. A.
1966 *An Appraisal of Tree-Ring Dated Pottery in the Southwest.* Anthropological Papers 10. Tucson, AZ: University of Arizona.

Brody, J. J.
1977 *Mimbres Painted Pottery*. Albuquerque, NM: Maxwell Museum of Anthropology and University of New Mexico Press.

Caperton, T. J.
1981 An Archaeological Reconnaissance of the Gran Quivira Area. In: *Contributions to Gran Quivira Archeology, Gran Quivira National Monument, New Mexico*, edited by A. C. Hayes, pp. 3-11. Publications in Archeology 17. Washington, DC: National Park Service.

Carlson, R. L.
1970 *White Mountain Red Ware: A Pottery Tradition of East-Central Arizona and Western New Mexico.* Anthropological Papers 19. Tucson, AZ: University of Arizona.

Carmichael, D. L.
1985 Transitional Pueblo Occupation on Dona Ana Range, Fort Bliss, New Mexico. In: *Views of the Jornada Mogollon: Proceedings of the Second Jornada Mogollon Conference*, edited by C. M. Beck, pp. 45-53. Contributions in Anthropology 12. Portales, NM: Eastern New Mexico University Press.
1986 *Archaeological Survey in the Southern Tularosa Basin of New Mexico.* Historic and Natural Resources Report 3. (University of Texas at El Paso, El Paso Centennial Museum, Publications in Anthropology 10.) Fort Bliss, TX: United States Army Air Defense Artillery Center, Directorate of Engineering and Housing, Environmental Management Office.

Corley, J. A.
1965 Proposed Eastern Extension of the Jornada Branch of the Mogollon Culture. *Transactions of the Regional Archeological Symposium for Southeastern New Mexico and Western Texas* 1:30-36.

Crown, P. L.
1994 *Ceramics and Ideology: Salado Polychrome Pottery.* Albuquerque, NM: University of New Mexico Press.

Del Bene, T., A. Rorex, and L. Brett
1986 *Report on Excavations at LA 30949 and 30951.* Report MN82.1. Portales, NM: Eastern New Mexico University, Agency for Conservation Archaeology.

DiPeso, C. C., J. B. Rinaldo, and G. J. Fenner
1974 *Casas Grandes, A Fallen Trading Center of the Gran Chichimeca*, Vol. 6. *Ceramics and Shell.* Amerind Foundation Series No. 9. Flagstaff, AZ: Northland Press.

Earles, A.
1987 *An Archaeological Assessment of "Las Huertas," Socorro, New Mexico.* Papers of the Maxwell Museum of Anthropology 3. Albuquerque, NM: University of New Mexico.

Farwell, R. E., Y. R. Oakes, and R. N. Wiseman
1992 *Investigations into the Prehistory and History of the Upper Rio Bonito, Lincoln County, New Mexico.* Laboratory of Anthropology Notes 297. Santa Fe, NM: Museum of New Mexico, Office of Archaeological Studies.

Habicht-Mauche, J. A.
1993 *The Pottery from Arroyo Hondo Pueblo, New Mexico.* Arroyo Hondo Archaeological Series 8. Santa Fe, NM: School of American Research.

Hammack, L. C.
1961 *Missile Range Archaeology.* Laboratory of Anthropology Notes 2. Santa Fe, NM: Museum of New Mexico, Office of Archaeological Studies.

Hayes, A. C. (editor)
1981 *Contributions to Gran Quivira Archeology, Gran Quivira National Monument, New Mexico.* Publications in Archeology 17. Washington, DC: National Park Service.

Hayes, A. C., J. N. Young, and A. H. Warren
1981 *Excavation of Mound 7, Gran Quivira National Monument, New Mexico.* Publications in Archeology 16. Washington, DC: National Park Service.

Jelinek, A. J.
1967 *A Prehistoric Sequence in the Middle Pecos Valley, New Mexico.* Anthropological Paper 31. Ann Arbor, MI: Museum of Anthropology, University of Michigan.

Kelley, J. H.
1979 The Sierra Blanca Restudy Project. In: *Jornada Mogollon Archaeology: Proceedings of the First Jornada Conference*, edited by P. H. Beckett and R. N. Wiseman, pp. 107-32. Las Cruces, NM: New Mexico State University, Department of Sociology and Anthropology, Cultural Resources Management Division, and Santa Fe, NM: State Planning Office, Historic Preservation Bureau.
1984 *The Archaeology of the Sierra Blanca Region of Southeastern New Mexico.* Anthropological Paper 74. Ann Arbor, MI: Museum of Anthropology, University of Michigan.

Kelley, J. H., and S. L. Peckham
1962 *Two Fragmentary Pit House Sites near Mayhill, New Mexico.* Laboratory of Anthropology Notes 201. Santa Fe, NM: Museum of New Mexico, Office of Archaeological Studies.

Lehmer, D. J.
1948 *The Jornada Branch of the Mogollon.* Social Science Bulletin 17. Tucson, AZ: University of Arizona.

Leslie, R. H.
1979 The Eastern Jornada Mogollon: Extreme Southeastern New Mexico (A Summary). In: *Jornada Mogollon Archaeology: Proceedings of the First Jornada Conference*, edited by P. H.

Beckett and R. N. Wiseman, pp. 179-99. Las Cruces, NM: Cultural Resources Management Division, New Mexico State University, and Santa Fe, NM: Historic Preservation Division, Office of Cultural Affairs, State of New Mexico.

Lintz, C. R.
1986 *Architecture and Community Variability within the Antelope Creek Phase of the Texas Panhandle.* Studies in Oklahoma's Past 14. Norman, OK: Oklahoma Archeological Survey.

Mera, H. P.
1931 *Chupadero Black-on-White.* Technical Series Bulletin 1. Santa Fe, NM: Laboratory of Anthropology.
1943 *An Outline of Ceramic Developments in Southern and Southeastern New Mexico.* Technical Series Bulletin 11. Santa Fe, NM: Laboratory of Anthropology.

Mera, H. P., and W. S. Stallings, Jr.
1931 *Lincoln Black-on-Red.* Technical Series Bulletin 2. Santa Fe, NM: Laboratory of Anthropology.

Miller, D. E.
1998 *A Study of the Ceramic Assemblage from the Late Prehistoric Site of Henderson (LA-1549), Southeastern New Mexico, and the Changes in Social Patterns Seen in the Assemblage.* Honors thesis, Department of Anthropology, University of Michigan, Ann Arbor, MI.

Parry, W. J., and J. D. Speth
1984 *The Garnsey Spring Campsite: Late Prehistoric Occupation in Southeastern New Mexico.* Technical Report 15. Ann Arbor, MI: Museum of Anthropology, University of Michigan.

Phillips, D. A., Jr.
1989 Prehistory of Chihuahua and Sonora, Mexico. *Journal of World Prehistory* 3(4):373-401.

Rautman, A. E.
1990 *The Environmental Context of Decision-Making: Coping Strategies Among Prehistoric Cultivators in Central New Mexico.* Ph.D. dissertation, University of Michigan, Ann Arbor, MI.
1993 Resource Variability, Risk, and the Structure of Social Networks: An Example from the Prehistoric Southwest. *American Antiquity* 58(3):403-24.

Reid, J. J., and S. M. Whittlesey
1992 New Evidence for Dating Gila Polychrome. Paper presented at the Second Salado Conference, Globe, AZ.

Seaman, T. J., and B. J. Mills
1988 What Are We Measuring? Rim Thickness Indices and Their Implications for Changes in Vessel Use. In: *Fourth Jornada Mogollon Conference (Oct. 1985): Collected Papers*, edited by M. S. Duran and K. W. Laumbach, pp. 163-94. Tularosa, NM: Human Systems Research.

Smiley, T. L., S. A. Stubbs, and B. Bannister
1953 *A Foundation for the Dating of Some Late Archaeological Sites in the Rio Grande Area, New Mexico: Based on Studies in Tree-Ring Methods and Pottery Analysis.* Research Bulletin 6. Tucson, AZ: University of Arizona, Laboratory of Tree-Ring Research.

Smith, W., R. B. Woodbury, and N. F. S. Woodbury
1966 *The Excavation of Hawikuh by Frederick Webb Hodge: Report of the Hendricks-Hodge Expedition, 1917-1923.* Contribution 20. New York: Museum of the American Indian, Heye Foundation.

Sokal, R. R., and F. J. Rohlf
1969 *Biometry: The Principles and Practice of Statistics in Biological Research.* San Francisco, CA: W. H. Freeman.

Stallings, W. S., Jr.
1931 *El Paso Polychrome.* Technical Series Bulletin 3. Santa Fe, NM: Laboratory of Anthropology.

Warren, A. H.
1979 The Glaze Paint Wares of the Upper Middle Rio Grande. In: *Archaeological Investigations in Cochiti Reservoir, New Mexico*, Vol. 4. *Adaptive Change in the Northern Rio Grande Valley*, edited by J. V. Biella and R. C. Chapman, pp. 187-216. Albuquerque, NM: University of New Mexico, Office of Contract Archaeology.
1992 Temper Analysis of the Pottery of Rio Bonito Valley. In: *Investigations Into the Prehistory and History of the Upper Rio Bonito, Lincoln County, Southeastern New Mexico*, by R. E. Farwell, Y. R. Oakes, and R. N. Wiseman, pp. 195-96. Laboratory of Anthropology Notes 297. Santa Fe, NM: Museum of New Mexico, Office of Archaeological Studies.

Watts, W. C.
1963 Distribution of Pottery in Surface Sites on the South Plains of Texas. *Bulletin of the South Plains Archeological Society* 1963:1-25 (Floydada, TX).

Way, K. L.
1979 Early Puebloan Occupation in the Southern Tularosa Basin, New Mexico. In: *Jornada Mogollon Archaeology: Proceedings of the First Jornada Conference*, edited by P. H. Beckett and R. N. Wiseman, pp. 41-52. Las Cruces, NM: New Mexico State University, Department of Sociology and Anthropology, Cultural Resources Management Division, and Santa Fe, NM: State Planning Office, Historic Preservation Bureau.

Wedel, W. R.
1982 Further Notes on Puebloan-Central Plains Contacts in Light of Archaeology. In: *Pathways to Plains Prehistory: Anthropological Perspectives on Plains Natives and Their Pasts*, edited by D. G. Wyckoff and J. L. Hofman, pp. 145-52. Oklahoma Anthropological Society Memoir 3. Duncan, OK: Cross Timbers Press.

West, K.
1982 *A Study of El Paso Brown Rim Form.* Master's thesis, Department of Sociology and Anthropology, University of Texas at El Paso, El Paso, TX.

Whalen, M. E.
1981 Origin and Evolution of Ceramics in Western Texas. *Bulletin of the Texas Archaeological Society* 52:215-29.
1993 El Paso Plain Brown Rims As Chronological Markers? New

Data on an Old Question. *Kiva* 58(4):475-86.

1994 *Turquoise Ridge and Late Prehistoric Residential Mobility in the Desert Mogollon Region.* University of Utah Anthropological Paper 118. Salt Lake City, UT: University of Utah Press.

White, D. E.

1992 Pinto Polychrome Petrography: A Clue to the Origin of the Salado Polychromes. Paper presented at the Second Salado Conference, Globe, AZ.

Wiseman, R. N.

1975 Test Excavations at Three Lincoln Phase Sites in the Capitan Mountains Region, Southeastern New Mexico. *Awanyu* 3(1):1-29.

1981 *Playas Incised, Sierra Blanca Variety: A New Pottery Type in the Jornada Mogollon.* Transactions of the 16th Regional Archaeological Symposium for Southeastern New Mexico and Western Texas. Midland, TX: Midland Archaeological Society.

1982 The Intervening Years: New Information on Chupadero Black-on-White and Corona Corrugated. *Pottery Southwest* 9(4):5-7.

1985 Proposed Changes in Some of the Ceramic Period Taxonomic Sequences of the Jornada Branch of the Mogollon. In: *Proceedings of the Third Jornada Mogollon Conference*, edited by M. S. Foster and T. C. O'Laughlin. *The Artifact* 23(1-2):9-17.

1986 *An Initial Study of the Origins of Chupadero Black-on-White.* Technical Note 2. Albuquerque, NM: Albuquerque Archaeological Society.

1991 Prehistoric Pottery of the Sierra Blanca-Roswell Region: Appraisal and Speculation. Paper presented at the 7th Jornada Conference, El Paso, TX/Juarez, Mexico, November 8-9, 1991.

n.d.a Introduction to Some Pottery Types of Southeastern and Central New Mexico: Jornada Brown (Sierra Blanca var.), South Pecos Brown, Corona Corrugated, Chupadero Black-on-white, Three Rivers Red-on-terracotta, and Lincoln Black-on-red. Volume of pottery descriptions to be published by the New Mexico Archaeological Council, Albuquerque, NM.

n.d.b Excavations at Rocky Arroyo (LA-25277). Manuscript.

n.d.c Excavations at the Fox Place. Manuscript.

n.d.d Excavations at Los Molinos and White Paint. Manuscript.

Wiseman, R. N., M. Y. El-Najjar, J. S. Bruder, M. Heller, and R. I. Ford

1976 *Multi-disciplinary Investigations at the Smokey Bear Ruin (LA 2112), Lincoln County, New Mexico.* Monograph 4. Las Cruces, NM: COAS Publishing and Research.

Zimmerman, L. E.

1996 *An Internal Chronology at the Late Prehistoric Henderson Site (LA-1549), New Mexico as Illustrated by El Paso Polychrome Rim Sherd Indices.* Honors thesis, Department of Anthropology, University of Michigan, Ann Arbor, MI.

Part II

The Animal Resources

4
Bison Hunting at the Henderson Site

John D. Speth
University of Michigan

Alison Rautman
Michigan State University

Introduction

As discussed in Chapter 2, one of the principal goals of the Henderson excavations in 1980-1981 was the recovery of economic data, particularly faunal and ethnobotanical material, from stratified trash deposits. However, inspection of the site revealed no obvious signs of extramural trash deposits, with the possible exception of sheet midden dumped down the slope on the north side of the pueblo. These deposits were shallow and disturbed by slumping and rodent activity, and appeared to offer little promise of being stratified. As a consequence, we focused our work during the entire 1980 season, and during a substantial part of the 1981 season, on the East Bar and Center Bar room blocks. Our hope was to find rooms that had been filled with trash following their abandonment as habitation or storage structures. Unfortunately, only Room C-5 in the Center Bar produced deeply stratified trash. The remaining rooms that we sampled in the first two seasons had been more heavily eroded and, as a consequence, contained much shallower deposits with only occasional pockets or lenses of ashy midden and relatively small quantities of animal bone.

Disappointed by the small amount of economic data that we were finding in the rooms, we decided midway through the second season to sample the more obvious swales and depressions outside the room blocks in the hope of locating a kiva. Again, beyond merely identifying the presence of such a structure, we hoped to find one that had been filled with trash after it ceased functioning in its ceremonial capacity. All but one of these depressions, however, turned out to be shallow natural features largely or entirely devoid of cultural material. The single exception was at the south end of the East Plaza (trench B/C). Though not a kiva, it was an elongated natural depression in the limestone bedrock filled to a depth of nearly a meter with fire-cracked rock and a truly remarkable faunal assemblage overwhelmingly dominated by bison. This huge earth oven complex was dated to the Late phase by several radiocarbon dates and by seriation of the El Paso Polychrome (EPP) jar rims (Zimmerman 1996; see discussion of the EPP rim seriation in Chapter 3). In 1994 we sampled a swale just north of the west end of the Main Bar which also proved to be a deep karstic sinkhole filled to a depth of over a meter with fire-cracked rock, ash, and large quantities of bison and other animal bones. This earth oven complex, referred to as the "Great Depression," was dated to the Early phase on the basis of the El Paso Polychrome jar rim seriation. Much of the discussion that follows focuses on these two fascinating samples. Limited testing in the West Plaza revealed no comparable deposits. It is important to point out that had we not located the East Plaza and Great Depression earth oven features, our faunal samples would have contained few bison. The fill in the rooms, especially the structures dating to the Late phase, contained mostly lagomorphs, antelope, a few deer, and occasional fish.

Treatment of the Bones

The bones from the rooms were, for the most part, in good condition and seldom needed special treatment. Particularly delicate fish bones, especially identifiable skull parts, were cleaned and coated with clear nail polish to strengthen them. Lagomorph and rodent mandibles and maxillae were also cleaned and the tooth rows treated with clear nail polish to keep the teeth from falling out. In contrast, the bones from the East

Plaza and Great Depression earth oven complexes were in much poorer shape and required extensive treatment to prevent them from disintegrating. These features formed large natural drainage sinks, collecting runoff from the surrounding elevated room blocks. Thus, the bones in these parts of the site had been subjected to repeated wetting and drying, which left them in an extremely fragile condition. Upon first exposure the bones appeared to be in almost pristine condition. Their surfaces were smooth, uncracked, and uncorroded, but they crumbled at the slightest touch. With extreme care, most bones could be removed and cleaned, but to keep them from disintegrating, all but the most dense bones (e.g., phalanges, calcanei, astragali, carpals, sesamoids) had to be treated with large amounts of preservative. In 1981, while working on the masses of bone in the East Plaza, and again in 1994 while working on the material in the Great Depression, we started out using Duco Cement diluted in acetone, but in both seasons after exhausting the supply of Duco in the entire city of Roswell, we experimented with a number of alternative techniques, settling on a polyvinyl acetate–based preservative that could be purchased locally in large quantities (Benwood's One Hour Clear Finish). We had used this same preservative successfully at the nearby Garnsey Bison Kill (Speth and Parry 1980), and we also used it to stabilize some of the human material from Henderson (Rocek and Speth 1986).

The use of a clear floor finish as a preservative is far from orthodox, and probably less than ideal from the perspective of the conservator. However, given time constraints and amount of preservative needed, this was the most expedient product that could be purchased locally in almost inexhaustible quantities and that dried quickly even when bones were saturated with moisture.

Garnsey Bison Kill

Before turning to the Henderson bison remains, we must digress briefly to describe the Garnsey Bison Kill, since this site will figure prominently in subsequent discussions. The Garnsey Site (LA-18399) is located on the eastern edge of the Pecos River valley about 20 km southeast of Roswell and approximately 32 km due east of Henderson. On a clear day the low red bluffs where Garnsey is located are easily visible from Henderson across the broad alluvial flats of the Pecos Valley.

Garnsey was excavated in 1977 and 1978 by the University of Michigan Museum of Anthropology, and details of this work have been published elsewhere (Speth and Parry 1978, 1980; Parry and Speth 1984; Speth 1983). The site dates to the mid- to late 1400s and is therefore anywhere from 50 to 200 years younger than Henderson. The Garnsey dating is based on a large series of conventional radiocarbon dates, and is supported by the presence of (basally notched) Harrell points, which are virtually absent at Henderson. As noted in Chapter 2, Harrell points probably do not become common in the Southern Plains and southeastern New Mexico until about A.D. 1450 (Parry and Speth 1984:31-32).

Garnsey was the scene of multiple kill events, which apparently always took place in the spring, around the time of calving (Wilson 1980). Each kill event involved only a few animals at a time, usually from 4 to 8 animals, but occasionally as many as 15 animals. The method of procurement is still uncertain, but probably involved ambushes or foot surrounds of small groups of animals that were grazing on the grass-covered floor of the wash. There is no evidence for the use of a corral or natural arroyo trap, and the slopes bounding the wash were too gentle to have permitted a successful jump. The paucity of projectile points (10) is perplexing, however, since they should be numerous in a kill site such as Garnsey that did not involve a lethal jump (see Frison 1978:245ff). Either the points, including fragments, were salvaged after each kill, which seems unlikely, or the hunters were using some sort of perishable point, perhaps wood, to arm their arrows, and those that were not salvaged have long since decayed. Wooden projectile points are widely documented in the North American ethnohistoric record (e.g., Mason 1893).

When compared to Northern Plains kills, many of which are well documented in the literature, the Garnsey Site is anomalous in certain respects that have proved to be extremely interesting (Speth 1983). First, all of the kill events at Garnsey occurred in the spring, whereas the vast majority of published kill sites in the Northern Plains have been attributed to the fall or winter. Second, the principal targets at Garnsey were adult and subadult bulls (about 60%), although cows were also taken, while in most Northern Plains sites cows were the preferred targets. Moreover, examination of element frequencies at Garnsey revealed that the hunters discriminated against the cows in their processing and transport decisions, such that an original kill population dominated by bulls was transformed into a residue of processed and discarded bones that was overwhelmingly dominated by female postcranial elements (70-100% depending on the specific element). Finally, the Garnsey hunters did relatively little on-site processing and selective culling of limb elements at the kill; instead, whole though not necessarily intact limbs were transported away from the kill. This pattern is strikingly different from the one seen in roughly contemporary late prehistoric kill sites in the Northern Plains, where extensive processing and culling were carried out by the hunters before they departed (Todd 1987, 1991).

An interesting question, of course, is why hunters would discard presumably edible portions of animals (the cows) that had already been killed, and at a time of year (the spring) when total food availability for the hunters would very likely have been low. The answer involves some interesting nutritional factors that have far-reaching implications for our understanding of the subsistence practices of both prehistoric and contemporary foragers. The animals that the Garnsey hunters were only partially and very selectively using appear to have been the pregnant and nursing cows (Speth 1983). Because these animals were either supporting full-term fetuses or nursing newborn calves at the time of the kill, they very likely were much leaner than the bulls or those cows that were not reproductively active that year. The Garnsey hunters, by killing mostly bulls, and by being extremely selective in processing cows, were deliberately targeting the most fat-rich cuts of meat and marrow bones.

The highly selective behavior of the Garnsey hunters might simply reflect the luxury of choice resulting from a series of particularly successful kills. But this strategy seems highly improbable in the Southern Plains during the spring, a time of shortage, not plenty. Moreover, innumerable ethnohistoric and ethnographic accounts parallel the behavior we see at Garnsey. Hunters have often been observed to abandon entire animals, if upon butchering they prove to be fat-depleted, even when the hunters themselves are short of food, and regardless of the fact that they may already have invested considerable effort to locate and kill the animals (Speth 1983; see also Speth and Spielmann 1983, and references therein). In other words, foragers often hunt for calories, and specifically for calories provided by a nonprotein source (i.e., fat). This behavior is evident year-round, but paradoxically it becomes most pronounced, not when food is abundant, but during periods of food shortage when the animals are leanest, the hunters' supply of plant foods has dwindled, and the hunters themselves are losing body weight. Since the nutritional basis for the behavior seen at Garnsey has been discussed elsewhere in detail, the arguments will be outlined only briefly here (see Speth 1983, 1987, 1989, 1990, 1991a; Cordain et al. 2000).

Fat is important to hunters for a variety of reasons. Fatty foods taste good and they produce a feeling of satiety. Fat is also a very concentrated source of energy, supplying twice as many kcal per gram as either protein or carbohydrate, and fat is more easily metabolized than protein. Finally, fatty foods carry important fat-soluble vitamins and essential fatty acids which, when eaten in sufficient quantity, maintain health (Speth 1989, 1990, 1991b).

But there is another very important reason why fat is critical to foragers (and farmers), particularly during times of stress when wild (or cultivated) plant foods become scarce or unavailable. There is an upper limit to the total amount of protein (plant or animal) that one can safely consume on a regular basis. This limit—best expressed as the total number of grams of protein per unit lean body mass that the body can safely handle—is about 300 g or roughly 50% of one's total calories under normal, nonstressful conditions. The upper limit may, in fact, be as low as about 35% of total calories (see Cordain et al. 2000). Protein intakes above this threshold, especially if they fluctuate sharply from day to day, may exceed the rate at which the liver can metabolize amino acids and the body can synthesize and excrete urea, leading to hypertrophy and functional overload of the liver and kidneys; elevated, perhaps toxic, levels of ammonia in the blood; and a variety of other serious, perhaps life-threatening, disorders (Cahill 1986; Cordain et al. 2000; McArdle et al. 1986; McGilvery 1983; Miller and Mitchell 1982; Rudman et al. 1973; Whitney and Hamilton 1984).

Thus, populations under normal conditions must find ways of reliably obtaining well over half of their daily caloric intake from nonprotein sources: in other words, from animal fat, plant oils, or carbohydrates. The serious negative consequences of a diet that fails to provide the needed nonprotein calories is strikingly illustrated by a condition known as "rabbit starvation" that confronted both arctic foragers and explorers when they were reduced to subsisting entirely on the fat-poor meat of rabbits and ptarmigan (Speth 1983). According to Stefansson (1944:234), a seasoned arctic explorer,

> if you are transferred suddenly from a diet normal in fat to one consisting wholly of rabbit you eat bigger and bigger meals for the first few days until at the end of about a week you are eating in pounds three to four times as much as you were at the beginning of the week. By that time you are showing both signs of starvation and of protein poisoning. You eat numerous meals; you feel hungry at the end of each; you are in discomfort through distention of the stomach with much food and you begin to feel a vague restlessness. Diarrhoea will start in from a week to 10 days and will not be relieved unless you secure fat. Death will result after several weeks.

While most foragers and small-scale horticulturalists undoubtedly faced occasional periods of severe food shortage, when stored foods were exhausted and their daily energy needs had to be provided largely by the meat of fat-depleted animals, conditions during most winters and springs were probably less stressful. During these times, keeping their protein intakes below 50% of calories may not have posed a serious problem. But there is a segment of the population for whom the safe upper threshold of protein intake must be kept considerably lower than 300 g or 50% of total calories—the pregnant women. While maternal protein intakes must be sufficient to avoid deficiencies, several studies suggest that supplementing maternal diets with protein in excess of about 25% of total calories (i.e., above about 100-150 g of protein) may lead to declines rather than gains in infant birth weight, and perhaps also to increases in perinatal morbidity and mortality as well as cognitive impairment. Infants who are born prematurely appear to be the most vulnerable to very high maternal protein supplements (Rush et al. 1980; Rush 1982, 1986, 1989; Sloan 1985; Kerr-Grieve et al. 1979; Worthington-Roberts and Williams 1989:88). Birth weights also decline when the mother's total calorie intake is restricted (Martorell and Gonzalez-Cossio 1987; National Academy of Sciences 1985; Rush 1989; Winick 1989), but declines appear to be particularly severe when the diet is both low in total energy and high in protein. This is strikingly demonstrated by data from Motherwell, a small community in Scotland, where for 30 years pregnant women were advised to consume a diet consisting of about 1,500 kcal and 85 g of protein (about 23% of total calories). Infant birth weights from Motherwell over this period were on average approximately 400 g lower than those of infants born in Aberdeen during the same period (Winick 1989:56). Declines in average birth weight of this magnitude are comparable to those seen during wartime famines (see discussion in Rush 1989; Speth 1990).

Thus, nonprotein sources of energy are extremely important to foragers and farmers alike, and the safe threshold for pregnant women, in particular, in these societies is clearly well below 50% of calories and may well be less than half this value. Protein intakes that exceed this threshold may have serious health consequences, including increased infant morbidity and mortality.

In light of this discussion, the behavior of prehistoric hunters at a spring-season bison kill such as Garnsey becomes more readily comprehensible. They preferentially targeted animals—adult males—that were in the best possible physical condition at that time of year; and they processed the carcasses for transport to another locality, a village or campsite, making very clear-cut choices in favor of portions of the animals that were high in both bulk and fat.

Now let us turn our focus to the bison remains from the Henderson Site. Using the bones discarded in the village, can we infer the nature of Henderson's kill sites? To what extent were their kills similar to those at Garnsey, and in what ways were they different? How far were they from the village? At what time or times of year did most bison hunting take place? What more general insights can these remains provide us concerning the role played by bison in Henderson's economy? In order to explore these and other issues, we begin first by looking in detail at the nature and composition of the total assemblage of bison remains from Henderson. We then turn to detailed comparisons between the major proveniences, focusing particularly on contrasts between the remains that were deposited in abandoned rooms and those that accumulated in more public, non-room contexts. The synopsis at the end of the chapter pulls together the principal conclusions that can be drawn from these analyses, and explores several of the more interesting implications in greater detail.

Total Henderson Bison Sample (1980-1981): Both Sexes Combined[1]

Introduction

As with other chapters in this volume, the discussion that follows focuses primarily on the material recovered in 1980-1981. In a few places, the bison remains from the excavations in 1994, 1995, and 1997 will also be discussed, but their detailed analysis must await a future publication. The 1980-1981 seasons of excavation at Henderson yielded a total of 2,027 bison bones. Of these, 1,665, or 82%, came from trench C at the south end of the East Plaza. Another 47 (2%) came from two other small trenches in the East Plaza (trenches B and D). Only 299 bison bones (less than 15%) came from the room blocks (128 or about 6% from trench A in the East Bar and 171 or about 8% from trench F in the Center Bar). The remaining 16 specimens (less than 1%) came from miscellaneous proveniences on the site, including surface debris from pothunter pits.

Tables A4.1-A4.5 in the appendix at the end of this chapter summarize the basic descriptive data for the bison material from the major 1980-1981 excavation units (trenches A, C, D, F). The following data are included in these tables (more fully explained in the tables themselves): total and immature NISP, total and immature MNE, total and immature MNI, total and immature %MNI, burned NISP, and % burned of total NISP.

Trenches B, E, G, H, and I were not tabulated. Trench E, a 1 m^2 unit in the Main Bar, and trench G, a 4 m^2 unit in the West Plaza, yielded no bison remains. Trench B, a shallow 4 m^2 unit at the south end of the East Plaza, produced only two bison bones—a fragmentary unburned adult calcaneus and an unburned adult distal metapodial. Trench H, a small test in a natural depression to the southwest of the Center Bar, and trench I, a small circular pile of burned limestone rock (lacking a central depression or ash-filled pit feature) to the north of the Main Bar, each yielded only one unburned bison-sized long-bone shaft fragment.

Element Frequencies

Utility Indices. Utility indices provide a valuable means of ordering and interpreting the frequencies of skeletal elements recovered from an archaeological site. First developed by Binford (1978) for caribou and sheep, these indices subsequently have been applied successfully to other taxa, including bison (e.g., Thomas and Mayer 1983; Speth 1983). Use of these indices for bison, even though they originally were intended for smaller animals, is justifiable (with reservation) because all are ungulates with broadly similar overall carcass proportions. Metcalfe and Jones (1988) subsequently modified and simplified Binford's principal index, the so-called "modified general utility index" or MGUI (see below), deriving a new index which they refer to as the "food utility index" or FUI (see also Lyman 1992). However, since the FUI and Binford's MGUI are highly correlated (Metcalfe and Jones 1988), we use Binford's original indices in subsequent discussion.

Emerson (1990) developed a utility index designed explicitly for bison—the "modified average total products index," or MAVGTP. Again, however, these values for the most part covary closely with those derived by Binford for sheep and caribou, and we therefore have opted here to rely on Binford's indices.

Binford's MGUI is a composite value built from three basic indices, the meat, marrow and grease indices. These indices express the amount of meat, marrow, and bone grease in each major anatomical segment of an ungulate carcass. Initial weight or volume measures are converted to indices by assigning the segment with the highest utility a value of 100%. Other segments are then scaled accordingly. A "general utility index" (GUI) is constructed by combining the meat, marrow, and grease values into a single composite index and again scaling the result to 100%. The MGUI, as the name implies, modifies the GUI to accommodate various small elements, or riders, that have little or no nutritional value (e.g., sesamoids, tarsals, carpals) but which nevertheless commonly are transported away from kill sites attached to more valuable elements.

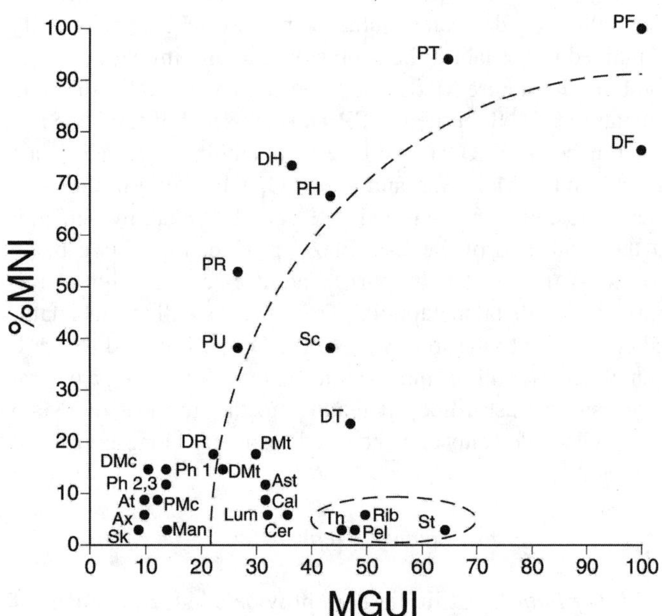

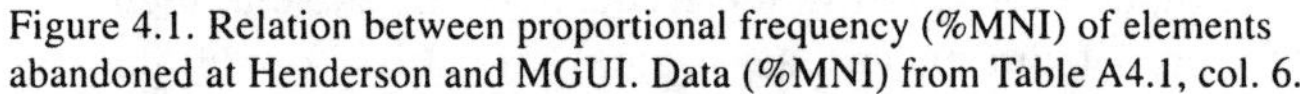

Figure 4.1. Relation between proportional frequency (%MNI) of elements abandoned at Henderson and MGUI. Data (%MNI) from Table A4.1, col. 6.

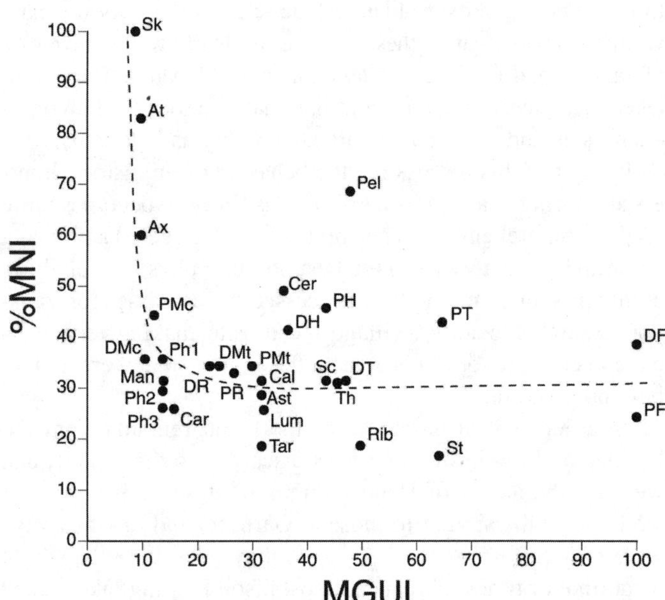

Figure 4.2. Relation between proportional frequency (%MNI) of elements abandoned at Garnsey Bison Kill and MGUI.

Typically, the MGUI is used as the independent variable against which the proportional representation of each skeletal element is plotted (see Binford 1978: Table 2.7 or Speth 1983: Table 13 for MGUI values). The measures of element frequency that we use here are NISP, MNE, and MNI. We also experimented with other measures, such as minimum animal units (see Frison and Todd 1986:69; Lyman 1992:9), but they yielded nearly identical results and we therefore did not employ them in the discussion that follows.

Binford (1978) defined three broad classes of curves that are likely to occur on kill sites. If elements are removed from the kill strictly according to their utility, the curve representing discarded bones should form a straight line, with low-utility parts abundant and high-utility parts rare. If only the highest-utility parts are taken and the remainder dumped at the kill, the result is a "gourmet" curve. Both of these curves are seldom observed in the real world. Typically, the element frequencies observed for kill sites, when plotted against the MGUI, form a curve that resembles a reversed "J" in which moderate-utility parts are somewhat underrepresented. Binford (1978) termed this a "bulk" curve.

Binford (1978) points out that semipermanent or permanent village sites should seldom be expected to produce curves that are simple mirror images of the bulk curves observed at kill sites. The principal reason is that intermediate stages of processing, culling, and consumption are likely to occur between the initial kill event and the final disposition of the bones in village refuse deposits. It therefore came as somewhat of a surprise to find that the Henderson bison assemblage from the 1980-1981 seasons, which is overwhelmingly dominated by the bones from the East Plaza, produced a curve that, in fact, broadly mirrors the Garnsey Kill Site curve (see Figs. 4.1, 4.2). In other words, parts common at Garnsey are rare at Henderson and vice versa. And, as will be discussed below, the two assemblages also mirror each other in the sex ratio of discarded limb elements—predominantly female bones left behind at Garnsey, mostly male bones brought into Henderson. And they have similar age structures—22% immature animals at Garnsey, 14% at Henderson in the Early phase and 22% in the Late phase (based on incompletely fused limb elements only). These results suggest that the Garnsey Site provides a reasonably good analog for the kill sites produced by the Henderson villagers, most particularly during the Late phase of the village occupation. Nevertheless, while the overall complementarity of the Henderson and Garnsey assemblages is striking, some interesting and informative discrepancies emerge when we compare the element frequencies at the village and kill more closely. These discrepancies are explored below.

As expected, in comparing Figures 4.1 and 4.2, high-utility elements, such as the femur and proximal tibia, are scarce at Garnsey and well represented at Henderson, while low-utility parts, such as the skull and neck vertebrae, are common at the kill and rare in the village.[2] However, a few elements at Henderson, particularly the sternum but also the pelvis, ribs, and thoracic vertebrae, deviate from the curve and deserve further comment. These elements have relatively high utility values in Binford's scheme but are underrepresented in the village. Let us begin with the pelvis.

As a glance at Figure 4.2 will show, the pelvis at the Garnsey Bison Kill was one of the more common elements left behind, despite the high utility value attributed to it by Binford's MGUI.

Moreover, the sex ratio of pelves at Garnsey was nearly identical to that of skulls, the element thought to provide the best indication of the sex ratio of the original kill population because of its excessive bulk in transport. In contrast, processing and culling had sharply biased the sex ratio of virtually every other postcranial element in favor of females. This implies that the pelvis of the bison, probably because of its large size, was stripped of meat in the field and, like the skull, was dumped at the kill site along with other low-utility parts (Speth 1983:90). The high utility assigned to the pelvis by Binford's MGUI is based on the much smaller and more transportable element in caribou and sheep. The scarcity of bison pelves at Henderson, therefore, is not surprising, and a utility value for this element in bison similar to the value assigned to the skull probably would be more appropriate.

The apparent scarcity of ribs at Henderson also deserves comment. In part, their scarcity may simply reflect the fact that only proximal ribs are included in Figure 4.1. Hundreds of medial and distal fragments of large-mammal (presumably bison) ribs are not included in the figure. However, as we will show, even when all of the fragmentary ribs are tabulated, this element is still underrepresented. Ribs are often poorly represented in archaeological sites, and their scarcity is commonly attributed to taphonomic factors such as trampling, decay, and the attritional impact of scavenging dogs, wolves, hyenas, or other predators (e.g., Marean et al. 1992). However, the fact that carnivore gnawing, puncturing, and pitting are rare throughout the Henderson bison assemblage, ribs included, suggests that their underrepresentation cannot be due solely to taphonomic factors. More importantly, as we show below, the smaller and much more delicate ribs of antelope and deer are better represented in the assemblage than are bison ribs. If taphonomic processes were eliminating them, ribs from smaller animals should be considerably less well represented than the far more robust bison ribs. Nor are high-utility rib units likely to have been left behind at the kill. At Garnsey, for example, ribs are also quite rare, and again their scarcity cannot be attributed entirely or even largely to carnivore destruction or fluvial sorting (Speth 1983). Hence, the systematic removal of dried bison rib slabs from Henderson for use in intervillage exchange or food sharing becomes a very real and likely possibility.

As already noted, the scarcity of ribs at Henderson might reflect, at least in part, the fact that the %MNI values used in Figure 4.1 were based solely on the number of proximal ends found in the collection. Since virtually all of these have been pulled from the faunal collection and tabulated, their scarcity is real and not an artifact of the incomplete tabulation of rib fragments. However, since a common field butchery practice is to break or chop the rib cage off close to the spine, leaving the proximal ends attached to the thoracic vertebrae (e.g., Binford 1978), proximal ribs should be quite scarce at Henderson, unless the entire thoracic column was transported to the village. The fact that thoracic vertebrae, as well as other axial elements, are also rare at Henderson suggests that vertebral columns were, in fact, either abandoned at the kill or, more likely, were exchanged along with the rib units to other communities in the region.

It should be noted that vertebral bodies of bison-sized animals are quite easily identified, even in highly fragmented condition. This is certainly true of the thoracic bodies, which have very distinctive overall shapes, as well as facets for the articulation of the ribs, which can be spotted even on very small fragments. Fragments of thoracic spinous processes, particularly the basal portions, are also readily identified. Thus, the scarcity at Henderson of thoracic vertebrae and other axial elements, like ribs, is almost certainly real, and not a reflection of their destruction by either taphonomic or human agents.

Interestingly, thoracic vertebrae were relatively uncommon at the Garnsey Bison Kill, with a %MNI value of only 31% (Speth 1983:86). Thus, thoracics were clearly being removed from this kill site in substantial numbers, in fact more so than many of the limb elements. This behavior is counterintuitive but has a logical explanation. O'Connell et al. (1988), working among Hadza foragers in Tanzania, documented that vertebral units, even from animals the size of giraffes, are often transported back to base camps. Vertebrae are important sources of edible tissue and grease in ungulates (Binford 1978; Blumenschine and Caro 1987), and bison vertebrae are apparently no exception (Emerson 1990). Moreover, along with ribs, they are among the more easily dried units (Binford 1978). Thus, if Garnsey does in fact provide a reasonable analog for kill sites made by the Henderson villagers, which certainly seems plausible given the overall complementarity of the bone assemblages from Henderson and Garnsey, then it is very likely that the villagers routinely brought back both thoracics and rib cage units, but subsequently traded them, once dried, to other communities in the region.

The idea of intervillage exchange in bison products is not as far-fetched or speculative as it might seem. Henderson (and nearby Rocky Arroyo Pueblo) trash contained large quantities of bison postcranial elements, but few ribs and axial elements. Conversely, contemporary villages in the uplands to the west and northwest—that is, in the Sierra Blanca–Sacramento Mountain region and in the Gran Quivira area—had primarily ribs and axial elements of bison (Driver 1990; Katherine A. Spielmann, pers. comm.). These could well have been obtained from the Pecos lowlands through exchange with villages like Henderson, Rocky Arroyo, Bloom Mound, and others.

An alternative though less plausible interpretation, of course, for the scarcity of axial elements at Henderson is that they were in fact routinely abandoned at kills, a pattern very different from that seen at Garnsey. If so, we would need to reduce the MGUI value for thoracics and other bulky axial elements, as was already suggested for the pelvis.

In order to add credence to the suggestion that bison rib units were used in intervillage trade, we must show that their scarcity at Henderson is neither an artifact of our reliance on just the proximal ends to estimate MNIs, nor a reflection of severe attritional processes (such as scavenging village dogs). To do this, we have followed the lead of Driver (1990), who measured the total length of all of the bison rib fragments in several Sacramento Mountain late prehistoric faunal assemblages, and then divided the total by the length of the longest rib in a modern adult male bison. This provided Driver with a figure for the total number of ribs in these assemblages (more than 75) that was more than double the value he obtained by relying solely on the most common epiphysis, that is, the proximal (or dorsal) end.

Like Driver, we sorted out all of the rib fragments in the 1980-1981 assemblage that could reasonably be classified as bison size, and that were clearly ribs and not pieces of vertebral processes. We then measured the maximum length of each fragment in centimeters using sliding dial calipers. We made no attempt when measuring the prehistoric rib fragments to account for the curvature of the specimens. Given the small size of most of the fragments, we felt this additional "accuracy" was unnecessary. However, the lengths of the complete ribs of modern comparative bison and antelope were measured using a flexible tape so that the very pronounced curvature of these specimens was taken into account. For rib segments that had spalled or broken apart longitudinally (lateral, medial, cranial, or caudal splinters of ribs), we divided their length by two, to compensate for the fact that more than one such fragment could have come from the same segment. We could, of course, have divided the total length of these splintered fragments by four (or more) to provide an even more conservative estimate of the total number of bison ribs in the assemblage. As will become obvious shortly, however, the most interesting insights come when we compare the estimated number of bison ribs with the value estimated for medium ungulates (antelope and deer). The results of this comparison remain the same, regardless of whether we divide by two or four, so long as we use the same figure for both taxa.

For the 1980-1981 Henderson assemblage as a whole, the total number of bison rib fragments was 824 (including the proximal ribs tallied in Fig. 4.1), with a total length of 4,449.4 cm. We then measured the ribs in a modern adult male bison in the comparative collections of the University of Michigan Museum of Anthropology. The longest rib in this skeleton was 68 cm, a value very similar to the one (70 cm) reported by Driver (1990:251). The total length of the 28 ribs in the modern bison was 1,482 cm, and the average length per rib was approximately 52.9 cm. Each of these values can be used to estimate the number of ribs represented in the Henderson assemblage. If we follow Driver in dividing the total length of the archaeological fragments by the length of the longest rib (68 cm) in the modern animal, we get a minimum of 65 ribs at the site or an MNI of 2.3 bison. If instead we total the length of the 28 ribs in the comparative skeleton and divide this value into the Henderson total, we arrive at a somewhat more realistic estimate for the MNI of 3 animals. We get the same result (MNI = 3) if we divide the total fragment length by the average length of a rib in the modern specimen. Given a minimum number of bison at Henderson of 34 (see Table A4.1), and using an MNI of 3 animals based on ribs, only about 8.8% of the expected number of ribs are represented in the assemblage. For comparison, the number of animals represented by proximal (dorsal) rib ends (MNI = 2; %MNI = 5.9%) is relatively close to the number represented by rib shaft fragments and splinters (Table A4.1), a result unlike the situation described by Driver at sites in the Sacramento Mountains. If we assume that rib units were generally broken or chopped off close to the spinal column at the kill, leaving proximal ends attached to the thoracics, this result provides intriguing indirect evidence that vertebral and rib units originally entered Henderson in similar numbers.

We can safely conclude, therefore, that bison ribs are poorly represented in the Henderson assemblage. Their scarcity is not an artifact of tabulating only proximal ends. But this in no way demonstrates that bison ribs were traded. Their underrepresentation might still be due largely to attritional processes, most notably scavenging by village dogs. We have already noted that signs of carnivore damage, such as gnawing and pitting, are rare in the bison assemblage, but it is conceivable that such obvious signs of scavenging might not provide a reliable measure of the real extent of carnivore destruction. An interesting and perhaps more reliable way of assessing the impact of attritional processes on the bison ribs is provided by examining the proportional representation of antelope and deer ribs. These much smaller and more delicate ribs should be far more vulnerable to carnivore damage than the robust rib shafts of bison. Thus, we repeated this same analysis with the sample of medium ungulate rib fragments.

According to Miracle (Chapter 5, Tables A5.4 and A5.6), there are a minimum of 21 antelope (*Antilocapra americana*) and 3 deer (*Odocoileus* sp.) in the 1980-1981 Henderson assemblage (to date, only a single phalanx of mountain sheep has been found at the site). There are 597 medium ungulate rib fragments in the assemblage (including the proximal ends tabulated by Miracle), which yield a total length of 2,286.1 cm (as in bison, in deriving this figure the length of split and splintered segments was divided by two). A modern comparative antelope skeleton of an adult male collected from a desiccated carcass found in 1980 near the Henderson Site yielded the following data: (1) longest rib, 28 cm; (2) total length of 28 ribs, 551 cm; (3) average length per rib, 19.7 cm. Using these values, between 12.5% and 17.3% of the expected number of ribs, or animals, are represented by the rib fragments. The specific value depends on how the percentages are calculated (i.e., 116 ribs out of 672, or 3 to 4 animals out of 24). Again, as in bison, the higher values (i.e., 116 ribs or 4 animals; 16.7-17.3%), derived by using either the total length of ribs in an antelope skeleton or the average length per rib, are probably more realistic than the figure obtained by using the longest rib.

These results show that antelope ribs are proportionately much better represented in the Henderson assemblage than are bison ribs, despite the fact that these bones are smaller and far more delicate in antelope and therefore should have been con-

Table 4.1. Frequency (NISP and MNE) of bison bones by major carcass unit at Henderson Site (1980-1981 only, all proveniences combined) and Garnsey Bison Kill.[a]

Carcass Unit	Henderson Site				Garnsey Bison Kill		Test Statistic (t_s)[f]
	NISP	%	MNE	%	MNE	(100-%MNE)[b]	
Axial	410	20.4	84	11.1	848	53.4	*22.24
Appendicular	1598	79.6	675	88.9	973	46.6	
Total	2008[c]		759		1821		
Front limb	527	48.0	239	44.4	327	44.2	0.07
Rear limb	571	52.0	299	55.6	259	55.8	
Total	1098[d]		538[e]		586		
Upper front limb	371	74.8	120	56.9	83	60.3	0.71
Lower front limb	125	25.2	91	43.1	126	39.7	
Total	496		211		209		
Upper rear limb	254	52.3	121	54.5	92	52.1	0.49
Lower rear limb	232	47.7	101	45.5	100	47.9	
Total	486		222		192		

[a]NISP, number of identifiable specimens; MNE, minimum number of elements; axial includes vertebrae, ribs, and sternum; appendicular includes all limbs elements, as well as carpals, tarsals, sesamoids, phalanges, and longbone shaft fragments; upper front limb includes scapula and humerus; lower front limb includes radius, ulna, and metacarpal; upper rear limb includes pelvis, femur, and patella; lower rear limb includes tibia and metatarsal.

[b]Second column of Garnsey entries obtained by subtracting % values given in Speth (1983:54-56) from 100 to approximate percentages of elements transported away from kill.

[c]Excludes 1 cancellous fragment and 18 fragments unidentifiable to specific element.

[d]Excludes 500 fragments of metapodials, phalanges, sesamoids, and long bone shafts that could not be assigned to front or rear of animal.

[e]Excludes 137 metapodials, sesamoids, and phalanges that could not be assigned to front or rear of animal.

[f]Test of equality of two percentages based on arcsine transformation (Sokal and Rohlf 1969:607-10; no asterisk, $p > .05$; single asterisk, $p < .001$); all comparisons are between %MNE values at Henderson and their counterparts, expressed as 100-%MNE, at Garnsey.

Table 4.2. Frequency (MNI) of major limb elements at Henderson Site (1980-1981 only, all proveniences combined) and Garnsey Bison Kill.

Limb Element	Henderson Site		Garnsey Bison Kill[a]		
	MNI[b]	%MNI[c]	MNI[b]	%MNI[d]	100-%MNI[e]
Scapula (Scap)	13	38.2	12	34.3	65.7
Prox. humerus (PH)	23	67.6	18	51.4	48.6
Dist. humerus (DH)	25	73.5	15	42.9	57.1
Prox. radius (PR)	18	52.9	13	37.1	62.9
Dist. radius (DR)	6	17.6	14	40.0	60.0
Prox. metacarpal (PMc)	3	8.8	18	51.4	48.6
Dist. metacarpal (DMc)	5	14.7	13	37.1	62.9
Prox. femur (PF)	34	100.0	9	25.7	74.3
Dist. femur (DF)	26	76.5	14	40.0	60.0
Prox. tibia (PT)	32	94.1	18	51.4	48.6
Dist. tibia (DT)	8	23.5	13	37.1	62.9
Prox. metatarsal (PMt)	6	17.6	14	40.0	60.0
Dist. metatarsal (DMt)	5	14.7	13	37.1	62.9

[a]Data from Speth (1983).

[b]MNI, minimum number of individuals.

[c]%MNI, MNI of each element observed at Henderson expressed as percent of maximum MNI value—34 animals (prox. femur).

[d]%MNI, MNI of each element observed at Garnsey expressed as percent of maximum MNI value—35 animals (skull).

[e]%MNI values at Garnsey subtracted from 100 to approximate values for elements transported away from kill.

siderably more susceptible to attritional processes.[3] Thus, while village dogs and other attritional processes may have removed or destroyed substantial numbers of ribs of both taxa, the significantly greater scarcity of bison ribs at Henderson lends credence to our suggestion that they were in fact removed from the village, possibly in the context of intervillage exchange or food sharing.

We are led to a very similar conclusion when we compare the proportional representation of bison versus antelope and deer thoracic vertebrae in the Henderson assemblage. As in the case of ribs, we began by sorting through all of the highly fragmentary remnants of axial elements, coding every piece that could be identified with reasonable certainty as deriving from either a large or a medium ungulate thoracic vertebra. The most commonly represented fragment was then used to estimate the minimum number of thoracics belonging to each taxon. In both taxa, the most common fragment proved to be the basal portion of the spinous process. Among the bison remains, there were only 12 elements (MNE) represented by these fragments. For the 34 animals at the site, there could have been up to 476. Thus, the observed frequency is only 2.5% of the maximum expected value (based on MNE's, not MNI's).

Among the antelope and deer, there were 23 thoracics represented by spinous processes. For the 24 individuals found at Henderson, there could have been up to 312 of these elements. Hence, for the medium ungulates, about 7.4% of the expected number of elements were recovered.

The bison and medium ungulate percentages for thoracics are significantly different ($t_s = 3.20, p = .001$), and the direction of the difference parallels the pattern seen in ribs—thoracic vertebrae are better represented in smaller ungulates than in bison. Interestingly, the same pattern holds across all of the vertebrae, and is statistically significant in all except the sacrum.[4] Hence, the underrepresentation of bison thoracic, and other, vertebrae at Henderson is unlikely to be due entirely, or even largely, to the scavenging activities of dogs. It is very likely, instead, that many of the bison vertebral units, like ribs, were removed from Henderson, possibly in the context of intervillage exchange or food sharing. The fact that antelope and deer vertebrae are also uncommon may, of course, indicate that axial units of these animals were also dispersed in a similar manner.

Let us return now to our discussion of elements of comparatively high utility that deviate from the curve in Figure 4.1. We have already considered the pelvis, ribs, and thoracic vertebrae. The final element that deserves comment is the sternum. Because of the particularly fragile nature of the sternebrae, their scarcity may reflect little more than the attritional effects of various taphonomic agents, or of the villagers themselves during the final stages of processing, cooking, and eating. It is also possible, however, that the sternebrae, like the ribs and axial elements, remained attached to rib units and were transported elsewhere as items of exchange.

Carcass Units. Table 4.1 summarizes the Henderson bison data (1980-1981 only, all proveniences combined) by major

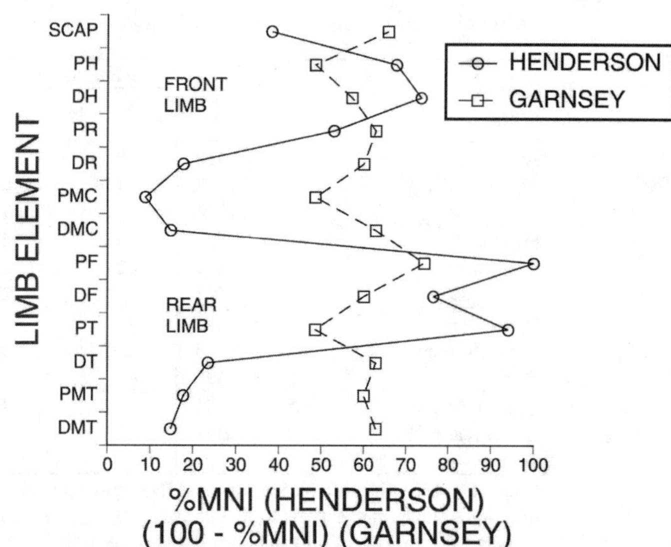

Figure 4.3. Frequency of major limb elements (MNI and %MNI) at the Henderson Site (1980-1981 only, all proveniences combined) and Garnsey Bison Kill.

carcass units using both NISP and MNE values. Data from the Garnsey Bison Kill are provided for comparative purposes (see Speth 1983). The Garnsey MNE percentages have been subtracted from 100 to approximate the assemblage that was transported away from the kill, thereby facilitating comparisons with Henderson. In most cases, the Henderson NISP and MNE values yield similar patterns, although in a few notable instances they deviate markedly from each other. These deviations should provide interesting insights in themselves, because the two measures reflect somewhat different aspects of the assemblage. The NISP values reflect the total number of fragments that could be identified to a particular element. The MNE values, in contrast, reflect the minimum number of elements represented by these fragments. Where the two measures are similar, the elements (e.g., proximal femur or distal tibia) are more or less intact; when they deviate sharply from each other, the elements have probably been broken apart into many small, but still recognizable, fragments. Obviously, the relationship between NISP and MNE is not straightforward, since some elements (e.g., tibia shafts) are much more easily identified than others (e.g., humerus shafts), even when broken into tiny pieces. Nevertheless, the deviations provide at least some indication of fragmentation patterns at the site. For the moment, however, we will be concerned primarily with the number of elements actually present in the assemblage, not with the degree to which they have been broken up. Hence, we will concentrate on the MNE values, deferring the discussion of the relationship between NISP and MNE until later.

The only significant difference in Table 4.1 between Henderson and Garnsey is the overwhelming predominance at the village of appendicular elements. This is not so at Garnsey, where axial and appendicular elements appear to have been removed in more nearly equal proportions. Two factors in particular may account for this difference. First, as already noted, axial elements originally may have been brought into the village in larger numbers than Table 4.1 might suggest, only to be dispersed elsewhere through gift-giving or exchange. Second, given the large body size of bison, and the fact that most of the carcass parts transported to Henderson were from adult males (see discussion below), it is very likely that the high proportion of appendicular elements reflects selective culling and transport decisions made by Henderson hunters at kills that were located far away from the village (see Binford 1978; Bunn et al. 1988; O'Connell et al. 1988). We will return to the question of transport distance shortly.

In other respects, Henderson and Garnsey are very similar. The meatier rear limb elements were brought into the village in greater numbers than front limb elements; and at Garnsey, rear limb bones were transported away from the kill in greater numbers than front limb elements. Similarly, meatier upper limb elements were brought into the village in greater numbers than less muscled lower limb elements, a pattern closely mirroring the assemblage transported away from Garnsey.

Thus, if one is willing to accept that the scarcity of axial parts at Henderson is a reflection of transport constraints and intercommunity exchange, then the assemblage from the village might easily have come from one or more kills much like the events documented at Garnsey. (The Garnsey Site itself could not have been the product of hunters from Henderson because the kill events postdate the Henderson occupation, very likely by over a century.) As already noted, the similarities extend well beyond the proportions of skeletal elements that were involved. The sites share nearly identical sex ratios and age structures (in the Late phase) as well.

However, there is also an interesting contrast between the two assemblages. As shown in Figure 4.3 (see also Table 4.2), the proportions (based on %MNI values) of the various limb elements transported away from Garnsey are amazingly uniform, with values for elements of both limbs clustering tightly around 60% (59.6% ± 7.5). The uniformity of these values suggests that whole limbs may often have been removed from the kill, with little selective culling or on-site processing prior to transport. This curious transport pattern was first pointed out by Todd (1987, 1991), who noted that in this regard Garnsey was more like Northern Plains Paleo-Indian kills than late prehistoric kills in the same region, in which on-site processing and culling is far more evident. The notable scarcity, and small size, of processing areas that were encountered during the excavations at Garnsey support this conclusion (Speth 1983).

Henderson, in contrast, shows a much more sinuous or "s"-shaped pattern, in which higher-utility upper limb elements vastly outnumber the more marginally useful lower limb elements. Whole limbs were apparently not being brought into the village; instead, the Henderson bison limbs had already undergone considerable culling and processing before the material reached the village, eliminating many of the marginal-utility distal limb and foot elements. This conclusion dovetails nicely with the sharply elevated proportions of appendicular elements compared to skulls, vertebrae, and pelves at the village. Thus, it seems very likely that the kill events documented at Henderson, on average, took place considerably farther from home than those seen at Garnsey.

Transport distance from kill to village was great enough to lead to the almost complete elimination of crania and pelves. Interestingly, there is also compelling evidence that average transport distance increased during the Late phase (i.e., after about A.D. 1270). This is suggested by the fact that the average marrow utility of limb elements brought into the village increased significantly in the Late phase, very likely because the hunters culled greater numbers of lower-utility parts prior to transport (average marrow utility: Early phase, 36.42 ± 25.99; Late phase, 40.03 ± 24.19; $t = -2.17$, $p < .05$).

Burning. The number of burned specimens recovered in 1980-1981 at Henderson is tabulated element by element in Table A4.1. Two different values are presented—the number of identifiable specimens that are burned ("NISP Burned"), and the number of burned fragments expressed as a percent of the total number of fragments of that element recovered ("% of Total NISP"). A total of 121 (5.97%) burned bison fragments were found out of a site-wide NISP of 2,027. These data, when summarized by three major subdivisions of the carcass—axial, front limb, and hind limb—again yield some interesting, though not unexpected, patterns (see Table 4.3). Appendicular elements show a higher incidence of burning than do axial elements, and a higher proportion of rear limb than front limb fragments are burned (both comparisons are statistically significant). While lower limb elements, especially those of the rear leg, are more likely than upper limb elements to be burned, these differences are not significant, perhaps due to the more modest sample sizes involved in these comparisons. In sum, processing and cooking that induced burning affected most notably the rear limb and especially the lower, less protected portion of that limb.

The burned bison bones from Henderson generally were only partly charred, not calcined, and the charring often amounted to little more than localized blackening rather than complete burning of the entire specimen. Moreover, burning was seldom so intense that it led to cracking or crazing of the surfaces of the bones. This pattern of patchy and comparatively mild charring most likely resulted from activities such as roasting, baking, or heating marrow bones, which only partially exposed bones to the fire, rather than from accidental or deliberate disposal of bones in the fire after cooking. We return later to this interesting issue.

The distribution of burning on the axial and limb bones can therefore provide a relatively clear indication of the segments into which carcasses had been butchered prior to cooking. The proportion of elements that are burned ranges from 0% for the proximal metatarsal and the distal end of both metapodials to a high of over 50% for the skull. It must be kept in mind, how-

Table 4.3. Frequency (NISP) of burned bison bones by major carcass unit at Henderson Site (1980-1981 only, all proveniences combined).[a]

Carcass Unit	Total NISP (Burned and Unburned)	Burned NISP	Burned % of Total NISP	Test Statistic (t_s)[b]
Axial	410	14	3.4	*2.57
Appendicular	1598	103	6.5	
Total	2008[c]	117[d]	5.8	
Front limb	527	28	5.3	**2.94
Rear limb	571	57	10.0	
Total	1098[e]	85[f]	7.7	
Upper limb	649	45	6.9	0.64
Lower limb	636	50	7.9	
Total	1285[g]	95[h]	7.4	
Upper front limb	371	21	5.7	0.56
Lower front limb	156	7	4.5	
Total	527	28	5.3	
Upper rear limb	278	24	8.6	1.05
Lower rear limb	293	33	11.3	
Total	571	57	10.0	

[a]NISP, number of identifiable specimens; % of Total NISP, percent burned of total NISP value given in first column of table; axial includes vertebrae, ribs, and sternum; appendicular includes all limbs elements, as well as carpals, tarsals, sesamoids, phalanges, and long bone shaft fragments; upper front limb includes scapula and humerus; lower front limb includes radius, ulna, and metacarpal; upper rear limb includes pelvis, femur, and patella; lower rear limb includes tibia and metatarsal.

[b]Test of equality of two percentages based on arcsine transformation (Sokal and Rohlf 1969:607-10; no asterisk, $p > .05$; single asterisk, $p = .01$; double asterisk, $p < .01$).

[c]Excludes 1 cancellous fragment and 18 fragments unidentifiable to specific element.

[d]Excludes 4 burned fragments unidentifiable to specific element.

[e]Excludes 500 fragments of metapodials, phalanges, sesamoids, and long bone shafts that could not be assigned to front or rear of animal.

[f]Excludes 18 burned fragments of metapodials, phalanges, sesamoids, and long bone shafts that could not be assigned to front or rear of animal.

[g]Excludes 313 long bone shaft fragments that could not be assigned to upper or lower limb of animal.

[h]Excludes 8 burned long bone shaft fragments that could not be assigned to upper or lower limb of animal.

ever, that the high frequency of burning seen in rare elements such as the skull (NISP = 11) may be more affected by small sample size than by prehistoric cooking patterns.

Most axial elements are so infrequent in the East Plaza trash or elsewhere on the site that no meaningful comments can be made about burning patterns. The one notable exception, however, are the ribs. Of the site-wide total of 824 specimens (NISP), 57 are burned (6.9%), a value that is very similar to the average incidence of burning (6.0%) for all bison elements combined (see Table A4.1).

In the front limb almost 5% of the scapulae, nearly 8% of the proximal humeri, and nearly 13% of the distal humeri are charred. Burning on the scapula tends to occur about equally on the edges of the blade and on the distal articulation. In contrast, on the humerus a different pattern of burning is evident. On the proximal humerus burning is generally restricted to the articular surface of the joint, while on the distal humerus it tends to be concentrated on the broken edges of the shaft and seldom on the distal epiphysis itself. This pattern suggests that the shoulder joint was sometimes, if not often, disarticulated and cooked as two separate units. However, the overall scarcity of scapulae in the East Plaza trash suggests that most were stripped of meat directly at the kill and discarded there.

It is worth noting that in five seasons of excavation at Henderson no tools were found that had been fashioned from the scapulae or from any other bones of bison. All of the bone tools and ornaments that have been recovered to date (e.g., awls, tubular beads, gaming pieces) were made from bones of deer or antelope, bird, and tortoise or turtle. Noteworthy by their absence are agricultural tools made from bison bones, such as tibia digging stick tips and scapula hoes, implements that are commonplace in contemporary Plains Village period farming communities farther to the east in the Southern Plains (e.g., Duffield 1970; Brooks et al. 1985).

Interestingly, many (at least 12) of the proximal humerus heads had been disarticulated from the scapula and then cleaved by an ax or chopper blow delivered parallel to the longitudinal axis of the shaft. Since no clear impact points could be identified on the epiphyses, it seems very likely that the blows were struck somewhere near the proximal end of the shaft. This suggestion can obviously be checked in the future by a closer look at the shaft fragments. The low incidence of burning on the cleaved surfaces indicates that these bones were broken open after they had been cooked and stripped of meat, presumably to gain access to the marrow or to prepare the epiphysis for grease-rendering. This is a somewhat unorthodox technique for gaining access to the marrow (see discussion in Binford 1981:148-66), but one which has been observed ethnographically, for example, among contemporary Hadza foragers in Tanzania (Henry T. Bunn, pers. comm.). Interestingly, similar split or cleaved proximal humerus heads were also noted at the Garnsey Bison Kill, providing clear evidence of on-site marrow processing, although the frequency of humeri processed in this way has not been tabulated. More orthodox methods were also used to open the humerus (and other elements) to get at the marrow cavity. Several of the humeri have clear circular or ovoid impact points on the proximal shaft just below (distal to) the proximal articulation. Several of these impacts display all of the classic fracture features, including flakes spalled from the interior of the shaft that originated at the point of impact, and fractures radiating out from, and concentric around, the point of impact (Bunn 1989).

The frequent traces of burning on the broken ends of the distal humerus shaft suggest that the humerus was often cooked as two distinct units, one consisting just of the proximal end and most of the shaft, the other consisting of the articulated elbow joint, of which the distal humerus forms an integral part.

The elbow joint itself, consisting of the proximal radius and ulna and the distal humerus, was commonly found as an articulated unit in the East Plaza trash. Burning is infrequent on the proximal ulna and on the articular surfaces of the proximal radius and distal humerus (2% in each), but is relatively common on the broken edges of the distal humerus shaft and distal radius shaft (13%). The articular surfaces of the distal radius (13%), the radial (14%) and ulnar carpals (17%), and the proximal metacarpal (20%) are also frequently burned, indicating that the lower leg and foot had been separated from the rest of the front limb before cooking by cutting through the carpal joint. These burning patterns indicate that the elbow joint was occasionally cooked with the entire radius apparently still attached and intact, although after cooking the radius was invariably broken open to extract the marrow. However, since many distal radius shafts are also burned, and since distal radii as well as metacarpals, carpals, and phalanges are quite scarce at Henderson, it appears that the distal radius was often simply broken off along with the foot at the kill and discarded there rather than being brought back to the village.

Several of the ulnae display classic impact fractures on the flat surface of the olecranon. Since the proximal ulna contains relatively little marrow, these fractures were probably made during butchering to facilitate stripping meat from the front leg. However, since proximal ulnae are quite common in the East Plaza trash, and since very few of the olecranons are burned, this stripping probably took place in the village after rather than before cooking. Like the proximal ulna, the head end of the calcaneus was also broken off, but since calcanei are quite scarce at Henderson and since several of them are burned (13%), it would appear that they were broken off during stages of dismemberment and butchering that took place before the rear leg was cooked and probably while the hunters were still at the kill.

Distal metacarpals and first phalanges (front vs. rear were not distinguished) are seldom burned (0% and <2%, respectively), while second and third phalanges are more often burned (11% each). Thus, the entire metacarpal, cut from the rest of the fore limb at the carpal joint, was probably cooked intact with the phalanges attached and then later broken open to extract the marrow. It is not entirely clear how or why third phalanges became burned, since this is unlikely to happen while the hoof is still in place. As already noted, however, lower fore limbs are relatively scarce at Henderson and were apparently seldom brought back to the village from the kill.

Let us turn briefly now to the rear leg. The proximal femur is seldom burned (<4%), and the part most often charred is the femur ball or head. In contrast, the distal femur is more commonly burned (nearly 16%), and most often directly on the surface of the epiphysis that articulates with the tibia and patella. Patellae, while quite common in the trash, are rarely burned. Femur balls are common in the midden, while pelves are not, implying that the proximal femur was disarticulated from the acetabulum at the kill by cutting, rather than breaking with a hammer or ax, leaving the head attached to the rest of the femur. The fact that few of the heads are burned is surprising, since one might expect them to have been exposed to the fire during cooking. The high incidence of burning on the distal epiphysis of the femur as well as on the proximal tibia (>14%), but rarely on the patella (<3%), indicates that the knee joint had been disarticulated prior to cooking. The knee joint was probably often still fully articulated when the rear legs were brought into the village.

Interestingly, like the heads of the humeri, many (at least 34) of the femur heads were cleaved longitudinally by an ax or chopper blow, presumably to open the shaft to extract the marrow. Impact points were again not obvious on the heads, implying that the blow was delivered to the proximal end of the shaft in such a way that the fracture continued through the attached ball. This conclusion is admittedly very sketchy and would benefit from direct replicative experimentation.

Metatarsals, distal tibiae, tarsals, and phalanges (front vs. rear not distinguished) are relatively scarce at Henderson. This implies that the lowermost portions of the hind legs together with the feet, like their counterparts in the fore limb, were often simply removed at the kill, either by cutting through the tarsal joint or by breaking off the tibia near the distal end. They were then discarded rather than being transported back to the village. It is of course likely that they were processed for their marrow content before being discarded. As noted earlier, the calcanei were often broken during this stage of butchering, probably to

Table 4.4. Fragmentation (FI) of bison bones by major carcass unit at Henderson Site (1980-1981 only, all proveniences combined) and Garnsey Bison Kill.[a]

Carcass Unit	Henderson Site			Garnsey Bison Kill		
	NISP[b]	MNE[c]	FI[d]	NISP[b]	MNE[c]	FI[d]
Axial	410	84	79.5	2660	848	68.1
Appendicular	1598	675	57.8	981	973	0.8
Total	2008	759		3641	1821	
Front limb	527	239	54.7	332	327	1.5
Rear limb	571	299	47.6	244	259	6.2
Total	1098	538		576	586	
Upper limb	649	278	57.2	190	146	23.2
Lower limb	636	397	37.6	791	827	4.6
Total	1285	675		981	973	
Upper front limb	371	120	67.7	116	83	28.5
Lower front limb	156	119	23.7	216	244	13.0
Total	527	239		332	327	
Upper rear limb	278	158	43.2	74	63	14.9
Lower rear limb	293	141	51.9	170	196	15.3
Total	571	299		244	259	

[a]Axial includes vertebrae, ribs, and sternum; appendicular includes all limbs elements, as well as carpals, tarsals, phalanges, and long bone shaft fragments (Henderson), excludes long bone shaft fragments (Garnsey); upper front limb includes scapula and humerus; lower front limb includes radius, ulna, and metacarpal; upper rear limb includes pelvis, femur, and patella; lower rear limb includes tibia and metatarsal.
[b]NISP, number of identifiable specimens.
[c]MNE, minimum number of elements.
[d]FI (fragmentation index) = 100 - (MNE/NISP × 100).

facilitate removal of the feet, but perhaps also to assist in stripping muscle from the rear leg. The few lower hind limb units that were brought back to the village display a pattern of burning somewhat analogous to that seen in the lower fore limb. The incidence of burning is moderately high on the distal tibia, especially on the edges of the broken shaft (8%), and moderately to very high on the tarsals (astragalus, 33%; calcaneus, 13%; lateral malleolus, 14%; naviculo-cuboid, 9%). An interesting contrast is seen in the treatment of the metapodials. Many proximal metacarpals are burned, but none of the proximal metatarsals show signs of burning. This contrast suggests that the lower hind leg and foot, when cooked, were usually still securely attached to the tarsals, and often probably to the distal tibia as well.

Fragmentation. The degree of fragmentation of different portions of the carcass provides additional insights into the processing activities carried out at Henderson. Ideally, such a study should include the many fragments and splinters of bone that almost certainly derive from bison. However, as noted previously, many of the fragments from the 1980-1981 seasons that could not be identified to specific element have not yet been analyzed. Instead, an alternative measure was needed that would provide a reasonable approximation of the degree of fragmentation. The approach used here is an index based on the ratio of MNE and NISP, devised by subtracting (MNE/NISP × 100) from 100.[5] This "fragmentation index" (FI) is tabulated below for each of the major portions of the bison carcass (Table 4.4). For comparative purposes, fragmentation values have also been tabulated for the Garnsey Bison Kill. The larger the value, the greater the degree of fragmentation. It must be borne in mind that all of the long bones recovered at the Henderson Site were broken. A fragmentation index of zero, therefore, does not mean that there was no breakage. It simply means that each identifiable fragment was sufficiently intact to be unambiguously counted in the MNE tallies.

At Henderson, axial elements are more highly fragmented than appendicular elements, although the difference is inflated by inclusion of many broken spines and processes of the vertebrae, as well as isolated unfused vertebral pads, in the axial NISP value. The difference in degree of fragmentation between the front and hind limb is not great, although the front limb tends to be more broken. Upper limbs are more highly fragmented than lower limbs. When examining upper and lower portions of the front and hind limbs separately, however, a pattern emerges. The upper front limb is highly fragmented, whereas the lower front limb shows little fragmentation. In contrast, the upper and lower portions of the rear limb are both similarly highly fragmented. In other words, processing that involved fragmentation focused on the upper front limb and the entire rear limb, but was less intense on the lower front limb.

Table 4.5. Age of bison mandibles from Henderson Site (1980-1981 only, all proveniences combined), based on tooth eruption and wear.[a]

Item No.	Grid Square (Level)	Locus	Side	Teeth	Age (Yrs.)	Comments
1571	509N549E (99.80-99.70)	East Plaza	L	dP_3, dP_4	< 1.0	dP_3 anterior facet just coming into wear; dP_4 unworn and just erupting; position of both with respect to alveolus displaced postmortem
1166	512N549E (100.02)	East Plaza	L	M_2, M_3	ca. 10	M_2 cupping but fossettes still present, enamel erupted above level of alveolus, metaconid height 8.20 mm; M_3 enamel erupted to level of alveolus, surface slightly bilophodont, ectostylid forms loop joined to main occlusal surface, metaconid height 22.00 mm.
1163	510N549E (99.50-99.44)	East Plaza	L	M_3	> 11	Fragment of M_3 in place, enamel fully erupted above level of alveolus; M_2 lost or missing; M_1 lost antemortem, root sockets resorbed

[a]See Speth and Parry (1980) for procedures and terminology.

Table 4.6. Age of immature bison bones from Henderson Site (all proveniences combined), based on stage of fusion of limb-element epiphyses.

Element	MNI		Age of Fusion	
	Unfused[a]	Fusing	Ox[b]	*Bison bonasus*[c]
Prox. humerus	4	2	3.5-4.0 yr.	—
Dist. humerus	0	0	15-20 mo.	3.0-4.0 yr.
Prox. radius	1	1	1.0-1.25 yr.	< 2.0 yr.
Dist. radius	1	0	3.5-4.0 yr.	Bulls 5.0 yr. Cows 6.0 yr.
Prox. ulna	1	0	3.5 yr.	6.0 yr.
Dist. metacarpal	1	1	2.0-2.5 yr.	3.0 yr.
Prox. femur	6	4	3.0 yr.	5.0-6.0 yr.
Dist. femur	2	3	3.5 yr.	5.0-6.0 yr.
Prox. tibia	5	1	4.0 yr.	6.0 yr.
Dist. tibia	1	1	2.0-2.5 yr.	Cows 3.0 yr.
Calcaneus	1	0	3.0 yr.	Bulls 5.0 yr. Cows 6.0 yr.
Dist. metatarsal	0	1	2.0-2.5 yr.	Cows 3.0 yr.
Phalanx 1	0	0	20 mo.-2.0 yr.	< 2.0 yr.
Phalanx 2	0	0	1.25-1.5 yr.	< 2.0 yr.

[a]Patella (1) from fetal or neonatal animal not listed in table.
[b]Data from Getty (1975:748, 756).
[c]Data from Empel and Roskosz (1963); these values differ slightly from those in Duffield (1973:133).

While the fragmentation values at Garnsey are lower in virtually every case than at Henderson, an expectable outcome for a kill site where comparatively little on-site processing seems to have taken place, the patterning among different limb units parallels what we found at the village. As at Henderson, the Garnsey fragmentation values for the front limb are similar to those for the hind limb. Also, as at Henderson, the upper front limb displays a much higher fragmentation index than does the lower front limb. And again, the upper and lower rear limbs have low and nearly identical values. These results indicate that on-site processing at Garnsey, while not extensive, tended to be focused on the upper front limb. The upper front limb continued to be the target of intense processing in the village.

While these results are interesting, and underscore another way in which Henderson and Garnsey are similar, they must be viewed with caution. The fragmentation index used here is far from ideal, and is sensitive to the degree to which the various elements can be identified from small pieces. For example, the higher values for the upper front limb may in part reflect the large size and highly fragmented state of the scapulae and the ease with which small pieces of this element can be recognized. Thus, until a better index is devised, these results must be evaluated by the extent to which they are compatible with conclusions drawn from other aspects of the data.

One other aspect of fragmentation at Henderson is considered here: the degree to which immature bones are broken in comparison with those of older animals. The average degree of fragmentation for the entire assemblage at Henderson (including immature bones) is 62.6. Interestingly, and perhaps counterintuitively, the FI value for immature elements alone is 40.2 (data from Table A4.1). While most taphonomists would expect the bones of immature animals to be more vulnerable to breakage or loss through a variety of attritional processes (e.g., Shipman 1981), at Henderson they are actually more intact than those of older animals. A very similar pattern was noted at the Garnsey Bison Kill, where immature elements in general were more likely to be found complete (Speth 1983:95). The principal reason, we believe, is that the carcasses of immature animals contain less body fat and less marrow fat than adult carcasses, and their bones therefore are much less likely to have been broken apart during butchering and subsequent processing. In fact, animals that are lean or "dry" are often cooked in stews together with other foods. Stewing or boiling would remove a significant proportion of the lipids from the cancellous tissues of the bones, making the bones, when discarded, much less interesting to scavenging village dogs (see discussion in Speth 2000).

Age Structure

Henderson in 1980-1981 yielded a minimum of 34 animals (maximum MNI based on the proximal femur); at least 10 (29.4%) of these are immature animals (maximum MNI for immature individuals also based on the proximal femur). The age structure of these animals is difficult to determine with any degree of precision, because the 1980-1981 excavations yielded no maxillaries with teeth, only three fragmentary loose teeth, and only three mandible fragments with one or more teeth still in place. The tiny sample of mandibles is described in Table 4.5.

In the absence of more precise indicators of age, the stage of fusion of limb element epiphyses can be used to divide the immature animals into broad age subgroups. The following fusion stages were recorded: fused, fusing, and unfused. Unfortunately, the fusion sequence for North American bison is unknown, necessitating the use of data from cattle (*Bos taurus*) and European bison (*Bison bonasus*) as approximations; though not ideal, the latter is considered the most suitable. These results are summarized in Table 4.6.

There are at least 10 immature bison in the Henderson faunal assemblage, based on counts of the proximal femur. Four of these individuals are represented by epiphyses that are just in the process of fusing, implying that these animals are approximately five to six years old. Unfused femoral epiphyses point to another six animals which are younger. One of these six animals is about three years old, based on the presence of single epiphyseal specimens, just in the process of fusing, from the distal metacarpal, distal metatarsal, and distal tibia. A fusing proximal radius indicates another animal approximately two years old, and a single unfused proximal radius points to a third individual less than two years old. A fetal or neonatal patella and a fragmentary mandible from an individual with an unworn deciduous premolar indicate at least one individual of less than a year old.

In sum, the Henderson Site produced a minimum of 24 (70.6%) adults and 10 (29.4%) immature animals, of which 4 (11.8% of the total MNI) were approximately 5-6 years old, 3 (8.8%) less than 5-6 years old but cannot be aged more precisely, 1 (2.9%) about 3 years old, 1 (2.9%) about 2 years old, and 1 (2.9%) less than a year.

For comparison, the Garnsey Bison Kill produced a total of 35 animals (based on skulls) of which 26 (74.3%) were adults and 9 (25.7%) were immature (based on unfused or fusing proximal tibias). These figures, similarly based on the fusion state of the limb epiphyses rather than on the eruption and wear state of the dentitions, are very close to those seen at Henderson, and indicate that both villagers and Garnsey hunters were taking animals that were nearly identical in terms of age structure. This, in turn, implies that the villagers employed strategies very similar to those used by the Garnsey hunters to trap the animals, and it also suggests that village hunting may have taken place at more or less the same time of year (in the spring; see Speth 1983). The issue of seasonality is discussed in more detail below.

If one determines the proportion of immature animals represented at Henderson by incompletely fused limb elements, but ignores differences in the timing of fusion among elements, the estimate is somewhat more conservative (20.5%). As indicated

Table 4.7. Frequency (NISP and MNE) of male and female bison limb elements from Henderson Site (1980-1981 only, all proveniences combined) and Garnsey Bison Kill.[a]

Element Sexed	Henderson Site					Garnsey Bison Kill				MGUI[e]	Marrow Index[f]	Grease Index[g]
	NISP[b]			MNE (%)[c]		MNE (%)[c]		(100 - %)[d]				
	M	F	% Sexed of Total NISP	M	F	M	F	M	F			
Dist. scap.	12	7	44.2	12 (63.2)	7 (36.8)	6 (30.0)	14 (70.0)	70.0	30.0	43.47	6.40	—
Prox. hum.	10	3	11.1	10 (76.9)	3 (23.1)	4 (25.0)	12 (75.0)	75.0	25.0	43.47	29.69	100.00
Dist. rad.	4	2	35.3	4 (66.7)	2 (33.3)	5 (38.5)	8 (61.5)	61.5	38.5	22.23	66.11	20.59
Prox. ulna[h]	7	2	20.9	4 (80.0)	1 (20.0)	8 (50.0)	8 (50.0)	50.0	50.0	26.64	43.64	17.69
Dist. mc.	4	1	55.6	4 (80.0)	1 (20.0)	4 (25.0)	12 (75.0)	75.0	25.0	10.50	67.08	6.04
Prox. fem.	29	14	38.7	29 (67.4)	14 (32.6)	1 (10.0)	9 (90.0)	90.0	10.0	100.00	33.51	46.55
Prox. tib.	33	10	29.9	33 (76.7)	10 (23.3)	3 (25.0)	9 (75.0)	75.0	25.0	64.73	43.78	40.09
Dist. mt.	9	1	41.7	9 (90.0)	1 (10.0)	5 (27.8)	13 (72.2)	72.2	27.8	23.93	100.00	8.31

[a]Specimens sexed in this table are the epiphyseal ends of limb elements that are the last to close; this permits the maturity of broken elements to be reliably assessed. For example, the distal humerus and distal femur were not sexed, because it is impossible to determine whether their corresponding proximal ends had been fused or unfused. Thus, a fused distal humerus or distal femur which falls within the size range of a female may in fact derive from an immature male.
[b]NISP, number of identifiable specimens.
[c]MNE, minimum number of elements.
[d]MNE (%) subtracted from 100 to approximate frequency of elements actually removed from Garnsey Bison Kill.
[e]MGUI, modified general utility index (see Binford 1978:74, Table 2.7; Speth 1983:97, Table 13).
[f]Marrow index (see Binford 1978:27, Table 1.9, col. 8).
[g]Grease index (see Brink and Dawe 1989:134, Table 20; note that their grease index values have been standardized by setting the highest value to 100.00 and scaling the remaining values accordingly).
[h]While the proximal ulna was the element sexed in this study, the MGUI, marrow, and grease index values given here are for the proximal radius; we assume that the ulna was often transported as a rider attached to the radius and hence serves as a close proxy for the frequency of male and female proximal radii.

Table 4.8. Frequency (NISP and MNE) of male and female bison carcass units at Henderson Site (1980-1981 only, all proveniences combined) and Garnsey Bison Kill.

Carcass Unit	Male Bison							Female Bison						
	Henderson Site				Garnsey Bison Kill[a]			Henderson Site				Garnsey Bison Kill[a]		
	NISP[b]	%	MNE[c]	%	MNE[c]	%	(100 - %)[d]	NISP[b]	%	MNE[c]	%	MNE[c]	%	(100 - %)[d]
Front limb	37	34.3	34	32.4	30	73.2	26.8	15	37.5	14	35.9	54	63.5	36.5
Rear limb	71	65.7	71	67.6	11	26.8	73.2	25	62.5	25	64.1	31	36.5	63.5
Total	108		105		41			40		39		85		
Upper limb	51	47.2	51	48.6	14	34.2	65.9	24	60.0	24	61.5	35	41.2	58.8
Lower limb	57	52.8	54	51.4	27	65.9	34.2	16	40.0	15	38.5	50	58.8	41.2
Total	108		105		41			40		39		85		
Upper front limb	22	59.5	22	64.7	13	43.3	56.7	10	66.7	10	71.4	26	48.2	51.9
Lower front limb	15	40.5	12	35.3	17	56.7	43.3	5	33.3	4	28.6	28	51.9	48.2
Total	37		34		30			15		14		54		
Upper rear limb	29	40.9	29	40.9	1	9.1	90.9	14	56.0	14	56.0	9	29.0	71.0
Lower rear limb	42	59.2	42	59.2	10	90.9	9.1	11	44.0	11	44.0	22	71.0	29.0
Total	71		71		11			25		25		31		

[a]Garnsey Bison Kill values represent total sexable MNE values for each element, regardless of whether they are proximal or distal portions (from Speth and Parry 1980:307-18).
[b]NISP, number of identifiable specimens.
[c]MNE, minimum number of elements.
[d]MNE(%) subtracted from 100 to approximate frequency of elements removed from Garnsey Bison Kill.

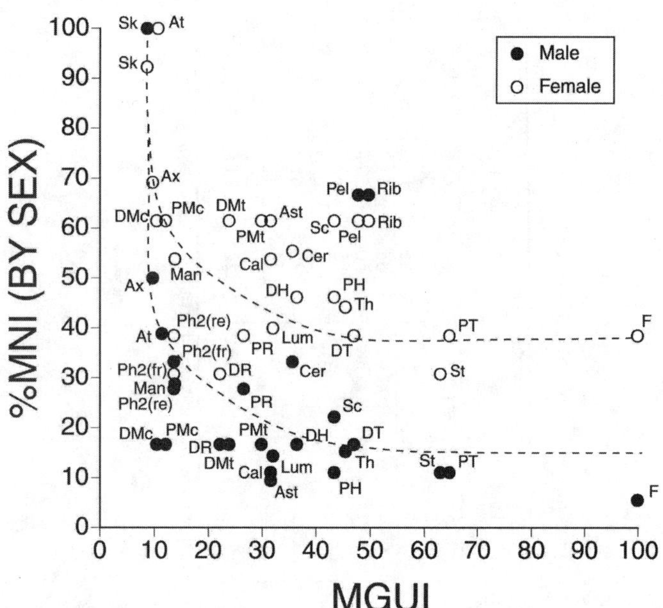

Figure 4.4. Relation between %MNI (male) and %MNI (female) and Binford's MGUI at Garnsey Bison Kill.

earlier, when broken down by phase, immatures comprise 13.6% of the Early phase sample and 21.9% of the Late phase sample. The Garnsey figure, computed in the same way, is 21.7%.

Total Henderson Bison Sample (1980-1981): By Sex

Introduction

The specific elements assigned to sex in this study were the distal scapula, proximal humerus, distal radius, proximal ulna, distal metacarpal, proximal femur, proximal tibia, and distal metatarsal. The procedures for sexing these particular elements in complete or fragmentary condition have been discussed at length elsewhere (see Speth and Parry 1980; Speth 1983:171-205, and references therein). One additional measurement has been added here. Since the only common and potentially sexable portion of the proximal femur was the head or ball, a variety of approaches were tried to separate specimens by sex. Kobrynczuk (1976) showed many years ago that the volume of the acetabulum could serve as a reliable indicator of sex in the European bison, *Bison bonasus*; we were successful in sexing the acetabuli of the Garnsey bison using the same technique. The volume was determined by building up the rim of the acetabulum with modeling clay to a uniform height and filling the enclosed depression with fine-grained sand. The volume of sand was then measured in a graduated cylinder. However, since bison innominates are extremely rare at Henderson, we reasoned that the volume of the femur ball might serve as a proxy for the volume of the acetabulum. Unfortunately, the femur-head volume proved too difficult to measure in a reliable manner. In the end, we used two partly redundant measurements taken on the femur ball that provided reasonably clear discrimination between males and females when cross-plotted against each other: the greatest craniocaudal diameter of the head (measurement C in Speth 1983:176), and the greatest craniocaudal circumference of the head (measured with a flexible or cloth tape measure, following the epiphyseal fusion line around the distal half of the circumference).

The sample of axial elements was too small to provide a reliable estimate of the proportion of male and female bison at Henderson. Analysis of the sex structure of the assemblage, therefore, considered only limb bones. Moreover, only the end of the element that is the last to fuse was sexed. This permitted the maturity of fragmentary specimens to be reliably assessed. Thus, for example, the distal portion of a broken humerus was not sexed, because it would be impossible to determine whether the corresponding proximal end had been fused or unfused. A fused distal humerus that fell within the size range of a female may in fact have come from an immature male. Interestingly, the appropriate articular ends of immature limb elements (i.e., those with unfused or fusing epiphyses) proved in most cases to be sexable, because their measurements almost invariably fell above the known range of mature female specimens, and often fell squarely within the male range. In other words, most of the immature specimens at Henderson turned out to be from male animals. Sexing the immature specimens at Henderson was possible primarily because these elements were from animals over about three years of age. By that age, male growth in bison has already begun to outstrip that of the female (see Halloran 1961).

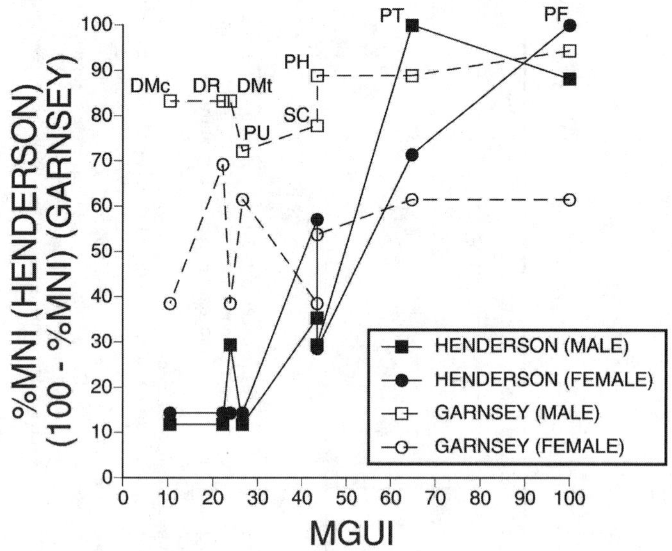

Figure 4.5. Relation between %MNI (male and female) from the Henderson Site and Garnsey Bison Kill and Binford's MGUI.

Table 4.9. Frequency (MNI) of male and female bison limb elements from Henderson Site (all proveniences combined) and Garnsey Bison Kill.[a]

Element Sexed	Henderson Site				Garnsey Bison Kill					
	MNI[b]		%MNI[c]		MNI[b]		%MNI[d]		(100-%MNI)[e]	
	M	F	M	F	M	F	M	F	M	F
Dist. scap.	6	4	35.3	57.1	4	8	22.2	61.5	77.8	38.5
Prox. hum.	5	2	29.4	28.6	2	6	11.1	46.2	88.9	53.8
Dist. rad.	2	1	11.8	14.3	3	4	16.7	30.8	83.3	69.2
Prox. ulna	2	1	11.8	14.3	5	5	27.8	38.5	72.2	61.5
Dist. mc.	2	1	11.8	14.3	3	8	16.7	61.5	83.3	38.5
Prox. fem.	15	7	88.2	100.0	1	5	5.6	38.5	94.4	61.5
Prox. tib.	17	5	100.0	71.4	2	5	11.1	38.5	88.9	61.5
Dist. mt.	5	1	29.4	14.3	3	8	16.7	61.5	83.3	38.5

[a]Specimens sexed in this table are those limb epiphyses that are last to close; this permits maturity of broken elements to be reliably assessed. For example, the distal humerus and distal femur were not sexed, because it is impossible to determine whether their corresponding proximal ends had been fused or unfused. Thus, a fused distal humerus or distal femur which falls within the size range of a female may in fact derive from an immature male.
[b]MNI, Minimum number of individuals.
[c]%MNI, MNI of each male and female element observed at Henderson, expressed as percent of maximum MNI value for each sex—17 male animals (prox. tibia) and 7 female animals (prox. femur).
[d]%MNI, MNI of each male and female element observed at Garnsey, expressed as percent of maximum MNI value for each sex—18 male animals (skull) and 13 female animals (atlas).
[e](100-%MNI), approximation of proportions of male and female elements in assemblage transported away from Garnsey Bison Kill.

The sex assignments for the combined Henderson limb bone sample are presented in Tables 4.7-4.9. Tables 4.7 and 4.9 provide counts and percentages for each sexed element. Table 4.8 groups the elements into major carcass units, using NISP and MNE values. The tables also provide comparative data from the Garnsey Bison Kill. In addition, Table 4.7 presents Binford's (1978) MGUI and marrow index values, as well as Brink and Dawe's (1989) grease index for the sexed elements.[6]

Sex Structure

The most striking aspect of the data in Tables 4.7 and 4.8 is the overwhelming predominance of males, even among the immature animals, regardless of which element is considered. Based on MNE values, the ratio of males to females ranges from a low of 63:37 for the distal scapula to a high of 90:10 for the distal metatarsal. The average ratio for all elements is 73:27; in just front limbs the ratio is 71:29, and in just rear limbs it is 74:26. The average sex ratio for all sexed elements from all five seasons of excavation at Henderson (1980-1997) is 67:33 in both the Early phase and the Late phase.

In broad outline, the patterning by sex seen at Henderson very closely complements the Garnsey Bison Kill. At the kill site, the proportion of female parts discarded vastly outnumbers discarded male parts. The average male:female ratio for appendicular elements at Garnsey is 30:70; in just front limb elements 33:67; and in just rear limb elements 23:77. If one expresses the Garnsey data in terms of carcass units removed from the kill rather than discarded there, the two sites display nearly identical patterns by sex.

At Henderson, rear leg parts outnumber front leg parts two to one (MNE) in both sexes, despite the greater number of different elements that could be sexed for the front limb. Clearly, many front limbs never made it into the Henderson trash. Some, perhaps most, were probably removed and discarded directly at the kill, although there is the possibility that some were removed from the kill and given or traded to other communities in the region. One reason for the obvious discrimination against front limbs is their lower bulk compared to that of rear limbs. But the front quarters, including the neck, are also more susceptible than the rear limbs to fat mobilization and depletion in the spring (the season when most bison hunting was probably done at Henderson; see below). Thus, lean or fat-depleted front limbs may simply have been dumped at the kill, a pattern strikingly similar to that seen at Garnsey (Speth 1983).

In the rear leg there is a strong tendency for the proportion (MNE) of male elements to increase as one moves distally down the limb (Table 4.7). A similar though less regular and pronounced trend is visible in the front leg. The predominance of males is most striking in the metapodials, and especially in the metatarsals, 90% of which are from male animals. Since the metapodials are important primarily as marrow bones, there was clear discrimination against females at Henderson when bones were transported for their marrow content.

The importance of male marrow bones in the culling and transport decisions of the village hunters is seen more clearly in the correlation between the proportion of male limb elements (MNE) and Binford's (1978) MGUI and marrow index, as well as Brink and Dawe's (1989) standardized grease index (%male vs. MGUI, $r = -.42, p = .31$; %male vs. marrow index, $r = +.71$,

$p = .05$; %male vs. grease index, $r = -.29$, $p = .55$). This result should not be taken to imply that bulk or general utility was unimportant in the villagers' transport decisions. In fact, quite the contrary, as we will demonstrate shortly.

Let us now look more closely at the patterning by sex of skeletal elements in the bone assemblage from the Garnsey Bison Kill. Figure 4.4 shows the relationship between %MNI and the MGUI for each sex at the kill (see also Speth 1983:94-96). The %MNI values represent the number of elements of a given sex removed from the kill calculated as a percentage of the expected number that should originally have been present based on the maximum number of individuals *of that sex* documented at the site. Shown here is a much wider array of elements than could be sexed at Henderson, including skulls, pelves, vertebrae, and many other parts of the skeleton. Both the male and female curves at Garnsey display the standard "bulk" form typical of many kill sites, in which high-utility elements are rare, low-utility elements are common, and parts of moderate utility are less well represented than might be expected just on the basis of their utility. The figure demonstrates that the utilities of various anatomical parts of females were ranked *with respect to each other* in much the same manner as were male parts, despite the high degree of sexual dimorphism in bison. It is worth noting, however, that while elements of both sexes form very similar overall distributions, female parts are much more widely scattered around their "regression line" than are male parts (both "regression lines" are hand-drawn approximations). Assuming this pattern is not merely an artifact of small sample sizes or errors in sexing female elements, it suggests that decisions regarding female parts tended to be more variable than those regarding male parts.

In addition, while the male and female "regression lines" in Figure 4.4 are close together for elements of low utility, they diverge from each other as one moves toward parts of moderate utility, and then remain widely separated but more or less parallel at the higher utilities. In other words, the higher the utility of a part, the greater the likelihood that the one discarded on the site will be female and the one transported will be male.

Figure 4.5 shows the same relationship displayed in Figure 4.4, but focuses on the eight limb elements that could be sexed at Henderson. We also have subtracted the %MNI values from 100 to approximate the proportions of elements that were transported away from the kill. (Although the ulna has very little usable marrow, we assume here that the ulna was frequently transported as a rider attached to the radius and hence serves as a close proxy for the frequency of male and female proximal radii.) At Garnsey, on average, 84.0% ± 6.9 of the expected number of male limb parts were transported away from the kill, compared to only 52.9% ± 12.6 of the expected number of female limb parts. The strikingly flat and widely separated male and female curves at Garnsey indicate that, among these limb elements, the hunters discriminated strongly against female elements regardless of their general utility. The flatness of the curves is also consistent with the evidence presented earlier that the hunters commonly removed whole limbs from the kill, with little or no on-site processing prior to transport. Interestingly, the female curve oscillates more markedly than the male curve in the low-utility range, suggesting that the criteria for accepting or rejecting these particular elements were more variable when preparing female limbs for transport.

Henderson yields a very different picture. The male and female curves are almost identical, with an average difference of only 0.4% ± 15.5 and, rather than forming an essentially flat distribution as was the case for Garnsey, the village %MNI values are strongly and positively correlated with the MGUI (see Fig. 4.5). This means that most of the elements brought into the village were high-utility ones, regardless of whether they derived from bulls or cows. This observation dovetails well with the conclusion reached earlier (see Fig. 4.3 and associated discussion) that village hunters transported a highly processed limb assemblage, one dominated by upper limbs, and particularly those of the meatier rear limb.

Earlier we said that the %MNE values for males at Henderson showed a strong positive correlation with marrow utility (which would mean that values for females were negatively correlated with marrow utility), and neither sex showed a significant correlation with the MGUI. Now we have presented data indicating that the %MNI values for males and females are both positively correlated with the MGUI. Why these seemingly contradictory results? To understand this, one has to keep in mind that the %MNE and %MNI values really measure two very different things. The %MNE values simply reflect the relative proportions of male elements compared to those of their female counterparts recovered at the site. The %MNE values, however, give no indication of how common a specific male element is relative to the number *of that sex* that would be expected on the basis of the estimated total number of *male* animals actually brought into the village. This information is conveyed by the %MNI values.

An example should make the distinction clearer. Looking first at MNE values, 90% of the distal metatarsals, an important marrow bone, are male, whereas only 63% of the scapulae, a poor marrow bone, are male. Thus, at Henderson the proportion of male elements is strongly correlated with marrow utility. However, there are only 10 sexed distal metatarsals from the site, and 19 sexed scapulae. Since there were a total of 24 individuals that could be sexed (17 males and 7 females), roughly 35% of the expected number of male scapulae and 57% of the expected female scapula were recovered, compared to only 29% of the male metatarsals and 14% of the female metatarsals. Thus, when %MNI values are considered, overall bulk utility, as measured by the MGUI, provides a strong predictor of what was transported to the site.

What do these data then tell us about the transport patterns of the village hunters? First, most of the carcass parts brought back to the community were from adult bulls. Second, regardless of sex the transported assemblage was overwhelmingly dominated by high-utility elements of the upper limbs, particularly those of the upper rear limbs. Third, while few bones that are useful primarily for their marrow content (e.g., metapodials) were brought back to the village, those that were transported were almost exclusively from males.

Earlier in this section we emphasized the striking similarity, or complementarity, between the Henderson and Garnsey bison assemblages in overall composition, sex structure, and age structure. We then introduced two subtle but interesting contrasts between the two sites: the removal of whole limbs units, both front and rear, from Garnsey; and the import of processed and selectively culled limb units, distinctly biased in favor of upper rear limbs, at Henderson. In light of these differences, are we justified in continuing to treat Henderson and Garnsey as components of broadly similar subsistence-settlement systems? While we cannot answer this question with any degree of certainty, the answer is at least a qualified "yes." The following are among the most likely factors that could lead to these differences.

1. Slightly different configurations of situational or logistical constraints that would alter the degree to which limbs had to be dismembered prior to transport, or that would change the value of front vs. rear limbs to the hunters. Such constraints include, for example, the distance between kill and village, the size of the task group participating in the kill, the nutritional condition of the animals, or the actual or anticipated degree of food insecurity facing the hunters at the time of the kill.

2. The presence of a secondary processing site between kill and village, where limb units were further butchered and unwanted bones, particularly those of the front limb, were discarded.

3. Food-processing and preparation techniques within the village that nonrandomly destroyed certain elements, particularly those of the front limb.

4. Differential discard patterns within the village such that front limb parts were less likely than other parts of the bison carcasses to end up in the trash.

5. Gift-giving or exchange that removed front limbs, along with ribs and axial elements, from the village.

6. Nonrandom loss of front limb elements through decay, trampling, carnivore destruction, or other taphonomic processes.

As already noted, there is no convincing evidence of severe taphonomic loss or bias (#6, above) in the Henderson assemblage. Carnivore gnawing, while present, is minimal on the bison bones. Complete loss of bison limb elements through decay, given their size and robustness, also seems unlikely. Moreover, the elements often cited in the literature as particularly sensitive indicators of attrition—the proximal tibia and proximal humerus—are among the most common and best preserved elements at the site (Speth 1983; Binford 1981).

The scarcity of ribs and vertebrae at Henderson, as suggested earlier, is very likely a reflection of exchange (#5). It is entirely plausible that many of the front limb units were also traded. We should note, however, that the contemporary communities to the west of Roswell in the foothills of the Sacramento Mountains not only have very few limb elements of bison in comparison to the number of ribs and vertebrae, but there also seems to be no clear bias at these upland sites in favor of elements of the front limb (e.g., Driver 1990). This in no way precludes the trade of front limbs by the Henderson villagers, but it would suggest that their trade partners did not reside in the Sacramento Mountains. As more faunal assemblages from upland sites find their way into print, we may be able to evaluate more precisely what bison parts were routinely involved in interregional exchange. Isotope and trace element studies may also help us pinpoint the most probable source areas for the traded parts.

Sampling bias (#4) is a possibility, but one that seems remote. In the 11 rooms that we examined in 1980-1981, we found very few bison bones. Virtually all of the bison remains that we did recover came from the midden in the East Plaza earth oven complex. Thus, it seems very likely that this assemblage should provide a fairly unbiased picture of the bison body parts that were brought into the village. Nevertheless, one remote possibility that has not yet been systematically explored is that some of the bison remains, biased in favor of elements of the front limb, were dumped down the slope behind (north of) the pueblo.[7]

Destructive food processing techniques, such as grease-rendering, at Henderson (#3) almost certainly contributed to differences in element frequencies between kill and village, but as discussed previously, this may have been a minor factor when dealing with bones as big and robust as those of bison. Even if bison bones were routinely broken up and boiled for grease, many of the fragments, including those from the front limb, would remain identifiable to element. Moreover, the fact that intact proximal epiphyses of the humerus are among the most common bones recovered at Henderson, despite the high rank of this element as a source of grease (Brink and Dawe 1989), suggests that the underrepresentation of front limb units is not due to grease-rendering activities.

In sum, Henderson and Garnsey may well have been parts of very similar subsistence-settlement systems, the differences in their bone assemblages stemming primarily from slightly different configurations of logistic constraints that altered the degree to which the bison had to be processed prior to transport, or the hunters' assessments of the utility of front limb units at the time of the kill (#1, above). What gave rise to these differences in logistic constraints is unknown. They could, for example, reflect shifts in the distance from home to the grazing areas of the target herds, or differences in the political climate of the region that encouraged or forced hunters to hunt closer to, or farther from, their village. However, the contrasts between Henderson and Garnsey could reflect real differences in mobility patterns, the Henderson hunters operating from a permanent or semi-permanent village, the Garnsey hunters operating from a temporary or seasonal encampment. Unfortunately, this last suggestion is difficult to evaluate.

Most archaeologists who work in southeastern New Mexico would probably rule out the possibility that the Garnsey hunters came from a village similar to Henderson. Most believe that by the mid-fifteenth century, when bison were being killed at Garnsey, the settled farming communities in the Roswell area had already been abandoned (e.g., Kelley 1984; Sebastian and Larralde 1989; Wiseman, Chapter 3). The most obvious farming villages that are known or believed to have had occupations more or less contemporary with Garnsey are located far to the west in the foothills of the Sierra Blanca–Sacramento Mountains, more than 100 km away (Kelley 1984). However, as noted before, these upland Pueblos had access mostly to bison ribs and axial elements; limb elements in these sites are exceedingly rare (Driver 1990). It seems unlikely, therefore, that the Garnsey hunters came from these communities, unless they routinely stopped at processing localities en route from the Pecos Valley back to the uplands where they culled most of the remaining bones. Such intermediate processing localities may remain to be discovered, but their existence seems unlikely.

But was the area around Roswell really already abandoned by sedentary or semisedentary farming peoples prior to the events at Garnsey? This traditional perception is based largely on two principal lines of evidence: (1) the scarcity of late prehistoric sites with permanent architecture in this stretch of the Pecos Valley; and (2) the absence, or rarity, in settlements such as Henderson, Rocky Arroyo, Bloom Mound, and Fox Place of ceramic types that were manufactured in the mid- to late 1400s.

A closer look at both of these lines of evidence shows that the date for the area's abandonment by village-dwelling farmers is, in fact, not as secure as it might seem, and that the Pecos or Hondo valleys could well have been the homeland of the Garnsey hunters. In the first place, the scarcity of late prehistoric farming communities in the Roswell area may be more apparent than real. The phenomenal growth of the city of Roswell, largely since World War II, has obliterated an unknown but possibly substantial number of small villages along the course of the Hondo. Many such settlements were still visible in the early 1930s (see Wolfe 1931) but are now destroyed. Interestingly, while a few of these sites had above-ground adobe structures (e.g., Henderson, Bloom Mound), the majority consisted entirely of pithouses, most of which were discovered fortuitously by arroyo-cutting, graveling operations, canal excavation, land-leveling, and so forth. The discovery and subsequent vandalism of the Rocky Arroyo Site in the 1970s, and more recently the discovery and systematic highway salvage excavation of the Fox Place Site (Regge N. Wiseman, pers. comm.), suggest that many more late prehistoric pithouse communities may remain undetected and protected beneath the alluvium that blankets the Pecos Valley and the lower reaches of its major tributaries such as the Hondo.

The Rocky Arroyo Site, despite its below-ground architecture, is very similar to Henderson's Late phase in age (see Chapter 3), artifactual content, and overall subsistence base, although the difference in architecture implies a fundamental difference in season of occupation, community organization, or mobility patterns (Regge N. Wiseman, pers. comm.; Gilman 1987). In any case, the Roswell area pithouse communities may not only have been developmental antecedents to later Pueblo villages such as Henderson and Bloom Mound; from about A.D. 1250 onward they may also have been one of the principal settlement types of the area's farmers, and one or more of these sites may well have been occupied into the mid-fifteenth century.

Another reason why we cannot rule out the Roswell area as the homeland for the Garnsey hunters is that the termination dates currently assigned to sites in the area are based on tenuous assumptions about when certain ceramic types ceased being manufactured. For example, none of Henderson's major ceramic types are thought to have been made past about A.D. 1400 (see Chapter 3). But in most cases it is not really known whether these types actually disappeared by A.D. 1400, or A.D. 1450, or even as late as A.D. 1500. In other words, given the current uncertainty about the appropriate end-dates for many of the principal ceramic types found in this part of the Southwest, it is possible that the Garnsey hunters came from a local settlement. Even the role of Henderson as their home base cannot confidently be ruled out on the basis of the ceramics alone.

Other lines of evidence from Henderson, Bloom Mound, Rocky Arroyo, and Fox Place, however, make it unlikely that the Garnsey hunters came from these particular communities. First, at Henderson almost all of the bison remains came either from the Great Depression, Main Bar East, or East Plaza, all of which appear to date entirely to the last third or half of the thirteenth century and perhaps the first decades of the fourteenth century, preceding the kill events at Garnsey by well over a century (see Chapter 2). The masses of bison bones found in 1994 in the Great Depression, though not yet radiocarbon dated, on stratigraphic grounds appear to be slightly earlier than those found in the East Plaza, and therefore considerably older than the Garnsey remains as well. Bison are also abundant at Rocky Arroyo, and perhaps also at Bloom Mound, but there is no evidence as yet that either of these sites lasted beyond A.D. 1400.

Perhaps more telling is the fact that out of the ten projectile points recovered from the Garnsey Site at least two were Harrell points (Speth 1983). In striking contrast, in a sample of several hundred identifiable points found at the Henderson Site, only one was a Harrell, and this specimen was found in disturbed deposits close to the surface (see Chapter 15). This style of projectile point also seems to be either rare or absent at Fox Place, Rocky Arroyo, and Bloom Mound. The Harrell point is a distinctive, small triangular arrowhead with a concave base, two side notches, and a third notch in the basal concavity itself (Bell 1958). This type does not appear in southeastern New Mexico until about A.D. 1400 at the earliest, and more likely not until ca. A.D. 1450 (Parry and Speth 1984:31-32). Its presence at Garnsey and its virtual absence at Henderson and the other known villages in the area, therefore, is consistent with the view that these communities were no longer occupied by the time hunters were active at Garnsey. Clearly, the Harrell point can serve as a valuable chronological marker, and its presence and frequency in other late prehistoric villages in the Roswell area may provide us with a better understanding of when farmers finally abandoned the Pecos Valley lowlands (or at least ceased being settled village farmers).

Thus, if the Garnsey hunters were operating from a base within easy reach of the kill, it seems likely that their settlement was an ephemeral encampment lacking permanent architecture. Many such sites exist in the Roswell area, judging by the numerous late prehistoric sherd and lithic scatters that have been reported over the years by both amateurs and professionals; many of these sites have yielded Harrell points, indicating that they fall within the appropriate time frame. Unfortunately, few of these sites have been professionally excavated, and even fewer have been systematically reported in the literature.

In sum, we do not know where the Garnsey hunters came from, but the pattern of whole-limb transport seen at the kill suggests that their final destination was not far away. In fact, it is likely that the home base for these hunters was an ephemeral encampment along one of the many drainages that once watered the Pecos Valley lowlands in the Roswell area. Since Garnsey is actually a palimpsest of many small kill events, it is possible that hunters from many different settlements used the same locality to hunt bison.

We turn now to one last issue that needs to be addressed in our discussion of the Henderson bison—the season or seasons of the year when most hunting occurred. We have already noted previously that the Henderson kills appear to have taken place during the spring. The next section provides the basis for this assertion.

Seasonality

Ideally, the seasonality of communal bison hunting events is determined by aging a large number of dentitions from young animals (e.g., Frison et al. 1976). Unfortunately, only three mandible fragments (and no maxillae) with one or more teeth in place were recovered at Henderson (in all five seasons of excavation). Only one of these (Lot No. 1166 in Table 4.5), a 10-year-old individual, could be aged with some degree of precision using crown height measurements. The degree of wear on both molars of this individual is nearly identical to that of a 10-year-old from the Garnsey Bison Kill (Wilson 1980:91), where multiple kill events all appear to have taken place in the late spring.

In the absence of an adequate sample of ageable dentitions, the high proportion of male limb elements at the Henderson Site provides strong indirect evidence that most, if not all, of the bison in the village were killed in the spring. As argued elsewhere (Speth 1983), bulls, on average, are likely to be in better shape than cows during the spring, because many of the cows at that time of year must support the high calorie demands of a full-term fetus or nursing calf. Moreover, in the spring new shoots of the preferred forage grasses, in particular the warm-season (C_4) species such as black grama (*Bouteloua eriopoda*) and buffalo grass (*Buchloe dactyloides*), have not yet emerged (Speth 1983). As a consequence, many of the cows by late spring may have become severely stressed, with much of their body and marrow fat mobilized or depleted. And, as discussed earlier, fat-depleted meat and marrow from stressed animals may be of limited value to hunters in the spring who might themselves be nutritionally stressed (Speth and Spielmann 1983; Speth 1987, 1989, 1990, 1991b; Cordain et al. 2000). Spring-season use of such parts, therefore, is likely to be minimized by hunters whenever a choice is possible. At Henderson, a procurement and processing pattern with an overall focus on male animals, and an increase in the proportion of male elements with high marrow utility, provides an indirect but nevertheless compelling argument that the villagers did most, if not all, of their bison hunting in the spring.

If the preferential targeting of bulls and the deliberate selection of male high-utility marrow bones are in fact signs that hunting took place during the spring, then the Henderson Site has produced little or no evidence of a fall or early winter bison hunt. Since ethnographically documented farmers in the Southwest and elsewhere in North America commonly hunted deer, bison, and other large mammals following the harvest (e.g., Speth and Scott 1989), the absence of clear evidence at Henderson for a fall bison hunt is surprising. The most obvious explanation is that bison were beyond the effective logistical range of the Henderson villagers at that time of year. Unfortunately, the seasonal movements of bison in and out of the Pecos Valley, particularly in its middle reaches between Fort Sumner and the New Mexico–Texas state line, remain far from clear, and historical data relevant to this issue are spotty and at times contradictory.

The three earliest Spanish expeditions to explore the Pecos Valley—Chamuscado in 1581, Espejo in 1582, and de Sosa in 1590—observed tracks, dung, and bones between the months of July and December, but never actually encountered living animals (Hammond and Rey 1966:88-90, 207, 259-64). These chronicles provide the strongest direct evidence that bison may not have been available in the Roswell area from at least mid-summer through the fall. Espejo's account and that of Luxan, a member of the expedition, disagree concerning the presence of bison in the Pecos Valley. Espejo claims to have seen many bison, whereas Luxan explicitly states that only tracks were observed. Hammond and Rey (1966) cogently argue that Luxan's diary is more reliable than Espejo's in this respect (see also Bamforth 1988).

Another expedition, the Mendoza-Lopez expedition, crossed the Pecos River just south of the New Mexico state line in mid-January 1684, observing numerous bison in and adjacent to the valley (Bolton 1946:328-33). This same expedition recrossed the Pecos somewhat farther south on its return in the latter part of May of 1684, again encountering bison throughout the region (Bolton 1946:342). The observations of this expedition, while interesting, tell us little about the availability of bison during the summer and fall. Moreover, their return in May took the expedition well south of the region of concern to us here.

A 1785-1786 Spanish account of attempts to establish peace with the Comanches and enlist their aid to subdue the Mescalero Apaches indicates that bison normally wintered in the Pecos Valley region:

> They next went on to confer about the proposed translation of the war to the neighborhood of the Rio del Norte to which Ecueracapa [Comanche chief] responded that the nation, being pleased, agreed to it. He was only awaiting the return of those who were going with our expedition to begin the campaigns through that region [Mescalero country] with ardor, assuring that they would be so much more active from October until spring because during this time the buffalo herds on which they subsisted particularly [ranged] from the Rio Pecos to the west. Thus they would have this source nearby to provide themselves with supplies so that he could always have parties combing the enemy country as they had resolved. [Thomas 1932:319-20]

While this report provides additional evidence that bison were present in the Pecos Valley during the fall, it appears to be referring to an area near, or south of, the New Mexico–Texas state line, again quite far for hunters operating out of a village in the Roswell area.

A report on a reconnaissance of the Sacramento Mountains in January of 1850 by a detachment of the United States Army indicated that the Mescalero Apaches had moved to the Pecos Valley or the country to the north to hunt "where the buffalo ranges at this season of the year" (Steen 1850, cited in Basehart 1974:23, 87). Unfortunately, the precise area referred to in this report is again unclear, and might well be as far north as the Canadian drainage in northeastern New Mexico or the Texas Panhandle.

A letter written on November 24, 1875, from Bosque Grande, New Mexico, a point on the Pecos River about 60 km north of Roswell, states:

> There are a great many buffalo on the Pecos all around Bosque. I went out the other day and killed one and it was very fat. Tell Add and Willie to come down and take a buffalo hunt. Billy Maxwell and some Mexicans are here from Fort Sumner hunting buffalo. [Klasner 1972:142]

Similarly, George Causey, a buffalo hunter on the Southern High Plains, reputedly observed bison sometime during the winter of 1878 in the sand hill country directly east-southeast of Roswell (Whitlock 1970:10-11).

Thus, the three earliest Spanish expeditions to explore the Pecos saw no actual herds of bison anywhere along the valley, including the Roswell area, between the months of July and December, but they did observe their tracks, dung, and skeletal remains, clear indications that bison made regular use of the valley at other times of year. Unfortunately, later accounts appear to contradict the earlier ones, reporting the presence of bison from October or November well into spring. Several of these later accounts, however, may be referring to portions of the Pecos well south of the New Mexico state line, while others may be referring to the Canadian drainage and adjacent areas of New Mexico and Texas well to the north of Roswell. The mid-nineteenth-century accounts—the letter from Bosque Grande and the Causey report—nonetheless clearly place bison within a few miles of the Roswell area during the fall and winter. These accounts must be viewed with particular caution, however, because in these two cases the presence of bison in the Pecos Valley area may reflect an anomalous situation brought about by the final slaughter of the southern herd. This tragic event was in full swing in the 1870s, and may have driven animals off the High Plains in search of refuge from the army of hunters that was pursuing them.

We are left with considerable uncertainty as to whether bison were actually present in the Roswell area during the fall and early winter prior to the Spanish entrada. Based on the earliest Spanish chronicles for the Pecos region, it is tempting to conclude that they were not. This conclusion must be viewed with caution, however, for several reasons. First, there are remains of female bison at Henderson, albeit not many, and without dentitions it is impossible to determine whether these animals were killed in the spring along with the bulls, or were taken during the fall. Second, if fall hunting took place far away from Henderson, far enough that an extended trek was necessary, few bones may have been transported back to the village, and the fall hunt might be virtually invisible archaeologically. Third, all of the historical accounts fall within the time frame of the so-called "Little Ice Age," a period which witnessed major climatic and environmental changes throughout the northern hemisphere (Lamb 1982; Sanchez and Kutzbach 1974). It is possible, therefore, that the fall and winter grazing range of bison during the thirteenth- and fourteenth-century Henderson occupation differed from the pattern which emerged during the subsequent "Little Ice Age."

The most parsimonious explanation for the absence of evidence at Henderson for a fall bison hunt is that bison were simply unavailable within a reasonable distance of the village at that time of year. Since farmers often engage in large-mammal hunting once the harvest is in, this might imply that the villagers shifted their efforts from bison to antelope, the other comparatively large species that is well represented in the Henderson faunal remains (deer are present but rare). However, as Chapters 5, 8, 9, and 12 will show, most or all of the antelope, lagomorphs, prairie dogs, and catfish were also hunted or caught in the spring or summer. Thus, if Henderson remained occupied throughout the year, meat from both large and small mammals, as well as catfish, probably formed only a minor part of the villagers' diet during the fall and winter months. But it is also possible that the villagers partially or totally abandoned Henderson after the harvest, in order to exploit bison or other resources elsewhere, not returning to the village until late in the winter or early the next spring, when they once again took up bison hunting in and near the Pecos Valley.[8] While speculative, this is an intriguing possibility, for it would mean that Henderson, despite its size (≈100 rooms), the amount of labor invested in its construction, and the obvious importance of maize in the villagers' diet, was either not a year-round settlement, or remained occupied for several months each year by only a fraction of its total population. This raises another issue—is it possible that late prehistoric Puebloan communities in other parts of the Southwest, often assumed to be fully sedentary on precisely the same criteria of size, permanence of architecture, and reliance on cultigens, might also be semisedentary? While this question is far from new, it is one that has not received the attention it deserves.

Henderson Bison Sample by Provenience (1980-1981): Both Sexes Combined

Introduction

Three major proveniences are considered in the next two sections: East Plaza (trenches B, C, D); East Bar room block (trench A; Rooms E-1 through E-6); and (3) Center Bar room block (trench F; Rooms C-1 through C-6). As noted earlier, the vast majority of the village's bison remains recovered in 1980-1981 came from a single trench (C) in the East Plaza (82%). This hinders comparisons with the room blocks, which produced extremely small samples of bison bone, and it all but precludes comparisons involving individual rooms. Bearing in mind these problems, the samples from the room block excavations nevertheless are large enough—128 bones from the East Bar and 171 bones from the Center Bar—to reveal several interesting contrasts with the remains in the East Plaza.

Element Frequencies

Carcass Units. As shown in Table 4.10, the element frequencies, grouped by major carcass units, are very similar in the room blocks and East Plaza (given the small sample sizes from the rooms, we are concerned here with the values for the "combined room blocks"). The only possible difference between the two contexts is seen in the rear limb, although the contrast is not statistically significant. In the East Plaza, upper and lower rear limb elements are represented in nearly identical frequencies, whereas in the room blocks, lower rear limb elements (tibia, tarsals, metatarsal, and phalanges) outnumber those from the upper rear limb (femur, patella) by a ratio of nearly three to two.

Burning. Table 4.11 compares the frequency of burned elements in the room blocks and East Plaza. Again, the elements are grouped by major carcass units. In most carcass units, the proportion of burned elements is higher in the room blocks than in the East Plaza. The difference is least marked in bones of the upper limb, especially in those of the upper front limb, and most pronounced in bones of the lower limb, particularly in those of the rear leg. As shown in the table, several of these contrasts are statistically significant.

Intuitively, one might expect the incidence of burning to be greater in the East Plaza than in trash dumped into rooms, given the presence of the massive earth oven complex in the plaza. This expectation would hold if roasting or pit-baking do, in fact, produce more burned bone than other cooking techniques. Unfortunately, archaeologists really understand very little about the relationship between cooking technique and the incidence of burning on bones (we return to this interesting issue in Chapter 14; for additional discussion of the relationship between cooking and charring of bones, see Binford 1978; Gifford-Gonzalez 1989, 1993; Jones 1993; Kent 1993; Oliver 1993; Vigne and Marinval-Vigne 1983; Yellen 1977, 1991a, 1991b). In fact, prehistorians often assume that most burning on bones is not produced when meat is cooked, but instead when bones are tossed into a fire, or a hearth is repositioned or rekindled over previously discarded debris (e.g., Stiner et al. 1995). This view has been stated most forcefully by Susan Kent (1993:348), based upon her ethnoarchaeological research among Kalahari San (Bushman) hunter-gatherers in the Kutse Game Reserve:

> I conclude that it is not appropriate to use burning as evidence of cooking. At least at Kutse, charring results more from noncooking activities, such as being trampled or pushed into the fire after deposition near a hearth than from cooking.

While Kent's conclusion may be entirely correct in the particular case she was examining, the patterning shown in Figure 4.6 suggests that a major part of the burning at Henderson is more likely the result of cooking than accidental post-discard exposure to fire. This is indicated by the fact that the probability of skeletal elements being burned varies in a systematic fashion across anatomical units, with the incidence of burning being low in axial parts, moderate in foot and front limb elements,

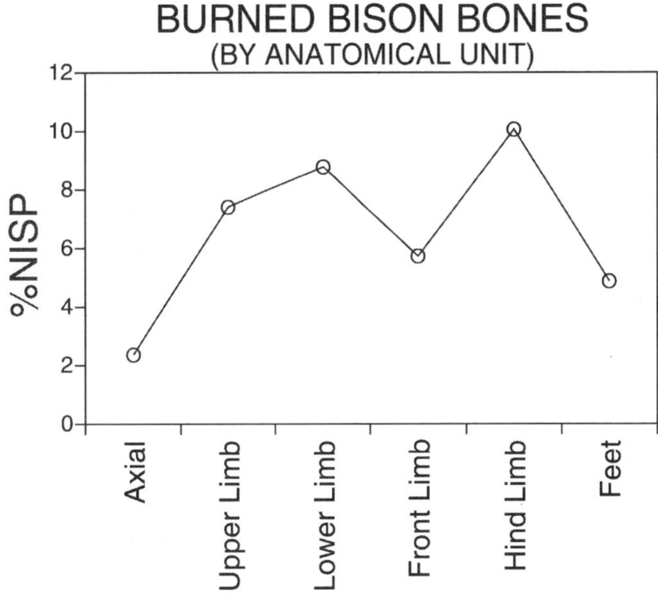

Figure 4.6. Frequency (NISP) of burned bison skeletal elements by major anatomical unit at the Henderson Site (all proveniences combined).

Table 4.10. Frequency (NISP) of bison carcass units by provenience at Henderson Site (1980-1981 only).[a]

Carcass Unit	East Bar (Trench A)		Center Bar (Trench F)		Combined Room Blocks (Tr. A, F)		East Plaza (Tr. B, C, D)		Test Statistic (t_s)[c]
	NISP[b]	%	NISP[b]	%	NISP[b]	%	NISP[b]	%	
Axial	11	8.7	40	23.8	51	17.5	359	21.1	1.52
Appendicular	115	91.3	128	76.2	243	82.7	1339	78.9	
Total	126		168		294		1698		
Front limb	38	52.8	37	55.2	75	54.0	449	47.2	1.49
Rear limb	34	47.2	30	44.8	64	46.0	502	52.8	
Total	72		67		139		951		
Upper limb	46	60.5	34	41.0	80	50.3	566	50.7	0.10
Lower limb	30	39.5	49	59.0	79	49.7	550	49.3	
Total	76		83		159		1116		
Upper front limb	32	84.2	22	59.5	54	72.0	316	70.4	0.29
Lower front limb	6	15.8	15	40.5	21	28.0	133	29.6	
Total	38		37		75		449		
Upper rear limb	14	41.2	12	40.0	26	40.6	250	49.8	1.39
Lower rear limb	20	58.8	18	60.0	38	59.4	252	50.2	
Total	34		30		64		502		

[a]Axial includes vertebrae, ribs, and sternum; appendicular includes all limbs elements, as well as carpals, tarsals, sesamoids, phalanges, and longbone shaft fragments; upper front limb includes scapula and humerus; lower front limb includes radius, ulna, and metacarpal; upper rear limb includes pelvis, femur, and patella; lower rear limb includes tibia and metatarsal.
[b]NISP, number of identifiable specimens.
[c]Test of equality of two percentages based on arcsine transformation (Sokal and Rohlf 1969:607-10; $p > .05$ in all cases).

Table 4.11. Frequency (NISP) of burned bison carcass units by provenience at Henderson Site (1980-1981 only).[a]

Carcass Unit	East Bar (Trench A)		Center Bar (Trench A, F)		Combined Room Blocks (Tr. A, F)		East Plaza (Tr. B, C, D)		Test Statistic (t_s)[d]
	NISP[b]	%[c]	NISP[b]	%[c]	NISP[b]	%[c]	NISP[b]	%[c]	
Axial	0	0.0	1	2.5	1	2.0	13	3.6	0.68
Appendicular	14	12.2	11	8.6	25	10.3	77	5.8	*2.42
Total	14		12		26		90		
Front limb	3	7.9	2	5.4	5	6.7	23	5.1	0.53
Rear limb	10	29.4	6	20.0	16	25.0	41	8.2	**3.52
Total	13		8		21		64		
Upper limb	4	8.7	2	5.9	6	7.5	39	6.9	0.20
Lower limb	10	33.3	7	14.3	17	21.5	32	5.8	**3.97
Total	14		9		23		71		
Upper front limb	2	6.3	1	4.6	3	5.6	18	5.7	0.04
Lower front limb	1	16.7	1	6.7	2	9.5	5	3.8	1.01
Total	3		2		5		23		
Upper rear limb	2	14.3	1	8.3	3	11.5	21	8.4	0.51
Lower rear limb	8	40.0	5	27.8	13	34.2	20	7.9	**3.90
Total	10		6		16		41		
Grand total	15	11.7	12	7.0	27	9.0	93	5.4	*2.23

[a]Axial includes vertebrae, ribs, and sternum; appendicular includes all limbs elements, as well as carpals, tarsals, sesamoids, phalanges, and long bone shaft fragments; upper front limb includes scapula and humerus; lower front limb includes radius, ulna, and metacarpal; upper rear limb includes pelvis, femur, and patella; lower rear limb includes tibia and metatarsal.
[b]NISP, number of identifiable specimens (burned).
[c]Percent burned of total NISP (burned and unburned) for each carcass unit (see Table 4.10 for total NISP values).
[d]Test of equality of two percentages based on arcsine transformation (Sokal and Rohlf 1969:607-10; no asterisk, $p > .05$; single asterisk, $p < .05$; double asterisk, $p < .001$).

especially those of the upper front limb, and highest in bones of the lower limb, particularly those of the lower rear limb (e.g., axial vs. front limb, $t_s = 2.69$, $p < .01$; axial vs. rear limb, $t_s = 5.25$, $p < .001$; axial vs. upper limb, $t_s = 3.89$, $p < .001$; axial vs. lower limb, $t_s = 4.38$, $p < .001$; front vs. rear limb, $t_s = 2.70$, $p < .01$; lower front vs. lower rear limb, $t_s = 3.03$, $p < .01$; head parts are omitted from consideration here because of sample-size limitations). If most burning occurred by accident after bones had been tossed aside, one would expect a random, or perhaps uniform, distribution across anatomical units. This is clearly not the case.

The nonrandom distribution of burning on bones at Henderson can be documented in three other ways as well. First, if we compare the proportion of articular ends (proximal and distal combined) of limb bones that are burned to the proportion of burned limb midshaft fragments, the values are significantly different (burned articular ends, 8.57%; burned midshaft fragments, 5.19%; $t_s = 2.06$, $p < .05$). If fragmentary bones were burned by accidental exposure to fire after they had been processed and discarded, shaft fragments and articular ends should have similar burning frequencies, but they do not.

Second, the average utility (MGUI) of burned bison bones ($\bar{x} = 55.66 \pm 26.96$) is significantly greater than that of unburned bones ($\bar{x} = 49.60 \pm 23.84$; $t = 2.09$, $p < .05$). Again, such a systematic discrepancy between the two categories would not be expected if burning were due largely to accidental post-discard exposure of bones to fire.

Third, the incidence of burning appears to be lower in juvenile than in adult bison (adult:juvenile, 7.9%:5.2%), although the difference is not statistically significant ($t_s = 1.16$, $p > .05$). Before rejecting this result, however, it is worth pointing out that the same patterning is present across all major taxa at Henderson, although none of the differences are significant (adult:juvenile rodents, 1.7%:1.5%; cottontail rabbit, 3.4%:2.1%; jackrabbit, 5.2%:4.8%; medium ungulate, 13.7%:11.1%; bison, 7.9%:5.2%). The failure of these comparisons to achieve statistical significance is undoubtedly due to the small percentage differences that are involved, as well as the very limited sample sizes of immature bones that are burned. If we nonetheless accept this patterning as real, and not merely a spurious artifact of inadequate samples, the results again imply that cooking, not accidental post-discard exposure to fire, produced much of the burning on the Henderson bones. Moreover, the lower incidence of burning in immature animals would also suggest that these animals were generally dismembered less thoroughly than adult carcasses prior to cooking, exposing less bone to fire, or that they were cooked in a different manner than adults. In light of their lower fat levels, immature animals often may have been cooked in stews.

Let us return now to the contrast between East Plaza and room block trash in the incidence of burned bone. If we accept that the incidence of burning on bones at Henderson is largely a product of the cooking technique that was being employed by the villagers, and not merely an accidental post-discard phenomenon, then the contrast between East Plaza and room blocks indicates that the character of the trash that was dumped into the rooms differed from the trash that accumulated in and around the East Plaza earth oven complex. A much higher degree of bone fragmentation in the room blocks than in the East Plaza also points toward the same general conclusion (see below). These differences in turn suggest that the processing and cooking activities reflected in room block trash differed in both type and intensity from those reflected in the East Plaza, a conclusion whose importance will become clearer in Chapter 14, when we compare the full suite of animal remains from plaza and room contexts.

Fragmentation. Table 4.12 summarizes the fragmentation data by provenience for the Henderson Site. As was done previously, the fragmentation index is calculated by taking the ratio of (MNE/NISP × 100) and subtracting the result from 100. The larger the value of the index, the greater the degree of fragmentation. Again, it should be borne in mind that all of the major limb elements recovered from Henderson were broken. Thus, an index of zero does not mean that the elements were complete. It simply indicates that the element portions were sufficiently complete to be included in the MNE tallies.

The most striking feature of Table 4.12 is the higher level of fragmentation, regardless of carcass unit, in the room blocks (combined) than in the East Plaza. Moreover, fragmentation is high in both upper and lower rear limb units, but high only in the upper front limb. By itself, the fragmentation index might reflect taphonomic or site formation processes, such as trampling or sweeping, that tended to bias the room block bone assemblage toward smaller, more highly fragmented pieces. However, it is hard to imagine processes of this nature that would lead to very different patterns in the hind and front limbs. Moreover, when looked at in conjunction with the burning data, the fragmentation index seems to point to real differences between room blocks and East Plaza in the way bison were processed.

Immature Elements. The proportion of immature bison elements (NISP) tabulated by carcass unit for different spatial contexts at Henderson is shown in Table 4.13. Unfortunately, the sample sizes from the room blocks (taken singly or together) are exceedingly small and, not surprisingly, none of the differences revealed by these comparisons is statistically significant. Nevertheless, the handling of the rear limb once again stands out as distinctive, and is therefore worth noting. In particular, the proportion of immature bones of the upper and lower rear leg is higher in the East plaza than in the room blocks. Also of interest is the comparatively low proportion of immature upper and lower front leg parts in both proveniences.

If the lower proportion of immature limb elements (especially those of the rear limb) in the room blocks is real and not merely an artifact of sample size, it could indicate that the bison in these deposits were procured during a different season (or seasons) of the year, or that the processing activities in the room blocks, while carried out at the same time of the year as those in the plaza, involved more stringent discrimination against

Table 4.12. Fragmentation (FI) of bison carcass units by provenience at Henderson Site (1980-1981 only).[a]

Carcass Unit	East Bar (Trench A)			Center Bar (Trench F)			Combined Room Blocks (Trench A, F)			East Plaza (Trench B, C, D)		
	NISP[b]	MNE[c]	FI[d]	NISP[b]	MNE[c]	FI[d]	NISP[b]	MNE[c]	FI[d]	NISP[b]	MNE[c]	FI[d]
Front limb	38	12	68.4	37	14	62.2	75	26	65.3	449	214	52.3
Rear limb	34	12	64.7	30	13	56.7	64	25	60.9	502	278	44.6
Total	72	24	66.7	67	27	59.7	139	51	63.3	951	492	48.3
Upper limb	46	11	76.1	34	11	67.7	80	22	72.5	566	257	54.6
Lower limb	30	16	46.7	49	29	40.8	79	45	43.0	550	360	34.6
Total	76	27	64.5	83	40	51.8	159	67	57.9	1116	617	44.7
Upper front limb	32	6	81.3	22	5	77.3	54	11	79.6	316	111	64.9
Lower front limb	6	6	0.0	15	9	40.0	21	15	28.6	133	103	22.6
Total	38	12	68.4	37	14	62.2	75	26	65.3	449	214	52.3
Upper rear limb	14	5	64.3	12	6	50.0	26	11	57.7	250	146	41.6
Lower rear limb	20	7	65.0	18	7	61.1	38	14	63.2	252	132	47.6
Total	34	12	64.7	30	13	56.7	64	25	60.9	502	278	44.6
Grand Total	87	34	60.9	123	50	59.4	210	84	60.0	1475	698	52.7

[a]Axial includes vertebrae, ribs, and sternum; appendicular includes all limbs elements, as well as carpals, tarsals, sesamoids, phalanges, and long bone shaft fragments; upper front limb includes scapula and humerus; lower front limb includes radius, ulna, and metacarpal; upper rear limb includes pelvis, femur, and patella; lower rear limb includes tibia and metatarsal.
[b]NISP, number of identifiable specimens; excludes long bone, cancellous, and indeterminate fragments.
[c]MNE, minimum number of elements.
[d]FI (fragmentation index) = 100 - (MNE/NISP × 100).

Table 4.13. Frequency (NISP) of immature bison carcass units by provenience at Henderson Site (1980-1981 only).[a]

Carcass Unit	East Bar (Trench A)		Center Bar (Trench F)		Combined Room Blocks (Trench A, F)		East Plaza (Tr. B, C, D)	
	NISP[b]	%[c]	NISP[b]	%[c]	NISP[b]	%[c]	NISP[b]	%[c]
Front limb	2	5.3	3	8.1	5	6.7	23	5.1
Rear limb	4	11.8	0	0.0	4	6.3	69	13.8
Total	6	8.3	3	4.5	9	6.5	92	9.7
Upper limb	4	8.7	1	2.9	5	6.3	51	9.0
Lower limb	2	6.7	2	4.1	4	5.1	45	8.2
Total	6	7.9	3	3.6	9	5.7	96	8.6
Upper front limb	2	6.3	1	4.6	3	5.6	14	4.4
Lower front limb	0	0.0	2	13.3	2	9.5	9	6.8
Total	2	5.3	3	8.1	5	6.7	23	5.1
Upper rear limb	2	14.3	0	0.0	2	7.7	37	14.8
Lower rear limb	2	10.0	0	0.0	2	5.3	32	12.7
Total	4	11.8	0	0.0	4	6.3	69	13.8
Grand total	6	7.9	3	3.6	9	5.7	96	8.6

[a]Upper front limb includes scapula and humerus; lower front limb includes radius, ulna, and metacarpal; upper rear limb includes pelvis, femur, and patella; lower rear limb includes tibia and metatarsal.
[b]NISP, number of identifiable specimens (immature).
[c]% of total NISP (mature and immature) for each carcass unit (see Table 4.10 for total NISP values); none of the percentage differences between the combined room blocks and the East Plaza is significantly different (significance evaluated using the test of equality of two percentages based on the arcsine transformation, t_s; $p > .05$ in all cases).

immature animals. The latter seems more likely for the following reason. As discussed earlier, the decided preference seen at Henderson for male animals, even among the immature age classes, and for male high-utility marrow bones, points to procurement and processing decisions strongly conditioned by both bulk and the lipid content of the animals. Since immature bison are smaller, and generally have smaller body fat reserves than adults (Speth 1983; Emerson 1990), it is not surprising that

Table 4.14. Frequency (MNE) of male and female bison carcass units by provenience at Henderson Site (1980 -1981 only).[a]

Carcass Unit	Combined Room Blocks (Trench A, F)				East Plaza (Trenches B, C, D)				Test Statistic (t_s)[c]
	Male MNE[b]	Female MNE[b]	Male %MNE	Female %MNE	Male MNE[b]	Female MNE[b]	Male %MNE	Female %MNE	
Front limb	7	1	87.5	12.5	64	15	81.0	19.0	0.48
Rear limb	4	5	44.4	55.6	96	21	82.1	18.0	*2.33
Total	11	6	64.7	35.3	160	36	81.6	18.4	1.53
Upper limb	4	5	44.4	55.6	94	22	81.0	19.0	*2.26
Lower limb	7	1	87.5	12.5	66	14	82.5	17.5	0.38
Total	11	6	64.7	35.3	160	36	81.6	18.4	1.53

[a]Upper front limb includes scapula and prox. humerus; Lower Front Limb includes dist. radius, prox. ulna, and dist. metacarpal; upper rear limb includes prox. femur; lower rear limb includes prox. tibia and dist. metatarsal.

[b]MNE, minimum number of elements.

[c]Test of equality of two percentages based on arcsine transformation (Sokal and Rohlf 1969:607-10; no asterisk, $p > .05$; single asterisk, $p < .05$).

young animals would be taken in smaller numbers than older ones, and that their carcasses would be subject to continued selective culling not only at the kill but at each subsequent stage of processing within the village.[9]

Henderson Bison Sample by Provenience (1980-1981): By Sex

One final way of comparing the room blocks and East Plaza earth oven complex is to examine the proportion of male and female elements in the two spatial contexts. Because of the extremely small number of sexable bones in the former, only data for the combined room blocks are considered. Table 4.14 summarizes these data (based on MNE) in terms of major limb units. Two interesting patterns are evident. First, more than 90% (NISP, 196 of 213) of the sexed bison limb elements from Henderson were concentrated in the East Plaza midden; fewer than 10% (17) of these limb bones ultimately found their way into room fill. Thus, most bison limbs appear to have been dismembered and processed, probably cooked, perhaps even consumed, and then discarded in and around the massive earth oven complex in the East Plaza.

Second, over 80% (MNE) of the sexed limb units in the East Plaza are from bulls, regardless of whether the unit is from an upper or lower portion of the front or rear leg. Undoubtedly, both their greater overall bulk and their more predictable spring season marrow-fat content contributed to the predominance of male limb bones in the plaza assemblage.

The pattern is somewhat different, however, in the assemblage of limb bones that found its way into room fill; in this case, the sex ratio varies in a more direct fashion with the utility of the part. Males again significantly outnumber females, but only among those limb parts that would have been comparatively low in bulk and most susceptible to spring season fat depletion in pregnant or nursing cows: that is, the front limbs and the lower or distal limbs. Among parts of higher bulk and potentially higher spring-season marrow-fat content—the rear limbs and upper limbs—females and males are more nearly equal in representation.

The clear contrasts between the bison assemblages in the combined room blocks and East Plaza—incidence of burning, degree of fragmentation, proportion of immature vs. adult animals, and proportion of male vs. female limb elements—all point to significant differences in the activity sets represented by the trash in the deposits from these two contexts. One likely reason for these differences is that the bones in the East Plaza reflect earlier stages in the processing of partially butchered carcasses brought into the village from the kill, while the less numerous, more highly fragmented, and more frequently burned remains in the room block deposits reflect later stages of processing and consumption.

But, as we shall explore more fully in Chapter 14, the differences appear to reflect more than just the temporal sequencing of steps in the handling of large, mostly male carcasses. Nothing shows this better than the average utility (MGUI) of male limb parts from the two contexts, which is significantly greater in the East Plaza ($\bar{x} = 61.1$) than in room fill ($\bar{x} = 42.2$, $t = 2.08$, $p < .05$). We would expect the utility of limb parts in the plaza area to be lower, on average, than in room fill, if the material in the East Plaza were merely debris left behind by the final stages in the dismembering and processing of carcass. Instead, it would appear that the activities recorded in the East Plaza differ from those reflected in room fill because they took place in a centralized and highly visible "public" or communal space, a context quite likely associated with important social and ritual observances, and one that probably involved the participation of most, if not all, of the community.

Table 4.15. Similarities and differences between Early phase and Late phase bison and medium ungulate assemblages.[a]

Comparison	Early Phase	Late Phase	Significance[b]
Bison			
Males (%)	67.4	67.2	$t_s = 0.03, p > .05$
Burned bones (%NISP)	5.4	7.3	$t_s = 2.38, p = .01$
Ribs (%NISP)	17.8	10.5	$t_s = 6.28, p < .001$
Room vs. non-room (%non-room)	54.5	80.6	$t_s = 17.1, p < .001$
Density (all proveniences) (NISP/m^3)	19.8	25.2	——
Density (non-room contexts) (NISP/m^3)	30.9	77.8	——
Marrow index (total NISP)	34.5	38.5	$t = 2.71, p < .01$
MGUI (%high utility)[c]	15.4	24.3	$t_s = 5.00, p < .001$
Phalanges (%)[d]	6.9	6.7	$t_s = 0.13, p > .05$
Medium Ungulates (Antelope and Deer)			
Room vs. non-room (%non-room)	44.0	45.0	$t_s = 1.01, p > .05$
Burned bones (%NISP)	13.9	7.1	$t_s = 7.52, p < .001$
Density (all proveniences) (NISP/m^3)	29.8	23.1	——
Density (non-room contexts) (NISP/m^3)	36.3	43.9	——
Marrow index (total NISP)	37.3	36.2	$t = 0.72, p > .05$
MGUI (%high utility)[c]	4.8	6.5	$t_s = 2.10, p < .05$
Phalanges (%)[d]	9.3	13.6	$t_s = 3.91, p < .001$
Projectile Points[e]			
Total points (items/m^3)	3.6	5.6	——

[a]The values presented in this table may differ somewhat from those given earlier in this chapter, because these analyses use all of the coded bison material from all five seasons of excavation.

[b]t_s, test of equality of two percentages based on arcsine transformation (Sokal and Rohlf 1969:607-10); t, standard unpaired t-test.

[c]High-utility elements, as defined here, include those with an MGUI greater than 60.0 (sternum, proximal and distal femur, and proximal tibia).

[d]Phalanges 1, 2, and 3 as percent of total NISP, excluding limb shaft fragments.

[e]Nearly 95% of the identifiable points are Washitas and Fresnos (see Chapt. 15).

Early Phase Bison: Great Depression vs. Main Bar East

Although detailed provenience-by-provenience tabulation of the bison assemblage recovered in 1994, 1995, and 1997 must await a future publication, these materials are of sufficient interest to warrant discussion here. Our excavations in 1980-1981 focused primarily on the Center Bar, East Bar, and East Plaza. Unknown to us at the time, all three of these proveniences dated to the Late phase. Most of the deposits we encountered in these first excavations were relatively shallow and therefore offered little in the way of stratigraphy. As a consequence, while we could examine many aspects of Henderson's economy in some detail, as we have been doing up to now in this chapter, we could say very little about how that economy might have changed over the century or so that the community was occupied. It was not until we returned to Henderson in 1994 that we sampled the Main Bar and Great Depression, and not until 1996 that we discovered, on the basis of the rim seriation of El Paso Polychrome jars, that these deposits predated those we had excavated previously (Zimmerman 1996; see also Chapter 3). Recognition that Henderson had two major occupational phases, separated from each other spatially rather than stratigraphically, permitted us for the first time to explore the temporal dimension of the community's economy. It quickly became apparent that there indeed had been significant changes, and that bison had played a pivotal role in these changes.

Some of the more striking similarities and differences between the Early phase and Late phase bison assemblages are outlined in Table 4.15. We include comparative data for the medium ungulate assemblages as well, because the role of antelope in Henderson's economy changed. Early and Late phase projectile point densities are also shown (see also Chapter 15).

The proportion of male bison is nearly identical (67%) in the Early phase and Late phase assemblages. (The figure for the proportion of male bison presented earlier in this chapter, based solely on the 1980-1981 data, is 73%.) If a predominance of bulls does, in fact, point to spring procurement, then there appears to have been no detectable change in the time of year when the Henderson villagers did their bison hunting. However, the proportion of high-utility elements (MGUI value >60.0) is significantly greater in bison than in antelope in both phases, with the difference becoming most striking in the Late phase. We take this to be the result of increasingly selective culling of lower-utility body parts of bison prior to transport, which in turn implies either that more bison were being taken per kill event, or that the kills occurred farther from home, or both. The average marrow index for bison also increases significantly in the Late phase, whereas the marrow index for medium ungulates shows little or no change over the same period. However, the ratio of cranial (upper head) parts to mandibular parts (NISP) in medium ungulates increases significantly in the Late phase, a strong indication that more complete antelope carcasses were being brought into the village (Early phase, 62%:38%; Late phase 77%:23%; $t_s = 3.19, p = .001$). Unfortunately, changes in the ratio of maxillary parts to mandibular parts cannot be checked in bison, because almost no skulls were brought to the village in either phase. However, the abundance of phalanges at the site provides an alternative way of comparing the treatment of bison and medium ungulates. In bison, these low-utility foot elements are comparatively rare, and show no significant change in proportional frequency from the Early phase to the Late phase. In contrast, foot bones of medium ungulates are significantly more abundant than those of bison in both time periods (Early phase: $t_s = 1.90, p \approx .05$; Late phase: $t_s = 7.47, p < .001$), and their proportion increases significantly in the Late phase (see Table 4.15). All of these contrasts between bison and medium ungulates, considered together, suggest that during the Late phase most antelope and deer were being procured closer to the village than during the preceding period, while bison were being hunted farther away.

The density of bison bones (NISP/m^3 of excavated deposit) increases about 27% in the Late phase, suggesting that more bison were brought to the community. In contrast, antelope show a striking decline in overall density, suggesting that their role in the village economy plummeted during the Late phase.

At the same time that bison appear to be increasing in importance in the village economy and medium ungulates are declining, the density of projectile points (nearly 95% of the identifiable points are Washitas and Fresnos) rises markedly, an independent, though indirect, indication of the increasing significance of bison hunting at Henderson.

Incidentally, in the Late phase, the vast majority of the bison bones occurred in non-room contexts, particularly in and around the huge earth oven complex in the East Plaza. Had we concentrated our excavations in the room blocks, we might have come to the conclusion that bison hunting was a very minor component of the village economy. However, the density of projectile points in the Late phase was high throughout the site, regardless of provenience, and would have clearly flagged the importance of large-mammal hunting in the village economy, even if our sampling design had inadvertently missed the masses of large-mammal bones in the earth oven complexes.

One of the most striking changes in the Late phase is the sharply increasing concentration of bison remains in non-room contexts. In the Early phase, roughly half of the bison came from the fill of rooms, especially those in the Main Bar East, and half came from non-room contexts, in particular the Great Depression. In the Late phase, the distribution pattern changed dramatically, such that fully 80% of the bison bones were encountered in non-room contexts, most notably in and around the East Plaza earth oven complex. This change is also clearly reflected in the density values (bones/m^3). The density of bison bones in non-room contexts more than doubles in the Late phase. In contrast, the distribution pattern for medium ungulates remains essentially unchanged from the Early phase to the Late phase. This is seen in the percentage values, and in the density of bones, in room versus non-room contexts. Thus, regardless of where bison and antelope were butchered and initially processed, during the Early phase roughly half of both taxa ended up discarded in room fill, whereas during the Late phase, antelope continued to be disposed of in the same manner, but bison increasingly became concentrated in and around a major public facility in the East Plaza.

The burning data further underscore the changes that were happening in the processing of bison and antelope. In bison the proportion of burned bones increases significantly in the Late phase, perhaps an indication that a greater proportion of the bison that came into the village were cooked in the East Plaza earth oven complex (we have already shown earlier that most burning is a direct product of food preparation and not the result of accidental post-discard exposure to fire). In contrast burning in antelope declined sharply in the Late phase, suggesting that meat from these animals was less likely to be roasted or pit-baked in the plaza facility.

Other changes are also noteworthy. Earlier we argued that the scarcity of bison ribs was most likely a reflection of their role as food items in intercommunity or interregional systems of exchange. The data presented in Table 4.15 show that the representation of ribs declined precipitously from the Early phase to the Late phase, suggesting that exchange involving dried bison meat intensified after about A.D. 1270.

A recently published meat drying index or MDI (Friesen 2001), a greatly streamlined and simplified version of the original drying utility index developed by Binford (1978), makes it possible to explore the role of dried-meat exchange in a more quantitative manner. Expressing skeletal element frequencies in terms of the percent observed out of the total number expected based on the maximum MNI value (%MNI), we find significant *positive* correlations, in both phases, between %MNI and Binford's (1978) marrow index (Early phase, $r_s = .39, p < .05$; Late phase, $r_s = .50, p = .01$), Binford's (1978) grease index (Early phase, $r_s = .44, p < .05$; Late phase, $r_s = .62, p = .001$), and Brink and Dawe's (1989) grease index (Early phase, $r_s = .75, p = .01$; Late phase, $r_s = .86, p < .01$). However, there is a significant *negative* correlation, in both phases, between %MNI and Friesen's MDI (Early phase, $r_s = -.45, p < .05$; Late phase, $r_s = -.48, p \approx .01$). As Friesen (2001:329) notes:

> Element distributions from dry-meat caches, and from camp sites at which large quantities of dry meat were consumed, are predicted to be positively correlated with the MDI, while ele-

> ment frequencies from kill or butchery sites at which dry meat was prepared for storage or consumption *elsewhere* are expected to be *negatively* correlated with the MDI [emphasis ours].

In contrast, %MNI values of medium ungulates (most of which are antelope) display no correlation with the MDI (Early phase, $r_s = .25$, $p > .05$; Late phase, $r_s = -.15$, $p > .05$). This result, of course, in no way precludes the possibility that some antelope meat was dried and exchanged with other communities, but the practice was not sufficient in frequency or quantity to bias the composition of the assemblage in the clear manner seen in bison.

Another line of evidence, this time ceramic in nature, underscores the sharply accelerating pace of westward-focused exchange in the Late phase. The five seasons of excavation at Henderson yielded a total of 1,560 sherds that came from distant source areas to the west and southwest of Roswell. Nearly 95% of these extraregional ceramics occurred in Late phase contexts (see Chapter 3). Thus, extraregional ceramic exchange appears to have been very limited in the Early phase, then increased explosively in the Late phase (i.e., after about A.D. 1270), and continued to intensify during the subsequent occupation at nearby Bloom Mound.

Synopsis

Excavations in 1980-1981 at the Henderson Site yielded over 2,000 bison bones, representing a minimum of 34 animals. More than 80% of these bones, from at least 31 animals, were recovered in a single large earth oven complex at the south end of the East Plaza. Had we not sampled this feature, we would have been led to the mistaken conclusion that bison played a very minor role in the diet and subsistence strategies of the Henderson villagers. The presence of this massive cooking feature in one of the village plazas was unexpected, as plazas in prehistoric Southwestern Pueblos were generally kept free of such debris.

The Henderson bison assemblage is analyzed in two principal steps. We begin by examining the nature and composition of the total assemblage from the village, first ignoring the sex of the animals and then looking specifically at differences in the treatment of males and females. We then compare the large collection of bones from the East Plaza midden with the much smaller sample from the combined room blocks, again first ignoring sex and then looking separately at males and females.

A number of characteristics of the material were considered at each step: (a) the composition of the sample (portion, state of epiphyseal fusion, presence or absence of burning), summarized element by element using NISP, MNE, and MNI values; (b) the frequency of elements grouped together by major units of the carcass (axial vs. appendicular, upper vs. lower limb, front vs. rear limb); (c) the frequency of burned elements, again grouped by major carcass units; (d) the degree of bone fragmentation, also by carcass units; and (e) the proportion of immature elements, once again by carcass unit.

Throughout the discussion, the Henderson material was compared to the bison remains from the nearby Garnsey Bison Kill, a mid-fifteenth-century kill site located on the east side of the Pecos River, approximately 32 km due east of the village. While the two sites are not contemporary, the kill being anywhere from 50 to 200 years younger than the village, the patterning at the two sites, in many respects, is so similar that it is very likely the two sites were components of similarly structured and organized subsistence-settlement systems. Nonetheless, some contrasts also emerge from the analyses and their implications are explored at some length.

We also briefly considered the bison remains recovered in the 1990s from Early phase contexts, particularly the Main Bar room block and the Great Depression, a massive earth oven complex located just north of the site. When compared to the bison remains from the Late phase, a number of interesting changes in Henderson's economy became apparent.

Looking first at the composition of the 1980-1981 assemblage as a whole, when element frequencies are plotted against Binford's modified general utility index (MGUI), the result is a curve that is a close inverse image of the bulk utility curve seen at Garnsey. In other words, elements of high utility are rare at the kill and common at Henderson and vice versa. The most striking differences between the two sites involve the pelvis, vertebrae, and ribs. The pelvis, despite the high utility assigned to it by Binford's MGUI, is common at the kill and rare at the village. But the MGUI was derived from studies of caribou and sheep, animals with small, easily transported pelves. The pelvis of bison is much heavier and bulkier and, like the skull, was probably stripped of edible tissue at the kill and dumped. Its scarcity at the village is therefore not surprising.

Ribs and vertebrae were both removed from Garnsey in substantial numbers, but were also rare in the village. Their scarcity at Henderson cannot be attributed entirely, or even largely, to on-site destructive processes, and instead very likely reflects intervillage exchange, gift-giving, or food sharing. This is shown, for example, by the fact that ribs and vertebrae of bison are both significantly less well represented at Henderson than are their much more fragile counterparts in deer and antelope, making it highly unlikely that the scarcity of these elements among the remains of the larger taxon can be attributed to the destructive proclivities of dogs. Bison bone assemblages from contemporary villages some 100 km and more to the west of Roswell in the Sierra Blanca–Sacramento Mountain area consist primarily of ribs and vertebrae, underscoring the probable importance of these elements in regional exchange systems.

The Garnsey hunters apparently transported whole limbs away from the kill, a pattern first noted by Lawrence Todd during a comparative analysis of Northern Plains bison kills. Moreover, they apparently made little or no distinction between front and rear limbs in their transport decisions. These observations suggest that the distance between Garnsey and the hunters' home base was not very far. In contrast, whole limbs were not being brought into Henderson. Instead, the villagers brought home primarily moderate- to high-utility elements of the upper limbs, having discarded most of the lower limbs and feet before the carcasses reached the village. And, unlike Garnsey, the village hunters brought in an assemblage that was distinctly biased in favor of the meatiest parts of the upper hind leg. These observations suggest that the distance, on average, between the kill or kills and Henderson was considerable.

On average, about 6% of the bison bones at Henderson are burned, although the incidence of burning varies considerably from element to element. Burning tends to be concentrated on the lower rear limbs. The incidence of burning varies in a systematic fashion across anatomical units, suggesting that charring resulted largely from exposure to heat during cooking. Had burning been the fortuitous product of post-discard exposure to fire, its incidence should either behave randomly, or perhaps uniformly, across anatomical units. In addition, epiphyses have a significantly higher incidence of burning than shaft fragments, an unexpected pattern if burning were largely accidental. Finally, mature elements are burned more often than immature animals. Again, if exposure to fire were largely accidental, there should be little or no difference between mature and immature elements.

The degree of fragmentation was approximated using a fragmentation index (FI), derived by subtracting (MNE/NISP × 100) from 100. The upper front limb was highly fragmented, while the lower portion of this limb was much less so. The degree of fragmentation in the rear leg was not quite as great as in the front leg, but the upper and lower portions of this limb were broken up to about the same extent. While all elements at Garnsey were less fragmented than at the village, no doubt a reflection of the limited amount of processing that went on at the kill, the patterning is still very similar to that seen at the village, with fragmentation being greatest in elements of the upper front limb.

Just over 29% of the animals at Henderson are immature, based on the state of epiphyseal fusion of limb elements. So few teeth were found at the village that age could not be determined in the standard way, using state of dental eruption and wear. At Garnsey, a nearly identical proportion (26%) of the animals are immature.

Another striking parallel between Henderson and Garnsey is in the sex ratio of the animals. At Henderson, 67% (73% using only the 1980-1981 data) of the limb elements are male. At Garnsey, over 60% of the appendicular elements transported away from the kill were male.

At Garnsey, kills took place year after year in the spring. The seasonality of these kill events was determined on the basis of the dental evidence. The hunters preferentially sought out bulls, killing on average about 60% males. As the animals were butchered, the hunters were much more selective in their choice of parts from cows than from bulls, abandoning many more of the female parts at the kill. For example, nearly 85% of the moderate- to high-utility male limb elements were removed from Garnsey compared to slightly over 50% of the female parts. The reason for this seemingly unusual behavior was that the hunters were selecting not just the parts with the highest total bulk or meat yield, but those parts with the highest total fat content (including marrow fat). In the spring, many of the cows would have been carrying a full-term fetus or nursing a young calf, placing a high calorie demand on the mother at a time of year when forage conditions were still poor. As a consequence, many of these females were likely to be nutritionally stressed and their body-fat deposits mobilized or perhaps even depleted. The Garnsey hunters were apparently keenly aware of this and chose animals and carcass parts accordingly.

If the preferential targeting of males at Garnsey is evidence of spring hunting, then, as at Garnsey, the Henderson villagers apparently also hunted bison largely, if not entirely, in the spring.

While Garnsey and Henderson are strikingly similar in many respects (e.g., overall assemblage composition, sex ratio), the two sites differ in two important respects (whole-limb transport at Garnsey, culled-limb transport at Henderson; similar treatment of front and rear limbs at Garnsey, bias against fore limbs at Henderson). Are these contrasts sufficient to suggest that Garnsey and Henderson were components of quite different subsistence-settlement systems? After discussing this issue at length, we conclude that these contrasts most likely reflect slightly different configurations of logistical constraints at the time of the kill, most notably short average transport distance in the case of Garnsey, long average transport distance in the case of Henderson. However, we also recognize the possibility that, by the mid-fifteenth century, the Garnsey hunters were part of a residentially more mobile system than had existed previously, as no settlement with permanent architecture has been securely identified in the Roswell area postdating about A.D. 1400.

The apparent absence at Henderson of a fall or early winter bison hunt, as suggested by the scarcity of female animals, raises the possibility that bison were not within range of the community at that time of year. This view is supported by the fact that the earliest Spanish explorers saw no bison in the Roswell area between the months of July and December. Unfortunately, the historic data on the seasonal movements of bison in this area of the Pecos Valley are not only spotty, but at times contradictory, as shown for example by the fact that nineteenth-century observers did encounter bison close to Roswell in the fall and early winter. This apparent discrepancy, however, could be due to the catastrophic disruption of the animals' seasonal movement patterns brought on by the final slaughter of the southern herd in the 1870s. Thus, while the most parsimonious explanation might conclude that bison were not hunted during the fall and early winter because the animals were beyond the effective range of the villagers at this time of the year, we cannot rule out the possibility that the village itself was seasonally abandoned. As subsequent chapters in this volume will show, a semisedentary settlement system is, in fact, a very real possibility, since not just bison hunting, but the hunting of antelope, cottontails, jackrabbits, prairie dogs, and catfish also took place largely, if not entirely, during the spring and summer months. It is hard to imagine that all of these animal resources would have been ignored by the villagers if the community remained fully occupied year-round.

Work in 1994, 1995, and 1997 revealed that several "Early phase" structures in the Main Bar began as domestic dwellings, but at some point in their domestic cycle were converted into store rooms. The evidence for this shift in function is provided largely by hearths, which were present on the primary floors of these rooms but absent in subsequent replasterings of the floors. If the village had been occupied only part of the year, and then totally abandoned for a period of several months, one might expect storage to be clandestine, perhaps hidden in subsurface pits located well away from the rooms. Widespread testing in non-room areas of the site in 1997 revealed no evidence of such hidden external storage features. Instead, we encountered many more bison earth oven complexes. The lack of hidden storage features, plus the presence of visible surface structures in the Main Bar apparently devoted largely or entirely to storage, suggests that Henderson was not totally abandoned after the harvest, but instead may have remained partially occupied by a segment of the population. This pattern of semi-sedentism is common in the ethnographic literature.

Comparisons of the 1980-1981 bison remains between proveniences within the village are hampered by the fact that more than 80% of these Late phase bones came from a single locus on the site—the East Plaza. Thus, it is necessary to combine the bones from all of the rooms into a single composite sample in order to make meaningful comparisons with the plaza assemblage. Looking first at carcass units, the principal difference between plaza and rooms is the greater proportion of lower rear limb bones in the latter. Burned elements, especially lower rear limbs, are also more numerous in the rooms. If we accept that the incidence of burning is not fortuitous, then the contrast between the two proveniences implies that radically different cooking techniques were employed in each. Unfortunately, zooarchaeologists still lack the ethnoarchaeological and experimental wherewithal to identify cooking techniques in the archaeological record with any degree of certainty. The degree of fragmentation is also greater in the room block assemblage than in the East Plaza remains. In contrast, the proportion of immature animals is lower in the rooms. Finally, over 80% of the sexed limb units in the East Plaza are from bulls, regardless of whether the unit is from an upper or lower portion of the front or rear leg. Both the greater overall bulk and the more predictable spring-season marrow-fat content of male limb bones contributed to their predominance in the plaza assemblage. In the room block assemblage, the sex ratio of the bison remains varies more directly with utility. Males again outnumber females, but only among those limb parts that would have been comparatively low in bulk and most susceptible to spring-season fat-depletion in pregnant or nursing cows—the front limbs and the lower or distal limbs. Among parts of higher bulk and potentially more reliable spring-season marrow-fat content—the rear limbs and upper limbs—females and males are more nearly equal in representation.

The clear contrasts between the bison assemblages in the trash of room blocks and the East Plaza in incidence of burning, degree of fragmentation, proportion of immature vs. adult animals, and proportion of male vs. female limb elements all point to significant differences in the activities performed there. One likely reason for these differences is that the bones in the East Plaza reflect earlier stages in the processing of partially butchered carcasses brought into the village from the kill, while the less numerous, more highly fragmented, and more frequently burned remains in the room block deposits reflect later stages of processing and consumption.

But, as we shall explore more fully in Chapter 14, the differences appear to reflect more than just the temporal sequencing of steps in the handling of large, mostly male carcasses. Nothing shows this better than the average utility (MGUI) of male limb parts from the two contexts, which is significantly greater in the East Plaza than in room fill. We would expect the utility of limb parts in the open plaza area to be lower, on average, than in room fill, if the material in the East Plaza were merely debris left behind by the final stages in the dismembering and processing of carcasses. Instead, it would appear that the activities recorded in the East Plaza differ from those reflected in room fill because they took place in a centralized and highly visible "public" or communal space, a context quite likely associated with important social and ritual observances, and one that probably involved the participation of most, if not all, of the community.

A brief discussion of the bison assemblage recovered in 1994, 1995, and 1997 was also presented. As these materials derive primarily from Early phase contexts, they allow us to discern several changes in Henderson's economy during the century or so that the village was occupied.

The proportion of male bison is nearly identical (67%) in the Early phase and Late phase assemblages. If a predominance of bulls points to procurement during the spring, then there appears to have been no detectable change in the time of year when the Henderson villagers did their bison hunting. The average marrow index for bison, however, increases significantly in the Late phase. We take this to be the result of increasingly selective culling of lower-utility body parts prior to transport, which in turns implies either that more animals were being taken per kill event, or that the kills occurred farther from home, or both. In contrast, the marrow index for medium ungulates shows little or no change over the same period. However, the ratio of cranial (maxillary) parts to mandibular parts in medium ungulates increases in the Late phase, indicating that more complete antelope carcasses were being brought into the village. These observations suggest that during the Late phase most antelope were procured closer to the village than during the preceding period, while bison were hunted farther away.

Bison density (bones/m^3 of excavated deposit) increases, albeit modestly, in the Late phase, suggesting that more bison were entering the community. In contrast, antelope show a striking decline in overall density, suggesting that their role in the village economy plummeted.

One of the most striking changes in the Late phase is the sharply increasing concentration of bison remains in non-room contexts. In the Early phase, roughly half of the bison came from the fill of rooms, especially those in the Main Bar East, and half came from non-room contexts, in particular the Great Depression. In the Late phase, the distribution pattern changed dramatically, such that fully 80% of the bison bones were encountered in non-room contexts. This change is also clearly reflected in the density (bones/m^3) of bison bones in non-room contexts, which more than doubles in the Late phase. In contrast, the distribution pattern for medium ungulates remains essentially unchanged from the Early phase to the Late phase. This is seen in the percentage values, and in the density of bones per m^3, in room versus non-room contexts. Thus, regardless of where bison and antelope were butchered and initially processed, during the Early phase roughly half of both taxa ended up discarded in room fill, whereas during the Late phase, antelope continued to be disposed of in the same manner, but bison increasingly became concentrated in and around a major public facility in the East Plaza.

The burning data further underscore the changes that were happening in the processing of bison and antelope. In bison the proportion of burned bones increases in the Late phase, perhaps an indication that a greater proportion of the bison that came into the village were cooked in the East Plaza earth oven complex. In contrast burning in antelope declined sharply in the Late phase, suggesting that meat from these animals was less likely to be roasted or pit-baked in the plaza facility.

Other changes are also noteworthy. The representation of bison ribs declined precipitously from the Early phase to the Late phase, suggesting that intra- and/or interregional exchange involving dried bison meat intensified after about A.D. 1270. Ceramic data underscore the sharply accelerating pace of westward-focused exchange in the Late phase. Nearly 95% of the extraregional ceramics that have been found at Henderson came from Late phase contexts.

In sum, the large assemblage of bison bones from the Henderson Site provides a number of valuable insights into the diet and subsistence strategies of these late prehistoric villagers in southeastern New Mexico. Some of these insights are straightforward, others more speculative, but all converge to form a remarkably coherent picture of hunting and processing decisions made by the village hunters. The following are the principal conclusions we feel reasonably secure in drawing from these analyses.

1. Bison formed a substantial part of the villagers' diet, outstripping antelope and deer, the only other large mammals at the site, in both absolute numbers of individuals and in total meat weight (see Chapters 5, 6 and 14).

2. In both phases, bison were hunted largely, if not entirely, during the spring of the year. Bulls were the principal targets of the hunters and, on average, probably comprised about 60% to 70% of the animals taken. Bison may have been beyond the effective range of the villagers at other times of year, although it is also likely that Henderson was at least partly abandoned for long-distance fall-winter bison hunting forays once the harvest was in.

3. Limbs were partially processed and selectively culled before they were brought into the village. Rear limbs were preferred over front limbs. The culling of front limbs probably reflects both their smaller bulk and their greater susceptibility to fat-depletion during the spring.

4. Rib and vertebral units may seldom have been brought into the village; or, as seems more likely, they were processed in the village and then taken as items of exchange or gift-giving to other communities in the area or to villages in the uplands far to the west of the Pecos Valley. Though less likely, front limbs may also have been items of exchange. Food exchange involving dried bison meat increased sharply in the Late phase. The ceramic evidence underscores the accelerating pace of westward-focused exchange in the Late phase. Virtually all of the extraregional ceramics occurred in Late phase contexts.

5. During the Early phase only about half of the bison remains were found in non-room contexts, such as the Great Depression, the other half coming from room fill in the Main Bar. In contrast, in the Late phase over 80% of the bison remains were concentrated in and around the East Plaza earth oven complex, with only 20% of the bones finding their way into room fill. This increasingly public handling of a large, communally procured resource underscores the growing community-wide social and ritual significance of bison to the Henderson villagers, a topic that is explored more fully in Chapter 14.

Acknowledgments

We were assisted in the analysis of the vertebrae by Lauren Bigelow. Our understanding of the bison materials recovered in the 1990s has benefited from work undertaken as part of two undergraduate honors theses, one by Erica Gooding (1995), the other by Laura Staro (1996), as well as lab analysis projects undertaken by Severin Fowles and Ramona Quesada. Our understanding of the extraregional ceramics recovered in the 1990s has benefited from work undertaken as part of an undergraduate honors thesis by Diane Miller (1998), as well as lab analysis projects undertaken by Heather Miljour and Julia Blough.

Notes

1. The excavations between 1994 and 1997 yielded an additional 1,785 bison bones. Of these, 694 came from the Early phase "Great Depression," 641 from the Early phase Main Bar East, and 281 came from the Late phase East Plaza (East). The remaining 10% came from the West Bar (32), Main Bar West (7), West Plaza (3), East Bar (75 or

4.2%), North Plaza test trench A (49), and small scattered tests elsewhere on the site (3).

Not all of the 1980-1981 fauna has been completely sorted as yet. However, virtually all of the identifiable bison have been pulled from the collection and are included here. The only obvious bison remains that are not included are small fragments of long-bone shafts, pieces of cancellous tissue, and very fragmentary vertebral processes. While proximal rib fragments were culled and tabulated along with other bison elements, and are included in the site-wide NISP of 2,027 bones, rib midsection and distal fragments were not sorted and tabulated until later, after all of the tables in this chapter had been completed. The frequency of ribs in the assemblage, however, became an important issue when we realized that they may have been removed from Henderson in the context of intervillage trade. As a consequence, it was decided to quantify all of the fragmentary ribs at the site; the results of this analysis are presented in the text but are not reflected in the site-wide NISP value or in the tables. While the many fragmentary pieces of limb shafts and other elements that have not yet been examined or counted ultimately will prove useful for resolving questions about the locus and intensity of various stages of processing and consumption, as well as aspects of site taphonomy or formation processes, their omission here should not seriously alter the conclusions of the present study. It should be noted that the total absence of identifiable remains of elk (*Cervus canadensis*) at the Henderson Site suggests that all of the fragmentary large mammal bones, including the rib fragments, derive from bison.

2. The high proportions of proximal tibias, proximal humeri, and distal femurs at Henderson, elements that are very susceptible to damage and loss, argue against severe biases in the assemblage arising from carnivore destruction or other noncultural biases. This conclusion is supported by the fact that signs of carnivore gnawing, puncturing, or pitting are rare on the bison bones. The abundance of epiphyses of tibiae, humeri, and femurs, however, also suggests that intensive grease rendering was not routinely practiced at the site, since these joints almost certainly would have been broken into small, often unidentifiable, fragments to extract the lipids (with the possible exception of the femur head or ball which is very durable and easily recognized even in very fragmentary condition). Other lines of evidence, discussed later in this chapter and in Chapter 5, lead to the same conclusion: grease production was not a major activity at Henderson. This conclusion, however, in no way precludes the frequent boiling of whole, or nearly whole, epiphyses in stews. Subsequent chapters, especially Chapter 14, will return to the issue of cooking technology at Henderson and to the apparent importance to the villagers of boiling as a means of food preparation.

3. The bison and antelope percentages are significantly different ($t_s = 5.04$, $p < .001$), provided that numbers of ribs rather than MNI are used in the calculation (test of equality of two percentages based on the arcsine transformation; Sokal and Rohlf 1969:607-10); the sample sizes are too small when MNI values are used.

4. The minimum number of elements (MNE) observed and the percent expected for the other vertebrae (bison and antelope, respectively) are as follows: atlas MNE = 3, 8.8% and MNE = 7, 29.1% ($t_s = 2.01$, $p < .05$); axis MNE = 3, 8.8% and MNE = 9, 37.5% ($t_s = 2.68$, $p < .05$); cervical MNE = 2, 3.5% and MNE = 3, 9.2% ($t_s = 2.01$, $p < .05$); lumbar MNE = 2, 4.1% and MNE = 3, 11.6% ($t_s = 2.41$, $p < .05$); sacrum MNE = 2, 5.9% and MNE = 2, 8.3% ($t_s = 0.35$, $p > .05$).

5. A similar fragmentation index, using the ratio of NISP to MNI, was used by Bunn (1983:145) in comparing bone assemblages from a modern San (Bushman) camp and a spotted hyena den.

6. Metcalfe and Jones (1988; see also Jones and Metcalfe 1988) have greatly simplified both Binford's MGUI, replacing it with a food utility index or FUI, and his marrow index. However, since both of the newer indices are highly correlated with Binford's original values, we continue to employ the older forms here. Use of the newer versions would lead to virtually identical results and conclusions.

7. Work at Henderson in 1994, 1995, and 1997 recovered a large number of Early phase bison remains in the Great Depression located just north of the Main Bar, and nearly comparable numbers of bones from Early phase structures in the Main Bar room block. Though the proportion of front limb elements (vs. rear limb elements) in these Early phase materials (54.1%) is somewhat greater than in the Late phase assemblage (48.4%), the difference is not statistically significant ($t_s = 1.80$, $p > .05$). Aside from the Great Depression, other test units excavated in the sheet midden north of the Main Bar produced very little bison bone, even though conditions for bone preservation were generally good.

8. Work in 1994, 1995, and 1997 revealed that several Early phase structures in the Main Bar began as domestic dwellings, but at some point in their use-life were converted into store rooms. The evidence for this shift in function is provided largely by hearths, which were present on the primary floors of these rooms but absent in subsequent replasterings of the floors. If a village were occupied only part of the year, and then totally abandoned for a period of months, one might expect storage to be clandestine, perhaps hidden in subsurface pits located well away from the rooms (e.g., DeBoer 1988). Widespread testing in non-room areas of the site in 1997 revealed no evidence of such hidden external storage features. Instead, we encountered many small- to moderate-sized bison earth oven complexes. The lack of hidden storage features, plus the presence of visible surface structures in the Main Bar apparently devoted largely or entirely to storage, suggests that Henderson was not totally abandoned after the harvest, but instead may have remained partially occupied by a segment of the population. This pattern of semi-sedentism is common in the ethnographic literature (see, for example, Murdock 1967, 1969; Murdock and Wilson 1972).

9. The greater selectivity exercised in transport decisions regarding juvenile animals brought to the village is clearly reflected in the fact that the average utility of the body parts of juveniles is significantly greater than that of adults (MGUI: immature $\bar{x} = 62.91 \pm 31.41$, mature $\bar{x} = 47.65 \pm 31.10$, $t = -5.31$, $p < .0001$; marrow index: immature $\bar{x} = 43.67 \pm 17.13$, mature $\bar{x} = 40.21 \pm 19.10$, $t = -2.00$, $p < .05$).

References Cited

Bamforth, D. B.

1988 Ethnohistory and Bison on the Southwestern Plains: A Minor Correction to Turpin. *Plains Anthropologist* 33(121):405-07.

Basehart, H. W.

1974 Mescalero Apache Subsistence Patterns and Socio-Political Organization. In: *Apache Indians XII*, edited by D. A. Horr, pp. 1-153. New York, NY: Garland Publishing.

Bell, R. E.

1958 *A Guide to the Identification of Certain American Indian Projectile Points*. Special Bulletin 1. Oklahoma City, OK: Oklahoma Anthropological Society.

Binford, L. R.

1978 *Nunamiut Ethnoarchaeology*. New York, NY: Academic Press.

1981 *Bones: Ancient Men and Modern Myths*. New York, NY: Academic Press.

Blumenschine, R. J., and T. M. Caro
1987 Unit Flesh Weights of Some East African Bovids. *African Journal of Ecology* 24:273-86.

Bolton, H. E. (editor)
1946 *Spanish Exploration in the Southwest, 1542-1706*. New York, NY: Barnes and Noble.

Brink, J., and B. Dawe
1989 *Final Report of the 1985 and 1986 Field Seasons at Head-Smashed-In Buffalo Jump, Alberta*. Archaeological Survey of Alberta, Manuscript Series 16. Edmonton, Alberta: Archaeological Survey of Alberta.

Brooks, R. L., R. R. Drass, and F. E. Swenson
1985 *Prehistoric Farmers of the Washita River Valley: Settlement and Subsistence Patterns During the Plains Village Period*. Archeological Resource Survey Report 23. Norman, OK: University of Oklahoma, Oklahoma Archeological Survey.

Bunn, H. T.
1983 Comparative Analysis of Modern Bone Assemblages from a San Hunter-Gatherer Camp in the Kalahari Desert, Botswana, and from a Spotted Hyena Den near Nairobi, Kenya. In: *Animals and Archaeology*, Vol. 1. *Hunters and Their Prey*, edited by J. Clutton-Brock and C. Grigson, pp. 143-48. BAR International Series 163. Oxford, England: British Archaeological Reports.
1989 Diagnosing Plio-Pleistocene Hominid Activity with Bone Fracture Evidence. In: *Bone Modification*, edited by R. Bonnichsen and M. H. Sorg, pp. 299-316. Orono, ME: University of Maine, Institute for Quaternary Studies, Center for the Study of the First Americans.

Bunn, H. T., L. E. Bartram, and E. M. Kroll
1988 Variability in Bone Assemblage Formation From Hadza Hunting, Scavenging, and Carcass Processing. *Journal of Anthropological Archaeology* 7(4):412-57.

Cahill, G. F.
1986 The Future of Carbohydrates in Human Nutrition. *Nutrition Reviews* 44(2):40-43.

Cordain, L., J. C. Brand Miller, S. B. Eaton, N. Mann, S. H. A. Holt, and J. D. Speth
2000 Plant-Animal Subsistence Ratios and Macronutrient Energy Estimations in Worldwide Hunter-Gatherer Diets. *American Journal of Clinical Nutrition* 71(3):682-92.

DeBoer, W. R.
1988 Subterranean Storage and the Organization of Surplus: The View from Eastern North America. *Southeastern Archaeology* 7(1):1-20.

Driver, J. C.
1990 Bison Assemblages from the Sierra Blanca Region, Southeastern New Mexico. *Kiva* 55(3):245-64.

Duffield, L. F.
1970 *Some Panhandle Aspect Sites: Their Vertebrates and Paleoecology*. Ph.D. dissertation, University of Wisconsin, Madison, WI.

1973 Aging and Sexing the Post-Cranial Skeleton of Bison. *Plains Anthropologist* 18(60):132-39.

Emerson, A. M.
1990 *The Archaeological Implications of Variability in the Economic Anatomy of Bison Bison*. Ph.D. dissertation, Washington State University, Pullman, WA.

Empel, W., and T. Roskosz
1963 Das Skelett der Gliedmassen des Wisents, *Bison Bonasus* (Linnaeus, 1758). *Acta Theriologica* 7(13):259-99.

Friesen, T. M.
2001 A Zooarchaeological Signature for Meat Storage: Rethinking the Drying Utility Index. *American Antiquity* 66(2):315-31.

Frison, G. C.
1978 *Prehistoric Hunters of the High Plains*. New York, NY: Academic Press.

Frison, G. C., and L. C. Todd
1986 *The Colby Mammoth Site: Taphonomy and Archaeology of a Clovis Kill in Northern Wyoming*. Albuquerque, NM: University of New Mexico Press.

Frison, G. C., M. C. Wilson, and D. Wilson
1976 Fossil Bison and Artifacts from an Early Altithermal Period Arroyo Trap in Wyoming. *American Antiquity* 41(1):28-57.

Getty, R.
1975 *Sisson and Grossman's the Anatomy of the Domestic Animals*, 5th Edition. Philadelphia, PA: W. B. Saunders.

Gifford-Gonzalez, D.
1989 Ethnographic Analogues for Interpreting Modified Bones: Some Cases from East Africa. In: *Bone Modification*, edited by R. Bonnichsen and M. H. Sorg, pp. 179-246. Peopling of the Americas Publications. Orono, ME: Center for the Study of the First Americans, Institute for Quaternary Studies, University of Maine.
1993 Gaps in Zooarchaeological Analyses of Butchery: Is Gender an Issue? In: *From Bones to Behavior: Ethnoarchaeological and Experimental Contributions to the Interpretation of Faunal Remains*, edited by J. Hudson, pp. 181-99. Occasional Paper 21. Carbondale, IL: Southern Illinois University, Center for Archaeological Investigations.

Gilman, P. A.
1987 Architecture as Artifact: Pit Structures and Pueblos in the American Southwest. *American Antiquity* 52:538-64.

Gooding, E. L.
1995 *Bison Remains in the Archaeological Record at the Henderson Pueblo (LA-1549), New Mexico*. Honors thesis, Department of Anthropology, University of Michigan, Ann Arbor, MI.

Halloran, A. F.
1961 American Bison Weights and Measurements from the Wichita Mountains Wildlife Refuge. *Proceedings of the Oklahoma Academy of Science* 41:212-18.

Hammond, G. P., and A. Rey
1966 *The Rediscovery of New Mexico, 1580-1594*. Coronado Cuarto Centennial Publication 3. Albuquerque, NM: University of New Mexico Press.

Jones, K. T.
1993 The Archaeological Structure of a Short-Term Camp. In: *From Bones to Behavior: Ethnoarchaeological and Experimental Contributions to the Interpretation of Faunal Remains*, edited by J. Hudson, pp. 101-14. Occasional Paper 21. Carbondale, IL: Southern Illinois University, Center for Archaeological Investigations.

Jones, K. T., and D. Metcalfe
1988 Bare Bones Archaeology: Bone Marrow Indices and Efficiency. *Journal of Archaeological Science* 15:415-23.

Kelley, J. H.
1984 *The Archaeology of the Sierra Blanca Region of Southeastern New Mexico*. Anthropological Paper 74. Ann Arbor, MI: Museum of Anthropology, University of Michigan.

Kent, S.
1993 Variability in Faunal Assemblages: The Influence of Hunting Skill, Sharing, Dogs, and Mode of Cooking on Faunal Remains at a Sedentary Kalahari Community. *Journal of Anthropological Archaeology* 12:323-85.

Kerr-Grieve, J. F., B. M. Campbell-Brown, and F. D. Johnstone
1979 Dieting in Pregnancy: A Study of the Effect of a High Protein Low Carbohydrate Diet on Birthweight in an Obstetric Population. In: *International Colloquium on Carbohydrate Metabolism in Pregnancy and the Newborn 1978*, edited by H. W. Sutherland and J. M. Stowers, pp. 518-34. New York, NY: Springer-Verlag.

Klasner, L.
1972 *My Girlhood Among Outlaws*, edited by E. Ball. Tucson, AZ: University of Arizona Press.

Kobrynczuk, F.
1976 Joints and Ligaments of Hind-Limbs of the European Bison in its Postnatal Development. *Acta Theriologica* 21(4):37-100.

Lamb, H. H.
1982 *Climate, History and the Modern World*. London, England: Methuen.

Lyman, R. L.
1992 Anatomical Considerations of Utility Curves in Zooarchaeology. *Journal of Archaeological Science* 19:7-22.

Marean, C. W., L. M. Spencer, R. J. Blumenschine, and S. D. Capaldo
1992 Captive Hyaena Bone Choice and Destruction, the Schlepp Effect and Olduvai Archaeofaunas. *Journal of Archaeological Science* 19:101-21.

Martorell, R., and T. Gonzalez-Cossio
1987 Maternal Nutrition and Birth Weight. *Yearbook of Physical Anthropology* 30:195-220.

Mason, O. T.
1893 North American Bows, Arrows and Quivers. *Annual Report of the Smithsonian Institution for 1893*, pp. 631-80. Annual Report for 1891-1892. Washington, DC: Smithsonian Institution.

McArdle, W. D., F. I. Katch, and V. L. Katch
1986 *Exercise Physiology: Energy, Nutrition, and Human Performance*. Philadelphia, PA: Lea and Febiger.

McGilvery, R. W.
1983 *Biochemistry: A Functional Approach*, 3rd Edition. Philadelphia, PA: W. B. Saunders.

Metcalfe, D., and K. T. Jones
1988 A Reconsideration of Animal Body-Part Utility Indices. *American Antiquity* 53:486-504.

Miller, D. E.
1998 *A Study of the Ceramic Assemblage from the Late Prehistoric Site of Henderson (LA 1549), Southeastern New Mexico, and the Changes in Social Patterns Seen in the Assemblage*. Honors thesis, Department of Anthropology, University of Michigan, Ann Arbor, MI.

Miller, S. A., and G. V. Mitchell
1982 Optimisation of Human Protein Requirements. In: *Food Proteins*, edited by P. F. Fox and J. J. Condon, pp. 105-20. London, England: Applied Science Publishers.

Murdock, G. P.
1967 *Ethnographic Atlas*. Pittsburgh, PA: University of Pittsburgh Press.
1969 Correlations of Exploitative and Settlement Patterns. In: *Contributions to Anthropology: Ecological Essays*, edited by D. Damas, pp. 129-50. Bulletin 230. Ottawa, Ontario: National Museums of Canada.

Murdock, G. P., and S. F. Wilson
1972 Settlement Patterns and Community Organization: Cross-Cultural Codes 3. *Ethnology* 11:254-95.

National Academy of Sciences
1985 *Preventing Low Birthweight*. Committee to Study the Prevention of Low Birthweight, Division of Health Promotion and Disease Prevention, Institute of Medicine. Washington, DC: National Academy Press.

O'Connell, J. F., K. Hawkes, and N. Blurton Jones
1988 Hadza Hunting, Butchering, and Bone Transport and Their Archaeological Implications. *Journal of Anthropological Research* 44:113-61.

Oliver, J. S.
1993 Carcass Processing by the Hadza: Bone Breakage from Butchery to Consumption. In: *From Bones to Behavior: Ethnoarchaeological and Experimental Contributions to the Interpretation of Faunal Remains*, edited by J. Hudson, pp. 200-227. Occasional Paper 21. Carbondale, IL: Southern Illinois University, Center for Archaeological Investigations.

Parry, W. J., and J. D. Speth
1984 *The Garnsey Spring Campsite: Late Prehistoric Occupation in Southeastern New Mexico*. Technical Report 15. Ann Arbor, MI: Museum of Anthropology, University of Michigan.

Rocek, T. R., and J. D. Speth
1986 *The Henderson Site Burials: Glimpses of a Late Prehistoric Population in the Pecos Valley*. Technical Report 18. Ann Arbor, MI: Museum of Anthropology, University of Michigan.

Rudman, D., et al.
1973 Maximal Rates of Excretion and Synthesis of Urea in Normal and Cirrhotic Subjects. *Journal of Clinical Investigation* 52:2241-49.

Rush, D.
1982 Effects of Changes in Protein and Calorie Intake During Pregnancy on the Growth of the Human Fetus. In: *Effectiveness and Satisfaction in Antenatal Care*, edited by M. Enkin and I. Chalmers, pp. 92-113. Clinics in Developmental Medicine 81/82. Philadelphia, PA: J. B. Lippincott.
1986 Nutrition in the Preparation for Pregnancy. In: *Pregnancy Care: A Manual for Practice*, edited by G. Chamberlain and J. Lumley, pp. 113-39. New York: John Wiley and Sons.
1989 Effects of Changes in Protein and Calorie Intake During Pregnancy on the Growth of the Human Fetus. In: *Effective Care in Pregnancy and Childbirth*, Vol. 1: *Pregnancy*, edited by I. Chalmers, M. Enkin, and M. J. N. Keirse, pp. 255-80. Oxford, England: Oxford University Press.

Rush, D., Z. Stein, and M. Sassier
1980 A Randomized Controlled Trial of Prenatal Nutritional Supplementation in New York City. *Pediatrics* 65:683-97.

Sanchez, W. A., and J. E. Kutzbach
1974 Climate of the American Tropics and Subtropics in the 1960s and Possible Comparisons with Climatic Variations of the Last Millennium. *Quaternary Research* 4:128-35.

Sebastian, L., and S. Lorralde
1989 *Living on the Land: 11,000 Years of Human Adaptation in Southeastern New Mexico: An Overview of Cultural Resources in the Roswell District, Bureau of Land Management*. Cultural Resources Series 6. Santa Fe, NM: Bureau of Land Management, New Mexico State Office.

Shipman, P.
1981 *Life History of a Fossil*. Cambridge, MA: Harvard University Press.

Sloan, N. L.
1985 *Effects of Maternal Protein Consumption on Fetal Growth and Gestation*. Ph.D. dissertation, Columbia University, New York, NY.

Sokal, R. R., and F. J. Rohlf
1969 *Biometry: The Principles and Practice of Statistics in Biological Research*. San Francisco, CA: W. H. Freeman.

Speth, J. D.
1983 *Bison Kills and Bone Counts: Decision Making by Ancient Hunters*. Chicago, IL: University of Chicago Press.
1987 Early Hominid Subsistence Strategies in Seasonal Habitats. *Journal of Archaeological Science* 14(1):13-29.
1989 Early Hominid Hunting and Scavenging: The Role of Meat as an Energy Source. *Journal of Human Evolution* 18(5):329-43.
1990 Seasonality, Resource Stress, and Food Sharing in So-Called "Egalitarian" Foraging Societies. *Journal of Anthropological Archaeology* 9(2):148-88.
1991a Some Unexplored Aspects of Mutualistic Plains-Pueblo Food Exchange. In: *Farmers, Hunters, and Colonists: Interaction Between the Southwest and the Southern Plains*, edited by K. A. Spielmann, pp. 18-35. Tucson, AZ: University of Arizona Press.
1991b Protein Selection and Avoidance Strategies of Contemporary and Ancestral Foragers. *Philosophical Transactions of the Royal Society* (London) B 334:265-70.
2000 Boiling vs. Baking and Roasting: A Taphonomic Approach to the Recognition of Cooking Techniques in Small Mammals. In: *Animal Bones, Human Societies*, edited by P. A. Rowley-Conwy, pp. 89-105. Oxford, England: Oxbow Books.

Speth, J. D., and W. J. Parry
1978 *Late Prehistoric Bison Procurement in Southeastern New Mexico: The 1977 Season at the Garnsey Site*. Technical Report 8. Ann Arbor, MI: Museum of Anthropology, University of Michigan.
1980 *Late Prehistoric Bison Procurement in Southeastern New Mexico: The 1978 Season at the Garnsey Site (LA-18399)*. Technical Report 12. Ann Arbor, MI: Museum of Anthropology, University of Michigan.

Speth, J. D., and S. L. Scott
1989 Horticulture and Large-Mammal Hunting: The Role of Resource Depletion and the Constraints of Time and Labor. In *Farmers as Hunters*, edited by S. Kent, pp. 71-79. New York, NY: Cambridge University Press.

Speth, J. D., and K. A. Spielmann
1983 Energy Source, Protein Metabolism, and Hunter-Gatherer Subsistence Strategies. *Journal of Anthropological Archaeology* 2(1):1-31.

Staro, L. E.
1996 *An Investigation of the Archaeological Bison Remains at Rocky Arroyo (LA-25277) and Henderson Pueblo (LA-1549), New Mexico*. Honors thesis, Department of Anthropology, University of Michigan, Ann Arbor, MI.

Steen, E.
1850 *Report to Lt. L. McLaws, Dona Ana, New Mexico, January 13, 1850*. Record Group No. 98. The National Archives. Washington, DC.

Stefansson, V.
1944 *Arctic Manual*. New York: Macmillan.

Stiner, M., S. Kuhn, S. Weiner, and O. Bar-Yosef
1995 Differential Burning, Recrystallization, and Fragmentation of Archaeological Bone. *Journal of Archaeological Science* 22:223-37.

Thomas, A. B.
1932 *Forgotten Frontiers*. Norman, OK: University of Oklahoma Press.

Thomas, D. H., and D. Mayer
1983 Behavioral Faunal Analysis of Selected Horizons. In *The Archaeology of Monitor Valley* 2: *Gatecliff Shelter*, edited by D. H. Thomas, pp. 353-90. Anthropological Paper 59(1). New York, NY: American Museum of Natural History.

Todd, L. C.
1987 Analysis of Kill-Butchery Bonebeds and Interpretation of Paleoindian Hunting. In: *The Evolution of Human Hunting*, edited by M. H. Nitecki and D. V. Nitecki, pp. 225-66. New York, NY: Plenum Press.
1991 Seasonality Studies and Paleoindian Subsistence Strategies. In: *Human Predators and Prey Mortality*, edited by M. C. Stiner, pp. 217-38. Boulder, CO: Westview Press.

Vigne, J.-D., and M.-C. Marinval-Vigne
1983 Méthode Pour la Mise en Evidence de la Consommation du Petit Gibier. In: *Animals and Archaeology*, Vol. 1. *Hunters and Their Prey*, edited by J. Clutton-Brock and C. Grigson, pp. 239-42. BAR International Series 163. Oxford, England: British Archaeological Reports.

Whitlock, V. H.
1970 *Cowboy Life on the Llano Estacado*. Norman, OK: University of Oklahoma Press.

Whitney, E. N., and E. M. N. Hamilton
1984 *Understanding Nutrition*, 3rd Edition. St. Paul, MN: West Publishing Company.

Wilson, M.
1980 Population Dynamics of the Garnsey Site Bison. In: *Late Prehistoric Bison Procurement in Southeastern New Mexico: The 1978 Season at the Garnsey Site (LA-18399)*, by J. D. Speth and W. J. Parry, pp. 88-129. Technical Report 12. Ann Arbor, MI: Museum of Anthropology, University of Michigan.

Winick, M.
1989 *Nutrition, Pregnancy, and Early Infancy*. Baltimore, MD: Williams and Wilkins.

Wolfe, W. L.
1931 Archaeological Report on the Hondo Sites. *El Palacio* 31(7):108-12.

Worthington-Roberts, B., and S. R. Williams
1989 *Nutrition in Pregnancy and Lactation*, 4th Edition. St. Louis, MO: Times Mirror/Mosby.

Yellen, J. E.
1977 Cultural Patterning in Faunal Remains: Evidence from the !Kung Bushmen. In: *Experimental Archaeology*, edited by J. E. Yellen, D. Ingersoll, and W. McDonald, pp. 271-331. New York, NY: Columbia University Press.
1991a Small Mammals: !Kung San Utilization and the Production of Faunal Assemblages. *Journal of Anthropological Archaeology* 10(1):1-26.
1991b Small Mammals: Post-Discard Patterning of !Kung San Faunal Remains. *Journal of Anthropological Archaeology* 10(2):152-92.

Zimmerman, L. E.
1996 *An Internal Chronology at the Late Prehistoric Henderson Site (LA-1549), New Mexico as Illustrated by El Paso Polychrome Rim Sherd Indices*. Honors thesis, Department of Anthropology, University of Michigan, Ann Arbor, MI.

Appendix to Chapter 4

Henderson Bison Assemblage

Table A4.1. Bison sample recovered from Henderson Site (all proveniences combined).

Element	Total Sample						Immature Only							Burned	
	NISP[a] (1)	% of Total NISP (2)	MNE[b] (3)	% of Total MNE (4)	MNI[c] (5)	% MNI[d] (6)	Unfus. NISP (7)	Fusing NISP (8)	Unfus. MNE[e] (9)	Fusing MNE (10)	Unfus. MNI[e] (11)	Fusing MNI (12)	Total Imm. %MNI[e] (13)	NISP (14)	% of Total NISP[f] (15)
Skull	11	0.54	1	0.13	1	2.94	—	—	—	—	—	—	—	6	54.55
Horn	1	0.05	1	0.13	1	2.94	—	—	—	—	—	—	—	—	0.00
Mandible	4	0.20	1	0.13	1	2.94	—	—	—	—	—	—	—	—	0.00
Teeth	3	0.15	1	0.13	1	2.94	—	—	—	—	—	—	—	—	0.00
Hyoid	2	0.10	1	0.13	1	2.94	—	—	—	—	—	—	—	—	0.00
Atlas	3	0.15	3	0.40	3	8.82	—	—	—	—	—	—	—	—	0.00
Axis	3	0.15	2	0.26	2	5.88	—	—	—	—	—	—	—	1	33.33
Cervical	21	1.04	10	1.32	2	5.88	—	—	—	—	—	—	—	1	4.76
Thoracic	70	3.45	6	0.79	1	2.94	—	—	—	—	—	—	—	1	1.43
Lumbar	13	0.64	6	0.79	2	5.88	—	—	—	—	—	—	—	—	0.00
Sacrum	2	0.10	2	0.26	2	5.88	—	—	—	—	—	—	—	—	0.00
Caudal	—	—	—	—	—	—	—	—	—	—	—	—	—	—	—
Vert. Frg.	36	1.78	—	—	1	2.94	—	—	—	—	—	—	—	—	0.00
Rib/Vert.	3	0.15	—	—	1	2.94	—	—	—	—	—	—	—	1	33.33
Rib	193	9.52	47	6.19	2	5.88	—	—	—	—	—	—	—	3	1.55
Cost. Crt.	29	1.43	—	—	1	2.94	—	—	—	—	—	—	—	—	0.00
Sternum	1	0.05	1	0.13	1	2.94	—	—	—	—	—	—	—	—	0.00
Scapula	172	8.49	25	3.29	13	38.24	—	—	—	—	—	—	—	8	4.65
Prx. Hum.	113	5.57	46	6.06	23	67.65	13	4	7	3	4	2	60.00	9	7.96
Dis. Hum.	77	3.80	49	6.46	25	73.53	—	—	—	—	—	—	—	4	13.33
H. Shaft	9	0.44	—	—	—	—	—	—	—	—	—	—	—	—	0.00
Prx. Rad.	48	2.37	36	4.74	18	52.94	1	1	1	1	1	1	20.00	1	2.08
Dis. Rad.	16	0.79	12	1.58	6	17.65	2	—	2	—	1	—	10.00	2	12.50
R. Shaft	3	0.15	—	—	—	—	—	—	—	—	—	—	—	—	0.00
Prx. Ulna	41	2.02	26	3.43	13	38.24	6	—	1	—	1	—	10.00	1	2.44
Dis. Ulna	3	0.15	3	0.40	2	5.88	—	—	—	—	—	—	—	—	0.00
Rad. Car.	7	0.35	5	0.66	3	8.82	—	—	—	—	—	—	—	1	14.29
Int. Car.	5	0.25	4	0.53	2	5.88	—	—	—	—	—	—	—	—	0.00
Uln. Car.	6	0.30	6	0.79	3	8.82	—	—	—	—	—	—	—	1	16.67
Acc. Car.	1	0.05	1	0.13	1	2.94	—	—	—	—	—	—	—	—	0.00
4th Car.	7	0.35	7	0.92	4	11.76	—	—	—	—	—	—	—	—	0.00
2-3 Car.	5	0.25	5	0.66	3	8.82	—	—	—	—	—	—	—	—	0.00
Prx. Mc.	5	0.25	5	0.66	3	8.82	—	—	—	—	—	—	—	1	20.00
Dis. Mc.	9	0.44	9	1.19	5	14.71	1	1	1	1	1	1	20.00	—	0.00
Innom.	15	0.74	2	0.26	1	2.94	—	—	—	—	—	—	—	1	6.67
Prx. Fem.	108	5.33	68	8.96	34	100.00	18	8	12	8	6	4	100.00	4	3.70
Dis. Fem.	114	5.62	51	6.72	26	76.47	8	5	4	5	2	3	50.00	18	15.79
F. Shaft	17	0.84	—	—	—	—	—	—	—	—	—	—	—	1	5.88

(cont.)

Element	Total Sample						Immature Only							Burned	
	NISP[a] (1)	% of Total NISP (2)	MNE[b] (3)	% of Total MNE (4)	MNI[c] (5)	% MNI[d] (6)	Unfus. NISP (7)	Fusing NISP (8)	Unfus. MNE[e] (9)	Fusing MNE (10)	Unfus. MNI[e] (11)	Fusing MNI (12)	Total Imm. %MNI[e] (13)	NISP (14)	% of Total NISP[f] (15)
Patella	39	1.92	39	5.14	20	58.82	1	—	1	—	1	—	10.00	1	2.56
Prx. Tib.	138	6.81	64	8.43	32	94.12	25	2	9	1	5	1	60.00	20	14.49
Dis. Tib.	25	1.23	16	2.11	8	23.53	3	1	2	1	1	1	20.00	2	8.00
T. Shaft	43	2.12	—	—	—	—	—	—	—	—	—	—	—	4	9.30
Lat. Mal.	7	0.35	4	0.53	2	5.88	—	—	—	—	—	—	—	1	14.29
Astrag.	9	0.44	7	0.92	4	11.76	—	—	—	—	—	—	—	3	33.33
Calc.	15	0.74	6	0.79	3	8.82	2	—	1	—	1	—	10.00	2	13.33
Nav.-Cub.	11	0.54	7	0.92	4	11.76	—	—	—	—	—	—	—	1	9.09
2-3 Tar.	19	0.94	16	2.11	8	23.53	—	—	—	—	—	—	—	—	0.00
Prx. Mt.	14	0.69	11	1.45	6	17.65	—	—	—	—	—	—	—	—	0.00
Dis. Mt.	11	0.54	10	1.32	5	14.71	—	1	—	1	—	1	10.00	—	0.00
Mt. Shaft	1	0.05	—	—	—	—	—	—	—	—	—	—	—	—	0.00
P. Mtpdl.	6	0.30	1	0.13	1	2.94	—	—	—	—	—	—	—	—	0.00
D. Mtpdl.	12	0.59	2	0.26	1	2.94	4	—	2	—	1	—	10.00	1	8.33
Mpd. Shaft	3	0.15	—	—	—	—	—	—	—	—	—	—	—	—	0.00
Prx. Sesa.	16	0.79	16	2.11	1	2.94	—	—	—	—	—	—	—	—	0.00
Dis. Sesa.	5	0.25	5	0.66	1	2.94	—	—	—	—	—	—	—	—	0.00
Sesamoid	13	0.64	13	1.71	1	2.94	—	—	—	—	—	—	—	—	0.00
Phal. 1	60	2.96	40	5.27	5	14.71	—	—	—	—	—	—	—	1	1.67
Phal. 2	36	1.78	32	4.22	4	11.76	—	—	—	—	—	—	—	4	11.11
Phal. 3	36	1.78	28	3.69	4	11.76	—	—	—	—	—	—	—	4	11.11
Longbone	313	15.44	—	—	—	—	—	—	—	—	—	—	—	8	2.56
Cancellous	1	0.05	—	—	—	—	—	—	—	—	—	—	—	—	0.00
Indeterm.	18	0.89	—	—	—	—	—	—	—	—	—	—	—	4	22.22
TOTAL	2027	100.04	759	100.00			84	23	43	21				121	5.97

[a]NISP, Number of identifiable specimens.
[b]MNE, Minimum number of elements.
[c]MNI, Minimum number of individuals.
[d]%MNI, MNI of each element observed expressed as percent of maximum MNI value—34 animals (prox. femur).
[e]Unfused NISP, Unfused MNE, Unfused MNI, and Total Immature %MNI tabulations include 1 (probable) fetal or neonatal patella. Total Immature %MNI calculated in same manner as %MNI (see note 4 above), based on maximum immature MNI value of 10 animals (prox. femur).
[f]Percent of NISP value in same row in Column (1).

Table A4.2. Bison Sample recovered from Henderson Site (Trench A, East Bar).

Element	Total Sample						Immature Only							Burned	
	NISP[a] (1)	% of Total NISP (2)	MNE[b] (3)	% of Total MNE (4)	MNI[c] (5)	% MNI[d] (6)	Unfus. NISP (7)	Fusing NISP (8)	Unfus. MNE[e] (9)	Fusing MNE (10)	Unfus. MNI[e] (11)	Fusing MNI (12)	Total Imm. %MNI[e] (13)	NISP (14)	% of Total NISP[f] (15)
Skull	—	—	—	—	—	—	—	—	—	—	—	—	—	—	—
Horn	—	—	—	—	—	—	—	—	—	—	—	—	—	—	—
Mandible	—	—	—	—	—	—	—	—	—	—	—	—	—	—	—
Teeth	1	0.78	1	2.94	1	50.00	—	—	—	—	—	—	—	—	—
Hyoid	1	0.78	1	2.94	1	50.00	—	—	—	—	—	—	—	—	—
Atlas	—	—	—	—	—	—	—	—	—	—	—	—	—	—	—
Axis	—	—	—	—	—	—	—	—	—	—	—	—	—	—	—
Cervical	—	—	—	—	—	—	—	—	—	—	—	—	—	—	—
Thoracic	1	0.78	1	2.94	1	50.00	—	—	—	—	—	—	—	—	—
Lumbar	1	0.78	1	2.94	1	50.00	—	—	—	—	—	—	—	—	—
Sacrum	—	—	—	—	—	—	—	—	—	—	—	—	—	—	—
Caudal	—	—	—	—	—	—	—	—	—	—	—	—	—	—	—
Vert. Frg.	1	0.78	1	2.94	1	50.00	—	—	—	—	—	—	—	—	—
Rib/Vert.	—	—	—	—	—	—	—	—	—	—	—	—	—	—	—
Rib	6	4.69	2	5.88	1	50.00	—	—	—	—	—	—	—	—	—
Cost. Crt.	—	—	—	—	—	—	—	—	—	—	—	—	—	—	—
Sternum	—	—	—	—	—	—	—	—	—	—	—	—	—	—	—
Scapula	18	14.06	1	2.94	1	50.00	—	—	—	—	—	—	—	—	—
Prx. Hum.	10	7.81	4	11.76	2	100.00	2	—	1	—	1	—	100.00	2	20.00
Dis. Hum.	4	3.13	1	2.94	1	50.00	—	—	—	—	—	—	—	—	—
H. Shaft	—	—	—	—	—	—	—	—	—	—	—	—	—	—	—
Prx. Rad.	3	2.34	3	8.82	2	100.00	—	—	—	—	—	—	—	—	—
Dis. Rad.	1	0.78	1	2.94	1	50.00	—	—	—	—	—	—	—	1	100.00
R. Shaft	—	—	—	—	—	—	—	—	—	—	—	—	—	—	—
Prx. Ulna	1	0.78	1	2.94	1	50.00	—	—	—	—	—	—	—	—	—
Dis. Ulna	—	—	—	—	—	—	—	—	—	—	—	—	—	—	—
Rad. Car.	—	—	—	—	—	—	—	—	—	—	—	—	—	—	—
Int. Car.	—	—	—	—	—	—	—	—	—	—	—	—	—	—	—
Uln. Car.	—	—	—	—	—	—	—	—	—	—	—	—	—	—	—
Acc. Car.	—	—	—	—	—	—	—	—	—	—	—	—	—	—	—
4th Car.	—	—	—	—	—	—	—	—	—	—	—	—	—	—	—
2-3 Car.	—	—	—	—	—	—	—	—	—	—	—	—	—	—	—
Prx. Mc.	—	—	—	—	—	—	—	—	—	—	—	—	—	—	—
Dis. Mc.	1	0.78	1	2.94	1	50.00	—	—	—	—	—	—	—	—	—
Innom.	—	—	—	—	—	—	—	—	—	—	—	—	—	—	—
Prx. Fem.	8	6.25	3	8.82	2	100.00	2	—	1	—	1	—	100.00	—	—
Dis. Fem.	3	2.34	1	2.94	1	50.00	—	—	—	—	—	—	—	2	66.67
F. Shaft	2	1.56	—	—	—	—	—	—	—	—	—	—	—	—	—

(cont.)

Element	Total Sample						Immature Only							Burned	
	NISP[a] (1)	% of Total NISP (2)	MNE[b] (3)	% of Total MNE (4)	MNI[c] (5)	% MNI[d] (6)	Unfus. NISP (7)	Fusing NISP (8)	Unfus. MNE[e] (9)	Fusing MNE (10)	Unfus. MNI[e] (11)	Fusing MNI (12)	Total Imm. %MNI[e] (13)	NISP (14)	% of Total NISP[f] (15)
Patella	1	0.78	1	2.94	1	50.00	—	—	—	—	—	—	—	—	—
Prx. Tib.	7	5.47	1	2.94	1	50.00	2	—	1	—	1	—	100.00	3	42.86
Dis. Tib.	2	1.56	2	5.88	1	50.00	—	—	—	—	—	—	—	1	50.00
T. Shaft	5	3.91	—	—	—	—	—	—	—	—	—	—	—	1	20.00
Lat. Mal.	2	1.56	2	5.88	1	50.00	—	—	—	—	—	—	—	—	—
Astrag.	4	3.13	2	5.88	1	50.00	—	—	—	—	—	—	—	3	75.00
Calc.	—	—	—	—	—	—	—	—	—	—	—	—	—	—	—
Nav.-Cub.	—	—	—	—	—	—	—	—	—	—	—	—	—	—	—
2-3 Tar.	—	—	—	—	—	—	—	—	—	—	—	—	—	—	—
Prx. Mt.	—	—	—	—	—	—	—	—	—	—	—	—	—	—	—
Dis. Mt.	—	—	—	—	—	—	—	—	—	—	—	—	—	—	—
Mt. Shaft	—	—	—	—	—	—	—	—	—	—	—	—	—	—	—
P. Mtpdl.	—	—	—	—	—	—	—	—	—	—	—	—	—	—	—
D. Mtpdl.	—	—	—	—	—	—	—	—	—	—	—	—	—	—	—
Mpd. Shaft	—	—	—	—	—	—	—	—	—	—	—	—	—	—	—
Prx. Sesa.	—	—	—	—	—	—	—	—	—	—	—	—	—	—	—
Dis. Sesa.	—	—	—	—	—	—	—	—	—	—	—	—	—	—	—
Sesamoid	—	—	—	—	—	—	—	—	—	—	—	—	—	—	—
Phal. 1	2	1.56	1	2.94	1	50.00	—	—	—	—	—	—	—	1	50.00
Phal. 2	—	—	—	—	—	—	—	—	—	—	—	—	—	—	—
Phal. 3	2	1.56	2	5.88	1	50.00	—	—	—	—	—	—	—	—	—
Longbone	39	30.47	—	—	—	—	—	—	—	—	—	—	—	—	—
Cancellous	—	—	—	—	—	—	—	—	—	—	—	—	—	—	—
Indeterm.	2	1.56	—	—	—	—	—	—	—	—	—	—	—	1	50.00
TOTAL	128	99.98	34	99.96			6	0	3	0				15	11.72

[a]NISP, Number of identifiable specimens.

[b]MNE, Minimum number of elements.

[c]MNI, Minimum number of individuals.

[d]%MNI, MNI of each element observed expressed as percent of maximum MNI value—34 animals (prox. femur).

[e]Unfused NISP, Unfused MNE, Unfused MNI, and Total Immature %MNI tabulations include 1 (probable) fetal or neonatal patella. Total Immature %MNI calculated in same manner as %MNI (see note 4 above), based on maximum immature MNI value of 10 animals (prox. femur).

[f]Percent of NISP value in same row in Column (1).

Table A4.3. Bison sample recovered from Henderson Site (Trench C, East Plaza).

Element	Total Sample						Immature Only							Burned	
	NISP[a] (1)	% of Total NISP (2)	MNE[b] (3)	% of Total MNE (4)	MNI[c] (5)	% MNI[d] (6)	Unfus. NISP (7)	Fusing NISP (8)	Unfus. MNE[e] (9)	Fusing MNE (10)	Unfus. MNI[e] (11)	Fusing MNI (12)	Total Imm. %MNI[e] (13)	NISP (14)	% of Total NISP[f] (15)
Skull	11	0.66	1	0.15	1	3.23	—	—	—	—	—	—	—	6	54.55
Horn	1	0.06	1	0.15	1	3.23	—	—	—	—	—	—	—	—	—
Mandible	4	0.24	1	0.15	1	3.23	—	—	—	—	—	—	—	—	—
Teeth	1	0.06	1	0.15	1	3.23	—	—	—	—	—	—	—	—	—
Hyoid	1	0.06	1	0.15	1	3.23	—	—	—	—	—	—	—	—	—
Atlas	2	0.12	2	0.29	2	6.45	—	—	—	—	—	—	—	—	—
Axis	2	0.12	2	0.29	2	6.45	—	—	—	—	—	—	—	1	50.00
Cervical	21	1.26	10	1.46	2	6.45	—	—	—	—	—	—	—	1	4.76
Thoracic	61	3.66	5	0.73	1	3.23	—	—	—	—	—	—	—	1	1.64
Lumbar	12	0.72	5	0.73	1	3.23	—	—	—	—	—	—	—	—	—
Sacrum	1	0.06	1	0.15	1	3.23	—	—	—	—	—	—	—	—	—
Caudal	—	—	—	—	—	—	—	—	—	—	—	—	—	—	—
Vert. Frg.	34	2.04	1	0.15	—	—	—	—	—	—	—	—	—	—	—
Rib/Vert.	3	0.18	1	0.15	—	—	—	—	—	—	—	—	—	1	33.33
Rib	164	9.85	41	5.99	2	6.45	—	—	—	—	—	—	—	3	1.83
Cost. Crt.	17	1.02	1	0.15	—	—	—	—	—	—	—	—	—	—	—
Sternum	1	0.06	1	0.15	1	3.23	—	—	—	—	—	—	—	—	—
Scapula	142	8.53	24	3.51	12	38.71	—	—	—	—	—	—	—	8	5.63
Prx. Hum.	85	5.11	37	5.41	19	61.29	10	4	6	3	3	2	50.00	6	7.06
Dis. Hum.	71	4.26	48	7.02	24	77.42	—	—	—	—	—	—	—	4	5.63
H. Shaft	6	0.36	—	—	—	—	—	—	—	—	—	—	—	—	—
Prx. Rad.	37	2.22	29	4.24	15	48.39	1	1	1	1	1	1	20.00	1	2.70
Dis. Rad.	12	0.72	9	1.32	5	16.13	1	—	1	—	1	—	10.00	1	8.33
R. Shaft	2	0.12	—	—	—	—	—	—	—	—	—	—	—	—	—
Prx. Ulna	37	2.22	25	3.65	13	41.94	4	—	1	—	1	—	10.00	1	2.70
Dis. Ulna	2	0.12	1	0.15	1	3.23	—	—	—	—	—	—	—	—	—
Rad. Car.	7	0.42	5	0.73	3	9.68	—	—	—	—	—	—	—	1	14.29
Int. Car.	5	0.30	4	0.58	2	6.45	—	—	—	—	—	—	—	—	—
Uln. Car.	5	0.30	5	0.73	3	9.68	—	—	—	—	—	—	—	—	—
Acc. Car.	1	0.06	1	0.15	1	3.23	—	—	—	—	—	—	—	—	—
4th Car.	7	0.42	7	1.02	4	12.90	—	—	—	—	—	—	—	—	—
2-3 Car.	5	0.30	5	0.73	3	9.68	—	—	—	—	—	—	—	—	—
Prx. Mc.	4	0.24	4	0.58	2	6.45	—	—	—	—	—	—	—	1	25.00
Dis. Mc.	7	0.42	7	1.02	4	12.90	1	1	1	1	1	1	20.00	—	—
Innom.	12	0.72	2	0.29	1	3.23	—	—	—	—	—	—	—	—	—
Prx. Fem.	93	5.59	60	8.77	30	96.77	16	8	12	8	6	4	100.00	3	3.23
Dis. Fem.	106	6.37	49	7.16	25	80.65	7	5	4	5	2	3	50.00	16	15.09
F. Shaft	12	0.72	—	—	—	—	—	—	—	—	—	—	—	1	8.33

(cont.)

Element	Total Sample						Immature Only							Burned	
	NISP[a] (1)	% of Total NISP (2)	MNE[b] (3)	% of Total MNE (4)	MNI[c] (5)	% MNI[d] (6)	Unfus. NISP (7)	Fusing NISP (8)	Unfus. MNE[e] (9)	Fusing MNE (10)	Unfus. MNI[e] (11)	Fusing MNI (12)	Total Imm. %MNI[e] (13)	NISP (14)	% of Total NISP[f] (15)
Patella	35	2.10	35	5.12	18	58.06	1	—	1	—	1	—	10.00	1	2.86
Prx. Tib.	121	7.27	61	8.92	31	100.00	23	2	9	1	5	1	60.00	12	9.92
Dis. Tib.	21	1.26	14	2.05	7	22.58	3	1	2	1	1	1	20.00	1	4.76
T. Shaft	33	1.98	—	—	—	—	—	—	—	—	—	—	—	3	9.09
Lat. Mal.	4	0.24	2	0.29	1	3.23	—	—	—	—	—	—	—	1	25.00
Astrag.	4	0.24	4	0.58	2	6.45	—	—	—	—	—	—	—	—	—
Calc.	12	0.72	5	0.73	3	9.68	2	—	1	—	1	—	10.00	2	16.67
Nav.-Cub.	10	0.60	7	1.02	4	12.90	—	—	—	—	—	—	—	1	10.00
2-3 Tar.	17	1.02	15	2.19	8	25.81	—	—	—	—	—	—	—	—	—
Prx. Mt.	14	0.84	11	1.61	6	19.35	—	—	—	—	—	—	—	—	—
Dis. Mt.	10	0.60	9	1.32	5	16.13	—	1	—	1	—	1	10.00	—	—
Mt. Shaft	1	0.06	—	—	—	—	—	—	—	—	—	—	—	—	—
P. Mtpdl.	6	0.36	1	0.15	—	—	—	—	—	—	—	—	—	—	—
D. Mtpdl.	10	0.60	2	0.29	1	3.23	4	—	2	—	1	—	10.00	—	—
Mpd. Shaft	2	0.12	—	—	—	—	—	—	—	—	—	—	—	—	—
Prx. Sesa.	12	0.72	12	1.75	1	3.23	—	—	—	—	—	—	—	—	—
Dis. Sesa.	4	0.24	4	0.58	1	3.23	—	—	—	—	—	—	—	—	—
Sesamoid	10	0.60	10	1.46	1	3.23	—	—	—	—	—	—	—	—	—
Phal. 1	55	3.30	41	5.99	6	19.35	—	—	—	—	—	—	—	—	—
Phal. 2	33	1.98	30	4.39	4	12.90	—	—	—	—	—	—	—	3	9.09
Phal. 3	32	1.92	24	3.51	3	9.68	—	—	—	—	—	—	—	4	12.50
Longbone	212	12.73	—	—	—	—	—	—	—	—	—	—	—	6	2.83
Cancellous	1	0.06	—	—	—	—	—	—	—	—	—	—	—	—	—
Indeterm.	12	0.72	—	—	—	—	—	—	—	—	—	—	—	3	25.00
TOTAL	1665	99.97	684	100.00			73	23	41	21				93	5.59

[a]NISP, Number of identifiable specimens.
[b]MNE, Minimum number of elements.
[c]MNI, Minimum number of individuals.
[d]%MNI, MNI of each element observed expressed as percent of maximum MNI value—34 animals (prox. femur).
[e]Unfused NISP, Unfused MNE, Unfused MNI, and Total Immature %MNI tabulations include 1 (probable) fetal or neonatal patella. Total Immature %MNI calculated in same manner as %MNI (see note 4 above), based on maximum immature MNI value of 10 animals (prox. femur).
[f]Percent of NISP value in same row in Column (1).

Table A4.4. Bison sample recovered from Henderson Site (Trench D, East Plaza).

Element	Total Sample						Immature Only							Burned	
	NISP[a] (1)	% of Total NISP (2)	MNE[b] (3)	% of Total MNE (4)	MNI[c] (5)	% MNI[d] (6)	Unfus. NISP (7)	Fusing NISP (8)	Unfus. MNE[e] (9)	Fusing MNE (10)	Unfus. MNI[e] (11)	Fusing MNI (12)	Total Imm. %MNI[e] (13)	NISP (14)	% of Total NISP[f] (15)
Skull	—	—	—	—	—	—	—	—	—	—	—	—	—	—	—
Horn	—	—	—	—	—	—	—	—	—	—	—	—	—	—	—
Mandible	—	—	—	—	—	—	—	—	—	—	—	—	—	—	—
Teeth	—	—	—	—	—	—	—	—	—	—	—	—	—	—	—
Hyoid	—	—	—	—	—	—	—	—	—	—	—	—	—	—	—
Atlas	—	—	—	—	—	—	—	—	—	—	—	—	—	—	—
Axis	—	—	—	—	—	—	—	—	—	—	—	—	—	—	—
Cervical	—	—	—	—	—	—	—	—	—	—	—	—	—	—	—
Thoracic	1	2.22	1	8.33	1	100.00	—	—	—	—	—	—	—	—	—
Lumbar	—	—	—	—	—	—	—	—	—	—	—	—	—	—	—
Sacrum	—	—	—	—	—	—	—	—	—	—	—	—	—	—	—
Caudal	—	—	—	—	—	—	—	—	—	—	—	—	—	—	—
Vert. Frg.	—	—	—	—	—	—	—	—	—	—	—	—	—	—	—
Rib/Vert.	—	—	—	—	—	—	—	—	—	—	—	—	—	—	—
Rib	9	20.00	2	16.67	1	100.00	—	—	—	—	—	—	—	—	—
Cost. Crt.	—	—	—	—	—	—	—	—	—	—	—	—	—	—	—
Sternum	—	—	—	—	—	—	—	—	—	—	—	—	—	—	—
Scapula	4	8.89	1	8.33	1	100.00	—	—	—	—	—	—	—	—	—
Prx. Hum.	7	15.56	1	8.33	1	100.00	—	—	—	—	—	—	—	—	—
Dis. Hum.	—	—	—	—	—	—	—	—	—	—	—	—	—	—	—
H. Shaft	1	2.22	—	—	—	—	—	—	—	—	—	—	—	—	—
Prx. Rad.	2	4.44	1	8.33	1	100.00	—	—	—	—	—	—	—	—	—
Dis. Rad.	—	—	—	—	—	—	—	—	—	—	—	—	—	—	—
R. Shaft	—	—	—	—	—	—	—	—	—	—	—	—	—	—	—
Prx. Ulna	—	—	—	—	—	—	—	—	—	—	—	—	—	—	—
Dis. Ulna	—	—	—	—	—	—	—	—	—	—	—	—	—	—	—
Rad. Car.	—	—	—	—	—	—	—	—	—	—	—	—	—	—	—
Int. Car.	—	—	—	—	—	—	—	—	—	—	—	—	—	—	—
Uln. Car.	—	—	—	—	—	—	—	—	—	—	—	—	—	—	—
Acc. Car.	—	—	—	—	—	—	—	—	—	—	—	—	—	—	—
4th Car.	—	—	—	—	—	—	—	—	—	—	—	—	—	—	—
2-3 Car.	—	—	—	—	—	—	—	—	—	—	—	—	—	—	—
Prx. Mc.	—	—	—	—	—	—	—	—	—	—	—	—	—	—	—
Dis. Mc.	—	—	—	—	—	—	—	—	—	—	—	—	—	—	—
Innom.	1	2.22	1	8.33	1	100.00	—	—	—	—	—	—	—	—	—
Prx. Fem.	1	2.22	1	8.33	1	100.00	—	—	—	—	—	—	—	—	—
Dis. Fem.	—	—	—	—	—	—	—	—	—	—	—	—	—	—	—
F. Shaft	2	4.44	—	—	—	—	—	—	—	—	—	—	—	—	—

(cont.)

Element	Total Sample						Immature Only							Burned	
	NISP[a] (1)	% of Total NISP (2)	MNE[b] (3)	% of Total MNE (4)	MNI[c] (5)	% MNI[d] (6)	Unfus. NISP (7)	Fusing NISP (8)	Unfus. MNE[e] (9)	Fusing MNE (10)	Unfus. MNI[e] (11)	Fusing MNI (12)	Total Imm. %MNI[e] (13)	NISP (14)	% of Total NISP[f] (15)
Patella	1	2.22	1	8.33	1	100.00	—	—	—	—	—	—	—	—	—
Prx. Tib.	2	4.44	1	8.33	1	100.00	—	—	—	—	—	—	—	—	—
Dis. Tib.	1	2.22	1	8.33	1	100.00	—	—	—	—	—	—	—	—	—
T. Shaft	—	—	—	—	—	—	—	—	—	—	—	—	—	—	—
Lat. Mal.	1	2.22	1	8.33	1	100.00	—	—	—	—	—	—	—	—	—
Astrag.	—	—	—	—	—	—	—	—	—	—	—	—	—	—	—
Calc.	—	—	—	—	—	—	—	—	—	—	—	—	—	—	—
Nav.-Cub.	—	—	—	—	—	—	—	—	—	—	—	—	—	—	—
2-3 Tar.	—	—	—	—	—	—	—	—	—	—	—	—	—	—	—
Prx. Mt.	—	—	—	—	—	—	—	—	—	—	—	—	—	—	—
Dis. Mt.	—	—	—	—	—	—	—	—	—	—	—	—	—	—	—
Mt. Shaft	—	—	—	—	—	—	—	—	—	—	—	—	—	—	—
P. Mtpdl.	—	—	—	—	—	—	—	—	—	—	—	—	—	—	—
D. Mtpdl.	—	—	—	—	—	—	—	—	—	—	—	—	—	—	—
Mpd. Shaft	—	—	—	—	—	—	—	—	—	—	—	—	—	—	—
Prx. Sesa.	—	—	—	—	—	—	—	—	—	—	—	—	—	—	—
Dis. Sesa.	—	—	—	—	—	—	—	—	—	—	—	—	—	—	—
Sesamoid	—	—	—	—	—	—	—	—	—	—	—	—	—	—	—
Phal. 1	—	—	—	—	—	—	—	—	—	—	—	—	—	—	—
Phal. 2	—	—	—	—	—	—	—	—	—	—	—	—	—	—	—
Phal. 3	—	—	—	—	—	—	—	—	—	—	—	—	—	—	—
Longbone	11	24.44	—	—	—	—	—	—	—	—	—	—	—	—	—
Cancellous	—	—	—	—	—	—	—	—	—	—	—	—	—	—	—
Indeterm.	1	2.22	—	—	—	—	—	—	—	—	—	—	—	—	—
TOTAL	45	99.97	12	99.97			0	0	0	0				0	0.00

[a]NISP, Number of identifiable specimens.
[b]MNE, Minimum number of elements.
[c]MNI, Minimum number of individuals.
[d]%MNI, MNI of each element observed expressed as percent of maximum MNI value—34 animals (prox. femur).
[e]Unfused NISP, Unfused MNE, Unfused MNI, and Total Immature %MNI tabulations include 1 (probable) fetal or neonatal patella. Total Immature %MNI calculated in same manner as %MNI (see note 4 above), based on maximum immature MNI value of 10 animals (prox. femur).
[f]Percent of NISP value in same row in Column (1).

Table A4.5. Bison sample recovered from Henderson Site (Trench F, Center Bar).

Element	Total Sample						Immature Only							Burned	
	NISP[a] (1)	% of Total NISP (2)	MNE[b] (3)	% of Total MNE (4)	MNI[c] (5)	% MNI[d] (6)	Unfus. NISP (7)	Fusing NISP (8)	Unfus. MNE[e] (9)	Fusing MNE (10)	Unfus. MNI[e] (11)	Fusing MNI (12)	Total Imm. %MNI[e] (13)	NISP (14)	% of Total NISP[f] (15)
Skull	—	—	—	—	—	—	—	—	—	—	—	—	—	—	—
Horn	—	—	—	—	—	—	—	—	—	—	—	—	—	—	—
Mandible	—	—	—	—	—	—	—	—	—	—	—	—	—	—	—
Teeth	1	0.58	1	2.00	1	50.00	—	—	—	—	—	—	—	—	—
Hyoid	—	—	—	—	—	—	—	—	—	—	—	—	—	—	—
Atlas	1	0.58	1	2.00	1	50.00	—	—	—	—	—	—	—	—	—
Axis	1	0.58	1	2.00	1	50.00	—	—	—	—	—	—	—	—	—
Cervical	—	—	—	—	—	—	—	—	—	—	—	—	—	—	—
Thoracic	7	4.09	1	2.00	1	50.00	—	—	—	—	—	—	—	—	—
Lumbar	—	—	—	—	—	—	—	—	—	—	—	—	—	—	—
Sacrum	1	0.58	1	2.00	1	50.00	—	—	—	—	—	—	—	—	—
Caudal	—	—	—	—	—	—	—	—	—	—	—	—	—	—	—
Vert. Frg.	1	0.58	1	2.00	1	50.00	—	—	—	—	—	—	—	—	—
Rib/Vert.	—	—	—	—	—	—	—	—	—	—	—	—	—	—	—
Rib	14	8.19	2	4.00	1	50.00	—	—	—	—	—	—	—	—	—
Cost. Crt.	12	7.02	1	2.00	1	50.00	—	—	—	—	—	—	—	—	—
Sternum	—	—	—	—	—	—	—	—	—	—	—	—	—	—	—
Scapula	8	4.68	1	2.00	1	50.00	—	—	—	—	—	—	—	—	—
Prx. Hum.	10	5.85	3	6.00	2	100.00	1	—	1	—	1	—	100.00	1	10.00
Dis. Hum.	2	1.17	1	2.00	1	50.00	—	—	—	—	—	—	—	—	—
H. Shaft	2	1.17	—	—	—	—	—	—	—	—	—	—	—	—	—
Prx. Rad.	5	2.92	2	4.00	1	50.00	—	—	—	—	—	—	—	—	—
Dis. Rad.	3	1.75	2	4.00	1	50.00	1	—	1	—	1	—	100.00	—	—
R. Shaft	1	0.58	—	—	—	—	—	—	—	—	—	—	—	—	—
Prx. Ulna	2	1.17	1	2.00	1	50.00	1	—	1	—	1	—	100.00	—	—
Dis. Ulna	1	0.58	1	2.00	1	50.00	—	—	—	—	—	—	—	—	—
Rad. Car.	—	—	—	—	—	—	—	—	—	—	—	—	—	—	—
Int. Car.	—	—	—	—	—	—	—	—	—	—	—	—	—	—	—
Uln. Car.	1	0.58	1	2.00	1	50.00	—	—	—	—	—	—	—	1	100.00
Acc. Car.	—	—	—	—	—	—	—	—	—	—	—	—	—	—	—
4th Car.	—	—	—	—	—	—	—	—	—	—	—	—	—	—	—
2-3 Car.	—	—	—	—	—	—	—	—	—	—	—	—	—	—	—
Prx. Mc.	1	0.58	1	2.00	1	50.00	—	—	—	—	—	—	—	—	—
Dis. Mc.	1	0.58	1	2.00	1	50.00	—	—	—	—	—	—	—	—	—
Innom.	2	1.17	1	2.00	1	50.00	—	—	—	—	—	—	—	1	50.00
Prx. Fem.	6	3.51	4	8.00	2	100.00	—	—	—	—	—	—	—	1	16.67
Dis. Fem.	4	2.34	1	2.00	1	50.00	—	—	—	—	—	—	—	—	—
F. Shaft	1	0.58	—	—	—	—	—	—	—	—	—	—	—	—	—

(cont.)

Element	Total Sample						Immature Only							Burned	
	NISP[a] (1)	% of Total NISP (2)	MNE[b] (3)	% of Total MNE (4)	MNI[c] (5)	% MNI[d] (6)	Unfus. NISP (7)	Fusing NISP (8)	Unfus. MNE[e] (9)	Fusing MNE (10)	Unfus. MNI[e] (11)	Fusing MNI (12)	Total Imm. %MNI[e] (13)	NISP (14)	% of Total NISP[f] (15)
Patella	1	0.58	1	2.00	1	50.00	—	—	—	—	—	—	—	—	—
Prx. Tib.	7	4.09	2	4.00	1	50.00	—	—	—	—	—	—	—	5	71.43
Dis. Tib.	—	—	—	—	—	—	—	—	—	—	—	—	—	—	—
T. Shaft	5	2.92	—	—	—	—	—	—	—	—	—	—	—	—	—
Lat. Mal.	—	—	—	—	—	—	—	—	—	—	—	—	—	—	—
Astrag.	1	0.58	1	2.00	1	50.00	—	—	—	—	—	—	—	—	—
Calc.	1	0.58	1	2.00	1	50.00	—	—	—	—	—	—	—	—	—
Nav.-Cub.	1	0.58	1	2.00	1	50.00	—	—	—	—	—	—	—	—	—
2-3 Tar.	2	1.17	1	2.00	1	50.00	—	—	—	—	—	—	—	—	—
Prx. Mt.	—	—	—	—	—	—	—	—	—	—	—	—	—	—	—
Dis. Mt.	1	0.58	1	2.00	1	50.00	—	—	—	—	—	—	—	—	—
Mt. Shaft	—	—	—	—	—	—	—	—	—	—	—	—	—	—	—
P. Mtpdl.	—	—	—	—	—	—	—	—	—	—	—	—	—	—	—
D. Mtpdl.	1	0.58	1	2.00	1	50.00	—	—	—	—	—	—	—	1	100.00
Mpd. Shaft	1	0.58	—	—	—	—	—	—	—	—	—	—	—	—	—
Prx. Sesa.	4	2.34	4	8.00	1	50.00	—	—	—	—	—	—	—	—	—
Dis. Sesa.	—	—	—	—	—	—	—	—	—	—	—	—	—	—	—
Sesamoid	3	1.75	3	6.00	1	50.00	—	—	—	—	—	—	—	—	—
Phal. 1	2	1.17	1	2.00	1	50.00	—	—	—	—	—	—	—	—	—
Phal. 2	3	1.75	2	4.00	1	50.00	—	—	—	—	—	—	—	—	—
Phal. 3	2	1.17	2	4.00	1	50.00	—	—	—	—	—	—	—	—	—
Longbone	45	26.32	—	—	—	—	—	—	—	—	—	—	—	2	4.44
Cancellous	—	—	—	—	—	—	—	—	—	—	—	—	—	—	—
Indeterm.	3	1.75	—	—	—	—	—	—	—	—	—	—	—	—	—
TOTAL	171	99.90	50	100.00			3	0	3	0				12	7.02

[a]NISP, Number of identifiable specimens.
[b]MNE, Minimum number of elements.
[c]MNI, Minimum number of individuals.
[d]%MNI, MNI of each element observed expressed as percent of maximum MNI value—34 animals (prox. femur).
[e]Unfused NISP, Unfused MNE, Unfused MNI, and Total Immature %MNI tabulations include 1 (probable) fetal or neonatal patella. Total Immature %MNI calculated in same manner as %MNI (see note 4 above), based on maximum immature MNI value of 10 animals (prox. femur).
[f]Percent of NISP value in same row in Column (1).

5
Antelope Procurement and Hunting Strategies at the Henderson Site

Preston T. Miracle
Cambridge University

Introduction

Pronghorn antelope (*Antilocapra americana*) remains are found in numerous archaeological sites in the American Southwest. Pronghorn congregate in large herds, enabling intensive and productive communal hunting, and they breed quickly (about twice as fast as North American deer) so that populations can sustain relatively high levels of predation pressure without declining significantly. Ethnographic accounts confirm these expectations. Pronghorn were pursued with both extensive (individual stalks) and intensive (communal hunts) strategies. Pronghorn, along with mule deer (*Odocoileus hemionus*), were a particularly important element of the diet in areas well beyond the normal range of the bison. They may also have become increasingly important to hunters within the range of bison at times when bison numbers declined, due perhaps to deteriorating range conditions or overhunting, or where the herds became less easily accessible (e.g., Davis and Fisher 1990). Despite the pronghorn's importance to ethnographically documented Southwestern societies, we know little about its economic role in the region's prehistory.

Geography, Climate, and Vegetation

The Henderson Site is situated on the southern edge of the Hondo River valley, on a small ridge at the point where the Hondo enters the alluvial flats of the Pecos Valley (Fig. 5.1; see also Rocek and Speth 1986:2-6). The topography of the immediate area varies from flat to rolling limestone hills, with elevations between 1135-1300 m. The annual precipitation in the area (measured at Roswell, ca. 17 km to the northeast of Henderson), ranges from 25 cm to 50 cm, with extremes of 12 cm and 84 cm in the 76 years on record (Kelley 1984:5). Kelley (1984:3) notes that dry-farming is considered "uncertain" when annual rainfall is below about 35 cm and "hazardous" when annual rainfall is below 25 cm. In the hilly terrain west of the Pecos Valley, only a thin layer of soil covers the rocky substrate; this soil supports an open vegetation of short grasses and perennial forbs and shrubs. Soils are deeper and more productive on the floodplain of the Hondo, but recent land leveling and irrigation activities have so altered the drainage that one can only guess at the farming potential of the valley in the distant past. Henderson is near, or within, the ecotone between mixed prairie and desert grassland (Howard and Bradybaugh 1983). Only a few trees are visible from the site today, and these are clustered along the old river channel.

Ecology of Medium Ungulates in Southeastern New Mexico

Antelope are primarily animals of grasslands and prairies. They avoid broken terrain or areas with vegetation over 75 cm tall (Howard et al. 1973; Wood 1989). Antelope are quite catholic in their diet, eating over 54 species of grasses, forbs, and shrubs (Howard et al. 1973), but prefer forbs. Mule deer, in contrast, prefer broken and covered terrain such as hardwood draws or wooded hills. Therefore, although antelope and deer food habits and habitat-use patterns overlap, there is a distinct spatial segregation between the two taxa due to their differing terrain and cover preferences (Wood 1989). The Henderson Site is located in good antelope country, and they are abundant in the

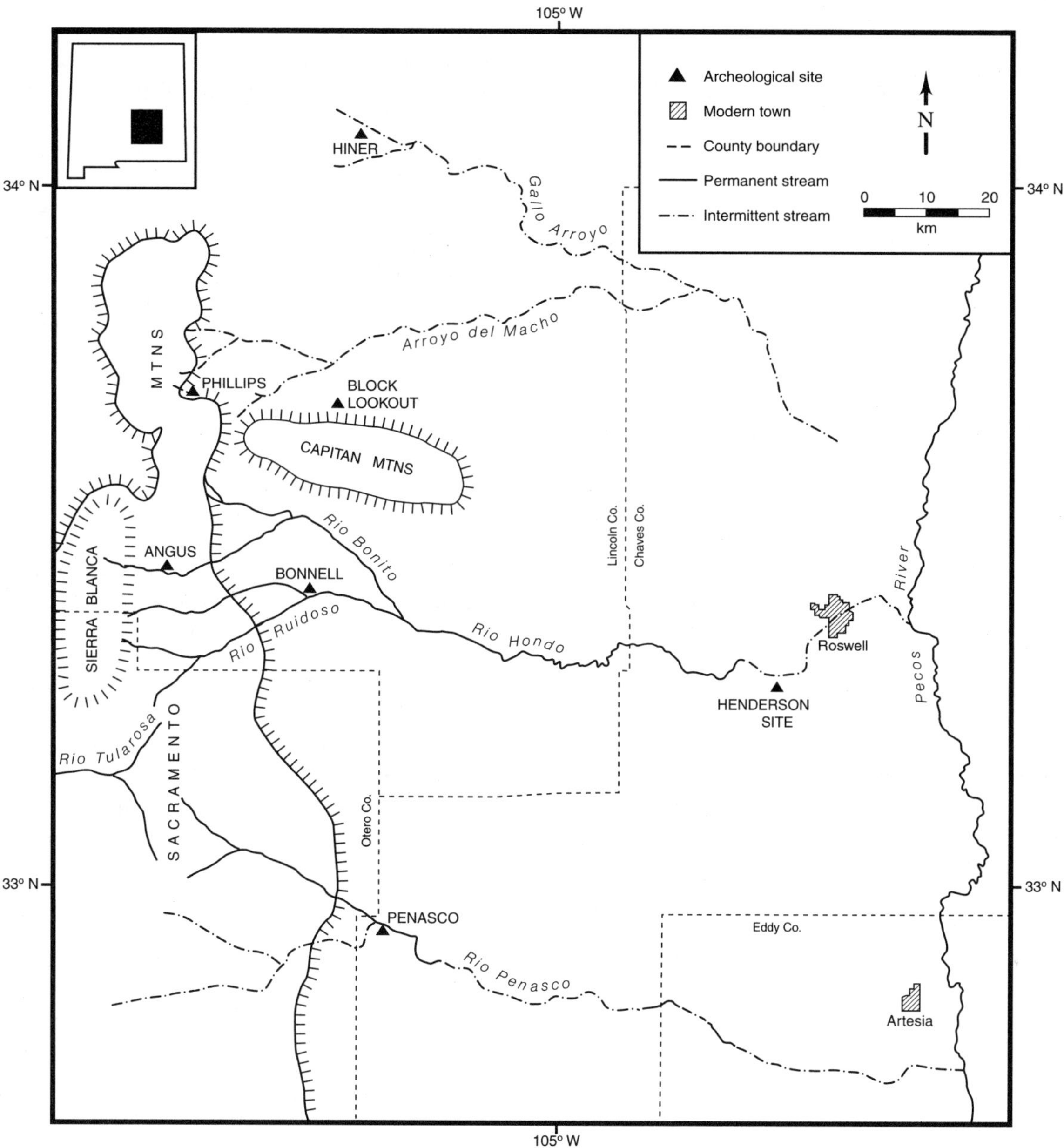

Figure 5.1. Map of principal late prehistoric archaeological sites in southeastern New Mexico.

region today (Howard and Bradybaugh 1983), although deer are also encountered, especially in the thickets along the Pecos and Hondo channels.

Methods

Identification

All excavated fill was screened in the field through quarter-inch mesh. Remains were roughly sorted by element and identifiability. Boxes of large fragments were also searched for identifiable remains. A fragment was considered "identifiable" if it could be identified to body-size category ("medium ungulate") and element and, in some cases, side (for long-bone shaft fragments, scapula fragments, and cranial fragments). Remains had been washed and labeled with either complete provenience information or lot numbers. Every coded element was assigned a sequential number (circled to distinguish it from the lot number). All remains from a particular element were coded at one time, with the exception of a sample of bones separated for isotopic analysis. Three bone tools were also coded and included in this analysis.

All identifications were made using modern comparative material curated in the zooarchaeology range of the University

Table 5.1. Degree of burning (NISP) of medium ungulate remains at Henderson Site.

Provenience	Total Burned NISP	Calcined	
		NISP	%
East Bar	25	15	60.0
Center Bar	35	15	42.8
Combined room blocks	60	30	50.0
East Plaza	46	21	45.6
Entire site	110	52	47.2

of Michigan Museum of Anthropology. The comparative material available included complete skeletons from the following taxa: one pronghorn antelope (male), one mule deer (female and fetus), two bighorn sheep (male and female), two wapiti or elk (male and female), and several white-tailed deer (male and female). Partial skeletons were available for one pronghorn antelope (female) and one mule deer (neonate). Reference was also made to Lawrence (1951) and Gilbert (1980) in the identification of remains.

Identifications to genus and species were only made if an identification was certain. Antelope identification was straightforward since there is only one species in the genus, *Antilocapra americana*. Most deer remains were too fragmentary to allow species identification. In a few cases, a tentative identification to species was possible, although these require larger comparative samples before we can make a positive identification. Remains not identifiable to genus were identified as "deer/antelope," since there were no positively identified remains of bighorn sheep in the material recovered from Henderson in 1980-1981.[1] However, a more accurate description would be "medium ungulate," allowing for the possibility of a few bighorn sheep remains among the fragments; this more inclusive grouping will be used in this chapter.

Coding

All identified remains were coded for element, species, side, end, fusion, and so forth using a numerical code adapted from "Bonesort" (Redding et al. 1975-77). More detailed notes were taken on mandibles and maxillae with teeth, cutmarks, patterns of burning, measurements, conjoins, and criteria for estimating the minimum number of elements (MNE).

The degree of burning was coded for all fragments. In the preliminary analysis of the data, the relative representation of calcined (gray to white) and charred (black) fragments were compared, but there were no striking differences by excavation area (Table 5.1), and sample sizes were too small to compare differential degrees of burning by body part. Therefore, the two categories were conflated into the category "burned."

All fragments were examined for traces of human modification. Only marks that were distinctly "V"-shaped in cross-section, narrow, and linear were identified as cutmarks. Most of these marks occurred in parallel sets. See Lyman (1987) for an overview of the growing literature on cutmark morphology and interpretation. Measurements taken on medium ungulate elements are described and defined in Table A5.1 at the end of the chapter. Guidelines and definitions developed by von den Driesch (1976) were followed whenever possible. Measurements were made with dial calipers and are recorded in millimeters to the nearest tenth. Identified cutmarks were noted and recorded by creating composite drawings for all cutmarks on an element. Tools made on medium ungulate bones that could be identified to body part were included in this analysis. Since only three elements were so identified (one proximal ulna and two proximal metacarpals), their inclusion or exclusion should not significantly affect the results of the analysis.

Measurement and Sexing of Antelope Remains

Standard measurements were taken of the Henderson antelope to allow comparison with other assemblages in the region. For the moment, such a comparison has been thwarted by the lack of published measurements from other sites or modern samples.[2] The Henderson measurements are presented in full in Tables A5.2 (antelope) and A5.3 (deer), in the appendix to this chapter, in the hope that others will be forthcoming with metric data. Stratified samples from the East Plaza were too small to test for a change in body size over time. Similarly, sample sizes of most elements were too small to allow a meaningful comparison between the room blocks and East Plaza. Except for the breadth of the trochlea of the distal humerus in antelope, the different areas of the site were not significantly different (one-tailed, two sample t-tests, $t = 0.89$, $p = 0.20$).

One of the primary goals of measurement was to attempt to distinguish between the sexes for different elements, as has been done for bison (Speth 1983). Pronghorn males average about 10% larger than females in body weight (Kitchen and O'Gara 1982). Males and females also differ in horn morphology (females lack the additional "prong"), but it is unclear how this difference is manifest in the underlying horn core. In the two modern antelope measured (a male and a female), the male's long bones were consistently longer than the female's but had smaller articular ends. Plots of measurements made on the Henderson archaeological material were neither bimodal nor easily interpretable as sexual dimorphism. Therefore, the sexing of individual elements was unsuccessful (excepting the innominate discussed below). At present, it is unclear whether this is because of the limited size of the sample of modern antelope available for measurement, or a limitation inherent in the species.

The innominate is sexually dimorphic in morphology in domestic sheep and goat, species similar in skeletal morphology and body size to the pronghorn (Boessneck 1969; Prummel and Frisch 1988). Two types of differences have been noted. First, there are contrasts in the subpubic border (ventral surface cau-

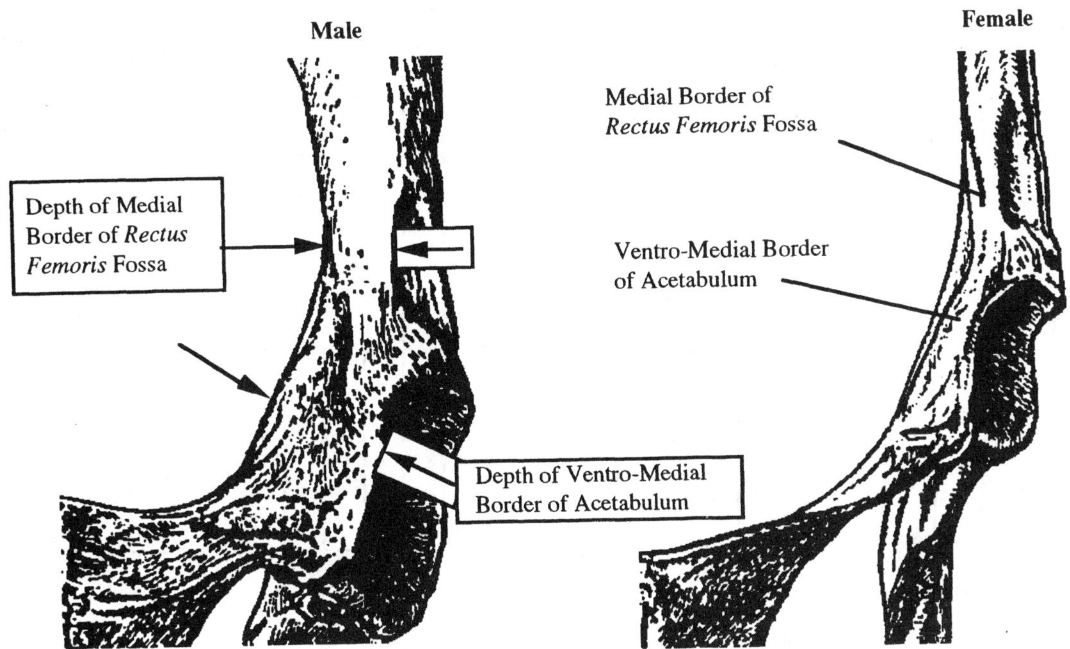

Figure 5.2. Sex differences in medium ungulate innominates and measurements made to sex innominates.

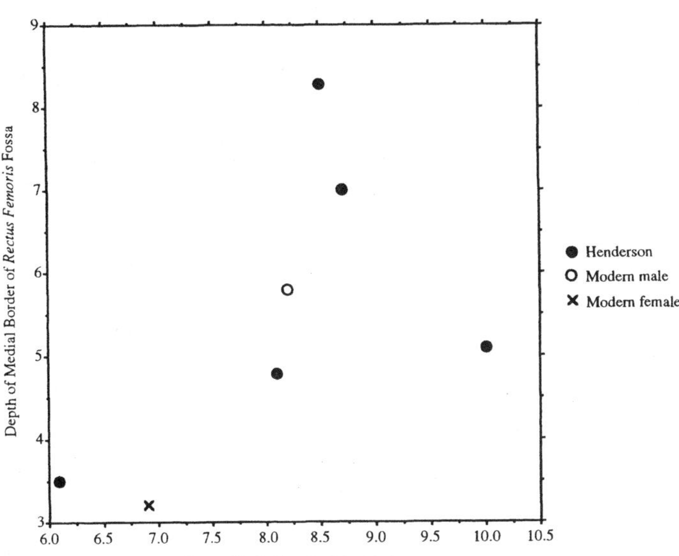

Figure 5.3. Correlation of sexually dimorphic features of the innominate in antelope.

dal to the pubic symphysis) due to the attachment of the penis in males (Taber 1956). However, I could not identify any subpubic portions of the pubis in the Henderson assemblages. Second, there are differences in the medial acetabular area of the ilium and pubis that most probably reflect the presence of a birth canal in females (Fig. 5.2). On the ilium immediately cranial from the acetabulum is an elongated pit for the origin of the rectus femoris (rectus femoris fossa). In males the medial border of the rectus femoris fossa is deep dorso-ventrally (roughly superior-inferior in ungulates due to the horizontal position of the pelvis), whereas in females the medial border is narrow dorso-ventrally. The ventro-medial border of the acetabulum (where the pubis and ilium fuse) is much deeper dorso-ventrally in males than in females of similar body size (Boessneck 1969:345). The male and female antelope specimens in the comparative collection unequivocally show these differences. Other differences that Boessneck (1969) and Prummel and Frisch (1988) observed in the shape and rugosity of the ilium and pubis in sheep/goat were not clearly marked in the comparative pronghorn specimens, and therefore were not used in the analysis of the archaeological remains.

Measurements were taken on the depth of the medial border of the rectus femoris fossa and the depth of the ventro-medial border of the acetabulum (Fig. 5.2). Measurements were also taken on the length (cranio-caudal) of the acetabulum to control for covariance with body size independent of sex. Plots of the depth of the medial border of the rectus femoris fossa and depth of the ventro-medial border of the acetabulum against the length of the acetabulum showed little relationship (Spearman's rank correlation, $r_s = 0.04$ and $r_s = 0.0$). On the other hand, the depth of the medial border of the rectus femoris fossa and the depth of the ventro-medial border of the acetabulum positively covary ($r_s = 0.71$), although the relationship is not statistically significant (Fig. 5.3). The frequency distributions of the depth of the medial border of the rectus femoris fossa and the depth of the ventro-medial border of the acetabulum are bimodal without overlap (Figs. 5.4 and 5.5). On the basis of this analysis, archaeological specimens with a rectus femoris fossa medial border less than 4 mm deep were classified as female. Also classed as female were specimens with

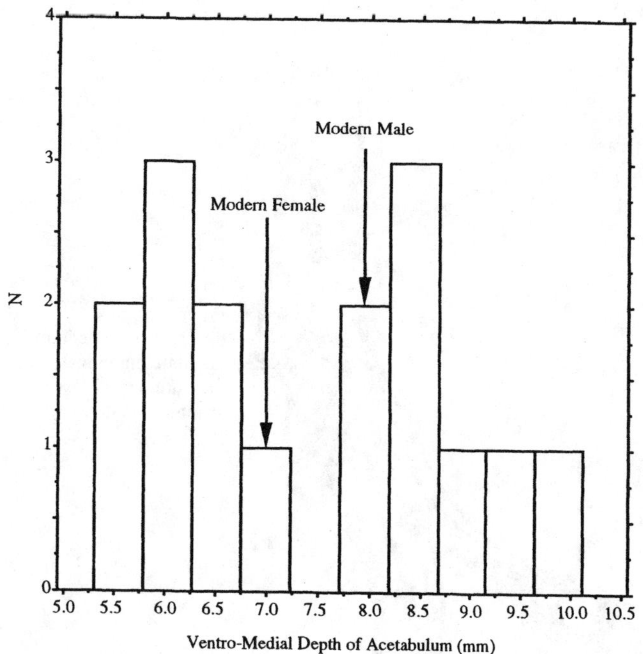

Figure 5.4. Ventro-medial depth of the acetabulum in Henderson and modern antelope.

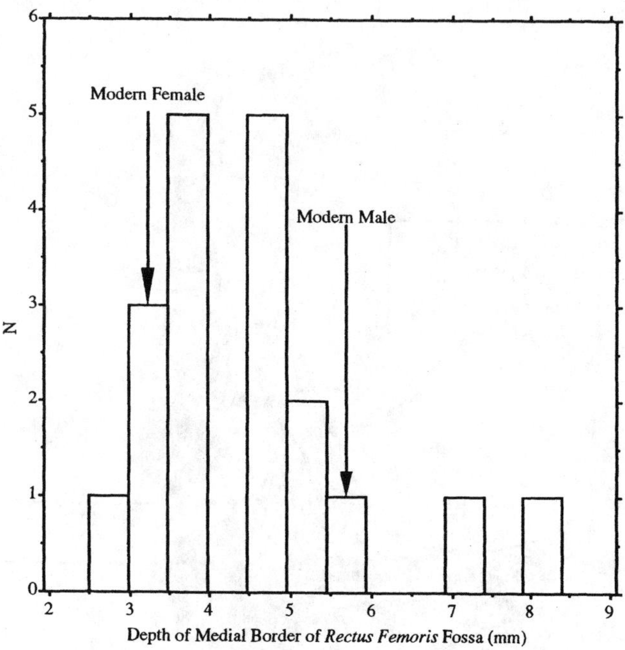

Figure 5.5. Depth of medial border of rectus femoris fossa in Henderson and modern antelope.

ventro-medial border of the acetabulum less than 7.5 mm deep. It should be noted that the five specimens that preserved both of these features produced internally consistent sex estimates.

Units of Quantification

Four units of quantification are used in this analysis. They are: (1) number of identifiable specimens (NISP); (2) minimum number of elements (MNE); (3) minimum number of individuals (MNI); and (4) minimum animal units (MAU). The NISP is simply the number of specimens identified to a taxonomic category (whether species, order, or class). The MNE controls for the differential fragmentation of skeletal elements and insures that samples are independent (otherwise a bone could be counted more than once if fragments were in different samples). It has been calculated by the presence of specific features on each element or portion of an element: M^2 of the skull, articular condyle of the mandible, head of the proximal femur, ischial portion of the acetabulum, distal end of first and second phalanges. The particular feature chosen for an element was the portion most represented in the assemblage. In some cases, different criteria were even used for lefts and rights of the same element (e.g., lateral condyle for right distal femur, medial condyle for left distal femur).

The MNI is then the minimum number of individuals that can account for the observed MNE, taking side and epiphyseal fusion into consideration. This assumes that in a given animal the rate of epiphyseal fusion will be bilaterally symmetrical; that is, if the right proximal humerus is fused, the left proximal humerus is also fused. The MNI was only calculated for the site as a whole. MNI's are sensitive to the lumping and splitting of samples (Grayson 1984:27-35). MNI's calculated separately for each excavation area would, when summed, probably give a larger total than MNI's calculated for the site as a whole. This is due to the interdependence of samples. Unless one is certain that the sampled populations are independent, one risks counting an animal twice if its elements are not evenly distributed within a site.

One way to control for the interdependence of samples from within the site is to standardize MNE's with respect to the body. This is done by dividing the MNE by the number of that element present in the skeleton. The resulting measure, the MAU, gives the most conservative estimates of abundance, since side and age are ignored (Frison and Todd 1986:69-71), but it can be safely summed and compared among different units. For these reasons, MAU was used instead of MNI for all intrasite comparisons.

The MNI and MAU are inherently conservative in giving "minimum" estimates, but differ in their underlying assumptions. The MNI asks "how many animals 'stand behind' the faunal assemblage" (Binford 1978:69). This assumes that faunal remains were introduced to the site and assemblage as parts of entire carcasses, of which the accurate estimation of the minimum number is one of the goals of the analysis. Built into the MAU, however, is the assumption that bones might have been introduced into the site and assemblage only as parts of carcasses. An analysis of the relative number of MAU's (usually standardized against the most abundant element as %MAU) for different elements should indicate whether entire carcasses or only parts of carcasses were introduced into a site and assemblage. One does not, however, have to assume this *a priori*.

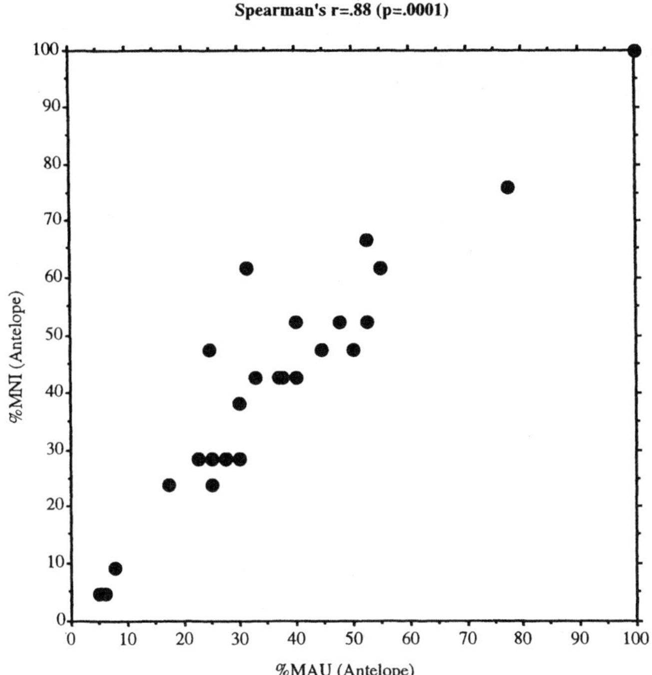

Figure 5.6. %MAU vs. %MNI for Henderson Site antelope (see text for definitions).

As shown in Figure 5.6, MNI and MAU give very similar results for the Henderson antelope when the assemblage is treated as a whole. For the reasons enumerated above, however, MAU is preferred for intrasite comparisons.

The samples from the East (n = 276) and Center bars (n = 458) were combined for the majority of the analysis and labeled "room blocks" or "combined room blocks," to alleviate the sample-size problem in comparisons between the assemblages.

Description of the Medium Ungulate Assemblage

Taxonomic Description

Only pronghorn and deer were identified in the medium ungulate assemblage. It was possible to distinguish with reasonable certainty between the two genera for all elements except thoracic vertebrae, lumbar vertebrae, caudal vertebrae, ribs, costal ribs, sesamoids, and the hyoid. Bones from both genera were found in all of the major excavation units (Tables 5.2a, 5.2b, A5.4-A5.19). Fetal remains (Table A5.20) were not identifiable to genera, but all were clearly from medium-sized ungulates.

Odocoileus. Both mule deer (*Odocoileus hemionus*) and white-tailed deer (*O. virginianus*) are present in the region today (Bailey 1931). Deer were frequently seen near the site during the five seasons of excavation (1980, 1981, 1994, 1995, 1997), and in all cases were mule deer. Unfortunately, deer remains from Henderson were not identifiable beyond the genus level. Describing archaeological remains from southeastern New Mexico that are roughly contemporaneous with those from Henderson, Driver (1985, 1989) also has not identified deer remains to species. A little farther to the northwest, and roughly contemporaneous with Henderson, at Gran Quivira Mound 7, both mule and white-tailed deer have been identified, although the criteria for identification are not given (McKusick 1981).

Antilocapra americana. Antelope are found in the Roswell area today (Howard and Bradybaugh 1983) and have been found in a number of archaeological sites in addition to Henderson in southeastern New Mexico (e.g., Driver 1985, 1989). McKusick (1981) identified pronghorn antelope at Gran Quivira Mound 7 as *Antilocapra americana americana*. No attempt was made to place the Henderson antelope in one of the five extant antelope subspecies due both to a lack of suitable comparative material

Table 5.2a. Species composition of medium ungulates by provenience (room blocks) at Henderson Site

Species	East Bar				Center Bar				Combined Room Blocks			
	NISP	%	MNE	%	NISP	%	MNE	%	NISP	%	MNE	%
Antelope	179	66.8	115	71.9	301	65.9	174	66.4	480	66.2	289	68.5
Deer	14	5.2	11	6.9	22	4.8	16	6.1	36	5.0	27	6.4
Antelope/deer	75	28.0	34	21.3	134	29.3	72	27.5	209	28.8	106	25.1
Total	268	100.0	160	100.0	457	100.0	262	100.0	725	100.0	422	100.0

Table 5.2b. Species composition of medium ungulates by provenience (East Plaza and entire site) at Henderson Site.

Species	East Plaza				Entire Site			
	NISP	%	MNE	%	NISP	%	MNE	%
Antelope	545	76.3	365	79.5	1095	71.6	696	74.8
Deer	27	3.8	19	4.1	66	4.3	47	5.1
Antelope/deer	142	19.9	75	16.3	369	24.1	187	20.1
Total	714	100.0	459	100.0	1530	100.0	930	100.0

and to serious doubts over the validity of these subspecies that have been expressed in the literature (see Kitchen and O'Gara 1982). Antelope are by far the most abundant taxon in the medium ungulate assemblage (Tables 5.2a, 5.2b). This is true for all excavation areas and levels.

In most of the analyses that follow, antelope, deer, and deer/antelope remains are treated together as "medium ungulates." Since mule/white-tailed deer and antelope are roughly similar in body size and proportions, and furthermore, since antelope constitute the vast majority of the identifiable specimens, lumping these categories loses little in general comparisons. Therefore, "medium ungulate" is a reasonable category for the taphonomic and economic analyses that follow.

Comparisons Between Different Proveniences

Tables 5.2a and 5.2b summarize antelope, deer, and deer/antelope remains from the major areas of the site excavated in 1980-1981. Measured by both NISP and MNE, antelope are more numerous in all areas than deer by a factor greater than 10. There is only a slight variation in the proportion of antelope and deer within the site; deer are more common in the combined room block assemblage than in the East Plaza, although the difference is not statistically significant. More important, remains identified as "deer/antelope" are much more numerous in the room blocks than in the East Plaza. The difference between the areas is statistically significant ($\chi^2 = 14.02, p = 0.001$ for MNE). The higher proportion of deer/antelope remains in the room blocks is probably due to increased fragmentation (hence reduced identifiability) of bones deposited in the structures compared to those in the East Plaza deposits. Burned bones of medium ungulates are present in modest numbers in the site (Table 5.3). Burned bones are slightly more frequent in the room blocks, and a greater proportion of the burned bones are calcined in the room blocks than in the East Plaza deposits, but neither difference is statistically significant. Thus, although the room blocks and East Plaza deposits differ slightly in composition, overall they are very similar, differing primarily in the greater degree of fragmentation of bones in the room blocks.

In Table 5.4, the NISP is divided by the volume of excavated fill to calculate NISP densities for different areas of the site. This brings out a contrast hidden by the simple NISP counts. The density of medium ungulate remains is almost six times greater in the East Plaza midden and Room C-5 deposits than in any of the other areas of the site sampled in 1980-1981. The high density of bones in Room C-5 confirms field impressions that this room contained a considerable amount of trash in the fill.

The medium ungulate remains in both the room blocks and East Plaza deposits represent either intentionally dumped refuse, accumulated refuse from proximate activities deposited *in situ*, or both. The similarity in assemblage composition between the deposits suggests that the sources of refuse in the two areas were similar. While they are qualitatively similar, they are quantitatively very different as shown by the contrast in NISP densities. Is the contrast in NISP density due to a difference in the rate of sediment deposition or trash deposition? In the former case, one would expect NISP density to increase proportionally as the rate of sediment deposition decreased. A test of this hypothesis requires precise chronological control of the duration of sediment accumulation. Unfortunately, the chronological resolution of the radiocarbon dates within the deposits is fairly poor. Nonetheless, the rate of sediment deposition would have to be six times faster in the room blocks (excluding Room C-5) to account for the contrast in NISP density. Rough calculations of sedimentation rates were made for Rooms E-4, C-5, and the East Plaza (grid squares 509N549-550E), using dates only from fill and excluding two chronologically inconsistent dates (Beta-3336 in Room E-4, and Beta-14071 in the East Plaza) (see Chapter 2). Assuming that the calibrated dates are correct, the maximum rates of sedimentation are: Room E-4, 0.57 cm/year; Room C-5, 2.86 cm/year; East Plaza, 2.00 cm/year. Contrary to the hypothesis of different rates of sedimentation, the deposits in the East Plaza and Room C-5 accumulated faster than those of the room blocks (excluding Room C-5). This strongly suggests that the contrast in NISP density in medium ungulates is due to differences in the rate of introducing trash into the deposits. In particular, trash was introduced at a much faster rate into the East Plaza and Room C-5 than it was in the room blocks (excluding Room C-5).

Sexing of Antelope

Using the measurement criteria on the pubis discussed above, it was possible to sex a number of the antelope remains. The NISP and MNI of antelope, by sex, are presented in Table 5.5. In addition, one deer pubis was sexed as female. In the site as a whole, nearly equal numbers of male and female antelope were killed, whether measured by NISP, MNE, or MNI. Broken down by area, there is no significant difference between the areas if remains are quantified by NISP, MNE, or MNI ($\chi^2 = 2.74, p = 0.10$ for NISP). These results are tenuous, however, due to the small absolute size of the samples. Females are slightly more abundant in the room blocks, while males are slightly more abundant in the East Plaza. Both sexes, however, are present in both assemblages.

Aging of Antelope

The mandibular teeth of antelope were aged using eruption and wear criteria developed by Dow and Wright (1962) and eruption times given by Hoover et al. (1959). Gilbert (1980:107) suggests that the M_3 erupts six months earlier in populations in Montana than in Colorado (Dow and Wright 1962), while the canine erupts six months earlier in populations in Colorado than in Montana (Hoover et al. 1959). A comparison of the eruption tables, however, shows considerable overlap in the eruption of the M_3. According to Dow and Wright (1962:3, Table 1), erup-

Table 5.3. Distribution of burned bones by provenience at Henderson Site.

Species	East Bar		Center Bar		Combined Room Blocks		East Plaza		Entire Site	
	NISP	%	NISP	%	NISP	%	NISP	%	NISP	%
Antelope	17	9.5	27	9.0	44	9.2	38	7.0	85	7.8
Deer	1	7.7	1	4.5	2	5.7	1	3.7	3	4.5
Antelope/ deer	7	9.3	7	5.2	14	6.7	7	4.9	22	6.0
Total	25	9.4	35	7.7	60	8.3	46	6.4	110	7.2

Table 5.4. Density (NISP/m^3 of excavated sediment) of medium ungulate remains by provenience at Henderson Site.[a]

Species	East Bar (34.85 m^3)		Center Bar (Excluding Room C-5) (16.99 m^3)		Center Bar (Including Room C-5) (8.77 m^3)		Combined Room Blocks (60.61 m^3)		East Plaza (16.20 m^3)		Entire Site (79.56 m^3)	
	NISP	Den.	NISP	Den.	NISP	Den.	NISP	Den.	NISP	Den.	NISP	Den.
Antelope	179	5.1	60	3.5	241	27.5	480	7.9	545	33.6	1095	13.8
Deer	14	0.4	5	0.3	17	1.9	36	0.6	27	1.7	66	0.8
Ant./deer	75	2.2	31	1.8	103	11.7	209	3.4	142	8.8	369	4.6
Total	268	7.7	96	5.7	361	41.3	725	12.0	714	44.1	1530	19.2

[a]Volume of excavated sediments for each provenience is provided in parentheses (1980 - 1981 seasons).

Table 5.5. Distribution of male and female antelope by provenience at Henderson Site.

Sex	Combined Room Blocks			East Plaza			Entire Site		
	NISP	MNE	MNI	NISP	MNE	MNI	NISP	MNE	MNI
Female	8	4	2	6	4	2	14	8	4
Male	3	2	2	9	7	4	12	9	6

Table 5.6. Age at death of Henderson antelope based on mandibular tooth eruption and wear.

Dental Age	NISP	MNI	Specimen Number[a]	Description of Teeth
3-6 mo.	2	1	1533	M_2 complete bud, erupting
4-9 mo.	1	1	1471	M_2 erupting, M_3 unerupted bud
6-12 mo.	2	1	1464	dP_4 anterior infundibulum absent, M_1 roots unformed
1-2 yr.	5	1	1491	M_3 erupting
2-3 yr.	4	1	1459	P_3 erupting
3+ yr.	12	1	1487	M_2 broken in alveolus, roots open
3-6 yr.	12	3	1466, 1467, 1469	M_2 and M_3 in alveolus, all infundibula present
6+ yr.	5	4	1493, 1517, 1540, 1541	M_2 (in alveolus or loose), all infundibula absent
Total	43	13		

[a]Sequential identification number assigned to each medium ungulate specimen included in MNI tabulation (circled on specimen to distinguish it from the lot number also written on each specimen).

tion begins between the eighth and twelfth month, and is finished before the twentieth month. Similarly, Hoover et al. (1959:46, Table 14) bracket the eruption of the M_3 between the ninth and twenty-third month. These dates, however, are the very earliest and latest possible. If, instead, one calculates the average dates for the commencement and completion of eruption, the range is from the eleventh to nineteenth month, dates almost identical to those given by Dow and Wright (1962). Data presented from hunter-killed antelope show the canine to be quite variable in its date of eruption (Dow and Wright 1962:14, Table 5). Considering this variability, it is uncertain if the contrast with the Colorado population is more than a sampling problem, and the eruption of the canine should not be used to age specimens. In any case, the Henderson mandibles were aged solely on the basis of molariform teeth.

Studies of incremental growth lines in the cementum of incisors (McCutchen 1969; Kerwin and Mitchell 1971) give reasonably similar results to wear-age estimates (60.9% agreement, n = 184). Agreement between the methods was higher for younger age classes (2.5 to 5.5 years), although wear-age techniques tended to underestimate the cementum age in younger age classes by several months. This systematic bias should not significantly affect the shape of a mortality curve based on wear-age estimates.

Table 5.7. Estimated epiphyseal fusion times (months) of long bones in mule deer (*Odocoileus hemionus*).

Skeletal Element	Fusion Times (months)		
	Unfused	Fusing	Fused
Prox. humerus	0 - 34	29 - 65	52+
Dist. humerus	0 - 14	8 - 14	14+
Prox. ulna	0 - 34	29 - 65	52+
Prox. radius	0 - 8	6 - 15	14+
Dist. radius	0 - 29	27 - 65+	65+
Dist. metacarpal	0 - 27	20 - 65+	65+
Prox. femur	0 - 29	27 - 65	52+
Dist. femur	0 - 34	29 - 65+	65+
Prox. tibia	0 - 34	29 - 52	34+
Dist. tibia	0 - 15	14 - 19	17+
Calcaneus	0 - 19	17 - 65+	65+
Dist. metatarsal	0 - 27	20 - 65	52+
Phalanx 1	0 - 14	8 - 15	14+
Phalanx 2	0 - 14	8 - 15	14+

Source: Lewall and Cowan (1963)

A more serious problem with wear-age techniques is a difference in rates of wear and eruption due to dietary or nutritional differences. Using incremental lines in cementum in molars as a control for age, Haynes (1984) found the rate of molar wear to be twice as fast in Southern Plains bison compared to Northern Plains bison, and suggested that the difference is due to a low grit/browsing diet of sedges in the north, as opposed to a high grit/grazing diet of grasses (high silica content) in the south. Keeping this in mind, I assume that rate of wear for prehistoric populations in southeastern New Mexico did not differ significantly from that of present-day Montana and Colorado.

Estimates of the age at death for the Henderson antelope are presented in Table 5.6. Age estimates were possible on mandibles and loose teeth from 13 individuals. MNI's were calculated after teeth were assigned to age classes and, as predicted by Grayson (1984:27-35), the resulting MNI's for a partitioned sample are greater than for the sample taken as a whole.

The epiphyseal fusion of long bones provides another method of calculating the age at death. Epiphyseal fusion of long bones allows only three categories—unfused, fusing, and fused—so that in the absence of articulated elements from a single skeleton it provides only rough information about the relative ages of animals represented. Silver (1969), however, has shown that fusion times are accelerated in domesticated wild sheep. Similarly, a well-fed population has accelerated fusion (Lewall and Cowan 1963; Silver 1969). Both of these factors suggest that precise age estimates are not possible on the basis of epiphyseal fusion in the absence of independent controls of nutritional state and domestication. Fusion times for mule deer were used in this analysis as an estimate for fusion times for pronghorn antelope since pronghorn data were not available. Mule deer fusion times were considered a better analog than those of domestic sheep due to the apparent effect of domestication on fusion time. In the absence of information about the overall nutritional state of prehistoric pronghorn populations in the area, I assume that the hunted populations were reasonably well fed.

The estimated times of epiphyseal fusion are presented in Table 5.7. These values were calculated for males in good condition. Fusion data for the Henderson antelope and deer/antelope (combined) are summarized in Table 5.8; fusion data for the Henderson deer are summarized in Table 5.9.

Fusion data for deer provide the best age data for this animal due to the paucity of teeth. Of the three individuals in the sample, one was younger than 15 months (based on the distal tibia), while the other two were older than 5.5 years (based on the distal metacarpal). Data from the other elements are consistent with these estimates, as is the single erupted M_3 (age greater than 2.5 years).

In the analysis of the antelope fusion data (Table 5.8), I have combined elements identified only as medium ungulate with

Table 5.8. Epiphyseal fusion data for antelope and deer/antelope at Henderson Site.

Skeletal Element	Epiphysis			Age Estimate in Months MNI		
	Unfused MNI	Fusing MNI	Fused MNI			
Prox. humerus	1	0	4	1: <34	4: >52	
Dist. humerus	1	1	15	1: <14	1: 8<<14	15: >14
Prox. ulna	6	0	3	6: <34	3: >52	
Prox. radius	0	0	13	13: >14		
Dist. radius	4	1	5	4: <29	1: 27<<65	5: >65
Dist. metacarpal	4	1	6	4: <27	1: 20<<65	6: >65
Prox. femur	4	1	6	4: <29	1: 27<<65	6: >52
Dist. femur	2	1	2	2: <34	1: 29<<65	2: >65
Prox. tibia	3	0	3	3: <34	3: >34	
Dist. tibia	3	0	6	3: <15	6: >17	
Calcaneus	2	0	7	2: <19	7: >65	
Dist. metatarsal	3	1	7	3: <27	1: 20<<65	7: >52
Phalanx 1	2	1	5	2: <14	1: 8<<15	5: >14
Phalanx 2	1	1	8	1: <14	1: 8<<15	8: >14

the antelope remains. Since over 90% of the elements identified to species were antelope, most of the remains identified as "medium ungulate" are probably antelope. The fusion data neatly complement the results based on mandibular dentitions. There are a moderate number of individuals younger than 15 months (MNI = 3 for distal tibia), and a large number of individuals older than 5.5 years (MNI = 7 for calcaneus). In both samples, very old individuals outnumber young individuals.

Carcass Units

In Tables 5.10-5.12, elements are grouped by major carcass unit for the "entire site" (all proveniences combined), combined room blocks, and East Plaza deposits. The carcass units are self-explanatory, with the following exceptions. The scapula is included with the appendicular elements, while the pelvis is included with the axial elements. The stylo-hyoid is included with the head. Upper front limb includes scapula and humerus; upper rear limb includes femur and patella. Foot elements that could not be identified to front or rear limb are only included in the upper/lower limb comparisons. Modified values for the front and rear limbs were used in the analysis since lower limb values are inflated by large numbers of small elements. This gives a truer comparison of the relative number of meat- and marrow-bearing elements within the limbs. The modified upper front limb includes scapula and humerus, while the modified lower front limb includes radius, ulna, and metacarpal. The modified upper rear limb includes only the femur, while the modified lower rear limb includes tibia and metatarsal.

Of the tabulated results, only the fragmentation index (FI) needs explication. The fragmentation index is a ratio of the MNE to NISP that can be calculated for any carcass unit or element. An alternative measure would be NISP/MNE or number of fragments per identified element. The problem with this measure is the division by zero that results when the MNE is 0. Speth and Rautman (see Chapter 4) develop and apply the fragmentation index in their analysis of the Henderson bison assemblages. The index increases in value with increased fragmentation (fewer MNE's relative to NISP). The FI, however, is only a rough measure of fragmentation since small fragments not identifiable to element were not included in its calculation. It is also important to note that all of the long bones were broken and MNE's were calculated separately for proximal and distal ends. A fragmentation index of zero only indicates each identifiable fragment from an element was sufficiently intact to be unambiguously tallied as an MNE.

In Table 5.13 elements from a complete antelope/deer skeleton are aggregated into the same carcass units that were used in Tables 5.10-5.12 above to provide expected values for comparison with the Henderson assemblage. In the Henderson medium ungulates, appendicular elements outnumber axial elements by over 3:1 in the East Plaza, while there are a few more axial elements (ratio of 2.7:1) in the combined room block assemblage. In a complete antelope skeleton, the ratio of appendicular to axial elements is 1.1:1. Chi-square tests show that the assemblages from both proveniences differ significantly from the expected frequency (p = 0.0001 in each case), but do not differ statistically from each other. When the axial skeleton is broken down into head vs. trunk elements, it is apparent that heads are present in the expected frequency, but that trunk elements are underrepresented. The slight contrast between the areas in carcass unit frequency is due to more trunk elements in the room blocks. Overall, however, this is a minor variation on a limb-dominated pattern.

Within the limbs, the frequency of front vs. rear and upper vs. lower elements varies slightly between the room blocks and

Table 5.9. Epiphyseal fusion data for deer at Henderson Site.

Skeletal Element	Epiphysis			Age Estimate in Months MNI	
	Unfused MNI	Fusing MNI	Fused MNI		
Dist. humerus	0	0	2	2: >14	
Prox. ulna	0	0	1	1: >52	
Prox. radius	0	0	1	1: >14	
Dist. radius	0	0	1	1: >65	
Dist. metacarpal	1	0	2	1: <27	2: >65
Prox. femur	1	0	0	1: <29	
Dist. femur	1	0	0	1: <34	
Prox. tibia	1	0	0	1: <34	
Dist. tibia	1	0	1	1: <15	1: >17
Dist. metatarsal	1	0	0	1: <27	
Phalanx 2	0	0	1	1: >14	

Table 5.10. Frequency of medium ungulate skeletal elements (NISP and MNE) by major carcass unit at Henderson Site (entire site).

Carcass Unit	Entire Site						
	NISP	%	MNE	%	Burned		FI[a]
					NISP	%	
Axial	514	33.6	236	26.3	27	5.3	54.1
Head	215	14.1	34	3.8	6	2.8	84.2
Trunk	299	19.5	202	22.5	21	7.0	32.4
Appendicular	1016	66.4	660	73.7	83	8.2	35.0
Total	1530		896		110	7.2	41.4
Front limb	356	52.4	237	55.9	19	5.3	33.4
Rear limb	323	47.6	187	44.1	27	8.4	42.1
Total	679		424		46	6.8	37.6
Upper limb	215	21.2	108	15.6	14	6.5	49.8
Lower limb	801	78.8	585	84.4	69	8.6	27.0
Total	1016		693		83	8.2	31.8
Upper front limb	129	36.2	64	27.0	10	7.8	50.4
Lower front limb	227	63.8	173	73.0	9	4.0	23.8
Total	356		237		19	5.3	33.4
Upper rear limb	86	25.6	44	22.0	4	4.7	48.8
Lower rear limb	250	74.4	156	78.0	23	9.2	37.6
Total	336		200		27	8.0	40.5
Mod. upper front limb	129	44.9	64	38.1	10	7.8	50.4
Mod. lower front limb	158	55.1	104	61.9	6	3.8	34.2
Total	287		168		16	5.6	41.5
Mod. upper rear limb	73	34.1	31	34.4	4	5.5	57.5
Mod. lower rear limb	141	65.9	59	65.6	14	9.9	58.2
Total	214		90		18	8.4	57.9

[a]FI (fragmentation index) = 100 - (MNE/NISP × 100).

Table 5.11. Frequency of medium ungulate skeletal elements (NISP and MNE) by major carcass unit at Henderson Site (combined room blocks).

Carcass Unit	Combined Room Blocks						
	NISP	%	MNE	%	Burned		FI[a]
					NISP	%	
Axial	262	36.1	114	27.0	17	6.5	56.5
Head	108	14.9	15	3.5	4	3.7	86.1
Trunk	154	21.2	99	23.5	13	8.4	35.7
Appendicular	463	63.9	308	73.0	43	9.3	33.5
Total	725		422		60	8.3	41.8
Front limb	151	53.2	104	60.1	6	4.0	31.1
Rear limb	133	46.8	69	39.9	11	8.3	48.1
Total	284		173		17	6.0	39.1
Upper limb	96	20.7	47	15.3	5	5.2	51.0
Lower limb	367	79.3	261	84.7	38	10.4	28.9
Total	463		308		43	9.3	33.5
Upper front limb	51	33.8	24	23.1	4	7.8	52.9
Lower front limb	100	66.2	80	76.9	2	2.0	20.0
Total	151		104		6	4.0	31.1
Upper rear limb	45	32.1	23	30.3	1	2.2	48.9
Lower rear limb	95	67.9	53	69.7	10	10.5	44.2
Total	140		76		11	7.9	45.7
Mod. upper front limb	51	44.0	24	34.8	4	7.8	52.9
Mod. lower front limb	65	56.0	45	65.2	2	3.1	30.8
Total	116		69		6	5.2	40.5
Mod. upper rear limb	38	39.2	16	40.0	1	2.6	57.9
Mod. lower rear limb	59	60.8	24	60.0	7	11.9	59.3
Total	97		40		8	8.2	58.8

[a]FI (fragmentation index) = 100 - (MNE/NISP × 100).

Table 5.12. Frequency of medium ungulate skeletal elements (NISP and MNE) by major carcass unit at Henderson Site (East Plaza).

Carcass Unit	East Plaza						
	NISP	%	MNE	%	Burned		FI[a]
					NISP	%	
Axial	229	32.1	113	24.6	10	4.4	50.7
Head	96	13.4	19	4.1	2	2.1	80.2
Trunk	133	18.6	94	20.5	8	6.0	29.3
Appendicular	485	67.9	346	75.4	36	7.4	28.7
Total	714		459		46	6.4	35.7
Front limb	181	51.3	119	50.9	13	7.2	34.3
Rear limb	172	48.7	115	49.1	14	8.1	33.1
Total	353		234		27	7.6	33.7
Upper limb	102	21.0	58	16.8	7	6.9	43.1
Lower limb	383	79.0	288	83.2	29	7.6	24.8
Total	485		346		36	7.4	28.7
Upper front limb	69	38.1	39	32.8	5	7.2	43.5
Lower front limb	112	61.9	80	67.2	8	7.1	28.6
Total	181		119		13	7.2	34.3
Upper rear limb	33	18.6	19	15.8	2	6.1	42.4
Lower rear limb	144	81.4	101	84.2	12	8.3	29.9
Total	177		120		14	7.9	32.2
Mod. upper front limb	69	45.4	39	43.3	5	7.2	43.5
Mod. lower front limb	83	54.6	51	56.7	5	6.0	38.6
Total	152		90		10	6.6	40.8
Mod. upper rear limb	28	27.5	14	28.0	2	7.1	50.0
Mod. lower rear limb	74	72.5	36	72.0	6	8.1	51.4
Total	102		50		8	7.8	51.0

[a]FI (fragmentation index) = 100 - (MNE/NISP × 100).

East Plaza, but in no case are the assemblages statistically different from each other or from the expected distribution of elements in a complete skeleton (Tables 5.10-5.13).

Patterns of burning on carcass units are summarized with the NISP of burned bones and the percentage of bones burned for each carcass unit. As discussed earlier, slightly more bones are burned in the room blocks than in the East Plaza. Comparing the major carcass units, in both areas the appendicular and trunk units are burned to a similar degree, while many fewer head elements are burned. Within the limb elements, however, the pattern of burning in the East Plaza is relatively uniform, while there is a bias for burning lower rear elements in the room blocks, although this difference is not statistically significant.

A comparison of fragmentation of the major carcass units (axial, head, trunk, appendicular) shows that remains from the room blocks are, in general, more fragmented than those from the East Plaza. This corroborates the previous observation that fewer remains could be identified to genus in the room blocks, and the corresponding interpretation of greater fragmentation in the room blocks. Therefore, the MNE is a more appropriate unit of measurement than NISP since it controls to some extent for differential fragmentation. The pattern of fragmentation in different carcass units, however, is fairly similar in the different areas. Trunk and appendicular elements are fragmented to a similar degree, while the head, not unexpectedly, is much more fragmented. This contrast may, in part, be due to the methods used in defining MNE's for the cranium. The cranium can fragment into many identifiable pieces (high NISP values), with only a few MNE's (in this case measured for maxillae and horn cores). No complete or even partially complete crania were recovered, however, suggesting the systematic processing or fragmentation of crania by human or natural agents. Fragmentation is the same in the front and rear limbs in the East Plaza, while in the room blocks the rear limbs are much more fragmented than the front limbs. Both areas show increased fragmentation in the upper limbs, but this is probably a product of the large number of small, compact elements in the lower limbs. When only the modified tallies for front and rear limbs are considered (i.e., excluding small, compact elements such as carpals and tarsals), the East Plaza shows increased fragmentation in the rear limbs relative to the front limbs, but similar degrees of fragmentation between upper and lower elements of front and rear limbs. In the room blocks, in contrast, the rear limbs are more fragmented than the front limbs than in the East Plaza, and the upper front limb elements are more fragmented than the lower front limb elements than in the East Plaza.

In summary, both East Plaza and room block assemblages are dominated by limb elements and underrepresented by trunk elements. When the different excavation areas are compared, however, in most cases chi-square tests show that the patterns in the two areas do not differ statistically. The major differences between the areas are in bone fragmentation, though they

Table 5.13. Expected frequencies (MNE) of elements by major carcass unit in a complete antelope/deer skeleton.

Carcass Unit	MNE	%
Axial	80	47.1
Head	7	4.1
Trunk	73	42.9
Appendicular	90	52.9
Total	170	
Front limb	46	51.1
Rear limb	44	48.9
Total	90	
Upper limb	14	15.6
Lower limb	76	84.4
Total	90	
Upper front limb	4	8.7
Lower front limb	42	91.3
Total	46	
Upper rear limb	2	4.6
Lower rear limb	42	95.5
Total	44	
Mod. upper front limb	2	40.0
Mod. lower front limb	3	60.0
Total	5	
Mod. upper rear limb	1	33.3
Mod. lower rear limb	2	66.7
Total	3	

Table 5.14. Number of fetal bones (NISP) by provenience at Henderson Site.

Provenience	Fetal NISP	Total NISP	Fetal %
East Plaza	9	714	1.3
Combined room blocks	7	725	1.0

are not statistically significant. Bones are more fragmented in the room block than in the East Plaza assemblages, and rear limbs and upper front limbs are more fragmented in the room block assemblages, while fragmentation in the limbs is constant in the East Plaza assemblages.

Taphonomy of Medium Ungulates at Henderson

Before considering behavioral or economic interpretations of faunal remains, it is important to consider the natural processes that might have modified and shaped the assemblage. The following natural processes were examined: bone preservation and weathering, carnivore/rodent destruction, and differential destruction mediated through bone density.

Bone preservation appears to have been quite good. As described in the analysis of the bison assemblage in Chapter 4, bones from the room blocks were in good to excellent condition. Bones from the East Plaza were in excellent condition at their initial exposure, but were demineralized and tended to disintegrate upon touch. While this necessitated the application of a preservative, all were recoverable. Body-part frequencies for different parts of the site (Tables A5.4-A5.20) show that the room blocks and East Plaza both contained low-density, easily destroyed elements as well as dense elements. This point is reinforced by the distribution of the particularly fragile fetal bones (Tables 5.14, A5.20). Although fetal bones are rare in the site in general, they are equally represented in the East Plaza and room blocks.

Bone weathering was not systematically coded for the assemblage, due to the difficulty in distinguishing unambiguously between bones damaged in excavation and those physically or chemically weathered. This was particularly a problem with the East Plaza assemblage. Preservative applied to specimens in the field, especially those from the East Plaza, altered the color of the bone and sometimes also obscured fine details on the surface of the bone, including traces of early weathering stages. Some elements displayed longitudinal cracks considered diagnostic of the early stages of weathering (Behrensmeyer 1978). A study controlling for the depositional area and bone preservation might reveal differences in the degree of weathering across the site. Nonetheless, the clear lack of evidence of Behrensmeyer's more advanced weathering stages suggests that weathering probably did not significantly alter the overall composition of the assemblage.

In six instances it was possible to conjoin medium ungulate remains with old breaks (as opposed to recent, excavation damage). In four cases, conjoined elements came from the same or adjacent excavation squares. In the remaining two cases, conjoined elements came from the same general excavation area, the East Plaza. The rarity of bone conjoins is probably due to the fragmentary nature of the assemblage, the exclusion of unidentified fragments from the analysis, and the partial sampling of archaeological deposits by excavation.

There is little evidence of either rodent or carnivore modification and destruction. Only one articular end, a distal humerus from a deer, displayed the substantial pitting and scoring diagnostic of carnivore, most likely canid, gnawing (Binford 1981; Haynes 1982). Other articular ends showed no evidence of carnivore gnawing. Examination of the smaller fragments suggested that a few were gnawed, but marks were not unequivocal and thus were left uncoded. Carnivores often enter long bones through articular ends, creating "long-bone cylinders" (Haynes 1982; Binford 1981:51). In contrast, humans typically break through long-bone shafts to open marrow cavities.[4] Therefore, the frequency of bone cylinders in an assemblage may be indicative of the importance of carnivores as agents of modification, although the preferential removal of articular ends by humans for grease rendering could lead to similar biases. In any case, long-bone cylinders are very rare in the medium ungulate assemblage (n = 6) at Henderson and exhibit no evidence of carnivore modification on either end. Studies of carnivore gnawing, however, suggest that the frequency and type of marks left by carnivores on bones is dependent on the context of consumption (Binford 1981:49). Furthermore, carnivores also modify assemblages by completely destroying bones and by transporting elements (Binford 1981:202-4; Haynes 1980, 1982). The

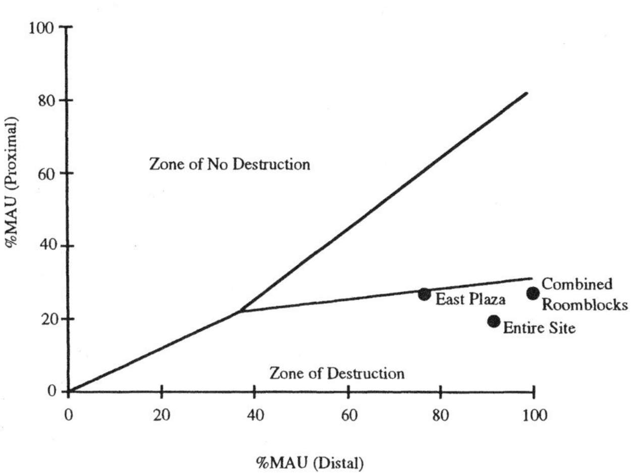

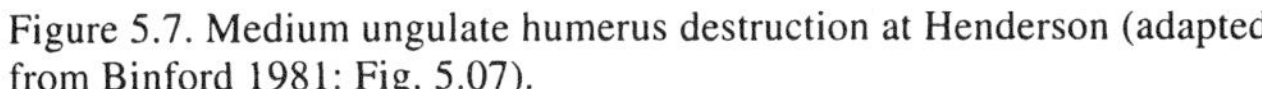

Figure 5.7. Medium ungulate humerus destruction at Henderson (adapted from Binford 1981: Fig. 5.07).

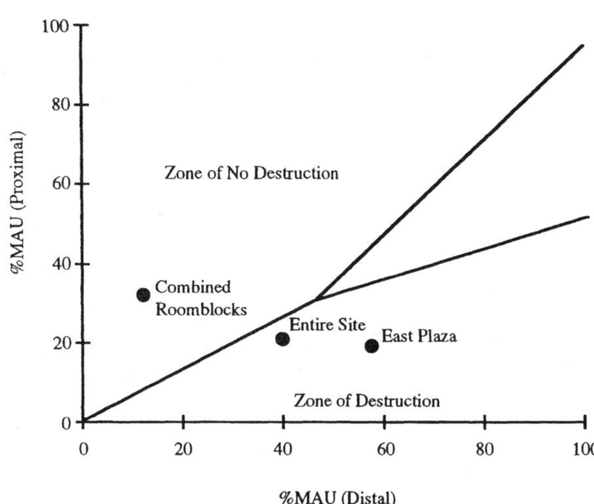

Figure 5.8. Medium ungulate tibia destruction at Henderson (adapted from Binford 1981: Fig. 5.08).

absence of evidence of carnivore damage, therefore, does not rule them out as modification agents. In particular, it is important to note that domestic dogs were present at the site (Chapter 7). Nevertheless, direct evidence of both weathering and carnivore modification of the Henderson medium ungulate assemblage is very slim.

The proportional representation of medium ungulate ribs provides another indication that carnivore damage has not totally altered the composition of the assemblage (see Chapter 4 for details of the rib analysis). All medium ungulate rib fragments were measured to determine the total length of ribs in the collection. For rib segments that had spalled longitudinally into cranial, caudal, lateral, or medial splinters, the length of each piece was first divided by two before being added to the total in order to compensate for the presence of multiple specimens that may have originated from the same segment. More conservative estimates of total rib length obviously would be obtained if the length of these individual splinters had been divided by four or even six. However, since one goal of the analysis was to compare the observed length of medium ungulate ribs against the value obtained for bison, the magnitude of this correction factor made little difference so long as both taxa were treated in the same manner. Once a figure for the total length of ribs in the assemblage was obtained, this value was divided by the total length of ribs in a modern antelope skeleton. The result was an estimate of the number of animals represented in the assemblage by ribs. In the case of medium ungulates, there are approximately 4 individuals or about 17% of the expected value for 24 animals (21 antelope and 3 deer). The same analysis was applied to the bison ribs, resulting in an estimate of 3 animals based on ribs or about 9% of the expected value for 34 animals. In other words, despite the fact that medium ungulate ribs are much smaller and far more delicate than the robust ribs of bison, they are proportionally better represented in the Henderson assemblage. While this result does not rule out the loss of medium ungulate ribs to the scavenging activities of village dogs or other carnivores, it does suggest that such attritional biases are not particularly severe.

Another method for assessing the amount of density-related attrition, perhaps due to carnivores, is to compare the proportions of proximal and distal articulations for the humerus and tibia (Binford 1981:217-19). Binford argues that the humerus and tibia are the most sensitive indicators of bone destruction; they show the greatest difference in survival potential between the proximal and distal ends, an observation clearly supported by Lyman's (1984) bulk density data. These expectations are strongly supported by assemblage data from the Nunamiut Eskimos. The relationship seen in the Nunamiut data is summarized in Figures 5.7 and 5.8, with data from the different Henderson assemblages plotted on the graphs. Assemblages that fall in the "zone of no destruction" have been commonly labeled "pristine," while those in the "zone of destruction" have been labeled "ravaged." The term "ravaged," however, may be misleading since it implies that carnivores are responsible for the modification and destruction. A similar bias against proximal ends may also be the result of grease rendering. With this in mind, it is interesting to note that caribou proximal humeri and tibiae have almost three times more grease utility than the distal ends (Binford 1978:33, Table 1.11). Thus, while retaining "pristine" as a category, I will use "destroyed" rather than "ravaged" to describe the Henderson assemblages in the zone of destruction.

Data for the humeri suggest that none of the Henderson medium ungulate assemblages are pristine; all have been heavily modified through bone destruction. In the entire site assemblage, the medium ungulate assemblage appears to be destroyed. Broken down into subareas, the East Plaza is just within the zone of destruction, while the combined room block assemblage appears more destroyed.

The tibia presents somewhat different results. The entire site assemblage appears intermediate between destroyed and pristine. Actually, however, it is composed of a pristine and a destroyed assemblage; the room blocks are well within the zone of no destruction, while the East Plaza is in the zone of destruction. Binford (1981:217-18) observed, in the case of the tibia, that some non-destroyed assemblages mixed with the destroyed assemblages below the diagonal line in the zone of destruction. He interpreted this mixture as a product of butchering a frozen carcass through the shaft of the tibia, resulting in the differential transport of different ends of the tibia. However, he noted no cases of destroyed assemblages above the diagonal line in the zone of no destruction. Therefore, on the basis of the tibia, I can safely conclude that the room blocks are less destroyed than the East Plaza.

Both the data on the humerus and tibia suggest that the East Plaza deposits were destroyed through some process of pre- or postdepositional attrition or destruction. Results for the combined room block assemblage are mixed. The humerus suggests destroyed, the tibia suggests pristine. Binford asserts (1981:218) that there is no empirical support for butchery through the shaft of the humerus. If he is right, the pattern at Henderson is probably not the result of the differential transport of the proximal versus distal ends. The destruction of the proximal humerus during butchery has also been suggested by Binford (1981:218). Another possibility, of course, is the preferential destruction of the proximal humerus in grease rendering. Interestingly, again looking at Binford's (1978:33, Table 1.11) grease utility index, the proximal humerus is six times as valuable as the distal end, while the proximal tibia is only twice as valuable as its distal end. Since grease rendering is essentially destructive, it would preferentially remove elements from an assemblage and might mimic the pattern that Binford attributes to differential transport. The room block pattern could have resulted from butchery through the proximal humerus, grease rendering, or a combination of both behaviors. These and other hypotheses will be examined in more detail below.

Economic Analysis of Medium Ungulates from Henderson

Introduction

A number of patterns have been described for the Henderson medium ungulates, and a series of simple tests were used to determine if observed variations in patterns were significant or products of sampling error. The taphonomic analysis was the first step in explaining the patterning in the assemblage. From it, I concluded that carnivores and weathering were most likely not major agents in the accumulation or modification of the assemblage. At the same time, however, several lines of evidence suggest that the degree of bone fragmentation and destruction varied within the site. In this section, I turn to humans as agents of bone collection, modification, and deposition.

Utility Indices

Utility indices were developed by Binford (1978) to provide a standard measure of the nutritional utility of meat (MUI or meat utility index), marrow, and grease, singularly or in combination (GUI or general utility index), associated with different bones in an ungulate skeleton. Binford further modified the GUI (creating the MGUI) to control for the transport of small bones attached as "riders" to higher-utility elements. Binford (1978) originally developed utility indices for caribou and domestic sheep, and others have since developed utility indices for other taxa (e.g., O'Connell and Marshall 1989). Utility indices are used as independent variables in comparisons with element frequencies (usually measured with %MNI or %MAU). Although these indices were developed for caribou and sheep, Speth (1983) showed that the caribou indices can be used effectively in the analysis of a bison assemblage due to the underlying similarity in body proportions in most ungulates.

Binford (1978) predicted that there should exist a family of curves relating element frequencies at kill sites to their nutritional utility. If only the highest-utility elements are taken and the rest are abandoned, the result is a so-called "gourmet" curve. When elements are removed proportional to their utility, the result is a straight line. If only the lowest-utility elements are systematically abandoned at the kill, while many elements of intermediate utility and most of the high-utility elements are taken, the result is a "bulk" curve (also called a "reverse utility" curve). At consumption sites, following transport from a kill, one might expect %MAU utility curves that are roughly a mirror image of those produced at kill sites, assuming of course that large-scale culling did not take place en route from kill to camp or village. These different curves reflect choices made by hunters about the type and quantity of carcass parts to transport, choices that are constrained by the nutritional status of the prey species and the hunters, logistical variables such as distance to camp, size of transport party, and means of transport, and proximate variables such as time of day and local environmental conditions.

Binford's GUI, however, is based on a complex quadratic formula with eight variables (gross weight of animal, gross weight of body part, dry bone weight of part, marrow cavity volume, percentage of oleic acid, grease value, bone volume, and bone density). Metcalfe and Jones (1988) convincingly argued that Binford's MUI can be more simply measured as meat weight (gross weight of part minus dry bone weight of part), and furthermore showed that marrow volume and grease value make little contribution to the GUI, since the GUI is primarily dependent on meat weight (GUI vs. meat weight: $r = 1.0$, $p < 0.0001$). Using Binford's corrections for low-utility riders and meat weight, they calculated a food utility index (FUI) that is significantly correlated with the original MGUI ($r = 0.99$, $p <$

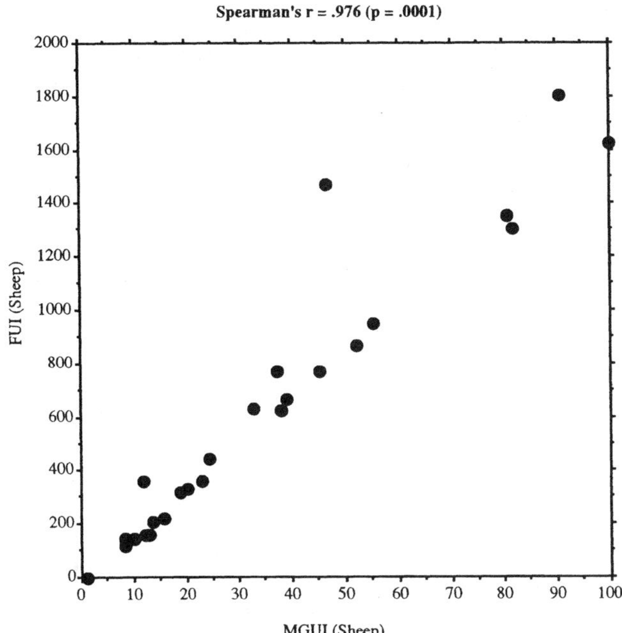

Figure 5.9. FUI (sheep) vs. MGUI (sheep).

Table 5.15. MGUI and FUI for domestic sheep.

Skeletal Element	Element Code	MGUI[a]	FUI[b]
Horn core	HC	1.0	1.0
Skull	SK	12.9	160.8
Mandible	MD	43.6	357.8
Atlas	AT	18.7	320.3
Axis	AX	18.7	320.3
Cervical vertebra	CV	55.3	951.2
Thoracic vertebra	TV	46.5	1469.6
Lumbar vertebra	LV	38.9	665.9
Pelvis	PEL	81.5	1303.8
Rib	RIB	100.0	1622.8
Sternebra	STM	90.5	1807.0
Scapula	SC	45.1	769.7
Proximal humerus	PH	37.3	769.7
Distal humerus	DH	32.8	629.7
Proximal radio-cubitus	PRC	24.3	443.1
Distal radio-cubitus	DRC	20.1	334.7
Carpals	CAR	13.4	209.2
Proximal metacarpal	PMC	10.1	146.4
Distal metacarpal	DMC	8.5	115.0
Proximal femur	PF	80.6	1353.2
Distal femur	DF	80.6	1353.2
Proximal tibia	PT	52.0	869.1
Distal tibia	DT	37.7	627.0
Tarsals	TAR	23.1	358.6
Astragalus	AST	23.1	358.6
Calcaneus	CAL	23.1	358.6
Proximal metatarsal	PMT	15.8	224.4
Distal metatarsal	DMT	12.1	157.3
Phalanx 1	P1	8.2	143.4
Phalanx 2	P2	8.2	143.4
Phalanx 3	P3	8.2	143.4

[a]MGUI values from Binford (1978: Table 2.7).
[b]FUI values derived from data in Binford (1978: Table 1.1).

0.0001). The FUI, therefore, measures essentially the same nutritional variables as the MGUI, without requiring the complicated mathematical transformations that Binford used to calculate the original MGUI.

Using a similar approach, Jones and Metcalfe showed that marrow utility, reflected in the Nunamiut choice of marrow bones and derived by Binford using another quadratic formula, is primarily dependent on the volume of the medullary cavity of bones ($r = 0.94$, including long bones, astragalus, tarsals and carpals). As with the FUI, marrow volume can be used to measure the marrow utility of an element, but does not require the complicated mathematical manipulations built into Binford's original marrow utility index.

A further benefit of using the FUI and marrow volume is that both require relatively simple data for a species that are sometimes already available in the wildlife literature. This may enable the calculation of these indices for taxa other than caribou. With this in mind, I searched the antelope literature for meat weight data. While several studies list dressed weights of entire antelope carcasses, in no case were meat weights broken down by element or body part. In the absence of meat weight data specific to a taxon, one can use utility indices from taxa of similar body proportions or body weight. Therefore, in the analysis of the Henderson medium ungulates, I used Binford's (1978) original data on a 90-month-old sheep to calculate the FUI following the procedures outlined by Metcalfe and Jones (1988). Sheep was preferred over caribou due to the very similar body weights of pronghorn and sheep, which allowed the use of unstandardized FUI values (Table 5.15). The sacrum and ulna are excluded from the FUI analysis since they were grouped by Binford with other elements (innominate and radius, respectively) in the calculation of meat weights.

Metcalfe and Jones (1988) further note, however, that both the MGUI and FUI assume that proximal and distal portions of a bone may be separated during butchery. This assumption reflects the butchering strategy used by ax-wielding Nunamiut when confronted with frozen carcasses. In other contexts it may be more appropriate to examine limb bones as complete elements. To this end, they recommend calculating a "complete-bone FUI." The procedure is similar, except that one adds the proximal and distal meat weights for each element before modifying the values to control for attached "riders." Derivation of a complete-bone FUI followed Metcalfe and Jones (1988) except for the phalanges. They calculated the FUI value of phalanges on the basis of the rear leg, resulting in FUI values for phalanges that were greater than those for carpals and metacarpals, bones that are more proximal in the carcass. To correct for this discrepancy, I calculated separate values for phalanges for the front and rear legs, and then averaged these values to arrive

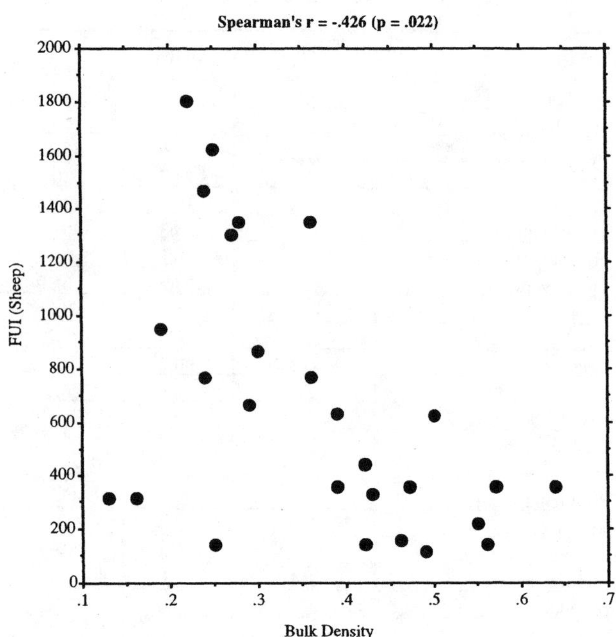

Figure 5.10. FUI (sheep) vs. bulk density.

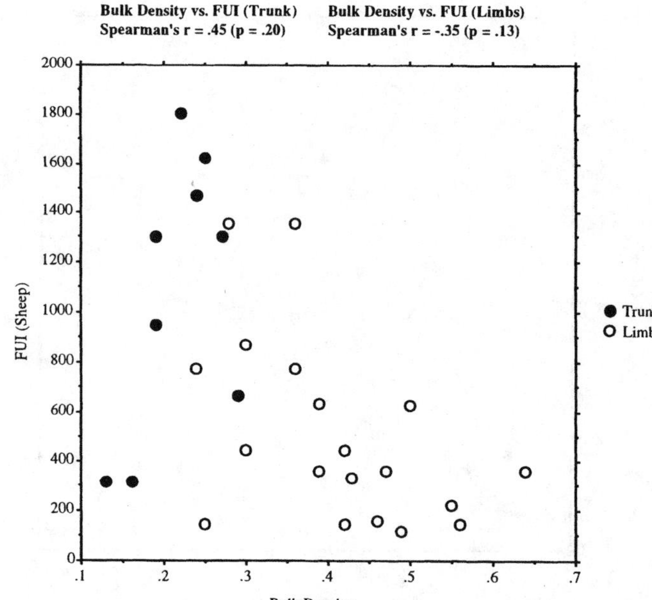

Figure 5.11. FUI (sheep) vs. bulk density, trunk compared to limb elements.

at a value for phalanges in general. As shown in Figure 5.9, the FUI and MGUI for sheep are very strongly correlated ($r_s = 0.98$, $p = 0.0001$).

The marrow cavity volumes of the 90-month-old sheep were used, but modified as suggested by Jones and Metcalfe: the astragalus, tarsals, and carpals were assigned a marrow volume of one. For grease utility, I used the index published by Binford (1978:33, Table 1.11).

As an alternative to nutritional utility, the bulk density of bones may also be an important source of patterning in faunal assemblages (Lyman 1984, 1985; Grayson 1988, 1989). Bulk density, as used by Lyman (1984), is the mass of a bone or bone portion divided by its volume (including pore space). As in Lyman's (1985) comparison of bulk density with the MGUI, the FUI for sheep and bulk density are significantly and negatively correlated (Fig. 5.10, $r_s = -0.43$, $p = 0.022$). Thus, *in situ* density-mediated destruction of elements could create an assemblage that would pattern significantly with the FUI. A correlation between %MAU and either bulk density or FUI may be measuring the effects of the same variable. If one distinguishes between trunk and limb elements in making FUI–bulk density comparisons, however, the pattern is slightly different (Fig. 5.11). Within limbs, the FUI decreases with increasing density, although the rank correlation is significant only at the $p = .10$ level. In contrast, for the trunk, the FUI increases with increasing bulk density, although this correlation is not statistically significant.

Neither marrow cavity volume and the complete-bone FUI for sheep ($r_s = 0.007$, $p = 0.972$) nor marrow volume and bulk density[5] ($r_s = 0.073$, $p = 0.794$) display any obvious relationship. Lyman (1985) found a positive but nonsignificant rank correlation between bulk density and grease utility ($r_s = 0.30$, $p = 0.11$). If one distinguishes between white (limb) and yellow (axial) grease (Binford 1978: Table 1.12), there is no relationship between the white grease index and bulk density ($r_s = -.02$, $p = 0.93$) and a clear, although not statistically significant, relationship between the yellow grease index and bulk density ($r_s = 0.52$, $p = 0.14$).

Element frequencies for medium ungulates at Henderson ("entire site" assemblage) are plotted against the FUI for sheep in Figure 5.12. The distal humerus and pelvis stand out with unusually high values. The distal humerus has relatively low food utility, while the pelvis is one of the richer elements in meat value. There is a tight cluster of low-utility elements and a more dispersed "cloud" of higher-utility elements. While the lower-utility elements are slightly more abundant than the higher-utility elements, overall there is little relationship between element frequency (%MAU) and food utility ($r_s = -0.279$, $p = 0.126$). If the pelvis and distal humerus are omitted from the comparison, the relationship becomes stronger and statistically significant ($r_s = -0.41$, $p = 0.03$). By excavation area, and with pelvis and distal humerus omitted, the relationship between %MAU and FUI is only statistically significant for the room blocks, excluding Room C-5 ($r_s = -0.525$, $p = 0.006$). The %MAU and FUI are uncorrelated in Room C-5 and weakly correlated in the East Plaza ($r_s = -0.288$, $p = 0.13$), although the East Plaza relationship is not statistically significant. The overall lack of significant patterning against food utility, however,

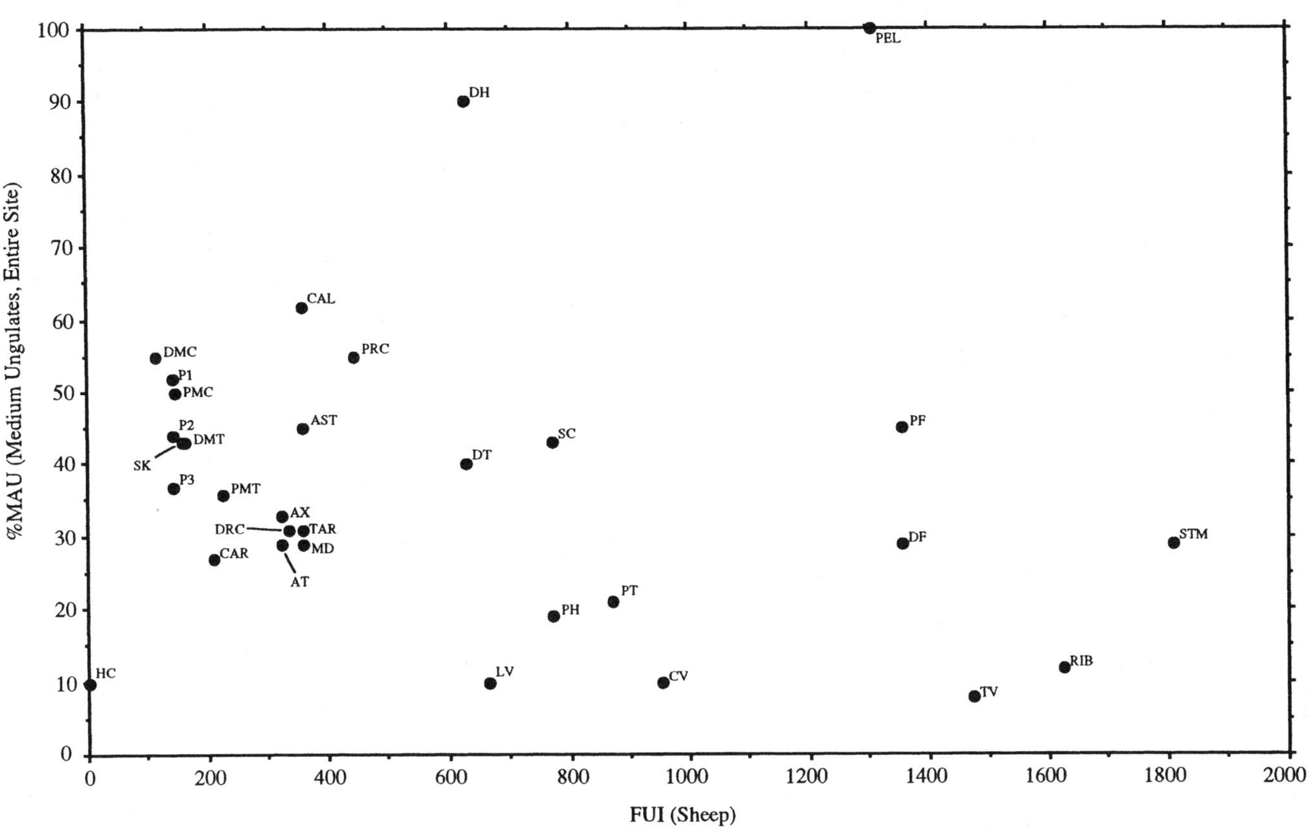

Figure 5.12. %MAU (entire site) vs. FUI (sheep) at the Henderson Site.

could be misleading. It is quite possible that clearer patterning might emerge if male and female elements could be plotted separately, as in the case of the Garnsey Site bison (Speth 1983). However, since it was impossible to sex the majority of medium ungulate elements at Henderson, significant patterns that differ by sex could be masked by the aggregate data. The utility curve for the total Henderson sample, as well as the curves for the assemblages separated by major proveniences within the site, do not fit any of the hypothetical family of curves for either kill sites or village sites. However, if the pelvis and distal humerus are omitted, some of the resulting curves appear to be a type of reverse-utility curve.

When assemblages are broken down by trunk and limbs, %MAU still does not significantly pattern with the FUI for the "entire site" assemblage (Fig. 5.13) or for any of the other assemblages. Although the trend for the trunk is positive and for the limbs negative, the difference may be a product of the inclusion of the unusually high value for the pelvis with the trunk elements. Removal of the pelvis and distal humerus from the analysis reveals an interesting contrast between the East Plaza and room blocks (excluding Room C-5). In the East Plaza (Fig. 5.14), while there is a negative correlation between %MAU trunk elements and the FUI (r_s = -0.66, p = 0.11), %MAU limb elements and the FUI are uncorrelated. In the room blocks (excluding Room C-5), in contrast, %MAU trunk elements and the FUI are uncorrelated (Fig. 5.15), while the relationship between %MAU limb elements and the FUI is statistically significant and negative (r_s = -.77, p = 0.001). Thus, removal of the pelvis and distal humerus produces reverse-utility curves for the trunk elements in the East Plaza and the limb elements in the room blocks (excluding Room C-5).

Medium ungulate element frequencies in the room blocks, East Plaza, and the site as a whole were not significantly rank-correlated with the complete-bone FUI (e.g., Fig. 5.16), grease index (e.g., Fig. 5.17), white grease index (not shown), or yellow grease index (not shown). The strongest relationship (Fig. 5.18) was between marrow volume and %MAU in Room C-5 (r_s = 0.78, p = 0.004), a pattern not present in the East Plaza (r_s = 0.197, p = 0.461) or in the remaining structures of the combined room blocks (r_s = -0.06, p = 0.82). This suggests a preferential disposal of marrow-processed elements in Room C-5. Otherwise, there is little evidence to support a preferential selection of skeletal elements on the basis of utility for the site as a whole, or within particular areas of the site.

It is important to note that the %MAU of the room blocks and East Plaza are significantly correlated with each other (r_s = 0.418, p = 0.018). Since neither assemblage is significantly correlated with the FUI, regardless of whether all elements are grouped together, or trunk and limb elements are compared separately, the major difference between the two proveniences ap-

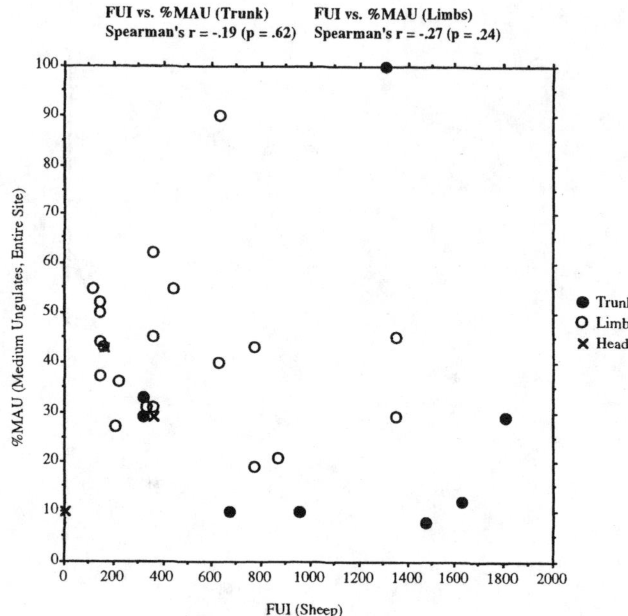

Figure 5.13. %MAU (entire site) vs. FUI (sheep) at the Henderson Site, trunk compared to limb elements.

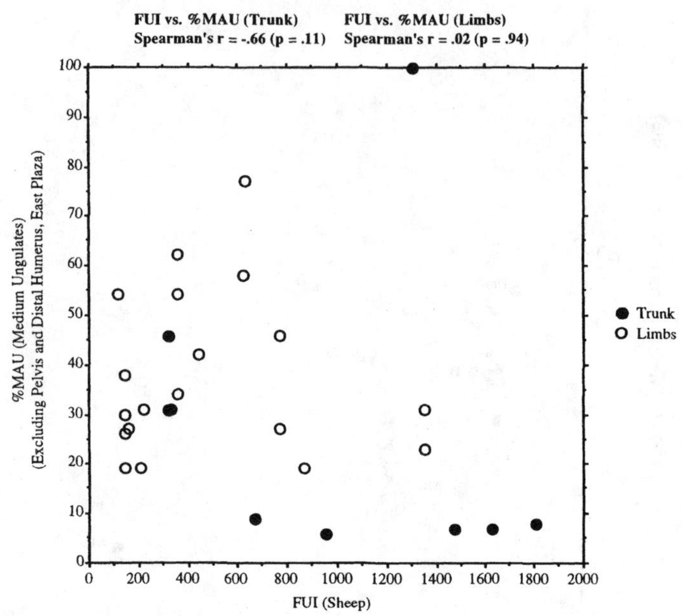

Figure 5.14. %MAU (East Plaza only) vs. FUI (sheep) at the Henderson Site, trunk compared to limb elements (excluding pelvis and distal humerus).

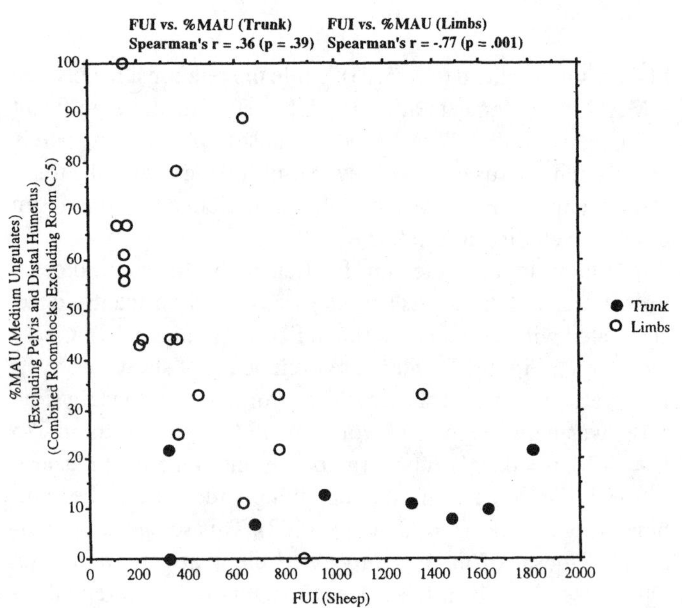

Figure 5.15. %MAU (combined room blocks only, excluding Room C-5) vs. FUI (sheep) at the Henderson Site, trunk compared to limb elements (excluding pelvis and distal humerus).

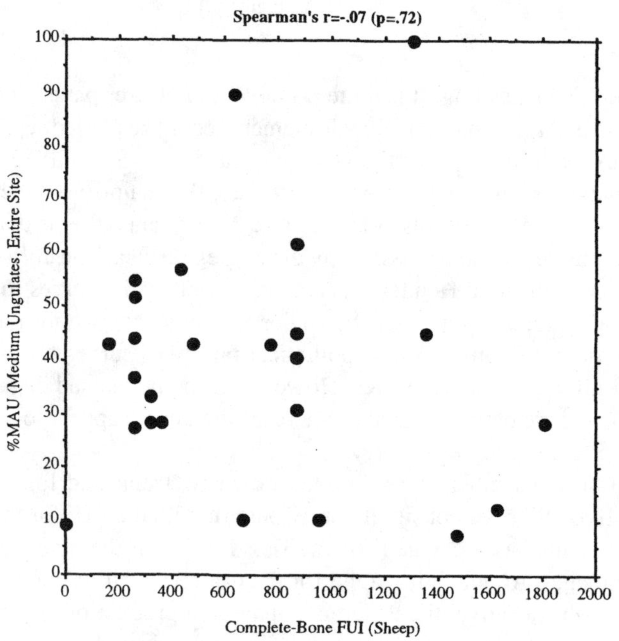

Figure 5.16. %MAU (entire site) vs. complete-bone FUI (sheep) at the Henderson Site.

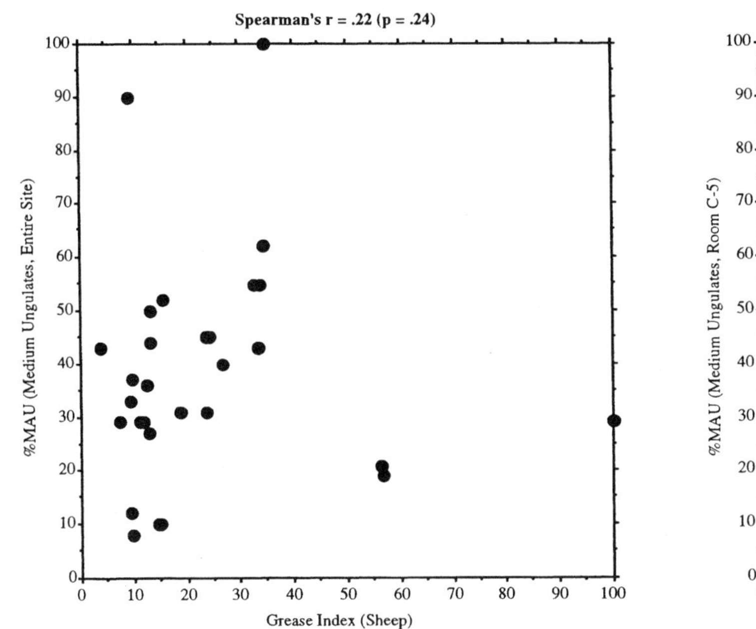

Figure 5.17. %MAU (entire site) vs. grease index (sheep) at the Henderson Site.

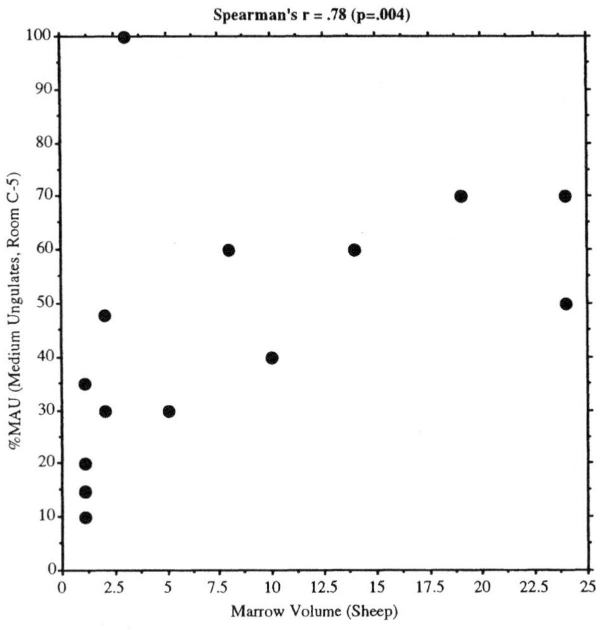

Figure 5.18. %MAU (Room C-5) vs. marrow volume (sheep) at the Henderson Site.

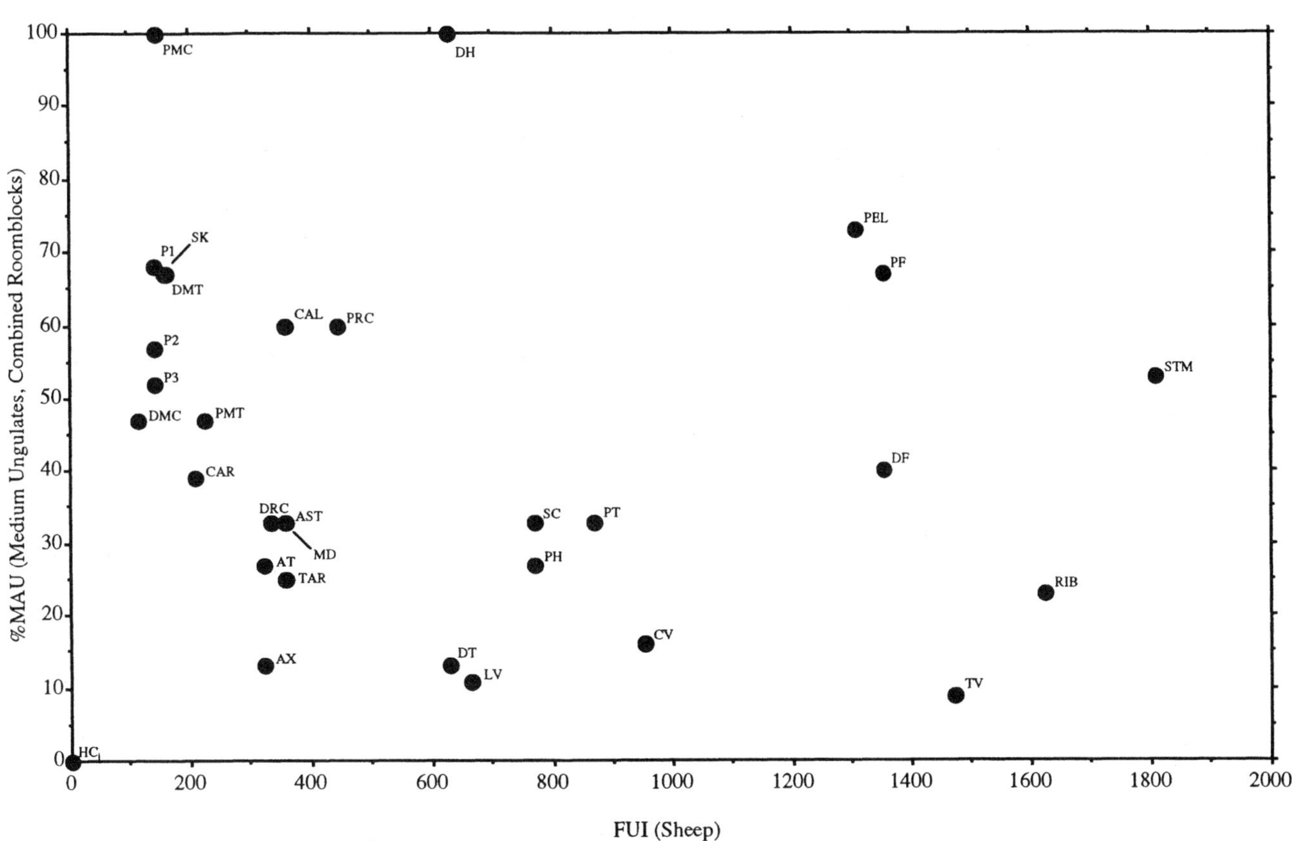

Figure 5.19. %MAU (combined room blocks) vs. FUI (sheep) at the Henderson Site.

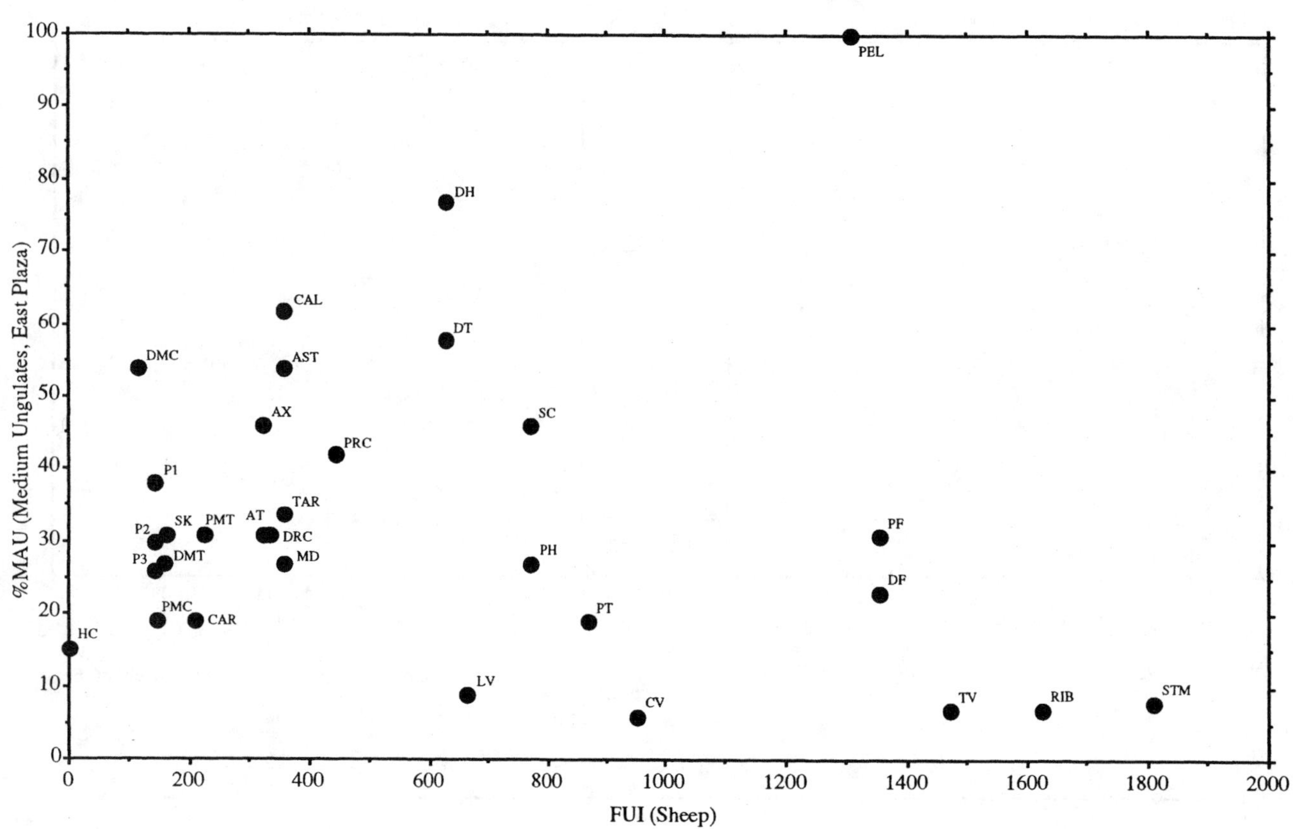

Figure 5.20. %MAU (East Plaza) vs. FUI (sheep) at the Henderson Site.

pears to be a better representation of skeletal elements in the room blocks overall rather than a bias based on utility of elements (Figs. 5.19-5.20).

Fragmentation values were also compared with utility indices. Positive correlations between bone fragmentation and nutritional utility would suggest a preferential processing of higher-utility elements as opposed to postdepositional attritional processes such as decay, trampling, or the like. One would expect especially strong correlations with the marrow and grease indices, since the processing of elements for marrow or grease necessitates bone breakage. However, at Henderson fragmentation of medium ungulate elements proved not to be correlated with the grease index, white grease index, or yellow grease index in any of the assemblages except the East Plaza. There is a strong correlation between the FI and the yellow grease index ($r_s = 0.65$, $p = 0.07$) in the East Plaza midden. Fragmentation, however, is significantly correlated with marrow cavity volume in the room blocks (Fig. 5.21, $r_s = 0.522$, $p = 0.05$), as well as in just Room C-5 ($r_s = 0.53$, $p = 0.05$) and in the remaining structures of the combined room blocks ($r_s = 0.52$, $p = 0.05$), but not in the East Plaza ($r_s = 0.35$, $p = 0.19$). Trash created in yellow grease processing may have been preferentially deposited in the East Plaza, while trash that resulted from marrow processing appears to have been preferentially deposited in room blocks.

In summary, the fragmentation data from the room blocks strongly suggest marrow processing, but does not correlate with any of the grease indices. In contrast, fragmentation in the East Plaza does not correlate strongly with marrow volume, but does suggest yellow grease processing. There is little direct evidence of grease processing at Henderson, but there is evidence of marrow processing. Analysis of the Henderson bison remains led to a very similar conclusion.

Bulk Density

In contrast to the utility indices, bulk density is significantly correlated with medium ungulate element frequency. For the assemblage as a whole, there appears to be a positive, linear relationship between bulk density and %MAU if one excludes the pelvis and distal humerus (Fig. 5.22). Both elements are more common than predicted by bulk density. Nonetheless, the pattern holds up statistically with a significant rank correlation between bulk density and %MAU ($r_s = 0.535$, $p = 0.004$) even when these two elements are included in the analysis.

The pattern for trunk vs. limb patterns is different (Fig. 5.23). Bulk density shows little relationship with %MAU values from the trunk. In fact, if one removes the pelvis from the analysis as an outlier, then trunk elements become less common as bulk

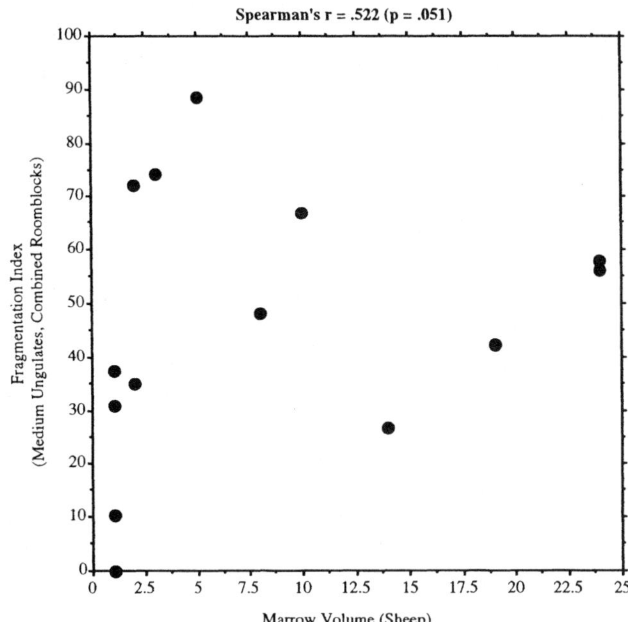

Figure 5.21. Fragmentation index (combined room blocks) vs. marrow volume (sheep) at the Henderson Site.

density increases. This is not the pattern that one would predict with density-mediated destruction. However, remembering that bulk density and the FUI are positively correlated for trunk elements, this is an expected pattern if elements were being removed from the assemblage, through transport or destruction, based on their food utility. The limbs, however, are positively correlated with bulk density, although the relationship is not statistically significant. Thus, limb elements may have been destroyed as a function of their bulk density, while trunk elements appear to have been destroyed or removed as a function of their food utility.

In the East Plaza, the pelvis and the distal humerus are more common than predicted by bulk density. In the room blocks, the overall fit with bulk density appears to be poorer than in the East Plaza (Figs. 5.24-5.25). Again, the distal humerus is more common than predicted by bulk density. The %MAU from both the room blocks and East Plaza assemblages is significantly rank correlated with bulk density ($r_s = 0.416$, $p = 0.025$ and $r_s = 0.454$, $p = 0.015$). The rank correlations with bulk density are very similar for the room block and East Plaza assemblages, suggesting that similar processes of accumulation or destruction were at work. I've already noted increased bone fragmentation in the room block deposits, possibly the reason that the rank correlation with bulk density in the room block deposits is

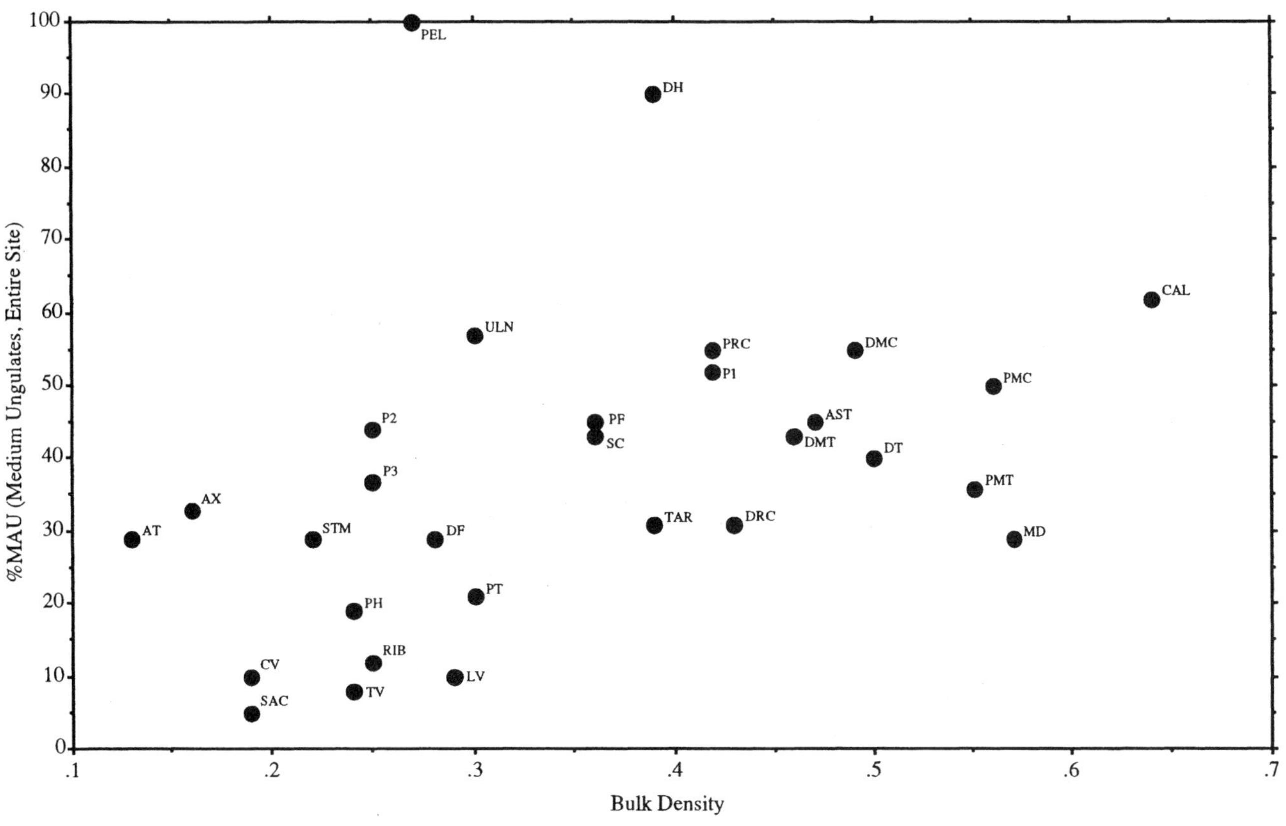

Figure 5.22. %MAU (entire site) vs. bulk density at the Henderson Site.

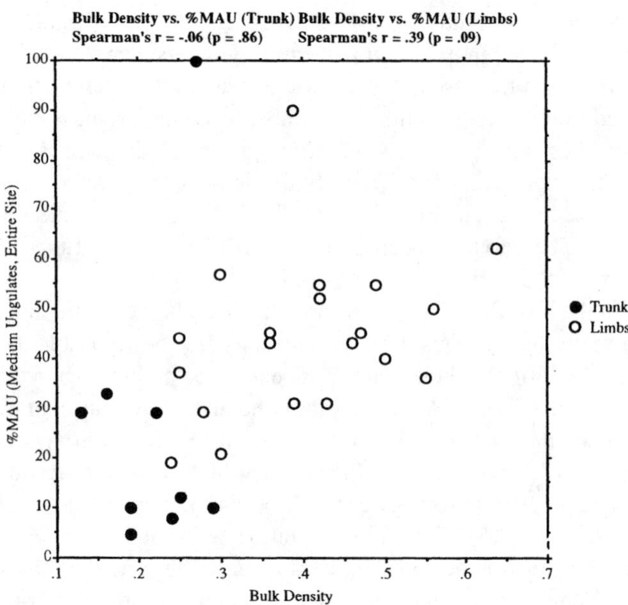

Figure 5.23. %MAU (entire site) vs. bulk density at the Henderson Site, trunk compared to limb elements.

weaker. In direct comparisons between bulk density and the FI in the combined room block, East Plaza, and "entire site" assemblages, rank correlations were not significant and scatter plots (not shown) showed no clear trends in the data. Bulk density and the FI, therefore, appear to measure different destructive processes since they do not covary in the Henderson assemblages.

Bone Transport vs. Destruction

There is little evidence to support the differential transport of medium ungulate elements, based on their food utility, either to or away from Henderson. Assuming that Henderson was not a kill site for medium ungulates (a safe assumption considering the architectural remains at the site), complete carcasses were probably brought to the site from kill sites in the surrounding region and consumed on site, leaving little intra-site differentiation other than increased evidence of marrow processing in the room block trash deposits. Differences in bone frequencies can best be understood as the result of destruction dependent on bulk density. The processes responsible for this destruction remain unknown, although trampling, weathering, carnivore attrition, butchery, and human consumption are all possibilities. Grease rendering does not seem a likely cause of the patterning, due to the lack of a relationship between element fre-

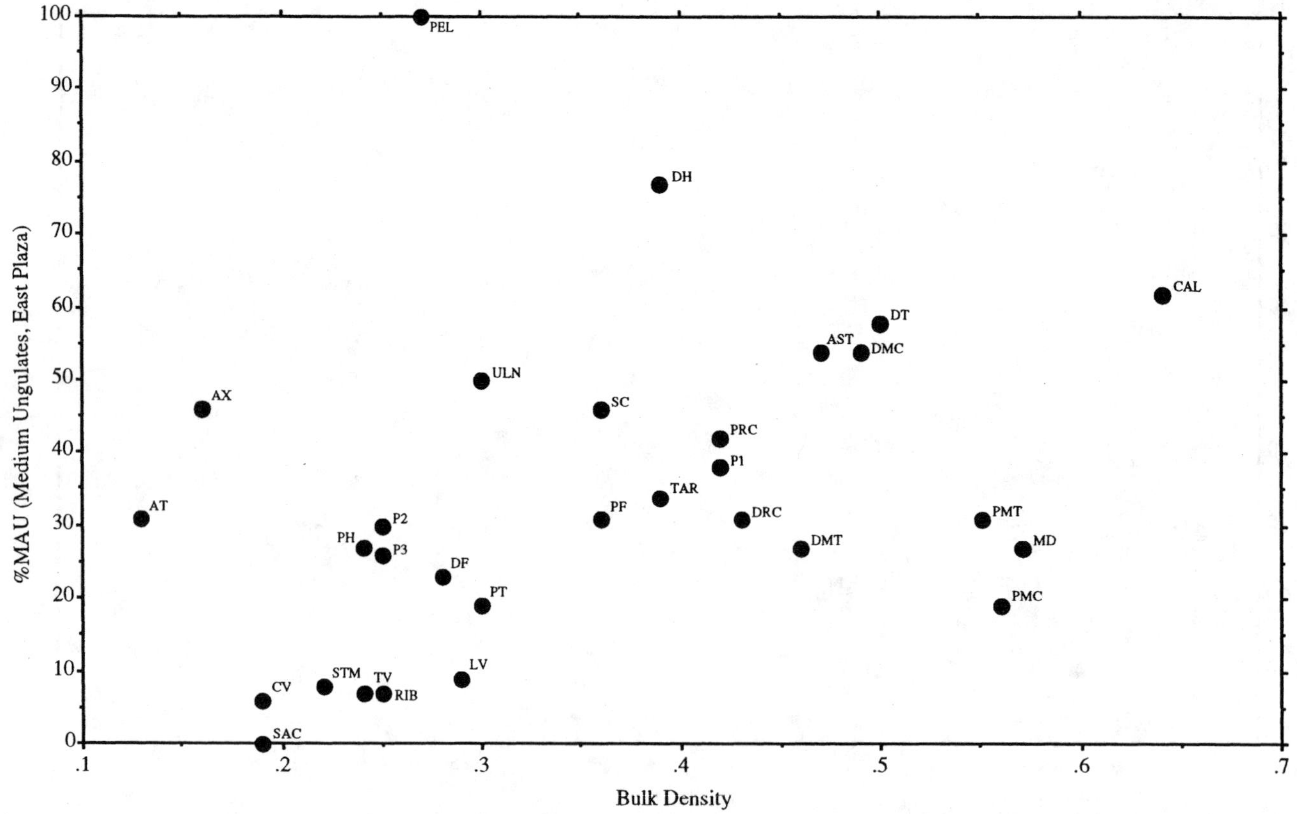

Figure 5.24. %MAU (East Plaza) vs. bulk density at the Henderson Site.

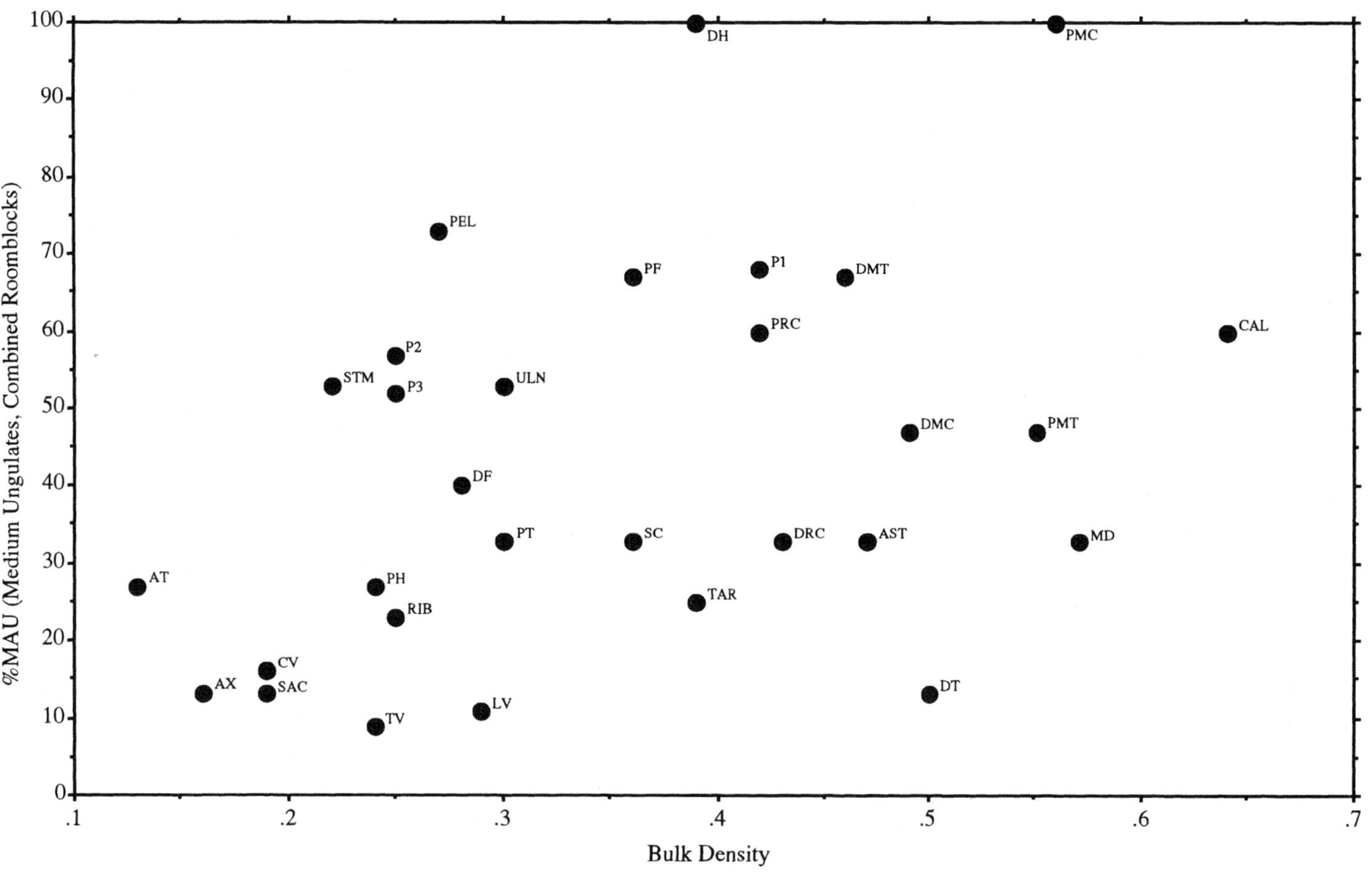

Figure 5.25. %MAU (combined room blocks) vs. bulk density at the Henderson Site.

quencies and grease utility. Similarly, carnivores seem unlikely agents of destruction due to the paucity of evidence of carnivore modification. The Henderson material, therefore, neatly fits Grayson's (1989) predictions for an assemblage modified by bone destruction and unmodified by differential transport.

However, assemblages of medium-sized ungulates (size classes 2 and 3, using criteria from Bunn et al. 1988) left at a kill by the Hadza (modern hunter-gatherers in Tanzania) after the removal of elements also fit Grayson's criteria for *in situ* destruction without bone transport (Miracle n.d.). One cannot rule out bone transport as a possible source of patterning in the Henderson assemblages.

There is, in fact, some evidence that heads of adult animals were differentially abandoned. If one assumes that the heads and postcranial remains came from the same individuals, then one can compare postcranial MNI estimates based on fusion data with those from heads based on aged mandibles. The head/postcrania ratio (MNI's) for animals less than 15 months old is 1.0, while the ratio for the oldest animals (older than 6 years for mandibles and older than 5.5 years for postcrania) is 0.57 (Fig. 5.26). Young animals are represented by equal numbers of heads and postcrania, while the oldest animals are underrepresented by heads.[6]

The bias against heads in the older animals is probably due to the differential transport of elements from kill/butchery to consumption sites. Heads contain little food value relative to their weight, and are thus often abandoned at kill/butchery sites. An alternative, the differential destruction of adult heads, is unlikely since teeth are the most durable and often the most diagnostic of elements. Heads that were preferentially attacked by carnivores, weathering, butchers, or cooks would still be identifiable on the basis of teeth. Another possibility would be the transport of carcasses intact to Henderson followed by the preferential disposal of heads away from the site. Among pueblo societies, heads, horns, antlers, and hides of antelope, deer, and mountain sheep were commonly used in rituals and were treated differently (e.g., Cordell 1977; Szuter 1991; Tyler 1975). Hunters ritually decorated the skull of an antelope and "took the head back to the mountains or the plain . . . [so] that it would come alive again" (Tyler 1975:33). Adult heads may have been preferentially abandoned either at the kill site or away from Henderson following ritual treatment.

MNI data suggest that entire carcasses of young animals were transported to Henderson from the kill site. It is possible, however, that the youngest animals suffered a preferential destruction of postcranial remains on site. Although unlikely, this al-

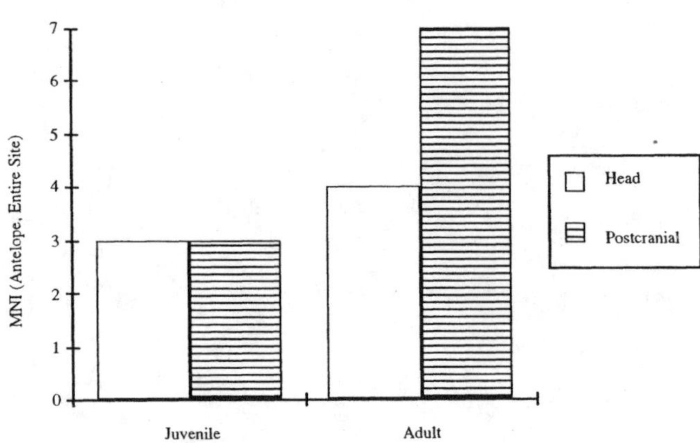

Figure 5.26. MNI (entire site) of antelope represented by head and postcranial elements at the Henderson Site.

ternative cannot be ruled out since immature bones are generally more susceptible than teeth to weathering, gnawing, and other destructive agents.

Cutmarks

Behavioral inferences based on the morphology and position of cutmarks are problematic (Lyman 1987a). We know little about the types of marks left by different activities or the range of variation in marks left by a single activity (e.g., Binford 1981, 1984). Many archaeologists have observed that cutmarks commonly represent mistakes, the slip of the knife in butchery, since the object of butchery is the dismemberment of a carcass and removal of meat; cutting into bone would dull or damage the cutting instrument, reducing efficiency by necessitating resharpening or repairs. Not surprisingly, traces of butchery left on a skeleton are often few in number. Fortunately for the faunal analyst, certain elements are more likely than others to be marked during butchery and consumption, and to be marked in fairly diagnostic ways.

Although butchery is a process, it is useful to distinguish between dismemberment and filleting of a carcass since the proximate goals of these activities are quite different (Binford 1981). Dismemberment is the separation of articulated bones or carcass units (when dealing with rib slabs, entire limbs, etc.); whereas filleting involves the removal of meat or tissue from bones. There is no necessary sequence in the performance of these activities; at times people fillet meat from complete carcasses or carcass units, or they may dismember part of a carcass with all, some, or no meat attached, although animal size, transport distance, time, and other factors may influence the pattern. Binford (1981, 1984) elegantly illustrated these differences in his observations of the Nunamiut Eskimos.

In dismemberment, the goal is to separate adjacent bones in order to break the carcass into more manageable units for further processing or transport. If one thinks of an ungulate carcass as a series of linearly arranged elements (in the axial skeleton, from the head to the tail; in the appendicular skeleton, each limb), the disarticulation will require transverse cuts through muscles and tendons connecting adjacent bones. Dismemberment marks, therefore, should tend to be transverse to the proximal-distal (cranial-caudal for the axial skeleton) axis of a bone (when an element is in anatomical position) and be clustered around joints (articular ends of long bones and carpals/tarsals in limbs).

In filleting, the goal is to separate meat from bone. This involves cutting back tissue from the periosteum, often accomplished with cuts longitudinal or oblique to the axis of a bone. Cuts may occur anywhere along the shaft or articular end of a bone. They are more likely to occur where bone morphology is complicated and nonlinear, or muscles are attached to bone.

The Henderson antelope appear to have been butchered with knives. A butcher using an ax may dismember a carcass by cutting through the shafts of bones (in particular, long bones) instead of cutting between them. Nothing in the breakage patterns of the medium ungulate remains at Henderson suggests ax use. In contrast, some of the proximal heads of bison femurs and humeri recovered from the East Plaza midden had been cleaved longitudinally by a stone ax or sharp-edged stone cleaver, apparently either in dismembering limbs or in opening the marrow cavity of these large and highly robust bones (see Chapter 4).

Bones were scanned visually and with the aid of a hand lens (10× magnification) once cutmarks had been located. While this technique will find most marks, it is possible for tiny marks to escape detection. Similarly, bone surfaces were sometimes eroded, weathered, obscured by preservative (especially those from the East Plaza), or otherwise modified to obliterate marks. Cutmark data by skeletal element and area of the site are presented in Tables 5.16-5.18.

Binford's system of classifying cutmarks (1981:136-42, Table 4.04), and his behavioral interpretations, with a few modifications, are used in the present study. For one cut rib head and shaft, reference is made to Grayson's (1988:63) analysis of the Last Supper Site assemblage of mountain sheep. Although Grayson does not provide an interpretation, the position of these marks on the dorsal surface of the rib shaft immediately distal to the tubercle and their short, "chevron" grouping suggest that they were produced during filleting. Another chevron grouping of cuts on an axis vertebra is also interpreted here as filleting. The marks on a skull fragment—the temporal process of a zygomatic—occur on the ridge produced by the masseter muscle. Binford (1984:104) notes that the disarticulation of the mandible tends to produce marks on the buccal surface of the alveolar process of the maxilla above the molar teeth (see also Grayson 1988:64, Fig. 13). These marks appear to be the result of the removal of the masseter muscle instead of the dismemberment of the mandible and are thus also interpreted as filleting.

Cutmarks occur on only 27 medium ungulate bones (1.8%

Table 5.16. Frequency of cutmarks (NISP and MNE) by skeletal element and provenience at Henderson Site.

Skeletal	Combined Room Blocks				East Plaza				Entire Site			
Element	NISP	%	MNE	%	NISP	%	MNE	%	NISP	%	MNE	%
SK	0	0.0	0	0.0	1	2.0	1	12.5	1	0.9	1	5.6
AT	0	0.0	0	0.0	2	40.0	1	25.0	2	20.0	1	16.7
AX	0	0.0	0	0.0	2	33.3	2	33.3	2	20.0	2	28.6
RIB	0	0.0	0	0.0	1	4.5	1	4.5	1	1.4	1	1.5
STM	1	25.0	1	25.0	0	0.0	0	0.0	1	16.7	1	16.7
SC	0	0.0	0	0.0	1	4.8	1	8.3	1	2.6	1	5.6
DH	5	26.3	5	33.3	1	4.3	0	0.0	6	13.0	5	13.2
ULN	1	10.0	0	0.0	1	5.9	1	7.7	3	9.7	2	8.3
PRC	4	44.4	4	44.4	5	35.7	5	45.5	9	32.1	9	39.1
PMC	1	5.6	1	6.7	0	0.0	0	0.0	1	3.8	1	4.8
Total	12	1.7	11	2.6	14	1.9	12	2.6	27	1.8	24	2.6

of total NISP) or 24 MNE's (2.6% of total MNE) in the Henderson assemblage. The frequency of cutmarked bones is almost identical for the East Plaza and combined room block assemblages (Table 5.16). Cutmarks are very unevenly distributed across skeletal elements. No cutmarks were observed on the rear leg or on most of the trunk (cervical, thoracic, lumbar, sacral, or caudal vertebrae, and innominate). Cutmarks are very rare on the front limb below the proximal radius-cubitus (a single proximal metacarpal). The uneven distribution of cutmarks on the skeleton is not a product of sample-size bias since many very common elements are completely free of marks. One can safely rule out differential weathering since nearly identical inventories of elements are present in the different areas of the site, yet the same elements are marked in each area. Furthermore, bone surfaces of lower limb elements and rear limbs were not significantly different in weathering from those of the upper front limb. By default, a behavioral explanation for this robust pattern seems the most likely.

The different areas of the site differ slightly in the distribution of cutmarks on elements. More axial elements and fewer humeri are marked in the East Plaza than the room blocks, while marks on the radius and ulna are similar. The contrast between the areas is heightened, however, when one considers the specific location of cuts on elements and the behavioral interpretation of these cuts. In Table 5.17, cutmarks are summarized by their particular form and location on an element, and in Table 5.18 cutmarks are tabulated as dismemberment vs. filleting. The totals are slightly larger in Table 5.17 than in Table 5.16, because several elements were marked in two distinct locations and hence are counted twice. The number of dismemberment and filleting cuts are nearly equal in the room blocks (53.8%, $n = 13$), but the majority of cuts on bones in the East Plaza are filleting cuts (66.7%, $n = 15$). This pattern, however, is not statistically significant ($\chi^2 = 1.2$, $p = 0.27$).

The pattern of differences between the two areas is much more complicated and interesting than simply a contrast between dismemberment and filleting. Dismemberment marks in the room blocks are limited to the elbow with the exception of one proximal metacarpal. These elements also bear marks of filleting. There are also dismemberment marks on bones from the East Plaza. They are concentrated on the atlas and axis, and are interpreted as the result of removing the head. Filleting marks also occur on the skull and axis. Cutmarks on the elbow joint, with a single exception, are all filleting marks. The evidence of filleting is similar for both assemblages. The difference, therefore, lies in dismemberment, of the head in the East Plaza, and of the front limb between the humerus and radius-ulna in the room blocks.

There are further contrasts in the location of dismemberment marks both within and between the assemblages. Binford (1981:124) observed that very different strategies of dismemberment of the front limb are used on supple (recently dead) vs. stiff (after rigor mortis has set in) carcasses. In the disarticulation of a supple limb, Nunamiut butchers cut along the anterior face between the distal humerus and proximal radius (marks RCp-5 on the proximal radius), and transversely across the medial surface of the distal humerus (marks Hd-2) to enable the twisting of the articulation out of its socket (Binford 1981:124). With a stiff joint, the first task is to make it flexible. This is accomplished by the Nunamiut by cutting between the olecranon process of the ulna and olecranon fossa of the distal humerus while attempting to flex the joint. This produces a series of short cuts on the anterior edge of the proximal ulna (RCp-5 on the olecranon process of the ulna)[7] and the posterior surface of the distal humerus on the olecranon fossa (Hd-3). Once sufficient amounts of connecting tissue have been severed to enable movement of the joint, disarticulation proceeds in a manner similar to a supple limb, with the exception that marks on the medial surface of the distal humerus (Hd-2) tended to be more oblique in orientation and proximal in location (Binford 1981:124).

At Henderson, the distal humerus and proximal radius and ulna from the room blocks are marked in a manner that suggests dismemberment of both supple and stiff joints. Three sets of marks suggest dismemberment of a supple limb (RCp-5 on the radius and Hd-2) and three sets of marks suggest dismem-

Table 5.17. Description and interpretation of cutmarks by skeletal element and provenience at Henderson Site.

Skeletal Element	Code Number[a] or Description	Cutmarks Comb. Rm Blks.	East Plaza	Entire Site	Behavioral Interpretation
SK	Temporal process of zygomatic	0	1	1	Filleting
AT	Cv-1	0	2	2	Disarticulation of head
AX	Cv-3	0	1	1	Disarticulation of head
	Chevrons on centrum	0	1	1	Filleting
RIB	Dorsal and distal to tubercle (Grayson 1988: Fig. 15d)	0	1	1	Filleting
STM	RS-4	1	0	1	Filleting
SC	S-1 but costal	0	1	1	Dismemberment
DH	Hd-2	1	0	1	Dismemberment of supple carcass
	Hd-3	2	0	2	Dismemberment of stiff carcass
	Hd-6	2	1	3	Filleting
ULN	RCp-5	1	0	1	Dismemberment of stiff carcass
	RCp-7	0	1	2	Filleting
PRC	RCp-5	2	1	3	Dismemberment of supple carcass
	RCp-6	3	5	8	Filleting
PMC	MCp-1	1	0	1	Dismemberment
Total		13	15	29	

[a]From Binford (1981: Table 4.04).

Table 5.18. Distribution of cutmarks by provenience at Henderson Site.

Type of Cutmark	Combined Room Blocks		East Plaza		Entire Site	
	NISP	%	NISP	%	NISP	%
Dismemberment	7	53.9	5	33.3	12	41.4
Filleting	6	46.2	10	66.7	17	58.6
Total	13		15		29	

berment of stiff joints (Hd-3 and RCp-5 on the proximal ulna). In the East Plaza, all dismemberment marks are supple limb types. This contrast suggests two patterns of dismemberment. In the first, carcasses were dismembered shortly after death, meaning the kill was close enough to Henderson to enable the transport of carcasses to Henderson for butchery, or it was dismembered at the kill sites before transport. The second pattern is consistent with significant time delay between death and butchery, most likely produced by the secondary dismemberment of limbs after they had been introduced to Henderson.

From the distribution of cutmarks on elements we can infer several things. First, there is no evidence to suggest the dismemberment of lower limbs either before or after the introduction of limbs to the site. Similarly, cuts characteristic of skinning an animal for its hide, often transverse cuts on the phalanges or metapodials, are completely lacking. Filleting marks are completely lacking on the meat-rich rear limbs and pelves. These parts were either abandoned unprocessed, or more likely, were processed in a manner that did not leave distinctive traces.

One possible explanation of the pattern of unmarked meaty elements would be the cooking/roasting of articulated limbs. If this were the case, then one would expect a very low frequency of burned bones from the meaty (hence protected from flames) upper limbs and a higher frequency of burned bones from the exposed, lower limbs. The %NISP of burned elements from the entire site assemblage is plotted for the front and rear limbs in Figures 5.27-5.28. With the exception of the scapula, the pattern of burning in the front and rear limbs supports this hypothesis.

Sample sizes are too small to interpret the slight contrast between the room blocks and East Plaza in frequency and location of cutmarks. I will only note that dismemberment marks in the East Plaza are concentrated on the upper neck (probably from removal of the head), while dismemberment marks in the room blocks are concentrated around the elbow (probably from the disarticulation of this joint). This may reflect slight differences in the sources of trash for these two areas; the East Plaza trash may have been produced at an earlier stage of disarticulation—the removal of the head—while the room block trash may have been produced at a later stage of joint disarticulation and secondary dismemberment. In this light, it is interesting that the disarticulation of joints in the room block trash is also correlated with greater evidence of marrow bone selection and fragmentation (see above).

Mortality Profile of Henderson Antelope

Age data for Henderson antelope were grouped into general age classes (Table 5.19) and used to construct a mortality graph (Fig. 5.29). The age classes were necessary due to the lack of

Table 5.19. Age classes by provenience of Henderson Site antelope.

Age Class (Years)	East Plaza		Combined Room Blocks		Entire Site	
	NISP	MNI	NISP	MNI	NISP	MNI
0 - 1	3	3	2	0	5	3
1 - 2	2	1	3	0	5	1
2 - 6	10	5	6	0	16	5
2+	5	0	2	0	12	0
6+	1	1	3	3	5	4
Total	21	10	16	3	43	13

Table 5.20. Antelope fawning dates at selected locations in western U.S.

Fawning Date	Location	Reference
1st week June	Moiese, Montana	Dow and Wright (1962)
1st week June	Eastern Colorado	Hoover et al. (1959)
4th week May	Central Idaho	Autenrieth and Fichter (1975)
3rd week May	Southeastern Oregon	Einarsen (1948)
3rd week May	Tucson, Arizona	Nichol (1942)
Mid-May-June	Roswell, New Mexico	Howard and Bradybaugh (1983)
April-May	Trans-Pecos Texas	Beuchner (1950)
Mid-March	South Texas	Lehman and Fuller (1943)

precision in aging isolated, permanent teeth. Individuals less than a year old are present, but are probably underrepresented due to the preferential destruction of immature elements. The poor representation of yearlings, however, cannot be attributed to differential destruction of immature remains. Adult remains and old individuals are more numerous. Antelope usually do not live beyond nine years (Kitchen and O'Gara 1982).

The resulting profile (Fig. 5.29) is problematic for several reasons. Lyman (1987b) suggests that a sample size of about 30 individuals, with individuals represented in most age classes, is needed for reliable results. Using his mortality data on elk killed by the Mount St. Helens eruption (1987b: Table 1), I randomly selected (with replacement) 10 samples each with a sample size of 10. Of these 10 samples, 8 were significantly rank-correlated (Spearman's r_s, one-tailed, $p < 0.05$) with a theoretical catastrophic mortality profile (TCMP). Thus, while the Henderson sample (MNI = 13) is considerably smaller than Lyman's recommended sample size, it may nevertheless be large enough to give reliable results.

A more serious problem is that the apparent abundance of adult and old individuals relative to the yearlings may be largely a product of grouping several different cohorts together. The inability to age dentitions and teeth to particular age classes prevents the calculation of a rank correlation with ideal mortality profiles as suggested by Lyman (1987b).[8]

Nonetheless, the relative abundance of old-adult remains, and the paucity of yearlings fits a U-shaped mortality profile better than the profile of a living population (Klein and Cruz-Uribe 1984:56-59; Stiner 1990:308). U-shaped profiles are also called "attritional" since they describe processes that target young and old individuals, such as selective predation, disease, and malnutrition. Profiles similar to a living population are called "catastrophic" since they appear to be generated by processes that are blind to the age of the prey, such as random predation, natural disasters, and game drives. In sum, I suggest that the mortality profile of the Henderson antelope more likely reflects attritional processes than catastrophic ones, although this conclusion should be considered tentative given the problems of the sample discussed above. The method of procurement will be considered in more detail below.

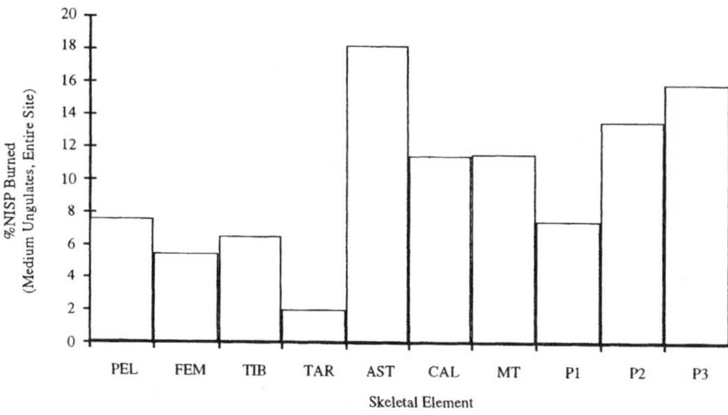

Figure 5.27. Frequency (%NISP) of burned bones in rear limb at the Henderson Site (entire site).

Seasonality

Animals that have restricted breeding and birthing seasons and bear only single litters during a year allow us to estimate the season of death by changes in the skeleton and dentition. To do this, we must have detailed information about the timing of reproduction for these taxa, and aging techniques reliable to within several months of accuracy. The eruption and wear of deciduous and permanent mandibular teeth is regular and time-specific enough in antelope to allow us to estimate the season of death for animals less than 18 months of age. At its best, this technique is accurate to a time span of several months. Since seasonally restricted breeders will produce cohorts of young approximately a year apart, similar tooth wear in older age classes would indicate animals killed at the same season of the year, whereas more variable wear states for similarly aged animals would indicate animals killed over several different seasons. This technique, however, could not be used reliably at Henderson due to the small size of the sample of mandibular dentitions. Fetal remains provide another indication of seasonality. Unfortunately, in the absence of known-age comparative fetal material for antelope, it was not possible to date the season of death of the Henderson remains more closely than a several-month period. A potentially powerful method of estimating the season of death is through the analysis of incremental lines in dental cementum. Although such analysis was beyond the present study, it would provide a very interesting check on

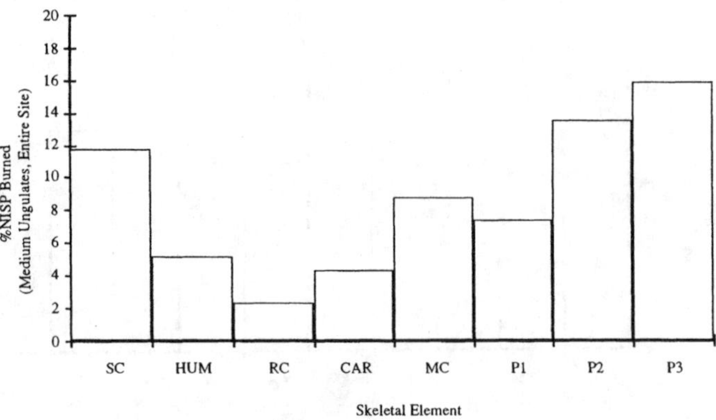

Figure 5.28. Frequency (%NISP) of burned bones in front limb at the Henderson Site (entire site).

the present estimates, as well as allow the examination of many teeth that could not be included here.

Antelope breed during a short rutting season in late September to early October, although the rut may begin as early as July in southern Texas (Beuchner 1950). The gestation length has been determined for captive animals to be 252 days (Kitchen and O'Gara 1982). Data on the birthing season are summarized in Table 5.20. As one would expect, given the variability in the timing of the rut, antelope fawn much earlier in southern Texas than in their more northern ranges. Birthing-date data display a rough gradient from later dates in the north to earlier dates in the south. This variation has not been explained, but is probably linked to climatic (temperature or moisture) or latitude (daylength) differences in cueing the commencement of the rut, since antelope will fawn regardless of the local weather conditions (Einarsen 1948:105). This variation in birthing dates is significant; seasonal estimates could differ by as much as two to three months.

Fortuitously, antelope have been studied in the immediate vicinity of the Henderson Site (Howard and Bradybaugh 1983). These authors report a birthing season of May to early June. Direct observation of the antelope, however, did not begin during the study years until the breeding season was almost finished (mid-June in 1979, late May in 1980). Aerial surveys were also conducted, but not during April and May. Therefore, it is not clear if the relatively long birthing season that they report is real, or a reflection of the lack of data for this time period. In populations to the north (Colorado), the birthing season is restricted to a two-week period centered on the first week of June (Hoover et al. 1959). To the west, in the Tucson area, the birthing season peaks during the third week of May. In the Trans-Pecos region of Texas to the south, births occur during April and May (Beuchner 1950). Roughly interpolating between these different data points to Roswell, I estimate that the birthing peak occurs in mid-May. Thus, in the analysis that follows, I assume a parturition date of mid-May for antelope in southeastern New Mexico.

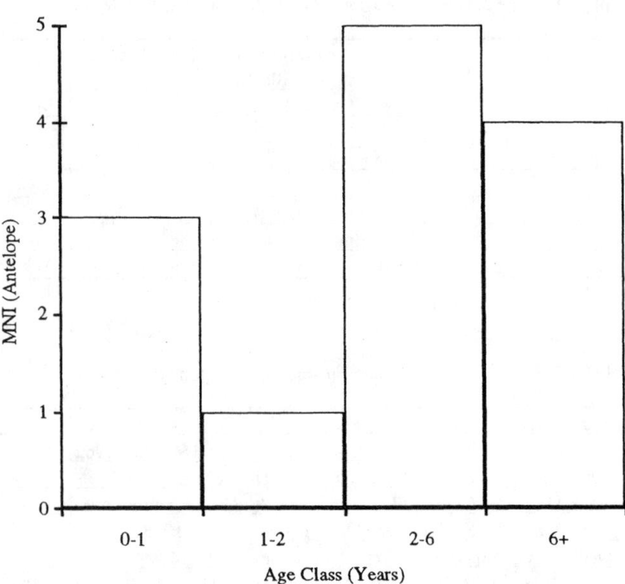

Figure 5.29. Mortality profile (MNI) of antelope at the Henderson Site (entire site).

The season of death for the Henderson antelope was estimated on the basis of mandibular dentitions and fetal remains. These data are presented in Tables 5.21-5.22. MNI's on dentitions are identical to those used in the analysis of the age structure, with the addition of one mandible from a full-term fetus. The four fetuses probably represent only two does since pronghorn females usually bear twins (Kitchen and O'Gara 1982).[9] The majority of animals at Henderson appear to have been killed during the winter-spring, although all seasons of the year may be represented (Fig. 5.30). The room blocks and East Plaza are quite similar in their seasonal indicators. Both show a strong dominance of winter-spring–killed antelope, with rare or no evidence of other seasons. On the basis of MNI's, there is one fall-killed individual from the room blocks, and one summer-killed and one fall-killed animal from the East Plaza, but each of these cases is based on a NISP of one. Sample sizes for both MNI and NISP are too small to conclude that the site areas differed in the seasonality of antelope procurement. The indication of more than one season of antelope procurement is compatible with the age-structure evidence for an attritional mortality profile. In conclusion, the majority of antelope at Henderson were killed during the winter-spring, while few antelope appear to have been killed during the summer and fall.

Summary of Analyses

Medium ungulates, predominantly antelope, were hunted mostly during the winter-spring months in the Lower Hondo region, although a few may have been taken during other seasons of the year. Roughly equal numbers of males and females were hunted. All ages were also hunted, although the death distribution is skewed in favor of very old individuals. With the

Table 5.21. Age at death and season of death of Henderson Site antelope.

Age	NISP	MNI	Date of Death	Specimen Number[a]	Description of Teeth and Postcranial Elements
Fetus	17	4[b]	Dec. - March	—	Proximal ulna
Full-term fetus	9	1	April - mid-May	1463	dP_2 - dP_4 unerupted
3-6 mo.	1	1	mid-Aug. - mid-Oct.	1533	M_2 complete bud, erupting
3-8 mo.	1		mid-Aug. - mid-Dec.	1486	dP_2 unworn, dP_3 slightly worn
4-9 mo.	1	1	mid-Sept.-mid-Jan.	1471	M_2 erupting, M_3 unerupted bud
6-12 mo.	2	1	mid-Nov. - mid-May	1464	dP_4 anterior infundibulum absent, M_1 roots unformed
12-16 mo.	1	1	mid-May - mid-Aug.	1491	M_3 erupting

[a]Sequential identification number assigned to each medium ungulate specimen included in MNI tabulation (circled on specimen to distinguish it from the lot number also written on each specimen).
[b]Represents two does.

Table 5.22. Seasonality indicators by provenience at Henderson Site.

Season	Room Blocks NISP	Room Blocks MNI	East Plaza NISP	East Plaza MNI	Entire Site NISP	Entire Site MNI
Winter-spring	15	2	14	3	29	5
Summer	0	0	1	1	1	1
Fall	1	1	1	1	2	1
Total	16	3	16	5	32	7

exception of adult heads, some of which were apparently abandoned at kill sites, entire carcasses were brought to Henderson for processing and consumption. The Henderson hunters did not differentially transport elements (excepting the head) to or from the site. There was minimal dismemberment of carcasses beyond a division into complete limbs and perhaps several axial portions prior to processing and consumption.

At Henderson, similar activities of medium ungulate processing and consumption appear to have created the trash deposited in the room blocks and the East Plaza. More trash from the secondary dismemberment of upper front limbs and processing for marrow was dumped in the room blocks than was dumped in the East Plaza. Trash from both places shows a consistent destruction of elements by bulk density. The agents of this destruction remain unknown, but probably was not due to either carnivores or bone-grease processing. The major contrast was a much higher concentration of medium ungulate bone trash in the East Plaza than in the room blocks, although the composition of the East Plaza trash did not differ significantly in most respects from that in the room blocks.

Antelope Procurement at Henderson

Introduction

It has sometimes been assumed (Speth and Scott 1989; Driver 1984, 1985, 2000) that faunal assemblages with more antelope than deer remains indicate the communal hunting of antelope herds. The goal of this section is to examine this assumption in light of the Henderson data. First, I examine seasonal changes in modern antelope herd composition in the Henderson area. Next, I briefly review several ethnographic descriptions of antelope hunting. Finally, I propose archaeological expectations for communal antelope hunting and compare these with the Henderson data.

Antelope Herd Organization at Different Seasons

Hunting strategies are constrained by the social organization of the prey species. Pronghorn antelope are herd animals. There is, however, considerable variation in herd composition and size that is dependent on seasonal variations in forage availability and the pronghorn's life cycle (fawning in the spring, mating in the fall). The following description of seasonal changes in pronghorn herd organization is based on observations made in the area of the Henderson Site in 1979-1980 (Howard and Bradybaugh 1983). As described above, antelope fawns in this part of New Mexico are normally born in mid-May. During the birthing season, females are either alone or in pairs of females, while males have dispersed into bachelor groups of two to eleven bucks. Females and fawns form nursery groups in July (average number of does is six). During August and September, the bachelor herds reduce in size (two to four animals) as males establish individual defended territories for the fall rut. There is some debate about whether or not pronghorn males herd harems during the rut (Kitchen and O'Gara 1982). In any case, there are mixed-sex groups during the fall. By mid-October, larger mixed-sex herds form. In the Henderson area, the average size of winter herds observed by Howard and Bradybaugh (1983) was 13, to a maximum 52 animals, with herd composition and size extremely variable. Winter herds lasted until February or March when separate bachelor herds were once again established.

Data from other field sites corroborate many of the observations made on the Henderson herds. In Colorado, Hoover et al. (1959:19) report that "pregnant does isolate themselves from other antelope about a week to ten days before fawning, and remain isolated until the young are about two weeks old. After that time, several does will run together with their fawns." In Idaho, Autenrieth and Fichter (1975:14-15) found that herds are maximally dispersed when does come into estrus (mid-fall) and when they give birth. Large groups form after the rut and continue into March or April, depending on local snow conditions. Nursery groups also form before the period of parturition ends, reaching a maximum size about six weeks after the peak birthing season. Essentially the same pattern of aggregation and dispersion is also reported by Kitchen (1974) for antelope in Montana.

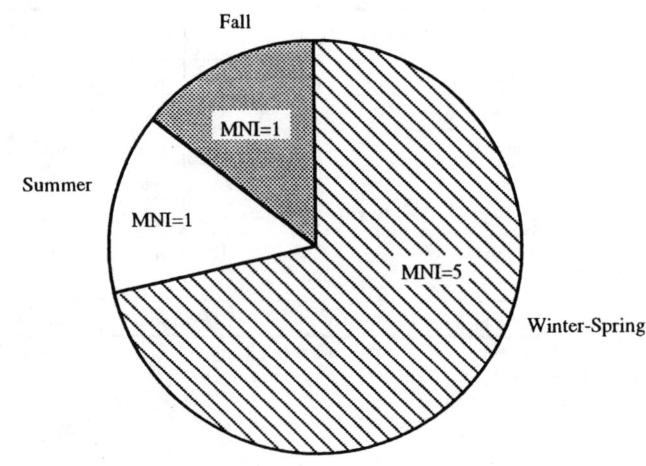

Figure 5.30. Seasonality of antelope procurement at the Henderson Site.

Ethnographic Descriptions of Antelope Hunting

Steward (1938, and references therein) gives some of the best descriptions of antelope hunting on foot. Steward (1938:34-36) asserts that individual antelope were taken "with considerable difficulty by lone hunters, . . . [who] usually stalked antelope wearing an antelope head and skin disguise." The difficulty was due to the pronghorn's preference for open terrain and its fast running speed. Among pueblo groups, at least three different hunting strategies were used: individual stalking, herd surrounds, and corral drives (Beaglehole 1936; Tyler 1975). Beaglehole (1936:6) reported for the Hopi that two men would cooperatively stalk antelope by running them down over several days. This method makes perfect sense, since although antelope can run very fast for short periods of time, they lack stamina and avoid prolonged or continuous travel (Howard and Bradybaugh 1983).

Both Steward and Beaglehole, however, suggest that communal hunting was the preferred method of procurement among Great Basin groups and Hopi. Groups of hunters would drive an antelope herd into a corral and kill with ease a large number of animals (Steward 1938:34-35) or, if mounted on horses, use a "true surround" technique by encircling a herd and then running it in circles to exhaustion (Steward 1938:36; Beaglehole 1936:6). There is little information about the size and composition of communal hunting groups. Steward (1938:128) estimated that 40 to 50 men and women, on foot, helped corral antelope in the Snake Valley, Nevada. White (quoted in Tyler 1975:37-38) recorded one report of a hunt in 1889, by mounted Acoma Indians, that involved 74 hunters, four cooks, and eight burros to carry the dried meat. More common in the literature are less precise estimates of several families or villages participating in a communal hunt. In any case, there was considerably more organization and ritual preparation for a communal hunt then for an individual stalk (Tyler 1975:35).

The seasonal timing of communal hunting appears to have depended on local environmental conditions. For example, Egan (quoted in Steward 1938:35) observed such a communal hunt in Antelope Valley (northeastern Nevada) during the colder months and commented that kills were usually all bucks or does. Antelope were communally hunted in June in the Owens Valley of eastern California (Steward 1938:81-82). In north-central Nevada (Battle Mountain), Steward (1938:163) reports communal antelope hunts during the winter. In south-central Idaho (Grouse Creek Valley), communal antelope hunts were held in the fall when antelope went south, and in early spring (Steward 1938:175). In Diamond Valley, Nevada, communal antelope hunts were held immediately prior to the fall harvest of pinyon nuts (Steward 1938:142). The Hopi hunted antelope in the fall when the animals were fattest, in the winter due to the ease of tracking, and in the spring after the young were born (Beaglehole 1936:4-5). The different hunting strategies were "to some extent influenced by the seasonal habits of the animal, as great surrounds were only practical when large numbers of antelope could be found together" (Tyler 1975:34). Therefore, herd surrounds and corral drives would have been limited to "winter after the rutting season was over . . . [when] smaller groups began to come together into large herds that numbered in the hundreds" (Tyler 1975:34). Antelope were too scattered to hunt during the summer. Within this small sample of ethnographic data, communal antelope hunts are reported for all seasons of the year, although the timing of hunts varied, perhaps due to local variations in the pronghorn's life cycle.

Frison (1971) offers a slightly different perspective on the suitability of hunting techniques during different seasons of the year.

> It is unwritten dogma in antelope country that they [antelope] are spring-of-the-year meat and should be taken shortly after the first grass appears. For a period of time before the fawns are born . . . and until they are two months or so old, the females with young and the males tend to remain singly or in small groups and are not too receptive to large scale trapping. They can, however, be very successfully hunted individually during this period. [Frison 1971:28]

Frison further argues that winter hunting in Wyoming would not have been feasible due to heavy snow cover, while the fall would have been the optimal time for communal hunting of antelope. Of interest in Frison's description is the reported feasibility of stalking antelope during the spring.

In sum, communal antelope hunting appears to have been most common during the fall and winter since these were seasons of herd aggregation. Individual stalking, on the other hand, would have been especially effective during the spring since does were, to some extent, tethered by their young. One might therefore expect, on the basis of these ethnographic accounts, that communal drives took place primarily during the fall and winter, and individual stalking during the spring.

Archaeological Markers of Communal Herd Hunting

Using the descriptions of antelope biology and ethnographic accounts of communal antelope hunting, one can develop criteria for identifying the archaeological remains.

Age profiles are useful. Since infant mortality is usually quite high in wild populations, the primary contrast between these age profiles is in the representation of adults. This point is especially important in species like the pronghorn, in which females usually bear more than one offspring per year—an attritional profile will more closely resemble a catastrophic profile due to the increased mortality of younger animals (Klein and Cruz-Uribe 1984:56-57). In these cases, however, the rise in mortality in the older age classes may only be perceptible in exceptionally large faunal samples (Klein and Cruz-Uribe 1984:57). Prime-age adults will be more numerous than old adults in a catastrophic profile, while the reverse is expected for an attritional profile. One would expect a catastrophic age profile of pronghorns if communal hunting drives were used (Klein and Cruz-Uribe 1984:56; Nimmo 1971). This assumes, of course, that hunters killed corralled antelope without selecting for age. An attritional profile, on the other hand, would imply a hunting method, such as stalking, to which the very young and old (due to inexperience, disease, or physical incapacity) would be more susceptible than prime-age adults.

Using the modern pronghorn herd composition in the Henderson area as an analog for prehistoric populations from the same region, one can make some predictions about the composition of herds available for communal hunting during different seasons of the year. During the fall and winter, communal hunting of mixed herds should create assemblages that contain both sexes. During the spring (as early as February), only single-sex herds could be hunted. Bachelor herds would be available throughout the spring and summer, while doe herds would only be available for four to eight weeks in the early spring. Nursery herds of does and fawns would be available July to August. Thus, any single communal hunt during the spring and summer would probably produce animals of a single sex. (This is excepting fawns, of course, but fawns cannot be accurately sexed in any case.) The accumulation of remains from several

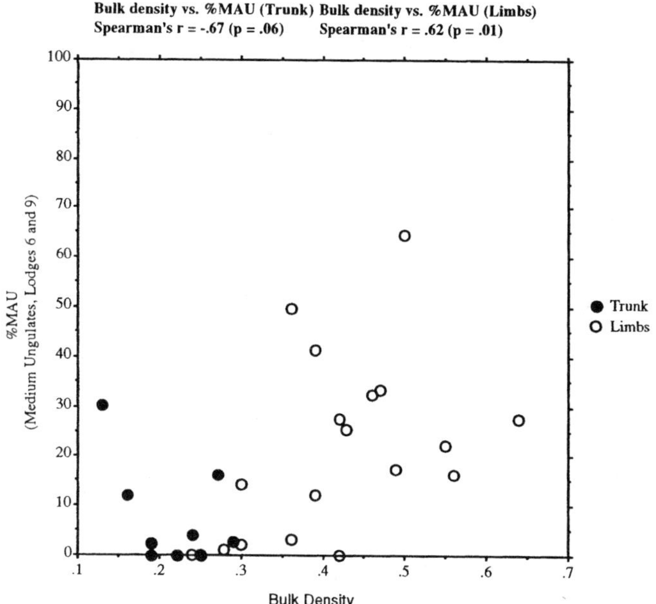

Figure 5.31. %MAU vs. bulk density at the Eden-Farson Site (Wyoming), trunk compared to limb elements (Lodges 6 and 9; n = 49.5).

"single-sex" communal hunts, however, could create mixed-sex assemblages if hunters were not consistent in targeting a single sex or if hunts from several different seasons were represented. Therefore, detailed data about the sex and age of animals killed and their season of death can be combined to test the above expectations, but due to the possible accumulation of remains from several distinct behavioral events (communal hunts), results may often be equivocal.

Carcass processing and differential transport of elements from kill sites may also vary between communal antelope drives and individual stalks. Antelope are small enough that a single hunter can transport a complete, or nearly complete, animal back to a residential site. The average live weight of antelope males and females in the Trans-Pecos region of Texas was 41 kg and 40 kg, respectively (Beuchner 1950). This yields average hog-dressed weights of 30.2 kg and 26.4 kg (Mitchell 1971). If large herds of animals are killed at once, however, one is faced with a surfeit of carcasses to process and meat to transport. A herd of 300 antelope was reported in Utah in 1911 (Steward 1938:34). Even larger herds may have been common prehistorically.

Ethnographic studies of the Nunamiut (Binford 1978) and Hadza (Bunn et al. 1988; O'Connell et al. 1988) show that as the amount to be transported increases, or the transport distance increases, carcasses are more likely to be field butchered and elements selectively transported with respect to food utility (Miracle n.d.). Therefore, assuming that communal hunts are likely to produce a number of kills (per hunter) at once, and that individual stalking usually results in only a single kill (per hunter), the pattern of transporting body parts from kill sites

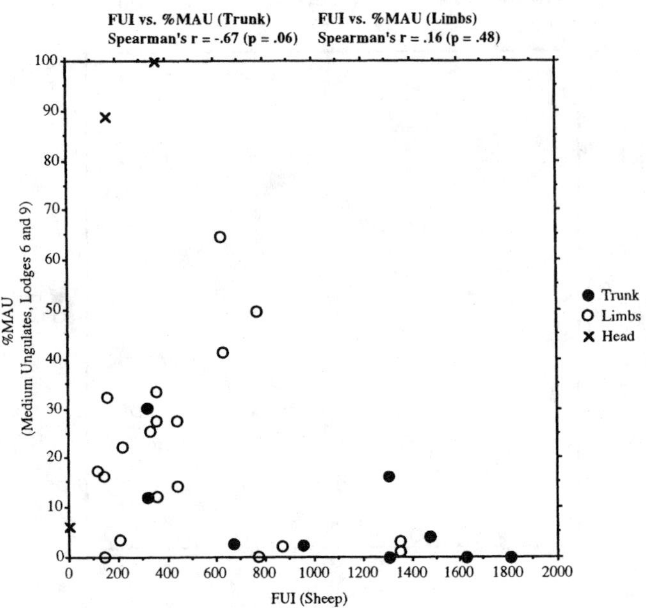

Figure 5.32. %MAU vs. FUI (sheep) at the Eden-Farson Site (Wyoming), trunk compared to limb elements (Lodges 6 and 9; $n = 49.4$).

may be indicative of hunting method. In residential assemblages, positive rank correlations between antelope element frequencies and food utility would suggest the field processing of carcasses and the preferential transport of higher-utility elements from the kill to residential site, i.e., communal hunts. Conversely, an individual hunt might be reflected by a relatively weak representation of the different body parts, and a lack of correlation with food utility. Perhaps an even better indication would be the evidence, through cutmark type and location, of the butchery of carcasses, in particular of feet (metapodials and phalanges) and possibly also heads, at residential sites. These are often among the first parts removed and abandoned in field butchery. Their presence in residential sites would indicate the transport of complete carcasses to residential sites for butchery and consumption.

In summary, a catastrophic mortality pattern, a sex ratio similar to that found in herds for the reconstructed season of procurement, and a clear-cut relationship between element frequency and food utility would be strong evidence of communal herd hunting. The demonstration of individual stalking is primarily dependent on an attritional mortality profile, and evidence of the initial butchering of animals at residential sites. Other combinations of these variables are more difficult to interpret in terms of hunting strategies.

Communal Hunting at Henderson?

The Henderson antelope do not fit any of the above expectations for communal hunting, but instead display a pattern that is very suggestive of individual stalking. First, the aged antelope mandibles suggest a selection for young and very old (age 6+) individuals. Communal hunting, or other tactics that are "blind" to the age of prey, would have produced an assemblage with many more young adults and prime-age adults. This pattern should be further exaggerated in pronghorn since females bear on average almost two young per year. Thus, I feel reasonably confident in the general pattern of the results, although I obviously would be more confident with a larger sample size.

Second, the seasonality data suggest that most animals were killed during the winter-spring, with an occasional antelope hunted during the summer and fall. Of the winter-spring kills, at least three of the five individuals were pregnant does, one killed late in term (May) and two killed slightly earlier in term (probably February to April). This is a time of year when antelope split into single-sex herds, and by May does have dispersed to give birth. On the other hand, a similar number of males and females are represented in the assemblage. A reasonable interpretation is that both males and females were hunted during the spring. This would imply either that several spring communal hunts of single sexes have been combined (excepting the late-term female), or that individual animals were stalked. The second interpretation is both more parsimonious and plausible, especially in light of the age-structure of the animals.

Finally, element frequencies of medium ungulates (overwhelmingly from antelope) at Henderson do not pattern closely with food utility (except for an underrepresentation of adult heads). The distribution and frequency of cutmarks suggest that complete and unprocessed limbs were transported to the site, bolstering the interpretation based on element frequencies.

Applying these same criteria to other antelope assemblages, it is possible to identify communal antelope hunting at other sites. For example, Nimmo (1971), using similar aging criteria for a large sample ($n = 79$ mandibles), found a catastrophic mortality curve for antelope from the Eden-Farson Site in Wyoming. Only one mandible was in the 6+ age class, while a total of nine mandibles (11%) were four years or older (4, 5, and 6+ age classes combined). In contrast, 31% of the Henderson individuals were in the 6+ age class. Furthermore, the dental eruption of the youngest age class at Eden-Farson suggests a fall kill, and mandibles from older age classes fall into discrete age groups, suggesting that these animals were also killed in the fall. Frison (1971) argues that the fall would have been the ideal time of the year to communally hunt antelope herds. Furthermore, element frequencies and the distribution of cutmarks at Eden-Farson suggest a bulk processing of meat for transport. I plotted (see Fig. 5.31) the combined element frequencies from Lodges 6 and 9 of the Eden-Farson Site against bulk density. In the assemblage as a whole, %MAU is positively correlated with bulk density ($r_s = 0.611$, $p = 0.001$). Broken down by trunk and limb elements (Fig. 5.31), however, there is little correlation (the trend is negative) between bulk density and trunk elements, while there is a strong, positive rank correlation between bulk density and limb elements. The %MAU-FUI curve (Fig. 5.32) clearly resembles a bulk curve and indicates the transport of higher-utility elements away from the site. Broken down by carcass unit, there is a strong negative correlation between %MAU and FUI of trunk elements (r_s = -0.67, p = 0.06). The limbs, in contrast, do not pattern against the FUI. Combining the bulk density and FUI results, trunk elements appear to have been selectively removed from the assemblage based on their food value, while limbs were not selectively transported and suffered destruction in proportion to their bulk density. Frison (1971) suggests that the antelope trap could have been located in the immediate vicinity of the site. This would make the Eden-Farson Site a field-processing site, an interpretation in agreement with the element frequency data. All lines of evidence indicate the communal hunting of antelope a short distance from the site, followed by the processing in bulk of carcasses for the further transport of meat.

Regional Comparisons

Introduction

There has been some debate (Driver 1985; Speth and Scott 1989) over the interpretation of faunal assemblages from other so-called "Lincoln phase" sites to the west of Henderson. Speth and Scott (1989) proposed that there was a temporal trend during the twefth to fifteenth centuries from sites dominated by small mammals to sites dominated by larger ungulates. They hypothesized that this shift to larger prey, and the implied increase in use of communal hunting strategies, might be indicative of more intensive horticultural economies together with depletion of preferred larger game resources close to home. Speth and Scott (1989:78) reported that communal hunting techniques are often less efficient, measured in return rates (kg of meat /person-hour of hunting), than individual techniques. Using the logic of optimal foraging theory—specifically central place foraging—and several ethnographic examples from Amazonia, they suggest that groups normally would only rarely hunt communally (e.g., for special intergroup feasts or periodic rituals). Communal hunting would emerge as a routine day-to-day economic strategy in response to local resource depletion or "commercial hunting" conditions (for example, to generate meat surpluses used in trade). Therefore, in Speth and Scott's scenario, one would expect communal hunting to become more important over time and covary with a general pattern of economic intensification.

Driver (1985) agreed that among Lincoln phase sites in southeastern New Mexico there are important contrasts in assemblage composition, but he argued that these contrasts primarily reflect differences in local site catchments, not temporal shifts in socioeconomy. Thus, in Driver's scenario communal techniques were used where and when antelope were locally abundant, as determined by environmental constraints. As an aside, Driver (1985:57) suggested that there was a direct trade-off between hunting and agricultural activities; an increase in communal hunting, because of the added organizational time required by such strategies, should covary with less intensive agricultural techniques. Thus, one would expect communal hunting in gentle, grassland habitats that would have supported relatively large antelope populations. These areas should also show evidence of less intensive agricultural practices.

Thanks to Driver's (1984, 1985, 1989, 2000) detailed work on the Phillips and Robinson sites in the Sierra Blanca region, there are published data on antelope assemblages contemporaneous with, and in a habitat similar to, Henderson. I will try to reconstruct the antelope procurement strategies at the Phillips and Robinson sites (both located on the east slope of the Sacramento Mountains about 100 km west of the Pecos Valley) and compare the results with Henderson to see if hunting strategies were similar at sites in similar habitats, and if not, how and why they differed.

Driver (1984, 1985, 2000) has demonstrated a strong relationship between site catchment and assemblage composition. His model predicts that within medium ungulate assemblages, antelope should predominate over deer in sites located in gentler terrain and grassland areas, while deer should predominate over antelope in broken terrain and wooded areas. In this respect, the Henderson medium ungulate assemblage neatly fits Driver's model; antelope predominate over deer (Table 5.23) and the site is located in a mixed prairie/desert grassland habitat on flat to rolling terrain. The local site catchment certainly helped to determine the target species at different sites.

Table 5.23. Antelope/deer ratio in some late prehistoric archaeological sites in southeastern New Mexico.[a]

Site	Antelope NISP	Deer NISP	Antelope/Deer Ratio	Reference
Penasco	9	56	0.2	Driver (1985: Table 26)
Bonnell	82	152	0.5	Driver (1985: Table 26)
CL-8	13	12	1.1	Driver (1989: Table 24)
Phillips	333	100	3.3	Driver (1985: Table 26)
Block	60	18	3.3	Driver (1985: Table 26)
Robinson	1318	299	4.4	Driver (1989: Table 23)
Hiner	47	6	7.8	Driver (1985: Table 26)
Henderson	1095	66	16.6	Miracle (this chapter)

[a]See Figure 5.1 for site locations.

Driver's model predicts that since Henderson, Phillips, and Robinson are all located in favorable antelope habitat, communal antelope hunting should have been practiced at all of the sites. Speth and Scott's model predicts that communal hunting might become more important over time, as a by-product of local depletion of preferred larger game stemming from the separate or combined effects of intensified agricultural techniques, decreased residential mobility, and local population aggregation.

Communal Hunting at Phillips and Robinson?

The Phillips Site is located on the east slope of the Sacramento Mountains in grassland close to the pinyon-juniper zone at an elevation of about 2000 m (Driver 1985:4). The site, excavated in 1955-1956 by Jane Holden Kelley (1984:200), contained a number of slab-lined rooms dating to the Corona (one room excavated) and Lincoln (16 rooms tested or excavated) phases (Kelley 1984:201-13). The Lincoln phase occupation at the site was broadly contemporary with the Henderson occupation (Speth, pers. comm.).

Driver (1985) analyzed the Phillips faunal data and suggested that the antelope were communally hunted. From the epiphyseal fusion data (medium ungulates combined), Driver (1985:37-38) inferred that animals over a range of age groups were killed, and that approximately half of the killed animals had not yet reached full skeletal maturity (about 5.0 to 5.5 years). The antelope dentitions showed that half of the individuals had been killed by their second year, concluding it to be "consistent with a communal hunting pattern in which a cohort is surrounded and slaughtered" (1985:38). The frequency of neonatal tibiae (16%) suggested to him that hunting took place in the spring.

These data, however, in some aspects also point to individual stalking and thus do not adequately distinguish between individually stalked and communally hunted patterns of procurement. As suggested previously, in a twinning species such as the antelope, one would expect a large number of neonate and yearling animals in both an attritional and catastrophic mortality profile (Klein and Cruz-Uribe 1984:57). Therefore, the key difference between these two types of mortality profile is in the oldest age class (better represented in an attritional profile). A simple mortality profile (Fig. 5.33) was made using Driver's (1985:38) age data.[10] The profile is diagnostic of neither a catastrophic nor an attritional pattern. Old individuals, however, are not as well represented in the sample as at Henderson.

The season of death was inferred by Driver (1985:36, 38) from dental eruption and fetal data. The "fetal" remains were assigned a season of death from February (if early fetal) to May (if neonatal). The estimation of MNE's is problematic, since females usually bear two young and the goal of the analysis is to estimate the number of pregnant does killed (otherwise values for spring will be twice as large relative to other seasons of the year). In this case, I used the fetal/neonate MNE of 6 (based on the tibia) to estimate an MAU of 1.5 and an MNE of 3 for does. If all of the fetal/neonate remains are neonate, then I have

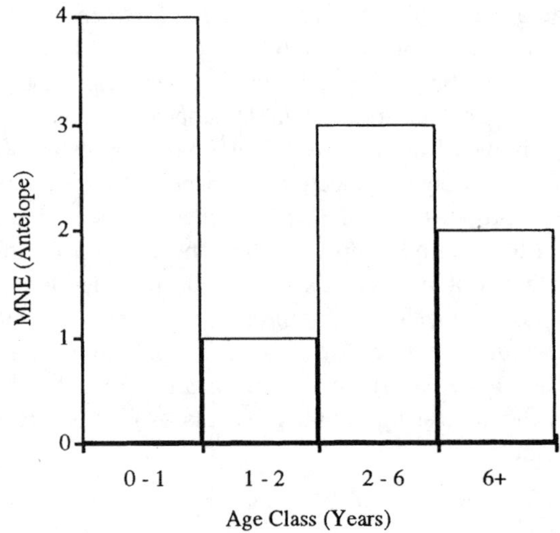

Figure 5.33. Mortality profile (MNE) of antelope at the Phillips Site.

underestimated by half. In either case, most of the animals were killed between the rut and the birthing season, October to May (Fig. 5.34). Like the age-structure data, the seasonality data are also ambiguous. From October to March, communal antelope hunting would have been possible, while from March to May communal hunting may have been difficult to impossible due to the dispersion of the herds (Frison 1971; Howard and Bradybaugh 1983). Thus, the mortality profile is intermediate between attritional and catastrophic and the seasonality data suggest significant hunting during the spring. Both lines of evidence suggest that some antelope were being stalked. Quite possibly, the Phillips hunters were using both strategies depending on the season of the year.

The results of the reanalysis of body-part frequencies, on the other hand, fit more closely the expected pattern of communally hunted animals. In the analysis of element frequencies, I combined antelope, deer, and medium ungulate data. A comparison of the MNE's for different deer and antelope elements shows that element frequencies are similar, which justifies combining the data (Fig. 5.35).[11] Bulk density is significantly rank-correlated with %MAU when the assemblage is taken as a whole ($r_s = 0.42$, $p = 0.04$). However, if one considers trunk and limb elements separately, then each group is negatively correlated with bulk density, although neither result is statistically significant (Fig. 5.36). Comparisons of the FUI against the %MAU for the entire assemblage are also not significant (Fig. 5.37). Broken down by carcass unit, the trunk is negatively rank correlated ($r_s = -.85$, $p = 0.04$), while the limbs are positively rank correlated ($r_s = 0.67$, $p = 0.007$). Through selective transport, processing, or both, meaty limb elements were preferentially added to the assemblage, while meaty trunk elements were removed. I interpret this pattern as evidence of selective transport

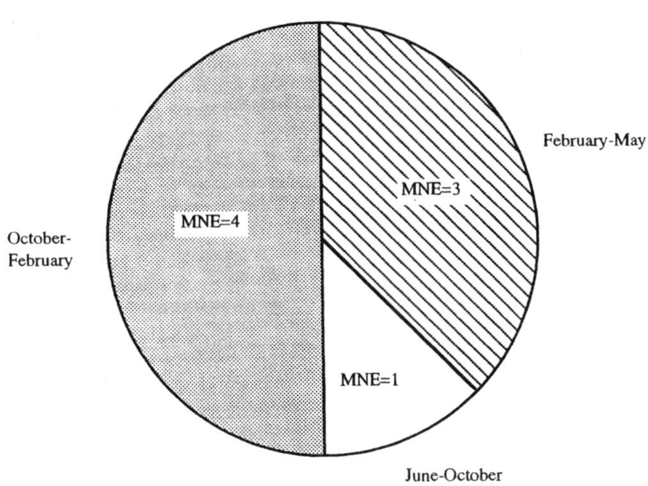

Figure 5.34. Seasonality of antelope procurement at the Phillips Site.

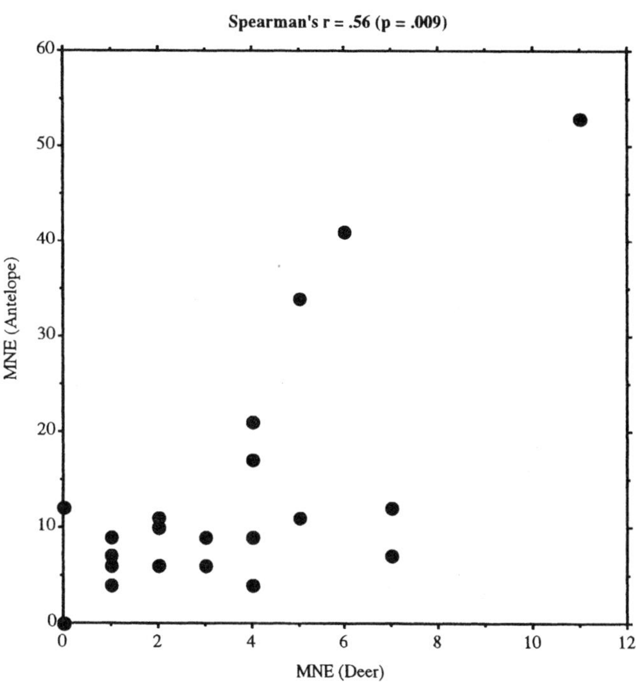

Figure 5.35. Frequency (MNE) of antelope vs. deer at the Phillips Site.

of meaty limbs to the site from kill sites. Remains of a number of animals were introduced as pieces (primarily limbs), although some carcasses were also transported whole. Once on site, there was a further destruction or removal of meaty trunk remains. This might be the result of intensive and destructive processing of these elements (e.g., for grease) or their removal through transport (as provisions or in trade).

In sum, the mortality and seasonality evidence from the Phillips Site do not provide an unambiguous picture of the hunting techniques used. The body-part data indicate a preferential transport of elements to the site based on food utility, a strategy that one might expect when large numbers of medium-sized animals are killed at once. Selective transport, however, is also an expectation when transport distances are long, even if handling only a single antelope carcass. The most plausible solution is to hedge all bets and conclude that the Phillips hunters used both communal and stalking techniques. In the absence of further data, we can do no better than that.

The Robinson Site is located on the east slope of Patos Mountain only a few kilometers to the north-northeast of the Phillips Site. The village, a comparatively large, rectangular structure with about 150 rooms surrounding a central plaza, sits in a sparsely wooded pinyon-juniper belt at an elevation of about 2000 m (Kelley 1984:251). Excavations from 1984 to 1986 exposed a series of room, plaza, and midden deposits with a rich faunal assemblage that has been analyzed by Driver (1989). A number of radiocarbon, archaeomagnetic, and obsidian hydration dates place the principal occupation at Robinson during the thirteenth, fourteenth, and perhaps fifteenth centuries, and ceramic and other artifactual data also point to an occupation roughly contemporary with Henderson (Stewart et al. 1991; see also Driver 1989: Table 21).

Driver (1989) suggests that antelope were communally hunted at Robinson to take "advantage of late winter/spring concentrations of animals, especially pronghorn" (Driver 1989:25). Since Robinson produced neonatal dentitions (deciduous premolars erupted but unworn) and relatively abundant neonatal bones (7%, NISP = 140), Driver (1989:19) concludes that the site was occupied during the late spring and further observes that "spring communal hunting is a well-established pattern in ethnographically known Southwestern cultures" (Driver 1989:25).

Robinson provides more convincing evidence of communal hunting of antelope herds than Phillips. The Robinson antelope mortality profile is based on mandibular dentitions that Driver (1989:19) aged as neonatal, immature (yearling), and mature. These age categories roughly correspond to the age classes 0-1 years, 1-2 years, and 2+ years (Fig. 5.38).[12] The mortality profile shows a large number of young and yearling remains, but few adult and old individuals. The profile is catastrophic in shape, and if the small sample is representative of the entire assemblage, then this catastrophic mortality curve would support an interpretation of communal antelope hunting.

Dentition and neonatal bones point to spring kills. Unworn deciduous premolars indicate animals killed shortly after birth, probably in the late spring. The "immature" animals had heavily worn deciduous premolars and some permanent teeth. Using Dow and Wright's (1962) criteria, these dentitions probably came from animals between 8 and 16 months of age, with a bias towards the older end of the age range. The yearling re-

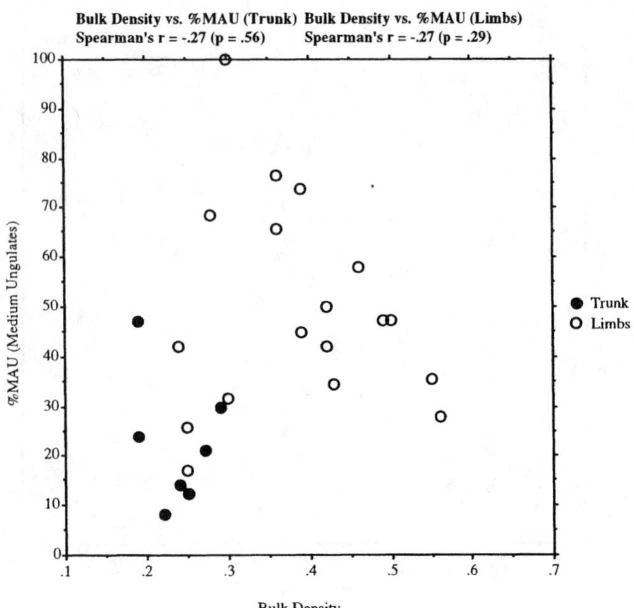

Figure 5.36. %MAU vs. bulk density at the Phillips Site, trunk compared to limb elements (n = 19).

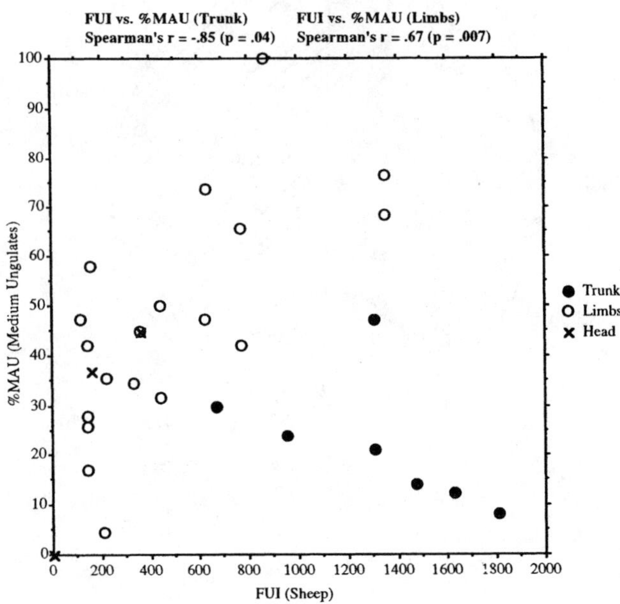

Figure 5.37. %MAU vs. FUI (sheep) at the Phillips Site, trunk compared to limb elements (n = 19).

mains also indicate late spring kills. It is not possible to estimate the season of death of the adult remains. In any event, antelope hunting was probably a late spring activity at the Robinson Site.

In the analysis of element frequencies, I combined antelope, deer, and medium ungulate data. A comparison of the MNE's for different deer and antelope elements shows similar element frequencies, which justify combining the data (Fig. 5.39). Bulk density is significantly rank-correlated with %MAU values (Fig. 5.40) for the assemblage as a whole ($r_s = 0.55, p = 0.003$), while there is no correlation between the FUI and the assemblage as a whole (Fig. 5.41). Considering the trunk and limb elements separately, bulk density and %MAU of trunk elements are not correlated, while there is a weak positive correlation with the %MAU of limb elements (Fig. 5.40). In the case of the FUI, however, there is a strong negative rank correlation with the %MAU of trunk elements and a strong positive rank correlation with the %MAU of limb elements (Fig. 5.41). This pattern is remarkably similar to that of the Phillips Site (see Fig. 5.37 above), and suggests the same interpretation. Through selective transport, processing, or both, meaty limb elements were preferentially added to the assemblage, while meaty trunk elements were removed from the assemblage through destruction (e.g., processing for grease) or transport (e.g., as provisions or in trade).

Each of these lines of evidence suggests the communal hunting of antelope herds. The mortality profile is catastrophic and, with the seasonality data, suggests that herds of antelope were

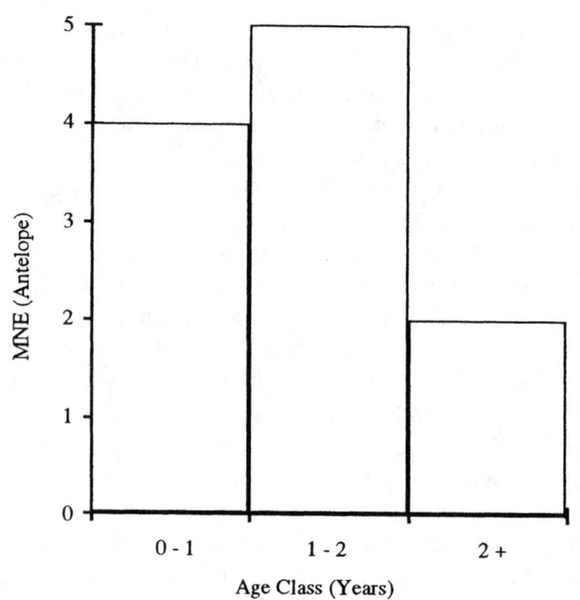

Figure 5.38. Mortality profile (MNE) of antelope at the Robinson Site.

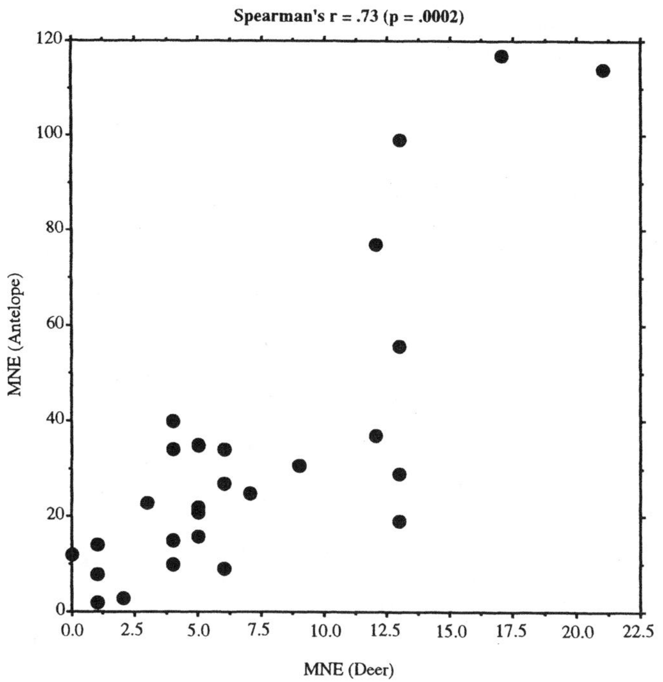

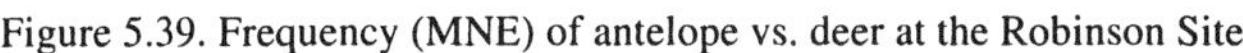
Figure 5.39. Frequency (MNE) of antelope vs. deer at the Robinson Site.

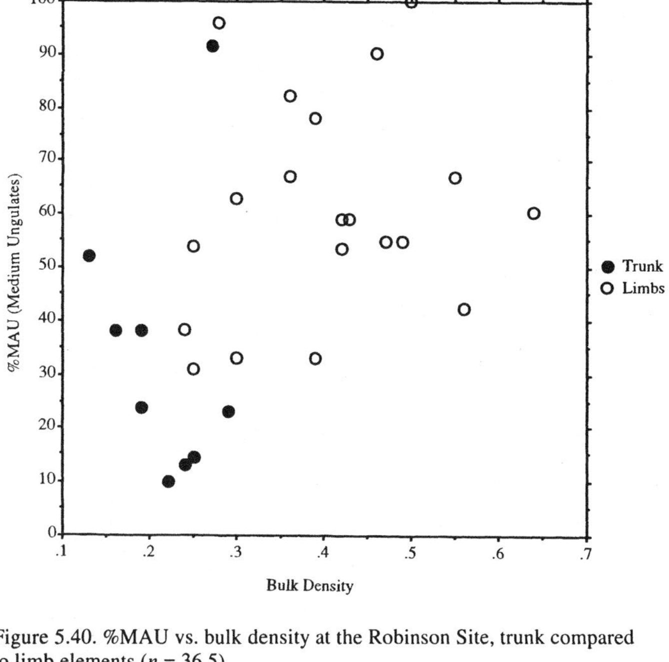

Figure 5.40. %MAU vs. bulk density at the Robinson Site, trunk compared to limb elements (n = 36.5).

taken during the late spring or early summer. The body-part data indicate the preferential transport of elements to the site based on food utility, a strategy that one might expect when large numbers of medium-sized animals are killed at once. As I have already suggested, communal hunting during the birthing season would probably not be feasible. By four to eight weeks after the birthing season, however, nursery herds have formed and communal hunts would have been possible. Thus, my interpretation of communal hunting pivots around the aging of the neonatal dentitions. If they show signs of wear, indicating animals at least a month or two old, then communal hunting makes perfect sense. On the other hand, truly unworn deciduous teeth would suggest fawns taken before nursery herds had formed. One might add that an attritional strategy during the spring would produce an abundance of neonatal remains due to their very high frequency in the natural populations. However, I favor a communal hunting interpretation due to the body-part evidence, and the likelihood that the antelope could have been hunted in the early summer after the formation of nursery herds.

I conclude that antelope were probably both stalked and communally hunted at Phillips during the fall, winter, spring and perhaps summer, but were primarily communally hunted at the Robinson Site, probably during the early summer. This is an interesting contrast since these sites are within a few kilometers of each other and the assemblages are similar in many ways, particularly in the ratio of antelope to deer and the frequency of different skeletal elements.

Implications of the Results

The medium ungulate assemblages from Henderson, Phillips, and Robinson are superficially similar—all dominated by antelope remains. The abundance of antelope remains has been taken by many as evidence of communal antelope hunting. Detailed analyses of these assemblages, however, suggest different patterns of antelope procurement and carcass use. Antelope were hunted communally at Robinson, individually at Henderson, and perhaps by both techniques at Phillips.

If geography were the primary factor influencing both animal distribution and procurement strategies, then one would expect communal antelope hunting at all three sites, since all are located in suitable antelope habitat.

The general contemporaneity of Henderson, Phillips, and Robinson makes temporal changes in socioeconomic strategies at the regional scale an unlikely explanation for the variation in antelope hunting strategies. At a more local scale, however, if depletion of preferred large-game resources in close proximity to an agriculturally based community favors the adoption of communal strategies, as suggested by Speth and Scott (1989), then the differences between these sites might reflect different settlement histories. The individual stalking of antelope at Henderson may be the product of a brief occupation, a low degree of dependence on cultivated crops, a small resident population, or some combination. The communal hunting at Robinson may reflect a longer duration of occupation at the site by a larger,

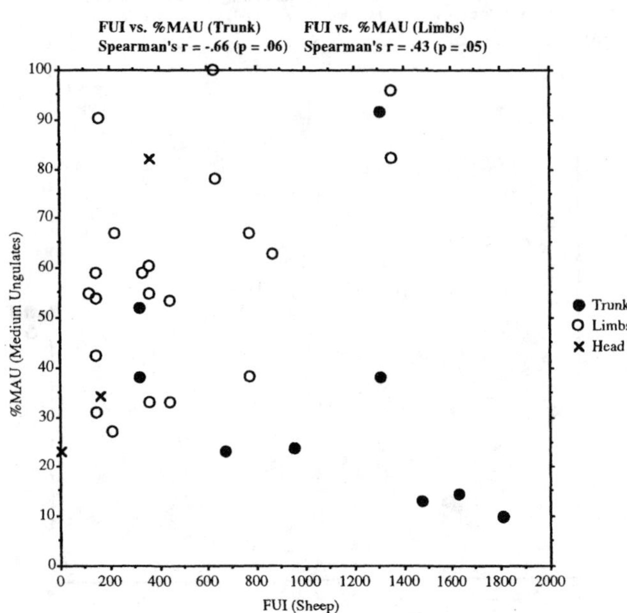

Figure 5.41. %MAU vs. FUI (sheep) at the Robinson Site, trunk compared to limb elements (n = 36.5).

more agriculturally dependent resident population, leading to greater local resource depletion. On the other hand, the inhabitants of Henderson appear to have communally hunted bison (Chapter 4), while bison remains are very rare at both Phillips and Robinson and do not support an interpretation of communal hunting at these sites (Driver 1985, 1989). The contrast in bison remains and procurement strategies between these sites might indicate a greater overall level of resource depletion at Henderson than at Phillips or Robinson, since communal bison hunting appears to have been so important at Henderson.

The different procurement strategies could also represent different facets of a larger sphere of interaction. At Henderson, bison appear to have been communally hunted and bison meat was traded (Chapter 4), while antelope were probably individually hunted and locally consumed. In contrast, Robinson appears to have received bison meat through trade and instead communally hunted antelope. The communal antelope hunting at Robinson may have been a technique to generate trade surpluses such as hides or a steady source of protein to supplement a perhaps less predictable flow of bison meat. Trade in antelope meat has yet to be documented archaeologically, although trade in deer meat has been documented ethnographically in the American Southwest (Ford 1983). Antelope skins were probably not traded for adult clothing since they are relatively poor in quality (Tyler 1975:37), but may have been traded for other uses, including ritual paraphernalia.

The possibility that antelope were communally hunted to insure a supplemental source of protein may have interesting implications for the scheduling and organization of hunting antelope versus bison. The Henderson hunters may have individually hunted antelope because of a time-conflict with communal bison hunts, or because it was a dependable alternative meat source. If one is going to invest the time and energy in a communal hunt, then it makes sense to maximize return rates by targeting the largest animals available, in this case, bison. Thus, the apparent nonintensive hunting of antelope during the winter-spring at Henderson may have been a by-product of the very intensive bison hunting practiced by the Henderson villagers. This does not explain why antelope were not communally hunted in the fall once the harvest was in. Bison may not have been present in the Pecos Valley during the fall (see discussion in Chapter 4); hence, bison procurement would not have presented a scheduling conflict. Other activities that might have interfered with communal antelope hunting remain to be identified.

At both Robinson and Phillips, in contrast, bison remains are rare, suggesting that bison were either not intensively hunted or were unavailable in the local region. At Robinson and Phillips, communal antelope hunting may have been practiced because there was no scheduling conflict with bison hunts, or because a protein deficit could best be filled by communally hunting antelope, or both. While antelope may have been a peripheral or at best a secondary hunting focus at Henderson, antelope may have been a crucial source of protein at Robinson and Phillips. In this case, Robinson and Phillips make an interesting contrast. Communal hunting at Robinson appears to have been limited to the early summer or late spring. At Phillips, antelope may have been hunted by both individual and communal techniques, and they were also hunted over more of the year. At Phillips, therefore, antelope may have been taken whenever they were available and with whatever techniques were required, while at Robinson, antelope hunting may have been limited by a more rigid seasonal schedule of economic activities. This could imply an even more intensive antelope procurement strategy at Phillips then at Robinson, or might instead indicate the intensive use of an as yet unidentified resource at Robinson that required the more rigid or fixed scheduling of communal antelope hunting. In any case, the role of antelope in hunting systems at the three sites appears to have differed and to have been strongly constrained by bison availability and procurement. Henderson hunters may have practiced a very intensive communal hunting, but of bison instead of antelope, while hunters at Robinson and Phillips appear to have focused more of their energies on antelope.

Conclusions

The Henderson Late phase medium ungulate assemblage is amazingly homogeneous within the site both spatially and temporally. Similar trash appears to have been dumped in abandoned rooms and in the East Plaza. The main contrast within the site was a much faster rate of accumulation of trash in the East Plaza and in Room C-5 than in the remaining rooms of the village. It appears that antelope were individually hunted, then butchered and processed (e.g., roasting whole limbs) in the East Plaza. They were then further processed (e.g., for marrow) in and around the room blocks. Trash was deposited in abandoned rooms or the East Plaza.

The economic analysis showed that medium ungulates, predominantly antelope, were hunted mostly during the winter-spring, with an occasional animal taken during other seasons of the year. Roughly equal numbers of males and females were hunted. An attritional form of mortality curve in conjunction with the seasonality indicators and evidence for the transport of essentially whole carcasses indicate the individual hunting of animals. The Henderson hunters did not differentially transport elements (excepting the head) on the basis of utility to or from the site. Prior to cooking, there was minimal dismemberment of carcasses beyond a division into limbs and perhaps several axial portions.

Through a review of the biological literature on antelope and the ethnographic literature on antelope hunting, I suggested a method for identifying communal and individual antelope hunting strategies. This method held up fairly well when examined against the well-known Eden-Farson Site assemblage, an assemblage that was very likely produced through communal antelope hunting. This method was then used in a reanalysis of the medium ungulate remains from the Phillips and Robinson Sites, two villages in southeastern New Mexico that are contemporary with Henderson, and the results suggest that antelope may have been communally hunted at the Robinson Site, but were probably pursued with a mixed strategy at the Phillips Site.

The proportion of antelope to deer remains at Henderson supports Driver's hypothesis of species selection constrained by habitat type, with antelope predominating in sites close to open grasslands. However, although Henderson, Phillips, and Robinson are all located in similar geographical settings, the prehistoric inhabitants of these three communities appear to have emphasized different hunting techniques. It was not possible to directly evaluate Speth and Scott's model, since a focus on medium ungulates represents only one of several avenues for hunting intensification. Variation in antelope hunting strategies between sites may be related to local resource depletion, intensified meat/hide production for trade, local shortages of protein or calories, or critical scheduling conflicts involving other resources that remain to be identified. Further exploration of these issues requires an integration of the results of the analysis of medium ungulates with those for bison and other subsistence and paleoenvironmental data.

Synopsis

This chapter presents the analysis of 1,530 medium ungulate bones recovered during two seasons of excavation at the Henderson Site (1980-1981). All of these remains date to the Late phase occupation of the village. The material discussed here represents all of the bones identifiable to at least genus as well as much of the material that could only be assigned to approximate body size (i.e., medium ungulate) and skeletal element. Not yet analyzed are several hundred miscellaneous limb-shaft fragments and broken vertebral processes. All of the medium ungulate rib fragments were culled and analyzed after the tables in this chapter had been completed, so the results of the rib analysis are discussed briefly in the text but the total rib count is not reflected in the tables.

Only pronghorn antelope (*Antilocapra americana*) and deer (*Odocoileus* sp.) were recognized in the medium ungulate assemblage. No evidence of mountain sheep was encountered during the 1980-1981 seasons. Given the fragmentary condition and small size of the medium ungulate sample from Henderson, no attempt was made to distinguish between mule deer (*O. hemionus*) and white-tailed deer (*O. virginianus*), both of which occur in the region today. At least 21 antelope (based on the pelvis) and 3 deer (based on the distal metacarpal) are represented in the assemblage. Antelope therefore clearly dominates the medium ungulate assemblage. To obtain adequate sample sizes, in several of the analyses the remains of deer, antelope, and those identified simply as "deer/antelope" have been lumped together and treated as a single group ("medium ungulate").

The medium ungulate bones in general are well preserved in all site proveniences, although, as with bison, some of the remains in the East Plaza had to be treated with preservative to facilitate their removal. There is little evidence to suggest that taphonomic processes significantly altered or biased the composition of the medium ungulate assemblage. For example, careful inspection of the surfaces of the bones revealed few recognizable traces of weathering. Signs of rodent or carnivore damage, such as gnawing, pitting, or crenulation, are also rare. In addition, the small, delicate ribs of medium ungulates are proportionately better represented than the far more robust ribs of bison, suggesting that destruction by village dogs or other carnivores did not severely alter the assemblage. Ratios of proximal to distal tibiae and humeri, and relationships between element frequencies and bulk density were also examined. Nothing in these analyses points to severe biases in the medium ungulate assemblage stemming from carnivore attrition, decay, trampling, or other taphonomic processes.

Antelope outnumber deer over 10:1 in the room blocks and in the East Plaza. Interestingly, remains identified as "deer/antelope" are much more numerous in the combined room block assemblage than in the East Plaza, a difference that appears to reflect greater fragmentation (and hence lower identifiability) of bones in the rooms.

Approximately 7.2% of the Late phase medium ungulate remains at Henderson are burned. The incidence of burning is higher in the rooms than in the East Plaza and more of the burned bones in the rooms are calcined. However, neither difference is statistically significant.

Antelope were sexed on the basis of measurements taken on the pelvis. For the site as a whole, there are nearly equal numbers of males (MNI = 6) and females (MNI = 4). The sample is too small to permit meaningful comparisons of the sex ratio between the room blocks and East Plaza. However, both sexes are represented in both proveniences.

Antelope were aged primarily on the basis of dental eruption and wear criteria. Age estimates were possible on mandibles and loose teeth from thirteen individuals. Epiphyseal fusion data provided complementary information on the age structure of the Henderson antelope. Based on dentitions, five animals were less than about three years old and eight animals more than three years old (of which four are more than six years old). The fusion data indicate that only three animals are under 15 months, while seven animals are older than 5.5 years. In other words, both aging criteria point to a sample dominated by old to very old individuals.

Looking at the proportional representation of various carcass units (axial vs. appendicular, front vs. rear limb, upper vs. lower limb), both room blocks and East Plaza are dominated by limb elements and underrepresented by trunk elements relative to the expected frequency in a complete antelope skeleton. Differences between proveniences in the proportional representation of different carcass units are not statistically significant. The major difference between room blocks and East Plaza is in the degree of bone fragmentation. Bones are more fragmented in the room blocks. In addition, in the room blocks rear limbs and upper front limbs are more fragmented than other limb units, while in the East Plaza, the degree of fragmentation among different limb units is relatively uniform.

Element frequencies (%MAU) for medium ungulates at Henderson, when plotted against Metcalfe and Jones's (1988) food utility index (FUI), and against Binford's (1978) grease index and marrow cavity volume, reveal little evidence of significant patterning, for the site assemblage as a whole, or for the separate East Plaza and room block assemblages. Similar results are obtained when the %MAU for trunk and limb elements are plotted separately against these same indices. The most striking exception is a significant relationship between %MAU and marrow cavity volume in the midden deposits of Room C-5. In addition, the degree of bone fragmentation in the room blocks proved to be uncorrelated with Binford's grease index, but was strongly correlated with marrow cavity volume. There appears to be little evidence, therefore, of grease rendering at Henderson, while there is evidence of marrow processing. A similar conclusion was reached in the analysis of the bison remains (Chapter 4).

The results of these analyses suggest that during the Late phase antelope (and probably deer) elements were not brought into or removed from the village on the basis of their food utility. Instead, the hunters appear to have transported complete young and nearly complete (minus the head) adult carcasses back to the village from kills in the surrounding region.

Only 27 medium ungulate bones (1.8% of total NISP) display cutmarks. The frequency of cutmarked bones in the room blocks and East Plaza is nearly identical. No cutmarks were observed on rear leg elements or on most of the trunk, and only one was noted on a lower front limb element. Most (nearly 7%) are concentrated on the upper fore limb. The distribution of cutmarks indicates that lower limbs were not dismembered either before or after their introduction into the village. Similarly, cuts characteristic of skinning an animal for its hide, often transverse cuts on the phalanges or metapodials, are absent. Following Binford's (1981) criteria for distinguishing cutmarks made on supple carcasses from those made on stiff ones, carcasses in both states appear to have been processed in the village. This suggests that at least some of the animals were killed quite close to the village. Filleting marks are completely lacking on the meat-rich rear limbs and pelves. These parts were presumably processed in a manner that did not leave distinctive traces. The concentration of signs of burning on the less meaty lower limbs is consistent with the absence of cutmarks on the meaty elements, pointing to the cooking or roasting of the meat while the limbs were still articulated. While sample sizes are exceedingly small, dismemberment marks in the East Plaza are concentrated on the axis and atlas, probably for removal of the head, while dismemberment marks in the room blocks are concentrated around the elbow, presumably for disarticulation of the joint. This may reflect slight differences in the sources of trash for these two areas. The East Plaza trash may have been produced at an earlier stage of disarticulation—removal of the head—while the room block trash may have been produced at a later stage of joint disarticulation and secondary dismemberment, perhaps in the context of marrow extraction and consumption.

Grouping of the Henderson antelope into age classes yields a mortality profile in which fawns and yearlings are poorly represented while prime adults and especially older individuals are more numerous. The underrepresentation of fawns may well be due to taphonomic factors, given the susceptibility of these small, unfused elements to attrition, but the poor representation of yearlings cannot be attributed to differential destruction of immature remains. Thus, despite the small number of ageable individuals, the Henderson sample resembles a U-shaped, or "attritional," mortality profile rather than a "catastrophic one," and suggests that procurement strategies employed by village hunters tended to select very old (and perhaps also very young) animals more often than prime adults.

In southeastern New Mexico, most antelope give birth to their young in mid-May. Given this parturition date, and using the aged dentitions and fetal remains to estimate season of death, most of the Henderson antelope appear to have been killed during the winter-spring, although all seasons of the year are represented. The season of death of antelope in the room blocks and East Plaza is very similar; both show a strong dominance of winter-spring kills, with rare or no evidence of other seasons. The indication of more than one season of antelope procurement is compatible with the age-structure evidence for an attritional mortality profile.

The herd organization of modern antelope in southeastern New Mexico, described by Howard and Bradybaugh (1983), undergoes regular and predictable changes over the course of the year. During the birthing period in mid-May, females are alone or in pairs, while males have dispersed into bachelor groups of two to about a dozen. In July females and fawns form nursery groups (averaging six does). During August and September, the bachelor herds reduce in size (two to four animals) as males establish individual defended territories for the fall rut. During the fall, mixed groups of males and females begin to form and by winter these groups have increased in size to about a dozen or more animals. These mixed herds last until February or March when separate bachelor herds are once again established.

Ethnohistoric and ethnographic descriptions of antelope hunting in western North America indicate that communal hunting took place at all seasons of the year, but was particularly common during the fall and winter when herds were aggregated. Individual stalking, on the other hand, appears to have been most effective in the spring, in part because does were, to some extent, tethered by their young.

Mortality profiles provide a useful tool for distinguishing in the archaeological record between communal hunting strategies, which are likely to produce catastrophic age curves, and individual stalking, which is more likely to produce an attritional age curve. The attritional nature of the Henderson mortality profile, therefore, suggests individual stalking rather than communal hunting. Moreover, during the spring and summer, antelope occur in single-sex groups and, as a consequence, any single communal hunt is likely to take just males or just females. The fact that the Henderson antelope assemblage contains nearly equal numbers of males and females again suggests individual stalking. Unfortunately, however, the sex data do not provide an unambiguous indictor of stalking because accumulation of remains from several single-sex communal hunts would also create mixed-sex assemblages if hunters were not consistent in targeting a single sex or if hunts from several different seasons were represented.

One other line of evidence also points to stalking as the dominant strategy used for the procurement of antelope at Henderson. If antelope were hunted communally, and especially if they were taken in large numbers at some distance from the village, initial processing and culling in the field would probably be necessary to facilitate transporting the meat and other products of the hunt back to the village. Field processing and culling are likely to produce an assemblage of elements whose frequencies are correlated with utility. In contrast, the Henderson medium ungulate data do not correlate with utility, and instead suggest that whole carcasses were brought into the village. This is the pattern one would expect if individual stalking were the principal method of procurement.

The chapter concludes with a look at the antelope procurement strategies employed by hunters at Robinson and Phillips, two late prehistoric communities in the Sierra Blanca region west of Henderson. Using data presented by Driver (1985, 1989, 2000), and employing the same criteria that were used to determine the hunting strategies at Henderson (seasonal timing of kills, mortality profiles, correlation of element frequencies with indices of utility), Phillips produces ambiguous results, supporting an interpretation of communal hunting in some respects and individual stalking in others; a mixed or varying strategy seems most likely. At Robinson, the indicators pattern more clearly and, in agreement with Driver's conclusion, suggest that antelope were taken communally. Thus, three sites, all roughly contemporary and all situated in or close to prime antelope habitat, display different strategies for procuring antelope. The Late phase Henderson villagers appear to have stalked antelope individually, those at Phillips may have hunted antelope both singly and communally, and those at Robinson relied primarily on communal techniques to take antelope.

The reasons for these differences remain unclear. One possible explanation, developed by Speth and Scott (1989), would posit that differences between these communities related to degree of exploitation. Depletion would be greatest near those communities with the largest and most residentially stable populations. According to Speth and Scott's model, as a community grows and stabilizes, the availability of large game close to a village declines, and communal hunting strategies, which were previously used for feasts, ceremonies, or other special occasions, become increasingly incorporated into routine subsistence activities. In this view, Robinson would be seen as the community experiencing the greatest local game depletion, a suggestion that fits well with the fact that Robinson is also the largest community of the three. However, the Henderson villagers were communally hunting bison, whereas the inhabitants of Phillips and Robinson were not. From this perspective, Henderson would have to be seen as the community that suffered from the most severe local game depletion. Unfortunately, until we find an independent way of monitoring the degree of local resource depletion, this model cannot be satisfactorily evaluated.

Another explanation would link the use of communal hunting strategies to the acquisition of meat and/or hides for use in trade with other communities. From this perspective, Robinson was targeting antelope for exchange while Henderson was focusing on bison. Perhaps the communal hunting of antelope by the Robinson villagers also assured them of a reliable supply of protein or calories to supplement a less predictable flow of bison meat from the Pecos lowlands. For the Henderson villagers, communal antelope hunting in the spring may have conflicted with communal bison hunting. This of course would not explain why antelope were not taken communally at Henderson during the fall. While bison may not have been present in the area following the harvest, antelope almost certainly were.

In sum, variation in antelope hunting strategies between sites may be related to local resource depletion, intensified meat/hide production for exchange, local shortages of protein or calories, or critical scheduling conflicts involving other resources that remain to be identified. Further exploration of these issues requires an integration of the results of the analysis of the medium ungulates with other subsistence and paleoenvironmental data.

Acknowledgments

I would like to thank Richard Ford, John O'Shea, Laura Ahearn, Jonathan Driver, and R. Lee Lyman for useful comments on earlier drafts of this paper. In particular, I thank John Speth for his support and inspiration at all stages of this project. Faults that remain are of course my own. Research summarized in this paper was partially supported by a University of Michigan Regent's Fellowship and a National Science Foundation Graduate Fellowship.

Notes

1. A single third phalanx of bighorn sheep (*Ovis canadensis*) was recovered at Henderson during the renewed excavations in the 1990s.

2. McKusick (1981) observed that antelope in the earlier levels at Gran Quivira are unusually large in body size (especially the males). In later levels, there is an overall decrease in body size that is particularly pronounced in males. Unfortunately, she did not publish any of the original metric data on which these conclusions were based.

3. The pronghorn male, on the basis of epiphyseal fusion, is probably a young adult (1-3 years), while the female specimen is from an older adult (all epiphyses well fused). The failure of criteria based on rugosity may be due to age-related changes in morphology (comparing a young male and an old female).

4. Brain (1981) notes that humans may also inflict considerable damage on bones with their teeth. In his observations of the Khoi, he noted that "fifteen tail vertebrae were chewed and swallowed, and limb bones such as femurs and metapodials suffered severely at their ends" (Brain 1981:18).

5. For the bulk density of complete long bones, I simply took the bulk density value of the denser articular end.

6. If one includes the 1-2 year old mandible in the sample of young animals, the head/postcrania ratio increases to 1.33. Although the representation of heads, as measured by MNI on aged teeth, varies dramatically between the room blocks and East Plaza, the NISP values are very similar, suggesting that this difference is a product of using the MNI. Comparisons of %MAU for head elements between the room blocks and East Plaza further support the NISP results.

7. Binford uses the same code number for the anterior face of the radius and the olecranon process of the ulna, although the interpretation of these marks is radically different.

8. If one chooses to calculate rank correlations with theoretical catastrophic mortality profiles (TCMP), then it only makes sense to also calculate rank correlations with theoretical attritional mortality profiles (TAMP). Since a TCMP must always contain fewer survivors in longer-lived age classes, for the purpose of rank correlations, any list of progressively decreasing values can be used. The shape of a TAMP, however, is dependent on the population dynamics of each species (actually each population) in question. Thus, a TAMP must be built from data on the mortality of a particular species.

9. Measurements of the fawn/doe ratio in living populations range from 1.6 (Hoover et al. 1959) to 1.75 (Beuchner 1950).

10. Driver (1985:38, and Table A57) does not provide MNI data; therefore, the data are graphed as MNE's. Dividing these estimates by two would give MAU's, which should be close to the MNI's.

11. Since the deposits were not screened, Driver (1985:27) suggests that many of the smallest medium ungulate bones—the carpals, smaller tarsals, third phalanges, and caudal vertebrae—were probably missed during excavation. These elements were excluded from the present analysis with the exception of the tarsals. Driver (1985) does not separate large (calcaneus, astragalus, naviculo-cuboid) from small tarsals (lateral malleolus, second-third tarsal, first tarsal) in his published tables. Since many of the small tarsals may have been lost in excavation, I assumed that mostly large tarsals were recovered and thus divided MNE values by eight (six large tarsals; and, assuming that two-thirds of small tarsals were missed in excavation, two small tarsals) instead of twelve (natural number of large and small tarsals in an antelope skeleton) to calculate the MAU for tarsals.

12. MNE's were used in these plots due to incomplete data to determine MNI's.

References Cited

Autenrieth, R. E., and E. Fichter
1975 On the Behavior and Socialization of Pronghorn Fawns. *Wildlife Monograph* 42:1-111.

Bailey, V.
1931 *Mammals of New Mexico*. North American Fauna 53. Washington, DC: U.S. Department of Agriculture, Bureau of Biological Survey.

Beaglehole, E.
1936 *Hopi Hunting and Hunting Ritual*. Yale University Publications in Anthropology 4.

Behrensmeyer, A. K.
1978 Taphonomic and Ecologic Information from Bone Weathering. *Paleobiology* 4:150-62.

Beuchner, H. K.
1950 Life History, Ecology, and Range Use of the Pronghorn Antelope in Trans-Pecos Texas. *American Midland Naturalist* 43:257-354.

Binford, L. R.
1978 *Nunamiut Ethnoarchaeology*. New York: Academic Press.
1981 *Bones: Ancient Men and Modern Myths*. New York: Academic Press.
1984 *Faunal Remains from Klasies River Mouth*. New York: Academic Press.

Boessneck, J.
1969 Osteological Differences Between Sheep (*Ovis aries* Linne) and Goat (*Capra hircus* Linne). In: *Science in Archaeology*, 2nd edition, edited by D. Brothwell and E. Higgs, pp. 331-58. New York: Praeger.

Bunn, H. T., L. E. Bartram, and E. M. Kroll
1988 Variability in Bone Assemblage Formation from Hadza Hunting, Scavenging, and Carcass Processing. *Journal of Anthropological Archaeology* 7:412-57.

Cordell, L. S.
1977 Late Anasazi Farming and Hunting Strategies: One Example of a Problem in Congruence. *American Antiquity* 42(3):449-61.

Davis, L. B., and J. W. Fisher, Jr.
1990 A Late Prehistoric Model for Communal Utilization of Pronghorn Antelope in the Northwestern Plains Region, North America. In: *Hunters of the Recent Past*, edited by L. B. Davis and B. O. K. Reeves, pp. 241-76. London, England: Unwin Hyman.

Dow, S. A., and P. L. Wright
1962 Changes in Mandibular Dentition Associated with Age in Pronghorn Antelope. *Journal of Wildlife Management* 26:1-8.

Driesch, A. von den
1976 *A Guide to the Measurement of Animal Bones from Archaeological Sites*. Bulletin of the Peabody Museum of Archaeology and Ethnology 1:1-136.

Driver, J. C.
1984 Zooarchaeology in the Sierra Blanca. In: *Recent Research in Mogollon Archaeology*, edited by S. Upham, F. T. Plog, D. G. Batcho, and B. E. Kauffman, pp. 140-55. Occasional Paper 10. Las Cruces, NM: New Mexico State University, The University Museum.
1985 *Zooarchaeology of Six Prehistoric Sites in the Sierra Blanca Region, New Mexico*. Technical Reports 17. Ann Arbor, MI: Museum of Anthropology, University of Michigan.
1989 Faunal Remains from the Robinson Site (LA46326) and Site CL-8, Capitan North Project, New Mexico. Report submitted to the Social Sciences and Humanities Research Council of Canada, Ottawa.
2000 Hunting Strategies and Horticultural Communities in Southeastern New Mexico. In: *Animal Bones, Human Societies*, edited by P. A. Rowley-Conwy, pp. 115-23. Oxford, England: Oxbow Books.

Einarsen, A. S.
1948 *The Pronghorn Antelope and Its Management*. Washington DC: The Wildlife Management Institute.

Ford, R. I.
1983 Inter-Indian Exchange in the Southwest. In: *Handbook of North American Indians*, Vol. 10. *Southwest*, edited by A. Ortiz, pp. 711-24. Washington, DC: Smithsonian Institution.

Frison, G. C.
1971 Shoshonean Antelope Procurement in the Upper Green River Basin, Wyoming. *Plains Anthropologist* 16:258-84.

Frison, G. C., and L. C. Todd
1986 *The Colby Mammoth Site*. Albuquerque, NM: University of New Mexico Press.

Gilbert, B. M.
1980 *Mammalian Osteology*. Laramie, WY (privately published).

Grayson, D. K.
1984 *Quantitative Zooarchaeology*. New York: Academic Press.
1988 *Danger Cave, Last Supper Cave, and Hanging Rock Shelter: The Faunas*. American Museum of Natural History Anthropological Paper 66(1).
1989 Bone Transport, Bone Destruction, and Reverse Utility Curves. *Journal of Archaeological Science* 16:643-52.

Haynes, G.
1980 Prey Bones and Predators: Potential Ecologic Information from Analysis of Bone Sites. *Ossa* 7:75-97.
1982 Utilization and Skeletal Disturbances of North American Prey Carcasses. *Arctic* 35:266-81.
1984 Tooth Wear Rate in Northern Bison. *Journal of Mammalogy* 65:487-91.

Hoover, R. L., C. E. Till, and S. Ogilvie
1959 *The Antelope of Colorado*. Technical Bulletin 4. Denver, CO: Department of Game and Fish, State of Colorado.

Howard, V. W., and J. S. Bradybaugh
1983 *Social Organization and Summer Behavior and Activity Patterns of Pronghorn Antelope in Southeastern New Mexico*. Research Report 497. Las Cruces, NM: New Mexico State University, Agricultural Experiment Station.

Jones, K. T., and D. Metcalfe
1988 Bare Bones Archaeology: Bone Marrow Indices and Efficiency. *Journal of Archaeological Science* 15:415-23.

Kelley, J. H.
1984 *The Archaeology of the Sierra Blanca Region of Southeastern New Mexico*. Anthropological Paper 74. Ann Arbor, MI: Museum of Anthropology, University of Michigan.

Kerwin, M. L., and G. J. Mitchell
1971 The Validity of the Wear-Age Technique for Alberta Pronghorns. *Journal of Wildlife Management* 35:743-47.

Kitchen, D. W.
1974 *Social Behavior and Ecology of the Pronghorn*. Wildlife Monograph 38:1-96.

Kitchen, D. W., and B. W. O'Gara
1982 Pronghorn. In: *Wild Mammals of North America: Biology, Management and Economics*, edited by J. A. Chapman and G. A. Feldhamer, pp. 960-71. Baltimore, MD: Johns Hopkins University Press.

Klein, R. G., and K. Cruz-Uribe
1984 *The Analysis of Animal Bones from Archeological Sites*. Chicago, IL: University of Chicago Press.

Lawrence, B.
1951 Postcranial Skeletal Characteristics of Deer, Pronghorn, and Sheep-Goat, with Notes on Bos and Bison. *Papers of the Peabody Museum of American Archaeology and Ethnology* 35(3, Part II):8-43.

Lewall, E. F., and I. M. Cowan
1963 Age Determination in Black-Tail Deer by Degree of Ossification of the Epiphyseal Plate in the Long Bones. *Canadian Journal of Zoology* 41:629-36.

Lyman, R. L.
1984 Bone Density and Differential Survivorship of Fossil Classes. *Journal of Anthropological Archaeology* 3:259-99.
1985 Bone Frequencies: Differential Transport, In Situ Destruction, and the MGUI. *Journal of Archaeological Science* 12:221-36.

1987a Archaeofaunas and Butchery Studies: A Taphonomic Perspective. In: *Advances in Archaeological Method and Theory*, Vol. 10, edited by M. B. Schiffer, pp. 249-337. New York: Academic Press.
1987b On the Analysis of Vertebrate Mortality Profiles: Sample Size, Mortality Type, and Hunting Pressure. *American Antiquity* 52(1):125-42.

McCutchen, H. E.
1969 Age Determination of Pronghorns by the Incisor Cementum. *Journal of Wildlife Management* 33:172-75.

McKusick, C. R.
1981 The Faunal Remains of Las Humanas. In: *Contributions to Gran Quivira Archeology*, edited by A. C. Hayes, pp. 39-65. Publications in Archeology 17. Washington, DC: U.S. Department of the Interior, National Park Service.

Metcalfe, D., and K. T. Jones
1988 A Reconsideration of Animal Body-Part Utility Indices. *American Antiquity* 53:486-504.

Miracle, P. T.
n.d. Bulk Density and the Interpretation of Skeletal Part Representation in Archaeological Faunal Assemblages. Manuscript.

Mitchell, G. J.
1971 Measurements, Weights, and Carcass Yields of Pronghorns in Alberta. *Journal of Wildlife Management* 35:76-85.

Nichol, A. A.
1942 Gathering, Transplanting, and Care of Young Antelope. *Journal of Wildlife Management* 6:281-87.

Nimmo, B. W.
1971 Population Dynamics of a Wyoming Pronghorn Cohort from the Eden-Farson Site, 48SW304. *Plains Anthropologist* 16:285-88.

O'Connell, J. F., and B. Marshall
1989 Analysis of Kangaroo Body Part Transport among the Alyawara of Central Australia. *Journal of Archaeological Science* 16:393-405.

O'Connell, J. F., K. Hawkes, and N. Blurton Jones
1988 Hadza Hunting, Butchering, and Bone Transport and Their Archaeological Implications. *Journal of Anthropological Research* 44:113-61.

Prummel, W., and H. J. Frisch
1988 A Guide for the Distinction of Species, Sex and Body Side in Bones of Sheep and Goat. *Journal of Archaeological Science* 13:567-77.

Redding, R. W., J. W. Pires-Ferreira, and M. A. Zeder
1975-77 A Proposed System for Computer Analysis of Identifiable Faunal Material from Archaeological Sites. *Paléorient* 3:190-203.

Rocek, T. R., and J. D. Speth
1986 *The Henderson Site Burials: Glimpses of a Late Prehistoric Population in the Pecos Valley*. Technical Report 18. Ann Arbor, MI: Museum of Anthropology, University of Michigan.

Silver, I. A.
1969 The Aging of Domestic Animals. In: *Science in Archaeology*, 2nd Edition, edited by D. Brothwell, pp. 283-302. New York: Praeger.

Speth, J. D.
1983 *Bison Kills and Bone Counts: Decision Making by Ancient Hunters*. Chicago, IL: University of Chicago Press.

Speth, J. D., and S. L. Scott
1989 Horticulture and Large-Mammal Hunting: The Role of Resource Depletion and the Constraints of Time and Labor. In: *Farmers as Hunters*, edited by S. Kent, pp. 71-79. Cambridge, England: Cambridge University Press.

Steward, J. H.
1938 *Basin-Plateau Aboriginal Sociopolitical Groups*. Bureau of American Ethnology Bulletin 120. Washington, DC: Smithsonian Institution.

Stewart, J. D., J. C. Driver, and J. H. Kelley
1991 The Capitan North Project: Chronology. In: *Mogollon V*, edited by P. H. Beckett, pp. 177-90. Las Cruces, NM: COAS Publishing and Research.

Stiner, M. C.
1990 The Use of Mortality Patterns in Archaeological Studies of Hominid Predatory Adaptations. *Journal of Anthropological Archaeology* 9(4):305-51.

Szuter, C. R.
1991 *Hunting by Prehistoric Horticulturalists in the American Southwest*. New York: Garland Publishing.

Taber, R. D.
1956 Characteristics of the Pelvic Girdle in Relation to Sex in Black-Tailed and White-Tailed Deer. *California Fish and Game* 42:15-21.

Tyler, H. A.
1975 *Pueblo Animals and Myths*. Norman, OK: University of Oklahoma Press.

Wood, A. K.
1989 Comparative Distribution and Habitat Use by Antelope and Mule Deer. *Journal of Mammalogy* 70:335-40.

Appendix to Chapter 5

Henderson Medium Ungulate Assemblage

Table A5.1. Definition of measurements taken on Henderson Site medium ungulate elements.[a]

Element/Measurements	*Element/Measurements*
Atlas	**Innominate**
BFcd: breadth of caudal artic. surface	LA: length of acetabulum (incl. lip)
GLv: greatest length on vent. centrum	SH: smallest height (depth) of iliac shaft
	SB: smallest breadth of iliac shaft
Scapula	**Femur**
GLP: length of artic. surface (incl. glenoid process)	Bp: breadth of prox. end
BG: breadth of artic. surface	DC: depth of femoral head
	Bd: breadth of dist. end
Humerus	Patella
BT: breadth of dist. trochlea	GB: greatest breadth
DTm: depth of medial surface of dist. trochlea	
DTl: depth of lateral surface of dist. trochlea	
Radius	**Tibia**
Bp: breadth of prox. end	Bp: breadth of prox. end
Dp: depth of prox. end	Bd: breadth of dist. end
Bd: breadth of dist. end	Dd: depth of dist. end
Ulna	**Lateral Malleolus**
BPC: breadth across coronoid process	GD: greatest depth
Radial Carpal	**Astragalus**
GD: greatest depth	GLl: greatest length of lateral half
	GLm: greatest length of medial half
	Dl: depth of lateral half
	Bd: breadth of dist. end
Intermed. Carpal	**Calcaneus**
GD: greatest depth	GL: greatest length
	GD: greatest depth of artic. surface with stragalus
Ulnar Carpal	**Naviculo-Cuboid**
GD: greatest depth	GB: greatest breadth
4th Carpal	**2nd-3rd Tarsal**
GD: greatest depth	GD: greatest depth
GB: greatest breadth	GB: greatest breadth
2nd-3rd Carpal	**Metatarsal**
GD: greatest depth	Bp: breadth of prox. end
GB: greatest breadth	Bd: breadth of dist. end
Metacarpal	**3rd Phalanx**
Bp: breadth of prox. end	DLS: diagonal length of sole
Bd: breadth of dist. end	Ld: length of dorsal surface
DD: smallest depth of diaphysis	MBS: middle breadth of sole
1st and 2nd Phalanx	**Teeth**
GLpe: greatest length of peripheral half	L: length
Bp: breadth of prox. end	Bd: breadth
SD: smallest breadth of diaphysis	
Bd: breadth of dist. end	

[a]Measurements follow von den Driesch (1976) wherever possible.

Table A5.2a. Measurements of Henderson Site antelope postcranial skeletal elements.

Element	*n*	*Mean*	*SD*	*Min.*	*Max.*
Atlas					
BFcd	1	50.0	-	-	-
GLv	1	32.3	-	-	-
Scapula					
GLP	6	41.1	2.1	37.3	43.5
BG	5	28.8	1.5	27.1	31.2
Humerus					
BT	17	35.7	1.9	33.2	39.4
DTm	10	31.7	1.7	29.8	34.0
DTl	8	20.4	1.2	18.9	22.7
Radius					
Bp	14	37.1	2.2	34.6	42.0
Dp	13	19.4	1.1	17.4	21.2
Bd	5	33.5	1.9	32.4	36.8
Ulna					
BPC	6	22.3	1.6	20.8	24.8
Radial Carpal					
GD	10	21.5	1.2	20.1	23.6
Intermed. Carpal					
GD	6	20.7	1.3	19.1	22.6
Ulnar Carpal					
GD	8	16.4	0.6	15.3	17.5
4th Carpal					
GD	8	17.8	0.8	17.0	19.4
GB	9	13.7	0.8	12.9	15.3
2nd-3rd Carpal					
GD	11	18.0	1.4	15.5	19.6
GB	11	16.8	1.5	14.4	19.3
Metacarpal					
Bp	5	29.1	1.6	27.1	31.0
Bd	7	28.7	2.1	25.6	30.8
DD	3	11.2	0.3	10.9	11.4
Innominate					
LA	7	32.7	1.4	30.4	34.4
SH	10	21.5	1.2	20.0	23.7
SB	10	10.2	1.1	7.9	11.4
Patella					
GB	7	24.1	0.6	23.2	24.7
1st Phalanx					
GLpe	33	50.2	2.0	46.4	53.8
Bp	45	13.9	0.6	12.4	15.2
SD	39	9.7	0.6	8.7	11.0
Bd	34	12.6	0.5	11.3	13.6
2nd Phalanx					
GLpe	50	29.9	1.2	27.6	32.0
Bp	51	12.5	0.6	11.2	14.3
SD	56	9.1	0.6	7.7	10.6
Bd	43	10.7	0.6	9.4	12.3
3rd Phalanx					

Table A5.2a (cont.)

DLS	38	31.5	2.5	26.3	36.8
Ld	39	26.3	2.6	20.5	30.4
MBS	44	6.8	0.8	4.4	8.5
Femur					
Bp	3	58.2	2.1	56.3	60.4
DC	6	23.4	0.4	22.9	23.8
Bd	2	47.3	0.1	47.2	47.3
Tibia					
Bp	3	48.3	1.5	47.3	50.0
Bd	8	31.8	1.3	29.9	33.4
Dd	8	25.2	1.0	24.0	26.8
Lateral Malleolus					
GD	10	17.9	1.2	14.9	19.0
Astragalus					
GLl	13	35.2	1.9	32.7	39.1
GLm	12	32.5	1.7	30.2	35.4
Dl	12	19.5	1.2	17.7	22.0
Bd	13	21.2	1.1	19.6	23.3
Calcaneus					
GL	7	77.3	3.1	72.3	82.1
GD	8	28.4	1.1	26.7	30.6
Naviculo-Cuboid					
GB	16	27.2	1.4	23.9	29.3
2nd-3rd Tarsal					
GD	12	19.0	0.9	17.3	20.4
GB	14	11.2	0.7	9.8	12.1
Metatarsal					
Bp	3	25.3	1.6	23.5	26.5
Bd	8	28.4	1.3	26.8	30.3

Table A5.2b. Measurements of Henderson Site antelope teeth.

Element	*n*	*Mean*	*SD*	*Min.*	*Max.*
$\mathbf{P_2}$					
L	1	6.1	-	-	-
B	1	3.3	-	-	-
$\mathbf{P_3}$					
L	5	8.8	1.1	8.0	10.4
B	6	5.2	0.4	4.9	5.9
$\mathbf{P_4}$					
L	4	9.3	0.9	8.2	10.4
B	4	5.7	0.7	4.7	6.1
$\mathbf{M_1}$					
L	7	12.6	0.9	11.4	14.1
B	7	6.5	0.3	6.0	6.8
$\mathbf{M_2}$					
L	5	13.7	1.3	12.3	15.8
B	3	7.4	0.3	7.2	7.7
$\mathbf{M_3}$					
L	5	21.6	1.2	20.3	23.6
B	5	7.5	0.4	7.2	8.1
$\mathbf{dP_3}$					
L	3	8.5	0.9	7.9	9.6
B	3	4.4	0.3	4.1	4.6
$\mathbf{dP_4}$					
L	3	14.5	0.5	14.1	15.1
B	3	6.1	0.4	5.8	6.5
$\mathbf{P^2}$					
L	6	7.8	1.0	6.3	9.4
B	7	5.6	0.4	5.0	6.2
$\mathbf{P^3}$					
L	3	7.9	0.8	7.2	8.8
B	3	6.2	0.5	5.7	6.7
$\mathbf{P^4}$					
L	2	10.3	2.0	8.9	11.7
B	2	8.9	0.7	8.4	9.4
$\mathbf{M^1}$					
L	7	13.0	1.4	11.5	14.8
B	5	9.9	0.3	9.5	10.2
$\mathbf{M^2}$					
L	6	15.0	0.9	13.8	16.5
B	5	9.9	1.0	8.9	11.3
$\mathbf{M^3}$					
L	4	16.2	0.7	15.7	17.2
B	4	9.7	0.9	9.2	11.0
$\mathbf{dP^2}$					
L	2	7.8	0.3	7.6	8.0
B	2	4.7	0.1	4.6	4.8
$\mathbf{dP^3}$					
L	4	9.2	1.6	7.9	11.5
B	4	6.7	0.9	5.5	7.7
$\mathbf{dP^4}$					
L	4	11.8	0.2	11.5	12.0
B	4	8.9	0.2	8.7	9.1

Table A5.3a. Measurements of Henderson Site deer postcranial skeletal elements.

Element	*n*	*Mean*	*SD*	*Min.*	*Max.*
Humerus					
BT	1	39.6	-	-	-
DTm	1	39.5	-	-	-
DTl	1	22.2	-	-	-
Intermed. Carpal					
GD	1	18.1	-	-	-
Ulnar Carpal					
GD	1	18.8	-	-	-
4th Carpal					
GD	1	18.6	-	-	-
GB	1	16.0	-	-	-
2nd-3rd Carpal					
GD	2	19.6	0.2	19.4	19.7
GB	2	17.3	0.8	16.7	17.8
Metacarpal					
Bp	-	-	-	-	-
Bd	1	29.0	-	-	-
DD	-	-	-	-	-
Innominate					
LA	-	-	-	-	-
SH	1	22.5	-	-	-
SB	1	9.6	-	-	-
Patella					
GB	1	30.1	-	-	-
2nd Phalanx					
GLpe	1	33.1	-	-	-
Bp	1	14.5	-	-	-
SD	1	10.7	-	-	-
Bd	1	11.2	-	-	-
3rd Phalanx					
DLS	3	32.9	1.7	31.4	34.8
Ld	3	30.2	1.0	29.1	31.0
MBS	2	7.8	1.1	7.0	8.6
Tibia					
Bp	-	-	-	-	-
Bd	1	36.8	-	-	-
Dd	1	29.7	-	-	-
Lateral Malleolus					
GD	1	19.0	-	-	-
Astragalus					
GLl	1	36.5	-	-	-
GLm	1	34.7	-	-	-
Dl	-	-	-	-	-
Bd	1	22.3	-	-	-
Calcaneus					
GL	-	-	-	-	-
GD	1	29.5	-	-	-
2nd-3rd Tarsal					
GD	1	20.7	-	-	-
GB	1	11.4	-	-	-

Table A5.3b. Measurements of Henderson Site deer teeth.

Element	*n*	*Mean*	*SD*	*Min.*	*Max.*
P_2					
L	-	-	-	-	-
B	1	5.2	-	-	-
P_3					
L	1	12.3	-	-	-
B	-	-	-	-	-
P^4					
L	1	11.7	-	-	-
B	1	9.4	-	-	-

Table A5.4. Antelope sample recovered from Henderson Site (all proveniences combined).

Body Part	Non-Immature				Immature							Burned Sample				Total Sample			
	Burned		Unburned		Burned Unfused		Unburned				Total MNE	Calcined		Total Burned					
							Unfused		Fusing										
	NISP	MNE	NISP	MNE	NISP	MNE	NISP	MNE	NISP	MNE		NISP	%	NISP	%	NISP	MNE	MNI	SIDE
HC	1	1	4	2	—	—	—	—	—	—	—	—	—	1	20.0	5	3	2	L
SK	3	—	103	16	—	—	2	—	—	—	—	1	33	3	2.8	107	16	9	R
MD	1	1	73	9	—	—	7	—	—	—	—	—	—	1	1.2	82	10	5	R
AT	1	—	8	5	—	—	—	—	—	—	—	—	—	1	11.1	9	5	5	—
AX	—	—	5	4	—	—	—	—	1	1	1	—	—	—	0.0	6	5	5	—
CV	—	—	5	4	—	—	2	2	—	—	2	—	—	—	0.0	7	6	1	—
TV	—	—	—	—	—	—	—	—	—	—	—	—	—	—	0.0	—	—	—	—
LV	—	—	—	—	—	—	—	—	—	—	—	—	—	—	0.0	—	—	—	—
SAC	—	—	2	1	—	—	—	—	—	—	—	—	—	—	0.0	2	1	1	—
PEL	7	2	77	32	—	—	12	6	—	—	6	2	29	7	7.3	96	40	21	L
RIB	—	—	—	—	—	—	—	—	—	—	—	—	—	—	0.0	—	—	—	—
STM	—	—	5	5	—	—	—	—	—	—	—	—	—	—	0.0	5	5	5	—
SC	3	2	20	9	—	—	1	1	—	—	1	1	33	3	12.5	24	12	8	R
PH	—	—	8	6	—	—	1	1	—	—	1	—	—	—	0.0	9	7	5	L
DH	3	3	29	26	—	—	1	1	2	2	3	1	33	3	8.6	35	32	17	R
ULN	1	1	13	10	—	—	7	7	—	—	7	1	100	1	4.8	21	18	10	L
PRC	1	1	24	21	—	—	—	—	—	—	—	—	—	1	4.0	25	22	13	L
DRC	—	—	8	6	—	—	8	5	1	1	6	—	—	—	0.0	17	12	6	L
CAR	3	3	56	56	—	—	—	—	—	—	—	3	100	3	5.1	59	59	10	L
PMC	2	2	22	17	—	—	—	—	—	—	—	2	100	2	8.3	24	19	11	R
DMC	1	—	15	11	1	1	13	7	2	1	9	1	50	2	5.9	34	20	10	R
PF	—	—	12	9	—	—	5	5	1	1	6	—	—	—	0.0	18	15	9	R
DF	1	1	5	5	—	—	3	3	2	2	5	1	100	1	9.1	11	11	6	L
PT	1	1	3	3	—	—	5	5	—	—	5	1	100	1	11.1	9	9	6	R
DT	1	1	9	9	—	—	5	5	—	—	5	—	—	1	6.7	15	15	9	L
TAR	1	1	49	49	—	—	—	—	—	—	—	1	100	1	2.0	50	50	13	R
AST	3	3	14	14	—	—	—	—	—	—	—	1	33	3	17.6	17	17	9	R
CAL	2	2	21	15	1	1	3	3	—	—	4	1	33	3	11.1	27	21	14	L
PMT	1	1	22	12	—	—	—	—	—	—	—	1	100	1	4.3	23	13	9	L
DMT	1	—	12	10	4	2	9	3	1	1	6	2	40	5	20.0	25	16	11	R
P1	9	5	82	61	—	—	19	14	4	4	18	5	56	9	7.9	114	84	11	LL/RM
P2	10	9	55	53	—	—	7	5	4	4	9	4	40	10	13.2	76	71	10	LL/RM
P3	9	9	48	48	—	—	2	2	—	—	2	2	22	9	15.3	59	59	9	LL/RM
PAT	—	—	12	12	—	—	—	—	—	—	—	—	—	—	0.0	12	12	6	L
DMP	2	—	4	—	2	—	1	—	—	—	—	3	75	4	44.4	9	—	—	—
MNB	1	1	2	2	—	—	—	—	—	—	—	—	—	1	33.3	3	3	3	—
STE	1	1	7	7	—	—	—	—	—	—	—	—	—	1	12.5	8	8	2	—
SES	—	—	—	—	—	—	—	—	—	—	—	—	—	—	0.0	—	—	—	—
HYO	—	—	—	—	—	—	—	—	—	—	—	—	—	—	0.0	—	—	—	—
SSC	2	—	2	—	—	—	—	—	—	—	—	—	—	2	50.0	4	—	—	—
SH	—	—	—	—	—	—	—	—	—	—	—	—	—	—	0.0	—	—	—	—
SRC	—	—	—	—	—	—	—	—	—	—	—	—	—	—	0.0	—	—	—	—
SMC	—	—	7	—	—	—	—	—	—	—	—	—	—	—	0.0	7	—	—	—
SF	—	—	—	—	—	—	—	—	—	—	—	—	—	—	0.0	—	—	—	—

(cont.)

Body Part	Non-Immature				Immature							Burned Sample				Total Sample			
	Burned		Unburned		Burned Unfused		Unburned				Total MNE	Calcined		Total Burned					
							Unfused		Fusing										
	NISP	MNE	NISP	MNE	NISP	MNE	NISP	MNE	NISP	MNE		NISP	%	NISP	%	NISP	MNE	MNI	SIDE
ST	—	—	1	—	—	—	—	—	—	—	—	—	—	—	0.0	1	—	—	—
SMT	5	—	35	—	—	—	—	—	—	—	—	4	80	5	12.5	40	—	—	—
CDV	—	—	—	—	—	—	—	—	—	—	—	—	—	—	0.0	—	—	—	—
COS	—	—	—	—	—	—	—	—	—	—	—	—	—	—	0.0	—	—	—	—
TOT.	77	51	879	549	8	4	113	75	18	17	96	38	45	85	7.8	1095	696	21	—

Table A5.5. Antelope/deer sample recovered from Henderson Site (all proveniences combined).

Body Part	Non-Immature				Immature									Burned Sample				Total Sample	
	Burned		Unburned		Burned		Unburned						Total MNE	Calcined		Total Burned			
					Unfused		Fetal		Unfused		Fusing								
	NISP	MNE	NISP	MNE	NISP	MNE	NISP	MNE	NISP	MNE	NISP	MNE		NISP	%	NISP	%	NISP	MNE
HC	-	-	-	-	-	-	-	-	-	-	-	-	-	-	-	-	-	-	-
SK	-	-	2	-	-	-	-	-	-	-	-	-	-	-	-	-	-	2	-
MD	-	-	-	-	-	-	1	1	-	-	-	-	1	-	-	-	-	1	1
AT	-	-	1	1	-	-	-	-	-	-	-	-	-	-	-	-	-	1	1
AX	1	-	3	2	-	-	-	-	-	-	-	-	-	1	100	1	25.0	4	2
CV	1	-	4	3	-	-	1	-	2	2	-	-	2	-	-	1	12.5	8	5
TV	2	2	28	18	-	-	-	-	6	1	1	-	1	2	100	2	5.4	37	21
LV	2	1	9	7	-	-	-	-	4	4	1	1	5	1	50	2	12.5	16	13
SAC	-	-	-	-	-	-	-	-	-	-	-	-	-	-	-	-	-	-	-
PEL	1	-	4	-	-	-	-	-	-	-	-	-	-	-	-	1	20.0	5	-
RIB	3	3	48	48	-	-	1	1	18	14	2	2	17	2	67	3	4.2	72	68
STM	-	-	1	1	-	-	-	-	-	-	-	-	-	-	-	-	-	1	1
SC	-	-	8	1	1	1	2	2	-	-	-	-	3	1	100	1	9.1	11	4
PH	-	-	6	1	-	-	-	-	1	-	-	-	-	-	-	-	-	7	1
DH	-	-	5	-	-	-	4	4	-	-	-	-	4	-	-	-	-	9	4
ULN	-	-	2	-	-	-	5	5	2	-	-	-	5	-	-	-	-	9	5
PRC	-	-	-	-	-	-	1	-	-	-	-	-	-	-	-	-	-	1	-
DRC	-	-	-	-	-	-	-	-	-	-	-	-	-	-	-	-	-	-	-
CAR	-	-	1	1	-	-	-	-	-	-	-	-	-	-	-	-	-	1	1
PMC	-	-	1	1	-	-	-	-	-	-	-	-	-	-	-	-	-	1	1
DMC	-	-	-	-	-	-	-	-	4	-	-	-	-	-	-	-	-	4	-
PF	-	-	4	1	-	-	-	-	2	2	-	-	2	-	-	-	-	6	3
DF	2	-	5	-	-	-	-	-	1	-	-	-	-	-	-	2	25.0	8	-
PT	-	-	-	-	-	-	-	-	2	-	-	-	-	-	-	-	-	2	-
DT	-	-	-	-	-	-	-	-	-	-	-	-	-	-	-	-	-	-	-
TAR	-	-	-	-	-	-	-	-	-	-	-	-	-	-	-	-	-	-	-
AST	1	-	3	1	-	-	-	-	-	-	-	-	-	-	-	1	25.0	4	1
CAL	-	-	2	2	1	-	2	2	2	-	-	-	2	-	-	1	14.3	7	4
PMT	-	-	-	-	-	-	-	-	-	-	-	-	-	-	-	-	-	-	-
DMT	-	-	-	-	-	-	-	-	-	-	-	-	-	-	-	-	-	-	-
P1	-	-	5	1	-	-	-	-	-	-	-	-	-	-	-	-	-	5	1
P2	-	-	2	1	-	-	-	-	-	-	-	-	-	-	-	-	-	2	1
P3	-	-	1	-	-	-	-	-	-	-	-	-	-	-	-	-	-	1	-
PAT	-	-	-	-	-	-	-	-	-	-	-	-	-	-	-	-	-	-	-
DMP	2	-	12	-	1	-	-	-	1	-	-	-	-	3	100	3	18.8	16	-
MNB	-	-	1	1	-	-	-	-	-	-	-	-	-	-	-	-	-	1	1
STE	-	-	4	4	-	-	-	-	-	-	-	-	-	-	-	-	-	4	4
SES	-	-	33	33	-	-	-	-	-	-	-	-	-	-	-	-	-	33	33
HYO	-	-	1	-	-	-	-	-	-	-	-	-	-	-	-	-	-	1	-
SSC	-	-	9	-	-	-	-	-	-	-	-	-	-	-	-	-	-	9	-
SH	1	-	15	-	-	-	-	-	-	-	-	-	-	1	100	1	6.3	16	-
SRC	-	-	8	-	-	-	-	-	-	-	-	-	-	-	-	-	-	8	-
SMC	-	-	1	-	-	-	-	-	-	-	-	-	-	-	-	-	-	1	-
SF	1	-	27	-	-	-	-	-	-	-	-	-	-	-	-	1	3.6	28	-
ST	1	-	15	-	-	-	-	-	-	-	-	-	-	1	100	1	6.3	16	-
SMT	-	-	-	-	-	-	-	-	-	-	-	-	-	-	-	-	-	-	-
CDV	-	-	2	2	-	-	-	-	2	2	1	1	3	-	-	-	-	5	5
COS	1	1	5	5	-	-	-	-	-	-	-	-	-	-	-	1	16.7	6	6
TOT.	19	7	278	135	3	1	17	15	47	25	5	4	45	12	55	22	6.0	369	187

Table A5.6. Deer sample recovered from Henderson Site (all proveniences combined).

Body Part	Non-Immature				Immature		Burned Sample				Total Sample			
	Burned		Unburned		Burned Unfused		Calcined		Total Burned					
	NISP	MNE	NISP	MNE	NISP	MNE	NISP	%	NISP	%	NISP	MNE	MNI	Side
ANT	1	-	6	1	-	-	-	-	1	14.3	7	1	1	R
SK	-	-	5	2	-	-	-	-	-	-	5	2	1	R
MD	-	-	5	1	-	-	-	-	-	-	5	1	1	R
AT	-	-	-	-	-	-	-	-	-	-	-	-	-	-
AX	-	-	-	-	-	-	-	-	-	-	-	-	-	-
CV	-	-	-	-	-	-	-	-	-	-	-	-	-	-
TV	-	-	-	-	-	-	-	-	-	-	-	-	-	-
LV	-	-	-	-	-	-	-	-	-	-	-	-	-	-
SAC	-	-	-	-	-	-	-	-	-	-	-	-	-	-
PEL	-	-	3	2	-	-	-	-	-	-	3	2	1	L
RIB	-	-	-	-	-	-	-	-	-	-	-	-	-	-
STM	-	-	-	-	-	-	-	-	-	-	-	-	-	-
SC	-	-	3	2	-	-	-	-	-	-	3	2	1	L
PH	-	-	-	-	-	-	-	-	-	-	-	-	-	-
DH	-	-	3	3	-	-	-	-	-	-	3	3	2	L
ULN	-	-	1	1	-	-	-	-	-	-	1	1	1	L
PRC	-	-	2	1	-	-	-	-	-	-	2	1	1	R
DRC	-	-	1	1	-	-	-	-	-	-	1	1	1	R
CAR	-	-	9	9	-	-	-	-	-	-	9	9	2	L
PMC	-	-	1	1	-	-	-	-	-	-	1	1	1	R
DMC	-	-	2	2	1	1	-	-	-	-	3	3	3	L
PF	-	-	-	-	1	1	-	-	-	-	1	1	1	L
DF	-	-	-	-	1	1	-	-	-	-	1	1	1	L
PT	-	-	-	-	1	1	-	-	-	-	1	1	-	-
DT	-	-	1	1	1	1	-	-	-	-	2	2	2	L
TAR	-	-	2	2	-	-	-	-	-	-	2	2	1	L
AST	-	-	-	-	-	-	1	100	-	-	-	-	1	L
CAL	-	-	1	1	-	-	-	-	-	-	1	1	1	R
PMT	-	-	2	2	-	-	-	-	-	-	2	2	1	L
DMT	-	-	1	-	2	2	-	-	-	-	3	2	1	L
P1	-	-	2	2	-	-	-	-	-	-	2	2	1	LL/RM
P2	1	1	2	1	-	-	1	100	1	33.3	3	2	1	LL/RM
P3	1	1	2	2	-	-	-	-	1	33.3	3	3	1	LL/RM
PAT	-	-	1	1	-	-	-	-	-	-	1	1	1	R
DMP	-	-	-	-	1	-	-	-	-	-	1	-	-	-
MNB	-	-	-	-	-	-	-	-	-	-	-	-	-	-
STE	-	-	-	-	-	-	-	-	-	-	-	-	-	-
SES	-	-	-	-	-	-	-	-	-	-	-	-	-	-
HYO	-	-	-	-	-	-	-	-	-	-	-	-	-	-
SSC	-	-	-	-	-	-	-	-	-	-	-	-	-	-
SH	-	-	-	-	-	-	-	-	-	-	-	-	-	-
SRC	-	-	-	-	-	-	-	-	-	-	-	-	-	-
SMC	-	-	-	-	-	-	-	-	-	-	-	-	-	-
SF	-	-	-	-	-	-	-	-	-	-	-	-	-	-
ST	-	-	-	-	-	-	-	-	-	-	-	-	-	-
SMT	-	-	-	-	-	-	-	-	-	-	-	-	-	-
CDV	-	-	-	-	-	-	-	-	-	-	-	-	-	-
COS	-	-	-	-	-	-	-	-	-	-	-	-	-	-
TOT.	3	2	55	38	8	7	2	50	3	4.5	66	47	3	-

Table A5.7. Medium ungulate sample recovered from Henderson Site (all proveniences combined).

Body Part	Non-Immature				Immature									Burned Sample				Total Sample			
	Burned		Unburned		Burned		Unburned						Total MNE	Calcined		Total Burned					
					Unfused		Fetal		Unfused		Fusing										
	NISP	MNE	NISP	MNE	NISP	MNE	NISP	MNE	NISP	MNE	NISP	MNE		NISP	%	NISP	%	NISP	MNE	MAU	%MAU
HC	2	1	10	3	-	-	-	-	-	-	-	-	-	-	-	2	16.7	12	4	2.0	9.5
SK	3	-	109	18	-	-	-	-	2	-	-	-	-	1	33	3	2.6	114	18	9.0	42.9
MD	1	1	79	10	-	-	1	1	7	-	-	-	1	-	-	1	1.1	88	12	6.0	28.6
AT	1	-	9	6	-	-	-	-	-	-	-	-	-	-	-	1	10.0	10	6	6.0	28.6
AX	1	-	8	6	-	-	-	-	-	-	1	1	1	1	100	1	10.0	10	7	7.0	33.3
CV	1	-	9	7	-	-	1	-	4	4	-	-	4	-	-	1	6.7	15	11	2.2	10.5
TV	2	2	28	18	-	-	-	-	6	1	1	-	1	2	100	2	5.4	37	21	1.6	7.7
LV	2	1	9	7	-	-	-	-	4	4	1	1	5	1	50	2	12.5	16	13	2.2	10.3
SAC	-	-	2	1	-	-	-	-	-	-	-	-	-	-	-	-	-	2	1	1.0	4.8
PEL	8	2	84	34	-	-	-	-	12	6	-	-	6	2	25	8	7.7	104	42	21.0	100.0
RIB	3	3	48	48	-	-	1	1	18	14	2	2	17	2	67	3	4.2	72	68	2.6	12.5
STM	-	-	6	6	-	-	-	-	-	-	-	-	-	-	-	-	-	6	6	6.0	28.6
SC	3	2	31	12	1	1	2	2	1	1	-	-	4	2	50	4	10.5	38	18	9.0	42.9
PH	-	-	14	7	-	-	-	-	2	1	-	-	1	-	-	-	-	16	8	4.0	19.0
DH	3	3	37	29	-	-	4	4	1	1	2	2	6	1	33	3	6.4	47	39	19.5	92.9
ULN	1	1	16	11	-	-	5	5	9	7	-	-	12	1	100	1	3.2	31	24	12.0	57.1
PRC	1	1	26	22	-	-	1	-	-	-	-	-	-	-	-	1	3.6	28	23	11.5	54.8
DRC	-	-	9	7	-	-	-	-	8	5	1	1	6	-	-	-	-	18	13	6.5	31.0
CAR	3	3	66	66	-	-	-	-	-	-	-	-	-	3	100	3	4.3	69	69	5.8	27.4
PMC	2	2	24	19	-	-	-	-	-	-	-	-	-	2	100	2	7.7	26	21	10.5	50.0
DMC	1	-	19	13	1	1	-	-	18	8	2	1	10	1	50	2	4.9	41	23	11.5	54.8
PF	-	-	16	10	-	-	-	-	8	8	1	1	9	-	-	-	-	25	19	9.5	45.2
DF	3	1	10	5	-	-	-	-	5	4	2	2	6	1	33	3	15.0	20	12	6.0	28.6
PT	1	1	3	3	-	-	-	-	8	6	-	-	6	1	100	1	8.3	12	10	5.0	23.8
DT	1	1	10	10	-	-	-	-	6	6	-	-	6	-	-	1	5.9	17	17	8.5	40.5
TAR	1	1	51	51	-	-	-	-	-	-	-	-	-	1	100	1	1.9	52	52	6.5	31.0
AST	4	3	17	15	-	-	-	-	-	-	-	-	-	2	50	4	18.2	21	18	9.0	42.9
CAL	2	2	24	18	2	1	2	2	5	3	-	-	6	1	25	4	11.4	35	26	13.0	61.9
PMT	1	1	24	14	-	-	-	-	-	-	-	-	-	1	100	1	4.0	25	15	7.5	35.7
DMT	1	-	11	10	4	2	-	-	11	5	1	1	8	2	40	5	17.9	28	18	9.0	42.9
P1	9	5	89	64	-	-	-	-	19	14	4	4	18	5	56	9	7.4	121	87	10.9	51.8
P2	11	10	59	55	-	-	-	-	7	5	4	4	9	5	45	11	13.6	81	74	9.3	44.0
P3	10	10	51	50	-	-	-	-	2	2	-	-	2	2	20	10	15.9	63	62	7.8	36.9
PAT	-	-	13	13	-	-	-	-	-	-	-	-	-	-	-	-	-	13	13	6.5	31.0
DMP	4	-	16	-	3	-	-	-	3	-	-	-	-	6	86	7	26.9	26	-	-	-
MNB	1	1	3	3	-	-	-	-	-	-	-	-	-	-	-	1	25.0	4	4	-	-
STE	1	1	11	11	-	-	-	-	-	-	-	-	-	-	-	1	8.3	12	12	2.4	11.4
SES	-	-	33	33	-	-	-	-	-	-	-	-	-	-	-	-	-	33	33	-	-
HYO	-	-	1	-	-	-	-	-	-	-	-	-	-	-	-	-	-	1	-	-	-
SSC	2	-	11	-	-	-	-	-	-	-	-	-	-	-	-	2	15.4	13	-	-	-
SMC	-	-	8	-	-	-	-	-	-	-	-	-	-	-	-	-	-	8	-	-	-
SF	1	-	27	-	-	-	-	-	-	-	-	-	-	-	-	1	3.6	28	-	-	-
ST	1	-	16	-	-	-	-	-	-	-	-	-	-	1	100	1	5.9	17	-	-	-
SMT	5	-	35	-	-	-	-	-	-	-	-	-	-	4	80	5	12.5	40	-	-	-
CDV	-	-	2	2	-	-	-	-	2	2	1	1	3	-	-	-	-	5	5	-	-
COS	1	1	5	5	-	-	-	-	-	-	-	-	-	-	-	1	16.7	6	6	-	-
TOT.	99	60	1212	722	11	5	17	15	168	107	23	21	148	52	47	110	7.2	1530	930	-	-

Table A5.8. Antelope and medium ungulate sample recovered from Henderson Site (East Bar).

Body Part	Antelope												Medium Ungulates				
	Non-Immature				Immature						Total Sample		Burned	Total Sample			
	Burned		Unburned		Burned		Unburned										
					Unfused		Unfused		Fusing								
	NISP	MNE	NISP	MNE	NISP	MNE	NISP	MNE	NISP	MNE	NISP	MNE	NISP	NISP	MNE	MAU	%MAU
HC	-	-	1	-	-	-	-	-	-	-	1	-	-	1	-	0.0	0.0
SK	1	-	24	7	-	-	1	-	-	-	26	7	1	28	8	4.0	100.0
MD	-	-	11	1	-	-	1	-	-	-	12	1	-	13	1	0.5	12.5
AT	1	-	-	-	-	-	-	-	-	-	1	-	1	1	-	0.0	0.0
AX	-	-	-	-	-	-	-	-	-	-	-	-	1	1	-	0.0	0.0
CV	-	-	-	-	-	-	1	1	-	-	1	1	-	2	2	0.4	10.0
TV	-	-	-	-	-	-	-	-	-	-	-	-	-	5	3	0.2	5.8
LV	-	-	-	-	-	-	-	-	-	-	-	-	1	2	2	0.3	8.3
SAC	-	-	1	1	-	-	-	-	-	-	1	1	-	1	1	1.0	25.0
PEL	-	-	7	1	-	-	1	-	-	-	8	1	-	9	1	0.5	12.5
RIB	-	-	-	-	-	-	-	-	-	-	-	-	-	10	8	0.3	7.7
STM	-	-	1	1	-	-	-	-	-	-	1	1	-	1	1	1.0	25.0
SC	-	-	1	1	-	-	-	-	-	-	1	1	-	3	1	0.5	12.5
PH	-	-	3	3	-	-	-	-	-	-	3	3	-	5	3	1.5	37.5
DH	2	2	3	3	-	-	-	-	-	-	5	5	2	5	5	2.5	62.5
ULN	-	-	-	-	-	-	1	1	-	-	1	1	-	2	2	0.0	0.0
PRC	-	-	1	1	-	-	-	-	-	-	1	1	-	1	1	0.5	12.5
DRC	-	-	2	2	-	-	-	-	-	-	2	2	-	3	3	1.5	37.5
CAR	-	-	12	12	-	-	-	-	-	-	12	12	-	16	16	1.3	33.3
PMC	-	-	6	5	-	-	-	-	-	-	6	5	-	7	6	3.0	75.0
DMC	-	-	5	4	-	-	1	1	1	-	7	5	-	10	6	3.0	75.0
PF	-	-	2	2	-	-	2	2	-	-	4	4	-	4	4	2.0	50.0
DF	-	-	1	1	-	-	-	-	-	-	1	1	-	1	1	0.5	12.5
PT	-	-	-	-	-	-	-	-	-	-	-	-	-	1	-	0.0	0.0
DT	-	-	-	-	-	-	1	1	-	-	1	1	-	1	1	0.5	12.5
TAR	1	1	5	5	-	-	-	-	-	-	6	6	1	7	7	0.9	21.9
AST	1	1	1	1	-	-	-	-	-	-	2	2	2	6	3	1.5	37.5
CAL	-	-	4	2	-	-	-	-	-	-	4	2	-	6	3	1.5	37.5
PMT	-	-	4	4	-	-	-	-	-	-	4	4	-	4	4	2.0	50.0
DMT	-	-	4	3	1	1	1	1	-	-	6	5	1	6	5	2.5	62.5
P1	4	2	19	14	-	-	2	-	-	-	25	16	4	27	17	2.1	53.1
P2	2	1	11	10	-	-	2	2	-	-	15	13	2	17	14	1.8	43.8
P3	3	3	10	10	-	-	1	1	-	-	14	14	4	17	16	2.0	50.0
PAT	-	-	-	-	-	-	-	-	-	-	-	-	-	-	-	0.0	0.0
DMP	1	-	-	-	-	-	-	-	-	-	1	-	3	7	-	0.0	0.0
MNB	-	-	-	-	-	-	-	-	-	-	-	-	-	-	-	0.0	0.0
STE	-	-	-	-	-	-	-	-	-	-	-	-	-	-	-	0.0	0.0
SES	-	-	-	-	-	-	-	-	-	-	-	-	-	14	14	0.0	0.0
HYO	-	-	-	-	-	-	-	-	-	-	-	-	-	-	-	0.0	0.0
SSC	-	-	-	-	-	-	-	-	-	-	-	-	-	3	-	0.0	0.0
SH	-	-	-	-	-	-	-	-	-	-	-	-	1	2	-	0.0	0.0
SRC	-	-	-	-	-	-	-	-	-	-	-	-	-	4	-	0.0	0.0
SMC	-	-	-	-	-	-	-	-	-	-	-	-	-	-	-	0.0	0.0
SF	-	-	-	-	-	-	-	-	-	-	-	-	-	2	-	0.0	0.0
ST	-	-	-	-	-	-	-	-	-	-	-	-	1	5	-	0.0	0.0
SMT	-	-	7	-	-	-	-	-	-	-	7	-	-	7	-	0.0	0.0
CDV	-	-	-	-	-	-	-	-	-	-	-	-	-	1	1	0.0	0.0
COS	-	-	-	-	-	-	-	-	-	-	-	-	-	-	-	0.0	0.0
TOT.	16	10	146	94	1	1	15	10	1	-	179	115	25	268	160		

Table A5.9. Deer sample recovered from Henderson Site (East Bar).

Body Part	Burned		Unburned		Total Sample	
	NISP	MNE	NISP	MNE	NISP	MNE
ANT	-	-	-	-	-	-
SK	-	-	1	1	1	1
MD	-	-	1	-	1	-
AT	-	-	-	-	-	-
AX	-	-	-	-	-	-
CV	-	-	-	-	-	-
TV	-	-	-	-	-	-
LV	-	-	-	-	-	-
SAC	-	-	-	-	-	-
PEL	-	-	-	-	-	-
RIB	-	-	-	-	-	-
STM	-	-	-	-	-	-
SC	-	-	1	-	1	-
PH	-	-	-	-	-	-
DH	-	-	-	-	-	-
ULN	-	-	-	-	-	-
PRC	-	-	-	-	-	-
DRC	-	-	1	1	1	1
CAR	-	-	3	3	3	3
PMC	-	-	-	-	-	-
DMC	-	-	1	1	1	1
PF	-	-	-	-	-	-
DF	-	-	-	-	-	-
PT	-	-	-	-	-	-
DT	-	-	-	-	-	-
TAR	-	-	1	1	1	1
AST	-	-	-	-	-	-
CAL	-	-	-	-	-	-
PMT	-	-	-	-	-	-
DMT	-	-	-	-	-	-
P1	-	-	1	1	1	1
P2	-	-	2	1	2	1
P3	1	1	1	1	2	2
TOT.	1	1	13	9	14	11

Table A5.10. Antelope/deer sample recovered from Henderson Site (East Bar).

Body Part	Non-Immature				Immature						Total Sample	
	Burned		Unburned		Burned		Unburned					
					Unfused		Fetal		Unfused			
	NISP	MNE	NISP	MNE	NISP	MNE	NISP	MNE	NISP	MNE	NISP	MNE
HC	-	-	-	-	-	-	-	-	-	-	-	-
SK	-	-	1	-	-	-	-	-	-	-	1	-
MD	-	-	-	-	-	-	-	-	-	-	-	-
AT	-	-	-	-	-	-	-	-	-	-	-	-
AX	1	-	-	-	-	-	-	-	-	-	1	-
CV	-	-	1	1	-	-	-	-	-	-	1	1
TV	-	-	5	3	-	-	-	-	-	-	5	3
LV	1	1	1	1	-	-	-	-	-	-	2	2
SAC	-	-	-	-	-	-	-	-	-	-	-	-
PEL	-	-	1	-	-	-	-	-	-	-	1	-
RIB	-	-	7	7	-	-	-	-	3	1	10	8
STM	-	-	-	-	-	-	-	-	-	-	-	-
SC	-	-	1	-	-	-	-	-	-	-	1	-
PH	-	-	1	-	-	-	-	-	1	-	2	-
DH	-	-	-	-	-	-	-	-	-	-	-	-
ULN	-	-	-	-	-	-	1	1	-	-	1	1
PRC	-	-	-	-	-	-	-	-	-	-	-	-
DRC	-	-	-	-	-	-	-	-	-	-	-	-
CAR	-	-	1	1	-	-	-	-	-	-	1	1
PMC	-	-	1	1	-	-	-	-	-	-	1	1
DMC	-	-	-	-	-	-	-	-	2	-	2	-
PF	-	-	-	-	-	-	-	-	-	-	-	-
DF	-	-	-	-	-	-	-	-	-	-	-	-
PT	-	-	-	-	-	-	-	-	1	-	1	-
DT	-	-	-	-	-	-	-	-	-	-	-	-
TAR	-	-	-	-	-	-	-	-	-	-	-	-
AST	1	-	3	1	-	-	-	-	-	-	4	1
CAL	-	-	1	1	-	-	-	-	1	-	2	1
PMT	-	-	-	-	-	-	-	-	-	-	-	-
DMT	-	-	-	-	-	-	-	-	-	-	-	-
P1	-	-	1	-	-	-	-	-	-	-	1	-
P2	-	-	-	-	-	-	-	-	-	-	-	-
P3	-	-	1	-	-	-	-	-	-	-	1	-
PAT	-	-	-	-	-	-	-	-	-	-	-	-
DMP	1	-	4	-	1	-	-	-	-	-	6	-
MNB	-	-	-	-	-	-	-	-	-	-	-	-
STE	-	-	-	-	-	-	-	-	-	-	-	-
SES	-	-	14	14	-	-	-	-	-	-	14	14
HYO	-	-	-	-	-	-	-	-	-	-	-	-
SSC	-	-	3	-	-	-	-	-	-	-	3	-
SH	1	-	1	-	-	-	-	-	-	-	2	-
SRC	-	-	4	-	-	-	-	-	-	-	4	-
SMC	-	-	-	-	-	-	-	-	-	-	-	-
SF	-	-	2	-	-	-	-	-	-	-	2	-
ST	1	-	4	-	-	-	-	-	-	-	5	-
SMT	-	-	-	-	-	-	-	-	-	-	-	-
CDV	-	-	1	1	-	-	-	-	-	-	1	1
COS	-	-	-	-	-	-	-	-	-	-	-	-
TOT.	6	1	59	31	1	-	1	1	8	1	75	34

Table A5.11. Antelope and medium ungulate sample recovered from Henderson Site (Center Bar, Rooms C-1 to C-6, excluding C-5).

Body Part	Antelope												Medium Ungulates				
	Non-Immature				Immature						Total Sample		Burned	Total Sample			
	Burned		Unburned		Burned		Unburned										
					Unfused		Unfused		Fusing								
	NISP	MNE	NISP	MNE	NISP	MNE	NISP	MNE	NISP	MNE	NISP	MNE	NISP	NISP	MNE	MAU	%MAU
HC	-	-	-	-	-	-	-	-	-	-	-	-	-	1	-	0.00	0.0
SK	-	-	5	-	-	-	-	-	-	-	5	-	-	5	-	0.00	0.0
MD	-	-	4	-	-	-	1	-	-	-	5	-	-	6	1	0.50	25.0
AT	-	-	1	1	-	-	-	-	-	-	1	1	-	1	1	1.00	50.0
AX	-	-	-	-	-	-	-	-	-	-	-	-	-	-	-	0.00	0.0
CV	-	-	-	-	-	-	-	-	-	-	-	-	-	2	1	0.20	10.0
TV	-	-	-	-	-	-	-	-	-	-	-	-	-	3	2	0.19	9.6
LV	-	-	-	-	-	-	-	-	-	-	-	-	-	-	-	0.00	0.0
SAC	-	-	-	-	-	-	-	-	-	-	-	-	-	-	-	0.00	0.0
PEL	-	-	1	-	-	-	-	-	-	-	1	-	-	1	-	0.00	0.0
RIB	-	-	-	-	-	-	-	-	-	-	-	-	1	6	4	0.17	8.5
STM	-	-	-	-	-	-	-	-	-	-	-	-	-	-	-	0.00	0.0
SC	-	-	-	-	-	-	-	-	-	-	-	-	1	2	1	0.50	25.0
PH	-	-	-	-	-	-	-	-	-	-	-	-	-	-	-	0.00	0.0
DH	-	-	1	1	-	-	-	-	1	1	2	2	-	6	3	1.50	75.0
ULN	-	-	-	-	-	-	-	-	-	-	-	-	-	-	-	0.00	0.0
PRC	-	-	1	1	-	-	-	-	-	-	1	1	-	2	2	1.00	50.0
DRC	-	-	-	-	-	-	1	1	-	-	1	1	-	2	1	0.50	25.0
CAR	-	-	7	7	-	-	-	-	-	-	7	7	-	7	7	0.60	30.0
PMC	1	1	2	2	-	-	-	-	-	-	3	3	1	3	3	1.50	75.0
DMC	-	-	1	-	-	-	-	-	-	-	1	-	-	1	-	0.00	0.0
PF	-	-	-	-	-	-	-	-	-	-	-	-	-	1	-	0.00	0.0
DF	-	-	1	1	-	-	-	-	-	-	1	1	-	3	1	0.50	25.0
PT	-	-	-	-	-	-	-	-	-	-	-	-	-	-	-	0.00	0.0
DT	-	-	-	-	-	-	-	-	-	-	-	-	-	-	-	0.00	0.0
TAR	-	-	2	2	-	-	-	-	-	-	2	2	-	2	2	0.25	12.5
AST	-	-	1	1	-	-	-	-	-	-	1	1	-	1	1	0.50	25.0
CAL	-	-	2	2	-	-	-	-	-	-	2	2	-	4	4	2.00	100.0
PMT	-	-	1	-	-	-	-	-	-	-	1	-	-	1	-	0.00	0.0
DMT	-	-	1	1	1	-	1	-	-	-	3	1	1	3	1	0.50	25.0
P1	1	-	4	2	-	-	2	2	-	-	7	4	1	9	5	0.63	31.3
P2	2	2	4	4	-	-	-	-	-	-	6	6	2	6	6	0.75	37.5
P3	1	1	4	4	-	-	-	-	-	-	5	5	1	5	5	0.65	32.5
PAT	-	-	-	-	-	-	-	-	-	-	-	-	-	-	-	0.00	0.0
DMP	-	-	-	-	-	-	-	-	-	-	-	-	-	1	-	0.00	0.0
MNB	-	-	-	-	-	-	-	-	-	-	-	-	-	-	-	0.00	0.0
STE	-	-	-	-	-	-	-	-	-	-	-	-	-	-	-	0.00	0.0
SES	-	-	-	-	-	-	-	-	-	-	-	-	-	3	3	0.00	0.0
HYO	-	-	-	-	-	-	-	-	-	-	-	-	-	-	-	0.00	0.0
SSC	-	-	-	-	-	-	-	-	-	-	-	-	-	1	-	0.00	0.0
SH	-	-	-	-	-	-	-	-	-	-	-	-	-	-	-	0.00	0.0
SRC	-	-	-	-	-	-	-	-	-	-	-	-	-	-	-	0.00	0.0
SMC	-	-	-	-	-	-	-	-	-	-	-	-	-	1	-	0.00	0.0
SF	-	-	-	-	-	-	-	-	-	-	-	-	-	1	-	0.00	0.0
ST	-	-	-	-	-	-	-	-	-	-	-	-	-	-	-	0.00	0.0
SMT	1	-	4	-	-	-	-	-	-	-	5	-	1	5	-	0.00	0.0
CDV	-	-	-	-	-	-	-	-	-	-	-	-	-	1	1	0.00	0.0
COS	-	-	-	-	-	-	-	-	-	-	-	-	-	-	-	0.00	0.0
TOT.	6	4	47	29	1	-	5	3	1	1	60	37	9	96	55		

Table A5.12. Deer sample recovered from Henderson Site (Center Bar, Rooms C-1 to C-6, excluding C-5).

Body Part	Non-Immature				Immature		Total Sample	
	Burned		Unburned		Unburned			
	NISP	MNE	NISP	MNE	NISP	MNE	NISP	MNE
ANT	-	-	1	-	-	-	1	-
SK	-	-	-	-	-	-	-	-
MD	-	-	1	1	-	-	1	1
AT	-	-	-	-	-	-	-	-
AX	-	-	-	-	-	-	-	-
CV	-	-	-	-	-	-	-	-
TV	-	-	-	-	-	-	-	-
LV	-	-	-	-	-	-	-	-
SAC	-	-	-	-	-	-	-	-
PEL	-	-	-	-	-	-	-	-
RIB	-	-	-	-	-	-	-	-
STM	-	-	-	-	-	-	-	-
SC	-	-	-	-	-	-	-	-
PH	-	-	-	-	-	-	-	-
DH	-	-	1	1	-	-	1	1
ULN	-	-	-	-	-	-	-	-
PRC	-	-	1	1	-	-	1	1
DRC	-	-	-	-	-	-	-	-
CAR	-	-	-	-	-	-	-	-
PMC	-	-	-	-	-	-	-	-
DMC	-	-	-	-	-	-	-	-
PF	-	-	-	-	-	-	-	-
DF	-	-	-	-	-	-	-	-
PT	-	-	-	-	-	-	-	-
DT	-	-	-	-	-	-	-	-
TAR	-	-	-	-	-	-	-	-
AST	-	-	-	-	-	-	-	-
CAL	-	-	-	-	-	-	-	-
PMT	-	-	-	-	-	-	-	-
DMT	-	-	-	-	-	-	-	-
P1	-	-	1	1	-	-	1	1
P2	-	-	-	-	-	-	-	-
P3	-	-	-	-	-	-	-	-
TOT.	-	-	5	4	-	-	5	4

Table A5.13. Antelope/deer sample recovered from Henderson Site (Center Bar, Rooms C-1 to C-6, excluding C-5).

Body Part	Non-Immature				Immature								Total Sample	
	Burned		Unburned		Burned		Unburned							
					Unfused		Fetal		Unfused		Fusing			
	NISP	MNE	NISP	MNE	NISP	MNE	NISP	MNE	NISP	MNE	NISP	MNE	NISP	MNE
HC	-	-	-	-	-	-	-	-	-	-	-	-	-	-
SK	-	-	-	-	-	-	-	-	-	-	-	-	-	-
MD	-	-	-	-	-	-	-	-	-	-	-	-	-	-
AT	-	-	-	-	-	-	-	-	-	-	-	-	-	-
AX	-	-	-	-	-	-	-	-	-	-	-	-	-	-
CV	-	-	1	1	-	-	-	-	-	-	-	-	1	1
TV	-	-	2	2	-	-	-	-	1	-	1	-	4	2
LV	-	-	-	-	-	-	-	-	-	-	-	-	-	-
SAC	-	-	-	-	-	-	-	-	-	-	-	-	-	-
PEL	-	-	-	-	-	-	-	-	-	-	-	-	-	-
RIB	1	1	1	1	-	-	-	-	3	1	1	1	6	4
STM	-	-	-	-	-	-	-	-	-	-	-	-	-	-
SC	-	-	1	-	1	1	-	-	-	-	-	-	2	1
PH	-	-	-	-	-	-	-	-	-	-	-	-	-	-
DH	-	-	3	-	-	-	-	-	-	-	-	-	3	-
ULN	-	-	-	-	-	-	-	-	-	-	-	-	-	-
PRC	-	-	-	-	-	-	-	-	-	-	-	-	-	-
DRC	-	-	-	-	-	-	1	-	-	-	-	-	1	-
CAR	-	-	-	-	-	-	-	-	-	-	-	-	-	-
PMC	-	-	-	-	-	-	-	-	-	-	-	-	-	-
DMC	-	-	-	-	-	-	-	-	-	-	-	-	-	-
PF	-	-	1	-	-	-	-	-	-	-	-	-	1	-
DF	-	-	1	-	-	-	-	-	1	-	-	-	2	-
PT	-	-	-	-	-	-	-	-	-	-	-	-	-	-
DT	-	-	-	-	-	-	-	-	-	-	-	-	-	-
TAR	-	-	-	-	-	-	-	-	-	-	-	-	-	-
AST	-	-	-	-	-	-	-	-	-	-	-	-	-	-
CAL	-	-	1	1	-	-	1	1	-	-	-	-	2	2
PMT	-	-	-	-	-	-	-	-	-	-	-	-	-	-
DMT	-	-	-	-	-	-	-	-	-	-	-	-	-	-
P1	-	-	1	-	-	-	-	-	-	-	-	-	1	-
P2	-	-	-	-	-	-	-	-	-	-	-	-	-	-
P3	-	-	-	-	-	-	-	-	-	-	-	-	-	-
PAT	-	-	-	-	-	-	-	-	-	-	-	-	-	-
DMP	-	-	1	-	-	-	-	-	-	-	-	-	1	-
MNB	-	-	-	-	-	-	-	-	-	-	-	-	-	-
STE	-	-	-	-	-	-	-	-	-	-	-	-	-	-
SES	-	-	3	3	-	-	-	-	-	-	-	-	3	3
HYO	-	-	-	-	-	-	-	-	-	-	-	-	-	-
SSC	-	-	1	-	-	-	-	-	-	-	-	-	1	-
SH	-	-	-	-	-	-	-	-	-	-	-	-	-	-
SRC	-	-	-	-	-	-	-	-	-	-	-	-	-	-
SMC	-	-	1	-	-	-	-	-	-	-	-	-	1	-
SF	-	-	1	-	-	-	-	-	-	-	-	-	1	-
ST	-	-	-	-	-	-	-	-	-	-	-	-	-	-
SMT	-	-	-	-	-	-	-	-	-	-	-	-	-	-
CDV	-	-	1	1	-	-	-	-	-	-	-	-	1	1
COS	-	-	-	-	-	-	-	-	-	-	-	-	-	-
TOT.	1	1	20	9	1	1	2	1	5	1	2	1	31	14

Table A5.14. Antelope and medium ungulate sample recovered from Henderson Site (Center Bar, Room C-5).

Body Part	Antelope												Medium Ungulates				
	Non-Immature				Immature						Total Sample		Burned	Total Sample			
	Burned		Unburned		Burned		Unburned										
					Unfused		Unfused		Fusing								
	NISP	MNE	NISP	MNE	NISP	MNE	NISP	MNE	NISP	MNE	NISP	MNE	NISP	NISP	MNE	MAU	%MAU
HC	-	-	1	-	-	-	-	-	-	-	1	-	-	1	-	0.0	0.0
SK	2	-	23	1	-	-	1	-	-	-	26	1	2	29	2	1.0	20.0
MD	1	1	21	2	-	-	-	-	-	-	22	3	1	24	3	1.5	30.0
AT	-	-	3	1	-	-	-	-	-	-	3	1	-	3	1	1.0	20.0
AX	-	-	2	1	-	-	-	-	-	-	2	1	-	3	1	1.0	20.0
CV	-	-	1	1	-	-	-	-	-	-	1	1	1	4	3	0.6	12.0
TV	-	-	-	-	-	-	-	-	-	-	-	-	-	10	4	0.3	6.2
LV	-	-	-	-	-	-	-	-	-	-	-	-	-	4	3	0.5	10.0
SAC	-	-	1	-	-	-	-	-	-	-	1	-	-	1	-	0.0	0.0
PEL	5	2	23	6	-	-	2	1	-	-	30	9	5	33	10	5.0	100.0
RIB	-	-	-	-	-	-	-	-	-	-	-	-	1	32	32	1.2	24.6
STM	-	-	2	2	-	-	-	-	-	-	2	2	-	3	3	3.0	60.0
SC	-	-	6	2	-	-	-	-	-	-	6	2	-	9	3	1.5	30.0
PH	-	-	1	1	-	-	-	-	-	-	1	1	-	2	1	0.5	10.0
DH	-	-	7	6	-	-	-	-	1	1	8	7	-	8	7	3.5	70.0
ULN	-	-	4	3	-	-	2	2	-	-	6	5	-	9	7	3.5	70.0
PRC	1	1	5	5	-	-	-	-	-	-	6	6	1	6	6	3.0	60.0
DRC	-	-	1	1	-	-	-	-	-	-	1	1	-	1	1	0.5	10.0
CAR	-	-	11	11	-	-	-	-	-	-	11	11	-	12	12	1.0	20.0
PMC	-	-	7	5	-	-	-	-	-	-	7	5	-	8	6	3.0	60.0
DMC	-	-	-	-	-	-	2	1	-	-	2	1	-	3	1	0.5	10.0
PF	-	-	7	5	-	-	1	1	-	-	8	6	-	9	6	3.0	60.0
DF	-	-	-	-	-	-	2	2	2	2	4	4	1	6	4	2.0	40.0
PT	1	1	1	1	-	-	3	3	-	-	5	5	1	5	5	2.5	50.0
DT	-	-	1	1	-	-	-	-	-	-	1	1	-	1	1	0.5	10.0
TAR	-	-	6	6	-	-	-	-	-	-	6	6	-	6	6	0.8	15.0
AST	-	-	1	1	-	-	-	-	-	-	1	1	-	1	1	0.5	10.0
CAL	-	-	1	1	-	-	-	-	-	-	1	1	-	3	2	1.0	20.0
PMT	1	1	3	2	-	-	-	-	-	-	4	3	1	4	3	1.5	30.0
DMT	1	-	2	1	-	-	1	-	1	1	5	2	1	7	4	2.0	40.0
P1	1	-	16	10	-	-	7	7	1	1	25	18	1	27	19	2.4	47.5
P2	2	2	9	8	-	-	1	1	1	1	13	12	3	15	14	1.8	35.0
P3	1	1	8	8	-	-	-	-	-	-	9	9	1	10	10	1.3	25.0
PAT	-	-	6	6	-	-	-	-	-	-	6	6	-	7	7	3.5	70.0
DMP	1	-	1	-	2	-	-	-	-	-	4	-	4	9	-	0.0	0.0
MNB	1	1	2	2	-	-	-	-	-	-	3	3	1	4	4	0.0	0.0
STE	-	-	3	3	-	-	-	-	-	-	3	3	-	4	4	0.0	0.0
SES	-	-	-	-	-	-	-	-	-	-	-	-	-	5	5	0.0	0.0
HYO	-	-	-	-	-	-	-	-	-	-	-	-	-	1	1	0.0	0.0
SSC	-	-	-	-	-	-	-	-	-	-	-	-	-	-	-	0.0	0.0
SH	-	-	-	-	-	-	-	-	-	-	-	-	-	5	-	0.0	0.0
SRC	-	-	-	-	-	-	-	-	-	-	-	-	-	1	-	0.0	0.0
SMC	-	-	1	-	-	-	-	-	-	-	1	-	-	1	-	0.0	0.0
SF	-	-	-	-	-	-	-	-	-	-	-	-	-	11	-	0.0	0.0
ST	-	-	-	-	-	-	-	-	-	-	-	-	-	3	-	0.0	0.0
SMT	-	-	6	-	-	-	-	-	-	-	6	-	-	6	-	0.0	0.0
CDV	-	-	-	-	-	-	-	-	-	-	-	-	-	1	1	0.0	0.0
COS	-	-	-	-	-	-	-	-	-	-	-	-	1	4	4	0.0	0.0
TOT.	18	10	193	103	2	-	22	18	6	6	241	137	26	361	207		

Table A5.15. Deer sample recovered from Henderson Site (Center Bar, Room C-5).

Body Part	Non-Immature				Immature		Total Sample	
	Burned		Unburned		Unburned			
	NISP	MNE	NISP	MNE	NISP	MNE	NISP	MNE
ANT	-	-	-	-	-	-	-	-
SK	-	-	2	1	-	-	2	1
MD	-	-	2	-	-	-	2	-
AT	-	-	-	-	-	-	-	-
AX	-	-	-	-	-	-	-	-
CV	-	-	-	-	-	-	-	-
TV	-	-	-	-	-	-	-	-
LV	-	-	-	-	-	-	-	-
SAC	-	-	-	-	-	-	-	-
PEL	-	-	2	1	-	-	2	1
RIB	-	-	-	-	-	-	-	-
STM	-	-	-	-	-	-	-	-
SC	-	-	1	1	-	-	1	1
PH	-	-	-	-	-	-	-	-
DH	-	-	-	-	-	-	-	-
ULN	-	-	1	1	-	-	1	1
PRC	-	-	-	-	-	-	-	-
DRC	-	-	-	-	-	-	-	-
CAR	-	-	1	1	-	-	1	1
PMC	-	-	1	1	-	-	1	1
DMC	-	-	-	-	-	-	-	-
PF	-	-	-	-	-	-	-	-
DF	-	-	-	-	-	-	-	-
PT	-	-	-	-	-	-	-	-
DT	-	-	-	-	-	-	-	-
TAR	-	-	-	-	-	-	-	-
AST	-	-	-	-	-	-	-	-
CAL	-	-	1	1	-	-	1	1
PMT	-	-	-	-	-	-	-	-
DMT	-	-	-	-	2	2	2	2
P1	-	-	-	-	-	-	-	-
P2	1	1	-	-	-	-	1	1
P3	-	-	1	1	-	-	1	1
PAT	-	-	1	1	-	-	1	1
DMP	-	-	-	-	1	-	1	-
TOT.	1	1	13	9	3	2	17	12

Table A5.16. Antelope/deer sample recovered from Henderson Site (Center Bar, Room C-5).

Body Part	Non-Immature				Immature								Total Sample	
	Burned		Unburned		Burned		Unburned							
					Unfused		Fetal		Unfused		Fusing			
	NISP	MNE	NISP	MNE	NISP	MNE	NISP	MNE	NISP	MNE	NISP	MNE	NISP	MNE
HC	-	-	-	-	-	-	-	-	-	-	-	-	-	-
SK	-	-	1	-	-	-	-	-	-	-	-	-	1	-
MD	-	-	-	-	-	-	-	-	-	-	-	-	-	-
AT	-	-	-	-	-	-	-	-	-	-	-	-	-	-
AX	-	-	1	-	-	-	-	-	-	-	-	-	1	-
CV	1	-	1	1	-	-	1	-	1	1	-	-	4	2
TV	-	-	8	4	-	-	-	-	1	-	-	-	9	4
LV	-	-	3	2	-	-	-	-	1	1	-	-	4	3
SAC	-	-	-	-	-	-	-	-	-	-	-	-	-	-
PEL	-	-	1	-	-	-	-	-	-	-	-	-	1	-
RIB	1	1	22	22	-	-	1	1	7	7	1	1	32	32
STM	-	-	1	1	-	-	-	-	-	-	-	-	1	1
SC	-	-	2	-	-	-	-	-	-	-	-	-	2	-
PH	-	-	1	-	-	-	-	-	-	-	-	-	1	-
DH	-	-	-	-	-	-	-	-	-	-	-	-	-	-
ULN	-	-	-	-	-	-	1	1	1	-	-	-	2	1
PRC	-	-	-	-	-	-	-	-	-	-	-	-	-	-
DRC	-	-	-	-	-	-	-	-	-	-	-	-	-	-
CAR	-	-	-	-	-	-	-	-	-	-	-	-	-	-
PMC	-	-	-	-	-	-	-	-	-	-	-	-	-	-
DMC	-	-	-	-	-	-	-	-	1	-	-	-	1	-
PF	-	-	1	-	-	-	-	-	-	-	-	-	1	-
DF	1	-	1	-	-	-	-	-	-	-	-	-	2	-
PT	-	-	-	-	-	-	-	-	-	-	-	-	-	-
DT	-	-	-	-	-	-	-	-	-	-	-	-	-	-
TAR	-	-	-	-	-	-	-	-	-	-	-	-	-	-
AST	-	-	-	-	-	-	-	-	-	-	-	-	-	-
CAL	-	-	-	-	-	-	-	-	1	-	-	-	1	-
PMT	-	-	-	-	-	-	-	-	-	-	-	-	-	-
DMT	-	-	-	-	-	-	-	-	-	-	-	-	-	-
P1	-	-	2	1	-	-	-	-	-	-	-	-	2	1
P2	-	-	1	1	-	-	-	-	-	-	-	-	1	1
P3	-	-	-	-	-	-	-	-	-	-	-	-	-	-
PAT	-	-	-	-	-	-	-	-	-	-	-	-	-	-
DMP	1	-	2	-	-	-	-	-	1	-	-	-	4	-
MNB	-	-	1	1	-	-	-	-	-	-	-	-	1	1
STE	-	-	1	1	-	-	-	-	-	-	-	-	1	1
SES	-	-	5	5	-	-	-	-	-	-	-	-	5	5
HYO	-	-	1	1	-	-	-	-	-	-	-	-	1	1
SSC	-	-	-	-	-	-	-	-	-	-	-	-	-	-
SH	-	-	5	-	-	-	-	-	-	-	-	-	5	-
SRC	-	-	1	-	-	-	-	-	-	-	-	-	1	-
SMC	-	-	-	-	-	-	-	-	-	-	-	-	-	-
SF	-	-	11	-	-	-	-	-	-	-	-	-	11	-
ST	-	-	3	-	-	-	-	-	-	-	-	-	3	-
SMT	-	-	-	-	-	-	-	-	-	-	-	-	-	-
CDV	-	-	-	-	-	-	-	-	-	-	1	1	1	1
COS	1	1	3	3	-	-	-	-	-	-	-	-	4	4
TOT.	5	2	79	43	-	-	3	2	14	9	2	2	103	58

Table A5.17. Antelope and medium ungulate sample recovered from Henderson Site (East Plaza).

Body Part	Antelope												Medium Ungulates				
	Non-Immature				Immature						Total Sample		Burned	Total Sample			
	Burned		Unburned		Burned		Unburned										
					Unfused		Unfused		Fusing								
	NISP	MNE	NISP	MNE	NISP	MNE	NISP	MNE	NISP	MNE	NISP	MNE	NISP	NISP	MNE	MAU	%MAU
HC	1	1	2	2	-	-	-	-	-	-	3	3	2	8	4	2.0	15.4
SK	-	-	48	8	-	-	-	-	-	-	48	8	-	50	8	4.0	30.8
MD	-	-	31	6	-	-	5	-	-	-	36	6	-	38	7	3.5	26.9
AT	-	-	4	3	-	-	-	-	-	-	4	3	-	5	4	4.0	30.8
AX	-	-	3	3	-	-	-	-	1	1	4	4	-	6	6	6.0	46.2
CV	-	-	4	3	-	-	1	1	-	-	5	4	-	6	4	0.8	6.2
TV	-	-	-	-	-	-	-	-	-	-	-	-	2	18	12	0.9	7.1
LV	-	-	-	-	-	-	-	-	-	-	-	-	1	9	7	1.2	9.0
SAC	-	-	-	-	-	-	-	-	-	-	-	-	-	-	-	0.0	0.0
PEL	2	-	39	20	-	-	9	5	-	-	50	25	3	54	26	13.0	100.0
RIB	-	-	-	-	-	-	-	-	-	-	-	-	1	22	22	0.8	6.5
STM	-	-	1	1	-	-	-	-	-	-	1	1	-	1	1	1.0	7.7
SC	3	2	11	5	-	-	1	1	-	-	15	8	3	21	12	6.0	46.2
PH	-	-	4	2	-	-	1	1	-	-	5	3	-	11	7	3.5	26.9
DH	1	1	17	16	-	-	1	1	-	-	19	18	1	23	20	10.0	76.9
ULN	1	1	8	6	-	-	4	4	-	-	13	11	1	17	13	6.5	50.0
PRC	-	-	14	11	-	-	-	-	-	-	14	11	-	14	11	5.5	42.3
DRC	-	-	5	3	-	-	7	4	1	1	13	8	-	13	8	4.0	30.8
CAR	3	3	21	21	-	-	-	-	-	-	24	24	3	29	29	2.4	18.6
PMC	1	1	6	4	-	-	-	-	-	-	7	5	1	7	5	2.5	19.2
DMC	1	-	7	6	2	2	9	4	1	1	20	13	3	22	14	7.0	53.8
PF	-	-	3	2	-	-	2	2	-	-	5	4	-	10	8	4.0	30.8
DF	1	1	3	3	-	-	1	1	-	-	5	5	2	9	6	3.0	23.1
PT	-	-	2	2	-	-	2	2	-	-	4	4	-	6	5	2.5	19.2
DT	1	1	8	8	-	-	4	4	-	-	13	13	1	15	15	7.5	57.7
TAR	-	-	34	34	-	-	-	-	-	-	34	34	-	35	35	4.4	33.7
AST	2	2	11	11	-	-	-	-	-	-	13	13	2	14	14	7.0	53.8
CAL	2	2	14	10	1	1	2	2	-	-	19	15	4	21	16	8.0	61.5
PMT	-	-	14	6	-	-	-	-	-	-	14	6	-	16	8	4.0	30.8
DMT	-	-	4	4	1	1	4	2	-	-	9	7	1	9	7	3.5	26.9
P1	2	2	37	31	-	-	6	4	3	3	48	40	2	49	40	5.0	38.5
P2	3	3	24	24	-	-	2	1	3	3	32	31	3	33	31	3.9	29.8
P3	4	4	22	22	-	-	1	1	-	-	27	27	4	27	27	3.4	26.0
PAT	-	-	5	5	-	-	-	-	-	-	5	5	-	6	5	2.5	19.2
DMP	-	-	3	-	-	-	1	-	-	-	4	-	-	9	-	0.0	0.0
MNB	-	-	-	-	-	-	-	-	-	-	-	-	-	-	-	0.0	0.0
STE	1	1	4	4	-	-	-	-	-	-	5	5	1	8	8	1.6	8.0
SES	-	-	-	-	-	-	-	-	-	-	-	-	-	9	9	0.0	0.0
HYO	-	-	-	-	-	-	-	-	-	-	-	-	-	-	-	0.0	0.0
SSC	1	-	2	-	-	-	-	-	-	-	3	-	1	8	-	0.0	0.0
SH	-	-	-	-	-	-	-	-	-	-	-	-	-	6	-	0.0	0.0
SRC	-	-	-	-	-	-	-	-	-	-	-	-	-	5	-	0.0	0.0
SMC	-	-	5	-	-	-	-	-	-	-	5	-	-	5	-	0.0	0.0
SF	-	-	-	-	-	-	-	-	-	-	-	-	-	9	-	0.0	0.0
ST	-	-	1	1	-	-	-	-	-	-	1	1	-	9	1	0.0	0.0
SMT	4	-	14	-	-	-	-	-	-	-	18	-	4	18	-	0.0	0.0
CDV	-	-	-	-	-	-	-	-	-	-	-	-	-	2	2	0.0	0.0
COS	-	-	-	-	-	-	-	-	-	-	-	-	-	2	2	0.0	0.0
TOT.	34	25	435	287	4	4	63	40	9	9	545	365	46	714	459		

Table A5.18. Deer sample recovered from Henderson Site (East Plaza).

Body Part	Non-Immature				Immature		Total Sample	
	Burned		Unburned		Unburned			
	NISP	MNE	NISP	MNE	NISP	MNE	NISP	MNE
ANT	1	-	4	1	-	-	5	1
SK	-	-	2	-	-	-	2	-
MD	-	-	1	-	-	-	1	-
AT	-	-	-	-	-	-	-	-
AX	-	-	-	-	-	-	-	-
CV	-	-	-	-	-	-	-	-
TV	-	-	-	-	-	-	-	-
LV	-	-	-	-	-	-	-	-
SAC	-	-	-	-	-	-	-	-
PEL	-	-	1	1	-	-	1	1
RIB	-	-	-	-	-	-	-	-
STM	-	-	-	-	-	-	-	-
SC	-	-	1	1	-	-	1	1
PH	-	-	-	-	-	-	-	-
DH	-	-	2	2	-	-	2	2
ULN	-	-	-	-	-	-	-	-
PRC	-	-	-	-	-	-	-	-
DRC	-	-	-	-	-	-	-	-
CAR	-	-	5	5	-	-	5	5
PMC	-	-	-	-	-	-	-	-
DMC	-	-	-	-	1	1	1	1
PF	-	-	-	-	1	1	1	1
DF	-	-	-	-	1	1	1	1
PT	-	-	-	-	1	1	1	1
DT	-	-	1	1	1	1	2	2
TAR	-	-	1	1	-	-	1	1
AST	-	-	-	-	-	-	-	-
CAL	-	-	-	-	-	-	-	-
PMT	-	-	2	2	-	-	2	2
DMT	-	-	-	-	-	-	-	-
P1	-	-	-	-	-	-	-	-
P2	-	-	-	-	-	-	-	-
P3	-	-	-	-	-	-	-	-
SMT	-	-	1	-	-	-	1	-
TOT.	1	-	21	14	5	5	27	19

Table A5.19. Antelope/deer sample recovered from Henderson Site (East Plaza).

Body Part	Non-Immature				Immature								Total Sample	
	Burned		Unburned		Burned		Unburned							
					Unfused		Fetal		Unfused		Fusing			
	NISP	MNE	NISP	MNE	NISP	MNE	NISP	MNE	NISP	MNE	NISP	MNE	NISP	MNE
HC	-	-	-	-	-	-	-	-	-	-	-	-	-	-
SK	-	-	-	-	-	-	-	-	-	-	-	-	-	-
MD	-	-	-	-	-	-	1	1	-	-	-	-	1	1
AT	-	-	1	1	-	-	-	-	-	-	-	-	1	1
AX	-	-	2	2	-	-	-	-	-	-	-	-	2	2
CV	-	-	1	-	-	-	-	-	-	-	-	-	1	-
TV	2	2	12	9	-	-	-	-	4	1	-	-	18	12
LV	1	-	5	4	-	-	-	-	2	2	1	1	9	7
SAC	-	-	-	-	-	-	-	-	-	-	-	-	-	-
PEL	1	-	2	-	-	-	-	-	-	-	-	-	3	-
RIB	1	1	16	16	-	-	-	-	5	5	-	-	22	22
STM	-	-	-	-	-	-	-	-	-	-	-	-	-	-
SC	-	-	3	1	-	-	2	2	-	-	-	-	5	3
PH	-	-	3	1	-	-	3	3	-	-	-	-	6	4
DH	-	-	2	-	-	-	-	-	-	-	-	-	2	-
ULN	-	-	1	-	-	-	2	2	1	-	-	-	4	2
PRC	-	-	-	-	-	-	-	-	-	-	-	-	-	-
DRC	-	-	-	-	-	-	-	-	-	-	-	-	-	-
CAR	-	-	-	-	-	-	-	-	-	-	-	-	-	-
PMC	-	-	-	-	-	-	-	-	-	-	-	-	-	-
DMC	-	-	-	-	-	-	-	-	1	-	-	-	1	-
PF	-	-	2	1	-	-	-	-	2	2	-	-	4	3
DF	1	-	2	-	-	-	-	-	-	-	-	-	3	-
PT	-	-	-	-	-	-	-	-	1	-	-	-	1	-
DT	-	-	-	-	-	-	-	-	-	-	-	-	-	-
TAR	-	-	-	-	-	-	-	-	-	-	-	-	-	-
AST	-	-	1	1	-	-	-	-	-	-	-	-	1	1
CAL	-	-	-	-	1	-	1	1	-	-	-	-	2	1
PMT	-	-	-	-	-	-	-	-	-	-	-	-	-	-
DMT	-	-	-	-	-	-	-	-	-	-	-	-	-	-
P1	-	-	1	-	-	-	-	-	-	-	-	-	1	-
P2	-	-	1	-	-	-	-	-	-	-	-	-	1	-
P3	-	-	-	-	-	-	-	-	-	-	-	-	-	-
PAT	-	-	-	-	-	-	-	-	-	-	-	-	-	-
DMP	-	-	5	-	-	-	-	-	-	-	-	-	5	-
MNB	-	-	-	-	-	-	-	-	-	-	-	-	-	-
STE	-	-	3	3	-	-	-	-	-	-	-	-	3	3
SES	-	-	9	9	-	-	-	-	-	-	-	-	9	9
HYO	-	-	-	-	-	-	-	-	-	-	-	-	-	-
SSC	-	-	5	-	-	-	-	-	-	-	-	-	5	-
SH	-	-	6	-	-	-	-	-	-	-	-	-	6	-
SRC	-	-	5	-	-	-	-	-	-	-	-	-	5	-
SMC	-	-	-	-	-	-	-	-	-	-	-	-	-	-
SF	-	-	9	-	-	-	-	-	-	-	-	-	9	-
ST	-	-	8	-	-	-	-	-	-	-	-	-	8	-
SMT	-	-	-	-	-	-	-	-	-	-	-	-	-	-
CDV	-	-	-	-	-	-	-	-	2	2	-	-	2	2
COS	-	-	2	2	-	-	-	-	-	-	-	-	2	2
TOT.	6	3	107	50	1	-	9	9	18	12	1	1	142	75

Table A5.20. Fetal medium ungulate sample by provenience recovered from Henderson Site.

Body Part	Center Bar		East Bar		East Plaza		Entire Site			
	NISP	MNE	NISP	MNE	NISP	MNE	NISP	MNE	MNI	Side
HC	-	-	-	-	-	-	-	-	-	-
SK	-	-	-	-	-	-	-	-	-	-
MD	-	-	-	-	1	1	1	1	1	R
AT	-	-	-	-	-	-	-	-	-	-
AX	-	-	-	-	-	-	-	-	-	-
CV	1	-	-	-	-	-	1	-	1	-
TV	-	-	-	-	-	-	-	-	-	-
LV	-	-	-	-	-	-	-	-	-	-
SAC	-	-	-	-	-	-	-	-	-	-
PEL	-	-	-	-	-	-	-	-	-	-
RIB	1	1	-	-	-	-	1	1	1	-
STM	-	-	-	-	-	-	-	-	-	-
SC	-	-	-	-	2	2	2	2	1	L
HUM	1	1	-	-	3	3	4	4	2	L
ULN	1	1	1	1	2	2	5	5	4	R
RC	1	-	-	-	-	-	1	-	1	L
CAR	-	-	-	-	-	-	-	-	-	-
MC	-	-	-	-	-	-	-	-	-	-
FEM	-	-	-	-	-	-	-	-	-	-
TIB	-	-	-	-	-	-	-	-	-	-
TAR	-	-	-	-	-	-	-	-	-	-
AST	-	-	-	-	-	-	-	-	-	-
CAL	1	1	-	-	1	1	2	2	2	L
MT	-	-	-	-	-	-	-	-	-	-
P1	-	-	-	-	-	-	-	-	-	-
P2	-	-	-	-	-	-	-	-	-	-
P3	-	-	-	-	-	-	-	-	-	-
TOT.	6	4	1	1	9	9	17	15	4	-

6

Scheduling Conflicts at the Henderson Site

Evidence for a Decline in Medium Ungulate Procurement and Use

Christina Waskiewicz
Washington University

James J. Noone
University of Michigan

John D. Speth
University of Michigan

Introduction and Expectations

Analysis of the bison remains, ceramics, and other classes of material from the Henderson Site suggests that the inhabitants of this Plains-margin community in the late thirteenth and early fourteenth century increasingly relied on long-distance procurement of bison and interregional exchange of bison products with Puebloan communities in the uplands to the west (see Chapters 3 and 4). The goal of this chapter is to examine how increasing reliance on long-range bison hunting, and the scheduling conflicts that most likely arose from intensification of this activity, may have affected the procurement and use of lower-ranked hunted resources, specifically the medium ungulates—deer and antelope.

Numerous lines of evidence point to the growing importance of bison in the village economy (see discussion in Chapter 4). For example, the proportion of high-utility elements (defined here as those elements with an MGUI value >60.0; Binford 1978:74) is significantly greater in the Late phase (24.3%) than in the Early phase (15.4%; $t_s = 5.00$, $p < .001$). The average marrow index (Binford 1978:27) for bison also increases (Early phase, 34.5l; Late phase, 38.5; $t = 2.71$, $p < .01$).[1] These data very likely reflect increasingly selective culling of lower-utility body parts of bison prior to transport, which in turn implies that more bison were being taken per kill event, or that the kills occurred farther from home, or both.

In addition, the density of bison bones increased by about 27% from the Early phase (19.8 bones/m^3) to the Late phase (25.2 bones/m^3), suggesting that more bison per unit time were brought into the community during the later period. The density of projectile points (nearly 95% of the identifiable points are Washitas and Fresnos; see Chapter 15) also rises markedly (Early phase, 3.6 points/m^3; Late phase, 5.6 points/m^3), an independent, albeit indirect, indication of the increasing importance of large-mammal hunting in the village economy.

One of the most striking changes in the Late phase handling of bison is the sharply increased concentration of their remains in non-room, or public, contexts. In the Early phase, roughly half (54.5%) of the bison came from the fill of rooms, especially those in the Main Bar East, and half came from non-room contexts, particularly the Great Depression. In the Late phase, the distribution pattern changed, such that fully 80% of the bison bones were encountered in non-room contexts, most notably in and around the East Plaza earth oven complex ($t_s = 17.1$, $p < .001$). This change is also clearly reflected in the density values. The density of bison bones in non-room contexts more than doubles from 30.9 bones/m^3 in the Early phase to 77.8 bones/m^3 in the Late phase. Thus, regardless of where bison were initially butchered and processed, during the Early phase roughly half of their remains ended up being discarded in room fill, whereas during the Late phase, discarded bison bones came to be concentrated in and around a single major public facility in the East Plaza.

The burning data further underscore the changes that were happening in the processing of bison. The proportion of burned bones rises significantly in the Late phase, indicating that a greater proportion of the bison that came into the village were cooked in the East Plaza earth oven complex (Early phase, 5.4%; Late phase, 7.3%; $t_s = 2.38$, $p = .01$).

Other changes are also noteworthy. In Chapter 4 it was shown that the scarcity of bison ribs at Henderson was most likely a reflection of their role as food items in intercommunity or interregional systems of exchange. When looked at over time, the representation of ribs declines precipitously from the Early phase (17.8%) to the Late phase (10.5%; $t_s = 6.28$, $p < .001$), suggesting that exchange involving dried bison meat intensified significantly after about A.D. 1270.

Ceramic evidence underscores the accelerating pace of westward-focused exchange in the Late phase. Five seasons of excavation at Henderson yielded a total of 1,560 sherds that came from distant source areas to the west and southwest of Roswell. Nearly 95% of these ceramics occurred in Late phase contexts (see Chapter 3). Thus, extraregional ceramic exchange appears to have been very limited in the Early phase, then increased explosively in the Late phase.

All of these lines of evidence, considered together, point to a shift in the role of bison in Henderson's economy during the Late phase. Larger numbers of animals were taken at increasingly greater distances away from the community, and their processing and consumption within the village became far more public and communal. The increasing focus on long-distance communal bison hunting appears to have gone hand-in-hand with an intensifying role of bison in interregional exchange systems.

Seasonality studies (see Chapters 4 and 5) indicate that both bison and antelope were taken primarily in the spring. Critical agricultural activities, such as field preparation and planting, would also have occurred at this time of year. Thus, there undoubtedly would have been scheduling conflicts among and between these subsistence pursuits that would have been exacerbated as long-distance bison hunting became increasingly important (e.g., Flannery 1968). Given the much higher ranking of bison compared to antelope and deer (O'Connell et al. 1988; Winterhalder 1981), we would expect that as bison became more important, the use of much lower-ranked medium ungulates would have changed in a series of predictable ways that would reflect their declining importance in the village economy. In the Henderson case, the difference in resource rank between bison and the medium ungulates is particularly marked, because most of the bison taken by the villagers were bulls (see Chapter 4). In brief, we would anticipate: (1) medium ungulates in the Late phase to become less abundant in village trash; (2) hunting, on average, to take place closer to the village; and (3) antelope and deer to become less important as public or communal resources.

Results

Abundance of Medium Ungulates

The analyses discussed here employ nearly the entire assemblage of medium ungulate remains recovered in all five seasons of excavation at the Henderson Site (1980, 1981, 1994, 1995, 1997). This assemblage consists of 4,673 medium ungulate bones, of which 2,089 derive from Early phase contexts and 2,584 derive from Late phase contexts. A small number of specimens, not tabulated here, came from contexts of uncertain temporal placement. Of the total, 714 came from the Center Bar, 530 from the East Bar, 1,022 from the East Plaza (trenches B and C), 740 from the Great Depression, and 1,364 from the Main Bar East. The remaining 303 bones came from a variety of small test excavations and less productive proveniences.

The frequency of medium ungulates as a proportion of the total village fauna declines sharply and significantly in the Late phase (NISP; taxa included are bison, antelope, deer, dogs, jackrabbits, cottontails, and prairie dogs; Early phase, 33.2%; Late phase, 19.5%; $t_s = 20.35$, $p < .001$). Likewise, the density of deer and antelope remains decreases by over 20% in the Late phase (Early phase, 29.8 bones/m^3; Late phase, 23.1 bones/m^3). These results strongly suggest that medium ungulates were being exploited far less heavily in the Late phase than in the preceding phase.

Transport Distance

Declining average transport distance for medium ungulates is evident in three different ways. First, in the Late phase there is a significant decline in the average utility (MGUI; Binford 1978) of elements being brought into the village, implying that there was less dismemberment and selective culling of the carcasses prior to transport (Early phase, 38.5; Late phase, 35.6; $t = 1.98$, $p = .05$; O'Connell et al. 1988, 1990, 1992; Bunn et al. 1988).

The second indication that dismemberment for transport decreased in the Late phase is a significant rise in the proportion of upper head parts or crania relative to jaws (Bunn et al. 1988; O'Connell et al. 1988, 1990, 1992; White 1952). The percentage of crania represented in the sample rises from 62.1% in the Early phase to 76.9% in the Late phase ($t_s = 3.19$, $p = .001$).

Third, the proportion of phalanges, low-utility elements that are often discarded at distant kill sites (White 1952; Binford 1978), increases significantly in the Late phase, another sign that average transport distance had declined (Early phase, 9.3%; Late phase, 13.6%; $t_s = 3.91$, $p < .001$).

The increase in the frequency of crania and phalanges and the decline in average utility taken together suggest that more complete animals were being transported back to the site, and that the average distance between kill and village had decreased, facilitating the hunter's return home with more complete carcasses.

Medium Ungulates as Public or Communal Resources

Miracle (Chapter 5) has suggested that most antelope at Henderson were not communally hunted, but instead were taken individually by stalking or encounter hunting. Bison, on the other hand, were very likely taken by long-distance communal efforts, particularly during the Late phase (see Chapter 4; see also Speth 1983). Given the differences between these two resources in rank and in the degree of communal involvement in their procurement, one would expect differences in the way these animals were processed and cooked in the village, differences that should become increasingly apparent in the Late phase as medium ungulates declined in economic importance. Such changes are in fact evident in a number of ways.

1. While the proportion of bison found in non-room or public contexts skyrockets in the Late phase (Early phase, 54.5%; Late phase, 80.6%; $t_s = 17.1$, $p < .001$), the proportion of medium ungulates found in such contexts is always much smaller than bison and does not change over time (Early phase, 44.0%; Late phase, 45.0%; $t_s = 1.01$, $p > .05$).

2. The average utility (MGUI) of skeletal elements found directly within public earth oven complexes (Great Depression, East Plaza) is not only much higher in bison than medium ungulates (Early phase, 51.8:36.5; Late phase, 51.0:34.1), but the Late phase value in medium ungulates declines significantly ($t = 2.02$, $p < .05$) while it remains unchanged in bison ($t = 0.52$, $p > .05$).

3. The incidence of burning increases significantly in Late phase bison (Early phase, 5.4%; Late phase, 7.3%; $t_s = 2.38$, $p = .01$), but declines sharply in medium ungulates (Early phase, 13.9%; Late phase, 7.1%; $t_s = 7.52$, $p < .001$). In Chapter 4, it was shown that most burning on bison bones is the result of food preparation, not accidental post-discard exposure to fire. The same is probably true of burning on medium ungulate bones. Burning tends to be concentrated on proximal and distal epiphyses rather than distributed equally over the entire element, as one might expect if burning were due largely to accidental exposure of already discarded bones (epiphyses, 11.1%; shaft, 7.9%; $t_s = 1.81$, $p = .07$). Thus, the decline in burning on medium ungulate bones likely reflects a shift in cooking technique away from the large-scale use of earth oven complexes for their preparation.

4. In the Early phase burning on medium ungulate bones is significantly higher in the East Plaza than in the rooms (East Plaza, 17.3%; room blocks, 11.0%; $t_s = 4.09$, $p < .001$). In the Late phase burning not only declines, but there is no longer any difference between plaza and room contexts (East Plaza, 7.0%; room blocks, 7.1%; $t_s = 0.14$, $p > .05$).

Though speculative, we may be able to say more about the kinds of changes that were taking place during the Late phase in the way antelope and deer were cooked. Elsewhere, one of us (Speth 2000) drew on comparative ethnographic observations to suggest that the task of cooking meat by boiling in traditional societies is generally performed by women, whereas the roasting or baking of meat may be done by either sex, depending on the particular animal being cooked, and especially on the social context in which the meat is being prepared. Men are much more likely to participate in cooking when the meat being prepared is for "large-scale extradomestic feasts or ceremonials" (Friedl 1975:59). More routine "domestic" food preparation, especially boiling, is generally done by women (see also Lowell 1991).

The decline already noted in the frequency of burning in Late phase medium ungulates is one line of evidence suggesting that these animals increasingly were prepared for consumption by boiling or stewing rather than roasting or pit-baking. Other lines of evidence point in the same direction. For example, if medium ungulates were roasted, the residual grease content in many of the bones would be greater than in bones that were boiled or stewed for extended periods (see discussion in Speth 2000). As a consequence, scavenging village dogs would find more edible tissue in discarded roasted or pit-baked bones than in ones that had been boiled. Put more explicitly as an expectation, if boiling increased in the Late phase, the proportion of medium ungulate skeletal elements damaged by carnivores should decline. Carnivore damage includes evidence on bones of gnawing, pitting, and punctures (e.g., Binford 1981; Lyman 1994). Since medium ungulates continued to be roasted or pit-baked in the plaza, but increasingly were boiled in room contexts, we should expect the decline in carnivore damage to be greatest in room block trash. That is precisely what we find. There is no significant change over time in the proportion of carnivore-damaged medium ungulate bones in non-room contexts (Early phase, 11.7%; Late phase, 14.6%; $t_s = 1.38$, $p > .05$). In room block trash, however, the proportion of carnivore-damaged bones declines sharply, from 16.6% in the Early phase to 11.4% in the Late phase ($t_s = 2.59$, $p < .01$).

We can look at this issue in another way as well. If village dogs scavenge bones because of their residual grease content, the percentage of bones displaying evidence of carnivore damage should be positively correlated with their grease content, or grease index (Binford 1978:33; Lyman 1994; Speth 2000). Hence, we would expect a significant correlation in the Early phase, when a higher proportion of the animals were roasted or pit-baked, and a weaker correlation, or no correlation at all, in the Late phase, when more of the animals were boiled or stewed. Again, our expectations are matched quite well by the evidence (Early phase, $r_s = 0.60$, $p = .001$; Late phase, $r_s = .25$, $p > .05$).[2]

The issue of medium ungulate processing can also be approached from another perspective, this time employing cutmark data (Binford 1981; Butterfield and May 1983). We have already suggested that antelope and deer were procured closer to home and more complete carcasses were brought back to the village during the Late phase. This would lead us to expect a decrease over time in the frequency of dismemberment cutmarks. What we in fact find is the opposite. The incidence of dismemberment marks increases significantly, from 2.3% in the Early phase to 5.3% in the Late phase ($t_s = 3.99, p < .001$). This seemingly contradictory result, however, is not necessarily incompatible with the suggestion that boiling increased in the Late phase. Cuts of meat that are to be boiled or stewed in ceramic pots may need to be much more thoroughly dismembered to fit them into the cooking vessels (i.e., pot-sizing; see Yellen 1977; Gifford-Gonzalez 1989, 1993) than cuts of meat prepared in large communal earth oven features.

Increasing emphasis on pot-sizing in the Late phase should also be reflected by the degree of fragmentation of the medium ungulate bones. Ideally, one should record the size of each bone, including the many uncoded limb-shaft splinters that almost certainly derive from antelope or deer. Unfortunately, such data were not recorded, and a much cruder proxy must be used to provide a reasonable approximation of the degree of fragmentation. The approach used here, as in Chapter 4, is a fragmentation index (FI) based on the ratio of MNE (minimum number of elements) and NISP (number of identifiable specimens), devised by subtracting (MNE/NISP × 100) from 100. The larger the value of FI, the greater the degree of fragmentation. The pattern of the results is as expected, although unfortunately the statistical significance of this index cannot be evaluated (Early phase FI = 52.1; Late phase FI = 57.0).

Filleting marks also yield interesting, albeit somewhat equivocal, insights into changing cooking practices at Henderson (Binford 1981). The incidence of filleting marks declines significantly over time in the room blocks (Early phase, 9.6%; Late phase, 6.0%; $t_s = 2.53, p = .01$), but not in the earth oven complexes (Early phase, 8.2%; Late phase, 9.4%; $t_s = 0.73, p > .05$). While other explanations cannot be ruled out, this result is again compatible with the view that antelope and deer meat were increasingly boiled in domestic contexts during the Late phase. Thoroughly cooking meat in this manner prior to removing the flesh from the bone generates very few cutmarks (Gifford-Gonzalez 1989, 1993).

Conclusion

The evidence outlined in this chapter, and in Chapter 5, suggests that medium ungulates, which were generally taken individually by stalking or encounter hunting, declined in both economic and social importance at Henderson as long-distance communal bison hunting, and interregional trade involving products of the bison hunt, became increasingly central. Many lines of evidence point to this conclusion. Medium ungulates as a proportion of the total fauna dropped precipitously in the Late phase, as did the density of antelope and deer bones per m^3 of excavated deposit. Hunting of these animals took place closer to the community, and more complete carcasses were brought home. Fewer antelope and deer were prepared in large public earth oven complexes, but instead appear increasingly to have been cooked by boiling or stewing in more "private" domestic contexts. The shift in the economic and social handling of antelope and deer at Henderson very likely occurred as a result of scheduling conflicts arising in the spring from the competing time and labor demands of long-range bison hunting and agricultural activities.

Synopsis

Medium ungulates, generally taken individually by stalking or encounter hunting, declined at Henderson in economic and social importance as long-distance communal bison hunting, and interregional trade involving products of the bison hunt, became central. Economic and social handling of antelope and deer probably shifted due to spring scheduling conflicts between long-range bison-hunting and agriculture. Many lines of evidence point to this conclusion.

1. Medium ungulates as a proportion of the total fauna dropped in the Late phase, as did the density of antelope and deer bones per m^3 of excavated deposit.
2. The average utility (MGUI) of skeletal elements brought into the village declined, implying less dismemberment and selective culling of the carcasses prior to transport. Also, the proportion of crania relative to mandibles increased, as did the proportional representation of low-utility phalanges. Hence, more complete animals were being transported back to the village, and the average distance between kill and village decreased.
3. The proportion of bison found in non-room or public contexts skyrockets in the Late phase; the proportion of medium ungulates found in such contexts is consistently much smaller and remains unchanged over time.
4. The MGUI of skeletal elements found in public earth oven complexes is much lower in medium ungulates than in bison; the Late phase value declines significantly while the value for bison remains unchanged.
5. The incidence of burning increases significantly in Late phase bison, but declines sharply in medium ungulates, most particularly in the East Plaza, reflecting a shift in cooking technique away from the large-scale use of public earth oven complexes toward boiling or stewing in more "private" domestic contexts.
6. Carnivore damage on medium ungulate bones declines sharply in Late phase room block trash, while it remains unchanged on bones from non-room areas. This suggests that bones from Late phase "domestic" contexts had been more thoroughly degreased before they were discarded and increasing numbers boiled or stewed rather than roasted or pit-baked.
7. The incidence of carnivore damage on medium ungulate bones is positively correlated with Binford's grease index in the Early phase, but uncorrelated in the Late phase, again suggesting more thorough degreasing of antelope and deer bones in the later period.

8. Dismemberment marks increase significantly in the Late phase. Other evidence clearly points to transport of more complete carcasses in the later period. This seemingly contradictory evidence could be interpreted as "pot-sizing" of cuts of meat to be boiled or stewed.

9. The degree of fragmentation of medium ungulate bones increases in the Late phase, supporting the "pot-sizing" explanation.

10. The incidence of filleting marks declines significantly over time in the room blocks, but not in the earth oven complexes. This result is again compatible with the view that antelope and deer meat were increasingly boiled in domestic contexts during the Late phase. Thoroughly cooking meat in this manner prior to removing the flesh from the bone generates very few cutmarks.

Acknowledgments

Preparation of this chapter has benefited from an undergraduate honors thesis on the Henderson medium ungulates by Tatum McKay (1996), as well as from independent research projects on various aspects of the prehistoric antelope and deer from Roswell area sites by Julie Solometo, Frank DeMita, Sara Olson, and Jessica de Young. We also thank Richard Ford and John O'Shea for their advice on the manuscript at various stages en route to completion.

Notes

1. t_s = test of equality of two percentages based on arcsine transformation (Sokal and Rohlf 1969:607-10); t = standard unpaired t-test.
2. r_s = Spearman's rank correlation coefficient (Siegel 1956).

References Cited

Binford, L. R.
1978 *Nunamiut Ethnoarchaeology*. New York: Academic Press.
1981 *Bones: Ancient Men and Modern Myths*. New York: Academic Press.

Bunn, H. T., L. E. Bartram, and E. M. Kroll
1988 Variability in Bone Assemblage Formation from Hadza Hunting, Scavenging, and Carcass Processing. *Journal of Anthropological Archaeology* 7:412-57.

Butterfield, R. M., and N. D. S. May
1983 *Muscles of the Ox*. St. Lucia, Queensland, Australia: University of Queensland Press.

Flannery, K. V.
1968 Archaeological Systems Theory and Early Mesoamerica. In: *Anthropological Archaeology in the Americas*, edited by B. J. Meggers, pp. 67-87. Washington, DC: Anthropological Society of Washington.

Friedl, E.
1975 *Women and Men: An Anthropologist's View*. New York: Holt, Rinehart and Winston.

Gifford-Gonzalez, D. P.
1989 Ethnographic Analogues for Interpreting Modified Bones: Some Cases from East Africa. In: *Bone Modification*, edited by R. Bonnichsen and M. H. Sorg, pp. 179-246. Peopling of the Americas Publications. Orono, ME: University of Maine, Institute for Quaternary Studies, Center for the Study of the First Americans.
1993 Gaps in Zooarchaeological Analyses of Butchery: Is Gender an Issue? In: *From Bones to Behavior: Ethnoarchaeological and Experimental Contributions to the Interpretation of Faunal Remains*, edited by J. Hudson, pp. 181-99. Occasional Paper 21. Carbondale, IL: Southern Illinois University, Center for Archaeological Investigations.

Lowell, J. C.
1991 Reflections of Sex Roles in the Archaeological Record: Insights from Hopi and Zuni Ethnographic Data. In: *The Archaeology of Gender: Proceedings of the Twenty-Second Annual Conference of the Archaeological Association of the University of Calgary*, edited by D. Walde and N. D. Willows, pp. 452-61. Calgary, Alberta: University of Calgary, Archaeological Association.

Lyman, R. L.
1994 *Vertebrate Taphonomy*. Cambridge, England: Cambridge University Press.

McKay, T. M.
1996 *The Effect of Increased Bison Hunting on Medium Ungulates at the Henderson Site, New Mexico (LA-1549)*. Honors thesis, Department of Anthropology, University of Michigan, Ann Arbor, MI.

O'Connell, J. F., K. Hawkes, and N. G. Blurton Jones
1988 Hadza Hunting, Butchering, and Bone Transport and Their Archaeological Implications. *Journal of Anthropological Research* 44(2):113-62.
1990 Reanalysis of Large Mammal Body Part Transport Among the Hadza. *Journal of Archaeological Science* 17(3):301-16.
1992 Patterns in the Distribution, Site Structure and Assemblage Composition of Hadza Kill-Butchering Sites. *Journal of Archaeological Science* 19(3):319-45.

Siegel, S.
1956 *Nonparametric Statistics for the Behavioral Sciences*. New York: McGraw-Hill.

Sokal, R. R., and F. J. Rohlf
1969 *Biometry: The Principles and Practice of Statistics in Biological Research*. San Francisco, CA: W. H. Freeman.

Speth, J. D.
1983 *Bison Kills and Bone Counts: Decision Making by Ancient Hunters*. Chicago, IL: University of Chicago Press.
2000 Boiling vs. Baking and Roasting: A Taphonomic Approach to the Recognition of Cooking Techniques in Small Mammals. In: *Animal Bones, Human Societies*, edited by P. A. Rowley-Conwy, pp. 89-105. Oxford, England: Oxbow Books.

White, T. E.
1952 Observations on the Butchering Techniques of Some Aboriginal Peoples: 1. *American Antiquity* 17 (4):337-38.

Winterhalder, B.
1981 Optimal Foraging Strategies and Hunter-Gatherer Research in Anthropology: Theory and Models. In: *Hunter-Gatherer Foraging Strategies: Ethnographic and Archaeological Analyses*, edited by B. Winterhalder and E. A. Smith, pp. 13-35. Chicago, IL: University of Chicago Press.

Yellen, J. E.
1977 Cultural Patterning in Faunal Remains: Evidence from the !Kung Bushmen. In: *Experimental Archaeology*, edited by D. W. Ingersoll, J. E. Yellen, and W. Macdonald, pp. 271-331. New York: Columbia University Press.

7

The Henderson Site Dogs

Lauren Bigelow
Northwestern University

John D. Speth
University of Michigan

Introduction

Five seasons of excavation at the Henderson Site yielded a small and fragmentary, but nevertheless interesting, collection of canid remains. The sample consists of 328 bones representing at least twelve individuals (pooled or site-wide MNI, based on mandibles and crania). Of these, 99 came from Early phase contexts (MNI = 5) and 229 from Late phase contexts (MNI = 9). All of the bones were disarticulated, most had been deliberately broken, and quite a few were burned (4.2%). Their disposal in trash-filled deposits along with the butchered and burned bones of bison, antelope, deer, rabbits, and other food debris make it clear that the dogs were the remains of meals. No articulated dog burials were encountered.

Taxonomic identification was handicapped by the fragmentary nature of the remains. Nevertheless, following criteria set out by Benecke (1987; dental crowding, size and shape of the tympanic bulla, shape of the sagittal crest, shape of the zygomatic process of the maxilla), it is clear that all of the identifiable cranial remains derive from domestic dogs (*Canis familiaris*) rather than wolves (*Canis lupus*) or coyotes (*Canis latrans*).

As is common elsewhere in the Southwest and Plains (Allen 1920; Colton 1970; Haag 1948; Olsen 1976), dogs of at least two distinct body sizes are represented in the assemblage, one averaging about 9 kg ("small"), the other averaging about 16 kg ("large").[1] Body size was estimated using the height (mm) of the mandible measured on the outer (labial) side at the center of the lower carnassial (M_1), as described by Clutton-Brock and Hammond (1994; see also Hamblin 1984); the results are presented in Table 7.1. Henderson's large dogs are similar in size to adult coyotes collected in the Roswell area. Based on NISP, approximately 82% derive from the small category.

The Henderson canid remains display almost no cutmarks. Only two examples were found, one on a lumbar vertebra, the other on a tibia shaft. Since the dogs were presumably raised in the village, and killed there, they would not have been transported and one would not expect cutmarks resulting from transport-related dismemberment. The absence of cutmarks related to processing and cooking, however, is another matter. Cutmarked dog remains are widely reported in the archaeological literature (e.g., Crockford 2000; Horard-Herbin 2000; Mick-O'Hara 1994; Olsen 1990; Parmalee 1965; Snyder 1991); their virtual absence at Henderson, therefore, implies that the dogs had been cooked prior to most dismemberment and flesh removal.

Traditionally, dogs were either roasted or boiled, generally with the hair singed off but the skin left intact (Gilmore 1934; Powers and Powers 1990; Schwartz 1997; Snyder 1991; Wing 1978). In light of the presence of burning on a number of the Henderson dog bones (4.3%), it would appear that some of these animals had been roasted, although the near absence of cutmarks suggests that the majority were boiled.

Most of the butchered remains derive from skeletally mature individuals (85.6%; based on NISP). The very limited amount of wear on the lower M_1's, however, indicates that many, perhaps most, of the mature animals were young when they were killed (Horard-Herbin 2000). None of the unfused bones were burned.

Table 7.1. Estimated body size of dogs from the Henderson Site.[a]

Provenience	Lot No.	Period	Mandibular Height (mm)	Weight (kg)	Body Size
East Plaza (B/C)	640	Late phase	23.8	15.1	large
East Plaza (B/C)	613	Late phase	23.3	14.4	large
Main Bar East	3714	Early phase	26.7	19.3	large
Main Bar East	3224	Early phase	18.5	8.9	small
East Bar	1115	Late phase	17.2	7.6	small
East Bar	342	Late phase	19.4	9.8	small
East Plaza (B/C)	711	Late phase	19.5	9.9	small

[a]Body size estimated using the height (mm) of the mandible measured on the outer (labial) side at the center of the lower carnassial (M_1), as described by Clutton-Brock and Hammond (1994).

Temporal Perspective

Handling of the dogs at Henderson underwent some interesting changes over time, although the patterning is not always clear-cut, and evaluation of the statistical significance of some of these changes is handicapped by small sample sizes. For example, the overall or site-wide density (NISP/m^3) of dog remains increases slightly from the Early phase (1.4 NISP/m^3) to the Late phase (2.0 NISP/m^3), with the most dramatic increase occurring in non-room contexts (Early phase, 1.0 NISP/m^3; Late phase, 4.3 NISP/m^3). The Late phase concentration of dog remains in "public" areas is also clearly reflected in the proportion of canid bones found in non-room contexts (Early phase, 23.3%; Late phase, 52.4%; $t_s = 5.10$, $p < .001$).[1] Thus, despite their generally small size, canids appear to have become a much more communal or public resource during the Late phase at Henderson.

At the same time, the method used to cook them may have shifted increasingly away from roasting toward boiling, as suggested by a decline in the incidence of burning (limbs only: Early phase, 6.4%; Late phase, 2.9%; $t_s = 1.12$, $p > .05$). Although the difference is not statistically significant, we believe that there was in fact a real change, and that the direction of this change was toward a decline in the incidence of burning. The reason we draw this conclusion, despite the lack of statistical significance, is that the proportion of burned bones declines in the Late phase in almost every anatomical unit (Early phase:Late phase; axial elements, 11.1%:4.2%; lower limbs, 7.0%:3.4%; upper limbs, 7.7%:5.9%; feet, 0%:0%).

A drop in burning frequency is not what we would have expected if dogs were becoming increasingly important as a communal resource. Quite the contrary, we would have expected more of the dogs to have been cooked in the massive East Plaza earth oven complex and the incidence of burning to have risen, not declined (see discussion in Chapters 4, 6, 8, and 9; see also Speth 2000). This apparent contradiction may be less problematic than it first appears, however. In traditional societies, foods that are boiled in public spaces most often are those that are being prepared for communal feasts or ceremonies (Speth 2000). And among Plains societies, boiled dog meat was often served at social gatherings and feasts, in special ceremonies, and as a food for honored guests (e.g., Gilmore 1934; Powers and Powers 1990; Schwartz 1997; Snyder 1991). Thus, what we may be seeing at Henderson is an increase in the importance of dogs in communal feasting and ceremony occurring hand-in-hand with an increase in the use of boiling or stewing to prepare these animals for consumption. Why such a change in cooking technique occurred is unfortunately not obvious, and remains an interesting but unresolved question.

Somewhat unexpectedly, the average utility (MGUI, limbs only) of the canid assemblage decreases significantly in the Late phase. Elsewhere in this volume, a decline in general utility has been seen as evidence for decreasing average transport distance (e.g., Chapters 4, 5, and 6). In the case of the dogs, however, where selective culling for transport presumably is not an issue, we have to seek another explanation. Some process *operating within the village* either increased the representation of low-utility parts in the Late phase or decreased the representation of high-utility parts (or some combination of the two). As the following comments attempt to show, the former scenario seems the most likely. If boiling became more important in the Late phase as a means of cooking dogs, the amount of edible tissue remaining in the bones at the time of discard very likely would have decreased (Speth 2000; Lupo 1995; see Kent 1993 for a different perspective). This should have favored the preservation, not the demise, of high-utility parts. Thus, an alternative explanation would involve some factor that increased the survivorship of low-utility parts, such as the head and feet. Again, the ethnographic and ethnohistoric literature provides a possible answer. Heads and feet of dogs were often cut off and discarded before the animals were cooked and, therefore, might well have been consumed by other village dogs. As more and more animals were boiled rather than roasted, the feet and heads might well have been included in the stew, and their survivorship, once defleshed and degreased by boiling, would have been substantially enhanced.

If this scenario is correct, we might expect there to be a *positive* correlation between grease utility and skeletal element frequency in the Early phase, when most of the low-utility parts were simply cut off, discarded, and destroyed by scavenging village dogs; and a weaker correlation, or no correlation at all, in the Late phase, when most bones, regardless of grease utility, were boiled, leaving the entire suite of elements with little remaining nutritional value at the time of discard (Lupo 1995). This is precisely what we find. Using Binford's (1978) grease utility index, in the Early phase $r_s = 0.43$ ($p < .05$), whereas in the Late phase $r_s = 0.05$ ($p > .05$). Similar results are obtained using Brink and Dawe's (1989) grease index—in the Early phase $r_s = 0.55$ ($p = .05$), whereas in the Late phase $r_s = 0.25$ ($p > .05$). Although these results are supportive, we must nonetheless view the interpretation offered here with caution, since other explanations might well lead to similar correlations.

Conclusions/Synopsis

While dogs were consumed on occasion throughout the prehistoric Southwest, their use as a food is generally seen as a short-term response to stress, a sign that normal or proper foods were not available in sufficient quantity (e.g., Mick-O'Hara 1994; Olsen 1990:115). While dogs were also used among Plains groups as a backup resource, what is most striking in traditional Plains societies is the role of dogs as a valued food for special occasions, ranging from greeting honored guests to community-wide feasts and ceremonies (Powers and Powers 1990; Snyder 1991). Henderson's use of dogs as a communal resource, particularly in the Late phase, appears to fall in with the Plains pattern. This is perhaps most clearly indicated by the concentration of dog remains in and around the huge earth oven complex in the East Plaza, the most public facility in the village.

In fact, the use of dogs as a communal resource is one of Henderson's most "Plains-like" features, one that intensified during the Late phase hand-in-hand with a growing focus on long-range bison hunting and interregional exchange (see Chapter 4). If one were to look at the community's artifactual record—at its ceramics, its groundstone, its stone tools—one would see only links to the Puebloan world. Almost none of the classic Plains artifact forms or raw materials are represented there—tools made on Alibates or Edwards Plateau chert, thumbnail endscrapers, bison tibia digging sticks, scapula hoes, beveled knives, bison rib rasps, cordmarked pottery (Kelley 1984). So one might be tempted to conclude that the Henderson people were migrants from the Puebloan heartland who, for climate-related or other reasons, struck out eastward into the grasslands to replicate their Pueblo world in an alien landscape, only to fail after a century or so and retreat back to their traditional homeland to the west. However, their skeletal biology, reported in detail over a decade ago by Rocek and Speth (1986), revealed that the Henderson folk were not merely transplanted Puebloan peoples, but in many respects displayed features that underscored their biological distinctiveness. Their communal use of dogs now stands as a cultural manifestation of this same distinctiveness, showing a pattern of behavior that one would not expect among traditional Puebloan peoples. In short, while the Henderson folk adopted a material inventory that was essentially Puebloan, many facets of their biology and their behavior set them clearly apart from their neighbors to the west.

Note

1. t_s = test of equality of two percentages based on arcsine transformation (Sokal and Rohlf 1969:607-10).

References Cited

Allen, G. M.
1920 Dogs of the American Aborigines. Harvard College, Museum of Comparative Zoology. *Bulletin* 63(9):431-517.

Benecke, N.
1987 Studies on Early Dog Remains from Northern Europe. *Journal of Archaeological Science* 14(1):31-49.

Binford, L. R.
1978 *Nunamiut Ethnoarchaeology*. New York: Academic Press.

Brink, J. W., and B. Dawe
1989 *Final Report of the 1985 and 1986 Field Seasons at Head-Smashed-In Buffalo Jump, Alberta*. Manuscript Series 16. Edmonton, Alberta: Archaeological Survey of Alberta.

Clutton-Brock, J., and N. Hammond
1994 Hot Dogs: Comestible Canids in Preclassic Maya Culture at Cuello, Belize. *Journal of Archaeological Science* 21(6):819-26.

Colton, H. S.
1970 The Aboriginal Southwestern Indian Dog. *American Antiquity* 35(2):153-59.

Crockford, S. J. (editor)
2000 *Dogs through Time: An Archaeological Perspective.* Proceedings of the 1st ICAZ Symposium on the History of the Domestic Dog (Eighth Congress of the International Council for Archaeozoology, August 23-29, 1998, Victoria, B.C. , Canada). BAR International Series 889. Oxford, England: British Archaeological Reports, Archaeopress.

Gilmore, M. R.
1934 The Arikara Method of Preparing a Dog for a Feast. *Papers of the Michigan Academy of Science, Arts and Letters* 19:37-38.

Haag, W. G.
1948 An Osteometric Analysis of Some Aboriginal Dogs. University of Kentucky, Department of Anthropology. *Reports in Anthropology* 7(3):107-264.

Hamblin, N. L.
1984 *Animal Use by the Cozumel Maya*. Tucson, AZ: University of Arizona Press.

Horard-Herbin, M.-P.
2000 Dog Management and Use in the Late Iron Age: The Evidence from the Gallic Site of Levroux (France). In: *Dogs through Time: An Archaeological Perspective.* Proceedings of the 1st ICAZ Symposium on the History of the Domestic Dog (Eighth Congress of the International Council for Archaeozoology, August 23-29, 1998, Victoria, B.C., Canada), edited by S. J. Crockford, pp. 115-21. BAR International Series 889. Oxford, England: British Archaeological Reports, Archaeopress.

Kelley, J. H.
1984 *The Archaeology of the Sierra Blanca Region of Southeastern New Mexico.* Anthropological Paper 74. Ann Arbor, MI: Museum of Anthropology, University of Michigan.

Kent, S.
1993 Variability in Faunal Assemblages: The Influence of Hunting Skill, Sharing, Dogs, and Mode of Cooking on Faunal Remains at a Sedentary Kalahari Community. *Journal of Anthropological Archaeology* 12(4):323-85.

Lupo, K. D.
1995 Hadza Bone Assemblages and Hyena Attrition: An Ethnographic Example of the Influence of Cooking and Mode of Discard on the Intensity of Scavenger Ravaging. *Journal of Anthropological Archaeology* 14(3):288-314.

Mick-O'Hara, L. S.
1994 *Nutritional Stability and Changing Faunal Resource Use in La Plata Valley Prehistory.* Ph.D. dissertation, University of New Mexico, Albuquerque, NM.

Olsen, J. W.
1990 *Vertebrate Faunal Remains from Grasshopper Pueblo, Arizona.* Anthropological Paper 83. Ann Arbor, MI: Museum of Anthropology, University of Michigan.

Olsen, S. J.
1976 The Dogs of Awatovi. *American Antiquity* 41(1):102-6.

Parmalee, P. W.
1965 The Food Economy of Archaic and Woodland Peoples at the Tick Creek Cave Site, Missouri. *Missouri Archaeologist* 27(2):1-34.

Powers, W. K., and M. N. Powers
1990 *Sacred Foods of the Lakota.* Kendall Park, NJ: Lakota Books.

Rocek, T. R., and J. D. Speth
1986 *The Henderson Site Burials: Glimpses of a Late Prehistoric Population in the Pecos Valley.* Technical Report 18. Ann Arbor: Museum of Anthropology, University of Michigan.

Schwartz, M.
1997 *A History of Dogs in the Early Americas.* New Haven, CT: Yale University Press.

Snyder, L. M.
1991 Barking Mutton: Ethnohistoric and Ethnographic, Archaeological, and Nutritional Evidence Pertaining to the Dog as a Native American Food Resource on the Plains. In: *Beamers, Bobwhites, and Blue-Points: Tributes to the Career of Paul W. Parmalee*, edited by J. R. Purdue, W. E. Klippel, and B. W. Styles, pp. 359-78. Illinois State Museum, Scientific Papers 23 and University of Tennessee, Department of Anthropology, Report of Investigations 52. Springfield, IL: Illinois State Museum.

Sokal, R. R., and F. J. Rohlf
1969 *Biometry: The Principles and Practice of Statistics in Biological Research.* San Francisco, CA: W. H. Freeman.

Speth, J. D.
2000 Boiling vs. Baking and Roasting: A Taphonomic Approach to the Recognition of Cooking Techniques in Small Mammals. In: *Animal Bones, Human Societies*, edited by P. A. Rowley-Conwy, pp. 89-105. Oxford, England: Oxbow Books.

Wing, E. S.
1978 Use of Dogs for Food: An Adaptation to the Coastal Environment. In: *Prehistoric Coastal Adaptations: The Economy and Ecology of Maritime Middle America*, edited by B. L. Stark and B. Voorhies, pp. 29-41. New York: Academic Press.

8
Rabbit Hunting by Farmers at the Henderson Site

Yun Kuen Lee
Harvard University

John D. Speth
University of Michigan

Introduction

Lagomorphs are among the most frequently recovered faunal remains in late prehistoric villages throughout the American Southwest, commonly outnumbering medium and large ungulates and often even rodents (see discussion in Flint and Neusius 1987; Szuter 1991). The many accounts of rabbit hunting in the ethnographic and ethnohistoric literature amply attest to their continuing importance into the historic period to Native Americans throughout the desert West and Southwest (see references in Szuter 1991:260-62; see also Beaglehole 1936; Buskirk 1986; Hill 1938; Lange 1968; Spier 1928, 1933; Steward 1938; Weber and Seaman 1985). Given their abundance in the archaeological record, and their documented importance in the "ethnographic present," it is not surprising that Southwestern faunal analysts have devoted considerable effort to their analysis and interpretation.

Lagomorph remains have often been studied as a means of gaining insight into past environmental conditions and to monitor changes in these conditions over time and space. Both the presence of species of rabbit and jackrabbit as well various ratios of cottontails and jackrabbits have been used to evaluate terrain and vegetation around a prehistoric site (e.g., Bayham and Hatch 1985a, 1985b; Flint and Neusius 1987; Shaffer 1991; Szuter 1991). In many early faunal studies, changes in the composition of the lagomorph assemblage over time were assumed to reflect vegetational changes brought about by fluctuations in precipitation (e.g., Harris 1963).

In a manner that is reminiscent of the history of the classic "*Dama-Gazella*" debate in the Near East (Bate 1937; Hooijer 1961; Davis 1977; Garrard 1982), more recent work with lagomorphs has increasingly focused on the complex interplay of factors in addition to paleoenvironment or paleoclimate that affect the composition of an archaeological lagomorph assemblage. These include the habitat preferences and behavior of the prey; the social and economic organization of the human community exploiting the prey; the technology and seasonal timing of procurement; the function and location of the settlement from which the hunting is being undertaken; the community's food, ritual, and other needs; the impact of cultivation, wood-cutting for construction and fuel, and other human activities on the local vegetation; and a variety of taphonomic and sampling factors (e.g., Akins 1985; Bayham and Hatch 1985a, 1985b; Bertram and Draper 1982; Binford et al. 1982; Cordell 1977; Driver 1985, 1991; Emslie 1977; Flannery 1966; Gillespie 1987, 1989; Lang and Harris 1984; Olsen 1990; Pippin 1987; Rohn 1971; Shaffer 1991, 1992; Speth and Scott 1989; Szuter 1991; Thomas 1969). Insights can be gained from the detailed analysis of lagomorph remains which, when combined with information from other classes of archaeological and paleoecological data, hold great promise for clarifying the nature and dynamics of past human adaptations.

Here we wish to provide a detailed record of the Henderson lagomorph assemblage that can be used by other researchers in comparative studies of hunting by prehistoric peoples in southeastern New Mexico and elsewhere in the Southwest, and to explore the lagomorph data for insights about the subsistence practices of the Henderson villagers themselves.

The 1980-1981 Henderson Lagomorph Assemblage

Two seasons of excavation at the Henderson Site (1980-1981) yielded a total of 5,804 lagomorph bones (NISP). Of these, 1,829 specimens (31.5%) are from jackrabbits (*Lepus* sp.) and 3,975 specimens (68.5%), are from cottontail rabbits (*Sylvilagus* sp.). Appendix tables A8.1 through A8.12 at the end of the chapter summarize the basic descriptive data for the lagomorph material from all major excavation units at the site. Data for jackrabbits and cottontails are tabulated in separate tables. The following data are included in these tables: number of identifiable specimens (NISP), minimum number of elements (MNE), and minimum number of individuals (MNI). Percentage values are also given. The first columns in the tables provide tabulations for mature and immature specimens together; subsequent columns give values for immature specimens alone (i.e., unfused and fusing limb elements). The last two columns provide information on the number and percentage of burned specimens (NISP). (The total number, or NISP, of lagomorph bones actually recovered at Henderson in 1980-1981 was 5,485. However, because the appendix tables provide tallies for the proximal and distal ends of the major limb elements separately, complete limb bones were counted twice, increasing the total NISP value to 5,804.)

The derivations of the values for "total skull" and "total mandible" in Tables A8.1-A8.12 need explanation. The NISP value for "total skull" is the sum of the individual values for the following portions of the skull: frontal, squamous-temporal, temporal-parietal, temporal-frontal, nasal, premaxilla, maxilla, maxilla-premaxilla, and complete skull. The MNE for "total skull" is the sum of the values for just maxilla, maxilla-premaxilla, and complete skull. Finally, the MNI for "total skull" is the sum of the MNI values for maxilla, premaxilla, and complete skull. The NISP for "total mandible" is the sum of the values for complete mandible, mandibular body, mandibular symphysis, mandibular border, and mandibular ramus. The MNE and MNI values for "total mandible" are the sum of the respective values for complete mandible and mandibular body.

The %MNI values in Tables A8.1-A8.12 are the proportion of the MNI value for a given element relative to the maximum MNI value for the total sample. For instance, the highest MNI value for jackrabbits at Henderson is given by the scapula (55), indicating that at least 55 animals are represented. Since there are only 39 individuals represented by jackrabbit skulls, the %MNI value for skulls is 70.9%.

The lagomorph materials from trenches G, H, and I are not tabulated in the Appendix because these units yielded very small numbers of bones. Trench G yielded 1 mandibular body, 1 proximal tibia, and 1 distal tibia of *Sylvilagus*. Only 1 *Sylvilagus* distal tibia was recovered from trench H. Trench I yielded a total of 13 lagomorph bones. These include 5 specimens of *Lepus:* 1 mandibular body, 1 scapula, 1 innominate, 1 astragalus, and 1 proximal second metatarsal. The remaining 8 specimens are bones of *Sylvilagus*: 2 mandibular bodies, 2 mandibular symphyses, 1 distal humerus, and 1 distal tibia. No *Lepus* bones were found in trenches G and H. One *Sylvilagus* individual (MNI) is represented by the remains in trench G, trench H, and trench I, and 1 *Lepus* individual (MNI) is represented by the bones in trench I.

In the total Henderson sample (all 1980-1981 proveniences combined), there are a minimum (MNI) of 55 jackrabbits and 128 cottontails (see Tables A8.1 and A8.2). Among the jackrabbits, at least 12 individuals (21.8%) are immature, based on the number of fusing or unfused limb elements. Among the cottontails, a minimum of 30 individuals (23.4%) are immature. Only 2.6% of the jackrabbit bones and 1.9% of the cottontail bones are burned.

The Henderson lagomorph assemblage appears to be composed of only two species: *Lepus californicus*, the black-tailed jackrabbit; and *Sylvilagus* sp., probably *S. audubonii*, the desert cottontail. Taxonomic identification of the jackrabbit remains is straightforward since only one species, *L. californicus*, occurs in southeastern New Mexico today (Findley et al. 1975; Bailey 1931). Taxonomic assignment of the cottontail remains is more complex. While only one species of rabbit, *S. audubonii*, occurs today in the Pecos Valley lowlands, the eastern cottontail, *S. floridanus*, has been reported in the Sacramento-Capitan mountain area less than 130 km west of Henderson (Findley et al. 1975), and it is widespread in the Texas Panhandle to the east of Henderson where its range overlaps that of the desert cottontail (Davis 1974; Hall 1981). While it is unlikely that small-bodied prey like rabbits were routinely transported to the village over such great distances (e.g., Speth and Scott 1989), it is conceivable that the range of the eastern cottontail encompassed more of southeastern New Mexico in the past (e.g., Hulbert 1984). Fortunately, using osteological criteria developed by Findley et al. (1975; see also Hoffmeister 1986:130; Flint and Neusius 1987; Neusius and Flint 1985), it is possible to establish empirically whether or not more than one species of cottontail is represented in the lagomorph assemblage at Henderson.

According to Findley et al. (1975:84-85), the depth of the lower jaw (measured at P_4) relative to the alveolar length of the cheek-tooth row (P_3–M_3) will separate *S. audubonii* from *S. floridanus* (and *S. nuttallii*, an upland cottontail species found today in northern New Mexico). Alveolar length is the distance between the anterior margin of the third premolar to the posterior margin of the third molar. Mandibular depth is the distance between the anterior border or alveolar notch of the fourth premolar and the ventral border of the mandible measured at right angles to the tooth row.

Measurements were made on 157 *Sylvilagus* mandibles (both left and right) from Henderson and the results are shown in Figure 8.1. An approximation of Findley et al.'s (1975:85) line

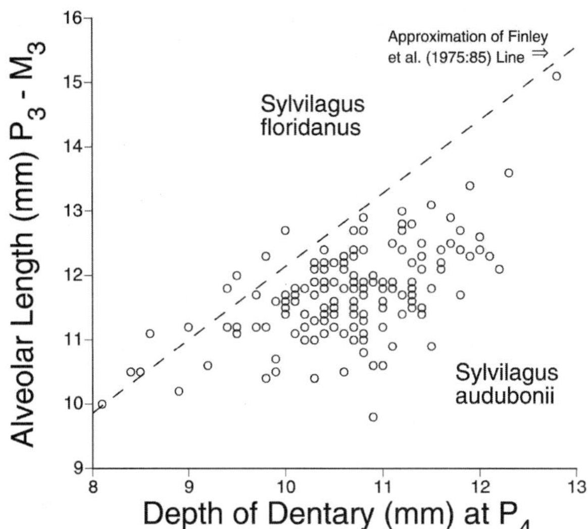

Figure 8.1. Bivariate plot of Henderson *Sylvilagus* mandible measurements (depth of dentary at P_4 vs. alveolar cheek-tooth row length P_3-M_3). Line (approximated from Findley et al. 1975:85) separates *S. audubonii* (below) from *S. floridanus* and *S. nuttallii* (above).

separating *S. audubonii* from *S. floridanus* and *S. nuttallii* is shown in the figure.[1] Mandibles falling below the line derive from *S. audubonii*; those falling above the line derive from the other two species of cottontail. All but nine of the Henderson specimens fall squarely below the line. These results indicate, not surprisingly, that most, if not all, of the Henderson rabbit remains are from the desert cottontail, *S. audubonii*. Thus, rabbits do not appear to have been transported back to Henderson from hunting treks in the uplands or out onto the High Plains of Texas, nor were they regularly obtained through trade with upland groups. The results also provide no evidence that the range of the eastern cottontail had expanded to include the Pecos Valley around Roswell during the thirteenth and fourteenth centuries.

The taxonomic identification of the postcranial elements deserves additional comment. In most cases, if a small-mammal bone could be identified to element, it was possible to determine whether the specimen was from a lagomorph or a rodent. Moreover, the lagomorph remains were easily separated into jackrabbit and cottontail on the basis of size. The principal lagomorph elements that have not been identified or tabulated are the ribs, phalanges, the smaller carpals and tarsals, and loose teeth. In addition, some of the more easily identifiable complete or nearly complete vertebrae have been tabulated, but numerous fragmentary specimens have not been recorded. Ribs are common in the collection and most probably derive from lagomorphs rather than rodents, since the latter are rare even in the flotation samples. Nevertheless, because rodent and lagomorph ribs cannot be distinguished reliably from each other, they have not been tabulated. Not surprisingly, very few phalanges or smaller carpals and tarsals were recovered in the screens or in the flotation samples, and no attempt has been made in the present study to identify and tabulate these either. Finally, while loose teeth of jackrabbits and cottontails are numerous, and identifiable, most of them became dislodged from their mandibles or maxillae during excavation or later while in storage; hence, these too have been omitted from the analysis.

Recovery Biases

Examination of the methods used to collect faunal remains is an essential first step in analyzing the composition of an assemblage (Shipman 1981). Assessing the nature and degree of recovery bias is particularly critical when dealing with the bones of very small-bodied mammals such as rodents, many of which will pass easily through the quarter-inch mesh screens used at Henderson (Thomas 1969; Shaffer 1992). Even when dealing with the bones of larger-bodied taxa such as lagomorphs, recovery biases must still be assessed, since bones of these animals, especially fragmentary ones, may also pass undetected through the screens. Such screening losses may affect not only the total recovery of lagomorph bones but also the ratio of cottontails to jackrabbits, because the bones of cottontails are much smaller. Thus, before we can explore the role of lagomorphs in the diet and subsistence strategies of the Henderson villagers, we must first show that the frequency of lagomorph remains, and particularly the ratio of cottontails to jackrabbits, is not merely an artifact of the screening methods that were used at the site.

First, we must digress briefly to describe the actual recovery procedures that were used at the site. All sediment not expressly saved for flotation, regardless of provenience, was passed through quarter-inch mesh screens suspended from tripods. The crew members were instructed to retrieve everything of an archaeological nature from the screens, regardless of size. Tiny or fragile items, including fragmentary bones, were put in plastic vials before being placed together with sherds, lithics, and other artifacts in paper bags. Items that were seen falling through the screen were retrieved. The sediments at Henderson generally were dry, loose, and passed quickly and easily through the screens. While there was a fair amount of pea-sized gravel in many of the excavation units, there were few rocks to contribute to fragmentation of small bones during the screening process. The obvious exception was in the East Plaza, where the deposits contained masses of fire-cracked rock. However, these rocks were generally hand-picked from the sediment before the fill was screened. Most of the flotation samples were processed in Michigan using a large washbasin lined on the bottom with mosquito netting supported from beneath by window screen. No lagomorph bones in the coarse fraction could pass through this mesh. After thorough drying, the coarse fraction was hand picked and all items of an archaeological nature, including tiny microfauna, were collected.

Table 8.1. Frequency (NISP and MNI) of *Lepus* and *Sylvilagus* remains by provenience in screened samples and flotation samples at Henderson Site.

Provenience	NISP				MNI			
	Jackrabbit (*Lepus*)	Cottontail (*Sylvi.*)	Total Lago.	% *Sylvi.* (Lago. Index)[a]	Jackrabbit (*Lepus*)	Cottontail (*Sylvi.*)	Total Lago.	% *Sylvi.* (Lago. Index)[a]
Screened Samples								
East Bar	529	1609	2138	0.75	16	59	75	0.79
Center Bar	553	1208	1761	0.69	20	50	70	0.71
Combined rooms	1082	2817	3899	0.72	36	109	145	0.75
Room C-5 only	358	649	1007	0.64	12	31	43	0.72
East Plaza[b]	534	834	1368	0.61	17	32	49	0.65
Entire site	1829	3975	5804	0.68	55	128	183	—
Flotation Samples[b]								
East Bar (0.43 m^3)	3	24	27	0.89	—	—	—	—
Center Bar (0.46 m^3)	16	42	58	0.72	—	—	—	—
Comb. rooms (0.89 m^3)	18	66	84	0.79	—	—	—	—
Room C-5 only (0.37 m^3)	14	31	45	0.69	—	—	—	—
East Plaza (0.23 m^3)	9	20	29	0.69	—	—	—	—
Entire site (1.17 m^3)	28	90	118	0.76	—	—	—	—

[a]See Szuter (1991:174-175) for discussion of lagomorph index.
[b]Volume of sediment processed by flotation in each provenience given in parentheses; total volume for "entire site" includes 0.05 m^3 of sediment processed by flotation from miscellaneous proveniences not listed in table.

Thus, while lagomorph remains caught in the screens were systematically collected, the question remains whether substantial numbers of bones, especially from cottontails, passed undetected through the quarter-inch mesh. One feature of the Henderson lagomorph assemblage that already argues against severe loss of smaller remains is the fact that cottontail bones outnumber jackrabbit bones by a ratio of over 2:1. If lagomorph bones were passing through the screens in large numbers, one might expect the smaller cottontail elements to be much less well represented.

Szuter (1991:49-55) examined the same issue, looking at the effect of different mesh sizes and screening practices on the recovery of lagomorph remains at sites in southern Arizona excavated and reported since 1970. Her conclusion was that with quarter-inch screening lagomorph remains were consistently and reliably recovered. Moreover, she also found that with the use of quarter-inch screens the bones of cottontails, despite their smaller size, were recovered about as consistently as those of jackrabbits.

Shaffer (1992) also explored the issue of screening bias, conducting a controlled experiment in which he repeatedly passed the bones (all unbroken) from disarticulated comparative skeletons of various rodents and lagomorphs (*S. audubonii* and *L. californicus*) through a quarter-inch screen. In this experiment he was able to determine for each element in the skeleton the likelihood that it would pass through the screen. Not unexpectedly, in the lagomorphs many of the elements which passed easily through the screen are those which archaeologists seldom tabulate, such as tiny carpals, tarsals, phalanges, ribs, sesamoids, patellae, and caudal vertebrae. Most other elements, with a few notable exceptions, were caught on the screens more than 70% of the time (precise figures are not given). The important elements that were recovered less than 70% of the time in Shaffer's experiments included the metacarpals and metatarsals (both species), pelvis (both species), and tibia (both species). That the unbroken metatarsals, pelvis, and tibia were recovered less than 70% of the time is a surprising result, even for the small-bodied cottontail, because these elements are relatively long and would probably only pass through the screen if they were tilted into an upright position. This of course may happen when the screen is shaken to force the sediment through but, as we will see shortly, the Henderson lagomorph data suggest that these elements were recovered consistently. The loss of cottontail metacarpals is not surprising, as these elements are very small. In sum, Shaffer's experiment shows that the rate of recovery for most elements, cranial and postcranial, is high in both lagomorph taxa. This encouraging result is very similar to the conclusion drawn by Szuter (1991).

Turning now to the Henderson data, one way of assessing the nature and extent of recovery biases is to compare the composition of the screening assemblage with that of the flotation assemblage. During the 1980-1981 seasons of excavation at Henderson, a total of 303 (average 3.88 liters) flotation samples, totaling 1.17 m^3 of sediment, were processed. Samples were taken from most levels in most grid squares, as well as from major cultural features, midden deposits, floor contacts, and ash lenses. Features and midden deposits, however, were preferentially sampled for flotation analysis, a bias that must be kept in mind when comparing the float remains to those from the screens. The flotation samples yielded a total (NISP) of 118 lagomorph bones. Of these, 28 (23.7%) were *Lepus* and 90 (76.3%) were *Sylvilagus*.[2] In the site-wide assemblage (which

Table 8.2. Proportion (%MNI) of major skeletal elements of *Lepus* and *Sylvilagus* in site-wide lagomorph assemblage at Henderson.

Skeletal Element	Jackrabbit (*Lepus*)		Cottontail (*Sylvilagus*)	
	MNI	%MNI	MNI	%MNI
Skull	39	70.9	100	78.1
Mandible	33	60.0	125	97.7
Atlas	4	7.3	3	2.3
Axis	3	5.5	3	2.3
Cervical	1	1.8	1	0.8
Thoracic	1	1.8	1	0.8
Lumbar	5	9.1	11	8.6
Scapula	55	100.0	128	100.0
Dist. humerus	54	98.2	111	86.7
Prox. radius	43	78.2	61	47.7
Metacarpal	17	30.9[b]	6	4.7[d]
Pelvis	24	43.6	107	83.6
Dist. femur	32	58.2	69	53.9
Tibia[a]	26	47.3	118	92.2
Calcaneus	23	41.8	93	72.7
Metatarsal	20	36.4[c]	58	45.3[e]

[a]Prox. tibia in *Lepus*; dist. tibia in *Sylvilagus*.
[b]Proximal mc. 4.
[c]Proximal mt. 2 and mt. 3.
[d]Proximal mc. 3.
[e]Proximal mt. 2.

includes both screening and flotation), 1,829 (31.5%) were *Lepus* and 3,975 (68.5%) were *Sylvilagus*. As expected, cottontails are somewhat better represented than jackrabbits in the flotation samples, perhaps indicating that some cottontail remains were lost in screening, but the difference is small and not statistically significant (test of equality of two percentages with arcsine transformation: $t_s = 1.88$, $p > .05$; Sokal and Rohlf 1969:607-10).

A more reliable way to assess the nature and degree of recovery losses is to compare flotation and screening samples from the same proveniences. These comparisons are presented in Table 8.1. The table lists the proportions of jackrabbits and cottontails for each major provenience unit at the site (i.e., East Bar, Center Bar, combined room blocks, and East Plaza), first for the screened assemblage and then for the flotation samples. The proportions in the screened materials are calculated using both NISP and MNI values. Only NISP values are used in the calculations for the flotation remains because the sample sizes are much too small to warrant the use of MNI values. Even the proportions based on NISP values for the flotation remains must be viewed with caution since the numbers are very small.

Table 8.1 shows that for each provenience the proportion of cottontails in the flotation samples, as expected, is somewhat higher than in the screened materials, pointing to the probable loss of bones of the smaller lagomorph. However, with the exception of the East Bar, the differences are very small, with values in the flotation samples ranging between only 3% and 8% above those in the screened samples. None of these provenience-by-provenience comparisons (including the East Bar) between flotation and screened samples is statistically significant (in all cases, $p > .05$; test of equality of two percentages based on the arcsine transformation; Sokal and Rohlf 1969:607-10). Thus, while screening biases are evident in the Henderson lagomorph assemblage, they appear to be minor.

The reason for the somewhat higher value in the East Bar flotation sample is unclear. It is hard to imagine that screening losses were more severe only in this one provenience, since the procedures for screening were the same everywhere, and the personnel doing the screening for the most part were also the same (crew members were periodically rotated among proveniences in order to gain experience in all parts of the site). Since the East Bar flotation sample is also the smallest one, with a total NISP of only 27 lagomorph bones (and only 3 jackrabbit bones), the somewhat higher cottontail percentage is probably an artifact of sample size rather than a reflection of screening biases (and as noted above the difference is not statistically significant).

Table 8.1 reveals the small magnitude of screening biases in another way. For the screened assemblage, the proportions of cottontails based on MNI values are always slightly higher than their proportions based on NISP values. Since the MNI values are derived from the most common skeletal element (generally the scapula, a large element that is unlikely to pass through the screens), whereas the NISP values include small elements that are much more likely to pass undetected through the screens, severe losses should lead to major differences between the percentages calculated using MNI values and those calculated using NISP values. Table 8.1 clearly shows this not to be the case.

Table 8.3. Density (NISP/m^3) of lagomorph bones by major provenience at Henderson Site.[a]

Taxon		Provenience: East Bar (All Rooms) (34.85 m^3)	Center Bar (Excluding Room C-5) (16.99 m^3)	Comb. Rooms (Excluding Room C-5) (51.90 m^3)	Room C-5 Only (8.77 m^3)	East Plaza (Tr. B, C) (12.73 m^3)	Flotation Samples (1.17 m^3)
Total Lagomorph	NISP	61.35	57.68	60.08	114.82	107.46	100.85
	MNE	52.63	42.55	49.27	86.20	77.69	73.51
	MNI	2.15	2.12	2.14	5.99	4.56	4.27
Lepus	NISP	15.18	15.60	15.30	40.82	41.95	23.93
	MNE	12.80	12.12	12.56	30.22	28.99	17.95
	MNI	0.46	0.59	0.50	1.82	1.89	0.85
Sylvilagus	NISP	46.17	42.08	44.78	74.00	65.51	76.92
	MNI	39.83	30.43	36.71	55.99	48.70	55.56
	MNI	1.69	1.53	1.64	4.16	2.67	3.42

[a]Volume of excavated sediment for tabulated proveniences given in parentheses.

Another way to assess the extent of screening biases in the lagomorph assemblage is to compare the proportional representation of various cottontail skeletal elements (%MNI) with the %MNI values of jackrabbit elements (Table 8.2). If screening biases were severe at Henderson, we would expect to see the lowest %MNI values in the smaller cottontail elements. In other words, if smaller elements of cottontails had been lost through screening at a greater rate than their larger counterparts in jackrabbits, observed element frequencies in cottontails should deviate more than jackrabbits from their expected frequencies (have lower %MNI values). This is generally not the case. With the obvious exception of the tiny cottontail metacarpal and radius, most other elements do not pattern in a way that would suggest biases from screening. Quite the contrary, the %MNI values for the mandible, tibia, pelvis, metatarsal, and even the tiny calcaneus are higher in the cottontail than in the jackrabbit and the values for other important elements, such as the scapula, femur, and humerus, are very similar. Among the limb elements, only the radius and metacarpal, both small, linear, and delicate bones, are significantly underrepresented in the cottontail. The overall similarity between the two species of lagomorph in the proportional representation of skeletal elements is underscored by the significant correlation between the %MNI values given in Table 8.2 (Spearman's r, $n = 16$, $r_s = .87$, $p < .01$).

The vertebrae deserve comment. It is clear from Table 8.2 that vertebrae of both species are very rare at Henderson. In contrast, Shaffer (1992) found in his screening experiments that all of the cottontail and jackrabbit vertebrae, except caudals, were recovered in the screens more than 70% of the time. However, Shaffer used only complete elements in his experiments, whereas most of the vertebrae that were recovered at Henderson were damaged or fragmentary, missing portions of their dorsal and transverse processes. More extensively broken vertebrae might well have passed undetected through the quarter-inch screens. Vertebrae, therefore, should be added to the list of elements that are probably underrepresented at the site due at least in part to recovery biases. Their underrepresentation also reflects the fact that many vertebral fragments could not be identified to taxon with confidence.

Another interesting way to examine the Henderson lagomorph assemblage for screening biases is to compare the density of lagomorphs in the flotation samples with the density of rabbits and jackrabbits recovered by screening. If lagomorphs were being lost in large numbers through screening, the density of remains in the flotation samples should be much greater than in samples that were collected from the screens. The density of total lagomorph remains in the flotation samples is approximately 101 specimens per m^3 (118 bones from a total flotation volume of 1.17 m^3). The density for the site-wide assemblage is considerably lower, about 73 specimens per m^3 (5,804 specimens from a total excavated volume of 79.56 m^3).

While this result might at first appear to be clear evidence that significant numbers of lagomorph remains have been lost in screening, a closer look at the strategy used at Henderson for selecting flotation samples suggests that the comparison may be misleading. As noted earlier, flotation samples, particularly large ones, were taken preferentially from deposits with a high potential for producing subsistence remains. Not surprisingly, therefore, many of the flotation samples were collected from midden deposits. Material collected from the screens, on the other hand, came from all proveniences and contexts—e.g., undifferentiated room fill, burial pits—many of which were virtually devoid of animal bones. Thus, it is not surprising that bone density is higher in the flotation samples. A more reasonable comparison, therefore, is between the density of lagomorphs recovered by flotation and the density of remains in screened assemblages that were obtained specifically from those areas of the site that were dominated by midden deposits—the East Plaza earth oven complex and Center Bar Room C-5. Screening in the East Plaza (trenches B and C) yielded 1,368 lagomorph bones for an overall density of about 107 specimens per

Table 8.4. Density (NISP/m³) of *Sylvilagus* skeletal elements in flotation samples, East Plaza, and Room C-5 at Henderson Site (1980-1981 only).[a]

Skeletal Element	Flotation (Vol. = 1.17 m³)		East Plaza[b] (Vol. = 11.90 m³)		Room C-5 (Vol. = 8.77 m³)	
	NISP	Density	NISP	Density	NISP	Density
Cranial	18	15.4	163	13.7	152	17.3
Mand. only	5	4.3	90	7.1	81	9.2
Scapula	6	5.1	66	5.2	71	8.1
Humerus	8	6.8	49	3.9	37	4.2
Radius	1	0.9	31	2.4	35	4.0
Ulna	3	2.6	33	2.6	37	4.2
Metacarpal	0	—	3	0.2	4	0.5
Pelvis	7	6.0	124	9.7	64	7.3
Femur	6	5.1	70	5.5	44	5.0
Tibia	11	9.4	103	8.1	74	8.4
Metatarsal	10	8.6	64	5.0	58	6.6

[a]Volume of sediment for combined flotation samples (n = 303) and tabulated proveniences given in parentheses.
[b]Trench C only.

m³; Room C-5 produced 1,007 lagomorph bones for a density of 115 specimens per m³. These results, shown in Table 8.3, again show that screening biases have not seriously affected the recovery of lagomorph remains.

However, since we are particularly concerned with assessing the extent of recovery biases against the smaller species, it is perhaps more informative to compare the density figures for just *Sylvilagus* rather than for total lagomorphs. The density of cottontail bones (NISP/m³) in the flotation samples is 76.9 specimens per m³. Their density in Room C-5 (74.0 bones per m³) is only slightly lower, whereas in the East Plaza their density (65.5 bones per m³) is noticeably lower (Table 8.3). While it is tempting to attribute the lower value in the East Plaza to screening biases, the fact that this provenience and Room C-5 were screened in exactly the same way suggests that factors other than recovery losses, perhaps taphonomic, perhaps cultural, may have contributed to the lower cottontail density in the East Plaza deposits. This suggestion gains plausibility when it is remembered that the density of total lagomorph remains in the East Plaza was entirely comparable to the density observed in the flotation samples.

If we repeat the same comparisons, this time looking at the density values for individual elements, it becomes clear that biases are present in only a few elements and that the differences are relatively minor (Table 8.4). The element-by-element density values shown in Table 8.4 for the flotation, East Plaza, and Room C-5 assemblages are all significantly and positively correlated, despite the small sample sizes (Spearman's r, n = 11: flotation and East Plaza, $r_s = .72, p < .05$; flotation and Room C-5, $r_s = .67$, $p < .05$; East Plaza and Room C-5, $r_s = .90$, $p < .01$). It must be kept in mind, of course, that these element-by-element comparisons are handicapped by the small sample sizes recovered by flotation. Interestingly, some of the elements which are poorly represented in the screened samples, such as the radius, ulna, and metacarpals, are also rare in the flotation samples. Their absence, therefore, may not be due to screening biases after all. It seems reasonable to conclude that while some cottontail bones have been lost through screening, the extent of loss has not been great across most elements.

In sum, there is very little evidence that screening bias has altered the composition of the jackrabbit assemblage. Given the large size of most *Lepus* elements, this result is not surprising. For cottontails, we cannot be quite as certain, but the results of several different analyses point toward the same general conclusion. While screening losses have almost certainly deleted many of the smallest *Sylvilagus* elements, such as the carpals, tarsals, sesamoids, and patella, most of the larger cottontail elements, including some that had low recovery rates in Shaffer's (1992) experiments, appear to have been recovered at Henderson with comparatively little bias stemming from the use of quarter-inch screens.

Taphonomy

While it seems unlikely that the Henderson lagomorph assemblage has been severely biased by recovery methods, we still face the problem of determining whether the majority of cottontail and jackrabbit remains at the site were brought there by the villagers or instead represent animals that died or were dragged into burrows in the site's deposits after the village had been abandoned. We also have to find a way to assess the extent to which the lagomorph assemblage has been altered by attritional processes, particularly the scavenging activities of predators such as village dogs. We first consider the issue of whether the lagomorphs represent human food remains or the carcasses of animals that had burrowed or were dragged into the deposits after the village had been abandoned. We then turn to the issue of attritional biases in the assemblage.

The black-tailed jackrabbit is the easiest case to examine. Many different lines of evidence point toward humans as the primary agent responsible for introducing the jackrabbit remains into the village. First, the highest densities of *Lepus* remains are found in trash deposits, particularly in the East Plaza and in Room C-5. Since this animal seldom uses burrows, either as a resting place or for escape, we cannot attribute their presence in these deposits to natural deaths (Bailey 1931; Dunn et al. 1982; Griffing and Davis 1976; Legler 1970; Orr 1940). In addition, none of the *Lepus* remains occurred as completely or partially articulated skeletons, which might be expected if animals died naturally in their burrows. While badgers, coyotes, and foxes are large enough to drag the carcass of a jackrabbit into their dens (Dunn et al. 1982), this is hardly likely to account for the many *Lepus* remains in the site. Moreover, the density of lagomorphs in the East Plaza trash was virtually identical to their density in the Room C-5 midden. While the latter deposits contained very little rock and therefore may have been attractive to burrowing or denning animals, the East Plaza midden was filled with fire-cracked rock, making it virtually impenetrable to all but the smallest burrowing rodents. Finally, 2.6% of the jackrabbit bones are burned, pointing toward a cultural origin for at least some of these remains. Taken together, it seems highly unlikely that the majority of *Lepus* remains represent natural deaths or the food remains of nonhuman predators.

The cottontail is more difficult to deal with. First, this animal does commonly use burrows for resting and escape, although it is still not entirely clear whether *Sylvilagus audubonii* excavates its own burrows or uses burrows made by other animals such as prairie dogs (Bailey 1931; Chapman et al. 1982; Chapman and Willner 1978; Orr 1940). Cottontails also are much smaller than jackrabbits and are more easily dragged into the dens of predators such as coyotes or foxes (Chapman et al. 1982). Nevertheless, some of the same arguments presented above for the cultural origin of the jackrabbit remains apply equally well to those of *Sylvilagus*. Cottontail skeletons were never found articulated or partially articulated at Henderson. Some of the cottontail bones, like jackrabbit bones, are burned, although as in *Lepus* the percentage is small (1.9%). The density of cottontails is highest in human-made trash deposits, including the rock-filled East Plaza midden, where burrowing by rabbits or predators would have been almost impossible.

While none of these arguments is convincing by itself, taken together it seems very likely that most, if not all, of the lagomorph remains, both *Lepus* and *Sylvilagus*, were brought into Henderson by the villagers themselves.

The other critical issue that needs to be addressed concerns the extent to which the lagomorph assemblage has been altered by attritional processes, such as weathering, trampling, or the scavenging activities of predators. Of most concern to us here is whether the skeletal element frequencies have been biased by the differential loss of the less resistant elements, and especially whether the overall ratio of cottontails to jackrabbits has been significantly altered by the selective destruction of the smaller, more delicate *Sylvilagus* remains. Several lines of evidence can be examined in an attempt to assess the impact of attritional processes. For example, we can note the presence on bone surfaces of cracking, splintering, exfoliation, or other telltale signs of weathering (e.g., Behrensmeyer 1978). We can also look for evidence of damage or destruction of bones by carnivores in the form of gnaw-marks, tooth pitting, crenulated edges, punctures, or other diagnostic forms of bone breakage, as well as acid-etching and polishing of the surfaces of bones that have passed through the gut of a predator (e.g., Andrews and Evans 1983; Binford 1981; Blumenschine and Selvaggio 1991; Hockett 1989; Horwitz 1990). Finally, the tendency for the observed element frequencies to covary with measures of bone density might also provide useful clues to the nature and extent of biases in the lagomorph assemblage, although such biases cannot automatically be assumed to reflect the operation of nonhuman taphonomic processes. The manner in which the villagers prepared, cooked, and consumed the lagomorphs may also have led to greater losses of less dense skeletal elements. We briefly consider each of these lines of evidence in the discussion that follows.

Loss through weathering does not appear to have played an important taphonomic role in the formation of the Henderson lagomorph assemblage. In general, the rabbit and jackrabbit bones are unweathered and in excellent condition, and none appear to have been exposed on the surface for prolonged periods of time according to the criteria outlined by Behrensmeyer (1978). Since most of the lagomorph remains were found in trash deposits, especially in Room C-5 and in the East Plaza midden, their excellent state of preservation suggests that burial in these deposits was quite rapid. This conclusion dovetails nicely with Miracle's (Chapter 5) reconstruction of deposition rates in different parts of the site based on the available radiocarbon dates. His analysis shows that sediments accumulated far more rapidly in the Room C-5 and East Plaza middens than elsewhere.

Severe attrition of the lagomorph assemblage at Henderson as a result of trampling is unlikely, because most of the remains were recovered from just two trash deposits, one that had been dumped into an abandoned room (Room C-5) and one that had accumulated in a gully or depression in the East Plaza. Both of these deposits are in places where heavy foot traffic would have been unlikely. Nevertheless, if trampling were a major process affecting the Henderson lagomorph assemblage, one possible indication might be a higher degree of bone breakage in jackrabbits, the larger species. A number of studies have shown that, under heavy trampling on a moderately soft substrate such as is found at Henderson, smaller bones (e.g., cottontails) are more likely than larger ones (e.g., jackrabbits) to become buried under a thin protective layer of sediment. This, in turn, subjects the larger bones that remain exposed on the surface to a greater rate of breakage (see, for example, Gifford 1980, 1981; Gifford and Behrensmeyer 1977; Nielsen 1991; Pintar 1987 [cited in Nielsen 1991]; Walters 1984; Yellen 1977). However, other studies of trampling have come up with contradictory results, finding no clear evidence that objects become sorted out by either size or weight as they penetrate into the substrate (e.g., Gifford-Gonzalez et al. 1985; Yellen 1991b). Thus, if differences do exist in the rate of bone breakage between the two lagomorph taxa, while interesting, it is not entirely clear whether these differences relate to trampling or to other factors. For example, the larger jackrabbit elements are also more likely to have been broken by humans in the process of butchering the animals, extracting marrow from the bones, and preparing the carcasses for cooking and consumption. Carnivores are also more likely to have broken the jackrabbit bones, because of their larger size, in order to get at the marrow or when attempting to consume the bones entirely (see Andrews and Evans 1983 for a discussion of the relationship between bone size and rate of breakage by carnivores).

The breakage data for the Henderson lagomorphs are summarized in Table 8.5. Interestingly, and perhaps counterintuitively, the table shows that the degree of bone breakage is nearly identical in the two species of lagomorph.[3] If vertical displacement of smaller bones does in fact protect them from breakage, these data suggest that trampling has probably not been a major force in the formation of the Henderson lagomorph assemblage, and therefore is unlikely to have led to major biases in the overall element or species composition of the assemblage. The unexpected patterning seen in Table 8.5 also suggests that carnivores may not have been a major factor in "ravaging" the lagomorph assemblage (see below), and also that humans may have processed cottontails and jackrabbits in much the same way, despite their different body size. We will return later to this last issue.

If bones were deleted from the Henderson lagomorph assemblage by attritional processes, the single most likely agent responsible for such losses would have been village dogs. In a village the size of Henderson, the only predator/scavenger with constant access to the trash deposits would have been domestic dogs (e.g., Kent 1981, 1993; Lyon 1970; Payne and Munson 1985; Walters 1984; see also Casteel 1971). Wild predator/scavengers, such as coyotes, wolves, foxes, and raptors, would have had much less frequent or direct access to village food remains so long as the community remained occupied (Yellen 1991a, 1991b). Moreover, even if the village had been abandoned seasonally, most lagomorph bones discarded by the villagers would have been defleshed prior to disposal, and such bones when exposed on the surface for more than a few weeks are unlikely to have been attractive to predators (e.g., Binford et al. 1988; Blumenschine 1986; Yellen 1991a, 199b). If the villagers had cooked the rabbit and jackrabbit bones in pots to make stews or broth rather than roasting or pit-baking them, the degreased bones would have been of little interest to scavengers from the moment they were discarded (e.g., Morey and Klippel 1991:17).

Obviously, one of the most clear-cut indications of scavenging by dogs is the presence on the bones of gnaw marks, pitting, crenulated edges, punctures, or traces of acid-etching and polishing on specimens that were actually ingested by a predator (e.g., Andrews and Evans 1983; Binford 1981; Horwitz 1990). At Henderson, however, such evidence is rare, not only on the lagomorph remains, but also on the bones of much larger species such as antelope and bison (see Chapters 4 and 5). This of course does not mean that village dogs played no role in the formation of the lagomorph assemblage (see Kent 1981, 1993). Given the small size of the bones of both cottontails and jackrabbits, access to marrow and cancellous tissue would not have required extensive gnawing and chewing. Instead, a scavenging dog could easily consume an entire element, if small enough, or bite off a portion of a larger element, leaving few or no clearly recognizable signs of their presence on the remaining fragments. Thus, documenting the taphonomic role of village dogs in the formation of the Henderson lagomorph assemblage must be approached through less direct means. One way has already been considered—differences in the degree of fragmentation of cottontail vs. jackrabbit bones—and the conclusion of this line of inquiry was that bones of both species were broken to the same extent (Table 8.5), making it unlikely that village dogs played a major role in the formation of the Henderson lagomorph assemblage.

Another approach to this issue, one which is now widely used by zooarchaeologists, is to examine the extent to which the observed lagomorph element frequencies covary with bone density.[4] Numerous studies have explored the relationship between bone survivorship and density (e.g., Behrensmeyer 1975; Binford 1981; Binford and Bertram 1977; Brain 1967, 1969, 1981; Brink and Dawe 1989; Grayson 1989; Kreutzer 1992; Lyman 1984, 1985, 1991, 1992; Lyman et al. 1992; Marshall and Pilgram 1991; Pavao 1996; Pavao and Stahl 1999). The less dense and more porous an element or portion of an ele-

Table 8.5. Degree of breakage of bones (NISP) of *Lepus* and *Sylvilagus* at Henderson Site (all 1980-1981 proveniences combined).

Taxon	Total NISP[a]	Complete or Nearly Complete Specimens[b]		Fragmentary Specimens[c]	
		NISP	%	NISP	%
Jackrabbit (*Lepus*)	1472	326	22.1	1146	77.9
Cottontail (*Sylvilagus*)	2886	690	23.9	2196	76.1
Total lagomorphs	4358	1016	23.3	3342	76.7

[a]The total NISP values shown here are lower than the site-wide values given in Tables A8.1 and A8.2, because certain elements, most notably skull parts, were not coded for degree of completeness.
[b]Includes all bones that were complete or more than 3/4 complete.
[c]Includes all identifiable fragments that were less than or equal to 3/4 complete.

Table 8.6. Proportion (%MNI) of *Lepus* and *Sylvilagus* skeletal elements (all 1980-1981 proveniences combined) and bulk (volume) density of lagomorph bones.[a]

Skeletal Element	Lago-morph Bulk (Volume) Density	Jackrabbit (*Lepus*) %MNI	Cottontail (*Sylvilagus*) %MNI
Mandible	0.27	60.0	97.7
Atlas	0.21	7.3	2.3
Axis	0.35	5.5	2.3
Cervical	0.30	1.8	0.8
Thoracic	0.30	1.8	0.8
Lumbar	0.30	9.1	8.6
Scapula	0.27	100.0	100.0
Prox. humerus	0.46	23.6	21.9
Dist. humerus	0.37	98.2	86.7
Prox. radius	0.16	78.2	47.7
Dist. radius	0.15	34.6	25.0
Prox. ulna	0.16	30.9	31.3
Prox. metacarpal	0.09	30.9[b]	4.7[f]
Dist. metacarpal	0.11	21.8[c]	3.9[g]
Pelvis	0.39	43.6	83.6
Prox. femur	0.28	47.3	35.9
Dist. femur	0.58	58.2	53.9
Prox. tibia	0.56	47.3	42.2
Dist. tibia	0.43	45.5	92.2
Astragalus	0.24	27.3	9.4
Calcaneus	0.38	41.8	72.7
Prox. metatarsal	0.13	36.4[d]	45.3[h]
Dist. metatarsal	0.12	16.4[e]	25.0[i]

[a]%MNI values for *Lepus* and *Sylvilagus* from Tables A8.1 and A8.2; Lagomorph (leporid) bulk (volume) density values are averages for four species (*Oryctolagus cuniculus*, *Sylvilagus floridanus*, *Lepus canadensis*, *Lepus californicus*; see Pavao and Stahl 1999).
[b]%MNI value for prox. mc. 4.
[c]%MNI value for dist. mc. 4.
[d]%MNI value for prox. mt. 2 or 3.
[e]%MNI value for dist. mt. 2.
[f]%MNI value for prox. mc. 3.
[g]%MNI value for dist. mc. 3.
[h]%MNI value for prox. mt. 2.
[i]%MNI value for dist. mt. 2.

ment, such as an epiphysis, the greater its susceptibility to destruction by attritional processes such as decay, trampling, sediment compaction, and consumption by carnivores. Thus, in an archaeological assemblage a high correlation between element frequency and density might be strong evidence that the assemblage has been biased by differential loss of those elements that are most vulnerable to attrition. However, several recent studies have shown that the interpretation of element frequency/ bone density plots may not be as straightforward as zooarchaeologists initially thought. Perhaps not surprisingly, various indices of food utility, such as Binford's (1978) MGUI and grease index and Metcalfe and Jones' (1988) FUI, also correlate with bone density (e.g., Brink and Dawe 1989; Grayson 1989; Lyman 1985, 1992; Klein 1989; Speth 1991). Thus, for example, many of the high-utility bones, parts that are most likely to be transported away from a kill by human hunters, are also ones with low densities and whose scarcity or absence at the kill might appear to be due to attritional losses. In sum, while the presence of a clear-cut correlation between element frequencies and bone density may be evidence of attrition, we cannot simply assume this. Such patterning may instead reflect past human food choices that focus on high-utility parts, as well as human techniques of food processing, such as bone-grease rendering, that destroy soft, porous bones rich in lipids.

Bulk (volume) density values are available for four taxa of lagomorph: *Oryctolagus cuniculus*, *Sylvilagus floridanus*, *Lepus canadensis*, *Lepus californicus* (Pavao 1996; Pavao and Stahl 1999). The values we use here are the combined averages for these four taxa. Using the %MNI values for 1 cranial (mandible) and 22 postcranial skeletal elements of *Lepus* and *Sylvilagus*, neither species shows a significant positive correlation between element frequency and bone density (Spearman's *r*: *Lepus*, $n = 23$, $r_s = .20$, $p > .05$; *Sylvilagus*, $n = 23$, $r_s = .29$, $p > .05$; see Table 8.6). These results suggest that lagomorph element frequencies at Henderson have not been heavily altered by attritional processes. In other words, village dogs, or other predator/scavengers, appear to have had little detectable impact on the overall composition of the lagomorph assemblage.

This conclusion may seem counterintuitive since many studies have noted the potential impact of dogs on the faunal remains discarded in villages and campsites (e.g., Kent 1981, 1993; Lyon 1970; Payne and Munson 1985; Walters 1984). The most likely explanation for the Henderson situation is that the vast majority of remains discovered in the 1980-1981 seasons came from contexts where deposition was quite rapid (Room C-5 in the Center Bar and the East Plaza midden), and where dogs may have had limited access to the bones. The situation in Room C-5 is the most clear-cut. Judging from the radiocarbon dates obtained from the floor and fill of this room, trash accumulated very soon after it had been abandoned. More importantly, the trash was dumped into the room while the walls were still standing at least 1.5 to 2 m high (it is not clear whether the roof was still in place or not). In addition, Room C-5 was surrounded on all four sides by other rooms. Thus, it may have been difficult for dogs to gain access to the discarded bones in this structure.

The situation in the East Plaza is less certain. Again, trash accumulated rapidly in the plaza, perhaps burying many of the lagomorph remains before dogs could get at them. The huge quantities of fire-cracked rock in the East Plaza may also have limited the ability of the dogs to dig into these deposits.

One other factor, alluded to earlier, may be especially relevant here. If most of the lagomorph bones are refuse from human meals, they would have been discarded in a largely defleshed condition. Furthermore, it is possible that many of the lagomorphs were cooked in pots rather than being roasted or baked. The low levels of burning seen in the lagomorph bones (*Lepus*, 2.6%; *Sylvilagus*, 1.9%) are certainly compatible with this suggestion.[5] Cooking in pots would not only have very effectively defleshed the lagomorph bones, but may also have degreased them and perhaps also removed the marrow (assum-

Table 8.7. Proportion (%MNI) of *Lepus* and *Sylvilagus* skeletal elements, marrow index, and grease index.

Skeletal Element	*Lepus* %MNI	*Sylvilagus* %MNI	Marrow Index[a]	Grease Index[b]
Mandible	60.0	97.7	5.74	—
Atlas	7.3	2.3	1.00	—
Axis	5.5	2.3	1.00	—
Cervical	1.8	0.8	1.00	—
Thoracic	1.8	0.8	1.00	—
Lumbar	9.1	8.6	1.00	—
Scapula	100.0	100.0	6.40	—
Prox. humerus	23.6	21.9	29.69	241.48
Dist. humerus	98.2	86.7	28.33	64.12
Prox. radius	78.2	47.7	43.64	42.71
Dist. radius	34.6	25.0	66.11	49.73
Prox. ulna	30.9	31.3	43.64	42.71
Prox. metacarpal	30.9	4.7	1.00	6.76
Dist. metacarpal	21.8	3.9	1.00	14.58
Pelvis	43.6	83.6	7.85	—
Prox. femur	47.3	35.9	33.51	112.41
Dist. femur	58.2	53.9	49.41	186.30
Prox. tibia	47.3	42.2	43.78	96.82
Dist. tibia	45.5	92.2	92.90	12.22
Astragalus	27.3	9.4	1.00	—
Calcaneus	41.8	72.7	1.00	—
Prox. metatarsal	36.4	45.3	1.00	7.44
Dist. metatarsal	16.4	25.0	1.00	20.07

[a]From Binford (1978:27, Table 1.9, col. 8); values for metapodials and large tarsals (astragalus and calcaneus) have been modified for lagomorphs (see text).
[b]From Brink and Dawe (1989:134, Table 20).

ing that most of the major marrow bones had been deliberately broken open before being put into the pot). While this scenario is obviously speculative, it is consistent with the data, and would suggest that most of the cottontail and jackrabbit bones may have been largely devoid of edible tissue by the time they became available to scavenging village dogs.[6]

This last observation suggests another way we might explore the impact of dogs on the Henderson lagomorph assemblage. If the bones had been discarded in defleshed condition, but had not had their marrow content and grease removed prior to discard, dogs should have depleted bones from the assemblage in a manner that would correlate with their marrow utility and possibly also with their grease utility. In other words, by destroying bones high in marrow or grease, the dogs should have left behind an assemblage that displays a *negative* correlation between element frequency, expressed in terms of %MNI values, and the marrow index (and perhaps also the grease index). Unfortunately, we must use marrow and grease indices derived from large ungulates as proxies for the indices in lagomorphs, for which values unfortunately have not been determined as yet. What we hope justifies the use of these proxies is the assumption that the anatomical proportions of lagomorph elements are sufficiently similar to those in medium to large ungulates to preserve the *relative ranking* of elements in terms of their marrow and grease content.

We use the standardized marrow index for caribou developed by Binford (1978:27, Table 1.9) with the following modifications. Given the small size, compact nature, and extremely tiny marrow cavities in lagomorph metapodials, astragali, and calcanei, we assign a marrow index value of 1.0 to each of these elements. For the grease index, we use the values derived for bison by Brink and Dawe (1989:134, Table 20). The %MNI values for the lagomorph elements used in these analyses, as well as the marrow and grease index values, are given in Table 8.7.

The %MNI values for both jackrabbits and cottontails are significantly and *positively* correlated with Binford's marrow index (Spearman's *r*, *Lepus*, $n = 23$, $r_s = .65$, $p < .01$; *Sylvilagus*, $n = 23$, $r_s = .58$, $p < .01$). This result is the reverse of what we would expect if the lagomorph assemblage had been ravaged by village dogs seeking scraps of marrow and grease in the discarded bones. It is possible that our inclusion of the vertebrae and mandible in this analysis, bones which have little or no useful marrow, creates a spurious correlation by forming a cluster of elements all with a marrow index of 1.0. We therefore recomputed the correlation with these elements omitted. This sharply reduces the total *n*, but despite this the jackrabbit %MNI

Table 8.8. Frequency (NISP) of complete vs. fragmentary *Lepus* and *Sylvilagus* bones by provenience at Henderson Site.[a]

Provenience	Complete		Fragmentary		Test Statistic (t_s)[c]
	NISP	%	NISP	%	
Jackrabbit (*Lepus*)					
East Bar	109	27.81	283	72.19	**4.18
Center Bar	115	24.78	349	75.22	**3.33
Combined room blocks[b]	249	26.63	686	73.37	**4.55
Room C-5 only	67	22.64	229	77.36	*2.29
East Plaza	68	15.85	361	84.15	
Entire site	325	22.66	1109	77.34	
Cottontail (*Sylvilagus*)					
East Bar	318	27.56	836	72.44	**4.71
Center Bar	200	22.25	699	77.75	*2.13
Combined room blocks[b]	537	25.33	1583	74.67	**4.03
Room C-5	110	21.96	391	78.04	1.73
East Plaza	112	17.83	516	82.17	
Entire site	690	23.91	2196	76.09	

[a]Most cranial elements other than mandibles are omitted from these tabulations.
[b]The value for "combined room blocks" includes a small number of lagomorph remains from a 1-m^2 unit excavated in the Main Bar (trench E).
[c]Comparison of proportion of fragmented lagomorph bones in East Plaza with proportions in various room block proveniences using test of equality of two percentages based on arcsine transformation (t_s; Sokal and Rohlf 1969:607-10; no asterisk, $p > .05$; single asterisk, $p < .05$; double asterisk, $p < .001$).

values continue to display a positive though weak correlation with the marrow index ($n = 17$, $r_s = .46$, $p = .07$). In *Sylvilagus* the correlation also remains positive, but is clearly no longer significant ($n = 17$, $r_s = .34$, $p = .18$). Using Brink and Dawe's (1989) grease index, no significant correlation is obtained for either species of lagomorph. In other words, there is no evidence that bones were ravaged by dogs on the basis of their grease content.

The positive correlation between skeletal element frequencies and the marrow index, together with other lines of evidence that have already been discussed, suggest that dogs have not seriously altered the composition of the lagomorph assemblage. For both species of rabbit, the element frequencies we observe appear to provide a reasonably unbiased record of the actual composition of the lagomorph assemblage that was discarded by the village's human inhabitants. But the positive correlation is somewhat surprising. We had expected to find little or no correlation, either positive or negative. A positive correlation in the site-wide antelope or bison assemblage might be evidence that the villagers selected elements at the kill on the basis of their marrow content, culling out the lower-utility bones before returning to the village. But it is hard to imagine the villagers doing this with lagomorphs. Most rabbits were probably brought into the village as whole carcasses. Once in the village, aside from removing the skin, innards, and perhaps lopping off the feet and head, the carcasses were most likely roasted or baked whole or cut up into manageable pieces and added to the stew pot. The positive correlation between the frequency of discarded elements and the marrow index suggests that the inhabitants discarded the lowest-utility parts, particularly the lower legs and feet, prior to cooking and consuming the rest. These would then have been destroyed by dogs, perhaps explaining why elements of the lower fore limbs and hind feet are underrepresented not just in the screened assemblage but also in the flotation samples.

Lagomorph Sample by Provenience

In the preceding section, we showed that neither the element nor the species composition of the lagomorph assemblage has been severely altered by recovery methods or taphonomic processes. This means that the assemblage provides a reasonably unbiased record of the cottontail and jackrabbit remains that were brought into Henderson and subsequently discarded there by the human inhabitants of the village. In the remaining sections, therefore, we explore the lagomorph data for insights into the role of these small mammals in the subsistence practices of the villagers. We begin by comparing the lagomorph assemblages recovered from each of the major provenience units at the site (East Bar, Center Bar, combined room blocks, and East Plaza). Of particular interest here is whether the remains discarded in the area of the huge East Plaza earth oven complex differ in any major way from the remains that ended up in the room blocks. The rationale here is that the East Plaza very likely constituted a more accessible and "public" locale in the com-

Table 8.9. Frequency (NISP) of burned *Lepus*, *Sylvilagus*, and total lagomorph bones by provenience at Henderson Site.

Provenience	Total NISP	Burned NISP	Burned %	Test Statistic (t_s)[a]
Jackrabbit (*Lepus*)				
East Bar	475	19	4.0	1.65
Center Bar	553	13	2.4	0.17
Combined room blocks	1028	32	3.1	1.06
Room C-5	358	5	1.4	0.87
East Plaza	502	11	2.2	
Entire site	1829	48	2.6	
Cottontail (*Sylvilagus*)				
East Bar	1495	20	1.3	**2.57
Center Bar	1208	28	2.3	0.87
Combined room blocks	2703	48	1.8	*1.92
Room C-5	649	16	2.5	0.57
East Plaza	776	23	3.0	
Entire site	3975	74	1.9	
Total Lagomorphs				
East Bar	1970	39	2.0	1.26
Center Bar	1761	41	2.3	0.58
Combined room blocks	3731	80	2.1	1.05
Room C-5	1007	21	2.1	0.89
East Plaza	1278	34	2.7	
Entire site	5804	122	2.1	

[a]Comparison of proportion of burned lagomorph bones in East Plaza with proportions in various room block proveniences using test of equality of two percentages based on arcsine transformation (t_s; Sokal and Rohlf 1969:607-10; no asterisk, $p > .05$; one asterisk, $p = .05$; two asterisks, $p = .01$).

munity than areas within the structures themselves. Thus, activities such as communal rabbit hunts that involved larger numbers of participants, and especially those that were linked to important calendrical ceremonies, are likely to be more clearly reflected in the East Plaza midden than in domestic room fill or trash.

Throughout this discussion, comparisons between the assemblages from the East Plaza and room blocks are made using proportions that are evaluated pairwise for statistical significance using Sokal and Rohlf's (1969:607-10) test of the equality of two percentages based on the arcsine transformation (t_s; a value of $p \leq .05$ is considered significant).

We consider first the ratio of cottontails to total lagomorphs (the "lagomorph index"; see Szuter 1991:174-75) in the rooms and the East Plaza. These data were presented earlier in the discussion of screening biases (see Table 8.1 above). When MNI values are considered, the proportion of cottontails in the East Plaza does not differ significantly from the proportion in any of the structures. This is not surprising given the small sample sizes. However, when NISP values are used instead, all but the Room C-5 sample differ significantly from the East Plaza sample, indicating that the proportion of jackrabbits is greater in the East Plaza than in the structures (Room C-5 only, $t_s = 1.74, p > .05$; combined room blocks, $t_s = 7.64, p < .001$; Center Bar, $t_s = 4.44, p < .001$; East Bar, $t_s = 8.91, p < .001$).

As discussed earlier, density values—NISP, MNE, or MNI per m^3 of deposit—are difficult to compare among proveniences because the values are obviously very sensitive to rates of deposition. The two most comparable proveniences in terms of depositional context are the ash-rich trash accumulations in Room C-5 and the East Plaza. Focusing on just these two samples (see Table 8.3 above), the densities of total lagomorph remains are very similar, regardless of whether NISP, MNE, or MNI values are used. However, while jackrabbit densities are virtually identical in these two proveniences, cottontail remains are more numerous per cubic meter of deposit in Room C-5. As noted earlier, this difference may reflect greater attritional losses of *Sylvilagus* bones, perhaps to village dogs, in the more exposed and accessible East Plaza. The difference, however, could indicate that jackrabbit remains were being discarded at comparable rates in both contexts, while remains of the much smaller cottontail rabbit accumulated more rapidly in the structure than in the plaza.

The degree of bone fragmentation (Table 8.8) is significantly greater in the East Plaza than in the rooms. The higher fragmentation values for both cottontails and jackrabbits in the East Plaza midden may again point to taphonomic processes at work: more trampling or scavenging by village dogs in this more exposed locale.[7] If the degree of bone fragmentation at the site were determined primarily by human food processing and consumption activities, we would expect remains discarded in the room blocks to be more comminuted, a pattern seen clearly in the bones of both bison and antelope (see Chapters 4 and 5).

Table 8.10. Frequency (NISP) of *Lepus* and *Sylvilagus* upper and lower limb bones by provenience at Henderson Site.[a]

Provenience	Upper Limb		Lower Limb		Test Statistic (t_s)[b]
	NISP	%	NISP	%	
Jackrabbit (*Lepus*)					
East Bar	126	30.07	293	69.93	**4.69
Center Bar	156	33.12	315	66.88	**3.86
Combined room blocks	282	31.69	608	68.31	**4.87
Room C-5	105	38.46	168	61.54	*1.91
East Plaza	187	45.83	221	54.17	
Cottontail (*Sylvilagus*)					
East Bar	462	38.40	741	61.60	**4.58
Center Bar	411	45.31	496	54.69	1.63
Combined room blocks	873	41.37	1237	58.63	**3.62
Room C-5	224	47.66	246	52.34	0.61
East Plaza	314	49.53	320	50.47	

[a]The upper limb includes the scapula, humerus, pelvis, and femur; the lower limb includes the radius, ulna, tibia, metapodials, calcaneus, and astragalus.

[b]Comparison of proportion of upper and lower lagomorph limb bones in East Plaza with proportions in various room block proveniences using test of equality of two percentages based on arcsine transformation (t_s; Sokal and Rohlf 1969:607-10; no asterisk, $p > .05$; one asterisk, $p = .05$; two asterisks, $p < .001$).

The proportion of burned jackrabbit bones in the East Plaza (2.19%) is very low and does not differ significantly from the value in any of the major room block proveniences (Table 8.9). In the cottontail samples, the incidence of burning in the East Plaza is again very low (2.96%), but is still significantly higher than the East Bar and the combined room block samples. This is the reverse of what we had anticipated on the basis of the large mammal evidence. As discussed in Chapters 4 and 5, much of the preliminary dismemberment, butchering, culling, and cooking of the bison and antelope carcasses appears to have taken place in the East Plaza. Some consumption of the large mammals very likely also took place there as well, perhaps in the context of hunt-related feasts or ceremonies. A small and highly select subset of skeletal elements, particularly marrow-rich lower limb bones, were then brought into the rooms, where further cooking, probably roasting, as well as marrow removal, produced a more highly burned and fragmented assemblage.

The cottontails, undoubtedly because of their much smaller body size, were handled differently from bison and antelope. First, most of the cottontails (and jackrabbits as well) appear to have been taken directly into the rooms for processing and cooking, bypassing entirely the large roasting/baking complex in the East Plaza. This is strongly suggested by the fact that only 26% of the lagomorph remains (based on NISP values) come from the East Plaza compared to some 80% of the bison and 50% of the medium ungulates (see Chapters 4 and 5). Second, the much lower incidence of burning in both jackrabbits and cottontails may indicate they were more often boiled, a suggestion made earlier in the taphonomic discussions to explain the limited evidence of attrition by village dogs. Of course, it very likely also reflects the fact that lagomorph carcasses, because of their small size, would have been less extensively dismembered than bison or antelope before roasting. In either case, the higher incidence of burned cottontail bones in the East Plaza may suggest that rabbits cooked in this part of the village were somewhat more likely to be roasted than those cooked in the rooms. This explanation is compatible with the greater bone fragmentation observed in the East Plaza lagomorph assemblage, since roasted bones discarded in the midden would have been more attractive to scavenging village dogs than bones that had been broken open and boiled.

Nevertheless, while the statistical tests may point to significant differences between the East Plaza and room blocks in the incidence of burned cottontail bones, the magnitude of these differences is so small that it is doubtful they are behaviorally important. This becomes more evident when the cottontail and jackrabbit remains are combined to enlarge the sample of burned bones (Table 8.9). In the combined sample, none of the pairwise comparisons with the East Plaza is significant. Thus, while lagomorphs may have been prepared more often by roasting or pit-baking in the East Plaza than in the room blocks, this cannot be convincingly demonstrated on the basis of the incidence of burned bones.

In both species of rabbit, lower limbs are significantly *less* well represented in the East Plaza than in most room block proveniences (Table 8.10). This was surprising since we had anticipated that, as in bison and antelope, many of the meat- and marrow-poor lower limbs and feet of lagomorphs would have been removed and discarded in the East Plaza before the carcasses were brought into the rooms for further processing and consumption. However, as noted above, much if not most of the processing of these small-bodied animals took place in the room blocks, not in the plaza. Thus, the underrepresentation of lower limbs and feet in the plaza, like the greater degree of

Table 8.11. Proportion (MNI) of immature *Lepus* and *Sylvilagus* remains by provenience at Henderson Site.

Provenience	Immature MNI	Total MNI	Immature%	Test Statistic (t_s)[a]
Jackrabbit (*Lepus*)				
East Bar	5	16	31.3	0.02
Center Bar	4	20	20.0	0.83
Combined room blocks	9	36	25.0	0.52
Room C-5	2	12	16.7	0.96
East Plaza	6	19	31.6	
Entire site	12	55	21.8	
Cottontail (*Sylvilagus*)				
East Bar	7	59	11.9	*2.12
Center Bar	8	50	16.0	1.46
Combined room blocks	15	109	13.8	*2.05
Room C-5	5	31	16.1	1.27
East Plaza	13	46	28.3	
Entire site	30	128	23.4	

[a]Comparison of proportion of immature lagomorph bones in East Plaza with proportions in various room block proveniences using test of equality of two percentages based on arcsine transformation (t_s; Sokal and Rohlf 1969:607-10; no asterisk, $p > .05$; one asterisk, $p < .05$).

bone fragmentation, may reflect the greater impact of scavenging village dogs in this open and highly accessible part of the site.

The lower limbs of lagomorphs are underrepresented in the room blocks as well, though less so than in the East Plaza. In addition to destruction by village dogs, especially in the plaza but elsewhere as well, they might also have been removed and discarded before the animals were brought into the village. The underrepresentation of lower limbs is clearly evident if one compares the observed proportions with those that would be expected in a complete skeleton. The elements that are tabulated in Table 8.10 include the scapula, humerus, pelvis, and femur for the upper limb, and the radius, ulna, tibia, metapodials, calcaneus, and astragalus for the lower limb. If whole elements are counted, there should be 8 upper limb elements (18.2%) and 36 lower limb elements (81.8%) in a complete skeleton. However, since we have used NISP values in Table 8.10, calculating the expected values is more complicated. Very few limb shafts were identified and tallied; thus we can assume that most broken limb bones are represented by two parts, one proximal and one distal. These values were then doubled to take into account the side of the element (left or right). In the case of the scapula, only bones with the distal portion largely intact were tallied, hence for this element the expected number is two (left and right). For ulnae, proximal ends and shafts were tabulated but distal fragments, which were very rare, were omitted. In the case of the pelvis, each innominate typically broke into about three identifiable fragments, the ilium, the ischium, and the acetabulum with varying proportions of the ilium and ischium attached. Given these estimates, we might expect a total identifiable NISP of 16 pieces (22.2%) for the upper limb and 56 pieces (77.8%) for the lower limb in a complete skeleton. These figures do not differ greatly from those obtained using whole elements.

While several of the comparisons made thus far seem to point to greater attritional losses in the plaza than in the room blocks, we cannot rule out the possibility that these differences stem from human rather than taphonomic sources. The Henderson villagers presumably discarded bones that were largely defleshed. If the bones weren't boiled, marrow and grease were the principal edible tissues remaining in these bones, and scavenging village dogs probably destroyed greater proportions of elements of higher marrow or grease utility. In other words, the correlations of %MNI values with marrow and grease utility should be negative if this was the case. We examined the correlation between the representation of lagomorph skeletal elements (expressed as %MNI) in the East Plaza assemblage with Binford's (1978) marrow utility index for caribou and Brink and Dawe's (1989) grease index for bison (see taphonomic discussion above on use of proxy indices).

In the taphonomic section, we noted that in the site-wide assemblage the correlations with marrow utility for both species of lagomorph were significant but *positive*. No significant correlations, positive or negative, were found with the grease index. A very similar result was obtained for just the East Plaza lagomorph assemblage. For marrow utility, both species yielded significant and *positive* correlations (Spearman's r, $n = 23$, *Lepus*, $r_s = .66, p < .01$; *Sylvilagus*, $r_s = .58, p < .01$). For grease utility, jackrabbits yielded a significant and again *positive* correlation ($n = 13$, *Lepus*, $r_s = .62, p < .05$; *Sylvilagus*, $r_s = .33, p > .05$). These results do not support the view that the East Plaza remains suffered unusually heavy attrition by village dogs, despite their potentially greater vulnerability. We remain uncertain, therefore, about the causes of the elevated fragmentation

Table 8.12. Proportion (NISP) of immature *Lepus*, *Sylvilagus*, and total lagomorph remains by provenience at Henderson Site.

Provenience	Immature NISP	Total NISP	Immature %	Test Statistic (t_s)[a]
	Jackrabbit (*Lepus*)			
East Bar	32	529	6.1	****3.25
Center Bar	36	601	6.0	****3.39
Combined room blocks	68	1130	6.0	****3.80
Room C-5	16	358	4.5	****3.95
East Plaza	60	513	11.7	
Entire site	141	1829	7.7	
	Cottontail (*Sylvilagus*)			
East Bar	103	1609	6.4	1.03
Center Bar	59	1267	4.7	**2.68
Combined room blocks	162	2876	5.6	*1.93
Room C-5	38	649	5.9	1.27
East Plaza	61	810	7.5	
Entire site	259	3975	6.5	
	Total Lagomorphs			
East Bar	135	2138	6.3	***3.05
Center Bar	95	1868	5.1	****4.44
Combined room blocks	230	4006	5.7	****4.12
Room C-5	54	1007	5.4	****3.52
East Plaza	121	1323	9.2	
Entire site	400	5804	6.9	

[a]Comparison of proportion of immature lagomorph bones in East Plaza with proportions in various room block proveniences using test of equality of two percentages based on arcsine transformation (t_s; Sokal and Rohlf 1969:607-10; no asterisk, $p > .05$; one asterisk, $p = .05$; two asterisks, $p < .05$; three asterisks, $p < .01$; four asterisks, $p < .001$).

levels and underrepresentation of lower limbs and feet in the East Plaza.

When we compare the proportions (based on MNI values) of immature lagomorphs recovered from the various proveniences, we encounter another interesting difference between the East Plaza and room block assemblages, one that is unlikely to derive from taphonomic processes (Table 8.11). Unfortunately, sample sizes based on MNI values are extremely small and hence the comparisons must be regarded with caution. Table 8.11 indicates that immature cottontails are significantly more numerous in the East Plaza than in the East Bar and combined room block samples. Immature jackrabbits are more common in the plaza than Room C-5, but this difference is not statistically significant.

To enlarge the sample sizes, Table 8.12 recomputes the proportion of immature animals from the various proveniences, this time using total NISP values rather than MNI values. While the NISP-based figures grossly underestimate the true proportion of immature animals in the assemblage, because they are inflated by cranial and other elements that cannot be aged, the results nevertheless reinforce Table 8.11. The proportions of immature jackrabbits and cottontails in the East Plaza sample are both significantly greater than the proportions in the room block samples.

When compared to the room block assemblages the East Plaza displays: (1) proportionately more jackrabbits, (2) a lower density of cottontail remains per cubic meter of deposit, (3) a greater degree of bone fragmentation, (4) proportionately fewer lower limb and foot elements, and (5) a greater proportion of immature animals. Taphonomic processes, in particular the scavenging activities of village dogs in the more open, accessible East Plaza locale might explain (1) through (4), but not (5). If village dogs were ravaging the bones in the plaza, the immature bones should have been the first to go. Thus, we conclude that the Henderson villagers discarded more immature animals in the East Plaza midden than in the room blocks. While less certain, it is also likely that the villagers discarded more jackrabbit remains in the plaza midden than in the rooms. The implications of these two observations will be explored later.

Seasonal Scheduling of Lagomorph Hunting

The seasonal timing of hunting activities is an important clue to prehistoric subsistence practices and mobility patterns. Archaeologists have devoted considerable effort and ingenuity to developing techniques for extracting seasonal information from animal remains (e.g., Monks 1981). For larger ungulates, such as bison, deer, and antelope, patterns of tooth eruption and wear provide the most reliable and precise information on seasonality (e.g., Frison 1978; Hillson 1986; Klein and Cruz-Uribe 1984). Ungulate dentitions are exposed to wear in predictable ways:

deciduous or "milk" premolars precede permanent ones and molars emerge stepwise (Smith 1992:137-38). The stage of wear on individual cusps of erupting teeth or the total height of enamel on an emerging or fully erupted tooth, provides an age for ungulate mandibles and maxillae. Since most ungulates in the temperate latitudes have calving seasons, usually a few weeks in the spring, tooth wear can be used to establish what time of year the animal was killed.

This approach cannot be used with lagomorphs because both cottontails and jackrabbits produce five or six litters each year, with the first births occurring as early as January and the last as late as September (Chapman and Willner 1978; Chapman et al. 1982; Dunn et al. 1982). Thus, even though techniques are well established for determining the age of lagomorph mandibles as well as other skeletal elements (Bothma et al. 1972; Broekhuizen and Maaskamp 1979; Cabon-Raczynska and Raczynski 1972; Connolly et al. 1969; Hale 1949; Iason 1988; Lechleitner 1959; Ohtaishi et al. 1976; Pascal and Kovacs 1983; Pepin 1973; Sullins et al. 1976; Taylor 1959; Thomsen and Mortensen 1946; Tiemeier et al. 1965; Tiemeier and Plenert 1964; Walhovd 1966), without some way of determining when an animal was born there is no way to use the animal's age to establish when it died. As a result, despite the obvious importance of lagomorphs as a prehistoric food resource in the American Southwest (and elsewhere), zooarchaeologists have either ignored them in assessments of site seasonality or have relied on untested analogies with the ethnographic present.

Fortunately, there may be another way to assess seasonality of lagomorph procurement (see also Whalen 1994:122-25; and Young 1996:127-37). This approach takes advantage of the fact that lagomorphs have multiple litters each year. Over a wide range of latitudes, total reproductive output in lagomorphs seems to be relatively constant, with species at lower latitudes producing more but smaller litters and those at higher latitudes producing fewer but larger litters (Flux 1981; Keith 1981). As a result, regardless of species or latitude, the proportion of immature individuals in the population changes in a predictable manner over the course of the year. Thus, early in the reproductive season, between about February and April, newborns are rarely encountered because they remain hidden and inactive for much of the day (Foster 1968:11; Flux 1970:113; Gross et al. 1974:42; Lord 1963). In the late spring and early summer, as the young of the first litters become more active and new litters are produced, the number of immature animals encountered in censuses rises rapidly. The proportion of juvenile animals continues to swell over the summer, so that by late summer or early fall they may comprise over 70% of the total population. During the fall and winter months the number of immature animals drops off precipitously as production of new litters stops and mortality takes its toll.

Numerous studies document this pattern in jackrabbits and hares. For example, in a study of black-tailed jackrabbits (*Lepus californicus*) in Kansas, Tiemeier et al. (1965:23) found that immature individuals (Age Class I, identified by having unfused proximal humeri) usually first appeared in field collections in May when they comprised less than about 10% of the population. The proportion of young rapidly increased over the summer to a peak of about 70% in August. Immatures then gradually declined in frequency until by December few were encountered.

Both black-tailed and white-tailed (*L. townsendi*) jackrabbit populations in the plains region of eastern Colorado showed a steady increase in the proportion of juveniles from May into the early fall, reaching a peak of between 70% and 90% in October (Gross 1969: Fig. 3).

Over a nine-year period, the average proportion of immature black-tailed jackrabbits in northern Utah rose from 1% in March to 5% in April, 31% in May, 56% in June, 79% in July, 83% in August, 88% in September, and 85% in October (Gross et al. 1974:42, Table 11).

Scottish mountain hares (*L. timidus scoticus*) display a similar trend. The proportion of immature animals in the population, assessed on the basis of the fusion of the proximal tibia, rose from about 22% in August to 55% in December (Flux 1970:113).

Walhovd (1966:125) found that immature Danish brown hares (*L. europaeus*), collected between early October and mid-December, comprised roughly 65% of the population.

Finally, Keith and Windberg (1978:42-44, see also Table 27), in a study of snowshoe hares (*L. americanus*) in Alberta, found that the proportion of juveniles rose from 0% in April to 56% in summer to a peak of 78% in October. Numbers then declined again, dropping to 68% in November and to between 45% and 52% in January.

Cottontail rabbits appears to follow a similar pattern, with low values in the spring and early summer and peak values in the late summer and fall. For example, in a study of a small sample of desert cottontails (*Sylvilagus audubonii*) near Fort Stanton, New Mexico, using the state of fusion of the distal radius to assess age, Foster (1968:11) found that the proportion of juveniles rose from just under 40% in August to 73% in September, reaching a peak of about 75% in October. The proportion dropped slightly in December to 73%, and then continued to decline over the late winter and spring.

Chapman et al. (1982) report that the proportion of juveniles in populations of eastern cottontails (*S. floridanus*) in Michigan and Ohio averaged over 80% in mid-November.

Among eastern cottontails taken in Wisconsin between October and December, Thomsen and Mortensen (1946: Table 1) found that over 87% of their sample was made up of juveniles.

In Illinois cottontail populations, Lord (1963:75) found that the proportion of immatures rose rapidly from zero or near zero in April and May to a peak of just over 70% in November and then fell off rapidly over the winter and spring.[8]

Finally, Sullins et al. (1976:21, Table 2) report that juveniles of *S. floridanus* captured in Oregon between late August and late September comprised nearly 50% of their sample.

These studies suggest a lagomorph pattern in which January

through April or May are characterized by low levels (less than about 30%) of immature animals, while June until as late as December are characterized by intermediate to high proportions of juveniles (more than 30% and typically over 50%). Thus, the proportion of immature animals, assessed for example by the proportion of unfused or fusing proximal humeri, may indicate whether an assemblage accumulated in either of these two broad seasonal periods.

However, before we can use these insights to assess the seasonality of lagomorph hunting in an archaeological context such as Henderson, there are three potential problems that must be addressed. First, we must know whether the stalking, snaring, trapping, and communal drives most commonly employed by Native American hunters to take rabbits and jackrabbits are likely to have produced a prey population whose age structure differed radically from that of the original wild population. Fortunately, wildlife biologists routinely assess the demographic structure of wild lagomorph populations by similar techniques: line transect counts, live trapping and snaring, shooting, netting, and various types of communal drive (e.g., Gross et al. 1974). Often several techniques are employed in the same study for the express purpose of establishing comparability of results. These studies show that the different census techniques produce broadly similar samples of the various age classes, with the possible exception of animals less than about two months old; these newborns remain hidden in burrows and are more likely to be taken by snaring than by driving or shooting (Foster 1968:11; Flux 1970:113; Gross et al. 1974:42).

The second problem is the degree to which the age structure of an archaeological faunal assemblage has been biased by attrition. This must be considered on a case by case basis. Numerous taphonomic studies have demonstrated the density-mediated vulnerability of the skeletal elements of immature animals to carnivore ravaging, leaching, trampling, and other attritional processes (e.g., Binford and Bertram 1977; Brain 1981; Lyman 1984). Thus, if an archaeological lagomorph assemblage contains only low to modest proportions of immature individuals, one cannot reliably draw conclusions about the seasonality of procurement events until the impact of taphonomic processes on the assemblage has been assessed. This is precisely the situation we encounter with the Henderson lagomorphs. Among the jackrabbit remains, immature individuals comprise approximately 22% of the sample, and among the cottontails, immatures comprise about 23% (Table 8.11).

The major conclusion of our earlier taphonomic analysis was that attritional losses of lagomorph remains, particularly due to the scavenging activities of village dogs, have been surprisingly minor. The reasons for the limited loss of bone through attrition included: (1) the likelihood that many of the lagomorph remains were defleshed and probably degreased by boiling before being discarded in the trash; (2) disposal of major quantities of trash in abandoned structures within the room blocks, such as Room C-5, that had standing walls and possibly intact roofs precluding access by scavengers other than small rodents to fresh remains; and (3) the large and extended village occupation limited access by wild predators and scavengers to freshly discarded lagomorph bones. We feel reasonably secure, therefore, in accepting the age structure of the Henderson lagomorph assemblage as a fairly reliable reflection of the demographic structure of the wild cottontail and jackrabbit populations encountered by the village hunters.

One last problem must be addressed before we can draw conclusions about the seasonality of lagomorph hunting at Henderson. Can we distinguish an archaeological assemblage that was produced largely or entirely by hunting events recurring annually during a single season of the year from one that is a palimpsest of hunting activities representing more than one season? Unfortunately, without some sort of additional information, the answer is probably no. In the case of Henderson, for example, the proportion of immatures of both jackrabbits and cottontails is relatively low, just under 25%.[9] This might imply that most or all hunting took place during the late winter or spring, sometime between about January and May. However, if half of the assemblage had been produced early in the year, so it contained few or no immatures, while the other half was produced during the late summer or fall, with high percentages of immatures, the resulting composite assemblage would also resemble the one seen at Henderson.

There may be a way out of this dilemma. Tiemeier et al. (1965:23, Table 15, Fig. 16), in their study of Kansas jackrabbits, recorded the proportion of fusing (Age Class II), not just unfused, proximal humeri. Individuals of this age class (10-12 months old) generally made up more than 20% of the population from January through April or May and again after July. The lowest levels, often below 10%, were most consistently found in June and July and occasionally in May. At Henderson, the proportion of Age Class II individuals, based on the presence of fusing proximal humeri and using MNI values, is about 4% in both taxa of lagomorphs (data from Tables A8.1 and A8.2). Such low values are unlikely to occur in an assemblage that is a product of hunting activities at more than one season of the year. Hence, combining these insights with the proportion of Age Class I (i.e., those with unfused proximal humeri) individuals discussed earlier, it would appear that most lagomorph hunting at Henderson took place during the late spring or early summer. Late summer, fall, and winter hunts are represented in the village lagomorph assemblage in much smaller numbers, if at all.

This conclusion was unexpected. A cursory glance at the Southwestern ethnographic literature shows that rabbit hunts, particularly communal drives, were commonplace among Puebloan farmers, not only in the spring, but also in the late summer and fall (e.g., Beaglehole 1936:11; Beckett 1974; Lange 1968:125-29, 333, 363; see also Neusius 1985, and Szuter 1991:260-62 for additional references to rabbit hunting in the Southwest). One would therefore expect late summer/fall hunts to be clearly in evidence at Henderson as well. Interestingly, their apparent scarcity, or absence, at Henderson parallels the

Table 8.13. Similarities and differences between Early phase and Late phase lagomorphs.[a]

Comparison	Early Phase	Late Phase	Significance[b]
Lepus			
Burned bones (%NISP)	7.7	2.6	$t_s = 5.31, p < .001$
Room vs. non-Room (%non-room)	40.6	33.4	$t_s = 3.36, p < .001$
Frequency (% of total fauna)[c]	11.0	14.8	$t_s = 7.38, p < .001$
Density (all proveniences) (NISP/m^3)	9.7	16.9	—
Density (non-room contexts) (NISP/m^3)	3.9	5.7	—
Age structure (%immature)	13.3	14.7	$t_s = 0.70, p > .05$
Marrow index (total NISP)	40.4	42.5	$t = -1.40, p > .05$
MGUI (%high utility)[d]	9.8	12.2	$t_s = 1.76, p > .05$
Sylvilagus			
Burned bones (%NISP)	3.8	1.8	$t_s = 4.19, p < .001$
Room vs. non-room (%non-room)	25.7	23.3	$t_s = 1.92, p \approx .05$
Frequency (% of total fauna)[c]	24.9	35.3	$t_s = 14.7, p < .001$
Density (all proveniences) (NISP/m^3)	22.1	40.4	—
Density (non-room contexts) (NISP/m^3)	5.7	9.4	—
Age structure (%immature)	16.1	12.7	$t_s = 2.49, p = .01$
Marrow index (total NISP)	37.8	38.9	$t = -1.02, p > .05$
MGUI (%high utility)[d]	14.3	14.2	$t_s = 0.19, p > .05$

[a]The values presented in this table are based on all of the coded lagomorph material from all five seasons of excavation (1980, 1981, 1994, 1995, 1997).
[b]t_s, test of equality of two percentages based on arcsine transformation (Sokal and Rohlf 1969:607-10); t, standard unpaired t-test.
[c]Taxa employed include bison, medium ungulates, dogs, jackrabbits, cottontails, and prairie dogs.
[d]High-utility elements, as defined here, include those with an MGUI greater than 60.0 (sternum, proximal and distal femur, and proximal tibia).

results of the bison and antelope analyses presented in Chapters 4 and 5. As with the lagomorphs, evidence for fall hunts of these larger mammals was also at best poorly represented. Increasingly, the Henderson faunal data seem to be pointing to a settlement pattern that is not thought to be typical of prehistoric Southwestern Puebloan farmers, one in which the village was partially, or possibly entirely, abandoned in the fall soon after the harvest was in, not to be fully reoccupied again until late winter or early spring.

In concluding, let us return briefly to one other aspect of seasonality. Earlier in this chapter, we noted that the proportion of both immature cottontails and jackrabbits was higher in the East Plaza than in the room blocks. Given the evidence just presented, this implies that the plaza assemblage contains a greater proportion of animals killed slightly later in the year, perhaps closer to the time of planting, than do the room block assemblages. In addition, the proportion of jackrabbits is higher in the East Plaza than in the room blocks, and the proportion of immature jackrabbits in the East Plaza is also significantly greater than the proportion of immature cottontails ($t_s = 2.52, p < .01$).[10] Since jackrabbits are more easily captured by communal drives than by other procurement techniques (see discussion in Szuter 1991:23; Flannery 1966; see also Henke and Demarais 1990), their elevated proportions in the East Plaza midden implies a greater representation of communal events there than in the room block deposits. These conclusions are not surprising given the open and "public" nature of the East Plaza earth oven complex.

The Temporal Perspective

Since completion of the original manuscript, we have finished coding most of the lagomorph remains recovered in all five seasons of excavation at Henderson (1980, 1981, 1994, 1995, 1997). This section briefly explores the temporal patterning in these data. The total sample consists of 8,668 lagomorph bones, of which 2,582 (29.8%) are *Lepus* and 6,086 (70.2%) are *Sylvilagus*. *Lepus* comprises 30.6% (NISP = 687) of the Early phase lagomorphs and 29.5% (NISP = 1,895) of the Late phase lagomorphs, indicating that the proportions of the two taxa remained unchanged over time. In both periods, cottontails vastly outnumber jackrabbits.

However, other data indicate that the role of lagomorphs in Henderson's economy changed through time (see Table 8.13). For example, expressed as a proportion of the total fauna (defined here as the total number of bones of bison, medium ungulates, dogs, jackrabbits, cottontails, and prairie dogs; NISP = 19,091), both lagomorph taxa increase significantly in the Late phase. This increase is also clearly reflected in the density values (NISP/m^3), which nearly doubled in the later period. In the Late phase more jackrabbits and cottontails were being taken by the villagers per unit time than in the preceding period.

Despite the sharp increase in the numerical importance of rabbits and jackrabbits, their social importance appears to have declined. In both taxa, the proportion of burned elements drops significantly in the Late phase, implying that fewer of these animals were prepared by roasting or pit-baking. Hand-in-hand with the change in cooking technique, the proportion of lagomorph bones found in "public" (non-room) contexts also declines. In light of arguments presented earlier in this chapter, it would appear that in the Late phase more of these animals were prepared in less public, "domestic" contexts and more often boiled or stewed rather than roasted or pit-baked.

Finally, there is some evidence for a change in the seasonality of procurement of the cottontails, though not of the jackrabbits. The proportion of immatures is low in both taxa, but declines even further in Late phase cottontails. In Chapters 4, 5, and 6, it has been argued that increasing emphasis during the Late phase on long-distance, spring-season communal bison hunting created or exacerbated scheduling conflicts among and between bison hunting and other subsistence pursuits. The decline in immature cottontails in the Late phase may indicate that rabbit hunting also came into increasing conflict with activities related to the bison hunt, and perhaps with agricultural activities as well, favoring their procurement even earlier in the spring.

Synopsis

Two seasons of excavation at the Henderson Site (1980-1981) yielded a total of 5,804 lagomorph bones (NISP). Of these, 1,829 specimens (31.5%) are from black-tailed jackrabbits (*Lepus californicus*) and 3,975 (68.5%) are from cottontail rabbits (*Sylvilagus* sp.). These remains represent a minimum (MNI) of 55 jackrabbits and 128 cottontails. Among the jackrabbits, at least 12 individuals (21.8%) are immature, based on the frequency of unfused and fusing limb epiphyses and calculated using MNI values. Among the cottontails, at least 30 individuals (23.4%) are immature. Only 2.6% of the jackrabbit bones and 1.9% of the cottontail bones are burned.

All of the rabbit remains recovered from Henderson appear to be from the desert cottontail (*Sylvilagus audubonii*) rather than the eastern cottontail (*S. floridanus*), the only other species of rabbit that might have been encountered in the Roswell area. The species determination is based on the depth of the mandible relative to the alveolar length of the cheek-tooth row (P_3-M_3), as described by Findley et al. (1975:84-85).

Before one can explore the role of lagomorphs in the diet and subsistence strategies of the Henderson villagers, potential recovery biases affecting the small-mammal remains must be systematically evaluated. During the excavations at Henderson, all sediments, except those saved for flotation, were passed through quarter-inch screens. Both Szuter (1991), in a literature review of screening biases reported for lagomorph bones recovered from sites in Arizona, and Shaffer (1992), in an experimental screening study, conclude that most skeletal elements of rabbits and jackrabbits will be reliably represented in samples recovered by conventional screening techniques.

The Henderson data appear to conform to these conclusions. First, the proportions of jackrabbits and cottontails in the screening samples do not differ significantly from their proportions in the assemblage recovered from the more than 300 flotation samples.

Second, when the proportions of the two lagomorph taxa in the screening samples are compared on a provenience-by-provenience basis (East Bar, Center Bar, East Plaza) with the values in the flotation samples from the corresponding locales, the differences are again not statistically significant.

Third, the proportion of cottontails calculated for each provenience using MNI values is very similar to the value obtained using NISP values. Since the MNI values are derived from the most common skeletal element (generally the scapula, pelvis, or tibia, all large elements that are unlikely to pass through the screens), whereas the NISP values include small elements that are much more likely to pass undetected through the screens, severe losses should lead to major differences between the percentages calculated using MNI values and those calculated using NISP values. This is not the case at Henderson.

Fourth, the observed frequencies of many of the smaller cottontail limb elements, expressed as percentages of their expected values (%MNI), are as large or larger than their corresponding values in jackrabbits. If screening biases had been severe at Henderson, we would expect the smaller elements of *Sylvilagus* to have much lower %MNI values, since these would have been lost at a greater rate than their larger counterparts in *Lepus*.

Fifth, the density of lagomorph remains in the flotation samples (101 bones/m^3), most of which were collected deliberately from trash-rich deposits, is comparable to the density of such remains recovered through quarter-inch screening of the East Plaza (107 bones/m^3) and Room C-5 (115 bones/m^3) midden deposits. When just the smaller lagomorph taxon is considered, the density in the flotation samples (76.9 bones/m^3) is virtually identical to the value in the Room C-5 deposit (74.0 bones/m^3), but noticeably higher than the East Plaza value (65.5 bones/m^3). While this result might point to recovery losses in the plaza, other observations, summarized below, suggest that the lower density of cottontail remains recovered from this provenience stems principally from cultural factors. In sum, there is very little evidence that the routine use of quarter-inch screening at Henderson has significantly affected the recovery rates of either jackrabbits or cottontails.

Two kinds of taphonomic bias were evaluated: whether the lagomorph bones are from animals that had been brought into the site by the villagers or instead are the remains of animals that had died naturally or were dragged by predators into burrows in the site's deposits after the village had been abandoned; and how much the assemblage has been altered by attritional processes, particularly by the scavenging activities of village dogs.

We conclude for the following reasons that most, if not all, of the jackrabbits were brought into Henderson by the villagers. The highest densities of *Lepus* bones were consistently found in trash deposits. Since black-tailed jackrabbits seldom use burrows for resting or escape, their abundance in the middens cannot be attributed to natural deaths. Also, the highest density of jackrabbit remains was encountered in the East Plaza midden. Since this midden was filled with fire-cracked rock, burrowing by predators large enough to drag the carcass of a jackrabbit into the deposit is unlikely. Jackrabbit remains never occurred as completely or even partially articulated skeletons. Finally, 2.6% of the *Lepus* bones were burned.

The same arguments are used for cottontails, but are less certain. *Sylvilagus* remains at Henderson were again most numerous in trash deposits. Articulated or semi-articulated skeletons were never encountered. High densities of cottontail bones were found in the East Plaza where burrowing by rabbits or by predators of rabbits was unlikely, if not impossible, because of the abundance of fire-cracked rock. Finally, some (1.9%) of the rabbit bones were burned.

Bias introduced by taphonomic processes such as weathering, trampling, or carnivore attrition appears to have been minimal.

Weathering damage on the bones is rare. Since most of the lagomorph bones were recovered from trash deposits, the absence of weathering damage implies rapid burial. Rapid accumulation of these deposits is also indicated by the radiocarbon dates.

Trampling also appears to have had a negligible effect on the lagomorph assemblage. Numerous taphonomic studies have shown that trampling on moderately soft substrates often leads to greater breakage of larger bones because they tend to remain exposed longer at or near the surface than smaller bones. The degree of fragmentation of the bones of both taxa of lagomorphs at Henderson is virtually identical, implying limited damage or loss due to trampling. Many of the lagomorph remains were recovered from trash dumped into an abandoned room within the confines of the Center Bar room block, as well as from a trash-filled gully in the East Plaza, both contexts where repeated trampling would be unlikely.

Surprisingly, the Henderson lagomorph assemblage appears to have been largely unaffected by scavenging dogs. Several lines of evidence point toward this conclusion. First, there is very little evidence of carnivore damage (e.g., gnaw-marks, punctures) on the bones. Second, the degree of fragmentation of jackrabbit and cottontail bones is virtually identical. In contrast, experimental taphonomic studies show that the bones of larger taxa (*Lepus*) should be more highly fragmented than those of smaller ones (*Sylvilagus*). Third, there is no statistically significant correlation between element frequency and bone density (i.e., bulk or volume density). Fourth, lagomorph element frequencies display a significant *positive* correlation with Binford's marrow utility index. If dogs had ravaged the defleshed but marrow-containing bones of jackrabbits and cottontails discarded by the villagers, one might expect a negative correlation—dogs would selectively destroy higher proportions of elements containing lots of marrow. The results of this analysis are inconclusive, since utility values for lagomorphs are unavailable and medium ungulate values (caribou) had to be used as proxies. Nevertheless, the convergence of evidence suggests that the Henderson lagomorph assemblage has not been seriously altered or biased by carnivore attrition.

Village dogs may have had only limited impact for several reasons. Most lagomorph bones were deposited in trash deposits that accumulated rapidly. Some of the trash was dumped into an enclosed structure within the Center Bar, inaccessible to dogs. Trash dumped in the East Plaza, with its high volume of fire-cracked rock, may not have been a very attractive locale for scavenging dogs. Though admittedly speculative, perhaps the most important reason for the low level of carnivore attrition is that most lagomorphs may have been cooked by boiling rather than roasting or pit-baking. This view is compatible with the low level of burning seen on the lagomorph bones, and the fact that less than about 30% of the lagomorph remains were found associated with the huge East Plaza earth oven complex. If most of the lagomorphs were in fact boiled, their discarded bones would have been degreased as well as defleshed, rendering them of little or no food value to scavenging dogs.

The minor impact of both recovery and taphonomic biases on the composition of the Henderson lagomorph assemblage allows us to focus on the place of these small mammals in the subsistence practices of the villagers. Comparing the lagomorph assemblage from the East Plaza with the remains from the room blocks shows that the former displays: (1) proportionately more jackrabbits, (2) a lower density of cottontail remains per cubic meter of deposit, (3) a greater degree of bone fragmentation, (4) proportionately fewer lower limb and foot elements, and (5) a greater proportion of immature animals. While (1) through (4) might all be attributed to taphonomic processes, in particular the scavenging activities of village dogs in the more open and accessible East Plaza locale, (5) cannot be explained in this manner. If the plaza assemblage had experienced greater attritional losses than the assemblage deposited within the room blocks, immature animals should be less well represented in the plaza. This is not the case, clearly indicating that the Henderson villagers discarded greater proportions of immature cottontails and jackrabbits in the East Plaza than in the room blocks. It is also very likely that the villagers discarded more jackrabbit remains in the East Plaza than in the rooms. This might be related to procurement techniques or seasonality.

In ungulates, seasonality is commonly established by determining the age at death of the animals on the basis of tooth eruption and wear patterns. Critical to the success of this approach is the existence of a single tightly constrained birth season for the species in question. Lagomorphs, unfortunately, produce multiple litters in the same year, and it is therefore impossible to determine to which of these litters a particular animal belongs.

Fortunately, there is an alternative approach to establishing the seasonal timing of lagomorph procurement. While this approach is unlikely to work in every context, it does produce an indication of the seasonality of rabbit and jackrabbit hunting at Henderson. Both taxa of lagomorph give birth to young between about February and July/August. During this period, the proportion of immature animals in the population rises from zero in the spring to 70% or 80% in the late summer and fall. The proportion of immature elements will be high in samples procured over the summer and fall and low in samples taken over the winter and spring.

This approach only works, however, if it can be shown that taphonomic processes have not selectively eliminated many of the immature elements. As already noted, this condition appears to be met in the Henderson case.

Another condition that must be met is that the hunting techniques used by the villagers would produce representative samples of the age structure of the wild populations. Numerous field studies of lagomorphs by wildlife biologists using analogous transect censusing, hunting, live-trapping, and driving techniques show this generally to be true.

Finally, a mixture of lagomorph remains killed during two or more seasons of the year can produce an assemblage that mimics the age structure of one that accumulated during a single season. In many archaeological situations, dealing with mixed assemblages may prove an insurmountable problem. Fortunately, at Henderson most rabbit hunting appears to have taken place between late winter and late spring or early summer. This conclusion is based on the low frequency of animals in the Henderson assemblage with *fusing* proximal humeri. Studies of wild lagomorph populations show that animals with fusing humeri are abundant throughout the year except during the spring.

In sum, most, if not all, lagomorph hunting at Henderson seems to have taken place during the late winter and spring. The somewhat higher proportion of immature animals and the higher ratio of jackrabbits to cottontails in the East Plaza midden suggest that: (1) more hunting events reflected by the plaza remains took place slightly later in the year (May/June) than those represented in the room blocks (later winter/spring); or (2) hunting techniques reflected by the plaza remains point to a greater use of communal methods. The absence of clear evidence for fall rabbit and jackrabbit hunts is surprising, but dovetails with the bison and antelope analyses (see Chapters 4 and 5) in suggesting that Henderson may have been partially, or perhaps entirely, abandoned by its residents each year following the harvest, not to be reoccupied again until late winter or spring.

Since completion of the original manuscript, almost all of the lagomorph remains recovered in all five seasons of excavation at Henderson (1980, 1981, 1994, 1995, 1997) have been coded and analyzed, making it possible to examine the data for temporal patterning. The total sample consists of over 8,600 lagomorph bones, of which 30% are *Lepus* and 70% are *Sylvilagus*. *Lepus* comprises roughly 31% of the Early phase lagomorphs and 30% of the Late phase lagomorphs indicating that the proportions of the two taxa remained unchanged over time. In both periods cottontails outnumber jackrabbits.

Other data, however, indicate changes in the role of lagomorphs in Henderson's economy. For example, the frequency of lagomorphs in the total faunal assemblage increases significantly in the Late phase. This increase is also clearly reflected in the density values (NISP/m^3), which nearly double in the later period.

Despite the sharp increase in the numerical importance of rabbits and jackrabbits, their social importance appears to have declined. In both taxa, the proportion of burned elements drops significantly in the Late phase, implying fewer of these animals were prepared by roasting or pit-baking. In addition, the proportion of lagomorph bones found in "public" contexts also declines. It appears that in the Late phase more of these animals were prepared in less public contexts and more often boiled or stewed rather than roasted or pit-baked.

Finally, there is some evidence for a change in the seasonality of procurement of the cottontails, though not of the jackrabbits. The proportion of immatures is low in both taxa, but declines even further in Late phase cottontails. In Chapters 4, 5, and 6, it has been argued that increasing emphasis during the Late phase on long-distance, spring-season communal bison hunting created or exacerbated scheduling conflicts among and between bison hunting and other subsistence pursuits. The decline in immature cottontails in the Late phase may indicate that rabbit hunting also came into increasing conflict with activities related to the bison hunt, favoring their procurement even earlier in the spring.

Acknowledgments

Our understanding of the lagomorph remains recovered from Henderson in 1994, 1995, and 1995 has benefited greatly from an undergraduate honors thesis by Rebecca Dean (1995) and from laboratory studies conducted by Sudha Shah and Amy Lawson.

Notes

1. There is some confusion in Findley et al. 1975:85 in the labeling of the *y* axis in their Figure 35. In the text, these authors make it clear that they are illustrating the cheek-tooth row length (P_3-M_3), but the axis in the figure is actually labeled "alveolar length" (P_3-M_1).

2. The small lagomorph sample recovered by flotation represents an MNI of four cottontails and one jackrabbit, both values based on the number of tibiae.

3. Breakage of the Henderson lagomorph bones was coded in terms of the fraction of the estimated total length of an unbroken element represented by the actual specimen. Six categories were coded: (1) complete; (2) nearly complete (very minor damage to the specimen); (3) more than.75 of the estimated length of an unbroken specimen; (4) between .75 and .5 of the estimated length; (5) between.5 and.25 and (6) less than .25. In Table 8.5, these six categories have been lumped together to form two: complete or nearly complete (categories 1, 2, and 3); and broken (categories 4, 5, and 6). This grouping in no way alters the result; cottontail and jackrabbit elements have strikingly similar breakage patterns despite the substantial differences in their body size and in the size of their individual skeletal elements.

4. In the archaeological literature, bone density has most commonly been referred to as "bulk density" but more recently the term "volume density" is being employed (see Kreutzer 1992; Lyman 1992). We use these terms interchangeably here, although they are not strictly speaking the same thing (see Lyman 1992).

5. Unfortunately, the low incidence of burning in no way proves that most lagomorphs at Henderson were prepared in pots. Even if small mammals were normally roasted in an open hearth, unlike bison, deer, or antelope they may not have been dismembered before being placed in the fire. They also could have been placed on preheated stones and baked in a pit, another technique unlikely to produce large numbers of charred bones (see also Kent 1993:348).

6. For similar conclusions concerning the survivorship of small mammal remains in !Kung San campsites that had been occupied for extended periods, see Yellen 1991a, 1991b.

7. Breakage due to trampling is likely to have been augmented in the East Plaza by the presence in the midden of thousands of sharp-edged pieces of fire-cracked rock.

8. Animals estimated to be less than or equal to six months in age on the basis of eye lens weight were counted as "immature" in these calculations (see also Young 1996:132).

9. When the fusion state of the lagomorph remains recovered from all five seasons of excavation is considered (NISP = 4,799), the proportion of immatures in both cottontails and jackrabbits is somewhat lower, ranging between about 13% and 16% depending on species and temporal phase (see Table 8.13 and associated text).

10. Test of equality of two percentages based on the arcsine transformation (Sokal and Rohlf 1969:607-10).

References Cited

Akins, N. J.
1985 Prehistoric Faunal Utilization in Chaco Canyon, Basketmaker III Through Pueblo III. In: *Environment and Subsistence of Chaco Canyon, New Mexico*, edited by F. J. Mathien, pp. 305-445. Publications in Archeology 18E, Chaco Canyon Studies. Albuquerque, NM: U.S. Department of the Interior, National Park Service.

Andrews, P., and E. M. N. Evans
1983 Small Mammal Bone Accumulations Produced by Mammalian Carnivores. *Paleobiology* (3):289-307.

Bailey, V.
1931 *Mammals of New Mexico*. North American Fauna 53. Washington, DC: U.S. Department of Agriculture, Bureau of Biological Survey.

Bate, D. M. A.
1937 Paleontology: The Fossil Fauna of the Wady el-Mughara Caves. In: *The Stone Age of Mount Carmel*, Vol. 1, edited by D. A. E. Garrod and D. M. A. Bate, pp. 139-240. Oxford, England: Clarendon Press.

Bayham, F., and P. Hatch
1985a Archaeofaunal Remains from the New River Area. In: *Hohokam Settlement and Economic Systems in the Central New River Drainage, Arizona*, edited by D. Doyel and M. D. Elson, pp. 405-33. Soil Systems Publications in Archaeology 4. Phoenix, AZ: Soil Systems, Inc.
1985b Hohokam and Salado Animal Utilization in the Tonto Basin. In: *Studies in the Hohokam and Salado of the Tonto Basin*, edited by G. Rice, pp. 191-210. Tempe, AZ: Arizona State University, Office of Cultural Resource Management.

Beaglehole, E.
1936 *Hopi Hunting and Hunting Ritual*. Yale University Publications in Anthropology 4.

Beckett, P. H.
1974 A Tiwa Rabbit Hunt as Held by the Tortugas Indians. *Awanyu* 2(1):40-46.

Behrensmeyer, A. K.
1975 The Taphonomy and Paleoecology of Plio-Pleistocene Vertebrate Assemblages East of Lake Rudolf, Kenya. *Harvard University, Museum of Comparative Zoology Bulletin* 146(10):473-578.
1978 Taphonomic and Ecologic Information from Bone Weathering. *Paleobiology* 4:150-62.

Bertram, J. B., and N. Draper
1982 The Bones from the Bis sa'ani Community: A Sociotechnic Archaeofaunal Analysis. In: *Bis sa'ani: A Late Bonito Phase Community on Escavada Wash, Northwest New Mexico*, Vol. 3, edited by C. D. Breternitz, D. E. Doyel, and M. P. Marshall, pp. 1015-65. Navajo Nation Papers in Anthropology 14. Window Rock, AZ: Navajo Nation Cultural Resource Management Program.

Binford, L. R.
1978 *Nunamiut Ethnoarchaeology*. New York: Academic Press.
1981 *Bones: Ancient Men and Modern Myths*. New York: Academic Press.

Binford, L. R., and J. B. Bertram
1977 Bone Frequencies—and Attritional Processes. In: *For Theory Building in Archaeology*, edited by L. R. Binford, pp. 77-153. New York: Academic Press.

Binford, L. R., M. G. L. Mills, and N. M. Stone
1988 Hyena Scavenging Behavior and Its Implications for the Interpretation of Faunal Assemblages from FLK 22 (the Zinj Floor) at Olduvai Gorge. *Journal of Anthropological Archaeology* 7(2):99-135.

Binford, M. R., W. H. Doleman, N. Draper, and K. B. Kelley
1982 Anasazi and Navajo Archeofauna. In: *Anasazi and Navajo Land Use in the McKinley Mine Area Near Gallup, New Mexico*, Vol. 1: *Archeology*, Part 1, edited by C. G. Allen and B. A. Nelson, pp. 448-507. Albuquerque, NM: University of New Mexico, Office of Contract Archeology.

Blumenschine, R. J.
1986 Carcass Consumption Sequences and the Archaeological Distinction of Scavenging and Hunting. *Journal of Human Evolution* 15:639-59.

Blumenschine, R. J., and M. M. Selvaggio
1991 On the Marks of Marrow Bone Processing by Hammerstones and Hyenas: Their Anatomical Patterning and Archaeological Implications. In: *Cultural Beginnings: Approaches to*

Understanding Early Hominid Life-Ways in the African Savanna, edited by J. D. Clark, pp. 17-32. Romisch-Germanisches Zentralmuseum, Forschungsinstitut f¸r Vor- und Fr¸geschichte, Monograph 19. Bonn, Germany: Dr. Rudolf Habelt GMBH.

Bothma, J. du P., J. G. Teer, and C. E. Gates
1972 Growth and Age Determination of the Cottontail in South Texas. *Journal of Wildlife Management* 36(4):1209-21.

Brain, C. K.
1967 Hottentot Food Remains and Their Meaning in the Interpretation of Fossil Bone Assemblages. *Namib Desert Research Station Scientific Papers* 32:1-11.
1969 The Contribution of the Namib Desert Hottentots to an Understanding of Australopithecine Bone Accumulations. *Namib Desert Research Station Scientific Papers* 39.
1981 *The Hunters or the Hunted? An Introduction to African Cave Taphonomy*. Chicago, IL: University of Chicago Press.

Brink, J., and B. Dawe
1989 *Final Report of the 1985 and 1986 Field Seasons at Head-Smashed-In Buffalo Jump, Alberta*. Manuscript Series 16. Edmonton, Alberta: Alberta Culture and Multiculturalism, Historical Resources Division, Archaeological Survey of Alberta.

Broekhuizen, S., and F. Maaskamp
1979 Age Determination in the European Hare (*Lepus europaeus* Pallas) in the Netherlands. *Zeitschrift fur Saugetierkunde* 44:162-75.

Buskirk, W.
1986 *The Western Apache: Living with the Land Before 1950*. Norman, OK: University of Oklahoma Press.

Cabon-Raczynska, K., and J. Raczynski
1972 Methods for Determination of Age in the European Hare. *Acta Theriologica* 17(7):75-86.

Casteel, R. W.
1971 Differential Bone Destruction: Some Comments. *American Antiquity* 36(4):466-69.

Chapman, J. A., J. G. Hockman, and W. R. Edwards
1982 Cottontails: *Sylvilagus floridanus* and Allies. In *Wild Mammals of North America: Biology, Management and Economics*, edited by J. A. Chapman and G. A. Feldhamer, pp. 83-123. Baltimore, MD: John Hopkins University Press.

Chapman, J. A., and G. R. Willner
1978 *Sylvilagus audubonii*. *Mammalian Species* 106:1-4.

Connolly, G. E., M. L. Dudzinski, and W. M. Longhurst
1969 The Eye Lens as an Indicator of Age in the Black-Tailed Jack Rabbit. *Journal of Wildlife Management* 33(1):159-64.

Cordell, L. S.
1977 Late Anasazi Farming and Hunting Strategies: One Example of a Problem in Congruence. *American Antiquity* 42(3):449-61.

Davis, S.
1977 The Ungulate Remains from Kebara Cave. In: *Moshe Stekelis Memorial Volume*, edited by B. Arensburg and O. Bar-Yosef, pp. 150-63. Eretz-Israel, Archaeological, Historical and Geographical Studies 13. Jerusalem, Israel: The Israel Exploration Society and The Institute of Archaeology of The Hebrew University of Jerusalem.

Davis, W. B.
1974 *The Mammals of Texas*. Bulletin 41. Austin, TX: Texas Parks and Wildlife Department.

Dean, R. M.
1995 *Lagomorph Remains from the Henderson Pueblo, New Mexico (LA-1549)*. Honors thesis, Department of Anthropology, University of Michigan, Ann Arbor, MI.

Driver, J. C.
1985 *Zooarchaeology of Six Prehistoric Sites in the Sierra Blanca Region, New Mexico*. Technical Report 17. Ann Arbor, MI: Museum of Anthropology, University of Michigan.
1991 Assemblage Formation at the Robinson Site (LA46326). In: *Mogollon V*, edited by P. H. Beckett, pp. 197-206. Las Cruces, NM: COAS Publishing and Research.

Dunn, J. P., J. A. Chapman, and R. E. Marsh
1982 Jackrabbits: *Lepus californicus* and Allies. In: *Wild Mammals of North America: Biology, Management and Economics*, edited by J. A. Chapman and G. A. Feldhamer, pp. 124-45. Baltimore, MD: Johns Hopkins University Press.

Emslie, S. D.
1977 *Interpretation of Faunal Remains from Archaeological Sites in Mancos Canyon, Southwestern Colorado*. Master's thesis, Department of Anthropology, University of Colorado, Boulder, CO.

Findley, J. S., A. H. Harris, D. E. Wilson, and C. Jones
1975 *Mammals of New Mexico*. Albuquerque, NM: University of New Mexico Press.

Flannery, K. V.
1966 The Postglacial "Readaptation" as Viewed from Mesoamerica. *American Antiquity* 31(6):800-5.

Flint, P. R., and S. W. Neusius
1987 Cottontail Procurement among Dolores Anasazi. In: *Dolores Archaeological Program—Supporting Studies: Settlement and Environment*, compiled by K. L. Peterson and J. D. Orcutt, pp. 255-73. Denver, CO: U.S. Department of the Interior, Bureau of Reclamation, Engineering and Research Center.

Flux, J. E. C.
1970 Life History of the Mountain Hare (*Lepus timidus scoticus*) in North-East Scotland. *Journal of Zoology (London)* 161:75-123.
1981 Reproductive Strategies in the Genus *Lepus*. In: *Proceedings of the First World Lagomorph Conference*, edited by K. Myers and C. D. MacInnes, pp. 155-74. Guelph, Ontario: University of Guelph.

Foster, R. C.
1968 *Reproductive Patterns of the Desert Cottontail of Fort Stanton, New Mexico.* Master's thesis, Department of Wildlife Management, New Mexico State University, Las Cruces, NM.

Frison, G. C.
1978 *Prehistoric Hunters of the High Plains.* New York: Academic Press.

Garrard, A. N.
1982 *The Environmental Implications of a Re-Analysis of the Large Mammal Fauna from Wadi el-Mughara Caves, Palestine.* BAR International Series 133. Oxford, England: British Archaeological Reports.

Gifford, D. P.
1980 Ethnoarchaeological Contributions to the Taphonomy of Human Sites. In: *Fossils in the Making: Vertebrate Taphonomy and Paleoecology*, edited by A. K. Behrensmeyer and A. P. Hill, pp. 93-106. Chicago, IL: University of Chicago Press.
1981 Taphonomy and Paleoecology: A Critical Review of Archaeology's Sister Discipline. *Advances in Archaeological Method and Theory* 4:365-438.

Gifford, D. P., and A. K. Behrensmeyer
1977 Observed Formation and Burial of a Recent Human Occupation Site in Kenya. *Quaternary Research* 8(3):245-66.

Gifford-Gonzalez, D. P., D. B. Damrosch, D. R. Damrosch, J. Pryor, and R. L. Thunen
1985 The Third Dimensions in Site Structure: An Experiment in Trampling and Vertical Displacement. *American Antiquity* 50(4):803-18.

Gillespie, W.
1987 Vertebrate Remains. In: *The Archaeology of the San Xavier Bridge Site (AZ BB:13:14), Tucson Basin, Southern Arizona*, Part 3: *Descriptions*, edited by J. Ravesloot, pp. 271-301. Archaeological Series 171. Tucson, AZ: University of Arizona, Arizona State Museum, Cultural Resource Management Division.
1989 Faunal Remains from Four Sites Along the Tucson Aqueduct: Prehistoric Exploitation of Jack Rabbits and Other Vertebrates in the Avra Valley. In: *Hohokam Archaeology Along Phase B of the Tucson Aqueduct Central Arizona Project*, Vol. 1: *Syntheses and Interpretations*, Part 1, edited by J. Czaplicki and J. Ravesloot, pp. 171-230. Archaeological Series 178. Tucson, AZ: University of Arizona, Arizona State Museum, Cultural Resource Management Division.

Grayson, D. K.
1989 Bone Transport, Bone Destruction, and Reverse Utility Curves. *Journal of Archaeological Science* 16:643-52.

Griffing, J. P., and C. A. Davis
1976 *Black-Tailed Jackrabbits in Southeastern New Mexico: Population Structure, Reproduction, Feeding, and Use of Forms.* Agricultural Experiment Station, Research Report 318. Las Cruces, NM: New Mexico State University.

Gross, J. E.
1969 *Jackrabbit Demographic and Life History Studies, Pawnee Site.* U.S. International Biological Program, Grassland Biome, Technical Report 16. Fort Collins, CO: Colorado State University, Natural Resource Ecology Laboratory.

Gross, J. E., L. C. Stoddart, and F. H. Wagner
1974 *Demographic Analysis of a Northern Utah Jackrabbit Population.* Wildlife Monograph 40. Washington, DC: Wildlife Society.

Hale, J. B.
1949 Aging Cottontail Rabbits by Bone Growth. *Journal of Wildlife Management* 13(2):216-25.

Hall, E. R.
1981 *The Mammals of North America*, Vol. 1, 2nd edition. New York: John Wiley and Sons.

Harris, A. H.
1963 *Vertebrate Remains and Past Environmental Reconstruction in the Navajo Reservoir District.* Museum of New Mexico Papers in Anthropology 11. Albuquerque, NM: Museum of New Mexico Press.

Henke, S. E., and S. Demarais
1990 Capturing Jackrabbits by Drive Corral on Grasslands in West Texas. *Wildlife Society Bulletin* 18(1):31-33.

Hill, W. W.
1938 *The Agricultural and Hunting Methods of the Navaho Indians.* Yale University Publications in Anthropology 18.

Hillson, S.
1986 *Teeth.* Cambridge, England: Cambridge University Press.

Hockett, B. S.
1989 Archaeological Significance of Rabbit-Raptor Interactions in Southern California. *North American Archaeologist* 10(2):123-39.

Hoffmeister, D. F.
1986 *Mammals of Arizona.* Tucson, AZ: University of Arizona Press and The Arizona Game and Fish Department.

Hooijer, D.
1961 The Fossil Vertebrates of Ksar Akil, A Paleolithic Rockshelter in Lebanon. *Zoologische Verhandelingen* 49:4-65.

Horwitz, L. K.
1990 The Origin of Partially Digested Bones Recovered from Archaeological Contexts in Israel. *Paléorient* 16:97-106.

Hulbert, R. C., Jr.
1984 Latest Pleistocene and Holocene Leporid Faunas from Texas: Their Composition, Distribution and Climatic Implications. *Southwestern Naturalist* 29(2):197-210.

Iason, G. R.
1988 Age Determination of Mountain Hares (*Lepus timidus*): A Rapid Method and When to Use It. *Journal of Applied Ecology* 25:389-95.

Keith, L. B.
1981 Population Dynamics of Hares. In: *Proceedings of the First World Lagomorph Conference*, edited by K. Myers and C. D. MacInnes, pp. 395-440. Guelph, Ontario: University of Guelph.

Keith, L. B., and L. A. Windberg
1978 *A Demographic Analysis of the Snowshoe Hare Cycle*. Wildlife Monograph 58. Washington, DC: Wildlife Society.

Kent, S.
1981 The Dog: An Archaeologist's Best Friend or Worst Enemy—The Spatial Distribution of Faunal Remains. *Journal of Field Archaeology* 8(3):367-72.
1993 Variability in Faunal Assemblages: The Influence of Hunting Skill, Sharing, Dogs, and Mode of Cooking on Faunal Remains at a Sedentary Kalahari Community. *Journal of Anthropological Archaeology* 12:323-85.

Klein, R. G.
1989 Why Does Skeletal Part Representation Differ between Smaller and Larger Bovids at Klasies River Mouth and Other Archaeological Sites? *Journal of Archaeological Science* 16:363-81.

Klein, R. G., and K. Cruz-Uribe
1984 *The Analysis of Animal Bones from Archeological Sites*. Chicago, IL: University of Chicago Press.

Kreutzer, L. A.
1992 Bison and Deer Bone Mineral Densities: Comparisons and Implications for the Interpretation of Archaeological Faunas. *Journal of Archaeological Science* 19:271-94.

Lang, R. W., and A. H. Harris
1984 *The Faunal Remains from Arroyo Hondo Pueblo, New Mexico: A Study in Short-Term Subsistence Change*. Arroyo Hondo Archaeological Series 5. Santa Fe, NM: School of American Research Press.

Lange, C. H.
1968 *Cochiti: A New Mexico Pueblo, Past and Present*. Carbondale, IL: Southern Illinois University Press.

Lechleitner, R. R.
1959 Sex Ratio, Age Classes and Reproduction of the Black-Tailed Jackrabbit. *Journal of Mammalogy* 40(1):63-81.

Legler, R. P., Jr.
1970 *Habitat Preference of the Desert Cottontail with Additional Notes on the Black-Tailed Jack Rabbit*. Master's thesis, Department of Wildlife Science, New Mexico State University, Las Cruces, NM.

Lord, R. D.
1963 *The Cottontail Rabbit in Illinois*. Illinois Department of Conservation, Technical Bulletin 3. Carbondale, IL: Southern Illinois University Press (Published for the Illinois Department of Conservation and Illinois Natural History Survey).

Lyman, R. L.
1984 Bone Density and Differential Survivorship of Fossil Classes. *Journal of Anthropological Archaeology* 3:259-99.
1985 Bone Frequencies: Differential Transport, In-Situ Destruction, and the MGUI. *Journal of Archaeological Science* 12:221-36.
1991 Taphonomic Problems with Archaeological Analyses of Animal Carcass Utilization and Transport. In: *Beamers, Bobwhites, and Blue-Points: Tributes to the Career of Paul W. Parmalee*, edited by J. R. Purdue, W. E. Klippel, and B. W. Styles, pp. 135-48. Scientific Papers 23. Springfield, IL: Illinois State Museum.
1992 Anatomical Considerations of Utility Curves in Zooarchaeology. *Journal of Archaeological Science* 19(1):7-22.

Lyman, R. L., L. E. Houghton, and A. L. Chambers
1992 The Effect of Structural Density on Marmot Skeletal Part Representation in Archaeological Sites. *Journal of Archaeological Science* 19(5):557-73.

Lyon, P. J.
1970 Differential Bone Destruction: An Ethnographic Example. *American Antiquity* 35(2):213-15.

Marshall, F., and T. Pilgram
1991 Meat Versus Within-Bone Nutrients: Another Look at the Meaning of Body Part Representation in Archaeological Sites. *Journal of Archaeological Science* 18:149-63.

Metcalfe, D., and K. T. Jones
1988 A Reconsideration of Animal Body-Part Utility Indices. *American Antiquity* 53:486-504.

Monks, G. G.
1981 Seasonality Studies. In: *Advances in Archaeological Method and Theory*, Vol. 4, edited by M. B. Schiffer, pp. 177-240. New York: Academic Press.

Morey, D. F., and W. E. Klippel
1991 Canid Scavenging and Deer Bone Survivorship at an Archaic Period Site in Tennessee. *Archaeozoologia* 4(1):11-28.

Neusius, S. W.
1985 Faunal Resource Use: Perspectives from the Ethnographic Record. In: *Dolores Archaeological Program: Studies in Environmental Archaeology*, compiled by K. L. Petersen, V. L. Clay, M. H. Matthews, and S. W. Neusius, pp. 101-15. Denver, CO: United States Department of the Interior, Bureau of Reclamation, Engineering and Research Center.

Neusius, S. W., and P. R. Flint
1985 Cottontail Species Identification: Zooarchaeological Use of Mandibular Measurements. *Journal of Ethnobiology* 5(1):51-58.

Nielsen, A. E.
1991 Trampling the Archaeological Record: An Experimental Study. *American Antiquity* 56(3):483-503.

Ohtaishi, N., N. Hachiya, and Y. Shibata
1976 Age Determination of the Hare from Annual Layers in the Mandibular Bone. *Acta Theriologica* 21(11):168-71.

Olsen, J. W.
1990 *Vertebrate Faunal Remains from Grasshopper Pueblo, Arizona*. Anthropological Paper 83. Ann Arbor, MI: Museum of Anthropology, University of Michigan.

Orr, R. T.
1940 *The Rabbits of California*. Occasional Paper 19. San Francisco, CA: California Academy of Sciences.

Pascal, M., and G. Kovacs
1983 La Determination de l'Age Individuel Chez le Lievre Europeen par la Technique Squelettochronologique. *Terre et Vie* 37:171-86.

Pavao, Barnet
1996 *Toward a Taphonomy of Leporid Skeletons: Photodensitometry Assays*. Senior honors thesis, Department of Anthropology, State University of New York, Binghamton, NY.

Pavao, Barnet, and Peter W. Stahl
1999 Structural Density Assays of Leporid Skeletal Elements with Implications for Taphonomic, Actualistic and Archaeological Research. *Journal of Archaeological Science* 26(1):53-66.

Payne, S., and P. J. Munson
1985 Ruby and How Many Squirrels? The Destruction of Bones by Dogs. In: *Palaeobiological Investigations: Research Design, Methods and Data Analysis*, edited by N. R. J. Fieller, D. D. Gilbertson, and N. G. A. Ralph, pp. 31-39. BAR International Series 266. Oxford, England: British Archaeological Reports.

Pepin, D.
1973 Recherche d'un Critere d'Age Chez le Lievre *Lepus europaeus*. *Annales de Zoologie-Ecologie Animale* 5(2):271-81.

Pintar, E.
1987 *Controles Experimentales de Desplazamientos y Alteraciones de Artefactos Liticos en Sedimentos Arenosos: Applicaciones Arqueologicas*. Tesis de licenciatura, Facultad de Filosofia y Letras, Universidad Nacional de Buenos Aires, Buenos Aires, Argentina.

Pippin, L. C.
1987 *Prehistory and Paleoecology of Guadalupe Ruin, New Mexico*. Anthropological Papers 112. Salt Lake City, UT: University of Utah

Rocek, T. R., and J. D. Speth
1986 *The Henderson Site Burials: Glimpses of a Late Prehistoric Population in the Pecos Valley*. Technical Report 18. Ann Arbor, MI: Museum of Anthropology,niversity of Michigan.

Rohn, A. H.
1971 *Mug House, Mesa Verde National Park, Colorado*. Archeological Research Series 7-D. Washington, DC: U.S. Department of the Interior, National Park Service.

Shaffer, B. S.
1991 *The Economic Importance of Vertebrate Faunal Remains from the Nan Ruin (LA 15049), A Classic Mimbres Site, Grant County, New Mexico*. Master's thesis, Department of Anthropology, Texas A & M University, College Station, TX.
1992 Quarter-Inch Screening: Understanding Biases in Recovery of Vertebrate Faunal Remains. *American Antiquity* 57(1):129-36.

Shipman, P.
1981 *Life History of a Fossil: An Introduction to Taphonomy and Paleoecology*. Cambridge, MA: Harvard University Press.

Smith, B. H.
1992 Life History and the Evolution of Human Maturation. *Evolutionary Anthropology* 1(4):134-42.

Sokal, R. R., and F. J. Rohlf
1969 *Biometry: The Principles and Practice of Statistics in Biological Research*. San Francisco, CA: W. H. Freeman and Company.

Speth, J. D.
1991 Taphonomy and Early Hominid Behavior: Problems in Distinguishing Cultural and Non-cultural Agents. In: *Human Predators and Prey Mortality*, edited by M. C. Stiner, pp. 31-40. Boulder, CO: Westview Press.

Speth, J. D., and S. L. Scott
1989 Horticulture and Large-Mammal Hunting: The Role of Resource Depletion and the Constraints of Time and Labor. In: *Farmers as Hunters*, edited by S. Kent, pp. 71-79. Cambridge, England: Cambridge University Press.

Spier, L.
1928 *Havasupai Ethnography*. American Museum of Natural History, Anthropological Paper 29 (Part 3):81-392.
1933 *Yuman Tribes of the Gila River*. Chicago, IL: University of Chicago Press.

Steward, J. H.
1938 *Basin-Plateau Aboriginal Sociopolitical Groups*. Bulletin 120. Washington, DC: Smithsonian Institution, Bureau of American Ethnology.

Sullins, G. L., D. O. McKay, and B. J. Verts
1976 Estimating Ages of Cottontails by Periosteal Zonations. *Northwest Science* 50(1)17-22.

Szuter, C. R.
1991 *Hunting by Prehistoric Horticulturalists in the American Southwest*. New York: Garland Publishing.

Taylor, R. H.
1959 Age Determination in Wild Rabbits. *Nature*184:1158-1159

Thomas, D. H.
1969 Great Basin Hunting Patterns: A Quantitative Method for Treating Faunal Remains. *American Antiquity* 34(4):392-401.

Thomsen, H. P., and O. A. Mortensen
1946 Bone Growth as an Age Criterion in the Cottontail Rabbit. *Journal of Wildlife Management* 10(2):171-76.

Tiemeier, O. W., M. F. Hansen, M. H. Bartel, E. T. Lyon, B. M. El-Rawi, K. J. McMahon, and E. H. Herrick
1965 *The Black-Tailed Jack Rabbit in Kansas*. Department of Zoology, Contribution 336, and Department of Bacteriology, Contribution 418. Manhattan, KS: Kansas Agricultural Experiment Station.

Tiemeier, O. W., and M. L. Plenert
1964 A Comparison of Three Methods for Determining the Age of Black-Tailed Jackrabbits. *Journal of Mammalogy* 45(3):409-16.

Walhovd, H.
1966 Reliability of Age Criteria for Danish Hares (*Lepus europaeus* Pallas). *Danish Review of Game Biology* 4 (Part 3):106-28.

Walters, I.
1984 Gone to the Dogs: A Study of Bone Attrition at a Central Australian Campsite. *Mankind* 14(5):389-400.

Weber, S. A., and P. D. Seaman (editors)
1985 *Havasupai Habitat: A. F. Whiting's Ethnography of a Traditional Indian Culture*. Tucson, AZ: University of Arizona Press.

Whalen, M. E.
1994 *Turquoise Ridge and Late Prehistoric Residential Mobility in the Desert Mogollon Region*. University of Utah Anthropological Paper 118. Salt Lake City, UT: University of Utah Press.

Yellen, J. E.
1977 Cultural Patterning in Faunal Remains: Evidence from the !Kung Bushmen. In: *Experimental Archaeology*, edited by D. W. Ingersoll, J. E. Yellen, and W. Macdonald, pp. 271-331. New York: Columbia University Press.
1991a Small Mammals: !Kung San Utilization and the Production of Faunal Assemblages. *Journal of Anthropological Archaeology* 10(1):1-26.
1991b Small Mammals: Post-Discard Patterning of !Kung San Faunal Remains. *Journal of Anthropological Archaeology* 10(2):152-92.

Young, L. C.
1996 *Mobility and Farmers: The Pithouse-to-Pueblo Transition in Northeastern Arizona*. Ph.D. dissertation, University of Arizona, Tucson, AZ.

Appendix to Chapter 8

Henderson Lagomorph Assemblage

Table A8.1. ***Lepus californicus*** **sample recovered from Henderson Site (all 1980-1981 proveniences combined).**

Element	Total Sample						Immature Only							Burned	
	NISP[a] (1)	% of Total NISP (2)	MNE[b] (3)	% of Total MNE (4)	MNI[c] (5)	% MNI[d] (6)	Unfus. NISP (7)	Fusing NISP (8)	Unfus. MNE (9)	Fusing MNE (10)	Unfus. MNI (11)	Fusing MNI (12)	Total Imm. %MNI[e] (13)	NISP (14)	% of Total NISP[f] (15)
Total Skull	145	7.9	77	5.2	39	70.9	—	—	—	—	—	—	—	1	0.69
Frontal	2	0.1	2	0.1	1	1.8	—	—	—	—	—	—	—	—	—
Squam.-Tem.	28	1.5	28	1.9	14	25.5	—	—	—	—	—	—	—	—	—
Tem.-Par.	4	0.2	4	0.3	2	3.6	—	—	—	—	—	—	—	—	—
Tem.-Frnt.	—	—	—	—	—	—	—	—	—	—	—	—	—	—	—
Nasal	14	0.8	14	1.0	7	12.7	—	—	—	—	—	—	—	—	—
Premax.	7	0.4	7	0.5	4	7.3	—	—	—	—	—	—	—	—	—
Maxilla	90	4.9	77	5.2	39	70.9	—	—	—	—	—	—	—	1	1.11
Max.-Prem.	—	—	—	—	—	—	—	—	—	—	—	—	—	—	—
Cmplt. Skull	—	—	—	—	—	—	—	—	—	—	—	—	—	—	—
Total Mand.	176	9.6	65	4.4	33	60.0	—	—	—	—	—	—	—	—	—
Cmplt. Man.	3	0.2	3	0.2	2	3.6	—	—	—	—	—	—	—	—	—
Man. Body	80	4.4	62	4.2	31	56.4	—	—	—	—	—	—	—	—	—
Man. Symph.	54	3.0	25	1.7	13	23.6	—	—	—	—	—	—	—	—	—
Man. Border	2	0.1	2	0.1	1	1.8	—	—	—	—	—	—	—	—	—
Man. Ramus	37	2.0	37	2.5	19	34.6	—	—	—	—	—	—	—	—	—
Atlas	4	0.2	4	0.3	4	7.3	—	—	—	—	—	—	—	—	—
Axis	3	0.2	3	0.2	3	5.5	—	—	—	—	—	—	—	—	—
Cervical	5	0.3	5	0.3	1	1.8	—	—	—	—	—	—	—	—	—
Thoracic	4	0.2	4	0.3	1	1.8	—	—	—	—	—	—	—	—	—
Lumbar	23	1.3	21	1.4	5	9.1	—	—	—	—	—	—	—	—	—
Sacrum	2	0.1	2	0.1	2	3.6	—	—	—	—	—	—	—	—	—
Scapula	151	8.3	110	7.4	55	100.0	2	—	2	—	1	—	8.3	4	2.65
Prx. Hum.	26	1.4	26	1.8	13	23.6	6	—	6	—	3	—	25.0	1	3.85
Dis. Hum.	109	6.0	108	7.3	54	98.2	10	—	10	—	5	—	41.7	10	9.17
H. Shaft	3	0.2	—	—	—	—	—	—	—	—	—	—	—	—	—
Prx. Rad.	86	4.7	86	5.8	43	78.2	1	1	1	1	1	1	16.7	5	5.81
Dis. Rad.	38	2.1	38	2.6	19	34.6	3	1	3	1	2	1	25.0	2	5.26
R. Shaft	49	2.7	—	—	—	—	—	—	—	—	—	—	—	2	4.08
Prx. Ulna	34	1.9	34	2.3	17	30.9	1	—	1	—	1	—	8.3	2	5.88
Dis. Ulna	9	0.5	9	0.6	5	9.1	—	—	—	—	—	—	—	—	—
Ulna Shaft	70	3.8	46	3.1	23	41.8	—	—	—	—	—	—	—	—	—
Prx. Mc. 2	26	1.4	26	1.8	13	23.6	—	—	—	—	—	—	—	1	3.85
Prx. Mc. 3	28	1.5	28	1.9	14	25.5	—	—	—	—	—	—	—	1	3.57
Prx. Mc. 4	34	1.9	34	2.3	17	30.9	—	1	—	1	—	1	8.3	—	—
Prx. Mc. 5	13	0.7	13	0.9	7	12.7	—	—	—	—	—	—	—	—	—
Dis. Mc. 2	14	0.8	14	1.0	7	12.7	4	—	4	—	2	—	16.7	—	—

(cont.)

Element	Total Sample						Immature Only							Burned	
	NISP[a] (1)	% of Total NISP (2)	MNE[b] (3)	% of Total MNE (4)	MNI[c] (5)	% MNI[d] (6)	Unfus. NISP (7)	Fusing NISP (8)	Unfus. MNE (9)	Fusing MNE (10)	Unfus. MNI (11)	Fusing MNI (12)	Total Imm. %MNI[e] (13)	NISP (14)	% of Total NISP[f] (15)
Dis. Mc. 3	15	0.8	15	1.0	8	14.6	3	—	3	—	2	—	16.7	—	—
Dis. Mc. 4	23	1.3	23	1.6	12	21.8	4	1	4	1	2	1	25.0	—	—
Dis. Mc. 5	13	0.7	13	0.9	7	12.7	—	—	—	—	—	—	—	—	—
Innom.	103	5.6	48	3.2	24	43.6	—	—	—	—	—	—	—	1	0.97
Prx. Fem.	53	2.9	52	3.5	26	47.3	3	—	3	—	2	—	16.7	—	—
Dis. Fem.	65	3.6	64	4.3	32	58.2	20	4	20	4	10	2	100.0	2	3.08
F. Shaft	22	1.2	—	—	—	—	—	—	—	—	—	—	—	—	—
Prx. Tib.	53	2.9	51	3.4	26	47.3	23	1	21	1	11	1	100.0	1	1.89
Dis. Tib.	50	2.7	50	3.4	25	45.5	14	—	14	—	7	—	58.3	1	2.00
T. Shaft	27	1.5	—	—	—	—	—	—	—	—	—	—	—	—	—
Astrag.	29	1.6	29	2.0	15	27.3	—	—	—	—	—	—	—	1	3.45
Calc.	46	2.5	46	3.1	23	41.8	7	4	7	4	4	2	50.0	5	10.87
Cen. Tar.	11	0.6	11	0.7	6	10.9	—	—	—	—	—	—	—	—	—
3rd Tar.	1	0.1	1	0.1	1	1.8	—	—	—	—	—	—	—	—	—
4th Tar.	4	0.2	4	0.3	2	3.6	—	—	—	—	—	—	—	—	—
Prx. Mt. 2	39	2.1	39	2.6	20	36.4	—	—	—	—	—	—	—	1	2.56
Prx. Mt. 3	39	2.1	39	2.6	20	36.4	—	—	—	—	—	—	—	1	2.56
Prx. Mt. 4	38	2.1	38	2.6	19	34.6	—	—	—	—	—	—	—	1	2.63
Prx. Mt. 5	28	1.5	28	1.9	14	25.5	—	—	—	—	—	—	—	1	3.57
Dis. Mt. 2	17	0.9	17	1.2	9	16.4	4	—	4	—	2	—	16.7	—	—
Dis. Mt. 3	14	0.8	14	1.0	7	12.7	4	1	4	1	2	1	25.0	—	—
Dis. Mt. 4	13	0.7	13	0.9	7	12.7	5	2	5	2	3	1	33.3	—	—
Dis. Mt. 5	14	0.8	14	1.0	7	12.7	1	1	1	1	1	1	16.7	—	—
Dis. Mt.	59	3.2	—	—	—	—	8	1	8	1	1	1	16.7	4	6.78
Mpd. Shaft	1	0.1	—	—	—	—	—	—	—	—	—	—	—	—	—
TOTAL	1829	100.0	1481	100.1	—	—	123	18	113	17	—	—	—	48	2.62

[a]NISP, Number of identifiable specimens.
[b]MNE, Minimum number of elements.
[c]MNI, Minimum number of individuals.
[d]%MNI, MNI of each element observed expressed as percent of maximum MNI value—55 animals (scapula).
[e]Total Immature %MNI calculated in same manner as %MNI (see note 4 above), based on maximum immature MNI value of 12 animals (dist. femur or prox. tibia).
[f]Percent of NISP value in same row in Column (1).

Table A8.2. ***Sylvilagus*** **sample recovered from Henderson Site (all 1980-1981 proveniences combined).**

Element	Total Sample						Immature Only							Burned	
	NISP[a] (1)	% of Total NISP (2)	MNE[b] (3)	% of Total MNE (4)	MNI[c] (5)	% MNI[d] (6)	Unfus. NISP (7)	Fusing NISP (8)	Unfus. MNE (9)	Fusing MNE (10)	Unfus. MNI (11)	Fusing MNI (12)	Total Imm. %MNI[e] (13)	NISP (14)	% of Total NISP[f] (15)
Total Skull	460	11.6	197	6.1	100	78.1	—	—	—	—	—	—	—	3	0.65
Frontal	—	—	—	—	—	—	—	—	—	—	—	—	—	—	—
Squam.-Tem.	46	1.2	46	1.4	23	18.0	—	—	—	—	—	—	—	—	—
Tem.-Par.	78	2.0	78	2.4	39	30.5	—	—	—	—	—	—	—	1	1.28
Tem.-Frnt.	1	0.0	1	0.0	1	0.8	—	—	—	—	—	—	—	—	—
Nasal	26	0.7	26	0.8	13	10.2	—	—	—	—	—	—	—	—	—
Premax.	28	0.7	28	0.9	14	10.9	—	—	—	—	—	—	—	—	—
Maxilla	279	7.0	195	6.0	98	76.6	—	—	—	—	—	—	—	2	0.72
Max.-Prem.	1	0.0	1	0.0	1	0.8	—	—	—	—	—	—	—	—	—
Cmplt. Skl.	1	0.0	1	0.0	1	0.8	—	—	—	—	—	—	—	—	—
Total Mand.	471	11.9	248	7.7	125	97.7	—	—	—	—	—	—	—	3	0.64
Cmplt. Man.	27	0.7	27	0.8	14	10.9	—	—	—	—	—	—	—	—	—
Man. Body	251	6.3	221	6.8	111	86.7	—	—	—	—	—	—	—	1	0.40
Man. Symph.	163	4.1	79	2.4	40	31.3	—	—	—	—	—	—	—	2	1.23
Man. Border	4	0.1	4	0.1	2	1.6	—	—	—	—	—	—	—	—	—
Man. Ramus	26	0.7	26	0.8	13	10.2	—	—	—	—	—	—	—	—	—
Atlas	3	0.1	3	0.1	3	2.3	—	—	—	—	—	—	—	—	—
Axis	3	0.1	3	0.1	3	2.3	—	—	—	—	—	—	—	—	—
Cervical	4	0.1	4	0.1	1	0.8	—	—	—	—	—	—	—	—	—
Thoracic	7	0.2	7	0.2	1	0.8	—	—	—	—	—	—	—	—	—
Lumbar	56	1.4	52	1.6	11	8.6	—	—	—	—	—	—	—	1	1.79
Sacrum	5	0.1	5	0.2	5	3.9	—	—	—	—	—	—	—	—	—
Scapula	297	7.5	255	7.9	128	100.0	—	—	—	—	—	—	—	6	2.02
Prx. Hum.	55	1.4	55	1.7	28	21.9	9	1	9	1	5	1	20.0	1	1.82
Dis. Hum.	222	5.6	222	6.9	111	86.7	2	—	2	—	1	—	3.3	4	1.80
H. Shaft	3	0.1	—	—	—	—	—	—	—	—	—	—	—	—	—
Prx. Rad.	121	3.0	121	3.7	61	47.7	1	—	1	—	1	—	3.3	5	4.13
Dis. Rad.	64	1.6	64	2.0	32	25.0	3	—	3	—	2	—	6.7	3	4.69
R. Shaft	25	0.6	—	—	—	—	—	—	—	—	—	—	—	1	4.00
Prx. Ulna	80	2.0	80	2.5	40	31.3	5	1	5	1	3	1	13.3	1	1.25
Dis. Ulna	25	0.6	5	0.2	3	2.3	7	1	5	—	3	—	10.0	—	—
Ulna Shaft	78	2.0	52	1.6	26	20.3	—	—	—	—	—	—	—	2	2.56
Prx. Mc. 2	4	0.1	4	0.1	2	1.6	—	—	—	—	—	—	—	—	—
Prx. Mc. 3	11	0.3	11	0.3	6	4.7	—	—	—	—	—	—	—	—	—
Prx. Mc. 4	3	0.1	3	0.1	2	1.6	—	—	—	—	—	—	—	—	—
Prx. Mc. 5	—	—	—	—	—	—	—	—	—	—	—	—	—	—	—
Dis. Mc. 2	3	0.1	3	0.1	2	1.6	1	—	1	—	1	—	3.3	—	—

(cont.)

Element	Total Sample						Immature Only							Burned	
	NISP[a] (1)	% of Total NISP (2)	MNE[b] (3)	% of Total MNE (4)	MNI[c] (5)	% MNI[d] (6)	Unfus. NISP (7)	Fusing NISP (8)	Unfus. MNE (9)	Fusing MNE (10)	Unfus. MNI (11)	Fusing MNI (12)	Total Imm. %MNI[e] (13)	NISP (14)	% of Total NISP[f] (15)
Dis. Mc. 3	9	0.2	9	0.3	5	3.9	—	—	—	—	—	—	—	—	—
Dis. Mc. 4	2	0.1	2	0.1	1	0.8	1	—	1	—	1	—	3.3	—	—
Dis. Mc. 5	—	—	—	—	—	—	—	—	—	—	—	—	—	—	—
Innom.	413	10.4	214	6.6	107	83.6	10	—	9	—	5	—	16.7	16	3.87
Prx. Fem.	92	2.3	92	2.8	46	35.9	21	—	21	—	11	—	36.7	2	2.17
Dis. Fem.	138	3.5	138	4.3	69	53.9	49	9	49	9	25	5	100.0	6	4.35
F. Shaft	50	1.3	—	—	—	—	—	—	—	—	—	—	—	—	—
Prx. Tib.	110	2.8	108	3.3	54	42.2	43	—	41	—	21	—	70.0	3	2.73
Dis. Tib.	235	5.9	235	7.3	118	92.2	36	1	36	1	18	1	63.3	7	2.98
T. Shaft	155	3.9	—	—	—	—	—	—	—	—	—	—	—	1	0.65
Astrag.	23	0.6	23	0.7	12	9.4	—	—	—	—	—	—	—	1	4.35
Calc.	185	4.7	185	5.7	93	72.7	5	—	5	—	3	—	10.0	4	2.16
Cen. Tar.	1	0.0	1	0.0	1	0.8	—	—	—	—	—	—	—	—	—
3rd Tar.	—	—	—	—	—	—	—	—	—	—	—	—	—	—	—
4th Tar.	—	—	—	—	—	—	—	—	—	—	—	—	—	—	—
Prx. Mt. 2	116	2.9	116	3.6	58	45.3	—	—	—	—	—	—	—	—	—
Prx. Mt. 3	88	2.2	88	2.7	44	34.4	—	—	—	—	—	—	—	2	2.27
Prx. Mt. 4	77	1.9	77	2.4	39	30.5	—	—	—	—	—	—	—	1	1.30
Prx. Mt. 5	77	1.9	77	2.4	39	30.5	—	—	—	—	—	—	—	—	—
Dis. Mt. 2	63	1.6	63	1.9	32	25.0	10	7	10	7	5	4	30.0	—	—
Dis. Mt. 3	47	1.2	46	1.4	23	18.0	7	5	7	5	4	3	23.3	—	—
Dis. Mt. 4	43	1.1	43	1.3	22	17.2	7	3	7	3	4	2	20.0	—	—
Dis. Mt. 5	43	1.1	43	1.3	22	17.2	9	3	9	3	5	2	23.3	—	—
Dis. Mt.	8	0.2	—	—	—	—	1	1	1	1	1	1	6.7	1	12.50
Mpd. Shaft	—	—	—	—	—	—	—	—	—	—	—	—	—	—	—
TOTAL	3975	100.0	3242	100.0	—	—	227	32	220	30	—	—	—	74	1.86

[a]NISP, Number of identifiable specimens.
[b]MNE, Minimum number of elements.
[c]MNI, Minimum number of individuals.
[d]%MNI, MNI of each element observed expressed as percent of maximum MNI value—128 animals (scapula).
[e]Total Immature %MNI calculated in same manner as %MNI (see note 4 above), based on maximum immature MNI value of 30 animals (dist. femur).
[f]Percent of NISP value in same row in Column (1).

Table A8.3. ***Lepus californicus*** **sample recovered from Henderson Site (Trench A, East Bar).**

Element	Total Sample						Immature Only							Burned	
	NISP[a] (1)	% of Total NISP (2)	MNE[b] (3)	% of Total MNE (4)	MNI[c] (5)	% MNI[d] (6)	Unfus. NISP (7)	Fusing NISP (8)	Unfus. MNE (9)	Fusing MNE (10)	Unfus. MNI (11)	Fusing MNI (12)	Total Imm. %MNI[e] (13)	NISP (14)	% of Total NISP[f] (15)
Total Skull	51	9.6	32	7.2	16	100.0	—	—	—	—	—	—	—	—	—
Frontal	1	0.2	1	0.2	1	6.3	—	—	—	—	—	—	—	—	—
Squam.-Tem.	7	1.3	7	1.6	4	25.0	—	—	—	—	—	—	—	—	—
Tem.-Par.	1	0.2	1	0.2	1	6.3	—	—	—	—	—	—	—	—	—
Tem.-Frnt.	—	—	—	—	—	—	—	—	—	—	—	—	—	—	—
Nasal	5	1.0	5	1.1	3	18.8	—	—	—	—	—	—	—	—	—
Premax.	—	—	—	—	—	—	—	—	—	—	—	—	—	—	—
Maxilla	37	7.0	32	7.2	16	100.0	—	—	—	—	—	—	—	—	—
Max.-Prem.	—	—	—	—	—	—	—	—	—	—	—	—	—	—	—
Cmplt. Skull	—	—	—	—	—	—	—	—	—	—	—	—	—	—	—
Total Mand.	42	8.0	23	5.2	12	75.0	—	—	—	—	—	—	—	—	—
Cmplt. Man.	2	0.4	2	0.5	1	6.3	—	—	—	—	—	—	—	—	—
Man. Body	25	4.7	21	4.7	11	68.8	—	—	—	—	—	—	—	—	—
Man. Symph.	10	1.9	6	1.4	3	18.8	—	—	—	—	—	—	—	—	—
Man. Border	1	0.2	1	0.2	1	6.3	—	—	—	—	—	—	—	—	—
Man. Ramus	4	0.8	4	0.9	2	12.5	—	—	—	—	—	—	—	—	—
Atlas	1	0.2	1	0.2	1	6.3	—	—	—	—	—	—	—	—	—
Axis	1	0.2	1	0.2	1	6.3	—	—	—	—	—	—	—	—	—
Cervical	2	0.4	2	0.5	1	6.3	—	—	—	—	—	—	—	—	—
Thoracic	—	—	—	—	—	—	—	—	—	—	—	—	—	—	—
Lumbar	7	1.3	5	1.1	1	6.3	—	—	—	—	—	—	—	—	—
Sacrum	—	—	—	—	—	—	—	—	—	—	—	—	—	—	—
Scapula	41	7.8	32	7.2	16	100.0	1	—	1		1	—	20.0	3	7.32
Prx. Hum.	4	0.8	5	1.1	3	18.8	3	—	3	—	2	—	40.0	1	25.00
Dis. Hum.	30	5.7	30	6.7	15	93.8	2	—	2	—	1	—	20.0	4	13.33
H. Shaft	1	0.2	—	—	—	—	—	—	—	—	—	—	—	—	—
Prx. Rad.	28	5.3	28	6.3	14	87.5	1	1	1	1	1	1	40.0	1	3.57
Dis. Rad.	7	1.3	7	1.6	4	0.3	2	—	2	—	1	—	20.0	—	—
R. Shaft	18	3.4	—	—	—	—	—	—	—	—	—	—	—	—	—
Prx. Ulna	8	1.5	8	1.8	4	0.3	—	—	—	—	—	—	—	—	—
Dis. Ulna	5	1.0	5	1.1	3	18.8	—	—	—	—	—	—	—	—	—
Ulna Shaft	19	3.6	10	2.2	5	31.3	—	—	—	—	—	—	—	—	—
Prx. Mc. 2	11	2.1	11	2.5	6	37.5	—	—	—	—	—	—	—	—	—
Prx. Mc. 3	11	2.1	11	2.5	6	37.5	—	—	—	—	—	—	—	—	—
Prx. Mc. 4	14	2.7	14	3.1	7	43.8	—	—	—	—	—	—	—	—	—
Prx. Mc. 5	3	0.7	3	0.7	2	12.5	—	—	—	—	—	—	—	—	—
Dis. Mc. 2	6	1.1	6	1.4	3	18.8	1	—	1	—	1	—	20.0	—	—

(cont.)

Element	Total Sample						Immature Only							Burned	
	NISP[a] (1)	% of Total NISP (2)	MNE[b] (3)	% of Total MNE (4)	MNI[c] (5)	% MNI[d] (6)	Unfus. NISP (7)	Fusing NISP (8)	Unfus. MNE (9)	Fusing MNE (10)	Unfus. MNI (11)	Fusing MNI (12)	Total Imm. %MNI[e] (13)	NISP (14)	% of Total NISP[f] (15)
Dis. Mc. 3	9	1.7	9	2.0	5	31.3	1	—	1	—	1	—	20.0	—	—
Dis. Mc. 4	11	2.1	11	2.5	6	37.5	1	—	1	—	1	—	20.0	—	—
Dis. Mc. 5	3	0.6	3	0.7	2	12.5	—	—	—	—	—	—	—	—	—
Innom.	15	2.8	12	2.7	6	37.5	—	—	—	—	—	—	—	—	—
Prx. Fem.	15	2.8	14	3.1	7	43.8	2	—	2	—	1	—	20.0	—	—
Dis. Fem.	15	2.8	15	3.4	8	50.0	7	2	7	2	4	1	100.0	—	—
F. Shaft	5	1.0	—	—	—	—	—	—	—	—	—	—	—	—	—
Prx. Tib.	14	2.7	13	2.9	7	43.8	7	—	6	—	3	—	60.0	1	7.14
Dis. Tib.	15	2.8	15	3.4	8	50.0	3	—	3	—	2	—	40.0	1	6.67
T. Shaft	6	1.1	—	—	—	—	—	—	—	—	—	—	—	—	—
Astrag.	8	1.5	8	1.8	4	25.0	—	—	—	—	—	—	—	1	12.50
Calc.	14	2.7	14	3.1	7	43.8	1	—	1	—	—	—	—	2	14.29
Cen. Tar.	3	0.6	3	0.7	2	12.5	—	—	—	—	—	—	—	—	—
3rd Tar.	—	—	—	—	—	—	—	—	—	—	—	—	—	—	—
4th Tar.	3	0.6	3	0.7	2	12.5	—	—	—	—	—	—	—	—	—
Prx. Mt. 2	12	2.3	12	2.7	6	37.5	—	—	—	—	—	—	—	—	—
Prx. Mt. 3	13	2.5	13	2.9	7	43.8	—	—	—	—	—	—	—	1	7.69
Prx. Mt. 4	10	1.9	10	2.2	5	31.3	—	—	—	—	—	—	—	—	—
Prx. Mt. 5	8	1.5	8	1.8	4	25.0	—	—	—	—	—	—	—	1	12.50
Dis. Mt. 2	9	1.7	9	2.0	5	31.3	—	—	—	—	—	—	—	—	—
Dis. Mt. 3	5	1.0	5	1.1	3	18.8	—	1	—	1	—	1	20.0	—	—
Dis. Mt. 4	5	1.0	5	1.1	3	18.8	1	—	1	—	1	—	20.0	—	—
Dis. Mt. 5	5	1.0	5	1.1	3	18.8	1	—	1	—	1	—	20.0	2	40.00
Dis. Mt.	16	3.0	—	—	—	—	—	—	—	—	—	—	—	—	—
Mpd. shaft	—	—	—	—	—	—	—	—	—	—	—	—	—	—	—
TOTAL	529	100.0	446	100.0	—	—	27	5	25	5	—	—	—	18	3.40

[a]NISP, Number of identifiable specimens.
[b]MNE, Minimum number of elements.
[c]MNI, Minimum number of individuals.
[d]%MNI, MNI of each element observed expressed as percent of maximum MNI value—16 animals (maxilla or scapula).
[e]Total Immature %MNI calculated in same manner as %MNI (see note 4 above), based on maximum immature MNI value of 5 animals (dist. femur).
[f]Percent of NISP value in same row in Column (1).

Table A8.4. ***Sylvilagus*** **sample recovered from Henderson Site (Trench A, East Bar).**

Element	Total Sample						Immature Only							Burned	
	NISP[a] (1)	% of Total NISP (2)	MNE[b] (3)	% of Total MNE (4)	MNI[c] (5)	% MNI[d] (6)	Unfus. NISP (7)	Fusing NISP (8)	Unfus. MNE (9)	Fusing MNE (10)	Unfus. MNI (11)	Fusing MNI (12)	Total Imm. %MNI[e] (13)	NISP (14)	% of Total NISP[f] (15)
Total Skull	195	12.1	78	5.6	40	67.8	—	—	—	—	—	—	—	—	—
Frontal	—	—	—	—	—	—	—	—	—	—	—	—	—	—	—
Squam.-Tem.	25	1.6	25	1.8	13	22.0	—	—	—	—	—	—	—	—	—
Tem.-Par.	35	2.2	35	2.5	18	30.5	—	—	—	—	—	—	—	—	—
Tem.-Frnt.	1	0.1	1	0.1	1	1.7	—	—	—	—	—	—	—	—	—
Nasal	15	0.9	15	1.1	8	13.6	—	—	—	—	—	—	—	—	—
Premax.	16	1.0	16	1.2	8	13.6	—	—	—	—	—	—	—	—	—
Maxilla	101	6.3	76	5.5	38	61.0	—	—	—	—	—	—	—	—	—
Max.-Prem.	1	0.1	1	0.1	1	1.7	—	—	—	—	—	—	—	—	—
Cmplt. Skull	1	0.1	1	0.1	1	1.7	—	—	—	—	—	—	—	—	—
Total Mand.	179	11.1	97	7.0	49	83.1	—	—	—	—	—	—	—	—	—
Cmplt. Man.	11	0.7	11	0.8	6	10.2	—	—	—	—	—	—	—	—	—
Man. Body	92	5.7	86	6.2	43	72.9	—	—	—	—	—	—	—	—	—
Man. Symph.	61	3.8	35	2.5	18	30.5	—	—	—	—	—	—	—	—	—
Man. Border	1	0.1	1	0.1	1	1.7	—	—	—	—	—	—	—	—	—
Man. Ramus	14	0.9	14	1.0	7	11.9	—	—	—	—	—	—	—	—	—
Atlas	2	0.1	2	0.1	1	1.7	—	—	—	—	—	—	—	—	—
Axis	—	—	—	—	—	—	—	—	—	—	—	—	—	—	—
Cervical	1	0.1	1	0.1	1	1.7	—	—	—	—	—	—	—	—	—
Thoracic	2	0.1	2	0.1	1	1.7	—	—	—	—	—	—	—	—	—
Lumbar	24	1.5	23	1.7	5	8.5	—	—	—	—	—	—	—	—	—
Sacrum	2	0.1	2	0.1	2	3.4	—	—	—	—	—	—	—	—	—
Scapula	96	6.0	80	5.8	40	67.8	—	—	—	—	—	—	—	1	1.04
Prx. Hum.	22	1.4	22	1.6	11	18.6	5	—	5	—	3	—	42.9	1	4.55
Dis. Hum.	94	5.8	94	6.8	47	79.7	—	—	—	—	—	—	—	—	—
H. Shaft	1	0.1	—	—	—	—	—	—	—	—	—	—	—	—	—
Prx. Rad.	68	4.2	68	4.9	34	57.6	1	—	1	—	1	—	14.3	2	2.94
Dis. Rad.	21	1.3	21	1.5	11	18.6	1	—	1	—	1	—	14.3	1	4.76
R. Shaft	10	0.6	—	—	—	—	—	—	—	—	—	—	—	1	10.00
Prx. Ulna	33	2.1	33	2.4	17	28.8	2	—	2	—	1	—	14.3	1	3.03
Dis. Ulna	14	0.9	14	1.0	7	11.9	4	1	2	—	1	—	14.3	—	—
Ulna Shaft	26	1.6	15	1.1	8	13.6	—	—	—	—	—	—	—	—	—
Prx. Mc. 2	2	0.1	2	0.1	1	1.7	—	—	—	—	—	—	—	—	—
Prx. Mc. 3	5	0.3	5	0.4	3	5.1	—	—	—	—	—	—	—	—	—
Prx. Mc. 4	1	0.1	1	0.1	1	1.7	—	—	—	—	—	—	—	—	—
Prx. Mc. 5	—	—	—	—	—	—	—	—	—	—	—	—	—	—	—
Dis. Mc. 2	1	0.1	1	0.1	1	1.7	1	—	1	—	1	—	—	—	—

(cont.)

Element	Total Sample						Immature Only							Burned	
	NISP[a] (1)	% of Total NISP (2)	MNE[b] (3)	% of Total MNE (4)	MNI[c] (5)	% MNI[d] (6)	Unfus. NISP (7)	Fusing NISP (8)	Unfus. MNE (9)	Fusing MNE (10)	Unfus. MNI (11)	Fusing MNI (12)	Total Imm. %MNI[e] (13)	NISP (14)	% of Total NISP[f] (15)
Dis. Mc. 3	4	0.3	4	0.3	2	3.4	—	—	—	—	—	—	—	—	—
Dis. Mc. 4	1	0.1	1	0.1	1	1.7	—	—	—	—	—	—	—	—	—
Dis. Mc. 5	—	—	—	—	—	—	—	—	—	—	—	—	—	—	—
Innom.	159	9.9	118	8.5	59	100.0	5	—	5	—	3	—	42.9	4	2.52
Prx. Fem.	37	2.3	36	2.6	18	30.5	9	—	9	—	5	—	71.4	1	2.70
Dis. Fem.	39	2.4	39	2.8	19	32.2	12	1	12	1	6	1	100.0	2	5.13
F. Shaft	14	0.9	—	—	—	—	—	—	—	—	—	—	—	—	—
Prx. Tib.	39	2.4	37	2.7	19	32.2	12	—	11	—	6	—	42.9	1	2.56
Dis. Tib.	106	6.6	106	7.6	53	89.8	16	—	16	—	8	—	57.1	4	3.77
T. Shaft	64	4.0	—	—	—	—	—	—	—	—	—	—	—	—	—
Astrag.	11	0.7	11	0.8	6	10.2	—	—	—	—	—	—	—	—	—
Calc.	71	4.4	71	5.1	36	61.0	1	—	1	—	1	—	14.3	—	—
Cen. Tar.	1	0.1	1	0.1	1	1.7	—	—	—	—	—	—	—	—	—
3rd Tar.	—	—	—	—	—	—	—	—	—	—	—	—	—	—	—
4th Tar.	—	—	—	—	—	—	—	—	—	—	—	—	—	—	—
Prx. Mt. 2	47	2.9	47	3.4	24	40.7	—	—	—	—	—	—	—	—	—
Prx. Mt. 3	41	2.6	40	2.9	20	33.9	—	—	—	—	—	—	—	—	—
Prx. Mt. 4	39	2.4	39	2.8	20	33.9	—	—	—	—	—	—	—	—	—
Prx. Mt. 5	36	2.2	36	2.6	18	30.5	—	—	—	—	—	—	—	—	—
Dis. Mt. 2	29	1.8	29	2.1	15	25.4	2	7	2	7	1	4	71.4	—	—
Dis. Mt. 3	23	1.4	22	1.6	11	18.6	4	2	4	2	2	1	42.9	—	—
Dis. Mt. 4	27	1.7	27	1.9	14	23.7	6	2	6	2	3	1	57.1	—	—
Dis. Mt. 5	21	1.3	21	1.5	11	18.6	5	2	5	2	3	1	57.1	—	—
Dis. Mt.	—	—	—	—	—	—	—	—	—	—	—	—	—	—	—
Mpd. Shaft	1	0.1	—	—	—	—	1	1	—	—	—	—	—	1	5.00
TOTAL	1609	100.0	1388	100.0	—	—	87	16	83	14	—	—	—	20	1.24

[a]NISP, Number of identifiable specimens.
[b]MNE, Minimum number of elements.
[c]MNI, Minimum number of individuals.
[d]%MNI, MNI of each element observed expressed as percent of maximum MNI value—59 animals (innominate).
[e]Total Immature %MNI calculated in same manner as %MNI (see note 4 above), based on maximum immature MNI value of 7 animals (dist. femur).
[f]Percent of NISP value in same row in Column (1).

Table A8.5. ***Lepus californicus*** **sample recovered from Henderson Site (Trench B/C, East Plaza).**

Element	Total Sample						Immature Only							Burned	
	NISP[a] (1)	% of Total NISP (2)	MNE[b] (3)	% of Total MNE (4)	MNI[c] (5)	% MNI[d] (6)	Unfus. NISP (7)	Fusing NISP (8)	Unfus. MNE (9)	Fusing MNE (10)	Unfus. MNI (11)	Fusing MNI (12)	Total Imm. %MNI[e] (13)	NISP (14)	% of Total NISP[f] (15)
Total Skull	34	6.6	16	4.0	8	42.1	—	—	—	—	—	—	—	1	2.94
Frontal	1	0.2	1	0.3	1	5.3	—	—	—	—	—	—	—	—	—
Squam.-Tem.	10	2.0	10	2.5	5	26.3	—	—	—	—	—	—	—	—	—
Tem.-Par.	1	0.2	1	0.3	1	5.3	—	—	—	—	—	—	—	—	—
Tem.-Frnt.	—	—	—	—	—	—	—	—	—	—	—	—	—	—	—
Nasal	2	0.4	2	0.5	1	5.3	—	—	—	—	—	—	—	—	—
Premax.	—	—	—	—	—	—	—	—	—	—	—	—	—	—	—
Maxilla	20	3.9	16	4.0	8	42.1	—	—	—	—	—	—	—	1	5.00
Max.-Prem.	—	—	—	—	—	—	—	—	—	—	—	—	—	—	—
Cmplt. Skull	—	—	—	—	—	—	—	—	—	—	—	—	—	—	—
Total Mand.	56	10.9	13	3.2	7	36.8	—	—	—	—	—	—	—	—	—
Cmplt. Man.	—	—	—	—	—	—	—	—	—	—	—	—	—	—	—
Man. Body	20	3.9	13	3.2	7	36.8	—	—	—	—	—	—	—	—	—
Man. Symph.	26	5.1	12	3.0	6	31.6	—	—	—	—	—	—	—	—	—
Man. Border	—	—	—	—	—	—	—	—	—	—	—	—	—	—	—
Man. Ramus	10	2.0	10	2.5	5	26.3	—	—	—	—	—	—	—	—	—
Atlas	1	0.2	1	0.3	1	5.3	—	—	—	—	—	—	—	—	—
Axis	1	0.2	1	0.3	1	5.3	—	—	—	—	—	—	—	—	—
Cervical	1	0.2	1	0.3	1	5.3	—	—	—	—	—	—	—	—	—
Thoracic	1	0.2	1	0.3	1	5.3	—	—	—	—	—	—	—	—	—
Lumbar	6	1.2	6	1.5	2	10.5	—	—	—	—	—	—	—	—	—
Sacrum	1	0.2	1	0.3	1	5.3	—	—	—	—	—	—	—	—	—
Scapula	48	9.4	30	7.4	15	79.0	—	—	—	—	—	—	—	1	2.08
Prx. Hum.	12	2.3	12	3.0	6	31.6	4	—	4	—	2	—	33.3	—	—
Dis. Hum.	33	6.4	33	8.2	17	89.5	2	—	2	—	1	—	16.7	2	6.06
H. Shaft	2	0.4	—	—	—	—	—	—	—	—	—	—	—	—	—
Prx. Rad.	24	4.7	24	5.9	12	63.2	—	—	—	—	—	—	—	1	4.17
Dis. Rad.	10	2.0	10	2.5	5	26.3	—	—	—	—	—	—	—	—	—
R. Shaft	15	2.9	—	—	—	—	—	—	—	—	—	—	—	1	6.67
Prx. Ulna	11	2.1	11	2.7	6	31.6	1	—	1	—	1	—	16.7	1	9.09
Dis. Ulna	—	—	—	—	—	—	—	—	—	—	—	—	—	—	—
Ulna Shaft	25	4.9	18	4.5	9	47.4	—	—	—	—	—	—	—	—	—
Prx. Mc. 2	4	0.8	4	1.0	2	10.5	—	—	—	—	—	—	—	—	—
Prx. Mc. 3	4	0.8	4	1.0	2	10.5	—	—	—	—	—	—	—	—	—
Prx. Mc. 4	7	1.4	7	1.7	4	21.1	—	—	—	—	—	—	—	—	—
Prx. Mc. 5	2	0.4	2	0.5	1	5.3	—	—	—	—	—	—	—	—	—
Dis. Mc. 2	2	0.4	2	0.5	1	5.3	2	—	2	—	1	—	16.7	—	—

(cont.)

Element	Total Sample						Immature Only							Burned	
	NISP[a] (1)	% of Total NISP (2)	MNE[b] (3)	% of Total MNE (4)	MNI[c] (5)	% MNI[d] (6)	Unfus. NISP (7)	Fusing NISP (8)	Unfus. MNE (9)	Fusing MNE (10)	Unfus. MNI (11)	Fusing MNI (12)	Total Imm. %MNI[e] (13)	NISP (14)	% of Total NISP[f] (15)
Dis. Mc. 3	—	—	—	—	—	—	—	—	—	—	—	—	—	—	—
Dis. Mc. 4	1	0.2	1	0.3	1	5.3	3	—	3	—	2	—	33.3	—	—
Dis. Mc. 5	2	0.4	2	0.5	1	5.3	—	—	—	—	—	—	—	—	—
Innom.	47	9.2	37	9.2	19	100.0	2	—	2	—	1	—	16.7	—	—
Prx. Fem.	16	3.1	15	3.7	8	42.1	1	—	1	—	1	—	16.7	—	—
Dis. Fem.	26	5.1	25	6.2	13	68.4	8	1	8	1	4	1	83.3	1	3.85
F. Shaft	3	0.6	—	—	—	—	—	—	—	—	—	—	—	—	—
Prx. Tib.	20	3.9	19	4.7	10	52.6	11	—	11	—	6	—	100.0	—	—
Dis. Tib.	10	2.0	10	2.5	5	26.3	4	—	4	—	2	—	33.3	—	—
T. Shaft	9	1.8	—	—	—	—	—	—	—	—	—	—	—	—	—
Astrag.	6	1.2	6	1.5	3	15.8	—	—	—	—	—	—	—	—	—
Calc.	9	1.8	9	2.2	5	26.3	5	1	5	1	3	1	66.7	1	11.11
Cen. Tar.	3	0.6	3	0.7	2	10.5	—	—	—	—	—	—	—	—	—
3rd Tar.	—	—	—	—	—	—	—	—	—	—	—	—	—	—	—
4th Tar.	1	0.2	1	0.3	1	5.3	—	—	—	—	—	—	—	—	—
Prx. Mt. 2	12	2.3	12	3.0	6	31.6	—	—	—	—	—	—	—	—	—
Prx. Mt. 3	8	1.6	8	2.0	4	21.1	—	—	—	—	—	—	—	—	—
Prx. Mt. 4	11	2.1	11	2.7	6	31.6	—	—	—	—	—	—	—	—	—
Prx. Mt. 5	6	1.2	6	1.5	3	15.8	—	—	—	—	—	—	—	—	—
Dis. Mt. 2	3	0.6	3	0.7	2	10.5	2	—	2	—	1	—	16.7	—	—
Dis. Mt. 3	1	0.2	1	0.3	1	5.3	3	—	3	—	2	—	33.3	—	—
Dis. Mt. 4	1	0.2	1	0.3	1	5.3	4	—	4	—	2	—	33.3	—	—
Dis. Mt. 5	1	0.2	1	0.3	1	5.3	—	—	—	—	—	—	—	—	—
Dis. Mt.	16	3.1	—	—	—	—	5	1	5	1	3	1	66.7	2	12.50
Mpd. Shaft	1	0.2	—	—	—	—	—	—	—	—	—	—	—	—	—
TOTAL	513	99.9	404	100.1	—	—	57	3	57	3	—	—	—	11	2.14

[a]NISP, Number of identifiable specimens.
[b]MNE, Minimum number of elements.
[c]MNI, Minimum number of individuals.
[d]%MNI, MNI of each element observed expressed as percent of maximum MNI value—19 animals (innominate).
[e]Total Immature %MNI calculated in same manner as %MNI (see note 4 above), based on maximum immature MNI value of 6 animals (prox. tibia).
[f]Percent of NISP value in same row in Column (1).

Table A8.6. ***Sylvilagus*** **sample recovered from Henderson Site (Trench B/C, East Plaza).**

Element	Total Sample						Immature Only							Burned	
	NISP[a] (1)	% of Total NISP (2)	MNE[b] (3)	% of Total MNE (4)	MNI[c] (5)	% MNI[d] (6)	Unfus. NISP (7)	Fusing NISP (8)	Unfus. MNE (9)	Fusing MNE (10)	Unfus. MNI (11)	Fusing MNI (12)	Total Imm. %MNI[e] (13)	NISP (14)	% of Total NISP[f] (15)
Total Skull	73	9.0	35	5.2	18	39.1	—	—	—	—	—	—	—	—	—
Frontal	—	—	—	—	—	—	—	—	—	—	—	—	—	—	—
Squam.-Tem.	2	0.3	2	0.3	1	2.2	—	—	—	—	—	—	—	—	—
Tem.-Par.	15	1.9	15	2.2	8	17.4	—	—	—	—	—	—	—	—	—
Tem.-Frnt.	—	—	—	—	—	—	—	—	—	—	—	—	—	—	—
Nasal	2	0.3	2	0.3	1	2.2	—	—	—	—	—	—	—	—	—
Premax.	1	0.1	1	0.2	1	2.2	—	—	—	—	—	—	—	—	—
Maxilla	53	6.5	35	5.2	18	39.1	—	—	—	—	—	—	—	1	1.89
Max.-Prem.	—	—	—	—	—	—	—	—	—	—	—	—	—	—	—
Cmplt. Skull	—	—	—	—	—	—	—	—	—	—	—	—	—	—	—
Total Mand.	90	11.1	47	6.9	24	52.2	—	—	—	—	—	—	—	1	1.11
Cmplt. Man.	3	0.4	3	0.4	2	4.4	—	—	—	—	—	—	—	—	—
Man. Body	50	6.2	44	6.5	22	47.8	—	—	—	—	—	—	—	1	2.00
Man. Symph.	33	4.1	15	2.2	8	17.4	—	—	—	—	—	—	—	1	3.03
Man. Border	—	—	—	—	—	—	—	—	—	—	—	—	—	—	—
Man. Ramus	4	0.5	4	0.6	2	4.4	—	—	—	—	—	—	—	—	—
Atlas	—	—	—	—	—	—	—	—	—	—	—	—	—	—	—
Axis	—	—	—	—	—	—	—	—	—	—	—	—	—	—	—
Cervical	1	0.1	1	0.1	1	2.2	—	—	—	—	—	—	—	—	—
Thoracic	2	0.3	2	0.3	1	2.2	—	—	—	—	—	—	—	—	—
Lumbar	9	1.1	9	1.3	2	4.4	—	—	—	—	—	—	—	1	11.11
Sacrum	1	0.1	1	0.2	1	2.2	—	—	—	—	—	—	—	—	—
Scapula	68	8.4	61	9.0	31	67.4	—	—	—	—	—	—	—	3	4.41
Prx. Hum.	15	1.9	15	2.2	8	17.4	1	—	1	—	1	—	7.7	—	—
Dis. Hum.	33	4.1	33	4.9	17	37.0	1	—	1	—	1	—	7.7	1	3.03
H. Shaft	1	0.1	—	—	—	—	—	—	—	—	—	—	—	—	—
Prx. Rad.	20	2.5	20	3.0	10	21.7	—	—	—	—	—	—	—	2	10.00
Dis. Rad.	9	1.1	9	1.3	5	10.9	—	—	—	—	—	—	—	1	11.11
R. Shaft	4	0.5	—	—	—	—	—	—	—	—	—	—	—	—	—
Prx. Ulna	15	1.9	15	2.2	8	17.4	1	1	1	1	1	1	15.4	—	—
Dis. Ulna	2	0.3	1	0.2	1	2.2	—	—	—	—	—	—	—	—	—
Ulna Shaft	16	2.0	12	1.8	6	13.0	—	—	—	—	—	—	—	1	6.25
Prx. Mc. 2	1	0.1	1	0.2	1	2.2	—	—	—	—	—	—	—	—	—
Prx. Mc. 3	2	0.3	2	0.3	1	2.2	—	—	—	—	—	—	—	—	—
Prx. Mc. 4	—	—	—	—	—	—	—	—	—	—	—	—	—	—	—
Prx. Mc. 5	—	—	—	—	—	—	—	—	—	—	—	—	—	—	—
Dis. Mc. 2	1	0.1	1	0.2	1	2.2	—	—	—	—	—	—	—	—	—

(cont.)

Element	Total Sample						Immature Only							Burned	
	NISP[a] (1)	% of Total NISP (2)	MNE[b] (3)	% of Total MNE (4)	MNI[c] (5)	% MNI[d] (6)	Unfus. NISP (7)	Fusing NISP (8)	Unfus. MNE (9)	Fusing MNE (10)	Unfus. MNI (11)	Fusing MNI (12)	Total Imm. %MNI[e] (13)	NISP (14)	% of Total NISP[f] (15)
Dis. Mc. 3	2	0.3	2	0.3	1	2.2	—	—	—	—	—	—	—	—	—
Dis. Mc. 4	—	—	—	—	—	—	—	—	—	—	—	—	—	—	—
Dis. Mc. 5	—	—	—	—	—	—	—	—	—	—	—	—	—	—	—
Innom.	126	15.6	91	13.4	46	100.0	3	—	3	—	2	—	15.4	4	3.17
Prx. Fem.	20	2.5	20	3.0	10	21.7	1	—	1	—	1	—	7.7	—	—
Dis. Fem.	45	5.6	45	6.6	23	50.0	21	4	21	4	11	2	100.0	3	6.67
F. Shaft	6	0.7	—	—	—	—	—	—	—	—	—	—	—	—	—
Prx. Tib.	29	3.6	28	4.1	14	30.4	7	—	7	—	4	—	30.8	1	3.45
Dis. Tib.	49	6.1	49	7.2	25	54.4	14	—	14	—	7	—	53.9	—	—
T. Shaft	30	3.7	—	—	—	—	—	—	—	—	—	—	—	1	3.33
Astrag.	2	0.3	2	0.3	1	2.2	—	—	—	—	—	—	—	—	—
Calc.	41	5.1	41	6.0	21	45.7	3	—	3	—	2	—	15.4	1	2.44
Cen. Tar.	—	—	—	—	—	—	—	—	—	—	—	—	—	—	—
3rd Tar.	—	—	—	—	—	—	—	—	—	—	—	—	—	—	—
4th Tar.	—	—	—	—	—	—	—	—	—	—	—	—	—	—	—
Prx. Mt. 2	20	2.5	20	3.0	10	21.7	—	—	—	—	—	—	—	—	—
Prx. Mt. 3	18	2.2	18	2.7	9	19.6	—	1	—	1	—	1	7.7	1	5.56
Prx. Mt. 4	15	1.9	15	2.2	8	17.4	—	—	—	—	—	—	—	1	6.67
Prx. Mt. 5	15	1.9	15	2.2	8	17.4	—	1	—	1	—	1	7.7	—	—
Dis. Mt. 2	10	1.2	10	1.5	5	10.9	1	—	1	—	1	—	7.7	—	—
Dis. Mt. 3	11	1.4	11	1.6	6	13.0	1	—	1	—	1	—	7.7	—	—
Dis. Mt. 4	1	0.1	1	0.2	1	2.2	—	—	—	—	—	—	—	—	—
Dis. Mt. 5	7	0.9	7	1.0	4	8.7	—	—	—	—	—	—	—	—	—
Dis. Mt.	—	—	—	—	—	—	—	—	—	—	—	—	—	—	—
Mpd. Shaft	—	—	—	—	—	—	—	—	—	—	—	—	—	—	—
TOTAL	810	100.0	679	100.0	—	—	54	7	54	7	—	—	—	24	2.96

[a]NISP, Number of identifiable specimens.
[b]MNE, Minimum number of elements.
[c]MNI, Minimum number of individuals.
[d]%MNI, MNI of each element observed expressed as percent of maximum MNI value—46 animals (innominate).
[e]Total Immature %MNI calculated in same manner as %MNI (see note 4 above), based on maximum immature MNI value of 13 animals (dist. femur).
[f]Percent of NISP value in same row in Column (1).

Table A8.7. ***Lepus californicus*** **sample recovered from Henderson Site (Trench D, East Plaza).**

Element	Total Sample						Immature Only							Burned	
	NISP[a] (1)	% of Total NISP (2)	MNE[b] (3)	% of Total MNE (4)	MNI[c] (5)	% MNI[d] (6)	Unfus. NISP (7)	Fusing NISP (8)	Unfus. MNE (9)	Fusing MNE (10)	Unfus. MNI (11)	Fusing MNI (12)	Total Imm. %MNI[e] (13)	NISP (14)	% of Total NISP[f] (15)
Total Skull	5	13.9	4	16.0	2	100.0	—	—	—	—	—	—	—	—	—
Frontal	—	—	—	—	—	—	—	—	—	—	—	—	—	—	—
Squam.-Tem.	1	2.8	1	4.0	1	50.0	—	—	—	—	—	—	—	—	—
Tem.-Par.	—	—	—	—	—	—	—	—	—	—	—	—	—	—	—
Tem.-Frnt.	—	—	—	—	—	—	—	—	—	—	—	—	—	—	—
Nasal	—	—	—	—	—	—	—	—	—	—	—	—	—	—	—
Premax.	—	—	—	—	—	—	—	—	—	—	—	—	—	—	—
Maxilla	4	11.1	4	16.0	2	100.0	—	—	—	—	—	—	—	—	—
Max.-Prem.	—	—	—	—	—	—	—	—	—	—	—	—	—	—	—
Cmplt. Skull	—	—	—	—	—	—	—	—	—	—	—	—	—	—	—
Total Mand.	6	16.7	2	8.0	1	50.0	—	—	—	—	—	—	—	—	—
Cmplt. Man.	—	—	—	—	—	—	—	—	—	—	—	—	—	—	—
Man. Body	2	5.6	2	8.0	1	50.0	—	—	—	—	—	—	—	—	—
Man. Symph.	4	11.1	1	4.0	1	50.0	—	—	—	—	—	—	—	—	—
Man. Border	—	—	—	—	—	—	—	—	—	—	—	—	—	—	—
Man. Ramus	—	—	—	—	—	—	—	—	—	—	—	—	—	—	—
Atlas	—	—	—	—	—	—	—	—	—	—	—	—	—	—	—
Axis	—	—	—	—	—	—	—	—	—	—	—	—	—	—	—
Cervical	—	—	—	—	—	—	—	—	—	—	—	—	—	—	—
Thoracic	—	—	—	—	—	—	—	—	—	—	—	—	—	—	—
Lumbar	—	—	—	—	—	—	—	—	—	—	—	—	—	—	—
Sacrum	—	—	—	—	—	—	—	—	—	—	—	—	—	—	—
Scapula	1	2.8	—	—	—	—	—	—	—	—	—	—	—	—	—
Prx. Hum.	1	2.8	1	4.0	1	50.0	—	—	—	—	—	—	—	—	—
Dis. Hum.	4	11.1	3	12.0	2	100.0	—	—	—	—	—	—	—	—	—
H. Shaft	—	—	—	—	—	—	—	—	—	—	—	—	—	—	—
Prx. Rad.	2	5.6	2	8.0	1	50.0	—	—	—	—	—	—	—	—	—
Dis. Rad.	1	2.8	1	4.0	1	50.0	—	—	—	—	—	—	—	—	—
R. Shaft	4	11.1	—	—	—	—	—	—	—	—	—	—	—	1	25.00
Prx. Ulna	—	—	—	—	—	—	—	—	—	—	—	—	—	—	—
Dis. Ulna	—	—	—	—	—	—	—	—	—	—	—	—	—	—	—
Ulna Shaft	2	5.6	2	8.0	1	50.0	—	—	—	—	—	—	—	—	—
Prx. Mc. 2	—	—	—	—	—	—	—	—	—	—	—	—	—	—	—
Prx. Mc. 3	1	2.8	1	4.0	1	50.0	—	—	—	—	—	—	—	—	—
Prx. Mc. 4	—	—	—	—	—	—	—	—	—	—	—	—	—	—	—
Prx. Mc. 5	1	2.8	1	4.0	1	50.0	—	—	—	—	—	—	—	—	—
Dis. Mc. 2	—	—	—	—	—	—	—	—	—	—	—	—	—	—	—

(cont.)

Element	Total Sample						Immature Only							Burned	
	NISP[a] (1)	% of Total NISP (2)	MNE[b] (3)	% of Total MNE (4)	MNI[c] (5)	% MNI[d] (6)	Unfus. NISP (7)	Fusing NISP (8)	Unfus. MNE (9)	Fusing MNE (10)	Unfus. MNI (11)	Fusing MNI (12)	Total Imm. %MNI[e] (13)	NISP (14)	% of Total NISP[f] (15)
Dis. Mc. 3	—	—	—	—	—	—	—	—	—	—	—	—	—	—	—
Dis. Mc. 4	—	—	—	—	—	—	—	—	—	—	—	—	—	—	—
Dis. Mc. 5	1	2.8	1	4.0	1	50.0	—	—	—	—	—	—	—	—	—
Innom.	3	8.3	2	8.0	1	50.0	—	—	—	—	—	—	—	—	—
Prx. Fem.	1	2.8	1	4.0	1	50.0	—	—	—	—	—	—	—	—	—
Dis. Fem.	—	—	—	—	—	—	—	—	—	—	—	—	—	—	—
F. Shaft	—	—	—	—	—	—	—	—	—	—	—	—	—	—	—
Prx. Tib.	—	—	—	—	—	—	—	—	—	—	—	—	—	—	—
Dis. Tib.	—	—	—	—	—	—	—	—	—	—	—	—	—	—	—
T. Shaft	1	2.8	—	—	—	—	—	—	—	—	—	—	—	—	—
Astrag.	1	2.8	1	4.0	1	50.0	—	—	—	—	—	—	—	—	—
Calc.	—	—	—	—	—	—	—	—	—	—	—	—	—	—	—
Cen. Tar.	—	—	—	—	—	—	—	—	—	—	—	—	—	—	—
3rd Tar.	—	—	—	—	—	—	—	—	—	—	—	—	—	—	—
4th Tar.	—	—	—	—	—	—	—	—	—	—	—	—	—	—	—
Prx. Mt. 2	1	2.8	1	4.0	1	50.0	—	—	—	—	—	—	—	—	—
Prx. Mt. 3	—	—	—	—	—	—	—	—	—	—	—	—	—	—	—
Prx. Mt. 4	—	—	—	—	—	—	—	—	—	—	—	—	—	—	—
Prx. Mt. 5	—	—	—	—	—	—	—	—	—	—	—	—	—	—	—
Dis. Mt. 2	—	—	—	—	—	—	—	—	—	—	—	—	—	—	—
Dis. Mt. 3	—	—	—	—	—	—	—	—	—	—	—	—	—	—	—
Dis. Mt. 4	—	—	—	—	—	—	—	—	—	—	—	—	—	—	—
Dis. Mt. 5	—	—	—	—	—	—	—	—	—	—	—	—	—	—	—
Dis. Mt.	—	—	—	—	—	—	—	—	—	—	—	—	—	—	—
Mpd. Shaft	—	—	—	—	—	—	—	—	—	—	—	—	—	—	—
TOTAL	36	100.0	25	100.0	—	—	—	—	—	—	—	—	—	1	2.78

[a]NISP, Number of identifiable specimens.
[b]MNE, Minimum number of elements.
[c]MNI, Minimum number of individuals.
[d]%MNI, MNI of each element observed expressed as percent of maximum MNI value—2 animals (maxilla or dist. humerus).
[e]Total Immature %MNI calculated in same manner as %MNI (see note 4 above), based on maximum immature MNI value.
[f]Percent of NISP value in same row in Column (1).

Table A8.8. ***Sylvilagus*** **sample recovered from Henderson Site (Trench D, East Plaza).**

Element	Total Sample						Immature Only							Burned	
	NISP[a] (1)	% of Total NISP (2)	MNE[b] (3)	% of Total MNE (4)	MNI[c] (5)	% MNI[d] (6)	Unfus. NISP (7)	Fusing NISP (8)	Unfus. MNE (9)	Fusing MNE (10)	Unfus. MNI (11)	Fusing MNI (12)	Total Imm. %MNI[e] (13)	NISP (14)	% of Total NISP[f] (15)
Total Skull	4	6.0	1	1.8	1	16.7	—	—	—	—	—	—	—	—	—
Frontal	—	—	—	—	—	—	—	—	—	—	—	—	—	—	—
Squam.-Tem.	—	—	—	—	—	—	—	—	—	—	—	—	—	—	—
Tem.-Par.	1	1.5	1	1.8	1	16.7	—	—	—	—	—	—	—	—	—
Tem.-Frnt.	—	—	—	—	—	—	—	—	—	—	—	—	—	—	—
Nasal	1	1.5	1	1.8	1	16.7	—	—	—	—	—	—	—	—	—
Premax.	—	—	—	—	—	—	—	—	—	—	—	—	—	—	—
Maxilla	2	3.0	1	1.8	1	16.7	—	—	—	—	—	—	—	—	—
Max.-Prem.	—	—	—	—	—	—	—	—	—	—	—	—	—	—	—
Cmplt. Skull	—	—	—	—	—	—	—	—	—	—	—	—	—	—	—
Total Mand.	6	9.0	4	7.1	2	33.3	—	—	—	—	—	—	—	—	—
Cmplt. Man.	—	—	—	—	—	—	—	—	—	—	—	—	—	—	—
Man. Body	4	6.0	4	7.1	2	33.3	—	—	—	—	—	—	—	—	—
Man. Symph.	2	3.0	—	—	—	—	—	—	—	—	—	—	—	—	—
Man. Border	—	—	—	—	—	—	—	—	—	—	—	—	—	—	—
Man. Ramus	—	—	—	—	—	—	—	—	—	—	—	—	—	—	—
Atlas	—	—	—	—	—	—	—	—	—	—	—	—	—	—	—
Axis	1	1.5	1	1.8	1	16.7	—	—	—	—	—	—	—	—	—
Cervical	—	—	—	—	—	—	—	—	—	—	—	—	—	—	—
Thoracic	—	—	—	—	—	—	—	—	—	—	—	—	—	—	—
Lumbar	1	1.5	1	1.8	1	16.7	—	—	—	—	—	—	—	—	—
Sacrum	—	—	—	—	—	—	—	—	—	—	—	—	—	—	—
Scapula	2	3.0	1	1.8	1	16.7	—	—	—	—	—	—	—	—	—
Prx. Hum.	—	—	—	—	—	—	—	—	—	—	—	—	—	—	—
Dis. Hum.	5	7.5	5	8.9	3	50.0	—	—	—	—	—	—	—	—	—
H. Shaft	—	—	—	—	—	—	—	—	—	—	—	—	—	—	—
Prx. Rad.	2	3.0	2	3.6	1	16.7	—	—	—	—	—	—	—	—	—
Dis. Rad.	—	—	—	—	—	—	—	—	—	—	—	—	—	—	—
R. Shaft	—	—	—	—	—	—	—	—	—	—	—	—	—	—	—
Prx. Ulna	—	—	—	—	—	—	—	—	—	—	—	—	—	—	—
Dis. Ulna	1	1.5	1	1.8	1	16.7	—	—	—	—	—	—	—	—	—
Ulna Shaft	1	1.5	1	1.8	1	16.7	—	—	—	—	—	—	—	—	—
Prx. Mc. 2	—	—	—	—	—	—	—	—	—	—	—	—	—	—	—
Prx. Mc. 3	—	—	—	—	—	—	—	—	—	—	—	—	—	—	—
Prx. Mc. 4	—	—	—	—	—	—	—	—	—	—	—	—	—	—	—
Prx. Mc. 5	—	—	—	—	—	—	—	—	—	—	—	—	—	—	—

(cont.)

Element	Total Sample						Immature Only							Burned	
	NISP[a] (1)	% of Total NISP (2)	MNE[b] (3)	% of Total MNE (4)	MNI[c] (5)	% MNI[d] (6)	Unfus. NISP (7)	Fusing NISP (8)	Unfus. MNE (9)	Fusing MNE (10)	Unfus. MNI (11)	Fusing MNI (12)	Total Imm. %MNI[e] (13)	NISP (14)	% of Total NISP[f] (15)
Dis. Mc. 2	—	—	—	—	—	—	—	—	—	—	—	—	—	—	—
Dis. Mc. 3	—	—	—	—	—	—	—	—	—	—	—	—	—	—	—
Dis. Mc. 4	—	—	—	—	—	—	—	—	—	—	—	—	—	—	—
Dis. Mc. 5	—	—	—	—	—	—	—	—	—	—	—	—	—	—	—
Innom.	7	10.5	4	7.1	2	33.3	1	—	1	—	1	—	100.0	—	—
Prx. Fem.	1	1.5	1	1.8	1	16.7	—	—	—	—	—	—	—	—	—
Dis. Fem.	2	3.0	2	3.6	1	16.7	1	—	1	—	1	—	100.0	—	—
F. Shaft	1	1.5	—	—	—	—	—	—	—	—	—	—	—	—	—
Prx. Tib.	3	4.5	2	3.6	1	16.7	1	—	1	—	1	—	100.0	—	—
Dis. Tib.	4	6.0	4	7.1	2	33.3	—	—	—	—	—	—	—	—	—
T. Shaft	2	3.0	—	—	—	—	—	—	—	—	—	—	—	—	—
Astrag.	—	—	—	—	—	—	—	—	—	—	—	—	—	—	—
Calc.	11	16.4	11	19.6	6	100.0	—	—	—	—	—	—	—	—	—
Cen. Tar.	—	—	—	—	—	—	—	—	—	—	—	—	—	—	—
3rd Tar.	—	—	—	—	—	—	—	—	—	—	—	—	—	—	—
4th Tar.	—	—	—	—	—	—	—	—	—	—	—	—	—	—	—
Prx. Mt. 2	4	6.0	4	7.1	2	33.3	—	—	—	—	—	—	—	—	—
Prx. Mt. 3	1	1.5	1	1.8	1	16.7	—	—	—	—	—	—	—	—	—
Prx. Mt. 4	1	1.5	1	1.8	1	16.7	—	—	—	—	—	—	—	—	—
Prx. Mt. 5	1	1.5	1	1.8	1	16.7	—	—	—	—	—	—	—	—	—
Dis. Mt. 2	3	4.5	3	5.4	2	33.3	—	—	—	—	—	—	—	—	—
Dis. Mt. 3	1	1.5	1	1.8	1	16.7	—	—	—	—	—	—	—	—	—
Dis. Mt. 4	1	1.5	1	1.8	1	16.7	—	—	—	—	—	—	—	—	—
Dis. Mt. 5	1	1.5	1	1.8	1	16.7	—	—	—	—	—	—	—	—	—
Dis. Mt.	—	—	—	—	—	—	—	—	—	—	—	—	—	—	—
Mpd. Shaft	—	—	—	—	—	—	—	—	—	—	—	—	—	—	—
TOTAL	67	100.0	56	100.1	—	—	3	—	3	—	—	—	—	—	—

[a]NISP, Number of identifiable specimens.
[b]MNE, Minimum number of elements.
[c]MNI, Minimum number of individuals.
[d]%MNI, MNI of each element observed expressed as percent of maximum MNI value—6 animals (calcaneus).
[e]Total Immature %MNI calculated in same manner as %MNI (see note 4 above), based on maximum immature MNI value of 1 animal (innominate, dist. femur, or prox. tibia).
[f]Percent of NISP value in same row in Column (1).

Table A8.9. ***Lepus californicus*** **sample recovered from Henderson Site (Trench E, Main Bar).**

Element	Total Sample						Immature Only							Burned	
	NISP[a] (1)	% of Total NISP (2)	MNE[b] (3)	% of Total MNE (4)	MNI[c] (5)	% MNI[d] (6)	Unfus. NISP (7)	Fusing NISP (8)	Unfus. MNE (9)	Fusing MNE (10)	Unfus. MNI (11)	Fusing MNI (12)	Total Imm. %MNI[e] (13)	NISP (14)	% of Total NISP[f] (15)
Total Skull	—	—	—	—	—	—	—	—	—	—	—	—	—	—	—
Frontal	—	—	—	—	—	—	—	—	—	—	—	—	—	—	—
Squam.-Tem.	—	—	—	—	—	—	—	—	—	—	—	—	—	—	—
Tem.-Par.	—	—	—	—	—	—	—	—	—	—	—	—	—	—	—
Tem.-Frnt.	—	—	—	—	—	—	—	—	—	—	—	—	—	—	—
Nasal	—	—	—	—	—	—	—	—	—	—	—	—	—	—	—
Premax.	—	—	—	—	—	—	—	—	—	—	—	—	—	—	—
Maxilla	—	—	—	—	—	—	—	—	—	—	—	—	—	—	—
Max.-Prem.	—	—	—	—	—	—	—	—	—	—	—	—	—	—	—
Cmplt. Skull	—	—	—	—	—	—	—	—	—	—	—	—	—	—	—
Total Mand.	1	25.0	—	—	—	—	—	—	—	—	—	—	—	—	—
Cmplt. Man.	—	—	—	—	—	—	—	—	—	—	—	—	—	—	—
Man. Body	—	—	—	—	—	—	—	—	—	—	—	—	—	—	—
Man. Symph.	1	25.0	—	—	—	—	—	—	—	—	—	—	—	—	—
Man. Border	—	—	—	—	—	—	—	—	—	—	—	—	—	—	—
Man. Ramus	—	—	—	—	—	—	—	—	—	—	—	—	—	—	—
Atlas	—	—	—	—	—	—	—	—	—	—	—	—	—	—	—
Axis	—	—	—	—	—	—	—	—	—	—	—	—	—	—	—
Cervical	—	—	—	—	—	—	—	—	—	—	—	—	—	—	—
Thoracic	—	—	—	—	—	—	—	—	—	—	—	—	—	—	—
Lumbar	—	—	—	—	—	—	—	—	—	—	—	—	—	—	—
Sacrum	—	—	—	—	—	—	—	—	—	—	—	—	—	—	—
Scapula	—	—	—	—	—	—	—	—	—	—	—	—	—	—	—
Prx. Hum.	—	—	—	—	—	—	—	—	—	—	—	—	—	—	—
Dis. Hum.	1	25.0	1	50.0	1	100.0	—	—	—	—	—	—	—	—	—
H. Shaft	—	—	—	—	—	—	—	—	—	—	—	—	—	—	—
Prx. Rad.	—	—	—	—	—	—	—	—	—	—	—	—	—	—	—
Dis. Rad.	1	25.0	—	—	—	—	—	—	—	—	—	—	—	—	—
R. Shaft	—	—	—	—	—	—	—	—	—	—	—	—	—	—	—
Prx. Ulna	—	—	—	—	—	—	—	—	—	—	—	—	—	—	—
Dis. Ulna	—	—	—	—	—	—	—	—	—	—	—	—	—	—	—
Ulna Shaft	—	—	—	—	—	—	—	—	—	—	—	—	—	—	—
Prx. Mc. 2	—	—	—	—	—	—	—	—	—	—	—	—	—	—	—
Prx. Mc. 3	—	—	—	—	—	—	—	—	—	—	—	—	—	—	—
Prx. Mc. 4	—	—	—	—	—	—	—	—	—	—	—	—	—	—	—
Prx. Mc. 5	—	—	—	—	—	—	—	—	—	—	—	—	—	—	—
Dis. Mc. 2	—	—	—	—	—	—	—	—	—	—	—	—	—	—	—

(cont.)

Element	Total Sample						Immature Only							Burned	
	NISP[a] (1)	% of Total NISP (2)	MNE[b] (3)	% of Total MNE (4)	MNI[c] (5)	% MNI[d] (6)	Unfus. NISP (7)	Fusing NISP (8)	Unfus. MNE (9)	Fusing MNE (10)	Unfus. MNI (11)	Fusing MNI (12)	Total Imm. %MNI[e] (13)	NISP (14)	% of Total NISP[f] (15)
Dis. Mc. 3	—	—	—	—	—	—	—	—	—	—	—	—	—	—	—
Dis. Mc. 4	—	—	—	—	—	—	—	—	—	—	—	—	—	—	—
Dis. Mc. 5	—	—	—	—	—	—	—	—	—	—	—	—	—	—	—
Innom.	—	—	—	—	—	—	—	—	—	—	—	—	—	—	—
Prx. Fem.	—	—	—	—	—	—	—	—	—	—	—	—	—	—	—
Dis. Fem.	—	—	—	—	—	—	—	—	—	—	—	—	—	—	—
F. Shaft	—	—	—	—	—	—	—	—	—	—	—	—	—	—	—
Prx. Tib.	—	—	—	—	—	—	—	—	—	—	—	—	—	—	—
Dis. Tib.	1	25.0	1	50.0	1	100.0	—	—	—	—	—	—	—	—	—
T. Shaft	—	—	—	—	—	—	—	—	—	—	—	—	—	—	—
Astrag.	—	—	—	—	—	—	—	—	—	—	—	—	—	—	—
Calc.	—	—	—	—	—	—	—	—	—	—	—	—	—	—	—
Cen. Tar.	—	—	—	—	—	—	—	—	—	—	—	—	—	—	—
3rd Tar.	—	—	—	—	—	—	—	—	—	—	—	—	—	—	—
4th Tar.	—	—	—	—	—	—	—	—	—	—	—	—	—	—	—
Prx. Mt. 2	—	—	—	—	—	—	—	—	—	—	—	—	—	—	—
Prx. Mt. 3	—	—	—	—	—	—	—	—	—	—	—	—	—	—	—
Prx. Mt. 4	—	—	—	—	—	—	—	—	—	—	—	—	—	—	—
Prx. Mt. 5	—	—	—	—	—	—	—	—	—	—	—	—	—	—	—
Dis. Mt. 2	—	—	—	—	—	—	—	—	—	—	—	—	—	—	—
Dis. Mt. 3	—	—	—	—	—	—	—	—	—	—	—	—	—	—	—
Dis. Mt. 4	—	—	—	—	—	—	—	—	—	—	—	—	—	—	—
Dis. Mt. 5	—	—	—	—	—	—	—	—	—	—	—	—	—	—	—
Dis. Mt.	—	—	—	—	—	—	—	—	—	—	—	—	—	—	—
Mpd. Shaft	—	—	—	—	—	—	—	—	—	—	—	—	—	—	—
TOTAL	4	100.0	2	100.0	—	—	—	—	—	—	—	—	—	—	—

[a]NISP, Number of identifiable specimens.
[b]MNE, Minimum number of elements.
[c]MNI, Minimum number of individuals.
[d]%MNI, MNI of each element observed expressed as percent of maximum MNI value—1 animal (dist. humerus or dist. tibia).
[e]Total immature %MNI calculated in same manner as %MNI (see note 4 above), based on maximum immature MNI value.
[f]Percent of NISP value in same row in Column (1).

Table A8.10. ***Sylvilagus*** **sample recovered from Henderson Site (Trench E, Main Bar).**

Element	Total Sample						Immature Only							Burned	
	NISP[a] (1)	% of Total NISP (2)	MNE[b] (3)	% of Total MNE (4)	MNI[c] (5)	% MNI[d] (6)	Unfus. NISP (7)	Fusing NISP (8)	Unfus. MNE (9)	Fusing MNE (10)	Unfus. MNI (11)	Fusing MNI (12)	Total Imm. %MNI[e] (13)	NISP (14)	% of Total NISP[f] (15)
Total Skull	3	9.1	1	3.2	1	50.0	—	—	—	—	—	—	—	—	—
Frontal	—	—	—	—	—	—	—	—	—	—	—	—	—	—	—
Squam.-Tem.	—	—	—	—	—	—	—	—	—	—	—	—	—	—	—
Tem.-Par.	1	3.0	1	3.2	1	50.0	—	—	—	—	—	—	—	—	—
Tem.-Frnt.	—	—	—	—	—	—	—	—	—	—	—	—	—	—	—
Nasal	—	—	—	—	—	—	—	—	—	—	—	—	—	—	—
Premax.	—	—	—	—	—	—	—	—	—	—	—	—	—	—	—
Maxilla	2	6.1	1	3.2	1	50.0	—	—	—	—	—	—	—	—	—
Max.-Prem.	—	—	—	—	—	—	—	—	—	—	—	—	—	—	—
Cmplt. Skull	—	—	—	—	—	—	—	—	—	—	—	—	—	—	—
Total Mand.	7	21.2	4	12.9	2	100.0	—	—	—	—	—	—	—	—	—
Cmplt. Man.	—	—	—	—	—	—	—	—	—	—	—	—	—	—	—
Man. Body	4	12.1	4	12.9	2	100.0	—	—	—	—	—	—	—	—	—
Man. Symph.	2	6.1	2	6.5	1	50.0	—	—	—	—	—	—	—	—	—
Man. Border	1	3.0	1	3.2	1	50.0	—	—	—	—	—	—	—	—	—
Man. Ramus	—	—	—	—	—	—	—	—	—	—	—	—	—	—	—
Atlas	—	—	—	—	—	—	—	—	—	—	—	—	—	—	—
Axis	—	—	—	—	—	—	—	—	—	—	—	—	—	—	—
Cervical	—	—	—	—	—	—	—	—	—	—	—	—	—	—	—
Thoracic	—	—	—	—	—	—	—	—	—	—	—	—	—	—	—
Lumbar	—	—	—	—	—	—	—	—	—	—	—	—	—	—	—
Sacrum	—	—	—	—	—	—	—	—	—	—	—	—	—	—	—
Scapula	2	6.1	2	6.5	1	50.0	—	—	—	—	—	—	—	—	—
Prx. Hum.	—	—	—	—	—	—	—	—	—	—	—	—	—	—	—
Dis. Hum.	1	3.0	1	3.2	1	50.0	—	—	—	—	—	—	—	—	—
H. Shaft	—	—	—	—	—	—	—	—	—	—	—	—	—	—	—
Prx. Rad.	2	6.1	2	6.5	1	50.0	—	—	—	—	—	—	—	—	—
Dis. Rad.	2	6.1	2	6.5	1	50.0	—	—	—	—	—	—	—	—	—
R. Shaft	—	—	—	—	—	—	—	—	—	—	—	—	—	—	—
Prx. Ulna	1	3.0	1	3.2	1	50.0	—	—	—	—	—	—	—	—	—
Dis. Ulna	—	—	—	—	—	—	—	—	—	—	—	—	—	—	—
Ulna Shaft	2	6.1	2	6.5	1	50.0	—	—	—	—	—	—	—	—	—
Prx. Mc. 2	—	—	—	—	—	—	—	—	—	—	—	—	—	—	—
Prx. Mc. 3	1	3.0	1	3.2	1	50.0	—	—	—	—	—	—	—	—	—
Prx. Mc. 4	—	—	—	—	—	—	—	—	—	—	—	—	—	—	—
Prx. Mc. 5	—	—	—	—	—	—	—	—	—	—	—	—	—	—	—

(cont.)

Element	Total Sample						Immature Only							Burned	
	NISP[a] (1)	% of Total NISP (2)	MNE[b] (3)	% of Total MNE (4)	MNI[c] (5)	% MNI[d] (6)	Unfus. NISP (7)	Fusing NISP (8)	Unfus. MNE (9)	Fusing MNE (10)	Unfus. MNI (11)	Fusing MNI (12)	Total Imm. %MNI[e] (13)	NISP (14)	% of Total NISP[f] (15)
Dis. Mc. 2	—	—	—	—	—	—	—	—	—	—	—	—	—	—	—
Dis. Mc. 3	—	—	—	—	—	—	—	—	—	—	—	—	—	—	—
Dis. Mc. 4	—	—	—	—	—	—	—	—	—	—	—	—	—	—	—
Dis. Mc. 5	—	—	—	—	—	—	—	—	—	—	—	—	—	—	—
Innom.	—	—	—	—	—	—	—	—	—	—	—	—	—	—	—
Prx. Fem.	1	3.0	1	3.2	1	50.0	—	—	—	—	—	—	—	—	—
Dis. Fem.	—	—	—	—	—	—	—	—	—	—	—	—	—	—	—
F. Shaft	—	—	—	—	—	—	—	—	—	—	—	—	—	—	—
Prx. Tib.	—	—	—	—	—	—	—	—	—	—	—	—	—	—	—
Dis. Tib.	2	6.1	2	6.5	1	50.0	1	—	1	—	1	—	100.0	—	—
T. Shaft	1	3.0	—	—	—	—	—	—	—	—	—	—	—	—	—
Astrag.	—	—	—	—	—	—	—	—	—	—	—	—	—	—	—
Calc.	3	9.1	3	9.7	2	100.0	—	—	—	—	—	—	—	—	—
Cen. Tar.	—	—	—	—	—	—	—	—	—	—	—	—	—	—	—
3rd Tar.	—	—	—	—	—	—	—	—	—	—	—	—	—	—	—
4th Tar.	—	—	—	—	—	—	—	—	—	—	—	—	—	—	—
Prx. Mt. 2	3	9.1	3	9.7	2	100.0	—	—	—	—	—	—	—	—	—
Prx. Mt. 3	1	3.0	1	3.2	1	50.0	—	—	—	—	—	—	—	—	—
Prx. Mt. 4	—	—	—	—	—	—	—	—	—	—	—	—	—	—	—
Prx. Mt. 5	—	—	—	—	—	—	—	—	—	—	—	—	—	—	—
Dis. Mt. 2	1	3.0	1	3.2	1	50.0	—	—	—	—	—	—	—	—	—
Dis. Mt. 3	—	—	—	—	—	—	—	—	—	—	—	—	—	—	—
Dis. Mt. 4	—	—	—	—	—	—	—	—	—	—	—	—	—	—	—
Dis. Mt. 5	—	—	—	—	—	—	—	—	—	—	—	—	—	—	—
Dis. Mt.	—	—	—	—	—	—	—	—	—	—	—	—	—	—	—
Mpd. Shaft	—	—	—	—	—	—	—	—	—	—	—	—	—	—	—
TOTAL	33	100.0	31	100.0	—	—	1	—	1	—	—	—	—	—	—

[a]NISP, Number of identifiable specimens.
[b]MNE, Minimum number of elements.
[c]MNI, Minimum number of individuals.
[d]%MNI, MNI of each element observed expressed as percent of maximum MNI value—2 animals (mandibular body, calcaneus, or prox. 2nd metatarsal).
[e]Total Immature %MNI calculated in same manner as %MNI (see note 4 above), based on maximum immature MNI value of 1 animal (dist. tibia).
[f]Percent of NISP value in same row in Column (1).

Table A8.11. *Lepus californicus* sample recovered from Henderson Site (Trench F, Center Bar).

Element	Total Sample						Immature Only							Burned	
	NISP[a] (1)	% of Total NISP (2)	MNE[b] (3)	% of Total MNE (4)	MNI[c] (5)	% MNI[d] (6)	Unfus. NISP (7)	Fusing NISP (8)	Unfus. MNE (9)	Fusing MNE (10)	Unfus. MNI (11)	Fusing MNI (12)	Total Imm. %MNI[e] (13)	NISP (14)	% of Total NISP[f] (15)
Total Skull	48	8.0	21	4.3	11	55.0	—	—	—	—	—	—	—	—	—
Frontal	—	—	—	—	—	—	—	—	—	—	—	—	—	—	—
Squam.-Tem.	9	1.5	9	1.8	5	25.0	—	—	—	—	—	—	—	—	—
Tem.-Par.	2	0.3	2	0.4	1	5.0	—	—	—	—	—	—	—	—	—
Tem.-Frnt.	—	—	—	—	—	—	—	—	—	—	—	—	—	—	—
Nasal	5	0.8	5	1.0	3	15.0	—	—	—	—	—	—	—	—	—
Premax.	7	1.2	7	1.4	4	20.0	—	—	—	—	—	—	—	—	—
Maxilla	25	4.2	21	4.3	11	55.0	—	—	—	—	—	—	—	—	—
Max.-Prem.	—	—	—	—	—	—	—	—	—	—	—	—	—	—	—
Cmplt. Skull	—	—	—	—	—	—	—	—	—	—	—	—	—	—	—
Total Mand.	60	10.0	22	4.5	11	55.0	—	—	—	—	—	—	—	—	—
Cmplt. Man.	1	0.2	1	0.2	1	5.0	—	—	—	—	—	—	—	—	—
Man. Body	27	4.5	21	4.3	11	55.0	—	—	—	—	—	—	—	—	—
Man. Symph.	10	1.7	4	0.8	2	10.0	—	—	—	—	—	—	—	—	—
Man. Border	1	0.2	—	—	—	—	—	—	—	—	—	—	—	—	—
Man. Ramus	21	3.5	—	—	—	—	—	—	—	—	—	—	—	—	—
Atlas	2	0.3	2	0.4	2	10.0	—	—	—	—	—	—	—	—	—
Axis	1	0.2	1	0.2	1	5.0	—	—	—	—	—	—	—	—	—
Cervical	2	0.3	2	0.4	1	5.0	—	—	—	—	—	—	—	—	—
Thoracic	2	0.3	2	0.4	1	5.0	—	—	—	—	—	—	—	—	—
Lumbar	9	1.5	9	1.8	2	10.0	—	—	—	—	—	—	—	—	—
Sacrum	—	—	—	—	—	—	—	—	—	—	—	—	—	—	—
Scapula	50	8.3	40	8.2	20	100.0	1	—	1	—	1	—	25.0	—	—
Prx. Hum.	7	1.2	7	1.4	4	20.0	—	—	—	—	—	—	—	—	—
Dis. Hum.	25	4.2	25	5.1	13	65.0	2	—	2	—	1	—	25.0	2	8.00
H. Shaft	—	—	—	—	—	—	—	—	—	—	—	—	—	—	—
Prx. Rad.	24	4.0	24	4.9	12	60.0	—	—	—	—	—	—	—	1	4.17
Dis. Rad.	16	2.7	16	3.3	8	40.0	1	1	1	1	1	1	50.0	2	12.50
R. Shaft	8	1.3	—	—	—	—	—	—	—	—	—	—	—	—	—
Prx. Ulna	12	2.0	12	2.4	6	30.0	—	—	—	—	—	—	—	1	8.33
Dis. Ulna	3	0.5	3	0.6	2	10.0	—	—	—	—	—	—	—	—	—
Ulna Shaft	20	3.3	15	3.1	8	40.0	—	—	—	—	—	—	—	—	—
Prx. Mc. 2	10	1.7	10	2.0	5	25.0	—	—	—	—	—	—	—	1	10.00
Prx. Mc. 3	11	1.8	11	2.2	6	30.0	1	—	1	—	1	—	25.0	1	9.09
Prx. Mc. 4	11	1.8	11	2.2	6	30.0	—	—	—	—	—	—	—	—	—
Prx. Mc. 5	7	1.2	7	1.4	4	20.0	—	—	—	—	—	—	—	—	—
Dis. Mc. 2	5	0.8	5	1.0	3	15.0	1	—	1	—	1	—	25.0	—	—

(cont.)

Element	Total Sample						Immature Only							Burned	
	NISP[a] (1)	% of Total NISP (2)	MNE[b] (3)	% of Total MNE (4)	MNI[c] (5)	% MNI[d] (6)	Unfus. NISP (7)	Fusing NISP (8)	Unfus. MNE (9)	Fusing MNE (10)	Unfus. MNI (11)	Fusing MNI (12)	Total Imm. %MNI[e] (13)	NISP (14)	% of Total NISP[f] (15)
Dis. Mc. 3	5	0.8	5	1.0	3	15.0	—	—	—	—	—	—	—	—	—
Dis. Mc. 4	10	1.7	10	2.0	5	25.0	—	1	—	1	—	1	25.0	—	—
Dis. Mc. 5	7	1.2	7	1.4	4	20.0	—	—	—	—	—	—	—	—	—
Innom.	28	4.7	20	4.1	10	50.0	—	—	—	—	—	—	—	—	—
Prx. Fem.	17	2.8	17	3.5	9	45.0	—	—	—	—	—	—	—	—	—
Dis. Fem.	20	3.3	20	4.1	10	50.0	5	1	5	1	3	1	100.0	1	5.00
F. Shaft	9	1.5	—	—	—	—	—	—	—	—	—	—	—	—	—
Prx. Tib.	16	2.7	16	3.3	8	40.0	5	1	5	1	3	1	100.0	—	—
Dis. Tib.	17	2.8	17	3.5	9	45.0	5	—	5	—	3	—	75.0	—	—
T. Shaft	10	1.7	—	—	—	—	—	—	—	—	—	—	—	—	—
Astrag.	12	2.0	12	2.4	6	30.0	—	—	—	—	—	—	—	—	—
Calc.	19	3.2	19	3.9	10	50.0	1	2	1	2	1	1	50.0	2	10.53
Cen. Tar.	5	0.8	5	1.0	3	15.0	—	—	—	—	—	—	—	—	—
3rd Tar.	1	0.2	1	0.2	1	5.0	—	—	—	—	—	—	—	—	—
4th Tar.	—	—	—	—	—	—	—	—	—	—	—	—	—	—	—
Prx. Mt. 2	9	1.5	9	1.8	5	25.0	—	—	—	—	—	—	—	—	—
Prx. Mt. 3	16	2.7	16	3.3	8	40.0	—	—	—	—	—	—	—	—	—
Prx. Mt. 4	13	2.2	13	2.7	7	35.0	—	—	—	—	—	—	—	1	7.69
Prx. Mt. 5	11	1.8	11	2.2	6	30.0	—	—	—	—	—	—	—	—	—
Dis. Mt. 2	3	0.5	3	0.6	2	10.0	2	—	2	—	1	—	25.0	—	—
Dis. Mt. 3	6	1.0	6	1.2	3	15.0	1	—	1	—	1	—	25.0	—	—
Dis. Mt. 4	6	1.0	6	1.2	3	15.0	—	2	—	2	—	1	25.0	—	—
Dis. Mt. 5	6	1.0	6	1.2	3	15.0	—	1	—	1	—	1	25.0	—	—
Dis. Mt.	21	3.5	—	—	—	—	2	—	2	—	1	—	25.0	—	—
Mpd. Shaft	1	0.2	—	—	—	—	—	—	—	—	—	—	—	—	—
TOTAL	601	100.0	491	100.0	—	—	27	9	27	9	—	—	—	12	2.00

[a]NISP, Number of identifiable specimens.
[b]MNE, Minimum number of elements.
[c]MNI, Minimum number of individuals.
[d]%MNI, MNI of each element observed expressed as percent of maximum MNI value—20 animals (scapula).
[e]Total Immature %MNI calculated in same manner as %MNI (see note 4 above), based on maximum immature MNI value of 4 animals (dist. femur or prox. tibia).
[f]Percent of NISP value in same row in Column (1).

Table A8.12. ***Sylvilagus*** **sample recovered from Henderson Site (Trench F, Center Bar).**

Element	Total Sample						Immature Only							Burned	
	NISP[a] (1)	% of Total NISP (2)	MNE[b] (3)	% of Total MNE (4)	MNI[c] (5)	% MNI[d] (6)	Unfus. NISP (7)	Fusing NISP (8)	Unfus. MNE (9)	Fusing MNE (10)	Unfus. MNI (11)	Fusing MNI (12)	Total Imm. %MNI[e] (13)	NISP (14)	% of Total NISP[f] (15)
Total Skull	165	13.0	73	7.1	37	74.0	—	—	—	—	—	—	—	—	—
Frontal	—	—	—	—	—	—	—	—	—	—	—	—	—	—	—
Squam.-Tem.	15	1.2	15	1.5	8	16.0	—	—	—	—	—	—	—	—	—
Tem.-Par.	23	1.8	23	2.2	12	24.0	—	—	—	—	—	—	—	—	—
Tem.-Frnt.	—	—	—	—	—	—	—	—	—	—	—	—	—	—	—
Nasal	8	0.6	8	0.8	4	8.0	—	—	—	—	—	—	—	—	—
Premax.	8	0.6	8	0.8	4	8.0	—	—	—	—	—	—	—	—	—
Maxilla	111	8.8	73	7.1	37	74.0	—	—	—	—	—	—	—	—	—
Max.-Prem.	—	—	—	—	—	—	—	—	—	—	—	—	—	—	—
Cmplt. Skull	—	—	—	—	—	—	—	—	—	—	—	—	—	—	—
Total Mand.	165	13.0	83	8.0	42	84.0	—	—	—	—	—	—	—	—	—
Cmplt. Man.	13	1.0	13	1.3	7	14.0	—	—	—	—	—	—	—	—	—
Man. Body	84	6.6	70	6.8	35	70.0	—	—	—	—	—	—	—	—	—
Man. Symph.	59	4.7	25	2.4	13	26.0	—	—	—	—	—	—	—	—	—
Man. Border	2	0.2	2	0.2	1	2.0	—	—	—	—	—	—	—	—	—
Man. Ramus	7	0.6	7	0.7	4	8.0	—	—	—	—	—	—	—	—	—
Atlas	1	0.1	1	0.1	1	2.0	—	—	—	—	—	—	—	—	—
Axis	2	0.2	2	0.2	1	2.0	—	—	—	—	—	—	—	—	—
Cervical	2	0.2	2	0.2	1	2.0	—	—	—	—	—	—	—	—	—
Thoracic	3	0.2	3	0.3	1	2.0	—	—	—	—	—	—	—	—	—
Lumbar	20	1.6	20	1.9	4	8.0	—	—	—	—	—	—	—	—	—
Sacrum	2	0.2	2	0.2	2	4.0	—	—	—	—	—	—	—	—	—
Scapula	115	9.1	99	9.6	50	100.0	—	—	—	—	—	—	—	2	1.74
Prx. Hum.	17	1.3	17	1.7	9	18.0	3	1	3	1	2	1	37.5	—	—
Dis. Hum.	73	5.8	73	7.1	37	74.0	1	—	1	—	1	—	12.5	3	4.11
H. Shaft	1	0.1	—	—	—	—	—	—	—	—	—	—	—	—	—
Prx. Rad.	29	2.3	29	2.8	15	30.0	—	—	—	—	—	—	—	1	3.45
Dis. Rad.	30	2.4	30	2.9	15	30.0	2	—	2	—	1	—	12.5	1	3.33
R. Shaft	9	0.7	—	—	—	—	—	—	—	—	—	—	—	—	—
Prx. Ulna	30	2.4	30	2.9	15	30.0	2	—	2	—	1	—	12.5	—	—
Dis. Ulna	6	0.5	6	0.6	3	6.0	—	—	—	—	—	—	—	—	—
Ulna Shaft	27	2.1	—	—	—	—	—	—	—	—	—	—	—	—	—
Prx. Mc. 2	1	0.1	1	0.1	1	2.0	—	—	—	—	—	—	—	—	—
Prx. Mc. 3	3	0.2	3	0.3	2	4.0	—	—	—	—	—	—	—	—	—
Prx. Mc. 4	2	0.2	2	0.2	1	2.0	—	—	—	—	—	—	—	—	—
Prx. Mc. 5	—	—	—	—	—	—	—	—	—	—	—	—	—	—	—
Dis. Mc. 2	1	0.1	1	0.1	1	2.0	—	—	—	—	—	—	—	—	—

(cont.)

Element	Total Sample						Immature Only							Burned	
	NISP[a] (1)	% of Total NISP (2)	MNE[b] (3)	% of Total MNE (4)	MNI[c] (5)	% MNI[d] (6)	Unfus. NISP (7)	Fusing NISP (8)	Unfus. MNE (9)	Fusing MNE (10)	Unfus. MNI (11)	Fusing MNI (12)	Total Imm. %MNI[e] (13)	NISP (14)	% of Total NISP[f] (15)
Dis. Mc. 3	3	0.2	3	0.3	2	4.0	—	—	—	—	—	—	—	—	—
Dis. Mc. 4	1	0.1	1	0.1	1	2.0	1	—	1	—	1	—	12.5	—	—
Dis. Mc. 5	—	—	—	—	—	—	—	—	—	—	—	—	—	—	—
Innom.	109	8.6	79	7.7	40	80.0	—	—	—	—	—	—	—	—	—
Prx. Fem.	39	3.1	39	3.8	20	40.0	7	—	7	—	4	—	50.0	1	2.56
Dis. Fem.	44	3.5	44	4.3	22	44.0	11	4	11	4	6	2	100.0	1	2.27
F. Shaft	13	1.0	—	—	—	—	—	—	—	—	—	—	—	—	—
Prx. Tib.	37	2.9	37	3.6	19	38.0	15	—	15	—	8	—	100.0	1	2.70
Dis. Tib.	60	4.7	60	5.8	30	60.0	3	—	3	—	2	—	25.0	3	5.00
T. Shaft	49	3.9	—	—	—	—	—	—	—	—	—	—	—	—	—
Astrag.	10	0.8	10	1.0	5	10.0	—	—	—	—	—	—	—	—	—
Calc.	49	3.9	49	4.8	25	50.0	—	—	—	—	—	—	—	2	4.08
Cen. Tar.	—	—	—	—	—	—	—	—	—	—	—	—	—	—	—
3rd Tar.	—	—	—	—	—	—	—	—	—	—	—	—	—	—	—
4th Tar.	—	—	—	—	—	—	—	—	—	—	—	—	—	—	—
Prx. Mt. 2	35	2.8	35	3.4	18	36.0	—	—	—	—	—	—	—	—	—
Prx. Mt. 3	19	1.5	19	1.8	10	20.0	—	—	—	—	—	—	—	1	5.26
Prx. Mt. 4	19	1.5	19	1.8	10	20.0	—	—	—	—	—	—	—	—	—
Prx. Mt. 5	22	1.7	22	2.1	11	22.0	—	—	—	—	—	—	—	—	—
Dis. Mt. 2	18	1.4	18	1.7	9	18.0	4	—	4	—	2	—	25.0	—	—
Dis. Mt. 3	8	0.6	8	0.8	4	8.0	—	1	—	1	—	1	12.5	—	—
Dis. Mt. 4	12	1.0	12	1.2	6	12.0	—	1	—	1	—	1	12.5	—	—
Dis. Mt. 5	12	1.0	12	1.2	6	12.0	3	—	3	—	2	—	25.0	—	—
Dis. Mt.	2	0.2	—	—	—	—	—	—	—	—	—	—	—	—	—
Mpd. Shaft	2	0.2	—	—	—	—	—	—	—	—	—	—	—	—	—
TOTAL	1267	100.0	1032	100.0	—	—	52	7	52	7	—	—	—	16	1.26

[a]NISP, Number of identifiable specimens.
[b]MNE, Minimum number of elements.
[c]MNI, Minimum number of individuals.
[d]%MNI, MNI of each element observed expressed as percent of maximum MNI value—50 animals (scapula).
[e]Total Immature %MNI calculated in same manner as %MNI (see note 4 above), based on maximum immature MNI value of 8 animals (dist. femur or prox. tibia).
[f]Percent of NISP value in same row in Column (1).

9

Prairie Dogs and Gophers

Food Resources or Taphonomic "Noise"?

John D. Speth
University of Michigan

Gudrun A. Scholler
University of Bonn

Introduction

The Henderson Site rodent assemblage is neither large nor diverse. The majority of specimens belong to a single species of rodent, the black-tailed prairie dog (*Cynomys ludovicianus*). There are 64 prairie dog individuals, based on the frequency of mandibles in the assemblage. Of these, 18 are immature animals. An additional 238 bones derive from the yellow-faced (or yellow-cheeked) pocket gopher (*Pappogeomys castanops*),[1] representing a minimum of 25 animals, based on the number of mandibles; 6 individuals are immature. Thirty-three specimens are from muskrats (*Ondatra zibethicus*), representing a minimum of 4 individuals, 2 immature. The remaining rodent bones, all from animals smaller than the pocket gopher have not as yet been identified to genus or species, and are treated in subsequent discussion as a single group ("misc. small rodents"). While this group undoubtedly includes several taxa, judging from the mandibles the majority of these specimens derive from only two or three species.

In addition, the excavations at Henderson yielded at least an incisor and four lower molars of beaver. Beaver were apparently present in the Roswell area until late in the nineteenth century, if not more recently, as indicated by various eye-witness accounts. For example, in the 1870s, a local farmer diverted water from a beaver dam on the North Spring River to his fields (Shinkle 1966:3). Beaver were also reported on the South Spring River (Poe 1981:263). No postcranial beaver bones have as yet been identified, although a few elements may yet be present in the small amount of 1980-1981 faunal material that remains to be identified.[2] Probably only one or two individuals are represented.

The black-tailed prairie dog, muskrat, and yellow-faced pocket gopher are all species that exist today in the Roswell area (Findley et al. 1975), although their numbers and distribution have been severely altered by decades of environmental abuse and systematic attempts at eradication. Their presence in the archaeological assemblage, therefore, is not surprising and in no way points to dramatically different climatic or environmental conditions in the past.

Element-by-element tabulations for the site-wide prairie dog and pocket gopher assemblages are presented in Tables A9.1 and A9.2 at the end of the chapter. The muskrats are not presented here because of the extremely small sample size, nor are the bones belonging to the "misc. small rodent" group, in this case because the assemblage, as will be seen below, was severely biased by recovery techniques in favor of mandibles and maxillae, which constitute nearly 60% of the remains in this category.

Interpreting the rodent remains from archaeological sites in the Southwest and elsewhere invariably poses a difficult taphonomic problem for zooarchaeologists, since we lack clear-cut criteria for distinguishing the remains that derive from human subsistence activities from those that derive from animals that died of natural causes within the archaeological deposits (see Driver 1985, 1991; Shaffer 1992b; Sobolik 1993; Szuter 1991; see also Yohe et al. 1991). In the Southwest, the ethnographic literature leaves no doubt that prairie dogs, gophers, ground squirrels, and other rodents figured in the diet of hunter-gatherers and farmers alike, not only as famine foods but often as "delicacies" and sometimes even as "normal" fare (e.g., Beaglehole 1936; Hill 1938; Spier 1928, 1933; Steward 1938; see also Shaffer 1992b; and Szuter 1991, and references therein).

But it is also obvious to archaeologists that rodents were frequent intruders in prehistoric sites, often riddling deposits with tunnels and dens, and occasionally dying in their burrows to be encountered by archaeologists as more or less fully articulated skeletons.

The problem then for the archaeologist is to find ways to distinguish culturally relevant rodent remains from those which are part of the site's taphonomic background. Unfortunately, there are as yet no simple and unambiguous criteria which can be applied to identify the remains of rodents that were consumed by a site's human inhabitants. Instead, each site (and each species) has to be argued separately, and the results are often frustratingly inconclusive. The Henderson rodents are no exception.

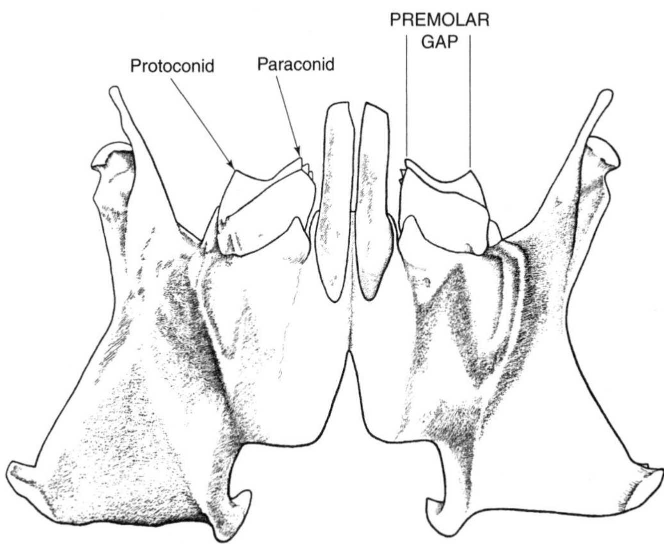

Figure 9.1. Frontal view of black-tailed prairie dog (*Cynomys ludovicianus*) mandible showing location of premolar gap. Measurement (mm) is taken between highest crest on paraconid and protoconid cusps (after Cox and Franklin 1990:144, Fig. 1).

Cultural vs. Natural Origin

The occurrence of fully or semi-articulated skeletons, particularly in dens or burrows, is perhaps one of the clearest indicators that rodent remains derive from noncultural sources (Driver 1985, 1991; Shaffer 1992b; Szuter 1991). However, in the case of Henderson, only one such skeleton was found in 1980-1981, that of an as yet unidentified "misc. small rodent" in a burrow in the East Bar. All of the prairie dog, gopher, and muskrat remains, as well as the other "misc. small rodent" bones, were totally disarticulated and widely dispersed throughout the deposits. The highly disarticulated and dispersed state of the vast majority of rodent bones at Henderson, therefore, at least tentatively points toward their role as human food remains.

Burning may indicate a cultural rather than taphonomic origin (Driver 1985, 1991; Shaffer 1992b; Szuter 1991). The problem at a site like Henderson, however, is that only a small fraction of bones, regardless of taxon, are burned (e.g., bison, 6.0%; antelope and deer, 7.2%; dog, 4.3%; jackrabbit, 2.6%; cottontail rabbit, 1.9%; prairie dog, 1.9%; gopher, 0.8%; "misc. small rodents," 0.6%), leaving the cultural status of the majority of small-mammal specimens in doubt. Nevertheless, the incidence of burning in prairie dogs, the largest and most common rodent at Henderson, is identical to the value observed in *Sylvilagus*, a similar-sized small mammal whose remains almost certainly owe their presence to the subsistence activities of the village's human inhabitants (see discussion in Chapter 8).

Interestingly, the Henderson faunal remains display a strong positive correlation between body weight and the proportion of bones that are burned. This relationship, discussed more fully in Chapter 14, holds across all mammalian taxa, from bison weighing hundreds of kilograms to rodents weighing less than 200 grams. This relationship indicates that the smaller the size of the prey the less likely its bones will be burned. While a number of factors, both cultural and taphonomic, may contribute to this intriguing patterning, cultural factors seem the most likely. Particularly important among these are: (1) the reduced need to dismember smaller carcasses prior to placing them in a cooking fire thereby exposing less bone to direct contact (either intentionally or by accident) with the flames, and (2) perhaps also a somewhat greater tendency to prepare small mammals in domestic contexts by boiling (stewing) rather than by roasting or pit-baking (the evidence for boiling is discussed in Chapters 6, 7, and 8). Thus, despite the comparatively low incidence of burned rodent bones, the observed values are nevertheless entirely compatible with the notion that most of these small mammals are human food remains.

Another line of evidence points in the same direction. The density of prairie dog bones, expressed as the number of specimens (NISP) per cubic meter of excavated deposit, is highest in the two major trash deposits sampled in 1980-1981: the East Plaza earth oven complex and the midden that accumulated in Room C-5 in the Center Bar (see Table 9.1). One might argue that the abundance of prairie dog remains in the room merely reflects the fact that these animals preferred to burrow (and hence also to die) in the soft, organic-rich sediments that filled this structure following its abandonment. However, this same argument cannot be used to account for their high density in the East Plaza midden, where closely packed masses of fire-cracked rock would have all but precluded burrowing by these relatively large-bodied rodents.

Unfortunately, interpreting the density values for the smaller-sized rodent taxa is more difficult. As shown in Table 9.1, the density values for these remains are high in the soft Room C-5 midden but low in the rocky East Plaza deposits. Thus, for these taxa the high value in the Center Bar structure could reflect either cultural or taphonomic processes.

Perhaps the most convincing evidence that many, if not all, of the prairie dogs were brought into the site by villagers is

Table 9.1. Density (NISP/m^3) of rodent bones in flotation samples and by major provenience at Henderson Site (1980-1981 only).

Provenience	Number of Identifiable Specimens (NISP)						Density (NISP/m^3)					
	Prairie Dog		Pocket Gopher		"Misc. Small Rodents"		Prairie Dog		Pocket Gopher		"Misc. Small Rodents"	
	Total NISP	Man./ Max.	Total NISP	Man./ Max.	Total NISP	Man./ Max.	Total NISP	Man./ Max.	Total NISP	Man./ Max.	Total NISP	Man./ Max.
East Bar	226	64	81	19	55	28	6.48	1.84	2.32	0.55	1.58	0.80
Center Bar	346	86	117	29	97	62	13.43	3.34	4.54	1.13	3.77	2.41
Comb. room blocks[a]	572	150	198	48	152	90	9.44	2.47	3.27	0.79	2.51	1.48
Room C-5	182	45	81	23	60	39	20.75	5.13	9.24	2.62	6.84	4.45
East Plaza[b]	242	81	35	18	10	6	20.34	6.81	2.94	1.51	0.84	0.50
Entire site	863	243	238	68	167	99	10.85	3.05	2.99	0.85	2.10	1.24
Flotation (n = 303)	11	4	8	0	16	7	9.40	3.42	6.84	0.00	13.68	5.98

[a]East Bar and Center Bar only.
[b]Trench C only.

provided by the age structure of the animals. Age in black-tailed prairie dogs can be estimated with reasonable precision based on the degree of wear of the lower premolar (Cox and Franklin 1990; see also Hoogland and Hutter 1987).[3] The method, referred to as the "premolar gap technique," is based on the breadth of the space or gap between the highest crest on the paraconid and protoconid cusps (see Fig. 9.1). Cox and Franklin (1990) found in a sample of 292 live, known-age prairie dogs from Scotts Bluff National Monument, Nebraska, that the breadth of the gap increased linearly up to about three years and then curvilinearly in older animals. They found no significant differences between males and females or among animals of different body weight.

We measured the premolar gaps in a sample of 68 well-preserved black-tailed prairie dog mandibles recovered in the 1980-1981 field seasons at the Henderson Site, using the average of three separate measurements taken on each specimen with dial calipers under low-power magnification. Accurately placing the tips of the calipers on the highest point on each cusp often proved to be very difficult, even under a microscope, because the surfaces were often broad and only slightly convex. Thus, we found it nearly impossible to replicate our own measurements consistently, nor could we match the level of precision (0.02 mm) reported by Cox and Franklin (1990:144). Not surprisingly, therefore, our initial results contained a great deal of "noise," a problem also clearly evident in the large standard errors reported by Cox and Franklin, who made their measurements on live animals and apparently without the aid of magnification.

We experimented with different ways of measuring the premolar gap, settling on a simple approach that yielded consistent, though less precise (0.1 mm) values. This technique involves holding the mandible upside down and gently touching the premolar cusps on an inked stamp pad. Keeping the mandible inverted, the cusps of the premolar are then pressed on a pad of paper producing a pair of tiny points. The diameter of these points can be minimized by using very little ink, pressing lightly on the paper, and making a series of impressions to use up excess ink. The premolar gap breadth is the center-to-center distance in mm between the two points. To make the measurements, we used a hand-held, transparent base, optical magnifier or comparator with a built-in "contact" reticule graduated to 0.1 mm.[4] We then used the linear regression results provided by Cox and Franklin (1990:145) to convert these gap values into approximate ages:

$$y = 1.541 + 0.013x,$$

where y is the premolar gap breadth in mm, and x is the known age in weeks of the animals in the Nebraska prairie dogs. These values must be regarded with caution, since the relationship has not been validated in other prairie dog samples, particularly among populations in the Southern Plains.

Studies of prairie dog demography typically report the ages of animals in just two broad classes, juveniles (animals less than a year old) and adults (yearlings and older animals). Grouped in this manner, Henderson yielded 27 juveniles (39.7%) and 41 adults (60.3%). For comparison, in a living population of black-tailed prairie dogs monitored over a period of fourteen years in Wind Cave National Park, South Dakota, Hoogland et al. (1987; see also Hoogland and Hutter 1987; Hoogland 1995) found that the average number of juveniles was 81 (37.9%) and the average number of yearlings and adults was 133 (62.1%). Vosburgh and Irby (1998) observed proportions of juveniles in both hunted and non-hunted Montana black-tailed prairie dog populations ranging from 29.6% to 49.0%, with a mean of about 38.9%. Similarly, Smith (1967:29) observed that there were about 33% juveniles and 67% yearlings and adults in a prairie dog colony in Kansas. These figures, based on living populations, are strikingly similar to the values seen in the faunal sample from Henderson, and strongly suggest that animals were being added to the deposits—by human or non-human agents—in proportions that closely approximate a living population.

The age structure of the animals that die each year in modern black-tailed prairie dog populations differs quite sharply

Table 9.2. Frequency (NISP) of bones of each rodent taxon recovered in quarter-inch screens and in flotation samples at Henderson Site (1980-1981 only).

Rodent Taxon	Screening Samples[a]		Flotation Samples[b]	
	NISP	%	NISP	%
Prairie dog	852	98.7	11	1.3
Pocket gopher	230	96.6	8	3.4
Muskrat	33	100.0	0	0.0
"Misc. small rodents"	151	90.4	16	9.6

[a]Quarter-inch-mesh screens (dry).
[b]$n = 303$ (vol. = 1.17 m^3).

Table 9.3. Frequency (NISP) of lagomorph and rodent dentitions (mandibles and maxillae) at Henderson Site (1980-1981 only).[a]

Small-Mammal Taxon	Total NISP	Mandibles and Maxillae	
		NISP	%
Jackrabbit	1269	321	25.3
Cottontail rabbit	3094	931	30.1
Prairie dog	863	243	28.2
Muskrat	33	10	30.3
Pocket gopher	238	68	28.6
"Misc. small rodents"	167	99	59.3

[a]Total NISP values for jackrabbit (*Lepus californicus*) and cottontail rabbit (*Sylvilagus audubonii*) are taken from Tables A8.1 and A8.2 (Chapter 8); lagomorph values shown here have been adjusted by deleting counts for vertebrae, metapodials, and tarsals, in order to make them comparable to NISP totals for rodents, which do not include these elements.

from the age structure of living populations. Juvenile mortality is very high (Hoogland 1985; Hoogland et al. 1987; Stockrahm and Seabloom 1988), as is clearly reflected, for example, in data from a population of black-tailed prairie dogs in the Black Hills. In this population, King (1955:48) found that, on average, about two-thirds of the animals that died in a given year were juveniles. Data provided by Menkens and Anderson (1991) on white-tailed prairie dogs (*Cynomys leucurus*) in Wyoming is similar—approximately two-thirds of the deaths per year were juveniles.[5]

If the values provided by these two studies of living prairie dog populations are in any way representative of the demographics of these animals during the thirteenth century in southeastern New Mexico, then the archaeological population that one might expect as a result of *natural* deaths at Henderson should be biased strongly toward animals less than a year old. Instead, the age structure suggests that the prairie dogs were deliberately hunted by the villagers, and that the techniques employed by the hunters captured juveniles and older animals in proportions similar to their expected natural abundance in the living population.

The prairie dog bones at Henderson are very likely the food remains of the site's human inhabitants, not background noise. This may also be true of the pocket gophers, and perhaps even many of the smaller rodents, but unfortunately the data at hand do not allow us to demonstrate this with any degree of certainty.

Recovery Biases

We will touch only briefly on the degree to which recovery biases stemming from the use of quarter-inch screens may have altered the composition of the rodent assemblage, both in terms of the proportions of the various taxa present and the representation of different skeletal elements. As discussed in Chapter 8, recovery of the bones of animals the size of *Sylvilagus* or larger is unlikely to be biased significantly by quarter-inch screening (Szuter 1991; Shaffer 1992a). The only bones of cottontails that are likely to be sharply underrepresented are the tiny carpals and tarsals—bones seldom tabulated by zooarchaeologists—and the metacarpals. Since the prairie dog, with an average body weight of 1.13 kg, is somewhat larger than the desert cottontail, which averages 0.92 kg, the recovery bias should be less against this rodent than the rabbit (see Table 14.1 in Chapter 14 for body-weight data and sources).

Taxonomic Representation

One way at Henderson to detect recovery biases against the smaller rodent taxa is to compare the density of bones (NISP/m^3 of deposit) recovered in the screens with their density in the flotation samples. As pointed out in Chapter 8, the most realistic comparisons involve the screening samples from the trash middens in Room C-5 and the East Plaza, since flotation samples were preferentially collected from features, middens, and other culturally rich deposits, whereas the screening samples include many cubic meters of artifact-poor room fill and overburden. A glance at Table 9.1 shows that the density of prairie dog remains is higher in these major trash deposits than in the flotation samples, arguing, as expected, against severe recovery losses of the bones of this relatively large-bodied rodent.

The picture is less clear-cut for the much smaller gopher (average body weight ca. 270 g). The East Plaza displays a density value that is considerably lower than the flotation value, perhaps a sign of recovery biases. On the other hand, the Room C-5 deposits display a much higher density value. Since the screening techniques used in both areas of the site were identical, it is unlikely that the low East Plaza value reflects problems in recovery.

A more reliable way to assess the degree of recovery bias against the pocket gopher is to compare the density of just mandibles and maxillae, two large and robust elements that are unlikely to have passed undetected through the screens (see Table

9.1). Unfortunately, when only these elements are considered, the flotation sample becomes very small. Nevertheless, the higher density of these elements in both the East Plaza and Room C-5 samples make it unlikely that gophers are severely underrepresented relative to the larger-bodied taxa as a result of screening losses.

Interestingly, screening biases do not even appear to be particularly severe against the smallest rodent taxa ("misc. small rodents") when comparisons are made using just mandibles and maxillae (Table 9.1). Again, the density of these cranial elements in the Room C-5 midden is similar to the value in the flotation samples.

Another way of examining recovery losses is simply to compare, for each rodent taxon, the proportion of bones recovered in the screens to the proportion found in the flotation samples. These comparisons are shown in Table 9.2. As expected, the proportion of the total NISP recovered in the flotation samples increases steadily with declining body size, a sign that more of the bones of smaller taxa were lost through the screens. All of the proportions shown in the table are significantly different.[6] Interestingly, however, even the "misc. small rodents" appear to be quite well represented in the screening samples: more than 90% of the remains of these tiny animals were recovered in the screens. Recovery biases, while clearly present, have not grossly distorted their proportional representation at Henderson.

Skeletal Element Representation

The nature and extent of screening biases against the smaller, less robust skeletal elements, particularly postcranial elements, of the various rodent taxa can be assessed by comparing the proportion of dentitions out of the total number of bones recovered for each taxon. These data are summarized in Table 9.3.

The patterning in Table 9.3 is quite striking. After a small but statistically significant increase ($t_s = 3.21$, $p < .001$) in the proportion of dentitions from about 25% in jackrabbits (average body weight 2.6 kg) to approximately 30% in cottontail rabbits (average weight 0.92 kg), the proportion then remains more or less constant across the rodent taxa until we reach the smallest size category, the "misc. small rodents" (average weight less than about 150-200 g). Among these tiny mammals, the proportion of dentitions jumps dramatically to comprise nearly 60% of the assemblage.

In sum, these comparisons indicate that recovery biases probably have had very little impact on the prairie dog, muskrat, and pocket gopher assemblages, either in terms of these taxa's abundance in the total Henderson fauna, or in terms of the proportional representation of most skeletal elements. The picture is more complex for the smallest rodent category. However, so long as mandibles and maxillae are the focus of analysis, screening does not appear to have biased their taxonomic abundance to any major degree. On the other hand, screening almost certainly has biased severely the proportional representation of the postcranial skeletal elements of these tiny animals.

Taphonomic Biases

Another important issue that needs to be considered is the extent to which the rodent assemblage has been altered by attritional processes, especially weathering, trampling, and the destructive activities of scavenging village dogs. Again, we draw heavily here on arguments that have been presented in greater depth in Chapter 8 in the discussion of the lagomorph remains.

Signs of severe weathering damage are rare among the rodent remains. Most bones are well preserved, with uncracked and unabraded surfaces, and show no evidence of extended exposure on the surface (Behrensmeyer 1978). The most notable exception to this generalization are bones exposed on the surface in the Center Bar by recent vandalism. The number of bones damaged in this way is small.

Although trampling may have contributed to bone breakage and perhaps to the selective loss of some of the most fragile elements (Gifford 1980, 1981; Gifford and Behrensmeyer 1977; Gifford-Gonzalez et al. 1985), it is unlikely to have been responsible for major biases in either the taxonomic or skeletal element composition of the rodent assemblage. This is most clearly the case for the rodent and other faunal remains in the Room C-5 midden, which accumulated in the structure while the walls and possibly even the roof were still intact. Trampling is more likely to have played a role in the East Plaza, given the much more open and accessible nature of this locale. Even here, though, trampling was probably not a major taphonomic force, since the midden accumulated largely within the confines of a bedrock depression that was unlikely to have been the locus of heavy foot traffic.

As argued in the discussion of the lagomorphs (Chapter 8), attrition by village dogs is the single most likely factor to have significantly altered the composition of the Henderson small-mammal assemblages (Kent 1981, 1993; Lyon 1970; Payne and Munson 1985; Walters 1984). In the case of the lagomorphs, two principal approaches were used in assessing the impact of dogs on the remains: (1) determining whether the observed skeletal element frequencies are significantly correlated with experimentally derived bulk (volume) density measures for these elements; and (2) examining the degree to which the observed element frequencies covary with marrow and grease utility. These same approaches will again be used here.

Numerous studies have documented the greater susceptibility of low-density skeletal elements, or parts of elements, to attritional losses (e.g., Behrensmeyer 1975; Brain 1967, 1969, 1981; Binford 1981; Binford and Bertram 1977; Grayson 1989; Kreutzer 1992; Lyman 1984, 1985, 1991, 1992; Lyman et al. 1992; Marshall and Pilgram 1991). Thus, a strong *positive* correlation between element frequency and bulk (volume) density suggests density-mediated attrition. Density values are now available for six taxa of small mammals, including two closely related fossorial species, the marmot and woodchuck (Behrensmeyer 1975; Binford and Bertram 1977; Brink and Dawe 1989; Kreutzer 1992; Lyman 1984, 1992; Lyman et al.

Table 9.4. Proportion (%MNI) of black-tailed prairie dog (*Cynomys ludovicianus*) and pocket gopher (*Pappogeomys castanops*) skeletal elements (all proveniences combined, 1980-1981 only), bulk (volume) density of marmot bones, marrow index, and grease index.

Skeletal Element[a]	Marmots (*Marmota*) Density[b]	Prairie Dog (*Cynomys*) %MNI	Pocket Gopher (*Pappogeomys*) %MNI	Marrow Index[c]	Grease Index[d]
Mandible	0.59	100.0	100.0	5.74	—
Scapula	0.58	53.1	8.0	6.40	—
Prox. humerus	0.37	7.8	4.0	29.69	241.48
Dist. humerus	0.62	54.7	48.0	28.33	64.12
Prox. radius	0.79	31.3	4.0	43.64	42.71
Dist. radius	0.51	9.4	40.0	66.11	49.73
Prox. ulna	0.66	64.1	28.0	43.64	42.71
Pelvis	0.44	67.2	64.0	7.85	—
Prox. femur	0.73	29.7	36.0	33.51	112.41
Dist. femur	0.48	9.4	32.0	49.41	186.30
Prox. tibia	0.45	3.1	12.0	43.78	96.82
Dist. tibia	0.56	48.4	60.0	92.90	12.22

[a]Table omits skeletal elements that were not identified and coded for black-tailed prairie dog and pocket gopher (i.e., vertebrae, metapodials, carpals, and tarsals).
[b]Bulk (volume) density values for marmots are averages for two closely related species (*Marmota monax* and *M. flaviventris*; see Lyman et al. 1992:566, Table 2).
[c]From Binford (1978:27, Table 1.9).
[d]From Brink and Dawe (1989:134, Table 20).

1992), and four lagomorph taxa: *Oryctolagus cuniculus*, *Sylvilagus floridanus*, *Lepus canadensis*, *Lepus californicus* (Pavao 1996; Pavao and Stahl 1999). We have opted to use the density values for marmots as proxies for the Henderson rodents, rather than those derived from lagomorphs, because, like marmots, both prairie dogs and gophers are fossorial animals. Obviously, regardless of which values we use as proxies, the results of such comparisons have to be regarded with caution, given the risks inherent in using density values derived from unrelated species.

The marmot bulk (volume) density values are presented in Table 9.4. Also presented in this table are the site-wide skeletal element frequencies, expressed as %MNI values, for both prairie dogs and gophers. Values for only twelve elements are given, since the vertebrae, metapodials, carpals, and tarsals of rodents were not identified and coded. The category of "misc. small rodents" is not considered here, because the element frequencies for these tiny animals have clearly been biased by the routine use of quarter-inch screens during the excavations.

Prairie dog skeletal element frequencies (%MNI) display a weak but positive correlation with marmot bone density; in contrast, gopher element frequencies show no correlation whatsoever. That the prairie dog correlation is not statistically significant is not surprising given the small number of elements involved in the comparisons (n = 12, Spearman's r, prairie dog vs. marmot density, $r_s = .38, p > .05$; pocket gopher vs. marmot density, $r_s = -.03, p > .05$). Thus, despite the lack of statistical significance, it is likely that density-mediated attrition, probably stemming in large part from the destructive activity of village dogs, has at least to some extent altered the composition of the prairie dog assemblage.

This conclusion is strikingly borne out for prairie dogs when element frequencies are correlated with marrow and grease utility. The rationale underlying these comparisons is as follows. In small mammals such as rodents, humans are unlikely to have made transport decisions of discrete carcass parts on the basis of utility. Instead, whole carcasses, or nearly whole carcasses minus the feet, were probably brought into the village for preparation and consumption. The defleshed bones of these rodents would then have been discarded. As discussed at length in Chapter 8, if the animals had been roasted or pit-baked, the discarded bones would still have contained grease and possibly some marrow as well, making them attractive to village dogs. On the other hand, if they had been broken open and then boiled or stewed, the discarded bones would have been largely or entirely degreased and stripped of their marrow content, making them of little or no interest to scavenging dogs (see Lupo 1995). Thus, if rodents at Henderson had been prepared primarily by roasting or pit-baking, one should expect a negative correlation between element frequency and both marrow and grease utility. In other words, the higher an element's marrow or grease utility, the more likely it would have been destroyed by village dogs. In contrast, if rodents generally had been boiled or cooked in stews, there should be little or no correlation between element frequency and either marrow or grease utility. Actually, in the case of the lagomorphs a clear-cut positive correlation was found with marrow utility. This unexpected result not only suggested that jackrabbits and cottontails were most often boiled or stewed rather than roasted or pit-baked, but also that the low-utility bones of the feet (including the metapodials) had been discarded prior to cooking, perhaps in fact before the animals were brought into the village, elevating the proportional representation of the higher-utility upper limb bones.

The marrow and grease indices have been included in Table 9.4. Again, values are presented only for the twelve skeletal elements that have been coded in rodents; other elements such as the vertebrae, metapodials, phalanges, carpals, and tarsals, while clearly present in the Henderson faunal collections, have not been identified to taxon or coded, and are therefore omitted from the table. Moreover, we are faced with the problem that marrow and grease utility have only been determined in medium and large ungulates such as sheep, caribou and bison (Binford 1978; Brink and Dawe 1989). We must therefore make do with proxies when analyzing the rodents. As in the case of the lagomorphs, what we hope justifies the use of these proxies is the assumption that the gross anatomical proportions of rodent elements are similar enough to their counterparts in ungulates that the relative ranking of elements, in terms of their marrow and grease content, is preserved.

In Table 9.4, we present the standardized marrow index for caribou developed by Binford (1978:27). For the grease index, we use the values developed for bison by Brink and Dawe (1989:134, Table 20). The sample sizes are obviously extremely small, especially for the grease index, but the results nevertheless are intriguing. Looking first at prairie dogs, the frequency of skeletal elements is significantly, and *negatively*, correlated with the marrow index ($n = 12$, Spearman's r, $r_s = -0.59$, $p < .05$). The %MNI values for this rodent are also negatively correlated with the grease index and again the value is significant ($n = 9$, $r_s = -0.66$, $p < .05$). In gophers the results are far less clear-cut, as neither of the correlations is significant, but in both cases the direction of the correlation is the same as in the prairie dog ($n = 9$, marrow utility, $r_s = -0.13$, $p > .05$; grease utility, $r_s = -0.35$, $p > .05$).

There are several factors that might explain why gophers pattern less clearly with utility than prairie dogs. Perhaps the most obvious is that gopher bones are much smaller and, when scavenged by dogs, are more likely to be consumed in their entirety without regard to the utility of the proximal or distal end. Another factor that cannot be ignored is the greater difficulty we experienced in assigning fragmentary gopher-sized postcranial elements to taxon. This uncertainty was not uniform across all elements and is very likely to have introduced greater inter-element variability into our gopher tallies. Finally, it is entirely possible that utility indices based on medium or large ungulate bones are poor proxies for the values in very small mammals.

In sum, the correlation between prairie dog element frequencies and marrow utility is diametrically opposite to the ones obtained for cottontails and jackrabbits. If the positive correlation found in the lagomorphs is indeed a sign of minimal attrition by village dogs, and this in turn is because these animals were usually boiled or stewed, then the prairie dog results must point to comparatively heavy attrition by village dogs, which in turn must be due to their being prepared more often by roasting or baking (see also Speth 2000). What this implies about the low incidence of burned bone in general at Henderson is explored in Chapter 14.

Cooking methods are reflected in the small-mammal data in another way. Taphonomists now routinely examine the ratio of proximal to distal humeri and tibiae as an index of the extent to which carnivores have altered an assemblage (e.g., Binford 1981). The logic is straightforward. The proximal epiphyses of these two elements are much more porous than the distal ones and contain more edible tissue that is attractive to predators or scavengers. Hence, the degree to which these articulations are underrepresented in an assemblage in comparison to their distal counterparts provides a useful measure of the degree of carnivore attrition.

We can use this same approach to see whether jackrabbit and cottontail humeri and tibiae show less evidence of attrition than those of prairie dogs and gophers, as would be expected if most of the lagomorphs had been boiled while most of the rodents had been roasted or baked. The relevant data are summarized in Table 9.5. Contrary to our expectations, proximal humeri of all four taxa, not just of rodents, are sharply underrepresented. Moreover, although the proximal humeri of jackrabbits and cottontails are proportionately slightly more numerous than those of rodents, as we had anticipated, the differences are very small and not statistically significant. However, if we combine the data for jackrabbits and cottontails into a single composite lagomorph value and do the same for the two rodent taxa, thereby providing larger sample sizes, the proximal humeri of the former are then significantly better represented than those of the latter ($t_s = 2.11$, $p < .05$).

The picture presented by the tibiae is more clear-cut. The proximal ends are much better represented in the lagomorphs than in the two rodent taxa, and all of the differences between taxa are significant (jackrabbit:prairie dog, $t_s = 5.59$, $p < .001$; jackrabbit:gopher, $t_s = 4.22$, $p < .001$; cottontail:prairie dog, $t_s = 3.55$, $p < .001$; cottontail:gopher, $t_s = 2.39$, $p < .05$).[7]

That lagomorphs and prairie dogs may have been cooked by different methods at Henderson is certainly not without ethnographic precedent in the Southwest. For example, Hill (1938:172) notes that, among the Navajo, prairie dogs

> were always cooked in the same way. They were cleaned; the liver, lungs and fat put back in the body cavity; salt added, and the opening pinned up with twigs. Then the hair was singed in an open fire and the animal buried in the ashes to roast.

Elmore (1938:152) makes similar observations concerning the Navajo method for preparing prairie dogs.

> After removing the entrails, the interior is sprinkled with salt and closed. It is then thrown on the fire and covered with embers. The hair is removed with a knife, and the dog eaten. The flesh is very greasy.

Table 9.5. Proportions of proximal and distal humeri and tibias of lagomorphs and rodents at Henderson Site (all proveniences combined).

Taxon	Humerus				Tibia			
	Proximal		Distal		Proximal		Distal	
	NISP	%	NISP	%	NISP	%	NISP	%
Jackrabbit	26	19.3	109	80.7	53	51.5	50	48.5
Cottontail	55	19.9	222	80.1	110	31.9	235	68.1
Prairie dog	10	12.7	69	87.3	9	12.9	61	87.1
Pocket gopher	2	7.7	24	92.3	5	14.3	30	85.7

While Hill offers no comments on Navajo methods for cooking rabbits and jackrabbits, Elmore (1938:153) states that in the pre-modern era

> rabbits were skinned, disemboweled, crushed between stones, bones and all, so that nothing might be lost. They were then put into earthen pots to boil.

Rabbits were usually boiled by the Havasupai, while most other animals, including rodents, were baked in earth ovens (Weber and Seaman 1985:62-64).[8]

Among Pueblo groups, boiling appears to have been a common, if not the preferred, method for cooking rabbit meat (e.g., Beaglehole 1936:14, 1937:68; Smith 1969:16). Unfortunately, there are very few equally explicit statements concerning the methods normally used by these groups for cooking prairie dogs. However, Richard I. Ford (pers. comm.), based on ethnographic fieldwork at Hopi, Zuni, and San Juan, believes that roasting was the traditional method for cooking prairie dogs, at least by these Pueblos.

The taphonomic analysis of the small-mammal remains from Henderson clearly had an unexpected dividend, one which archaeologists may find worthwhile pursuing further in the future. In exploring the patterning between element frequencies and various indices of utility, relationships that we examined initially primarily as a way of assessing the extent to which the rodent and lagomorph assemblages had been altered by village dogs, we inadvertently found a method that may also allow us to determine whether small mammals were most often boiled or instead roasted or baked. This fortuitous discovery in turn may provide archaeologists with a useful addition to the growing array of techniques and approaches that now exist for investigating the spatial organization of subsistence activities.

This approach may also offer a means for identifying an activity that, in the ethnographic realm at least, appears to be closely linked to gender, namely, boiling (see also Speth 2000). The task of cooking meat by boiling is usually performed by women, whereas the roasting or baking of meat may be done by either sex, depending on the particular animal being cooked, and especially on the social context in which the meat is being prepared.[9] Men are much more likely to participate in cooking when the meat being prepared is for "large-scale extradomestic feasts or ceremonials" (Friedl 1975:59). More routine "domestic" food preparation, especially boiling, is generally done by women (see also Lowell 1991).

Given that the very close links between gender and the preparation and distribution of food have been a topic of discussion for years by ethnologists (e.g., Friedl 1975; Levi-Strauss 1975; Dumont 1972), and given the fact that activities related to subsistence and food preparation are among the most highly visible and accessible in the prehistoric record, it is surprising that archaeologists have devoted so little attention to food preparation, especially to cooking. Fortunately, this situation is now changing with the recent explosion of interest among archaeologists in finding ways to recognize and study gender systems in the past (e.g., Gero and Conkey 1991; Walde and Willows 1991; Claassen 1992; Bacus et al. 1993). While the relationship between gender and food is only one small part of this burgeoning research, nonetheless it is a topic which is beginning to draw serious attention (e.g., Brumfiel 1991; Hastorf 1991; Gifford-Gonzalez 1993; Sassaman 1992).

Before the approach presented here can be used with confidence, we need further experimental and ethnoarchaeological studies of the differential fate, upon discard, of roasted, baked, and boiled small-mammal bones in the presence of scavenging village dogs. We also need utility indices designed explicitly for small mammals such as lagomorphs and rodents. And we need a much closer look at the relationship between method of cooking and gender among ethnographically documented small-scale societies, in order to better understand how real and widespread this pattern actually is, and the circumstances in which it occurs.

Seasonal Scheduling of Prairie Dog Hunting

If we accept the arguments made earlier that most, if not all, of the prairie dogs at Henderson were brought into the site by the villagers themselves and are not the fortuitous remains of noncultural taphonomic processes, then the seasonality of prairie dog hunting becomes a matter of considerable interest. Unlike the lagomorphs and pocket gophers, which both produce two or more litters over the course of the breeding season, black-tailed prairie dogs give birth to a single litter of four or five young early in the spring (Anthony and Foreman 1951; Burt

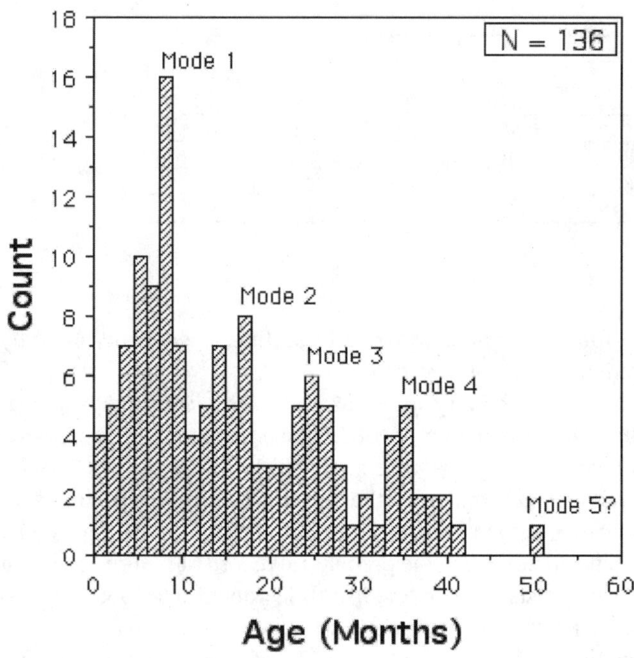

Figure 9.2. Black-tailed prairie dog age structure (months) at the Henderson Site (n = 136, 1980-1997 seasons).

and Grossenheider 1976:95, 124, 132; Costello 1970; Davis 1974:156, 171; King 1955; Schmidly 1977:74, 79). This means that if the age at death of the prairie dogs can be determined on the basis of tooth eruption or wear, then, as in larger ungulates, the approximate time of year when these rodents were killed can be estimated.

Fortunately, as discussed earlier, the age of black-tailed prairie dog mandibles can be estimated by measuring the width of the gap between the highest crest on the paraconid and protoconid cusps of the premolar (see Fig. 9.1; Cox and Franklin 1990). One hundred thirty-six *Cynomys* lower premolars from the 1980-1997 field seasons at Henderson were well enough preserved to be measured. Using Cox and Franklin's (1990:145) linear regression model (see above), we converted the premolar gap breadths into monthly values.[10] The histogram of ages for these specimens displays four, possibly five, unambiguous peaks or modes (Fig. 9.2). In other words, certain ages are conspicuously overrepresented while others are underrepresented, indicating that much of the prairie dog hunting at Henderson took place during a seasonally restricted part of the year.

We then calculated the mean age in months for the individuals represented in each of the five modes. These are: 6.1 ± 2.6 months (mode 1, n = 58), 15.5 ± 2.6 months (mode 2, n = 35), 25.3 ± 2.5 months (mode 3, n = 25), and 36.1 ± 2.5 months (mode 4, n = 17). Only a single specimen falls in the fifth mode, with an age of approximately 49 months. The means for the five age cohorts or modes are separated from each other by intervals that roughly approximate twelve months. Greater precision in our estimates cannot be expected for several reasons: (1) the small sample sizes and measurement error involved in the Henderson calculations; (2) substantial measurement error built into the original data collected by Cox and Franklin (1990); and (3) increasingly variable and distinctly nonlinear rates of tooth wear in the older age classes sampled by Cox and Franklin (1990; see discussion of tooth-wear rates in Lowe 1967; Murie 1951).

To determine the approximate time of year when most prairie dog hunting took place at Henderson, we need to know the season when prairie dogs in this region are born. Unfortunately, there is surprisingly little precise information on the timing of prairie dog births (Davis 1974:156). Most authors agree that the young are born in March or April, with the pups first emerging from their burrows when they are about six to eight weeks old (Costello 1970; Davis 1974; King 1955). The timing varies with both latitude and altitude. The best data for the Southern Plains region are provided by Anthony and Foreman (1951:248) for prairie dogs in the Wichita Mountains Wildlife Refuge at Cache in western Oklahoma. Births among these animals take place over two to three weeks in early March, with the pups first emerging above ground about six to eight weeks later. If most prairie dog births in the Roswell area were similarly timed, the mean value for the youngest age cohort would suggest that most hunting at Henderson took place during the period between about June and October, or during the summer and early fall. Given the multiple sources of error associated with the age determinations, we must regard this conclusion with caution.

Stockrahm and Seabloom (1990) have recently published a schedule of tooth eruption for the black-tailed prairie dog, which allows us to be somewhat more precise about the onset of prairie dog hunting at Henderson. All of the Henderson mandibles with teeth still in place have lower third molars that are fully erupted and in wear. This means that all of the animals were at least 2.5 months old when they were killed. Only one mandible has a deciduous premolar still in place (the M_3 of this specimen is erupted and in full wear). All of the other Henderson specimens have fully erupted permanent P_4's. This single immature mandible must come from an animal between about 2.5 and 3.2 months old. Thus, the entire Henderson sample consists of animals that were more than about 2.5 months old when they were killed, pointing to the onset of hunting sometime in May.

In sum, premolar gap measurements of prairie dog mandibles from the Henderson Site display clear-cut multimodality, indicating that these animals were not hunted with the same intensity year-round. Determining the actual time of year represented by these remains is more complicated. However, if we accept the validity of Cox and Franklin's (1990) regression equation for animals in the Roswell area, then prairie dog hunting probably took place largely, if not entirely, in the late spring, summer, and early fall. Few, if any, animals were taken in the late fall and winter, despite the fact that these rodents probably would have been available year-round. (While black-tailed prairie dogs hibernate during periods of harsh winter weather, they commonly reemerge from their burrows on sunny winter days [Anthony and Foreman 1951; Costello 1970; King 1955]). If correct, this conclusion dovetails closely with the data provided by the bison, antelope, and lagomorphs; few or none of these animals appear to have been hunted in the late fall or early winter by the Henderson villagers.

Temporal Perspective

Since completion of the original manuscript on the prairie dogs from the 1980-1981 seasons at Henderson, we have coded the remaining *Cynomys* bones allowing us to examine, briefly, the temporal dimension in this assemblage. Prairie dog density increases fairly substantially over time, rising from 6.3 NISP/m^3 in the Early phase to 9.8 NISP/m^3 in the Late phase. The increase is most dramatic in non-room contexts, where the density increases from only 4.1 NISP/m^3 in the Early phase to 10.7 NISP/m^3 in the Late phase. Clearly, more prairie dogs per unit time were brought into the community in the later period, and more of these rodents were processed and discarded in non-room contexts. This latter point is underscored by the significant increase in the proportion of *Cynomys* remains that were encountered in non-room contexts (Early phase, 22.0%; Late phase, 31.0%; $t_s = 3.59$, $p < .001$).

Earlier in this chapter we noted that a significant *negative* correlation (Spearman's *r*) between prairie dog skeletal element frequencies and grease utility pointed to attrition of the rodent assemblage, very likely by village dogs. Based on this evidence and parallels drawn from the ethnographic literature, we then argued that most of the Henderson prairie dogs had probably been cooked by roasting rather than boiling. When we examine the prairie dog remains by chronological phase, the negative correlations with grease utility persist, regardless of whether we use Binford's (1978) or Brink and Dawe's (1989) indices (Early phase: Binford, $r_s = -.56$, $p = .05$, Brink and Dawe, $r_s = -.70$, $p = .05$; Late phase, Binford, $r_s = -.73$, $p = .01$, Brink and Dawe, $r_s = -.77$, $p < .05$). It would appear, therefore, that roasting or pit-baking persisted as the preferred means of cooking prairie dogs throughout the community's existence.

The seasonality of prairie dog procurement appears to have remained the same over time as well. The mean ages (in months) for each of the four principal age cohorts in the two chronological phases are very similar, and none of the differences are statistically significant (Early phase:Late phase: mode 1, 6.1:6.1; mode 2, 15.1:15.8; mode 3, 24.6:25.6; mode 4, 35.7:36.2).

Synopsis

The 1980-1981 rodent assemblage from the Henderson Site is neither large nor taxonomically diverse. Most of the identifiable remains are from the black-tailed prairie dog (*Cynomys ludovicianus*), a relatively large rodent similar in live weight to the desert cottontail. Bones of the much smaller-bodied yellow-faced or yellow-cheeked pocket gopher (*Pappogeomys castanops*) are also relatively common. Muskrats (*Ondatra zibethicus*), while present, are rare. The remaining rodent bones, the vast majority of which are mandibles and maxillary fragments, are all from animals smaller than the pocket gopher. These have not yet been identified to taxon and are treated here as a single group, "misc. small rodents." Only a few species make up most of this group.

Distinguishing in the archaeological record between rodents that were consumed by people and those that represent part of the natural taphonomic background of a site is problematic.

The following lines of evidence suggest that the prairie dogs, muskrats, and probably also the pocket gophers are the remains of human subsistence. Even the smallest class of rodents may be mostly human food remains, but this is less certain.

Only a single articulated rodent skeleton, in the "misc. small rodent" category, was encountered in the first two seasons of excavation. All of the other remains were disarticulated and widely dispersed within the deposits.

Approximately 1.9% of the prairie dog bones are burned, identical to the incidence of burning in the cottontail rabbit. Burning evidence on gopher bones is lower still, but in line with the incidence that would be predicted based on body size (see Chapter 14 for correlation of body weight and burning.)

The highest densities (NISP/m^3) of prairie dog remains were found in the midden deposits in Room C-5 and the East Plaza. While the abundance of these animals in the room might reflect the fact that they preferred to burrow into the soft, organic-rich midden that filled this structure after its abandonment, this same argument does not apply to the East Plaza, where burrowing by these large-bodied rodents would have been much impeded by densely packed masses of fire-cracked rock. Thus, the abundance of prairie dog remains in the midden deposits almost certainly reflects their importance as a food source for the villagers. As in the case of the prairie dogs, the highest densities of gopher and smaller rodent bones are also encountered in a midden context, but in these smaller taxa only in Room C-5, not in the East Plaza. Thus, while their abundance is probably also a reflection of their role in the diet of the villagers, we cannot rule out the possibility that their presence is due instead to natural taphonomic processes.

That the prairie dogs are human food remains and not background "noise" is most clearly shown by the age structure of the recovered animals. Aging of the mandibles using the "premolar gap technique" shows that about one-third of the Henderson animals are juveniles and two-thirds are yearlings and adults. Nearly identical proportions of juveniles and older animals are seen in living prairie dog populations. In contrast, juveniles make up about two-thirds of the animals that die each year in modern *Cynomys* populations, a value that is nearly double the value seen at Henderson. These data indicate that the Henderson villagers hunted the prairie dogs, and used techniques such as traps or snares, that captured juveniles and adults in proportions very similar to their natural abundance in living populations.

The nature and extent of recovery bias introduced by the routine use of quarter-inch screens at Henderson had to be assessed. Two forms of bias were considered—bias in the proportional representation of different rodent taxa, and bias in the representation of various skeletal elements within each rodent taxon. Taxonomic bias was considered first.

The flotation samples provide an excellent standard against which to compare the screened assemblages. Lower densities in the latter may imply higher loss rates, especially if the difference between the flotation and screening assemblages becomes greater the smaller the taxon. Because flotation samples were preferentially taken from deposits rich in organic and archaeological remains, while screening samples included many cubic meters of nearly sterile overburden and room fill, the flotation samples are best compared with screening assemblages from midden deposits, particularly those from Room C-5 and the East Plaza. Both of these middens display considerably higher prairie dog densities than do the flotation samples. Prairie dog remains, therefore, do not appear to have been lost in significant quantities through the quarter-inch screens. Room C-5, but not the East Plaza, also has higher densities of gophers and "misc. small rodents." Since both proveniences were screened using the same techniques, it is unlikely that the lower densities of the smaller taxa in the East Plaza are due to screening losses.

More reliable comparisons between flotation and screening assemblages are obtained by looking at the densities of mandibles and maxillae, since these elements are relatively large, robust, and easily recognized, and they are therefore less likely than fragmentary postcranial elements to pass undetected through the screens. When just these two cranial elements are considered, the screening samples from Room C-5 and the East Plaza have comparable or higher densities than the flotation samples for all taxa, including even the "misc. small rodents." Again, the conclusion is that the proportional representation of even the smallest rodent taxa is faithfully reflected in the screening samples.

When the proportion of all bones of a given taxon (% of NISP) found in the screens is compared to the proportion recovered in the flotation samples, the latter increases steadily from 1.3% in prairie dogs to 3.4% in gophers to 9.6% in the "misc. small rodents." All of the percentages are significantly different, suggesting greater screening losses of postcranial elements in the smaller taxa but the magnitude of the losses, even in the smallest category, is surprisingly small.

In sum, recovery losses have biased the taxonomic composition of the Henderson rodent assemblage against the smaller species. However, the magnitude of this bias appears to be small. Moreover, so long as taxonomic abundance is assessed on the basis of the frequency of mandibles and maxillae, even the smallest rodent taxa are faithfully represented in the screens.

The magnitude of recovery bias affecting the proportional representation of different skeletal elements proved to be small in all but the smallest taxonomic category, the "misc. small rodents." This is shown by the proportion of dentitions out of the total number of bones (NISP) recovered for each taxon. There is a small but statistically significant increase in the proportion of dentitions from about 25% in jackrabbits to 30% in cottontails. The proportion remains more or less constant in prairie dogs, muskrats, and pocket gophers. Only in the "misc. small rodents" does the percentage of dentitions jump sharply to comprise nearly 60% of the assemblage.

Taphonomic biases were also examined. The rodent bones in general are well preserved, showing very few signs of weathering. Trampling damage or loss is also thought to be minor at Henderson, since much of the rodent assemblage comes from middens where heavy foot traffic was probably limited. This is particularly true of the materials from the trash in Room C-5, which accumulated in an abandoned structure while the walls and possibly even the roof were intact. Trampling may have been more important in the East Plaza, but the accumulation of the midden in a gully within the plaza may have protected these bones from heavy trampling as well.

If the Henderson rodent assemblage has suffered attritional losses, the single most likely cause would have been the scavenging activities of village dogs. The same assumptions, caveats, and provisos applying to lagomorphs apply here (see Chapter 8). Both prairie dogs and gophers show weak positive correlations between element frequencies and the bulk, or volume, density of the elements. The lack of statistical significance is thought to be due primarily to the small number of skeletal elements involved in the correlations. The "misc. small rodents" were not included in this analysis because recovery losses have already severely biased their element frequencies. Unlike the lagomorphs, these results suggest that density-mediated attrition has altered the element frequencies of both prairie dogs and gophers.

In the discussion of the lagomorphs in Chapter 8, it was suggested that dogs would be attracted primarily to bones that were discarded with some amount of edible tissue still remaining. The positive correlation between element frequency and utility suggests that dogs did not ravage the rabbit and jackrabbit assemblages, which in turn implies that most of the bones of these animals had been boiled before they were discarded.

Analysis of the rodent bones produced the opposite result. At least in the prairie dogs, element frequencies are negatively correlated with both marrow and grease utility. The higher the utility of the element the less common the bone in the assemblage. A similar pattern was observed in the gophers, but the correlations do not attain statistical significance. These results suggest that prairie dogs, and possibly gophers and other rodents, were scavenged by village dogs, which in turn implies that these animals were commonly prepared by roasting or baking rather than boiling. Henderson is not unusual in this regard; comparable practices are well documented in the ethnographic record of the Southwest.

While the covariation of element frequencies with various indices of utility was initially examined as a way of assessing losses due to scavenging village dogs, the results suggest an interesting way for distinguishing between boiled and roasted (or baked) small mammal food remains. This approach in turn may provide a useful additional tool for investigating the spatial organization of subsistence-related activity areas. It may also one day contribute to studies of gender in the archaeological record, since in the ethnographic realm boiling most commonly is done by women. However, before this technique can be applied with confidence, we need further experimental and ethnoarchaeological studies of the fate, upon discard, of boiled, roasted, and baked small mammal bones, utility indices developed explicitly for small mammals, and the posited relationship between gender and mode of cooking.

Since the prairie dog is an important food resource at Henderson, the seasonal timing of prairie dog hunting by the villagers is also important. The season of death of these animals was estimated by the "premolar gap technique" developed by Cox and Franklin (1990). They found that the breadth of the gap between the protoconid and paraconid cusps of the mandibular premolar was significantly correlated with age in a sample of black-tailed prairie dogs from Nebraska. The relationship was linear in animals less than about three years of age and curvilinear in older adults. Since prairie dogs have only a single litter of four to five young each breeding season, with most births in Southern Plains populations occurring over a two to three week period in early March, the age distribution of the mandibles provides a basis for determining whether hunting was seasonal or year-round, and for estimating the time of year when most animals were killed.

The premolar gap data in a sample of 136 black-tailed prairie dog mandibles from Henderson showed four, possibly five, distinct modes representing different age classes. Each mode is separated from adjacent modes by intervals of roughly twelve months. This result indicates that prairie dog hunting at Henderson was in fact seasonal, not year-round, taking place between late spring and early fall.

Chronologically, the density of *Cynomys* remains per cubic meter of excavated deposit increases over time, rising from 6.3 NISP/m^3 in the Early phase to 9.8 NISP/m^3 in the Late phase. The increase is most dramatic in non-room contexts, where the density increases from only 4.1 NISP/m^3 in the Early phase to 10.7 NISP/m^3 in the Late phase.

The seasonality of prairie dog procurement appears to have remained the same over time. The mean ages for each of the four principal age cohorts in the two chronological phases are very similar, and none of the differences are statistically significant.

Acknowledgments

The analyses and conclusions presented here benefited from an undergraduate honors thesis on the Henderson rodents by Amelia M. Natoli (1995), as well as from independent laboratory research projects, focused primarily on the question of seasonality, conducted by Jennifer L. Bragg, Linda K. Gebric, and Stephanie C. Pinsky.

Notes

1. *Pappogeomys* is easily distinguished from other pocket gophers because it possesses a single groove on the outer surface of each upper incisor (Findley et al. 1975:154; Hall 1981:515).
2. No additional beaver remains were encountered in the 1994, 1995, and 1997 excavations at Henderson.
3. The black-tailed prairie dog has a single lower premolar which is designated as P_4 (Stockrahm and Seabloom 1990:105).
4. Available from Edmund Scientific Company, Barrington, New Jersey.
5. Menkens and Anderson (1991) provide demographic data for three prairie dog colonies that were severely affected by disease, and for one colony that was apparently healthy. Only the values from the latter are considered here.
6. Test of equality of two percentages based on arcsine transformation (Sokal and Rohlf 1969:607-10); prairie dog vs. pocket gopher, $t_s = 1.95$, $p = .05$; prairie dog vs. "misc. small rodents," $t_s = 4.77$, $p < .001$; pocket gopher vs. "misc. small rodents," $t_s = 2.58$, $p < .01$. Muskrats were omitted from statistical comparisons because of small sample sizes.
7. The better representation of proximal humeri and tibiae in lagomorphs is not simply a function of larger body size, since the prairie dog is slightly larger on average than the desert cottontail.
8. Prairie dogs are not listed as a food resource of the Havasupai (Weber and Seaman 1985:39).
9. The Havasupai provide a clear-cut Southwestern example of the association of boiling with women (Weber and Seaman 1985:64). While intriguing, a single case such as this one remains little more than an anecdote until a systematic cross-cultural study shows this aspect of the division of labor to be a recurrent and predictable phenomenon. We are grateful to Susan Kent and John Parkington for bringing this interesting facet of gender to our attention.
10. Cox and Franklin's (1990) linear regression expresses the relationship between premolar gap and age in terms of weeks. The estimated age of an animal in weeks was divided by 4.29 to derive the corresponding age in months.

References Cited

Anthony, A., and D. Foreman
1951 Observations on the Reproductive Cycle of the Black-Tailed Prairie Dog (*Cynomys ludovicianus*). *Physiological Zoology* 24(3):242-48.

Bacus, E. A., et al. (editors)
1993 *A Gendered Past: A Critical Bibliography of Gender in Archaeology*. Technical Report 25. Ann Arbor, MI: Museum of Anthropology, University of Michigan.

Beaglehole, E.
1936 *Hopi Hunting and Hunting Ritual*. Yale University Publications in Anthropology 4.
1937 *Notes on Hopi Economic Life*. Yale University Publications in Anthropology 15.

Behrensmeyer, A. K.
1975 The Taphonomy and Paleoecology of Plio-Pleistocene Vertebrate Assemblages East of Lake Rudolf, Kenya. *Harvard University, Museum of Comparative Zoology Bulletin* 146(10):473-578.
1978 Taphonomic and Ecologic Information from Bone Weathering. *Paleobiology* 4:150-62.

Binford, L. R.
1978 *Nunamiut Ethnoarchaeology*. New York: Academic Press.
1981 *Bones: Ancient Men and Modern Myths*. New York: Academic Press.

Binford, L. R., and J. B. Bertram
1977 Bone Frequencies—and Attritional Processes. In: *For Theory Building in Archaeology*, edited by L. R. Binford, pp. 77-153. New York: Academic Press.

Brain, C. K.
1967 Hottentot Food Remains and Their Meaning in the Interpretation of Fossil Bone Assemblages. *Namib Desert Research Station Scientific Papers* 32:1-11.
1969 The Contribution of the Namib Desert Hottentots to an Understanding of Australopithecine Bone Accumulations. *Namib Desert Research Station Scientific Papers* 39.
1981 *The Hunters or the Hunted? An Introduction to African Cave Taphonomy*. Chicago, IL: University of Chicago Press.

Brink, J., and B. Dawe
1989 *Final Report of the 1985 and 1986 Field Seasons at Head-Smashed-In Buffalo Jump, Alberta*. Manuscript Series 16. Edmonton, Alberta: Alberta Culture and Multiculturalism, Historical Resources Division, Archaeological Survey of Alberta.

Brumfiel, E. M.
1991 Weaving and Cooking: Women's Production in Aztec Mexico. In: *Engendering Archaeology: Women and Prehistory*, edited by J. M. Gero and M. W. Conkey, pp. 224-51. Oxford, England: Basil Blackwell.

Burt, W. H., and R. P. Grossenheider
1976 *A Field Guide to the Mammals of America North of Mexico* (3rd Edition). The Peterson Field Guide Series. Boston, MA: Houghton Mifflin.

Claassen, C. (editor)
1992 *Exploring Gender Through Archaeology: Selected Papers from the 1991 Boone Conference*. Monographs in World Archaeology 11. Madison, WI: Prehistory Press.

Costello, D. F.
1970 *The World of the Prairie Dog*. Philadelphia, PA: J. B. Lippincott.

Cox, M. K., and W. L. Franklin
1990 Premolar Gap Technique for Aging Live Black-Tailed Prairie Dogs. *Journal of Wildlife Management* 54(1):143-46.

Davis, W. B.
1974 *The Mammals of Texas* (Revised). Bulletin No. 41. Austin, TX: Texas Parks and Wildlife Department.

Driver, J. C.
1985 *Zooarchaeology of Six Prehistoric Sites in the Sierra Blanca Region, New Mexico*. Technical Report 17. Ann Arbor, MI: University of Michigan, Museum of Anthropology.
1991 Assemblage Formation at the Robinson Site (LA46326). In: *Mogollon V*, edited by P. H. Beckett, pp. 197-206. Las Cruces, NM: COAS Publishing and Research.

Dumont, J.-P.
1972 *Under the Rainbow: A Structural Analysis of the Concepts of Nature, Culture and Supernature Among the Panare Indians*. Ph.D. dissertation, University of Pittsburgh, Pittsburgh, PA.

Elmore, F. H.
1938 Food Animals of the Navajo. *El Palacio* 44(22-24): 149-54.

Fehrenbacher, L. H., and E. Fleharty
1976 Body Composition, Energy Content, and Lipid Cycles of Two Species of Pocket Gophers (*Geomys bursarius* and *Pappogeomys castanops*) in Kansas. *Southwestern Naturalist* 21(2):185-98.

Findley, J. S., A. H. Harris, D. E. Wilson, and C. Jones
1975 *Mammals of New Mexico*. Albuquerque, NM: University of New Mexico Press.

Friedl, E.
1975 *Women and Men: An Anthropologist's View*. New York: Holt, Rinehart and Winston.

Gero, J. M., and M. W. Conkey (editors)
1991 *Engendering Archaeology: Women and Prehistory*. Oxford, England: Basil Blackwell.

Gifford, D. P.
1980 Ethnoarchaeological Contributions to the Taphonomy of Human Sites. In: *Fossils in the Making: Vertebrate Taphonomy and Paleoecology*, edited by A. K. Behrensmeyer and A. P. Hill, pp. 93-106. Chicago, IL: University of Chicago Press.
1981 Taphonomy and Paleoecology: A Critical Review of Archaeology's Sister Discipline. *Advances in Archaeological Method and Theory* 4:365-438.

Gifford, D. P., and A. K. Behrensmeyer
1977 Observed Formation and Burial of a Recent Human Occupation Site in Kenya. *Quaternary Research* 8(3):245-66.

Gifford-Gonzalez, D. P.
1993 Gaps in Zooarchaeological Analyses of Butchery: Is Gender an Issue? In: *From Bones to Behavior: Ethnoarchaeological and Experimental Contributions to the Interpretation of Faunal Remains*, edited by J. Hudson, pp. 181-99. Occasional Paper 21. Carbondale, IL: Southern Illinois University, Center for Archaeological Investigations.

Gifford-Gonzalez, D. P., D. B. Damrosch, D. R. Damrosch, J. Pryor, and R. L. Thunen
1985 The Third Dimensions in Site Structure: An Experiment in Trampling and Vertical Displacement. *American Antiquity* 50(4):803-18.

Grayson, D. K.
1989 Bone Transport, Bone Destruction, and Reverse Utility Curves. *Journal of Archaeological Science* 16:643-52.

Hall, E. R.
1981 *The Mammals of North America*, Vol. 1 (2nd Edition). New York: John Wiley and Sons.

Hastorf, C. A.
1991 Gender, Space, and Food in Prehistory. In: *Engendering Archaeology: Women and Prehistory*, edited by J. M. Gero and M. W. Conkey, pp. 132-59. Oxford, England: Basil Blackwell.

Hill, W. W.
1938 *The Agricultural and Hunting Methods of the Navaho Indians*. Yale University Publications in Anthropology 18.

Hoogland, J. L.
1985 Infanticide in Prairie Dogs: Lactating Females Kill Offspring of Close Kin. *Science* 230:1037-40.
1995 *The Black-Tailed Prairie Dog: Social Life of a Burrowing Mammal*. Chicago, IL: University of Chicago Press.

Hoogland, J. L., D. K. Angell, J. G. Daley, and M. C. Radcliffe
1987 Demography and Population Dynamics of Prairie Dogs. In: *Eighth Great Plains Wildlife Damage Control Workshop Proceedings, Rapid City, South Dakota*, pp. 18-21. General Technical Report RM-154. Fort Collins, CO: U.S. Department of Agriculture, Forest Service, Rocky Mountain Forest and Range Experiment Station.

Hoogland, J. L., and J. M. Hutter
1987 Using Molar Attrition to Age Live Prairie Dogs. *Journal of Wildlife Management* 51(2):393-94.

Kent, S.
1981 The Dog: An Archaeologist's Best Friend or Worst Enemy—The Spatial Distribution of Faunal Remains. *Journal of Field Archaeology* 8(3):367-72.
1993 Variability in Faunal Assemblages: The Influence of Hunting Skill, Sharing, Dogs, and Mode of Cooking on Faunal Remains at a Sedentary Kalahari Community. *Journal of Anthropological Archaeology* 12:323-85.

King, J. A.
1955 *Social Behavior, Social Organization, and Population Dynamics in a Black-Tailed Prairie dog Town in the Black Hills of South Dakota*. Contributions from the Laboratory of Vertebrate Biology 67. Ann Arbor, MI: University of Michigan.

Kreutzer, L. A.
1992 Bison and Deer Bone Mineral Densities: Comparisons and Implications for the Interpretation of Archaeological Faunas. *Journal of Archaeological Science* 19:271-94.

Levi-Strauss, C.
1975 *The Raw and the Cooked*. New York: Harper Colophon Books.

Lowe, V. P. W.
1967 Teeth as Indicators of Age with Special Reference to Red Deer (*Cervus elaphus*) of Known Age from Rhum. *Journal of Zoology (London)* 152:137-53.

Lowell, J. C.
1991 Reflections of Sex Roles in the Archaeological Record: Insights from Hopi and Zuni Ethnographic Data. In: *The Archaeology of Gender: Proceedings of the 22nd Annual Chacmool Conference*, edited by D. Walde and N. D. Willows, pp. 452-61. Calgary, Alberta: University of Calgary, Archaeological Association.

Lupo, K. D.
1995 Hadza Bone Assemblages and Hyena Attrition: An Ethnographic Example of the Influence of Cooking and Mode of Discard on the Intensity of Scavenger Ravaging. *Journal of Anthropological Archaeology* 14(3):288-314.

Lyman, R. L.
1984 Bone Density and Differential Survivorship of Fossil Classes. *Journal of Anthropological Archaeology* 3:259-99.
1985 Bone Frequencies: Differential Transport, In-Situ Destruction, and the MGUI. *Journal of Archaeological Science* 12:221-36.
1991 Taphonomic Problems with Archaeological Analyses of Animal Carcass Utilization and Transport. In: *Beamers, Bobwhites, and Blue-Points: Tributes to the Career of Paul W. Parmalee*, edited by J. R. Purdue, W. E. Klippel, and B. W. Styles, pp. 135-48. Scientific Papers 23. Springfield, IL: Illinois State Museum.
1992 Anatomical Considerations of Utility Curves in Zooarchaeology. *Journal of Archaeological Science* 19:7-22.

Lyman, R. L., L. E. Houghton, and A. L. Chambers
1992 The Effect of Structural Density on Marmot Skeletal Part Representation in Archaeological Sites. *Journal of Archaeological Science* 19(5):557-73.

Lyon, P. J.
1970 Differential Bone Destruction: An Ethnographic Example. *American Antiquity* 35(2):213-15.

Marshall, F., and T. Pilgram
1991 Meat Versus Within-Bone Nutrients: Another Look at the Meaning of Body Part Representation in Archaeological Sites. *Journal of Archaeological Science* 18:149-63.

Menkens, G. E., and S. H. Anderson
1991 Population Dynamics of White-Tailed Prairie Dogs During an Epizootic of Sylvatic Plague. *Journal of Mammalogy* 72(2):328-31.

Murie, O. J.
1951 *The Elk of North America*. Harrisburg, PA: Stackpole.

Natoli, A. M.
1995 *Pueblo Exploitation of Prairie Dogs as Food Resources: Fauna from the Henderson Site*. Honors thesis, Department of Anthropology, University of Michigan, Ann Arbor, MI.

Pavao, B.
1996 *Toward a Taphonomy of Leporid Skeletons: Photodensitometry Assays.* Senior honors thesis, Department of Anthropology, State University of New York, Binghamton, NY.

Pavao, B., and P. W. Stahl
1999 Structural Density Assays of Leporid Skeletal Elements with Implications for Taphonomic, Actualistic and Archaeological Research. *Journal of Archaeological Science* 26(1):53-66.

Payne, S., and P. J. Munson
1985 Ruby and How Many Squirrels? The Destruction of Bones By Dogs. In: *Palaeobiological Investigations: Research Design, Methods and Data Analysis*, edited by N. R. J. Fieller, D. D. Gilbertson, and N. G. A. Ralph, pp. 31-39. BAR International Series 266. Oxford, England: British Archaeological Reports.

Poe, S. A.
1981 *Buckboard Days.* Albuquerque, NM: University of New Mexico Press.

Sassaman, K. E.
1992 Gender and Technology at the Archaic-Woodland "Transition." In: *Exploring Gender Through Archaeology: Selected Papers from the 1991 Boone Conference*, edited by C. Claassen, pp. 71-79. Monographs in World Archaeology 11. Madison, WI: Prehistory Press.

Schmidly, D. J.
1977 *The Mammals of Trans-Pecos Texas.* College Station, TX: Texas A & M University Press.

Shaffer, B. S.
1992a Quarter-Inch Screening: Understanding Biases in Recovery of Vertebrate Faunal Remains. *American Antiquity* 57(1):129-36.
1992b Interpretation of Gopher Remains from Southwestern Archaeological Sites. *American Antiquity* 57(4):683-91.

Shinkle, J. D.
1966 *Reminiscences of Roswell Pioneers.* Roswell, NM: Hall-Poorbaugh Press.

Smith, M. E.
1969 *Governing at Taos Pueblo.* Contributions in Anthropology 2(1). Portales, NM: Eastern New Mexico University, Paleo-Indian Institute.

Smith, R. E.
1967 *Natural History of the Prairie Dog in Kansas.* Miscellaneous Publication 49. Lawrence, KS: University of Kansas, Museum of Natural History.

Sobolik, K. D.
1993 Direct Evidence for the Importance of Small Animals to Prehistoric Diets: A Review of Coprolite Studies. *North American Archaeologist* 14(3):227-44.

Sokal, R. R., and F. J. Rohlf
1969 *Biometry: The Principles and Practice of Statistics in Biological Research.* San Francisco, CA: W. H. Freeman and Company.

Speth, J. D.
2000 Boiling vs. Baking and Roasting: A Taphonomic Approach to the Recognition of Cooking Techniques in Small Mammals. In: *Animal Bones, Human Societies*, edited by P. A. Rowley-Conwy, pp. 89-105. Oxford, England: Oxbow Books.

Spier, L.
1928 *Havasupai Ethnography.* American Museum of Natural History, Anthropological Paper 29 (Part 3):81-392.
1933 *Yuman Tribes of the Gila River.* Chicago, IL: University of Chicago Press.

Steward, J. H.
1938 *Basin-Plateau Aboriginal Sociopolitical Groups.* Bulletin 120. Washington, DC: Smithsonian Institution, Bureau of American Ethnology.

Stockrahm, D. M. B., and R. W. Seabloom
1988 Comparative Reproductive Performance of Black-Tailed Prairie Dog Populations in North Dakota. *Journal of Mammalogy* 69(1):160-64.
1990 Tooth Eruption in Black-Tailed Prairie Dogs from North Dakota. *Journal of Mammalogy* 71(1):105-8.

Szuter, C. R.
1991 *Hunting by Prehistoric Horticulturalists in the American Southwest.* New York: Garland Publishing.

Vosburgh, T. C., and L. R. Irby
1998 Effects of Recreational Shooting on Prairie Dog Colonies. *Journal of Wildlife Management* 62(1):363-72.

Walde, D., and N. D. Willows (editors)
1991 *The Archaeology of Gender: Proceedings of the 22nd Annual Chacmool Conference.* Calgary, Alberta: University of Calgary, Archaeological Association.

Walters, I.
1984 Gone to the Dogs: A Study of Bone Attrition at a Central Australian Campsite. *Mankind* 14(5):389-400.

Weber, S. A., and P. D. Seaman (editors)
1985 *Havasupai Habitat: A. F. Whiting's Ethnography of a Traditional Indian Culture.* Tucson, AZ: University of Arizona Press.

Yohe, R. M., M. E. Newman, and J. S. Schneider
1991 Immunological Identification of Small-Mammal Proteins on Aboriginal Milling Equipment. *American Antiquity* 56(4):659-66.

Appendix to Chapter 9

Henderson Rodent Assemblage

Table A9.1. Black-tailed prairie dog (*Cynomys ludovicianus*) sample recovered from Henderson Site (all proveniences combined, 1980-1981 only).

Element	Total Sample						Immature Only							Burned	
	NISP[a] (1)	% of Total NISP (2)	MNE[b] (3)	% of Total MNE (4)	MNI[c] (5)	% MNI[d] (6)	Unfus. NISP (7)	Fusing NISP (8)	Unfus. MNE (9)	Fusing MNE (10)	Unfus. MNI (11)	Fusing MNI (12)	Total Imm. %MNI[e] (13)	NISP (14)	% of Total NISP[f] (15)
Total Skull	181	20.64	113	13.55	57	89.06	—	—	—	—	—	—	—	—	—
Frontal	—	—	—	—	—	—	—	—	—	—	—	—	—	—	—
Squam.-Tem.	69	7.87	68	8.15	34	53.13	—	—	—	—	—	—	—	—	—
Tem.-Par.	—	—	—	—	—	—	—	—	—	—	—	—	—	—	—
Tem.-Frnt.	—	—	—	—	—	—	—	—	—	—	—	—	—	—	—
Nasal	—	—	—	—	—	—	—	—	—	—	—	—	—	—	—
Premax.	—	—	—	—	—	—	—	—	—	—	—	—	—	—	—
Maxilla	101	11.52	96	11.51	48	75.00	—	—	—	—	—	—	—	—	—
Max.-Prem.	5	0.57	5	0.60	3	4.69	—	—	—	—	—	—	—	—	—
Cmplt. Skull	6	0.68	6	0.72	6	9.38	—	—	—	—	—	—	—	—	—
Total Mandible	131	14.94	128	15.35	64	100.00	—	—	—	—	—	—	—	—	—
Cmplt. Man.	49	5.59	49	5.88	25	39.06	—	—	—	—	—	—	—	—	—
Man. Body	82	9.35	79	9.47	40	62.50	—	—	—	—	—	—	—	—	—
Man. Symph.	—	—	—	—	—	—	—	—	—	—	—	—	—	—	—
Man. Border	—	—	—	—	—	—	—	—	—	—	—	—	—	—	—
Man. Ramus	—	—	—	—	—	—	—	—	—	—	—	—	—	—	—
Atlas	—	—	—	—	—	—	—	—	—	—	—	—	—	—	—
Axis	—	—	—	—	—	—	—	—	—	—	—	—	—	—	—
Cervical	—	—	—	—	—	—	—	—	—	—	—	—	—	—	—
Thoracic	—	—	—	—	—	—	—	—	—	—	—	—	—	—	—
Lumbar	—	—	—	—	—	—	—	—	—	—	—	—	—	—	—
Sacrum	—	—	—	—	—	—	—	—	—	—	—	—	—	—	—
Scapula	71	8.10	68	8.15	34	53.13	—	—	—	—	—	—	—	1	1.41
Prx. Hum.	10	1.14	10	1.20	5	7.81	5	3	5	3	3	2	27.78	—	—
Dis. Hum.	69	7.87	69	8.27	35	54.69	5	—	5	—	3	—	16.67	2	2.90
H. Shaft	18	2.05	18	2.16	9	14.06	—	—	—	—	—	—	—	—	—
Prx. Rad.	40	4.56	40	4.80	20	31.25	—	—	—	—	—	—	—	1	2.50
Dis. Rad.	11	1.25	11	1.32	6	9.38	14	—	14	—	7	—	38.89	1	9.09
R. Shaft	—	—	—	—	—	—	—	—	—	—	—	—	—	—	—
Prx. Ulna	81	9.24	81	9.71	41	64.06	29	5	29	5	15	3	100.00	3	3.70
Dis. Ulna	4	0.46	4	0.48	2	3.13	—	—	—	—	—	—	—	—	—
Ulna Shaft	3	0.34	3	0.36	2	3.13	—	—	—	—	—	—	—	—	—
Prx. Mc. 2	—	—	—	—	—	—	—	—	—	—	—	—	—	—	—
Prx. Mc. 3	—	—	—	—	—	—	—	—	—	—	—	—	—	—	—
Prx. Mc. 4	—	—	—	—	—	—	—	—	—	—	—	—	—	—	—
Prx. Mc. 5	—	—	—	—	—	—	—	—	—	—	—	—	—	—	—
Dis. Mc. 2	—	—	—	—	—	—	—	—	—	—	—	—	—	—	—
Dis. Mc. 3	—	—	—	—	—	—	—	—	—	—	—	—	—	—	—

(cont.)

Element	Total Sample						Immature Only							Burned	
	NISP[a] (1)	% of Total NISP (2)	MNE[b] (3)	% of Total MNE (4)	MNI[c] (5)	% MNI[d] (6)	Unfus. NISP (7)	Fusing NISP (8)	Unfus. MNE (9)	Fusing MNE (10)	Unfus. MNI (11)	Fusing MNI (12)	Total Imm. %MNI[e] (13)	NISP (14)	% of Total NISP[f] (15)
Dis. Mc. 4	—	—	—	—	—	—	—	—	—	—	—	—	—	—	—
Dis. Mc. 5	—	—	—	—	—	—	—	—	—	—	—	—	—	—	—
Innom.	108	12.32	85	10.19	43	67.19	—	—	—	—	—	—	—	6	5.56
Prx. Fem.	38	4.33	38	4.56	19	29.69	1	1	1	1	1	1	11.11	—	—
Dis. Fem.	12	1.37	12	1.44	6	9.38	10	—	10	—	5	—	27.78	—	—
F. Shaft	13	1.48	13	1.56	7	10.94	—	—	—	—	—	—	—	1	7.69
Prx. Tib.	9	1.03	4	0.48	2	3.13	6	2	6	2	3	1	22.22	—	—
Dis. Tib.	61	6.96	61	7.31	31	48.44	17	1	17	1	9	1	55.56	1	1.64
T. Shaft	17	1.94	14	1.68	7	10.94	—	—	—	—	—	—	—	—	—
Astrag.	—	—	—	—	—	—	—	—	—	—	—	—	—	—	—
Calc.	—	—	—	—	—	—	—	—	—	—	—	—	—	—	—
Cen. Tar.	—	—	—	—	—	—	—	—	—	—	—	—	—	—	—
3rd Tar.	—	—	—	—	—	—	—	—	—	—	—	—	—	—	—
4th Tar.	—	—	—	—	—	—	—	—	—	—	—	—	—	—	—
Prx. Mt. 2	—	—	—	—	—	—	—	—	—	—	—	—	—	—	—
Prx. Mt. 3	—	—	—	—	—	—	—	—	—	—	—	—	—	—	—
Prx. Mt. 4	—	—	—	—	—	—	—	—	—	—	—	—	—	—	—
Prx. Mt. 5	—	—	—	—	—	—	—	—	—	—	—	—	—	—	—
Dis. Mt. 2	—	—	—	—	—	—	—	—	—	—	—	—	—	—	—
Dis. Mt. 3	—	—	—	—	—	—	—	—	—	—	—	—	—	—	—
Dis. Mt. 4	—	—	—	—	—	—	—	—	—	—	—	—	—	—	—
Dis. Mt. 5	—	—	—	—	—	—	—	—	—	—	—	—	—	—	—
Dis. Mt.	—	—	—	—	—	—	—	—	—	—	—	—	—	—	—
Mpd. Shaft	—	—	—	—	—	—	—	—	—	—	—	—	—	—	—
TOTAL	877	100.02	834	100.00	—	—	87	12	87	12	—	—	—	16	1.82

[a]NISP, Number of identifiable specimens.
[b]MNE, Minimum number of elements.
[c]MNI, Minimum number of individuals.
[d]%MNI, MNI of each element observed expressed as percent of maximum MNI value—64 animals (mandible).
[e]Total Immature %MNI calculated in same manner as %MNI (see note 4 above), based on maximum immature MNI value of 18 animals (prox. ulna).
[f]Percent of NISP value in same row in Column (1).

Table A9.2. Yellow-cheeked pocket gopher (*Pappogeomys castanops*) sample recovered from Henderson Site (all proveniences combined, 1980-1981 only).

Element	Total Sample						Immature Only							Burned	
	NISP[a] (1)	% of Total NISP (2)	MNE[b] (3)	% of Total MNE (4)	MNI[c] (5)	% MNI[d] (6)	Unfus. NISP (7)	Fusing NISP (8)	Unfus. MNE (9)	Fusing MNE (10)	Unfus. MNI (11)	Fusing MNI (12)	Total Imm. %MNI[e] (13)	NISP (14)	% of Total NISP[f] (15)
Total Skull	16	6.67	16	6.69	8	32.00	—	—	—	—	—	—	—	—	—
Frontal	—	—	—	—	—	—	—	—	—	—	—	—	—	—	—
Squam.-Tem.	—	—	—	—	—	—	—	—	—	—	—	—	—	—	—
Tem.-Par.	—	—	—	—	—	—	—	—	—	—	—	—	—	—	—
Tem.-Frnt.	—	—	—	—	—	—	—	—	—	—	—	—	—	—	—
Nasal	—	—	—	—	—	—	—	—	—	—	—	—	—	—	—
Premax.	—	—	—	—	—	—	—	—	—	—	—	—	—	—	—
Maxilla	14	5.83	14	5.86	7	28.00	—	—	—	—	—	—	—	—	—
Max.-Prem.	2	0.83	2	0.84	1	4.00	—	—	—	—	—	—	—	—	—
Cmplt. Skull	—	—	—	—	—	—	—	—	—	—	—	—	—	—	—
Total Mandible	49	20.42	49	20.50	25	100.00	—	—	—	—	—	—	—	—	—
Cmplt. Man.	21	8.75	21	8.79	11	44.00	—	—	—	—	—	—	—	—	—
Man. Body	28	11.67	28	11.72	14	56.00	—	—	—	—	—	—	—	—	—
Man. Symph.	1	0.42	1	0.42	1	4.00	—	—	—	—	—	—	—	—	—
Man. Border	2	0.83	2	0.84	1	4.00	—	—	—	—	—	—	—	—	—
Man. Ramus	—	—	—	—	—	—	—	—	—	—	—	—	—	—	—
Atlas	—	—	—	—	—	—	—	—	—	—	—	—	—	—	—
Axis	—	—	—	—	—	—	—	—	—	—	—	—	—	—	—
Cervical	—	—	—	—	—	—	—	—	—	—	—	—	—	—	—
Thoracic	—	—	—	—	—	—	—	—	—	—	—	—	—	—	—
Lumbar	—	—	—	—	—	—	—	—	—	—	—	—	—	—	—
Sacrum	—	—	—	—	—	—	—	—	—	—	—	—	—	—	—
Scapula	3	1.25	3	1.26	2	8.00	—	—	—	—	—	—	—	—	—
Prx. Hum.	2	0.83	2	0.84	1	4.00	—	—	—	—	—	—	—	—	—
Dis. Hum.	24	10.00	24	10.04	12	48.00	5	—	5	—	3	—	50.00	—	—
H. Shaft	3	1.25	3	1.26	2	8.00	—	—	—	—	—	—	—	—	—
Prx. Rad.	2	0.83	2	0.84	1	4.00	—	—	—	—	—	—	—	—	—
Dis. Rad.	19	7.92	19	7.95	10	40.00	11	—	11	—	6	—	100.00	—	—
R. Shaft	—	—	—	—	—	—	—	—	—	—	—	—	—	—	—
Prx. Ulna	13	5.42	13	5.44	7	28.00	6	1	6	1	3	1	66.67	—	—
Dis. Ulna	3	1.25	3	1.26	2	8.00	—	—	—	—	—	—	—	—	—
Ulna Shaft	—	—	—	—	—	—	—	—	—	—	—	—	—	—	—
Prx. Mc.2	—	—	—	—	—	—	—	—	—	—	—	—	—	—	—
Prx. Mc.3	—	—	—	—	—	—	—	—	—	—	—	—	—	—	—
Prx. Mc.4	—	—	—	—	—	—	—	—	—	—	—	—	—	—	—
Prx. Mc.5	—	—	—	—	—	—	—	—	—	—	—	—	—	—	—
Dis. Mc.2	—	—	—	—	—	—	—	—	—	—	—	—	—	—	—

(cont.)

Element	Total Sample						Immature Only							Burned	
	NISP[a] (1)	% of Total NISP (2)	MNE[b] (3)	% of Total MNE (4)	MNI[c] (5)	% MNI[d] (6)	Unfus. NISP (7)	Fusing NISP (8)	Unfus. MNE (9)	Fusing MNE (10)	Unfus. MNI (11)	Fusing MNI (12)	Total Imm. %MNI[e] (13)	NISP (14)	% of Total NISP[f] (15)
Dis. Mc.3	—	—	—	—	—	—	—	—	—	—	—	—	—	—	—
Dis. Mc.4	—	—	—	—	—	—	—	—	—	—	—	—	—	—	—
Dis. Mc.5	—	—	—	—	—	—	—	—	—	—	—	—	—	—	—
Innom.	32	13.33	31	12.97	16	64.00	—	—	—	—	—	—	—	1	3.13
Prx. Fem.	17	7.08	17	7.11	9	36.00	3	—	3	—	2	—	33.33	—	—
Dis. Fem.	15	6.25	15	6.28	8	32.00	9	—	9	—	5	—	83.33	—	—
F. Shaft	—	—	—	—	—	—	—	—	—	—	—	—	—	—	—
Prx. Tib.	5	2.08	5	2.09	3	12.00	4	—	4	—	2	—	33.33	—	—
Dis. Tib.	30	12.50	30	12.55	15	60.00	5	—	5	—	3	—	50.00	1	3.33
T. Shaft	4	1.67	4	1.67	2	8.00	—	—	—	—	—	—	—	—	—
Astrag.	—	—	—	—	—	—	—	—	—	—	—	—	—	—	—
Calc.	—	—	—	—	—	—	—	—	—	—	—	—	—	—	—
Cen. Tar.	—	—	—	—	—	—	—	—	—	—	—	—	—	—	—
3rd Tar.	—	—	—	—	—	—	—	—	—	—	—	—	—	—	—
4th Tar.	—	—	—	—	—	—	—	—	—	—	—	—	—	—	—
Prx. Mt.2	—	—	—	—	—	—	—	—	—	—	—	—	—	—	—
Prx. Mt.3	—	—	—	—	—	—	—	—	—	—	—	—	—	—	—
Prx. Mt.4	—	—	—	—	—	—	—	—	—	—	—	—	—	—	—
Prx. Mt.5	—	—	—	—	—	—	—	—	—	—	—	—	—	—	—
Dis. Mt.2	—	—	—	—	—	—	—	—	—	—	—	—	—	—	—
Dis. Mt.3	—	—	—	—	—	—	—	—	—	—	—	—	—	—	—
Dis. Mt.4	—	—	—	—	—	—	—	—	—	—	—	—	—	—	—
Dis. Mt.5	—	—	—	—	—	—	—	—	—	—	—	—	—	—	—
Dis. Mt.	—	—	—	—	—	—	—	—	—	—	—	—	—	—	—
Mpd. Shaft	—	—	—	—	—	—	—	—	—	—	—	—	—	—	—
TOTAL	240	99.99	239	100.03	—	—	43	1	43	1	—	—	—	2	0.83

[a]NISP, Number of identifiable specimens.
[b]MNE, Minimum number of elements.
[c]MNI, Minimum number of individuals.
[d]%MNI, MNI of each element observed expressed as percent of maximum MNI value—25 animals (mandible).
[e]Total Immature %MNI calculated in same manner as %MNI (see note 4 above), based on maximum immature MNI value of 6 animals (dist. radius).
[f]Percent of NISP value in same row in Column (1).

10
The Henderson Birds

John D. Speth
University of Michigan

Steven D. Emslie
University of North Carolina, Wilmington

Sara Olson
University of Otago, Dunedin

Introduction

The avifauna from the 1980-1981 seasons at the Henderson Site, as well as the material from the nearby and roughly contemporary Rocky Arroyo Site, have been described in detail elsewhere (Emslie et al. 1992) and only a brief overview is presented here, updated to include the bones recovered at Henderson in 1994, 1995, and 1997. The village produced a small but diverse assemblage of bird bones, representing at least 129 individuals and a minimum of 48 taxa (see Table 10.1). All species are currently found in New Mexico (Hubbard 1978), although the cardinal (*Cardinalis cardinalis*) may not have been present in the state until early in the twentieth century.

Passeriformes comprise 25.0% of the assemblage and at least 27.0% of the individuals. Unfortunately, over 80% of the Passeriformes specimens could not be assigned to genus or species. Thus, the true MNI value for these birds is undoubtedly much higher than 35. Included in the identified passerine bones are species such as icterids, corvids, and sparrows that are commonly associated with agricultural fields (Emslie 1981a, 1981b, 1983). Nearly a third of the assemblage is made up of aquatic, non-passerine specimens that could be assigned to a taxonomic level more precise than Aves, such as coots (*Fulica americana*), various ducks, sandhill crane, egret, ibis, and dowitcher. Included as aquatic taxa are bones of Gaviiformes, Podicipediformes, Anseriformes, Gruiformes, Ciconiiformes (egret and ibis), and Charadriiformes. Predatory birds, including several species of hawk, osprey, northern harrier, golden eagle, kestrel, and six species of owl, make up 27.8% of the bones. Turkey vulture (*Cathartes aura*) is also included with the predatory birds.

In addition to the disarticulated avian remains, four complete bird skeletons were uncovered. Three of these were turkeys (*Meleagris gallopavo*). All three were burials of immature birds in Early phase non-room contexts, two (both unburned and found in 1994) from the base of the earth oven complex in the Great Depression (Lot No. 3500, grid square 553N512E, elevation = 99.15 m; Lot No. 3494, grid square 554N512E, elevation = 99.06 m), the third (also unburned and found in 1997) from an elongated roasting or baking pit dug into an early plaza surface beneath the Main Bar East room block (Lot No. 5181, grid square 541N534E, elevation = 100.28 m). An unburned human infant burial (age probably less than one year) was found in 1994 directly adjacent to the two turkey burials at the base of the Great Depression. This infant was not excavated and was left in place when we backfilled the feature. The undisturbed and unburned condition of all three turkey burials at the base of earth oven features suggests that they served as some form of "closure offering" (e.g., Walker 1995) placed into the emptied pit shortly after its last use and subsequently covered over with fire-cracked rock and other debris as the pit was deliberately

Figure 10.1. Sealed cylindrical pit beneath Room M-1 in the Main Bar East capped by "closure offering" of red-winged blackbird.

sealed. How the human infant came to be buried at the base of the Great Depression earth oven complex is not known, but a nonviolent death coincident in time with the closure of the pit seems the most likely scenario.

The fourth bird burial, found in 1995, was a red-winged blackbird (*Agelaius phoeniceus*) that had been placed directly over a sealed cylindrical storage(?) pit beneath Room M-1 in the Main Bar East room block (Lot No. 4019, Feature 146, grid square 538N536E, elevation = 100.09 m; see Fig. 10.1). The rim of the cylindrical pit was encircled with small, tabular, upright limestone rocks, and the seal of the pit itself was formed by a disk-shaped limestone slab that had been set directly within, and wedged snugly against, the base of the circle of upright stones. The blackbird was placed directly on the slab, and the slab and bird were then covered with ash, giving the sealed mouth of the feature the look of a rock-encircled hearth. The entire feature was subsequently buried under a conical mound of fire-cracked rock that contained bones of bison, antelope, lagomorph, fish, and other species (a number of which were burned), as well as many charred yucca seeds (*Yucca baccata*) and burned corn cobs. However, neither the limestone slab nor the bird skeleton showed any signs of having been burned, suggesting that the hearth and overlying mound of fire-cracked rock had been deliberately piled there to seal, and perhaps hide, the underlying pit. Unfortunately, despite the intact seal, nothing was preserved inside the pit. Several sediment samples were taken but have not been analyzed.

The density of avian bones recovered from the Henderson Site is 3.50 NISP/m^3. The density in non-room or plaza contexts (3.73 NISP/m^3) is somewhat greater than in room fill (3.41 NISP/m^3). Overall density declines somewhat over time, from 3.76 NISP/m^3 in the Early phase to 3.33 NISP/m^3 in the Late phase. When looked at by major habitat groupings, aquatic birds increase slightly in density (Early phase, 0.89 NISP/m^3; Late phase, 1.09 NISP/m^3), non-aquatic birds increase as well (Early phase, 0.82 NISP/m^3; Late phase, 1.49 NISP/m^3), and predatory birds decline sharply (Early phase, 1.24 NISP/m^3; Late phase, 0.62 NISP/m^3). The habitat groupings used in this chapter are defined as follows. Aquatic birds include Gaviiformes, Podicipediformes, Anseriformes, Gruiformes, Ciconiiformes (egret and ibis), and Charadriiformes. Non-aquatic birds include Caprimulgiformes, Ciconiiformes, Columbiformes, Cuculiformes, Galliformes, Passeriformes, and Piciformes. Day predators include Accipitriformes, as well as one member of Ciconiiformes, the turkey vulture (*Cathartes aura*); night predators include Strigiformes.

Table 10.2 shows the frequency of Early phase and Late phase avian remains by order. Perhaps the most dramatic changes are the sharp decline in Accipitriformes and the equally dramatic increase in Passeriformes in the Late phase ($t_s = 6.28, p < .001$). The drop in Accipitriformes is most clear-cut in the rooms, where Passeriformes come to predominate in the Late phase (Table 10.3). In the plazas and earth oven complexes, however, the picture is somewhat different. Again, Accipitriformes decline, as in the rooms, but less dramatically so, and Passeriformes

Table 10.1. Avifauna (NISP and MNI) from the Henderson Site (all proveniences combined).

Taxon	NISP (MNI)
Aves (NISP = 72)	
Unidentifiable bird bones	72 (5+)
Gaviiformes (NISP = 1)	
Common loon (*Gavia immer*)	1 (1)
Podicipediformes (NISP = 8)	
Horned grebe (*Podiceps auritus*)	2 (1)
Pied-billed grebe (*Podilymbus podiceps*)	6 (1)
Ciconiiformes (NISP = 15)	
Great egret (*Casmerodius albus*)	1 (1)
White ibis (*Eudocimus albus*)	2 (1)
Turkey vulture (*Cathartes aura*)	12 (3)
Anseriformes (NISP = 46)	
Mallard (*Anas platyrhynchos*)	7 (1)
Duck (*Anas* sp.)	4 (2)
Teal (*Anas* sp.)	9 (2)
Canvasback (*Aythya* cf. *A. valisineria*)	5 (2)
Duck (*Aythya* sp.)	4 (1)
Ruddy duck (*Oxyura jamaicensis*)	2 (1)
Common merganser (*Mergus merganser*)	2 (1)
Anatidae, indet.	13 (3)
Accipitriformes (NISP = 127)	
Swainson's hawk (cf. *Buteo swainsoni*)	25 (4)
Red-tailed hawk (*Buteo jamaicensis*)	17 (2)
Hawk (*Buteo* sp.)	55 (4)
Cooper's hawk (*Accipiter cooperii*)	2 (1)
Red-shouldered hawk (*Buteo* cf. *B. lineatus*)	1 (1)
Rough-legged hawk (*Buteo lagopus*)	1 (1)
Black hawk (*Buteogallus anthracinus*)	1 (1)
Northern harrier (*Circus cyaneus*)	2 (1)
Osprey (*Pandion haliaetus*)	4 (1)
Golden eagle (*Aquila chrysaetos*)	7 (2)
American kestrel (*Falco sparverius*)	4 (2)
Accipitridae, indet.	8 (1)
Galliformes (NISP = 32)	
Turkey (*Meleagris gallopavo*)[a]	15 (6)
Quail (Odontophorinae, indet.)	13 (3)
Gambel's quail (*Callipepla* cf. *C. gambelii*)	1 (1)
Scaled quail (*Callipepla* cf. *C. squamata*)	3 (2)
Gruiformes (NISP = 126)	
Common moorhen (*Gallinula chloropus*)	2 (2)
American coot (*Fulica americana*)	120 (14)
Sandhill crane (*Grus canadensis*)	4 (1)
Charadriiformes (NISP = 1)	
Dowitcher (*Limnodromus* sp.)	1 (1)
Columbiformes (NISP = 9)	
Mourning dove (*Zenaida macroura*)	9 (3)
Strigiformes (NISP = 31)	
Screech owl (*Otus* sp.)	2 (1)
Great horned owl (*Bubo virginianus*)	15 (2)
Saw-whet owl (*Aegolius acadicus*)	1 (1)
Burrowing owl (*Athene cunicularia*)	9 (3)
Long-eared owl (*Asio* cf. *A. otus*)	1 (1)
Short-eared owl (*Asio flammeus*)	2 (1)
Owl (*Asio* sp.)	1 (1)
Cuculiformes (NISP = 1)	
Road-runner (*Geococcyx californianus*)	1 (1)
Caprimulgiformes (NISP = 1)	
Nighthawk (*Chordeiles minor*)	1 (1)
Piciformes (NISP = 7)	
Northern flicker (*Colaptes auratus*)	7 (2)
Passeriformes (NISP = 159)	
Flycatcher (*Tyrannus* sp.)	1 (1)
Chihuahuan raven (*Corvus cryptoleucus*)	7 (1)
Northern cardinal (*Cardinalis cardinalis*)	1 (1)
Lark sparrow (*Chondestes grammacus*)	1 (1)
Sparrow (*Zonotrichia* sp.)	2 (2)
Emberizinae, indet.	1 (1)
Red-winged blackbird (*Agelaius phoeniceus*)[b]	3 (2)
Meadowlark (*Sturnella* sp.)	4 (2)
Brewer's blackbird (*Euphagus cyanocephalus*)	2 (1)
Common grackle (*Quiscalus quiscula*)	1 (1)
Pinyon jay (*Gymnorhinus cyanocephalus*)	1 (1)
cf. Parulidae (Warblers)	1 (1)
Passeriformes, indet.	134 (20)
TOTAL	**636 (129)**

[a]NISP = 15 bones, representing 3 MNI; total MNI also includes 3 complete articulated skeletons (burials) that are not tallied in the NISP value.

[b]NISP = 3 bones, representing 1 MNI; total MNI also includes 1 complete articulated skeleton (burial) that is not tallied in the NISP value.

increase, such that in Late phase non-room contexts the two orders come to be represented in nearly equal proportions.

Table 10.4 summarizes the data for the proportion of wing versus non-wing elements (NISP) for each major habitat grouping. For comparative purposes, data are provided for the expected proportion of wing versus non-wing elements in a complete bird skeleton, using the same elements that were tabulated in the archaeological assemblage (i.e., ignoring elements that have not been fully identified as yet, such as vertebrae, ribs, and some of the phalanges). It is obvious from the table that wing and non-wing parts are represented in all habitat groups, except the non-aquatic one, in proportions that one would expect if whole birds had been brought into the community. The non-aquatic group, made up primarily of Passeriformes (71.1%) and Galliformes (15.6%; quail and turkey), are overwhelmingly represented by wing elements, indicating that they were generally not used for food, and instead were brought into the village most often as wing fans (obvious exceptions, of course, are the three complete turkeys and the red-winged blackbird that were buried as closure offerings in the Early phase). The proportion of wing elements in the non-aquatic group in both phases significantly exceeds the proportion (32.14%) that would be expected had whole birds been brought into the village (Early phase, CR = 3.76, $p < .001$; Late phase, CR = 7.01, $p < .001$; Garrett 1967:238-39). Whether the wing fans were obtained from locally captured birds or were received through

Table 10.2. Frequency of Early phase and Late phase avian remains (NISP) by order at the Henderson Site.

Order	Total		Early Phase		Late Phase	
	NISP	%	NISP	%	NISP	%
Accipitriformes	126	22.22	77	36.84	49	13.69
Anseriformes	46	8.11	15	7.18	31	8.66
Caprimulgiformes	1	0.18	1	0.48	0	0.00
Charadriiformes	1	0.18	0	0.00	1	0.28
Ciconiiformes	15	2.65	11	5.26	4	1.12
Columbiformes	9	1.59	1	0.48	8	2.23
Cuculiformes	1	0.18	1	0.48	0	0.00
Galliformes	35	6.17	21	10.05	14	3.91
Gaviiformes	1	0.18	1	0.48	0	0.00
Gruiformes	126	22.22	45	21.53	81	22.63
Passeriformes	160	28.22	23	11.00	137	38.27
Piciformes	7	1.23	1	0.48	6	1.68
Podicipediformes	8	1.41	1	0.48	7	1.96
Strigiformes	31	5.47	11	5.26	20	5.59
TOTAL	567	100.00	209	100.00	358	100.00

exchange from other communities, or some combination of the two, is unknown. The proportion of wing fans of non-aquatic birds in the Early phase does not differ statistically from the Late phase value ($t_s = 0.31, p > .05$).

Pulling some of the previous insights together, several points are noteworthy. Although the raptors were obtained by the villagers as whole birds, ethnographic evidence from the Southwest suggests that these birds were seldom if ever eaten (Ladd 1963; Tyler 1991). Most of the passerines and Galliformes (turkey, quail) at Henderson do not appear to have been eaten either, because they are represented largely by wing fans.

Also, only eight bird bones (1.25%) are burned. Of the burned specimens that can be assigned to genus and species, four are hawks (*Buteo* sp.) and one is a raven (*Corvus cryptoleucus*). None of these birds are likely to have been used for food, hence the reason they are burned is unknown. Two of the remaining burned specimens could only be identified as passerines and are therefore also unlikely to have been food birds. The last burned specimen could only be identified as Aves.

Over time the influx of avian remains into village deposits declined slightly. However, when looked at by major habitat grouping, it is clear that not all categories declined. What declined most noticeably was the influx of predatory birds into the village. At the same time, the density of passerines and Galliformes increased. Thus, we appear to have the partial replacement of one non-food category by another. The only birds that might have served as a source of food, as well as a source of feathers, are the aquatic species, particularly coots and ducks, and their density increased by about 20% in the Late phase. Most waterfowl in both phases were found in room contexts (Early phase, 85.7%; Late phase, 73.8%), but the proportion of waterfowl occurring in public contexts increased significantly in the Late phase ($t_s = 1.93, p \approx .05$). In contrast, the proportion of non-food birds, most particularly the predatory species, in plaza contexts declined sharply (Early phase, 50.7%; Late phase, 19.9%; $t_s = 6.99, p < .001$).

What might have led to a decline in the ritual or ceremonial importance of predators, particularly day-predators such as hawks? We have no definitive answer, but we are willing to speculate a little (see also Olson 2001). The hawks are commonly associated with hunting, among other functions (Tyler 1991). But as hunters they are far surpassed by eagles, and particularly by large mammalian predators like mountain lions. Thus, their hunting association is most clearly with smaller game such as rabbits:

> [M]any hawks and falcons are great hunters, at least of small game. There is even a Hawk deity specialized for rabbit hunting. For the most part, however, the great beasts of prey have preempted the field as patrons of hunting. After all, no small hawk is equal to Mountain Lion as a symbol of this power. [Tyler 1991:193]

If, as is argued in Chapter 4, Henderson was undergoing a major social and economic transformation toward intensification of long-distance communal bison hunting, hand-in-hand with a decline in the communal importance of smaller animals, then perhaps the apparent decline in the ceremonial and ritual importance of hawks and other predatory birds reflects these changes. The underlying logic here is that the economic and social importance of a particular hunted resource is linked to the frequency, intensity, and social scale of ceremonies and rituals related to that resource, which in turn should affect the frequency with which particular birds would be brought into the village for use in costumes, prayer sticks, and other paraphernalia needed for those ceremonies and rituals.

Tempting as such a scenario might be, however, it oversimplifies the multifaceted symbolic role played by birds in Pueblo ritual and ceremony (e.g., Tyler 1991; Hibben 1975). Moreover,

Table 10.3. Frequency of Early phase and Late phase Accipitriformes and Passeriformes in room and non-room contexts.

Period	Room				Non-Room			
	Accipitriformes		Passeriformes		Accipitriformes		Passeriformes	
	NISP	%	NISP	%	NISP	%	NISP	%
Early phase	36	85.71	6	14.29	41	70.69	17	29.31
Late phase	30	19.87	121	80.13	19	54.29	16	45.71

Table 10.4. Frequency of Early phase and Late phase wing and non-wing bones (NISP) by major habitat group.

Habitat	Early Phase				Late Phase			
	Wing		Non-Wing		Wing		Non-Wing	
	NISP	%	NISP	%	NISP	%	NISP	%
Aquatic	19	30.16	44	69.84	47	38.52	75	61.48
Non-aquatic	32	55.17	26	44.83	96	57.49	71	42.51
Predator (day)[a]	23	29.87	54	70.13	16	32.65	33	67.35
Predator (night)[b]	3	27.27	8	72.73	5	25.00	15	75.00
Whole bird[c]	18	32.14	38	67.86	18	32.14	37	67.86

[a]Includes all predatory birds except owls.
[b]Includes owls only.
[c]In determining the expected number of bones in a whole bird, the following guidelines were followed: (1) each major limb element is assumed to consist of 4 parts (left, right, proximal, distal); (2) vertebrae, ribs, and carpals were not included; (3) it is assumed that there are only 2 wing phalanges (1 left and 1 right) and 12 lower limb phalanges (many lower limb phalanges of birds have not yet been identified).

it makes the simplistic assumption that numerical importance reflects symbolic importance. In essence, therefore, the declining number of predatory birds at Henderson might reflect changes in symbolic domains unrelated to hunting. Moreover, even if the scenario we offer here is correct, at least in broad outline, it does not explain why passerine wing fans increased in importance, at least numerically. Unfortunately, we are hampered by the fact that so few of the passerine bones could be identified to genus and species, precluding a more detailed exploration of the probable symbolic functions of these ritually important birds.

Northern Cardinal

The presence at Henderson of the northern cardinal (*Cardinalis cardinalis*) is a possible example of a passerine obtained by intercommunity exchange. This species was rare in Arizona and apparently absent in New Mexico prior to the 1870s, but expanded its range northward and eastward in the following decades (Phillips 1968:151; Hubbard 1978:86-87; Ferg and Rea 1983). It apparently did not become established in New Mexico until the early part of the twentieth century. We know of no other archaeological records of the cardinal in New Mexico, although there are at least three records of this species in Arizona, with the earliest dating from A.D. 850-950 (Ferg and Rea 1983). These authors suggest that the brightly feathered cardinal, like the macaw, may have been brought into the Southwest from Mesoamerica through trade. This suggestion assumes, of course, that the species only recently expanded its range northward into the American Southwest and was not present there prior to the historic period.

Turkey

Aside from the three complete burials of immature turkeys discussed earlier, apparently sacrificed as closure openings when earth oven complexes were sealed, bones of *Meleagris gallopavo* are infrequent at Henderson (NISP = 15). There is no evidence that turkeys constituted a food source for the villagers, nor is there any evidence that they were raised in the village. A small number of tiny eggshell fragments (NISP = 27; mean fragment size 1.10 ± 0.31 cm), from eggs perhaps large enough to be those of turkey, were encountered during the excavations, but the villagers could easily have collected them from wild turkeys or, more likely, from waterfowl. Most of these shell fragments were found in the room blocks (88.5%, NISP = 23); only three specimens (11.5%) were found in non-room contexts. Microscopic study might clarify whether the eggshell fragments derive from turkey, waterfowl, or other comparatively large birds (e.g., Keepax 1981; Sidell 1993).

Seasonality of Bird Hunting

Unfortunately, the species of birds encountered at Henderson provide little information about the seasonality of the village occupation. The best seasonal indicators are likely to be the aquatic species, particularly the coots and ducks, since many of the passerines, and possibly also the hawks, owls, and other predatory birds, may have been obtained by the villagers through exchange with other communities. However, as indicated by a leaflet distributed by the Bitter Lake National Wildlife Refuge (U.S. Department of the Interior 1984; see also Hubbard 1978), most of these aquatic birds, particularly those that are likely to have been important subsistence items at Henderson, can be found in the refuge over much of the year. For example, the most common aquatic species at Henderson, the American coot, can be seen in the refuge throughout most of the year and is abundant there in the spring, fall, and winter. Many of the other species of waterfowl found at Henderson are also frequent inhabitants or visitors of the refuge wetlands during the spring, fall, and winter. The only period when many of these birds are absent or uncommon in the area is during the summer. Thus, the avian species that were most likely hunted locally by the villagers could have been acquired over much of the year, and neither support nor contradict the view, suggested by the bison, antelope, lagomorph, prairie dog, and catfish remains, that the village was at least partly abandoned following the harvest in the fall (see Chapters 4-9, 12). The presence of bones of fledgling red-tailed hawk, quail, and burrowing owl at Henderson suggest at least some late spring/summer exploitation of these species, but the small number of immature specimens in no way precludes their exploitation at other times of year as well.

Synopsis

Henderson produced a small but diverse assemblage of bird bones, representing at least 129 individuals and 48 taxa. All species are currently found in New Mexico, although the cardinal may not have been present in the state until the twentieth century. Passeriformes comprise 25.0% of the assemblage, 27.0% of the individuals. Aquatic forms, especially coots, make up nearly a third of the assemblage. Predatory birds make up 27.8%.

Four complete bird skeletons were uncovered. Three of these were turkey. All three were burials of immature birds in Early phase non-room contexts, probably closure offerings. The fourth bird burial was a red-winged blackbird (*Agelaius phoeniceus*) placed directly over a sealed cylindrical storage(?) pit,

The overall density of avian bones recovered from the Henderson Site is 3.50 NISP/m^3. The density in non-room or plaza contexts is somewhat greater than in room fill. Density declines over time, but when looked at by major habitat groupings, both aquatic and non-aquatic birds increase in density, while the density of predatory birds declines sharply.

Accipitriformes drop sharply in the Late phase, while Passeriformes increase. The decline in hawks and other predators is most clear-cut in the rooms, where Passeriformes come to predominate in the Late phase. In the plazas and earth oven complexes, Accipitriformes also decline, but less dramatically. Passeriformes increase.

Wing and non-wing parts are represented in all habitat groups, except the non-aquatic one, in proportions that one would expect if whole birds were brought into the community. Passerines, quail and turkey are overwhelmingly represented by wing elements, indicating non-food use, probably as wing fans. Whether the wing fans were obtained from locally captured birds or were received through exchange from other communities, or some combination of the two, is unknown. The proportion of wing fans of non-aquatic birds remains constant over time.

Pulling some previous insights together, several points are noteworthy. Although the raptors were obtained by villagers as whole birds, ethnographic evidence from the Southwest suggests they were seldom eaten. Most quail and turkey at Henderson do not appear to have been eaten either. Over time, the avian remains in village deposits decline slightly. However, when looked at by major habitat grouping, predatory birds declined but passerines and Galliformes increased, suggesting the partial replacement of one non-food category by another. The only birds that might have served as a source of both food and feathers are the aquatic species, particularly coots and ducks, and their density increased by about 20% in the Late phase. Most waterfowl in both phases were found in room contexts, but waterfowl in public contexts increased in the Late phase. Predators and other non-food birds declined sharply in plaza contexts in the Late phase.

Why the decline in ritual importance of predators? If Henderson was intensifying long-distance communal bison hunting, it suggests there was a decline in the communal importance of smaller animals, hence, a decline in the ceremonial and ritual importance of hawks and other predatory birds. This oversimplifies the multifaceted symbolic role played by birds in Pueblo ritual and ceremony. Moreover, it assumes that numerical importance reflects symbolic importance. The declining number of predatory birds at Henderson might reflect changes in symbolic domains unrelated to hunting. Even if this broad scenario is correct, it does not explain why passerine wing fans increased in importance, at least numerically. Because most passerine bones could not be identified to genus or species, a more detailed exploration of this issue is not possible.

Henderson birds provide little insight into the seasonality of village occupation. The best seasonal indicators are likely to be the aquatic species, particularly the coots and ducks, since passerines, and possibly hawks, owls and other predatory birds, may have been obtained through exchange. Most aquatic birds can be found today at Bitter Lake National Wildlife Refuge over much of the year except the summer. That Henderson may have been abandoned in the fall after the harvest can neither be supported nor contradicted by the avian evidence.

References Cited

Emslie, S. D.
1981a Birds and Prehistoric Agriculture: The New Mexican Pueblos. *Human Ecology* 9(3):305-29.

1981b Prehistoric Agricultural Ecosystems: Avifauna from Pottery Mound, New Mexico. *American Antiquity* 46(4):853-61.

1983 Cultural and Climatic Implications in Anasazi Faunal Exploitation: A Review and Perspectives. In: *Proceedings of the Anasazi Symposium 1981*, edited by J. E. Smith, pp. 119-23. Mesa Verde National Park, CO: Mesa Verde National Park and Museum Association.

Emslie, S. D., J. D. Speth, and R. N. Wiseman
1992 Two Prehistoric Puebloan Avifaunas from the Pecos Valley, Southeastern New Mexico. *Journal of Ethnobiology* 12(1):83-115.

Ferg, A., and A. M. Rea
1983 Prehistoric Bird Bone from the Big Ditch Site, Arizona. *Journal of Ethnobiology* 3(2):99-108.

Garrett, H. E.
1967 *Statistics in Psychology and Education*. New York: David McKay Company.

Hibben, F. C.
1975 *Kiva Art of the Anasazi at Pottery Mound*. Las Vegas, NV: KC Publications.

Hubbard, J. P.
1978 Revised Check-List of the Birds of New Mexico. *New Mexico Ornithological Society Publication* 6.

Keepax, C. A.
1981 Avian Egg-Shell from Archaeological Sites. *Journal of Archaeological Science* 8:315-35.

Ladd, E. J.
1963 *Zuni Ethno-Ornithology*. Master's thesis, Department of Anthropology, University of New Mexico, Albuquerque, NM.

Ligon, J. S.
1961 *New Mexico Birds and Where to Find Them*. Albuquerque, NM: University of New Mexico Press.

Olson, S. C.
2001 *A Wing and a Prayer: Ritual Use of Birds at the Henderson Site*. Senior honors thesis, Department of Anthropology, University of Michigan, Ann Arbor, MI

Phillips, A. R.
1968 The Instability of the Distribution of Land Birds in the Southwest. *Papers of the Archaeological Society of New Mexico* 1:129-62.

Sidell, E. J.
1993 *A Methodology for the Identification of Archaeological Eggshell*. MASCA Research Papers in Science and Archaeology 10, Supplement. Philadelphia, PA: University of Pennsylvania, University Museum.

Tyler, H. A.
1991 *Pueblo Birds and Myths*. Flagstaff, AZ: Northland Publishing Co.

U.S. Department of the Interior
1984 *Birds of Bitter Lake National Wildlife Refuge*. Leaflet RF-22510-2. Roswell, NM: U.S. Department of the Interior, Fish and Wildlife Service.

Walker, W. H.
1995 *Ritual Prehistory: A Pueblo Case Study*. Ph.D. dissertation, University of Arizona, Tucson, AZ.

11
Fish and Fishing at Henderson

John D. Speth
University of Michigan

Susan L. Scott
University of Southern Mississippi

Ralph F. Stearley
Calvin College

Introduction

Most visitors to Roswell today have no idea, as they drive south along Main Street through the heart of the city, that several of the dry, concrete-walled ditches and culverts they cross were once sparkling rivers that until the late nineteenth century flowed year-round and made the Roswell area a veritable oasis in an otherwise vast, dry, and barren landscape. Even the Pecos River itself, which passes just east of Roswell as it winds its way southward toward the Texas state line, hardly impresses today's visitor as much more than a low-lying expanse of red mud and a tangle of salt cedar and weeds; only the occasional trickle of red soupy water and signs on the bridges serve as reminders that this is in fact a river.

This part of southeastern New Mexico didn't impress the earliest Anglo visitors either. In 1855, before the city of Roswell existed, James Bennett, a dragoon involved in military campaigns against the Mescalero Apaches, described the Pecos River between the mouth of the Hondo and the present-day town of Artesia in less than laudatory terms:

> The soil is filled with vermin. Thousands of rattlesnakes, tarantulas, and centipedes are running over the ground throughout this region. . . . It is dry barren soil. The banks are so high and steep that we can hardly find a place to water our animals. The water of the Pecos is quite brackish, not good water. [Brooks and Reeve 1948:75-76, cited in Jelinek 1967:25-26]

This is hardly the kind of landscape where one would expect to find fish in any abundance. But today's waterless landscape bears little resemblance to what it looked like only a century ago. Before 1900, Roswell in fact could boast of six permanently flowing rivers (not counting the Pecos itself), teeming with fish, and providing what seemed to the early settlers to be an inexhaustible water supply. F. H. Newell (1891:285), in the Annual Report of the U.S. Geological Survey, described Roswell as having "the finest and most easily controlled supply of water in the [New Mexico] territory, and an equally good body of land to be irrigated." Already by 1930, however, almost all had been destroyed.

These six rivers, all western tributaries of the Pecos, from north to south included the North, Middle, and South Berrendo, North Spring, Hondo, and South Spring. The character of these rivers, and the remarkable fish resources they once possessed, is beautifully described in a letter written in 1876 by one of Roswell's early settlers, Marshall Ashley Upson. His description is so vivid that it is worth quoting at length.

> [The North Spring] river is as transparent as crystal and about forty feet wide. . . . The Pecos is fully as large as the Rio Grande, although the Rio Grande is several hundred miles longer. . . .
>
> Besides North Spring River there is South Spring River which has its rise just four miles south of this house, and makes its junction with the Hondo at its mouth, where they both, or rather all three [including North Spring] empty into the Pecos. . . . [Shinkle 1966:16]
>
> Besides these four rivers, there are two smaller ones, their rise being from springs not more than two and one-half and three and one-half miles from this house, and emptying into the Pecos

> two and three and one-half miles below the mouth of the Hondo. Six rivers within four miles of our door—two within pistol shot—literally alive, all of them with fish. Catfish, sunfish, bull pouts, suckers, eels, and in the two Spring Rivers and the two Berrendo (Antelope) splendid bass. These four rivers are so pellucid that you can discern the smallest object at their greatest depth. The Hondo is opaque and the Pecos is so red with mud that any object is obscured as soon as it strikes the water. Here is where the immense catfish are caught. I pulled one out four and one-half years ago that weighed fifty seven pounds. Eels five and six feet long are common. Bass in the clear streams from two to four pounds is an average. [Shinkle 1966:16; see also Wiseman 1985]

Later in the same letter, Upson goes on to provide additional fascinating details about fishing in Roswell, and again his comments are worth quoting in full.

> Fishing will be my amusement, as well as profit. We have two dams in the acequia, about twenty yards apart. We have eight catfish there now, which will average sixteen pounds each. We set out lines in Spring River at night, visit them in the morning, carry our fish 200 or 300 yards, and drop them between the dams. When we want them to ship, we open the gate of the lower dam, running off the water, pick up the fish, take out the entrails, and ship them to Fort Stanton and Las Vegas [New Mexico] where they are worth twenty cents per pound. We could by labor ship 500 pounds per week. We will send off 100 pounds tonight all caught by two visits per day to only three lines. [Shinkle 1966:18]

That Roswell was well known in the late nineteenth century for its fishing is shown by the reminiscences of another early Roswell settler, Amelia Bolton Church. As recorded in Shinkle (1966:93), she said:

> the first time I saw Roswell was in August 1880. At that time I lived in White Oaks, in Lincoln County. We had heard so much of the wonderful fishing there was in the rivers around Roswell that we made up a party of friends and came down to fish and camp.

Other somewhat later descriptions echo the same sentiments about the incredible water resources of the Roswell area. For example, Cecil Bonney (1971:35) remembered that in the early days,

> North Spring River headed near the old pest house, formed by more than twenty large springs bubbling up out of the ground to start a river. The temperature of the North Spring River was the same year-round. It teemed with various game fish—large-mouth black bass, sunfish, bream, and others.

Bonney (1971:16) provides a striking photograph of North Spring River as it appeared in 1910. An even more remarkable photograph of the head of North Spring River in 1887, showing its great size, is shown in Roche (1978:6).

The listing of fish species, particularly in post-nineteenth-century descriptions of the area, must be used with caution, since deliberate attempts to stock fish such as bass occurred within the first decade of the twentieth century and possibly earlier (e.g., Adams 1983:32; see also Dills 1933; Carman 1974:88ff).

Bonney (1971:36) goes on to note that

> those were the days when there was not a well in the Pecos Valley. Five rivers flowed within six miles of each other—each with a large head of pure, crystal water—providing life-giving moisture for thousands of acres of rich land lying between, to the west and to the east. Here is where the pioneers built their homes; plowed and tilled their acres; and planted their orchards, their grains, their alfalfa, and later their cotton. Water was taken from the North and South Spring Rivers and the three Berrendos by ditches . . . to irrigate the various farms.
>
> In the days of the old-timers, all of those rivers teemed with fish: large-mouth bass, perch, bream, catfish, buffalo, eel, and rainbow trout.

Lucius Dills also commented on the rivers and fish resources in Roswell:

> In the earlier period, the Berrendos, the Spring Rivers, and the Hondo, below its confluence with North Spring, teemed with Bass, Catfish and Perch, with some Eel and Buffalo, to say nothing of an unappreciated quantity of Suckers.
>
> This was before a washout on the Texas Pacific Railroad, west of Toyah, made it seemingly necessary for our Paternal Federal Government to dump a carload of Carp fingerlings into the Pecos River, to the eternal despoilment of that stream and its tributaries for real fishing. [Dills 1933: unpaginated]

Thus, before 1900 the Roswell area was probably one of the best-watered areas in the Southwest, with seven major rivers all flowing within a few kilometers of each other. Eye-witness accounts agree that these rivers once teemed with fish, enough in fact to support a small fishing industry that at least for a brief period supplied markets as far afield as Fort Stanton and Las Vegas, New Mexico. Given these historical accounts, the presence of fish at Henderson, Rocky Arroyo, Fox Place, and other prehistoric villages along the banks of the Hondo is not surprising, although they would certainly not have been anticipated if the prehistoric resource base had been modeled solely on the basis of what one sees there today.

Assemblage Composition

The Henderson fish assemblage recovered during the 1980-1981 field seasons is large (NISP = 1,847), and most of the bones, including delicate cranial elements, are extremely well preserved (see Tables A11.1-A11.3 at the end of the chapter).[1] At least ten taxa (genera and species) are represented in the collection. The vast majority of the identifiable bones are from catfish. Included are headwater catfish (*Ictalurus lupus*), channel catfish (*I. punctatus*), black bullhead (*I. melas*), and flathead catfish (*Pylodictis olivaris*). *Ictalurus lupus* and *I. punctatus* are morphologically very similar and, as a consequence, many of the ictalurid bones could not be assigned with certainty to one or the other species (see Kelsch and Hendricks 1990; Yates et al. 1984).The nearby, quasi-contemporary Rocky Arroyo village, which yielded an even larger (NISP = 4,300+ bones and scales) collection of fish remains (Wiseman 1985), also produced these same species of catfish, plus a small number of bones of two additional forms—blue catfish (*I. furcatus*) and Chihuahua catfish (*I. chihuahuensis*).[2]

The next most common fishes at Henderson, after the catfish, are suckers and buffalo; at least two species are present—gray redhorse (*Moxostoma congestum*) and smallmouth buffalo (*Ictiobus bubalus*).

The remaining taxa are represented by only one or two bones each and include longnose gar (*Lepisosteus osseus*), represented by a single scale), white bass (*Morone chrysops*), spotted bass (*Micropterus punctulatus*), and sunfish or bluegill (*Lepomis* sp.). At least one Cyprinidae (the family that includes carps and minnows) is also present.

The absence of eels (*Anguilla rostrata*) at both Henderson and Rocky Arroyo is curious given their frequent mention by early Roswell settlers as part of the local fish fauna (e.g., Shinkle 1966:16).

Unfortunately, over one-third of the Henderson fish bones could not be identified even to family or order; the vast majority of these remains, however, are very likely from catfish, although suckers are probably also represented.

Excluding the unidentifiable fish bones, and using NISP values, catfish comprise 92.9% of the Henderson assemblage. Using MNI values, and again excluding the unidentifiable bones, the proportion of catfish falls to 76.9%. It is clear that catfish overwhelmingly dominate the Henderson fish assemblage. To some extent this is because many catfish bones are distinctive and easily identified, at least to the family or generic level, whereas in most other taxa only a much narrower range of elements are diagnostic. We see this clearly in the drop in the proportion of ictalurids compared to non-ictalurids when MNI values are used instead of NISP values. Nevertheless, the excellent state of preservation of delicate cranial elements that serve as diagnostics for identifying not only catfish but many of the other taxa as well suggests that the preponderance of Ictaluridae is real, and not merely a by-product of zooarchaeological procedures.

Recovery Biases and Taphonomy

Fish bones are notoriously underrepresented in Southwestern archaeological sites, even in riverine contexts where their presence is expected on the basis of ethnohistoric and ethnographic accounts (e.g., Adams and Chavez 1956; Hill 1982:59-61; Lange 1968:140-41; Schroeder and Matson 1965:62; see also Snow 1976). Their scarcity or absence is often attributed to recovery biases, especially in sites where screening was not routinely practiced, as well as to the fragility of most fish bones, which renders them susceptible to attritional losses. Another factor may be that many skeletal elements of fish, particularly when broken, are less easily recognized than mammal bones in the screens as something worth saving. Why fish bones are so abundant and well preserved at Henderson, as well as at Rocky Arroyo[3] and the Fox Place Site[4], another thirteenth-century village site about 15 km downstream from Henderson on the Hondo River, is therefore somewhat of a mystery. We suspect the answer may lie in the way the fish were cooked by the inhabitants of these communities. Although we did not formally tabulate the incidence of burning on fish bones, only a few of the nearly 2,000 Henderson specimens showed any evidence of direct contact with fire. Roasting or pit-baking, therefore, may not have been a common method of preparing fish at Henderson, or it was done in such a way that bones were seldom burned. It seems far more likely that fish were generally either baked or boiled; both of these cooking techniques would rarely have exposed bones to charring. And if boiling was a common method used by the villagers, then the discarded fish bones, like rabbit and jackrabbit bones, would not have been very attractive to scavenging village dogs (see discussion in Chapters 6-9).

Nevertheless, despite the abundance and excellent state of preservation of the fish remains at Henderson, recovery methods may have altered the composition of the assemblage and must therefore be considered. The best way to assess the degree of recovery bias at Henderson is to compare the density of fish bones in the flotation samples with the density of bones in the screening assemblage. As noted in previous chapters, the flotation samples were taken from midden deposits, ash lenses, hearth and pit fill, and other contexts having a high probability of yielding animal bones and other economic remains, whereas screening was routinely done for virtually all deposits, including nearly sterile overburden and room fill. Quarter-inch screens were used in all seasons of excavation at Henderson; almost no sediment was discarded without being screened, regardless of context. Hence, the most realistic density comparisons are between the float samples and those screening samples that were recovered from trash middens, in other words, the deposits in Room C-5 in the Center Bar and in the East Plaza.

Beginning first with Room C-5, 792 fish bones were recovered by screening from a total of 8.77 m^3 of excavated deposit, yielding a density of 90 bones per m^3. In contrast, flotation of 0.37 m^3 of sediment from this structure produced 177 fish bones, for a density of 478 bones per m^3. A similar picture emerges from the East Plaza midden. Screening yielded 233 bones from the 12.73 m^3 of deposit excavated, for a density of 18 specimens per m^3, while flotation of 0.23 m^3 of deposit from this midden yielded 26 bones, for a density of 113 specimens per m^3. These results indicate that the routine use of quarter-inch screens at Henderson almost certainly has biased the site-wide fish assemblage against smaller bones, and hence against both smaller taxa and smaller individuals of a given taxon. Unlike mammals, fish grow throughout their lifespan (Casteel 1976; Wheeler and Jones 1989). These biases obviously limit the kinds of issues that we can explore with the data. Fortunately, however, in both contexts the float densities are approximately five

Table 11.1. Proportion (NISP) of Ictalurid versus non-Ictalurid remains in East Plaza and combined room blocks at Henderson Site.[a]

Provenience	Ictalurid		Non-Ictalurid	
	NISP	%	NISP	%
East Plaza	174	97.21	5	2.79
Combined room blocks	902	92.13	77	7.87
Entire Site	1087	92.91	83	7.09

[a]The proportions in the East Plaza and combined room blocks differ significantly from each other (test of equality of two percentages based on arcsine transformation, $t_s = 2.87$, $p < .01$; Sokal and Rohlf 1969:607-10).

to six times greater than the screening densities, indicating, perhaps not surprisingly, that the degree of recovery bias in both assemblages is comparable. This means that, despite the recovery losses, we can at least make reliable comparisons between the East Plaza and combined room block assemblages.

East Plaza vs. Room Block Fish Assemblages

Slightly over 86% of the fish remains recovered in 1980-1981 came from Late phase deposits in the East Bar and Center Bar room blocks, and of these, nearly two-thirds (61%) came from the trash midden in Center Bar Room C-5. Thus, when fish were brought into Henderson, most ended up being discarded within the room blocks. Only about 14% found their way into the Late phase deposits in the East Plaza.

In comparing the East Plaza remains with those from the rooms, the first contrast that emerges is a small but statistically significant difference between the two proveniences in the proportion of ictalurids vs. other fish taxa. This contrast is shown in Table 11.1. The proportion of non-ictalurids relative to catfish is slightly higher in the rooms than in the plaza.

One of the most striking and intriguing differences between the fish remains in the East Plaza and room blocks is size; the fish in the former, on average, are larger than those in the latter. This is clearly shown, for example, by comparing the average weight per bone in the two contexts. In the East Plaza, the mean is 0.34 ± 0.97 g compared to only 0.15 ± 0.18 g in the combined room blocks. The difference is highly significant ($t = 7.01$, $p < .001$, df = 1,830).

One might argue that the presence of larger bones in the East Plaza is largely a function of site formation processes (e.g., Schiffer 1987), in which greater numbers of large bones were removed from the houses and disposed of in the plaza midden, while smaller bones were more often left behind in the rooms. We can easily check for this by comparing the East Plaza sample with just the bones discarded in the midden in Room C-5. The size difference persists, indicating that it is not due to site formation processes (Room C-5: average weight per bone = 0.15 ± 0.14 g, $t = 5.83$, $p < .001$, df = 1,226).

Obviously, bone weights provide a rather crude approximation of fish size, since there is no way to control adequately for differences in the degree of fragmentation among the bones. A more reliable approach is based on estimates of the actual length of the Henderson fish, which is obtained by comparing the size of the prehistoric skeletal elements with their counterparts in modern fish of known length (e.g., Wheeler and Jones 1989; Casteel 1976). Length as used here refers to the "standard length," the distance from the tip of the snout to the hypural fold or end of the hypural plate (see Wheeler and Jones 1989:139; Casteel 1976:50). Using this approach, the average length of the fish in the 1980-1981 assemblage from Henderson, combining all taxa and all proveniences, is 27.73 ± 13.83 cm (NISP = 1,451). The average length for just ictalurids (28.75 ± 12.35 cm, NISP = 1,003) is virtually identical. The non-ictalurids are somewhat longer on average (36.62 ± 14.40 cm) than the catfish, and the difference is statistically significant ($t = 5.32$, $p < .001$, df = 85).

The difference in the average size of the fish between East Plaza and rooms persists and remains highly significant when estimated length is used instead of weight per bone. Thus, the mean length of fish in the East Plaza (all taxa combined) is 34.49 ± 17.00 cm (NISP = 222), compared to only 26.50 ± 12.82 cm (NISP = 1,214) in the combined room blocks and 27.02 ± 12.53 cm (NISP = 760) in the Room C-5 midden (East Plaza vs. combined room blocks: $t = 8.07$, $p < .001$, df = 269; East Plaza vs. Room C-5 only: $t = 7.16$, $p < .001$, df = 295).

Very similar results are obtained when only ictalurid bones are considered. The mean length of catfish in the East Plaza is 36.47 ± 16.33 cm (NISP = 173), while in the combined room blocks the value is 28.60 ± 11.80 cm (NISP = 900). The difference is again highly significant ($t = 7.49$, $p < .001$, df = 208).

So far we have compared average fish size in the two contexts only in terms of the overall or grand mean. If we now compare the proportions of remains in the two contexts by 20-cm size classes, a surprising pattern emerges: the larger the size class, the greater the proportion of the remains (NISP) in the East Plaza (see Table 11.2). Essentially the same pattern holds regardless of whether we use total fish remains or only those identified as ictalurids (not shown in Table 11.2).

Amazingly, despite some minor irregularities introduced by small sample sizes, the pattern even holds when we tabulate the fish by 5- and 10-cm size classes (Table 11.3). Moreover, when broken down by these smaller classes, an interesting size threshold becomes apparent that was not as clearly evident in Table 11.2. Among fish smaller than 50 cm in length, less than 15% to 20% of the bones are found in the East Plaza. Above 50 cm, the proportion of remains found in the plaza approximately doubles to between 30% and 40%. We will defer further discussion of this intriguing patterning until Chapter 14, where the issue is addressed more broadly, showing that mammals and birds also display the same finely graded size-frequency contrast between non-room and room contexts.

While the East Plaza and room blocks differ in the proportions of fish of different sizes, there is no significant difference between the two contexts in the proportion of cranial to postcranial elements (Table 11.4). In making these comparisons, el-

Table 11.2. Proportion (NISP) of fish (all taxa combined) by 20-cm size classes in combined room blocks and East Plaza at Henderson Site.

Size Class[a] (cm)	Combined Room Blocks		East Plaza	
	NISP	%	NISP	%
0-20	352	90.72	36	9.28
20-40	666	84.52	122	15.48
40-60	107	71.81	42	28.19
> 60	25	52.08	23	47.92

[a]Standard length.

Table 11.3. Proportion (NISP) of fish (all taxa combined) by 5- to 10-cm size classes in combined room blocks and East Plaza at Henderson Site.

Size Class[a] (cm)	Combined Room Blocks		East Plaza	
	NISP	%	NISP	%
0-5	2	100.00	0	0.00
5-10	20	90.90	2	9.09
10-15	42	93.33	3	6.67
15-20	116	92.80	9	7.20
20-25	177	85.51	30	14.49
25-30	178	87.25	26	12.75
30-35	101	82.11	22	17.89
35-40	69	80.23	17	19.77
40-50	56	86.15	9	13.85
50-60	20	62.50	12	37.50
60-70	14	66.67	7	33.33
70-80	3	100.00	0	0.00
80-90	0	0.00	1	100.00

[a]Standard length.

Table 11.4. Proportion (NISP) of cranial to postcranial elements of fish (all taxa combined) in East Plaza and combined room blocks at Henderson Site.[a]

Provenience	Cranial Elements		Postcranial Elements	
	NISP	%	NISP	%
East Plaza	109	43.78	140	56.22
Combined room blocks	714	47.00	805	53.00
Room C-5 only	457	48.31	489	51.69
Entire site	828	46.44	955	53.56

[a]Skeletal elements of fish have been assigned to cranium or postcranium (i.e., pectoral, trunk, and fin elements) following definitions given by Wheeler and Jones (1989:122-24), Courtemanche and Legendre (1985), and Mundell (1975). Table includes all bones identifiable to element, including those not assigned to taxon. There are no significant differences between proveniences in the proportion of cranial to postcranial skeletal parts (test of equality of two percentages based on arcsine transformation; Sokal and Rohlf 1969:607-10).

ements have been assigned to the cranium or postcranium following the definitions given by Wheeler and Jones (1989:122-24), Courtemanche and Legendre (1985), and Mundell (1975). Cranial parts are well represented in both proveniences. It should be borne in mind that Table 11.4 does not take fish size into account. As will become clear shortly, once size enters into the picture, the proportion of cranial and postcranial elements displays definite patterning by provenience.

The data in Table 11.4 suggest several things. First, the overall abundance of delicate cranial bones supports the argument made earlier that scavenging dogs have not thoroughly ravaged the Henderson fish assemblage. Second, the fact that the proportion of cranial remains in the East Plaza is nearly the same as in the rooms, despite the greater accessibility of the plaza to village dogs, further underscores the limited role of these carnivores as taphonomic agents in the formation of the fish bone assemblage. For the fragile elements of the cranium to have survived in such numbers relative to the more robust elements of the postcranium, it seems likely that many of the heads must have been boiled, largely defleshing and degreasing them before they were discarded. Third, the abundance of heads also suggests, not surprisingly, that many, perhaps most, of the fish were brought into the village whole.

This last suggestion deserves further examination. In Table 11.5, we have tabulated the proportions of cranial and postcranial elements (all taxa combined) by 20-cm size classes. When fish length is taken into account, head elements turn out to be well represented only in the two intermediate size classes. In the smallest and largest size classes, they are sharply underrepresented. We believe the underrepresentation of heads in the smallest group of fish may be largely a function of recovery losses, either because their tiny cranial elements may have passed through the quarter-inch screens more readily than the more robust vertebral bodies, or because vertebrae were more easily recognized in the screens by the excavators than small cranial elements. This is certainly not the case, however, for the cranial parts of the largest class of fish, those individuals exceeding 60 cm in length. The underrepresentation of these crania suggests that the heads were cut off and discarded before the fish were brought back to the village.

In Table 11.6 we present the proportion of head to trunk elements, again for all taxa combined, but this time subdivided by provenience as well as by size class. In the rooms, the proportions are virtually indistinguishable from the site-wide values shown in the previous table. Heads of the smallest and largest size classes are underrepresented. The patterning is also similar in the East Plaza, except that the heads of the 40-60 cm fish are also underrepresented; the proportion of heads for this size class in the plaza differs significantly from the value in the rooms (test of equality of two percentages based on arcsine transformation, $t_s = 2.43$, $p = .01$; Sokal and Rohlf 1969:607-10). The plaza sample for this size class is very small, however, and it is therefore not clear whether this difference, while significant statistically, is culturally meaningful. Table 11.6 makes it clear that there is no tendency, regardless of size, for heads to be overrepresented in the plaza, a pattern that might be expected if many of the Henderson fish had been prepared there for drying.

Briefly summarizing these last points, it appears that most fish were brought to the village whole, with the notable exception of the largest size classes, those greater than about 60 cm in length. The heads of these individuals were apparently cut off and discarded outside the village.

Table 11.5. Proportion (NISP) of cranial and postcranial fish elements (all taxa combined) by 20-cm size classes at Henderson Site (all proveniences combined).

Size Class[a] (cm)	Cranium		Postcranium	
	NISP	%	NISP	%
0-20	80	19.66	327	80.34
20-40	420	50.30	415	49.70
40-60	82	51.90	76	48.10
> 60	12	23.53	39	76.47

[a]Standard length.

Table 11.6. Proportion (NISP) of cranial and postcranial fish elements (all taxa combined) by 20-cm size classes by provenience at Henderson Site.[a]

Size Class[b] (cm)	Cranium		Postcranium	
	NISP	%	NISP	%
Combined Room Blocks				
0-20	74	20.16	293	79.84
20-40	355	50.43	349	49.57
40-60	66	*57.39	49	42.61
> 60	6	21.43	22	78.57
East Plaza				
0-20	5	13.89	31	86.11
20-40	62	51.24	59	48.76
40-60	15	*35.71	27	64.29
> 60	6	26.09	17	73.91

[a]Significance evaluated by test of equality of two percentages based on arcsine transformation (Sokal and Rohlf 1969:607-10); values flagged with asterisk denote proportions which differ significantly from each other ($t_s = 2.43$, $p = .01$).
[b]Standard length.

Catfish pectoral spines are distinctive and robust elements, and their proportions in the East Plaza and room blocks provide interesting additional insights into the nature of the Henderson fish assemblage. Pectoral spines are proportionately better represented in the plaza than in the rooms, and the difference is statistically significant (Table 11.7). Many of the spines from both proveniences have been snapped off, probably deliberately, although we have not tabulated the actual incidence of this practice in either context, nor have we determined whether larger spines were more likely to have been broken off than smaller ones. The overrepresentation of spines in the plaza suggests that many of the Henderson fish destined for the rooms were first gutted in the plaza. However, as noted earlier, the heads of these fish were not removed and discarded in the plaza.

Table 11.8 shows the same data that was presented in the previous table, but this time broken down by size class. The samples for most size classes, unfortunately, are rather small, hampering comparison. Nevertheless, these data show that pectoral spines are overrepresented in the East Plaza primarily for the 20-40 cm fish, a difference that is statistically significant ($t_s = 2.67$, $p < .01$). Spines in the 40-60 cm size class may also be overrepresented in the plaza, but the difference is not large enough to be significant given the small sample sizes.

Next, we calculated the average length of the fish in the combined room blocks and East Plaza using just the pectoral spines, and compared these values with the averages derived by using the full array of bones identified as ictalurids. The results are interesting. For the combined room blocks, the spine-based estimate is 27.25 ± 9.38 cm (NISP = 70), a value that is very close to the one estimated for this provenience using the total ictalurid sample (28.60 ± 11.80 cm, NISP = 900). In contrast, the spine-based estimate for the East Plaza (29.79 ± 10.32 cm, NISP = 24) is significantly smaller than its counterpart based on the entire ictalurid sample (36.47 ± 16.33 cm, NISP = 173). This implies that the pectoral spines of the largest individuals are underrepresented in the East Plaza, a conclusion that dovetails well with two observations made earlier: that larger fish tend to be concentrated in the plaza, and that many of the larger fish had been beheaded before they were brought into the community.

Fishing at Henderson

The average size of the fish at Henderson, most of which are catfish, is about 28 cm. A channel catfish of this length would weigh about 0.18 to 0.23 kg and be between three and four years old (Davis 1959:13; Simco and Cross 1966:217). Carlander (1969:539) provides slightly higher weight estimates, closer to 0.25 or even 0.30 kg. The relationships among length, weight, and age in catfish are complex and depend on a number of factors including the condition of the physical environment (water temperature, food, turbidity), population density, interspecific competition, and of course whether the fish is wild or was raised in a hatchery or managed impoundment. The figures provided here are approximations intended to give a rough idea of the size of the Henderson fish. The largest fish found at the site in the 1980-1981 seasons—a flathead catfish (*Pylodictis olivaris*)—was between 80 and 90 cm in length. An individual of this size would probably weigh about 4 to 6 kg, or more, and be at least twelve to thirteen years old (Piper et al. 1982:406, 434-35, Appendix I-4; Davis 1959:13). Again, Carlander provides a much higher weight estimate: from 9.5 to 20 kg or more.

Table 11.7. Proportion (NISP) of catfish pectoral spines in East Plaza and combined room blocks at Henderson Site.

Provenience	Pectoral Spines		Ictaluridae Total NISP	Test Statistic[a] (t_s)
	NISP	%		
East Plaza	24	13.79	174	
Combined room blocks	70	7.76	902	2.37*
Room C-5 Only	44	7.52	585	2.38*

[a]Test of equality of two percentages based on arcsine transformation (Sokal and Rohlf 1969:607-10); values flagged with asterisk denote proportions which differ significantly from East Plaza value ($p < .05$).

Table 11.8. Proportion (NISP) of catfish pectoral spines by 20-cm size classes in the combined room blocks and East Plaza at Henderson Site.

Size Class[a] (cm)	Combined Room Blocks			East Plaza			Test Statistic[b] (t_s)
	Spines		Total Ictal. NISP	Spines		Total Ictal. NISP	
	NISP	%		NISP	%		
0-20	11	5.95	185	1	6.67	15	0.11
20-0	55	9.23	596	20	18.87	106	*2.67
40-0	3	3.06	98	3	9.68	31	1.36
> 60	1	4.76	21	0	0.00	21	1.43

[a]Standard length.
[b]Test of equality of two percentages based on arcsine transformation (Sokal and Rohlf 1969:607-10); statistic flagged with asterisk denotes proportions which differ significantly from each other.

Davis (1959:15), in his study of Kansas channel catfish, notes that few individuals live longer than seven years. This means that few exceed 40 or 50 cm in length. Interestingly, this same approximate threshold is apparent in the lengths of the Henderson fish (all taxa combined), with 86% of the bones (NISP = 1,242 of 1,451) deriving from individuals less than 40 cm long and 65% coming from individuals less than 30 cm long. According to Carlander (1969:551; see also Cole et al. 1991:80), fish less than about 30 cm are probably immature.

There is no evidence that the villagers were selectively targeting large fish. Whatever method or methods were being used to capture catfish took in primarily small- to moderate-sized individuals between 10 and 40 cm.

The flotation samples provide additional insights into the capture techniques used by the Henderson villagers. Although this assemblage is small (total NISP = 165 bones for which body-size could be estimated), the smallest size classes are well represented (see Table 11.9). In fact, fully 55% of the analyzed bones of fish under 20 cm fall within the 5-10 cm size class. While these small fish could have been taken one at a time by hook and line, spearing, clubbing, or other similar methods, it seems more likely that they would have been captured by techniques such as baited traps that were unlikely to discriminate against the taking of small fish (see Rau 1884; Rostlund 1952). Nets are also a possibility, but one might then expect the Henderson fish remains to also include a much larger number of nonpredatory species.

Finally, if one looks at Figure 11.1, which shows the frequency distribution of fish lengths at Henderson, it is clear that we are not dealing with a normal distribution. The falloff above 40 cm is too abrupt (the drop below 10 cm almost certainly reflects the lack of analysis of the smallest remains). Instead, the distribution is precisely what one might expect if baited traps had been used to capture catfish. Fish larger than about 40 cm were unable to enter the trap. These larger individuals were probably taken by spear or net. A gill net might also produce a sharp falloff such as that shown in Figure 11.1, but such nets are unlikely to have taken so many tiny fish as well (e.g., Hamley 1975).

Table 11.9. Proportion (NISP) of fish (all taxa combined) by 20-cm size classes in flotation samples at Henderson Site.

Size Class (cm)[a]	NISP	%
0-20	78	47.27
20-40	69	41.82
40-60	17	10.30
> 60	1	0.61
TOTAL	165	

[a]Standard length.

Identifying the locale or locales where the Henderson villagers did most of their fishing is difficult with the limited information at hand. Nevertheless, the location of the village, together with information provided in the early historic accounts, allows us to at least make some reasonable guesses. The straight-line distances from Henderson to the various rivers provide a starting point (Table 11.10). All of the rivers, except the Hondo itself, are at least 20 km from Henderson. The distances shown in the table are to the nearest point on the river; suitable fishing locales on these rivers may actually have been farther away. A round-trip in excess of 40 km almost certainly would have required an overnight stay. Hence, these distance considerations suggest that most of the fishing would have been done in the Hondo, which was just a few hundred meters from the village, assuming of course that it provided suitable habitat for the catfish and other species found at the village.

The historic accounts, particularly the detailed description of the Roswell rivers and their fish provided by Upson's letter of 1876 (Shinkle 1966, cited above), make it clear that catfish were available in all of the rivers, but that the largest individuals were generally caught in the Pecos and possibly also in the Hondo. There are two reasons why these two rivers would have offered particularly suitable habitat for catfish (Cole et al. 1991; Davis 1959; Koster 1957; Lee et al. 1980; Minckley 1973; Simco and Cross 1966; Sublette et al. 1990). First, several of the catfish species adapt well to turbid waters, and some actually thrive under these conditions: channel catfish[5], flathead catfish, and black bullhead, for example. Moreover, both channel and flathead catfish feed actively during periods of rising water and flooding. When we examine the nature of the rivers, the Pecos and Hondo best fulfill these conditions. The three Berrendos

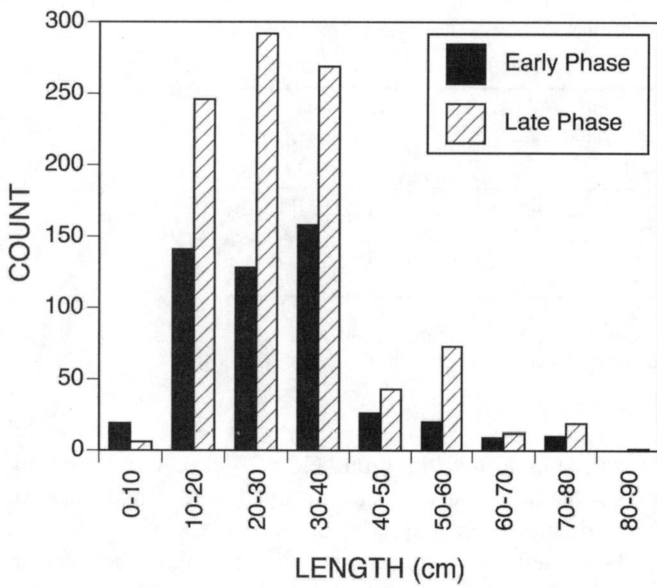

Figure 11.1. Frequency distribution of fish lengths (cm) by phase at the Henderson Site.

and the two Spring Rivers, all now defunct, were fed by springs located very close to Roswell. Thus, they drained very small areas of low relief and normally carried minimal sediment loads. Upson described them as "so pellucid that you can discern the smallest object at their greatest depth" (Shinkle 1966:16). In contrast, the Pecos and the Hondo arise in upland areas many miles from Roswell and drain vast areas. In addition, until they were totally altered by dam construction and massive water diversion projects, both rivers were subject to much greater seasonal variation in runoff and generally carried much higher sediment loads, a point also noted by Upson: "the Hondo is opaque and the Pecos is so red with mud that any object is obscured as soon as it strikes the water. Here is where the immense catfish are caught" (Shinkle 1966:16). This last statement, unfortunately, is ambiguous since it could mean that the really large catfish were caught in the turbid waters of both rivers or only in the Pecos. In any case, there seems little doubt that the Hondo, at least until the 1870s, contained catfish as well as other species.

Unfortunately, Upson's letter is much more detailed about North Spring River, where his small-scale fishing enterprise was based, than about the Hondo and its fish resources. Were fish available more or less anywhere along the Hondo in the Roswell area? Or were they only found in the lowermost reaches of the river, "below its confluence with North Spring," as remembered in the 1930s by Lucius Dills when reminiscing about the mid- to late 1880s (Shinkle 1966:116)? The confluence of the Hondo with North Spring River is 20 km downstream from Henderson. If Dills' description applied to the aboriginal period as well, then all of the rivers, including the Hondo, would have been largely out of reach for routine fishing by the Henderson villagers. The implication of Dills' statement is that the Hondo in the

Table 11.10. Distance and approximate direction from Henderson Site to major rivers in Roswell area.[a]

River	Distance		Approx. Direction
	Miles	Kilometers	
Pecos	17.6	28.9	East
South Spring	13.5	22.1	East-northeast
North Spring	11.5	18.9	Northeast
South Berrendo	10.5	17.2	North-northeast
Middle Berrendo	14.0	23.0	Northeast
North Berrendo	16.5	27.1	Northeast
Hondo	0.1	0.2	North

[a]Distance is to nearest point on river, not to a specific fishing locale that may have been used prehistorically by Henderson villagers.

1880s was an intermittent stream, which only flowed year-round below its junction with North Spring, a tributary fed by numerous permanently flowing springs.

A study by Newell (1891:285) confirms that the Hondo above the confluence was, in fact, intermittent in the 1880s, and therefore probably unsuitable for fishing:

> The Hondo, formed by the confluence of numerous brooks rising in the White Mountains, flows for some distance through the foothills, and then enters the prairie country west of Roswell. Just before emptying into the Pecos it receives the water of the Berenda [*sic*] and North Spring rivers. In the summer above the mouth of these rivers it becomes very low and the bed even dries. In 1886 it was dry for two months; in 1887 for three weeks; in 1888 for only one. On the prairie it flows in a tortuous course through a narrow channel, cut in loose gravel, from 8 to 15 feet deep.

But by the 1880s water use along the entire course of the Hondo was already extremely heavy, making observations from this period of dubious value for understanding the aboriginal river. To clarify this issue further, we examined the Government Land Office (GLO) Survey plat records for the State of New Mexico (Chaves County) housed in Santa Fe. To our knowledge, these provide the earliest existing descriptions of the Hondo in the general vicinity of the Henderson Site. To our surprise, they show that as early as 1868 this stretch of the valley was already being heavily irrigated. Over and over again the documents mention acequias or ditches that were being used to divert water away from the main channel. More importantly, they mention a sizable settlement known as Plaza San Jose, with "about 30 houses and some 200 inhabitants," located in T. 12 S., R. 22 E., Section 5, only about 8 km upstream from Henderson. This community, as well as numerous other settlements and farmsteads along the Hondo's entire course, must have placed extremely heavy demands on the river, undoubtedly reducing its flow and making it much less predictable.

This community, also referred to as "Missouri Plaza," was apparently abandoned in the early 1870s as increased water use farther upstream on the Hondo reduced its flow below the level needed to sustain irrigation in the Roswell area (Schaafsma et al. 1967).

Despite the heavy water use in the 1860s, the documents suggest that the river was still a perennial stream. For example, in T. 11 S., R. 21 E., just a few kilometers west of the site, the Hondo is described as "not subject to overflow," certainly not the characterization one would expect of an intermittent stream subject to flash-flooding as it is today. Similarly, the river in T. 11 S., R. 22 E., even closer to Henderson, is described as "a deep, rapid stream, affording a sufficient supply of water for all purposes of irrigation." This would hardly be the case if the river dried up every summer, as it apparently did only two decades later.

The size of the river is also described in the GLO documents. For example, in T. 12 S., R. 21.5 E., again quite near the site, the river was "60 links wide" (1 link = 7.92 in). Somewhat closer still (T. 12 S., R. 22 E.) the river was "40 links wide." Unfortunately, the documents say nothing about the depth of the river in the vicinity of Henderson.

While we may never be sure what the Hondo was really like in aboriginal times, based on the GLO documents it seems very likely that prior to the 1860s the river flowed year-round over its entire length, not just below its confluence with North Spring River. If so, the Hondo was probably the principal river fished by the Henderson villagers, although from time to time the other rivers may have been exploited.

Why are catfish so abundant at Henderson? Perhaps the Henderson fish assemblage mirrors the natural species composition of the river. This seems unlikely, however, for two reasons. First, although we lack detailed information on the natural populations of fish in the Hondo prior to Anglo settlement of the area, the early accounts mention quite a diversity of species in the local rivers, including buffalo, bass, eel, and others. Moreover, Hatch (1985: Appendix) and Sublette et al. (1990:3-4) provide detailed lists and distributional maps of the species thought to be native to the Pecos drainage at the start of the historic era. Their information illustrates the great diversity that must have characterized these drainages in the past.

Second, the numerically preeminent catfish in the Henderson assemblage are predators which, as discussed earlier, were most likely taken by baited trap, a technique that by its very nature is selective in terms of species (Jackson 1986:471-81 makes a very similar argument for selective catfish procurement at the Copes Site, a Poverty Point period site in the Lower Mississippi Valley; see also Jackson 1989:193-94). A more plausible interpretation, therefore, is that the Henderson fish remains reflect deliberate selection on the part of the villagers.

Why were catfish preferred over other species? Catfish are comparatively easy to catch, but there is another, perhaps less obvious, reason why they were targeted by the Henderson villagers, as well as by many other Native American groups (Rostlund 1952:33-34). In prime condition, catfish are among the fattiest freshwater species in North America and therefore would have been a valuable source of calories (see discussion in Jackson 1986, 1989). While the published data on fat levels in catfish span a considerable range, individuals with lipids comprising 10% or more of total body weight are not uncommon (e.g., Ammerman 1985:572, Table 12.4; Atwater 1892; Clark and Clough 1926:505; Magee 1976; Murray et al. 1977:276; Page and Andrews 1973:1343, Table 4; Piper et al. 1982; Stickney and Andrews 1971). Such values match or even exceed the fat levels found in bison, antelope, and other mammals in peak physical condition (Speth and Spielmann 1983:10-11, Table 2). Catfish, therefore, not only offered an important resource to supplement the lean fare provided by larger mammals, they were also a resource that could be taken close to home and, if they were captured using baited traps, their procurement would have conflicted little with agricultural activities or other subsistence pursuits (Speth 1991; Speth and Scott 1989). The seasonality of catfish exploitation at Henderson is examined in Chapter 12.

Temporal Perspective

None of the fish remains recovered during the 1994, 1995, and 1997 excavations at Henderson have been identified to taxon as yet. However, to allow us to look at whether the use of fish changed in any significant way over time, we have inventoried all of the bones from the 1994 and 1995 seasons by grid square and elevation, but ignoring taxonomic identification.[6] While less than ideal, this at least permits us to look at broad changes in the density of remains per cubic meter of excavated deposit, incidence of burning, and average fish size.

The total number of fish bones recovered in the first four seasons of excavation at Henderson (1980, 1981, 1994, 1995) is 2,774. The overall density of fish remains (NISP/m^3) declines sharply from the Early phase (24.4/m^3) to the Late phase (17.3/m^3).[7] The falloff in density affects fish remains in both room (Early phase, 25.5/m^3; Late phase, 16.7/m^3) and non-room contexts (Early phase, 22.6/m^3; Late phase, 18.3/m^3), but the decline is most marked in the rooms. Thus, substantially fewer fish were brought into the village in the Late phase, but of those that were, a somewhat higher proportion ended up in more public contexts.

Average fish size increased slightly in the Late phase, the difference almost achieving statistical significance (Early phase, 26.8 ± 13.7 cm; Late phase, 28.2 ± 13.8 cm; $t = -1.86$, $p = .06$). However, when looked at by spatial provenience, there is no difference in average fish size between room and non-room contexts in the Early phase (room, 26.8 ± 13.8 cm; non-room, 28.8 ± 9.9 cm; $t = 0.52$, $p > .05$), but a highly significant difference in the Late phase (room, 26.3 ± 12.0 cm; non-room, 34.4 ± 16.9 cm; $t = 8.08$, $p < .0001$). The results thus far indicate that while fewer fish were brought into the village in the Late phase, a greater proportion of them ended up in plaza contexts, and the average size of these "plaza" fish was larger.

Very few of Henderson's fish bones are burned (0.68%). When looked at chronologically, there is a significant decline in the incidence of burning, from 1.03% in the Early phase to 0.31% in the Late phase ($t_s = 2.42$, $p \approx .01$). This decline appears to have affected primarily fish in non-room or plaza contexts (Early phase, 2.02%; Late phase, 0.34%; $t_s = 1.96$, $p = .05$). While there also is a decline in the incidence of burning in the rooms, the change is much smaller and not statistically significant (Early phase, 0.82%; Late phase, 0.30%; $t_s = 1.69$, $p > .05$). It has been argued elsewhere in this volume (see Chapters 6, 8, and 9) that a decline in burning may indicate an increase in the use of boiling in food preparation, and it would appear that by this logic, boiling increased in Late phase plaza contexts, but probably not in rooms.

Synopsis

The 1980-1981 field season at Henderson yielded a large and well-preserved assemblage of fish remains representing at least 10 taxa (genera and species). Most of the identifiable remains recovered in 1980-1981 are from ictalurids, particularly channel catfish (*I. punctatus*), but also headwater catfish (*I. lupus*), black bullhead (*I. melas*), and flathead catfish (*Pylodictis olivaris*). Other fish present in much smaller numbers are gray redhorse (*Moxostoma congestum*), smallmouth buffalo (*Ictiobus bubalus*), longnose gar (*Lepisoteus osseus*), white bass (*Morone chrysops*), spotted bass (*Micropterus punctulatus*), sunfish or bluegill (*Lepomis* sp.), and at least one Cyprinidae. Eel (*Anguilla rostrata*), though commonly mentioned in the historical accounts, was not identified in the prehistoric collections.

Based on NISP values, ictalurids comprise 92.9% of the total assemblage; using MNI values, ictalurids make up 76.9% of the assemblage. Regardless of which measure of abundance is used, Ictaluridae clearly dominate the fish remains from the village.

While fish bones are both abundant and well preserved at Henderson, many of the smaller bones may have passed through the quarter-inch screens that were routinely used during the excavations, biasing the assemblage in favor of larger taxa and larger individuals within each taxon. Recovery biases therefore have to be assessed before other aspects of the assemblage can be considered. As with small mammals, screening losses can best be examined by looking at the composition of the assemblage recovered by flotation. As expected, the density of fish bones per cubic meter of excavated sediments is much lower in the screening samples than in those recovered by flotation, a clear indication that many smaller bones have been lost.

More than 86% of all fish remains came from the room blocks, compared to only about 14% from the plaza. Thus, most fish remains ended up being discarded within the structures. However, the mean (standard) length of fish (all taxa combined) is significantly greater in the plaza (34.5 cm) than in the rooms (26.5 cm). This difference is not an artifact of site formation processes, such as sweeping, which might bias the remains that were inadvertently left behind in the rooms in favor of smaller elements and hence smaller individuals. The fish in the Room C-5 trash midden are also smaller, on average, than those in the plaza.

When the proportions of remains in the two contexts are tallied by discrete 20 cm size classes, a striking pattern emerges: the larger the size class, the greater the proportion of the remains in the East Plaza. This same pattern persists even when 5- and 10-cm size classes are used. In addition, there is a clear size threshold, such that for fish smaller than about 50 cm in length, less than 15% to 20% of the bones are found in the plaza, while for larger fish the proportion found in the plaza nearly doubles to between 30% and 40%. Further discussion of this intriguing pattern is deferred until Chapter 14, where it is shown that the same finely graded size-frequency contrast between plaza and room blocks cross-cuts the mammals and birds as well.

When size is ignored, cranial parts are equally well represented in the plaza and structures. The overall abundance of cranial parts at Henderson, somewhat unusual in Southwestern archaeological sites, suggests that scavenging dogs have not seriously ravaged the fish assemblage, perhaps an indication that fish, like lagomorphs, were generally boiled rather than baked or roasted, making their discarded bones of little interest to dogs. The abundance of heads at Henderson also indicates that most fish were brought into the village whole.

When the proportions of cranial and postcranial elements are examined by 20-cm size classes, head elements turn out to be well represented only in the two intermediate groups. Heads are sharply underrepresented in the smallest and largest (>60 cm) size classes. Their poor representation in the smallest class is almost certainly due to a combination of attritional losses and recovery bias. In contrast, the scarcity of cranial parts among the largest fish indicates that the heads of these individuals were cut off before the fish were brought back to the village. Underrepresentation of the pectoral spines of the largest fish points to the same conclusion.

The average length of the fish at Henderson, most of which are catfish, is about 28 cm. A channel catfish of this size would weigh about 0.18 to 0.23 kg. In the 1980-1981 assemblage, the largest fish taken by the villagers—a flathead catfish (*Pylodictis olivaris*)—was 80-90 cm in length. This individual probably weighed at least 4-6 kg, or more, and was at least twelve to thirteen years old (a pectoral spine from a catfish that measured over 110 cm in length was recovered in 1997). In the wild, few catfish live past seven years, and hence few exceed about 40 cm in length. Interestingly, this same length threshold is seen in the Henderson remains, with over 85% of the bones from fish less than 40 cm long. Moreover, the flotation samples indicate that fish less than 15 cm long were also well represented at the site. Thus, the Henderson villagers were using a fishing technique that targeted catfish, but that did not exclude the smaller individuals in favor of large fish. Since catfish are predators, these observations suggest that the villagers probably used some form of baited trap to catch them.

Catfish may have been targeted for several reasons. First, the Hondo was a turbid river, providing suitable habitat for catfish. Second, catfish are comparatively easy to catch. Third, in peak condition catfish are among the fattiest freshwater fish in North America, making them a valuable source of calories to supplement the normally lean fare provided by larger mammals. Finally, they were a resource that could be taken close to home and, if captured using baited traps, their procurement would have conflicted little with agricultural activities or other subsistence pursuits.

None of the fish remains recovered during the 1994, 1995, and 1997 excavations at Henderson have been identified to taxon as yet. However, to allow us to look at whether the use of fish changed in any significant way over time, we inventoried all of the bones from the 1994 and 1995 seasons by grid square and elevation, ignoring taxonomic identification. This permitted us to look at broad changes in the density of remains, incidence of burning, and average fish size.

The total number of fish bones recovered in the first four seasons of excavation at Henderson (1980-1995) is 2,774. The overall density of fish remains (NISP/m^3) declines sharply from the Early phase (24.4/m^3) to the Late phase (17.3/m^3). The falloff in density affects fish remains in both room and non-room contexts, but the decline is most marked in the rooms. Thus, substantially fewer fish were brought into the village in the Late phase, but of those that were, a somewhat higher proportion ended up in more public contexts.

Average fish size increased slightly in the Late phase. However, when looked at by spatial provenience, there is no difference in average fish size between room and non-room contexts in the Early phase, but a highly significant difference in the Late phase. The results thus far indicate that, while fewer fish were brought into the village in the Late phase, a greater proportion of them ended up in plaza contexts, and the average size of these "plaza" fish was larger.

Very few of Henderson's fish bones are burned (0.68%). When looked at chronologically, however, there is a significant decline in the incidence of burning, from 1.03% in the Early phase to 0.31% in the Late phase. This decline appears to have affected primarily fish in non-room or plaza contexts. While there also is a decline in the incidence of burning in the rooms, the change is much smaller and not statistically significant. It has been argued elsewhere in this volume that a decline in burning may indicate an increase in the use of boiling in food preparation, and it would appear that by this logic, boiling increased in Late phase plaza contexts, but probably not in rooms.

Notes

1. With the exception of catfish pectoral spines (see Chapter 12) and vertebrae, the fish bones from the 1994, 1995, and 1997 field seasons at Henderson have not been analyzed.

2. Identification of the bones of the Chihuahua catfish (*Ictalurus chihuahuensis*) in the Rocky Arroyo faunal material was made by Robert R. Miller of the Museum of Zoology, University of Michigan. According to Miller, Rocky Arroyo is the first reported archaeological occurrence of this species in New Mexico.

3. More than 4,000 fish bones, as well as hundreds of delicate scales, were recovered from a small wedge of fill that was salvaged by Regge N. Wiseman of the Museum of New Mexico from a badly vandalized thirteenth-century pit structure at Rocky Arroyo. Preservation of these fragile remains was undoubtedly enhanced by the fact that the bones had been dumped into a below-ground structure, but other factors, such as the method of cooking, almost certainly contributed to the survival of this unusual assemblage.

4. Because a large part of the Fox Place Site was slated to be destroyed or indirectly impacted by construction of a "hazardous-materials" truck bypass around the western side of the city of Roswell, the endangered part was recently excavated by the Museum of New Mexico and a final report is now being prepared (Wiseman n.d.).

5. According to Davis (1959:16, 20), channel catfish grow larger and faster in clear water than in turbid water, but their reproductive success is lower in the former than in the latter, perhaps because the young are more vulnerable to predation.

6. We were assisted in compiling the inventory by Angela Schmorrow (1997), who completed a Senior Honors Thesis on the 1994 and 1995 fish remains. The bones from the 1997 excavations have not been tallied as yet.

7. Excavated sediment volumes used to calculate densities here are values for the 1980 through 1995 seasons only.

References Cited

Adams, C. S.
1983 *Little Town West of the Pecos—1909.* Roswell, NM: Pioneer Printing.

Adams, E. B., and F. A. Chavez
1956 *The Missions of New Mexico, 1776: A Description by Fray Francisco Atanasio Dominguez with Other Contemporary Documents.* Albuquerque, NM: University of New Mexico Press.

Ammerman, G. R.
1985 Processing. In: *Channel Catfish Culture*, edited by C. S. Tucker, pp. 569-620. Amsterdam, The Netherlands: Elsevier.

Atwater, W. O.
1892 *The Chemical Composition and Nutritive Values of Food Fishes and Aquatic Invertebrates.* Report of the U.S. Commissioner of Fisheries for 1888:679-868.

Bonney, C.
1971 *Looking Over My Shoulder: Seventy-Five Years in the Pecos Valley.* Roswell, NM: Hall-Poorbaugh Press.

Brewer, D. J.
1987 Seasonality in the Prehistoric Faiyum Based on the Incremental Growth Structures of the Nile Catfish (Pisces: *Clarias*). *Journal of Archaeological Science* 14:459-72.

Brooks, C. E., and F. D. Reeve (Editors)
1948 *Forts and Forays, James A. Bennett: A Dragoon in New Mexico 1850-1856.* Albuquerque, NM: University of New Mexico Press.

Carlander, K. D.
1969 *Handbook of Freshwater Fishery Biology*, Vol. 1. *Life History Data on Freshwater Fishes of the United States and Canada, Exclusive of the Perciformes*. Ames, IA: Iowa State University Press.

Carman, L. Q.
1974 U.S. Fish Hatchery. In: *As We Remembered It*, by "Dexter Old Timers," pp. 88-91. Roswell, NM: Hall-Poorbaugh Press.

Casteel, R. W.
1976 *Fish Remains in Archaeology*. New York: Academic Press.

Clark, E. D., and R. W. Clough
1926 Chemical Composition of Fish and Shellfish. In: *Nutritive Value of Fish and Shellfish*. Department of Commerce, Bureau of Fisheries, Appendix X to the Report of the U. S. Commissioner of Fisheries for 1925, Bureau of Fisheries Document 1000, Technological Contribution 27:502-26. Washington, DC: Government Printing Office.

Cole, R. A., R. A. Deitner, R. J. Tafanelli, and G. A. Desmare
1991 Habitat, Fish Community, and Stocking Effects on Channel Catfish Stock Density, Growth, and Harvest in New Mexico Warmwater Reservoirs. In *Warmwater Fisheries Symposium I*, edited by J. L. Cooper and R. H. Hamre, pp. 79-90. General Technical Report RM-207. Fort Collins, CO: U.S. Department of Agriculture, Forest Service, Rocky Mountain Forest and Range Experiment Station.

Courtemanche, M., and V. Legendre
1985 *Os de Poissons: Nomenclature Codifieé, Noms Français et Anglais*. Rapport Technique 06-38. Montréal, Québec: Gouvernement du Québec, Ministère du Loisir, de la Chasse et de la Pêche, Direction Régionale de Montréal.

Davis, J.
1959 *Management of Channel Catfish in Kansas*. Miscellaneous Publication 21. Lawrence, KS: University of Kansas, Museum of Natural History.

Dills, L.
1933 *Roswell: Some Facts and Observations Relative to Its Settlement and Early Growth*. Roswell, NM: Chaves County Archaeological and Historical Society.

Hamley, J. M.
1975 Review of Gillnet Selectivity. *Journal of Fisheries Research Board Canada* 32:1943-69.

Hatch, M. D.
1985 *The Native Fish Fauna of Major Drainages East of the Continental Divide in New Mexico*. Master's thesis, Graduate Faculty of Biology, Eastern New Mexico University, Portales, NM.

Hill, W. W.
1982 *An Ethnography of Santa Clara Pueblo, New Mexico*, edited and annotated by C. H. Lange. Albuquerque, NM: University of New Mexico Press.

Jackson, H. E.
1986 *Sedentism and Hunter-Gatherer Adaptations in the Lower Mississippi Valley: Subsistence Strategies during the Poverty Point Period*. Ph.D. dissertation, University of Michigan, Ann Arbor, MI.
1989 Poverty Point Adaptive Systems in the Lower Mississippi Valley: Subsistence Remains from the J. W. Copes Site. *North American Archaeologist* 10(3):173-204.

Jelinek, A. J.
1967 *A Prehistoric Sequence in the Middle Pecos Valley, New Mexico*. Anthropological Paper 31. Ann Arbor, MI: University of Michigan, Museum of Anthropology.

Kelsch, S. W., and F. S. Hendricks
1990 Distribution of the Headwater Catfish *Ictalurus lupus* (Osteichthyes: Ictaluridae). *Southwestern Naturalist* 35(3): 292-97.

Koster, W. J.
1957 *Guide to the Fishes of New Mexico*. Albuquerque, NM: University of New Mexico Press.

Lange, C. H.
1968 *Cochiti: A New Mexico Pueblo, Past and Present*. Carbondale, IL: Southern Illinois University Press.

Lee, D. S., C. R. Gilbert, C. H. Hocutt, R. E. Jenkins, D. E. McAllister, and J. R. Stauffer, Jr.
1980 *Atlas of North American Freshwater Fishes*. North Carolina Biological Survey Publication 1980-12. Raleigh, NC: North Carolina State Museum of Natural History.

Magee, J. B.
1976 *Some Effects of Size, Source, and Season of Harvest on Nutritional Composition of Catfish*. Ph.D. dissertation, Mississippi State University, Mississippi State, MS.

Minckley, W. L.
1973 *Fishes of Arizona*. Phoenix, AZ: Sims Printing Company.

Morey, D. F.
1983 Archaeological Assessment of Seasonality from Freshwater Fish Remains: A Quantitative Procedure. *Journal of Ethnobiology* 3(1):75-95.

Mundell, R. L.
1975 *An Illustrated Osteology of the Channel Catfish (Ictalurus punctatus)*. Midwest Archeological Center Occasional Studies in Anthropology 2. Lincoln, NE: National Park Service, Midwest Archeological Center. Reprinted in *Reprints in Anthropology*, Volume 21, 1980, pp. 1-11, by J & L Reprint Company, Lincoln, NE.

Murray, M. W., J. W. Andrews, and H. L. DeLoach
1977 Effects of Dietary Lipids, Dietary Protein and Environmental Temperatures on Growth, Feed Conversion and Body Composition of Channel Catfish. *Journal of Nutrition* 107:272-80.

Newell, F. H.
1891 Hydrography of the Arid Regions. *Twelfth Annual Report of the United States Geological Survey to the Secretary of the Interior, 1890-1891*, Part II. *Irrigation*, by J. W. Powell, pp. 282-90. Washington, DC: Government Printing Office.

Page, J. W., and J. W. Andrews
1973 Interactions of Dietary Levels of Protein and Energy on Channel Catfish (*Ictalurus punctatus*). *Journal of Nutrition* 103(9):1339-46.

Piper, R. G., I. B. McElwain, L. E. Orme, J. P. McCraren, L. G. Fowler, and J. R. Leonard
1982 *Fish Hatchery Management*. Washington, DC: U.S. Department of the Interior, Fish and Wildlife Service.

Roche, B. F.
1978 The Pioneer Period, 1866-1890. In: *Roundup on the Pecos*, edited by E. E. Fleming and M. S. Huffman, pp. 6-15. Roswell, NM: Chaves County Historical Society.

Rau, C.
1884 *Prehistoric Fishing in Europe and North America*. Smithsonian Contribution to Knowledge 25. Washington, DC: Smithsonian Institution.

Rostlund, E.
1952 *Freshwater Fish and Fishing in Native North America*. University of California Publications in Geography 9. Berkeley, CA: University of California Press.

Schaafsma, C. F., M. Mayer, and J. P. Wilson
1967 *La Plaza de San Jose: Excavations in the Two Rivers Reservoir*. Laboratory of Anthropology Note 160. Santa Fe, NM: Museum of New Mexico, Laboratory of Anthropology, Research Section.

Schiffer, M. B.
1987 *Formation Processes of the Archaeological Record*. Albuquerque, NM: University of New Mexico Press.

Schmorrow, A.
1997 *Fish Remains and Subsistence Changes at the Henderson Site*. Undergraduate honors thesis, Department of Anthropology, University of Michigan, Ann Arbor, MI.

Schroeder, A. H., and D. S. Matson
1965 *A Colony on the Move: Gaspar CastaÒo de Sosa's Journal, 1590-1591*. Santa Fe, NM: School of American Research.

Shinkle, J. D.
1966 *Reminiscences of Roswell Pioneers*. Roswell, NM: Hall-Poorbaugh Press.

Simco, B. A., and F. B. Cross
1966 *Factors Affecting Growth and Production of Channel Catfish,* Ictalurus punctatus. University of Kansas Publication 17(4):191-256. Lawrence, KS: University of Kansas, Museum of Natural History.

Snow, D. H.
1976 Notes from a New Mexico Piscatory. *New Mexico Wildlife* 21(2):11-14.

Sokal, R. R., and F. J. Rohlf
1969 *Biometry: The Principles and Practice of Statistics in Biological Research*. San Francisco, CA: W. H. Freeman.

Speth, J. D.
1991 Some Unexplored Aspects of Mutualistic Plains-Pueblo Food Exchange. In: *Farmers, Hunters, and Colonists: Interaction Between the Southwest and the Southern Plains*, edited by K. A. Spielmann, pp. 18-35. Tucson, AZ: University of Arizona Press.

Speth, J. D., and S. L. Scott
1989 Horticulture and Large-Mammal Hunting: The Role of Resource Depletion and the Constraints of Time and Labor. In: *Farmers as Hunters*, edited by S. Kent, pp. 71-79. New York: Cambridge University Press.

Speth, J. D., and K. A. Spielmann
1983 Energy Source, Protein Metabolism, and Hunter-Gatherer Subsistence Strategies. *Journal of Anthropological Archaeology* 2(1):1-31.

Stickney, R. R., and J. W. Andrews
1971 Combined Effects of Dietary Lipids and Environmental Temperature on Growth, Metabolism and Body Composition of Channel Catfish (*Ictalurus punctatus*). *Journal of Nutrition* 101:1703-1710.

Sublette, J. E., M. D. Hatch, and M. Sublette
1990 *The Fishes of New Mexico*. Albuquerque, NM: University of New Mexico Press.

Wheeler, A., and A. K. G. Jones
1989 *Fishes*. Cambridge: Cambridge University Press.

Wiseman, R. N.
1985 Bison, Fish and Sedentary Occupations: Startling Data from Rocky Arroyo (LA 25277), Chaves County, New Mexico. In: *Views of the Jornada Mogollon: Proceedings of the Second Jornada Mogollon Archaeology Conference*, edited by C. M. Beck, pp. 30-32. Contributions in Anthropology 12. Portales, NM: Eastern New Mexico University Press.
n.d. *The Fox Place (LA 68188), a Late Prehistoric Hunter-Gatherer Pithouse Village Near Roswell, New Mexico*. Manuscript.

Yates, T. L., M. A. Lewis, and M. D. Hatch
1984 Biochemical Systematics of Three Species of Catfish (Genus *Ictalurus*) in New Mexico. *Copeia* 1984(1):97-101.

Appendix to Chapter 11

Henderson Fish Assemblage

Table A11.1. Fish remains (NISP and MNI) from Henderson Site (all proveniences combined, 1980-1981 only).

Taxon	NISP(MNI)	Size-Class[a](MNI)
Semionotiformes		
Longnose Gar (*Lepisosteus osseus*)	1 (1)	Unknown
Cypriniformes		
Carps and Minnows (Cyprinidae)	1 (1)	Unknown
Suckers and Buffalofish (Catostomidae)	35 (2)	1(35-40), 1(40-50)
Smallmouth Buffalo (*Ictiobus bubalus*)	9 (5)	1(30-35), 1(35-40), 1(40-50), 1(50-60), 1(60-70)
Gray Redhorse (*Moxostoma congestum*)	26 (6)	1(25-30), 1(30-35), 1(35-40), 1(40-50), 1(50-60), 1(60-70)
Siluriformes		
Catfishes (Ictaluridae)	395 (38)	1(5-10), 4(10-15), 5(15-20), 5(20-25), 5(25-30), 4(30-35), 1(35-40), 9(20-40), 2(40-50), 1(50-60), 1(70-80)
Catfishes (*Ictalurus* spp.)	285 (35)	5(10-15), 6(15-20), 7(20-25), 7(25-30), 6(30-35), 2(35-40), 1(40-50), 1(50-60)
Headwater Catfish (*Ictalurus lupus*)	23 (12)	2(15-20), 3(20-25), 3(25-30), 3(30-35), 1(35-40)
Channel Catfish (*Ictalurus punctatus*)	21 (5)	1(20-25), 1(25-30), 1(40-50), 1(50-60), 1(60-70)
Headwater/Channel Catfish (*I. lupus/punct.*)	273 (40)	3(10-15), 4(15-20), 8(20-25), 9(25-30), 9(30-35), 4(35-40), 2(40-50), 1(50-60)
Black Bullhead (*Ictalurus melas*)	9 (3)	1(15-20), 1(20-25), 1(25-30)
Flathead Catfish (*Pylodictis olivaris*)	81 (11)	1(20-25), 1(25-30), 1(30-35), 1(35-40), 3(40-50), 1(50-60), 1(60-70), 1(70-80), 1(80-90)
Total Ictalurids	1087 (60)	1(5-10), 8(10-15), 10(15-20), 8(20-25), 10(25-30), 9(30-35), 5(35-40), 5(40-50), 1(50-60), 1(60-70), 1(70-80), 1(80-90)
Perciformes		
Basses, Sunfishes, etc. (Perciformes)	6 (3)	2(0-20), 1(20-40)
White Bass (*Morone chrysops*)	1 (1)	1(25-30)
Spotted Bass (*Micropterus puntulatus*)	1 (1)	1(25-30)
Sunfishes (*Lepomis* spp.)	3 (3)	1(10-15), 1(15-20), 1(20-25)
Indeterminate		
Non-Identifiable	677 (-)	
TOTAL	1847 (78)	

[a]Standard length.

Table A11.2. Fish remains (NISP and MNI) from Henderson Site (East Plaza).

Taxon	NISP(MNI)	Size-Class[a](MNI)
Semionotiformes		
Longnose Gar (*Lepisosteus osseus*)	0 (0)	
Cypriniformes		
Carps and Minnows (Cyprinidae)	0 (0)	
Suckers and Buffalofish (Catostomidae)	2 (1)	Unknown
Smallmouth Buffalo (*Ictiobus bubalus*)	1 (1)	1(40-50)
Gray Redhorse (*Moxostoma congestum*)	2 (2)	1(35-40), 1(60-70)
Siluriformes		
Catfishes (Ictaluridae)	57 (9)	2(15-20), 1(20-25), 2(25-30), 1(30-35), 1(35-40), 1(40-60), 1(>60)
Catfishes (*Ictalurus* spp.)	41 (8)	1(10-15), 1(15-20), 2(20-25), 1(25-30), 1(30-35), 1(35-40), 1(50-60)
Headwater Catfish (*Ictalurus lupus*)	2 (2)	1(20-25), 1(35-40)
Channel Catfish (*Ictalurus punctatus*)	0 (0)	
Headwater/Channel Catfish (*I. lupus/punct.*)	46 (8)	2(20-25), 2(25-30), 2(30-35), 1(35-40), 1(50-60)
Black Bullhead (*Ictalurus melas*)	3 (2)	1(15-20), 1(20-25)
Flathead Catfish (*Pylodictis olivaris*)	25 (5)	1(30-35), 1(40-50), 1(50-60), 1(60-70), 1(80-90)
Total Ictalurids	174 (15)	1(10-15), 2(15-20), 2(20-25), 2(25-30), 3(30-35), 1(35-40), 1(40-50),
1(50-60), 1(60-70), 1(80-90)		
Perciformes		
Basses, Sunfishes, etc. (Perciformes)	0 (0)	
White Bass (*Morone chrysops*)	0 (0)	
Spotted Bass (*Micropterus puntulatus*)	0 (0)	
Sunfishes (*Lepomis* spp.)	0 (0)	
Indeterminate		
Non-Identifiable	80 (-)	
TOTAL	259 (18)	

[a]Standard length.

Table A11.3. Fish remains (NISP and MNI) from Henderson Site (combined room blocks).

Taxon	NISP(MNI)	Size-Class[a](MNI)
Semionotiformes		
Longnose Gar (*Lepisosteus osseus*)	1 (1)	Unknown
Cypriniformes		
Carps and Minnows (Cyprinidae)	0 (0)	
Suckers and Buffalofish (Catostomidae)	33 (2)	1(35-40), 1(40-50)
Smallmouth Buffalo (*Ictiobus bubalus*)	8 (5)	1(30-35), 1(35-40), 1(40-50), 1(50-60), 1(60-70)
Gray Redhorse (*Moxostoma congestum*)	24 (6)	1(25-30), 1(30-35), 1(35-40), 1(40-50), 1(50-60), 1(60-70)
Siluriformes		
Catfishes (Ictaluridae)	334 (37)	1(5-10), 4(10-15), 5(15-20), 5(20-25), 4(25-30), 4(30-35), 1(35-40), 9(20-40), 2(40-50), 1(50-60), 1(70-80)
Catfishes (*Ictalurus* spp.)	243 (29)	4(10-15), 5(15-20), 6(20-25), 6(25-30), 5(30-35), 2(35-40), 1(40-50)
Headwater Catfish (*Ictalurus lupus*)	21 (11)	2(15-20), 2(20-25), 3(25-30), 3(30-35), 1(35-40)
Channel Catfish (*Ictalurus punctatus*)	21 (5)	1(20-25), 1(25-30), 1(40-50), 1(50-60), 1(60-70)
Headwater/Channel Catfish (*I. lupus/punct.*)	222 (35)	3(10-15), 4(15-20), 6(20-25), 9(25-30), 6(30-35), 4(35-40), 2(40-50), 1(50-60)
Black Bullhead (*Ictalurus melas*)	6 (3)	1(15-20), 1(20-25), 1(25-30)
Flathead Catfish (*Pylodictis olivaris*)	55 (9)	1(20-25), 1(25-30), 1(30-35), 1(35-40), 3(40-50), 1(50-60), 1(70-80)
Total Ictalurids	902 (52)	1(5-10), 7(10-15), 8(15-20), 7(20-25), 10(25-30), 6(30-35), 5(35-40), 5(40-50), 1(50-60), 1(60-70), 1(70-80)
Perciformes		
Basses, Sunfishes, etc. (Perciformes)	6 (3)	2(0-20), 1(20-40)
White Bass (*Morone chrysops*)	1 (1)	1(25-30)
Spotted Bass (*Micropterus puntulatus*)	1 (1)	1(25-30)
Sunfishes (*Lepomis* spp.)	3 (3)	1(10-15), 1(15-20), 1(20-25)
Indeterminate		
Non-Identifiable	594 (-)	
TOTAL	1573 (69)	

[a]Standard length.

12
Seasonality of Catfish Procurement at the Henderson Site

Kristen K. Arntzen
Washington University

John D. Speth
University of Michigan

Introduction

The thousands of bison bones recovered from the Henderson Site (Chapter 4), as well as hundreds of projectile points (Chapter 15), underscore the tremendous importance of large-mammal hunting in the community's economy. The faunal evidence also indicates that bison hunting intensified in the Late phase, after about A.D. 1275, with hunts taking place more frequently, and kills occurring farther, on average, from home. At the same time, the overwhelming predominance of bulls in the assemblage suggests that most, if not all, of the bison hunting took place in the spring; surprisingly absent at Henderson is any clear evidence of fall or winter hunts. Thus, in the fall and winter months either the villagers focused on animal resources other than bison, or the community was partially, or possibly even entirely, abandoned, so that the villagers could pursue bison herds that were too far away from the Pecos Valley to be reached by hunting parties from Henderson.

Seasonality studies of the antelope (Chapter 5), lagomorphs (Chapter 8), and prairie dogs (Chapter 9) also fail to produce clear evidence of late fall or winter procurement, although none of these analyses is precise enough to rule out the possibility that some hunting activity did take place during the colder months of the year. Thus, the mammalian fauna raise the distinct possibility that Henderson, despite its seeming architectural permanence, may not have been occupied year-round, or at least was not occupied year-round by its full contingent of able-bodied adults. In other words, Henderson may have been a semi-sedentary community, fully occupied each year only from sometime in the late winter or early spring until after the fall harvest was in, whereupon many, perhaps all, of its able-bodied adults left home to hunt bison far from the village, and perhaps also to participate in long-distance exchange with Puebloan communities to the west. The presence of above-ground storage rooms at the site (Chapter 4), and the apparent scarcity of clandestine subsurface storage pits in plazas and other non-room contexts (DeBoer 1988), lead us to believe that the community was probably seldom, if ever, completely abandoned. Thus, hunting activities probably did continue year-round at the village, but the faunal remains suggest that the vast majority of the hunting took place between late winter or spring and early fall.

Channel catfish (*Ictalurus punctatus*) remains from Henderson offer another taxon for which seasonality of procurement can be estimated with at least a fair degree of reliability. Over 90% of the nearly 3,000 fish bones recovered from Henderson in the first four seasons of excavation (1980, 1981, 1994, 1995) are from catfish.[1] While at least four different species of catfish are represented (see Chapter 11)—channel catfish (*I. punctatus*), headwater catfish (*I. lupus*), black bullhead (*I. melas*), and flathead catfish (*Pylodictis olivaris*)—the vast majority in fact are channel catfish. The technique for determining season of death is based on the study of growth annuli visible in thin-sections of the pectoral spines, elements that were both numerous and reasonably well preserved at the site. As the following presentation attempts to show, the catfish appear to have been procured primarily during the summer or early fall, perhaps close to harvest time. None of the catfish examined to date appear to have been taken in late fall, winter, or early spring, adding credence to the view that at least a sizeable number of the community's able-bodied members left Henderson each year after the harvest and did not return home until sometime in the latter part of winter or early the following spring.

Seasonality of Catfish Procurement

Fish are particularly amenable to studies of seasonality, because distinct annual growth rings (annuli) form in bony tissues, such as pectoral spines, in response to seasonal changes in water temperature and food availability (e.g., Cailliet et al. 1986; Casteel 1972, 1975a, 1975b, 1976; Morales-Nin 1992). Moreover, growth continues throughout most of their lives with little or no resorption of bony tissues once they are laid down (Casteel 1972:404-5; Wheeler and Jones 1989:154-55).

Thus, in temperate environments where annual variations in water temperature and food availability are reasonably pronounced, fish experience a seasonal growth cycle in which an increase in growth rate is correlated with increasing day length, warming waters, and greater abundance of food (Wheeler and Jones 1989:154). In addition, it is thought that growth is recorded in tissues in increments representing specific, regular intervals of time, perhaps even individual days (Wheeler and Jones 1989:154, and references therein; Osten 1977:6-7). During periods of rapid growth, such as spring and summer, these increments are laid down at greater distances from each other than in periods of slower growth, such as winter, when the accumulation of increments is much denser. It is this differential seasonal deposition of tissue that produces "annuli"—distinctive contrasts in the denseness of small increments that usually mark the transition from warm-weather, rapid-growth seasons, to cooler periods of reduced growth.

These annuli are observable in many elements of the fish skeleton, including scales, vertebrae, otoliths, and pectoral and dorsal spines (e.g., Artz 1980; Cailliet et al. 1986; Cannon 1988; Casteel 1972, 1976; Colley 1990; Marzolf 1955; Monks 1981; Morales-Nin 1992; Rojo 1987; Smith 1983; Van Neer et al. 1993). In studies of seasonality done on catfish, the main element of analysis is the pectoral spine (e.g., Brewer 1987, 1988; Luff and Bailey 2000; Marzolf 1955; Morey 1983; Osten 1977, 1980; Sneed 1951). Bony, and often well preserved, these elements are easy to recognize on archaeological sites and form the sample that we analyzed from the Henderson Site. Dorsal spines offer similar information, and also have a more regular shape in cross-section, but they are generally less sturdy and seem to be found less often in archaeological contexts, or so was the case at Henderson.

It must be noted, however, that other circumstances besides the changing of the seasons can affect the rate of growth in fish, and in turn alter the appearance of annuli (Wheeler and Jones 1989:156-57). The most notable of these is the stress of spawning, in which demands for calcium metabolism by developing gonads may interrupt the regular growth cycle by diverting the deposition of bony tissue. This can result in confusing "false annuli." Scales are particularly susceptible to such stress, but the effects may be observed in other tissues as well (e.g., Marzolf 1955:244). Such limitations, as with any approach to seasonality determination, must be kept in mind.

Season of death using pectoral spines is assessed by determining the ratio of the width of the fraction of the final year's growth completed by the time of capture to the previous full year's growth, as seen in transverse thin-sections of the spines. This ratio or "growth index" is then compared to values determined using spines from modern catfish of known season of capture. Obviously, to maximize the reliability of this technique, the modern spines should derive not only from the same species of catfish, but also from the same general environment as the archaeological specimens. Unfortunately, at this stage of the research in southeastern New Mexico, we have not yet established a modern comparative series for channel catfish, and have had to rely instead on data published by Morey (1983) for this same species from similar latitudes in the southeastern U.S. While less than ideal, Morey's data provide a reasonable first approximation that can be modified by future research in New Mexico.

Morey used modern comparative data to derive a regression equation which he could then use to predict the season of death of archaeological specimens. However, Morey's initial plot of the growth index against date of death displayed a substantial expansion of the error variance with time of death. To stabilize the error variance, Morey (1983:80-83) transformed the growth indices using a technique known as "Taylor's power law," in which each index value was raised to a power based on a slope coefficient derived by regression (the power value was .363 in Morey's analysis). The regression generated using the transformed data is the one Morey then used to interpret his archaeological specimens, and we use the same regression here to interpret the Henderson material.

Preparing and Measuring the Thin Sections

Before discussing the results, the procedures we employed for preparing and measuring the thin sections deserve comment. When we first began the project, we adopted methods that are widely used for making petrographic thin sections. Unfortunately, when applied to nonfossilized but weathered archaeological bone, these procedures did not work well, forcing us to experiment with alternative means for sectioning and mounting the specimens (see Arntzen 1995 for a more detailed discussion of these problems and our solutions to them).

We followed Sneed (1951) and Marzolf (1955:243, Fig. 1) in sectioning the pectoral spines at the distal end of the basal recess or groove (see Fig. 12.1). Spines were cut using a Buehler Isomet low-speed wafering saw. After making the initial cut, the spine was embedded in a mold using Castolite-AC clear casting plastic resin and hardener. The Castolite was allowed to set at room temperature for twenty-four hours and then removed from the mold cup. Next, the Castolite block with embedded spine was ground using a slurry of water and 400-size (400 par-

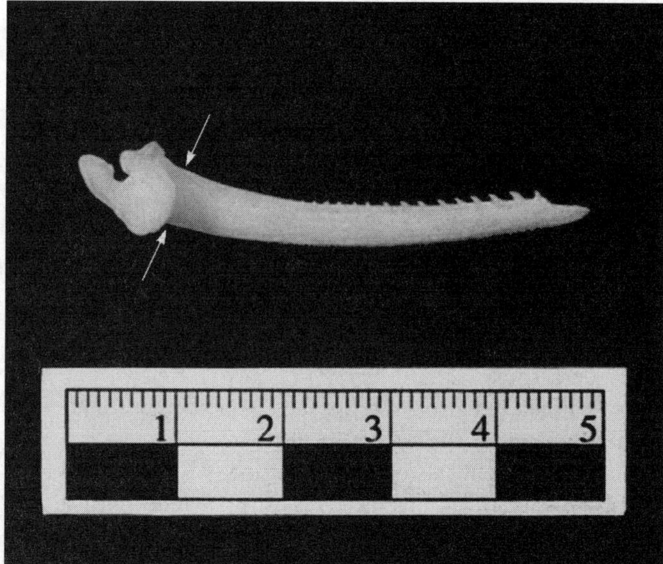

Figure 12.1. Modern channel catfish pectoral spine showing location of thin section.

ticles per cm) silicon carbide grit on a low-speed lap wheel. When the entire sectioned face of the spine was smooth and free of striations made by the saw, the block was ground manually on a glass plate with 600-size grit in a water slurry. The Castolite block was then mounted on a glass slide using Hillquist epoxy. The mounted slide was kept at 100° F for the first half-hour in order to initiate curing; it was then allowed to set for twenty-four hours at room temperature. The block was then cut off using the low-speed saw, leaving a section with a thickness between 500 and 1,000μ (1 mm) attached to the slide. The section was ground down on a lap wheel to around 200μ using 400-size grit in a water slurry. The final thinning was done by hand on a glass plate using 600-size grit in a water slurry. The section was then brought to a glassy polish using 5μ grit and kerosene on a high-speed, cloth-covered polishing wheel.

One difficulty became apparent the moment we attempted to cut the spines. Most were quite fragile and splintered during the cutting process. To prevent such splintering at the key point for observing the annuli, spines were pre-cut at a point proximal to the desired plane of the final thin section. They were then embedded in Castolite before the remainder of the basal groove was cut off and the Castolite block prepared for mounting. This procedure, of course, significantly increased preparation time, as it takes much longer to cut through one inch of hardened plastic than through a thin piece of porous bone, but kept the spine from splintering.

Other difficulties also became apparent. For example, during the final cleaning of the thin sections just prior to using the high-speed polisher, the Castolite peeled away from some of the slides because the epoxy bond had not cured adequately. To achieve a stronger bond, subsequent specimens were allowed to cure for a minimum of three days before sectioning.

In addition, the bond that formed between the spines and the surrounding Castolite resin was also inadequate. Apparently the water used in grinding, polishing, and cleaning the specimens caused the archaeological bone to swell in the Castolite. Since the Castolite is a solid unyielding material, the spine forced its way up and out of the surrounding plastic once the entire section had been ground thin enough. To allay this problem, we substituted kerosene in all steps where we had previously used water, as kerosene does not cause the expansion that water does when drawn into porous bone.

We also found that the Castolite had not infused thoroughly into the porous structure of some of the spines. This was evidenced by distorted visual properties of the Castolite near the spine and, in some cases, actual gaps between plastic and bone. The presence of air and traces of kerosene within the porous bone may have prevented the Castolite from fully penetrating. To remove any residual kerosene, we placed the spines in an acetone bath for several hours, or even overnight, prior to embedding. In order to force Castolite into the pores within the spines, we placed the specimens in a vacuum for about two minutes. This caused the air in the bone to first expand and bubble, but when the pressure under the pump was returned to normal, the air contracted again, pulling Castolite into the pores.

Embedding specimens in a vacuum helped in many cases but not all, for in some the Castolite still pulled away from the spine as it set. Because of this, we finally abandoned the use of Castolite altogether, turning instead to commercial epoxy as an embedding medium (see also Kaminski et al. 1990). To prevent bubbles from forming, embedding was again done under a vacuum, reducing the pressure for two minutes and then bringing it back to normal.

One final problem should be noted. The archaeological spines were considerably softer than either the Castolite or the commercial epoxy in which they were embedded. Thus, when they were ground and polished using loose grit, particularly the larger 400-size, the bone was reduced faster than the surrounding embedding medium. This created a small recess at the point where the spine was exposed on the surface, and the grit would accumulate there, exacerbating the effect. To avoid this, we substituted grit paper (like sandpaper, but with carbide grit of the necessary size) for loose grit. This somewhat lengthened the time needed for reducing the sections to the desired thickness, but helped to preserve the specimens within the embedding matrix. Final polishing was still done using the cloth-covered wheel and loose 5μ grit.

Once prepared, the thin sections were viewed under normal illumination with a Leitz Laborlux 12 Pol light microscope. Annuli measurements were made along the postero-dorsal and anterior axis or radius (see Sneed 1951; Marzolf 1955; Morey 1983). These measurements were used to calculate the raw growth indices, which were then transformed according to the procedures outlined by Morey (1983). Measurements were taken using an ocular micrometer that was calibrated to a stage micrometer.

A slight change was made in the method of measuring growth increments. Unlike Morey's (1983) schematic of a pectoral spine

Table 12.1. Transformed "growth indices" derived from measurements of thin sections of catfish (*Ictalurus punctatus*) pectoral spines from the Henderson Site.

Lot No.	Grid North	Grid East	Upper Elevation (m)	Lower Elevation (m)	Side	Age	Transformed Growth Index[a]		Radius of Postero-dorsal Lobe[b]	Fish Length (mm)	Comments
							Postero-dorsal (Large) Lobe	Anterior Lobe			
1194	515	535	100.90	100.70	Right	4+	5.72	5.93	164.75	205	
0851	516	535	101.00	100.80	Right	4+?	5.95	6.40	214.56	270	
0850	515	535	101.10	100.90	Left	5+	4.85	4.21	268.20	351	
1472	516	533	101.35	101.10	Right	5+?	4.41	3.85	214.56	270	
1064	511	547	100.20	100.10	Left	5+	N/A	4.94	N/A	N/A	
1523	513	534	100.85	100.72	Right	5+?	4.46	3.61	160.92	205	
0286	516	534	101.20	101.00	Right	4+?	3.16	3.69	222.22	267	
1775	525	565	101.30	101.25	Right	3+	4.53	4.69	214.56	270	
0941	511	550	100.00	99.90	Right	4+	4.65	4.60	199.23	242	Displayed false annulus
1732a	517	534	100.95	100.85	Right	4-5+	N/A	4.90	N/A	N/A	More proximal section
1732b	517	534	100.95	100.85	Right	4-5+	4.60	4.96	206.90	252	More distal section
1355	507	550	100.00	99.90	Right	4+?	N/A	4.64	218.01	270	
0652	527	567	101.21	101.20	Right	3+?	4.76	3.65	206.90	252	
1173	517	533	101.05	100.95	Right	4+	4.91	4.78	245.21	300	Displayed false annulus
1426	508	550	99.90	99.80	Left	5+	4.68	5.32	199.23	242	Displayed false annulus

[a]See Morey (1983:80-83).
[b]mm × 100.

thin section, the annuli in the Henderson specimens were very thin and light when viewed under the microscope. Changes in luminosity that produced the annuli were gradual, and in most cases it was an arbitrary decision as to where each annulus began. Much clearer, however, was the contrast between the outer edge of the annulus and the darker bone representing the resumption of rapid growth.

Thus, in order to make more consistent measurements, we decided to measure yearly growth increments from the outer edge of one annulus to the outer edge of the next. This method will always result in a smaller measurement for the last partial year of growth than does Morey's method, as it does not include the last complete annulus, while his method does. The measurement of the last complete year of growth would be essentially the same using either method, though, as both include one annulus (Morey's measurement starts with the second to last complete annulus while ours ends with the last complete annulus). Thus, growth indices calculated using our approach will be smaller than if the measurements had followed Morey's procedure, and in turn the date of death may be underpredicted.

The actual magnitude of this discrepancy, however, is small. Henderson's annuli are very thin; hence, error in estimation works out to be only a few weeks at most—outside the resolution of the model. In addition, this underprediction may be counterbalanced by another discrepancy that could lead to slight overprediction when using the model. This discrepancy is the difference in latitude between the area of origin of Morey's modern sample (Tennessee and Kentucky), and southeastern New Mexico—nearly four degrees. When Morey applied his model to archaeological specimens from Nebraska, he suggested that the growing season might start later in more northerly latitudes, and proposed adding an extra few weeks to his estimates of seasonality in order to avoid underprediction (1983:91-92). An adjustment of this sort might also be appropriate for seasonality estimates of the Henderson pectoral spines, only in this case one might expect the growing season to start sooner than for the specimens in Morey's model. Perhaps a correction factor in which a few weeks were subtracted from predictions would be in order. However, given the many other potential sources of error in the model, it is probably not prudent to consider adjustments of this sort. It is merely suggested that the slight underprediction of date of death for the Henderson specimens resulting from minor differences in measurement techniques might be counterbalanced by overprediction in date of death due to latitudinal differences.

In addition to taking measurements from the large posterior lobe of the thin section, we also recorded growth increments in the anterior portion of the spine (see Table 12.1). This area has promise for allowing more consistent measurements, as it is generally more symmetrical in shape than either posterior lobe. It is not certain, however, if results comparable in reliability to those from the large posterior lobe can be obtained from this region.

We also determined the age of each specimen. In several cases, however, it was difficult to tell whether the central lumen had absorbed all of the first year's growth, thus making the second year's annulus the first visible line, or if the first year's growth was only partially resorbed and the first line seen was actually the first annulus. In either case, the estimated age for each specimen is not likely to be off by more than one year.

Finally, we estimated the length of each fish, based on the radius of the pectoral spine at the point of sectioning, following procedures outlined by Sneed (1951) and Marzolf (1955). These authors measured the radii of spines from the center of the lumen to the outer edge of the large posterior lobe. Sneed (1951:177, Table 1) produced a detailed table giving the average total length of fish for each of thirty-two divisions of spine radius. This table allowed us to estimate the length of the Henderson catfish from the radii of their thin-sectioned pectoral spines.

Results and Discussion

In all, nineteen thin sections with intact posterior lobes, all dating to Henderson's Late phase (see Chapter 2), were analyzed. Four of these, unfortunately, produced aberrant results and were rejected, their final year's growth already having exceeded the previous year's without formation of a visible annulus. However, the remaining 15 thin sections, from 14 different spines, fall in a surprisingly tight cluster along Morey's regression line (see Table 12.1 and Fig. 12.2). All fall between the months of June and October, with 9 of the 14 (64%) grouped in the two months of August and September. None fall between the months of November and May. Given the many uncertainties and assumptions involved in these seasonality determinations, not to mention the relatively small number of thin sections that have been analyzed to date, one should not view these results as definitive. But they are surprisingly congruent with the seasonality patterning indicated by the bison, antelope, lagomorphs, and prairie dogs: all point to a concentration of hunting activity between spring and late summer or early fall, and a much lower level of hunting, or possibly none at all, following the harvest (see Chapters 4-9).

How might one account for this tight clustering of fishing activity in the late summer or early fall? Why not a more uniform distribution spanning much or all of the year? Two principal factors may be involved in this unexpected result. First, catfish are particularly easy to catch during times of rising water levels (e.g., Koster 1957:75; Davis 1959:7-8). Peak stream flow in the Hondo probably occurred at two principal times during the year, once in the spring, when snow melt in the Sacramento Mountains swelled the downstream reaches of the river, the second toward the end of the summer when monsoonal thunderstorms once again increased the level of runoff. Thus, we might expect the seasonal distribution of fishing to be distinctly bimodal, with one peak in the spring, the other in late summer. The scarcity or absence of catfishing during the first of these two high-water periods is therefore perplexing. One possible scenario to account for this unexpected absence is that conflicts in scheduling may have arisen between fishing and spring-season agricultural activities, such as field preparation, planting, and early weeding. Conflicts may also have arisen between fishing and intensive hunting focused on bison, antelope, and rabbits, activities that may have taken place in conjunction with important community-wide rituals and ceremonies (e.g., communal rabbit drives). During the second period of high runoff in late summer, scheduling conflicts may have been reduced as bison, antelope, and rabbit hunting tapered off; more effort could then be devoted to catfishing until the time and labor demands of the harvest once again created serious scheduling conflicts (Speth and Scott 1989). An explanation based on putative scheduling conflicts is not very compelling, however, since it would appear that most catfish were caught using some form of baited trap, a "passive" technology that by its very nature would have minimized scheduling conflicts.

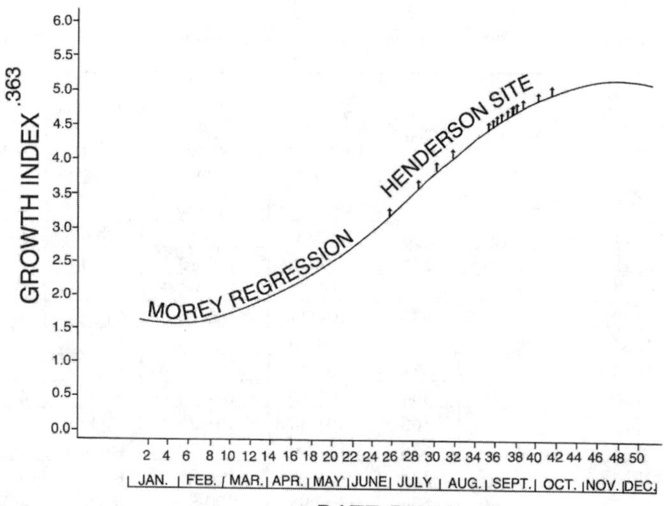

Figure 12.2. Plot of Morey's (1983:82) regression of transformed pectoral spine growth index by date of death for modern channel catfish (*Ictalurus punctatus*) from the southeastern U.S. showing transformed growth index values for Henderson Site specimens.

The second and probably more important reason for the apparent concentration of fishing activity in the late summer is the fact that this species is one the fattest freshwater fishes in North America, comparing in caloric yield to salmon and eel (e.g., Atwater 1891; Clark and Clough 1926; Jaramillo et al. 1994; Kim and Lovell 1995; Magee 1976; Murray et al. 1977; Mustafa and Medeiros 1985; Nettleton et al. 1990; Nettleton and Exler 1992; Page and Andrews 1973; Stickney and Andrews 1971). Prior to the harvest, many ethnographically documented small-scale farming communities experience food shortages (Cadeliña 1982; Dugdale and Payne 1987; Huss-Ashmore et al. 1989; Nurse 1968; Ogbu 1973; Speth 1991; Wandel and Holmboe-Ottesen 1992). Resources stored over the winter and spring are often in short supply by late summer, while labor demands associated with gardening are on the increase. Catfish and prairie dogs (another species with considerable body fat in late summer; see Chapter 9), therefore, may have been critical resources for the villagers, helping to "tide them over" until the arrival of a successful harvest.

Conclusions

Preliminary thin-section analysis of catfish pectoral spines from the Henderson Site in southeastern New Mexico has revealed a pattern emphasizing late summer procurement. These results add further credence to the view that Henderson, despite its permanent Puebloan-style architecture, was a semi-sedentary community, occupied between planting and harvest and then partially, perhaps entirely, abandoned for the remainder of the year. The targeting of catfish, a calorically rich food source, prior to the harvest may have been a strategy employed by the villagers to sustain them until the maize harvest was in. This was also a time of year when catfish may have been particularly easy to catch, because of high water levels in the Hondo River, and when their procurement did not seriously conflict with other critical subsistence or ceremonial activities. The possibility of late prehistoric semi-sedentism in the Pecos Valley, in the context of considerable architectural investment, may have significance for examining anew the links between architectural permanence and occupational mobility elsewhere in the Southwest.

Synopsis

Seasonality studies of bison, antelope, rabbits, and prairie dogs fail to produce evidence of late fall or winter procurement, although these analyses are not sufficiently precise to rule out the possibility that some hunting activity did take place during the colder months of the year. Thus, the mammalian fauna raise the possibility that Henderson, despite its seeming architectural permanence, may not have been occupied year-round, or at least was not occupied year-round by its full contingent of able-bodied adults. The presence of above-ground storage rooms at the site, and the scarcity of clandestine subsurface storage pits in non-room contexts, lead us to believe that the community was probably seldom, if ever, completely abandoned. Thus, hunting activities probably did continue year-round at Henderson, but the faunal remains suggest that most hunting took place between late winter or spring and early fall.

At Henderson, channel catfish (*Ictalurus punctatus*) are amenable to studies of seasonality because annual growth rings (annuli) form in their pectoral spines in response to seasonal changes in water temperature and food availability. During periods of rapid growth, such as spring and summer, these increments are laid down at greater distances from each other than in periods of slower growth, such as winter, when the accumulation of increments is much denser. This seasonal deposition of tissue produces "annuli," distinctive contrasts in the denseness of small increments that usually mark the transition from warm-weather, rapid-growth seasons, to cooler periods of reduced growth.

Season of death using pectoral spines is assessed by determining the ratio of the width of the fraction of the final year's growth completed by the time of capture to the previous full year's growth, as seen in transverse thin sections of the spines. This ratio or "growth index" should then be compared to values determined using spines from modern catfish of known season of capture. Unfortunately, we have not yet established a modern comparative series for New Mexican channel catfish, and have had to rely instead on data published by Morey (1983) for this same species from similar latitudes in the southeastern U.S. Morey's data provide a reasonable first approximation that can be modified by future research in the Southwest.

Using modern comparative data, Morey derived a regression equation which he could use to predict the season of death of archaeological specimens. However, his initial plot of the growth index against date of death displayed substantial expansion of the error variance with time of death. To stabilize the error variance, Morey transformed the growth indices using "Taylor's power law," in which each index value was raised to the .363 power. We use the same regression to interpret the Henderson material.

We sectioned the pectoral spines at the distal end of the basal recess or groove. We then made numerous unsuccessful attempts to mount the cut specimens in Castolite, a clear casting plastic resin and hardener commonly used as an embedding medium in thin-section work. The Castolite did not fully infuse the archaeological spines with plastic and often pulled away from the specimen. After much experimentation, we found that we had to use kerosene instead of water in all stages of cutting, grinding, and polishing; commercial epoxy rather than Castolite as the embedding medium; and that embedding had to be done under a vacuum. Once these procedures were incorporated into the thin-sectioning process, we were able to obtain stable mounts that could be cut to between 100 and 200μ, allowing us to observe the growth annuli with reasonable clarity.

In all, nineteen thin sections, all dating to Henderson's Late phase, were analyzed. Four of these produced aberrant results and were rejected. However, the remaining 15 thin sections, from 14 different spines, fall in a surprisingly tight cluster along Morey's regression line. All fall between the months of June and October, with 9 of the 14 grouped in the two months of August and September. None fall between the months of November and May. These results are surprisingly congruent with the seasonality patterning indicated by the bison, antelope, lagomorphs, and prairie dogs: all point to a concentration of hunting activity between spring and late summer or early fall, and a much lower level of hunting, or possibly none at all, following the harvest.

How might one account for this tight clustering of fishing activity in the late summer or early fall, rather than a more uniform distribution spanning much or all of the year? We might expect the seasonal distribution of fishing to be bimodal, with one peak in the spring, the other in late summer, times of rising water levels when catfish are most easily caught. The scarcity or absence of catfishing during the first of these periods is therefore perplexing. One possible scenario to account for this unexpected absence is that conflicts in scheduling may have arisen between fishing and spring-season agricultural activities, such as field preparation, planting, and early weeding. Conflicts may also have arisen between fishing and intensive hunting focused on bison, antelope, and rabbits, activities that may have taken place in conjunction with important community-wide rituals and ceremonies. During the second period of high runoff, in late summer, scheduling conflicts may have been reduced as bison, antelope, and rabbit hunting tapered off; more effort could then be devoted to catfishing until the time and labor demands of the harvest once again created serious scheduling conflicts.

A more important reason for the apparent concentration of fishing activity in the late summer may be that this species is one the fattest freshwater fishes in North America, comparable in caloric yield to salmon and eel. Prior to the harvest, many ethnographically documented small-scale farming communities experience food shortages. Resources stored over the winter and spring are often in short supply by late summer, while labor demands associated with gardening arc on the increase. Catfish may have been a critical resource for the villagers, helping to "tide them over" until the arrival of a successful harvest.

Acknowledgments

We thank Daniel Fisher and Bill Sanders for generously providing us the use of their labs, and for their invaluable help in working out suitable methods for embedding the spines.

Note

1. The fish bones recovered in 1997 have not been inventoried as yet.

References Cited

Arntzen, K. K.
1995 *Support for Semi-Sedentism at the Late Prehistoric Henderson Site (LA-1549): Evidence from Analysis of Catfish Pectoral Spine Thin-Sections*. Honors thesis, Department of Anthropology, University of Michigan, Ann Arbor, MI.

Artz, J. A.
1980 Inferring Season of Occupation from Fish Scales: An Archaeological Approach. *Plains Anthropologist* 25(87):47-61.

Atwater, W. O.
1891 *The Chemical Composition and Nutritive Values of Food Fishes and Aquatic Invertebrates*. Report of the U.S. Commissioner of Fisheries for 1888:679-868. Washington, DC: Government Printing Office.

Brewer, D. J.
1987 Seasonality in the Prehistoric Faiyum Based on the Incremental Growth Structures of the Nile Catfish (Pisces: *Clarias*). *Journal of Archaeological Science* 14(5):459-72.
1988 A Comment on Methodology and Seasonality of the Nile Catfish in the Prehistoric Faiyum. *Journal of Archaeological Science* 15(5):583-85.

Cadeliña, R. V.
1982 *Batak Interhousehold Food Sharing: A Systematic Analysis of Food Management of Marginal Agriculturalists in the Philippines*. Ph.D. dissertation, University of Hawaii, Honolulu, HI.

Cailliet, G. M., M. S. Love, and A. W. Ebeling
1986 *Fishes: A Field and Laboratory Manual on Their Structure, Identification, and Natural History*. Belmont, CA: Wadsworth Publishing Company.

Cannon, A.
1988 Radiographic Age Determination of Pacific Salmon: Species and Seasonal Inferences. *Journal of Field Archaeology* 15(1):103-8.

Casteel, R. W.
1972 Some Archaeological Uses of Fish Remains. *American Antiquity* 37(3):404-19.
1975a Estimation of Size, Minimum Numbers of Individuals, and Seasonal Dating by Means of Fish Scales from Archaeological Sites. In: *Archaeozoological Studies*, edited by A. T. Clason, pp. 70-86. Amsterdam: North-Holland Publishing Company.
1975b On the Remains of Fish Scales from Archaeological Sites. *American Antiquity* 39(4):557-81.
1976 *Fish Remains in Archaeology*. New York: Academic Press.

Clark, E. D., and R. W. Clough
1926 Chemical Composition of Fish and Shellfish. In: *Nutritive Value of Fish and Shellfish*. Department of Commerce, Bureau of Fisheries, Appendix X to the Report of the U.S. Commissioner of Fisheries for 1925, Bureau of Fisheries Document 1000, Technological Contribution 27:502-26. Washington, DC: Government Printing Office.

Colley, S. M.
1990 The Analysis and Interpretation of Archaeological Fish Remains. *Archaeological Method and Theory* 2:207-53.

Davis, J.
1959 *Management of Channel Catfish in Kansas*. Miscellaneous Publication 21. Lawrence, KS: University of Kansas, Museum of Natural History.

DeBoer, W. R.
1988 Subterranean Storage and the Organization of Surplus: The View from Eastern North America. *Southeastern Archaeology* 7(1):1-20.

Dugdale, A. E., and P. R. Payne
1987 A Model of Seasonal Changes in Energy Balance. *Ecology of Food and Nutrition* 19(3):231-45.

Huss-Ashmore, R., J. J. Curry, and R. K. Hitchcock (editors)
1989 *Coping With Seasonal Constraints*. MASCA Research Papers in Science and Archaeology 5. Philadelphia, PA: University of Pennsylvania, The University Museum, MASCA.

Jaramillo, F., S. C. Bai, B. R. Murphy, and D. M. Gatlin
1994 Application of Electrical Conductivity for Non-destructive Measurement of Channel Catfish, *Ictalurus punctatus*, Body Composition. *Aquatic Living Resources* 7(2):87-91.

Kaminski, M. T., E. J. Peters, and R. S. Holland
1990 Pectoral-Spine Embedding to Facilitate Sectioning for Age Analysis of Young Channel Catfish (*Ictalurus punctatus*). *Transactions of the Nebraska Academy of Sciences* 18:99-100.

Kim, M. K., and R. T. Lovell
1995 Effect of Overwinter Feeding Regimen on Body Weight, Body Composition and Resistance to *Edwardsiella ictaluri* in Channel Catfish, *Ictalurus punctatus. Aquaculture* 134:237-46.

Koster, W. J.
1957 *Guide to the Fishes of New Mexico.* Albuquerque, NM: University of New Mexico Press.

Luff, R. M., and G. N. Bailey
2000 Analysis of Size Changes and Incremental Growth Structures in African Catfish *Synodontis schall* (schall) from Tell el-Amarna, Middle Egypt. *Journal of Archaeological Science* 27(9):821-35.

Magee, J. B.
1976 *Some Effects of Size, Source and Season of Harvest on Nutritional Composition of Catfish.* Ph.D. dissertation, Food Science and Technology, Mississippi State University, Mississippi State, MS.

Marzolf, R. C.
1955 Use of Pectoral Spines and Vertebrae for Determining Age and Growth of the Channel Catfish. *Journal of Wildlife Management* 19:243-49.

Monks, G. G.
1981 Seasonality Studies. In: *Advances in Archaeological Method and Theory*, Vol. 4, edited by M. B. Schiffer, pp. 177-240. New York: Academic Press.

Morales-Nin, B.
1992 *Determination of Growth in Bony Fishes from Otolith Microstructure.* FAO Fisheries Technical Paper 322. Rome, Italy: United Nations, Food and Agriculture Organization.

Morey, D. F.
1983 Archaeological Assessment of Seasonality from Freshwater Fish Remains: A Quantitative Procedure. *Journal of Ethnobiology* 3(1):75-95.

Murray, M. W., J. W. Andrews, and H. L. DeLoach
1977 Effects of Dietary Lipids, Dietary Protein and Environmental Temperatures on Growth, Feed Conversion and Body Composition of Channel Catfish. *Journal of Nutrition* 107:272-80.

Mustafa, F. A., and D. M. Medeiros
1985 Proxiпate Composition, Mineral Content, and Fatty Acids of Catfish (*Ictalurus punctatus*, Rafinesque) for Different Seasons and Cooking Methods. *Journal of Food Science* 50(3):585-88.

Nettleton, J. A., W. H. Allen, L. V. Klatt, W. M. N. Ratnayake, and R. G. Ackman
1990 Nutrients and Chemical Residues in One- to-Two-Pound Mississippi Farm-Raised Channel Catfish (*Ictalurus punctatus*). *Journal of Food Science* 55(4):954-58.

Nettleton, J. A., and J. Exler
1992 Nutrients in Wild and Farmed Fish and Shellfish. *Journal of Food Science* 57(2):257-60.

Nurse, G. T.
1968 Seasonal Fluctuations in the Body Weight of African Villagers. *Central African Journal of Medicine* 14:122-27, 147-50.

Ogbu, J.
1973 Seasonal Hunger in Tropical Africa as a Cultural Phenomenon: The Onicha Ibo of Nigeria and the Chakka Poka of Malawi Examples. *Africa* 43:317-32.

Osten, L. W.
1977 *The Use of the Pectoral Fin Spines of Channel Catfish* (Ictalurus punctatus) *in Order to Estimate Paleoclimates.* Master's thesis, Department of Geology, Southern Methodist University, Dallas, TX.
1980 An Estimate of the Climate Along the Nile Valley between 18,000 and 14,000 B.P. Based on Pectoral Fin Spines of Catfish. In: *Loaves and Fishes: The Prehistory of Wadi Kubbaniya*, edited by F. Wendorf, R. Schild, and A. E. Close, pp. 331-34. Dallas, TX: Southern Methodist University.

Page, J. W., and J. W. Andrews
1973 Interactions of Dietary Levels of Protein and Energy on Channel Catfish (*Ictalurus punctatus*). *Journal of Nutrition* 103(9):1339-46.

Rojo, A. L.
1987 Excavated Fish Vertebrae as Predictors in Bioarchaeological Research. *North American Archaeologist* 8(3):209-26.

Smith, H. A.
1983 Determination of Seasonality in Archaeological Sites through Examination of Fish Otoliths: A Case Study. *Journal of Field Archaeology* 10(4):498-500.

Sneed, K. E.
1951 A Method for Calculating the Growth of Channel Catfish, *Ictalurus lacustris punctatus. Transactions of the American Fisheries Society* 80:174-83.

Speth, J. D.
1991 Some Unexplored Aspects of Mutualistic Plains-Pueblo Food Exchange. In: *Farmers, Hunters, and Colonists: Interaction Between the Southwest and the Southern Plains*, edited by K. A. Spielmann, pp. 18-35. Tucson, AZ: University of Arizona Press.

Speth, J. D., and S. L. Scott
1989 Horticulture and Large-Mammal Hunting: The Role of Resource Depletion and the Constraints of Time and Labor. In: *Farmers as Hunters*, edited by S. Kent, pp. 71-79. New York, NY: Cambridge University Press.

Stickney, R. R., and J. W. Andrews
1971 Combined Effects of Dietary Lipids and Environmental Temperature on Growth, Metabolism and Body Composition of Channel Catfish (*Ictalurus punctatus*). *Journal of Nutrition* 101:1703-10.

Van Neer, W., S. Augustynen, and T. Linkowski
1993 Daily Growth Increments on Fish Otoliths as Seasonality Indicators on Archaeological Sites: The Tilapia from Late Palaeolithic Makhadma in Egypt. *International Journal of Osteoarchaeology* 3:241248.

Wandel, M., and G. Holmboe-Ottesen
1992 Food Availability and Nutrition in a Seasonal Perspective: A Study from the Rukwa Region in Tanzania. *Human Ecology* 20(1):89-107.

Wheeler, A., and A. K. G. Jones
1989 *Fishes*. Cambridge, England: Cambridge University Press.

13
Freshwater Mollusks
A Source of Food or Just Ornaments?

John D. Speth
University of Michigan

Tatum M. McKay

The Henderson Bivalve Assemblage (1980-1981)

The total sample of 1980-1981 bivalve remains consists of 1,403 pieces (NISP), including a minimum of 264 hinge/umbo fragments (Table 13.1). Only two complete shells were encountered. The larger of these, measuring about 11.5 cm in length by 7.0 cm in breadth, came from the East Bar and had clearly been used as a tool (see Fig. 13.3 below). The other, measuring 10.7 cm by 6.5 cm, came from the Center Bar and showed no obvious evidence of either use or modification. An additional 33 specimens comprise at least a third or more of a complete valve. Most of the remaining 1,368 fragments are very small, with many of the pieces <1 cm in maximum length. The average weight per fragment is only 1.24 g.

Ninety-three of the specimens are complete enough to identify to taxon. All of these are from a single freshwater Unionacean species, *Cyrtonaias tampicoensis* (Fuller 1975; Metcalf 1982). Seventeen specimens were probably not from this species, but were too fragmentary for more precise identification. Most of the remaining pieces, though too small to be assigned to species, very likely derive from *C. tampicoensis*.

Metcalf (1982:52) notes that *C. tampicoensis* today is restricted to the lower Rio Grande and the lowermost reaches of the Pecos River in Texas, but that until about 3,000 years B.P. its distribution extended well up the Pecos into southeastern New Mexico. Since the publication of Metcalf's synthesis, the recovery of *C. tampicoensis* from several late prehistoric archaeological sites in the Roswell area (e.g., Henderson, Rocky Arroyo, Fox Place, Townsend) demonstrates that this species of bivalve remained common as far north as Chaves County until at least the end of the thirteenth century, if not later (Regge N. Wiseman, pers. comm.; Maxwell 1986).

Although we did not examine the Henderson material with the explicit goal of determining the number of individuals represented, the site-wide MNI value can at least be approximated. There are many hinge/umbo fragments that are <2 cm in length. When broken into small fragments, a moderately large *C. tampicoensis* valve would produce four to six such pieces. Dividing the total number of hinge/umbo fragments ($n = 264$) by either 4 or 6, we arrive at a range of 44 to 66 valves, or 22 to 33 individuals.

The number of valves, and individuals, in the Henderson collection can be estimated in another way, as well. The total weight of all of the shell fragments recovered from the site is 1,739.7 g. The complete shell from the East Bar noted earlier, one of the largest specimens in the collection, weighs 56.5 g. If all of the shells weighed this amount when they were complete, there would be at least 31 valves or 16 individuals represented in the collection. Many shell fragments clearly derive from smaller valves, though, so the true number of individuals must be greater. While we cannot determine the original valve weight of the broken shells, many derive from individuals that were between about a third and half the size of the East Bar specimen. Thus, if we reduce the 56.5 g figure by these amounts, we get a range of between 46 and 62 valves, or 23-31 individuals. These figures are similar to those derived from estimates of the number of hinge/umbo fragments, and suggest that the fragmentary shells recovered at Henderson represent the remains of between 20 and 40 mollusks. A figure of 30 individuals will be used in subsequent discussion.

Given that the average weight of the shell fragments at Henderson is barely 1.25 g, it is clear that the valves have been broken up into many very tiny pieces. The average, in fact, is about 50 fragments per valve (based on a total NISP of 1,403

Table 13.1. Freshwater mollusk shell remains by provenience from the Henderson Site (1980-1981 only).[a]

Provenience	Total Shell	Valve Part				Burned		Valve Symmetry				Utilized Margin		Mean Weight[b] (g)
		Hinge/Umbo		Body				Left		Right				
	NISP	NISP	%	NISP	%	NISP	%	NISP	%	NISP	%	NISP	%	Mean±1σ
Site (all proveniences)	1403	264	18.8	1139	81.2	83	5.9	137	49.6	139	50.4	7	0.5	1.24±3.61
Combined room blocks	892	155	17.4	737	82.6	26	2.9	75	48.4	80	51.6	3	0.3	1.09±3.39
East Bar	347	64	18.4	283	81.6	11	3.2	29	42.6	39	57.4	1	0.3	1.18±4.28
East Plaza (B/C)	417	88	21.1	329	78.9	53	12.7	52	52.0	48	48.0	3	0.7	1.66±4.38
East Plaza (D)	43	10	23.3	33	76.7	2	4.7	5	50.0	5	50.0	1	2.3	0.92±1.43
Center Bar	545	91	16.7	454	83.3	15	2.8	46	52.9	41	47.1	2	0.4	0.99±2.58
Ring midden	2	—	—	2	100.0	—	—	—	—	—	—	-	—	0.06±0.03

[a]All identifiable specimens are freshwater Unionidae bivalves of the species *Cyrtonaias tampicoensis* (Lea, 1838); most if not all of the smaller fragments tabulated here are believed to derive from this same species; identifications of complete or nearly complete valves made by John B. Burch, Museum of Zoology, University of Michigan.

[b]Tiny shell fragments with weights less than 0.01 g were arbitrarily assigned a weight of 0.001 g.

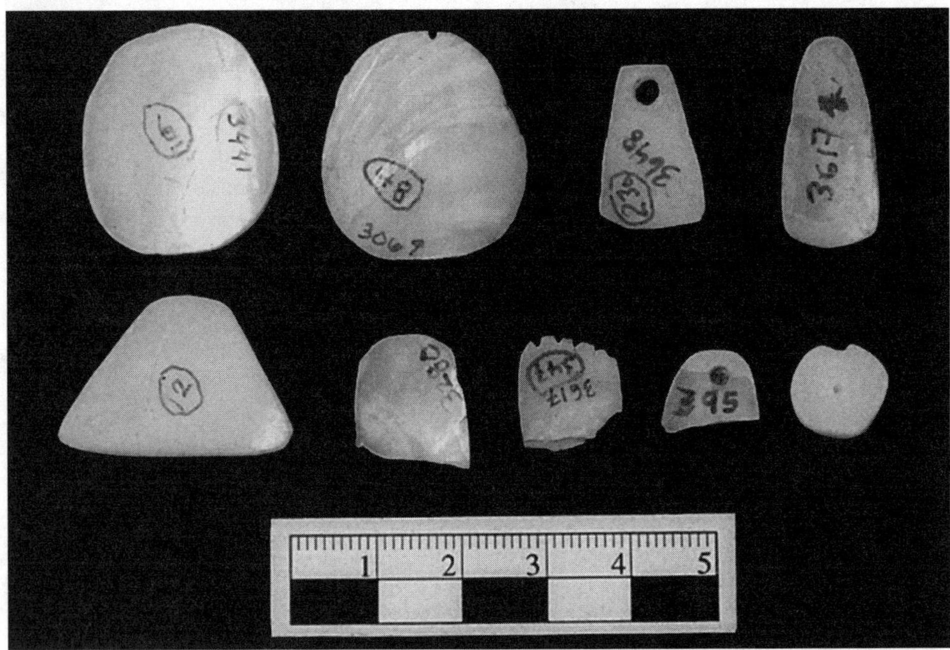

Figure 13.1. Examples of complete and fragmentary ornaments manufactured at the Henderson Site from the shells of freshwater bivalves.

pieces and a site-wide MNI value of 30 mollusks). In some contexts, for example the East Plaza, this high degree of breakage might be attributed to trampling, and possibly also to gradual postdepositional compaction of the midden that crushed some of the shells between the masses of fire-cracked rock. However, these processes are unlikely to have played much of a role in the Room C-5 midden in the Center Bar, where essentially rock-free trash accumulated within the protective confines of an abandoned room; yet even here most of the shell fragments are tiny. We suspect extensive fragmentation occurred in the process of on-site ornament manufacture, an activity amply attested to at Henderson by the presence of numerous complete, as well as unfinished and broken, ornaments cut from what appear to be the shells of freshwater bivalves, presumably *C. tampicoensis* (Figs. 13.1, 13.2). A few of the shells (0.5%; NISP = 7; see Table 13.1) were also clearly used as cutting or scraping tools and, as will be discussed below, this too may have contributed to the breakage (Fig. 13.3).

While many of the *Cyrtonaias* shells were probably used for making ornaments, and at least some were also used as tools, what evidence do we have that these animals were also collected by the villagers for their food value? This has proven to be a difficult question to answer. Even if we could show the animals were alive when collected, this would not prove conclusively that they were eaten. The one thing that we can say with certainty about the Henderson shells is that many display an amazingly standardized pattern of breakage, in which the posterior third to half of the valve was broken off, leaving just

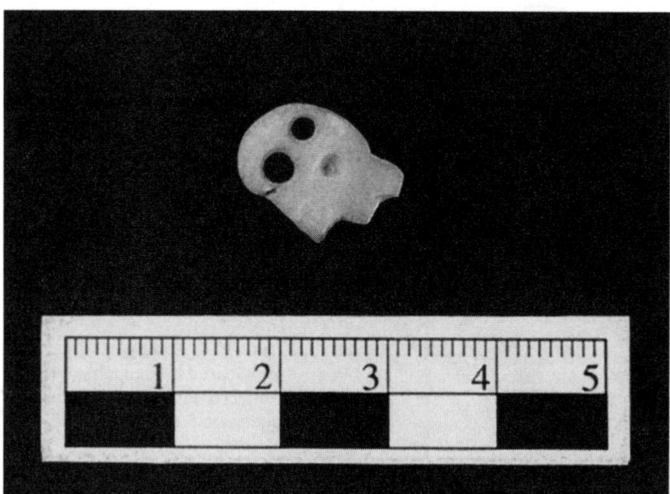

Figure 13.2. Probable freshwater shell cut into the shape of a mountain sheep (Lot 385, Main Bar East, Room M-2, grid square 535N542E, elevation = 100.80 m).

the umbo or beak, the complete anterior margin, and the anterior half (more or less) of the ventral margin (Fig. 13.4). But it is not easy to determine whether this breakage occurred while using the shell as a tool, or instead while prying open a living animal to get at the edible tissues inside. Let us briefly look at each of these possibilities.

Regge N. Wiseman first drew our attention to this interesting breakage pattern, which he also observed at the Fox Place Site, a roughly contemporary pithouse village located a few kilometers downstream from Henderson on the Hondo. The shell terminology used in this discussion follows Solem (1974:70).

The posterior margin of the *C. tampicoensis* shell is the sharpest edge and hence the one best suited for cutting or scraping soft materials such as hair or fat from bison or antelope hides, scales from fish, or maize kernels from the cob. However, this margin is also the thinnest, and thus most prone to breakage under pressure. It is plausible that the characteristic breakage pattern seen in many of the Henderson shells is due to their use as tools.

The most obvious problem with this argument is that only seven specimens of over 1,400 display unambiguous evidence of use. This assessment is based largely on a visual inspection of the fragments. We have not systematically examined the shells under a microscope, nor have we conducted replicative experiments with *C. tampicoensis* valves to determine the kinds of edge damage that one should expect from different kinds of cutting and scraping activities (see, for example, Toth and Woods 1989). A much closer look at the collection is needed in order to determine the extent to which the villagers used shell tools.

Another explanation for the breakage pattern is that the villagers gathered living mollusks for food, extracting the edible tissues inside by driving a wedge or lever between the valves at the posterior end, breaking this end of the shells in the process. If the villagers had collected shells solely for tools or ornaments, it is far more likely that they would have picked up valves of dead animals that were already open.

The problem with this argument is that it is much easier to open the valves by simply placing them in a fire or by steaming or boiling them. In either case, most of the shells would prob-

Figure 13.3. Examples of freshwater bivalve shells probably used as cutting or scraping tools at the Henderson Site.

Figure 13.4. Examples of standardized breakage pattern of freshwater bivalve shells at the Henderson Site.

ably have opened without breaking (see, for example, Meehan 1982:86ff). Breakage would only be likely if the villagers had eaten the mollusks raw. If mollusks were opened by placing them in the fire, then, given their lack of a protective outer covering of flesh, we might expect a fairly high proportion of the valves to show evidence of burning (e.g., Coutts 1970:59). Interestingly, this is precisely what we see in the Henderson shells, but only in those from the East Plaza midden. There, the incidence of burning is nearly 13%, a value higher than the average seen in any other animal at the site. By comparison, the incidence of burning on shells in the combined room block assemblage is less than 3% (Table 13.1). This difference is highly significant ($t_s = 6.51, p < .001$).[1] Mollusks might have been initially opened by placing them on or near a fire in the plaza, and many of the unburned shells then taken into the rooms for use there as tools and for making ornaments. It is also possible that mollusks were cooked in the rooms by steaming or boiling.

In order to better understand why the Henderson valves were so fragmented, we decided to determine how many of the pieces could be identified unambiguously as debris from ornament manufacture. We started by examining the details of the broken edges under low-power magnification, attempting to identify pieces that had been deliberately cut. As the work progressed, however, we lost confidence in our criteria, and we decided instead to adopt a much more conservative approach, focusing solely on the one feature that we felt could be recognized with certainty—the presence of holes that had been deliberately drilled through the valves. Sorting through the hundreds of shell fragments from Henderson, we found many pieces with remnants of perforations along their margins that looked as if they had broken while being drilled. Upon closer inspection, many of these "drill" holes displayed the characteristic features of carnivore punctures (Blumenschine and Selvaggio 1991; Bunn 1989). The holes invariably originated from a single surface, flaring outward to form a broad Hertzian cone (Speth 1972) that detached a series of flakes and spalls from the opposite face. In contrast, the perforations made in pieces that were unquestionably shell ornaments appear to have been drilled from both surfaces, with little evidence of spalling, creating a hole that in profile resembles an hourglass. The most compelling evidence was the discovery of a valve fragment with two parallel grooves or gouges on the interior surface, U-shaped in cross-section, that terminated at the edge of the piece in a pair of unambiguous punctures. This specimen is illustrated in Figure 13.5.

There seems little doubt that many of the perforations in the Henderson shell fragments were made by a small-bodied predator rather than drilled by human artisans. The question is which predator? A number of North American small mammals consume mollusks on occasion. Three species in particular are prime candidates, because they are frequent predators of bivalves, and because all three are found today in New Mexico or have been reported there in the recent past (Bailey 1931; Findley et al. 1975). These are muskrat (*Ondatra zibethicus*), striped skunk, (*Mephitis mephitis*), and mink (*Mustela vison*) (Bee et al. 1981:197; Bovbjerg 1956; Davis 1974:100; Ewer 1973:187; Manville 1948:637; O'Neil 1949:66). The black-footed ferret (*Mustela nigripes*) and long-tailed weasel (*Mustela frenata*) are also possible candidates, because both are small-bodied carnivores that occur in southeastern New Mexico, although neither

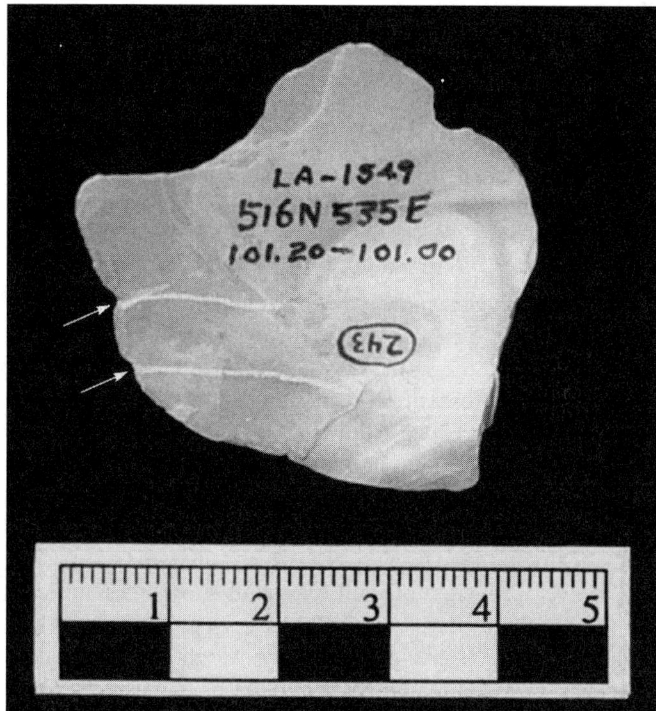

Figure 13.5. *Cyrtonaias tampicoensis* valve fragment with parallel grooves and punctures made by the incisors of a small-bodied carnivore.

is reported to consume mollusks (e.g., Ewer 1973; Hall 1951; King 1989; Svendsen 1982).

The muskrat can be ruled out. The marks left by the incisors of this rodent are easily distinguished from the punctures and U-shaped grooves seen on the Henderson shells. There is no doubt that the predator is a carnivore, not a rodent.

The gap between the paired grooves and punctures on the specimen illustrated in Figure 13.5 is only 6.3 mm. Since the marks were made on the interior surface of the shell, it is likely they were produced by the predator's lower jaw as it was forced between the valves to break them apart. We compared the value from the Henderson specimen with average intercanine gap values determined on mandibles of several small-bodied carnivore species housed in the comparative collections of the Museum of Zoology at the University of Michigan. Using comparative specimens as a basis for identifying the carnivore responsible for the damage on the prehistoric shells presents a few problems. First, none of the comparative specimens were collected in New Mexico; second, we cannot be certain that the grooves were produced by the lower jaw; and third, the archaeological specimen is a single example produced by an animal of unknown age and sex. Nevertheless, the measurements taken on the modern skeletons allow us to rule out the striped skunk with reasonable confidence, because this predator has an average intercanine gap nearly double that seen in the Henderson specimen, in excess of 11 mm in both males and females. The black-footed ferret can be eliminated for the same reason.

This leaves just two carnivores, the long-tailed weasel and the mink. The comparative mink specimens (14 males, 12 females) displayed average intercanine gaps (8.4 mm and 7.4 mm, respectively) that were somewhat larger than the archaeological specimen, while the long-tailed weasels (9 males, 4 females) yielded values that were slightly smaller (5.6 mm and 4.7 mm).

Thus, both predators remain potential candidates and deciding between them is not possible with the limited information at hand. The long-tailed weasel, though well-documented in the Roswell area, has not been reported, to the best of our knowledge, to prey on mollusks. The mink, on the other hand, while a well-known consumer of bivalves, has never been reported in southeastern New Mexico (Bailey 1931; Findley et al. 1975). The closest historical record is from the Rio Grande Valley near Las Lunas, just south of Albuquerque, some 400 m higher in elevation than Roswell and 250 km to the northwest (Findley et al. 1975:308). However, given the wholesale destruction of the many springs and rivers that once made Roswell one of the best watered areas in the Southwest, a process that was well underway before the end of the nineteenth century (see Chapter 11), it is possible that mink were once present near Henderson. Thus, while we cannot identify the predator with certainty, we feel that the mink is the most likely candidate.

Regardless of which predator was responsible for the punctures, their presence on shells from all major proveniences at the site indicates that some, perhaps many, of the mollusks were already dead when they were picked up by the villagers. Neither the mink nor the weasel would have consumed the mollusks within the village. This means that many of the bivalves were brought into Henderson as raw material for ornaments or tools, not food. Moreover, if predators opened these bivalves before they were collected by the villagers, then it is also possible that many were already broken before they were brought back to the site. The characteristic breakage seen in many of the shells, in which only the umbo and anterior third to half of the valve remain intact, may have been produced by predators, not by village artisans roughing out blanks for ornaments or employing shells as tools.

In sum, the high incidence of burning seen on the shells in the East Plaza is probably the result of placing animals on or near a fire to open them. If this interpretation is correct, then at least some of the mollusks at Henderson were eaten by the villagers. On the other hand, the presence of carnivore punctures on many of the unburned valves indicates that some, perhaps many, were picked up already dead, presumably for use by village artisans in the manufacture of ornaments. Unfortunately, we have no way at present to determine how many of the mollusks at Henderson actually fall within either of these categories.

Bivalve Assemblage by Provenience

In order to facilitate comparisons between the rooms and the East Plaza, and to assure adequate sample sizes, the assemblages from the East Bar and Center Bar were combined into a single composite sample ("combined room blocks"). In addition, NISP rather than MNI values are used here, again in order to maximize sample sizes. Most of the data discussed in this section are taken from Table 13.1.

Roughly two-thirds of the mollusk remains were found in the rooms. A very similar result is obtained if only hinge/umbo fragments are considered.

As noted above, many of the shells in the East Plaza are burned, whereas traces of burning are rare on room block specimens. One interpretation of this difference is that mollusks were cooked in the plaza by being placed near or directly in the fire, and the unburned valves were then taken into the rooms where they were used as tools or for making ornaments. An alternative interpretation is that mollusks were prepared in the rooms as well as in the plaza, but by boiling or steaming; shells cooked in either of these ways would bear few traces of burning.

One might expect the higher incidence of burning in the plaza to be accompanied by greater fragmentation. This is not the case. The average weight of the fragments in the plaza is significantly greater than that of the pieces in the rooms ($t = 2.65$, $p < .01$). This result could be misleading, however, since the presence of a few complete or nearly complete valves in the plaza sample could skew the mean weight. To check for this, we began systematically removing outliers from the room block and plaza assemblages and then checking the significance of the difference between the mean weights in the two proveniences. In the first run, the heaviest shells, those greater than 50 g ($n = 2$), were removed. The difference not only remained significant but in fact became somewhat more pronounced ($t = 2.86$, $p < .01$). We then considered only shells less than 10 g. Again, the difference between the two proveniences persisted and again became stronger ($t = 3.97$, $p < .001$). Only when the sample was reduced to pieces less than 5 g, a cutoff that eliminated 8.6% of the plaza specimens and 4.0% of the room block specimens, did the difference drop to the point where it was no longer statistically significant ($t = 1.82$, $p = .07$). These results show that the plaza sample contains a significantly greater proportion of heavier, presumably larger and more complete, shell fragments than the rooms.

Put another way, approximately 8.6% of the plaza sample consists of fragments greater than 5 g in weight, whereas only 4.0% of the combined room block assemblage consists of shell fragments this heavy. These proportions are significantly different ($t_s = 3.20$, $p = .001$).

These results, when considered together with the burning evidence, imply that early stages in the preparation of the mollusks are better represented in the plaza than in the rooms. This suggestion in turn dovetails best with the view that live mollusks, when brought into Henderson, were cooked in the plaza. Many of the unburned valves were then taken into the rooms for further use as raw material for making ornaments or as tools.

Temporal Perspective

Since this chapter was written, the freshwater shells recovered at Henderson in 1994 and 1995 have also been analyzed, and these new data are discussed briefly here. The enlarged sample consists of 1,935 pieces, of which 495 (25.6%) derive from Early phase contexts and 1,440 (74.4%) from Late phase contexts. Density (NISP/m^3) more than doubles in the later period (Early phase, 8.3/m^3; Late phase, 19.0/m^3). In both periods density is substantially higher in non-room than in room contexts (Early phase, 15.8/m^3 vs. 6.7/m^3; Late phase, 28.6/m^3 vs. 16.1/m^3).

For the enlarged sample as a whole, and ignoring the temporal dimension, the proportion of burned shell is 5.79%. In the earlier period, 5.86% of the fragments are burned, and the proportion remains essentially unchanged in the later period (5.76%). In the Early phase the proportion of fragments that are burned is nearly identical in both room (5.92%) and non-room (5.75%) contexts. However, in the Late phase the incidence of burning drops in the rooms (2.87%; $t_s = 2.35$, $p \approx .01$) and rises dramatically in the plazas (11.85%; $t_s = 2.46$, $p = .01$).

The average weight of shell fragments shows no significant change over time (Early phase, 1.14 ± 2.73 g; Late phase, 1.26 ± 3.60 g; $t = -0.68$, $p > .05$). Average weight per fragment is consistently greater in non-room contexts than in rooms (Early phase, $t = -1.77$, $p = .08$; Late phase, $t = -2.86$, $p < .01$).

Perhaps the most important conclusion to be drawn from the chronological data is that importation of bivalves into Henderson increased dramatically in the Late phase, with a much greater number of these animals being baked or roasted in public contexts.

Synopsis

A total of 1,403 freshwater bivalves, mostly small fragments averaging 1.24 g, were recovered at the Henderson Site in the first two seasons of excavation. Only two shells were complete. Ninety-three of the specimens have been identified as *Cyrtonaias tampicoensis*, today found only in the lower Rio Grande and the Pecos River in Texas. Seventeen pieces are from a different freshwater species, too fragmentary to identify further.

About 40 to 80 valves, 20 to 40 individuals, are represented by the fragments. Using an intermediate MNI figure of 30 means the valves on average have been broken into about 50 pieces. The fragmentation probably comes from use of the shells as raw material for ornament manufacture and as tools; many remains of both tools and ornaments were found.

Demonstrating that these mollusks were also collected for food is less straightforward. Many of the shells were broken apart in the same distinctive way, with the posterior third to half of the valve broken off, leaving the umbo, the complete anterior margin, and the anterior half of the ventral margin. This pattern of breakage could have been produced by using the valve as a tool, or by prying open the valves of living mollusks with a lever or wedge to get at the edible tissues.

Used as tools, this thin posterior margin of the shell would be most likely to break. Unfortunately, few of the edge fragments in the collection display traces of use visible to the naked eye. A systematic microscopic study of the shell margins for traces of use-related damage, aided by replicative experiments with *C. tampicoensis* valves, is needed to clarify the extent to which the shells of this mollusk were used as tools by the villagers.

The other explanation for the breakage pattern—that they were used as food—is equally problematic. Bivalves are most easily opened by placing them in or near a fire or by steaming or boiling them. None of these methods is likely to produce the kind of breakage seen at Henderson. But shells opened in a fire should show at least some evidence of burning. The East Plaza shells do: the incidence of burning there is nearly 13%, a value higher than in any other animal at the site. The East Plaza also contained a significantly higher proportion of larger fragments than did the room blocks. Given these observations, it seems very likely that at least some of the mollusks were collected for food.

In examining the shell fragments for traces of ornament manufacture, tiny perforations were noted that were at first interpreted as drill holes, but which subsequently proved to be punctures made by the canines of a small-bodied predator. On the interior surface of one specimen, two parallel grooves or gouges, U-shaped in cross-section and puncturing the shell, provided evidence of a predator with a 6-7 mm gap between mandibular canines. Only two New Mexican carnivores have canines this close together, the long-tailed weasel (*Mustela frenata*) and the mink (*Mustela vison*). The mink is a well-known bivalve predator and hence the most likely candidate. However, there are no historic reports of them in southeastern New Mexico. The closest known occurrence of this carnivore is in the Rio Grande Valley, nearly 250 km to the northwest of Roswell. The severe depletion of Roswell's many springs and rivers by the late nineteenth century may have obliterated the habitat for mink.

The presence of puncture marks indicates at least some of the mollusks were already dead when collected, and therefore that they were used by humans as raw material for ornaments or tools, not as food. It may also mean that the characteristic breakage pattern seen at Henderson could have been produced by predators.

Since this chapter was written, the freshwater shells recovered at Henderson in 1994 and 1995 have also been analyzed. The enlarged sample consists of 1,935 pieces, of which 25.6% derive from Early phase contexts and 74.4% from Late phase contexts. Density more than doubles in the later period, and in both periods density is substantially higher in non-room than in room contexts.

In the earlier period, 5.9% of the fragments are burned. The proportion of burned fragments remains essentially unchanged in the later period (5.8%). In the Early phase the proportion of fragments that are burned is nearly identical in both room and non-room contexts. However, in the Late phase the incidence of burning drops in the rooms and rises dramatically in the plazas.

The average weight of shell fragments shows no significant change over time. Average weight per fragment is consistently greater in plazas than in rooms.

Perhaps the most important conclusion to be drawn from the chronological data is that importation of bivalves into Henderson increased dramatically in the Late phase, with a much greater number of these animals being baked or roasted in public contexts.

Acknowledgments

We are grateful to John B. Burch of the Museum of Zoology, University of Michigan for identifying these bivalves.

Note

1. Test of the equality of two percentages based on the arcsine transformation (Sokal and Rohlf 1969:607-10).

References Cited

Bailey, V.
1931 *Mammals of New Mexico*. North American Fauna 53. Washington, DC: U.S. Department of Agriculture, Bureau of Biological Survey.

Bee, J. W., G. E. Glass, R. S. Hoffmann, and R. R. Patterson
1981 *Mammals in Kansas*. Public Education Series 7. Lawrence, KS: University of Kansas, Museum of Natural History.

Blumenschine, R. J., and M. M. Selvaggio
1991 On the Marks of Marrow Bone Processing by Hammerstones and Hyenas: Their Anatomical Patterning and Archaeological Implications. In: *Cultural Beginnings: Approaches to Understanding Early Hominid Life-Ways in the African Savanna*, edited by J. D. Clark, pp. 17-32. Romisch-Germanisches Zentralmuseum, Forshungsinstitut für Vor- und Frühgeschichte. Bonn, Germany: Dr. Rudolf Habelt GMBH.

Bovbjerg, R.
1956 Mammalian Predation on Mussels. *Proceedings of the Iowa Academy of Science* 63:737-40.

Bunn, H. T.
1989 Diagnosing Plio-Pleistocene Hominid Activity with Bone Fracture Evidence. In: *Bone Modification*, edited by R. Bonnichsen and M. H. Sorg, pp. 299-316. Orono, ME: University of Maine, Institute for Quaternary Studies, Center for the Study of the First Americans.

Coutts, P. J. F.
1970 *The Archaeology of Wilson's Promontory*. Australian Aboriginal Studies 28, Prehistory and Material Culture Series 7. Canberra, Australia: Australian Institute of Aboriginal Studies.

Davis, W. B.
1970 *The Mammals of Texas* (revised). Bulletin 41. Austin, TX: Texas Parks and Wildlife Department.

Ewer, R. F.
1973 *The Carnivores*. Ithaca, NY: Cornell University Press.

Findley, J. S., A. H. Harris, D. E. Wilson, and C. Jones
1975 *Mammals of New Mexico*. Albuquerque, NM: University of New Mexico Press.

Fuller, S. L. H.
1975 The Systematic Position of *Cyrtonaias* (Bivalvia: Unionidae). *Malacological Review* 8:81-89.

Hall, E. R.
1951 *American Weasels*. University of Kansas Publication 4. Lawrence, KS: University of Kansas, Museum of Natural History.

King, C.
1989 *The Natural History of Weasels and Stoats*. Ithaca, NY: Comstock Publishing Associates.

Manville, R. H.
1948 The Vertebrate Fauna of the Huron Mountains, Michigan. *American Midland Naturalist* 39: 615-40.

Maxwell, T. D.
1986 *Archaeological Test Excavations at the Townsend Site (LA 34150), Chaves County, New Mexico*. Laboratory of Anthropology Note 344. Santa Fe, NM: Museum of New Mexico, Laboratory of Anthropology, Research Section.

Meehan, B.
1982 *Shell Bed to Shell Midden*. Canberra, Australia: Australian Institute of Aboriginal Studies.

Metcalf, A. L.
1982 Fossil Unionacean Bivalves from Three Tributaries of the Rio Grande. In: *Proceedings of the Symposium on Recent Benthological Investigations in Texas and Adjacent States*, edited by J. R. Davis, pp. 43-58. Austin, TX: Texas Academy of Science, Aquatic Sciences Section.

O'Neil, T.
1949 *The Muskrat in the Louisiana Coastal Marshes: A Study of the Ecological, Geological, Biological, Tidal, and Climatic Factors Governing the Production and Management of the Muskrat Industry in Louisiana*. New Orleans, LA: Louisiana Department of Wild Life and Fisheries, Fish and Game Division, Federal Aid Section.

Sokal, R. R., and F. J. Rohlf
1969 *Biometry: The Principles and Practice of Statistics in Biological Research*. San Francisco, CA: W. H. Freeman.

Solem, G. A.
1974 *The Shell Makers: Introducing Mollusks*. New York: John Wiley and Sons.

Speth, J. D.
1972 Mechanical Basis of Percussion Flaking. *American Antiquity* 37(1):34-60.

Svendsen, G. E.
1982 Weasels. In: *Wild Mammals of North America: Biology, Management, and Economics*, edited by J. A. Chapman and G. A. Feldhamer, pp. 613-28. Baltimore, MD: Johns Hopkins University Press.

Toth, N., and M. Woods
1989 Molluscan Shell Knives and Experimental Cut-Marks on Bones. *Journal of Field Archaeology* 16:250-55.

14
Interspecific Comparisons
Evidence for Cooking Methods and Communal Food Sharing

John D. Speth
University of Michigan

Introduction

Previous chapters have each been devoted to a single species, such as bison or pronghorn antelope, or to a group of closely related animals, such as lagomorphs, rodents, or fish. In this chapter, I focus instead on interspecific comparisons, looking in particular at two attributes of the fauna that are significantly correlated with the body size of the animals; these are the incidence of burning, and the proportion of remains discarded in non-room versus room contexts. These comparisons provide useful insights into cooking methods used by the villagers; they also reveal a striking pattern of food sharing that crosscuts virtually every class of animal food brought into the community.

Body Weight

The average body size (live weight in kg) for each major animal taxon is listed in Table 14.1. Sixteen different taxa, or groups of closely related taxa, are tabulated, ranging from bison which weigh over 700 kg to bird eggs estimated to weigh only about 60 g. The table also provides the sources for these data, and explains in detailed footnotes how these averages were obtained. Only a brief description of these procedures is presented here.

In bison, male and female weights have been combined to calculate the average. However, since the proportion of male to female bison in the Henderson sample deviates sharply from 50:50, and since bulls and cows are very different in body weight, the figure has been adjusted to reflect the actual proportions of the two sexes in the assemblage. In most other species the animals could not be sexed and a 50:50 sex ratio has been assumed in computing the average.

The medium ungulate bones recovered in 1980-1981, whenever possible, were identified to the level of genus or species (i.e., *Odocoileus* sp. and *Antilocapra americana*; see Chapter 5). However, in order to expedite the coding and analysis of the material recovered in the 1995 and 1997 field seasons, no attempt was made to distinguish deer and antelope, and all of these materials were simply coded together as "medium ungulates." Hence, the rather small NISP values for deer and antelope in Table 14.1 reflect only the 1980, 1981, and 1994 material; the much larger NISP values for "medium ungulates" in the same table reflect all of the material recovered in all five seasons, including the specimens identified as deer and antelope.

Dogs of at least two distinct body sizes are represented in the assemblage, one averaging about 9 kg ("small"), the other averaging about 16 kg ("large"). Body size was estimated using the height (mm) of the mandible measured on the outer (labial) side at the center of the lower carnassial (M_1), as described by Clutton-Brock and Hammond (1994). Henderson's "large" dogs are similar in size to adult coyotes collected in the Roswell area. The vast majority of the remains (over 80%, based on NISP) derive from individuals of the "small" category, and the estimated weight for this size category is the value used in Table 14.1.

The weights for the birds are given by order (Anseriformes, Gruiformes, and Passeriformes). These figures are "grand means" obtained by combining the average weights (assuming a 50:50 sex ratio) for each taxon in an order that is represented in the Henderson material. The resulting averages are fairly crude

Table 14.1. Proportion (NISP) of bones by species and body size in room and non-room contexts at Henderson Site (1980-1997).

Taxon	Ave. Weight (kg)	References	Combined Room Blocks		Non-Room Contexts		Burned[a] %
			NISP	%	NISP	%	
MAMMALS							
Bison (*Bison bison*)	726.90[b]	Jones et al. (1983:336)	1143	28.02	2936	71.98	5.97
Mule deer (*Odocoileus hemionus*)	66.50[c]	Mackie et al. (1982:863)	36	57.14	27	42.86	4.55
Antelope (*Antilocapra americana*)	40.50[c]	Kitchen and O'Gara (1982:962)	480	46.83	545	53.17	7.76
Medium ungulate (*A. amer. + O. hem.* + "Medium ungulate")	40.50	Kitchen and O'Gara (1982:962)	2589	55.04	2115	44.96	9.95
Dog (*Canis familiaris*)	9.00	See Chapter 7	185	55.89	146	44.11	4.23
Jackrabbit (*Lepus californicus*)	2.58[c]	Griffing (1974:676)	1130	68.78	513	31.22	3.98
Prairie dog (*Cynomys ludovicianus*)	1.13[c]	Bailey (1931:119)	575	70.38	242	29.62	1.70
Cottontail (*Sylvilagus audubonii*)	0.92[c]	Chapman and Willner (1978:1)	2876	78.02	810	21.98	2.29
Muskrat (*Ondatra zibethicus*)	0.84[d]	Davis (1974:225)	24	85.71	4	14.29	0.00
Pocket gopher (*Pappogeomys castanops*)	0.27[c]	Davis (1974:170)	188	84.30	35	15.70	0.84
Misc. small rodents	< 0.10[e]		150	93.75	10	6.25	0.60
BIRDS							
Anseriformes (Various ducks)	0.88[f]	Dunning (1984)	16	76.19	5	23.81	0.00
Gruiformes (Moorhen, coot, crane)	0.80[g]	Dunning (1984)	63	85.14	11	14.86	0.00
Passeriformes (Various perching birds)	0.10[h]	Dunning (1984)	148	91.93	13	8.07	1.88
Avian eggshell	0.06[i]	Harrison (1978)	23	88.46	3	11.54	0.00
FISH							
Various Fish Species	0.21[j]	Davis (1959:35)	1575	85.88	259	14.12	0.46
MOLLUSKS							
Unionidae (*Cyrtonaias tampicoensis*)	< 0.20[k]	Parmalee and Klippel (1974:424)	892	68.14	417	31.86	5.79

[a]Number of burned bones expressed as percentage of total NISP (all proveniences combined).
[b]Average of mean adult male and female weights, assuming sample consists of 75% males and 25% females (see Chapter 4).
[c]Average of mean adult male and female weights, assuming sample consists of 50% males and 50% females.
[d]Average weight for female only (based on populations in Texas); muskrats in southern New Mexico and west Texas are unusually small and true weight may therefore be lower than the state-wide value given here (see Bailey 1931:209; Schmidly 1977:123).
[e]Includes several unidentified species of rodents, all of which are significantly smaller in body size than yellow-faced pocket gopher (*Pappogeomys castanops*).
[f]Average of mean adult male and female weights, assuming sample consists of 50% males and 50% females and weighted according to MNI of each taxon as shown in Table 10.1 (see Chapter 10); average incorporates the following taxa: mallard (*Anas platyrhynchos*), pintail (*A. acuta*), shoveler (*A. clypeata*), teal (*A. discors*), canvasback (*Aythya valisineria*), and common merganser (*Mergus merganser*).
[g]Average of mean adult male and female weights, assuming sample consists of 50% males and 50% females and weighted according to MNI of each taxon as shown in Table 10.1 (see Chapter10); average incorporates the following taxa: common moorhen (*Gallinula chloropus*), American coot (*Fulica americana*), and sandhill crane (*Grus canadensis*).
[h]Average of mean adult male and female weights, assuming sample consists of 50% males and 50% females and weighted according to MNI of each taxon as shown in Table 10.1 (see Chapter 10); average incorporates the following taxa: flycatcher (*Tyrannus* sp.), Chihuahuan raven (*Corvus cryptoleucus*), northern cardinal (*Cardinalis cardinalis*), lark sparrow (*Chondestes grammacus*), sparrow (*Zonotrichia* sp.), red-winged blackbird (*Agelaius phoeniceus*), meadowlark (*Sturnella* sp.), and Brewer's blackbird (*Euphagus cyanocephalus*).
[i]Avian eggshell fragments from unidentified species of bird; radius of curvature and thickness of fragments indicate eggs were relatively large and probably from wild ducks or other aquatic species; eggshells probably not from domestic or wild turkey, given scarcity of bones of this species in Henderson faunal assemblage; weight provided in this table is for commercial domestic chicken egg ("Grade A," 5.8 × 4.4 cm), which is similar in size to eggs of mallard, canvasback, merganser, and wild turkey (see Harrison 1978), and therefore provides reasonable "ball park" estimate for weight of Henderson specimens.
[j]Average maximum length of fish (all taxa combined) recovered from Henderson, estimated from size of various skeletal elements, is 27.7 cm (NISP = 1,451); average maximum length of just catfish (Ictaluridae, all taxa combined), which makes up over half of the total fish assemblage, is 28.8 cm (NISP = 1,003); estimated weight value used here is based on 30-cm long channel catfish (*Ictalurus punctatus*), the most common species of catfish at Henderson.
[k]Weight of largest complete valve of *Cyrtonaias tampicoensis* recovered at Henderson was 56.5 g; approximate live weight of this individual (i.e., two valves plus soft body parts) was probably less than ca. 200 g, based on weights provided by Parmalee and Klippel (1974:424, Table 1).

estimates, but they reflect the fact that most of the waterfowl at Henderson are larger than most of the passerines, and they place the birds in their proper relationship with other animals. It is assumed here that most, if not all, of the waterfowl served as sources of food as well as feathers for the Henderson villagers. As discussed in Chapter 10, the passerines present a more complex situation. Wing elements for these birds significantly outnumber leg elements, suggesting that for many of the passerines only wings were brought into the village. However, since many leg elements are also present in the assemblage, it is likely that at least some of these birds were brought whole into the village and perhaps eaten.

The avian eggshell fragments at Henderson, though tiny pieces, are from relatively large eggs, most likely from waterfowl. Based on the radius of curvature of the fragments and their thickness, the eggs appear to have been similar in size to modern commercially farmed chicken eggs weighing approximately 0.06 kg.

Many of the Henderson fish remains are from ictalurids, especially channel catfish (*Ictalurus punctatus*). Based on the size of various skeletal elements in the faunal assemblage, the average length of the Henderson catfish, and other fish at the site as well, is about 30 cm. A channel catfish 30 cm long weighs about 0.21 kg.

Most of the mollusk shell fragments recovered at Henderson are from a freshwater species (*Cyrtonaias tampicoensis*) that is no longer present in this stretch of the Pecos River. The live weight of the individual represented by the largest complete valve in the collection (11.5 cm long by 7.0 cm wide at the umbo) was estimated on the basis of the live weight of several different freshwater mollusk species of roughly comparable valve size collected by Parmalee and Klippel (1974) from rivers in the midwestern United States.

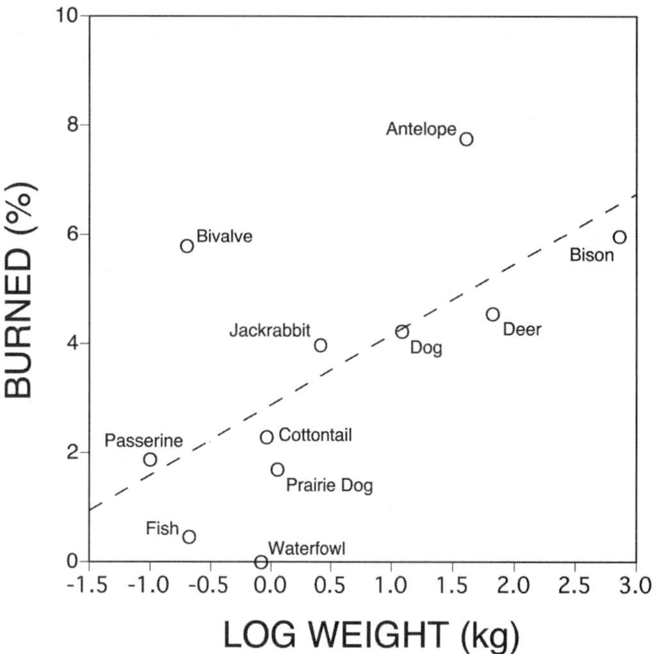

Figure 14.1. Incidence of burning (%NISP) plotted against log of body weight.

Incidence of Burning vs. Body Weight

The incidence of burning ("%burned") simply refers to the percentage of bones, out of the total NISP for a given taxon, that is burned. I am concerned here only with this percentage, not with the extent or intensity of burning (e.g., calcined vs. charred) nor its precise anatomical location. The correlation between the log of body weight (kg) and %burned, using eleven major taxa or closely related groups of taxa—bison, deer, antelope, small dog, jackrabbit, prairie dog, cottontail, waterfowl, passerines, fish, and mollusks—is positive but not significant ($r_s = .45, p > .05$; see Fig. 14.1). However, one of these categories—mollusks—clearly differs from the others in an important way; their shells lack an external covering of flesh to protect them from becoming burned if they are prepared by roasting or baking in or close to a fire. This almost certainly accounts for their unexpectedly high incidence of burning (5.8%). Once mollusks are eliminated from consideration, the correlation becomes significant ($r_s = .79, p < .05$). In other words, the incidence of burning tends to increase with the body size of the animal.

Using these same taxa, the correlation between body size and incidence of burning remains significant and positive in both temporal periods (Early phase, $r_s = .72, p < .05$; Late phase, $r_s = .85, p \approx .01$).[1]

These results raise two interesting and undoubtedly interrelated questions. Why is the overall incidence of burning at Henderson comparatively low in all species? And why is the incidence of burning positively correlated with body size? To answer these questions, we must consider different techniques of cooking meat, and how they might result in charred bones. Unfortunately, there is surprisingly little ethnoarchaeological or experimental research to turn to for insights in this matter. Most studies of animal use among contemporary hunter-gatherers and small-scale farmers have focused primarily on the early stages in the handling of an animal, from its initial procurement and field butchering at the kill site to the transport of dismembered carcass units back to a camp or village (e.g., Binford 1978; Bunn et. al. 1988; O'Connell et al. 1988, 1992). With the notable exception of marrow extraction (e.g., Binford 1978, 1981), which has received a lot of attention, little research has been devoted to subsequent stages in the processing of the animal and, in particular, to the handling and fate of bones during cooking (see Binford 1978; Gifford-Gonzalez 1989, 1993; Jones 1993; Kent 1993; Oliver 1993; Vigne and Marinval-Vigne 1983; Yellen 1977, 1991a, 1991b). Gifford-Gonzalez (1993:182) summarizes the current state of affairs:

> the full range of activities that incorporate animal resources into human nutrition—and the material effects of such tasks on bone—are not being sufficiently studied. Specifically, culinary strategies and tactics are intimately tied to the nutritional benefits derived from faunal resources, they can drive field butchery decisions, and they determine the patterning of faunal refuse, even in field situations.

Even among the handful of studies that have focused explicitly on burning, few have examined the relationship between methods of cooking and the incidence of charring. Instead, most have been concerned either with developing criteria for recognizing traces of burning in fossil bones, or with investigating the effects of burning on bone fracture properties (e.g., Buikstra and Swegle 1989; Shipman et al. 1984). Thus, the following discussion is somewhat speculative, underscoring the need for more ethnoarchaeological research focused directly on the cooking of hunted foods (Gifford-Gonzalez 1989:206, 1993; Kent 1993).

Not surprisingly, a cursory survey of the ethnographic literature on hunter-gatherers and small-scale subsistence farmers shows that meat and associated bones are generally boiled in a pot or other suitable liquid-filled container; roasted directly on, above, or next to the fire; or baked in a pit or earth oven. Presumably, bones cooked by boiling are unlikely to be burned (I omit discussion here of the many ways that bones can become burned after being cooked, for example by being deliberately tossed, kicked, or swept into the fire; or by being accidentally discarded in a place that later becomes the locus of a new hearth).

Roasting, on the other hand, is much more likely to produce burned bone, especially if animals are first skinned and dismembered, and the cuts of meat placed directly on or above the flames of the fire or buried within live coals. Not surprisingly, when animals are merely gutted but not skinned or butchered prior to cooking, roasting produces lower levels of burning (e.g., Jones 1993:108). Charring will be most evident on those bones or parts of bones that are not protected by surrounding tissue. Particularly vulnerable are the mandibular and maxillary teeth, the articular surfaces of dismembered joints, and the protruding ends of limb shafts and other bones that have been broken during skinning and butchering.

The high incidence of burning produced by roasting meat directly on an open fire is clearly shown in ethnoarchaeological data provided by Gifford-Gonzalez (1989:186, 223-24) for the Dassanetch, a group of pastoralists in northern Kenya. While the Dassanetch often boil the meat of zebra, large bovids, and caprines, they also frequently roast the heads and limbs of these animals directly in the coals of a fire. As a consequence of being roasted,[1] nearly 30% of the zebra bones, 40% of the bovid bones and over 50% of the caprine bones show evidence of burning.[2]

The incidence of burning that we might expect to be produced by pit-baking is less obvious, but probably falls somewhere between the levels produced by open-fire roasting and boiling in a pot, the actual value depending in large part on the nature of the oven, for instance, whether the meat is placed directly on live coals or on preheated stones. In a recent quantitative study of pit-roasting by Kalahari San, Kent (1993:348) found that fewer than 1% of the bones displayed any evidence whatsoever of charring. Not unexpectedly, Kent found that the incidence of burning resulting from boiling was even lower, and may in fact have been produced largely or entirely by accidental exposure to fire after the bones had been cooked.

If the Dassanetch data are in any way typical of the incidence of burning that can be expected from placing dismembered body parts of animals directly on the live coals of a fire, which is in excess of 20% or 30% (see also Vigne and Marinval-Vigne 1983 for a probable archaeological case), then the very low incidence at Henderson suggests that this method of cooking was not commonly employed. Instead, it would appear that the villagers boiled or stewed much of their meat in pottery vessels, or baked it in pits or earth ovens. Some of the smallest animals may have been roasted, but if so it was probably done with skins intact and with little or no prior dismemberment. The use of pots for stewing or boiling is amply attested to at Henderson. More than half of the site's total ceramic assemblage is sherds from large, thin-walled El Paso Polychrome jars, many of which, despite their painted decorations, are heavily sooted on the exterior from being placed directly on or above a fire (see Chapter 3). And, of course, there is clear evidence for the use of earth ovens at Henderson, strikingly evidenced by the huge masses of fire-cracked rock and ash concentrated at the south end of the East Plaza and in the Great Depression.[3]

If the likelihood that a bone will become charred during pit-baking or roasting is at least in part a function of the amount of bone exposed by skinning, dismemberment, and butchery, then the positive correlation of the incidence of burning with body size at Henderson is very likely a reflection of the greater need to reduce larger-bodied animals to more manageable pieces (see, for example, Yellen 1977).[4] In contrast, small mammals, such as prairie dogs, can be cooked effectively with virtually no prior butchery other than perhaps gutting the animal before placing it in the hearth or pit (e.g., Hill 1938:172).

In sum, the very low incidence of burning across all species at Henderson probably reflects the fact that the villagers boiled much of their meat or baked it with heated rocks in earth ovens. Direct roasting of meat in open fires was probably done primarily with small mammals, which were neither skinned, nor dismembered first. Larger carcasses required more dismemberment and butchering prior to cooking than did smaller ones, increasing the chances for their bones to become burned.

Species Abundance in Non-Room Contexts vs. Body Weight

Before looking at the abundance of the various animal taxa in non-room contexts, such as the Great Depression and East

Plaza, it is necessary to comment on the nature of trash disposal at Henderson. The village is small and it would be naive to assume that all residues of activities that were carried out in the rooms were discarded exclusively within the room blocks. It is quite likely that part of this "domestic" trash was, in fact, also dumped in depressions and elsewhere outside the rooms, contributing to the buildup of midden in plazas and other non-room contexts. While the West Plaza has not been systematically sampled, it is clear from several trenches and smaller exposures that the East Plaza, at least, was never kept free of debris from earth oven complexes and other activities. Fire-cracked rock, animal bones, lithics, and other cultural material were encountered virtually everywhere we sampled. But as the analyses in the previous chapters have shown repeatedly, the composition of non-room trash is far from a carbon copy of room block trash. Some of the differences are obvious, such as the masses of fire-cracked rock and the many large limestone "choppers" in the plazas (Chapter 2). Other contrasts are more subtle, such as the small but statistically significant differences in the degree of bone fragmentation, the incidence of burning, and the age structure of the animal remains discarded in the two proveniences. Additional contrasts are discussed in this chapter and in subsequent ones as well. Given the many ways in which the plaza and room block trash accumulations differ, it is clear that the activities reflected in the two contexts are far from identical.

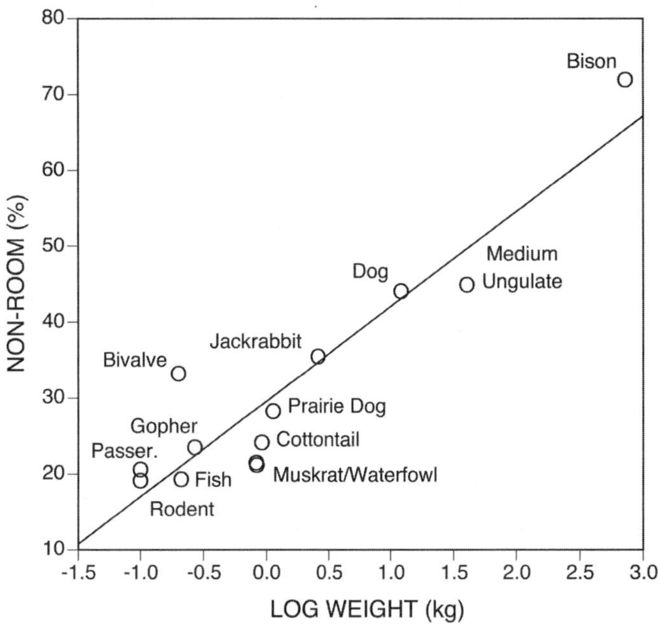

Figure 14.2. Abundance of species in non-room contexts, expressed as a percentage of total NISP of that species, plotted against log of body weight.

With these comments in mind, let us return now to the topic at hand. The abundance of a species in non-room contexts, expressed as the percentage of the total NISP of that species recovered at the site, proved to be positively and significantly correlated with the log of body weight ($r_s = .85$, $p = .003$).[5] In other words, the larger the animal, the proportionately more abundant are its remains in non-room contexts (see Fig. 14.2). The mollusks are anomalous; despite their small size, many occurred in non-room contexts. As noted in Chapter 13, however, an unknown but significant number of shells appear to have been scavenged by the villagers from the food remains of a small-bodied carnivore, likely the mink (*Mustela vison*). These bivalves, therefore, were brought back to the site for use in making ornaments or for use as shell tools, not food. Unfortunately, we have no way at present to determine how many of the valves at Henderson actually represent human food remains. If mollusks are omitted from the correlation, the relationship is even stronger ($r_s = .96$, $p = .001$).

This result might seem obvious. Given their size, bison, and possibly also antelope and deer, were almost certainly butchered in open areas such as plazas, not within the confined spaces of the room blocks. Thus, it is hardly surprising that the bones of these animals are most abundant in non-room contexts. Similarly, we might expect the majority of remains of small mammals to be found in the room blocks, and this in fact is also the case. Following this same logic a step further, we would expect the correlation to diminish, or vanish entirely, if the large-bodied mammals are dropped from the analysis, so that the focus is only on animals the size of jackrabbits and smaller. Surprisingly, however, when this is done the positive correlation still persists and remains significant ($r_s = .66$, $p < .05$). And, if we again drop the anomalous mollusks, the correlation rises markedly ($r_s = .90$, $p = .01$).

In these correlations, we used a single value for fish which represented the average size of all species of fish brought into the community. However, when just the fish are examined, and broken down by 5- and 10-cm size classes, we see the same body-size patterning with respect to provenience: the larger the fish, the more likely its remains are to be found in non-room contexts (Fig. 14.3). One could argue that this pattern is an artifact of site formation processes (Schiffer 1987), in which larger fish bones (which generally come from larger individuals) were routinely cleaned out of the rooms and dumped in open areas, while smaller bones were inadvertently left behind in the rooms and gradually became concentrated there. However, almost none of the debris in rooms is floor-contact material, but trash that had been deliberately dumped into abandoned structures. So the sharp bias in favor of larger animals in the plazas does not appear to be a by-product of room cleaning. Thus, the same decision-making process that concentrated the remains of larger mammals in non-room contexts were also systematically applied to the fish that were brought into the village, such that the bigger the fish the more likely it was processed in plaza areas and its bones discarded there. The relationship shown in Figure 14.3 is clearly nonlinear, the effect becoming most pronounced in fish greater than about 50 cm in length.

This size-frequency patterning in Henderson's animal remains was completely unexpected. While I have tried repeat-

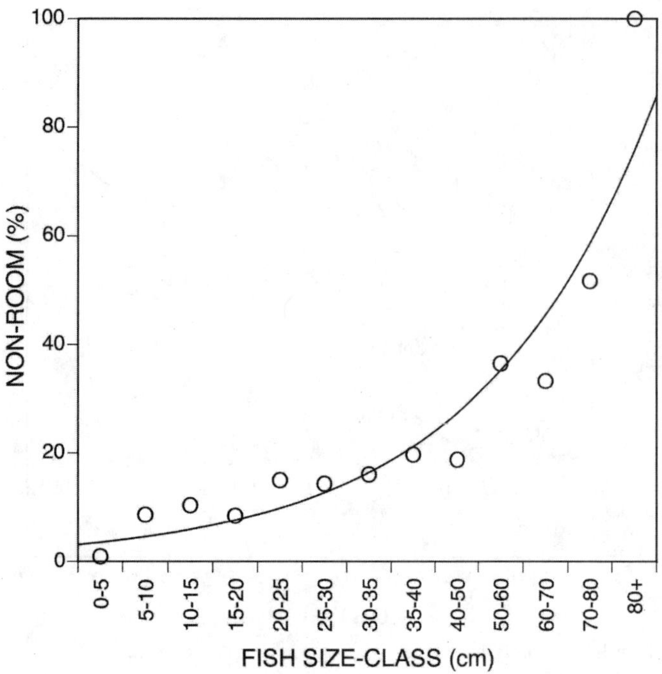

Figure 14.3. Abundance of fish remains in non-room contexts plotted against 5- to 10-cm size classes.

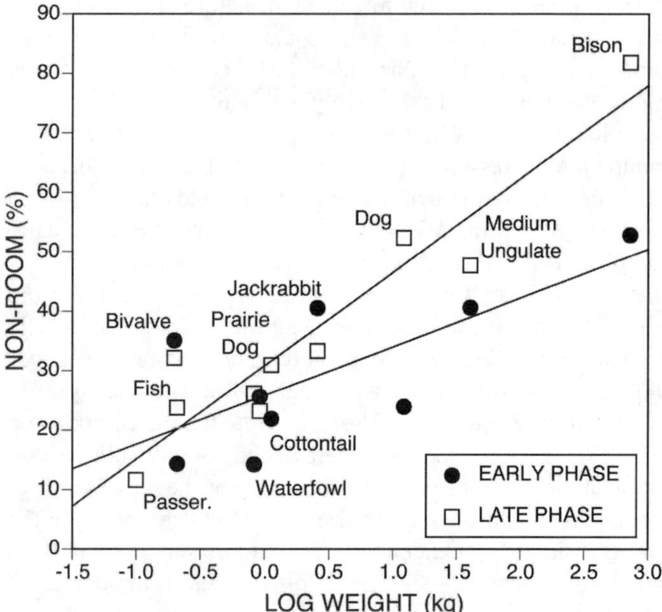

Figure 14.4. Abundance of taxa in non-room contexts by temporal phase plotted against log of body weight.

edly to convince myself that the patterning is a by-product of site formation processes produced by dumping larger debris away from dwellings, the many differences between the two contexts, in addition to size, argue otherwise. Instead, this striking patterning seems to suggest that decisions by the villagers whether to process and dispose of animal bones in plazas, or instead to take them into more private, domestic contexts, were graded on an extraordinarily fine scale that differentiated even among the smaller mammals, fish, and food birds. Before discussing the implications of these results, however, let us first look at this same issue from a chronological perspective. This exercise, quite surprisingly, shows that the behavior that concentrated animals in open areas according to their size actually intensified significantly in the Late phase, reflecting major changes in community-wide patterns of food preparation and sharing.

Figure 14.4 examines the same relationship shown in Figure 14.2—the abundance of species in non-room contexts, expressed as the percentage of the total NISP of species recovered at the site—but this time the data are subdivided by phase. Muskrats, gophers, and "misc. small rodents" have been eliminated from this figure because most of the Early phase bones of these taxa that were recovered in the 1990s have not been analyzed as yet. In addition, only the Late phase passerine value is plotted; the Early phase non-room value (73.9%) clearly falls way off the regression line. The reason for this marked deviation is not known, but it perhaps reflects the fact that very few passerines were actually used as food at Henderson (see Chapter 10). The same positive correlation emerges in both time periods, but with two notable changes: (1) for almost all taxa, the proportion occurring in non-room contexts is higher in the Late phase than in the Early phase, and (2) the slope of the Late phase regression line is much steeper. The change is most dramatic in bison, the species that increasingly became the economic focus of the community, and dog, an animal that commonly served as an important ceremonial food among historically documented Plains bison-hunting populations.

The Henderson fish display an even more striking distributional change in the Late phase (Fig. 14.5) than was apparent in Figure 14.4. In the Early phase there is almost no difference between room and non-room contexts in the proportions of fish of differing sizes. However, in the Late phase the proportion of fish above about 40 cm in length increases markedly in plaza areas. Clearly, whatever governed the disposal patterns of fish changed dramatically in the Late phase, concentrating most of the larger individuals in public contexts.

Before discussing the implications of these results in greater detail, we will examine the faunal data from one other angle, in order to further clarify the nature of the activities that took place in the village plazas. This last analysis compares the average utility of remains found in non-room contexts with the utility of bones from the room blocks, to determine whether the body parts processed and discarded in the two contexts were roughly equivalent in terms of their overall food worth.

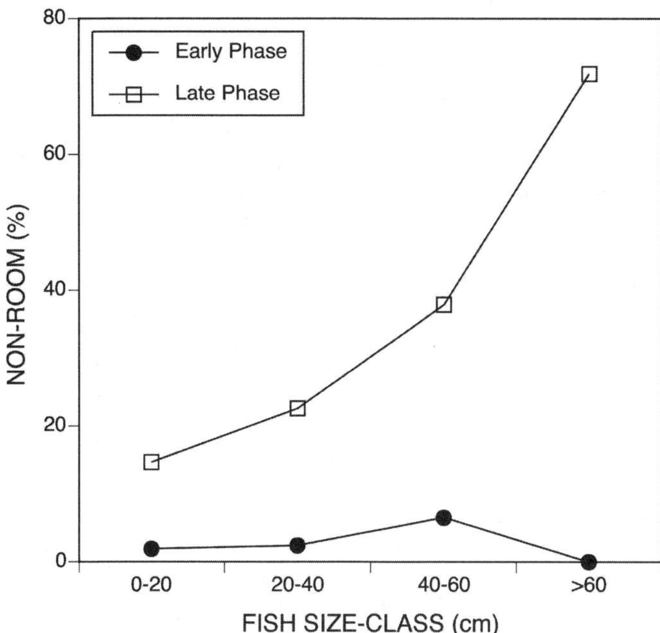

Figure 14.5. Abundance of fish remains in non-room contexts by temporal phase plotted against 20-cm size classes.

Utility of Mammal Remains in Room and Non-Room Contexts

For the three largest taxa with adequate sample sizes—bison, medium ungulates, and jackrabbits—I have calculated the average modified general utility index (MGUI; Binford 1978:74, Table 2.7) of the major limb elements recovered in each temporal period in room and non-room contexts. (Dogs are omitted here because of extremely small sample sizes when considering only major limb elements.) The results are summarized in Table 14.2.

One might question the appropriateness of Binford's MGUI values for these comparisons, particularly for elements such as the metapodials of jackrabbits, which differ in structure from those of ungulates and are clearly of much lower utility. It must be kept in mind, however, that the goal of this analysis is to compare the average utility of the remains of a given taxon in plazas with the remains *of the same taxon* in the room blocks; I am not concerned here with interspecific comparisons. The much higher average MGUI for bison than for the other two taxa almost certainly reflects the fact that these massive animals, most of which were adult bulls, were selectively culled prior to transport from the locus of the kill to the village (see Chapter 4).

In doing this analysis, I originally expected that the average utility in the two contexts would differ, with higher overall utilities occurring in the room block trash. The reason for this expectation was simply that, regardless of whether the animals were initially butchered in plazas or in rooms, many of the higher-utility bones would ultimately have been brought into the rooms for cooking, consumption, or at least for marrow extraction, whereupon the majority would have been discarded, along with other domestic trash, in nearby abandoned rooms. If a fair amount of the trash generated in the rooms also ended up being dumped in the plazas, one might expect the utility values in the two contexts to be more or less equivalent.

However, as Table 14.2 shows, the results are again quite different from what I had originally anticipated, particularly for the Late phase. Two of the taxa—bison and jackrabbits—display significantly higher average utility values in non-room contexts than in room block trash. This would seem to imply that greater numbers of the higher-utility limb elements of these animals were processed, perhaps cooked, and then discarded in plaza areas, without ever having been taken into the rooms. Bison were most often handled in this manner. In fact, during the Late phase over 80% of the bones of this species, most of which are moderate- to high-utility elements, ended up in non-room areas. Interestingly, although only one-third of the Late phase jackrabbit remains ended up in non-room contexts, this species also shows a significant bias toward higher-utility parts in plaza areas. Medium ungulates, on the other hand, display no contrast.

While the utility data are intriguing, their interpretation is not obvious. Why should the more valuable limb bones of both bison and jackrabbits be concentrated more heavily in public areas, while medium ungulate limb bones are not? Body size is not the answer. What bison and jackrabbits do share in common, however, is the fact that both were almost certainly taken by communal hunting methods involving the cooperation of

Table 14.2. Average utility (MGUI) of major limb elements by taxon in room and non-room contexts at Henderson Site.[a]

Taxon	Early Phase			Late Phase		
	Room	Non-Room	Significance[b]	Room	Non-Room	Significance[b]
Bison	50.6±24.0	57.2±27.5	$t = -1.95, p = .05$	52.5±25.3	57.0±27.4	$t = -1.89, p \approx .05$
Medium Ungulates	40.6±25.1	42.9±22.1	$t = -1.01, p > .05$	41.7±25.2	41.7±19.7	$t = +0.05, p > .05$
Jackrabbits	38.7±22.2	39.6±23.8	$t = -0.41, p > .05$	39.4±24.0	42.6±23.5	$t = -2.43, p = .01$

[a]Modified general utility index (after Binford 1978:74, Table 2.7).
[b]Standard unpaired t-test.

many, if not most, of the able-bodied members of the village. In contrast, antelope (and probably deer) were apparently hunted individually (see Chapter 5). Thus, the concentration of higher-utility body parts of certain taxa in public areas of the village probably reflects the fact that the entire community, or some sizeable portion thereof, was involved in the procurement of those taxa and hence in their subsequent preparation and consumption.

In summary, most meat at Henderson was either boiled or pit-baked. Roasting meat directly on an open fire was apparently not a common method of cooking. The larger the animal, the more likely it was processed, cooked, probably consumed, and then discarded in non-room contexts. The villagers appear to have been concerned about the body size of their prey on an exceedingly fine-grained scale, making distinctions even among the smaller mammals, birds, and fish. Finally, in bison and jackrabbits significantly greater proportions of higher-utility limb elements were processed and deposited in plaza areas than in room blocks. These data appear to suggest that the higher-utility elements most likely to end up in plaza trash are from animals that were hunted, processed, and probably shared communally.

What conclusions can we reasonably draw from these results concerning the handling and distribution of meat at Henderson? First, given the open and presumably very public nature of the plaza areas, and the obvious prominence and accessibility of their massive earth oven complexes (Great Depression in the Early phase; East Plaza in the Late phase), I suspect that animals processed in these areas of the village would not only have been highly visible to all members of the community, but also the ones most subject to the pressures and demands of interhousehold meat sharing. And since foods that come in comparatively large "packages," and whose acquisition occurs at irregular intervals, are generally shared more frequently and more widely among households than smaller ones, a pattern well documented ethnographically among both foragers and small-scale horticulturalists (e.g., Aspelin 1979; Cadelina 1982; Hames 1990; Heinen 1994:287; Kaplan and Hill 1985; Kaplan et al. 1990; Lee 1979; Marshall 1993, 1994:74), it is no surprise that the remains of larger animals are much more abundant in the plazas than in enclosed disposal contexts directly associated with particular structures or room blocks. What is particularly unusual about Henderson, aside from the fact that sharing can be recognized in the archaeological record at all, is the extraordinarily fine-grained scale of discrimination among body sizes exercised by the villagers, involving smaller fish and birds as well as mammals, a pattern that has yet to be reported by ethnographers. Finally, the fact that higher-utility elements of communally hunted animals appear to be better represented in the plazas than in the room blocks adds further weight to the suggestion that plazas, most particularly in the Late phase, were a locus of communally focused activities in which meat sharing and consumption played a prominent role.

Synopsis

This chapter compares taxa or groups of taxa, looking in particular at: (1) the overall incidence of burning, and the relationship between the percentage of remains that are burned and average body size; (2) the relationship between the proportion of remains found in non-room contexts and body size; and (3) the average food utility of bison, medium ungulate, and jackrabbit remains found in plazas compared to the utility of their remains in room blocks.

The incidence of burning is surprisingly low in all of the Henderson taxa. The highest values are about 6% in bison and 10% in medium ungulates. The other taxa, with the exception of mollusks, have much lower values. Two particularly useful studies, one among Dassanetch pastoralists in Kenya, the other among Ache foragers in Amazonia, suggest that over 20% or even 30% of the bones cooked directly over an open fire are likely to become charred. If these values are true for Henderson, open-fire roasting was not a major method for cooking meat at Henderson. The huge quantities of fire-cracked rock in the Great Depression and East Plaza suggest that pit-baking was one of the principal techniques. Heavy sooting on the exterior of most sherds of El Paso Polychrome, the dominant jar form at Henderson, indicates that boiling may also have been important.

The average body weight of animals belonging to eleven different taxa (or groups of similar taxa) is positively correlated with burning. The taxa involved are bison, deer, antelope, dog, jackrabbit, cottontail rabbit, prairie dog, Passeriformes (various perching birds), waterfowl, fish, and freshwater bivalves. If burning results primarily from exposure of unprotected bone to flames or glowing coals, the positive correlation with body size means larger animals were more completely dismembered and processed prior to being cooked than smaller ones.

The larger the animal, the more abundant its remains in plazas (expressed as percent of total NISP). For bison, deer, and antelope this result is expected. Because of their large size, these animals are likely to have been butchered in open areas, and many of the bones processed and discarded there rather than being taken into the rooms. However, the same weight/abundance relationship still holds when the medium and large mammals are excluded and only animals the size of jackrabbits and smaller are considered. The relationship even persists when just fish are considered by themselves.

This pattern could be an artifact of room-cleaning, in which larger bones (generally from larger-sized individuals and taxa) were routinely removed from rooms and dumped in plazas, while smaller bones were inadvertently left behind in the structures. However, most trash in rooms is not floor-contact material, but debris deliberately dumped into abandoned structures.

This striking size-frequency patterning implies that decisions by the villagers whether to process and dispose of animal bones in the plaza, or to take them instead into the rooms, were graded on an extraordinarily fine scale that differentiated even among the smaller mammals, fish, and birds.

Chronologically, the same positive correlation emerges in both time periods, but with two notable changes: (1) for almost all taxa, the proportion in non-room contexts is higher in the Late phase than in the Early phase, and (2) the slope of the Late phase regression line is much steeper. The change is most dramatic in bison, the species that increasingly became the economic focus of the community, and dog, an animal that commonly served as an important ceremonial food among historically documented Plains bison-hunting populations.

Finally, the average utility (MGUI) of bison, medium ungulate, and jackrabbit remains found in non-room contexts is compared with the utility of bones of these taxa found in room blocks, in order to determine whether the body parts processed and discarded in the two contexts were roughly equivalent in terms of their overall food worth.

The results differ from what had been anticipated, particularly for the Late phase. Bison and jackrabbits display significantly higher average utility values in non-room contexts than in room block trash. This would seem to imply that greater numbers of the higher-utility limb elements of these animals were processed, perhaps cooked, and then discarded in plaza areas, without ever having been taken into the rooms. Bison were most often handled in this manner. In fact, during the Late phase more than 80% of the bones of this species ended up in non-room contexts. Interestingly, although only one-third of the Late phase jackrabbit remains ended up in non-room contexts, this species also shows a significant bias toward higher-utility parts in plaza areas. Medium ungulates, on the other hand, display no contrast.

Why should the more valuable limb bones of both bison and jackrabbits be concentrated more heavily in public areas, while medium ungulate limb bones are not? What bison and jackrabbits share in common is that both were taken by communal methods involving the cooperation of many members of the village. In contrast, antelope (and probably deer) were apparently hunted individually.

The concentration of larger animals, and of higher-utility body parts, in and around major earth oven complexes very likely reflects the fact that these areas of the village were the locus of repeated events of interhousehold, perhaps community-wide, meat sharing. Given the open and presumably very public nature of these cooking features, animals processed in them would have been highly visible to all members of the community and hence the ones most subject to the pressures and demands of sharing. What is particularly unusual about the pattern of sharing seen at Henderson, aside from the fact that it can be seen at all, is the extraordinarily fine-grained scale of discrimination among body sizes exercised by the villagers, involving smaller fish and birds as well as mammals. Nothing comparable to this has yet been documented ethnographically.

Notes

1. In this chronological comparison, the single category "medium ungulate" were used instead of separate values for deer and antelope, because none of the medium ungulates from the 1995 and 1997 field seasons have been identified to the level of genus or species as yet, thereby eliminating a substantial portion of the Early phase material.

2. These figures were derived by combining the values in Tables 3a and 3b of Gifford-Gonzalez (1989:223-24).

3. While thousands of bison, antelope, and other animal bones are clearly associated with the spoils of the East Plaza and Great Depression earth oven complexes, it is very likely that plant foods were also cooked in these features.

4. Interestingly, Gifford-Gonzalez's (1989) data on the incidence of burning produced by open-fire roasting behaves in the opposite manner, with somewhat lower values in zebra and large bovids, and the highest values in caprines. Since she was unable to observe the actual roasting of the large-bodied species, the reasons for this are unknown.

5. Taxa included bison, medium ungulates, dogs, jackrabbits, prairie dogs, cottontails, muskrats, gophers, "misc. small rodents," ducks and coots, passerines, fish, and bivalves.

References Cited

Aspelin, P. L.

1979 Food Distribution and Social Bonding among the Mamainde of Mato Grosso, Brazil. *Journal of Anthropological Research* 35(3):309-27.

Bailey, V.

1931 *Mammals of New Mexico*. North American Fauna 53. Washington, D.C.: U.S. Department of Agriculture, Bureau of Biological Survey.

Binford, L. R.

1978 *Nunamiut Ethnoarchaeology*. New York, NY: Academic Press.

1981 *Bones: Ancient Men and Modern Myths*. New York, NY: Academic Press.

Buikstra, J. E., and M. Swegle

1989 Bone Modification Due to Burning: Experimental Evidence. In: *Bone Modification*, edited by R. Bonnichsen and M. H. Sorg, pp. 247-58. Peopling of the Americas Publications. Orono, ME: Center for the Study of the First Americans, Institute for Quaternary Studies, University of Maine.

Bunn, H. T., L. E. Bartram, and E. M. Kroll

1988 Variability in Bone Assemblage Formation from Hadza Hunting, Scavenging, and Carcass Processing. *Journal of Anthropological Archaeology* 7(4):412-57.

Cadeliña, R. V.

1982 *Batak Interhousehold Food Sharing: A Systematic Analysis of Food Management of Marginal Agriculturalists in the Philippines*. Ph.D. dissertation, University of Hawaii, Honolulu, HI.

Chapman, J. A., and G. R. Willner

1978 *Sylvilagus audubonii*. *Mammalian Species* (American Society of Mammalogists) 106:1-4.

Clutton-Brock, J., and N. Hammond
1994 Hot Dogs: Comestible Canids in Preclassic Maya Culture at Cuello, Belize. *Journal of Archaeological Science* 21(6):819-26.

Davis, J.
1959 *Management of Channel Catfish in Kansas*. University of Kansas Museum of Natural History Miscellaneous Publication 21. Topeka, KS: State Biological Survey and Forestry, Fish and Game Commission of Kansas.

Davis, W. B.
1974 *The Mammals of Texas*. Bulletin 41. Austin, TX: Texas Parks and Wildlife Department.

Dunning, J. B., Jr.
1984 *Body Weights of 686 Species of North American Birds*. Western Bird Banding Association Monograph 1. Cave Creek, AZ: Eldon Publishing.

Gifford-Gonzalez, D.
1989 Ethnographic Analogues for Interpreting Modified Bones: Some Cases from East Africa. In: *Bone Modification*, edited by R. Bonnichsen and M. H. Sorg, pp. 179-246. Peopling of the Americas Publications. Orono, ME: Center for the Study of the First Americans, Institute for Quaternary Studies, University of Maine.
1993 Gaps in Zooarchaeological Analyses of Butchery: Is Gender an Issue? In: *From Bones to Behavior: Ethnoarchaeological and Experimental Contributions to the Interpretation of Faunal Remains*, edited by J. Hudson, pp. 181-99. Occasional Paper 21. Carbondale, IL: Southern Illinois University, Center for Archaeological Investigations.

Griffing, J. P.
1974 Body Measurements of Black-Tailed Jackrabbits of Southeastern New Mexico with Implications of Allen's Rule. *Journal of Mammalogy* 55(3):674-78.

Hames, R.
1990 Sharing among the Yanomamo, Part I. The Effects of Risk. In: *Risk and Uncertainty in Tribal and Peasant Economies*, edited by E. Cashdan, pp. 89-106. Boulder, CO: Westview Press.

Harrison, C.
1978 *A Field Guide to the Nests, Eggs and Nestlings of North American Birds*. Glasgow, Scotland: William Collins Sons and Company.

Heinen, H. D.
1994 More On Why Hunter-Gatherers Work. *Current Anthropology* 35(3):287-89.

Hill, W. W.
1938 *The Agricultural and Hunting Methods of the Navaho Indians*. Yale University Publications in Anthropology 18.

Jones, J. K., D. M. Armstrong, R. S. Hoffmann, and C. Jones
1983 *Mammals of the Northern Great Plains*. Lincoln, NE: University of Nebraska Press.

Jones, K. T.
1993 The Archaeological Structure of a Short-Term Camp. In: *From Bones to Behavior: Ethnoarchaeological and Experimental Contributions to the Interpretation of Faunal Remains*, edited by J. Hudson, pp. 101-14. Occasional Paper 21. Carbondale, IL: Southern Illinois University, Center for Archaeological Investigations.

Kaplan, H., and K. Hill
1985 Food Sharing among Ache Foragers: Tests of Explanatory Hypotheses. *Current Anthropology* 26(2):223-46.

Kaplan, H., K. Hill, and A. M. Hurtado
1990 Risk, Foraging and Food Sharing among the Ache. In: *Risk and Uncertainty in Tribal and Peasant Economies*, edited by E. Cashdan, pp. 107-44. Boulder, CO: Westview Press.

Kent, S.
1993 Variability in Faunal Assemblages: The Influence of Hunting Skill, Sharing, Dogs, and Mode of Cooking on Faunal Remains at a Sedentary Kalahari Community. *Journal of Anthropological Archaeology* 12:323-85.

Kitchen, D. W., and B. W. O'Gara
1982 Pronghorn (*Antilocapra americana*). In: *Wild Mammals of North America: Biology, Management, and Economics*, edited by J. A. Chapman and G. A. Feldhamer, pp. 960-71. Baltimore, MD: Johns Hopkins University Press.

Lee, R. B.
1979 *The !Kung San: Men, Women, and Work in a Foraging Society*. Cambridge, England: Cambridge University Press.

Mackie, R. J., K. L. Hamlin, and D. F. Pac
1982 Mule Deer (*Odocoileus hemionus*). In: *Wild Mammals of North America: Biology, Management, and Economics*, edited by J. A. Chapman and G. A. Feldhamer, pp. 862-77. Baltimore, MD: Johns Hopkins University Press.

Marshall, F.
1993 Food Sharing and the Faunal Record. In: *From Bones to Behavior: Ethnoarchaeological and Experimental Contributions to the Interpretation of Faunal Remains*, edited by J. Hudson, pp. 228-46. Occasional Paper 21. Carbondale, IL: Southern Illinois University, Center for Archaeological Investigations.
1994 Food Sharing and Body Part Representation in Okiek Faunal Assemblages. *Journal of Archaeological Science* 21(1):65-77.

O'Connell, J. F., K. Hawkes, and N. G. Blurton Jones
1988 Hadza Hunting, Butchering, and Bone Transport and Their Archaeological Implications. *Journal of Anthropological Research* 44(2):113-61.
1992 Patterns in the Distribution, Site Structure and Assemblage Composition of Hadza Kill-Butchering Sites. *Journal of Archaeological Science* 19(3):319-45.

Oliver, J. S.
1993 Carcass Processing by the Hadza: Bone Breakage from Butchery to Consumption. In: *From Bones to Behavior:*

Ethnoarchaeological and Experimental Contributions to the Interpretation of Faunal Remains, edited by J. Hudson, pp. 200-227. Occasional Paper 21. Carbondale, IL: Southern Illinois University, Center for Archaeological Investigations.

Parmalee, P. W., and W. E. Klippel
1974 Freshwater Mussels as a Prehistoric Food Resource. *American Antiquity* 39(3):421-34.

Schiffer, M. B.
1987 *Formation Processes of the Archaeological Record*. Albuquerque, NM: University of New Mexico Press.

Schmidly, D. J.
1977 *The Mammals of Trans-Pecos Texas*. College Station, TX: Texas A & M University Press.

Shipman, P., G. Foster, and M. J. Schoeninger
1984 Burnt Bones and Teeth: An Experimental Study of Color, Morphology, Crystal Structure and Shrinkage. *Journal of Archaeological Science* 11:307-25.

Speth, J. D., and G. A. Johnson
1976 Problems in the Use of Correlation for the Investigation of Tool Kits and Activity Areas. In: *Cultural Change and Continuity*, edited by C. E. Cleland, pp. 35-57. New York: Academic Press.

Vigne, J.-D., and M.-C. Marinval-Vigne
1983 Methode pour la Mise en Evidence de la Consommation du Petit Gibier. In: *Animals and Archaeology: 1. Hunters and Their Prey*, edited by J. Clutton-Brock and C. Grigson, pp. 239-42. BAR International Series 163. Oxford, England: British Archaeological Reports.

Yellen, J. E.
1977 Cultural Patterning in Faunal Remains: Evidence from the !Kung Bushmen. In: *Experimental Archaeology*, edited by J. E. Yellen, D. Ingersoll, and W. McDonald, pp. 271-331. New York: Columbia University Press.
1991a Small Mammals: !Kung San Utilization and the Production of Faunal Assemblages. *Journal of Anthropological Archaeology* 10(1):1-26.
1991b Small Mammals: Post-Discard Patterning of !Kung San Faunal Remains. *Journal of Anthropological Archaeology* 10(2):152-92.

Part III

The Stone Tools

15
Projectile Points from the Henderson Site (1980-1981)

Michael A. Adler
Southern Methodist University

John D. Speth
University of Michigan

Introduction

The small excavations at Henderson in 1980 and 1981 yielded an unexpectedly large sample of projectile points (*n* = 529). Of these, 472 were recovered during the excavations in the Center Bar, East Bar, and East Plaza; the remaining specimens were found on the surface of the site, either eroding from the room blocks or from disturbed deposits in the plazas. The greater part of these projectile points were broken. Only about 30% of the points were complete or had minimal damage; the remaining specimens were fragments.

The sample discussed here focuses on a subset of 458 specimens. An additional 28 points[1] were retrieved after the analysis had been completed, while processing flotation and geological samples, and sorting through the thousands of tiny pieces of debitage from the site. Also excluded here is a cache of 43 projectile points and hafted knives buried with a thirteenth-century adult male (Feature 36) beneath the floor of Room E-3 in the East Bar of the site. Many of these points are well-known archaic forms, such as Marshalls and Shumlas, and were manufactured from distinctive Texas lithic materials, such as Alibates chert, Tecovas jasper, and Edwards Plateau chert. One large biface, almost identical in form to the classic "turkey tail" of the Late Archaic in eastern North America, is made of a distinctive wavy banded brown material that has been identified as Tiger "chert" from southwestern Wyoming (Whittaker et al. 1988). These interesting specimens have been described in detail elsewhere (see Rocek and Speth 1986).

Excluding the "archaic" types found with the Feature 36 burial, as well as a handful of dart points and hafted knives recovered from nonburial contexts, the vast majority of the Henderson projectile points fall into two widely recognized small triangular arrowhead types, Washita and Fresno (see Table 15.1 and Figs. 15.1-15.3). In addition, there are three small, thin, corner-notched arrowheads, one Harrell point base, one Garza-like point, and a few unusual points that do not fall easily into any of the more common categories found in the region.

Our type designations broadly follow those of Suhm and Jelks (1962) and Bell (1958, 1960). The Washita, as used here, is a small triangular projectile point with small side notches and a straight to concave base. We also include as Washitas a small number of specimens with slightly convex bases. Although Suhm and Krieger (1954:500) classified the Washita as a subtype of the Harrell point, Bell (1958) classified it as a separate type of small side-notched point lacking a basal notch. We follow Bell's system here.

Washita points are by far the most numerous type at Henderson, comprising 46.7% of the total point assemblage (62.2% if the large number of unidentifiable fragments comprising the "indeterminate" category are excluded; see Fig. 15.1). Most of the Henderson specimens have concave bases (82.5% of the 103 measurable bases are concave, 17.5% are straight to slightly convex). Their side notches are consistently placed approximately one-third of the way from the base to the tip (the ratio of blade length to maximum length in a sample of 114 complete or nearly complete Washita points is 0.68 ± .08). In some of the points, the side notches are deep, narrow, and parallel-sided, while in others the notches are more open and rounded or "U"-shaped. However, when examined statistically, these two notch forms appear to be arbitrary endpoints of a continuum in notch shapes (expressed by the ratio of notch breadth to depth) rather than discrete stylistic variants of the Washita.

Three points are unusual variants of the typical Washita (Fig. 15.3a, b). One of these, from Room E-4 in the East Bar, is thick in cross-section and has broad, shallow notches, a slightly convex base, and a deliberately serrated blade. Two multi-notched

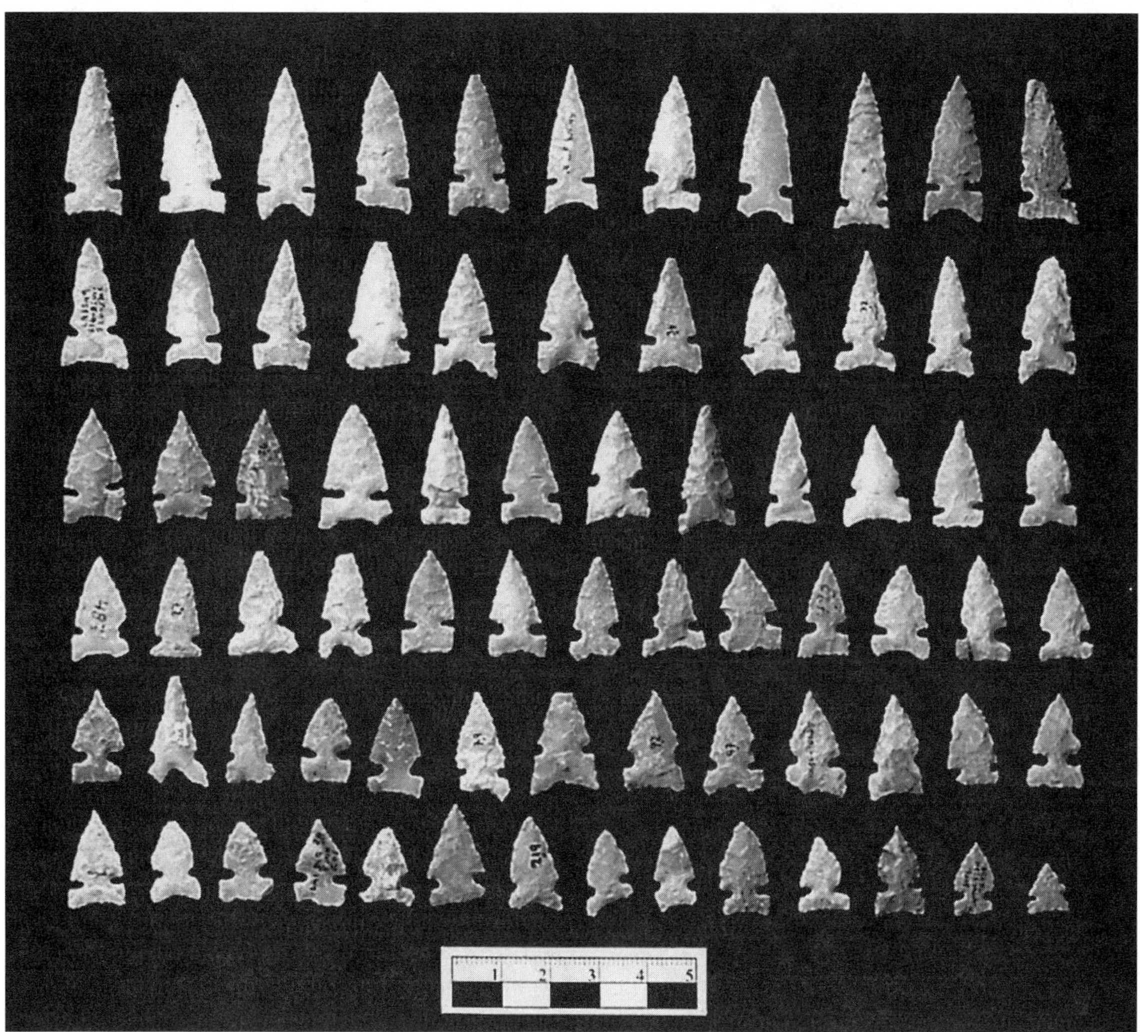

Figure 15.1. Washita points from the Henderson Site.

points were also recovered. The first example, again found in Room E-4, has a broken notch and base on one half of the point, and two notches on the other intact side of the point. The second multi-notched point, recovered in the East Plaza, has two notches on each side of the blade. One pair of notches is located just above the base in the normal position for small side-notched points. The second notch is half way between the blade tip and the first set of notches. The blade tip of this second point has been sharpened, and wear on the tip indicates the possible use of the point as a drill.

The second most common point form at Henderson is the Fresno (Fig. 15.2). Comprising 24.9% of the sample (33.1% excluding the "indeterminates"), Fresnos are small triangular points which generally have straight to concave bases and which lack side notches. Like the Washitas (82.5%), most of the Fresnos from the site have concave bases (73.8% of 61 specimens with measurable bases).[2] Not surprisingly, the Fresno has been characterized in the literature both as a distinctive projectile point type, and as an unfinished blank or preform for the manufacture of Washita points, and probably also Harrell and Garza points (e.g., Whittaker 1987:470; Jelks 1993:10-11). We will return to this issue shortly.

Only a single basal fragment of a Harrell point was found at Henderson (Fig. 15.3). This specimen was recovered from disturbed surface deposits overlying Room E-2 in the East Bar. The Harrell, as used here, is a small side-notched point with a third notch placed in the middle of the base. It should be noted that several of the Washita points in this assemblage resemble Harrell points due to their deep basal indentations. However, the Harrell point is distinguished by a clearly defined notch in the base, not just a deep, but broad basal concavity.

Like the Harrell, only one Garza point was recovered at Henderson (Fig. 15.3). Garza points are small triangular points lacking side notches but having a single notch in the center of the base. Again, like the Harrell, the sole Garza was found in highly disturbed surficial deposits overlying the floor of Room C-2 in the Center Bar. There is extensive wear on the blade tip, indicating the possible use of this biface as a drill.

Table 15.1. Frequency of projectile point types by provenience at the Henderson Site.

Projectile Point Type	Provenience							
	Combined Room Blocks	Center Bar	Room C-5	East Plaza	East Bar	Other Areas	Entire Site	
	n	*n*	*n*	*n*	*n*	*n*	*n*	%
Washita	150	76	33	32	74	32	214	46.7
Serrated "Washita"[a]	1	-	-	-	1	-	1	0.2
Multi-notched "Washita"[b]	1	-	-	1	1	-	2	0.4
Fresno	94	48	23	12	46	8	114	24.9
Harrell	1	-	-	-	1	-	1	0.2
Garza	1	1	-	-	-	-	1	0.2
Corner-notched[c]	2	1	-	1	1	-	3	0.7
Dart point/hafted knife	7	-	-	1	7	-	8	1.7
Indeterminate	82	48	19	15	34	17	114	24.9
TOTAL	339	174	75	62	165	57	458	99.9

[a]An unusual specimen with extremely broad, shallow notches and a slightly convex base.
[b]Washita-like points, one specimen with a single side notch on one lateral edge and two side notches on the opposite edge, the other specimen with two notches on each edge.
[c]Arrowheads.

Three small, triangular, corner-notched arrowheads were also recovered in the excavations (Fig. 15.3). We have not assigned these points to a formal type. One of the specimens, from the Center Bar, is missing the base, but may have had corner notches. The other examples, one from the East Plaza and one from the East Bar, are complete.

The final category of points found at Henderson includes several relatively large, thick dart points or hafted knives (Fig. 15.3). No attempt is made here to assign these to type. Two of these points—a deeply corner-notched specimen of dark brown chert and a shallowly side-notched specimen with rounded base of "fingerprint" chert—were found directly on the floor of Room E-3, the pitroom which also yielded the burial cache of 43 dart points/knives (i.e., Feature 36; see Rocek and Speth 1986). These specimens may well have been part of the same set, which for some reason were either not placed into the grave or became displaced at some later date.

There are 114 fragments of points which, due to their incomplete nature, cannot be assigned to type. Projectile point tips comprise 111 of these. Judging by their size and shape, most of these tip fragments probably derive from Washita and Fresno points. The unclassifiable fragments do not include many of the basal fragments, for these could often be identified to a specific point type.

Comparison of Washita and Fresno Point Attributes

Two projectile point forms—Washita and Fresno—comprise the vast majority of the Henderson assemblage. Interestingly, there is considerable uncertainty among archaeologists whether the Fresno, or its unnamed Southwestern counterpart, should be treated as a distinct point type in its own right, or should instead be seen as an unfinished "blank" designed for the manufacture of Washitas, Harrells, and Garzas (e.g., Christenson 1997; Jelks 1993:10-11; Whittaker 1987:470). In an attempt to clarify this issue, nineteen size attributes and several shape indices for the Henderson Washitas and Fresnos were systematically compared. Most of the measurements are self-explanatory and only a brief description is provided here.

Maximum length of complete point was measured parallel to the long axis of the specimen from the tip to the most proximal extremity of the base. Maximum thickness was taken wherever it occurred on the point, which in many cases proved to be in the neck or base area. Blade length was measured parallel to the long axis of the point from the tip to the shoulder. Shoulder width was taken perpendicular to the point's long axis just above (distal to) the notches. Stem length is the portion of the specimen from the shoulder to the proximal extremity of the base. It includes the neck and base, and in complete points is identical to the value obtained by subtracting blade length from maximum length. Base width is the maximum width of the haft element, taken at the most proximal extremity of the base. Neck width is the minimum distance between the notches. On Washita points, notch breadth and notch depth were recorded for each notch. The two notches were distinguished from each other on the basis of their breadth, the more constricted one being referred to as the "narrow" notch, the more open one as the "other" notch. Notch depth was measured perpendicular to the long axis of the point, and in most cases from the lateral edge of the shoulder to the neck. Notch width was measured perpendicular to depth. Basal concavity (or convexity) was measured perpendicular to an imaginary line drawn between the most proximal corners of the base. The degree of concavity was measured from this line to the maximum extent of the concavity, and was assigned a negative value. Convexity of the base was measured in the opposite direction from the line and

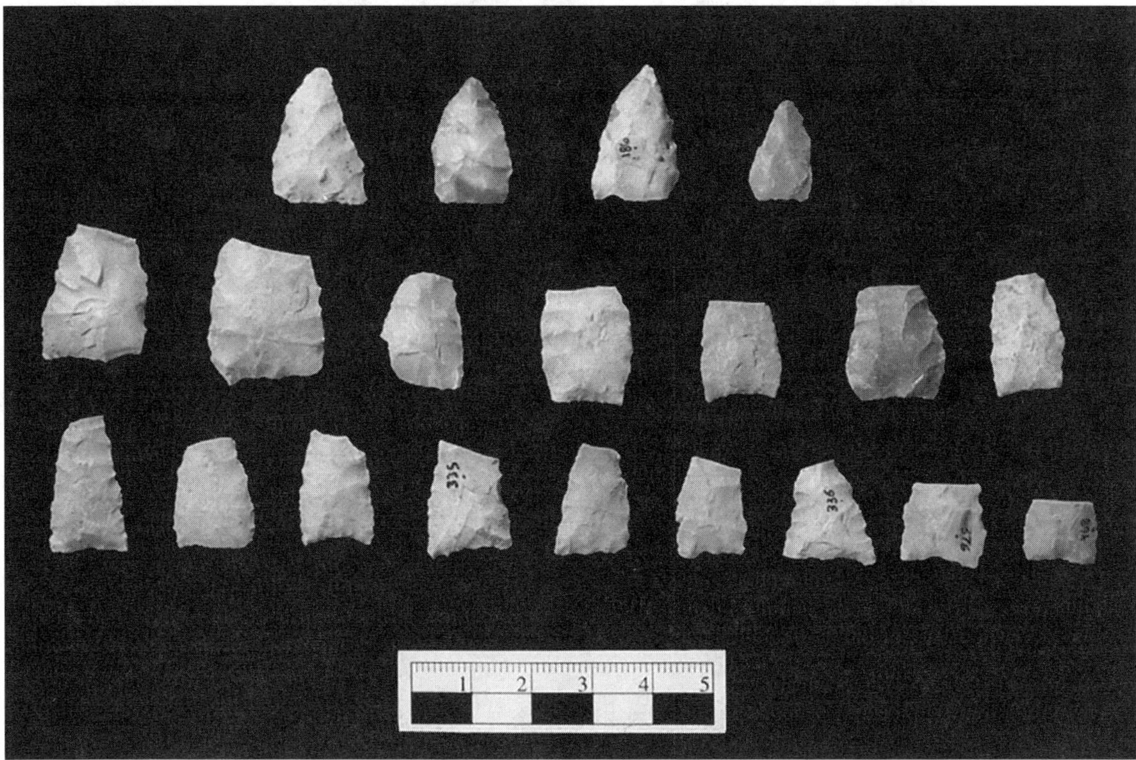

Figure 15.2. Fresno points from the Henderson Site.

was assigned a positive value. Only a few specimens had either straight or convex bases.

The summary descriptive data for the Henderson Washitas and Fresnos, as well as the results of the statistical analyses, are summarized in Table 15.2. Significance was assessed using the Mann-Whitney U-test (Siegel 1956), a nonparametric test which does not require the assumption of normally distributed samples. As the following discussion will attempt to show, the two types differ consistently and significantly in size, shape, quality of retouch, and raw material selection. All but the last of these differences are consistent with the view that the Fresnos at Henderson are unfinished blanks or preforms. Only the difference in raw material selection might point toward the opposite conclusion, namely that the two forms constitute distinct and legitimate projectile point types. Even if one adopts the latter position, and sees the two forms as discrete types, the results of these, and subsequent, analyses fail to provide any clear evidence that Washitas and Fresnos were used by the villagers for different purposes, or that they represent stylistic variants that were associated with the residents of different room blocks.

Overall, Fresno points are larger than their notched counterparts, a generalization which holds for all attributes except maximum length. Washita points tend to have slightly longer maximum lengths ($\bar{x}$ = 2.23 cm) than Fresno points ($\bar{x}$ = 2.14 cm), although the difference is not significant. Fresno points are significantly thicker ($\bar{x}$ = 0.35 cm) than Washitas ($\bar{x}$ = 0.30 cm); and they also have larger base widths (Fresno, $\bar{x}$ = 1.27 cm; Washita, $\bar{x}$ = 1.19 cm). Given these size differences, it is not surprising that Fresnos are also significantly heavier than Washitas (Fresno, $\bar{x}$ = 0.92 g; Washita, $\bar{x}$ = 0.66 g). As might be expected, the differences between the two point types also extend to their overall shape, as expressed by the ratio of maximum length to base width. The closer the measure approaches 1.0, the more the point shape approximates an equilateral triangle. Washitas have a longer, more streamlined shape ($\bar{x}$ = 1.92), while Fresno points are "squatter" in overall shape ($\bar{x}$ = 1.73). The difference is statistically significant (p = .044, U-test; not shown in Table 15.2). Finally, while the majority of specimens of both point types have indented or concave bases, the depth of the concavity is greater on average in the Washita points than in the unnotched Fresnos.

In sum, Washita and Fresno points at Henderson differ significantly from each other in both size and shape. While Washita points are comparable in length to Fresno points, Fresnos tend to be thicker, wider, heavier, and squatter in overall shape. Fresno points also have a less pronounced basal concavity than Washita points. And, as alluded to earlier, most Fresnos are less finely flaked than Washitas. All of these differences, with the possible exception of length, are compatible with the view that many, perhaps all, of the Fresnos were merely blanks or preforms waiting to be made into Washita points. The only evidence that might point in the opposite direction is the fact that nearly 86% of the Fresnos are made of a locally available gray chert (see below), whereas fewer than 75% of the Washitas are made of

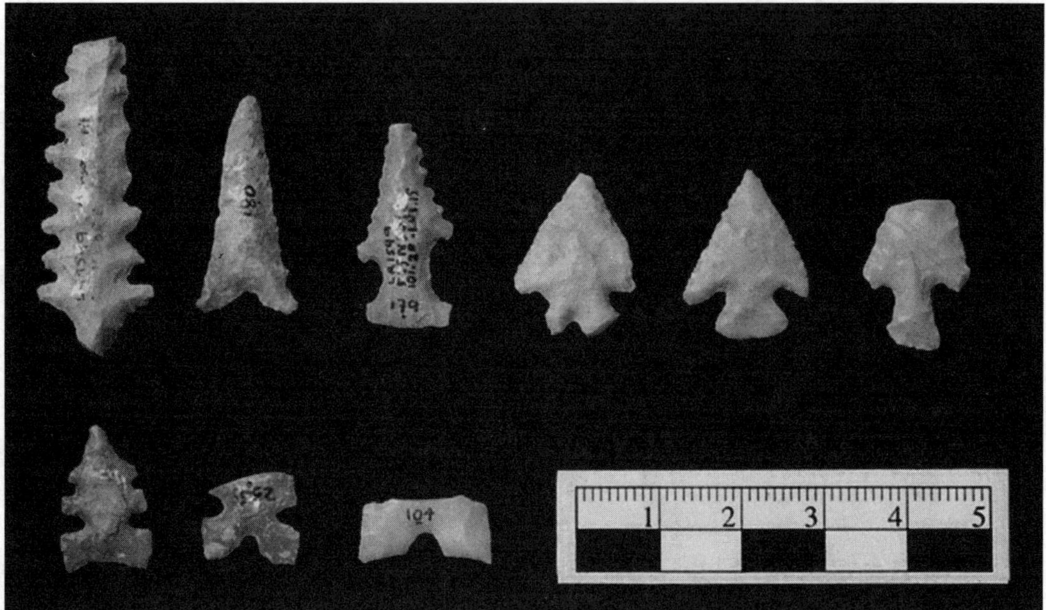

Figure 15.3. Miscellaneous projectile point types from the Henderson Site.

this same material, a difference that is statistically significant ($t_s = 2.64; p < .01$).[3] One would not expect any major difference in raw material selection if Fresnos were merely unfinished Washitas. This of course assumes that all of the Washitas were made on-site. If the villagers made some of the Washitas elsewhere and brought them into the community in finished form, or if they received some of them as gifts or through exchange, the proportions of the various raw materials might then be expected to differ from those seen in the Fresnos. Thus, while we cannot resolve the issue conclusively, we feel that the preponderance of the measurement evidence presented here supports the view that the Fresno at Henderson is an unfinished Washita point and not a distinct point type in its own right. This conclusion must not be taken to mean that all Fresnos, at all times, and in all places were unfinished projectile points. Christenson (1997) cites several ethnohistoric cases where Fresnos were hafted and used as projectile tips.

Lithic Materials Utilized at Henderson

Nine clearly different types of lithic material were used at Henderson for the manufacture of projectile points (Table 15.3). Additional material types (e.g., Edwards Plateau chert, Tiger "chert") were recognized in the cache of points found with the burial in Feature 36 in the East Bar (see Rocek and Speth 1986); these are not included in Table 15.3. A tenth "miscellaneous" category was needed as a catchall for those lithic materials which were not readily classifiable in one of the other categories.

The vast majority of the points at Henderson ($n = 360$) were made from a light gray material, here called "local gray" chert. This material is abundantly available eroding from the bedrock limestone outcrops to the west of Henderson, as well as in the gravels exposed along the channel of the Hondo and Rocky Arroyo. There is some variation in the shades of light gray chert at the site, but overall the material is a consistent, rather than heterogeneous, category.

The next most common lithic type ($n = 42$) is identified as "Tecovas-like" jasper (red variety). This material comprises about ten percent of the entire projectile point assemblage. The label "Tecovas-like" is used because the source of the material remains to be securely identified. Tecovas jasper occurs along the eastern escarpment of the Llano Estacado south of Amarillo in the Texas Panhandle (Hughes 1978:20-21; Katz and Katz 1976:70; see also Mallouf 1989). According to Banks (1984:72), material closely resembling Tecovas jasper is also found in the Oklahoma Panhandle in tributary areas of the North Canadian River and in the headwaters of the Cimarron River in New Mexico. Tecovas-like materials also outcrop west of the "Caprock" or Llano Estacado, approximately 70 km east-northeast of Henderson (Donald E. Clifton, pers. comm.). Finally, Tecovas look-alikes can occasionally be found in gravels along the Pecos River near Roswell, although these nodules are generally small and of poor quality. Thus, the Tecovas-like materials found at Henderson could have come from any of these sources, including local gravels, although the latter seems the least likely. A small proportion of the assemblage ($n = 6$, 1.3%) was classified as a pink variety of Tecovas-like jasper. The source of this material is also uncertain.

The next most common lithic types at Henderson are chalcedonies which, like the Tecovas materials, are present in two different color variations: clear ($n = 8$) and red ($n = 8$). The reddish chalcedony appears to be an iron-rich variety of the clear chalcedony, and may well have come from the same, currently unidentified, lithic source.

Table 15.2. Summary descriptive data for Washita and Fresno points from the Henderson Site (all proveniences combined)[a]

Attribute	Washita			Fresno			Signif.[c]
	n	Mean±1σ	CV[b]	*n*	Mean±1σ	CV[b]	
Max. length	87	2.23±.46	20.5	31	2.14±.53	24.1	.231
Max. thickness	87	0.30±.05	16.6	31	0.35±.10	25.7	.000
Blade length	129	1.53±.42	27.4	—	—	—	—
Shoulder width	157	1.06±.13	12.3	—	—	—	—
Stem length	109	0.70±14	20.0	—	—	—	—
Basal width	106	1.19±.18	15.1	81	1.27±.23	18.1	.006
Neck width	192	0.65±.12	18.4	—	—	—	—
Narrow notch width	147	0.21±.06	33.0	—	—	—	—
Narrow notch depth	144	0.20±.06	30.0	—	—	—	—
Other notch width	75	0.23±.06	33.0	—	—	—	—
Other notch depth	76	0.21±.07	35.0	—	—	—	—
Basal concavity	103	0.09±.14	158.8	61	0.05±.08	177.5	.001
Weight	87	0.66±.24	34.0	31	0.93±.51	54.3	.048

[a]All lengths in cm; weight in g; entries of "—" denote measurements not applicable to the Fresno type (e.g., various notch measurements).

[b]Coefficient of variation.

[c]Statistical significance (probability level) based on Mann-Whitney U-test (Siegel 1956).

Several points (n = 7) were made of so-called fingerprint chert, a distinctive opaque, gray-and-white-banded material. This material is abundant in the Sacramento Mountains west of Roswell, although cobbles and pebbles of fingerprint chert are fairly common in gravels along the channel of Rocky Arroyo only a few kilometers downstream from Henderson.

Two points were made of light tan chert and five were made of dark brown chert. The source of these materials is unknown. The former could be either local or nonlocal in origin; the latter is probably nonlocal.

Only five points are made of Alibates chert, a material that is clearly nonlocal in origin. This highly distinctive material comes from quarries along the Canadian River in the Texas Panhandle, north of Amarillo (Shaeffer 1958).

Finally, fifteen points and fragments were unclassifiable as to lithic type. The source of these cherts is unknown but it is entirely possible that many or all could have been found locally in the gravels of the Pecos, Hondo, or Rocky Arroyo.

The distribution of lithic materials by point type is shown in Table 15.4. Most of the Washita and Fresno points, the two types that comprise the vast majority of the Henderson assemblage, are made of locally obtainable gray chert. As noted earlier, however, the proportion of this chert type is significantly greater among the Fresnos (86.0%) than among the Washitas (73.8%). In other words, more of the Washitas are made of raw materials that had been obtained from sources beyond the Pecos Valley. Among the nonlocal materials used to make Washitas, the red variety of Tecovas-like jasper is the most common; a few are also made of Alibates. Both of these material types point to sources out in the grasslands to the east or northeast of Henderson. Two other potentially nonlocal raw materials, though uncommon at the site, are noteworthy because they occur primarily among point types that on stylistic grounds were probably manufactured either before or after the principal late thirteenth-century occupation at the site. Thus, two of the eight "archaic" dart points found outside of mortuary contexts at Henderson are made of dark brown chert. Likewise, of the two pieces of tan chert that were recovered, one had been fashioned into the site's only Harrell point, a type that probably postdates A.D. 1400 in the Southern Plains region (Parry and Speth 1984:31-32).

Observations on Blade Breakage

Slightly fewer than one-third (n = 129) of the 458 projectile points recovered at Henderson were complete. The rest of the assemblage consisted of point fragments, ranging from tiny pieces of bases and tips to relatively complete specimens missing only part of the blade or haft element. In the site-wide assemblage, 156 fragments were complete basal elements, all of which were identifiable to type (Washita, n = 85; Fresno, n = 71). There were also 111 isolated tips from small triangular arrow points. Not surprisingly, many of these were from Washita points that had broken off directly at the notches; many others, broken from the point more distally along the blade, could not be confidently assigned to type, although virtually all of them, based on their thickness, probably came from either Washita or Fresno points.

Among the Washitas, 87 of the 214 classifiable specimens were complete or nearly complete, whereas among the Fresnos,

Table 15.3. Frequency of lithic raw material types used for the manufacture of projectile points at the Henderson Site.[a]

Raw Material Type	Provenience					
	Center Bar	East Plaza	East Bar	Other Areas	Entire Site	
	n	*n*	*n*	*n*	*n*	%
Local gray chert	137	54	131	38	360	78.6
"Fingerprint" chert	5	1	1	0	7	1.5
Alibates chert	3	1	1	0	5	1.1
Tecovas-like jasper (pink)	2	0	3	1	6	1.3
Tecovas-like jasper (red)	15	5	9	13	42	9.2
Chalcedony (red)	4	0	3	1	8	1.7
Chalcedony (clear)	3	0	5	0	8	1.7
Dark brown chert	2	0	2	1	5	1.1
Tan chert	0	0	2	0	2	0.4
"Miscellaneous" chert	3	1	8	3	15	3.3

[a]Excludes material types (e.g., Edwards Plateau chert, Tiger "chert") found in projectile point cache associated with Feature 36 burial in East Bar (see Rocek and Speth 1986).

only 31 of the 114 classifiable specimens were complete, a difference that is statistically significant ($t_s = 2.46, p = .01$). Given the more delicate nature of the Washitas, we had expected that a greater proportion of them would have been broken during the final stages of manufacture, especially during the notching process, and of course during use. The fact that more of the Fresnos were broken would appear to be at odds with this expectation. Two explanations for this counterintuitive result come to mind, although neither is particularly convincing. First, if we accept the view that Fresnos were merely preforms for Washitas, these results might imply that breakage was more likely to occur early in the manufacturing process, perhaps because the local gray chert, the material most commonly used at the site, was commonly flawed or otherwise of poor quality. Hence, once a suitable piece was found and successfully transformed into a preform, its chances of breaking during later manufacturing stages sharply declined.

On the other hand, the breakage data may reflect little more than screening and sampling biases that favored the recovery of Fresno points. The small, delicate bases of Washita points, once broken from the rest of the point, could easily have passed unnoticed through a quarter-inch screen. This problem may have been exacerbated by the fact that the bases themselves often split through the basal concavity into two smaller fragments or "ears" that are even less likely to have been recovered by routine screening. Moreover, while initial sorting of the thousands of tiny flakes from Henderson almost certainly retrieved most of the whole Washita bases, some, perhaps many, isolated basal "ears" may have been overlooked.

In sum, while we still lean toward the Fresno-as-preform perspective, there are problems with this interpretation, and the verdict, at least in the case of Henderson, remains uncertain.

Intrasite Comparisons

In this section, we compare the projectile points recovered from the principal units excavated: Center Bar, East Bar, and East Plaza. We focus our discussion primarily on the Washita and Fresno points, since these are by far the most common forms regardless of provenience. We begin by systematically comparing the projectile point assemblages from the East Bar and Center Bar in order to determine whether there are any major differences in either the overall typological composition of their assemblages, or in the size and shape of the Washitas and Fresnos. We then compare the combined room block assemblage with the much smaller sample from the East Plaza to determine whether there are contrasts in the projectile point assemblages that in any way mirror the striking differences between these two areas of the village in their faunal assemblages.

Typologically, the projectile point assemblages from the Center Bar and East Bar are very similar. Both are dominated by Washita and Fresno points, and the proportions of these two forms are virtually identical in both room blocks. In the Center Bar, 43.7% of the points are Washitas while in the East Bar 44.8% are Washitas (see Table 15.1 above). Fresnos are uniformly less common at Henderson, regardless of provenience, making up 27.6% of the Center Bar assemblage and 27.9% of the East Bar assemblage. Obviously, these differences are not statistically significant. If the Fresnos are Washita preforms, these results indicate that point manufacturing was carried out in both room blocks with nearly equal frequency.

The inhabitants of both room blocks also made use of virtually identical proportions of local versus nonlocal raw materials for the manufacture of their points. Thus, in the Center Bar, 78.7% of the points (all types combined) are made of local gray chert. In the East Bar, the figure is 79.4%.

Table 15.4. Frequency of lithic raw material types by projectile point type at the Henderson Site.

Raw Material Type	Arrowhead							Dart Point/ Hafted Knife	Indet.	Total
	Washita	Fresno	Harrell	Serrated Washita	Multi-Notched Washita	Corner-Notched	Garza			
Local gray chert	158	98	-	1	2	3	1	4	93	360
"Fingerprint" chert	2	1	-	-	-	-	-	1	3	7
Alibates chert	4	-	-	-	-	-	-	-	1	5
Tecovas-like chert (pink)	3	1	-	-	-	-	-	-	2	6
Tecovas-like chert (red)	30	7	-	-	-	-	-	-	5	42
Chalcedony (red)	5	2	-	-	-	-	-	-	1	8
Chalcedony (clear)	5	2	-	-	-	-	-	-	1	8
Dark brown chert	1	1	-	-	-	-	-	2	1	5
Tan chert	-	1	1	-	-	-	-	-	-	2
"Miscellaneous" chert	6	1	-	-	-	-	-	1	7	15
TOTAL	214	114	1	1	2	3	1	8	114	458

Table 15.5. Summary measurement data for Washita and Fresno points from the Center Bar and East Bar at the Henderson Site.[a]

Attribute[b]	Washita			Fresno		
	Center Bar Mean±1σ	East Bar Mean±1σ	Signif.[c]	Center Bar Mean±1σ	East Bar Mean±1σ	Signif.[c]
Max. length	2.33±.49	2.21±.44	.181	2.16±.47	2.17±.63	.550
Max. thickness	0.29±.06	0.28±.05	.722	0.34±.09	0.34±.08	.898
Blade length	1.59±.45	1.49±.38	.331	—	—	—
Shoulder width	1.09±.12	1.02±.10	.002	—	—	—
Stem length	0.75±.14	0.69±.15	.158	—	—	—
Neck width	0.64±.11	0.66±.13	.460	—	—	—
Base width	1.22±.15	1.20±.18	.599	1.30±.21	1.28±.27	.838
Narrow notch width	0.22±.06	0.21±.06	.603	—	—	—
Narrow notch depth	0.22±.07	0.18±.06	.017	—	—	—
Other notch width	0.23±.06	0.24±.06	.496	—	—	—
Other notch depth	0.22±.08	0.19±.05	.136	—	—	—
Basal concavity	0.11±.14	0.07±.15	.190	0.04±.06	0.05±.09	.369
Weight	0.68±.23	0.66±.26	.474	1.02±.52	0.91±.47	.448
Blade shape[d]	1.51±.38	1.48±.38	.529	—	—	—
Point shape[e]	2.01±.52	1.86±.32	.219	1.70±.23	1.73±.42	.500*

[a]Entries of "—" denote measurements not applicable to the Fresno type (e.g., various notch measurements).
[b]All lengths in cm; weight in g.
[c]Statistical significance (probability level) based on Mann-Whitney U-test (Siegel 1956); entries accompanied by "*" indicate small samples requiring use of median test.
[d]Ratio of blade length to shoulder width.
[e]Ratio of maximum length to base width.

Included with the Washitas and Fresnos were modest numbers of specimens with straight to slightly convex bases. The proportions of these basal variants in the two room blocks, combining Washitas and Fresnos to maximize sample sizes, are statistically indistinguishable. Thus, in the Center Bar, 23.1% of the specimens have straight to slightly convex bases, compared to 22.2% of the East Bar sample.

The Washita and Fresno points from the two room blocks are also very similar in size and shape (see Table 15.5). For the Washitas, a total of thirteen size attributes and two shape indices were compared. Of these, only two achieve statistical significance: shoulder width and notch depth. The Center Bar points tend to be slightly broader at the shoulder than those from the East Bar, and their notches are deeper. All of the other attributes, as well as overall point shape and blade shape, exhibit remarkable uniformity across the site, underscoring the tremendous internal homogeneity of the Henderson Washita points. Even the shoulder width and notch depth that appear to distinguish the Washitas in the two room blocks turn out to be significantly correlated with each other, indicating that they are more or less redundant expressions of the same component of projectile point size ($r_s = 0.49, p < .01$). In essence, therefore, the Washitas from the Center Bar and East Bar really only differ from each other in a single dimension, and the magnitude of that difference is so small that it may be of no cultural or behavioral significance.

The Fresnos are also remarkably uniform across the site, showing no significant differences between the two room blocks in either mean attribute measurements or in overall shape. Average values of maximum length, maximum thickness, basal width, basal concavity, weight, and point shape all seem to come from the same homogeneous population of points.

In sum, both in terms of typological composition and in terms of size and shape, the projectile point assemblages from the Center Bar and East Bar are remarkably similar. If these two room blocks were occupied by discrete corporate groups, bounded to any significant degree by social, economic, or other criteria of membership, their existence is not reflected by any clear patterning in the projectile point assemblages, aside perhaps from a tiny difference among the Washitas in average shoulder width.

We now turn to a comparison of the projectile points from the room blocks with the sample recovered from the East Plaza. Since no major distinctions were found between either the Washitas or the Fresnos in the two room blocks, in the discussion that follows we have combined the Center Bar and East Bar samples for each form. Unfortunately, there is no way to augment the small size of the East Plaza sample.

As shown in Table 15.1 above, the proportion of Washitas in the East Plaza midden assemblage is higher, and the proportion of Fresnos lower, than in the combined room block assemblage, but neither difference is statistically significant (Washitas, $t_s = 1.07, p > .05$; Fresnos, $t_s = 1.44, p > .05$).

Nor was there any significant difference between the two proveniences in the proportion of Washita and Fresno points with concave as opposed to straight or convex bases. Thus, among the Washitas, 81.8% of the East Plaza specimens have concave bases compared to 82.1% in the combined room block assemblage. Similarly, among the Fresnos, 87.5% of the East Plaza specimens have indented bases, compared to 70.8% in the room block sample ($t_s = 1.10, p > .05$).

Although we had no reason *a priori* to expect the plaza and room block projectile point assemblages to differ typologically from each other, we did expect them to differ in the ratio of tips to bases. To our surprise, however, this was not the case. Of the 62 points recovered from the East Plaza, 22.6% were isolated tips. The proportion of tips in the room blocks was nearly identical. Thus, despite evidence discussed in previous chapters that most, if not all, of the large- and medium-size mammals, particularly bison and antelope, were initially processed in the plaza, there is no evidence in the 1980-1981 assemblage to suggest that isolated point tips that may still have been embedded in the carcasses when the animals were brought into the village were systematically removed and discarded there before the meat was taken into the rooms.

Perhaps not surprisingly, the Washitas and Fresnos from the room blocks are both strikingly similar in size and shape to their counterparts from the East Plaza (Table 15.6). Only a single measurement turned out to differ significantly between the two proveniences—the base width of Fresno points. The specimens from the rooms are on average about 1.5 mm wider at their base than are those from the plaza midden. However, since none of the other measurements or shape indices for the Fresnos differ significantly between the two proveniences, it is unlikely that this single contrast is behaviorally or culturally of much import.

Thus, while the East Plaza and room blocks differ dramatically from each other in their faunal content, with 80% of the bison remains ending up in the plaza and most small-mammal remains being discarded in the structures (see Chapter 14), there are no parallel contrasts between these two proveniences in either the typological composition of their projectile point assemblages or in the average size or shape of the specimens that comprise the two principal point types.

Projectile Points and Hunting

The thousands of bison and medium ungulate bones encountered at Henderson testify to the importance of hunting in the village economy. Interestingly, however, had we not excavated in the East Plaza, we would have found almost no evidence of bison, and we would have grossly underestimated the importance of antelope. Finding the remains of the medium and large mammals was not simply a matter of excavating in the East Plaza. Over 80% of the bison remains and roughly half of the antelope bones came from a single 20 m^2 concentration near the southern margin of the East Plaza, a peripheral area that we tested upon the advice of a knowledgeable local amateur archaeologist, Robert Leslie. Prior to his visit, we had made a number of test excavations in both plazas and in every case had encountered bedrock within a few centimeters of the surface. We had decided therefore to abandon work in the plazas and concentrate on the room blocks. Leslie directed our attention to an isolated mesquite bush growing near the south end of the East Plaza. He pointed out that its presence implied relatively deep deposits in this particular area of the plaza, because the mesquite was large and must have had a substantial root system. He was correct; our excavation revealed an ancient karstic depression in the bedrock that was filled with more than a meter of ash and fire-cracked rock, as well as thousands of antelope and bison bones.

The systematic disposal of medium- to large-mammal remains in concentrated areas outside of the rooms, and even outside of the pueblo, is not unique to Henderson. For example, Driver (1991:200-201) reported a similar pattern at the Robinson Site near Capitan, New Mexico, and Alison E. Rautman (pers. comm.) found an analogous situation at a pueblo site near Gran Quivira. There is more than one formation process that might

Table 15.6. Summary measurement data for Washita and Fresno points from the combined room blocks and East Plaza at the Henderson Site.[a]

Attribute[b]	Washita			Fresno		
	Combined Room Blks. Mean±1σ	East Plaza Mean±1σ	Signif.[c]	Combined Room Blks. Mean±1σ	East Plaza Mean±1σ	Signif.[c]
Max. length	2.27±.47	2.07±.28	.130	2.16±.54	1.75±.04	.241*
Max. thickness	0.29±.05	0.29±.04	.713	0.34±.08	0.30±.03	.119
Blade length	1.54±.42	1.43±.41	.154	—	—	—
Shoulder width	1.06±.12	1.07±.13	.691	—	—	—
Stem length	0.71±.15	0.69±.13	.503	—	—	—
Neck width	0.65±.12	0.64±.10	.621	—	—	—
Base width	1.21±.17	1.15±.17	.143	1.29±.24	1.14±.11	.053*
Narrow notch width	0.22±.06	0.19±.05	.109	—	—	—
Narrow notch depth	0.20±.07	0.20±.05	.597	—	—	—
Other notch width	0.24±.06	0.21±.04	.138	—	—	—
Other notch depth	0.21±.07	0.22±.06	.566	—	—	—
Basal concavity	0.09±.14	0.08±.14	.700	0.04±.08	0.08±.08	.627*
Weight	0.68±.25	0.63±.20	.524	0.96±.52	0.45±.07	.241*
Blade shape[d]	1.49±.38	1.40±.33	.263	—	—	—
Point shape[e]	1.93±.43	1.92±.24	.500*	1.71±.34	1.62	—[f]

[a]Entries of "—" denote measurements not applicable to the Fresno type (e.g., various notch measurements).
[b]All lengths in cm; weight in g.
[c]Statistical significance (probability level) based on Mann-Whitney U-test (Siegel 1956); entries accompanied by "*" indicate small samples requiring use of median test.
[d]Ratio of blade length to shoulder width.
[e]Ratio of maximum length to base width.
[f]Too few cases (n = 1 in East Plaza).

give rise to such a disposal pattern. For example, routine household cleaning would very likely bias the distribution of faunal remains, with bulkier bones and other trash being discarded in localized middens away from dwellings (Schiffer 1987). Bones of larger mammals might also accumulate in extramural areas simply because these are convenient places in which to butcher large animals. In addition, ritual practices related to hunting may lead to the selective disposal of the bones of larger mammals in shrines or other special contexts within and even beyond the village precincts (e.g., Cordell 1977). And, in the Henderson case, communal patterns of food sharing, cooking, and possibly even consumption apparently led to the accumulation of thousands of bison and antelope bones in a singe large spoil heap in the earth oven complex at the southern end of the East Plaza (see Chapter 14).

Whatever the reason, there is a real possibility that the bones of larger mammals will be underrepresented in faunal samples from Pueblo village sites, particularly samples that derive largely from room block excavations (e.g., Driver 1991). To detect this sort of bias, we need an independent way to measure the degree to which the inhabitants of a prehistoric community engaged in big-game hunting, one that works even if the excavations do not adequately sample the nonresidential portions of the site. Perhaps the most obvious candidate for such a measure, though a crude one, is the number of projectile points that a site yields, ideally expressed in a standardized form to facilitate intersite comparisons, such as the number of points per unit volume of excavated sediment or the number of points per excavated structure. While this approach is not a new one (e.g., Nelson 1984:231; Bayham 1982:368-69; Head 1988; Bradley 1988:22-23), it has yet to be widely or systematically explored in the Southwest.

The Henderson case illustrates the potential of this approach. Though a small excavation by Southwestern standards, with barely 160 m^2 (80 m^3) opened and twelve rooms partially sampled, Henderson yielded an astounding number of bison, antelope, and deer bones (over 3,500) and an equally astounding number of complete and fragmentary projectile points (nearly 500 in nonmortuary contexts).[4] In other words, for every seven larger-mammal bones, one point or point fragment was found. Expressed in terms of density, Henderson yielded more than five points per cubic meter of excavated fill and overburden.

Finding suitable comparative data is very difficult. While many Southwestern excavation reports provide tabulations of the total number of points that were recovered, very few provide volumetric data that would allow one to determine the average density of points per cubic meter of deposit (e.g., Bradley 1988:22). This of course means that projectile point totals are heavily influenced by the overall scale of the excavations; big excavations tend to produce more points than small ones. There are obviously many other potential biases in these data as well,

Table 15.7. Frequency of projectile points from major Pueblo excavation and survey projects in the American Southwest.

Site	Points n	Reference
	New Mexico	
Pueblo Alto	104	Cameron (1987:271)
Salmon Ruin	282	Shelley (1983:73)
Gran Quivira, Mound 7	298	Young (1981:108-9)
Galaz Ruin[a]	249	LeBlanc (1984:236-45)
Arroyo Hondo	488	Phagan (1993:238)
Tijeras Pueblo	603	Judge (1974:47)[b]
Henderson (total)	529	Adler and Speth (this volume)
Henderson (surface)	57	Adler and Speth (this volume)
Pajarito Arch. Res. Project (surface)	327	Head (1988:22)
	Arizona	
Awatovi	208	Woodbury (1954:124-32)
Antelope House	54	Linford (1986:523)
Homolovi III	240	Lisa C. Young (pers. comm.)
Grasshopper[c]	±1000	Whittaker (1987:475)
Snaketown[d]	2159	Haury (1976:296)
	Colorado	
Mug House	19	Rohn (1971:107)
Wallace Ruin	355	Bradley (1988:23)[e]
	Chihuahua (Mexico)	
Casas Grandes (Medio Period)	98	DiPeso et al. (1974:389)

[a]Includes points recovered by Mimbres Foundation and University of Minnesota excavations.

[b]Cited in Phagan (1993:238).

[c]Whittaker (1987:475) examined over 500 points, which he estimates "to be roughly half of those recovered."

[d]Includes points recovered from the 1934-1935 and 1964-1965 excavations; many of these points came from cremations (Haury 1976:296).

[e]Bradley (1988:22-23) provides projectile point totals for several other Four Corners area sites; all produced fewer points than Wallace Ruin.

such as the failure in some excavations to use screens; reporting of only complete or identifiable specimens; sampling different disposal contexts or sites of different function; differences among sites in the frequency or intensity of warfare or in the manufacture of points specifically for use in mortuary ritual; greater reliance in some regions on perishable projectile tips; and so forth. Despite these and other potential problems, the abundance of points recovered in the modest excavations at the Henderson Site nonetheless stands out when compared with the tallies reported from many other, often vastly larger, excavations elsewhere in the Southwest (see Table 15.7; additional data from sites in the Four Corners area can be found in Bradley 1988:22-23).

We also include in Table 15.7 the number of points recovered on the surface by the Pajarito Archaeological Research Project (PARP), a large-scale survey that systematically covered 66 km^2 of terrain and examined a total of 880 sites (Head 1988:22). All points that were encountered during the PARP survey were collected. Despite this massive effort, the project yielded only 327 identifiable points (283 points from 153 sites, plus 44 isolated finds). For comparison, 57 projectile points were picked up from the surface of the Henderson Site. Again, there are innumerable factors that complicate the comparison, such as differences in surface visibility, intensity of local amateur collecting, and degree of disturbance by rodents and pothunters. But the magnitude of the difference is what is striking. The Pajarito survey produced on average fewer than two points per site, if we focus just on the 153 sites that yielded at least one point. The figure would be dramatically reduced if we included all 880 sites, many of which produced no points whatsoever. The yield of points from the surface of Henderson was over thirty times greater.

There seems little doubt that the quantity of points at Henderson faithfully reflects the tremendous importance of big-game hunting in the community's economy. (Importance here refers to the presumed contribution of large-mammal hunting to the villagers' diet in calories or kilograms of meat, not to the ritual or social significance that may have been accorded by the villagers to this activity.) However, in order for projectile points to provide a useful independent measure of the degree to which a community engaged in hunting, their distribution within the site must not be isomorphic with larger-mammal bone distribution. In other words, one should not have to find the particular places where the bones of the larger mammals were discarded in order to obtain a reliable estimate of the abundance of projectile points at the site.

This condition appears to be well satisfied at Henderson. We found no correlation, either positive or negative, between the frequency per grid unit of projectile points and the abundance of larger-mammal remains ($r_s = .03, p > .05$).[5] In fact, the density of points in the room blocks was comparable to, or even higher than, the value in the East Plaza midden (East Plaza midden, 5.21 points/m^3; total room block overburden and fill, 5.59 points/m^3; Room C-5 trash midden, 8.55 points/ m^3). Thus, even if we had totally missed the accumulation of bison and antelope bones in the East Plaza, and instead had confined our excavations entirely to the room blocks, we would still have recovered an extremely large number, and high density, of projectile points. While encouraging, these results of course do not mean that projectile points will work as effectively elsewhere in the Southwest. Our results do suggest, however, that an approach such as this, using density values to adjust for differing excavation scales, is well worth exploring further.

Temporal Perspective

Since completion of the original manuscript over a decade ago, in which we dealt only with the points recovered in the 1980-1981 field seasons, we have analyzed all of Henderson's projectile points, and present here a brief update on this material, with particular emphasis on similarities and contrasts between the Early phase and Late phase assemblages.

Projectile point density increases in the younger period, with by far the sharpest increase occurring in non-room contexts (Table 15.8). It is probably no coincidence that this increase parallels the Late phase increase in both the density and proportion of bison remains found in plaza as opposed to room block contexts (see Chapter 4).

Table 15.9 summarizes the frequency and proportions of the various types of projectile points recovered from Henderson broken down by temporal phase. Bifaces have been included in this table. They may be early-stage preforms for the manufacture of Washitas or other point types (possibly via the Fresno as an intermediate stage). Most of the bifaces are ovate and quite thick, averaging 3.87 ± 1.05 cm in length ($n = 55$), 2.35 ± 0.48 cm in width ($n = 65$), 0.82 ± 0.25 cm in thickness ($n = 87$), and 7.03 ± 5.37 g in weight ($n = 87$).

Particularly noteworthy in Table 15.9 is the significant increase in the proportion of Washitas in the Late phase ($t_s = 2.03$, $p < .05$), and the concomitant decline in all other point types, but most especially Fresnos. When looked at spatially, there is no significant change over time in the proportion of Washitas in the rooms ($t_s = 0.59, p > .05$), but their frequency jumps sharply in the plazas ($t_s = 3.37, p < .001$).

It is important to point out that the "decline" at Henderson in the popularity of Fresnos is relative, not absolute. Because percentages must sum to 100, when one percentage goes up, at least one other one must come down. Thus, from the percentages alone, it is impossible to determine whether Fresnos actually decline or merely fail to increase as rapidly as Washitas. Density measures provide the simplest way out of this dilemma. When looked at using density values, Fresnos entered both the Early and Late phase deposits at essentially the same rate (1.15 points/m^3 vs. 1.11 points/m^3). Washita points entered the record at an increased rate over time.

The data presented in Table 15.9 raise some intriguing questions. If, as we have suggested earlier in this chapter, the Fresno point represents an intermediate stage in the manufacture of Washitas, rather than a distinct projectile point form in its own right, then its relative decline, in the face of increasing numbers of Washitas, might imply that proportionately fewer Washita points were manufactured on-site in the Late phase than during the preceding period. This in turn might be an indication that the hunters' mobility had increased in the Late phase, such that more of their projectile points were made elsewhere. If so, then we would expect the proportion of Washitas made on local gray chert to decrease in the younger period. This however is not what happens. The proportion remains unchanged over time (Early phase, 74.0%; Late phase, 74.0%), casting doubt on the Fresno-as-preform perspective.

Table 15.8. Density of projectile points by provenience and chronological phase (all excavation seasons).[a]

Phase/Provenience	n	Excavated Volume (m^3)	Density (n/m^3)
Entire Site			
Early phase	248	70.7	3.51
Late phase	480	111.9	4.29
Room vs. Non-Room			
Early phase (room)	197	46.8	4.21
Early phase (non-room)	51	23.9	2.13
Late phase (room)	377	83.8	4.50
Late phase (non-room)	103	28.1	3.67

[a]Dart points and bifaces excluded.

Likewise, if Washitas increasingly were manufactured elsewhere in the Late phase, one might expect the proportions of complete vs. fragmentary points in the Henderson assemblage to change over time, although we are unable to specify the precise nature and direction such change should take. Instead, what we observe at Henderson is a pattern of breakage that remains virtually unchanged over time again casting doubt on the likelihood that significantly fewer Washitas were manufactured onsite in the later period.

	Complete	Tips	Bases
Early phase	32.1%	48.5%	19.4%
Late phase	32.5%	47.0%	20.5%

Thus, it is now beginning to seem increasingly likely that many of Henderson's Fresnos may, in fact, represent a distinct projectile point form, rather than a preform or blank for the manufacture of Washitas, as we believed when we first prepared the manuscript for this chapter. If so, their proportional decline in the Late phase might imply a change in the popularity of one style over another that might in turn serve, locally at least, as a valuable temporal marker. Such a change in popularity might, for example, reflect an increasing preference for notched over unnotched arrow points, because village hunters desired projectile tips that were more prone to shattering in a wound upon impact, or that were less likely to detach from the shaft (or foreshaft) when the arrow hit the intended target or when it was subsequently removed from the prey (see discussion and references in Christenson 1997). Unfortunately, we presently lack sufficient data from younger sites in the region to explore this expectation further. However, ongoing work at Bloom Mound, a nearby site that is demonstrably younger than Henderson's Late phase (see Chapter 3), may in the not-too-distant future yield an assemblage large enough to allow us to determine whether Fresno points do, in fact, continue to decline in relative popularity following Henderson's abandonment.

Basic metric data for the Washita points, broken down by phase, are provided in Table 15.10. The points from the two phases are strikingly similar in most respects, with very few differences achieving statistical significance. The exceptions are maximum thickness (measured anywhere on the point), neck width (measured between the notches), the ratio of neck width to maximum thickness, and the ratio of maximum point length to blade length. These differences are so slight, however, that it is difficult to believe they reflect conscious stylistic choices on the part of the knappers. Nevertheless, neck width and the ratio of maximum length to blade length both yield essentially the same ordering of Henderson's major proveniences as the one generated by seriating the El Paso Polychrome jar rims (see Chapter 3). Moreover, Bloom Mound, which postdates Henderson, yields a mean value for neck width of 0.72 ± .14 cm ($n = 23$), a result that makes sense in terms of its ceramically based temporal placement. The ratio of maximum length to blade length also yields the proper ordering, with Bloom Mound's

Table 15.9. Frequency of projectile point types by provenience at the Henderson Site (1980-1997)[a]

Projectile Point Type	Early Phase		Late Phase		Early Phase				Late Phase				Entire Site[b]	
					Room		Non-Room		Room		Non-Room			
	n	%	*n*	%	*n*	%	*n*	%	*n*	%	*n*	%	*n*	%
Washita	100	35.09	231	42.31	85	37.61	15	25.42	173	39.95	58	51.33	336	39.86
Serrated "Washita"	0	0.00	2	0.37	0	0.00	0	0.00	2	0.46	0	0.00	2	0.24
Multi-notched "Washita"	0	0.00	3	0.55	0	0.00	0	0.00	2	0.46	1	0.88	3	0.36
Fresno	81	28.42	124	22.71	65	28.76	16	27.12	106	24.48	18	15.93	209	24.79
Harrell	0	0.00	1	0.18	0	0.00	0	0.00	1	0.23	0	0.00	1	0.12
Garza	0	0.00	1	0.18	0	0.00	0	0.00	1	0.23	0	0.00	1	0.12
Corner-notched arrowhead	2	0.70	3	0.55	2	0.88	0	0.00	2	0.46	1	0.88	6	0.71
Dart point/hafted knife	4	1.40	12	2.20	4	1.77	0	0.00	10	2.31	2	1.77	17	2.02
Indeterminate	65	22.81	115	21.06	45	19.91	20	33.90	90	20.79	25	22.12	181	21.47
Biface	33	11.58	54	9.89	25	11.06	8	13.56	46	10.62	8	7.08	87	10.32
TOTAL	285	100.00	546	100.00	226	100.00	59	100.00	433	100.00	113	100.00	843	100.00

[a]Excludes 43 points/hafted knives recovered from Feature 36 burial (Rocek and Speth 1986).
[b]Totals for "entire site" differ from sum of Early phase and Late phase assemblages, because a number of projectile points were found on the surface or in excavation contexts where chronological placement could not be determined.

Table 15.10. Metric attributes of Henderson Site Washita points by chronological phase (1980-1997).

Attribute	Early Phase			Late Phase			Signif.[a]
	Mean	±1σ	n	Mean	±1σ	n	
Max. length (cm)	2.15	.47	55	2.20	.46	120	$t = -0.70, p > .05$
Max. thickness (cm)	.30	.05	100	.29	.05	231	$t = +1.95, p = .05$
Blade length (cm)	1.59	.41	61	1.52	.42	163	$t = +1.03, p > .05$
Shoulder width (cm)	1.05	.12	77	1.05	.15	191	$t = +0.12, p > .05$
Base width (cm)	1.15	.14	66	1.17	.19	142	$t = -0.82, p > .05$
Neck width (cm)	.62	.13	84	.66	.13	212	$t = -2.29, p < .05$
Concavity (cm)[b]	-.11	.11	56	-.08	.13	150	$t = -1.16, p > .05$
Weight (g)	.55	.20	100	.57	.25	231	$t = -0.57, p > .05$
Max. length/base width	1.86	.39	49	1.90	.42	111	$t = -0.46, p > .05$
Max. length/blade length	1.42	.16	53	1.50	.18	120	$t = -2.70, p < .01$
Neck width/thickness	2.14	.57	84	2.31	.52	212	$t = -2.55, p = .01$

[a]Standard unpaired t-test.
[b]Minus value (-) denotes concave base.

mean (1.61 ± .20, n = 10) significantly larger than either of Henderson's values. Unfortunately, Rocky Arroyo, another nearby site that appears to be roughly contemporary with Henderson's younger occupation, must be omitted from these comparisons, because its sample of measurable projectile points is too small to permit statistical evaluation.

While these attributes of the Washita points do appear to seriate chronologically at both Henderson and Bloom Mound, we must emphasize that there is no reason to assume that they will work equally well outside of the immediate area. The differences are extremely small and most likely reflect very localized changes in such things as the materials or techniques used for making the points, arrow shafts, or hafts, or shifts in the frequency or intensity with which points were resharpened.

There are other aspects of Henderson's assemblage of Washita points, the dominant form at the site, that are worth noting. For example, the proportion of point fragments (bases and tips combined) is significantly higher in non-room contexts (65.5%) than in rooms (47.4%; $t_s = 2.42, p \approx .01$). This statement applies with certainty only to the Late phase material, as the Early phase sample, although patterned in a similar way, is too small for meaningful analysis.

Even more intriguing is the fact that broken Washita points (for the purposes of this analysis, all tips of "indeterminate" type are assumed to derive from Washita points) are made from local cherts significantly less often (tips only, 69.2%; bases only, 67.7%; tips and bases combined 68.3%) than are complete points (79.9%; complete points vs. combined fragments, $t_s = 2.43, p \approx .01$).[6] Thus, fragmentary points not only tend to be more heavily concentrated in non-room areas, but a substantial proportion of these fragments, tips and bases alike, derive from points that were made elsewhere and presumably were already broken when they were transported into the village. The implications of these observations are that many of the fragmentary points entered Henderson as broken tips embedded in bison and antelope carcasses, and as broken point bases on arrows that were refurbished in the village. As already noted, however, there appears to be no temporal trend in the breakage patterns to indicate that in the Late phase a significantly greater proportion of Henderson's projectile points were made off-site.

Synopsis

The comparatively small excavations at the Henderson Site in 1980-1981 yielded nearly five hundred complete and fragmentary projectile points from nonmortuary contexts. The vast majority of the identifiable specimens fall into two well-known late prehistoric types: Washita and Fresno. The Washita is a small triangular arrowhead with side notches and a straight to slightly concave base. The Fresno is essentially a Washita point minus the notches. Washita points comprise nearly 50% of the Henderson assemblage; Fresnos comprise another 25%. In addition to these, the 1980-1981 excavations at Henderson produced a single Harrell point (a Washita-like point with an additional notch in the base), a Garza point (a basally notched triangular arrowhead lacking side notches), three small corner-notched arrowheads, and several dart points or hafted knives. There were also, of course, many fragmentary tips and blades that could not be assigned confidently to type. Their size and shape, however, suggest that most, if not all, come from Washitas or Fresnos.

There is considerable uncertainty among Southern Plains and Southwestern archaeologists concerning the typological status of the Fresno. Many view the Fresno as a legitimate type, while others feel that it is merely a blank or preform waiting to be transformed into a Washita (or Harrell) point. In an attempt to clarify this issue, we measured the Henderson Washitas and Fresnos, recording a suite of size attributes and several shape indices. These data reveal that the Henderson Fresnos differ significantly from the Washitas in both size and shape. While Washitas are comparable in length to Fresnos, the latter on average are thicker, wider, heavier, and squatter in overall shape, and their bases are less deeply indented. In addition, most Fresnos are less finely flaked than Washitas. All of these differences are compatible with the view that many, perhaps all, of the Fresnos at Henderson are Washita blanks or preforms. Only one line of evidence might be taken to suggest that the Fresno is a legitimate point type in its own right—a significantly greater proportion of the Fresnos are made on local materials (Fresno, 86%; Washita, 75%). However, if the villagers made some of the Washitas elsewhere and brought them into the community in finished form, or if they received some of the Washitas as gifts or through exchange from other communities, one might expect this raw-material difference. The evidence, therefore, seems to best support the view that the Fresno, at least at Henderson, is an unfinished Washita rather than a distinct point type.

While at least eleven different raw material types were used at Henderson in the manufacture of projectile points, nearly 80% of the points are made on "local gray" chert, a poor to moderate quality light gray to bluish-gray material that is readily available as small nodules throughout the area. The second most common lithic material at the site, comprising only about 10% of the assemblage, is a red to pink jasper that closely resembles the Tecovas jaspers found along the eastern escarpment of the Llano Estacado in the Texas Panhandle. Regardless of whether these materials are genuine Tecovas, or merely Tecovas look-alikes, they almost certainly come from nonlocal sources. The remaining raw material types are each represented by only a few specimens. Some of these materials are clearly nonlocal in origin (e.g., Alibates chert from the Texas Panhandle, Edwards Plateau chert from west-central Texas, Tiger chert from south-western Wyoming), while others may be either local or nonlocal (e.g., fingerprint chert, dark-brown chert, tan chert).

While 70% of the Washita points at Henderson are broken, a significantly greater proportion of Fresnos are fragmentary. Given the thinner, more delicate nature of the Washita, as well as the presence of side notches, we had expected Washitas to have been more susceptible to breakage during manufacture and use. Either breakage was more likely to occur early in the making of the preform, perhaps as the knapper encountered unseen flaws in the emerging biface, or screening and other recovery biases failed to recover significant numbers of broken Washitas, particularly the tiny, delicate fragments of the base or haft element. We favor the latter explanation, although we acknowledge that the Fresno-as-preform interpretation is far from conclusive.

Comparisons of the projectile points from the Center Bar and East Bar reveal no significant differences between the two proveniences in either the typological composition, or in size and shape. Thus, if these two room blocks had been occupied by discrete corporate groups, bounded by social, economic, or other criteria of membership, their existence is not reflected by any patterning in the projectile point assemblages.

Similarly, there were no differences between the combined room block assemblages and the points from the East Plaza in either typology or size/shape characteristics. Surprisingly, there was also no difference between structures and plaza in the ratio of tips to bases. Thus, despite the masses of bones of larger mammals in the plaza, there is no evidence to suggest that isolated point tips still embedded in the carcasses when the animals were brought into the village were systematically removed and discarded in the plaza before the meat was taken into the rooms.

One of the striking features of the Henderson excavation was the great quantity of bison and antelope bones recovered from what is a comparatively small excavation by Southwestern standards. These remains underscore the importance of big game hunting in the village economy. However, over 80% of the bison bones and half of the antelope bones came from a single 20 m^2 concentration near the southern margin of the East Plaza. Had we excavated only in the rooms we would have found almost no evidence of bison and we would have grossly underestimated the importance of antelope. Finding the remains of these larger mammals, however, was not simply a matter of excavating in the plaza. In fact, we did systematically investigate the plaza, but encountered bedrock just beneath the surface almost everywhere we tested. The bison and antelope remains had been dumped into a deep, elongated depression at the perimeter of the plaza, an area that we tested only on the advice of a visitor who noted a large, isolated mesquite bush growing there. He pointed out that a bush of this size possessed a large root system which in turn implied that bedrock in this area of the plaza was unlikely to lie just below the surface.

The pattern of systematically dumping the bones of larger mammals beyond the confines of the structures, and possibly even outside of the village itself, is not unique to Henderson. Similar disposal patterns have been reported from sites elsewhere in the Southwest, as well as in the ethnographic literature. The bones of larger mammals might well be underrepresented in faunal samples from Southwestern village sites, particularly in samples from excavations that focused most heavily on residential areas.

As a check on such bias, we need an independent way to estimate the importance of big-game hunting in a site's economy. Perhaps the most obvious candidate for such a measure is the number of projectile points a site yields, ideally expressed in some standardized form such as density. Henderson provides a clear example of the potential value of this approach. Though barely 160 m^2 were opened and only twelve rooms were partially sampled, Henderson in 1980-1981 yielded 3,500 bison, antelope, and deer bones and 529 projectile points, or more than five points or point fragments per cubic meter of deposit. While few published reports from elsewhere in the Southwest provide density data, an omission that makes intersite comparisons extremely difficult, a cursory survey of the literature shows that the abundance of projectile points at Henderson is unusual. There seems little doubt that the great quantity of points at Henderson reflects the tremendous importance of big-game hunting in the community's economy. Moreover, we found no correlation at Henderson, either positive or negative, between the spatial distribution of the larger-mammal bones and projectile points. In fact, the density of points in the room blocks was comparable to, or even higher than, their density in the East Plaza midden, indicating that had we missed the plaza midden entirely and concentrated our excavations entirely within the structures, we would nevertheless have recovered a large number of projectile points, large enough to show big-game hunting had played a prominent role in the Henderson economy.

Since completion of the original manuscript over a decade ago, in which we dealt only with the Late phase points recovered in the 1980-1981 field seasons, we have analyzed all of the site's projectile points, and conclude the chapter with a brief update on this material, contrasting the Early phase and Late phase assemblages.

Projectile point density increases in the younger period, with the sharpest increase occurring in non-room contexts. It is probably no coincidence that this increase parallels the Late phase increase in both the density and proportion of bison remains found in plaza as opposed to room block contexts.

The proportion of Washitas increases significantly in the Late phase, while the proportions of all other point types decline, especially Fresnos. When looked at spatially, there is no significant change over time in the proportion of Washitas in the rooms, but their frequency jumps sharply in the plazas. When densities of points per m^3 of excavated deposit are examined, there is a major increase over time in the rate at which Washita points enter the record, while the rate that Fresnos enter the deposits remains essentially unchanged.

The decline in the proportional representation of Fresnos relative to Washitas raises some interesting questions. If, as we suggested earlier in the chapter, the Fresno point represents an intermediate stage in the manufacture of Washitas, rather than a distinct projectile point form in its own right, then its relative decline, in the face of increasing numbers of Washitas, might imply that proportionately fewer Washita points were manufactured on-site in the Late phase than in the preceding period. This in turn might be an indication that the hunters' mobility had increased in the Late phase, such that a greater proportion of their projectile points were made elsewhere. If so, then we would expect the percentage of Washitas made on materials *other than* the common local gray chert to increase in the younger period. This is not what happens. The proportion remains absolutely unchanged over time, casting doubt on the Fresno-as-preform perspective.

Likewise, if Washitas increasingly were manufactured elsewhere in the Late phase, one might expect the proportions of complete vs. fragmentary points in the Henderson assemblage to change over time, although we are unable to specify the precise nature and direction such change should have taken. Instead, what we observe at Henderson is a pattern of breakage that remains virtually unchanged over time, again casting doubt on the likelihood that significantly fewer Washitas were manufactured on-site in the later period.

Thus, many of Henderson's Fresnos may, in fact, represent a distinct projectile point form after all, rather than a preform or blank for the manufacture of Washitas, as we first believed. If so, their proportional decline in the Late phase might imply a change in the popularity of one style over another that might serve, locally at least, as a valuable temporal marker.

The points from the two phases are strikingly similar in their metrics, with very few differences achieving statistical significance. The exceptions are maximum thickness, neck width, the ratio of neck width to maximum thickness, and the ratio of maximum point length to blade length. These differences are so slight, however, that it is difficult to believe they reflect conscious stylistic choices on the part of the knappers. Nevertheless, neck width and the ratio of maximum length to blade length both yield essentially the same ordering of Henderson's major proveniences as the one generated by seriating the El Paso Polychrome jar rims. We must emphasize, however, that there is no reason to assume that these attributes will seriate assemblages equally well outside of the immediate area.

Other aspects of Henderson's assemblage of Washita points are worth noting. The proportion of point fragments (both bases and tips combined) is significantly higher in non-room contexts than in rooms. Even more intriguing is the fact that broken Washita points are made from local cherts significantly less often than are complete points. Thus, fragmentary points tend to be more heavily concentrated in non-room areas and a substantial proportion of these fragments, tips and bases alike, derive from points made elsewhere and presumably already broken when transported into the village. The implications of these observations are that many of the fragmentary points entered Henderson as broken tips embedded in bison and antelope carcasses, and as broken point bases on arrows that were refurbished in the village. As already noted, however, no temporal trend can be found in the breakage patterns to indicate that in the Late phase a greater proportion of Henderson's projectile points were made off-site.

Acknowledgments

Preliminary analysis of the 1980-1981 projectile points was undertaken as part of an undergraduate honors thesis by Gretchen Neve (1981). Analysis of the 1994, 1995, and 1997 materials has benefited from undergraduate honors thesis research conducted by Gwendolyn M. Bell (1995), Ellen Haskell (1997), and Richard Raffaelli (1998) as well as from an independent research project by Kendall Eccleston in 1993. We thank the late Robert H. (Bus) Leslie of Hobbs, New Mexico, for directing us to the East Plaza Midden. It is doubtful that we would have found these important deposits had it not been for his familiarity with the growth habits of mesquite.

Notes

1. Among the 28 points are 14 Washitas (3 complete or nearly complete; 3 blades broken at the notches; 8 basal fragments), 3 basal fragments of Fresnos, 7 fragmentary tips of either Washitas or Fresnos, 1 thick corner-notched arrow point or small dart point, 1 elongated blade sharply serrated on both edges (Fig. 15.3f), and 2 dart points or hafted knives (both corner-notched). In addition, there are two unusual tanged knives, both from the Center Bar (Fig. 15.3i). Not counted here are 23 complete and 18 broken bifaces. Most of these are thick, crudely flaked, oval to quasi-triangular preforms. A few still preserve traces of cortex. Almost all of the bifaces are made on local gray chert.

2. The difference between the two point forms in the proportion of specimens with concave bases is not statistically significant ($t_s = 1.32$, $p > .05$, test of the equality of two percentages based on the arcsine transformation, Sokal and Rohlf 1969:607-10).

3. Test of equality of two percentages based on the arcsine transformation (Sokal and Rohlf 1969:607-10).

4. These figures are based solely on the 1980-1981 excavations.

5. In calculating the correlation, only excavated squares were included and only squares which contained at least one point and one bone of bison, antelope, or deer.

6. The proportion of complete points made on local gray chert (79.9%) does not differ significantly from the proportion of gray chert (75.0%; CR = 1.44, $p > .05$, one-tailed test) in the total lithic sample studied by Brown (see Chapter 16).

References Cited

Banks, L. D.
1984 Lithic Resources and Quarries. In: *Prehistory of Oklahoma*, edited by R. E. Bell, pp. 65-5. Orlando, FL: Academic Press.

Bayham, F. E.
1982 *A Diachronic Analysis of Prehistoric Animal Exploitation at Ventana Cave*. Ph.D. dissertation, Arizona State University, Tempe, AZ.

Bell, G. M.
1995 *An Analysis of the Projectile Points from the Henderson Site (LA-1549)*. Honors thesis, Department of Anthropology, University of Michigan, Ann Arbor, MI.

Bell, R. E.
1958 *Guide to the Identification of Certain American Indian Projectile Points*. Special Bulletin 1. Oklahoma City, OK: Oklahoma Anthropological Society.
1960 *Guide to the Identification of Certain American Indian Projectile Points*. Special Bulletin 2. Oklahoma City, OK: Oklahoma Anthropological Society.

Bradley, B. A.
1988 Wallace Ruin Interim Report. *Southwestern Lore* 54(2):8-33.

Cameron, C. M.
1987 Chipped Stone from Pueblo Alto. In: *Investigations at the Pueblo Alto Complex, Chaco Canyon*, Vol. 3, Part 1. *Artifactual and Biological Analyses*, edited by F. J. Mathien and T. C. Windes, pp. 231-90. Publications in Archeology 18F, Chaco Canyon Studies. Santa Fe, NM: U. S. Department of the Interior, National Park Service.

Chayes, F.
1971 *Ratio Correlation: A Manual for Students of Petrology and Geochemistry*. Chicago, IL: University of Chicago Press.

Christenson, A. L.
1997 Side-Notched and Unnotched Arrowpoints: Assessing Functional Differences. In: *Projectile Technology*, edited by H. Knecht, pp. 131-42. New York: Plenum Press.

Cordell, L. S.
1977 Late Anasazi Farming and Hunting Strategies: One Example of a Problem in Congruence. *American Antiquity* 42(3):449-61.

DiPeso, C. C., J. B. Rinaldo, and G. J. Fenner
1974 *Casas Grandes: A Fallen Trading Center of the Gran Chichimeca*, Vol. 7. *Stone and Metal*. Amerind Foundation Series 9. Flagstaff, AZ: Northland Press.

Driver, J. C.
1991 Assemblage Formation at the Robinson Site (LA46326). In: *Mogollon V*, edited by P. H. Beckett, pp. 197-206. Las Cruces, NM: COAS Publishing and Research.

Haskell, E.
1997 *Projectile Points at the Henderson Pueblo (LA-1549): Indications of a Mutual Subsistence Economy*. Honors thesis, Department of Anthropology, University of Michigan, Ann Arbor, MI.

Haury, E. W.
1976 *The Hohokam, Desert Farmers and Craftsmen: Excavations at Snaketown, 1964-1965*. Tucson, AZ: University of Arizona Press.

Head, G. N.
1988 *Hunting Intensification on the Pajarito Plateau, North Central New Mexico*. Master's thesis, Department of Anthropology, University of California, Los Angeles, CA.

Hughes, J. T.
1978 Geology. In: *Archeology at Mackenzie Reservoir*, edited by J. T. Hughes and P. S. Willey, pp. 16-23. Archeological Survey Report 24. Austin, TX: Texas Historical Commission, Office of the State Archeologist.

Jelks, E. B.
1993 Observations on the Distribution of Certain Arrow-Point Types in Texas and Adjoining Regions. *Lithic Technology* 18(1-2):9-15.

Judge, W. J.
1974 *The Excavation of Tijeras Pueblo, 1971-1973: Preliminary Report, Cibola National Forest, New Mexico*. Archeological Report 3. Albuquerque, NM: USDA Forest Service, Southwestern Regional Office.

Katz, S. R., and P. R. Katz
1976 *Archeological Investigations in Lower Tule Canyon, Briscoe County, Texas*. Archeological Survey Report 16. Austin, TX: Texas Historical Foundation, Texas Tech University, Texas Historical Commission.

LeBlanc, S. A.
1984 The Structure of Projectile Point Form. In: *The Galaz Ruin: A Prehistoric Mimbres Village in Southwestern New Mexico*, edited by R. Anyon and S. A. LeBlanc, pp. 236-46. Albuquerque, NM: Maxwell Museum of Anthropology and University of New Mexico Press.

Linford, L. D.
1986 The Stone Artifacts. In: *Archeological Investigations at Antelope House*, edited by D. P. Morris, pp. 514-41. Washington, D.C.: U.S. Department of the Interior, National Park Service.

Mallouf, R. J.
1989 Quarry Hunting with Jack T. Hughes: Tecovas Jasper in the South Basin of the Canadian River, Oldham County, Texas. In: *In the Light of Past Experience: Papers in Honor of Jack T. Hughes*, edited by D. C. Roper, pp. 307-26. Publication 5. Amarillo, TX: Panhandle Archeological Society.

Nelson, M. C.
1984 Food Selection at Galaz: Inferences from Chipped Stone Analysis. In: *The Galaz Ruin: A Prehistoric Mimbres Village in Southwestern New Mexico*, edited by R. Anyon and S. A. LeBlanc, pp. 225-36. Albuquerque, NM: Maxwell Museum of Anthropology and University of New Mexico Press.

Neve, G.
1981 *Style: An Experiment in Projectile Point Attribute Analysis*. Honors thesis, Department of Anthropology, University of Michigan, Ann Arbor, MI.

Parry, W. J., and J. D. Speth
1984 *The Garnsey Spring Campsite: Late Prehistoric Occupation in Southeastern New Mexico*. Technical Report 15. Ann Arbor, MI: Museum of Anthropology, University of Michigan.

Phagan, C. J.
1993 *The Stone Artifacts from Arroyo Hondo Pueblo*. Arroyo Hondo Archaeological Series 8 (Part II). Santa Fe, NM: School of American Research Press.

Raffaelli, R.
1998 *Projectile Points at Henderson (LA-1549): A Study of Subsistence through Time*. Honors thesis, Department of Anthropology, University of Michigan, Ann Arbor, MI.

Rocek, T. R., and J. D. Speth
1986 *The Henderson Site Burials: Glimpses of a Late Prehistoric Population in the Pecos Valley*. Technical Report 18. Ann Arbor, MI: Museum of Anthropology, University of Michigan.

Rohn, A. H.
1971 *Mug House: Wetherill Mesa Excavations, Mesa Verde National Park—Colorado*. Washington, D.C.: U.S. Department of the Interior, National Park Service.

Shaeffer, J. B.
1958 The Alibates Flint Quarry, Texas. *American Antiquity* 24(2):189-91.

Schiffer, M. B.
1987 *Formation Processes of the Archaeological Record*. Albuquerque, NM: University of New Mexico Press.

Shelley, P. H.
1983 *Lithic Specialization at Salmon Ruin, San Juan County, New Mexico*. Ph.D. dissertation, Washington State University, Pullman, WA.

Siegel, S.
1956 *Nonparametric Statistics for the Behavioral Sciences*. New York: McGraw-Hill Publishing.

Sokal, R. R., and F. J. Rohlf
1969 *Biometry: The Principles and Practice of Statistics in Biological Research*. San Francisco, CA: W. H. Freeman.

Suhm, D. A., and E. B. Jelks (editors)
1962 *Handbook of Texas Archaeology: Type Descriptions*. Special Publication 1. Austin, TX: Texas Archaeological Society and Texas Memorial Museum.

Suhm, D. A., and A. D. Krieger
1954 *An Introductory Handbook of Texas Archaeology*. Bulletin 25. Austin, TX: Texas Archaeological Society.

Whittaker, J. C.
1987 Individual Variation as an Approach to Economic Organization: Projectile Points at Grasshopper Pueblo, Arizona. *Journal of Field Archaeology* 14:465-79.

Whittaker, J. C., A. Ferg, and J. D. Speth
1988 Arizona Bifaces of Wyoming Chert. *Kiva* 53(4):321-34.

Woodbury, R. B.
1954 *Prehistoric Stone Implements of Northeastern Arizona*. Reports of the Awatovi Expedition 6, Papers of the Peabody Museum of American Archaeology and Ethnology 34. Cambridge, MA: Harvard University, Peabody Museum of American Archaeology and Ethnology.

Young, J. N.
1981 Stone Artifacts of Mound 7. In: *Excavation of Mound 7, Gran Quivira National Monument, New Mexico*, edited by A. C. Hayes, J. N. Young, and A. H. Warren, pp. 105-39. Publications in Archeology 16. Washington, D.C.: U.S. Department of the Interior, National Park Service.

16
The Lithic Assemblage from the Henderson Site

Jody L. Brown

Introduction

This study focuses on a sample of 5,516 lithic pieces selected from two major midden deposits excavated in 1980-1981 at the Henderson Site, out of a total assemblage estimated to be over 30,000 specimens, most of which remain to be analyzed. These deposits were the trash in Room C-5 in the Center Bar and the midden in the earth oven complex at the southern end of the East Plaza. The lithic samples analyzed from these two middens encompass all of the debitage and flaked stone tools from 8 m^2 near the center of Room C-5 and 17 m^2 from the deepest central portion of the East Plaza midden.

In addition to thousands of flakes of chert, jasper, and other cryptocrystalline materials, the East Plaza midden produced a large number of crude, heavy-duty limestone choppers and cleaverlike tools, presumably used in butchering the many bison and antelope that were brought into the village. Some of these tools were then incorporated into the earth oven where they burned and fractured much like the masses of ordinary fire-cracked rock that filled the midden (for an analogous example from the Great Plains, see Lovick 1983). Most of these heavy-duty tools were not included in the present study, although numerous limestone flakes, either detached deliberately when these expedient tools were made or accidentally spalled from them during use, are tabulated. Some of these limestone flakes may have been produced during the manufacture of metates, all of which were fashioned, probably on-site, from local bedrock (see Chapter 17).

Strikingly different faunal assemblages were encountered in the room blocks and the East Plaza midden (see Chapter 14). The East Plaza midden produced masses of bison and antelope bones, while the room blocks yielded much higher proportions of smaller mammals. One of the principal goals of this analysis is to determine whether there are parallel contrasts in the range or frequency of flaked stone tool types and raw materials that might shed further light on the nature of the activities that were carried out in these two contexts.

The two lithic samples that are the focus of study here are random only in the sense that almost everything recovered from the selected grid squares was analyzed. Excluded from analysis are hundreds of tiny flakes and pieces of microdebitage recovered from flotation and geological samples. Of course they are anything but random in terms of the proveniences they represent. They derive entirely from two spatially restricted midden deposits; lithics from other contexts are not represented. In addition, the room block material examined here comes only from a single structure in the Center Bar, while the thousands of specimens from the East Bar are omitted entirely. (Almost no excavation was conducted in 1980-1981 in the Main Bar of the village.) Nevertheless, despite these obvious limitations, the two subsamples provide valuable insights into the overall character of the Henderson lithics, as well as a firm baseline for future, more extensive studies.

Terms and Procedures

Brief definitions and explanations of the terms employed in recording the lithic material, as well as the procedures used in measuring the specimens, are provided below.

Table 16.1. Artifact counts and percentages by provenience at the Henderson Site (1980-1981 only).

Artifact Type	Center-Bar		East Plaza		Total Sample	
	n	%	*n*	%	*n*	%
Unmodified flake	1322	53.41	1611	52.98	2933	53.17
Utilized flake	414	16.73	515	16.94	929	16.84
Unifacially retouched flake	184	7.43	222	7.30	406	7.36
Bifacially retouched flake	13	0.53	15	0.49	28	0.51
Side-scraper	184	7.43	202	6.64	386	7.00
End-scraper	27	1.09	46	1.51	73	1.32
Biface	34	1.37	43	1.41	77	1.40
Knife	0	0.00	3	0.10	3	0.05
Drill	3	0.12	3	0.10	6	0.11
Core	122	4.93	176	5.79	298	5.40
Block	82	3.31	87	2.86	169	3.06
Notch	45	1.82	52	1.71	97	1.76
Core-scraper	34	1.37	41	1.35	75	1.36
Lozenge scraper	8	0.32	8	0.26	16	0.30
Gouge	2	0.08	12	0.39	14	0.25
Chopper	1	0.04	5	0.16	6	0.11
TOTAL	2475	100.00	3041	100.00	5516	100.00

Raw Material Type. Sixteen lithic raw material types were designated. These types are based entirely on characteristics of the material that are visible with the naked eye, such as color and texture. No Alibates chert or obsidian were found in the samples analyzed, although both materials were present in small quantities at the site. At times it was difficult to assign a piece to one specific type because of mottling or intergrading of colors or textures; in such cases, the piece was classified according to the dominant color or texture.

Flake Type. Five principal categories are recognized.

1. *BRF (biface reduction flake).* A flake that results from the manufacture of a biface. Platform formed by the intersection of two faces of a biface. Platform usually small and faceted. Bulb usually diffuse; scars on dorsal face from previous removals. Flake distinctly curved in profile (Parry 1987:36).

2. *BPO (bipolar reduction flake).* Distinctive ventral face with "sheared cone" (flat ventral face with diffuse bulb and closely spaced ripples from point of impact). Platform crushed with small flakes on ventral face; distal end may also display crushing. Scars on dorsal face from previous removals that originated at both proximal and distal ends (Parry 1987:36).

3. *PRB (platform remnant-bearing flake).* Simple flake with preserved platform, bulb of percussion, and recognizable dorsal and ventral faces.

4. *NPRB (non-platform remnant-bearing flake).* Flake with no trace of platform (either flake fragment or flake so modified that original platform is indistinguishable).

5. *SHA (shatter).* Small fragment distinguished from NPRB by our inability to identify dorsal/ventral faces or other distinctive markings (e.g., ripples); arbitrarily distinguished from "block/fragment" (see below) on the basis of its smaller size.

Artifact Type. Sixteen distinct categories are recognized.

1. *Unmodified flake/piece.* A flake or fragment with no sign of consistent retouch or utilization (small, irregular flake scars) using a 10× hand lens. It was often difficult to identify utilization on coarser-grained materials such as basalt, quartzite, and granite.

2. *Utilized flake/piece.* A flake or fragment with small, relatively continuous flake scars along one or more edges (scars 2 mm long or more). No attempt was made to determine presence/absence of use polishes on any of the artifacts.

3. *Unifacially retouched flake/piece.* A flake or fragment with continuous, regular flake scars along one or more edges on one face, either dorsal or ventral. Flake scars do not significantly alter the shape of the edge or edges of the piece.

4. *Bifacially retouched flake/piece.* A flake or fragment with continuous, regular flake scars occurring on both faces along one or more edges. Flake scars do not significantly alter the overall shape of the edge or edges of the piece.

5. *Side-scraper (unifacial and bifacial).* Unifacial or bifacial retouch along one or both lateral edges of a flake which substantially alters both the shape of the edge and its edge angle. For flakes that exhibit chipping on both a side and the distal end, a judgment was made as to the edge with the greatest amount of alteration and the tool was classified accordingly.

6. *End-scraper (unifacial and bifacial).* Unifacial or bifacial retouch on the distal end of a flake that substantially alters both the shape of the edge and its edge angle. None of the tools so classified were of the "traditional" end-scraper type (i.e., flakes with thick, rounded distal ends and steep working edges).

7. *Biface.* Tool with retouch on both dorsal and ventral face; retouch invasive, extending inward from the edge at least 5 mm. Retouch substantially alters the original shape of the piece,

Table 16.2. Expedient nature of the Henderson Site lithic assemblage.[a]

Measures of Expedient Core Technology	Lower Chaco Drainage		Black Mesa				Henderson Site
	Preceramic	Puebloan	Archaic	BMII	PI	PII	
Biface to core ratio[b]	0.80	0.13	5.75	2.38	0.45	0.04	0.22
% tools with facial retouch[c]	22	6	29	14	14	2	6
% flakes with faceted platforms[d]	7	3	41	41	34	22	23
% bifacial thinning flakes[e]	—	—	15	19	2	0	4

[a]Chaco (New Mexico) and Black Mesa (Arizona) data from Parry and Kelly (1987:291-92).
[b]Bifaces at Henderson include both finished and unfinished specimens, as well as drills; cores include all cores, as well as the small subset of limestone choppers that has been analyzed.
[c]Facially retouched tools at Henderson include finished bifaces and heavily retouched unifaces. "Non-retouched" artifacts include all utilized flakes, utilized cores, and choppers, as well as all side- and end-scrapers, since these latter two categories generally have only minimal retouch.
[d]At Henderson, faceted platforms are those with PLSC ≥3.
[e]Bifacial thinning flakes are equivalent to bifacial reduction flakes (BRF) at Henderson.

whether flake or small core, generally forming an ovate specimen with lenticular cross-section. Projectile points have not been included in this study; see Chapter 15.

8. *Knife.* Flake or fragment exhibiting one edge that has been heavily but noninvasively retouched to produce a steep, blunt edge; opposing edge sharp and unmodified.

9. *Drill.* Bifacially flaked piece with deliberately retouched elongated projection. Base generally expanding.

10. *Core.* Raw material from which one or more flakes have been removed. Usually large and bulky pieces with no evidence of use other than as a source for flakes.

11. *Block/fragment.* Specimen that lacks identifiable or complete scars from previous flake removals. Derived from cores that were shattered beyond recognition. Larger than pieces classified as shatter.

12. *Notched flake/piece.* Specimen with one or a series of small, usually lateral, notches formed by retouch. In a few specimens, proximity of multiple notches produces a somewhat serrated edge.

13. *Core-scraper (planer?).* Usually a relatively large core, with much of the original cortex present, that exhibits marginal retouch or heavy use along an edge.

14. *Lozenge-shaped scraper.* Small lozenge-shaped tool, with steep dorsal retouch along one edge and finer retouch along all other edges. Possible projectile point blanks transformed into scrapers.

15. *Gouge (perforator).* Tool with pointed projection formed by purposeful retouch along one edge. Gouge distinguished from drill because projection is relatively short and formed entirely by retouch on dorsal face.

16. *Core-chopper.* Large, heavy, crudely flaked chopper with unifacial or bifacial flaking along one margin to form a deeply sinuous cutting or chopping edge. Working edge often heavily battered from use.

Cortex Amount. Four arbitrary categories are distinguished.

1. *0%.* No cortex present.
2. *≤50%.* Cortex extends over less than half of the surface.
3. *>50%.* Cortex extends over more than half of the surface, but not over the entire surface.
4. *100%.* Cortex covers all of the dorsal face of the flake (excluding small utilization scars or small unifacial and bifacial retouch scars), or all of the surface of a block or piece (rare).

Platform Scar Count (PLSC). This attribute records the number of scars, regardless of size, on the striking platform of a flake (see Magne 1985:113). It does not include platform preparation scars formed on the dorsal surface of a flake adjacent to the platform. The value of this measure should increase as reduction proceeds. Only four states were recorded: 0, 1, 2, ≥3. A value of PLSC = 0 means the platform retains the original unmodified cortical surface of the nodule or cobble.

Dorsal Scar Count (DSC). This attribute records the number of flake scars visible on the dorsal face of a flake or on the entire surface of a core (see Magne 1985:113). Flake scars from subsequent retouch of the piece are not included. The measure is expected to increase as reduction proceeds. Only four states were recorded: 0, 1, 2, ≥3. A value of DSC = 0 means the specimen retains the original unmodified cortex over the entire surface.

Weight. The weight of each piece was taken to the nearest 0.10 g using an electronic digital balance. Those pieces registering 0.0 g on the scale (e.g., microdebitage) were arbitrarily assigned a weight of 0.10 g.

Maximum Dimension. This measurement records the maximum size of a flake or core independent of its orientation. Values were determined using a nested circle graph, with diameters increasing in 0.5 cm increments.

Tool and Debitage Types

The inventory of chipped stone artifact types from Room C-5 in the Center Bar and the East Plaza midden are tabulated in

Table 16.3. Raw material counts and percentages by provenience at the Henderson Site.

Raw Material Type	Center-Bar *n*	Center-Bar %	East Plaza *n*	East Plaza %	Total Sample *n*	Total Sample %
Limestone	381	15.39	852	28.02	1233	22.35
Basalt	44	1.78	68	2.24	112	2.03
Quartzite (white)	13	0.53	4	0.13	17	0.31
Quartzite (red)	21	0.85	31	1.02	52	0.94
Quartz	1	0.04	1	0.03	2	0.04
Siltstone	22	0.89	21	0.69	43	0.78
Granite	5	0.20	6	0.20	11	0.20
Chert (white)	214	8.65	276	9.08	490	8.88
Chert (red)	90	3.64	108	3.55	198	3.59
Chert (gray)	897	36.24	912	29.99	1809	32.80
Chert (brown/tan)	623	25.17	602	19.80	1225	22.21
Chert (fingerprint)	59	2.38	50	1.64	109	1.98
Chert (mottled)	104	4.20	108	3.55	212	3.84
Chert (green)	1	0.04	2	0.07	3	0.05
TOTAL	2475	100.00	3041	100.00	5516	100.00

Table 16.1. Using the chi-square statistic and a .05 level of significance, the values from the structure and plaza are not significantly different (chi square = 15.99, df = 15). In fact, both raw counts and percentage frequencies are amazingly similar in the two assemblages across the entire suite of artifact types. Slightly over half of the assemblage as a whole consists of unmodified flakes, and nearly identical values appear in both subsampled areas. The next most common artifact type is the utilized flake/piece, making up almost 17% of the assemblage as a whole (as well as in the two separate areas). Unifacially retouched flakes comprise just over 7% of the assemblage, while side-scrapers are almost as frequent at approximately 7% for both areas. Cores (5.4%) and blocks (3.1%) are the next most numerous lithic artifact type. Notches, core-scrapers, end-scrapers, and bifaces each comprise less than 2% of the total sample assemblage. The remaining artifact types (knives, drills, bifacially retouched flakes, lozenge-shaped scrapers, and gouges) are rare. (As already mentioned, while "classic" end-scrapers with rounded, steeply retouched distal margins are present at Henderson, they are extremely rare, and none were encountered in the samples analyzed here. Most of the choppers and other heavy-duty tools of limestone from the East Plaza midden have not been analyzed.)

The striking similarity of the lithic assemblages from the East Plaza and Center Bar middens suggests that both loci received a substantial part of their trash from comparable, if not identical, sources. This result parallels observations made in Chapter 15 concerning the projectile points; both proveniences yielded point assemblages that were virtually indistinguishable. The similarity of the flaked stone tool assemblages from the plaza and Center Bar stands in stark contrast to the differences that characterize the faunal assemblages from these two areas. Most of the bones from the plaza midden were from large mammals, particularly bison and antelope, while the room blocks produced mostly small-mammal bones (see Chapter 14). Thus, the formation processes that led to the accumulation of lithic material in these two middens do not appear to have been very closely linked to those that led to the accumulation of the faunal remains.

Parry and Kelly (1987) speculate that as communities in the Southwest and elsewhere became increasingly sedentary there was a corresponding change in their lithic assemblages towards a more expedient core technology. The sample of lithics from Henderson, a community that may have been semi-sedentary, appears to align with their findings. In Table 16.2, values derived from the Henderson data are compared with data provided by Parry and Kelly (1987:291-92). These data suggest a trend over time toward more expedient technologies in the ratios and percentages of certain tool and flake types in the Southwest. For Henderson, the ratio of bifaces to cores is 0.22, and the

Table 16.4. Density (items/m^3) of artifacts at the Henderson Site[a]

Artifact Type	Center Bar	East Plaza
Unmodified flake	144.5	144.2
Utilized flake	45.3	46.1
Unifacially retouched flake	20.1	19.9
Bifacially retouched flake	1.4	1.3
Side-scraper	20.1	18.1
End-scraper	3.0	4.1
Biface	3.7	3.9
Knife	0.0	0.3
Drill	0.3	0.3
Core	13.3	15.8
Block	9.0	7.8
Notch	4.9	4.7
Core-scraper	3.7	3.7
Lozenge scraper	0.9	0.7
Gouge	0.2	1.1
Chopper	0.1	0.5
TOTAL DENSITY	270.5	272.2

[a]Volume of excavated sediment yielding lithic samples was 9.15 m^3 and 11.17 m^3 from Room C-5 and the East Plaza, respectively.

percentage of tools with facial retouch is 6%; both values fall within Parry and Kelly's Pueblo period category which is based on data from the Lower Chaco drainage (northwestern New Mexico) and from Black Mesa (northeastern Arizona). Although the flake type and platform scar count data will be discussed later, it is clear from Table 16.2 that the percentage of bifacial thinning flakes and the percentage of flakes with faceted platforms also reflect the expedient nature of the Henderson lithic sample.

Raw Materials

The lithic assemblages from the Center Bar and East Plaza are mostly made of local raw materials (Table 16.3). Absent in these two samples are extra-local materials, such as obsidian from New Mexican or other sources, Alibates from the Texas Panhandle, and Edwards Plateau chert from central Texas. These materials are present at the site, however, especially among the projectile points, though in very small numbers (see Chapter 15). Local gray and brown (tan) cherts are by far the most common lithic raw materials at Henderson, and nodules of these can be found within a few hundred meters of the site. Limestone, the other common material at the site, is ubiquitous in the area. Several, perhaps most, of the remaining material types probably originated from alluvial gravels associated with the present and former channels of the Pecos and Hondo rivers. The most likely exceptions to this generalization are basalt and granite, and possibly the red chert or jasper, some of which resembles Tecovas jasper from the eastern escarpment of the Caprock or Llano Estacado in the Texas Panhandle (e.g., Banks 1984:72; Hughes 1978:20-21; Katz and Katz 1976:70; Mallouf 1989; see also Chapter 15).

The distinction between the two most common material types at the site, gray and brown (tan) chert, is arbitrary; these two types can be lumped together since they almost certainly are variants of the same chert and probably derive from the same local sources. In fact, they occur together in bands or zones on a large number of specimens. In the study of the projectile points, Adler (see Chapter 15) treated these variants as a single type, which he referred to as "local gray" chert.

When the samples from the Center Bar and East Plaza are compared, there are interesting differences in the proportions of the various material types. The biggest differences are in the percentage frequencies for limestone (Center Bar, 15.4%; East Plaza, 28.0%), and brown and gray cherts (both varieties combined; Center Bar, 61.4%; East Plaza, 49.8%). While all, or nearly all, of the limestone flakes from both proveniences are included in these figures, most of the heavy-duty tools of limestone encountered in the East Plaza are not. Had these also been included in the tallies, the contrast between the two proveniences would be far greater.

After the gray and brown cherts and limestone, the next most common raw material type within both areas is white chert, 8.7% in the Center Bar and 9.1% in the East Plaza. Red chert (Tecovas-like) and mottled chert each account for slightly over 3.5% in each area. Finally, in descending order of abundance in each of the subsample areas are basalt, fingerprint chert, red quartzite, siltstone, granite, white quartzite, green chert, and quartz.

The hundreds of flakes and other worked pieces of limestone in the East Plaza are clearly the major contributor to the differences between the two proveniences in the proportions of raw material types. This becomes apparent when the limestone specimens are omitted, and the percentages recomputed; the differences between the Center Bar and East Plaza then all but disappear. Most notably, the percentage frequencies for gray and brown (tan) chert become statistically indistinguishable (Center Bar/East Plaza: gray chert, 42.8%/41.7%; brown chert, 29.8%/27.5%).

Aside from the hundreds of limestone flakes and numerous heavy-duty chopping and cutting tools that were discarded in the East Plaza, the two proveniences yielded lithic assemblages that are virtually identical, both in the array of tool types they contain and in the proportional representation of raw material types. And, as subsequent discussion will show, other comparisons further underscore the similarity of these two assemblages. Thus, it seems reasonable to conclude that the East Plaza was used routinely as a locus for dumping domestic trash in much the same way that abandoned rooms were, and that the unusual assemblage of limestone tools in the plaza was employed in butchering the many bison, antelope, and deer carcasses that were brought into the village, ultimately becoming incorporated, along with the large-mammal bones, into what otherwise was typical household trash. In addition, as noted earlier, some of the limestone flakes in the plaza may be the by-products of on-site manufacture of metates, all of which were fashioned from the local limestone bedrock (see Chapter 17).

Density of Artifacts

The densities of artifact types are given in Table 16.4. The excavated volume that produced each of the lithic samples is 9.15 m^3 for Room C-5 and 11.17 m^3 for the East Plaza. Table 16.4 shows that the two proveniences yielded amazingly similar density values for total artifacts, as well as for specific artifact types. In some cases, such as unmodified flakes, the figures are virtually identical. As expected, unmodified flakes exhibit the highest density in both samples, followed by utilized flakes, unifacially retouched flakes and side-scrapers, cores, blocks, notches, bifaces and end-scrapers, and core-scrapers, and limited numbers of the other types.

Artifact Types by Raw Material Type

Counts and percentage frequencies of artifact types within each raw material type have been calculated in Tables 16.5 and

Table 16.5. Counts of artifact types by raw material type.

Artifact Type	Area	Coarse-Grained							Fine-Grained						
		Ls	Bas	Q (wh)	Q (rd)	Qtz	Sltst	Gran	Ch (wh)	Ch (rd)	Ch (gry)	Ch (br)	Ch (fng)	Ch (mot)	Ch (grn)
Unmod. flake	Center Bar	284	34	10	16	1	17	3	102	45	459	294	21	35	1
	East Plaza	623	48	3	19	1	16	4	118	51	417	269	16	25	1
Util. flake	Center Bar	31	5	0	2	0	0	0	42	14	168	119	15	18	0
	East Plaza	69	11	1	5	0	1	0	61	20	179	125	21	22	0
Unifac. ret. flake	Center Bar	10	0	0	0	0	0	1	19	9	71	58	7	9	0
	East Plaza	18	3	0	3	0	1	1	26	13	81	57	3	16	0
Bifac. ret. flake	Center Bar	0	0	0	0	0	0	0	0	3	3	4	2	1	0
	East Plaza	0	0	0	0	0	1	0	1	1	6	5	0	1	0
Side-scraper	Center Bar	3	0	1	0	0	0	0	17	8	81	51	5	18	0
	East Plaza	17	1	0	0	0	0	1	33	9	73	50	2	15	1
End-scraper	Center Bar	1	0	0	0	0	0	0	2	1	7	12	0	4	0
	East Plaza	1	0	0	0	0	0	0	7	0	26	10	0	2	0
Biface	Center Bar	0	0	0	0	0	0	0	4	0	13	10	2	5	0
	East Plaza	0	0	0	2	0	0	0	2	1	19	11	3	5	0
Knife	Center Bar	0	0	0	0	0	0	0	0	0	0	0	0	0	0
	East Plaza	0	0	0	0	0	0	0	0	0	2	1	0	0	0
Drill	Center Bar	0	0	0	0	0	0	0	0	0	1	2	0	0	0
	East Plaza	0	0	0	0	0	0	0	0	0	2	1	0	0	0
Core	Center Bar	14	3	1	2	0	1	0	11	3	40	37	2	8	0
	East Plaza	61	4	0	1	0	2	0	12	8	45	28	4	11	0
Block	Center Bar	36	1	0	1	0	4	1	4	3	19	11	2	0	0
	East Plaza	51	0	0	0	0	0	0	4	2	16	10	1	3	0
Notch	Center Bar	0	1	1	0	0	0	0	8	1	17	15	2	0	0
	East Plaza	5	1	0	1	0	0	0	6	2	23	12	0	2	0
Core-scraper	Center Bar	1	0	0	0	0	0	0	3	3	13	8	1	5	0
	East Plaza	2	0	0	0	0	0	0	5	0	14	15	0	5	0
Lozenge scraper	Center Bar	0	0	0	0	0	0	0	1	0	5	1	0	1	0
	East Plaza	0	0	0	0	0	0	0	1	1	3	2	0	1	0
Gouge	Center Bar	0	0	0	0	0	0	0	1	0	0	1	0	0	0
	East Plaza	0	0	0	0	0	0	0	0	0	6	6	0	0	0
Chopper	Center Bar	1	0	0	0	0	0	0	0	0	0	0	0	0	0
	East Plaza	5	0	0	0	0	0	0	0	0	0	0	0	0	0

Table 16.6. Percentage frequencies of artifact types by raw material type.

Artifact Type	Area	Coarse-Grained							Fine-Grained						
		Ls	Bas	Q (wh)	Q (rd)	Qtz	Sltst	Gran	Ch (wh)	Ch (rd)	Ch (gry)	Ch (br)	Ch (fng)	Ch (mot)	Ch (grn)
Unmodified flake	Center Bar	74.5	77.3	76.9	76.2	100.0	77.3	60.0	47.7	50.0	51.2	47.2	35.6	33.7	100.0
	East Plaza	73.1	70.6	75.0	61.3	100.0	76.2	66.7	42.8	47.2	45.7	44.7	32.0	23.1	50.0
Utilized flake	Center Bar	8.1	11.4	0	9.5	0	0	0	19.6	15.6	18.7	19.1	25.4	17.3	0
	East Plaza	8.1	16.2	25.0	16.1	0	4.8	0	22.1	18.5	19.6	20.8	42.0	20.4	0
Unifac. ret. flake	Center Bar	2.6	0	0	0	0	0	20.0	8.9	10.0	7.9	9.3	11.9	8.7	0
	East Plaza	2.1	4.4	0	9.7	0	4.8	16.7	9.4	12.0	8.9	9.5	6.0	14.8	0
Bifac. ret. flake	Center Bar	0	0	0	0	0	0	0	0	3.3	0.3	0.6	3.4	1.0	0
	East Plaza	0	0	0	0	0	4.8	0	0.4	0.9	0.7	0.8	0	0.9	0
Side-scraper	Center Bar	0.8	0	7.7	0	0	0	0	7.9	8.9	9.0	8.2	8.5	17.3	0
	East Plaza	2.0	1.5	0	0	0	0	16.7	12.0	8.3	8.0	8.3	4.0	13.9	50.0
End-scraper	Center Bar	0.3	0	0	0	0	0	0	0.9	1.1	0.8	1.9	0	3.8	0
	East Plaza	0.1	0	0	0	0	0	0	2.5	0	2.9	1.7	0	1.9	0
Biface	Center Bar	0	0	0	0	0	0	0	1.9	0	1.4	1.6	3.4	4.8	0
	East Plaza	0	0	0	4.7	0	0	0	0.7	0.9	2.1	1.8	6.0	4.6	0
Knife	Center Bar	0	0	0	0	0	0	0	0	0	0	0	0	0	0
	East Plaza	0	0	0	0	0	0	0	0	0	0.2	0.2	0	0	0
Drill	Center Bar	0	0	0	0	0	0	0	0	0	0.1	0.3	0	0	0
	East Plaza	0	0	0	0	0	0	0	0	0	0.2	0.2	0	0	0
Core	Center Bar	3.7	6.8	7.7	9.5	0	4.5	0	5.1	3.3	4.5	5.9	3.4	7.7	0
	East Plaza	7.2	5.9	0	3.2	0	9.5	0	4.3	7.4	4.9	4.7	8.0	10.2	0
Block	Center Bar	9.4	2.3	0	4.8	0	18.2	9.2	1.9	3.3	2.1	1.8	3.4	0	0
	East Plaza	6.0	0	0	0	0	0	0	1.4	1.9	1.8	1.7	2.0	2.8	0
Notch	Center Bar	0	2.3	7.7	0	0	0	0	3.7	1.1	1.9	2.4	3.4	0	0
	East Plaza	0.6	1.5	0	3.2	0	0	0	2.2	1.9	2.5	2.0	0	1.9	0
Core-scraper	Center Bar	0.3	0	0	0	0	0	0	1.4	3.3	1.4	1.3	1.7	4.8	0
	East Plaza	0.2	0	0	0	0	0	0	1.8	0	1.5	2.5	0	4.6	0
Lozenge scraper	Center Bar	0	0	0	0	0	0	0	0.5	0	0.6	0.2	0	1.0	0
	East Plaza	0	0	0	0	0	0	0	0.4	0.9	0.3	0.3	0	0.9	0
Gouge	Center Bar	0	0	0	0	0	0	0	0.5	0	0	0.2	0	0	0
	East Plaza	0	0	0	0	0	0	0	0	0	0.7	1.0	0	0	0
Chopper	Center Bar	0.3	0	0	0	0	0	0	0	0	0	0	0	0	0
	East Plaza	0.6	0	0	0	0	0	0	0	0	0	0	0	0	0

Table 16.7. Percentage frequencies of artifact types for coarse- vs. fine-grained raw material types.

Artifact Type	Raw Material Type: Coarse-grained %	Raw Material Type: Fine-grained %
Unmodified flake	73.4	45.8
Utilized flake	8.5	19.9
Unifacially retouched flake	2.5	9.1
Bifacially retouched flake	0.1	0.7
Side-scraper	1.5	9.0
End-scraper	0.1	1.8
Biface	0.1	1.9
Knife	0.0	0.1
Drill	0.0	0.1
Core	6.1	5.2
Block	6.4	1.9
Notch	0.6	2.2
Core-scraper	0.2	1.8
Lozenge scraper	0.0	0.4
Gouge	0.0	0.3
Chopper	0.4	0.0

16.6. These highly detailed data are then summarized for the combined assemblages in Table 16.7. The Center Bar and East Plaza display no substantial differences in percentage frequencies of artifact types within each raw material type (Table 16.6). However, in examining these tables, one notices immediately a clear difference between the "coarse-grained" raw materials (i.e., limestone, basalt, quartzites, granite, siltstone) and the "fine-grained" cherts in the proportion of flakes that are unmodified. Forty percent or less (usually less than 30%) of the coarse-grained raw materials are modified by either utilization or formal retouch, regardless of provenience, whereas generally over 50% of the finer-grained materials (cherts) are modified. This is undoubtedly because many of the coarse-grained flakes, most particularly those of limestone, are unmodified debitage from the manufacture of heavy-duty tools or spalls that accidentally came off the working edge of these tools during use, while others are debris from roughing out metates. Some of the limestone flakes, however, have been utilized and others have been deliberately retouched.

Table 16.8. Flake types by raw material type.

Raw Material Type	Area	Flake Type[a]: BRF n	BRF %	BPO n	BPO %	PRB n	PRB %	NPRB n	NPRB %	SHA n	SHA %	Total n
Limestone	Center Bar	0	0	0	0	285	86.9	30	9.1	13	4.0	328
	East Plaza	1	0.1	0	0	667	90.6	47	6.4	21	2.9	736
Basalt	Center Bar	0	0	0	0	36	90.0	3	7.5	1	2.5	40
	East Plaza	0	0	0	0	60	93.8	3	4.7	1	1.6	64
Quartzite (white)	Center Bar	0	0	0	0	11	91.7	1	8.3	0	0	12
	East Plaza	1	25.0	0	0	3	75.0	0	0	0	0	4
Quartzite (red)	Center Bar	0	0	0	0	15	83.3	1	5.6	2	11.1	18
	East Plaza	0	0	0	0	27	93.1	2	6.9	0	0	29
Quartz	Center Bar	0	0	0	0	1	100.0	0	0	0	0	1
	East Plaza	0	0	0	0	1	100.0	0	0	0	0	1
Siltstone	Center Bar	0	0	0	0	14	82.4	2	11.8	1	5.8	17
	East Plaza	0	0	0	0	15	78.9	4	21.1	0	0	19
Granite	Center Bar	0	0	0	0	4	100.0	0	0	0	0	4
	East Plaza	0	0	0	0	5	83.3	1	16.7	0	0	6
Chert (white)	Center Bar	11	5.7	2	1.0	156	81.3	22	11.5	1	0.5	192
	East Plaza	27	10.7	1	0.4	202	79.8	19	7.5	4	1.6	253
Chert (red)	Center Bar	7	8.6	1	1.2	61	75.3	8	9.9	4	5.0	81
	East Plaza	13	13.4	1	1.0	76	78.4	6	6.2	1	1.0	97
Chert (gray)	Center Bar	24	2.9	4	0.5	665	81.7	98	12.0	23	2.9	814
	East Plaza	58	7.0	9	1.1	649	78.9	84	10.2	23	2.8	823
Chert (brown)	Center Bar	24	4.3	6	1.1	452	80.7	62	11.1	16	2.8	560
	East Plaza	37	6.8	6	1.1	440	80.9	53	9.7	8	1.5	544
Chert (fingerprint)	Center Bar	2	3.7	2	3.7	44	81.5	4	7.4	2	3.7	54
	East Plaza	3	7.0	0	0	37	86.0	3	7.0	0	0	43
Chert (mottled)	Center Bar	3	3.4	1	1.1	71	79.8	13	14.6	1	1.1	89
	East Plaza	3	3.6	1	1.2	72	85.7	7	8.3	1	1.2	84
Chert (green)	Center Bar	0	0	0	0	1	100.0	0	0	0	0	1
	East Plaza	0	0	0	0	2	100.0	0	0	0	0	2
TOTAL	Center Bar	71	3.2	16	0.7	1816	82.1	244	11.0	64	3.0	2211
	East Plaza	143	5.3	18	0.7	2256	83.4	229	8.4	59	2.2	2705
	combined	214	4.4	34	0.7	4072	82.8	473	9.6	123	2.5	4916

[a]BRF, bifacial reduction flake; BPO, bipolar flake; PRB, platform remnant-bearing flake; NPRB, non-platform remnant-bearing flake; SHA, shatter.

Table 16.9. Amount of cortex (counts) by raw material type.[a]

Raw Material Type	Center Bar Amount of Cortex				East Plaza Amount of Cortex			
	0%	≤50%	>50%	100%	0%	≤50%	>50%	100%
Limestone	134	78	51	68	322	173	124	122
Basalt	24	7	3	6	35	8	12	9
Quartzite (white)	7	4	1	0	3	0	0	1
Quartzite (red)	13	1	2	2	17	4	4	5
Quartz	1	0	0	0	1	0	0	0
Siltstone	4	4	4	5	7	2	3	7
Granite	2	1	0	1	0	2	2	2
Chert (white)	157	24	13	5	190	54	15	2
Chert (red)	57	15	12	0	75	18	1	4
Chert (gray)	594	167	58	19	626	164	45	16
Chert (brown/tan)	418	110	35	12	392	106	46	20
Chert (fingerprint)	38	16	1	0	38	5	2	0
Chert (mottled)	69	22	4	1	63	18	10	3
Chert (green)	1	0	0	0	2	0	0	0
TOTAL COUNT	1519	449	184	119	1771	550	264	191
PERCENTAGE	66.9	19.8	8.1	5.2	63.8	19.8	9.5	6.9

[a]Cores and blocks have been omitted form these tabulations.

Table 16.10. Amount of cortex (percentage frequencies) by raw material type.[a]

Raw Material Type	Center Bar Amount of Cortex				East Plaza Amount of Cortex			
	0%	≤50%	>50%	100%	0%	≤50%	>50%	100%
Limestone	40.5	23.6	15.4	20.5	43.5	23.3	16.7	16.5
Basalt	60.0	17.5	7.5	15.0	54.7	12.5	18.8	14.0
Quartzite (white)	58.3	33.3	8.3	0	75.0	0	0	25.0
Quartzite (red)	72.2	5.6	11.1	11.1	56.7	13.3	13.3	16.7
Quartz	100.0	0	0	0	100.0	0	0	0
Siltstone	23.5	23.5	23.5	29.5	36.8	10.5	15.9	36.8
Granite	50.0	25.0	0.0	25.0	0	33.3	33.3	33.3
Chert (white)	78.9	12.1	6.5	2.5	72.8	20.7	5.7	0.8
Chert (red)	67.9	17.9	14.3	0	76.5	18.4	1.0	4.1
Chert (gray)	70.9	19.9	6.9	2.3	73.6	19.3	5.3	1.9
Chert (brown/tan)	72.7	19.1	6.1	2.1	69.5	18.8	8.2	3.5
Chert (fingerprint)	69.1	29.1	1.8	0	84.4	11.1	4.5	0
Chert (mottled)	71.9	22.9	4.2	1.0	67.0	19.2	10.6	3.2
Chert (green)	100.0	0	0	0	100.0	0	0	0

[a]Cores and blocks have been omitted from the tabulations.

Flake Types

Of the 5,516 lithic pieces from the Center Bar and the East Plaza included in this analysis, 89.0% are identified as flakes, shatter, or flake tools (Table 16.8). This proportion is virtually the same when the East Plaza and the Center Bar are examined separately. The vast majority of the debitage and flake tools consist of platform remnant–bearing flakes. The next most common flake type is the non-platform remnant–bearing flake. Biface reduction flakes are not well represented in the samples. Only two examples of non-chert biface reduction flakes are present, one of limestone and one of white quartzite. All of the bipolar flakes, 0.7% of the total sample, are of chert.

While the percentages for these five flake-type categories are broadly similar in the Center Bar and East Plaza, the differences in the values for two of the categories nonetheless are large enough to attain statistical significance.[1] The proportion of biface reduction flakes in the East Plaza is greater than in the Center Bar ($t_s = 3.62$, $p < .001$), and the proportion of non-platform remnant–bearing flakes is lower ($t_s = 3.03$, $p < .01$). Both of these differences might indicate that later stages of lithic reduction proportionately are slightly better represented in the

Table 16.11. Amount of cortex (counts) for coarse- vs. fine-grained raw material types.

Raw Material Type	Center Bar Amount of Cortex				East Plaza Amount of Cortex			
	0%	≤50%	>50%	100%	0%	≤50%	>50%	100%
Fine-grained	1334	354	123	37	1386	361	119	45
Coarse-grained	184	95	61	82	385	189	145	146
TOTAL	1519	449	184	119	1771	550	264	191

Table 16.12. Amount of cortex (percentage frequencies) for coarse- vs. fine-grained raw material types.

Raw Material Type	Center Bar Amount of Cortex				East Plaza Amount of Cortex			
	0%	≤50%	>50%	100%	0%	≤50%	>50%	100%
Fine-grained	72.2	19.1	6.7	2.0	72.5	18.9	6.2	2.4
Coarse-grained	43.7	22.5	14.4	19.4	44.5	21.8	16.8	16.9

Table 16.13. Amount of cortex by raw material type on non-retouched and retouched artifacts (Center Bar).

Raw Material Type		Non-Retouched				Retouched			
		0%	≤50%	>50%	100%	0%	≤50%	>50%	100%
Limestone	*n*	130	72	46	66	4	7	1	1
	%	41.4	22.9	14.6	21.0	30.8	53.8	7.7	7.7
Basalt	*n*	23	7	3	6	1	0	0	0
	%	59.0	17.9	7.7	15.4	100.0	0	0	0
Quartzite (white)	*n*	7	2	1	0	0	1	0	0
	%	70.0	20.0	10.0	0	0	100.0	0	0
Quartzite (red)	*n*	13	1	2	2	0	0	0	0
	%	72.2	5.6	11.1	11.1	0	0	0	0
Quartz	*n*	1	0	0	0	0	0	0	0
	%	100.0	0	0	0	0	0	0	0
Siltstone	*n*	4	4	4	5	0	0	0	0
	%	23.5	23.5	23.5	29.4	0	0	0	0
Granite	*n*	1	1	0	1	1	0	0	0
	%	33.3	33.3	0	33.3	100.0	0	0	0
Chert (white)	*n*	113	18	8	5	40	4	4	0
	%	78.5	12.5	5.5	3.5	83.4	8.3	8.3	0
Chert (red)	*n*	40	11	8	0	16	2	4	0
	%	67.8	18.6	13.6	0	72.7	9.1	18.2	0
Chert (gray)	*n*	447	115	47	18	133	40	10	1
	%	71.3	18.3	7.5	2.9	72.3	21.7	5.4	0.5
Chert (brown/tan)	*n*	309	75	21	8	93	31	14	0
	%	74.8	18.2	5.1	1.9	67.4	22.5	10.1	0
Chert (fingerprint)	*n*	26	10	0	0	10	5	0	0
	%	72.2	27.8	0	0	66.7	33.3	0	0
Chert (mottled)	*n*	40	11	2	0	22	8	2	1
	%	75.5	20.8	3.8	0	66.7	24.2	6.1	3.0
Chert (green)	*n*	1	0	0	0	0	0	0	0
	%	100.0	0	0	0	0	0	0	0

plaza midden, although most other comparisons do not support this (see below).

Amount of Cortex

As can be seen from Tables 16.9 and 16.10, the percentage occurrences of the various amounts of cortex remaining on lithic pieces in the two samples are very similar, with roughly 65% of all pieces exhibiting no cortex at all. When the figures within each area are combined into simply two states, ≤50% or >50%, the resemblance between the two proveniences is even more pronounced, with pieces exhibiting 50% or less cortex constituting 86.7% of the Center Bar sample and 83.6% of the plaza sample, and those with greater than 50% cortex making up 13.3% and 16.4% of the samples, respectively. These values are very similar, again suggesting that the trash in the two areas of the village came from comparable sources.

Table 16.14. Amount of cortex by raw material type on non-retouched and retouched artifacts (East Plaza).

Raw Material Type		Non-Retouched				Retouched			
		0%	≤50%	>50%	100%	0%	≤50%	>50%	100%
Limestone	*n*	309	157	108	118	13	15	10	3
	%	44.7	22.7	15.6	17.1	31.5	36.6	24.4	7.3
Basalt	*n*	35	9	7	8	1	1	2	1
	%	59.3	15.3	11.9	13.5	20.0	20.0	40.0	20.0
Quartzite (white)	*n*	3	0	0	1	0	0	0	0
	%	75.0	0	0	25.0	0	0	0	0
Quartzite (red)	*n*	15	3	3	3	1	0	1	2
	%	62.5	12.5	12.5	12.5	25.0	0	25.0	50.0
Quartz	*n*	1	0	0	0	0	0	0	0
	%	100.0	0	0	0	0	0	0	0
Siltstone	*n*	6	1	3	7	1	1	0	0
	%	35.3	5.9	17.6	41.2	50.0	50.0	0	0
Granite	*n*	0	1	1	2	0	1	1	0
	%	0	25.0	25.0	50.0	0	50.0	50.0	0
Chert (white)	*n*	136	31	11	1	48	22	3	1
	%	76.0	17.3	6.1	0.6	64.9	29.7	4.1	2.0
Chert (red)	*n*	54	15	0	2	20	3	1	2
	%	76.1	21.1	0	2.8	76.9	11.5	3.9	7.7
Chert (gray)	*n*	445	101	37	13	161	47	7	3
	%	74.7	16.9	6.2	2.2	73.8	21.6	3.2	1.4
Chert (brown/tan)	*n*	278	67	32	17	86	31	12	3
	%	70.6	17.0	8.1	4.3	67.6	21.8	8.5	2.1
Chert (fingerprint)	*n*	33	3	1	0	3	1	1	0
	%	89.2	8.1	2.7	0	60.0	20.0	20.0	0
Chert (mottled)	*n*	30	9	6	2	26	6	4	1
	%	63.8	19.1	12.8	4.3	70.3	16.2	10.8	2.7
Chert (green)	*n*	1	0	0	0	1	0	0	0
	%	100.0	0	0	0	100.0	0	0	0

In Tables 16.11 and 16.12, the raw material types have been grouped into coarse- and fine-grained states. The percentage frequencies of cortex amount within each raw material state are again strikingly similar in the Center Bar and East Plaza samples: roughly 90% of fine-grained and 65% of the coarse-grained specimens exhibit 50% or less cortex on their surfaces. Not surprisingly, on average, much less cortex remains on the fine-grained flakes and tools than on the coarse-grained specimens.

When divided simultaneously by presence or absence of retouch and by raw material type, the data on cortex amounts display no major differences between modified and unmodified pieces that are not merely the product of small sample sizes (Tables 16.13, 16.14). This similarity holds true for both coarse- and fine-grained materials and in both proveniences. These broadly comparable cortex amounts very likely reflect the expedient nature of the Henderson lithic assemblage in that, on the whole, retouched pieces were not extensively worked, but instead were modified just enough to perform a specific task and then discarded.

Dorsal Scars

Table 16.15 provides a summary of dorsal scar counts, regardless of raw material type, for four broad artifact categories: unmodified, utilized, unifacially retouched, and bifacially retouched. The scar patterns were examined to determine whether specific flake types (measured by the number of dorsal scars) were preferentially selected by the Henderson villagers for modification or use. In both areas of the site, unmodified flakes most commonly display only one or two dorsal scars (Center Bar, 52.4%; East Plaza, 53.8%). Utilized flakes, unifacially retouched flakes, and bifacially retouched flakes show great similarities in dorsal scar frequency, with most displaying three or more scars (Center Bar, $\bar{x}$ = 59.9%; East Plaza, $\bar{x}$ = 56.4%). Since the unmodified category includes many flakes that were removed during the initial stages of core preparation, it is not surprising that there are many flakes displaying only one to two dorsal scars. However, it is also clear from the above tabulations that the villagers preferred the products from later stages of core reduction when choosing flakes for immediate use or further modification.

Platform Scars

Table 16.16 utilizes the same four artifact categories as in the previous section. From these data, it is clear that, in both samples, platforms with one or two scars are the most common, regardless of category (60-70% of specimens). Platform faceting (platforms with three or more scars) is not particularly common at Henderson. In both proveniences, faceted platforms are more likely to be found on utilized and unifacially retouched flakes than on unmodified flakes (the bifacially retouched category is too small for meaningful comment). In the Center Bar, however, only the proportion of utilized flakes with faceted platforms differs significantly from the value seen in unmodified flakes (t_s = 4.05, $p < .001$). The value for unifacially retouched flakes, while greater than the figure seen in the unmodified category, does not differ significantly ($t_s = 1.48$, $p > .05$), perhaps because the sample size of these retouched pieces is relatively small.

In the East Plaza, the unmodified, utilized, and unifacially retouched flakes all differ significantly from each other in the proportion of faceted platforms, the proportion increasing with degree of modification (again, bifacially retouched flakes are excluded because of the extremely small sample size; utilized vs. unmodified: $t_s = 2.95$, $p < .01$; unifacially retouched vs. unmodified: $t_s = 6.03$, $p < .001$; unifacially retouched vs. utilized: $t_s = 3.62$, $p < .001$).

If one can assume that flakes with faceted platforms were produced later in the reduction process than flakes with fewer platform scars, these data suggest that the Henderson villagers preferred to make their tools on flakes that were produced during more advanced reduction stages. A broadly similar trend was reflected in the dorsal scar counts (see Table 16.15).

Artifact Weight and Size

The weight of all lithic specimens was measured to the nearest 0.10 g. Tables 16.17-16.19 summarize the weight data in terms of coarse- vs. fine-grained materials for each artifact type in the Center Bar and East Plaza, as well as for the total sample. As expected, the mean weights of tools made of coarse materials are heavier than the mean weights of comparable tools made of fine materials. Also as expected, the tools in the Center Bar are similar in average weight to their counterparts in the East Plaza, with one notable exception—the cores made on fine-grained materials are heavier (and slightly larger) in the East Plaza (weight, $\bar{x} = 25.8$ g; maximum length, $\bar{x} = 3.3$ cm) than in the Center Bar (weight, $\bar{x} = 12.9$ g; maximum length, $\bar{x} = 2.7$ cm), and the difference is significant (weight, $t = 1.97$, $p < .05$; maximum length, $t = 3.04$, $p < .01$). The cores made of coarse-

Table 16.15. Dorsal scars (counts and percentage frequencies) by provenience at the Henderson Site.

Artifact Type	Center Bar						East Plaza					
	None		1-2		≥3		None		1-2		≥3	
	n	%	*n*	%	*n*	%	*n*	%	*n*	%	*n*	%
Unmodif. flake	109	8.6	665	52.4	494	39.0	158	10.0	839	53.8	562	36.0
Utilized flake	5	1.2	155	37.8	250	61.0	15	2.9	207	40.4	290	56.7
Unifac. ret. flake	5	2.8	71	40.1	101	57.1	9	4.1	89	40.5	122	55.4
Bifac. ret. flake	0	0	4	33.3	8	66.7	0	0	6	40.0	9	60.0
TOTAL	119	6.4	895	47.9	853	45.7	182	7.9	1141	49.5	983	42.6

Table 16.16. Platform scars (counts and percentage frequencies) by provenience at the Henderson Site.

Artifact Type	Center Bar								East Plaza							
	None		1-2		≥3		Crushed		None		1-2		≥3		Crushed	
	n	%	*n*	%	*n*	%	*n*	%	*n*	%	*n*	%	*n*	%	*n*	%
Unmod. flake	98	8.5	788	68.1	268	23.1	4	0.3	147	10.2	1021	71.1	255	17.8	13	0.9
Utilized flake	24	6.6	213	59.0	123	34.1	1	0.3	37	7.7	323	67.2	116	24.1	5	1.0
Unifac. ret. flake	11	7.5	93	63.7	42	28.8	0	0	5	2.6	111	58.4	73	38.4	1	0.6
Bifac. ret. flake	1	13.0	6	75.0	1	12.5	0	0	2	20.0	7	70.0	1	10.0	0	0
TOTAL	134	8.0	1100	65.8	434	25.9	5	0.3	191	9.0	1462	69.1	445	21.0	19	0.9

Table 16.17. Average weight (g) of artifacts made of coarse- vs. fine-grained raw materials (Center Bar).

Artifact Type	Coarse-Grained			Fine-Grained		
	n	Mean	±1σ	*n*	Mean	±1σ
Unmodified flake	365	3.3	11.2	957	1.5	7.8
Utilized flake	38	4.4	6.8	376	2.3	4.7
Unifacially retouched flake	11	3.4	5.5	173	2.0	3.3
Bifacially retouched flake	0	0	0	13	3.6	2.4
Side-scraper	4	11.1	7.2	180	4.1	4.6
End-scraper	1	6.1	0	26	4.7	6.5
Biface	0	0	0	34	7.0	5.1
Knife	0	0	0	0	0	0
Drill	0	0	0	3	1.6	1.8
Core	21	63.4	82.4	101	12.9	37.1
Block	43	4.7	6.5	39	2.1	2.5
Notch	2	10.6	11.2	43	2.0	1.9
Core-scraper	1	4.0	0	33	6.4	5.2
Lozenge scraper	0	0	0	8	6.2	5.6
Gouge	0	0	0	2	3.1	3.8
Chopper	1	552.0	0	0	0	0

Table 16.18. Average weight (g) of artifacts made of coarse- vs. fine-grained raw materials (East Plaza).

Artifact Type	Coarse-Grained			Fine-Grained		
	n	Mean	±1σ	*n*	Mean	±1σ
Unmodified flake	714	4.5	10.5	897	1.7	8.3
Utilized flake	87	9.6	15.4	428	2.6	4.8
Unifacially retouched flake	26	14.4	18.5	196	2.5	5.9
Bifacially retouched flake	1	22.5	0	14	6.2	7.5
Side-scraper	19	19.5	36.3	183	4.4	6.4
End-scraper	1	46.6	0	45	4.4	4.5
Biface	2	24.2	14.1	41	10.3	11.0
Knife	0	0	0	3	8.8	12.3
Drill	0	0	0	3	3.1	1.5
Core	68	107.1	176.3	108	25.8	54.6
Block	51	9.3	21.1	36	2.0	1.5
Notch	7	14.9	11.8	45	3.9	3.5
Core-scraper	2	98.2	18.7	39	15.9	23.6
Lozenge scraper	0	0	0	8	13.2	18.9
Gouge	0	0	0	12	5.3	7.5
Chopper	5	396.0	171.8	0	0	0

grained materials are also heavier, on average, in the plaza than in the rooms, but the difference is not significant, perhaps because the sample sizes are very small ($t = 1.09$, $p > .05$). The reason for this difference is not evident, given the absence of major differences in virtually every other parameter considered (e.g., amount of cortex, number of dorsal scars, frequency of platform faceting).

The average size of the various artifact classes at Henderson, determined using the maximum dimension of the specimens, is presented in Table 16.20. Only the results for the combined sample are given since the size data mirror very closely the observations made using specimen weights. As expected, in every case where sample sizes permit meaningful comparisons, the average size of artifacts made on coarse-grained materials is greater than that of artifacts made on chert. Perhaps the most interesting observation that can be made from the data in Table 16.20 is that most formal tools made on cherts (side-scrapers, end-scrapers, bifaces, bifacially retouched flakes, notches, and knives) are significantly larger, on average, than either utilized or unifacially retouched flakes made of these materials.[2] This result parallels the ethnographic observations of White and Thomas (1972) which showed that flake size among New Guinea Highlanders was a primary determinant in the selection of flake blanks for subsequent modification.

Table 16.19. Average weight (g) of artifacts made of coarse- vs. fine-grained raw materials (total sample).

Artifact Type	Coarse-Grained			Fine-Grained		
	n	Mean	±1σ	*n*	Mean	±1σ
Unmod. flake	1079	4.1	10.7	1854	1.6	8.0
Utilized flake	125	8.0	13.6	804	2.5	4.8
Unifacially retouched flake	37	11.2	16.5	369	2.3	4.8
Bifacially retouched flake	1	22.5	0	27	4.9	5.7
Side-scraper	23	18.1	33.0	363	4.3	5.6
End-scraper	2	26.4	28.6	71	4.5	5.3
Biface	2	24.2	14.1	75	8.8	9.0
Knife	0	0	0	3	8.8	12.3
Drill	0	0	0	6	2.4	1.7
Core	89	96.8	159.8	209	19.6	47.3
Block	94	7.2	16.3	75	2.1	2.0
Notch	9	13.9	11.2	88	2.9	3.0
Core-scraper	3	66.8	55.9	72	11.6	18.3
Lozenge scraper	0	0	0	16	9.7	13.9
Gouge	0	0	0	14	5.0	7.0
Chopper	6	422.0	166.4	0	0	0

Conclusions

What is perhaps most surprising about the Henderson lithics is the striking similarity of the assemblages from room and non-room contexts, despite the tremendous differences in their faunal assemblages. The proportional representation of artifact types in the East Plaza and Center Bar middens, with one notable exception, are virtually identical. In both assemblages, slightly over half of the artifacts are unmodified flakes, followed by utilized flakes, unifacially retouched flakes and side-scrapers, cores, and blocks. The remaining tool types, including notches, core-scrapers, end-scrapers, bifaces, knives, drills, bifacially retouched flakes, lozenge scrapers, and gouges, are very poorly represented in both proveniences. The single noteworthy contrast is the presence in the East Plaza midden of crude, unifacial and bifacial choppers, most made on irregular blocks of limestone. These tools are rare in the Center Bar.

The surprising degree of similarity in the array of tool and debitage types from these two proveniences is underscored repeatedly in comparisons of other features of the assemblages. For example, if one excludes the artifacts made of limestone and other coarse-grained materials, both assemblages display virtually identical proportions of fine-grained raw material types, with local gray and brown (tan) cherts overwhelmingly predominating. The density of artifacts in the two middens, expressed as the number of specimens per cubic meter of deposit, are also nearly identical. In addition, the proportions of flakes with recognizable, intact, platforms are indistinguishable, as are the percentage frequencies of artifacts with little vs. abundant remnant cortex. Flakes with faceted platforms are more or less equally well represented in the Center Bar and East Plaza, as are flakes with three or more dorsal scars. Finally, average weights and artifact sizes are also very similar in the two proveniences.

All of these comparisons point to the same conclusion: the bulk of the lithics in the two middens derive from similar, if not identical, sources. The only notable difference between them that might parallel the striking contrast seen in the faunal assemblages is in the abundance of heavy-duty limestone choppers. These clearly expedient cutting tools are found primarily in the plaza, and may well be tools that were used for the initial butchering and processing of the many bison and antelope carcasses that were brought into the village.

Synopsis

This chapter analyzes a subsample of 5,516 lithic artifacts (formal tools, cores, and debitage) from the two principal midden deposits encountered during the 1980-1981 excavations at the Henderson Site. These deposits are the trash in the fill of Center Bar Room C-5 and the deep ashy midden in the earth oven complex at the southern end of the East Plaza. All of the chipped stone artifacts recovered from these two proveniences, either *in situ* or in the quarter-inch screens, are included in the present study. Excluded here, however, are hundreds of pieces of microdebitage that were found in flotation and geological samples, as well as many crude, heavy-duty limestone choppers that were encountered in the East Plaza midden. The samples analyzed here are estimated to represent roughly 10% to 20% of the total assemblage of some 30,000 to 40,000 pieces recovered during the two seasons of excavation.

In view of the strikingly different faunal assemblages that were encountered in these two midden deposits, with thousands of bison and antelope bones in the East Plaza and mostly the remains of small mammals, particularly cottontails, jackrabbits, and prairie dogs, in Room C-5, one of the principal goals of this analysis was to determine whether there are parallel contrasts

Table 16.20. Average maximum dimensions (cm) of artifact types for coarse- vs. fine-grained raw materials (total sample).

Artifact Type	Coarse-Grained			Fine-Grained		
	n	Mean	±1σ	*n*	Mean	±1σ
Unmod. flake	1079	2.3	1.2	1854	1.6	0.8
Utilized flake	125	3.0	1.3	804	2.2	0.9
Unifacially retouched flake	37	3.3	1.4	369	2.1	0.9
Bifacially retouched flake	1	5.5	0	27	2.7	1.0
Side-scraper	23	4.0	2.0	363	2.7	0.9
End-scraper	2	5.3	2.5	71	2.6	0.9
Biface	2	4.5	1.4	75	3.3	1.0
Knife	0	0	0	3	3.7	1.6
Drill	0	0	0	6	2.6	0.9
Core	89	5.1	2.4	209	3.0	1.4
Block	94	2.6	1.2	75	1.9	0.6
Notch	9	3.8	1.2	88	2.4	0.8
Core-scraper	3	5.2	2.8	72	3.1	1.2
Lozenge scraper	0	0	0	16	3.4	1.3
Gouge	0	0	0	14	2.8	1.2
Chopper	6	9.9	1.4	0	0	0

between these two proveniences in their flaked stone tool assemblages.

The proportional representation of artifact types in the East Plaza and Center Bar middens, with one notable exception, proved to be virtually identical. In both assemblages, slightly over half of the artifacts are unmodified flakes (53%), followed by utilized flakes (17%), unifacially retouched flakes and side-scrapers (7%), cores (5% to 6%), and blocks (3%). The remaining tool types, including notches, core-scrapers, end-scrapers, bifaces, knives, drills, bifacially retouched flakes, lozenge scrapers, and gouges, are very poorly represented in both proveniences. The single noteworthy contrast is the presence in the East Plaza midden of numerous, very crude, unifacial and bifacial choppers, most made on irregular blocks of limestone. These tools are rare in the Center Bar. Most of these pieces remain to be analyzed.

The surprising degree of similarity in the array of tool and debitage types from these two proveniences is underscored repeatedly in comparisons of other features of the assemblages. For example, if one excludes the artifacts made of limestone and other coarse-grained materials, both assemblages display virtually identical proportions of fine-grained raw material types, with local gray and brown (tan) cherts overwhelmingly predominating (Center Bar/East Plaza: gray chert, 43%/42%; brown chert, 30%/28%). The density of artifacts in the two middens, expressed as the number of specimens per cubic meter of deposit, are also nearly identical (Center Bar/East Plaza: 271 items per m^3/272 items per m^3). In addition, the proportions of flakes with recognizable, intact, platforms are indistinguishable (Center Bar/East Plaza: 82%/83%), as are the percentage frequencies of artifacts with less than 50% cortex (Center Bar/East Plaza: fine-grained materials, 91%/91%; coarse-grained materials, 66%/66%). Flakes with faceted platforms (three or more platform scars) are similarly represented in the Center Bar and East Plaza (26%/21%), as are flakes with three or more dorsal scars (Center Bar/East Plaza: 46%/43%). Finally, average weights and artifact sizes are also very similar in the two proveniences. These results were foreshadowed by the analysis of the projectile points in Chapter 15; both proveniences yielded very similar assemblages.

All of these comparisons point to the same conclusion: the bulk of the lithics in the two middens derive from similar, if not identical, sources. The only notable difference between them that might parallel the striking contrast seen in the faunal assemblages is in the abundance of heavy-duty limestone choppers found primarily in the plaza. These may be tools that were used for the initial butchering and processing of bison and antelope carcasses brought into the village. Some of the limestone flakes may also be debris from the manufacture of metates, all of which appear to have been fashioned on-site from the local bedrock.

Notes

1. Test of the equality of two percentages based on the arcsine transformation (Sokal and Rohlf 1969:607-10).

2. All comparisons between the mean size of these tool types and the average size of both utilized and unifacially retouched flakes, using *t*-tests, were statistically significant, most at $p < .01$.

References Cited

Banks, L. D.
1984 Lithic Resources and Quarries. In: *Prehistory of Oklahoma*, edited by R. E. Bell. Orlando, FL: Academic Press.

Hughes, J. T.
1978 Geology. In: *Archeology at Mackenzie Reservoir*, edited by J. T. Hughes and P. S. Willey, pp. 16-23. Archeological Survey Report 24. Austin, TX: Texas Historical Commission, Office of the State Archeologist.

Katz, S. R., and P. R. Katz
1976 *Archeological Investigations in Lower Tule Canyon, Briscoe County, Texas*. Archeological Survey Report 16. Austin, TX: Texas Historical Foundation, Texas Tech University, Texas Historical Commission.

Lovick, S. K.
1983 Fire-Cracked Rock As Tools: Wear-Pattern Analysis. *Plains Anthropologist* 28(99):41-52.

Magne, M. P. R.
1985 *Lithics and Livelihood: Stone Tool Technologies of Central and Southern Interior British Columbia*. Mercury Series, Archaeological Survey of Canada Paper 133. Ottawa, Ontario: National Museum of Man.

Mallouf, R. J.
1989 Quarry Hunting with Jack T. Hughes: Tecovas Jasper in the South Basin of the Canadian River, Oldham County, Texas. In: *In the Light of Past Experience: Papers in Honor of Jack T. Hughes*, edited by D. C. Roper, pp. 307-26. Publication 5. Amarillo, TX: Panhandle Archeological Society.

Parry, W. J.
1987 *Chipped Stone Tools in Formative Oaxaca, Mexico: Their Procurement, Production and Use*. Memoir 20. Ann Arbor, MI: Museum of Anthropology, University of Michigan.

Parry, W. J., and R. L. Kelly
1987 Expedient Core Technology and Sedentism. In: *The Organization of Core Technology*, edited by J. K. Johnson and C. A. Morrow, pp. 285-304. Boulder, CO: Westview Press.

Rocek, T. R., and J. D. Speth
1986 *The Henderson Site Burials: Glimpses of a Late Prehistoric Population in the Pecos Valley*. Technical Report 18. Ann Arbor, MI: Museum of Anthropology, University of Michigan.

Sokal, R. R., and F. J. Rohlf
1969 *Biometry: The Principles and Practice of Statistics in Biological Research*. San Francisco, CA: W. H. Freeman.

White, J. P., and D. H. Thomas
1972 What Mean These Stones? Ethno-Taxonomic Models and Archaeological Interpretations in the New Guinea Highlands. In *Models in Archaeology*, edited by D. L. Clarke, pp. 275-308. London, England: Methuen.

17
The Groundstone Evidence

John D. Speth
University of Michigan

Tatum M. McKay

Kristen K. Arntzen
Washington University

Introduction

More than fifty years ago, Katharine Bartlett (1933:3) wrote:

> In the last fifty years or more that American archaeologists have been interested in the Southwest remarkably little attention has been given to the corn grinding stones of the prehistoric Pueblos. In very early reports—when all objects discovered were new in the experience of the finders—fairly detailed descriptions were given of metates and manos. After that milling stones were no novelty, and moreover, they were too cumbersome to be taken back to the laboratory for study, and so we have the beginning of the long period, which has lasted well into the last decade, when metates were described as being "of the usual type."

Unfortunately, had Bartlett's comments been written half a century later they still would have provided a fairly accurate characterization of the continuing disinterest shown by Southwestern archaeologists in these "cumbersome" objects. (There were some notable exceptions such as Woodbury 1954.) In fact, manos and metates are one of the few classes of artifact that many Southwestern archaeologists still discard today without the slightest compunction.

Fortunately, a growing number of Southwestern archaeologists are beginning to explore the intriguing relationships between the form and size of grinding stones and the degree to which their prehistoric makers were dependent on maize. These relationships stem in large measure from the fact that as a society's dependence on corn or other starchy cereals increases, more time and effort have to be expended grinding the kernels into flour. These growing time and labor demands favor improvements in the effectiveness and efficiency of the grinding equipment (and in many other technological and social domains as well). Significant improvements can be achieved simply by augmenting the amount of grinding surface of both mano and metate (e.g., Adams 1989, 1993; Calamia 1983, 1991; Hard 1984, 1986, 1990; Katz et al. 1974; Lancaster 1983, 1984, 1986; Mauldin 1991, 1993; Molleson 1994; Morris 1990; Nelson and Lippmeier 1993; Stahl 1989; Vierra 1993; Wright 1994).

In the case of the mano, breadth is constrained by the size of the grinder's hand. Thus, significant increases in surface area can be achieved primarily by lengthening the tool, a change which favors a shift from one-handed to two-handed mano forms. Further increases in efficiency can be obtained by changing the design of the mano from a tool with a single grinding surface to one with two or more working faces. This change reduces the frequency with which the mano has to be roughened to maintain its grinding effectiveness and prevents the grinding faces from wearing unevenly (Adams 1993).

Changes in the shape and size of the mano are accompanied by corresponding changes in the form and size of the metate as well. These changes are well documented in the Southwest. The earliest metates used by archaic foragers and the first maize cultivators were basin-shaped. These were generally positioned horizontally and grinding was done using a one-handed mano moved around the basin in a rotary fashion. Over much of the Southwest, basin-shaped metates gradually gave way to trough forms to accommodate the use of broader, two-handed manos. The trough metate was placed in a tilted position with the working surface sloping away from the grinder who moved the mano

Figure 17.1. Complete metate from Room C-2 at the Henderson Site.

back and forth using a reciprocal motion. Finally, in many parts of the Southwest, trough metates were supplanted by slab forms that maximized the breadth of the grinding surface while minimizing the amount of energy-wasting contact between the ends of the mano and the sides of the metate.

These changes in mano and metate form did not take place at the same time everywhere in the Southwest, nor did earlier forms entirely disappear as newer ones came into common use. Nevertheless, by about A.D. 700-900 very few Puebloan communities were using basin-shaped metates and one-handed manos as their primary type of milling equipment (e.g., Woodbury 1954). Thus, at a late thirteenth-century Pueblo village like Henderson, one would certainly expect most of the metates to be either trough or slab forms, and most of the manos to be two-handed forms with at least two opposing grinding surfaces.

Neither is the case. Almost all of the metates recovered to date from Henderson are roughly shaped, massive blocks of limestone with extremely shallow, ovoid grinding basins; and most of the manos are one-handed forms, with a single working face, that have been crudely fashioned from heavy granitic or metamorphic river cobbles. If the form and grinding surface area of the milling equipment does in some way reflect the contribution of maize to the diet, as the many studies just cited would suggest, then one must conclude that the Henderson villagers were at best only moderately dependent on this crop. The manos and metates from Henderson, therefore, provide remarkably clear signals, unaffected by the preservation biases that plague reconstructions based on perishable food remains, that the economy of this Plains-margin village may have been quite different from the sedentary, maize-based pattern so typical of Puebloan communities elsewhere in the Southwest at this time period.

Metates

Metates, whether broken or complete, were uncommon at Henderson. Only 21 metates were recovered in the 164 m^2 of the site sampled in 1980 and 1981. This figure includes two large complete metates that were found lying on the surface of the Center Bar, undoubtedly dumped there by vandals who had excavated a fairly substantial pit in the north end of this room block. Fragments of very small grinding stones, clearly used for purposes other than food processing, are excluded from discussion in this chapter. The metates recovered in the 1990s (1994, 1995, 1997) have not been analyzed as yet, but they were uncommon artifacts, as was the case in 1980-1981, and they were massive, basin-shaped, and made of local limestone. Also as in the first two seasons of work, most of the metates found in the 1990s were broken, probably deliberately, and either discarded or incorporated into wall foundations. None were found *in situ* in their place of use and none had been cached for future use.

Curiously, most of the metates recovered in 1980-1981 were broken (n = 16; 76%), despite the fact that many had been made

Figure 17.2. Complete metate found on surface of Center Bar at the Henderson Site.

on very thick and sometimes massive blocks of limestone. Even among the six most substantial metates, that is, specimens made on blocks that were at least 20 cm thick, four were broken. Not only were the metates very thick, but most had extremely shallow—less than 3 cm deep—grinding basins when they broke. In fact, only a single metate had a grinding surface sufficiently deep to have made the tool somewhat fragile during use. This specimen, made on a 12-cm thick slab, had a 9-cm deep grinding surface at the time it broke. Thus, most of the Henderson metates appear to have been deliberately broken, and they were broken long before they were in any functional sense exhausted.

This conclusion is reinforced by the fact that many of the broken metates had been incorporated, together with unmodified limestone slabs, as "uprights" in the bases of walls when the rooms were first constructed or remodeled. Several metate fragments were found *in situ* in their upright position in eroded wall stubs, while others were found "floating" just above the floors in room fill in positions clearly indicating that they had been displaced from their original location when the walls collapsed. Thus, many of the metates may have been broken deliberately to produce slabs small enough to be used in the walls.

This suggestion leaves unanswered the intriguing question of why the Henderson villagers chose to break what appear to have been fully functional metates, when unmodified rocks would have fulfilled the same architectural function equally well. Outcrops of tabular limestone were readily accessible on the slopes surrounding the village as well as on neighboring hilltops. Securing suitable blocks for either wall construction or metate-making was probably not difficult. But transforming a massive limestone block into a functioning metate required at least a modicum of flaking to trim the block to its proper shape; and it of course required considerably more effort to peck out a grinding basin of suitable size, curvature, and abrasiveness (e.g., Aschmann 1949; Hayden 1987; Horsfall 1987; Huckell 1986; Pastron 1974). Why break a massive metate, long before it ceased to be usable as a grinding slab, to use it as an upright in the base of a wall? Why not simply use an unmodified piece of rock for this purpose?

At present, we see no simple mechanical or technological reason for this curious practice. It seems more likely to us that the explanation will be found in the ideological realm than in the contingencies of the milling process itself. In other words, metates may have been broken deliberately, and new ones made, not because they became exhausted or too costly to refurbish, but for example as part of a New Year's or world renewal rite, or a pre-harvest ritual. While these suggestions are plausible, we see no direct way to evaluate them with the data at hand.

Since so many of the metates are broken, it is difficult to provide meaningful summary statistics for the sample. Average values and ranges are provided for the primary dimensions of the few specimens that are complete enough to allow measurement. Five of the metates from 1980-1981 are fully intact and one nearly so; most of the measurements are taken from these. Three of the complete specimens are illustrated in Figures 17.1-17.3. The average maximum length of the metate blocks, measured on six specimens, is 55.7 cm (range, 47-59 cm). The maximum breadth of these same metates is 39.2 cm (range, 28-50 cm). Thickness could be estimated on eighteen of the metates, yielding a mean of 15.1 cm (range, 7-28 cm). The true value of the mean is undoubtedly somewhat greater than this figure, however, since the thickness values taken on the broken specimens generally underestimate the maximum values, probably substantially in several instances. As noted earlier, many of the metates are made on blocks that are 20 cm or more in thickness.

Figure 17.3. *In situ* limestone metate on primary floor in southwest corner of East Bar Room E-4 (photo looking to south). Note fragmentary metate incorporated into wall base immediately to right (west) of complete metate.

The grinding basins of the Henderson metates are circular to strongly ovoid. A few of the deeper basins at first glance appear troughlike, but even these have grinding surfaces that are deeply concave in both transverse and longitudinal section. None of the Henderson metates are true trough forms. In the six specimens for which the basins can be accurately measured, the mean length is 36.5 cm (range, 33-43 cm) and the mean width is 28.0 cm (range, 21-34 cm). Most of the metate basins are also very shallow (n = 10; mean depth below rim, 2.7 cm; range, 1.5-9.0 cm). The grinding surface area of each of the six measurable basins, estimated using the formula for the area of an ellipse, is 577 cm^2, 641 cm^2, 700 cm^2, 895 cm^2, 961 cm^2, and 1,081 cm^2, with an overall mean of 809 cm^2. This average figure may seem surprisingly small when compared to the size of the blocks on which the six metates were made (average area of blocks 2,205 cm^2, range 1,316-2,950 cm^2). Part of the reason that the basins are so much smaller than the blocks on which they are made is because most metates have a broad unmodified platform left at one end that may have served as a "mano rest." In addition, the blocks have been very crudely shaped, leaving substantial bulges and irregularities on the sides and ends that often extend well beyond the margins of the basin; these bulges inflate considerably the maximum length and width measurements of the blocks.

Given the recent focus among Southwestern archaeologists on the relationship between average grinding surface area and degree of commitment to maize agriculture, it would be interesting to compare the value for the Henderson basin metates with values for basin, trough, and slab metates from sites elsewhere in the Southwest. Unfortunately, so few values have been published as yet that such a comparison would not be very productive (see for example Bartlett 1933; Lancaster 1984, 1986; Shelley 1983; Vierra 1993). We are in much better shape when it comes to manos, for which there now exists a much more substantial body of data. We will turn to the Henderson manos shortly.

The striations visible on the grinding surfaces of the Henderson metates are almost invariably oriented parallel to the long axis of the block, indicating that the dominant strokes used in the milling process were reciprocal rather than rotating. Wear on the manos, whether one-handed or two-handed, points to the same conclusion (see below).

Many of the metates, even those with very shallow grinding basins, display a smooth band of from one to several centimeters wide around the upper margin of the basin, while the remainder of the basin has a much rougher texture. This implies, not surprisingly, that most metates underwent at least one, and perhaps many, episodes of refurbishing or roughening before they were abandoned or broken. Without experimental studies using comparable manos and limestone blocks, it is difficult to estimate how long a basin metate of this kind might be used before it became necessary to roughen the grinding surface. Studies of this sort might clarify whether it's possible that the Henderson metates were ritually broken after only a single year of use.

Three of the complete metates were found in primary use context within structures. No metates were tipped over in "storage" position, nor were they found in contexts that might imply they had been cached for later use. One of the complete metates (see Fig. 17.1) was found in Room C-2 in the Center Bar. It was in the northeast quarter of the room, parallel to, and within about 15 cm of, the room's east wall, and about 1.5 m south of the room's north wall. The "mano rest" was on the north end, implying that the grinder positioned himself/herself to the north of the metate. The metate had been carefully propped up into a nearly horizontal position by placing a mano under its southwest corner and a grooved maul under its southeast corner. Propping in this manner was necessary to attain a horizontal position, because the slab's underside was highly irregular and would have tilted steeply to the south without the props. There is no doubt that the desired orientation of the metate was horizontal or nearly so (the slab tilted very slightly to the south). The mano used as a prop did not fit in the grinding basin and was clearly not the tool used with this metate.

A second complete metate was found in southwest quarter of Room E-4 in the East Bar. This massive piece of milling equipment was also oriented parallel to the long axis of the room, but in this case was situated within about 10 cm of the room's west wall and about 75 cm north of the room's south wall. Like the metate in Room C-2, this one had also been propped up into a nearly horizontal position by placing a thin limestone slab under the south end. The desired position actually tilted the slab very slightly to the north. While both ends of the slab have broad platforms that could have served as mano rests, the shelf at the south end is the broadest. In addition, the southern mano rest is slightly higher than its counterpart at the other end. The prominence of the shelf at the south end of the metate, together with the slight northward tilt of the entire slab, suggest that the grinder was positioned at the southern end.

The third complete metate found in primary use context came from the southeast quarter of Room E-5, a badly eroded room built directly over the pitroom in the East Bar (Room E-3). This metate was again oriented parallel to the long axis of the room, about 50 cm west of the room's east wall and one meter north of the room's south wall. The mano rest on this specimen was to the south and presumably the grinder worked from the south end. The grinding basin is about 7 cm deep and appears to be a trough, although the bottom of the basin rises noticeably at the end opposite the mano rest and the sides of the basin converge in that direction. Thus, while superficially resembling a trough metate, the tool was employed in a manner more typical of a basin metate. As in the other metates, this specimen was oriented more or less horizontally, in this case however without the aid of props.

Summarizing the metate data, the following points are the most noteworthy. Metates are not common at Henderson. All of the specimens recovered are basin or "basinoid" metates, not true trough or slab forms. They are all crudely shaped from locally available tabular limestone blocks. Many are more than half a meter long and 20 cm thick. Their grinding basins are circular to ovoid, and generally quite shallow. Manos were used in a reciprocal rather than a rotary fashion. Few of the metates can in any sense be considered spent. Despite their size and limited wear, most of the metates were broken, presumably deliberately. Most of the broken metates, along with hundreds of unmodified pieces of limestone, were used as uprights in the bases of walls. No mechanical or technical reasons for the breakage of these massive tools are immediately apparent, and it seems more likely that breakage had a ritual cause. Only three metates were found in their primary use context, one in the Center Bar and two in the East Bar. While hardly much of a sample upon which to base generalizations, the following patterns are worth keeping in mind in future excavations at Henderson or at contemporary villages elsewhere in the area. Metates were positioned in corners of rooms and oriented parallel to the room's long axis. The proximity of the metate to a wall may have provided the grinder with a rigid foot support. Metates were positioned horizontally, or nearly so, using props when necessary. When not in use, metates were neither turned over in storage position, nor were they cached. Perhaps the most speculative suggestion given the minuscule sample of *in situ* metates, but also potentially the most interesting, is that grinders in the East Bar may have worked in the opposite direction from grinders in the Center Bar, a contrast that might mark important social dimensions within the organizational structure of the community.

Manos

Like metates, manos were not very common at Henderson. The assemblage from all five seasons of excavation consists of only 76 specimens, of which only 43 are complete or nearly so. Many of the manos had been recycled once they were no longer needed for grinding purposes. Several had been roughly notched on each edge at or near the midpoint of the long axis and then hafted for use as a crude hammer or maul. Many were tossed into the earth oven complexes as heating stones, where they became reddened and often fractured in the process. Some had also been used to grind red pigment.

Average dimensions for the manos, both for the site as a whole and broken down by chronological phase, are provided in Table 17.1. Perhaps the most striking aspect of the Henderson manos is the high degree of variability in shape. There has been little or no attempt at standardization in this assemblage. Some of the manos are made on massive, egg-shaped or globular water-

Table 17.1. Metric data for the Henderson Site manos (1980-1997).

Attribute	Total Sample			Early Phase			Late Phase		
	n	Mean ± 1σ	CV	*n*	Mean ± 1σ	CV	*n*	Mean ± 1σ	CV
Max. length (cm)	43	16.7±4.4	.26	10	14.1±3.7	.26	33	17.5±4.4	.25
Max. width (cm)	76	10.4±2.7	.25	20	10.2±2.7	.27	55	10.6±2.6	.24
Max. thick. (cm)	76	5.7±2.1	.37	20	5.2±1.6	.30	55	6.0±2.2	.37
Weight (g)	43	1795.9±961.1	.54	10	1453.4±767.2	.53	33	1899.7±1000.0	.53
Surface area (cm^2)	43	189.8±71.5	.38	10	168.4±63.3	.38	33	196.3±73.4	.37

worn cobbles, the largest among them weighing well over 4 kg, while others are made on much flatter, almost tabular pieces of stone. The majority have only one working surface (n = 64 or 84.2%), and none evidence any deliberate attempt at shaping the cobble. Six of the manos have breadths equal to or greater than 14 cm, the maximum width that any of us were able to grasp securely. The materials used for making the manos are also quite varied. Most are made of igneous or metamorphic river cobbles, probably Plio-Pleistocene in age, and very likely collected from eroded cobble exposures capping some of the nearby hills. Sandstone was rarely used for manos, and limestone was never employed.

When looked at by phase, average maximum length differs significantly, with the longest manos in the Late phase (t = -.21, $p < .05$). None of the remaining attributes, however, differ significantly from each other. Interestingly, although mean grinding-surface area is larger in the Late phase than in the Early phase, as expected given the greater mean length in the younger period, the difference fails to achieve statistical significance. This failure may simply be a product of the very small sample size in the Early phase (n = 10). Nevertheless, we are left with ambiguous results. If we accept that mano length and grinding-surface area broadly track a community's dependence on maize (holding other variables such as raw material type, shape, and size constant), then we might have tentative evidence for some degree of agricultural intensification at Henderson (e.g., Adams 1989, 1993; Calamia 1983, 1991; Hard 1984, 1986, 1990; Mauldin 1991, 1993). Such a scenario is supported by the fact that the density of manos per m^3 of excavated deposit increases by about 75%, from 0.28 manos/m^3 in the Early phase to 0.49 manos/m^3 in the Late phase. However, since the absolute change in mano surface area is not very great (about 17%), since manos are very scarce in both periods, and since the sample sizes on which these comparisons are based are very small, there seems to be little secure evidence to support the view that maize became increasingly important in the villagers' diet during the latter part of the occupation.[1]

Conclusions

A number of salient aspects of Henderson's metate and mano assemblage are worth reiterating here. First, judging by the three cases in which metates were found *in situ* (all in Late phase contexts), corn grinding appears to have been done individually within separate households, not in clustered or communal grinding areas.

Second, all of the metates (and probably the manos as well) were made of locally available materials (tabular limestone blocks for the metates; igneous or metamorphic waterworn cobbles for the manos). Most, if not all, of these tools were manufactured right at the village, as evidenced by many large limestone flakes and spalls found in plaza trash.

Third, most of the metates were deliberately broken long before they had been exhausted, reflecting in our view some sort of ritual practice, perhaps related to an annual renewal cycle.

Finally, neither type of tool is common at Henderson. Either the villagers processed much of their corn using wooden mortars and pestles, tools which have not survived, or their dependence on maize was lower than in most contemporary Pueblos in the heartland of the Southwest. We favor the latter view for several reasons: (1) the manos are crude and unstandardized, (2) most manos have only one working surface, (3) most metates have very shallow, basin-shaped grinding surfaces, (4) carbon- and nitrogen-isotope signatures determined on human skeletal remains from Henderson indicate a lower dependence on C_4 plants, probably maize among them, than at quasi-contemporary Pueblos like Pecos, Gran Quivira, and Hawikuh (see Chapter 20), and (5) Henderson's human dentitions display a low incidence of dental caries, more typical of hunter-gatherers than farmers (Rocek and Speth 1986). Thus, it seems reasonable to conclude that maize was not as important a staple at Henderson as it was elsewhere in the late prehistoric Southwest (Habicht-Mauche et al. 1994; Spielmann et al. 1990).

Synopsis

Both metates and manos were uncommon at Henderson. Most of the metates were broken, despite the fact that many had been made on massive blocks of limestone, and most had extremely shallow grinding basins when they broke. Thus, most of the Henderson metates appear to have been deliberately broken, and they were broken long before the tools were in any functional sense "exhausted." Many of the broken metates had been incorporated, together with unmodified limestone slabs, as "uprights" in the bases of walls when the rooms were first constructed or remodeled. Thus, many of the metates may have been broken deliberately to produce slabs small enough to be used in the walls.

Why did the Henderson villagers break what appear to have been fully functional metates, when unmodified rocks would have fulfilled the same architectural function equally well? Outcrops of tabular limestone were readily accessible on the slopes surrounding the village as well as on neighboring hilltops. Thus, securing suitable blocks for either wall construction or metate-making would not have been difficult. Transforming a massive limestone block into a functioning metate required at least a modicum of flaking to trim the block to its proper shape; and it of course required considerably more effort to peck out a grinding basin of suitable size, curvature, and abrasiveness.

It seems more likely that the explanation will be found in the ideological realm than in the contingencies of the milling process itself. Metates may have been broken deliberately, and new ones made, not because they became exhausted or too costly to refurbish, but as part of an annual renewal rite, or a pre-harvest ritual.

The average maximum length of the metate blocks, measured on six specimens, is 55.7 cm. The maximum breadth of these same metates is 39.2 cm. Thickness could be approximated on 18 of the metates, yielding a mean of 15.1 cm. Several of the metates are made on blocks that are 20 cm or more in thickness.

The grinding basins of the Henderson metates are circular to strongly ovoid. A few of the deeper basins appear troughlike, but even these have grinding surfaces that are deeply concave in both transverse and longitudinal section. None of the Henderson metates are true trough forms. Most of the metate basins are very shallow. The average grinding-surface area of six measurable specimens is 809 cm^2. Most metates have a broad unmodified platform left at one end that may have served as a "mano rest."

Three of the complete metates were found in primary use context within structures. None were tipped over in "storage" position, and none were found in contexts that might imply they had been cached for later use. Metates were positioned in corners of rooms and oriented parallel to the room's long axis. The proximity of the metate to a wall may have provided the grinder with a rigid foot support. Metates were positioned horizontally, or nearly so, using props when necessary.

Like metates, manos were not very common at Henderson. The assemblage from all five seasons of excavation consists of only 76 specimens, nearly half of which are broken. Many of the manos had been recycled once they were no longer needed for grinding purposes. Several had been roughly notched on each edge at or near the midpoint of the long axis and then hafted for use as a crude hammer or maul. Many were tossed into the earth oven complexes as heating stones, where they became reddened and often fractured in the process. Some had also been used to grind red pigment.

Perhaps the most striking aspect of the Henderson manos is their high degree of variability in shape. There has been little or no attempt at standardization in this assemblage. Some of the manos are made on massive, egg-shaped or globular waterworn cobbles, the largest among them weighing well over 4 kg, while others are made on much flatter, almost tabular pieces of stone. Nearly 85% have only one working surface, and none evidence any deliberate attempt at shaping the cobble. Most manos are made of igneous or metamorphic river cobbles, probably Plio-Pleistocene, and very likely collected from eroded cobble exposures capping some of the nearby hills. Sandstone was rarely used for manos, and limestone was never employed.

When the manos are looked at by phase, average maximum length differs significantly, with the longest manos in the Late phase. None of the remaining metric attributes, however, differ significantly from each other. Although mean grinding-surface area is larger in the Late phase than in the Early phase, the difference fails to achieve statistical significance. This failure may simply be a product of the very small sample size in the Early phase. If we accept that mano length and grinding-surface area broadly track a community's dependence on maize, then we might have weak and tentative evidence for some degree of agricultural intensification at Henderson. Such a scenario is supported by the fact that the density of manos per m^3 of excavated deposit increases by about 75% from the Early phase to the Late phase. However, carbon isotope data (see Chapter 20), the low incidence of caries, and the use of basin-shaped metates and unformalized one-handed manos all point to an economy in which maize played a much less prominent role than it did in the communities farther west in the heart of the pueblo world.

Note

1. A doctoral dissertation, recently completed by Gina S. Powell (2001) of Washington University in St. Louis, has explored the issue of maize use during Henderson's Early and Late phase and finds no compelling evidence of intensified production or use.

References Cited

Adams, J. L.
1989 Experimental Replication of the Use of Ground Stone Tools. *Kiva* 54(3):261-72.
1993 Toward Understanding the Technological Development of Manos and Metates. *Kiva* 58(3):331-44.

Aschmann, H.
1949 A Metate Maker of Baja California. *American Anthropologist* 51: 682-86.

Bartlett, K.
1933 Pueblo Milling Stones of the Flagstaff Region and Their Relation to Others in the Southwest: A Study in Progressive Efficiency. *Museum of Northern Arizona Bulletin* 3:3-32.

Calamia, M. A.
1983 *Interpreting Human Mobility through the Analysis of Ground Stone Implements.* Master's thesis, Department of Anthropology, University of Illinois, Urbana, IL.
1991 Ground Stone Variability among Jornada Mogollon Sites and Its Implications for Interpreting Residential Mobility. In: *Mogollon V*, edited by P. H. Beckett, pp. 119-32. Las Cruces, NM: COAS Publishing and Research.

Habicht-Mauche, J. A., A. A. Levendosky, and M. J. Schoeninger
1994 Antelope Creek Phase Subsistence: The Bone Chemistry Evidence. In: *Skeletal Biology in the Great Plains: Migration, Warfare, Health, and Subsistence*, edited by D. W. Owsley and R. L. Jantz, pp. 291-304. Washington, DC: Smithsonian Institution Press.

Hard, R. J.
1984 Settlement and Subsistence in the Chihuahuan Desert. *Proceedings of the American Society for Conservation Archaeology* 2:234-51.
1986 *Ecological Relationships Affecting the Rise of Farming Economies: A Test from the American Southwest*. Ph.D. dissertation, University of New Mexico, Albuquerque, NM.
1990 Agricultural Dependence in the Mountain Mogollon. In: *Perspectives on Southwestern Prehistory*, edited by P. E. Minnis and C. L. Redman, pp. 122-34. Boulder, CO: Westview Press.

Hayden, B.
1987 Traditional Metate Manufacturing in Guatemala Using Chipped Stone Tools. In: *Lithic Studies among the Contemporary Highland Maya*, edited by B. Hayden, pp. 8-119. Tucson, AZ: University of Arizona Press.

Horsfall, G. A.
1987 Design Theory and Grinding Stones. In: *Lithic Studies Among the Contemporary Highland Maya*, edited by B. Hayden, pp. 332-77. Tucson, AZ: University of Arizona Press.

Huckell, B. B.
1986 *A Ground Stone Implement Quarry on the Lower Colorado River, Northwestern Arizona*. Cultural Resources Series 3. Phoenix, AZ: U.S. Department of the Interior, Bureau of Land Management.

Katz, S. H., M. L. Hediger, and L. A. Valleroy
1974 Traditional Maize Processing Techniques in the New World. *Science* 184:765-73.

Lancaster, J. W.
1983 *An Analysis of Manos and Metates from the Mimbres Valley, New Mexico*. Master's thesis, Department of Anthropology, University of New Mexico, Albuquerque, NM.
1984 Groundstone Artifacts. In: *The Galaz Ruin: A Prehistoric Mimbres Village in Southwestern New Mexico*, by R. Anyon and S. A. LeBlanc, pp. 247-62. Albuquerque, NM: Maxwell Museum of Anthropology and the University of New Mexico Press.
1986 Ground Stone. In: *Short-Term Sedentism in the American Southwest: The Mimbres Valley Salado*, edited by B. A. Nelson and S. A. LeBlanc, pp. 177-90. Albuquerque, NM: University of New Mexico Press.

Mauldin, R. P.
1991 Agricultural Intensification in the Mogollon Highlands. In: *Mogollon V*, edited by P. H. Beckett, pp. 62-74. Las Cruces, NM: COAS Publishing and Research.
1993 The Relationship between Ground Stone and Agricultural Intensification in Western New Mexico. *Kiva* 58(3):317-30.

Molleson, T.
1994 The Eloquent Bones of Abu Hureyra. *Scientific American* 271(2):70-75.

Morris, D. H.
1990 Changes in Groundstone Following the Introduction of Maize into the American Southwest. *Journal of Anthropological Research* 46(2):177-94.

Nelson, M. C., and H. Lippmeier.
1993 Grinding-Tool Design as Conditioned by Land-Use Pattern. *American Antiquity* 58(2):286-305.

Pastron, A. G.
1974 Preliminary Ethnoarchaeological Investigations among the Tarahumara. In: *Ethnoarchaeology*, edited by C. B. Donnan and C. W. Clewlow, pp. 93-114. Monograph 4. Los Angeles, CA: University of California, Institute of Archaeology.

Powell, G. S.
2001 *Hunting and Farming between the Plains and the Southwest: Analysis of Archaeobotanical Remains from the Henderson Site, Roswell, New Mexico*. Ph.D. dissertation, Washington University, St. Louis, MO.

Shelley, P. H.
1983 *Lithic Specialization at Salmon Ruin, San Juan County, New Mexico*. Ph.D. dissertation, Washington State University, Pullman, WA.

Spielmann, K. A., M. J. Schoeninger, and K. Moore
1990 Plains-Pueblo Interdependence and Human Diet at Pecos Pueblo, New Mexico. *American Antiquity* 55(4):745-65.

Stahl, A. B.
1989 Plant-Food Processing: Implications for Dietary Quality. In: *Foraging and Farming: The Evolution of Plant Exploitation*, edited by D. R. Harris and G. C. Hillman, pp. 171-94. London, England: Unwin Hyman.

Vierra, B. J.
1993 Lithic Synthesis and Conclusions. In: *Across the Colorado Plateau: Anthropological Studies for the Transwestern Pipeline Expansion Project*, Vol. XVII, Book 1, Parts 1 and 2. *Architectural Studies, Lithic Analyses, and Ancillary Studies*, by B. J. Vierra, T. W. Burchett, K. L. Brown, M. E. Brown, P. T. Kay, and C. J. Phagan, pp. 353-81. Albuquerque, NM: University of New Mexico, Office of Contract Archaeology and Maxwell Museum of Anthropology.

Woodbury, R. B.
1954 *Prehistoric Stone Implements of Northeastern Arizona*. Reports of the Awatovi Expedition 6, Papers of the Peabody Museum of American Archaeology and Ethnology 34. Cambridge, MA: Harvard University.

Wright, K. I.
1994 Ground-Stone Tools and Hunter-Gatherer Subsistence in Southwest Asia: Implications for the Transition to Farming. *American Antiquity* 59(2):238-63.

Part IV

Ethnobotany

18
Archaeobotanical Maize
The Screened Sample (1980-1981)

Sandra L Dunavan
University of Michigan

Introduction

While numerous archaeological and ethnobotanical studies show that maize was the dominant plant food resource throughout much of the American Southwest in late prehistoric times, there are few details concerning its role in prehistoric subsistence economies in southeastern New Mexico. This chapter helps to fill this gap by providing a detailed description and analysis of the maize remains recovered from the Henderson Site. Maize was clearly an important food resource to the Henderson villagers, as shown by the near ubiquity of carbonized cob and cupule fragments in the site. Although taphonomic biases preclude a quantitative assessment of the caloric contribution of maize, it is safe to say that corn was an important component of the villagers' diet during the late thirteenth and fourteenth centuries (see also Rocek and Speth 1986).

The Henderson maize offers valuable insights into many other archaeological issues besides diet. For example, the site-wide distribution of maize remains can be used to explore site formation processes, and both local and regional variability in cob and kernel size and morphology can provide important clues to patterns of social interaction, local agricultural productivity, and the nature and degree of environmental stress. Following a description of recovery techniques and the methods by which the maize remains were measured and classified, maize deposition and spatial patterning at Henderson are examined, and the cobs and kernels are described and statistically summarized. Finally, cob variability, both intrasite and regional, is discussed (see also Adams 1994). In the hope that others will find innovative ways to use these data, detailed measurements for all maize remains examined are included (see also Dunavan 1994).

Methods

In 1980 and 1981, fill from all excavation areas and features was screened through quarter-inch mesh or separated for flotation samples. Recognizable maize fragments, particularly carbonized cobs and kernels, were picked from screens or hand-collected *in situ*, and bagged and labeled with separate field specimen numbers. These materials are the focus of the chapter.

For many decades, agronomists and botanists have described and classified cobs as a basis for understanding maize variation and evolution (Anderson and Brown 1948; Anderson and Cutler 1942; Bird and Goodman 1977; Carter and Anderson 1945; Goodman and Paterniani 1969; Nickerson 1953; Wellhausen et al. 1952:26-33). Pioneering botanists and paleoethnobotanists, including Cutler (1964), Cutler and Meyer (1965), Galinat and Gunnerson (1963), Jones (1949), and Jones and Fonner (1954), also used various morphological traits in their descriptions of maize as products of temporally and geographically distinct human selection. Because of the maize cob's complex morphology and the numerous attributes used by various specialists, methods for analyzing prehistoric maize have only recently begun to be standardized (Bird 1994). King (1987:81-120) evaluates many of the morphological attributes most commonly used by paleoethnobotanists by examining their variation in prehistoric and historic cobs, their potential for archaeological preservation, and their genetic and environmental underpinnings. In general, her terminology and measures have been used in this analysis. Several additional, largely qualitative, cob characteristics, including many of those used by Ford (1973:188-89), were also recorded. It should be noted again that all attributes were observed on carbonized material, and that these quantitative measures are not directly comparable to those taken from desiccated or modern specimens. In general, cobs shrink 15-30% when carbonized (Caddell 1983:250; Cutler and Blake 1973a; Goette et al. 1994; King 1987:147-48), but different parts of cobs may vary in shrinkage, which may in turn vary according to how dry the cob was at the time it was burned.

A number of quantitative variables were recorded. All measurements were taken with digital calipers and recorded in millimeters and tenths of millimeters. Fragment length is the length of the cob, cob fragment, or cupule segment (a fragment of at least three linked cupules) along the long axis of the cob. Cob rachis diameter (minimum, maximum, and average) was measured on exposed cob cross-sections, and measures the distance from opposite cupule lips (Bird 1994; King 1987:92; Caddell 1983:250). Glume diameter (maximum, minimum, average) was measured between opposite lower glumes on cobs with unbroken glumes. Pith diameter (maximum, minimum, average) measures the distance from the bases of opposite cupules (King 1987:93). All diameters were recorded from complete cobs, or cob fragments which had a complete diameter, and all diameters were recorded from breaks near the middle of the cob, or as near to it as possible. Stalk diameters were taken in the few instances in which stalk remnants were still attached to cob bases.

Cupule width was measured on large, complete cupules in the middle of all fragments. In general, only one cupule per cob, or cob fragment, was measured. Cupule width measures the space from the outside of one cupule wing, also called the rachis flap, to the other. Cupule height, measured at right angles to cupule width, corresponds to King's (1987:89) kernel thickness or alicole length, or rachis segment length, although rachis segment length is usually computed as an average of three cupules. Wing width, or rachis flap length (King 1987:87), measures the extension from the outside of the cupule wing to the aperture where the kernels once sat. Aperture length (King's 1987:93 internal cupule width) measures the span in which the kernels sat in the cupule, and corresponds to the cupule width minus the wing width. Aperture height extends perpendicular to this measure (Doebley and Bohrer 1983:24). Aperture depth, often impossible to determine in these carbonized, sometimes eroded and internally distorted cupules, was measured with a needlelike extension of the calipers, and extended from the cupule lip to the bottom of the cupule aperture. Lower glume length, measured parallel to cupule width, records the length of the thin flaplike piece that partially encloses the kernel and holds it in place in the cupule.

Cob row number is one of the most commonly recorded nominal characteristics of archaeological cobs. As with diameter, row number was recorded only from complete cobs or fragments with complete diameters. Although row number has been estimated from loose kernels or cupules (e.g., Cutler and Blake 1973a:4-5, 1973b:3-4), carbonization adds to the problems inherent in this technique (Pearsall 1980; Bohrer 1986:30; King 1987:128-32), and for this reason it was not used to estimate row number at Henderson.

When possible, the section of cob (base, midsection, or tip), the amount of cob curvature (weak, strong, or none), cross-section shape (circular, elliptical, or square), and the presence of irregular rows, spiraling rows, row pairing, and incomplete pollination were also noted. If the cob appeared to be a nubbin (a diminutive cob formed on tillers or side stalks), this was also noted. Although the proportion of nubbins in a maize population can be a useful indicator of agricultural practices and environment, the definition of nubbins remains a subjective matter (Brugge 1965; Jessup 1982:44, 49, 52). Small but complete or mostly complete cobs, often incompletely pollinated, usually with row numbers of eight or less, were designated as "nubbins" in the Henderson maize population.

Fewer variables were recorded for maize kernels. Kernel height was measured on all specimens, measuring from the base of the kernel where attached in the cupule, to the top or cap, the part seen when kernels are still attached to cobs. Kernel width, perpendicular to kernel height (and parallel to cupule width), and kernel thickness (corresponding to cupule height or alicole length) was also taken on all kernels. Germ (or embryo) height and width could only be obtained from the one kernel that still retained a complete embryo. Kernel shape, corresponding to Johannessen and Hastorf's (1989) cap shape, was recorded for all kernels. Kernel and cob colors could not be determined, since all samples were carbonized.

Deposition and Spatial Patterning

None of the maize cobs or fragments recovered in 1980-1981 at Henderson retained any kernels, and isolated kernels were rare at the site. Only 42.2% (n = 158) of the specimens examined had complete cross-sections, and just nine of these were complete cobs (all classified as nubbins). The remaining 57.8% of the cob sample analyzed (n = 216) consisted of "cupule segments," or linear pieces of maize cobs or rachises with at least three complete cupules. Five isolated kernels found in the screens are also described here. Many more kernel fragments and smaller cob fragments, especially cupules, were found in the flotation samples, but their morphology has not been described, due to their small size and high degree of fragmentation.

Fragmentation of charred cobs may have occurred during carbonization and deposition, or in the postdepositional environment. Because they are not edible, have a tough, woody structure, and were commonly used for fuel, corn cobs are more commonly carbonized and preserved than many other plant foods or plant wastes which may only be accidentally charred when being cooked or dried (Miksicek 1987:220; Toll 1985:259-60; Wetterstrom 1973:12, 1986). Cobs and fragments recovered from the screens ranged from 0.4 cm to 4.1 cm in length, and the mean fragment length was 1.5 cm for both the entire site-

Table 18.1. Density of maize fragments from the Henderson Site.

Provenience	*n*	Volume[a] (m^3)	Density (n/m^3)
East Plaza (B/C)	31	12.73	2.4
East Bar (all rooms)	48	34.85	1.4
Room E-1	5	5.07	1.0
Room E-2	1	5.12	0.2
Room E-3	23	5.04	4.6
Room E-4	19	9.98	1.9
Center Bar (all rooms)	298	25.76	11.6
Room C-1	2	2.12	0.9
Room C-2	1	4.89	0.2
Room C-3	25	3.09	8.1
Room C-4	15	6.71	2.2
Room C-5	252	8.77	28.7
Room C-6	3	0.18	16.7
All rooms (excl. C-5)	46	16.99	2.7
TOTAL	377	73.34	5.1

[a]Values for volume of excavated deposit are for 1980-1981 seasons only.

wide assemblage, and for separate excavation areas of the Center Bar, East Bar, and East Plaza. The distribution of fragment lengths is skewed, with few fragments under 0.7 cm in length, reflecting a bias against smaller fragments presumably introduced by the quarter-inch screen size and my decision not to measure cupule segments with fewer than three linked cupules.

The scarcity of complete cobs, as well as the small mean fragment size, suggest that the maize remains were subjected to a fair amount of fragmentation. The cause of this extensive breakage is not entirely clear, however. Some, perhaps most, probably occurred when the cobs were burned. Trampling may also have contributed to the breakage, although its role is likely to have been relatively minor, since many broken specimens came from the midden in Center Bar Room C-5, an enclosed context where foot traffic is not likely to have been very heavy. Breakage may also have occurred, at least in some areas of the site, when structures were modified or remodeled. Unless immediately covered, carbonized cobs on or near the surface were also subjected to freeze-thaw cycles, repeated wetting and drying, and other destructive weathering processes.

Interestingly, almost 80% of the recovered maize remains came from the Center Bar, and about 85% of the those were found in a single deposit—the stratified trash midden in Room C-5. Only 12.7% of the cob fragments came from the East Bar; the remaining 8.2% were recovered in the East Plaza. Clearly, maize deposition was not uniform in different rooms, room blocks, and plaza areas. Density indices, which average the number of measurable fragments per cubic meter of fill for a given area (Miller 1989), provide an easy way to visualize these differences, and are shown in Table 18.1 for the different excavation areas and for individual rooms in the Center Bar.

Obviously, the high density of maize found in the Center Bar is largely a result of the exceptionally high density of remains in Room C-5, although Room C-3 also had a considerable quantity of charred cob fragments. The high density value for Room C-6, a badly vandalized structure near the north end of the Center Bar, may be an artifact of sample size; only 0.18 m^3 was excavated from this structure but three cob fragments were recovered, yielding a density index (16.7/m^3) that is second only to Room C-5.

The correlation between the number of fragments and the volume of excavated sediment for the East Bar, East Plaza, and Center Bar (except Room C-5) is significant ($r = .62, p \approx .05$); the number of fragments recovered increases with the volume of sediment excavated. Smaller fill volumes show the most variability, almost certainly reflecting sampling error. The sample from Room C-5 is clearly an outlier, however, since when quantities from this room are added to the calculations r drops to .36 ($p > .05$).

That maize was far more abundant in Room C-5 than elsewhere in the Center Bar or in the East Bar room block is not particularly surprising, since this room contained the largest stratified trash deposit encountered within the structures that were excavated in 1980 and 1981. What is striking, however, is the scarcity of maize remains in the East Plaza, since significant deposits of trash also accumulated in this area of the village (see Chapters 2 and 14). Carbonized maize was apparently discarded far more often in room block trash than in plaza trash.

As noted earlier, the mean length of cob fragments was virtually identical in both room blocks and plaza (1.5 cm). The same seems to be true of the portions of maize cobs that were discarded in the different proveniences (see Table 18.2). In all three excavation areas, cob midsections (the longest part of the

Table 18.2. Frequency (*n*) of cob sections by provenience at the Henderson Site.

Cob Section	Provenience						Site-Wide Total	
	East Plaza		East Bar		Center Bar			
	n	%	*n*	%	*n*	%	*n*	%
Midsection	9	56.3	20	64.5	128	72.3	157	70.1
Base	1	6.3	3	9.7	2	1.1	6	2.7
Tip	6	37.5	5	16.1	41	23.2	52	23.2
Complete	—	—	3	9.7	6	3.4	9	4.0
TOTAL	16		31		177		224	

cob) comprise between half and 75% of the pieces recovered. Cob bases make up less than 10% of the sample in all areas, and cob tips constitute between 15% and 40% of the sample. Only nine complete cobs (all classified as nubbins) were recovered, and these were found in roughly similar proportions in all three areas (chi square; $.05 > p > .025$).

Thus, although there are major differences between room block and plaza trash in the density of maize remains, there seem to be no differences between these two proveniences in the degree to which the cobs were fragmented or in the proportions of different cob sections (or nubbins). This suggests that, while maize remains were far less likely to accumulate in the East Plaza than in the room blocks, the cobs that did end up there had been treated in much the same way.

Cob Morphology

Traditionally, a few measures and several qualitative attributes which are clearly distinguishable on carbonized cobs, such as row number, cupule width, and cob shape, have been used to demonstrate distinctive types of archaeological maize (e.g., Cutler 1964; Cutler and Blake 1974; Jones and Fonner 1954:106-15). This description of archaeological maize was generally carried out at the same time as, and often closely linked with, the description of varieties or races of maize grown by modern Native American populations in the Southwest and northern Mexico (Anderson and Cutler 1942; Wellhausen et al. 1952). Archaeological races of maize in the Southwest are thus generally recognized on the basis of perceived similarities to modern varieties, especially those recorded in *Races of Maize in Mexico* (Wellhausen et al. 1952).

This approach presumes that archaeological varieties of maize are the same as those grown today, and that these ancient cultivars can be traced in an unbroken (if not immutable) line. However, given the genetic plasticity of maize and the rapidity with which it changes with cultural selection, there is no reason to assume that all of the types identified archaeologically have direct genetic relationships with morphologically similar modern races, or that each archaeological race represents a separate introduction that has diffused through the American Southwest without alteration. Jones (1968:85) and Winter (1973:440, 1983:428-33) describe at greater length some of the problems inherent in the idea of identifying maize races in archaeological samples.

Even with complete, modern, uncarbonized specimens, it is not always possible to distinguish genetic effects from variation in cob morphology caused by a multitude of environmen-

Table 18.3. Henderson Site cob summary statistics (including nubbin cobs).

Cob Statistics	Provenience			Entire Site	
	East Plaza	East Bar	Center Bar	Total	%
Row no.					
2	—	1	—	1	0.7
4	—	1	—	1	0.7
8	2	1	34	37	24.5
10	2	14	52	68	45.0
12	1	1	39	41	27.2
14	—	—	3	3	2.0
Mean row no.	9.6	9.2	10.2	10.0	
n	5	128	128	151	
SD	1.7	2.4	1.7	1.8	
CV	17.7	26.1	16.7	18.0	
Mean glume diameter (mm)	9.5	10.6	10.4	10.4	
n	5	13	93	111	
SD	6.0	3.3	2.2	2.6	
CV	63.1	31.1	21.2	25.0	
Mean rachis diameter (mm)	6.2	6.0	4.9	5.1	
n	7	15	139	156	
SD	3.0	2.3	1.5	1.7	
CV	48.4	38.3	30.6	33.3	
Mean pith diameter (mm)	3.5	3.1	2.6	2.7	
n	7	16	132	155	
SD	2.1	1.4	0.9	1.1	
CV	60.0	45.2	34.6	40.7	

n = number, SD = standard deviation, CV = coefficient of variation

Table 18.4. Henderson Site cob summary statistics (excluding nubbin cobs).

Cob Statistics	Provenience			Entire Site	
	East Plaza	East Bar	Center Bar	Total	%
Row no.					
2	—	—	—	—	—
4	—	—	—	—	—
8	—	—	26	26	20.5
10	—	13	49	62	48.8
12	1	1	34	36	28.3
14	—	—	3	3	2.4
Mean row no.	12.0	10.1	10.2	10.2	
n	1	14	112	127	
SD	—	0.5	1.6	1.5	
CV	—	5.0	15.7	14.7	
Mean glume diameter (mm)	14.7	11.7	10.7	10.9	
n	2	10	81	93	
SD	4.6	2.9	2.1	2.3	
CV	31.3	24.8	19.6	21.2	
Mean rachis diameter (mm)	9.8	6.4	5.1	5.3	
n	2	12	115	129	
SD	1.3	2.3	1.4	1.7	
CV	13.2	35.9	27.4	32.1	
Mean pith diameter (mm)	5.6	3.5	2.7	2.9	
n	2	12	113	127	
SD	2.3	1.1	0.9	1.0	
CV	41.1	31.4	33.3	34.5	

tal factors (Cervantes et al. 1978; Donaldson and Toll 1982:1132; Benz 1985; Mackey 1985). Additionally, small samples of archaeological maize may not be fully representative of the complete range of variation present in prehistoric populations. Given these and other problems, no attempt has been made to assign the maize from the Henderson Site to a particular historic race or races.

Descriptive statistics for the cobs from the Henderson Site are presented in Table 18.3. The mean value, the number of fragments measured for each particular statistic, standard deviation, and coefficient of variation, a standard measure of dispersion illustrating the percentage of the mean represented by the standard deviation, are listed for the site as a whole and separately for each major excavation area.

In the East Bar and Center Bar, it appears that a majority of the maize was 10-rowed (about 40% to 75%), with the remaining cobs almost evenly divided between 8- and 12-rowed forms, and less than 3% 14-rowed. Unfortunately, the East Plaza sample is too small to allow meaningful comparisons with the cobs from the room blocks, but two anomalous nubbins, both incompletely pollinated, one with only two rows, the other with four rows, were found among the cobs and cob fragments recovered from the East Plaza. Also, a "feminized" maize tassel, a not uncommon genetic mutation, was also recovered from this area (but is not listed in Table 18.3).

All of the diameters analyzed here are weakly but significantly correlated with cob row number (glume diameter, $r = .30, p < .01$; rachis diameter, $r = .22, p < .01$; pith diameter, $r = .27, p = .001$). Goodman and Paterniani (1969) found that cob diameter (with kernels), rachis diameter, and row number were only moderately affected by environmental differences, implying that these were the best indicators of genetic difference. Mackey (1983) found that cob diameter (with kernels) was affected by the amount of precipitation, although the differences were not great—on the order of a few millimeters. Thus, it appears that both genetic and environmental factors may have played a role in the diameters shown in Table 18.3.

The fact that mean diameter varies by over 30%, depending on whether cobs with glumes still attached or eroded rachises were measured (i.e., mean glume diameter vs. mean rachis diameter), emphasizes the need to publish descriptions of measurements rather than unspecified—"cob diameters." Sometimes "cob diameters" even refers to the diameter of cobs with kernels, such as those published by Harvey and Galinat (1984) and Mackey and Holbrook (1978).

The mean diameters summarized in Table 18.3 may be influenced by the inclusion of the invariably smaller diameters exhibited by nubbins (Jessup 1982:49, 52), perhaps inordinately so, since nubbins constitute a large portion of the total sample of cob fragments with measurable diameters, especially in the East Bar and East Plaza. Therefore, the same measurements, calculated without nubbins, are presented in Table 18.4, and the statistical summary for nubbins alone is presented in Table 18.5.

Although cupules represent a very small portion of the morphological attributes that differentiate maize cobs, cupules are

Table 18.5. Henderson Site nubbin cob summary statistics.

Nubbin Cob Statistics	All Proveniences Combined		
	n	%	Cum.%
Row no.			
2	1	4.2	4.2
4	1	4.2	8.4
8	11	45.8	54.2
10	6	25.0	79.2
12	5	20.8	100.0
Attributes	*n*	Mean	SD
row no.	24	8.9	2.5
glume diameter (mm)	18	7.6	2.3
rachis diameter (mm)	27	4.0	1.4
pith diameter (mm)	28	2.0	1.0
cupule width (mm)	36	4.9	1.2
cupule height (mm)	36	2.6	0.7
wing width (mm)	35	1.1	0.4
aperture height (mm)	34	0.8	0.3
aperture depth (mm)	23	1.1	0.3
lower glume length (mm)	20	2.9	0.9

more commonly preserved at archaeological sites than are larger cob fragments. King (1987:116) found that wing width, aperture height, and aperture depth show little variation, and probably are not best used to describe differences in maize populations. However, cupule width, cupule height (King's alicole length, kernel thickness, or rachis segment length), and lower glume length seem to "show potential for the study of carbonized archaeological specimens" (King 1987:118), and the first two measures seem to be relatively unaffected by environmental variation (Benz 1985; Mackey 1983). Furthermore, Johannessen et al. (n.d.) show that cupule measurements can be used to distinguish some modern races of maize, and may be useful in describing prehistoric variability, as long as cupule placement on the cob is standardized. Summary statistics for cupule morphology (including nubbins) for the entire site and the separate excavation areas are given in Table 18.6. Since nubbins exhibit significantly smaller measures for some cupule attributes, such as cupule width, cupule height, and lower glume length ($p < .05$ for t-tests comparing nubbin cupules and other cupules), nubbin cupule statistics are given separately (see Table 18.5).

Table 18.7 presents summary data on the qualitative characteristics recorded for cob fragments, again, for the site as a whole and for the different excavation areas. Row pairing is significantly associated with row number. Irregular rows, incomplete pollination, and nubbins are also positively associated. Spiral rows are commonly associated with cob curvature. Some of the elliptical cobs and cob curvature may be a product of postdepositional deformation, but elliptical cob shape may also result from patterns of growth against the stalk or from a genetic predisposition.

Measurable stalk fragments were only found on six cobs: one from the East Plaza, two from the East Bar, and three from the Center Bar. Stalk diameters ranged from 3.6 to 8.2 mm, with a mean diameter of 5.8 mm.

Overall, the amount of variation present in cob and cupule variables, both in the site-wide assemblage and in the different excavation areas, is not very great. Relatively small standard deviations and coefficients of variation indicate a fairly uniform maize population. As shown by the CV's in Tables 18.4 and 18.6, cob and cupule variation within the Center Bar is lower for almost all variables than within the other two areas. The maize in the Center Bar rooms may have been deposited over a shorter period of time, or this maize may represent fewer episodes of deposition in the same span of time, where greater quantities of morphologically similar cobs were deposited.

Kernel Morphology

Only five measurable, slightly fragmented carbonized kernels were recovered *in situ* or from the screens (a few others were found in the flotation samples). Three of these kernels were found in Room C-5 in the Center Bar; one of these had husk impressions and a piece of charred husk attached, suggesting that it came from a cob with kernels that were accidentally burned, perhaps while in storage. The other two kernels were recovered from the East Plaza. Measurements and the shape of the kernel tops, where distinguishable, are shown in Table 18.8. The kernels were almost as thick as they were high. Kernel width was slightly larger than height or thickness, undoubtedly due to the predominance of 8- and 10-rowed cobs at the site.

Intrasite Variation

Paleoethnobotanists examining archaeological maize in the Southwest suggest that within-site variation in cob morphology may be caused by a number of different factors. Among these are: (1) the social distance of different lineages or corporate groups within a pueblo, as reflected by their use of different varieties of corn, or corn grown in different fields, within different microenvironments (e.g., Wetterstrom 1973:17-23, 1986); (2) the use of different varieties, or larger, more perfect cobs in ceremonial contexts or for different types of processing activities (e.g., Cutler and Meyer 1965:140-41; Doebley and Bohrer 1983; Jessup 1982); and (3) temporal change (e.g., Doebley and Bohrer 1983; Hall 1975). The number of episodes of deposition of cobs can be thought of as a variant of temporal change. This presumes that a single depositional episode usually involved cobs from only one or a few processing events (probably from fewer types of maize grown under more similar field conditions), which would therefore be somewhat less variable in morphology than would an accumulation of cobs representing multiple depositional episodes.

Assuming that all of the maize recovered from the Henderson Site in 1980-1981 is roughly contemporaneous (from the Late phase, see Chapter 2), any significant differences that might

Table 18.6. Henderson Site cupule summary statistics.

Cupule Statistics	Provenience			Site-Wide Total
	East Plaza	East Bar	Center Bar	
Mean cupule width (mm)	6.6	5.9	5.7	5.8
n	31	48	297	376
SD	1.7	1.3	1.2	1.3
CV	25.7	22.0	21.1	22.4
Mean cupule height (mm)	3.4	2.9	2.7	2.8
n	31	48	297	376
SD	0.8	0.7	0.6	0.7
CV	23.5	24.1	22.2	25.0
Mean wing width (mm)	1.3	1.0	1.2	1.2
n	28	47	296	371
SD	0.3	0.2	0.4	0.4
CV	23.1	20.0	33.3	33.3
Mean aperture height (mm)	1.3	0.8	0.9	0.9
n	26	46	295	367
SD	0.6	0.3	0.2	0.3
CV	46.1	37.5	22.2	33.3
Mean aperture depth (mm)	1.2	1.1	1.0	1.1
n	23	27	231	281
SD	0.6	0.5	0.3	0.4
CV	50.0	45.4	30.0	36.4
Mean lower glume length (mm)	3.9	3.5	3.3	3.4
n	20	36	208	264
SD	0.8	0.7	0.7	0.7
CV	20.5	20.0	21.2	20.6

exist in cob or cupule characteristics between different excavation contexts are likely to stem from the first two factors described above. Unfortunately, comparisons of features of cob size and morphology between proveniences are hindered by the very small samples recovered from the East Bar and East Plaza. Nevertheless, it is clear that mean row number and the means of the various diameters are not significantly different in the three areas (*t*-tests: *p* values range from .08 to .88). When the same variables are compared, but with nubbins excluded (as in Table 18.4 above), the East Plaza has to be dropped entirely because only a few measurable cobs remain in the sample from this part of the site. For the East Bar and Center Bar room blocks, where sample sizes remain adequate despite the exclusion of nubbins, mean row number and glume diameter are again not significantly different, although rachis diameter and pith diameter do show a slight but statistically significant difference; *p* values obtained from *t*-tests comparing rachis and pith diameters are .06 and .03, respectively, implying that there may be some slight differences in cob morphology in these two areas.

Due to the fragmentary nature of the maize, there is a much larger sample of cupule measurements than cob measurements. Unlike row numbers and most cob diameters, some cupule dimensions do vary significantly across the site. Cupule width in the East Plaza averages almost a millimeter larger than in the Center Bar, and about 0.7 mm larger than in the East Bar ($p < .01$), despite the fact that the East Plaza sample is composed of proportionately more nubbins (which should have smaller cupules). Similarly, cupule heights and lower glume lengths are significantly larger in the East Plaza than in the East Bar or Center Bar ($p < .01$).

Despite the fact that these differences are statistically significant, their magnitude is quite small (less than a millimeter in most cases), making it unlikely that they reflect the use of different varieties of maize. These size differences more likely reflect the use of maize grown under slightly different field conditions, or perhaps maize that was selected for use in the plaza because the cobs were slightly larger or better shaped than other cobs.

These spatial comparisons demonstrate that the East Plaza midden is distinctive, both because it contains very little corn (only 8.2% of the total remains), and because the corn that does occur there is slightly larger than the maize recovered in the room blocks. The scarcity of maize in the plaza raises the interesting possibility that this resource, at least in an unprocessed state, played a limited role in community-wide patterns of food sharing. The justification for this assertion follows the same arguments offered in Chapter 14 to account for the abundance of various animal taxa in the East Plaza. Only a brief sketch of these arguments is provided here. The animal remains found in the plaza midden differ in many respects from the remains that accumulated in the room blocks. The plaza contains the vast majority of the large and medium ungulates, particularly bison

Table 18.7. Henderson Site cob qualitative characteristics.

Cob Characteristics	Provenience						Site-Wide Total	
	East Plaza		East Bar		Center Bar			
	%	*n*	%	*n*	%	*n*	%	*n*
Cob curvature								
strong	27.3	3	15.0	3	46.8	37	39.1	43
weak	—	—	5.0	1	26.6	21	20.0	22
none	72.7	8	80.0	16	26.6	21	40.9	45
Row pairing								
strong	56.3	9	75.0	18	55.6	85	58.0	112
weak	43.7	7	25.0	6	44.4	68	42.0	81
Row form								
irregular rows	8.3	2	6.7	3	9.8	17	9.1	22
spiral rows	25.0	6	15.6	7	35.3	60	30.5	73
Pollination								
incomplete	—	—	6.3	3	8.2	24	7.3	27
Nubbin cobs								
nubbins	22.6	7	10.4	5	8.2	24	9.7	36
Cross-section								
elliptical	100.0	1	63.6	7	39.5	49	42.2	57
circular	—	—	36.4	4	59.7	74	57.8	78
square	—	—	—	—	0.8	1	—	—

and antelope, while the rooms contain most of the jackrabbits, cottontails, prairie dogs, and other small mammals. Thus, in terms of its faunal content, the plaza midden is not merely an accumulation of household trash that ended up being dumped outside rather than within an abandoned structure. The presence of the massive earth oven in the East Plaza also indicates that many animals were butchered, cooked and probably consumed there as well. Since the East Plaza was an open, readily accessible, and presumably very public area, animal foods prepared, eaten, and discarded in this part of the village would have been visible to all members of the community and would therefore have been most subject to the pressures and demands of interhousehold meat sharing.

The obvious scarcity of corn in the East Plaza suggests that maize still on the cob, like the smaller animals, may not have been heavily involved in community-wide patterns of food sharing. This does not imply that corn was never shared among village households, nor that it was of little symbolic importance. It simply means that the quantity of unprocessed corn shared in this public manner was not great. This would not surprise ethnographers who have done quantitative studies of food sharing among contemporary small-scale horticultural societies; such studies repeatedly show that plant foods, cultivated as well as wild, are generally shared less frequently, and less widely, than animal foods (e.g., Aspelin 1979; Hames 1990). The fact that the few maize fragments found in the East Plaza midden were very slightly, but significantly, larger on average than those from the room blocks suggests that some corn may have been deliberately chosen for use in special events or ceremonies held in the plaza, events that very likely did involve the interaction of households on a broader, perhaps community-wide, level.

Regional Variation

Although regional patterns of maize variation, especially comparisons of row numbers and postulated races of maize, have traditionally been the focus of analyses of archaeological maize in the American Southwest, little is known about prehistoric maize in southeastern New Mexico (see discussion in Adams 1994). Harvey and Galinat (1984) wrote a brief description of the maize found at the nearly contemporaneous Block Lookout Site, which was published in Kelley's (1984) report on the archaeology of the Sierra Blanca region of southeastern New Mexico. The Block Lookout cobs seem to have been less fragmented than those from the Henderson Site, since the average complete cob length was 4.29 cm, compared to an average of 1.58 cm for the fragments from Henderson, where the longest complete cob was only 4.14 cm.

Row numbers for the 242 cobs recovered from Block Lookout are different, but not dramatically so, from those at the Henderson Site. About 45% of the maize at Block Lookout was 8-rowed (compared to a little less than 25% at Henderson), while around 42% was 10-rowed (compared to 45%), and only 12% was 12-rowed (compared to 27% at Henderson).

Harvey and Galinat (1984:282) note that cob diameters at Block Lookout (with or without kernels and/or glumes is not specified) ranged from 10 to 22 mm, but averaged about 15 mm. Glume diameters at Henderson average only 10.4 mm, while the largest is just under 18 mm. Harvey and Galinat also note, however, that one of the striking characteristics of the maize from Block Lookout was "the apparent homogeneity of the population" (Kelley 1984:269); the same characterization also fits the Henderson material. This low level of intrasite maize

Table 18.8. Henderson Site kernel summary statistics.

Kernel Statistics	Provenience					Summary Values
	East Plaza		Center Bar			
Kernel						
no.	(1)	(2)	(3)	(4)	(5)	(1-5)
height (mm)	6.7	5.5	5.4	7.0	7.4	6.4
width (mm)	9.5	8.6	7.6	9.5	8.4	8.7
thickness (mm)	5.2	6.6	4.9	6.9	7.2	6.2
Embryo						
height (mm)	-	-	-	5.8	-	5.8
width (mm)	-	-	-	3.8	-	3.8
Top shape						
square	X	-	-	-	-	
oval	-	X	X	X	X	

variability not only implies that everyone at Henderson grew the same types of maize, but that they only had (or only chose to use) a rather narrow range of genetic variation in maize. Historically, the diffusion of genetically different maize varieties from different ethnic groups has contributed to hybrid vigor and increased variability. The lack of evidence for this kind of variation at Henderson may imply that little trade in new seed stock took place.

The small size of the maize cobs at the Block Lookout Site was the other characteristic that most impressed Harvey and Galinat (1984). Interestingly, the cobs from the Henderson Site are even smaller. When compared with more or less contemporary maize from other parts of New Mexico, the small size of the cobs is even more striking. Mackey and Holbrook (1978), for instance, describe archaeological maize from the Largo-Gallina area of north-central New Mexico (dating to the latter part of the thirteenth century) as environmentally stressed compared to maize from earlier sites in this area, reasoning that slight decreases in row number, cob diameters, and cupule width reflect a drier environment. Their smallest mean cob diameter for any site, however, is 13.3 mm, and their smallest mean cupule width is 7.7 mm (Mackey and Holbrook 1978:35); these values are well above the average glume diameter (excluding nubbins) of 10.9 mm and the average cupule width of 5.8 mm found at Henderson.

Similarly, maize cob and cupule averages reported by Wetterstrom (1973, 1986) from Arroyo Hondo, a large site near Santa Fe in north-central New Mexico but dating to the fourteenth century, are smaller on average than those described by Mackey and Holbrook (1978), but are still substantially larger than those from the Henderson Site. At Arroyo Hondo, mean cob diameter was 12.8 mm and mean cupule width was 6.4 mm.

Most maize that has been documented from more or less contemporary archaeological sites in other parts of the Southwest exhibits substantially larger cobs and cupules than at Henderson (e.g., Doebley and Bohrer 1983; Hall 1975; Winter 1973). Cobs with external dimensions (e.g., diameter) most similar to those at Henderson occur in sites that date almost two centuries earlier, for example, at sites in Chaco Canyon and at several outliers (Donaldson and Toll 1982; Pippin 1987; Toll 1985; Winter 1983:440). Toll (1985:261) suggests that the small maize at some of these sites may "reflect environmental factors which we know to be poorer in the Chaco area," since cobs from some other Chacoan sites and outliers in better watered areas are substantially larger (e.g., Doebley and Bohrer 1983).

The small cobs from the Henderson Site are especially interesting because the mean row number for these cobs is not very high (10.0). Smaller cupule size is usually associated with higher row-numbered cobs, which are more common in Basketmaker sites in the Southwest, or with prehistoric maize varieties classified as "Chapalote" or "Reventador" or as "Small Cob Flints" (Cutler 1964; Cutler and Blake 1974; Cutler and Meyer 1965). Most Pueblo II and III period maize, including maize from the few sites that have been documented in eastern New Mexico and west Texas, is characterized by lower mean row numbers (Cutler and Blake 1973b:51, 69). Winter (1973, 1974, 1983:430) describes variation in the proportion of 8-rowed maize cobs after A.D. 1000 across the northern southwest as a gradient, with lower mean row numbers in the east near Mesa Verde (reflecting higher proportions of 8-rowed cobs), and higher mean row numbers at Fremont sites like Evans Mound in southwestern Utah. The row numbers from the Henderson Site seem to fit the general pattern of low mean row numbers for late Pueblo sites, especially for those on the eastern edge of the Southwest, although the cobs (and cupules) are unusually small.

The temporal decrease in mean row number just described has been viewed as a reflection of increasing maize productivity, since late prehistoric 8-rowed cobs have larger cupules (and kernels) with comparatively smaller rachises than do higher-rowed cobs (Galinat and Gunnerson 1963; Jessup 1982:52), thus producing proportionately more kernel. On this basis, Jessup (1982:52) has suggested that the ratio between rachis diameter and cupule width could be used as a rough index for comparing productivity. Lower ratios indicate more kernel compared to cob and more productive corn, although of course cob length, and the number of cobs per plant, which are important factors in agricultural productivity, cannot be considered with this ratio.

At the Henderson Site this ratio averages 0.9. The well-described maize cobs from the late thirteenth-century secondary occupation at Salmon Ruin (Doebley and Bohrer 1983), though larger than those from Henderson, also have a larger ratio (1.4), implying that they did not necessarily produce more food. Several small sites along the Lower Chaco River that predate Henderson by a few centuries yielded cobs that have similar diameters but rachis diameter/cupule width ratios that are even larger, ranging from 1.8 to 2.0 (Winter 1983:441), hinting that these cobs may have been even less efficient at producing usable grain.

The small cob diameters and cupule widths exhibited by the maize at Henderson may indicate diminished yields when compared to other late prehistoric maize varieties described in the Southwest, especially in the absence of any evidence for increased cob length. Unfortunately, the only complete cobs recovered from Henderson were nubbins, and these are poorly suited for determining average cob length. However, the Henderson corn also had a smaller cob rachis in relation to cupule width than is seen at other sites, and hence may have produced proportionately more grain per cob. Thus, it is not possible to conclude that the maize grown at Henderson was less productive, or yielded fewer calories per cob, than did maize grown elsewhere in the Southwest. All that can be stated with certainty is that the Henderson cobs are smaller than those reported from other sites of roughly the same age, though they display an appropriate array of row numbers for this part of the Southwest and time period.

Additional research in southeastern New Mexico and elsewhere in the Southwest, with well-described maize, including quantitative measures of such attributes as glume and rachis diameter, cob length, cupule width, height, and lower glume length, as well as proportions of nubbins and other qualitative characteristics, may help determine if the small maize from Henderson was environmentally stressed, because of either climate or agricultural practices, or if it was a genetically isolated variety. This issue of course cannot be resolved solely on the basis of the maize remains. Particularly critical to our understanding of why the Henderson cobs were diminutive is a better grasp of the climatic and environmental conditions that prevailed in southeastern New Mexico during the late thirteenth and early fourteenth centuries. Unfortunately, such information is woefully inadequate at present. Regardless of whether the small maize from Henderson ultimately proves to be the result of environmental stress or genetic isolation, both possibilities have interesting implications for the villagers' use of the environment, their subsistence practices, and their social and economic interactions with other parts of the Southwest and Southern Plains.

Synopsis

This chapter examined the 377 complete and fragmentary maize cobs recovered from Late phase deposits during the 1980-1981 excavations at the Henderson Site. Only those remains that were found *in situ* or in the quarter-inch screens are considered here.

A wide range of quantitative and qualitative information was recorded for the cobs and cob fragments. Quantitative measurements included cob (or cob fragment) length; cob rachis, glume, and pith diameter; cupule width and height; wing width; aperture length, depth, and height; and lower glume length. Nominal characteristics included cob row number; portion of cob represented; amount of cob curvature; cross-section shape; and presence of irregular or spiraling rows, row pairing, and incomplete pollination. The presence of nubbins was also noted. Kernel features that were documented included height, width, and thickness, as well as shape.

All of the Henderson maize was carbonized. None of the cobs retained any kernels. Most cobs were very fragmented and the nine complete specimens that were recovered were all classified as nubbins.

Almost 80% of the maize remains came from the Center Bar, and nearly 85% of these came from a single deposit within this room block, the trash midden in Room C-5. Just under 13% of the corn came from the East Bar and barely 8% came from the midden at the southern end of the East Plaza. The scarcity of maize in the East Bar was not unexpected, since no major trash accumulations were encountered in any of the rooms that were sampled in this room block. However, the small amount of maize in the East Plaza midden is surprising. The contrast between Room C-5 and the East Plaza in their yield of maize remains is underscored when the number of cobs and cob fragments from each provenience is expressed in terms of density. In Room C-5 the density is over 28 pieces per m^3, whereas in the plaza the density is less than 2.5 per m^3. While the density values are strikingly different, there seem to be no significant differences between these two proveniences in the degree of fragmentation, or the proportions of cob bases, tips, or midsections (or nubbins).

Most of the maize from Henderson is 10-rowed (about 40% to 75% depending on provenience), with the remaining cobs almost evenly divided between 8- and 12-rowed forms. Less than 3% are 14-rowed.

Overall, the amount of variation reflected in both cob and cupule measurements is not very great, indicating that the maize grown by the Henderson villagers was fairly uniform. Comparisons of mean row number and the means of the various cob diameters, though hampered by the small sample from the East Plaza, reveal no significant differences between the major proveniences. However, cupule dimensions, particularly cupule width, height, and lower glume length, are all significantly greater in the plaza sample, though the magnitude of the differences are slight (less than a millimeter in most cases). These small size differences are unlikely to reflect different varieties of maize, and instead probably indicate the use of maize grown under slightly different field conditions, or perhaps maize that was chosen for use in the plaza because the cobs were slightly larger or better shaped than other cobs.

The East Plaza midden is distinctive, both because it contains very little corn, and because the corn that does occur there is slightly larger than the maize recovered in the room blocks. The scarcity of maize in this open, accessible, and presumably very public area of the village stands in stark contrast to the large quantity of bison and antelope bones found there, and raises the interesting possibility that corn, at least in an unprocessed state, played a much more limited role in community-wide patterns of food-sharing than did animal foods (the basis for this argument is presented more fully in Chapter 14). This observation of course finds numerous parallels in the ethnographic literature, where it is well documented that plant foods are less often and less widely shared than meat.

The fact that the few maize fragments found in the East Plaza midden are slightly larger on average than those from the room blocks suggests that some corn may have been deliberately chosen for use in special events or ceremonies held in the plaza, events that very likely did involve the interaction of households on a broader, perhaps community-wide, level.

One of the most striking features of the Henderson maize is the small size of the cobs. The cobs in fact are smaller, on average, than those that have been reported from most other roughly contemporary sites in the Southwest, including cobs that are believed to have been grown under environmentally stressed conditions. Cobs with external dimensions most similar to those from Henderson come from sites that date almost two centuries earlier.

While the Henderson maize is smaller than contemporary varieties elsewhere in the Southwest, the mean row number is more or less what one would expect for a site of this time period in the eastern part of the Southwest.

When compared to other late prehistoric maize varieties reported from the Southwest, the small size of the Henderson corn may indicate diminished yields, perhaps because the crops were grown under environmentally stressful conditions. On the other hand, the small maize may reflect a genetically isolated variety, one in fact that may have been relatively productive. This is hinted at by the fact that the Henderson corn has a smaller cob rachis in relation to cupule width than is seen at other sites, and hence may have produced proportionately more grain per cob. This assumes, of course, that the cobs were comparable in length to cobs from contemporary sites elsewhere in the Southwest, an assumption that unfortunately cannot be evaluated at present given the fragmentary nature of the Henderson maize. Whether the small maize from Henderson ultimately proves to be the result of environmental stress or genetic isolation, both possibilities have interesting implications for the villagers' use of the environment, their subsistence practices, and their social and economic interactions with other parts of the Southwest and Southern plains.

References Cited

Adams, K. R.
1994 A Regional Synthesis of *Zea mays* in the Prehistoric American Southwest. In: *Corn and Culture in the Prehistoric New World*, edited by S. Johannessen and C. A. Hastorf, pp. 273-302. Boulder, CO: Westview Press.

Anderson, E., and W. L. Brown
1948 A Morphological Analysis of Row Number in Maize. *Annals of the Missouri Botanical Garden* 35:323-36.

Anderson, E., and H. C. Cutler
1942 Races of *Zea mays*: Their Recognition and Classification. *Annals of the Missouri Botanical Garden* 29:69-86.

Aspelin, P. L.
1979 Food Distribution and Social Bonding among the Mamainde of Mato Grosso, Brazil. *Journal of Anthropological Research* 35(3):309-27.

Benz, B. F.
1985 Maize in Paleoenvironmental Reconstruction: A Cautionary Note. *Plains Anthropologist* 30:145-47.

Bird, R. McK.
1994 Manual for the Measurement of Maize Cobs. In: *Corn and Culture in the Prehistoric New World*, edited by S. Johannessen and C. Hastorf, pp. 5-22. Boulder, CO: Westview Press.

Bird, R. McK., and M. M. Goodman
1977 The Races of Maize V: Grouping Maize Races on the Basis of Ear Morphology. *Economic Botany* 31:471-78.

Bohrer, V.
1986 Guideposts in Ethnobotany. *Journal of Ethnobiology* 6(1):27-43.

Brugge, D. M.
1965 Charred Maize and "Nubbins." *Plateau* 38(2):49-51.

Caddell, G. M.
1983 Floral Remains from the Lubbub Creek Archaeological Locality. In: *Studies of Material Remains from the Lubbub Creek Archaeological Locality*, edited by C. S. Peebles, pp. 274-381. Prehistoric Agricultural Communities in West Alabama, Volume II. Report submitted to the U. S. Army Corps of Engineers, Mobile District, by the University of Michigan Museum of Anthropology, Ann Arbor, MI.

Carter, G., and E. Anderson
1945 A Preliminary Survey of Maize in the Southwestern U.S. *Annals of the Missouri Botanical Garden* 32:297-323.

Cervantes, T. S., M. M. Goodman, E. Casas D., and J. O. Rawlings
1978 Use of Genetic Effects and Genotype by Environmental Interactions for the Classification of Mexican Races of Maize. *Genetics* 90:339-48.

Cutler, H. C.
1964 Appendix A. Plant Remains from the Carter Ranch Site. In: *Chapters in the Prehistory of Eastern Arizona II*, by P. S. Martin et al., pp. 174-83. Fieldiana Anthropology Series 55. Chicago, IL: Field Museum of Natural History.

Cutler, H. C., and L. W. Blake
1973a Corn from Cahokia Sites. In: *Explorations into Cahokia Archaeology*, edited by M. L. Fowler, pp. 122-36. Illinois Archaeological Survey Bulletin 7.
1973b *Plants from Archaeological Sites East of the Rockies*. St. Louis, MO: Missouri Botanical Garden.
1974 Corn from Casas Grandes. In: *Casas Grandes: A Fallen Trading Center of the Gran Chichimeca*, Vol. 8, by C. C. Di Peso, J. B. Rinaldo, and G. J. Fenner, pp. 308-14. Amerind Foundation Series 9. Flagstaff, AZ: Northland Press.

Cutler, H. C., and W. Meyer
1965 Corn and Cucurbits from Wetherill Mesa. In: *Contributions of the Wetherill Mesa Archeological Project*, edited by D. Osborne, pp. 136-52. Memoir 19. Washington, DC: Society for American Archaeology.

Doebley, J., and V. L. Bohrer
1983 Maize Variability and Cultural Selection at Salmon Ruin, New Mexico. *Kiva* 49(1-2):19-37.

Donaldson, M. L., and M. S. Toll
1982 Prehistoric Subsistence in the Bis Sa'ani Area: Evidence from Flotation, Macrobotanical Remains, and Wood Identification. In: *Bis Sa'ani: A Late Bonito Phase Community on Escavada Wash, Northwest New Mexico*, Vol. 3, edited by C. D. Breternitz, D. E. Doyel, and M. P. Marshall, pp. 1099-1180. Navajo Nation Papers in Anthropology 14. Window Rock, AZ: Navajo Nation Cultural Resource Management Program.

Dunavan, S. L.
1994 Maize on the Middle Pecos River: An Analysis of Cobs from the Henderson Pueblo. In: *Corn and Culture in the Prehistoric New World*, edited by S. Johannessen and C. A. Hastorf, pp. 303-14. Boulder, CO: Westview Press.

Ford, R. I.
1973 The Moccasin Bluff Corn Holes. In: *The Moccasin Bluff Site and the Woodland Cultures of Southwestern Michigan*, by R. L. Bettarel and H. G. Smith, pp. 188-97. Anthropological Paper 49. Ann Arbor, MI: University of Michigan, Museum of Anthropology.

Galinat, W. C., and J. A. Gunnerson
1963 *Spread of Eight-Rowed Maize from the Prehistoric Southwest*. Leaflet 20(5). Cambridge, MA: Harvard University, Botanical Museum.

Goette, S., M. Williams, S. Johannessen, and C. A. Hastorf
1994 Toward Reconstructing Ancient Maize: Experiments in Processing and Charring. *Journal of Ethnobiology* 14(1):1-21.

Goodman, M. M., and E. Paterniani
1969 The Races of Maize III: Choice of Appropriate Characters for Racial Classification. *Economic Botany* 23:265-73.

Hall, R. L.
1975 Cultivars from Antelope House. *Kiva* 41(1):49-56.

Hames, R.
1990 Sharing Among the Yanomamo, Part I. The Effects of Risk. In: *Risk and Uncertainty in Tribal and Peasant Economies*, edited by E. Cashdan, pp. 89-106. Boulder, CO: Westview Press.

Harvey, H. R., and W. C. Galinat
1984 Corn. In: *The Archaeology of the Sierra Blanca Region of Southeastern New Mexico*, by J. H. Kelley, pp. 269-283. Anthropological Paper 74. Ann Arbor, MI: Museum of Anthropology, University of Michigan.

Jessup, D.
1982 *Some Cultural Implications of Botanical Remains From Black Mesa, Arizona*. Senior honors thesis, Department of Anthropology, University of Michigan, Ann Arbor, MI.

Johannessen, S., S. Goette, and C. Hastorf
n.d. Ancient and Modern Maize Fragments: An Experiment in Variability. Paper presented at the "Conference on Corn and Culture in the Prehistoric New World," University of Minnesota, Minneapolis, May 11-13, 1990.

Johannessen, S., and C. A. Hastorf
1989 Corn and Culture in Central Andean Prehistory. *Science* 244:690-92.

Jones, V. H.
1949 Maize from the Davis Site: Its Nature and Interpretations. In: *The George C. Davis Site, Cherokee County, Texas*, edited by H. P. Newell and A. D. Krieger, pp. 241-49. Memoir 5. Washington, DC: Society for American Archaeology.
1968 Corn from the McKees Rocks Village Site. *Pennsylvania Archaeologist* 38(1-4):81-86.

Jones, V. H., and R. L. Fonner
1954 Plant Materials from Sites in the Durango and La Plata Areas, Colorado. In: *Basket-Maker II Sites near Durango, Colorado*, by E. H. Morris and R. F. Burgh, pp. 93-115. Publication 604. Washington, DC: Carnegie Institution of Washington.

Kelley, J. H.
1984 *The Archaeology of the Sierra Blanca Region of Southeastern New Mexico*. Anthropological Paper 74. Ann Arbor, MI: Museum of Anthropology, University of Michigan.

King, F. B.
1987 *Prehistoric Maize in Eastern North America: An Evolutionary Evaluation*. Ph.D. dissertation, University of Illinois, Urbana, IL.

Mackey, J. C.
1983 The Documentation of Environmental Control of Morphological Variability in Archaeological Maize: A Paleoenvironmental Reconstruction Technique. *Plains Anthropologist* 28:209-17.
1985 A Thirteenth Century A.D. Example of the Successful Use of Archaeological Corn Collections for Paleoenvironmental Reconstruction: A Reply to Benz. *Plains Anthropologist* 30:149-59.

Mackey, J. C., and S. J. Holbrook
1978 Environmental Reconstruction and the Abandonment of the Largo-Gallina Area, New Mexico. *Journal of Field Archaeology* 5:29-49.

Miksicek, C. H.
1987 Formation Processes of the Archaeobotanical Record. In: *Advances in Archaeological Method and Theory*, Vol. 10, edited by M. B. Schiffer, pp. 211-47. New York: Academic Press.

Miller, N. F.
1989 Ratios in Paleoethnobotanical Analysis. In: *Current Paleoethnobotany*, edited by C. A. Hastorf and V. S. Popper, pp. 72-85. Chicago, IL: University of Chicago Press.

Nickerson, N. H.
1953 Variation in Cob Morphology among Certain Archaeological and Ethnological Varieties of Maize. *Annals of the Missouri Botanical Garden* 40:79-111.

Pearsall, D. M.
1980 Analysis of an Archaeological Maize Kernel Cache From Manabi Province, Ecuador. *Economic Botany* 34:344-51.

Pippin, L. C.
1987 Botanical Remains. In: *Prehistory and Paleoecology of Guadalupe Ruin, New Mexico*, pp. 139-40. Anthropological Paper 112. Salt Lake City, UT: University of Utah.

Rocek, T. R., and J. D. Speth
1986 *The Henderson Site Burials: Glimpses of a Late Prehistoric Population in the Pecos Valley*. Technical Report 18. Ann Arbor, MI: Museum of Anthropology, University of Michigan.

Toll, M. S.
1985 An Overview of Chaco Canyon Macrobotanical Materials and Analysis to Date. In: *Environment and Subsistence of Chaco Canyon, New Mexico*, edited by F. J. Mathien, pp. 247-77. Publications in Archeology 18E, Chaco Canyon Studies. Albuquerque, NM: National Park Service.

Wellhausen, E. J., L. M. Roberts, and E. Hernanadez X.
1952 *Races of Maize in Mexico: Their Origin, Characteristics and Distribution*. Cambridge, MA: Harvard University, Bussey Institute.

Wetterstrom, W. E.
1973 *The Paleoethnobotany of the Arroyo Hondo Site: Preliminary Report on the Edible Plant Remains*, pp. 12-24. Report submitted to the School of American Research, Santa Fe, NM.
1986 *Food, Diet, and Population at Prehistoric Arroyo Hondo Pueblo, New Mexico*. Arroyo Hondo Archaeological Series 6. Santa Fe, NM: School of American Research.

Winter, J. C.
1973 The Distribution and Development of Fremont Maize Agriculture: Some Preliminary Interpretations. *American Antiquity* 38(4):439-54.
1974 Cultivated Plants. In *Hovenweep 1974*. Archeological Report No. 1. San Jose, CA: San Jose State University, Department of Anthropology.
1983 A Comparative Study of Prehistoric, Historic, and Contemporary Agriculture along the Lower Chaco, I. The Anasazi. In: *Economy and Interaction along the Lower Chaco River: The Navajo Mine Archeological Program, Mining Area III, San Juan County, New Mexico*, edited by P. Hogan and J. C. Winter, pp. 421-44. Albuquerque, NM: University of New Mexico, Office of Contract Archaeology and Maxwell Museum of Anthropology.

19
Fuel Exploitation at the Henderson Site

Marie S. Harris

Steven Archer
University of California, Berkeley

Introduction

By analyzing charcoal, we can examine fuel use by the Henderson villagers over the course of the site's thirteenth- and fourteenth-century occupation. Hypothetically, inhabitants of a village such as Henderson might be expected to select the most efficient or the highest and steadiest heat-producing fuels that were available close to the community. However, in semi-arid open-grassland habitats such as southeastern New Mexico, where potential fuel sources are very limited to start with, such preferred fuels are quickly depleted, and the inhabitants are forced either to exploit less preferred sources available nearby, or travel farther to obtain preferred materials. Presumably, a limit exists as to how far the inhabitants will travel before they begin shifting to less desirable fuels in the immediate area (e.g., Shackleton and Prins 1992).

This perspective emphasizes efficiency, and ignores the possibility that preferred fuel resources may be selected on the basis of cultural factors other than heat value or travel distance. If fuel resources were culturally selected, the use or avoidance of a particular species would not necessarily reflect local availability. In any case, preferred fuels should be identifiable by examining the species that predominate in the charcoal of the Early phase of the occupation. Any subsequent degradation of these preferred fuels should be discernible in the archaeological record by a shift to other resources in the Late phase.

Modern Vegetation

Currently the region is dominated by short-grass prairie and desert shrub (Rangeland Resources International 1977). Vegetation in the vicinity of the Henderson Site includes grama grass (*Bouteloua* sp.), snakeweed (*Gutierrezia sarothrae*), four-wing saltbush (*Atriplex canescens*), greasewood (*Sarcobatus vermiculatus*), mesquite (*Prosopis juliflora*), Mormon tea (*Ephedra* sp.), yucca (*Yucca* spp.), and cholla and prickly pear (*Opuntia* spp.). Dense stands of sacaton grass (*Sporobolus wrightii*) are found in wetter areas along the floor of the Hondo. Aside from recently planted ornamentals around ranch houses, the only native trees in the area today occur as a thin line along the banks of the Hondo channel. Among these are walnut (*Juglans major*), hackberry (*Celtis reticulata*), cottonwood (*Populus* sp.), willow (*Salix* sp.), and ash (*Fraxinus velutina*).

The landscape today is strikingly similar to the one described by Government Land Office (GLO) surveyors in 1867 and 1868 (Government Land Office Survey plat records for the State of New Mexico, Chaves County).[1] A few direct quotes from the surveyors' field notebooks provide a vivid description of the appearance of the area more than 130 years ago.

> The Hondo River running through a portion of this Township is a deep rapid stream, affording a sufficient supply of water for all purposes of irrigation. . . . The uplands produce grama and other grasses, which makes rich pasturage. . . . There is no timber in this Township excepting a little scattered along the river banks. [T. 11 S., R. 22 E., 1867]

> The timber consisting of black walnut, ash, red bud and willow is confined to a narrow fringe along the Rio Hondo. [T. 12 S., R. 22 E., 1868]

> The land suitable for cultivation in this Township is confined to the irrigable land of the Rio Hondo, of which there is sufficient to support a large settlement. The land on either side of the Hondo bottom is broken limestone ground, and is only valu-

able for grazing purposes. The timber is confined to the banks of the Hondo, and consists of a few, scattering [*sic*] willow, red bud, and black walnut trees. [T. 11 S., R. 19 E., 1868]

It is clear from these descriptions that the only trees in the area in the 1860s, as today, grew along the Hondo, and would not have provided much wood for either construction or fuel. Projecting conditions as they were in the 1860s back into the thirteenth and fourteenth centuries is fraught with uncertainty, yet it seems highly unlikely that fuel (or construction timber) would have been vastly more abundant to Henderson's Native American inhabitants than they were to the first European settlers in the Roswell area.

Methods

In all, we analyzed the wood charcoal from 33 flotation samples (see Toll 1988) taken from stratified columns in four distinct areas of the site: 7 from the Great Depression earth oven complex (Early phase), 6 from Main Bar East Room M-1 (Early phase), 10 from plaza deposits beneath Center Bar Room C-5 (Early phase), and 10 from the East Plaza earth oven complex (Late phase). Several of these samples had already been sorted to separate wood charcoal from other botanical remains. We sorted the remaining samples, removing all nonwood materials, such as monocot stems, seeds, and maize cupules/kernels. We then sieved the flotation samples through a 2.0 mm geological screen. Only charcoal pieces greater than 2.0 mm were analyzed. These pieces were dumped into a box that contained a grid of 20 equally sized squares. One piece of charcoal was blindly chosen from each square in order to obtain a random subsample.

Each piece of charcoal was broken to expose a fresh transverse section and examined under 10-40× magnification using a dissecting microscope. Identification was based on pore pattern, ray width, and similarity to reference specimens housed in the Ethnobotany Laboratory of the Museum of Anthropology at the University of Michigan (e.g., Core et al. 1979; Harrar 1957; Hoadley 1990; Minnis 1987; Rossen and Olson 1985). Identifications were made only to the level of genus.

After the microscope examination, each piece was assigned to a specific category. If identification was possible, it was grouped according to its genus; if identification was not possible, it was assigned to an unidentified category based on its pore pattern. In all, there were five "unidentified" categories: (1) unidentified ring porous; (2) unidentified semi-ring porous; (3) unidentified diffuse porous; (4) unidentified conifer; and (5) nonidentifiable. Ring porous, semi-ring porous, and diffuse porous types are hardwoods. Ring porous taxa display an abrupt transition between larger early-wood pores and smaller late-wood pores. Ring porous species at Henderson include *Fraxinus*, *Quercus*, and *Prosopis*. Semi-ring porous woods show a gradual transition between early- and late-wood pores. The relevant genus occurring at Henderson is *Juglans*. Diffuse porous woods display pores of similar and consistent size throughout the growth season. Henderson species include *Acer* and possibly *Populus*, although *Populus* has not been positively identified in the flotation samples under analysis here.

Gymnosperms are significantly different in appearance under the microscope (e.g., Core et al. 1979; Harrar 1957; Hoadley 1990; Minnis 1987; Rossen and Olson 1985). Conifers are marked by the presence of distinct square-shaped tracheids and have a gridlike appearance. *Pinus* and *Juniperus* have both been identified at the site. *Pinus* is distinguished by the presence of resin ducts that are visible with a binocular metallurgical microscope under 200-400× magnification. *Juniperus*, in contrast, is distinguished by its lack of resin ducts.

Taxa Recovered

In all, nine taxa were identified in the flotation samples examined here: *Acer* sp. (maple or box elder), *Fraxinus* sp. (ash), *Juglans* sp. (walnut), *Quercus* sp. (oak), *Juniperus* sp. (juniper), *Pinus* sp. (pine), *Atriplex/Sarcobatus* sp. (saltbush/greasewood), *Prosopis* sp. (mesquite), and *Ephedra* (Mormon tea). Of these, ash and saltbush/greasewood consistently rank as the most abundant taxa recovered from the flotation samples, regardless of phase or spatial context, and regardless of whether the data are expressed as percentages, counts per liter, or grams per liter (see below). Other taxa appear in smaller amounts, most notable of which are oak, mesquite, and juniper.

Fraxinus sp. (Ash)

Ash is commonly identified at other late prehistoric sites in the Roswell area (see Toll, in press). It is present at Henderson in significant amounts as charcoal, and it was used for roof support beams as well, four unburned examples of which were found *in situ* in Room E-4 in the East Bar (Rocek and Speth 1986). While there are a number of species of ash found in the Southwest, the only one that occurs today in Chaves County is *F. velutina* (Martin and Hutchins 1981). Velvet ash grows to about 10 m or more in height, and is present along stream banks or in mountain canyons at altitudes above about 600 m (Lamb 1975; Vines 1960).

Atriplex/Sarcobatus sp. (Saltbush/Greasewood)

Atriplex/Sarcobatus makes up a large percentage of the Henderson charcoal. Morphologically the two genera are not easily distinguishable from each other under the microscope, although their common pore pattern is very distinctive. These easily identified woods are hard and often used for fuel. Black greasewood (*Sarcobatus vermiculatus*) is the only Southwestern species that Vines (1960) identifies in the *Sarcobatus* genus. Black greasewood is a shrub that grows up to about 3 m in height, and is commonly found on alkaline soils (Elmore and Janish 1976; Lamb 1975; Vines 1960). Scattered greasewood bushes are common today on the low hills surrounding the Henderson Site. Several species of *Atriplex* are present in the region, although four-wing saltbush (*A. canescens*) is by far the most common one today in the vicinity of Henderson. These shrubs grow to a height of about 2 m.

Quercus sp. (Oak)

Oak is another common wood identified in the flotation samples. The wood is dense and durable and in many parts of North America was used for fuel and posts. Local species, however, are generally too small to have been used prehistorically for construction timbers (Lamb 1975). Common varieties in southeastern New Mexico include: chinquapin oak (*Q. muehlenbergii*), wavyleaf oak (*Q. undulata*), Gambel's oak (*Q. gambelii*), gray oak (*Q. grisea*), and shinnery oak (*Q. havardii*). None of these species occurs in the vicinity of the site. Shinnery oak grows today on sand dunes between the Pecos Valley and the Llano Estacado, at least 50 km to the east of Henderson, while the other oaks would only have been available in the uplands to the west. During periods of peak runoff, however, oak driftwood may have been washed down the Hondo River.

Acer sp. (Box Elder or Big-Tooth Maple)

The *Acer* specimens recovered from Henderson appear to derive from either of two species: *A. negundo* (box elder) or *A. grandidentatum* (big-tooth maple). Interestingly, neither of these two species grows in Chaves County today, although they do grow in surrounding counties. Both species normally grow at elevations higher than Henderson, generally above about 1,400 m (Elmore and Janish 1976). The lowest elevation reported in Martin and Hutchins (1981) for either of the two species is about 1,600 m, which is significantly higher than Henderson's elevation (1,186 m). The species are common in valleys, canyons, and along mountain stream banks. Box elder can grow up to a height of about 20 m, and big-tooth maple can reach a maximum height of about 9 m. As was the case with ash, *Acer* is common at Henderson as wood charcoal, and it was also used at the site for construction, as evidenced by several burned roof beams collapsed on to the floor of Center Bar Room C-2. Both species are found today in the Capitan and Sacramento mountains to the west of Roswell. The residents of Henderson may have made long-distance forays to the uplands to procure trees for construction timbers; however, smaller pieces suitable at least for firewood could have been scavenged as driftwood from the Hondo.

It is difficult to determine which species is represented in the Henderson samples. Interestingly, a 1932 brochure cited by Shinkle (1966:115) claims that "boxwood" was occasionally present along the Rio Hondo when Roswell was first settled in the nineteenth century. Toll (in press) has also reported the presence of "cf. *Acer negundo*" from the nearby quasi-contemporary Fox Place (LA-68188), although she notes that it could possibly be *A. grandidentatum*.

Prosopis sp. (Mesquite)

Mesquite grows as a shrub or small tree and today is found throughout the area. Its distribution and, even more so, its density of coverage in the past, however, are far less certain, because mesquite is notorious for spreading under conditions of heavy overgrazing and suppressed range fires (Fisher 1977). The wood makes an excellent fuel and can also be used for posts (Vines 1960). Mesquite is fairly common in the Late phase samples, but does not appear in any of the Early phase samples that we analyzed. There are several possible reasons for this discrepancy: identifier caution, sampling bias, or that, for either cultural or environmental reasons, mesquite was not heavily utilized as a fuel resource in the Early phase. We were extremely cautious during the process of identifying semi-ring porous woods such as *Prosopis* when the charcoal specimens were small. If there was only one ring on which to base an identification, and the pore pattern was not absolutely clear, we did not assign the piece to genus but instead placed it in the more inclusive category. Consequently, it is possible that many of the pieces that were assigned to the semi-ring porous group are in actuality mesquite. It is also likely, however, that mesquite was not very heavily utilized in the Early phase as a fuel. Mesquite very likely was used as firewood in the Early phase, but it was used more heavily during the later period.

Juglans sp. (Walnut)

Walnut was recovered at Henderson in small amounts. The local species is *Juglans microcarpa* (Texas black walnut), which is a strong-scented shrub or small tree attaining a height of 9 m (Vines 1960). *Juglans* has not been identified in any structural samples from the site, although it would be a suitable construction material. However, walnut has been identified in the flotation samples, albeit in small amounts. In addition, a walnut "prayer stick" was recovered from the Feature 25 burial in the East Bar (Rocek and Speth 1986).

Juniperus sp. (Juniper)

The species present at Henderson is likely to be *Juniperus monosperma*, or one-seed juniper. Juniper is an evergreen tree that can attain 15 m in height. It usually grows on mountain slopes or on lower hills above elevations of about 900 m (Mohlenbrock and Thieret 1987). Henderson's inhabitants could have gathered juniper driftwood from the Hondo River as it washed down from the Sacramento Mountains. The wood is used locally for both fuel and posts (Vines 1960).

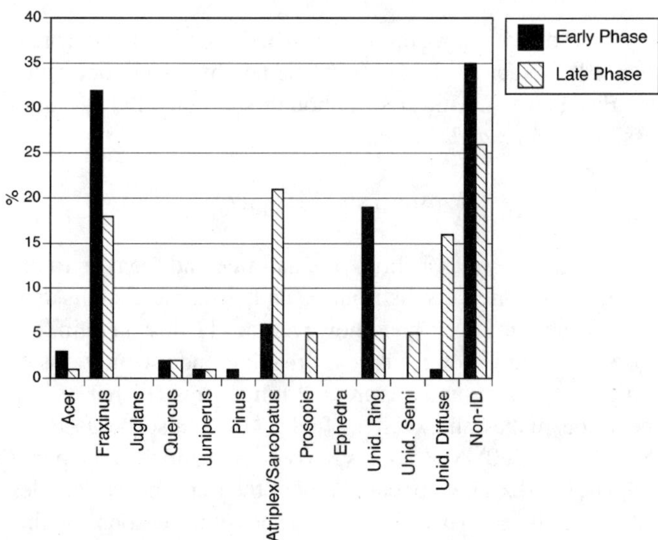

Figure 19.1. Abundance of taxa, expressed as percentages, in Early phase and Late phase charcoal samples from the Henderson Site.

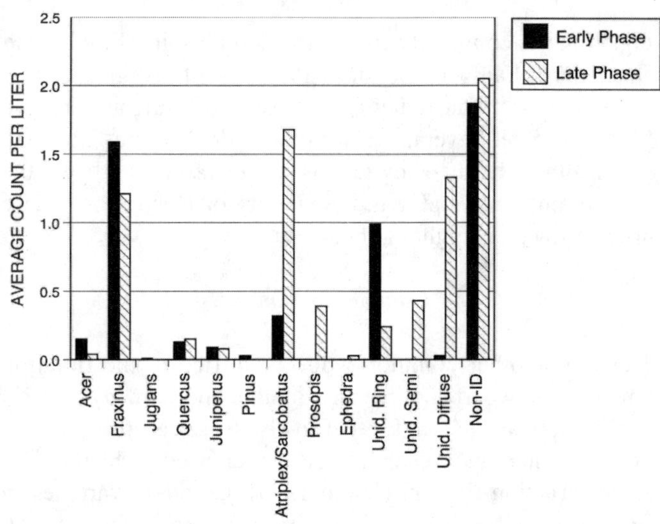

Figure 19.2. Abundance of taxa, expressed as counts per liter, in Early phase and Late phase charcoal samples from the Henderson Site.

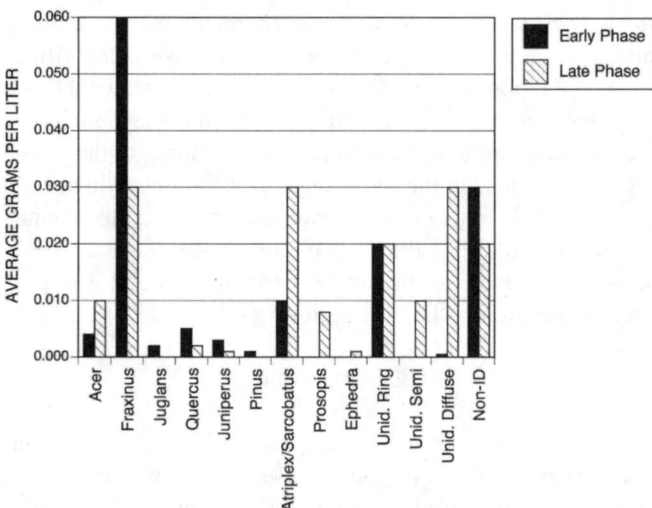

Figure 19.3. Abundance of taxa, expressed as grams per liter, in Early phase and Late phase charcoal samples from the Henderson Site.

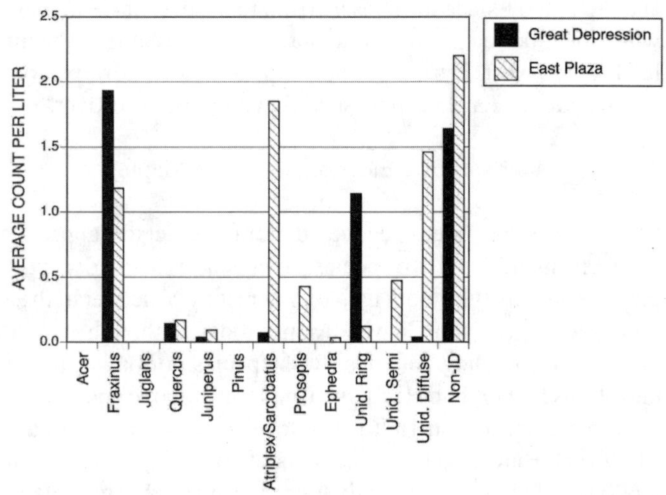

Figure 19.4. Abundance of taxa, expressed as counts per liter, in charcoal samples from Early phase and Late phase earth oven complexes.

Pinus sp. (Pine)

Potential *Pinus* species include ponderosa *(P. ponderosa)* and pinyon pine *(P. edulis)*. Both species grow at higher altitudes, and neither would have been available in the vicinity of Henderson. Pine can be used for construction and as a fuel. Driftwood may have been gathered from the Hondo River as it washed down from higher elevations.

Ephedra sp. (Mormon Tea)

Ephedra, or Mormon tea, grows as a small shrub on dry alkaline soils. While present in the vicinity of the site today, *Ephedra* is not common.

Populus sp. (Cottonwood)

Populus has been identified among the artifactual remains from Henderson. A small, flat "prayer stick," cut or carved in the form of a stylized corn plant, was found with the Feature 3 burial in Room E-4 in the East Bar (Rocek and Speth 1986). Cottonwood is often used for fuel and posts. Its absence in both the structural and flotation samples at Henderson is therefore surprising, especially since cottonwood/willow is listed among the primary building materials at nearby Fox Place (Toll, in press.). Cottonwood may have been scarce in the local environment around Henderson. It is also possible that its absence is an artifact of sampling bias. Even so, it is unlikely that cottonwood was ever a major source of fuel at Henderson.

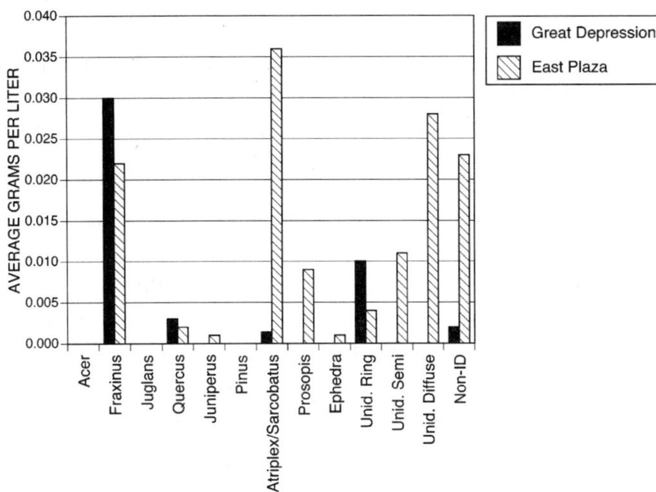

Figure 19.5. Abundance of taxa, expressed as grams per liter, in charcoal samples from Early phase and Late phase earth oven complexes.

Results

Overall, the unidentifiable material makes up the largest percentage of both the Early phase (35.0%) and Late phase (26.0%) samples (Fig. 19.1). Many pieces were extremely small and so badly weathered that identification was not possible. Of the identifiable species in the Early phase sample, *Fraxinus* ranks first at 32.0%, unidentified ring porous is second at 19.0%, and *Atriplex/Sarcobatus* ranks third at 6.0%. Some of the ring porous specimens may also be *Fraxinus*, in which case the true value for ash would be even higher. In the Late phase samples, *Atriplex/Sarcobatus* is the largest identifiable category (21%). The percentage of *Fraxinus* decreases from 32% in the Early phase to 18% in the Late phase. Interestingly, the diffuse porous category increases from 1% to 16% in the Late phase. Possible diffuse porous species at Henderson include *Acer* and *Populus*.

Similar results are obtained when the phases are compared using counts per liter (Fig. 19.2) or grams per liter (Fig. 19.3). In both figures, *Fraxinus* predominates in the Early phase, and then declines in the Late phase, while *Atriplex/Sarcobatus* increases. The same trends appear when just the samples from the earth oven complexes are considered, facilities that presumably employed substantial amounts of fuel when they were fired (Figs. 19.4, 19.5).

In sum, *Fraxinus* (ash) appears to have been the most heavily utilized fuel resource at Henderson in the Early phase, but it appears to have been superseded by *Atriplex/Sarcobatus* in the Late phase. The use of other shrubby species—mesquite and Mormon tea—also increases in the Late phase. Another interesting feature of this Early/Late phase comparison is that the unidentified ring porous category decreases significantly in the Late phase. There is a good possibility that this category is largely made up of ash as well.

Conclusions

There is evidence of a change in fuel exploitation over time at Henderson. Early phase villagers used *Fraxinus*, one of the principal trees that grew along the Hondo, while Late phase villagers used *Atriplex/Sarcobatus* and other shrubby taxa, such as *Prosopis* and *Ephedra*. There are various scenarios that might account for this shift in strategies (e.g., Smart and Hoffman 1988). The change could be the result of preferred fuel degradation. During the early decades of the occupation, Henderson's inhabitants may have depleted a significant portion of the ash that was available in the vicinity of the village, forcing them to utilize greater amounts of wood from smaller, shrubbier species. Alternatively, local environmental deterioration, caused for example by drought, may have reduced the growth of trees along the Hondo. However, nothing has been found at Henderson as yet that points to significant environmental change, although detailed pollen studies remain to be undertaken (J. D. Speth, pers. comm.). Thus, at present we are unable to determine what specific factor or factors led to the change in fuel use at Henderson. Whatever the underlying cause—climate change or local degradation of preferred fuel supplies—Henderson underwent a major shift in selected fuel resources, from trees to much smaller shrubs.

Synopsis

This charcoal analysis examines the fuel used by the Henderson villagers in the thirteenth and fourteenth century. Hypothetically, inhabitants of a village such as Henderson might be expected to select the most efficient or the highest and steadiest heat-producing fuels available close to the community. However, in open grasslands such as southeastern New Mexico, where potential fuel sources were very limited to start with, such preferred fuels may have become depleted quickly, and the inhabitants forced either to exploit less preferred sources that remained available nearby, or travel farther to obtain preferred materials. Presumably, a limit exists as to how far the inhabitants will travel before they begin shifting to less desirable fuels in the immediate area.

This perspective emphasizes efficiency, and ignores the possibility that preferred fuel resources may be selected for cultural reasons other than heat value or travel distance. If fuel resources were culturally selected, the use or avoidance of a particular species would not necessarily reflect local availability. Nevertheless, identification of "preferred" fuels should be possible by examining the species that predominate in the Early phase; any subsequent degradation of these preferred fuels should be discernible by a shift to other resources in the Late phase.

Currently the region is dominated by short-grass prairie and desert shrub. Vegetation in the vicinity of the Henderson Site includes grama grass, snakeweed, four-wing saltbush, greasewood, mesquite, Mormon tea, yucca, cholla, and prickly pear. Aside from recently planted ornamentals around ranch houses, the only native trees in the area today occur as a thin line along the banks of the Hondo channel. Among these are walnut (*Juglans major*), hackberry (*Celtis reticulata*), cottonwood (*Populus* sp.), willow (*Salix* sp.), and ash (*Fraxinus velutina*).

The landscape today is very similar to the one described by GLO surveyors in the 1860s. It is clear from these descriptions that the only trees in the area 130 years ago, as today, grew along the Hondo, and would not have provided a great deal of wood for either construction or fuel. Projecting conditions as they were in the 1860s back into the thirteenth and fourteenth centuries is risky, yet it seems highly unlikely that fuel (or construction timber) would have been more abundant to Henderson's Native American inhabitants than they were to the first European settlers in the Roswell area.

We analyzed the wood charcoal from 33 flotation samples taken from four different areas of the site: 7 from the Great Depression earth oven complex (Early phase), 6 from Main Bar East Room M-1 (Early phase), 10 from plaza deposits beneath Center Bar Room C-5 (Early phase), and 10 from the East Plaza earth oven complex (Late phase). In all, nine taxa were identified in the flotation samples examined here: *Acer* sp. (maple or box elder), *Fraxinus* sp. (ash), *Juglans* sp. (walnut), *Quercus* sp. (oak), *Juniperus* sp. (juniper), *Pinus* sp. (pine), *Atriplex/Sarcobatus* sp. (saltbush/greasewood), *Prosopis* sp. (mesquite), and *Ephedra* (Mormon tea). Of these, ash and saltbush/greasewood consistently rank as the most abundant taxa recovered from the flotation samples, regardless of phase or spatial context, and regardless of whether the data are expressed as percentages, counts per liter, or grams per liter. Other taxa appear in smaller amounts, notably oak, mesquite, and juniper.

Of the identifiable species in the Early phase sample, *Fraxinus* ranks first at 32.0%, unidentified ring porous is second at 19.0%, and *Atriplex/Sarcobatus* ranks third at 6.0%. Some of the ring porous specimens may also be *Fraxinus*, in which case the true value for ash would be even higher. In the Late phase samples, *Atriplex/Sarcobatus* is the largest identifiable category (21%). The percentage of *Fraxinus* decreases from 32% in the Early phase to 18% in the Late phase.

Very similar results are obtained when the phases are compared using counts per liter or grams per liter. *Fraxinus* predominates in the Early phase, and then declines in the Late phase, while *Atriplex/Sarcobatus* increases. The same trends are clearly apparent when just the samples from the earth oven complexes are considered, facilities that presumably employed substantial amounts of fuel.

There is evidence of change in fuel exploitation over time at Henderson. Early phase strategies focused on the use of ash, one of the principal trees that grew along the Hondo, while Late phase strategies concentrated much more heavily on the use of saltbush/greasewood and other shrubby taxa, such as mesquite and Mormon tea. Various scenarios might account for this shift in strategies. The change could be the result of preferred-fuel degradation. During the early decades of the occupation, Henderson's inhabitants may have depleted a significant portion of the ash that was available in the vicinity of the village, forcing them to utilize greater amounts of wood from smaller, shrubbier species. Alternatively, local environmental deterioration, caused for example by drought, may have reduced the growth of trees along the Hondo. However, nothing has been found at Henderson as yet that points to significant environmental change, although detailed pollen studies remain to be undertaken. Thus, at present we are unable to determine what specific factor or factors led to the change in fuel use at Henderson. Whatever the underlying cause—climate change or local degradation of preferred fuel supplies—Henderson underwent a major shift in selected fuel resources, from trees to much smaller shrubs.

Acknowledgments

We are grateful to Richard I. Ford, Gina S. Powell, Heather Trigg, and Sandra L. Dunavan for their assistance in identifying the Henderson charcoal.

Note

1. Available through the U.S. Department of the Interior, Bureau of Land Management, P. O. Box 1449, Santa Fe, NM 87504-1449.

References Cited

Core, H. A., W. A. Côté, and A. C. Day
1979 *Wood Structure and Identification* (2nd ed.). Syracuse, NY: Syracuse University Press.

Elmore, F. H., and J. R. Janish
1976 *Shrubs and Trees of the Southwest Uplands*. Popular Series 19. Tucson, AZ: Southwest Parks and Monuments Association.

Fisher, C. E.
1977 Mesquite and Modern Man in Southwestern North America. In: *Mesquite: Its Biology in Two Desert Scrub Ecosystems*, edited by B. B. Simpson, pp. 177-88. US/International Biological Program Synthesis Series 4. Stroudsburg, PA: Dowden, Hutchinson and Ross.

Harrar, E. S.
1957 *Hough's Encyclopaedia of American Woods*. New York: Robert Speller.

Hoadley, R. B.
1990 *Identifying Wood: Accurate Results with Simple Tools*. Newtown, CT: Taunton Press.

Lamb, S. H.
1975 *Woody Plants of the Southwest*. Santa Fe, NM: Sunstone Press.

Martin, W. C., and C. R. Hutchins
1981 *A Flora of New Mexico*. Vaduz, Liechtenstein: J. Cramer.

Minnis, P. E.
1987 Identification of Wood from Archaeological Sites in the American Southwest, 1. Keys for Gymnosperms. *Journal of Archaeological Science* 14(2):121-32.

Mohlenbrock, R. H., and J. W. Thieret
1987 *Trees: A Quick Reference Guide to Trees of North America*. New York: Collier Books, Macmillan Publishing Company.

Rangeland Resources International
1977 *Final Report for Eastside Roswell Vegetation Inventory (YA-512-CT7-182)*. Report Presented to the Bureau of Land Management, Roswell District Office, Roswell, NM.

Rocek, T. R., and J. D. Speth
1986 *The Henderson Site Burials: Glimpses of a Late Prehistoric Population in the Pecos Valley*. Technical Report 18. Ann Arbor, MI: Museum of Anthropology, University of Michigan, .

Rossen, J., and J. Olson
1985 The Controlled Carbonization and Archaeological Analysis of SE U.S. Wood Charcoals. *Journal of Field Archaeology* 12(4):445-56.

Shackleton, C. M., and F. Prins
1992 Charcoal Analysis and the "Principle of Least Effort" — A Conceptual Model. *Journal of Archaeological Science* 19(6):631-37.

Shinkle, J. D.
1966 *Reminiscences of Roswell Pioneers*. Roswell, NM: Hall-Poorbaugh Press.

Smart, T. L., and E. S. Hoffman
1988 Environmental Interpretation of Archaeological Charcoal. In: *Current Paleoethnobotany: Analytical Methods and Cultural Interpretations of Archaeological Plant Remains*, edited by C. A. Hastorf and V. S. Popper, pp. 167-205. Chicago, IL: University of Chicago Press.

Toll, M. S.
1988 Flotation Sampling: Problems and Some Solutions, with Examples from the American Southwest. In: *Current Paleoethnobotany: Analytical Methods and Cultural Interpretations of Archaeological Plant Remains*, edited by C. A. Hastorf and V. S. Popper, pp. 36-52. Chicago, IL: University of Chicago Press.
in press Plant Utilization at the Fox Place. In: *The Fox Place (LA 68188): A Late Prehistoric Hunter-Gatherer Pithouse Village Near Roswell, New Mexico*, edited by R. N. Wiseman. Santa Fe, NM: Museum of New Mexico.

Vines, R. A.
1960 *Trees, Shrubs, and Woody Vines of the Southwest*. Austin, TX: University of Texas Press.

Part V

Skeletal Indicators of Diet

20
The Stable Isotope Results

Margaret J. Schoeninger
University of California, San Diego

Introduction

A small number of samples of bone, both human and bison, were prepared to determine carbon- and nitrogen-stable isotope ratios in bone collagen as an independent measure of diet among the inhabitants of the Henderson Site. For carbon, the stable isotope ratios $^{13}C/^{12}C$, represented as $\delta^{13}C$ values in parts per thousand (per mil, or ‰) in bone collagen reflect the $^{13}C/^{12}C$ ratio in the diet of the individual (DeNiro and Epstein 1978). The utility of this method is based on an average 1% (10 per mil) difference in stable carbon isotope δ (delta) values between plants that synthesize a three-carbon molecule during the first phase of photosynthesis (referred to as C_3 plants) and other plants (referred to as C_4 plants) such as tropical grasses that synthesize a four-carbon molecule in the first phase (O'Leary 1988). The difference in plant δ values is reflected in the tissues of animals, including humans, that eat them. Humans or animals such as antelope that eat C_3 plants have tissues with a "C_3 signature" because their tissues reflect the $\delta^{13}C$ values of the C_3 plants they consume. Similarly, humans or animals such as bison on the southern Great Plains that eat C_4 plants have tissues with a "C_4 signature." As one moves from the southern Great Plains to the northern Great Plains, the grass cover includes increasingly more C_3 grasses (Barnes et al. 1983). This change has been shown to be reflected in the bone collagen of bison dwelling in the north versus those that live farther south (Pratt n.d.; Stafford et al. n.d.). For this reason, several bison samples were included in this project.

Stable nitrogen isotope ratios $^{15}N/^{14}N$ in bone collagen, presented as $\delta^{15}N$ values in per mil (‰) notation, also reflect the values in the individual's diet (DeNiro and Epstein 1981). Among terrestrial plants (see Delwiche et al. 1979; Virginia and Delwiche 1982), those such as legumes which fix atmospheric nitrogen tend to have stable isotope values which differ from those that use soil nitrates. A previous study, however, revealed that, contrary to expectation, domestic beans did not carry a diagnostic $\delta^{15}N$ signature and thus cannot be detected as a component of human diet (Spielmann et al. 1990).

Methods

Thirteen samples of human bone and three bison samples were prepared for stable carbon- and nitrogen-isotope ratio

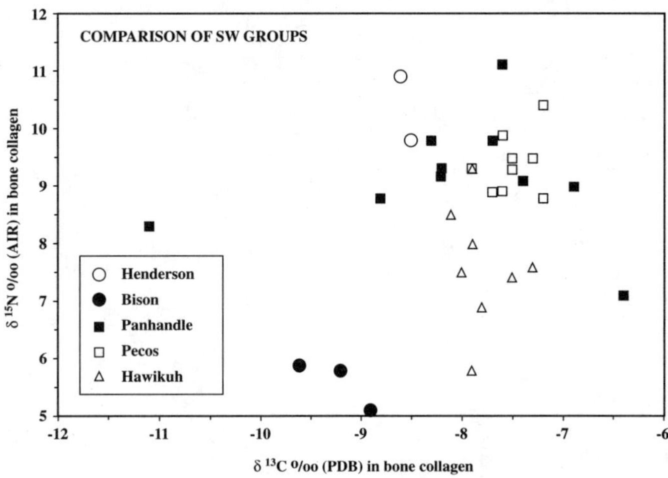

Figure 20.1. Henderson Site human (and bison) stable isotope values compared with values from other Southwestern human groups.

Table 20.1. Stable isotope ratios in Henderson Site human and bison bone samples.

Specimen	Sample I.D.[a]	Provenience[b]	$\delta^{13}C$ ‰ (PDB)	$\delta^{15}N$ ‰ (Air)
Human (adult male)	Feat. 41	Center Bar	-9.0	—[c]
Human (adult female)	Feat. 8	East Bar	-8.5	9.8
Human (adult male)	Feat. 29	East Bar	-8.6	10.9
Bison	Item 1279	East Plaza	-8.9	5.1
Bison	Item 1473	East Plaza	-9.6	5.9
Bison	Item 1304	East Plaza	-9.2	5.8

[a]Henderson Site burial features are described in detail in Rocek and Speth (1986); I.D. numbers listed here for bison are sequential item numbers assigned to each bison bone, not lot numbers as listed in Chapter 2.
[b]All specimens date to Henderson's Late phase (see Chapter 2).
[c]N_2 lost.

analysis (Table 20.1). Of the 13 human samples, only three retained enough collagen for such analysis; all of the bison samples retained adequate collagen. Briefly, the samples were prepared as follows. All samples were cleaned mechanically of surface debris and then ultrasonicated in double distilled water. Bone was ground, passed through a 0.71 mm mesh screen, demineralized in hydrochloric acid, and the resultant organic fraction (mainly the protein collagen) was dissolved (i.e., hydrolyzed) in a weak, hot hydrochloric acid solution (following Longin 1971, with modifications for humic acid removal by DeNiro and Epstein 1981, and Schoeninger and DeNiro 1984). The organic fraction was lyophilized to dryness and weighed into clean quartz tubing with excess cupric oxide, elemental copper, and elemental silver. The tubing was sealed under vacuum, combusted at 800°C, and allowed to cool to room temperature. The resulting H_2O, CO_2, and N_2 were separated cryogenically in a glass vacuum line and the carbon dioxide and nitrogen gas were analyzed mass spectrometrically. The gas fractions were prepared in the author's then-laboratory at Harvard University. The N_2 was measured in Dr. Jim McCarthy's laboratory at Harvard University on a V.G.602E mass spectrometer. The CO_2 was measured in Dr. John Hayes's laboratory at Indiana University on a Finnegan MAT Delta E mass spectrometer. Standard preparations of proline yielded a precision of less than 0.1 per mil for carbon and less than 0.2 per mil for nitrogen.

Results

Both the human and the bison samples display a C_4 signature. Even so, the more negative values in bison indicate that a smaller proportion of their calories and/or protein came from foods that had a C_4 signature than was true for the humans. If the human samples from Henderson are compared with other human samples from the American Southwest (Fig. 20.1), however, those from Henderson appear to have eaten less C_4 foods than did the settled maize agriculturalists from Pecos Pueblo (data redrawn from Spielmann et al. 1990) or from Hawikuh (data redrawn from Habicht-Mauche et al. 1994). The data from Henderson fall at the negative end of the distribution for a group of part-time horticulturalists from the Panhandle region of Texas (data redrawn from Habicht-Mauche et al. 1994). In the case of the inhabitants of the Panhandle, the authors concluded that the people were eating some combination of cactus, bison, and maize (see also Huebner 1991). The data in the present study suggest that the people buried at Henderson had, during life, eaten a significant amount of bison and some combination of plants with a C_4 signature. A rough estimate of diet can be made if two assumptions are made. First, that a diet without any plants or animals with a C_4 signature produces a value in bone collagen of approximately -21 per mil and that a diet consisting of 100% plants and animals with a C_4 signature produces a value of around -6 to -7 per mil. Second, that a linear increase in the amount of foods with a C_4 signature results in a linear increase in the δ value in bone collagen. Given these two assumptions, the data from Henderson indicate that approximately 85% of the people's calories and/or protein came from C_4 foods compared to 90-95% among the settled maize agriculturalists from Pecos and Hawikuh.

Synopsis

A small number of samples of bone, both human (n = 13) and bison (n = 3), were analyzed to determine carbon- and nitrogen-stable isotope ratios in bone collagen as an independent measure of diet among the inhabitants of the Henderson Site. Only three of the human samples retained enough collagen for such analysis; all of the bison samples retained adequate collagen. Both the human and the bison samples display a C_4 signature. Even so, the more negative values in bison indicate that a smaller proportion of their calories and/or protein came from foods that had a C_4 signature than was true for the humans. If the human samples from Henderson are compared with other human samples from the American Southwest, however, those from Henderson appear to have eaten less C_4 foods than did the settled maize agriculturalists from Pecos Pueblo or from Hawikuh. The data from Henderson fall at the negative end of the distribution for a group of part-time horticulturalists from the Panhandle region of Texas. In the case of the inhabitants of the Panhandle, the authors concluded that the people were eating some combination of cactus, bison, and maize. The data in the present study suggest that the people buried at Henderson had, during life, eaten a significant amount of bison and some combination of plants with a C_4 signature. A rough estimate of diet can be made if two assumptions are made. First, that a diet without any plants or animals with a C_4 signature produces a value in bone collagen of approximately -21 per mil and that a diet consisting of 100% plants and animals with a C_4 signature produces a value of around -6 to -7 per mil. Second, that a linear increase in the amount of foods with a C_4 signature results in a linear increase in the δ value in bone collagen. Given these two assumptions, the data from Henderson indicate that approximately 85% of the people's calories and/or protein came from C_4 foods compared to 90-95% among the settled maize agriculturalists from Pecos and Hawikuh.

References Cited

Barnes, P. W., L. L. Tieszen, and D. J. Ode
1983 Distribution, Production, and Diversity of C_3- and C_4-Dominated Communities in a Mixed Prairie. *Canadian Journal of Botany* 61:741-51.

Delwiche, C. C., P. J. Zinke, C. M. Johnson, and R. A. Virginia
1979 Nitrogen Isotope Distribution as a Presumptive Indicator of Nitrogen Fixation. *Botanical Gazette* S65-S69.

DeNiro, M. J., and S. Epstein
1978 Influence of Diet on the Distribution of Carbon Isotopes in Animals. *Geochimica et Cosmochimica Acta* 42:495-506.
1981 Influence of Diet on the Distribution of Nitrogen Isotopes in Animals. *Geochimica et Cosmochimica Acta* 45:341-51.

Habicht-Mauche, J. A., A. A. Levendosky, and M. J. Schoeninger
1994 Antelope Creek Phase Subsistence: The Bone Chemistry Evidence. In: *Skeletal Biology in the Great Plains: Migration, Warfare, Health, and Subsistence*, edited by D. W. Owsley and R. L. Jantz, pp. 291-304. Washington, DC: Smithsonian Institution Press.

Huebner, J. A.
1991 Cactus for Dinner, Again! An Isotopic Analysis of Late Archaic Diet in the Lower Pecos Region of Texas. In: *Papers on Lower Pecos Prehistory: Studies in Archeology*, edited by S. A. Turpin, pp. 175-90. Austin, TX: University of Texas.

Longin, R.
1971 New Method of Collagen Extraction for Radiocarbon Dating. *Nature* 230:241-42.

O'Leary, M. H.
1988 Carbon Isotopes in Photosynthesis. *BioScience* 38:328-36.

Pratt, D. R.
n.d. *Carbon/Nitrogen Isotope Assay of 61 Burials from the Upper Mississippi River Valley*. Master's thesis, University of Minnesota, Minneapolis, MN.

Rocek, T. R., and J. D. Speth
1986 *The Henderson Site Burials: Glimpses of a Late Prehistoric Population in the Pecos Valley*. Technical Report 18. Ann Arbor, MI: Museum of Anthropology, University of Michigan.

Schoeninger, M. J., and M. J. DeNiro
1984 Nitrogen and Carbon Isotopic Composition of Bone Collagen from Marine and Terrestrial Animals. *Geochimica et Cosmochimica Acta* 48:625-39.

Spielmann, K. A., M. J. Schoeninger, and K. Moore
1990 Plains-Pueblo Interdependence and Human Diet at Pecos Pueblo, New Mexico. *American Antiquity* 55(4):745-65.

Stafford, T. W., M. L. Fogel, K. Brendel, and P. E. Hare
n.d. Late Quaternary Paleoecology of the Southern High Plains Based on Stable Carbon and Nitrogen Analyses of Fossil Bison Collagen. Manuscript.

Virginia, R. A., and C. C. Delwiche
1982 Natural ^{15}N Abundance of Presumed N_2-Fixing and Non-N_2-Fixing Plants from Selected Ecosystems. *Oecologia* 54:317-25.

Part VI

Concluding Remarks

21
Life on the Periphery
Economic and Social Change in Southeastern New Mexico

John D. Speth
University of Michigan

Introduction

The preceding twenty chapters have presented a great deal of information about the material and economic life of a small, isolated community of farmer-hunters who lived some seven centuries ago along the semi-arid grassland margins between the Southwest and Southern Plains. This little village flourished for little more than a hundred years before it was abandoned and its gradually decaying mud walls melted into obscurity. Yet, despite its small size, isolated location, and brief existence, this community has provided tantalizing glimpses of a way of life that disappeared long before the first Europeans entered New Mexico and began chronicling the region's Native American cultures. Thus, my first goal in this chapter is essentially one of culture history, to pull together what seem to be the most interesting of the many details that have been presented in the preceding chapters in order to integrate them into a more coherent picture of what Henderson was like as a community, and how its economy changed during its comparatively brief existence.

But the events and forces that propelled Henderson toward increasing dependence on bison also have relevance beyond local culture history. Despite its isolation, Henderson clearly did not exist in a vacuum. What happened there very likely reflects not only the local political, social, and environmental milieu, but also pressures and opportunities emanating from the heartland of the Southwest as well. Thus, my second goal in this chapter, and by far the more speculative of the two, is to explore some of the possible reasons why Henderson's economy might have undergone such dramatic changes during the late thirteenth and early fourteenth century. The scenarios put forth in this second part are not intended as definitive explanations for the changes that we see at Henderson—we still know far too little about the site, or about its place within the broader region. Instead, our attempts here should be seen as a first step toward identifying and delineating a set of interesting issues that can then serve as targets for future problem-oriented research in southeastern New Mexico.

Henderson as a Village

By Southwestern standards, Henderson was a modest-sized community. I estimate that it had between 105 and 130 rooms: a guess, because most rooms are difficult to identify on the surface and only a small portion of the village has actually been excavated. Even less is known about Henderson's population. Not knowing the total number of rooms makes population estimates tenuous at best. Not all rooms were used as domestic dwellings, and it is equally clear that not all structures were contemporary. Perhaps the best one can do, given all these unknowns, is to say that Henderson's population at any point in time was probably small.

But this is not a very satisfying answer. Perhaps we can tweak the data a bit more and at least provide a crude ball-park estimate of the upper limit of Henderson's population. If we assume that all structures of a given phase were in use at the same time, that no Early phase structures remained in use during the Late phase, that all were used for domestic purposes, and that none had a second story, we can make the following calculations. Structures in the Early phase portion of the site (Main

Bar and perhaps West Bar) are roughly square and average about 3.5 m on a side, or 12.25 m^2. Many of the Late phase rooms of the Center Bar and East Bar are larger, some substantially so, but the overall average is about 3.5 m in width by 4.5 m in length, or roughly 15.75 m^2. The total estimated area of the Early phase portions of the site is 1,068 m^2 (or 854 m^2 if reduced by 20%; see Chapter 2). At an average of 12.25 m^2 per room, I would estimate there were between 70 and 87 Early phase rooms. During the Late phase, the estimated area for the Center Bar and East Bar is 878 m^2 (702 m^2 if reduced by 20%). At about 15.75 m^2 per room, I would estimate there were between 35 and 43 rooms in the Late phase. The real number of rooms in this period was probably somewhat greater, because at least some of the structures in the Main Bar continued to be used during the Late phase. Thus, the total number of rooms at Henderson, both phases combined, lies somewhere between about 105 and 130. I suspect the smaller value is more realistic.

Next, we can make crude estimates of the upper limit to total population in each phase by assuming that each person occupied about 10 m^2 of roofed-over living space (Naroll 1962), a value that has been in wide use in the anthropological and archaeological literature for many years, and one that has seen numerous attempts at refinement but also a great deal of criticism (e.g., Brown 1987; Cameron 1999; Casselberry 1974; Casteel 1979; Cook and Heizer 1965; De Roche 1983; Dohm 1990; Kolb 1985; Kramer 1982; LeBlanc 1971; Read 1978; Wiessner 1974). Using this figure, we arrive at a maximum population estimate of 85 to 107 people for the Early phase, and more than 70 to 88 people for the Late phase. These figures suggest that Henderson's inhabitants probably numbered fewer than 100 in both phases, and probably closer to 70 or 80.

We also know that the village developed in two principal phases of occupation. The first, or Early phase, which probably began between about A.D. 1250 and A.D. 1275, saw the construction of the Main Bar, and perhaps also the West Bar, forming a multi-tiered linear or "L"-shaped block of rooms. Most of these rooms appear to have been roughly square with rounded corners, their floors set well below ground level, upright roof-support posts near each corner, and entry through a hatch in the (presumably flat) roof. A large earth oven complex, the so-called "Great Depression," served as the principal communal and ritual focus for the village during the Early phase. This feature, a large karstic depression situated just north of the Main Bar at it western end, was filled with thousands of pieces of fire-cracked rock, as well as thousands of animal bones ranging from huge bison to tiny rodents and fish. The presence of unburned and fully articulated turkey burials at the base of this feature indicates that it was emptied after its last use and ritually closed or sealed.

During the Late phase, which we guess began in the early 1300s, several structures in the Main Bar were converted from domestic dwellings into storage facilities, and two large room blocks, the East Bar and Center Bar, were added on, giving the village its final "E"-shaped layout. Whether the West Bar remained in use during the Late phase is uncertain, and it is possible that the Late phase village more closely resembled an "F" or even a squared "U". The community's orientation shifted from the north, and perhaps west, to the south, and perhaps east, with the earth oven complex in the East Plaza becoming the principal communal and ritual focus. The last portion of the village to be occupied appears to have been the East Bar. Henderson was finally abandoned sometime during the mid- to late fourteenth century, although sporadic visits to the hilltop location may have continued for some time thereafter.

The villagers grew maize and other crops in fields along the floodplain of the Hondo, and collected a wide range of wild plants from the surrounding area as well as from the uplands to the west (Powell 2001). While maize was clearly a staple crop, as burned cobs, cob fragments, and small numbers of kernels are nearly ubiquitous in the deposits of both phases, its contribution to the villagers' diet was significantly less than at quasi-contemporary Puebloan communities like Pecos, Gran Quivira, and Hawikuh. Several lines of evidence point to this conclusion. First, Henderson's manos are crude, often massive, and utterly unstandardized, and most have only a single working surface. Second, the metates have very shallow, basin-shaped grinding surfaces, quite unlike the trough and slab forms so common elsewhere in the Southwest at the same time period. Third, carbon- and nitrogen-isotope signatures from Henderson's human skeletal remains (all dating to the Late phase) indicate a modest dependence on C_4 plants, maize very likely among them. Finally, Henderson's human dentitions display a low incidence of dental caries, more typical of hunter-gatherers than farmers (Rocek and Speth 1986).

Henderson's heavy reliance on bison is one of the community's most striking features. Nearly a quarter of all mammal remains found at the site are from this huge herbivore (about 4,100 bones). While the remains of medium ungulates, most of which are antelope, are slightly more numerous (4,700 bones), the fact that an adult pronghorn weighs less than 6% of the weight of a full-grown male bison indicates the tremendous contribution the latter made to Henderson's economy. While cottontails were numerically the most frequently hunted animals at Henderson (about 6,100 bones), it would take nearly 800 of these tiny animals to equal the weight of a single bison bull. It is sobering to note that the tremendous importance of bison would not have been evident had our excavations focused solely on Henderson's room blocks. Bison remains in these parts of the site were quite scarce, particularly in the Late phase. Only when we encountered the deposits in and around the earth oven complexes did the real importance of these animals become apparent.

The bison bones that villagers transported back to the village were primarily of moderate to high utility, especially the upper hind limbs, the hunters having discarded most of the bones of the lower limbs and feet, many of the upper front-limb elements, and almost all of the skulls and pelves. This highly selective assemblage of body parts indicates that the hunters killed most of their bison quite far from the village, and focused their transport efforts on those parts of the carcasses, including marrow bones, that had the highest food value.

Two-thirds of the bison brought back to the village were males, an indication that most if not all of the bison hunting was done in the spring. The scarcity or absence of fall and winter bison hunts strongly suggests that the herds had moved beyond the effective range of village hunters during these months of the year. Seasonality studies of other important animal taxa at Henderson, including antelope, cottontails, jackrabbits, prairie dogs, and catfish, suggest that most of these animals were procured during the spring, summer, or early fall, raising the possibility that the village may have been abandoned after the harvest. However, the fact that a number of the Main Bar dwellings had been converted into store rooms in the Late phase (visible structures that would have been easy targets for marauding strangers), as well as our failure to find evidence of clandestine storage features, such as bell-shaped pits, in areas away from the dwellings, make it unlikely that the village was entirely vacated (see DeBoer 1988). The most parsimonious interpretation of the evidence, therefore, would seem to be that some members of the community were resident year-round, but that during the late fall and winter months many of the able-bodied adults left home for an extended period to pursue bison and other resources in areas remote from this part of the Pecos Valley.

Dried bison meat was extensively traded by the villagers. This is indicated by the fact that bison ribs and vertebrae, two elements frequently involved in the production of dried meat, were both sharply underrepresented at Henderson, much more so than their smaller and far more fragile counterparts in antelope and deer, ruling out a simple taphonomic explanation for their scarcity. Interestingly, bison bone assemblages from quasi-contemporary villages in the uplands west of the Pecos Valley are dominated by ribs and vertebrae, underscoring the probable importance of these anatomical units in regional and interregional exchange systems.

One of the most fascinating discoveries at Henderson was the striking relationship between the body size of an animal resource and the abundance of its remains in domestic vs. public contexts. Thus, the larger the animal, the more likely it was processed, cooked, probably consumed, and then discarded in and around the massive earth oven complexes in the plazas. What is particularly surprising about this finding is the fact that the villagers appear to have been concerned about the body size of their prey on an exceedingly fine-grained scale, making distinctions even among smaller mammals, birds, and fish. Moreover, significantly greater proportions of higher-utility limb elements of bison and jackrabbits, the only two animal resources that were communally hunted by the villagers, were processed and discarded in plaza areas. The concentration of larger animals, and of higher-utility body parts, in and around major earth oven complexes very likely reflects the fact that these areas of the village were the locus of repeated events of interhousehold, perhaps community-wide, meat sharing and feasting. Given the open and presumably very public nature of these cooking features, animals processed in them would have been highly visible to all members of the community and hence the ones most subject to the pressures and demands of sharing.

Perhaps the most important discovery at Henderson, one that only became evident once we found that we could internally seriate the El Paso Polychrome jar rims, was the dramatic economic change that took place within the community during its comparatively brief existence. Bison hunting became far more important in the Late phase, as evidenced by an increase in the overall density of both bison bones and projectile points in the younger deposits. At the same time, the average utility of body parts brought back to the village increased, very likely reflecting more selective culling of carcasses prior to transport. Such a shift in transport decisions is precisely what one would expect if the average number of animals taken per kill event, or the distance separating kill from village, had increased. Of course, these two possibilities need not be mutually exclusive. In either case, in the Late phase we seem to be witnessing an increasing investment by village hunters in logistically organized bison hunting, targeting herds that were located much farther from home.

The communal importance of bison also increased dramatically within the village, as evidenced most clearly by the fact that during the Early phase only about half of the bison were processed, cooked, and consumed in communal spaces, whereas during the Late phase this figure skyrocketed to over 80%, with the highest-utility parts becoming concentrated in and around major public facilities. At the same time, the communal importance of antelope appears to have plummeted, as many fewer animals were brought to the village, more of the hunting was done by individual stalking close to home, and more of the meat was cooked by boiling in domestic contexts rather than by baking or roasting in the public earth oven complexes.

Hand-in-hand with the increasing importance of bison as a communal resource, we also see a dramatic jump in the intensity of regional and interregional exchange involving dried bison meat and probably other products of the hunt as well. This is strikingly shown by the precipitous decline in the proportional representation of bison ribs and vertebrae in the early 1300s. Henderson's ceramic assemblage underscores the sharply accelerating pace of westward-focused exchange in the Late phase. Nearly 95% of the extraregional ceramics that have been found at the village come from Late phase contexts.

The growing importance of interregional exchange can be seen in two other ways as well. One piece of evidence is provided by our recent work at Bloom Mound, a neighboring village that was occupied only a generation or two after Henderson. This small site is justly famous for its extraordinary assemblage of nonlocal ceramics, copper bells, obsidian flakes and points, and other items imported from distant areas (Kelley 1984), a clear indication that the pace of exchange between villages in this stretch of the Pecos Valley and communities in the heartland of the Southwest continued to accelerate after Henderson had been abandoned.

The second bit of evidence is less clear-cut but nonetheless interesting. Most ornaments made on demonstrably nonlocal materials, such as turquoise beads and pendants, *Olivella* shell beads, and *Glycymeris* shell bracelets, were found in burials that date to the Late phase. A similar number of burials was found in Early phase contexts, but the vast majority of these were infants and children that were unaccompanied by grave goods. While this striking difference could reflect a much greater influx of nonlocal ornaments into the village during the Late phase, it could equally well be the result of changing mortuary practices or sampling bias. The way around this impasse is to focus on ornaments and other unusual items that were found in nonburial contexts (we include here items such as fluorite and quartz crystals, twin-terminated quartz crystals known locally as "Pecos diamonds," obsidian flakes, and selenite plaques). Some of these items may have been lost or deliberately discarded in the trash, while others may have been inadvertently removed from burials by later construction activities or by the destructive proclivities of burrowing rodents. In either case, the abundance of such items found in fill from Early vs. Late phase contexts should provide at least a crude index of the total quantity that were brought into the community in each period. The results are as expected: in the Early phase, 19.3% of the ornaments and other unusual items are of clearly nonlocal origin, whereas in the Late phase the proportion jumps to 28.1%, a difference that is statistically significant ($t_s = 1.93, p = .05$).

Despite the many changes taking place at Henderson, particularly the growing importance of communal bison hunting and vastly intensified interregional exchange, there seems to be little detectable change in the agricultural component of the economy. Statistical analyses fail to reveal any major change over time in the density of small starchy seeds such as chenopods or amaranths, or in the density of maize cobs, cob fragments, or kernels (Powell 2001). Thus, Henderson's increasing emphasis on long-distance bison hunting does not appear to have been at the expense of maize cultivation.

That said, there are nevertheless several subtle hints that point to emerging or intensifying scheduling conflicts among key subsistence pursuits, agricultural activities almost certainly among them. Perhaps the most obvious locus of conflict centered on bison itself. While we are unable to pinpoint the specific months when long-distance hunting forays were launched from Henderson, we do know that most of these activities took place during the spring, probably centered on the calving season, as at the nearby Garnsey bison kill (Speth 1983). As a consequence, village bison hunting almost certainly came into direct conflict with critical farming activities such as field preparation, planting, and early weeding.

Antelope hunting at Henderson very likely reflects another locus of increasing spring-season scheduling conflict during the Late phase, as evidenced by their decline in sheer quantity and communal or public importance, as well as the fact that most Late phase antelope hunts were conducted much closer to home than during the preceding period.

The least convincing piece of evidence for increasing scheduling conflicts in Late phase subsistence pursuits is the decline in the proportion of immature cottontails. This decline could imply that Late phase procurement of many of these animals took place somewhat earlier in the year than during the preceding phase, a shift that also may have been motivated by the competing time and labor demands of both bison hunting and farming.

Henderson may also have undergone some fascinating but still very poorly understood changes in community organization. The clearest suggestion of this is provided by the faunal remains themselves. As already noted, the quantity of an animal's bones that ended up in and around the public earth oven complexes is closely predicted by its body size—the larger the animal, the more likely it was processed, cooked, probably consumed, and then discarded in non-room contexts. This pattern of discrimination on the basis of body size was already clearly evident in the Early phase but was greatly accentuated in the Late phase, most especially for bison, where the proportion of remains, particularly high-utility ones, jumped in public areas from roughly 50% to over 80%. If the Great Depression and East Plaza earth oven complexes were the loci of repeated events of interhousehold, perhaps community-wide, food sharing and feasting, it is clear that such activities became far more important after about A.D. 1300 (see Hayden 1995, 1997 for interesting discussions of the role of communal feasting in egalitarian and emerging transegalitarian societies; see also Potter 1997a, 1997b for a faunal perspective on feasting in a Puebloan context).

There is another possible sign of village-wide organizational change, although its nature and significance are less obvious. We have already noted that the size of the average house at Henderson increased in the Late phase from about 12.25 m^2 to 15.75 m^2, an increase in floor area of nearly 30%. Use of average values may in fact be misleading and underestimate the magnitude of the change, as a number of the houses in the Late phase are substantially larger than any of their Early phase predecessors, attaining lengths as great as 6 m. While recognizing the danger of equating house with household, it is tempting nonetheless to suggest that the increase in structure size reflects an increase in commensal unit size and perhaps, therefore, a fundamental change in family form.

What sort of change in family organization we might be seeing at Henderson, and why such a change might have come about, are, of course, the interesting questions, but we can do little more than speculate at the moment. One interesting possibility, discussed many years ago by Pasternak et al. (1976, 1983, 1997; see also Crown and Kohler 1994), is a shift from nuclear family units to extended family households in response to changing activity patterns that regularly required men or women to be in two places at once:

> We suggest here that, in the absence of an ability to replace family labor with hired or slave labor, extended family households will develop when work done by a mother away from home (cultivating or gathering far away) makes it difficult for her to tend her children and/or perform her other regular, time-consuming domestic tasks; or when outside activities of a father (distant warfare, trading trips, migratory wage labor) make it difficult for him to perform his subsistence work. That is, we suggest that extended family households emerge when there are "incompatible" activity requirements that cannot be met by a mother or father in a one-family household. [Pasternak et al. 1976:110]

The increasing importance of long-range communal bison hunts and interregional exchange during the Late phase might have provided precisely the sort of "activity requirement" incompatibilities envisioned by Pasternak and colleagues, in which many adult men, and perhaps many adult women as well, were away from the village for extended periods of time.

There are a number of ways that one might go about evaluating this more thoroughly, but unfortunately not with the data at hand. For example, if commensal unit site increased, as might be expected with a shift from nuclear family units to some more inclusive family form, the average volume of domestic cooking pots might be expected to increase (Mills 1999; Smith 1985). The principal cooking vessels used by the Henderson villagers were the large globular El Paso Polychrome jars, a function that is clearly indicated by the heavy sooting on many sherd exteriors (see also Seaman and Mills 1988; Whalen 1994). Unfortunately, the small size of most El Paso rim sherds has made it impossible to obtain reliable estimates of rim diameter, a decidedly crude but perhaps workable proxy for overall vessel size.

A much less reliable approach, the ratio of El Paso rim sherds to body sherds, might also provide evidence for a change in average vessel size (Scarborough 1992), but we have not yet faced the daunting task of coding the estimated 60,000+ El Paso body sherds recovered in the five seasons of excavation. Moreover, for this ratio to work, the average size of the body sherds in both phases must be comparable, so that an increase in the number of body sherds relative to rim sherds reflects larger vessel size, not smaller average sherd size. This assumption may not hold, however. The mean thickness of the walls of the El Paso jars (measured on the rim sherds) decreases significantly from the Early phase to the Late phase (Early phase, $\bar{x} = 4.76 \pm 1.02$ mm; Late phase, $\bar{x} = 4.47 \pm 1.16$ mm; $t = 2.98$, $p = .003$). In addition, research by Whalen (1996) in south-central New Mexico suggests that both the quantity and frequency of different size classes of temper particles in at least the earlier portion of the El Paso brownware series changed over time, trends that might well have continued into the later polychromes. It is hard to believe that such changes would not have affected the size of the sherds that were produced when the thinner-walled Late phase vessels broke. Thus, at the moment we are less than optimistic about the feasibility of estimating the average volume of Henderson's cooking pots, either via measurements of rim diameter or via the ratio of rim to body sherds.

One might also expect that an increase in commensal unit size would be paralleled by an increase in the number of household fireplaces, or in their average diameter, or both (see Whalen 1994; Scarborough 1992). Unfortunately, we are again stymied, in this case by our very small sample of hearths. We would have had to excavate much more of the site than we did in order to obtain an adequate sample; and our priority, as well as that of the Archaeological Conservancy, was to preserve for future generations as much of Henderson as possible.

There is another way that one might be able to detect changes in commensal unit size. If more adult women co-resided in Late phase households than in earlier ones, we might expect to find an increase in the number of metates in or adjacent to the younger structures (e.g., Ortman 1998; Spielmann 1995). Unfortunately, we found almost none of these massive grinding tools *in situ* in either phase. Most had been deliberately broken and incorporated into the foundations of walls.

The bottom line is that we know frustratingly little about the nature of the organizational changes that took place at Henderson during the opening decades of the fourteenth century. These changes are among the most fascinating aspects of our research at the site, and we will continue to seek new and better ways to both identify and explain them.

Forces beyond Southeastern New Mexico

As one explores the economic changes that were going on at Henderson in the late 1200s and early 1300s, one cannot help but wonder why they took place. What pushed, or enticed, the villagers to increase their reliance on long-range bison hunting? And what encouraged them to become closely enmeshed in a network of exchange with the Pueblo world to the west? As I indicated at the outset of this chapter, these are questions with no simple or obvious answers, at least not yet, but they are certainly among the most interesting issues raised by the work at Henderson.

It has been known for many years that bison became more prominent in Southern Plains archaeological assemblages after about A.D. 1250 (e.g., Baugh 1986; Bozell 1995; Bryson and Murray 1977; Collins 1971; Creel et al. 1990; Dillehay 1974; Drass and Flynn 1990; Greer 1976; Huebner 1991; Jelinek 1966, 1967; Lensink 1993; Lynott 1980; Ricklis 1992; Tiffany 1982). But why this should be so remains shrouded in uncertainty. The simplest and most obvious answer, suggested by many, is that bison numbers in the Southern Plains were simply very low prior to the mid-1200s (Dillehay 1974; Jelinek 1966, 1967). Their numbers then increased either because conditions in the Southern Plains improved, attracting or supporting larger numbers of animals, or because conditions farther to the north deteriorated, forcing bison herds southward into the Southern Plains. In either case, the underlying assumption is that bison numbers in archaeological sites are a reflection of their actual numbers in the region.

While the simplicity of an environmental explanation of this sort is appealing, one can also explain the increasing importance of bison in Southwestern and Southern Plains economies using socioeconomic rather than environmental factors (see Speth 1991; Speth and Scott 1985, 1989). A socioeconomic model would be structured something like this. In the late 1200s and early 1300s, following the abandonment of the Four Corners area, large numbers of immigrants poured into the northern and central Rio Grande (Ahlstrom and Van West 1995; Cameron 1995; Cordell 1995; Cordell et al. 1994; Lekson and Cameron 1995; Lipe 1995; Spielmann 1998). Partly as a result of the burgeoning populations in the Rio Grande, and partly in response to the changing political climate (LeBlanc 1997, 1999; Schaafsma 1999), these communities began to aggregate on an unprecedented scale. These large, rapidly agglomerating farming communities, many with hundreds and even thousands of rooms, almost certainly depleted their readily accessible sources of animal protein within a matter of decades, forcing their inhabitants to seek alternative sources. In part this could be accomplished locally, by altering crop mixes in favor of more protein-rich plant foods, raising turkeys, or fishing (see discussion in Speth and Scott 1989). These communities probably also turned to more distant protein sources, undertaking long-distance forays into the mountains to procure deer and mountain sheep or out into the grasslands to hunt antelope and bison. An efficient alternative for communities situated along the margins of the Southern Plains, whose hunting had become constrained by the time and labor demands of their farming activities, was to enter into regular, complementary exchange relationships with groups who resided closer to the major bison herds, the farmers providing carbohydrates, the bison hunters providing high-quality protein (as well as hides and other byproducts of the hunt).

Farmers, however, might not seek such "mutualistic" exchange relationships with hunting populations until the level of horticultural commitment, village permanence, and local resource depletion had crossed some critical, but as yet unknown, threshold, increasing the villagers' dependence on large mammals to the point where they could only procure sufficient quantities of these resources in distant hunting zones (Speth 1991:27-28).

Similarly, the extent to which Southern Plains groups could focus their subsistence efforts on just bison was very likely constrained by the scarcity of abundant, predictable carbohydrate resources on the High Plains and by the low levels of fat provided by the region's bison, even when the animals were in peak physiological condition (Speth 1983; Speth and Spielmann 1983). Thus, the mutualistic exchange ties that were observed between Plains and Pueblo groups when the Spanish first entered the American Southwest may not have emerged until Southwestern farmers actively sought a protein source that had to be procured far out in the Plains and, at the same time, were able to provide their Plains trading partners with a reliable source of carbohydrates sufficient to offset the nutritional constraints of a hunting economy heavily focused on a fat-poor animal resource (Speth 1983, 1991; Cordain et al. 2000). These conditions apparently were not met until the late 1200s or early 1300s, and were probably triggered by the influx of new populations into the Rio Grande following the abandonment of the Four Corners area (Spielmann 1986, 1991).

In reality, of course, the socioeconomic and environmentally based models of the sort outlined here should not be viewed as mutually exclusive or contradictory. Exchange relationships would not have emerged if climatic and environmental conditions in the grasslands had not supported bison herds of sufficient size and number, nor were they likely to develop if conditions for agriculture precluded the reliable production of carbohydrate surpluses. In other words, conditions had to be such that both sides could afford to specialize and produce a surplus, and stable enough to permit continuity of the relationship over a period of years (Spielmann 1986). Thus, a favorable environment is clearly necessary for the development of mutualism, but by itself is not sufficient to account for the actual emergence of such relationships; socioeconomic factors are also a necessary part of the equation.

So where do these musings take us with regard to Henderson? At a nearby village known as Fox Place, whose major occupation probably predates Henderson's by at most a few generations, recent excavations have shown that bison were hunted but only in small numbers (Wiseman, in press; Akins, in press). Thus, between the abandonment of Fox Place, which probably occurred in the mid-1200s, and the founding of Henderson shortly thereafter, the importance of bison in local economies increased markedly. And by the first decades of the 1300s, during Henderson's Late phase, exchange ties to the west increased explosively, almost certainly signaling the emergence of mutualistic relationships that began to draw together the Southern Plains and Pueblo worlds in a manner that was without precedent in the region.

The forces that began to tightly enmesh the economies of Plains and Pueblo groups undoubtedly involved more than just a need for protein and carbohydrate. The political climate in the Southwest was also changing radically during the late thirteenth and early fourteenth centuries, creating new economic opportunities for populations that had ready access to the bison herds of the Southern Plains. LeBlanc (1997, 1999; see also Schaafsma 1999) has built a convincing case that warfare between Pueblo groups increased dramatically after about A.D. 1300, at the end of the so-called "Medieval Warm Period." In LeBlanc's view, intensified conflict was fostered by high human population levels in a context of increasingly unfavorable agricultural conditions. The instability of the time may have been exacerbated by the introduction of a new shock weapon, the sinew-backed recurved bow (the "Turkish" bow of the Spanish chronicles), in combination with solid-wood arrows, which together rendered traditional basketry or wicker shields obsolete and ushered in a new form of shield made from bison hide. According to LeBlanc (1999:107),

> the hides had to be heated, pounded, and shaped to produce a tough shield, and it's unclear whether these production techniques would have required the skills of specialists. But, if every adult male needed such a shield, then the consequences for exchange with the Plains people in order to obtain buffalo hides must have been significant.

Henderson may well have been swept up in this newly emerging economic activity, becoming a source of hides for the manufacture of Pueblo shields, as well as providing dried meat, robes, and other more traditional products of the hunt.

Now that I have ventured out to the end of the proverbial limb, I may as well go one step farther and saw it off. As will shortly become obvious, my comments here are pure conjecture, as there is no hard evidence as yet to back them up. What was the fate of Henderson? What was all this economic change leading to? My hunch is that Henderson's occupants were well on their way toward becoming full-fledged bison hunting specialists, perhaps even "dog nomads" of the sort described less than two centuries later by the first Spanish explorers to enter the Southwest (Hammond and Rey 1940, 1953; see also Spielmann 1991). Many of the changes that we see at Henderson seem to point in that direction. Long-distance communal bison hunting was intensifying rapidly and becoming a central economic focus of the community, hand-in-hand with close economic ties to the Puebloan world. In pursuit of these activities, each spring many of Henderson's able-bodied adults left the community on long-distance bison hunts, and each autumn following the harvest the village was almost completely abandoned. It is a short step from this sort of semi-sedentary hunting-farming economy to a semi-nomadic or fully nomadic lifeway specializing on the dual activities of bison hunting and exchange.

Unfortunately, we did not actually observe such a transition at Henderson, although the village's abandonment might mark not just a physical relocation of the community but the final step in its economic and social transformation. What was happening in the last decades of Henderson's existence is critical to understanding the whole process. But in order to see more precisely what was taking place as the occupation drew to a close, we need to find a way to break apart the entity that in the present study we have simply lumped together as "Late phase." Unfortunately, we presently lack the means to accomplish this. Deeply stratified deposits are rare. Radiocarbon and archaeomagnetic dating produce results with error factors as great as the brief period we are trying to examine. And our El Paso rim seriation, productive as it was, is not sensitive enough to give us the needed resolution. Nevertheless, I remain confident that we one day will find a way to tease apart Henderson's Late phase and begin to probe the final stages of the occupation in much greater detail. Work at nearby Bloom Mound may help in this process, as the occupation at this small village may have outlasted Henderson's by a few generations.

Clearly, much remains to be learned about the region's late prehistoric inhabitants. The work done thus far at Henderson has clarified many aspects of the lives and economy of these ancient New Mexicans, but it is also eminently clear that many new questions have surfaced, interesting and important ones that we are not yet able to address. Many of these can probably be answered by new or more detailed studies of existing collections. Others, however, can only be answered through renewed excavations at Henderson and elsewhere. Tragically, the archaeological record of southeastern New Mexico is disappearing before our eyes at an unbelievable rate, through urban expansion, mineral exploitation, widespread misuse and abuse of the landscape, and sheer vandalism. We can only hope that sites like Henderson, Garnsey, Bloom Mound, Rocky Arroyo, Fox Place, and a handful of others demonstrate just how valuable the area's archaeological record really is, and that Southwestern archaeologists will take full advantage of that potential before the record is irretrievably lost.

References Cited

Ahlstrom, R. V. N., and C. R. Van West
1995 Environmental and Chronological Factors in the Mesa Verde-Northern Rio Grande Migration. *Journal of Anthropological Archaeology* 14(2):125-42.

Akins, N. J.
in press Fox Place Fauna. In: *The Fox Place (LA 68188), A Late Prehistoric Hunter-Gatherer Pithouse Village Near Roswell, New Mexico*, by Regge N. Wiseman. Santa Fe: Museum of New Mexico, Office of Archaeological Studies.

Baugh, S. T.
1986 Late Prehistoric Bison Distributions in Oklahoma. In: *Current Trends in Southern Plains Archaeology*, edited by T. G. Baugh, pp. 83-96. Memoir 21. Lincoln, NE: Plains Anthropological Society.

Bozell, J. R.
1995 Culture, Environment, and Bison Populations on the Late Prehistoric and Early Historic Central Plains. *Plains Anthropologist* 40(152):145-63.

Brown, B. M.
1987 Population Estimation from Floor Area: A Restudy of "Naroll's Constant." *Behavior Science Research* 22(1-4):1-49.

Bryson, R. A., and T. J. Murray
1977 *Climates of Hunger: Mankind and the World's Changing Weather*. Madison, WI: University of Wisconsin Press.

Cameron, C. M.
1995 Migration and the Movement of Southwestern Peoples. *Journal of Anthropological Archaeology* 14(2):104-24.
1999 Room Size, Organization of Construction, and Archaeological Interpretation in the Puebloan Southwest. *Journal of Anthropological Archaeology* 18(2):201-39.

Casselberry, S. E.
1974 Further Refinement of Formulae for Determining Population from Floor Area. *World Archaeology* 6:116-22.

Casteel, R. W.
1979 Relationships between Surface Area and Population Size: A Cautionary Note. *American Antiquity* 44(4):803-7.

Collins, M. B.
1971 A Review of Llano Estacado Archaeology and Ethnohistory. *Plains Anthropologist* 16:85-104.

Cook, S. F., and R. F. Heizer
1965 *The Quantitative Approach to the Relation between Population and Settlement Size*. Reports of the University of California Archaeology Survey 64. Berkeley, CA: University of California Archaeological Research Facility, Department of Anthropology.

Cordain, L., J. B. Miller, S. B. Eaton, N. Mann, S. H. A. Holt, and J. D. Speth
2000 Plant-Animal Subsistence Ratios and Macronutrient Energy Estimations in Worldwide Hunter-Gatherer Diets. *American Journal of Clinical Nutrition* 71(3):682-92.

Cordell, L. S.
1995 Tracing Migration Pathways from the Receiving End. *Journal of Anthropological Archaeology* 14(2):203-11.

Cordell, L. S., D. E. Doyel, and K. W. Kintigh
1994 Processes of Aggregation in the Prehistoric Southwest. In: *Themes in Southwest Prehistory*, edited by G. J. Gumerman, pp. 109-33. School of American Research Advanced Seminar Book. Santa Fe, NM: SAR Press.

Creel, D. G., R. F. Scott, and M. B. Collins
1990 A Faunal Record from West Central Texas and Its Bearing on Late Holocene Bison Population Changes in the Southern Plains. *Plains Anthropologist* 35(127):55-69.

Crown, P. L., and T. A. Kohler
1994 Community Dynamics, Site Structure, and Aggregation in the Northern Rio Grande. In: *The Ancient Southwestern Community: Models and Methods for the Study of Prehistoric Social Organization*, edited by W. H. Wills and R. D. Leonard, pp. 103-17. Albuquerque, NM: University of New Mexico Press.

DeBoer, W. R.
1988 Subterranean Storage and the Organization of Surplus: The View from Eastern North America. *Southeastern Archaeology* 7(1):1-20.

De Roche, C. D.
1983 Population Estimates from Settlement Area and Number of Residences. *Journal of Field Archaeology* 10(2):187-92.

Dillehay, T. D.
1974 Late Quaternary Bison Population Changes on the Southern Plains. *Plains Anthropologist* 19:180-96.

Dohm, K. M.
1990 Effect of Population Nucleation on House Size for Pueblos in the American Southwest. *Journal of Anthropological Archaeology* 9(3):201-39.

Drass, R. R., and P. Flynn
1990 Temporal and Geographic Variations in Subsistence Practices for Plains Villagers in the Southern Plains. *Plains Anthropologist* 35(128):175-90.

Greer, J. W.
1976 Notes on Bison in Val Verde County, Texas: Additions to Dillehay. *Plains Anthropologist* 21:237-39.

Hammond, G. P., and A. Rey
1940 *Narratives of the Coronado Expedition, 1540-1542*. Coronado Historical Series 2. Albuquerque, NM: University of New Mexico Press.

Hammond, G. P., and A. Rey
1953 *Don Juan de Oñate: Colonizer of New Mexico, 1595-1628*. Coronado Cuarto Centennial Publications 5-6. Albuquerque, NM: University of New Mexico Press.

Hayden, B.
1995 Pathways to Power: Principles for Creating Socioeconomic Inequalities. In: *Foundations of Social Inequality*, edited by T. D. Price and G. M. Feinman, pp. 15-86. New York, NY: Plenum Press.
1997 Observations on the Prehistoric Social and Economic Structure of the North American Plateau. *World Archaeology* 29(2):242-61.

Huebner, J. A.
1991 Late Prehistoric Bison Populations in Central and Southern Texas. *Plains Anthropologist* 36(137):343-58.

Jelinek, A. J.
1966 Correlation of Archaeological and Palynological Data. *Science* 152:1507-9.
1967 *A Prehistoric Sequence in the Middle Pecos Valley, New Mexico*. Anthropological Paper 31. Ann Arbor, MI: Museum of Anthropology, University of Michigan.

Kelley, J. H.
1984 *The Archaeology of the Sierra Blanca Region of Southeastern New Mexico*. Anthropological Paper 74. Ann Arbor, MI: Museum of Anthropology, University of Michigan.

Kolb, C. C.
1985 Demographic Estimates in Archaeology: Contributions from Ethnoarchaeology on Mesoamerican Peasants. *Current Anthropology* 26(5):581-99.

Kramer, C.
1982 *Village Ethnoarchaeology: Rural Iran in Archaeological Perspective*. New York, NY: Academic Press.

LeBlanc, S. A.
1971 An Addition to Naroll's Suggested Floor Area and Settlement Population Relationship. *American Antiquity* 36(2):210-11.
1997 Modeling Warfare in Southwestern Prehistory. *North American Archaeologist* 18(3):235-76.
1999 *Prehistoric Warfare in the American Southwest*. Salt Lake City, UT: University of Utah Press.

Lekson, S. H., and C. M. Cameron
1995 The Abandonment of Chaco Canyon, the Mesa Verde Migrations, and the Reorganization of the Pueblo World. *Journal of Anthropological Archaeology* 14(2):184-202.

Lensink, S. C.
1993 Episodic Climatic Events and Mill Creek Culture Change: An Alternative Explanation. *Plains Anthropologist* 38(145):189-97.

Lipe, W. D.
1995 The Depopulation of the Northern San Juan: Conditions in the Turbulent 1200s. *Journal of Anthropological Archaeology* 14(2):143-69.

Lynott, M. J.
1980 Prehistoric Bison Populations of Northcentral Texas. *Bulletin of the Texas Archaeological Society* 50:89-101.

Mills, B. J.
1999 Ceramics and the Social Contexts of Food Consumption in the Northern Southwest. In: *Pottery and People: A Dynamic Interaction*, edited by J. M. Skibo and G. M. Feinman, pp. 99-114. Foundations of Archaeological Inquiry. Salt lake City, UT: University of Utah Press.

Naroll, R.
1962 Floor Area and Settlement Population. *American Antiquity* 27(4):587-89.

Ortman, S. G.
1998 Corn Grinding and Community Organization in the Pueblo Southwest, A.D. 1150-1550. In: *Migration and Reorganization: The Pueblo IV Period in the American Southwest*, edited by K. A. Spielmann, pp. 165-92. Anthropological Research Papers 51. Tempe, AZ: Arizona State University.

Pasternak, B., C. R. Ember, and M. Ember
1976 On the Conditions Favoring Extended Family Households. *Journal of Anthropological Research* 32(2):109-23.
1983 On the Conditions Favoring Extended Family Households. In: *Marriage, Family, and Kinship: Comparative Studies of Social Organization*, by M. Ember and C. R. Ember, pp. 125-49. New Haven, CT: HRAF Press.
1997 *Sex, Gender, and Kinship: A Cross-Cultural Perspective*. Upper Saddle River, NJ: Prentice-Hall.

Potter, J. M.
1997a *Communal Ritual Feasting, and Social Differentiation in Late Prehistoric Zuni Communities*. Ph.D. dissertation, Arizona State University, Tempe, AZ.
1997b Communal Ritual and Faunal Remains: An Example from the Dolores Anasazi. *Journal of Field Archaeology* 24(3):353-64.

Powell, G. S.
2001 *Hunting and Farming between the Plains and the Southwest: Analysis of Archaeobotanical Remains from the Henderson Site, Roswell, New Mexico*. Ph.D. dissertation, Washington University, St. Louis, MO.

Read, D. W.
1978 Towards a Formal Theory of Population Size and Area of Habitation. *Current Anthropology* 19:312-17.

Ricklis, R. A.
1992 The Spread of a Late Prehistoric Bison Hunting Complex: Evidence from the South-Central Coastal Prairie of Texas. *Plains Anthropologist* 37(140):261-73.

Rocek, T. R., and J. D. Speth
1986 *The Henderson Site Burials: Glimpses of a Late Prehistoric Population in the Pecos Valley*. Technical Report 18. Ann Arbor, MI: Museum of Anthropology, University of Michigan.

Scarborough, V. L.
1992 Ceramics, Sedentism, and Agricultural Dependency at a Late Pithouse/Early Pueblo Period Village. In: *Long-Term Subsistence Change in Prehistoric North America*, edited by D. R. Croes, R. A. Hawkins and B. L. Isaac, pp. 307-33. Research in Economic Anthropology, Supplement 6. Greenwich, CT: JAI Press.

Schaafsma, P.
1999 *Warrior Shield and Star: Imagery and Ideology of Pueblo Warfare*. Santa Fe, NM: Western Edge Press.

Seaman, T. J., and B. J. Mills
1988 What Are We Measuring? Rim Thickness Indices and Their Implications for Changes in Vessel Use. In: *Fourth Jornada Mogollon Conference (Oct. 1985): Collected Papers*, edited by M. S. Duran and K. W. Laumbach, pp. 163-94. Tularosa, NM: Human Systems Research, Inc.

Smith, M. F.
1985 Toward an Economic Interpretation of Ceramics: Relating Vessel Size and Shape to Use. In: *Decoding Prehistoric Ceramics*, edited by B. A. Nelson, pp. 254-309. Carbondale, IL: Southern Illinois University Press, Center for Archaeological Investigations.

Speth, J. D.
1983 *Bison Kills and Bone Counts: Decision Making by Ancient Hunters*. Chicago, IL: University of Chicago Press.
1991 Some Unexplored Aspects of Mutualistic Plains-Pueblo Food Exchange. In: *Farmers, Hunters, and Colonists: Interaction Between the Southwest and the Southern Plains*, edited by K. A. Spielmann, pp. 18-35. Tucson, AZ: University of Arizona Press.

Speth, J. D., and S. L. Scott
1985 Late Prehistoric Subsistence Change in Southeastern New Mexico: The Faunal Evidence from the Sacramentos. In: *Proceedings of the Third Jornada-Mogollon Conference*, edited by M. S. Foster and T. C. O'Laughlin, pp. 137-48. The Artifact 23(1-2). El Paso, TX: El Paso Archaeological Society.
1989 Horticulture and Large-Mammal Hunting: The Role of Resource Depletion and the Constraints of Time and Labor. In *Farmers as Hunters*, edited by S. Kent, pp. 71-79. New York, NY: Cambridge University Press.

Speth, J. D., and K. A. Spielmann
1983 Energy Source, Protein Metabolism, and Hunter-Gatherer Subsistence Strategies. *Journal of Anthropological Archaeology* 2(1):1-31.

Spielmann, K. A.
1986 Interdependence Among Egalitarian Societies. *Journal of Anthropological Archaeology* 5(4):279-312.
1995 Glimpses of Gender in the Prehistoric Southwest. *Journal of Anthropological Research* 51(2):91-102.

Spielmann, K. A. (Editor)
1991 *Farmers, Hunters, and Colonists: Interaction between the Southwest and the Southern Plains*. Tucson, AZ: University of Arizona Press.
1998 *Migration and Reorganization: The Pueblo IV Period in the American Southwest*. Anthropological Research Papers 51. Tempe, AZ: Arizona State University.

Tiffany, J. A.
1982 *Chan-ya-ta: A Mill Creek Village*. Report 15. Iowa City, IA: Office of the State Archaeologist.

Whalen, M. E.
1994 *Turquoise Ridge and Late Prehistoric Residential Mobility in the Desert Mogollon Region*. University of Utah Anthropological Paper 118. Salt Lake City, UT: University of Utah Press.
1996 Ceramic Technology and the Seriation of El Paso Plain Brown Pottery. *Kiva* 62(2):171-84.

Wiessner, P.
1974 A Functional Estimator of Population from Floor Area. *American Antiquity* 39(2):343-50.

Wiseman, R. N.
in press *The Fox Place (LA 68188), A Late Prehistoric Hunter-Gatherer Pithouse Village Near Roswell, New Mexico*. Santa Fe: Museum of New Mexico, Office of Archaeological Studies.